SEVENTH EDITION

Strategies for Teaching Students with Learning and Behavior Problems

Sharon Vaughn

University of Texas–Austin

Candace S. Bos

Late of University of Texas–Austin

Upper Saddle River, New Jersey

Columbus, Ohio

Library of Congress Cataloging in Publication Data

Vaughn, Sharon.
   Strategies for teaching students with learning and behavior problems
/ Sharon S. Vaughn, Candace S. Bos.—7th ed.
      p.   cm.
   Bos's name appears first on the earlier edition.
   Includes bibliographical references and index.
   ISBN-13: 978-0-205-60856-0 (pbk.)
   ISBN-10: 0-205-60856-6 (pbk.)
   1. Learning disabled children—Education—United States.   2. Problem
children—Education—United States.   3. Remedial teaching—United
States.   I. Bos, Candace S.   II. Title.
   LC4705.B67 2009
   371.9—dc22

                                                    2008001814

Executive Editor: Virginia Lanigan
Editorial Assistant: Matthew Buchholz
Director of Marketing: Quinn Perkson
Development Editor: Shannon Steed
Marketing Manager: Kris Ellis-Levy
Production Editor: Janet Domingo
Composition Buyer: Linda Cox
Manufacturing Manager: Megan Cochran
Editorial Production Service: Omegatype Typography, Inc.
Electronic Composition: Omegatype Typography, Inc.
Interior Design: Carol Somberg
Photo Researcher: Omegatype Typography, Inc.
Cover Administrator: Kristina Mose-Libon

This book was set in PhotinaMT by Omegatype Typography, Inc. It was printed and bound by R. R. Donnelley, MO. The cover
was printed by Phoenix Color Corp.

Pearson Education Ltd.
Pearson Education Singapore Pte. Ltd.
Pearson Education Canada, Ltd.
Pearson Education–Japan

Pearson Education Australia Pty. Limited
Pearson Education North Asia Ltd.
Pearson Educación de Mexico, S. A. de C. V.
Pearson Education Malaysia Pte. Ltd.

Photo Credits: p. xxxii, Ariel Skelley/Corbis; p. 30, Michael Newman/PhotoEdit; p. 64, Gabe Palmer/Corbis; p. 84, Frank
Siteman; p. 148, Will Hart; p. 194, © 2002 Tom Lindfors/Lindfors Photography; p. 240, Michael Newman/PhotoEdit; p. 292,
Scholastic Studio 10/Index Stock; p. 360, Richard Orton/Index Stock Imagery; p. 406, Michael Newman/PhotoEdit; p. 460,
Richard Hutchings/PhotoEdit; p. 506, Michelle D. Bridwell/PhotoEdit

Merrill
is an imprint of

www.pearsonhighered.com

10 9 8 7 6 5 4 3 2 1
ISBN 13: 978–0–205–60856–0
ISBN 10:   0–205–60856–6

Dedication

To Jim and Bob and Jon

ABOUT THE AUTHOR

Sharon Vaughn (Ph.D., University of Arizona) holds the H. E. Hartfelder/ Southland Corporation Regents Chair in Human Development and is a recipient of the AERA Special Education SIG distinguished researcher award. She was the editor-in-chief of the *Journal of Learning Disabilities* and the coeditor of *Learning Disabilities Research and Practice.* Dr. Vaughn is the author of numerous books and research articles that address the reading and social outcomes of students with learning difficulties including *Teaching Students Who Are Exceptional, Diverse, and At Risk in the General Education Classroom,* with Jeanne Schumm and Candace Bos (4th ed., Allyn & Bacon). Currently she is the principal or co-principal investigator on several Institute for Education Science, National Institute for Child Health and Human Development, and Office of Special Education Programs research grants investigating effective interventions for students with learning disabilities and behavior problems as well as students who are English language learners.

Brief Contents

Contents

I. UNDERSTANDING and PLANNING INSTRUCTION for STUDENTS WITH LEARNING and BEHAVIOR PROBLEMS

Part I introduces the characteristics of students with learning and behavior problems as well as the procedures for identifying and planning a special educational program for students who are eligible. General considerations for assessing students, designing instruction, and delivering effective instruction are addressed. In addition, the theoretical approaches to teaching and applications for the classroom are fully explored. Part I also presents issues beyond the curriculum: social behaviors and intervention approaches, coordinating instruction, creating a conducive learning environment, and communication with other professionals and families. These strategies enable teachers to serve the full range of students' educational needs.

Chapter 1

Planning and Teaching for Understanding   1

Chapter 2

Approaches to Learning and Teaching   30

Chapter 3

Response to Intervention   64

Chapter 4

Promoting Social Acceptance and Managing Behavior   84

Chapter 5

Communicating, Collaborating, and Coteaching: Working with Professionals and Families   148

II INSTRUCTING STUDENTS with LEARNING and BEHAVIOR PROBLEMS

Part II covers the topic of instruction in the basic skill and content areas, including oral language, reading, written expression, content area learning, and mathematics. Numerous effective teaching strategies are provided for each to prepare teachers to teach all students, including those with learning and behavior disorders.

Chapter 6

Assessing and Teaching Oral Language   194

Chapter 7

Assessing and Teaching Reading: Phonological Awareness, Phonics, and Word Recognition   240

Chapter 8

Assessing and Teaching Reading: Fluency and Comprehension   292

Chapter 9
Assessing and Teaching Writing and Spelling   360

Chapter 10

Assessing and Teaching Content Area Learning and Vocabulary Instruction   406

Chapter 11

Assessing and Teaching Mathematics   460

Chapter **12**
Transition Planning Process   506

Appendix A

CEC Knowledge and Skill Base for All Beginning Special Education Teachers of Students with Learning Disabilities

Appendix B

CEC Knowledge and Skill Base for All Beginning Special Education Teachers of Students with Emotional and Behavioral Disabilities

List of Features

APPLY the CONCEPT

CLASSROOM APPLICATIONS

INSTRUCTIONAL ACTIVITIES

SPOTLIGHT on DIVERSITY

TECH TIPS

Preface

hile traveling by car on a typical Arizona scorcher between Phoenix and Tucson after attending a state Association for Children and Adults with Learning Disabilities meeting, we were discussing the content and assignments for the methods courses we taught at our respective universities. The conversation inevitably drifted to what we would like to do better. Because both of us were responsible for preparing teachers and potential teachers to work effectively with students who have learning and behavior problems, we spent a considerable amount of time considering the content of our classes. We concluded that we would like the class and the textbook for the class to provide adequate background in procedures for teaching skill and content areas such as reading, math, oral and written expression, and social and study skills. We also would like our students to understand which methods are most effective with what types of students and why.

Chapter **4**

Promoting Social Acceptance and Managing Behavior

The first edition of this book was the result of that initial lengthy discussion, which focused on the ideal content that would prepare teachers to meet the needs of elementary and secondary students with learning and behavior problems. With each new edition, we continue to present fresh ideas and information but always while keeping sight of our original purpose. Recent research and policy have provided new guidance, such as response to intervention, for improving instruction and outcomes for students with learning and behavior problems, and we have integrated this new content into each chapter.

Audience and Purpose

We have written this book for undergraduate and graduate students who are developing expertise in teaching students with learning and behavior problems. This book is also intended for professionals in the field, including general and special education teachers, school psychologists, speech/ language specialists, and school administrators who are interested in learning more about working successfully with students who have learning and behavior problems.

The purpose of this book is threefold; we seek to provide

1. *Foundations.* Information about general approaches to learning and teaching so that the foundation for the methods and procedures for teaching all learners can be better understood.
2. *Detailed methods.* Descriptions of methods and procedures that include sufficient detail so that teachers and other professionals know how to use them.
3. *Organization and planning.* Information about classroom and behavior management, consultation, and collaboration with families and professionals so that beginning teachers can develop a plan of action for the school year and experienced teachers can refine these skills.

New to This Edition

This edition reflects a revision of the book with an emphasis on reading instruction, scientifically based instructional practices, response to intervention, progress monitoring, technology, and diversity.

- A new chapter on response to intervention, contributed by Janette Klingner at the University of Colorado, reflects the increased importance of this model in prevention and intervention by discussing the key components of RTI and its implementation, how RTI is facilitated by effective screening and progress monitoring, and the special educator's role in the RTI process.

- New text organization highlights assessment and RTI and we have dedicated a full chapter to promoting social acceptance and managing behavior.

- Additional methods for communicating and working effectively with families are included throughout the chapters.

- Spotlight on Diversity features incorporate the most current methods for teaching diverse student populations, including students from culturally and linguistically diverse backgrounds.

- Expanded Tech Tips in each chapter, contributed by Jean Ulman at Ball State University, highlight software and other technologies that can enhance teaching and learning.

- New practical Instructional Activities sections have been added throughout the book to provide examples of classroom activities that emphasize the chapter topic.

- Classroom Applications features discuss the use of in-depth teaching methods in the classroom by analyzing their procedures and providing commentary on their effectiveness.

Special Features in This Edition

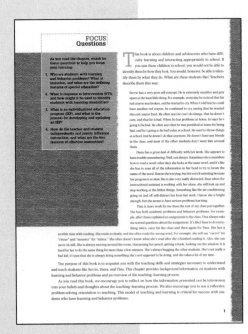

◀ Focus Pedagogy

At three points in each chapter, the key ideas are called out and reinforced to focus student learning. The **Focus Questions** are listed at the beginning of each chapter to help students predict the central concepts. These Focus Questions are repeated at appropriate points in the chapter to highlight those key concepts where they are presented. Each chapter-closing section includes brief **Focus Answers** to reinforce the key concepts; more detailed answers are available on the companion Website.

Apply the Concept ▶

These boxes address practical issues surrounding the concepts and approaches discussed throughout the chapters.

◀ Tech Tips

These features highlight software and other technologies that assist with instruction and student learning.

Spotlight on Diversity ▶

These sections spotlight methods for teaching student populations who are culturally and linguistically diverse, including English language learners.

◀ Instructional Activities

These sections include many classroom activities that may teach new skills or practice and reinforce already acquired skills. For each activity, the objective, materials, and teaching procedures are described.

Classroom Applications ▶

These features discuss the classroom implementation of the major teaching strategies presented in the chapters. The procedures are discussed, followed by commentary on the factors necessary for the success of the strategy.

◀ Chapter-Closing Resources

The closing section of each chapter contains several resources to help readers understand how to teach students with learning and behavior problems and expand on what they have learned in each chapter. The **Summary** is a helpful recap of the central chapter topics. The **Focus Answers** provide brief answers to the chapter **Focus Questions. Think and Apply** includes questions and activities to apply what was learned in the chapter. **Apply the Standards** is a resource for preservice teachers of general and special education. It explains which Council for Exceptional Children (CEC) standards the chapter reflects, and it gives activities to help readers understand how those standards relate to the chapter contents.

The **Websites as Resources** section lists useful online resources related to the chapter topics.
MyEducationLab activities and exercises that correlate to chapter topics conclude each chapter.

Supplements

The following supplements provide an outstanding array of resources that facilitate learning about students with disabilities and their families. For more information, ask your local Pearson Higher Education sales representative or contact the Allyn & Bacon Merrill Faculty Field Support Department at 1-800-526-0485.

For technology products, please contact technical support directly at 1-800-677-6337 or http://247.pearsoned.com.

To view our online product catalogs, go to www.pearsonhighered.com.

Resources for Instructors

Instructor's Manual. The Instructor's Manual includes a wealth of interesting ideas and activities designed to help instructors teach the course. Each chapter includes a chapter-at-a-glance grid, chapter overview, key topics, lecture-discussion outlines, invitation for learning activities, think and apply questions, and suggested readings and media. (Available for download from the Instructor Resource Center at www.pearsonhighered.com/irc.)

Test Bank. The Test Bank includes more than a thousand questions, including multiple-choice, short answer, true/false, and essay questions. Page references to the main text, suggested answers, skill types, plus correlations to the CEC Standards have been added to each question to help instructors create and evaluate student tests. (Available for download from the Instructor Resource Center at www.pearsonhighered.com/irc.)

Computerized Test Bank. The printed Test Bank is also available electronically through the Allyn & Bacon computerized testing system, TestGen. Instructors can use TestGen to create exams in just minutes by selecting from the existing database of questions, editing questions, and/or writing original questions. (Available for download from the Instructor Resource Center at www.pearsonhighered .com/irc.)

PowerPoint™ Presentation. Ideal for lecture presentations or student handouts, the PowerPoint™ Presentation created for this text provides dozens of ready-to-use graphic and text images. (Available for download from the Instructor Resource Center at www.pearsonhighered.com/irc.)

Resources for Students

PEARSON **myeducationlab**   *Your Class. Your Career. Everyone's Future.*
Where the Classroom Comes to Life

MyEducationLab is a research-based learning tool that brings teaching to life. Through authentic in-class video footage, interactive simulations, rich case studies, examples of authentic teacher and student work, and more, MyEducationLab prepares you for your teaching career by showing what quality instruction looks like.

MyEducationLab is easy to use! At the end of every chapter in the textbook, you will find the MyEducationLab logo adjacent to activities and exercises that correlate material you've just read in the chapter to your reading/viewing of multimedia assets on the MyEducationLab site. These assets include the following:

- **Video.** The authentic classroom videos in MyEducationLab show how real teachers handle actual classroom situations.

- **Case Studies.** A diverse set of robust cases illustrates the realities of teaching and offer valuable perspectives on common issues and challenges in education.

- **Simulations.** Created by the IRIS Center at Vanderbilt University, these interactive simulations give you hands-on practice at adapting instruction for a full spectrum of learners.

- **Readings.** Specially selected, topically relevant articles from ASCD's renowned *Educational Leadership* journal expand and enrich your perspectives on key issues and topics.

- **Student & Teacher Artifacts.** Authentic preK–12 student and teacher classroom artifacts are tied to course topics and offer you practice in working with the actual types of materials you will encounter daily as teachers.

- **Lesson & Portfolio Builders.** With this effective and easy-to-use tool, you can create, update, and share standards-based lesson plans and portfolios.

Acknowledgments

From Sharon Vaughn—This seventh edition was the second time I revised the book without my dear friend and colleague Candace S. Bos. I knew what an outstanding writer and teacher educator she was; I know even better now. I miss her daily, and working on this book was a clear reminder of how much she taught me and how hard it is to work without her. Virginia Lanigan, editor, provided more than her usual excellent support and good ideas, and she convinced me of the importance of continuing the book without Candy. Shannon Steed, developmental editor, provided valuable suggestions and advice. Shannon is so capable and supportive that her assistance has made this the best edition yet.

Many people deserve a great deal more acknowledgment than their names appearing here will provide. I wish to acknowledge and thank the teachers whom Candy and I have written about in this book. The time we have spent in their classrooms—observing, discussing, and teaching—has afforded us the ability to write a book that is grounded in classroom experiences and practices. These teachers include Juan Caberra, Judy Cohen, Joan Downing, Mary Lou Duffy, Joyce Duryea, Jane Eddy, Louise Fournia, Joan Gervasi, Sally Gotch, Linda Jones, Sharon Kutok, Tom Lebasseur, Tiffany Royal, Marynell Schlegel, Mary Thalgott, and Nina Zaragoza.

I also thank Jean G. Ulman of Ball State University for contributing the completely new Tech Tips, Janette Klingner of University of Colorado at Boulder for contributing the new RTI chapter, and James R. Patton of University of Texas–Austin for contributing and revising the transition chapter. I would also like to thank several individuals whose expert support and assistance in previous editions remain in this edition: Paulette Jackson, Dr. Ae-hwa Kim, and Dr. Jeannie Wanzek.

From the author team—We especially wish to acknowledge the following individuals for their reviews for the seventh edition: Kathleen Brown, Purdue University, Calumet; Doug Carothers, University of Hawaii at Hilo; Pat Edelen-Smith, University of Hawaii at Manoa; Kimberly Fields, Albany State University; DiAnne B. Garner, Virginia Commonwealth University; Brenda Gilliam, University of Texas at Tyler; Marie K. Hopkins, University of Hartford; Linda Metzke, Lyndon State College; W. Drue Narkon, University of Hawaii at Manoa; Catherine A. Shea, Indiana University Southeast; Judy L. Stuart, Furman University; Kevin Sutherland, Virginia Commonwealth University; Claire Verden, West Chester University; Maureen P. Walsh, Bloomsburg University; and Charmayne Zieziula, Buffalo State College. A special thank you for the contributions of Dr. Alison Gould Boardman and Katie Klingler Tackett who provide outstanding suggestions and practical ideas.

Special thanks also to our husbands, Jim and Bob, who wondered if we would ever come out from behind our computers.

Most important of all, we would like to thank the teacher whose observations, research, and thinking has done more to guide our development and the field of special education than any other: Samuel A. Kirk.

Chapter 1

Planning and Teaching for Understanding

As you read the chapter, watch for these questions to help you focus your learning:

1. Who are students with learning and behavior problems? What is inclusion, and what are the defining features of special education?

2. What is response to intervention (RTI), and how might it be used to identify students with learning disabilities?

3. What is an individualized education program (IEP), and what is the process for developing and updating an IEP?

4. How do the teacher and student independently and jointly influence instruction, and what are the key features of effective instruction?

This book is about children and adolescents who have difficulty learning and interacting appropriately in school. If you saw these children in school, you would not be able to identify them by how they look. You would, however, be able to identify them by what they do. What are these students like? Teachers describe them this way:

Servio has a very poor self-concept. He is extremely sensitive and gets upset at the least little thing. For example, yesterday he noticed that his red crayon was broken, and he started to cry. When I told him he could have another red crayon, he continued to cry, saying that he wanted this red crayon fixed. He often says he can't do things, that he doesn't care, and that he is bad. When he has problems at home, he says he's going to be bad. He often says that he was punished at home for being bad, and he's going to be bad today at school. He used to throw things at school, but he doesn't do that anymore. He doesn't have any friends in the class, and most of the other students don't want him around them.

Dana has a great deal of difficulty with her work. She appears to have trouble remembering. Well, not always. Sometimes she remembers how to read a word; other days she looks at the same word, and it's like she has to scan all of the information in her head to try to locate the name of the word. I know she is trying, but it is very frustrating because her progress is so slow. She is also very easily distracted. Even when the instructional assistant is working with her alone, she will look up and stop working at the littlest things. Something like the air-conditioning going on and off will distract her from her work. I know she is bright enough, but she seems to have serious problems learning.

Tina is more work for me than the rest of my class put together. She has both academic problems and behavior problems. For example, after I have explained an assignment to the class, Tina always asks me several questions about the assignment. It's like I have to do everything twice, once for the class and then again for Tina. She has a terrible time with reading. She reads so slowly, and she often reads the wrong word. For example, she will say "carrot" for "circus" and "monster" for "mister." She often doesn't know what she's read after she's finished reading it. Also, she can never sit still. She is always moving around the room, sharpening her pencil, getting a book, looking out the window. It is hard for her to do the same thing for more than a few minutes. She's always bugging the other students. She's not really a bad kid, it's just that she is always doing something she's not supposed to be doing, and she takes a lot of my time.

The purpose of this book is to acquaint you with the teaching skills and strategies necessary to understand and teach students like Servio, Dana, and Tina. This chapter provides background information on students with learning and behavior problems and an overview of the teaching–learning process.

As you read this book, we encourage you to reflect on how the information presented can be interwoven into your beliefs and thoughts about the teaching–learning process. We also encourage you to use a reflective, problem-solving orientation to teaching. This model of teaching and learning is critical for success with students who have learning and behavior problems.

FOCUS
Question | **1.** Who are students with learning and behavior problems? What is inclusion, and what are the defining features of special education?

Students with Learning and Behavior Problems

Most teaching professionals are able to recognize with little difficulty those students who have learning and behavior problems. They are students who call attention to themselves in the classroom because they have difficulty learning and interacting appropriately. Students with learning and/or behavior problems manifest one or more of the following behaviors:

- *Poor academic performance.* Students display significant problems in one or more academic areas such as spelling, reading, and mathematics. The key to understanding students with learning disabilities is that they display unexpected underachievement.
- *Attention problems.* Many students seem to have difficulty working for extended periods of time on a task. They may have trouble focusing on the teacher's directions. These students are often described by teachers as being easily distracted.
- *Hyperactivity.* Some students are overactive and have a difficult time staying in their seats and completing assigned tasks. They move from task to task, and often from location to location in the classroom. When working on an assignment, the least little noise will distract them.
- *Memory.* Many students have a hard time remembering what they were taught. Often their difficulty remembering is associated with symbols such as letters and numbers. These students may remember something one day but not the next.
- *Poor language abilities.* Many students have language difficulties that are manifested in a number of ways. As toddlers, these students may have taken longer in learning to talk. Often these language problems can be corrected through speech therapy. Many also have difficulty developing phonological awareness skills (Torgesen, Wagner, and Rashotte, 1997). Students may have difficulty with vocabulary, understanding the concept, using language to adequately express themselves, or producing correct sounds.
- *Aggressive behavior.* Some students are physically or verbally assaultive. They may hit, kick, get into fights, and/or verbally threaten or insult others. These children are easily upset and cope with being upset by acting out.
- *Withdrawn behavior.* Some students seldom interact with others. Unlike shy students, who may have one or two friends, these students are real loners who avoid involvement with others.
- *Bizarre behavior.* Some students display unusual patterns of behavior. They may stare for long periods of time at objects that they hold in the light, they may sit and rock, or they might display aggressive behaviors at times and withdrawn behaviors at other times.

Students with learning and/or behavior problems often exhibit more than one of these behaviors. Yet some students exhibit these behaviors and are not identified as having learning or behavior problems. There are other factors that teachers consider when determining how serious a learning and behavior problem is.

Factors to Consider in Determining How Serious a Learning or Behavior Problem Is

Fifteen to 25 percent of all students have some type of learning or behavior problem. Students with learning disabilities are five times more prevalent than those with behavior disorders. There are several factors to consider when you are determining how serious a problem is:

1. *Persistence of the problem.* Sometimes a student has a learning or behavior problem for a short period of time, perhaps while there is some type of crisis in the family, and then it disappears. These behaviors and feeling states are not considered problems if they occur occasionally. Other students display persistent learning and behavior problems throughout their schooling experience. These problems have more serious consequences for the students.

2. *Severity of the problem.* Is the student's learning or behavior problem mild, moderate, or severe? Is the student performing slightly below or significantly below what would normally be expected of him or her? Is the behavior slightly different or substantially different from that of the student's peers?

3. *Speed of progress.* Does the student appear to be making steady progress in the classroom despite the learning and behavior problem? We do not expect all students to learn at the same rate. In fact, in an average fourth-grade classroom, the range of performance varies from second-grade level to seventh-grade level.

4. *Motivation.* Is the student interested in learning? Does the student persist at tasks and attempt to learn? Does the student initiate and complete tasks without continual praise and encouragement?

5. *Parental response.* How do family members feel about a child's academic and/or behavioral progress? How do they think it compares with the child's progress in the past? Are they concerned about how their child's abilities compare with those of other children the same age? How have siblings performed in school?

6. *Other teachers' responses.* How did the student perform in previous classes? What do previous or other teachers say about the student's learning style, academic abilities, and behavior?

7. *Relationship with the teacher.* What type of relationship does the student have with his or her present teacher? Sometimes there is a poor interpersonal match between the student and the teacher that may interfere with the student's academic performance and/or behavior.

8. *Instructional modifications and style.* What attempts has the teacher made to modify the student's academic and/or behavioral program? Does the student seem responsive to attempts at intervention? If the student is not performing well in a traditional reading program, has the teacher tried other instructional approaches to reading? Has the student had opportunities to work with different students in the class? If the problem is behavior, what behavior change programs have been implemented? Have any been successful?

Is there a good match between the student and the classroom setting? Some children function best in a highly structured classroom where the rules, expectations, and assignments are very clearly stated. Other children function better in a learning environment where there is more flexibility.

9. *Adequate instruction.* Has the student had adequate exposure to the material and enough time to learn? Some students have little experience with formal learning situations before coming to school. Other students have multiple experiences, including preschool programs that teach letters and letter sounds. Students who have less exposure to school learning situations or whose parents provide few school-like learning experiences may need more time and exposure to the learning environment before they make gains. Determine what prerequisite skills are missing and how they can be acquired.

10. *Behavior–age discrepancy.* Does the student display problems that are unusual or deviant for the student's age? For example, many preschoolers will whine and withdraw to another room, but few children do so after grade 2.

11. *Other factors.* Are there other factors that might be contributing to the student's learning and/or behavior problems? For example, how closely do the student's background experiences, culture, and language match those of the teacher and other students in the class? Are there any health-related factors that may be interfering with the student's learning or behavior? Have the student's vision and hearing been adequately assessed to determine whether they might be affecting the student's learning or behavior?

Considering these factors will help you to identify the severity of the student's problems and whether the student may need additional classroom supports.

The Defining Features of Special Education

How does special education for students with learning and behavior problems differ from a good general education? Recently, individuals have addressed this issue to help teachers identify practices that promote learning for students with special needs (Landrum, Tankersley, and Kauffman, 2003; Vaughn and Linan-Thompson, 2003; Zigmond and Baker, 1994). Consider the following six features of instruction that, according to Heward (2003), define effective instruction for students with learning and behavior problems:

1. *Individually planned.* Instruction, materials, and setting of instruction are selected or adapted on the basis of student needs.
2. *Specialized.* Instruction and adaptations include related services and assistive technology that are not often a part of the general education curriculum.
3. *Intensive.* Precise, targeted instruction is designed to assist students in making efficient progress toward gaining necessary skills and strategies.

4. *Goal-directed.* Instruction focuses on individual goals and objectives necessary for student success.
5. *Employ research-based methods.* Selection and application of effective teaching methods are supported by research.
6. *Guided by student performance.* Student response to instruction is continually assessed for use in evaluating the effectiveness of instruction and adjusting instruction when necessary.

Heward (2003) further states that many misunderstandings about teaching and learning interfere with successful delivery of special education for students with disabilities. For example, many educators and administrators are taught that a structured curriculum including instruction and practice in individual skills is unnecessary and harmful to students' general learning. Contrary to this belief, students with learning and behavior problems often need academic tasks broken down into smaller, obtainable skills in order to progress.

Some educators also believe that student performance cannot be measured. As Heward points out, a hallmark of special education is that it is goal-directed and guided by student performance. Therefore, assessment of student outcomes is needed to guide appropriate instruction and to move students as quickly as possible through instruction to ensure student success in academics and related areas. This means that instruction must be focused and provided with a sense of urgency. Unstructured lessons and activities that are developed for the sole purpose of creativity and fun without regard for effectiveness can be detrimental to students with learning and behavior problems. These students need the very best instruction using research-supported techniques to ensure that time is not wasted and teachers are providing opportunities for students to gain the necessary abilities and obtain the motivating experience of success. Throughout this book, we will demonstrate effective instructional techniques in reading, written expression, math, and other content areas for students with learning and behavior problems.

Learning and Educational Environments for Students with Learning and Behavior Problems

Most students with learning and behavior problems are educated in the general education classroom. But students who have severe learning and behavior problems may receive a range of support services, including reading or math support, counseling, individualized instruction with a teaching assistant, and special education.

In many schools, reading or math specialists assist students with learning problems. These specialists typically provide supplemental instruction to the regular reading or math instruction the students receive in the general education classroom. Such additional instruction can help students with learning problems make sufficient progress in reaching expected performance levels. Often, specialists and classroom teachers collaborate to ensure that the instruction they provide is consistent and follows a similar sequence of skills.

Some classroom teachers have a teaching assistant who provides supplemental instruction for students with learning problems. These services are provided similarly to the services of the reading or math specialist. However, teaching assistants often do not have the instructional background that specialists do. Therefore, it is imperative that teachers provide teaching assistants with sufficient guidance. This includes planning lessons, training in effective instruction for students with learning problems, and monitoring instruction. When teaching assistants are given appropriate instructional tools for teaching students with learning problems, the supplemental help they provide often helps students to make the necessary progress to learn at expected levels.

Students with disabilities receive services through special education. PL 94-142, reauthorized as the Individuals with Disabilities Education Act (IDEA), ensures that a continuum of placements is available for students. This continuum is conceptualized as proceeding from the least to the most restrictive. The term *restrictive*, in an educational sense, refers to the extent to which students are educated with nondisabled peers. A more restrictive setting is one in which students spend no part of their educational program with nondisabled peers. In a less restrictive setting, students may spend part of their educational day with nondisabled peers. IDEA mandates that all students should be educated in the least-restrictive educational environment possible (IDEA, 2004).

Including Students with Learning and Behavior Problems

When students with special needs are included in the general education classroom, either their specialized services are provided within the general education class, or they are pulled out of the classroom for a portion of the day to receive the services.

The decision to include a student with special needs is made by an individual educational planning and placement committee. This committee is typically made up of one or both of the child's guardians, the special education teacher, the general education teacher, relevant professionals such as the school psychologist, and the administrator who supervises the special education program in which the student participates. At the recommendation of the special education and general education teachers and the professionals who evaluate the student's progress, the committee collectively decides whether the student's social and educational needs would best be met in the regular classroom and writes up the individualized education program (IEP) accordingly.

Most students with emotional and learning disabilities spend at least some of their school day in general education classrooms with their nondisabled peers. Therefore, both general education and special education teachers are often responsible for the instruction and outcomes of students with disabilities.

Almost 2.7 million students with disabilities, or 47 percent of the special education population, received instruction in general education settings for 80 percent of the day during the 2002 school year (U.S. Department of Education, April 2006). Where were students with learning disabilities and behavior disorders educated? Almost 47 percent of students identified as severely learning disabled spent 80 percent of their time in general education classrooms, whereas only 29 percent of students identified as seriously emotionally disturbed were in regular classrooms for that same amount of time. It is quite likely that fewer students identified as seriously emotionally disturbed are in general education because their behavior interferes significantly with the academic progress of others in the classroom.

IDEA introduced the concept of a continuum of placements, including the *least restrictive environment* (LRE). Since its passage in 1997, there has been a growing interest in educating students with disabilities with their peers who are nondisabled. IDEA contained a strong mandate to provide greater access to the general education curriculum. As more students with special needs are placed in general education classrooms, with special education teachers consulting or collaborating with classroom teachers, the emphasis on consultation/collaborative models has grown (see Chapter 5 on coordinating instruction with families and other professionals). The latest reauthorization of IDEA in 2004 puts an increased emphasis on academic performance goals and measures of accountability for students with disabilities that are consistent with standards for students without disabilities.

There are several reasons why inclusion is important for students with learning and behavior problems. First, the research has not clearly demonstrated either the academic or social benefits of placing students in segregated special education classrooms in comparison to regular classrooms. Second, students are likely to be viewed as more socially and academically acceptable when they remain in the regular classroom. Third, court decisions have encouraged placement of students with learning disabilities in the regular classroom to the extent possible (Hallahan, Keller, McKinney, Lloyd, and Bryan, 1988; McKinney and Hocutt, 1988; Prillaman, 1981; Schultz and Turnbull, 1984).

Students with learning disabilities and behavior problems have not always received the specific academic and behavioral supports they require in general education classrooms. Thus, inclusion may not always work as well as was intended by the law, or as was envisioned by the families of special education students and by the schools that serve them (McIntosh, Vaughn, Schumm, Haager, and Lee, 1993; Schumm and Vaughn, 1991, 1992a, 1992b; Schumm, Vaughn, Haager, McDowell, Rothlein, and Saumell, 1995; Vaughn and Schumm, 1994).

Lawmakers intended for students with special needs who are included in the general education classroom to receive accommodations for their learning and/or emotional needs within the classroom. The special education teacher, as consultant/collaborator with regular classroom teacher, is to help the general education teacher become familiar with the student's IEP and then help that teacher to plan and, in some cases, deliver appropriate instruction. The general classroom teacher is responsible for planning and delivering the instruction or intervention the student needs.

Most secondary-level (middle and high school) classroom teachers stated that they had not used IEPs or psychological reports to guide their planning for special education students. They had, however, gathered information from the families and former teachers of students with special needs. Some teachers said that they had very little contact with the special education teacher who monitored their students with special needs and they were not aware that the students had IEPs.

A few teachers had no contact with a special education teacher and were unaware that they even had a student with special needs in their class. In such cases, there was clearly a lack of communication between the special education teacher responsible for monitoring the progress of the students with special needs and the regular classroom teacher.

FOCUS Question 2. What is response to intervention (RTI), and how might it be used to identify students with learning disabilities?

Response to Intervention (RTI) as a Means of Identifying Students with Learning Disabilities

Individuals with learning disabilities have typically been identified through referral by classroom teachers or families, followed by a complete battery of assessments designed to identify whether the students qualify as learning disabled. Typically, these assessments included an IQ and an achievement test. If students' IQ scores were a certain number of points above their achievement scores (in other words, there is a large discrepancy between the IQ and achievement scores), the students would be identified as having a learning disability due to their "unexpected underachievement." Recently, there has been considerable concern about the appropriateness of administering IQ tests to all students, particularly minority students, and the extent to which the IQ–achievement discrepancy is an appropriate measure for identification of learning disabilities (Bradley, Danielson, and Hallahan, 2002; Donovan and Cross, 2002; Stuebing, Fletcher, LeDoux, Lyon, Shaywitz, and Shaywitz, 2002).

What is IQ–achievement discrepancy, and what are the concerns about using it? To reiterate, IQ–achievement discrepancy is the common practice by which the IQ and standardized achievement scores of students are compared, in the belief that a significant discrepancy (higher IQ scores than achievement scores on one or more relevant outcomes) is a strong indicator of learning disabilities.

The four specific concerns about this practice are as follows:

1. The discrepancy is difficult to determine with young children and may unnecessarily postpone identification until second grade or later; this concern highlights why some refer to the IQ–achievement discrepancy as the "wait to fail" model.
2. Many young children ages five to seven benefit greatly from prevention programs, particularly in reading, that could keep them from developing greater difficulties in reading.
3. Formal IQ and achievement tests are expensive to administer and interpret, and the money might be better used to provide instruction.
4. IQ tests provide little information to teachers to assist them in improving or modifying their instruction.

What alternatives are there to traditional IQ–achievement discrepancy approaches for identifying students with learning disabilities? The most frequently suggested alternative is response to intervention (RTI). What is RTI? Though the exact use and application of RTI varies somewhat depending on who is describing it, RTI typically involves a multitiered system of interventions, a data collection system that informs decision making, and ongoing progress monitoring. The number of tiers, what data are collected, and the measures used to determine if a child is "responding" to an intervention might differ depending on the school and content area. RTI can also be conceptualized as a systematic application of data-based decision making to enhance outcomes for all children (Burns and Ysseldyke, 2005). RTI provides a preventative approach to special education and promotes early screening and interventions so that students at risk for academic or behavior difficulties are provided with timely and appropriate services.

Progress Monitoring

For example, Cherry Tree School utilizes a three-tier RTI model. All students are screened three times a year to determine who is meeting benchmarks in reading and math. Carlos's and Lynn's scores show that they are reading below grade level. In addition to receiving reading instruction in their general education classroom (Tier I), they both receive 25 extra minutes of reading instruction in a small group of students from their general education teacher during center time. This "extra boost" of reading instruction helps Carlos begin to read on grade level; because he "responds to the intervention," he does not need additional help. However, Lynn does not respond to this intervention as evidenced by her continued low scores on progress monitoring measures. Lynn moves to Tier III where she receives 50 minutes a day of extra reading instruction; this time, Lynn is taught in a smaller group by the reading specialist. If Lynn continues to not respond adequately to this intervention, she may be referred to special education. It is important to note that RTI can be done in many content areas (including behavior) and at all grade levels.

RTI addresses concerns about the IQ–achievement discrepancy because students begin to receive help as soon as they start demonstrating academic or behavior difficulties, regardless of what grade they are in. In addition, many students, such as Carlos, need only an "extra boost" in order to be successful in the general education classroom. For students like Carlos, future reading difficulties are prevented by early intervention. Students who respond adequately to the intervention and are able to make appropriate progress in the classroom are considered high-responders to the intervention; typically, they do not need further intervention and are unlikely to require special education. Students like Lynn whose response to the intervention is low may be referred for further evaluations and considered for special education (Vaughn and Fuchs, 2006). In order to determine if a student has responded to an intervention, the measures used for screening and progress monitoring are typically quick and easy to administer and are directly related to skills needed for academic or behavior success in the classroom. Therefore, these measures help teachers pinpoint where a student is having difficulties and alter or improve their instruction accordingly (see Apply the Concept 1.1).

In August 2006, regulatory guidelines for implementing RTI were published (USED, 2006). Key aspects of the guidelines include the following:

- State criteria must not utilize a severe discrepancy between intellectual ability and achievement.
- State criteria must permit the use of a process based on children's responses to scientific, research-based intervention.
- When determining specific learning disabilities (SLD), personnel must determine whether children are making age-appropriate progress or making progress to meet state-approved grade-level standards.
- Lack of achievement may not be due to lack of appropriate instruction in reading or math.
- There are many models of RTI.
- Though specific procedures are not described, the importance of timelines and structured communication with family members is emphasized.
- Frequent and ongoing assessments to determine response to intervention can be determined by the state.
- RTI is not a substitute for a comprehensive evaluation.
- No single procedure can be relied on to determine special education.

How can funds for "early intervening services" be used within an RTI framework? Fifteen percent of IDEA funds can be used by a school district for early intervening services. This use is discretionary except in the case of local education agencies (LEAs) who have been determined to have engaged in significant racial or ethnic disproportionality in special education identification or placement. Funds can be used for a wide array of

Apply the Concept 1.1

Adopting an RTI Model to Identify Students with Learning Disabilities

The 2004 reauthorization of IDEA, the Individuals with Disabilities Education Improvement Act, recommends that states and schools abandon the IQ–achievement discrepancy to identify students with learning disabilities and

instead use an RTI approach. However, IDEA 2004 does not require that schools use RTI. Your principal asks your opinion on what your school should do in terms of identifying students with learning disabilities.

What are the pros and cons of the IQ–achievement discrepancy and RTI? Which model do you recommend that your school use in determining special education eligibility?

supports including early intervention, professional development, behavioral services, and other education supports (Zirkel, 2007).

Is RTI effective? Initial research suggests that English language learners who receive scientifically based reading instruction early on are likely to maintain gains and those who are low-responders can be identified through RTI approaches (Linan-Thompson, Cirino, and Vaughn, 2007; Linan-Thompson, Vaughn, Prater, and Cirino, 2006).

Challenges to Implementing an RTI Approach

Possible difficulties with implementing an RTI approach include questions about who provides the interventions (a paraprofessional, general education teacher, special education teacher, or other specialist) and the extent to which validated instructional practices exist in fields other than reading, such as math or writing. Nevertheless, this approach appears to be a path for prevention of academic and behavioral difficulties that will increasingly be used by school districts (Vaughn and Fuchs, 2003). Another challenge involves defining "response to intervention" so that practicing school districts are able to determine: (1) responders from nonresponders, (2) the necessary professional development for practicing professionals, and (3) the role of families. Ensuring family involvement in RTI can be challenging initially as it may require adjustments to new practices.

Other issues and perceived barriers to implementation of RTI include:

- Personnel may not be adequately trained to implement RTI.
- High-quality instruction in early reading is well understood, however, other academic domains and other grade levels are less well developed.
- Leaders at the school, district, and state levels are inadequately prepared to implement RTI practices.
- Many folks perceive RTI as a special education initiative rather than a combined general and special education initiative.
- Inadequate local and state level policies and resources may compromise effective implementation of RTI.

The National Association of State Directors of Special Education (NASDSE) has developed a readily accessible guide to RTI that is available on their Website (www.nasdse.org) entitled *Response to Intervention: Policy Considerations and Implementation* (NASDSE, 2006).

FOCUS Question 3. What is an individualized education program (IEP), and what is the process for developing and updating an IEP?

Developing an Individualized Education Program

For students who have been identified as requiring special education services (including students with learning or emotional disabilities), procedures for setting goals and planning instruction are designated by law. IDEA requires that an IEP be developed for each student with special educational needs. A multidisciplinary team develops, implements, and reviews the IEP, which is both a process and a document. The process involves a group of individuals, often referred to as the IEP team, using assessment information, eligibility, and the needs of the student to establish an appropriate specialized educational program for a student with disabilities. The document is a record of the decisions that have been agreed upon by the team (Johns, Crowley, and Guetzloe, 2002). The IEP must be reviewed annually and can be revised at any time to address lack of expected progress, the results of any reevaluations, or other relevant information provided by either the school or family members. Figure 1.1 presents a sample IEP completed for John, a fifth grader with learning disabilities.

The members of the multidisciplinary team include the following people:

- A representative of the local education agency—an administrator who is qualified to supervise services to students with disabilities and who is knowledgeable about the general education curriculum as well as resources and services available
- Parent(s) or guardian(s)
- Special education teacher
- At least one general education teacher if the student is participating or is likely to participate in general education classes
- Evaluative personnel—someone who can interpret the results from the student's

FIGURE 1.1

Individualized Education Program

I. Demographic Information

Last	First	M.I.		Date
Smith, John E.				May 12, 2007

Student I.D.	Address	Home Phone	Work Phone
2211100	23 Lakeview St. Collier, MN 32346	(459)555-5555	(459)555-5000

Date of Birth	Grade Level	Home School	Program Eligibility
03-02-96	5	Lakeview Elementary	Learning Disabilities

Reason for Conference: ❏ Staffing   ☑ Review

II. Conference

Parent Notification

Attempt #1:	Attempt #2:	Attempt #3:
Letter: 3-02-07	Phone call: 3-13-07	Notice sent home with student: 3-22-07

Parent Response: Will attend as per phone call on 3-13-07

III. Present Levels of Educational Performance

John is a 5th grade student whose disability inhibits his ability to read required material. John can read 35/100 in two minutes from a 4.0 grade level paragraph and 45/100 in two minutes from a 3.0 grade level paragraph. John can answer 8/10 literal questions and 4/10 inference questions from a 4.0 grade level passage read to him.

IV. Annual Goals and Short-Term Benchmarks

1. John will increase reading fluency to the 4.0 grade level.

    John will read orally a passage at the 4.0 grade level in 2 minutes with 50 or more words correct.

    John will use correct intonation and prosody when reading orally a passage at the 4.0 grade level 50% of the time.

2. John will improve the percentage of accuracy when responding to literal and inferential questions.

    John will answer literal questions from a 4.0 grade level passage read to him with 75% accuracy.

    John will answer inferential questions from a 4.0 grade level passage read to him with 90-100% accuracy.

Describe the extent to which the student will not participate in general education settings and explain why the student cannot be placed in general education settings.

John will not participate in general education settings for language arts, science, and social studies instruction. John requires close supervision when completing tasks, high levels of assistance, and intensive, systematic instruction.

V. Related Services

Type of Service, Aid or Modification			Location	Time per day/week
Assistive Technology:	❏ Yes	☑ No		
Adaptive PE:	❏ Yes	☑ No		
Audiology Services:	❏ Yes	☑ No		
Counseling:	❏ Yes	☑ No		
Interpreter:	❏ Yes	☑ No		
Medical Services:	❏ Yes	☑ No		
Occupational Therapy:	❏ Yes	☑ No		*(continued)*

FIGURE 1.1

Continued

Orientation/Mobility:	☐ Yes	☑ No	
Physical Therapy:	☐ Yes	☑ No	
Psychological Services:	☐ Yes	☑ No	
Special Transportation:	☐ Yes	☑ No	
Speech/Lang. Therapy:	☑ Yes	☐ No	Self-contained class, 30 min./wk

VI. Assessment Participation

Will the student participate in state and district assessments: ☑ Yes   ☐ No

If yes, what accommodations or modifications will be provided?

☐ None   ☑ Flexible Setting   ☐ Flexible Presentation   ☑ Flexible Scheduling
☐ Flexible Responding

If no, indicate why state and district assessments are inappropriate:

VII. Transition Planning/Statement

☑ Under 14: Transition planning not needed.

☐ 14–15 years old: Statement of transition services needed that focuses on student's course of study.

☐ 16 years old: Outcome statement that describes a direction and plan for the student's post-high school years from the perspective of student, parent, and team members.

VIII. Scheduled Report to Parents/Guardians

John's parents will be informed of progress toward his annual goals via parent/teacher conferences and interim report cards (4 times per year). Parents will be notified of goals that have been met and the rate of progress toward meeting all of the annual goals.

IX. Initiation/Duration Dates

Special education and related services will initiate _September 2007_, through _June 2008_
                                      (MM/YY)   (MM/YY)

IX. Persons Attending Conference

Signature	Position	Date
Mary Smith	Parent	May 12, 2007
Jonathan Smith	Parent	May 12, 2007
Laura Jones	Special Education Teacher	May 12, 2007
Rafael Gonzalez	General Education Teacher	May 12, 2007
Larry Brick	LEA Representative	May 12, 2007
Harrison Washington	School Psychologist	May 12, 2007
John Smith	Student	May 12, 2007

educational, psychological, and/or behavioral evaluations

- Student, if the teachers and parents determine that it is appropriate for the student to attend the IEP meeting. If transition services are being discussed, the student must be invited to participate.
- Other professionals as appropriate. Parents or the school may invite others who can provide information or assistance such as an interpreter, therapists or other personnel who work with the student, or a student advocate such as parents' friends or lawyers.

What should be included in the IEP? According to Section 514(*d*)(1)(A) of IDEA (2004), as of July 1, 2005, the IEP must include the following nine elements:

1. The student's current levels of educational performance and social-emotional functioning, including how the student's disability affects the student's involvement and progress in general education settings
2. Measurable annual goals that address the student's individual learning needs and that, to the extent possible, enable the student to participate in and progress in the general education classroom
3. Special education, related services, and supplementary aids and services to be provided to the student, including program modifications or supports for school personnel that will be provided for the student
4. An explanation of the extent to which the student will not participate in general education classes
5. A statement indicating how the student will participate in state- or districtwide assessments and outlining any modifications and accommodations to be provided during testing. If the student will not participate in state or district assessments, the IEP must include an explanation of why the student will not participate and how the student will be assessed.
6. When services will begin, as well as the frequency, location, and duration of services and modifications
7. How progress toward annual goals will be measured and how the family will be regularly informed of progress toward these goals. IDEA mandates that parents/guardians be updated on their children's progress toward IEP goals and objectives at the same time as report cards are issued for all students.

8. Explanation of transition services at age 16, including measurable postsecondary goals, to help the student prepare for a job or college by taking appropriate classes and/or accessing services outside of school
9. A list and signatures of the committee members present

Writing Effective IEP Goals

A major part of the IEP involves the annual goals. An annual goal usually covers an entire school year. According to IDEA (2004), short-term objectives are also included for students who take alternate assessments aligned to alternate achievement standards. Short-term objectives are smaller steps that help the student reach the annual goal. Completion of related sets of short-term objectives should lead to accomplishment of the annual goals developed by the multidisciplinary team. Figure 1.2 shows an example of an annual goal and short-term objectives. Goals can address academic, social-emotional, or functional needs. The written statements of annual goals must meet

FIGURE 1.2

Sample Goal and Short-Term Objectives in an IEP

Annual Goal:
Lisa McKinney will achieve a math score at the fourth-grade level or above on the Mathematics Achievement Assessment.

Short-Term Objectives
1. Lisa will demonstrate mastery of multiplication and division facts (0–10) by completing weekly one minute timed multiplication and division fact math tests with 90% accuracy.
2. Given 10 three-digit by two-digit multiplication problems, Lisa will solve the problems with 90% accuracy.
3. Given 10 two-digit by one-digit division problems, Lisa will use long division to solve the problems with 90% accuracy.
4. Given 10 one-step word problems, Lisa will identify the operation (addition, subtraction, multiplication, or division) and solve with 90% accuracy.
5. After correctly solving five one-step word problems, Lisa will describe (either orally to the teacher or in writing) how she got her answers with 80% accuracy.
6. Given daily teacher prepared "problem-of-the-day" assignments, Lisa will copy each problem into her math notebook and work cooperatively with a partner to solve it, showing work and the correct solution four out of five times.

certain requirements. According to Gibb and Dyches (2000), annual goals must:

- Be measurable
- Tell what the student can reasonably achieve in a year
- Relate to helping the student be successful in general education settings and/or address other educational needs ensuing from the disability
- Include short-term objectives

For IEPs that also include short-term objectives, Gibb and Dyches (2000) suggest the following:

- Describe the behavior in an observable, measurable way (e.g., "Luis will add two-digit numbers").
- Include the circumstances under which the behavior will take place (e.g., "given manipulatives and peer assistance").
- State the criterion for mastery (e.g., "with 85% accuracy").

Because the IEP-writing process is complicated, several software programs are available to help teachers. These programs are showcased in Tech Tips 1.1.

During the IEP conference, family members and professionals work together to identify appropriate accommodations and modifications that will assist the student in learning skills in class. It is important that teachers be included in the decisions about accommodations and modifications because they are the ones responsible for implementing these in the classroom. For example, if the IEP team decides that a student needs a highlighted textbook in science, someone must be available to do the highlighting, or the accommodation cannot be carried out. Furthermore, effective communication systems must be in place so that all teachers and support personnel who will work with the student are aware of the accommodations and modifications that will be implemented. The processes involved in designing and implementing effective accommodations and modifications are discussed further in this chapter as well as in following chapters.

Family Involvement

The IEP meeting is a way for family members and school personnel to communicate about the education of a student with disabilities. According to IDEA, "parents are considered equal partners with school personnel" in the IEP process. The IEP serves as a safeguard not only for students but also for families and the education team. All reasonable attempts to ensure the participation of family members in the IEP process should be taken:

- Schedule IEP meetings at times that are convenient for families, checking with them in advance to determine a suitable date, time, and location.
- Notify families well in advance of the meeting. Include in the notice the purpose, time, and location of the meeting and the names and positions of the people who will be in attendance. Parents/guardians should be involved in the decision about whether the student will attend.
- If family members choose not to attend even after reasonable efforts have been made to accommodate their schedules, the school should use other methods to involve them, including telephone calls or home visits. The school must document its attempts to involve family members.
- The school must take measures to ensure that families understand IEP proceedings, including providing an interpreter if English is not their first language.
- Family involvement in the development of the IEP should be documented, and parents/guardians should receive a copy of the IEP.

Remember that often too much emphasis is placed on compliance rather than on genuine communication (Harry, Allen, and McLaughlin, 1995). Dettmer, Thurston, and Dyck (1993) suggest that those involved in the IEP process consider the following:

- Educators and parents are working as a team for a common goal—the student's success.
- Pay attention to when and why defensive behavior arises. Put your feelings aside, and help others, including family members, to build positive relationships. If the team is unable to act positively, postpone interactions until the defensiveness can be handled.
- Remember that the family's values are not what is being addressed, only the needs and interests of parents/guardians and their child. Consider what the problem is, not who the person is.
- Do not waste time wishing that the people would be different. Accept them as they are. Respect a family's rights to have their own values and opinions.
- Remember that most families are doing the best that they can under the circumstances of their life. People do not decide to be poor parents/guardians.

TECHTips

1.1 IEP Management Software

Throughout the book you will find Tech Tips features containing helpful information on instructional and assistive technology related to the content of the chapter. This Tech Tip suggests ways to make the writing and updating of the individualized education program (IEP) more time-efficient and easier overall. The most useful IEP software programs allow a teacher to select from skill sequences and write long-term and short-term objectives, freely customizing skills and objectives to meet individual needs.

Often school systems or special education units adopt one particular IEP software application for use by its entire staff. You may find that to be the case in your school district. Some programs are installed in individual computers; others are Web-based. Web-based systems are especially useful because you can access the data from any on-line computer. It is also easier to transfer records as the child moves along in his or her education, from teacher to teacher and school to school.

Following is a list of IEP management software names along with their primary Web addresses:

IEP Writer Supreme II
www.superschoolsoftware.com

IEPMaker Pro
www.iepware.com

SEMSNet
www.eutactics.com

STAR
www.specialsolutions.com/
softwaresolutions.htm

Class IEP Program
www.classplus.com

SEAS
www.computerautomation.com/

PennSTAR
diskbooks.org/pstar.html

SpEd Forms
www.spedforms.com/products.asp

When a functional behavioral assessment is required for an IEP, see these Websites:

www.pbis.org/english/Functional_Assessment
_of_Behavior.htm

http://cecp.air.org/fba/default.asp

A broader tool for helping to make placement decisions, developing IEPs, and developing behavior intervention plans (BIPS) is the *Behavioral Objective Sequence* (BOSR) from Research Press (www.researchpress.com). Designed to help educators assess behavioral problems and deficits in social skills, BOSR is an observation-based, CD-ROM assessment tool for use with learners from elementary grades through adolescence.

Teacher Preparing an IEP

Chapter 5 describes strategies you can use for actively involving families in their child's education, including planning and implementing programs.

Student Involvement and Self-Determination

The self-directed IEP is designed to facilitate students' participation in IEP meetings (Arndt, Konrad, and Test, 2006). By law, students need to attend IEP meetings only if appropriate. In practice, many students with learning and emotional disabilities do not attend these meetings, even when the students are in secondary-level settings. Yet involving students in this decision-making process helps them develop a commitment to learning and a sense of responsibility and control over the decisions made regarding their learning.

Why do many students not attend the conference? In interviewing junior high students with learning disabilities and their parents, two major reasons are evident (Van Reusen and Bos, 1990). First, parents frequently are not aware that students can attend. Second, even when students are invited to attend, they choose not to because they feel that they do not know what to say or do, and they are afraid that the major topic of discussion will be "how bad they are doing."

To alleviate these two concerns, Van Reusen and his colleagues developed a self-advocacy strategy that is designed to inform students and prepare them to participate in educational planning or transition planning conferences (Van Reusen, Bos, Schumaker, and Deshler, 1994). Teachers can teach students this strategy in about five to six hours over a one- to two-week period. We have found that junior high and high school students with learning disabilities who learn this strategy provide more information during IEP conferences than do students who are only told about the IEP conference but not taught the strategy (Bos and Van Reusen, 1986; Van Reusen and Bos, 1990).

What is self-determination? It is the opportunity for individuals to make important decisions about their own lives. For individuals with disabilities, it refers to the opportunity to be actively involved in decisions about their own learning. Self-determination is important because students who engage in self-determination have improved academic performance. How can teachers improve self-determination of students in the IEP process? Teachers can actively engage students in the IEP development and the monitoring of their progress toward meeting IEP goals. This ensures that students are actively involved in the process. The following prompts and activities facilitate student engagement (Arndt, Konrad, and Test, 2006):

1. Ask students to think about their instructional and behavioral goals prior to the IEP meeting. Meet to discuss and brainstorm goals so that students are prepared for the meeting.
2. Ask students at the IEP meeting to indicate the purpose of the meeting.
3. Consider asking students the following questions:
   - What are your goals in school?
   - How successful have you been in meeting them?
   - Are you working hard to meet goals?
   - What are you doing well? What would you like to do better?

4. Prompt students to ask others at the meeting what they think of stated goals, progress, and future goals.
5. Ask students to work with the committee to develop goals for transition, academics, social, and other related areas.
6. Check frequently with students to determine if they have questions or other issues.
7. Ask students to specify the support needed to meet the agreed upon goals.
8. Summarize and close the meeting.

FOCUS Question 4. How do the teacher and student independently and jointly influence instruction, and what are the key features of effective instruction?

Teaching Students with Learning and Behavior Problems

Instruction for students like Servio, Dana, and Tina, described at the beginning of the chapter, needs to be carefully orchestrated to take into account the interactive nature of the teaching–learning process. The *teaching–learning process* is a model of teaching and learning that takes into account the complexity of the learning environment or context, the beliefs and characteristics of the learner and teacher, and the instructional cycle the teacher orchestrates to facilitate learning. It is based on notions of *individual programming*. Although students may be instructed in groups, the teacher studies and plans for each student's needs, realizing that students have both common and unique needs. The teaching–learning process is shown in Figure 1.3. It is the foundation on which the rest of this book rests in that it presents a reflective, problem-solving approach to teaching students with learning and behavior problems. Let us look first at the key players in this process: the learner and the teacher.

The Learner

The learner brings to school beliefs and attitudes about learning and the world in which he or she lives, a variety of skills and knowledge on which to build, and strategies to assist in the learning process. In a way, we are speaking of the *characteristics of the learner.* As teachers, we often seem most concerned about the *skill level* of students. Our assessment process focuses on determining the level at which the student is functioning and what skills the student can and cannot perform. However, *knowledge, attitudes,* and *strategic learning* can also provide us with a wealth of information concerning the learner and may prove to be critical features when determining how to facilitate learning. If a learner has little knowledge of the topic being studied, the teacher can assist the student by providing activities that build background knowledge and help the student to link this new knowledge to current knowledge.

Skills and knowledge not only play an important role in learning, but also influence the learner's attitudes about learning and the world. Randy and Tamara illustrate this point. In fifth grade, Randy was determined to learn how to read, although at the time he was struggling with beginning reading books. He worked all year on his reading, and at the end of the year, he had grown in his reading skill by about one grade level. Still, he carried with him the attitude that reading was important and that he should continue to struggle with a process that for him was quite difficult. Tamara, on the other hand, was a sixth grader who was reading at about the third-grade level. For her, learning to read was a much easier process, yet she finished the year making only marginal gains. Why? She believed that reading simply was not necessary for her life and that her future goal, being a mother, just didn't require her to be a good reader. These students' attitudes influenced their rate of learning.

A student's strategies for learning also affect the teaching–learning process. When you are told to read a chapter in a textbook and study for a test, what strategies do you employ? Do you preview the chapter before reading? Do you ask questions as you read to check your comprehension? Do you underline or take notes? Do you review your notes before the test, rehearsing the important points? These are all strategies that make you a more effective student.

The Teacher

The second player in the teaching–learning process is the teacher. The teacher brings to the learning situation teaching knowledge and skills; beliefs and attitudes about teaching, learning, and the world; and strategies for teaching. One purpose of this chapter is to heighten your awareness of your beliefs and attitudes about teaching.

As you read this section, reflect on your beliefs and attitudes about teaching, learning, and

FIGURE 1.3

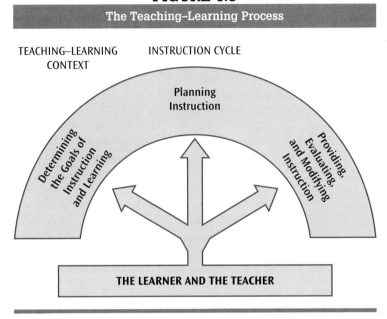

The Teaching–Learning Process

students who experience learning and behavior problems. What is the nature of learning and what is the role of the teacher?

Learning can be perceived as changes in behavior that result in students demonstrating new knowledge and skills. The role of the teacher is that of an educational technician who engineers instruction or arranges the environment so that the probability of learning is increased. This is accomplished by providing students with effective instruction and rewards for learning. An effective teacher conveys knowledge and skills in a systematic, explicit manner. This perception of learning and teaching is probably best reflected in behavior theory and cognitive behavior modification, both of which are discussed in Chapter 2. It is also reflected in instructional strategies and materials that are based on systematic ordering and teaching of skills. Some of the strategies and materials presented in the content chapters reflect this perspective on learning and teaching.

Learning can also be perceived as a dynamic process in which students play an active role, constantly interacting with the environment and people around them. Not only do students' notions, ideas, and skills change in the learning process, but so does the environment in which learning takes place. Thus, learning is not merely the accumulation of knowledge and skills but it is also the active construction and transformation of ideas based on observations and experiences. This perception of learning is represented in information-processing and schema theories, which are presented in Chapter 2. The teacher creates an environment in which students can take risks and develop flexible learning and thinking strategies as they acquire skills and knowledge. You will also find this perspective represented in the content chapters, Chapters 6 through 11.

Just as the characteristics of the learner affect the teaching–learning process, so will the *teacher's beliefs and attitudes.* And because the teaching–learning process is dynamic and interactive, a teacher's beliefs and attitudes will change, depending on the needs of learners. For example, Ms. Kranowski, a special education teacher who works with students who have learning and behavior problems, has 11 students—fourth through sixth grade—in her self-contained class. Each day after lunch, they practice writing. Ms. Kranowski uses a process approach to teaching writing in which students select their own topics and write about them, sometimes taking several weeks to complete a piece. Students usually write multiple drafts, sharing their work with other students and the teacher.

At first, the learners in Ms. Kranowski's class needed to develop a process for writing. They needed to develop purposes for their writing other than to please the teacher or to complete the worksheets. As the students became more confident of their drafts, they needed to learn such skills as how to organize a descriptive paragraph and a story and how to use dialogue and quotation marks. Although Ms. Kranowski continues with this process approach to writing, she now also spends time teaching skills to small groups. She uses systematic skill lessons whereby she models a skill, then has the students practice it in their own writing and in published and teacher-made materials. Whereas the first approach to teaching represents an interactive model of teaching and learning, during skill lessons Ms. Kranowski serves as the conveyor of knowledge by explicitly teaching systematic skill sequences. Ms. Kranowski's instruction shifts to reflect the needs of the students in her class.

How does Ms. Kranowski explain her simultaneous use of these different approaches to the teaching–learning process?

Well, when I first began using a process approach to teaching writing, I found that the students really learned to like writing. For me, that was a big accomplishment, since most of these kids had previously hated writing. But I also found that because these students have so many learning problems and take so much practice to learn a new skill, they just weren't getting enough opportunities to practice intensely a new writing skill when they were first trying to learn it. Consequently, they never learned the skills very well. Now, two days a week, we take about 20 minutes for a skill lesson. I select the skill according to the needs of the students as a group. Right now we are working on dialogue and quotation marks. I introduce the skill and show how I use it in my writing. Then several of the students demonstrate how they can use it in their writing. We use an overhead projector, and they project their writing on the screen. We talk about how to add quotation marks, and they add them right then. For the next several weeks when they are writing their pieces, I encourage them to use dialogue, and we make an effort to compliment each other when the quotation marks are right. If the students need additional practice, I provide them with stories in which they have to add quotation marks to the writing. We also take turns reading stories and books that have lots of dialogue, and the students identify the dialogue and tell where the quotes go. I realize that this is really mixing two philosophies of teaching and learning, but for me it's the best way to get the job done.

The Instructional Cycle

Within the teaching–learning process, the *instructional cycle* helps to shape and sequence teaching and learning (refer to Figure 1.3 again). Ms. Kranowski uses this cycle in her teaching as she sets instructional goals; plans instruction; and provides, evaluates, and modifies instruction based on evaluation. She uses this cycle in a flexible way, taking into account the *characteristics of the learner,* her *teaching beliefs and attitudes,* and the *context* in which the teaching and learning are happening. Sometimes she changes her instructional goals on the basis of input from the students or feedback about rate of learning. Sometimes she modifies her plans and the way in which she instructs to reach her instructional goals more effectively. When Ms. Kranowski added skill lessons to the writing curriculum, she changed her plans, which resulted in changes in instruction. The features of effective instruction should be considered in developing and implementing each part of the instructional cycle.

Features of Effective Instruction

Effective instruction is tantamount to a balancing act. Some teachers appear to be magicians because they seem to effortlessly balance the various features of effective instruction. However, keeping this balance requires a clear understanding of each feature as well as knowledge about how and when to implement them. Following are some of the features of effective instruction that should be present in all teaching:

1. Assessing progress
2. Designing instruction
   - Determining goals of instruction
   - Flexible grouping
   - Adaptations
   - Scaffolding
   - Careful use of instructional time
3. Delivering instruction
   - Quick pacing
   - Sufficient opportunities for student response
   - Error correction

These features will benefit all the students in a classroom, but they are particularly helpful for students with learning and behavior problems.

Assessing Progress

Assessment is an essential component of instruction for students with learning and behavior difficulties. Assessing progress means continually examining data from both formal and informal assessments to determine students' knowledge and skills. It is recommended that a variety of assessment tools be used in assessing students. You can obtain information from reading inventories, standardized tests, observations, and student work samples to assist you in monitoring students' progress and to guide your planning. Monitoring students' learning will help you to determine when students require extra assistance, and you will be able to adjust instruction accordingly. Monitoring of student progress should be frequent (one to three times per week) and ongoing.

Progress Monitoring

According to the instructional cycle (Figure 1.3), instruction is implemented after learning and instructional goals have been established and instruction has been planned. However, instruction is more effective and efficient if, at the same time the instruction is being implemented, it is also being evaluated and—based on the evaluation—modified.

As we evaluate, it is crucial to keep a written record of student progress. The written record provides a means for objectively reflecting on the data to determine whether progress is evident (e.g., Deno, Fuchs, Marston, and Shin, 2001; Fuchs and Deno, 1991; Fuchs and Fuchs, 1996; Green,

2001; Madelaine and Wheldall, 1999). This written record also provides a means for communicating with others regarding student progress. Sharing progress with parents, principals, other teachers, and—most important—the student provides a sense of accomplishment and satisfaction for all involved. Having students monitor their own progress can increase their motivation for learning and give them a sense of pride in learning. Self-monitoring procedures have been used with students who have learning and behavior problems (e.g., Frith and Armstrong, 1986; Hallahan, Lloyd, Kosiewicz, Kauffman, and Graves, 1979; Jackson and Boag, 1981; Swanson, 1985).

Types of Evaluation Measures

Progress Monitoring

Although a teacher or student can use many methods to evaluate progress, generally one or more of three basic types are used: progress graphs and charts, performance records, and process records. Progress graphs are frequently used for measuring daily progress on individual skills or knowledge. Performance records are usually used for measuring progress across time (e.g., grading period, semester, and year). Curriculum-based measurement (Fuchs and Deno, 1991) is an example of a performance record that is closely tied to the curriculum being taught. Process records not only focus on the progress that is evident in the products, but also document progress in the learning process. Portfolios, learning logs, and dialogue journals can be used for this purpose.

Progress Graphs and Charts

Progress graphs and charts are generally used to measure progress on one behavior or skill. Graphs seem particularly well suited for self-monitoring because the results are displayed in such a manner that they are easy to interpret (see Figures 1.4 and 1.5). To be suitable for a progress graph, the behavior, skill, or knowledge must be quantifiable, either by time or by occurrence. For example, Ms. Shiller, the junior high teacher for a self-contained classroom of students with emotional disabilities, uses progress graphs for the following activities:

- Silent reading rate
- Speed in completing math facts
- Percentage of questions answered correctly for the social studies assignment

FIGURE 1.4
Timing Chart Using a Line Graph

Student Name: Hector

Task: x facts, 50 facts

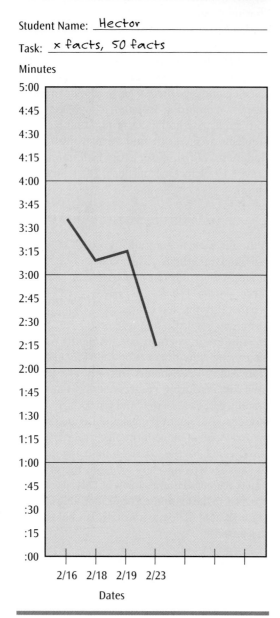

Dates

FIGURE 1.5
Timing Chart Using a Bar Graph

Student Name: Hector

Task: x facts, 50 facts

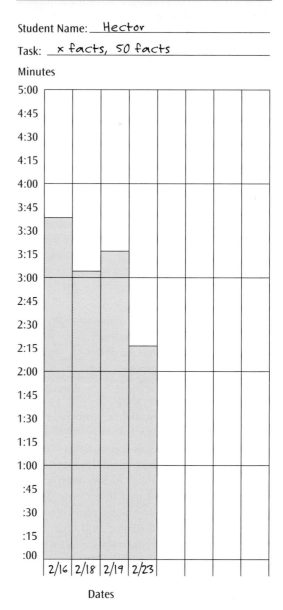

Dates

- Number of times the student disrupted other students during the morning independent learning activity
- Student and teacher rating of written pieces based on interest and readability

With a progress graph, the measurement unit is marked on the vertical axis. For example, *time* for graphing silent reading rate, *speed* for graphing math facts completed, and *percent* for graphing the percentage of social studies questions answered correctly would be marked on the vertical axis. On the horizontal axis, the occurrence unit is marked (e.g., date, teaching session, social studies assignment number). It is relatively easy to plot progress data on either a line graph, as depicted in Figure 1.4, or a bar graph, as shown in Figure 1.5.

Progress charts are usually used in the same manner as progress graphs: to measure progress on one skill or behavior. The difference between a progress chart and a progress graph is that with a chart, the score is reported but is not presented in a relational manner (see Figure 1.6).

Although progress charts are generally more efficient in the use of space, they do not provide the clear visual representation of student performance; therefore, student progress or lack of it is not so readily apparent. Consequently, graphing is generally recommended over charting for student self-monitoring.

Performance Records

Performance records are often used to record student progress across a set of skills or knowledge and for a significant length of time. An IEP is a performance record in that annual goals and short-term objectives are written, and evaluation of the goals and objectives is recorded in the IEP (see Figure 1.1). Many school districts have developed skill and knowledge competencies or objectives that students need to attain at various grade levels. These are often arranged on an individual student performance record so that as a student becomes proficient in a listed competency, it can be noted (see Figure 1.7). Many commercial reading, math, writing, and other content area programs publish performance records so student progress can be recorded. One caution in using such performance records is that although most of them measure proficiency, they do not measure maintenance, generalization, or application. Consequently, a teacher may receive a performance record on a student and find that the student cannot perform some of the skills that are listed as mastered.

In addition to collecting permanent products, the teacher and/or the students may want to keep a progress journal. Usually, this journal accompanies the performance record or progress graphs and charts and provides the student or teacher with space in which each can write comments about progress. Ms. Shiller found that progress journals were particularly helpful for documenting progress regarding students' behavior. She used this method in combination with graphs to evaluate several students' progress. She found that her dated journal entries provided insights into how she might modify the instructional context and the instruction.

Curriculum-based measurement (CBM) is one system of performance records that highlights the close tie between curriculum and student performance, using frequent samplings from curriculum materials to assess students' academic performance (e.g., Fuchs and Deno, 1991; Tindal and Marston, 1990). CBM has been used successfully for students who have learning and behavior problems to improve reading fluency, reading

FIGURE 1.6
Progress Chart for Sight Words

Name: Lisa	3/12	3/14	3/15	3/18
sometimes	+ + +	+ + +	+ + +	+ + +
everyone	− − o	− o +	o + +	+ + +
when	− − −	o o +	− o +	o + +
themselves	− o +	o + +	o + +	+ + +
mystery	− o o	o o +	+ o +	+ o +
hurry	o o +	+ + +	+ + +	+ + +
their	− o −	o + o	+ o +	+ + +
friend	+ o +	+ + +	+ + +	+ + +
mountain	− o o	o o +	+ + o	+ + +
trail	− + −	− o −	− + +	+ o +
route	− − o	o + o	o + o	o o +

+ Correct and automatic
o Correct but not automatic
− Incorrect

FIGURE 1.7
Competency-Based Performance Record

Student: Karen

Competency Area and Skill	Mastery
Early Reading	
Identifies letters of alphabet	10/00
Names letters of alphabet	12/00
Holds book, turns pages one at a time	9/00
Looks first at left page, then at right	9/00
Distinguishes print from pictures	9/00
Scans left to right, top to bottom	9/00
Reads along listening to a familiar book	9/00
Rhymes words	11/00
Identifies words in a familiar book	10/00
Beginning Reading	
Reads simple stories (preprimer/primer)	3/01
Identifies consonant sounds	2/01
Identifies short vowel sounds	2/01
Identifies long vowel sounds	4/01
Identifies simple sight words in isolation	2/01
Recognizes that "s" makes words plural etc.	4/01

comprehension, spelling, and arithmetic computation in both general education and special education classrooms (e.g., Conte and Hintze, 2000; Deno, 1998; Fuchs, Fuchs, Hamlett, and Allinder, 1991; Fuchs, Fuchs, Hamlett, Phillips, and Karns, 1995). For example, reading fluency in a third-grade class can be measured each week by having each student read 100-word passages from the reading curriculum and graphing fluency rates across time. This type of measurement provides ongoing data for making instructional decisions. Mercer and Mercer (1993) suggest that the teacher can assess changes in student performance over time by considering level of performance as affected by instructional change, rate of learning (as reflected by changes in the slope of the trend line) compared to the goal or aim rate, and variability in the consistency of the performance.

Process Records: Portfolios, Learning Logs, and Dialogue Journals

Portfolios, learning logs, and dialogue journals not only highlight task performance across time but also document progress in the learning process. In

FIGURE 1.8

Learning Log Entry for Jose and Dialogue Journal Entry for Tamara on "Harassing Miss Harris" from *The Great Gilly Hopkins* (not corrected for spelling)

Jose

I like this chapter of the book. Even thow it was hard to read, I liked it. I think that is becuase the auther lets you know just how terrible Gilly feels in her new school. I think that letting you know feelings makes writing more interesting.

Tamara

I just read the chapter on Harassing Miss Harris. I liked it a lot because sometimes I feel like Gilly. I feel so mad that I just want to get mad and not do the work. I really like the way the author lets you know just how Gilly feels. I guess that is why I liked it so much. You know Gilly's feelings.

a portfolio, samples are collected across the semester or year (e.g., Paulson, Paulson, and Meyer, 1991; Tierney, Carter, and Desai, 1991). Not only are the final products collected, but so are rough drafts, planning or brainstorming sheets, and practice sheets. For example, a student's writing portfolio might contain five stories and essays as well as the brainstorm sheets, research notes, rough drafts, revisions, and edited drafts associated with each piece of writing. Whereas reading samples (including oral reading and discussions) can be collected on audiotape, written products can be collected for writing and math. Photographs of projects in subject areas as well as the associated written work can be collected for content area work such as social studies and science. The teacher may want to set up a portfolio for each student in the class, have the students help select which pieces to place in the portfolio, and then review the portfolios with the students to identify areas of progress and assist in targeting other areas on which to work.

The teacher can also use learning logs or dialogue journals (e.g., Atwell, 1987; Harste, Shorte, and Burke, 1988) to share thoughts about projects on which the students are working. Learning logs allow the students to reflect on their learning and the processes they have used in learning. In the context of reading and writing, Harste and his colleagues (1988) note, "When learners reflect, they come to value the strategies they are developing through engaging in reading and writing and through observing the demonstrations of other readers and writers around them" (p. 286). Because learning logs focus on communicating ideas or problems the students are having, the focus is not on correct spelling or grammar. The entry of Jose (see Figure 1.8), a fifth-grade student with written expression difficulties, reflects what he is learning as a reader and author after reading the chapter entitled "Harassing Miss Harris" in the book *The Great Gilly Hopkins* (Paterson, 1978).

Dialogue journals also provide a means of evaluation and the opportunity for students to carry on a written conversation with their teacher. Ms. Shiller regularly uses a dialogue journal to communicate with Tamara, a sixth-grade student with conduct disorders, about what Tamara is reading. Tamara's journal entry about the same chapter in *The Great Gilly Hopkins* reflects how she uses the journal to communicate both her learning processes and her sense of identification with Gilly (see Figure 1.8).

One of the major obstacles in evaluating student progress is planning and organizing an evaluation system. Early in the school year, the teacher should do the following:

1. Determine what is to be evaluated.
2. Determine how it is to be evaluated (e.g., progress graphs, charts, permanent product records, portfolios).
3. Determine whether and when student self-monitoring will be used (e.g., learning logs and dialogue journals).
4. Develop the forms needed for evaluation.
5. Set up the system so that it is easy to collect, file, and retrieve progress data.

The teacher should coordinate the evaluation system with the school system and then collect and use the data to make instructional decisions.

When a teacher approaches instruction with a plan of action, it is important to remember that the plan will need to be modified. Effective instruction takes place when the instructional procedures and content match the overall teaching–learning process. Because the teaching–learning process is dynamic and flexible, the instructional process must also be dynamic and flexible.

Designing Instruction

Once objectives have been set and students' skills have been assessed, you can begin designing instruction. Designing instruction refers to using student data to plan for effective instruction (University of Texas Center for Reading and Language Arts, 2000a, 2000b). When teachers systematically adjust instruction in response to assessment information, students' rate of learning increases (Fuchs et al., 1995).

How can teachers design instruction so that the needs of all the students in a classroom are met? Many teachers find it difficult to teach the wide range of skills their students lack. Because these deficits are so many and so varied in level, it seems impossible to cover them all. The steps to designing instruction are as follows:

1. Use the information gathered from various assessment tools. Curriculum-based measurements are particularly suited for this purpose because they are ongoing and closely aligned with curricular goals (University of Texas Center for Reading and Language Arts, 2000a, 2000b).
2. Group students with similar instructional needs.
3. Set specific instructional targets that focus on particular concepts using curricular objectives and annual goals as a guideline.

4. Prepare a schedule, and choose and sequence appropriate activities and tasks.
5. Set up a group management system that is specifically designed to provide instruction in a variety of grouping patterns.
6. Identify students who need additional, more intensive instruction.

Determining Goals of Instruction

Setting goals for instruction helps a teacher know where he or she is going. Several questions a teacher may ask in setting goals for instruction and learning are as follows:

- Have I used the information I have about the characteristics of the learner?
- Have I taken into account my beliefs and attitudes?
- Have I involved the students in setting the goals?
- Have I set goals that are realistic yet challenging to both the learner and myself?
- How do these goals fit within the larger teaching–learning context (e.g., goals of the school, curriculum, long-range career goals of the student)?

When Ms. Kranowski set her instructional goals for writing, she decided that she had two major objectives: to have the students experience successful writing in a variety of forms and to have the students develop writing skills that would help them in school and later in life. She wanted very much to involve the students in setting goals, believing that the students would then have a greater commitment to reaching those goals. She began the year by telling the students about "the way that writing works" in the classroom. She shared the importance of supporting each other, for she wanted students to set a goal of working together. As they worked together, shared their writing, and got to know each other better, Ms. Kranowski sat down with each one of the students and helped them select skills for improvement. By analyzing the students' written products, observing the students as they wrote, talking with the students about their writing, and using her knowledge about the scope and sequence of writing skills, she felt comfortable working with students in selecting goals. In this way, Ms. Kranowski's instructional goals were interwoven with her students' learning goals.

Flexible Grouping

Deciding what type of grouping pattern to use is also part of designing instruction. Because of the large range of abilities, interests, and background knowledge in most classrooms, it is best to use flexible grouping. Flexible grouping, another component of effective instruction, refers to the use of a variety of grouping practices that change depending on the goals and objectives for the lesson. Mixed-ability groups, same-ability groups, whole groups, pairs, and individualized instruction can be used to meet different student and instructional needs. Groups should be flexible, and students should be regrouped on a regular basis.

Adaptations

"The goal of adaptations is to provide all students with the opportunity to participate to the maximum extent possible in typical activities of the classroom" (Deschenes, Ebeling, and Sprague, 1994, p. 13). The use of adaptations enhances learning for all students, not only those with learning and behavior problems (Roller, 2002). Adaptations can be divided into three categories:

1. Instructional design (e.g., accessing resources, collaborating with other professionals, having a plan for adaptations, and integrating technology)
2. Instructional and curricular (e.g., making learning visible and explicit; using clear, simple language; breaking a task or activity into steps; and providing multiple ways of demonstrating learning)
3. Behavioral support (e.g., teaching alternative behaviors, being consistent, providing structure, and being proactive)

The use of adaptations is one way to demonstrate acceptance, respect, and interest for individual learning differences. When determining whether adaptations are necessary, consider the demands of the lesson and the skills of the learner. If there is a mismatch between the abilities required by the lesson and the student's skills, adaptations may be necessary. The adaptations that are used should create a better match between the student's skills and the task. For example, if a lesson on main ideas will require students to write the main idea of a story and a student with a reading disability has difficulty writing letters or words quickly, there may be a mismatch between the demands of the lesson and the student's abilities. If the instruction on main ideas is at the correct level for the student, adaptations to the lesson can allow the student to benefit more from the instruction. One adaptation may be to give the student extra time to write the main idea sentence. A second possible adaptation may be to have the student work with a partner to develop a main idea sentence. In this case, the student with the reading disability can be fully involved in creating the main idea sentence, but the partner can write the sentence.

Scaffolding

An essential element of effective instruction for students with learning and behavior problems is the use of scaffolding (Coyne, Kame'enui, and Simmons, 2001; Torgesen, 2002). *Scaffolding* means adjusting and extending instruction so that the student is challenged and able to develop new skills. The teacher can scaffold instruction to meet the needs of the students by manipulating the task, materials, group size, pace, presentation, and so on. The metaphor of a scaffold captures the idea of an adjustable and temporary support that can be removed when it is no longer needed. Vygotsky (1978) describes learning as occurring in the *zone of proximal development*: "the distance between the actual developmental level as described by independent problem solving and the level of potential development as determined through problem solving under adult guidance or in collaboration with more capable peers" (p. 86). Important to promoting development within the students' zones of proximal development is the teacher's ability to relinquish control of the strategies to the students (Johnson Santamaria, Fletcher, and Bos, 2002). To scaffold instruction effectively, teachers must teach new content in manageable steps, use explicit, systematic instruction for each step, and provide practice and review until students are independent and confident (see Apply the Concept 1.2).

Teaching in manageable steps involves breaking complex tasks into smaller steps to allow students to master each step of the task. Each step should be slightly more difficult than the previous one and should lead up to the full, complex skill the students are to learn. Providing specific instruction for each step of a complex task not only allows student success, but also creates a clear picture of what subskills students have mastered and what still needs further instruction or practice.

In addition to teaching in small segments, each step must be taught by using explicit, systematic instruction. Explicit instruction includes modeling, guided and independent practice, and use of consistent instructional procedures. Systematic instruction refers to sequencing instruction from easier to more difficult and teaching the easier skills to mastery before introducing more complex skills. Many reading strategies require complex

Apply the Concept 1.2

Scaffolding Instruction

Use the following guidelines to scaffold instruction for students with learning and behavior problems:

- Break the task into small steps.
- Teach easier skills first, then more difficult skills.
- Slow the pace of new skill introduction to allow for more practice of a task.

- Use a small group size.
- Make thought process for accomplishing tasks overt by talking to students about what you are thinking when you engage in the task. Have students share what they are thinking when they practice the task.
- Teach strategies for completing complex skills.

- Model all steps involved in completing tasks.
- Provide teacher assistance during the first student attempts at skills.
- Praise the accomplishment of each small step.
- Use concrete materials during initial skill instruction.
- Vary the materials used.

---

thought processes and quick decision making. Students with reading difficulties or disabilities often do not automatically infer the thought processes that good readers use. Therefore, strategies for reading words and comprehending text must be taught in an overt way. Modeling strategies and guiding students through new tasks assist them in acquiring new skills without frustration. As each step is mastered, students become more independent in their ability to perform the skill or strategy.

Scaffolding reading instruction is analogous to the process many parents use when teaching their child to ride a bike. Although most children have seen many models of other adults and children riding bikes, a model of the whole bike-riding process by itself is probably not enough for a child to understand all the tasks that go into riding a bike successfully. Consequently, many parents divide riding a bike into smaller steps and teach each step explicitly, while allowing the child sufficient opportunities to practice and master each step. For example, as a first step, a parent may model and provide guided practice for sitting on the bike. The parent may provide explicit instruction by telling the child where to place feet and hands and how to work the pedals for moving forward and braking. Second, the materials may be scaffolded by attaching training wheels. This allows the child to practice what the parent has taught about sitting and pedal movement without having to deal with balancing the bike too. After the child has mastered riding with training wheels, the next step may be for the parent to take the training wheels off and hold the bike while running with the child as the child rides the bike. This allows the child to begin getting a feel for the balance needed to ride

the bike independently. Parents can also assist the child in the thought processes for bike riding—look straight ahead, don't lean to one side, and so on. This explicit instruction helps the child learn techniques for balancing on the bike. The next step may be to slowly remove the scaffold by holding the bike less and less tightly and finally letting go while the child rides. The final step for the child is to learn to start pedaling the bike and balancing without the parent holding on to get the bike started.

Dividing bike riding into manageable steps not only helps the child learn a new, complex skill with less frustration (or in this case less injury), but also allows faster learning because the steps of the process are made explicit and practiced to mastery. Reading instruction should be similarly broken down into manageable steps, and each step should be taught explicitly and practiced to mastery. Independent reading is the ultimate result, but independent reading requires many, many steps and thought processes. For students with reading difficulties or disabilities to succeed, all of these must be taught explicitly and effectively.

Time Management

One of the most powerful tools for improving learning is *careful use of instructional time.* For teachers working with students who are functioning below grade level, effective time management becomes

Progress Monitoring

an essential part of designing and providing instruction. In addition to avoiding wasting time, teachers must decide how much time to give to each activity or concept. Good and Brophy

(1997) found that as much as 70 percent of the school day is spent doing seatwork. When deciding how to sequence activities and how much time to spend on each, the teacher must think about the learner, the materials, and the task (Kame'enui and Carnine, 1998; Rosenshine, 1997). As was discussed earlier, the features of effective instruction must be balanced carefully, and their implementation must be ongoing. Assessment is a necessary step in designing instruction; similarly, instruction is an integral part of assessment and student monitoring.

Ms. Kranowski watched and listened to the students and analyzed their written products over time. She used curriculum-based measures to gauge skills in capitalization, punctuation, spelling, and grammar. All these evaluative measures led her to the same conclusion: Her students' writing skills were not improving at a rate that she considered adequate. Ms. Kranowski decided to compile all the data using a class summary sheet. She then examined the data to find similar needs among her students. Estrella, Aileen, Luther, Jacqueline, and Sally were having difficulty capitalizing proper nouns. While the rest of the class completed a first draft of a story, Ms. Kranowski spent 10 minutes with these students providing direct and explicit instruction on the rules of capitalization. She had prepared several examples of proper nouns, which she used to monitor her students' understanding by asking them to think aloud about why the nouns were or were not capitalized.

In determining how to modify her instruction, Ms. Kranowski thought about the ideas presented in Figure 1.9. She felt that she had adequately addressed the first four questions. Student motivation, attention, encouragement, and modeling had been good. She did not feel as comfortable about her answers to the next three questions: prior knowledge, manner of presentation, and practice. Sometimes she thought she wasn't focusing enough on one or two writing skills. She tended to present too much and not allow for enough practice and feedback. Ms. Kranowski decided that her modifications had to alleviate the problems with presentation, practice, and feedback. Her solution was the skill lessons that focused on teaching specific writing skills twice a week. For Ms. Kranowski and her students, this solution was successful. Her students began acquiring and maintaining the targeted writing skills. Now she is asking questions and planning for generalization and application.

FIGURE 1.9

Questions for Evaluating the Instructional Process

- *Student motivation.* Am I creating a context in which learning is valued?
- *Student attention.* Am I creating an environment in which students can and are encouraged to attend to the learning task?
- *Encouragement.* Am I creating a setting in which students are encouraged to take risks and be challenged by learning?
- *Modeling.* Are the students given the opportunity to watch, listen, and talk to others so that they can see how the knowledge or skill is learned?
- *Activating prior knowledge.* Am I getting the students to think about what they already know about a skill or topic, and are they given the opportunity to build upon that information in an organized fashion?
- *Rate, amount, and manner of presentation.* Are the new skills and knowledge being presented at a rate and amount that allows the students time to learn, and in a manner that gives them enough information yet does not overload them?

- *Practice.* Are the students given ample opportunity to practice?
- *Feedback.* Are the students given feedback on their work so they know how and what they are learning?
- *Acquisition.* Are the students given the opportunity to learn skills and knowledge until they feel comfortable with them and to the point they do or know something almost automatically?
- *Maintenance.* Are the students given the opportunity to continue to use their skills and knowledge so that they can serve as tools for further learning?
- *Generalization.* Are the students generalizing the skills and knowledge to other tasks, settings, and situations? Are the students, other teachers, or parents seeing the learning?
- *Application.* Are the students given the opportunity to apply their skills and knowledge in new and novel situations, thereby adapting their skills to meet the new learning experiences?

Delivering Instruction

In addition to planning and designing effective instruction for students with reading problems, the delivery of the instruction must be considered. Several features occur during the delivery of effective instruction, including use of a quick pace, providing sufficient opportunities for students to respond, and error correction. Many of these same instructional practices are beneficial for students who are English language learners (ELLs) and also have learning problems. See Apply the Concept 1.3 for a description.

Quick Pacing

Quick pacing refers to instruction and student response that move at a manageable pace for students while taking full advantage of every minute of instruction. A quick pace eliminates unnecessary teacher talk and minimizes the amount of time between activities, allowing for more instructional time. For students who are behind in their reading skills, increased instructional time is essential. To catch up to expected levels of reading, students with reading problems have to make more progress than an average reader. A quick pace also keeps students actively engaged in the lesson. There is very little time for them to do anything other than the lesson at hand. This, in turn, increases their instructional time. When the scaffolding techniques discussed earlier are used effectively, students can be successful, and the lesson can move at a quick pace.

Sufficient Opportunities for Student Response

When delivering a lesson, the teacher's focus should be on allowing students to practice and review the skills and subskills being taught. Therefore, lessons should be filled with opportunities for students to respond and demonstrate what they are learning. There are several ways to increase the number of opportunities to respond within a lesson:

1. *Limit teacher talk.* Limiting the length of teacher talk can be accomplished by breaking up teacher modeling or explanations of concepts with questions for the students. Students can replicate teacher models or respond to related questions as each step of a process or strategy is taught.

2. *Use choral and individual responding.* Choral responding permits all students participating in the lesson to answer at the same time. Its use,

Apply the Concept 1.3

Designing Instruction for English Language Learners (ELLs) with Learning Disabilities

Students with learning disabilities who are English language learners (ELLs) benefit from many of the same instructional practices associated with improved outcomes for monolingual students with learning disabilities. Effective teachers adjust their instruction to consider the language and concept demands of their instruction. These teachers realize that ELLs' understanding of new concepts may be enhanced through instruction that uses routines, embeds redundancy in lessons, and provides explicit discussion of vocabulary and the structure of language required to complete the task, as well as lessons that are organized to teach students to be aware of what they are learning and where they are confused. Haager and colleagues (Graves, Gersten, and Haager, 2004; Haager, Gersten, Baker, and Graves, 2003) conducted an observational study in 20 classrooms that included students who were ELLs, representing more than 10 different language groups. They identified effective teachers based on students' academic outcomes. They then looked at the instructional practices of these teachers. Effective teachers of ELLs:

- Used explicit teaching
- Monitored student progress
- Provided opportunities to practice new learning
- Incorporated strategies that supported student acquisition of English language skills

Which instructional practices should you use in your teaching to ensure that English language learners have opportunities to learn? Providing clear, specific, and easy-to-follow procedures helps students learn new skills and strategies. It is also important to provide opportunities for students to acquire the language associated with these new skills and strategies. Teaching explicitly assists students; this includes identifying and using the structural and visual cues present in words making relationships among concepts, words, or ideas visible and connected.

followed by individual responses of students, increases the number of opportunities a particular student has to practice skills within a lesson.

3. *Use a variety of grouping formats.* Teaching students in small groups or using structuring lessons for pairs of students gives each student more turns to practice new skills. Students who have reading difficulties or disabilities often need extensive practice to learn new concepts. Providing additional practice opportunities within the lesson is an effective way to increase student skill levels.

Error Correction

Error correction refers to the teacher assistance that is provided when students respond incorrectly during a lesson or while reading a passage. Students with reading difficulties or disabilities need teachers to assist them with errors immediately and to provide additional opportunities to practice the skill correctly after assistance (Parker, Hasbrouck, and Denton, 2002). When students read or answer questions incorrectly without immediate error correction, they practice the skill incorrectly. The effects of inaccurate practice can add up quickly, allowing the student to learn the skill incorrectly. This means that the student will have to spend a significant amount of time relearning the skill in the future.

SUMMARYfor Chapter 1

Students with learning and behavior problems are distinguished by difficulties that make it hard for them to succeed in school. Before referring a child for special education services, teachers and professionals must consider a host of factors, including the severity and persistence of the problem, the speed of learning, motivation, the instructional modifications that have been tried, and the quality of the instruction that the child has received.

A relatively new model for prevention and facilitating the identification of students with learning disabilities works by determining their response to increasingly intensive, research-based interventions. Response to intervention (RTI) uses data based on how a student responds to a treatment or intervention in order to make important educational decisions, such as whether students need more intensive intervention or if they should receive special education services. The National Association of State Directors of Special Education (NASDSE) has developed a readily accessible guide to RTI entitled *Response to Intervention: Policy Considerations and Implementation* (NASDSE, 2006).

Each student who is eligible for special education services has an individualized education program (IEP) that is developed by parents/guardians and professionals to establish and document specific information related to that student's individual needs, such as the current levels of performance, measurable goals, and the modifications and services that will be necessary to carry out the education plan in the least restrictive environment (LRE).

To teach students with learning and behavior problems, teachers must attend to the learning environment, as well as the beliefs and characteristics of both the learner and the teacher. Teachers can use the instructional cycle to set goals and plan instruction, provide instruction, and then evaluate learning and make modifications based on student progress.

By continually assessing and analyzing students' knowledge and skills, teachers can adjust instruction to support learning. Methods for assessing progress include progress charts and graphs to measure progress on one behavior or skill such as reading fluency; performance records such as the IEP; progress journals and curriculum-based measurements that record ongoing documentation and evidence of progress; and records of the process of learning such as portfolios, learning logs, and dialogue journals.

Once a teacher has determined what students know and what they should learn, the teacher is ready to design the instruction. Considerations at this phase include how to group students, what adaptations will be needed, how to scaffold instruction, and the careful use of instructional time to meet the needs of various learners. Next, to facilitate learning during the delivery of instruction, teachers must maintain a manageable but quick pace that minimizes teacher talk and time between activities, provide ample opportunities for students to participate and to demonstrate what they are learning, and incorporate error correction procedures.

This chapter introduces students to the kinds of learning and behavior problems that teachers will find in their classrooms, the characteristics they are likely to display, and procedures that are involved in identifying these students for a special education program. The importance of both student and teacher factors in the instructional cycle is considered. Finally, the chapter presents the features of effective instruction and the importance of evaluating progress. The remaining chapters will focus more specifically on how to apply the methods of effective instruction and ongoing assessment to specific skills and content areas to meet the individual needs of students with behavior and learning problems.

FOCUS
Answers

FOCUS Question 1. Who are students with learning and behavior problems? What is inclusion, and what are the defining features of special education?

Answer: In general, *inclusion* refers to full-time placement in a general education classroom with support services provided within the classroom from a special education teacher. A key element of inclusion is collaboration between the special education teacher and the general education teacher. If this collaboration is unsuccessful, the system may not work to benefit the student. Ensuring that students with disabilities receive a special education and that the IEPs of students are fulfilled is still the responsibility of teachers, even when students are fully included.

FOCUS Question 2. What is response to intervention (RTI), and how might it be used to identify students with learning disabilities?

Answer: Response to intervention (RTI) is a preventative approach to academic and behavioral problems that uses a multitiered intervention model and ongoing systematic data collection to determine whether students are making adequate progress in the general education classroom. These data sources may be used to facilitate referral and identification for learning disabilities or behavior problems.

FOCUS Question 3. What is an individualized education program (IEP), and what is the process for developing and updating an IEP?

Answer: The IEP is both a process and a document. The process involves a group of individuals who establish an appropriate specialized educational program. At the IEP meeting, the team determines and documents whether a student is eligible for special education services; which services will be provided, the amount of services, and where they will occur; and the goals and objectives, adaptations needed, and additional considerations as necessary, such as accommodations to statewide assessments.

FOCUS Question 4. How do the teacher and student independently and jointly influence instruction, and what are the key features of effective instruction?

Answer: Both the teacher and the student bring into the classroom knowledge and skills, as well as beliefs about school and about the world. Therefore, learning involves the accumulation of knowledge and skills, but it is also the active construction and transformation of ideas based on observations and experiences. Research has been conducted that supports the use of the following instructional features to meet the needs of students with learning and behavior problems: assessing progress, designing instruction, delivering instruction, and error correction.

THINKand
APPLY

- What are some of the characteristics of students with learning and behavior problems?
- What factors should be considered when the teacher is determining how serious a learning or behavior problem is?
- What is the teaching–learning process, and how can the teacher apply it to students with learning and behavior problems?

- How do the individualized educational program (IEP) and student and teacher involvement relate to the instructional cycle?
- What measures can be used to evaluate student progress?
- What are some of the features of effective instruction?
- What is scaffolding?
- What adaptations can be made to promote learning for students with learning or behavior problems?

APPLYthe
STANDARDS

 Council for Exceptional Children

1. Consider the CEC standards (BD2K3, LD2K3) that ask the teacher to recognize the characteristics of students with learning and behavior problems. Briefly describe the characteristics of students who demonstrate severe behavior and learning problems and how these characteristics may

prompt a teacher to refer a student who demonstrated them for special services.

Standard BD2K3: Social characteristics of individuals with emotional/behavioral disorders.

Standard LD2K3: Psychological, social, and emotional characteristics of individuals with learning disabilities.

2. How do response to intervention (RTI) models differ from traditional methods of identifying and providing services to students with learning disabilities (LD1K2, LD1K3, LD1K4)?

    Standard LD1K2: Philosophies, theories, models, and issues related to individuals with learning disabilities.

    Standard LD1K3: Impact of legislation on the education of individuals with disabilities.

    Standard LD1K4: Laws and policies regarding pre-referral, referral, and placement procedures for individuals who may have learning disabilities.

3. Identify a student with whom you have worked or whom you know personally who exhibits characteristics of a learning disability or emotional/behavioral disorder. Use the instructional cycle to identify an appropriate educational or social goal for this child, to make a plan to implement effective instructional practices, and to evaluate progress toward this goal (BD4K4, LD4S1, LD7K3, LD8S1).

    Standard BD4K4: Prevention and intervention strategies for individuals who are at risk of emotional/behavioral disorders.

    Standard LD4S1: Use of research-supported methods for academic and nonacademic instruction of individuals with learning disabilities.

    Standard LD7K3: Interventions and services for children who may be at risk for learning disabilities.

    Standard LD8S1: Choosing and administering assessment instruments appropriate to the individual with learning disabilities.

WEBSITES as RESOURCES | to Assist in the Teaching–Learning Process

The following Websites provide extensive resources to expand your understanding of the teaching–learning process:

- The National Association of State Directors of Special Education www.nasdse.org
- The International Dyslexia Association www.interdys.org
- Hello Friend: Ennis William Cosby Foundation www.hellofriend.com
- New Circle of Inclusion Home Page http://circleofinclusion.org
- LD OnLine www.ldonline.org
- National Research Center on Learning Disabilities Resource Kit http://nrcld.org/resource_kit
- Center on Instruction www.centeroninstruction.org
- Intervention Central www.interventioncentral.com

PEARSON myeducationlab
Where the Classroom Comes to Life

Case Study Homework Exercise Go to MyEducationLab and select the topic "INCLUSIVE PRAC-TICES," then read the case study "He's Just a Goofy Guy" and complete the activity questions below.

Jake is an energetic first grader with a learning disability. The teachers in this case study consider the least restrictive environment and the issues related to having Jake included in the general education 1st grade classroom.

1. How does the least restrictive environment (LRE) relate to this scenario?
2. Why do you think Betty is resistant to having Jake in her class?
3. Use information from the chapter and the case study to create a list of ideas that could be used to support Jake's transition into the general education classroom.

Module Homework Exercise Go to MyEducationLab and select the topic "LEGAL AND POLICY IS-SUES," then read the module "RTI (Part I): An Overview" and complete the activity questions below.

This module outlines the differences between the IQ-achievement discrepancy model and the Response-to-Intervention (RTI) model. It also offers a brief overview of each tier in the RTI model and explains its benefits.

1. After reading the section on RTI in the chapter and the module, summarize your understanding of RTI.

2. How can RTI benefit students who have not yet been determined to have a disability?

Case Study Homework Exercise Go to MyEducationLab and select the topic "PRE-REFERRALS, PLACEMENT, AND IEP PROCESS," then read the case study "Is This Child Mislabled?" and complete the activity questions below.

Serge Romanich, a third-grade student and refugee from Serbia, spoke limited English. His education had been sporadic at best and the new elementary school he was attending had tested and classified him as having learning disabilities. Now the professionals who work with Serge wonder if he is appropriately placed in special education.

1. Review the IEP steps outlined in the chapter. How could the information provided in the case study be used to qualify Serge for special education services and to develop his IEP?

2. Do you think Serge's skills were adequately assessed? Provide a rationale for your response.

Chapter **2**

Approaches to Learning and Teaching

1. What are operant learning and applied behavioral analysis, and how can teachers manipulate antecedents and implement consequences to increase desirable behaviors or decrease undesirable behaviors?

2. What is cognitive strategy instruction, and how is it used to teach academic, cognitive, or social skills?

3. How can teachers use the features of sociocultural theory to make instruction more effective for the students they teach?

4. How can knowledge of information-processing and schema theories assist teachers in meeting the needs of students with learning and behavior problems?

Meaghan knew by the time she was a senior in college that she wanted to be a special education teacher, but was close to finishing her psychology degree and did not want to change majors. Instead, Meaghan completed her undergraduate degree in psychology and then returned to school to pursue a degree with certification in special education. While going to school part-time she was also working as a teaching assistant in a middle school. Fortunately, much of what she learned in psychology was directly applicable to the work she was doing with a team of special education teachers. She had learned a great deal about various learning theories as a psychology major and in particular how to use applied behavior analysis. Now, much of what she was asked to implement as schoolwide behavior support was based on the applied behavior analysis she had learned as an undergraduate. She understood the importance of looking for positive behaviors and providing reinforcement to students when they exhibited them. She also understood how to be consistent in her application of rules. Furthermore, her coursework that addressed cognitive behavioral theories also assisted her in effectively implementing many of the cognitively based math and reading strategies that she was encouraged to use by the special education teachers. All in all, the longer she worked as a special education teaching assistant the more she appreciated her strong background in learning theory.

This chapter highlights some of the critical features of learning theory that apply to delivering effective instruction and providing classroom management. Models and theories of learning can assist teachers in understanding and explaining how students learn. They also guide teachers in modifying their teaching to promote effective and efficient learning. This chapter surveys four theories or approaches to learning and teaching: operant learning and applied behavior analysis, cognitive strategy instruction, sociocultural theory of learning, and information-processing and schema theories. The chapter is sequenced to move from less to more cognitively oriented models. Many of the general principles that are presented in this chapter will be applied to specific content areas in subsequent chapters. As you read this chapter, we encourage you to think about students who you know are not succeeding in school and who have learning and behavior problems. How are their learning patterns and habits explained by the various approaches to learning described in this chapter? What general teaching principles do the different approaches suggest to help such students? How can technology assist in the teaching–learning process (see Tech Tips 2.1)?

TECHTips

2.1   Guidelines for Computer-Assisted Instruction

Educators have long recognized the value of educational computer software to supplement and enhance classroom instruction. For learners with special needs, computer-assisted instruction can provide the support required to be successful with the general education curriculum.

Sometimes it can be difficult for a teacher to decide how to use computer software. Ascertaining the category a program falls into is often a key to how it could be used. All educational software falls within nine basic categories suggested by Ulman (2005):

- *Reinforced practice.* Allows for practice and strengthening of previously learned skills, often in a game format. Learner responses are reinforced in various ways for both correct and incorrect answers. Most educational software falls into this category.
- *Tutorial.* Teaches new concepts, often with guided steps, multimedia presentation, and much repetition. Tutorials usually have a management system that keeps track of learner progress and achievement.
- *Simulation.* Simulates some aspect of real life. Simulations allow learners to make virtual real-life decisions and observe the likely consequences of those decisions. They also provide opportunities for learners to work cooperatively.
- *Problem solving.* Gives learners the opportunity to solve instructionally relevant problems. Often skills include geometry, spatial relations, sequencing, and cause and effect.

- *Graphics.* Software that learners can use to create and manipulate images—including paint and draw programs; page layout programs; photo editing software; and programs with templates for greeting cards, banners, and other graphics products.
- *Reference.* Electronic versions of more traditional printed reference materials such as a dictionary, thesaurus, and encyclopedia.
- *Teacher utility.* Software programs that make a teacher's job easier, such as grade books, spreadsheets, IEP software, word processing, databases, and presentation software.
- *Student utility.* Software programs that make the learner's job easier, such as simplified spreadsheet and database software, calculators, talking word processors—usually with fewer and less complex features.
- *Authoring.* Tools for creating interactive, multimedia instructional materials—*Classroom Suite* (*IntelliTalk 3, IntelliPics Studio 3*, and *IntelliMathics 3*) from IntelliTools, Inc.

In the upcoming chapters, the Tech Tips features will offer suggestions for educational software to supplement the traditional classroom curriculum, along with activities available on the Internet. As with any materials that they use in their classrooms, teachers should always preview the software, determine what prerequisite skills are necessary for learner success, and decide upon a specific use for the program that fits into the educational plan of the learner.

FOCUS Question

1. **What are operant learning and applied behavioral analysis, and how can teachers manipulate antecedents and implement consequences to increase desirable behaviors or decrease undesirable behaviors?**

Operant Learning and Applied Behavior Analysis

Operant learning theorists, teachers, and other professionals who use applied behavior analysis believe that behavior is learned and therefore can be unlearned, or the student can be taught new behaviors. Operant learning and applied behavior analysis focus on identifying observable behaviors and manipulating the antecedents and consequences of these behaviors to change behavior. Operant learning theory, for the most part, is not concerned with what you think or tell yourself during the learning process.

In this section on operant learning and applied behavior analysis, we will discuss how to manipulate antecedents and use consequences to increase behaviors that we want to see continued and how to eliminate undesirable behaviors. We also discuss how to teach to different levels of learning.

Manipulating Antecedents

An *antecedent* is an environmental event or stimulus that precedes a behavior and influences the probability that it will recur in the future. Antecedents influence desirable and undesirable behaviors. It is relatively easy for teachers to manipulate antecedents to change student behaviors. Teachers can analyze the environment and identify factors that contribute to desirable and undesirable behaviors. By identifying and changing these factors, teachers can increase student learning and minimize or eliminate antecedents that interfere. In observing antecedent behaviors, the teacher usually considers instructional content, classroom schedule, classroom rules, classroom arrangement, and peer interactions.

Instructional Content

Teachers can consider a number of ways to manipulate instructional content to control behavior: make activities more interesting, incorporate student preferences, reduce task difficulties or length, provide choices, and develop functional or age-appropriate activities. By modifying educational programs, teachers can prevent students' inappropriate or undesirable behavior, and establish a pleasant classroom environment. For example, Blair (1996) found that incorporating the students' activity preferences into circle time and academic activities in a preschool/kindergarten essentially eliminated the undesirable behavior of young students who had significant behavior problems.

Classroom Schedule

A well-designed schedule allows everyone to predict what will occur during the school day and assist with the allocation of instructional time. Teachers can involve students in planning the daily schedule. In addition, it is important to avoid revising a schedule because changes can be disruptive, undermining students' ability to predict what will happen during the day.

Classroom Rules

When properly developed and stated, carefully selected rules can contribute to a positive classroom atmosphere. They help students understand what will and will not be accepted in the classroom. It is important to select a limited number of rules to make it easier for students to remember them. Seek the class's input on the rules to increase students' commitment to following them. State rules positively to help students identify the acceptable behavior, and post the rules so students can refer to them.

Room Arrangement

Noises and crowding in a classroom sometimes increase undesirable behaviors. Arranging the furniture in the classroom to partition some areas can reduce noise levels, and limiting the number of students in any area can reduce crowding. See Chapter 4 for additional information on classroom arrangement and sample room arrangements.

Peer Interactions

The classroom and the school are important social communities, and peer interactions play a significant role in determining the levels of desirable and undesirable behaviors. Teachers can facilitate peer interaction by pairing students who have good social skills with students who have more difficulty in prosocial skills, encouraging interaction between students with and without disabilities, and teaching prosocial skills to decrease inappropriate behaviors and to increase appropriate behaviors. For more information on teaching prosocial skills, refer to Chapter 4.

Increasing Desirable Behaviors through Consequences

Progress Monitoring

During the past few weeks, Ms. Glenn has focused on teaching Marjorie, Sheila, and Ali subtraction with regrouping. During this time, she demonstrated many of the principles by using 10 packs of sticks. The students practiced applying the principles on the chalkboard. Ms. Glenn then asked the students to practice the skills independently by completing a math sheet with 12 subtraction-with-regrouping problems. She watched them complete the first problem correctly. She then needed to teach another group, yet she wanted to be sure that these three students would continue to work on their math.

According to operant learning principles, behavior is controlled by the consequences that follow it. Ms. Glenn needed to decide what consequences would follow appropriate math performance to maintain or increase its occurrence. She told Marjorie, Sheila, and Ali, "If you get nine or more problems correct on this math sheet, I will let you have five minutes of free time in the Fun Corner." Free time in the Fun Corner was a big reinforcement for all three students, and they accurately completed the math sheet while she worked with other students.

There are four principles to apply in attempting to maintain or increase behavior:

1. The behavior must already be in the student's repertoire. In the preceding example,

Ms. Glenn's students knew how to perform the math task. To maintain or increase social or academic behaviors, the teacher must first be sure that the student knows how to perform the target behaviors.

2. A consequence must follow the precise behavior to be changed or must be linked to the behavior through language. For example, the teacher may say, "Because you completed all of your math assignments this week, I'll let you select a movie to watch."

3. A reinforcer is whatever follows a behavior and maintains or increases the rate of the behavior.

4. To be most powerful, reinforcement should occur immediately following the behavior.

Thus, to increase the frequency of a behavior, we can manipulate the consequence that follows the behavior. Consequences that increase behavior, such as reinforcement and the Premack principle, will be discussed next.

Reinforcement

Reinforcement is the most significant way to increase desirable behavior. There are two types of reinforcement: positive and negative; both increase responding. How do they differ? The major difference between positive and negative reinforcement is that *positive reinforcement* is the *presentation* of a stimulus to increase responding, whereas *negative reinforcement* is the *removal* of a stimulus to increase responding.

Positive reinforcement increases responding by following the behavior with activities, objects, food, and social rewards that are associated with increasing the behavior. Toys, games, and privileges such as helping the teacher or having extra recess time are examples of positive reinforcers.

The effectiveness of a reinforcement program depends on selecting reinforcers that actually do reinforce. The use of a reinforcer preference checklist is recommended for identifying reinforcers. Activities and events that a student selected when given a wide choice are more likely to be strongly reinforcing. To prevent students from being satiated with the reinforcer, reinforcement menus are recommended. Instead of providing one reinforcer over time, giving a choice of reinforcers increases their value and prevents the satiation.

In using reinforcers, it is important to start with more *intrinsic reinforcers* such as using activities that are reinforcing to the student (e.g., listening to music, coloring) and move to more *tangible reinforcers* such as tokens and food only as necessary. For example, Christian (1983) suggests a seven-level hierarchy of reinforcers, ranging from food and hugs to internal self-reinforcement ("I did a good job"). This hierarchy is presented in Table 2.1.

The practice of negative reinforcement is often misused because the term *negative* is misinterpreted to mean harmful or bad, and therefore, the implication is that positive reinforcement is good and negative reinforcement is bad. Negative reinforcement simply means taking away something unpleasant if a specific behavior is exhibited. If a teacher scowls at a student until the student works, removing the scowl is negative reinforcement. The learning that takes place through negative reinforcement is avoidance learning. A common use in schools is the completion of work assignments to

TABLE 2.1

Practical Reinforcement Hierarchy for Classroom Behavior Modification		
	Consequence Level	**Examples**
Concrete, Tangible ↕ Abstract, Intrinsic	Positive physical contact	Hugs, pats, proximity
	Food	Milk, raisins, crackers, gum
	Toys	Balloon, marbles, kite, clay
	School implements	Eraser, ruler, notepad, pencil
	Privilege	Free time, errands, computers, eat lunch with teacher
	Praise	Positive comments, grades, certificate
	Internal self-reinforcement	"I did well." "My work is complete."

Source: Adapted from B. T. Christian (1983). A practical reinforcement hierarchy for classroom behavior modification. *Psychology in the Schools, 20,* pp. 83–84. Used with permission.

avoid staying after school. Students often use negative reinforcement with adults. An example is a child who throws a temper tantrum until he or she gets what he or she wants.

How we select reinforcers has considerable influence on the extent to which they are effective. Hall and Hall (1998) provide the following suggestions for selecting reinforcers:

- Consider the age and interests of the person whose behavior you want to improve.
- Specify the behavior you want to improve through reinforcement.
- After you consider what you know about the person, his or her age, interests, and what he or she likes and dislikes, identify a list of potential reinforcers.
- Use the behaviors that the person likes to engage in as reinforcers for the behaviors that he or she likes less.
- Interview the person about the things that he or she likes and would be reinforcing to that person.
- Try something new as a reinforcer.
- Consider using reinforcers that occur naturally in the environment.
- Be sure to keep a record of the target behavior and the extent to which it is influenced by the reinforcers.

Secondary Reinforcers

A *secondary reinforcer* is a previously neutral behavior that is paired with a reinforcer and therefore takes on reinforcing properties of its own. Thus, if the teacher always calls a student up to the teacher's desk before rewarding the student, then being called to the teacher's desk becomes a secondary reinforcer.

Sincere praise and attention are the most frequently used secondary reinforcers. Teachers are often quite skillful at using such subtle but effective secondary reinforcers as a hand on the shoulder, a pat on the head, a smile, or a wink. Many teachers position themselves carefully in the room to be near students whose behavior they want to reinforce with their attention. Figure 2.1 provides options for letting students know you value their good work and behavior.

Special education teachers frequently use token reinforcement systems. A *token system* is an economy in which a symbol (e.g., points, chips, or stars) is given if a designated behavior is exhibited. Tokens are symbols in that they usually have little inherent value but can be exchanged for valuable things or privileges. Token systems can be

FIGURE 2.1

33 Ways to Say "Very Good"

1. Exactly right.
2. Keep working on it, you're getting better.
3. You outdid yourself today.
4. Great!
5. You figured that out fast!
6. Good work!
7. You really make my job fun.
8. Fantastic!
9. I knew you could do it!
10. You are doing much better today.
11. Way to go!
12. Perfect!
13. That's the way to do it!
14. You are good.
15. Congratulations!
16. You got that down pat.
17. Wow!
18. That's right!
19. That's much better.
20. Wonderful!
21. That's quite an improvement!
22. That's great!
23. One more time and you will have it.
24. Tremendous!
25. You did it that time.
26. You've got your brain in gear today.
27. Nothing can stop you now.
28. Terrific!
29. Now you have it!
30. You make it look easy.
31. Sensational!
32. Good for you!
33. You are learning fast.

simple, such as receiving stars for completing writing assignments, with each star worth three minutes of extra recess. Figure 2.2 presents several cards that could be used with younger students to record points. Token economies can also be quite complicated as in a level system with rewards and privileges that vary according to the level the student is on. Students are assigned to levels contingent on their behavior. Being raised or lowered to a different level occurs as points are accumulated. Points are awarded and deducted for a full range of behaviors. More complicated token systems are typically used to manage aggressive behaviors displayed by severely disturbed students.

Shaping

If reinforcement maintains or increases the rate of behavior, what does a teacher do if a target behavior is occurring at a very low rate or not at all?

FIGURE 2.2

Forms for Recording Points Earned in a Token Economy

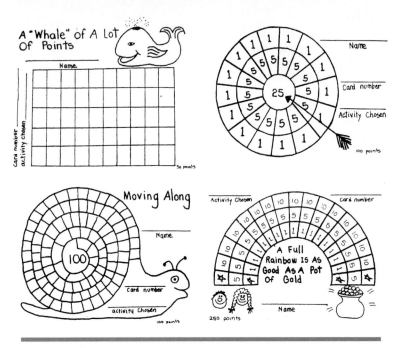

Source: P. Kaplan, J. Kohfeldt, and K. Sturla, *It's Positively Fun: Techniques for Managing the Learning Environment* (Love, 1975), pp. 15–16. Reproduced by permission of Love Publishing Company.

For example, Mr. Kladder's goal is to shape Rhonda's behavior so that she is performing multiplication facts quickly and automatically. During the initial teaching phase, Mr. Kladder rewards Rhonda for computing 3 × 5 by adding five 3s. After Rhonda demonstrates that she can perform this behavior with a high degree of accuracy, Mr. Kladder no longer reinforces her for adding the numbers but reinforces her only for skip counting 5, 10, 15 and then writing the answer. After Rhonda is successfully able to skip count, she is reinforced for computing the answer in her head and writing it down. Now Mr. Kladder begins to give Rhonda timed tests in which she is reinforced only for beating her best time. Mr. Kladder is *shaping* Rhonda's behavior by reinforcing responses that more and more closely approximate the target response.

The Premack Principle

If one activity occurs more frequently than another, the more frequently occurring activity can be used as a reinforcer to increase the rate of the less frequently occurring activity (Premack, 1959). For example, Adam more frequently participates in outdoor play than in writing stories. His teacher can make outdoor play contingent on completing writing assignments. The advantage of the Premack principle is that a teacher can use events that are already occurring in the classroom. For example, a teacher might inventory a student's behaviors and rank them from most liked to least liked: (1) reading, (2) math, (3) spelling. Thus, reading could be contingent on completing spelling. A more appropriate list for most students with learning and behavior problems might include five minutes of free time contingent on completing spelling. Reinforcing activities such as talking quietly with friends or listening to music can be used to increase the rate of less desirable activities such as completing a book report.

Group Contingencies

Group contingencies can be used to increase desirable behavior or decrease undesirable behavior. When *group contingencies* are used, a group of students is either reinforced or loses reinforcement, contingent on the behavior of the entire group or of a target student in the group. For example, a teacher could establish a 20-minute block of free time at the end of the school day. Every time the noise level in the classroom exceeds the teacher's limits, she subtracts 1 minute from the allocated free time. Group contingencies can also be used to change the behavior of a particular student in the class. For instance, Carla is a 12-year-old child who has been mainstreamed into a sixth-grade class. During Carla's first couple of weeks in the class, she continually got into fights with her classmates during recess. The teacher told the class that she would extend their recess by 10 minutes if Carla did not get into any fights during recess. The class included Carla in their group play, and fighting was eliminated. However, there are dangers in group contingencies being dependent on the behavior of an individual. The individual could use his or her position to manipulate the behavior of others in the class. It is also possible that the individual will view himself or herself negatively because of this position.

Axelrod (1998) defines group contingencies by identifying a 10-step program for their use:

1. Select only one behavior to change.
2. Carefully specify in a written format the behavior that you want to change.
3. Determine through careful observation how often and when the behavior occurs.
4. Think about what might be reinforcing to all members of the group.
5. Decide what the group contingency will be for the reinforcer.

6. Be sure to identify a behavior that everyone in the group is capable of performing.
7. Provide the reinforcer contingent on a reasonable improvement in the target behavior.
8. Let each member of the group as well as the group as a whole know when they are behaving appropriately.
9. Monitor the progress of the group and each member of the group.
10. Revise the program as needed.

Contingency Contracting

Contingency contracting is an agreement between two or more persons that specifies their behaviors and consequences. A common example of a contingency contract is the agreement between parent and child regarding an allowance. The child agrees to perform certain behaviors in return for a specified amount of money each week. The contingency contract should specify who is to do what, when, under what conditions, and for what consequences (see Figure 2.3).

Decreasing Undesirable Behaviors through Consequences

Unfortunately, students manifest behaviors that interfere with their learning or the learning of others. Techniques for decreasing these undesirable behaviors include extinction, differential reinforcement, punishment, and time-out.

FIGURE 2.3
Sample Contingency Contract Form

Source: P. Kaplan, J. Kohfeldt, and K. Sturla, *It's Positively Fun: Techniques for Managing the Learning Environment* (Love, 1975), p. 21. Reproduced by permission of Love Publishing Company.

Extinction

Extinction is the removal of reinforcement following a behavior. For example, a teacher wants to extinguish a student's shouting out and determines that telling the student to raise his hand is reinforcing the shouting behavior. To extinguish shouting out, the teacher removes the reinforcer ("Raise your hand") and ignores the student's shouting out.

Extinction can be an effective means of decreasing undesirable behaviors, but it is often slow and can be impractical for many behaviors that occur within the classroom because the reinforcers for the undesirable behavior are often difficult for the teacher to control. For example, the student who continually shouted out in class was being reinforced not only by the classroom teacher's attention ("Raise your hand"), but also by other students who attended to him when he shouted out. A teacher who wants to reduce this behavior through extinction has to eliminate both the teacher's reinforcement and the reinforcement of others in the class. To compound the difficulty, slip-ups by a teacher or students intermittently reinforces the behavior and maintains it for a long time.

Another characteristic of extinction is its effect on the rate at which the target behavior continues to occur. During extinction, the target behavior will increase in rate or intensity before decreasing. Thus, a teacher who is attempting to eliminate tantrums through extinction will observe the tantrums occurring more frequently at first, lasting longer, and perhaps even being louder and more intense than before extinction. If the teacher continues to withhold reinforcement, usually attention, the rate and intensity will decrease, and tantrums can be eliminated. For this reason, it is extremely important to chart behavior when using extinction. To document behavior change, take *baseline data*, a record of the frequency and/or duration of the behavior before implementing the intervention, and continue to record data after intervention is implemented.

Although extinction can be an effective way to decrease undesirable behaviors, it requires patience and the ability to control all of the reinforcers. Ignoring, the most frequently applied form of extinction in the classroom, is an important skill for teachers to learn. Three points to remember about using ignoring as a means of decreasing undesirable behavior are:

1. Ignoring can be effective when the behavior is being reinforced by teachers or students who are willing to discontinue reinforcement.

2. If a teacher attempts to eliminate a behavior through ignoring, the behavior must be ignored *every* time it occurs.
3. Ignoring will not be effective if the behavior is being maintained by other reinforcers, such as the attention of selected classmates.

Differential Reinforcement

Differential reinforcement involves strengthening one set of responses in contrast to another. It is an effective procedure for developing a positive behavior management plan. The main advantage of differential reinforcement is that positive consequences are used to reduce the strength of undesirable behavior. Therefore, negative side effects associated with punishment procedures are avoided. There are several forms of differential reinforcement.

Differential Reinforcement of Incompatible Behaviors and Alternative Behaviors. Differential reinforcement of incompatible behaviors (DRI) involves identifying desirable behaviors. Reinforcement is then provided contingent on the occurrence of the targeted desirable behaviors. For example, while ignoring the out-of-seat behavior of a student, the teacher targets and reinforces the desirable behavior that is incompatible with it— in this case, in-seat behavior. Therefore, when Scott is sitting in his seat, the teacher is quick to catch his appropriate behavior and reinforce it. In addition, the teacher would intermittently reinforce Scott for being in his seat. In the case of DRI, the new response (incompatible behavior) is selected because it represents an incompatible alternative to the disruptive behavior; the two behaviors cannot occur simultaneously. In differential reinforcement of alternative behaviors (DRA), the alternative behavior is not necessarily incompatible with the disruptive response, and it can occur at the same time as the undesirable behavior. The goal of using DRA is to strengthen a range of appropriate behaviors that teachers will attend to naturally, thereby reinforcing a broad repertoire of appropriate behavior. Careful planning should ensure that the reinforcers selected are sufficiently attractive and delivered with sufficient frequency to motivate student performance while removing reinforcers from the undesirable behavior. Both DRI and DRA ensure that new behaviors are fostered at the same time that undesirable behaviors are being diminished.

Differential Reinforcement of Other Behaviors. Differential reinforcement of other behaviors (DRO) is the reinforcement of the nonoccurrence of target behavior during a specified time period; reinforcers are delivered following time intervals in which the target behavior does not occur. For example, a teacher may allow a student free time at the end of each 30-minute scheduled period in which no target behavior occurred. Therefore, determining the length of the reinforcement period before using DRO is important. Brief intervals of 1 to 10 minutes may be selected for high-rate behaviors, and intervals up to a day in length may be used for low-rate behaviors. DRO may be most effective when used in combination with a DRA procedure by reinforcing occurrences of alternative behavior as well as providing reinforcement for intervals in which a zero rate of the target behavior occurred. When combined with other methods, DRO can be a powerful procedure (Sulzer-Azaroff and Mayer, 1991).

Regardless of the type of differential reinforcement, reinforcing behavior through consequences requires the teacher to do four things:

1. Identify the behavior that is to change (interfering behavior).
2. Identify the incompatible behavior.
3. Stop reinforcing the interfering behavior.
4. Reinforce the desirable behavior.

Response Cost

Response cost is a procedure in which a specified amount of a reinforcer is removed after each occurrence of the target behavior. Withdrawal of favored activities and tangible reinforcers are common response strategies for young children. For example, a student is not allowed to play during free-choice session because of his or her aggression toward peers. One of the most common response cost strategies for older students is the use of withdrawal of tokens following a target behavior. For example, say students earn 20 points for completing each assignment throughout the day. Points can be exchanged for primary reinforcers at the end of the day. Engaging in a target behavior may result in a response cost of 30 points. Response cost is an aversive procedure that should be used carefully because it can inadvertently be used to punish positive behaviors. For example, teachers may be tempted to ask students to complete additional work if assignments are completed before the end of the class period, but additional work requirements may act as a response cost for early assignment completion.

Thibadeau (1998) provides the following suggestions for implementing response cost:

- Provide a description of the behavior that will allow the teacher to determine whether there has been any change.
- Collect measures of students' current levels of performance.
- Identify which reinforcers will be removed following the target undesirable behavior.
- Specify the amount of the reinforcer that will be removed.
- Be sure that students understand the rules of response cost.
- Implement the response cost strategy with limited attention.
- When appropriate behaviors occur, be certain to reinforce them.
- Monitor the progress of the response cost on an ongoing basis.
- Make appropriate changes to the response cost system when needed.

Punishment

Punishment, the opposite of reinforcement, is following a behavior with a consequence that decreases the strength of the behavior or reduces the likelihood that the behavior will continue to occur. Unfortunately, punishment does not ensure that desired behavior will occur. For example, a student who is punished for talking in class might stop talking but may not attend to his or her studies for the remainder of the day.

There are many significant arguments against the use of punishment:

- Punishment is ineffective in the long run.
- Punishment often causes undesirable emotional side effects, such as fear, aggression, and resentment.
- Punishment provides little information about what to do, teaching the individual only what not to do.
- The person who administers the punishment is often associated with it and also becomes aversive.
- Punishment frequently does not generalize across settings, thus it needs to be readministered.
- Fear of punishment often leads to escape behavior.

If there are so many arguments against using punishment, why is it so often chosen as a means for changing behavior? There are many explanations, including lack of familiarity with the consequences of punishment and the inability to effectively use a more positive approach. Also, punishment is often reinforcing to the punisher, reducing the occurrence of the undesirable behavior, therefore reinforcing its use.

Punishment should be used only to stop behaviors that are harmful to the child or others. In this case, students should be told ahead of time what the consequences (punishment) for exhibiting undesirable behavior will be. When undesirable behavior occurs, punishment should be delivered quickly and as soon as the inappropriate behavior is initiated. Punishment should be applied consistently every time the designated behavior occurs. Teachers who choose to use punishment should identify several other behaviors they would like to see maintained and give extensive reinforcement for occurrence of these behaviors.

Time-Out

Time-out involves removing a student from the opportunity to receive any reinforcement. For example, to impose a time-out, the teacher asks a student to sit in the hall during the remainder of a lesson, or asks a young child to leave a group, or asks a student to sit in a quiet chair until he or she is ready to join the group.

Unfortunately, time-out is frequently used inappropriately. The underlying principle behind the successful use of time-out is that the environment the student is leaving must be reinforcing and the time-out environment must be without reinforcement. This is not as easy to achieve as one might think. For example, when Elizabeth was talking and interfering with others during a science lesson, her teacher thought she would decrease Elizabeth's behavior by sending her to time-out, which was a chair in the back of the room away from the group. The teacher became discouraged when Elizabeth's inappropriate behavior during science class increased in subsequent lessons rather than decreased. A likely explanation is that Elizabeth did not enjoy science class and found sitting in a chair in the back of the room looking at books reinforcing. The efficacy of time-out is strongly influenced by environmental factors. If the environment the student is leaving is unrewarding, then time-out is not an effective means of changing the student's behavior.

Teachers who use secluded time-out areas or contingent restraint (holding the student down plus withdrawal, exclusion, and seclusion) should be aware of the legal implications of such intervention and should obtain the necessary authorization from school administrators and from parents or guardians. A position paper on the use of behavior

Apply the Concept 2.1

Guidelines for Implementing Time-Out

Time-out, like punishment, should be used as a last resort. Teachers should discuss this intervention with school administrators and parents before implementing it, and follow these steps:

1. Students should be told in advance which behaviors will result in time-out.
2. The amount of time students will be in time-out should be specified ahead of time.
3. The amount of time students are in time-out should be brief (one to five minutes).
4. Students should be told once to go to time-out. If a student does not comply, the teacher should unemotionally place the student in time-out.
5. Time-out must occur every time an undesirable behavior occurs.
6. Contingencies should be set in advance for students who fail to comply with time-out rules.

7. The time-out area should be constantly monitored.
8. When time-out is over, a student should return to the group.
9. Positive behaviors that occur after time-out should be reinforced.

Hall and Hall (1998) provide helpful suggestions about how to handle the potential problems that occur with time-out. Several of their suggestions follow:

- Add time to a student's time-out for refusing to go to time-out or displaying other inappropriate behaviors such as screaming, yelling, and kicking.
- Students should be required to clean up any mess made during time-out before they return from time-out.
- Be sure to have a backup consequence if a student refuses to go to time-out and the amount of

time added reaches 30 minutes (usually considered the maximum amount).

- Do not argue with individuals when they either try to talk you out of time-out or indicate that you have no right to put them in time-out. Ignore their comments.
- If the inappropriate behavior involves two students and it is not possible to determine the source of the problem, do not argue; put both students in time-out.
- If the student displays the behavior in a place where it is not possible to use time-out, indicate that time-out will be provided when you return to the classroom.
- Be sure to chart the effects of time-out so that you can determine whether it is working.

---

reduction strategies has been issued by the Council for Children with Behavior Disorders (CCBD, 2002). Recommended procedures for successfully implementing time-out are listed in Apply the Concept 2.1.

Peer Confrontation System

Peers as well as a teacher can serve as behavior controllers for students. In a procedure referred to as the *peer confrontation system* (Salend, Jantzen, and Giek, 1992), the teacher and students identify behavior problems in the group. The teacher helps the students in the group to respond to students who are having a behavioral problem in the following way: The teacher says, "Mark seems to be having some difficulty. Who can tell Mark what the problem is?" Selecting a student from the group, the teacher says, "Can you tell Mark what the problem is?" The teacher follows with "What does Mark need to do to solve the problem?" In the Salend et al. (1992) study, 12 of the 13 students indicated that they would like to continue using the peer confrontation system.

Stages of Learning

One way in which the principles of operant learning can be applied is through *stages of learning*. The stages of learning (see Figure 2.4) are the levels a student moves through in acquiring proficiency in learning (Rivera and Smith, 1997). For example, the first stage of learning, *entry*, is the level of performance the student is currently exhibiting. During the second stage, *acquisition*, the components of the target behavior are sequenced into teachable elements. Each teachable element is taught to mastery through a high rate of reinforcement, shaping, and consistent use of cues. When the behavior is occurring at a high level of accuracy, the focus of the learning is on *proficiency*. During this stage, the teacher's goal is to increase the student's accuracy and fluency in performing the behavior. At the next stage, *maintenance*, the goal is for the behavior to be maintained at the target level of accuracy and proficiency with intermittent reinforcement and a reduction in teacher assistance and cues. The next stage is *generalization*,

FIGURE 2.4

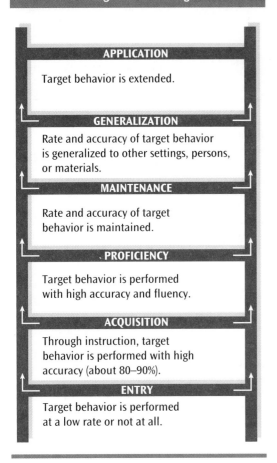

Stages of Learning

APPLICATION

Target behavior is extended.

GENERALIZATION

Rate and accuracy of target behavior is generalized to other settings, persons, or materials.

MAINTENANCE

Rate and accuracy of target behavior is maintained.

PROFICIENCY

Target behavior is performed with high accuracy and fluency.

ACQUISITION

Through instruction, target behavior is performed with high accuracy (about 80–90%).

ENTRY

Target behavior is performed at a low rate or not at all.

Source: Adapted from D. P. Rivera and D. D. Smith, *Teaching Students with Learning and Behavior Problems,* 3rd ed. (Boston: Allyn & Bacon, 1997).

in which the target behavior transfers across settings, persons, and materials. Stokes and Baer (1977) suggest that generalization may be a separate skill that needs to be taught. Apply the Concept 2.2 provides further information on how to teach for generalization. At the final stage, *application,* the learner is required to extend and utilize the learning in new situations. Application is a difficult skill for special learners, and the teacher's role is to demonstrate and provide a range of opportunities for applying the newly acquired skill.

In summary, teachers can apply the principles of operant learning and applied behavior analysis for both instructional and classroom management purposes. In a classroom based on operant learning theory, the teacher has behavioral objectives that specify the behaviors students need to perform to be judged successful. If a target response does not occur naturally, the teacher must develop a method of shaping the behavior.

The behaviors are sequenced from simple to more difficult. A full range of reinforcers is used, such as verbal praise, smiles from the teacher, gold stars, tokens, free time, and other specialized reinforcers that are effective with students. Students are dealt with individually, and target behaviors reflect the students' needs. Behaviors are initially taught through continuous reinforcement; after these behaviors have been acquired, they are maintained through intermittent reinforcement. Teachers reduce inappropriate behavior by ignoring it and reinforcing incompatible behavior. Teachers avoid the use of punishment. Behaviors are discussed in observable terms, and learning is measured by the acquisition of new behaviors.

FOCUS Question 2. What is cognitive strategy instruction, and how is it used to teach academic, cognitive, or social skills?

Cognitive Strategy Instruction

Cognitive strategy instruction (CSI) integrates ideas from operant, social, and cognitive learning theories and assumes that cognitive behavior (thinking processes), like observable behaviors, can be changed. This model of instruction is based on the earlier work from social learning theory (Bandura, 1977, 1986) and cognitive behavior modification (Harris, 1985; Meichenbaum, 1977). CSI incorporates principles of operant learning but adds principles from social learning theory and cognitive theory that are important to consider when the goal of instruction is to change the way the student thinks. In numerous research studies, cognitive strategy instruction has been shown to be particularly effective with students who have learning and behavior problems (Swanson, 1999a, 1999b).

Let's look at how Ms. Neal helps Marlow and his classmates better understand the science concepts and textbook she is using in her seventh-grade resource science class. Even though Marlow, a student with behavior disorders, can identify most of the words in the text, he remembers only a few details from what he reads. Ms. Neal wants to teach Marlow and his classmates how to understand and remember the major points of a reading. She decides that if she wants to teach the students this cognitive behavior, she will have to give them a consistent set of steps to

Apply the Concept 2.2

Generalization Strategies

Change Reinforcement

Description/Methods	Examples
Vary amount, power, and type of reinforcers.	
• Fade amount of reinforcement.	• Reduce frequency of reinforcement from completion of each assignment to completion of day's assignment.
• Decrease power of reinforcer from tangible reinforcers to verbal praise.	• Limit use of stars/stickers and add more specific statements, e.g., "Hey, you did a really good job in your math book today."
• Increase power of reinforcer when changing to mainstreamed setting.	• Give points in regular classroom although not needed in resource room.
• Use same reinforcers in different settings.	• Encourage all teachers working with a student to use the same reinforcement program.

Change Cues

Description/Methods	Examples
Vary instructions systematically.	
• Use alternate/parallel directions.	• Use variations of cue, e.g., "Find the . . ."; "Give me the . . ."; "Point to the. . . ."
• Change directions.	• Change length and vocabulary of directions to better represent the directions given in the regular classroom, e.g., "Open your book to page 42 and do the problems in set A."
	• Move from real objects to miniature objects.
• Use photograph.	• Use actual photograph of object or situation.
• Use picture to represent object.	• Move from object/photograph to picture of object or situation.
• Use line drawing or symbol representation.	• Use drawings from workbooks to represent objects or situations.
• Use varying print forms.	• Vary lower- and uppercase letters; vary print by using manuscript, boldface, primary type.
	• Move from manuscript to cursive.

Change Materials

Description/Methods	Examples
Vary materials within task.	
• Change medium.	• Use unlined paper, lined paper; change size of lines; change color of paper.
	• Use various writing instruments such as markers, pencil, pen, computer.
• Change media.	• Use materials such as films, microcomputers, filmstrips to present skills/concepts.
	• Provide opportunity for student to phase into mainstream.

Apply the Concept 2.2

Generalization Strategies   (continued)

Change Response Set	
Description/Methods	**Examples**
Vary mode of responding.	
• Change how student is to respond.	• Ask student to write answers rather than always responding orally.
	• Teach student to respond to a variety of question types such as multiple choice, true-false, short answer.
• Change time allowed for responding.	• Decrease time allowed to complete math facts.

Change Some Dimension(s) of the Stimulus	
Description/Methods	**Examples**
Vary the stimulus systematically.	
• Use single stimulus and change size, color, and shape.	• Teach colors by changing the size, shape, and shade of "orange" objects.
• Add to number of distractors.	• Teach sight words by increasing number of words from which student is to choose.
• Use concrete (real) object.	• Introduce rhyming words by using real objects.
• Use toy or miniature representation.	• Use miniature objects when real objects are impractical.

Change Setting(s)	
Description/Methods	**Examples**
Vary instructional work space.	
• Move from structured to less structured work arrangements.	• Move one-to-one teaching to different areas within classroom.
	• Provide opportunity for independent work.
	• Move from one-to-one instruction to small group format.
	• Provide opportunity for student to interact in large group.

Change Teachers	
Description/Methods	**Examples**
Vary instructors.	
• Assign student to work with different teacher.	• Select tasks so that student has opportunities to work with instructional aide, peer tutor, volunteer, regular classroom teacher, and parents.

Source: S. Vaughn, C. S. Bos, and K. A. Lund (1986, Spring). But they can do it in my room. *Teaching Exceptional Children*, pp. 177–178. Copyright © 1986 by the Council for Exceptional Children. Reprinted with permission.

use in completing the process, in much the same way that we use a consistent set of steps to tie shoes. She also knows that for the students to learn what to do, they need to observe someone else. But how can she do this?

First, she selects the steps she wants to teach Marlow and the other students to use when they read their science text. Next, she and the students discuss the strategies the students currently use and their effectiveness. They also discuss the importance of improving their skills and the payoff for improvement. Ms. Neal then tells the students about the steps she uses when she reads. To model these steps, she reads and explains what she is thinking (i.e., cognitive modeling). Then she talks them through the steps as the students try them. Finally, Ms. Neal gives the students lots of opportunities to practice the steps when reading their textbooks, encouraging them at first to say the steps aloud as they work through them. She provides feedback on how they are doing, and she teaches them how to evaluate their own performance.

Using these systematic techniques, Ms. Neal finds that in several weeks, Marlow and his classmates are improving in their ability to remember the important information from their science text. In addition, they are beginning not to rely so much on the strategy she taught them. It is almost as if they are using it automatically, without having to consciously remember to use it. Ms. Neal believes that she has taught her students a good strategy for thinking about what they are reading and that she has changed their cognitive behavior (thinking processes). To promote generalization, Ms. Neal discusses with Marlow and his classmates other opportunities they have for using the strategy. The students begin keeping a list on the board of occasions when the strategy can be used. They also begin using the strategy on these different occasions (e.g., reading the newspaper during current events, reading other textbooks, editing each others' stories and essays) and discussing how useful the strategy was in helping them.

Ms. Neal used *cognitive strategy instruction* (CSI). This approach includes an analysis of the task as well as an analysis of the thinking processes that are involved in performing the task. It also includes teaching routines that utilize cognitive modeling, self-instructional techniques, and evaluation of performance (Meichenbaum, 1977; Meichenbaum and Biemiller, 1998).

Several key learning and teaching principles are associated with CSI. One principle is *cognitive modeling*, or "thinking aloud." When Ms. Neal explained what she was thinking as she read, she was using cognitive modeling. Another principle is *guided instruction.* Ms. Neal used this principle when she guided the students through the reading task by telling them the steps in the process as they read. *Self-instruction* is another principle. When learners use language to guide their own performance, they are using self-instruction. For instance, if you talk or think through the steps in solving a complex algebra problem while completing it, you are using self-instruction.

Self-evaluation and self-regulation are two additional principles. *Self-evaluation* refers to making judgments about the quality or quantity of performance. Ms. Neal had Marlow and his classmates judge the quality of their performance by having them pause at the end of each section of the science text and comment on how they were doing. *Self-regulation* refers to the learners' monitoring of their own thinking strategies through language mediation. Self-regulation also occurs when learners correct or use fix-up strategies when they detect a problem. For example, Ms. Neal taught Marlow and his classmates to say to themselves what the main idea was when they finished reading each paragraph or section of the text. If the students could not give the main idea, then she demonstrated and encouraged them to use a fix-up strategy. In this case, she showed them how to go back and reread the first sentence in the paragraph to see whether that helped them to remember the main idea. If this did not work, she demonstrated how to review the paragraph quickly.

Common Features of Cognitive Strategy Instruction

Cognitive strategy instruction has been used to develop a range of academic and social skills. Common features of CSI include strategy steps, modeling, self-regulation, verbalization, and reflective thinking.

Strategy Steps

A series of steps are usually identified for the student to work through when solving a problem or completing a task. These steps are based on an analysis of the cognitive and observable behaviors needed to complete the task. Before Ms. Neal began teaching, she determined the steps in the reading strategy she wanted to teach Marlow and his classmates.

Graham and Harris and their colleagues have developed a series of writing strategies to assist students in writing stories and other pieces (Graham and Harris, 1993; Graham, MacArthur, and Schwartz, 1995; MacArthur, Graham, Schwartz, and Schafer, 1995; MacArthur,

Schwartz, Graham, Molloy, and Harris, 1996). Each strategy has steps that the students learn to assist them with specific aspects of writing. For example, to help students write a story, Graham and Harris (1989) used the following strategy steps:

1. Look at the picture (picture prompts were used).
2. Let your mind be free.
3. Write down the story part reminder. The questions for the story part reminder were as follows:
   - Who is the main character? Who else is in the story?
   - When does the story take place?
   - Where does the story take place?
   - What does the main character want to do?
   - What happens when he or she tries to do it?
   - How does the story end?
   - How does the main character feel?
4. Write down the story part ideas for each part.
5. Write your own story; use good parts and make sense.

Modeling

In CSI, modeling is used as a primary means of instruction. Research in social learning theory as well as in cognitive behavior modification supports the notion that modeling is an effective teaching technique. With CSI, students are asked not only to watch observable behaviors as the instructor performs a task, but also to listen to the instructor's self-talk. In this way, the instructor models both observable behaviors and the unobservable thinking processes associated with those behaviors. Being able to model thinking processes is an important component for teaching such cognitive skills as verbal math problem solving, finding the main idea in a paragraph, editing written work, and solving social problems. In most instances, the person who does the modeling is the teacher or a peer, but video and puppets have also been used. For example, Vaughn, Ridley, and Bullock (1984) used puppets to teach interpersonal social skills to young, aggressive children. The puppets were used to model appropriate social behaviors and strategies for solving interpersonal problems.

Self-Regulation

Self-regulation refers to learners' monitoring their thinking and actions through language mediation. Students first use language to mediate their actions by overtly engaging in self-instruction and self-monitoring. Later, this language mediation becomes covert.

Using self-regulation, students act as their own teachers. Students are expected to take active roles in the learning process and to be responsible for their own learning (Harris and Pressley, 1991; Meichenbaum and Biemiller, 1998; Pressley, Brown, El-Dinary, and Afflerbauch, 1995). Although they work under the guidance of a teacher, students are expected to monitor their learning, change or modify strategies when difficulties arise, evaluate their performance, and in some cases provide self-reinforcement.

Peers have also been used to promote student regulation and monitoring. For example, MacArthur, Graham, and their colleagues (MacArthur, Schwartz, and Graham, 1991) used a peer editing strategy to increase students' knowledge about writing and revising and to increase their revising activity. The strategy was taught by special education teachers who were using a process approach to teaching writing (see Chapter 9) and word processing. The steps in the peer editing strategy were as follows:

1. *Listen* and read along as the author reads.
2. *Tell* what it was about and what you like best.
3. *Read* and make *Notes. Clear?* Is there anything that is difficult to understand? *Details?* Where could more information be added?
4. *Discuss* your suggestions with the author.
5. The author makes revisions on the computer (MacArthur et al., 1995, p. 234).

The procedure involved peers in that steps 1 and 2 were completed by pairs of students. Then the two students worked independently to complete step 3 and then met together again for step 4 to discuss each paper and the suggested revisions. For step 5, each author worked at the computer to make the revisions that he or she thought were useful.

Classwide peer tutoring (Greenwood, Delquadri, and Hall, 1989) and peer-assisted learning (Fuchs, Fuchs, Mathes, and Simmons, 1997) have been used extensively with students who are

Progress Monitoring

low achievers and/or have learning and behavior problems. These procedures allow students to support each other in practicing skills such as solving math word problems or building reading fluency and to assist each other in setting goals and monitoring progress.

Aggression replacement theory (Glick and Goldstein, 1987) uses self-regulation as an effective procedure for assisting students with behavior disorders, particularly those with conduct disorders, in controlling their anger. Through aggression replacement theory, students learn to identify anger-producing situations (triggers) and to recognize their responses to these situations (cues). They then learn a number of techniques that are designed to assist them in relaxing and cognitively handling the situation. In reviewing self-regulation outcome research conducted with students with behavior disorders, Nelson, Smith, Young, and Dodd (1991) found numerous studies indicating that self-regulation procedures can be extremely effective in enhancing both the academic and social behavior of these students.

Verbalization

Verbalization is typically a component of self-instruction and self-monitoring in which overt verbalization is faded to covert verbalization. Many CSI programs rely on a talk-aloud or think-aloud technique (e.g., Deshler, Ellis, and Lenz, 1996; Harris and Graham, 1992; Montague and Bos, 1990; Swanson, 1999b). After listening to the teacher think aloud as he or she performs the targeted processes and task, students are encouraged to talk aloud as they initially learn the strategy. For example, Ramon might say the following as he completes a two-digit subtraction problem without regrouping: "Start at the ones place, and take the bottom number away from the top. Write the answer in the ones place. Now go to the tens place. Do the same thing." Usually, these overt verbalizations occur only during the initial stages of learning. As the strategy becomes more automatic, students are encouraged to think to themselves instead of thinking aloud.

In addition to verbalization about the learning processes, students are also encouraged to make self-statements about their performance. For example, "That part is done. Now go to the next part" or "I'm getting much faster at this" or "I need to think about all my choices before I decide."

Meichenbaum (1977) has suggested three ways to encourage students to use self-talk:

1. Teachers can model self-talk and self-statements as they perform tasks.
2. Teachers can begin with tasks at which students are already somewhat proficient. Later, as students become comfortable with self-talk, teachers can switch to targeted tasks.
3. Students can develop and use cue cards to help them remember the steps they are to talk through.

As an example of the third method, Camp, Blom, Herbert, and Van Doorninck (1977) used the pictures in Figure 2.5 as cue cards when teaching

FIGURE 2.5

Cue Cards Used for Teaching Self-Control

1

What am I supposed to do?

2

What are some plans?

3

How is my plan working?

4

How did I do?

Source: B. W. Camp and M. A. S. Bash, *Think Aloud: Increasing Social and Cognitive Skills—A Problem-Solving Program for Children. Classroom Program: Grades 1–2* (Champaign, IL: Research Press, 1985), pp. 48–51. Reprinted with permission.

self-control to 12 aggressive second-grade boys. The cue cards were used as reminders to self-verbalize as the boys applied these questions first to cognitive and then to interpersonal tasks.

Reflective Thinking

Reflective thinking requires students to take the time to think about what they are doing. Teaching students who have learning and behavior problems to stop and think is an important skill to include in instruction (Troia, Graham, and Harris, 1999). Many of these students are impulsive and seem to act without thinking (Kauffman, 2001; Lerner, 2000). These students have limited and ineffective strategies for approaching academic tasks and social situations. They approach these tasks and situations in a disorganized, haphazard way, often without thinking about the consequence of their actions. In using cognitive strategy instruction, teachers assist students in using reflective thinking.

Let's look at how Wong, Wong, Perry, and Sawatsky (1986) encouraged reflective thinking when they taught seventh-grade students to use self-questioning when summarizing social studies texts. After teaching the students how to identify the main idea of paragraphs and how to summarize paragraphs, Wong and colleagues taught the students a summarization strategy. The questions the students asked themselves were as follows:

1. In this paragraph, is there anything I don't understand?
2. In this paragraph, what's the most important sentence (main-idea sentence)? Let me underline it.
3. Let me summarize the paragraph. To summarize, I rewrite the main-idea sentence and add important details.
4. Now, does my summary statement link up with the subheading?
5. When I have written summary statements for a whole subsection:
   a. Let me review my summary statements for the whole subsection. (A subsection is one with several paragraphs under the same subheading.)
   b. Do my summary statements link up with one another?
6. At the end of an assigned reading section: Can I see all the themes here? If yes, let me predict the teacher's test question on this section. If no, let me go back to step 4. (Wong et al., 1986, pp. 25–26)

The specificity of the questions and cues can be important for success. For example, Graham, MacArthur, et al. (1995) found that cueing students to revise to add specific information resulted in better-quality writing than did telling students to revise to make the paper better.

Teaching Implications of Cognitive Strategy Instruction

Cognitive strategy instruction is designed to actively involve students in learning. Meichenbaum and Biemiller (1998) characterize the student as a collaborator in learning. General guidelines to consider for doing so include the following:

- Analyze the target behavior carefully.
- Determine what strategies students are already using if any.
- Select strategy steps that are as similar as possible to the strategy steps that good problem solvers use.

- Work with students to develop strategy steps.
- Teach prerequisite skills.
- Teach strategy steps, using modeling, self-instruction, and self-regulation.
- Give explicit feedback.
- Teach strategy generalization.
- Help students maintain the strategy.

Guidelines for monitoring the effects of instruction (see Table 2.2) have also been suggested (Rooney and Hallahan, 1985). A growing body of research supports the use of cognitive strategy instruction for developing academic, cognitive, and social skills (Deshler et al., 1996; Graham, Harris, and Troia, 1998; Pressley, 1998), and recent reviews of research on students with learning and behavior problems consistently identify CSI as one of the most effective instructional strategies for teachers to use (Gersten, Schiller, and Vaughn, 2000; Mastropieri and Scruggs, 1997; Swanson, 1999b). As discussed in Apply the Concept 2.3, researchers at the Center for Research on Learning at the University of Kansas have developed a learning strategy curriculum as well as a number of task-specific strategies (e.g., finding the main idea, word identification, test taking, listening and taking notes) that employ cognitive strategy instruction.

> **FOCUS Question** 3. How can teachers use the features of sociocultural theory to make instruction more effective for the students they teach?

Sociocultural Theory of Cognitive Development

The sociocultural theory of cognitive development (Vygotsky, 1978) is similar to cognitive strategy instruction in that it highlights the importance of modeling and the use of language to facilitate learning. However, the theory assumes that learning is socially constructed and, as a social activity, is highly influenced by the funds of knowledge that learners bring to situations. Knowledge is meaningfully constructed in these social activities (Englert, Rozendal, and Mariage, 1994; Moll, 1990; Rogoff, 1990; Tharp, Estrada, Dolton, and Yamauchi, 1999; Trent, Artiles, and Englert, 1998).

Vygotsky was a Russian psychologist who conducted his most important work during the 1920s

TABLE 2.2

Guidelines for Assessing Strategy Effectiveness

Behavior	Assessment Questions
Independence	Can the student use the strategy without cues or assistance?
	Can the student match the appropriate strategy to the task?
	Can the student adapt the strategy if necessary?
Spontaneity	Does the student use the strategy without being asked or cued to do so?
Flexibility	Can the student modify and adapt the strategy to match the situation?
	Can the student pick out the cues in the situation to guide strategy use?
Generalization	Does the student use the strategy appropriately in various situations?
	Does the student use the strategy across different class periods?
Maintenance	Does the student continue to use the strategy after direct instruction of the strategy has stopped?
Reflective thinking	Does the student stop and think about how to do a task before beginning?
	Does the student think about which strategy to use before beginning?
	Does the student reflect on his or her performance and adjust the strategy if necessary?
Improved performance	Has the student's performance on the targeted task improved?
	Is there improvement in the student's productivity, accuracy, and task completion?
Improved self-concept	Does the student see himself or herself as an active participant in learning?
	Does the student see himself or herself in control of his or her learning?
	Does the student regard himself or herself as more successful?

Progress Monitoring

Source: Adapted from K. J. Rooney and D. P. Hallahan (1985). Future direction for cognitive behavior modification research: The quest for cognitive change. *Remedial and Special Education 6* (2), p. 49. Copyright © 1985 by PRO-ED. Used with permission.

and 1930s. However, owing to the popularity of behavioral theories, Piaget's theory, and information-processing theory, his work did not attract great interest until the last 20 years (Byrnes, 1996). Cognitive Strategy Instruction in Writing (Englert, Raphael, Anderson, Anthony, and Stevens, 1991), the Early Literacy Project (Englert, Garmon, Mariage, Rozendal, Tarrant, and Urba, 1995), and the Optimal Learning Environment (Ruiz, Garcia, and Figueroa, 1996) are highlighted in this section because they focus directly on students with disabilities or young children who are at risk for developing academic learning disabilities. Although Vygotsky's theory of cognitive development embraces many concepts, we have highlighted three that are particularly important in using this theory for teaching students who may have special needs or are from diverse cultural and linguistic backgrounds: the use of resources, the social nature of learning (including the use of interactive dialogue), and the use of scaffolded instruction.

Use of Resources

A key concept of sociocultural theory is that teachers need to consider and use the resources that the students bring to learning (Diaz, Moll, and Mehan, 1986). These include such things as culture and language as well as background knowledge the **Diversity** learners can apply to the problem that is being solved or the knowledge being constructed. For example, in assisting Mexican American elementary students to develop literacy, Moll and Greenberg (1990) began by first exploring the *funds of knowledge* that could be gained from the community and the Hispanic and Southwestern cultures. They also examined how literacy functioned as a part of community and home life. They brought this information into the schools and used it to build a literacy program. In this way, students who are culturally diverse were given the opportunity to use sources of knowledge that are not often highlighted in traditional school curriculums.

Social Nature of Learning and Interactive Dialogue

Another important aspect of sociocultural theory is the premise that learning occurs during social interactions; that is, learning is a social event in

Apply the Concept 2.3

Application of Cognitive Strategy Instruction: The Learning Strategies Curriculum

Can the principles of cognitive strategy instruction be applied to academic tasks in such a way that adolescents with learning disabilities can be successful in performing the skills required for secondary school settings? This is one of the major questions that was addressed by Don Deshler, Jean Schumaker, and their colleagues at the Kansas University Center for Research on Learning. The Strategies Intervention Model (Deshler et al., 1996; Lenz, Ellis, and Scanlon, 1996) is a comprehensive example of an intervention model based on cognitive strategy instruction.

The goal of the Strategies Intervention Model is "to teach learning disabled adolescents strategies that will facilitate their acquisition, organization, storage, and retrieval of information, thus allowing them to cope with the demands of social interaction" (Alley and Deshler, 1979, p. 8). Learning strategies are techniques, principles, or routines that enable students to learn to solve problems and complete tasks independently. Strategies include how a person thinks and acts when planning, executing, and evaluating performance on a task and its outcomes. Broadly, a learning strategy (1) includes a general approach to solving a set of problems, (2) promotes goal-directed behavior, (3) teaches selection of appropriate procedures, (4) guides implementation of a procedure, (5) shows how to monitor progress, (6) can be controlled, and (7) provides and focuses on cues to take action. Learning strategies instruction focuses on how to learn and how to use what has been learned.

The Learning Strategies Curriculum contains three strands of academic, task-specific strategies. The Acquisition Strand enables students to gain information from written materials and includes such strategies as the Word Identification Strategy

(Lenz, Schumaker, Deshler, and Beals, 1993) and the Paraphrasing Strategy (Schumaker, Denton, and Deshler, 1993). The Storage Strand consists of strategies to assist students in organizing, storing, and retrieving information. The First-Letter Mnemonic Strategy (Nagel, Schumaker, and Deshler, 1994) is an example of a storage strategy. The Expression and Demonstration of Competence Strand contains strategies that enable students to complete assignments, express themselves, and take tests. The Test Taking Strategy (Hughes, Schumaker, Deshler, and Mercer, 1993), the Paragraph Writing Strategy (Lyerla, Schumaker, and Deshler, 1994), and the Error Monitoring Strategy (Schumaker, Nolan, and Deshler, 1994) are examples of strategies that assist students in taking tests, writing cohesive paragraphs, and editing written work.

Each strategy uses a teaching model that incorporates principles of cognitive behavior modification. The stages in the model are:

Acquisition

Stage 1   Pretest and Make Commitments

Obtain measure(s) of current functioning.

Make students aware of inefficient/ineffective habits.

Obtain students' commitments to learn.

Stage 2   Describe the Strategy

Ensure that students have rationales for strategy use.

Ensure that students know characteristics of situations for when and where to use the strategy.

Describe results that can be expected.

Supervise goal setting.

Describe and explain the strategy steps.

Present the remembering system.

Stage 3   Model the Strategy

Demonstrate the entire strategy "thinking aloud."

Involve the students in a demonstration.

Stage 4   Elaboration and Verbal Rehearsal

Assist students to verbally rehearse the strategy steps and what each step means.

Require students to memorize the strategy.

Stage 5   Controlled Practice and Feedback

Supervise practice in "easy" materials.

Provide positive and corrective feedback.

Move from guided practice to independent practice.

Require mastery.

Stage 6   Advanced Practice and Feedback

Supervise practice in materials from regular coursework.

Provide positive and corrective feedback.

Fade prompts and cues for strategy use and evaluation.

Move from guided practice to independent practice.

Require mastery.

Stage 7   Confirm Acquisition and Make Generalization Commitments

Obtain measure(s) of progress.

(continued)

Apply the Concept 2.3

Application of Cognitive Strategy Instruction   (continued)

Make students aware of progress.

Obtain the students' commitment to generalize.

Phase I   Orientation

Discuss situations, settings, and materials in which the strategy can be used.

Evaluate appropriateness of strategy in various settings and materials.

Identify helpful aspects of the strategy and adjustments.

Make students aware of cues for using the strategy.

Phase II Activation

Program the students' use of the strategy in a variety of situations.

Provide feedback.

Reinforce progress and success.

Phase III Adaptation

Identify cognitive processes.

Discuss how the strategy can be modified to meet differing demands.

Assist students in applying the modifications.

Phase IV Maintenance

Set goals related to long-term use.

Conduct periodic reviews.

Identify self-reinforcers and self-rewards.

Provide feedback.

This teaching model relies heavily on modeling, self-instruction, and self-regulation. It encourages students to assume an active and collaborative role in learning. The teaching model has been validated with a number of specific learning strategies (e.g., Bulgren, Hock, Schumaker, and Deshler, 1995; Hughes and Schumaker, 1991; Lenz and Hughes, 1990; Schumaker, Deshler, Alley, Warner, and Denton, 1982). Several of the specific learning strategies are presented in the chapters on reading, written expression, and content areas learning and study skills.

Note: The University of Kansas Center for Research on Learning requires that persons planning to implement the Learning Strategies Model obtain training available through the Center for Research on Learning, 1122 West Campus Road, University of Kansas, Lawrence, KA 66045, 785-864-4780, www.ku-crl.org.

which language plays an important role. Applying this concept, teachers and students discuss what they are learning and how they are going about learning. Such interactive dialogue or instructional conversations between teachers and learners provide language models and tools for guiding one's inner talk about learning (Bos and Reyes, 1996; Englert et al., 1995; Mariage, 2000; Moll, 1990). Initially, a more expert person may model the self-talk and vocabulary related to the cognitive processes. However, this gives way to a collaborative or interactive dialogue in which the learner assumes increasing responsibility. This type of teaching allows for the instruction of cognitive and metacognitive strategies within purposeful, meaningful discussions and provides a means for selecting, organizing, and relating the content matter being discussed. For example, in reciprocal teaching (Palincsar and Brown, 1984), a technique designed to foster comprehension and comprehension monitoring, the teacher and students take turns leading dialogues that focus on their knowledge of the information they are studying and on the processes they are using for understanding and for checking their understanding (see Chapter 8).

Englert et al. (1991) designed an instructional writing program based on a sociocultural theory of cognitive development entitled Cognitive Strategy Instruction in Writing. The program (see Chapter 9) fosters interactive dialogue among teachers and students about the writing process and problem-solving strategies (Englert et al., 1991; Englert, Raphael, and Anderson 1992). In the program, think sheets help the teacher and students see, discuss, and think about the questions, text structures, and problem-solving strategies that good writers use in planning, drafting, editing, redrafting, and final drafting a written piece. In this program, interactive dialogue plays a critical role in successful instruction. For example, Ms. Patrick and her students discuss editing a piece of her writing on how to plant bulbs. Ms. Patrick's goal is to demonstrate for students and guide them in how to reread their texts for meaning and organization from the perspective of a reader and how to examine their texts to see whether they accomplished their goals related to purpose and text structure (Englert, 1992). During this discussion, Ms. Patrick has put her writing on the overhead for students to comment on and edit.

T: Okay, as I read my paper . . . listen for several things. Listen for key words. [Check for] clear steps. Ask, "Does it make sense?" *She reads her own story.*

Jim: It has five key words. First, next, then, then, next. *Two students reread her paper aloud and another goes up spontaneously and circles her key words on the overhead. As students begin to circle her key words, she responds.*

T: Go ahead and circle my key words, that's just a draft; I'll be revising it anyway. *The students count five key words.*

T: Was it clear?

Ss: Yes.

T: What was clear about it?

Meg: You said how to put it in the pot and then how to do it . . . [You said] put soil in the pot.

T: Was anything unclear?

Roy: If you added more, it would be awful. I think it was perfect.

T: Even my writing isn't perfect all the time. I never said what kind of soil to put in there. And when I said pour half the soil in the pot, I wonder if they know to buy a bag.

Roy: You need to say, "First, you need to tell them to go to the store and buy [a] pot, soil, and bulbs." They are going to say, "Where do I get this stuff?"

T: You are right . . . I think I'll write in the margins. (Englert, 1992, p. 159)

In this example, Ms. Patrick guides the students to demonstrate and discuss editing strategies. She creates a context in which students come to understand and negotiate the meaning of text and to share their understandings about writing. She thinks aloud, for example, "I think I'll write [notes] in the margin," and then demonstrates on her draft.

Scaffolded Instruction

Another concept of the sociocultural theory of learning relates to the role of the teacher or the expert, who encourages learners by providing temporary and adjustable support as they develop new skills, strategies, and knowledge. The instruction is referred to as *scaffolded instruction* (Tharp and Gallimore, 1988) or *mediated learning* (Kozulin and Presseisen, 1995). The concepts of scaffolding and zones of proximal development were explained in Chapter 1. In the example of Ms. Patrick, Englert (1992) discusses how she relinquishes control of her paper by letting the students circle the key words. Englert (1992) notes that this "transfer of

control was prompted in earlier lessons when Ms. Patrick instructed her students to take the overhead marker and mark up texts" (p. 163). In fact, research on this program in fourth- and fifth-grade general education classrooms with students who have learning disabilities demonstrated that the teachers who were most effective in promoting student gains and transfer in writing modeled the writing strategies, involved students in classroom dialogues about writing, promoted strategy flexibility, and relinquished control of strategies to students (Anderson, Raphael, Englert, and Stevens, 1991).

In the Early Literacy Project (ELP; Englert et al., 1994, 1995; Mariage, 2000), the literacy curriculum is structured to include activities that provide opportunities for scaffolded instruction and the teaching of strategies. Figure 2.6 provides an overview of these activities and the principles of the ELP. Important to promoting development within the students' zones of proximal development is the teacher's ability to relinquish control of the strategies to the students. To illustrate the dialogue that works within the zone of proximal development, Englert and her colleagues (1994) describe the interactive dialogues among the teacher and students, including students at risk for learning disabilities, during the morning news. In this lesson, the class constructed a morning news about the information from their thematic unit on dinosaurs. Each student took responsibility for drafting a section of the story, and the class reread and edited the various sections. The teacher (T) used this opportunity to model specific writing and editing conventions and to highlight the multiple sources and classroom resources that can be employed in the literacy process.

T: Lauren, you wrote this part. Would you like to read this part for us?

L: I need help with it.

T: Okay, would you like to pick somebody to read that part with you? *Lauren picks a student to help her pronounce unfamiliar words that she can't read.*

T: Does anyone have a question for Lauren about cavemen? *When no one responds, the teacher proceeds to illustrate.* Where did you get the idea about cavemen? When we were talking [referring to the time when she interacted with Lauren as she wrote this section], did we say that dinosaurs ate cavemen?

Ss: No.

T: You know what Lauren told me as she wrote that idea? She got it out of her imagination. But this paper is kind of

FIGURE 2.6

Early Literacy Project Principles and Activities

Silent Reading

Description
Independent reading
Reading to an adult
Listening to new story at listening center

Purpose: Work on fluency for author's chair; provide experience with varied genres

Thematic Unit

Description
Teacher and students brainstorm, organize, write drafts, read texts, or interview people to get additional information about a topic or theme from multiple sources, and use reading/writing strategies flexibly to develop and communicate their knowledge
Oral/written literacy connections are made apparent

Purpose: Model learning processes; introduce literacy language, genre, and strategies; model reading/writing processes and connections; provide interrelated and meaningful contexts for acquisition and application of literacy knowledge; conventionalize and develop shared knowledge about the purpose, meaning, and self-regulation of literacy acts

Morning News

Description
Students dictate personal experience stories
Teacher acts as a scribe in recording ideas and as a coach in modeling, guiding, and prompting literacy strategies

Purpose: To model and conventionalize writing and self-monitoring strategies; demonstrate writing conventions; provide additional reading and comprehension experiences; promote sense of community; empower students; provide meaningful and purposeful contexts for literacy strategies

Principles of the Early Literacy Project

Using Meaningful Activities

Teaching to Self-Regulate

Apprenticing Students in the Dialogue

Empowering Students in the Community

Literature/Story Response

Description
Students read stories and respond to them in various ways (e.g., sequence stories, illustrate story events, map story events or story structure, summarize story, etc.)
Students make a personal affective response to stories
Students work with partners or small groups to develop response

Purpose: To promote students' application of literacy strategies; present varied genres to students; promote students' ownership of the discourse about texts; futher students' enjoyment of texts; make text structure visible to students

Choral and Partner Reading/ Writing

Description
Choral reading & taped story reading
Partner reading & partner writing

Purpose: To provide opportunities for students to fluently read & write connected texts; to provide opportunities for students to use literacy language and knowledge; to develop reading/ writing vocabulary and enjoyment of reading

Sharing Chair

Description
Read books, poems, personal writing
Students control discourse and support each other
Students ask questions, answer questions, and act as informants to peers and teacher

Purpose: Promote reading/writing connection; empower students as members of the community; allow students to make public their literacy knowledge and performance; develop shared knowledge

Author's Center

Description
Process Writing Approach (students plan, organize, draft, edit texts)
Students partner-write and work collaboratively to brainstorm ideas, gather additional information, write drafts, share drafts, receive questions, and write final draft
Students use literacy strategies modeled in thematic units

Purpose: To develop a sense of community; develop shared knowledge; provide opportunities for students to rehearse literacy strategies; empower students in appropriating and transforming strategies

Source: C. S. Englert, M. S. Roszendal, and M. Mariage (1994). Fostering the search for understanding: A teacher's strategies for leading cognitive development in "zones of proximal development." *Learning Disability Quarterly. 17.* p. 191. Reprinted by permission of Council for Learning Disabilities.

telling true things, so I'm wondering if we should leave it in or take it out. SH, what do you think?

SH: There was cavemen. See that book right there? *Points to book.*

T: You can get it. I guess what I'm wondering is if we know for sure if they [dinosaurs] ate cavemen?

A: I saw it in a movie.

T: Was it a real movie or a cartoon movie? *Ss talks about movie and book.* All right. Do we want to leave that [part] in?

Ss: U-huh!

B: Didn't dinosaurs eat other dinosaurs?

T: We have to ask Meg because she was the writer. *B turns to Meg and repeats comment. Meg agrees that B's idea can go in the story. Then the teacher turns to ask the opinion of the class.* What do you think about adding that idea [to our story], boys and girls? "Dinosaurs eat other dinosaurs." I want you to put your thumb up if you think that is a good idea. *Surveys students.* So I'm going to put a caret here and I'm going to say, "Dinosaurs eat other dinosaurs." (Englert et al., 1994, p. 198)

This dialogue illustrates how the teacher uses interactive discussion and classroom resources to support scaffolded instruction. "For example, she encouraged Lauren to select a peer to help her read and asked students to turn to each other in making final decisions about the text. She also acknowledged the contribution of movies, texts, and students' own imagination in the writing process" (Englert et al., 1994, p. 198).

Instructional Implications

There are many instructional implications from the sociocultural theory of cognitive development. The following four are particularly important:

1. Instruction is designed to facilitate scaffolding and cooperative knowledge sharing among students and teachers within a context of mutual respect and critical acceptance of others' knowledge and experiences.
2. Learning and teaching should be meaningful, socially embedded activities.
3. Instruction should provide opportunities for mediated learning, with the teacher or expert guiding instruction within the students' zones of proximal development.
4. Students' sociocultural backgrounds should provide the basis on which learning is built.

This last implication of sociocultural theory is highlighted in the Optimal Learning Environment (Ruiz et al., 1996), which was designed for students with disabilities who are from culturally and linguistically diverse backgrounds. Apply the Concept 2.4 describes this curriculum. Research suggests that this approach is particularly effective for culturally and linguistically diverse students with disabilities (e.g., Ruiz and Figueroa, 1995; Ruiz, Figueroa, and Boothroyd, 1995). Many of the strategies that are incorporated into the curriculum are further described in Chapters 7 through 9.

> **FOCUS Question** 4. **How can knowledge of information-processing and schema theories assist teachers in meeting the needs of students with learning and behavior problems?**

Information-Processing and Schema Theories

Whereas the operant learning and applied behavior analysis model focuses on observable behaviors and views learning as establishing functional relationships between a student's behavior and the stimuli in the environment, cognitive learning theory focuses on what happens in the mind, and views learning as changing the learner's cognitive structure.

Information-processing theory, one of the dominant cognitive theories since the 1970s, attempts to describe how sensory input is perceived, transformed, reduced, elaborated, stored, retrieved, and used (Anderson, 1990; Atkinson and Shiffrin, 1968; Ericsson and Kintsch, 1995; Massaro and Cowan, 1993). Figure 2.7 presents a simplified model of the sequence of stages in which information is processed or learned. Although the figure implies that each activity is relatively separate, these processes are highly interactive, with a gradual increase in the amount of integrative and higher-order processing used. This processing system is controlled by *executive functioning* or *metacognition*, which assists the learner in coordinating, monitoring, and determining which strategies the learner should employ for effective learning (Brown, 1980).

We can use this model to explain how Greg, a high school student with learning disabilities, might acquire and remember some new information about the concept of *seizure* as it relates to the

Apply the Concept 2.4

Optimal Learning Environment (OLÉ)

Diversity

Optimal Learning Environment (OLÉ) is built on Vygotsky's sociocultural theory (1978) and Krashen's (1985) concept of comprehensible input. These suggest that for culturally and linguistically diverse students who may or may not have learning disabilities, it is important for teachers to provide learning environments that enable students to go beyond their actual levels of performance with deliberate scaffolding. Krashen's concept of comprehensible input (e.g., visual cues, regalia, total physical response) acts as a scaffold for students who are learning English as a second language.

OLÉ is a flexible literature-based language arts curriculum that integrates reading, listening, speaking, and writing. Using OLÉ, teachers create a learning situation that is highly contextualized under optimal conditions where teachers employ instructional strategies to promote 12 optimal learning conditions:

- Student choice
- Student-centered
- Whole-part-whole approach
- Active student participation
- Focus on ideas before mechanics
- Authentic purposes for learning
- Immersion in language and print
- Teacher and peer demonstrations
- Approximation
- Immediate response
- Classrooms as learning communities
- High expectations

The optimal conditions are based on the work of Cambourne and Turnbill (1987) and classroom research with culturally and linguistically diverse students in general or special educational environments (e.g., Echevarria and McDonough, 1996; Ruiz and Figueroa, 1995).

The OLÉ curriculum integrates the teaching and use of nine strategies or activities that are often used in process-oriented, learning strategies classrooms. They include the following:

- Interactive journals
- ABC wall chart or class book
- Shared reading with decodable and predictable texts
- Pocket chart reading with decodable and predictable texts
- Patterned writing with decodable and predictable texts
- DEAR (Drop Everything and Read) time
- Literature study
- Creating texts from wordless books
- Writers' workshop

Each strategy is a collaborative undertaking. Students as well as teachers write in *interactive journals* on a daily basis, independently choosing topics. These journals function as a record of their writing development, and students receive a response each time they write. Emergent readers and writers "read" their entries to the teacher so that the teacher can respond with a vocalized written question for students to answer.

ABC wall charts or *class books* ensure that students are learning the letters that will enable them to decode with better accuracy. Creating their own pictures and key words for each letter gives students the opportunity to relate the letters to their own knowledge and thus remember them more easily. Posting these personal letter representations in place of a conventional letter chart gives students ownership of the alphabet and boosts their self concept.

In *shared reading*, students read alone or in a small group with an expert who assists them in unlocking the alphabetic code. Fluency, automaticity, and strategic reading are the goals of shared reading, especially when decodable texts are used. Reading the text using various methods (e.g., echo reading, choral reading, reader's Theater, see Chapter 8) allows for automaticity

and opportunities for readers to develop strategies such as predicting a word's meaning from the context or detecting the mood of the story.

Pocket chart reading supports students in developing word recognition skills. With words written on sentence strips or tagboard cards, students work with the text without depending on pictures to decode.

To develop writing skills, predictable texts are used to assist in *patterned writing*. New books can be created by taking students directly through the writing process in a safe environment that is teacher-assisted. Patterned writing involves taking a piece of the predictable text and allowing students to complete the sentence or phrase with their own words.

During the 10 to 15 minutes of *DEAR (Drop Everything and Read)* time, students and teachers alike act as avid readers, either alone or sharing a favorite story with a friend. Students are encouraged to discuss story elements, illustrations, or interesting vocabulary words.

Literature studies are a natural progression from shared reading and DEAR time. In small groups, students are encouraged to construct meanings, interpret text, and respond to literature in many other ways. Teachers act as facilitators during these literature discussions.

Creating texts from wordless books, and *writers' workshop*, go side by side in providing teachers opportunities to demonstrate and scaffold the writing process. OLÉ encourages students to use their funds of knowledge about literacy and life to develop knowledge and skills in reading and writing. Within the OLÉ framework, it is important to provide learning opportunities that are sequentially ordered so that students are continually stretched to learn within their zones of proximal development but not unduly frustrated (Johnson Santamaria et al., 2002).

FIGURE 2.7

An Information-Processing Model of Learning

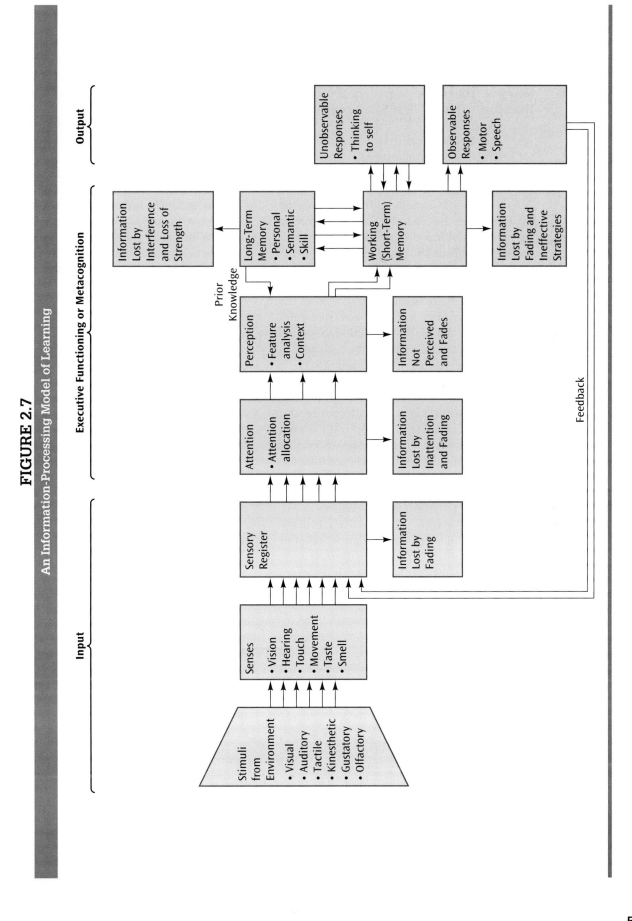

Fourth Amendment of the U.S. Constitution. Mr. Gomez is explaining the concepts of search and seizure to Greg and the rest of the students in government class. Mr. Gomez writes the word *seizure* on the board and says, "Seizure is when the police take your possessions away from you because those possessions are illegal. Sometimes the police need a search warrant to seize your possessions, and sometimes they do not. As you read this chapter, see if you can determine the rules for when the police need a search warrant."

According to the model presented in Figure 2.7, the first step in learning and remembering the information on the concept of *seizure* is to receive the information through the senses. Mr. Gomez exposed Greg to both visual and auditory information by writing the word on the board and by talking about it.

Next, the information is transported to the sensory register. Here, both the visual representation of *seizure* and the auditory information are stored. At this point, Greg has neither attended to the information nor connected meaning to it.

Now Greg can attend to the information, but because he cannot attend to all sensory information, he must screen out some to attend to specific parts. If Greg is attending to the hum of the air conditioner or thinking about a Friday night date rather than purposefully listening to the teacher, the information that Mr. Gomez shared cannot be learned because Greg has not selectively attended to it.

Next, Greg can recognize or perceive the information by detecting the salient features in the information and using the context and his prior knowledge to assist in perception. For example, Greg can use salient visual features in the word *seizure*, his sight word recognition for the word (prior knowledge), and Mr. Gomez's discussion of seizure (context) to perceive the word that was written on the board as *seizure* rather than *leisure* or *search*.

Once the information has been perceived, it can be held for a short period of time in working, or short-term, memory. If Greg wants to learn the information, he can either transfer and store the information in long-term memory or use a strategy to keep the information active in short-term memory. Unless some effort is made to remember the information, it will fade in about 15 seconds. We can use a variety of memory strategies to keep information active. For example, we can rehearse it (repeat it aloud or silently to ourselves), chunk it (group it together to make fewer pieces of information to remember), or elaborate on it (expand on it by using information we already know). Greg

rehearses the word and its definition by saying it several times to himself.

Greg is aware that the information related to the term *seizure* needs to be remembered for a long time or at least until the test next week. Therefore, the information must be meaningfully stored in long-term memory to become part of his cognitive structure. This way, he should be able to retrieve the information for the test next week. One efficient means of storing new information is to relate the new information to old information. Greg retrieves from his memory a story about a senior who tried to raise marijuana in his backyard. The police found it, arrested him, and seized the marijuana. When he hears or reads the word *seizure*, Greg can think of the senior having the marijuana seized. He also retrieves from his memory that search and seizure are discussed in the Fourth Amendment. He can relate the new information to old information almost as if he were filing it in an organized filing system. When the test is given next week and Mr. Gomez asks for the definition of *seizure*, Greg should be able to retrieve the information from long-term memory into working memory and then write the definition because he filed it in a meaningful way.

Throughout the process, learning is orchestrated by executive functioning or metacognition. For example, when Greg decided to rehearse the word and its definition rather than writing them down, he was using his executive functioning to coordinate the learning process.

Although we process information in a logical sequence (see Figure 2.7), we generally process information very quickly and don't think consciously about what we are doing. We do not necessarily say to ourselves, "Now I need to rehearse this so I won't forget it" or "I have to relate this information to what I already know so that I can remember it." Information processing is also very interactive. Feedback is possible both from observable responses we make and unobservable thinking responses. These interactions are depicted by the bidirectional arrows in Figure 2.7. Let's explore information processing further by looking at each component and at the overall coordinating processes of executive functioning and metacognition.

Sensing

Sensing involves the use of one or more of our senses to obtain information. It refers to our system's capacity to use the sensory processes to obtain information, not our system's ability to attend or discriminate. Stimuli from the environment are received through all our senses. However, much of the information we learn in school-related tasks is received through visual and auditory senses.

Attention

Most of us use the term *attention* to refer to a wide range of behaviors. We speak of attending to details when we are concerned about the quality of a job, we ask people whether they are attending to us when we want them to hear what we are about to say, and we measure students on the amount of time they attend to tasks. *Selective attention* is the capacity to focus awareness on selected incoming stimuli. As depicted in Figure 2.7, we attend only to some of the information, depending on the task demands.

The importance of selective attention can be demonstrated in relation to the reading process. You have probably had the experience of reading a text by going through the mechanical motions (identifying the words) only to realize suddenly that you are not attending and cannot remember what you were reading. Instead, your mind has drifted to thoughts about a friend's problems, the music playing in the background, or how good the apple pie baking in the oven smells. An effective learner must selectively attend to the relevant stimuli.

Attention is a limited resource and can be allocated to only a few cognitive processes at a time. However, the more proficient you are at a process, the less attention it will require. Well-practiced processes require little attention and are said to be *automatic*, whereas processes that require considerable attention have been referred to as *deliberate* or *purposive* (Hasselbring, Goin, and Bransford, 1987; Swanson, 1996). LaBerge and Samuels (1974; Samuels, 1987) have applied these principles to the reading process. Poor readers, including many students with learning and behavior problems, must allocate so much of their attention to identifying the words in the text that little is left to allocate to comprehension. Good readers, however, have word recognition at an automatic level and therefore have more attentional capacity to allocate to understanding what they read (Adams, 1990).

Not only do students with learning disabilities have to allocate more attention to some tasks than nondisabled students do, they also have difficulty selectively attending to the relevant stimuli and attending for sustained periods of time (Hynd, Obrzut, and Bowen, 1987; Richards, Samuels, Turnure, and Ysseldyke, 1990; Swanson, 1996). Teachers help students with learning disabilities when they gain their attention and direct it to the relevant information. Teachers can then check with students to ensure understanding and make further adjustments as needed (Lerner, 2000).

Perception

Once we allocate our attention to incoming stimuli, the next step in processing is to recognize or perceive the information. *Perception* can be defined as "the process of 'recognizing' a raw, physical pattern in sensory store as representing something meaningful" (Loftus and Loftus, 1976, p. 23). Students who have perceptual disabilities usually have trouble interpreting and obtaining meaning from the stimuli in the environment.

One explanation of how perception works involves the perceiver's using feature analysis and the context in which a stimulus is presented to give the stimulus meaning. An example of *feature analysis* is that we process more slowly and are prone to confuse letters that have minimal feature differences, such as *C* and *G* or *b* and *d*. Similar findings have been shown with speech sounds (phonemes).

Read the two words presented in Figure 2.8. Did you have any difficulty reading *THE CAT*? Now look closely at the *H* and the *A*. They are the exact same visual image. The context provided by the words facilitates the appropriate interpretation (Neisser, 1967). Context also plays an important role in perceiving auditory stimuli. Our store of background information, as represented in long-term memory (see Figure 2.7), interacts with the incoming stimuli to assist us in the perception process.

Short-Term or Working Memory

Short-term, or *working*, *memory* can be thought of as activated memory, since it contains information that is easily accessible. Working memory has a limited capacity; we have the ability to store only a small amount of information in working memory at any one time, that is, seven bits of information plus or minus two bits (Anderson, 1995). In contrast, long-term memory represents information that is stored outside the attentional spotlight (Ericsson and Kintsch, 1995; Rumelhart, 1977). Working memory is similar to the material on a computer screen in that it will be lost when the

FIGURE 2.8

Effect of Context on Letter Recognition

THE CAT

power is turned off unless the information has been saved (Anderson, 1995). An example can clarify the difference between short-term and long-term memory.

Study the following numbers so that you can remember them: 9–6–5–8–2–4–1–7. Now cover the numbers, wait for at least 15 seconds, and then write them. After you attended and perceived the numbers, you probably studied them to keep them active in your working memory, and then you wrote them. To keep the numbers active, you might have rehearsed the numbers, closed your eyes and tried to visualize them, or used some other memory strategy.

Now write the phone numbers of your two best friends. This information is stored in long-term memory. You had to search your long-term memory for your two best friends. You probably used their names in searching, although you could have used their appearances or an idiosyncratic characteristic. Then you retrieved their phone numbers and transferred these to working memory. Once the information was in working memory, you were ready to use the information, so you wrote the phone numbers.

Now, without looking back, write the eight numbers you were asked to remember earlier. You will probably have difficulty with this task. Because information fades from working memory if you do not work with it, and because you filled your working memory with the phone numbers of your two best friends, you probably cannot write the original numbers. If you had stored the original numbers in long-term memory, you might be able to retrieve them, but the task did not require you to do this. Consequently, they are lost forever.

A number of concepts were demonstrated by this example:

1. Working, or short-term, memory is activated memory.
2. Working memory has a limited capacity. We can keep a limited amount of information in working memory (i.e., seven pieces of information plus or minus two pieces). These pieces may vary in scope or size. For example, they may be seven single digits, seven phone numbers, or seven major concepts.
3. The more we cluster or group information into larger related concepts, the more information we can keep in working memory. For example, we can cluster information for a shopping list by meats: chicken, hamburger, pork chops; bread: wheat, white, rye; and fruit: apple, orange, banana.

4. If we do not actively work with the information in working memory, it fades rapidly (in about 30 seconds).
5. We can use various strategies to keep information active in working memory. For example, we can rehearse the information, elaborate on it, or create visual images of it.
6. Information in working memory is easily replaced by new incoming information (e.g., recalling your friends' phone numbers).
7. Information that is not transferred to long-term memory cannot be retrieved.
8. Information that is stored in long-term memory is sometimes retrievable. How information is organized in long-term memory affects how easily it can be retrieved.
9. Information from long-term memory is transferred to working memory. Then you can use that information (e.g., writing the phone numbers of your best friends).

Some students with learning and behavior problems have difficulties with tasks requiring them to listen to or look at numbers, pictures, letters, words, or sentences; hold them in working memory; and then recall them (e.g., Brainerd and Reyna, 1991; Howe, Brainerd, and Kingma, 1985; Swanson, 1991, 1996; Torgesen, Rashotte, Greenstein, Houck, and Portes, 1987). However, the more a person knows about something, the better able the person is to organize and absorb information on that topic. Furthermore, students with learning and behavior problems can be taught strategies to make more efficient use of their working memory (Mastropieri and Scruggs, 1998; Pressley, 1998; Slavin, 2000).

Long-Term Memory and Schemas

We have already discussed the role that long-term memory plays in learning. Using Figure 2.7 as a reference, we see that *long-term memory* aids us in perceiving incoming stimuli. It provides the context that allows us to use top-down processing in perceiving information (e.g., to perceive the stimuli *THE CAT* in Figure 2.8 even though the visual images of the *H* and the *A* are the same). It helps us to fill in the words or speech sounds of a conversation that we do not fully hear when we are at a noisy party. Information is retrieved from long-term memory and transferred to working memory before it can be used to make responses.

If long-term memory plays such an important part in the information-processing system, how is it organized? If it has to hold all the information we know, including our store of knowledge about the world, procedural information on how to do numerous skills such as tie shoes and play basketball, and information about our goals and values, how does long-term memory keep all this information straight? Cognitive psychologists do not know just how this vast array of information is organized, but they do have some logical hunches.

According to schema theory, our knowledge is organized into schemas. *Schemas* can be defined as organized structures of stereotypic knowledge (Schank and Abelson, 1977). They are higher-order cognitive structures that assist in understanding and recalling events and information. Researchers hypothesize that we have innumerable schemas or scripts for events and procedures and that it is our schemas that allow us to make inferences about the events that happen around us (Anderson, 1995; Rumelhart, 1980).

Read the following short passage about an event that John experienced:

> John had been waiting all week for Friday evening. He skipped lunch just to get ready for the occasion. At 6:30 P.M., he got in his car and drove to the restaurant. He planned to meet several friends. When he arrived, he got out of his car and waited outside for his friends.

At this point, you are probably using a general schema for restaurants. You could answer such questions as "Is John going to eat dinner?" and "Will John eat dinner with his friends?" However, you have not been given enough information to utilize a more specific restaurant schema. Now read on to see how your schema is sharpened:

> After a few minutes, John's friends arrived. They entered the restaurant and walked up to the counter. John placed his order first. After everyone ordered, they carried the trays of food to a booth.

How has your schema changed? You should be using a more specific schema, one for fast-food restaurants. Now you can probably answer more specific questions such as "What kind of food did John and his friends probably eat?" and "Did John leave a tip?" Utilizing schemas (e.g., our prior knowledge about stereotypic events) allows us to make inferences, thereby filling in the gaps and giving meaning to incoming information. Schemas serve a crucial role in providing an account of how old or prior knowledge interacts with new or incoming information (Anderson, 1990, 1995; Rumelhart, 1985).

Within and across schemas, concepts or ideas are organized so as to promote understanding and retrieval. Information can be stored in semantic networks composed of concepts and relationships between concepts (Ericsson and Kintsch, 1995; Rumelhart, 1980). Figure 2.9 presents a representation of the concept of "bird." (Your network for "bird" is probably more extensive than the one presented in this figure.) The closer together the concepts are in the network, the better they serve as cues for each other's recall (Anderson, 1995; Swanson and Cooney, 1996). For example, "wings" should serve as a better recall cue for "bird" than should "two." A concept does not exist in isolation in semantic memory but is related to other concepts at higher, lower, or the same levels. In the case of "birds," it could be filed along with "reptile" and "mammal" under the superordinate concept of animals.

Schemas and semantic networks allow us to organize our knowledge in such a way that we can retrieve information and effectively add new information to long-term memory. They also assist us in determining the relationships among ideas. However, students with learning and behavior problems may not spontaneously use their prior knowledge, and teachers must link new knowledge to existing knowledge.

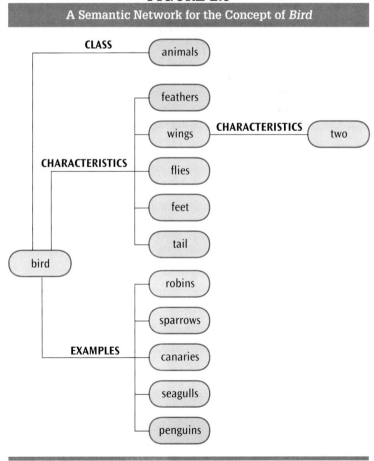

FIGURE 2.9

A Semantic Network for the Concept of *Bird*

Apply the Concept 2.5

Comprehension Monitoring

Read the following short essay:

There are some things that almost all ants have in common. For example, they are all very strong and can carry objects many times their own weight. Sometimes they go very, very far from their nest to find food. They go so far away that they cannot remember how to go home. So, to help them find their way home, ants have a special way of leaving an invisible trail. Everywhere they go, they put out an invisible chemical from their bodies. This chemical has a special odor. Another thing about ants is they do not have noses to smell with. Ants never get lost (Bos and Filip, 1984, p. 230).

As you read the first part of this essay, you probably read along smoothly and quickly, comprehending the information and confirming that in fact what you are reading makes sense. However, when you read the last couple of lines of the essay, you probably slowed your reading rate, possibly went back and reread, and/or stopped and thought about what you were reading. If these are the types of cognitive strategies in which you engaged, then you were using your executive functioning or metacognition to monitor your information processing system.

Executive Functioning or Metacognition

The specific processes in the information-processing system (i.e., attention, perception, working memory, and long-term memory) are controlled or coordinated by what has been referred to as *executive functioning* (see Figure 2.7). For example, as learners, we must decide which stimuli to attend to (e.g., the book we are reading and/or the smell of the apple pie baking), whether to rely more on feature analysis or context and prior knowledge when perceiving information, what memory strategies are most effective for keeping the information active in working memory, and what is an effective and efficient way to store the information so we can retrieve it later. Making decisions allows us to control the learning process.

This executive functioning has also been referred to as *metacognition* (Brown, 1980; Flavell, 1976). Metacognition is generally considered to have two components (Brown, 1980):

1. An awareness of what skills, strategies, and resources are needed to perform a cognitive task
2. The ability to use self-regulatory strategies to monitor the thinking processes and to undertake fix-up strategies when processing is not going smoothly

In many ways, metacognition and executive functioning are similar to the concepts of self-evaluation and self-regulation that we presented in the section on cognitive strategy instruction (Hacker, Dunlosky, and Graesser, 1998). Metacognition and executive functioning require learners to monitor the effectiveness of their learning and, on the basis of feedback, regulate learning by activating task-appropriate strategies. Read the short essay in Apply the Concept 2.5, and see how you use your metacognition.

Students with learning and behavior problems certainly have potential for difficulties with executive functioning or metacognition. For example, the essay that you read in Apply the Concept 2.5 was also read by groups of seventh graders, some of whom had reading disabilities and others who were average achievers. They were asked to read the essay and decide whether it made sense. Although most of the average-achieving students recognized the inconsistency, most of the students with learning disabilities reported that there was nothing wrong with the essay (Bos and Filip, 1984). Wong suggests that because most students with reading disabilities have difficulty with decoding, many of their cognitive resources are allocated to this task, leaving limited resources for comprehension. Others have found similar metacognitive deficits for these students on reading, writing, and math tasks (Cherkes-Julkowski, 1985; Montague and Bos, 1986a,1986b; Swanson, 1996; Swanson and Trahan, 1992; Torgesen, 1985; Welch, 1992).

Teaching Implications of Information-Processing and Schema Theories

As you read the content chapters in this book, think about how information-processing theory helped to shape the instructional techniques. When teaching, think about how you can modify your teaching and the learning environment to facilitate directing students' attention to relevant stimuli and their perception of incoming information. For example, teachers who frequently made suggestions about students using metamemory strategies and gave cues for their use found that the students showed better maintenance and more deliberate use of the strategies than students whose teachers rarely made such suggestions (Lucangeli, Galderisi, and Cornoldi, 1995). What strategies can you teach students so that information can stay active in working memory, and how can you present information to facilitate its storage and organization of long-term memory? How can you teach students to use executive functioning to coordinate the various learning and memory strategies?

Several general implications are as follows:

1. *Provide cues to students so that they can be guided to the relevant task(s) or salient features of the task.* For instance, when giving a lecture, provide cues to assist students in attending to the key points by giving an overview of the lecture, writing important concepts on the board, providing students with a written outline of the lecture, or teaching students how to listen and look for behaviors that signal important information (e.g., raised voice, repetition).

2. *Have students study the critical feature differences between stimuli when trying to perceive differences.*

For example, highlight the "stick" part of the letters *b* and *d*, or provide instances and noninstances when discussing a concept.

3. *Have the students use the context to aid in perception.* Students are not likely to substitute *bog* for *dog* if they are reading a story or sentence about a dog.

4. *Facilitate the activation of schemas, and provide labeled experiences.* In this way, students can develop adequate schemas and modify their current schemas for better understanding of the concepts being presented in both skill and content area subjects.

5. *Teach students to use specific memory strategies.* These could include association, visualization, chunking, and rehearsal.

6. *Use organization techniques to assist students in organizing their long-term memories*, using such content enhancements as semantic maps, relationship charts, and concept diagrams.

7. *Teach students how to be flexible thinkers and to solve problems, thereby encouraging them to use executive functioning.*

SUMMARY for Chapter 2

This chapter presents several models to learning and teaching for guiding the teaching–learning process. The models provide principles that influence the way you, as a teacher, observe, record, interact, and evaluate the teaching–learning process with students.

The first model—operant learning theory and applied behavior analysis—focuses on observed behavior and the antecedents and consequences that control the behavior. In this model, the teacher is able to modify the antecedents by adjusting such variables as the class climate and schedule. The teacher can also increase or maintain desirable behaviors through positive and negative reinforcement, secondary reinforcers, the Premack principle, shaping, and group contingencies. Through operant learning, the teacher is also able to decrease undesirable behaviors by using extinction, differential reinforcement, punishment, and time-out. Teachers can use the principles from operant learning to enhance students' progress through the stages of learning. These include entry, acquisition, proficiency, maintenance, generalization, and application. The teaching–learning process in the operant learning model is highly teacher-directed.

The second model—cognitive strategy instruction—uses principles from both operant learning theories and cognitive-oriented theories. Key features of cognitive strategy instruction are that they include strategy steps, modeling, self-regulation, verbalization, and reflective thinking. Through cognitive

strategy instruction, the student and the teacher have a more interactive role in the teaching–learning process.

The third model—a sociocultural theory of learning—emphasizes the social nature of learning and encourages interactive discussions between students and teachers. In these discussions, the teacher is encouraged to use the students' funds of knowledge and to provide the needed support for students to acquire new strategies, skills, and knowledge.

The fourth model—information-processing and schema theories—explains how information is received, transformed, retrieved, and expressed. Key features of information processing are sensing, sensory register, attention, perception, memory, and executive functioning or metacognition. The information-processing model focuses on an interactive role between teachers and students, with the concentration on activating prior background knowledge in the students, relating new learning to information that learners have already learned, and maintaining students as active learners who think about how they think, study, and learn.

Throughout the remaining chapters, you will see many examples of the principles for teaching and learning covered in this chapter. These examples will assist you in understanding how the different approaches to learning and teaching can be applied when interacting with students. In a sense, this chapter provides the theoretical underpinnings for the strategies that are presented in subsequent chapters. As you read, think about how theory guides instructional practices and how it will guide your teaching as you work with students experiencing learning and behavior problems.

FOCUS Answers

FOCUS Question 1. What are operant learning and applied behavioral analysis, and how can teachers manipulate antecedents and implement consequences to increase desirable behaviors or decrease undesirable behaviors?

Answer: Operant learning is based on the notion that behaviors are learned. In this way, individuals can either unlearn undesirable behaviors or be taught new behaviors. The first step to helping students learn and use appropriate behaviors is to manipulate antecedents, or to attend to the events or stimuli that precede certain behaviors. When undesirable behaviors do occur, using consequences can help students to unlearn or replace selected behaviors.

FOCUS Question 2. What is cognitive strategy instruction, and how is it used to teach academic, cognitive, or social skills?

Answer: Cognitive strategy instruction (CSI) is a systematic method that is used to change thinking processes by organizing the teaching and monitoring of task completion or skill development and by actively involving students in learning. Examples of strategies or skills that are taught in CSI are finding the main idea, decoding unknown words, and taking notes. In brief, the teacher selects a target strategy, works with the student to develop the strategy steps, and gives feedback.

FOCUS Question 3. How can teachers use the features of sociocultural theory to make instruction more effective for the students they teach?

Answer: Sociocultural theory is based on the notion that learning occurs through personal interactions. Therefore, an emphasis is placed on language as a teaching tool and the instructional conversations that occur between teachers and students (as well as between students). There is also a focus on students' resources or background knowledge, language, and culture.

FOCUS Question 4. How can knowledge of information-processing and schema theories assist teachers in meeting the needs of students with learning and behavior problems?

Answer: Information-processing theory emphasizes the components of the brain that are used to manage information in terms of input, metacognition, and output. Schema theory posits that our knowledge is organized into schemas, or organized structures of knowledge, that assist in understanding and recalling events and information. Information-processing and schema theories call our attention to various components of the brain that are activated during learning. Examples of instructional features that incorporate these theories are activating prior knowledge; relating new learning to existing schemas; and teaching and monitoring the use of metacognitive strategies to organize task completion and to check for understanding.

THINK and APPLY

- Within the operant learning model, what procedures can be used to increase desirable behavior? To decrease undesirable behavior?
- What are the stages of learning, and how can they be applied using the operant learning model?
- What are the common characteristics of cognitive strategy instruction?
- Using principles associated with cognitive strategy instruction, design a strategy that one could use to solve subtraction problems with regrouping.
- What implications does a sociocultural perspective have for teaching and learning?

- Why does a sociocultural theory provide particularly relevant support and scaffolds for students who are culturally and linguistically diverse?
- How does long-term memory relate to working memory and perception?
- Using ideas from information-processing and schema theories, what could you do to assist a student who is having difficulties remembering the information needed to pass an objective social studies test?

APPLY the STANDARDS

 Council for Exceptional Children

1. Consider the CEC standards related to using educational theories to guide instruction (BD1K5, BD4S1, LD1K2, LD4S1, LD9S2). Select one theoretical approach presented in this chapter, and explain how you could use that theory to guide instruction for individuals with learning or behavior problems.

Standard BD1K5: Theory of reinforcement techniques in serving individuals with emotional/behavioral disorders.

Standard BD4S1: Use strategies from multiple theoretical approaches for individuals with emotional/behavioral disorders.

Standard LD1K2: Philosophies, theories, models, and issues related to individuals with learning disabilities.

Standard LD4S1: Use research-supported methods for academic and nonacademic instruction of individuals with learning disabilities.

Standard LD9S2: Use research findings and theories to guide practice.

WEBSITESas RESOURCES | for Approaches to Learning and Teaching

The following Websites provide extensive resources to expand your understanding of the approaches to teaching and learning:

- Memory Experiments and Games http://faculty.washington.edu/chudler/chmemory.html
- Behavior Management www.geocities.com/Athens/Styx/7315/subjects/behavior.html
- Operant Conditioning and Behaviorism—An Historical Outline http://genetics.biozentrum.uni-wuerzburg.de/behavior/learning/behaviorism.html
- Socio-Cultural Theory at University of Colorado at Denver http://carbon.cudenver.edu/~mryder/itc_data/soc_cult.html

Where the Classroom Comes to Life

Video Homework Exercise Go to MyEducationLab and select the topic "INSTRUCTIONAL PRACTICES AND LEARNING STRATEGIES," then watch the video "Cooperative Learning" and complete the activity questions below.

A fifth grade math class uses cooperative learning groups to develop story problems. The teacher discusses some of the issues involved in cooperative learning.

1. What are the benefits of cooperative learning in this video?
2. What are the potential problems associated with cooperative learning?
3. How is cooperative learning related to the elements of sociocultural theory outlined in the chapter?

Video Homework Exercise Go to MyEducationLab and select the topic "INSTRUCTIONAL PRACTICES AND LEARNING STRATEGIES," then watch the video "Memory Part 2" and complete the activity questions below.

In this video, two adolescents share their strategies for remembering information.

1. What evidence is provided in the video that these two children are beginning to develop metacognitive skills?
2. What strategies from information-processing and schema theories could you use to support the students in the video to increase their memory and understanding of new material?

Chapter 3

Response to Intervention

Janette Klingner
University of Colorado at Boulder

Katie Kelly has been a special education teacher at Morning Glory Elementary School for six years. She primarily works with students with learning disabilities, but her caseload also includes some students with behavior problems. Part of the Westside School District, Morning Glory is a semi-urban school located within a large metropolitan area. The school's demographics have been shifting over the last several years, from a predominately white middle-class student body to one that is generally working-class and culturally and linguistically diverse. The ethnic makeup of the school's 700 students is now 40 percent White, 40 percent hispanic, 15 percent African American, 3 percent Asian, and 2 percent other. Morning Glory just became a Title I school for the first time, with 70 percent of the students receiving free or reduced-price lunches. About 18 percent of the students are designated as English language learners (ELLs), meaning that they are not yet fully proficient in English. Almost all of the ELLs speak Spanish as their first language, though a few speak Eastern European languages.

In keeping with recommendations from the state department of education, Westside School District is in the process of transitioning to a response to intervention (RTI) model. The district's two primary goals are: (1) to provide students with early support when they first show signs of struggling, and (2) to determine which students should be considered for special education by assessing their response to research-based interventions. Westside has selected Morning Glory as one of the first schools to implement RTI for several reasons. First, the principal is enthusiastic about the new model and would like to try it; she is hopeful that the additional professional development and resources the district has promised will benefit the school. Second, the school has had low test scores on the state's accountability test. Third, the school has a disproportionate number of culturally and linguistically diverse students in its special education programs.

Katie is excited about the potential of RTI to make a real difference for children. She has always worried about those students who did not qualify for special education and seemed to fall through the cracks, as well as about those students who were placed in special education but did not really seem to have disabilities. Yet she is also apprehensive about what her changing roles and responsibilities will be. She attended a summer workshop on RTI sponsored by her district, and she has also been reading books, articles, and online resources about the model to increase her understanding of what is involved.

In this chapter, you will learn more about the challenges Katie and her colleagues will face as they embark on this new journey. But first, let us find out more about response to intervention.

FOCUS Question 1. What past challenges does RTI address?

Past Challenges and Legislation

The field of learning disabilities is in the middle of a transformation. The term *learning disability* was first coined by Samuel Kirk in 1962. In 1965, Barbara Bateman defined students with learning disabilities as manifesting "an educationally significant discrepancy between their estimated potential and actual level of performance related to basic disorders in the learning process" (p. 220). Since then, learning disabilities have been identified primarily by determining a student's potential or ability, usually with an intelligence test, and comparing that with the student's achievement, as measured by reading or math tests. Students who were assessed as being low in both ability and achievement could not qualify for special education services unless they were so low they were determined to have mental retardation. Thus, many students who did not qualify for special education seemed to languish in general education without extra help.

Now, the federal government, professional organizations, and experts in the field are recommending that educators drop the use of discrepancy criteria and instead determine eligibility through a process that focuses on a student's response to research-based instruction and interventions. In the Individuals with Disabilities Improvement Education Act (IDEA; 2004 reauthorization), eligibility and identification criteria for learning disability are described as follows [614(b)(6)(A)-(B)]:

> When determining whether a child has a specific learning disability:
>
> - The LEA [local education agency] is not required to consider a severe discrepancy between achievement and intellectual ability.
> - The LEA may use a process that determines if a child responds to scientific, research-based intervention as part of the evaluation.

Response to intervention, or RTI, is the new model for identifying students who need special education services. In addition to replacing discrepancy criteria, RTI diverges from previous practice in another significant way. In the past, when students first showed signs of struggling, the prevailing approach was to wait and see how they did over time. The idea was that students might simply be slow to achieve academically because of normal developmental or experiential differences, and that it would be a disservice to assess them prematurely and place them in special education. Yet when students struggled, there were few avenues for providing them with extra support. Also, when young students were evaluated for possible special education placement, they sometimes did not yet exhibit enough of a discrepancy between their ability and their achievement to qualify for special education services. For these reasons, this approach was often referred to as the "wait to fail" model.

RTI is different. All students are screened in kindergarten and their progress is assessed frequently so that those students who do not seem to be making adequate progress are provided with timely interventions, before they have a chance to fall further behind. Thus, RTI is a *prevention and intervention model.* As you read this chapter, think about what these changes mean for special educators—and for students.

Challenges Related to Previous Identification Procedures

Over the past 30 years, the field of learning disabilities has struggled with numerous challenges related to its definition and identification procedures. Vaughn and Klingner (2007) note that these challenges include:

- An increase of more than 200 percent since the category was established
- Questionable procedures for determining learning disabilities through emphasis on an IQ–achievement discrepancy and processing disorders
- Students identified using a "wait to fail" model rather than a prevention–early intervention model
- Subjectivity in student referral for services with teachers' and others' perceptions sometimes weighing too heavily in the process
- Students' opportunities to learn not adequately considered during the referral and identification process
- Considerable variation from state to state concerning identification procedures and prevalence rates for learning disabilities
- An identification process that provides little information to guide instructional decision making

- Problematic assessment practices, particularly for culturally and linguistically diverse students
- Disproportionate numbers of culturally and linguistically diverse students inappropriately identified for and served in special education

The overview in Table 3.1 compares identification of students with learning disabilities before IDEA 2004 to the identification process with RTI.

Contemporary Initiatives

Recently, three contemporary major initiatives set the stage for changes in how we think about learning disabilities. First, the President's Commission on Excellence in Special Education held public hearings throughout the United States and received hundreds of written comments (President's Commission, 2002) about the state of special education in the nation's education system. They concluded that special educators were spending too much time on paperwork and not

TABLE 3.1
Identifying Students with Learning Disabilities Prior to IDEA 2004 and with RTI

Prior to IDEA 2004	RTI
No universal academic screening.	All students are screened.
Little progress monitoring.	Progress monitoring assesses whether students are reaching benchmarks—multiple data points are collected over an extended period of time across different tiers of intervention.
"Wait to fail" model—students not provided with interventions until they have qualified for special education.	Students are provided with interventions at the first sign they are struggling; there is an increased focus on proactive responses to students' difficulties.
Focus on within-child problems or deficits.	Ecological focus. Systems approach to problem solving, focused on instruction and interventions varied in time, intensity, and focus.
Clear eligibility criteria (i.e., a child either did or did not qualify for special education services). Categorical approach—targeted, intensive interventions typically not provided unless a student was found eligible for special education.	Tiered model of service delivery with interventions provided to all students who demonstrate a need for support, regardless of whether they have a disability label.
Multidisciplinary team mostly made up of special education professionals; individual students typically referred by classroom teachers with academic and/or behavioral concerns.	Problem-solving (or intervention) teams include general and special educators; teams consider progress monitoring data and all students who are not reaching benchmarks.
Reliance on assessments, particularly standardized tests.	Collaborative educational decisions based on ongoing school, classroom, and individual student data; adjustments to instruction/intervention based on data.
Assessment data collected during a limited number of sessions.	Multiple data points collected over time and in direct relationship to the intervention provided.
"Comprehensive evaluation" consisting mainly of formal assessments conducted by individual members of the multidisciplinary team, often the same battery of tests administered to all referred children.	"Full and individualized evaluation" relies heavily on existing data collected throughout the RTI process; evaluation includes a student's response to specific validated interventions and other data gathered through observations, teacher and parent checklists, and diagnostic assessments.
LD construct of "unexpected underachievement" indicated by low achievement as compared to a measure of the child's ability (i.e., IQ–achievement discrepancy)	LD construct of "unexpected underachievement" indicated by low achievement and insufficient response to validated interventions that work with most students ("true peers"), even struggling ones.

enough time teaching. The commission also noted that general education and special education seemed to be operating as two separate systems rather than a coherent whole. In their report, they recommended shifting to a prevention model that takes into account the fact that students with disabilities are also part of general education and that requires special and general educators to work together more closely.

Second, in August 2001, the Office of Special Education Programs brought together leading researchers to discuss numerous issues related to learning disabilities identification (Bradley, Danielson, and Hallahan, 2002). The team reached consensus on eight principles related to learning disabilities and the eventual use of RTI to facilitate more appropriate identification of students with learning disabilities (Vaughn and Klingner, 2007):

1. The concept of learning disabilities is a valid construct.
2. Students with learning disabilities require a special education.
3. Individuals with LD have a disorder that is experienced across the life span.
4. The exact prevalence of learning disabilities is unknown. The rate may be as high as 6 percent.
5. IQ–achievement discrepancy is not adequate for identifying students with learning disabilities.
6. Linking processing disabilities to learning disabilities has not been adequately established; also, most processing disabilities are difficult to measure and link to treatment.
7. RTI is the most promising method of identifying individuals with learning disabilities.
8. We know much about effective interventions for students with learning disabilities and yet ineffective interventions continue to be used.

Third, the National Research Council report on the disproportionate representation of culturally and linguistically diverse students in special education provided similar recommendations (Donovan and Cross, 2002). The council promoted widespread use of early screening and intervention practices and RTI models. Their premise was that if schoolwide behavior and early reading programs help culturally and linguistically diverse students receive the support they need and improve their opportunities to learn, then the number of students who exhibit ongoing problems will decrease and the students who continue to struggle will more likely be those who require a special education.

With these three initiatives serving as a backdrop, Congress passed the Individuals with Disabilities Education Improvement Act (IDEA 2004). The new law promoted RTI as a way to identify students with LD, as well as *early intervening services* (EIS) to provide students with support as soon as they show signs of struggling. IDEA 2004:

- Recommends but does not require abandoning use of the IQ–achievement discrepancy criterion
- Urges early screening and intervention so that students who show signs of struggling do not fall further behind
- Recommends a multitiered intervention strategy
- Asks districts to review practices to accelerate learning so that students make adequate progress in special education
- Recommends ongoing systematic progress monitoring of students' responses to high-quality, research-based interventions
- Requires better integration of services between general and special education
- Emphasizes the role of context when referring, identifying, and serving students in special education

IDEA 2004 represents a dramatic shift in how we think about supporting student learning. RTI requires collaboration among general educators, special educators, and, where relevant, Title 1 support personnel. As such it is quite different from previous models in which each group tended to carry out its work separately. Greater emphasis is placed on providing students with improved instruction and supplemental supports within general education rather than on finding within-child deficits. According to Alexa Posny, director of the U.S. Department of Education's Office of Special Education Programs, "RTI and EIS are absolutely the future of education—not the future of special education, but of education" (cited in Burdette, 2007, p. 3).

FOCUS Question 2. What are the key components of RTI and how are they implemented?

Components of RTI

Response to intervention is a way to help all students who show signs of struggling and also to determine who may have learning disabilities. RTI is a schoolwide model that starts with students in kindergarten. No single model of RTI is currently accepted as the "gold standard" (Bradley, Danielson, and Doolittle, 2005). Nevertheless, RTI programs commonly include four key components (National Association of State Directors of Special Education, 2006; Vaughn and Fuchs, 2003):

1. *They implement high-quality, research-based instruction matched to the needs of students.* Only instructional practices that generally produce high learning rates for students, as demonstrated by scientific research, are used. The implementation of high-quality instructional practices and interventions is intended to increase the probability of positive student responses.

2. *They monitor students' learning over time to determine their level and rate of performance (for ongoing decision making).* Educators assess all students' learning to determine if they are making progress toward meeting expected benchmarks at a rate commensurate with that of similar peers. Students who do not seem to be progressing are provided with extra assistance in the form of interventions targeted to their needs.

3. *They provide interventions of increasing intensity when students continue to struggle.* The intensity of instruction can be enhanced by reducing group size, increasing time, and/or making sure that interventions are even more carefully tailored to the students' instructional needs.

4. *They make important educational decisions based on data.* Decisions about which interventions to use, the intensity of the interventions, and the duration of the interventions are based on students' responses to the interventions. Results may inform educators about a possible learning disability.

See Tech Tips 3.1 for software, assessment tools, and a list of Websites to help you better understand and implement a response to intervention model.

Layers of Intervention

RTI models include various tiers or layers of intervention (see Figure 3.1). As students move through the tiers, the intensity of the interventions they receive increases. Some models include three tiers, while others include a fourth tier. Estimates in the area of reading are that approximately 80 percent of all learners make adequate progress in Tier 1; 15 percent to 20 percent may require some supplemental instruction in Tier 2, while about 5 percent to 6 percent need intensive intervention implemented in Tier 3.

Tier 1

Progress Monitoring

Tier 1 involves all students. In Tier 1, general education teachers provide evidence-based instruction. Classroom teachers or support personnel screen students and regularly monitor their progress using assessments designed for that purpose. Teachers differentiate instruction as needed and strive to provide appropriate, effective instruction for their students.

Tier 2

Tier 2 is only for those students who are not making adequate progress in Tier 1—in other words, those who are not responding to instruction. Tier 2 interventions are provided in small groups, and therefore are more intensive than Tier 1 instruction. Tier 2 interventions *supplement* rather than supplant the core curriculum taught in Tier 1 general education classrooms and are intended to reinforce the concepts and skills taught there. Yet the support that students receive in Tier 2 is still under the domain of general education. It is *not* special education. All children who appear to be struggling, as evidenced by their slow rate of progress and low assessment scores, are entitled to this support. Researchers refer to this consideration of both the rate of progress and absolute levels of learning as a *dual discrepancy model* (Fuchs, Fuchs, and Speece, 2002).

Interventionists continue to monitor the progress of students while they are receiving Tier 2 support. Tier 2 interventions are provided for a fixed duration (e.g., 10 weeks). After this time, educators examine progress monitoring and other data to decide whether the student is making good progress and should return to Tier 1–only instruction, is making some but not sufficient progress and should receive another dose of Tier 2 intervention, or is making very little progress and should be moved to Tier 3.

Tier 3

In Tier 3, those students who continue to experience difficulties and show minimal progress with Tier 2 interventions are provided with more intensive support. Depending on the number of tiers in

3.1 Using Technology to Implement RTI

A key objective of RTI is to select an instructional strategy to match a student's specific needs. Universal design, authoring software, and assessment software are aspects of technology that might facilitate RTI.

Universal design is a growing movement toward designing products and environments to accommodate the diverse needs and abilities of all people. Here is an example: Imagine the curb along the sidewalk edge of a busy street. To make the intersection navigable by persons in wheelchairs, ramped concrete replaces the curb. Not only can persons in wheelchairs easily navigate the intersection, but people pushing strollers, riding bicycles, walking with bulky packages, or people with poor balance or limited vision also have easier access.

The concept of universal design can be applied to instructional materials to meet the varied needs of all learners. Instead of making "curb cuts" in traditionally designed curricula materials, we need materials that increase the usability for everyone, appealing to different learning styles, methods of input, learner backgrounds, and abilities and disabilities. Such classroom materials may have varying levels of difficulty, multiple means of input, various modes of presentation, and features to customize pace and feedback.

A program that exemplifies the concept of universal design is the Early Learning Series from Marblesoft (www.marblesoft.com). The programs feature multiple difficulty levels; support of all popular input and scanning devices; a built-in record-keeping system; and teacher control of the problems being practiced, prompting, and reinforcement. Teachers can customize the learning environment to meet the specific needs of each individual child. For more about universal design for learning see the CAST Website (www.cast.org).

There is computer software called *authoring* that offers teachers ways to customize curriculum content to maximize the success of every student. *BuildAbility* from Don Johnston Incorporated (www.donjohnston.com) enables teachers to make curriculum and stories accessible to all students and is easy enough for young learners to create their own multimedia reports. IntelliTools, Inc. (www.intellitools.com), has marketed three of its most effective classroom programs with a single interface, *Classroom Suite*. The new suite contains *IntelliTalk 3*—a talking word processor and authoring program, *IntelliMathics 3*—an arithmetic authoring program, and *IntelliPics Studio*—a multimedia authoring program. Recommended for Grades PreK–8,

these programs offer tremendous possibilities for customizing the curriculum for all learners. For a terrific collection of free teacher-made activities, locate the Activities Exchange area of the IntelliTools Website. From this site, you can also download the entire *Classroom Suite* program free for 90 days.

Beyond the traditional assessment software, several assessment packages may be beneficial to teachers practicing RTI. The *Language Arts Objective Sequence* (LOSR), available from Research Press (www.researchpress.com), helps teachers evaluate current language arts performance levels and identify specific goals and objectives. *Spell 2* by Learning by Design, Inc., available from Don Johnston Incorporated (www.donjohnston.com), is a spelling assessment tool that can recommend the type of spelling instruction needed to improve spelling and decoding skills.

The following Web links offer useful resources for various aspects of RTI:

Scientifically Based Research
    http://jimwrightonline.com/php/rti/rti_wire.php
Specific research-based interventions for reading, math, and writing in addition to assessment, screening, and progress monitoring.

Intervention Central
    http://interventioncentral.org
Academic and behavioral intervention strategies, publications on effective teaching practices, and tools that streamline classroom assessment and intervention.

Least Restrictive Behavioral Interventions
    www.usu.edu/teachall/text/behavior/LRBI.htm
Utah rules for selection of behavioral interventions for use with students with disabilities; checklists and videos.

Florida Center for Reading Research
    www.fcrr.org/curriculum/curriculum.htm
Disseminates information about research-based practices related to literacy instruction and assessment for children in preschool through 12th grade.

Sample Screens from Marblesoft's Early Learning Series

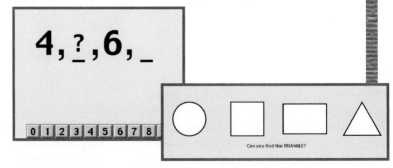

the RTI model, this tier may or may not be special education. Tier 3 students receive explicit instruction individually or in small groups of two or three students. Reading instruction typically focuses on word study, vocabulary, application of word study and vocabulary to text reading, fluency, and comprehension.

Implementing Interventions

Not everyone agrees on who should decide which interventions to implement in an RTI model, or how these decisions should be made. Some researchers recommend a standard treatment protocol model (Fuchs and Fuchs, 2006). Others prefer a problem-solving model (Marston, Muyskens, Lau, and Canter, 2003). Still others favor a hybrid model that is a combination of these two approaches (Vaughn, Linan-Thompson, and Hickman, 2003). As the National Association of State Directors of Special Education noted, "Some . . . have suggested that multi-tier systems might use *either* a problem-solving method . . . *or* a standard treatment protocol approach. This is an artificial distinction. All RTI systems must consider implementing the best features of both approaches" (Batsche et al., 2005).

Standard Treatment Protocol

With the standard treatment protocol model, the same empirically validated treatments are used for all children with similar problems (Batsche et al., 2005). The standard treatment protocol does not differ from child to child. The interventions are chosen from an approved list, and instructional decisions follow a standard protocol. Possible approaches might include explicit instruction in phonological awareness or in phonics skills, peer-assisted learning strategies, or computer programs (Case, Speece, and Molloy, 2003). Specific research-based interventions for students with similar difficulties are provided in a standardized format to ensure fidelity of implementation. Proponents argue that this is the most research-based of the approaches to RTI, and leaves less room for error in professional judgment (Fuchs and Fuchs, 2006).

Problem-Solving Model

The problem-solving model is a more individualized or personalized approach. For each child who is not progressing, a problem-solving team meets to consider all of the data available so that they can come up with an intervention plan for the child. Interventions are planned specifically for

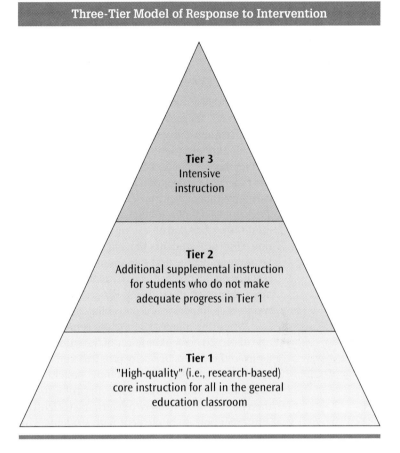

FIGURE 3.1
Three-Tier Model of Response to Intervention

Tier 3
Intensive instruction

Tier 2
Additional supplemental instruction for students who do not make adequate progress in Tier 1

Tier 1
"High-quality" (i.e., research-based) core instruction for all in the general education classroom

the targeted student and are provided over a reasonable period of time. The process typically follows these steps:

1. Define the problem
2. Analyze the problem
3. Develop a plan
4. Implement the plan
5. Evaluate the plan

This approach maximizes problem-solving opportunities by allowing teams to be flexible. Professional expertise is valued.

Differences between the Two Models

Christ, Burns, and Ysseldyke (2005) note that the fundamental difference between the standard treatment protocol and the problem-solving model is the extent to which decision-making teams engage in analyzing individual student data before selecting and implementing interventions. With a standard treatment protocol, there is little examination of the reasons for a child's struggles. In contrast, the problem-solving model is more flexible. The emphasis is on individualized, targeted interventions based on an analysis of the learning context, environmental conditions, and instructional variables as well as on a student's progress monitoring and other assessment data (Tilly, Reschly, and Grimes, 1999).

Decision-Making Teams

There are different names for the decision-making teams in RTI models. They might be called "intervention teams," "problem-solving teams," or "RTI teams." Schools might have one or more teams, and membership might be flexible, depending on the expertise needed for a given situation. Teams can have different purposes. One purpose at the Tier 1 level might involve reviewing progress monitoring data and observing classroom instruction. If several students in a class do not seem to be progressing, the first step should be to help the teacher modify his or her instruction to be more appropriate for all students. Observing in classrooms is an important responsibility of the team.

When the majority of a class is progressing and about 20 percent or fewer of the students differ from their peers in rate of progress and the extent to which they are reaching benchmarks (Compton, Fuchs, Fuchs, and Bryant, 2006), then the role of the team is to determine which Tier 2 interventions to implement with students who are slower to respond. This process is more elaborate and focused on individual student needs when the school is using a problem-solving model, and less involved when the school is implementing a standard treatment protocol model.

When students who are receiving Tier 2 interventions continue to experience difficulty, the decision-making team convenes to determine which steps to take next. The team might decide to try different Tier 2 interventions, or perhaps more intensive Tier 3 interventions. The team might decide to initiate a more comprehensive evaluation for possible special education identification. When this is the case, due process safeguards apply. Families must provide permission for an evaluation to take place. As before the passage of IDEA 2004, families may request an evaluation for their child.

Decision-making teams should include members with relevant expertise. One team member must have expertise in learning disabilities. Another should be an expert in the targeted area of concern (e.g., reading, mathematics, behavior). If the student is an English language learner, it is critical that someone on the team have expertise in language acquisition, and if relevant, bilingual education. In addition, families should be included, as well as general education teacher(s) and special education teacher(s).

"Non-Responders" in an RTI Model

Students who make expected gains are said to "respond" to instruction and are projected to continue to make progress when evidence-based instruction is provided in their general education classrooms. An example of a good response is when the gap narrows between a student's rate and level of progress and that of her or his peers. In other words, the student seems to be catching up. An example of a questionable response is when the rate at which the gap is widening slows down, but the gap is still increasing (Batsche et al., 2005).

On the other hand, students who make minimal or no gains after being taught with high-quality, validated interventions are considered to be inadequately responding to intervention; in other words, they are "non-responders." The gap keeps growing without a change in rate. According to researchers (e.g., Fuchs, Mock, Morgan, and Young, 2003), these students may need more intensive long-term interventions, most likely through special education services.

Non-responders do not seem to progress even when instructed with a research-based approach. However, it is important to remember that not all students learn in the same way. Thus, one student may respond well to a given research-based intervention and another student may not. Research can only help us make educated guesses about which instructional practices are most likely to benefit the greatest number of children. But even in the best research studies, some students might actually respond better to an alternative approach. Therefore, when a child does not seem to be responding to an instructional method, it is important to try a different approach. RTI researcher Amanda VanDerHayden defines non-responders as "students for whom we have not yet found the right intervention" (personal communication, February 2006). Before educators conclude that a child is a non-responder who needs more intensive services, they should consider that there are many reasons the child may not be responding to instruction, such as:

- The method is not an effective one with this child, and a different approach would yield better results.
- The level of instruction might not be a good match for the child.
- The environment might not be conducive to learning.

Similarly, we know that teachers vary a great deal in how they apply different instructional approaches. How well a teacher implements a practice affects how well students learn (Al Otaiba and Fuchs, 2006). This common sense finding has important implications for anyone implementing RTI. Before deciding that a student is not responding to an intervention, it is essential to observe instruction to get a sense for how well it is being implemented. Another way to think about this is that the very notion that a child's "non-response" is meaningful and indicative that she or he needs more intensive intervention is based on the idea that *most* of the child's peers receiving the same instruction are thriving. If the majority of the students in the class are struggling, then the first step must be to improve instruction.

In other words, classroom observations must be part of every RTI model (Vellutino, Scanlon, Small, Fanuele, and Sweeney 2007; Fuchs et al., 2003; Vaughn and Fuchs, 2003). Vellutino and colleagues (2007) note that, "Intervention at this level is based on the assumption that many if not most struggling readers will be able to profit from relevant modifications in classroom literacy instruction, despite the fact that they were (apparently) less well equipped than their normally achieving classmates to compensate for inadequacies in reading instruction" (p. 186). This recognition that many students struggle when their instruction is inadequate is an important one, with significant implications for culturally and linguistically diverse students who often are educated in high-poverty, high-needs schools in which teachers are sometimes not as qualified as in more affluent schools (Darling Hammond, 1995; Harry and Klingner, 2006; Oakes, Franke, Quartz, and Rogers, 2002).

 Spotlight on Diversity

RTI and Students Who Are Culturally and Linguistically Diverse

RTI has the potential to improve outcomes for students who are culturally and linguistically diverse and to more accurately determine which students need special education services (Klingner and Edwards, 2006). Yet it will take a great deal of professional development and support to help those implementing RTI move away from the deficit-based model of the past. Many practitioners assume that children must have an internal deficit of some kind if they are not progressing, or perhaps they come from a supposedly "disadvantaged" background and their underachievement cannot be improved (Harry and Klingner, 2006). According to previous learning disabilities identification criteria, students presumably could not be identified as having a disability if their difficulties could be attributed to environmental factors. In reality, though, it can be quite challenging to determine the reasons for a student's struggles. The RTI model addresses this challenge by focusing on students' needs for support, regardless of the reason, rather than on whether they have a disability.

Similarly, a significant assumption underlying RTI models is that a stronger focus on classroom instruction, progress monitoring, and early intervention services will suffice to properly address the problem of students being inappropriately referred to and placed in special education. Yet the quality of RTI depends on the quality of preparation of the individuals involved. Without sufficient knowledge about cultural and linguistic diversity, for example, educators implementing RTI may presume that a child who does not make progress at a certain pace must have a disability rather than recognize that the child may need additional time and support while learning English. Although the process of learning to read in one's second language is similar to learning to read in one's first language, there also are important differences of which teachers may not be aware (August and Shanahan, 2006). Or teachers may equate cultural differences with cultural deficits, which may influence their interpretations of their diverse students' behaviors (Klingner and Solano-Flores, 2007). Second language acquisition, best practices for English language learners, and cultural variations should be considered when assessing student progress, designing interventions, and interpreting English language learners' responses to interventions.

Problem-solving RTI approaches appear to be more appropriate for use with culturally and linguistically diverse students because the focus is on understanding external or environmental factors that affect their opportunity to learn in addition to personal factors. For RTI to work, team members must have expertise in cultural and linguistic diversity and be knowledgeable about interventions that have been effective with culturally and linguistically diverse students with different needs.

Working with Families

As with previous versions of the Individuals with Disabilities Education Act, families *must* be involved when a school is considering whether to conduct comprehension evaluations of children to determine whether they have a disability. Just as before, families can request a formal evaluation for a disability at any time. A family should also be notified early in the RTI process that a child seems to be struggling and that the school plans to try specific interventions to help. The Council for Exceptional Children (2006–2007) suggests that schools let families know about their child's participation in the RTI process at least by Tier 2. Schools should describe the RTI process, provide families with written intervention plans that are clearly explained, obtain families' consent, and provide families with regular updates about their child's progress. The National Center for Learning Disabilities (Cortiella, 2006) advises including the following information in written intervention plans:

- A description of the specific intervention;
- The length of time (such as the number of weeks) that will be allowed for the intervention to have a positive effect;
- The number of minutes per day the intervention will be implemented (such as 30 to 45 minutes);
- The persons responsible for providing the intervention;
- The location where the intervention will be provided;
- The factors for judging whether the student is experiencing success;
- A description of the progress monitoring strategy or approach, such as CBM, that will be used;
- A progress monitoring schedule;
- How frequently (the parents) will receive reports about (their) child's response to the intervention. (p. 5)

FOCUS Question 3. **How do screening and progress monitoring of students facilitate RTI?**

Universal Screening

Universal screening in reading, and sometimes in math, is an essential component of RTI models at the Tier 1 level. This process involves administering the same test to all students to determine who is likely to be at risk for academic difficulties, in the same way that schools have checked children's vision for years to screen students for potential problems. In many schools, screening is carried out three times a year: in the fall, winter, and spring. Screening instruments usually have few items and are short in duration. Screening is used to determine if additional testing is needed. Schoolwide academic screening was rarely implemented with previous models. Instead, it was typically the classroom teacher who first noticed that students were struggling and referred them for an evaluation. Invariably some students were overlooked. With universal screening, however, everyone is tested.

Universal screening is a quick way to identify general performance levels and determine whether students are on track to developing proficiency in the fundamental skills of reading and math. We know much more than we used to about how to predict future reading levels, for example, using phonological awareness and rapid naming tasks. Thus, we can determine with some accuracy which students are at risk and require additional intervention (Vellutino et al., 2007). Foorman and Ciancio make the point that "the purpose of early screening could be identifying students *not* at risk so that instructional objectives can be established for students potentially at risk" (2005, p. 494). Screening also provides valuable information about class performance and identifies teachers who might need further professional development. Once students have been identified as needing additional assistance using a screening measure, interventions are provided.

Numerous assessments can be used as screening instruments (see Table 3.2 for a list of possible reading measures). Some tests assess only one or two elements of reading (such as the C-TOPP, which only tests phonological processing), while others tap into several reading components. Some are quite quick to administer, such as the TOWRE, while others take much longer, such as the QRI-4 (Rathvon, 2004).

Using Screening to Make Educational Decisions

Screening is useful for providing quick information at the classroom or group level as well as at the student level (Ikeda, Rahn-Blakeslee, Niebling, Allison, and Stumme, 2006). When all of the students in a school are screened, school administrators can examine assessment results for patterns across as well as within classrooms. When problems are widespread across classrooms, schoolwide interventions are called for. Or it could be that most of the students

TABLE 3.2
Possible Screening Measures for Reading

Assessment	Publisher and Website	Grades or Ages	Oral Lang.	PA	Phon.	Word ID	Flu.	Voc.	Comp.	Comments
AIMSweb Curriculum-Based Measurement (CBM)	Edformation www.aimsweb.com	K–12	No	Yes	Yes	No	Yes	No	Yes	Offers Web-based data management
Basic Early Assessment of Reading (BEAR)	Riverside www.riverpub.com	K–3	No	Yes	Yes	Yes	Yes	Yes	Yes	Pencil-paper and computerized versions
Comprehensive Test of Phonological Processing (CTOPP)	PRO-ED www.proedinc.com	K–3	No	Yes	No	No	No	No	No	Phonological processing only
Dynamic Indicators of Basic Early Literacy Skills (DIBELS)	Sopris West/Cambium www.dibelsassessment.com	K–3, 4–6	No	Yes	Yes	No	Yes	No	Yes (4–6 only)	Grade 4–6 students assessed only in fluency and comprehension
Fox in a Box-2	CTB McGraw-Hill www.ctb.com	PreK–3	Yes	Yes	Yes	Yes	Yes	Yes	Yes	Includes PreK
Qualitative Reading Inventory-4 (QRI-4)	Allyn & Bacon/ Longman www.ablongman.com	K–12	No	Yes	No	Yes	Yes	No	Yes	Informal Assessment Instrument
Slosson Oral Reading Test (SORT-R3)	Slosson www.slosson.com	K–12	No	No	No	Yes	No	No	No	Word ID only
Scholastic Reading Inventory (SRI)	Scholastic teacher.scholastic.com	K–12	No	No	No	No	No	No	Yes	Computer Adaptive; Includes Data Management System
Test of Early Reading Ability (TERA-3)	Pearson http://ags.pearsonassessments.com PRO-ED www.proedinc.com	Ages 3.6–8.6	No	No	No[1]	Yes[2]	No	Yes	Yes	Assesses letter knowledge and environmental print
Texas Primary Reading Inventory (TPRI)	Texas Education Agency www.tpri.org	K–2	Yes	Yes	Yes	Yes	Yes	Yes	Yes	Includes screening section and inventory section
Test of Word Reading Efficiency (TOWRE)	Pearson http://ags.pearsonassessments.com	Ages 6.0–24.11	No	No	Yes	Yes	No	No	No	Pseudo-word reading and Word ID only

Note: Lang. = language; PA = phonological awareness; Phon. = phonics; ID = identification; Flu. = fluency; Voc. = vocabulary; Comp. = comprehension.
[1] Letter knowledge only.
[2] Environmental print only.

in the majority of classrooms do well, whereas in one or two classrooms a lot of students seem to be struggling. When this is the case, data indicate a classwide problem in which it may be most appropriate to provide interventions at the class level. When only a few students are struggling relative to their peers, then problems seem to be at an individual level, and individual interventions are warranted.

Progress Monitoring
Whereas screening is used to assess *all* students to determine who might need additional support, progress monitoring is applied with individual students to assess their response to interventions. Like screening measures, progress monitoring instruments are quick to administer and focus on targeted skills in the

Apply the Concept 3.1

Steps in Conducting Progress Monitoring

There are a number of steps to follow when screening students and conducting progress monitoring. Deno, Lembke, and Reschly Anderson (no date) describe one way to apply these concepts:

1. Screen all students in the fall.
2. Rank students by grade level and by classroom. In other words, compile assessment results so that patterns of achievement within classrooms and across classrooms at every grade level can be examined.

3. Identify lower-achieving students in each grade or classroom.
4. Set goals for individual students.
5. Use frequent progress monitoring with students identified as low achievers. Progress monitoring might occur monthly or as often as every week, particularly with the lowest students, on targeted skills (e.g., oral reading fluency).
6. Students who score at adequate levels or higher on the screening instrument can be assessed less

frequently, for example, three times a year (i.e., in the fall, winter, and spring).
7. Create graphs that provide visual displays of students' progress.
8. Evaluate progress monitoring data regularly using a systematic set of decision rules to determine whether interventions seem to be effective for individual students.
9. Revise interventions as necessary in response to the data.

core curriculum. The purposes of progress monitoring are to closely monitor students' progress, to develop profiles of students' learning, and to assess the effectiveness of interventions so that changes can be made if necessary. These data can be quite useful if children continue to struggle and the decision is made to conduct a comprehensive evaluation of their strengths and needs. Progress monitoring measures are administered frequently, perhaps once a month, or as often as once a week in some cases. For more information on progress monitoring measures and procedures specific to reading and mathematics, see Chapters 7, 8 and 11 in this book. For a list of steps to follow in completing progress monitoring, see Apply the Concept 3.1.

> **FOCUS Question 4.** What is the role of the special educator in an RTI model?

Role of Special Education Teachers

The special education teacher plays several important roles in a multitiered RTI model: collaborating with general education and providing consultation services, helping to identify children with disabilities, offering intensive interventions to

Tier 3 students, and helping Tier 3 students access the general education curriculum. Special educators may work with struggling students who have not been labeled as having disabilities. In some ways these are similar to the roles special education teachers assumed in the past, and in other ways they are quite different. These shifting roles will require some fundamental changes in the way general education and special education personnel do their work (National Association of School Psychologists, 2006).

Collaborating and Consulting with General Educators

As with previous models, particularly coteaching and inclusion, one role of the special education teacher in an RTI model is to collaborate with general education teachers and other teachers (e.g., English language development teacher, reading specialist) to provide students who have special needs with a seamless set of services. Special education teachers may still spend part of their day coteaching or meeting with general education teachers as part of a collaborative-consultation model (see Chapter 5 for a full explanation of collaborative models). The purpose of these efforts is to make sure students with disabilities receive accommodations and adaptations so that they have access to the general education curriculum and can participate in the general education program to the extent they are able.

Another way that special education teachers collaborate is by serving on RTI problem-solving (or intervention) teams that consider progress monitoring and other data and make decisions about teacher and student needs. Special education teachers provide their expertise when planning interventions or assessments. They are most likely the team member with the greatest expertise about learning disabilities and can offer insights about individual cases.

Identifying Students with Disabilities

When students have participated in targeted interventions at the Tier 2 level and still do not seem to progress, the problem-solving team may conclude that a comprehensive evaluation is needed to determine if the students have learning disabilities. Not all researchers agree about how much and what kind of additional data are needed to make this determination. The National Association of School Psychologists emphasizes that RTI requires a "shift from a within-child deficit paradigm to an eco-behavioral perspective" (Canter, 2006). In other words, the data collected should include information about the instructional environment as well as within-child factors.

Most experts agree that RTI data by themselves are not sufficient to identify learning disabilities, but that RTI data should serve as the core of a comprehensive evaluation. Most likely the special education teacher would administer formal and informal measures of the child's academic skills (in addition to the screening measures, progress monitoring, and other assessment data already collected). The focus should be to develop a profile that includes information about the student's strengths as well as areas of need. The special education teacher and/or other members of the team would observe the child in different contexts to better understand the instructional environment and how appropriate it seems, as well as under what conditions the student seems to thrive or struggle. Observations should include a focus on how well the child is doing in comparison with similar peers.

A psychologist may or may not conduct an evaluation of the student's intellectual ability and cognitive functioning. Just how this is done depends on the state's and district's policies and what the problem-solving team decides is useful data. If the team has concerns about the child's mental and emotional health, the psychologist also conducts assessments in this area. A social worker interviews the parents about the child's background and developmental milestones. The team collects additional information, such as about the child's attendance patterns. The family members are involved in the process as valued team members.

The special education teacher then works with the team to review and analyze all relevant data to make decisions about the best course of action for the child. They develop an intervention plan and set learning and, if appropriate, behavioral goals. If the team determines that the student has a disability, then they develop an individualized educational plan (see Chapter 1 to review the IEP process).

Providing Intensive Interventions

Much of a special education teacher's time should be devoted to providing intensive individualized instruction to students identified as having learning disabilities. Many consider this "the hallmark of special education" (Division for Learning Disabilities, 2006). Yet as the numbers of students identified as having disabilities has increased over the last few decades and instructional group sizes have grown, in many schools the special education teacher has lost this role. Experts believe that many of the students placed in special education in the learning disabilities category probably did not truly have a disability, but instead had not received sufficient opportunities to learn through effective, appropriate instruction. With RTI, the hope is that teams will accurately identify students with learning disabilities, and these will be the students who receive intensive, individualized support.

Special education teachers work one-on-one or with small groups of students in reading, math, or other content areas (Vaughn and Linan-Thompson, 2003), using techniques described in Chapters 6 through 11 of this text. Instruction is intense, frequent, and of a longer duration than at previous tiers in the RTI model. The special education teacher controls task difficulty and provides ongoing systematic and corrective feedback; progress monitoring continues. See Apply the Concept 3.2 for an example of how Katie Kelly conducts intensive interventions with her reading class.

Helping Students Access the General Education Curriculum

Another critical role of special education teachers is helping students with learning disabilities access the general education curriculum, as stipulated by

Apply the Concept 3.2

Intensive Interventions in Reading

Katie is teaching a 30-minute lesson to a group of 4 fourth- and fifth-grade students who are all reading at an upper-first or a second-grade level. This instruction is considered special education, at the third tier of the school's RTI model. Progress monitoring data indicate that all four students need to build their word study skills. Class begins and students immediately get to work. Their first task is one they know well, and enjoy. They have one minute to think of and write down all of the words that have the –ide or –ike rime, or, in other words, are in the same word families. Katie lets them know when time is up, and they count up all of the words they have listed. The student with the most words reads them aloud, while other students check their lists to see if they have written down any words not stated by the first student, and read these aloud. This is a quick warm-up activity that also serves as a review of previously learned material.

Next Katie introduces two syllable words that have an open, vowel-silent *e* pattern: be-side, a-like, lo-cate, fe-male, e-rase, do-nate, re-tire, ro-tate, pro-vide, and mi-grate. The last two are "challenge" words because they include blends. Before the lesson began, Katie had written the words on the whiteboard at the front of the classroom, each with a hyphen between syllables. Each student also has a list of the words at his or her desk, one row with the hyphens in each word and another without them. Katie directs students to count how many syllables they see in each word. Next she has them mark vowels and consonants. She asks them what they notice about the first syllable in each word, and then what they notice about the second syllable in each word (i.e., that all have the vowel-silent *e* pattern). She points out that they have learned the syllables before, and probably recognize most of them. She asks them to look for syllables

they know. Then together Katie and the students read the words.

Katie explains and demonstrates what the words mean. For example, for the word *erase*, she erases a word on the board, and for *retire*, she reminds the students that one of their previous teachers has retired. Students practice reading the words, first with the entire group, and then taking turns with a partner. Katie and the students next play a game of Concentration, using the same words. Before students arrived, she had set the cards out on a table, ready to go for the game. Some cards have a first syllable on them, and others a second syllable. The goal is for students to match the syllables to make the target words. Finally, for the last six minutes of the lesson, students read connected text with the target words. Before students leave, Katie asks them to look for and bring in any books or magazine or newspaper articles that have one or more of the target words.

IDEA 2004. Special education teachers rely on data collected by the problem-solving or intervention team and work with general educators to develop accommodations, modifications, and/or learning supports to help students experience success in general education classrooms. Special education teachers may also work with students with disabilities and others who are struggling with similar skills and concepts on learning strategies and study skills, or on reinforcing key concepts through preteaching or review.

Specialized Knowledge

Teachers who work with students who have learning disabilities need specialized knowledge so that they can match students' needs with the most appropriate interventions and recommend

modifications, adaptations, and accommodations that support students' success with the general education curriculum. Thus, according to the Division for Learning Disabilities (2006) special educators should:

- Understand and be able to apply pedagogy related to cognition, learning theory, language development, behavior management, and applied behavioral analysis
- Be knowledgeable about criteria for identifying and selecting research-based instructional programs to use with students who have learning disabilities
- Be able to individualize instruction by conducting a task analysis and determining what a child already knows and can do and needs to learn next

- Be able to provide explicit instruction in reading, writing, spelling, math, and listening and learning strategies
- Be able to adjust instruction and learning supports based on student progress, observation, and clinical judgment
- Be able to conduct comprehensive evaluations that include standardized assessment measures, informal assessment, and behavioral observations, and be able to develop meaningful educational recommendations
- Be able to explain test results to help parents and teachers understand students'

needs and the recommendations the special educator has generated during the assessment process

- Possess strong communication and collaboration skills so that they can function as effective members of problem-solving teams
- Understand and apply the legal requirements of IDEA 2004 and federal and state regulations

See Apply the Concept 3.3 to reflect on RTI and how teachers at Morning Glory Elementary address challenges with RTI.

Apply the Concept 3.3

Addressing Challenges with RTI

The teachers at Morning Glory Elementary School are confused about different aspects of RTI and uncertain how to deal with some of the challenges they are facing. What would you recommend to help them address each of these challenges?

Challenge #1: According to progress monitoring data, more than half of the students in some classes are not reaching benchmarks. What should they do?

Possible Response: When many students are not progressing with a particular instructional program or in certain classrooms, the first step is to look for ways to improve instruction. Perhaps the teachers need more professional development on how to use designated research-based instructional practices. Or perhaps the teachers should try different approaches. It is important: (1) to examine the program to determine if it has been validated with students like those in the class, (2) to determine whether instruction is at an appropriate level for students and the program is well-implemented, and (3) to establish whether teachers are sufficiently differentiating instruction to meet diverse student needs.

Determining whether a program is well implemented and appropriate

for students requires observing in classrooms. The program might be an appropriate one, but the teacher could be having trouble applying it with fidelity. Maybe the teacher is struggling with classroom management and needs assistance in this area before being able to focus more on instruction. Or perhaps the teacher lacks the knowledge and skills to differentiate instruction (Klingner, Méndez Barletta, and Hoover, in press). In any case, it is important to explore what can be done to improve instruction and to provide group interventions before providing individual interventions.

Challenge #2: RTI problem-solving meetings look very much like the Child Study Team Meetings of previous years, focused on possible reasons for a child's struggles from a deficit perspective. For example, teachers talk of "referring students to RTI" (Orosco, 2007). The teachers and other school personnel are not clear how the RTI process is similar to and different from the Pre-Referral Process. What would you recommend?

Possible Response: RTI differs significantly from previous models in thinking about supporting struggling students. It is to be expected that it will take some time for school

personnel to shift from focusing on figuring out what is wrong with a student to looking more broadly at the instructional context and ways to make it better, as well as at how to provide support for all students who need help, regardless of label (Klingner et al., in press). One option during this transition period is to focus on making sure Tier 1 instruction and Tier 2 interventions are as strong as possible.

Challenge #3: School personnel are unclear about what it means to provide "evidence-based" or "research-based" instruction and the extent to which instruction should be differentiated to meet students' needs in the first tier. How would you explain this?

Possible Response: "Research-based" means that an instructional practice has been validated by testing it in comparison with different practices and finding it to be the most effective. Research can help us make an educated guess about which practice is most likely to work well with the majority of our students, but it does *not* tell us which practice will work with everyone. In fact, we know that not all students learn the same way and students' learning needs vary.

(continued)

Apply the Concept 3.3

Addressing Challenges with RTI *(continued)*

"Research-based" implies that we can generalize from the findings of original research studies to our own teaching situations. Yet it is important to remember that it is only possible to generalize to other student populations and contexts like those in these studies. This is not always the case, as with English language learners who are often left out of studies because they are not yet fully proficient in English. Numerous instructional approaches recommended as being research-based have not actually been validated or tried out with English language learners or in school contexts similar to those in which many English language learners are educated (Klingner and Edwards, 2006).Vaughn and Fuchs (2003) have noted that research on interventions with culturally and linguistically diverse students is very limited. Nevertheless, district and school personnel should make every effort to select research-based interventions that actually have been tried and found to be effective with students similar to those with whom they will be used.

Challenge #4: School personnel are confused about Tier 2 interventions. They wonder what should "count" as a secondary intervention and whether the special education teacher can provide Tier 2 interventions. They also are not sure what to do about those students who seem to need secondary interventions for an indefinite period of time. How would you respond?

Possible Response: Only those small group interventions that are supplemental to the core curriculum and based on students' needs as assessed by universal screening and progress monitoring can be considered Tier 2 interventions. Some practitioners struggle with the idea that secondary interventions are provided as part of general education. Yet this notion is fundamental to RTI.

Although special education teachers can serve as consultants regarding Tier 2 interventions, and may even provide Tier 2 interventions from time to time, this should not be their primary role, and they should not be a school's main Tier 2 intervention providers.

Some students progress enough with the interventions in Tier 2 that they return to Tier 1, but then their progress slows down, and they once again need Tier 2 support. When they receive Tier 2 interventions they once more do well. Our position is that these students should consider participating in Tier 2 as needed, and when needed, based on ongoing progress monitoring data. Tier 2 interventions are always of a fixed duration, but if it should appear that a student requires this level of support again, it should be offered. The important point is that Tier 2 interventions seem to be meeting the student's needs.

SUMMARY for Chapter 3

RTI must be a schoolwide approach, one that is designed and implemented as part of a complex process of school improvement. This entails coordinating curriculum and assessment considerations, addressing teachers' professional development needs, attending to school climate issues that might constrain change efforts, and enhancing leaders' capacities to orchestrate and respond to multiple (often contradictory) reforms. Adelman and Taylor (no date) caution that if RTI is treated simply as a way to provide more and better instruction, it is not likely to be effective for many students. Instead, RTI must be understood as part a comprehensive system of classroom and schoolwide learning supports. With broad-based schoolwide models, schools are in a better position not only to address problems successfully when they are first detected, but also to prevent many problems from occurring. Adelman and Taylor note that an effective RTI model reduces the numbers of students who are inappropriately referred for special education and also enhances attendance, reduces misbehavior, closes the achievement gap, and increases graduation rates. Sustained implementation of RTI will require strong leadership, collaboration among special educators and general educators, and a well-established infrastructure (Burdette, 2007).

FOCUS Answers

FOCUS Question 1. What past challenges does RTI address?

Answer: RTI addresses numerous challenges associated with past procedures for supporting student learning and identifying students with learning disabilities. Previous identification criteria focused on establishing a discrepancy between achievement and potential as measured with an IQ test. Yet this way of determining who qualified for special education turned out to be problematic for multiple reasons. Not all students who struggle and need special education demonstrate an IQ–achievement discrepancy. Also, it can be difficult to assess accurately the potential of students, particularly culturally and linguistically diverse students. The identification process was quite subjective, and varied a great deal across schools, districts, and states. Not enough attention was given to making sure students had received an adequate opportunity to learn. In addition, by the time students demonstrated enough of a discrepancy to qualify for special education services, they were already quite far behind, and years had passed in which they could have been receiving intensive assistance.

FOCUS Question 2. What are the key components of RTI and how are they implemented?

Answer: RTI includes several key components. The first is high-quality, research-based instruction that is well-matched to students' needs and implemented with fidelity by skilled, caring teachers. Additional components include schoolwide screening to assess the learning levels of all students, and progress monitoring designed to assess individual students' learning over time. Thus, an important aspect of RTI is data-based decision making. Data are used to make decisions about which interventions to use, the intensity of interventions, and the duration of the interventions.

FOCUS Question 3. How do screening and progress monitoring of students facilitate RTI?

Answer: Universal screening and progress monitoring are essential components of RTI. It is through these assessment procedures that data-based decisions can be made about which research-based instructional practices should be used to teach students. Screening is done as part of the first tier of an RTI model. All students are screened. Progress monitoring can also be part of the first tier, but it is an essential component of Tiers 2 and 3. The progress of all students who receive interventions targeted to their instructional needs is monitored frequently. The purposes of progress monitoring are to assess the effectiveness of the interventions so that changes can be made if necessary and also to develop a profile of the student's learning. These data can be quite useful when determining whether a student has a learning disability.

FOCUS Question 4. What is the role of the special educator in an RTI model?

Answer: Special education teachers play several important roles in an RTI model. They collaborate with general education teachers and other service providers, offering consultation services and helping to identify children with disabilities. They also provide intensive interventions to special education students to help them reach learning objectives in targeted areas, such as in reading and/or math. In addition, they help special education students access the general education curriculum. Special educators might also work with struggling students who have not been labeled as having disabilities.

THINKand APPLY

- How are RTI models different frame previous prereferral and special education models?
- What are the benefits of universal screening?
- What are the benefits of progress monitoring?
- Observe a problem-solving (or intervention) team meeting at a local school. What kinds of data do team members consider? What do you notice about the decision-making process?

- Why might RTI models be more appropriate for and useful with culturally and linguistically diverse students than previous models?
- What considerations are important when using RTI with culturally and linguistically diverse populations?
- What kinds of specialized knowledge should special education teachers have?

- What challenges might schools face when they are implementing RTI?
- Observe Tier 2 and Tier 3 instruction in a nearby school. What do you notice about the similarities and differences between the two? Who provides the interventions in each case?
- How should families be involved in an RTI model?

APPLYthe STANDARDS

Use the information presented in this chapter and your knowledge of the CEC standards (LD1K5, LD4K2, LD7K1, LD8K2, LD8K3, CC10K1) to describe the strengths of an RTI model in meeting the needs of struggling readers in elementary school.

Standard LD1K5: Current definitions and issues related to the identification of individuals with learning disabilities.

Standard LD4K2: Methods for ensuring individual academic success in one-to-one, small group, and large group settings.

Standard LD7K1: Relationships among reading instruction methods and learning disabilities.

Standard LD8K2: Factors that could lead to misidentification of individuals with learning disabilities.

Standard LD8K3: Procedures to identify young children who may be at risk for learning disabilities.

Standard CC10K1: Models and strategies of consultation and collaboration.

WEBSITESas RESOURCES | for Response to Intervention

The following Websites provide extensive resources to expand your understanding of response to intervention:

- Center on Instruction www.centeroninstruction.org
- Council for Exceptional Children (CEC) www.cec.sped.org
- Council for Exceptional Children (CEC), Division for Learning Disabilities www.teachingld.org
- Focus on Response to Intervention: RTI Resource Library www.reading.org/resources/issues/focus_rti_library.html
- National Association of School Psychologists www.nasponline.org
- National Association of State Directors of Special Education (NASDSE) www.nasdse.org
- National Center for Culturally Responsive Educational Systems www.nccrest.org
- National Center for Learning Disabilities www.ncld.org
- National Research Center on Learning Disabilities www.nrcld.org
- Regional Resource and Federal Center (RRFC) Network www.rrfcnetwork.org
- RTI Resource Center www.autoskill.com/intervention/rti.php
- U.S. Department of Education, Office of Special Education and Rehabilitative Services www.ed.gov/about/offices/list/osers/index.html

Where the Classroom Comes to Life

Module Homework Exercise Go to MyEducationLab and select the topic "LEGAL AND POLICY ISSUES," then read the module "RTI (Part I): An Overview" and complete the activity questions below.

This module outlines the differences between the IQ–achievement discrepancy model and the response-to-intervention (RTI) model. It also offers a brief overview of each tier in the RTI model and explains its benefits.

1. How might the identification process influence which students might be identified with a learning disability in classrooms similar to Katie Kelly's from the opening case study in Chapter 3?

2. Which components of RTI appear to be the most challenging to implement? Review the chapter and the module and brainstorm solutions to the challenges you identified.

Module Homework Exercise Go to MyEducationLab and select the topic "ASSESSMENT," then read the module "RTI (Part II): Assessment" and complete the activity questions below.

This module explores in detail the assessment procedures integral to RTI. It also outlines how to use progress monitoring data to determine if a student is meeting the established performance criteria or if more intensive intervention is needed.

1. Based on the chapter and the information provided in the module, how can teachers initially identify struggling readers?

2. How will teachers determine which students need more intensive instruction?

Chapter 4

Promoting Social Acceptance and Managing Behavior

As you read the chapter, watch for these questions to help you focus your learning:

1. How should teachers arrange the physical and instructional environment of the inclusive classroom to promote prosocial behavior?

2. How can teachers use classroom management and positive behavior support to promote prosocial behavior?

3. What is the purpose of a functional behavioral assessment (FBA), and what are the procedures for developing an effective FBA?

4. What do we know about how students with behavior and learning difficulties feel about themselves, are perceived by others, and interact socially with others?

As Donna Douglas listened to her son, Jeff, playing with a classmate in his room, she closed her eyes and flinched when Jeff said, "That's not how you do it. I know how to do it. Give it to me." She hoped that the classmate would understand Jeff and not find her son's difficulty in interacting with others so disagreeable that the classmate would not return. Donna knew that Jeff was not mean or cruel, but he had a difficult time with interpersonal communication. He had trouble making and maintaining friends. He didn't seem to know how to listen and respond to others, and he often expressed himself harshly and inconsiderately.

At their weekly meeting, Malik's special education teacher's first comment to the school counselor was "I feel let down. Malik and I had an agreement that I would give him free time at the end of the day if he brought a signed note from his regular classroom teachers that indicated his behavior was appropriate in class. After three days of signed notes and free time, I checked with his regular classroom teachers only to find out that Malik had his friends forge the teachers' initials. The teachers had not seen the note. Though this experience is discouraging, I remind myself that two years ago, Malik was incapable of spending even 30 minutes in a regular classroom without creating havoc. He has improved, and he even has a friend in the regular classroom. It is comforting to know that despite periodic setbacks, his social skills have gradually improved."

Jeff and Malik both have difficulties with social skills. Many students with learning and behavior problems have a hard time in school, at home, and work because of how they interact with others. This chapter will help you to understand the social characteristics of students who have learning and behavior problems. This chapter will explore how these students are perceived by others and how they respond to others. In addition, interventions that can be used to improve the social behaviors of students will be presented, along with programs and activities that can assist in teaching interpersonal social skills. First we discuss how teachers can effectively arrange the physical and instructional environment of the special education classroom to promote success.

FOCUS
Question | **1.** How should teachers arrange the physical and instructional environment of the inclusive classroom to promote prosocial behavior?

Preparing the Physical and Instructional Environment

As she completed her first year of teaching as a junior high special education teacher, Ms. Habib commented,

> I'm really looking forward to next year. The first year of teaching has to be the hardest. There is so much to get organized at the beginning of the year, so many decisions to be made, and so many new routines and procedures to learn. You have to figure out what your resources are as well as the students' needs. You also have to decide what type of instructional program you want. Based on this, you need to determine how to arrange the room to facilitate learning, what materials to select or develop, and how to organize the materials so that the students can find them easily. You must decide how to group the students and how to schedule them into the room. In comparison to this year, next year should be a breeze. I'll be able to spend much more time refining my teaching skills, focusing on the students, and strengthening the program.

In many ways, Ms. Habib is a manager, as are all teachers. At the beginning of the year, management decisions are made at a fast and furious pace. We will explore some of the decisions that teachers have to consider in getting started and look at some options they might consider in making those decisions. Additionally, promoting social acceptance of students and managing the classroom to ensure positive behavior is a critical part of every teacher's job and will be described in this chapter.

Arranging the Environment

In Chapter 1, we discussed how the teaching–learning process takes place within a specific context. Making this context or environment pleasant and conducive to learning can facilitate the teaching–learning process. Teachers should consider both the instructional arrangement and the physical arrangement of that context.

Instructional Arrangement

The term *instructional arrangement* refers to the manner in which a teacher groups students and the learning format the teacher selects. Inclusive settings require arranging grouping instruction with general education teachers. Generally, there are six instructional arrangements: large group instruction, small group instruction, one-to-one instruction, independent learning, collaborative learning, and peer teaching (Mercer and Mercer, 2005). Most teachers want to have the flexibility to provide for several different instructional arrangements within their classrooms.

Large Group Instruction. In large group instruction, a teacher usually provides support or explicit instruction to a group of six or more students. Large group instruction is appropriate when the goal of instruction is similar for all students. Teachers often use this type of instructional arrangement when preteaching vocabulary, introducing reading comprehension strategies, reading aloud and asking questions, or proving information that may be useful to a large group of students. This arrangement can be used both for didactic instruction (i.e., instruction in which one person, usually the teacher, provides information) and for interactive instruction (i.e., when students and teachers discuss and share information). In large group instruction, students generally have less opportunity to get feedback about their performance and less opportunity to receive corrective feedback. Because large group instruction is the most frequently used arrangement in general education classrooms, students with reading difficulties can benefit from opportunities to learn in other grouping formats, particularly small group instruction.

Following are some activities that teachers can implement to make large group instruction as effective as possible:

- Ask all students a comprehension question, and then ask them to discuss their answer with a partner. This gives all students in the group an opportunity to reflect and comment on the question.
- Provide a whiteboard and a marker or paper and pencil to all students in the large group. Ask them to write words, sentences, letters, or answers as you instruct the group as a whole.
- Use informal member checks to determine whether students in the group agree, disagree, or have a question about an issue related to comprehension or story retelling.

- Ask selected students to provide in their own words a summary of points of view that have been expressed by several different students in the group.
- Distribute lesson reminder sheets that provide students with a structure for answering questions about what they learned from a lesson, what they liked about what they learned, and what else they would like to learn. This increases the likelihood that students will attend to lessons and learn more.

Small Group Instruction. Small group instruction usually consists of groups of three to five students and is used when a teacher wants to provide very specific instruction, feedback, and support. Teachers form small groups of students who either are at different ability levels (heterogeneous groups) or have similar abilities in a particular curriculum area (homogeneous groups). One benefit of using small groups is that a teacher can individualize instruction to meet each group's specific needs. For example, during a cooperative learning activity in which students are grouped heterogeneously, the teacher is able to give a mini-lesson to a group that is having difficulty working together.

Same-ability, or homogeneous, groups are often used for teaching specific reading skills, because students can be grouped by reading level, particularly for beginning reading instruction. In using small group instruction, a teacher usually involves one group of students while the remaining students participate in independent learning, cooperative learning, or peer tutoring. Sometimes teachers who work in resource rooms schedule students so that only two to five students come at one time; thus, all the students can participate in small group instruction at once. Many teachers prefer using a horseshoe table arrangement for small group instruction because it allows them to easily reach the materials in front of each student in the group.

See the section on coteaching at the end of this chapter for more ideas about how a reading specialist and/or special education teacher and general education teacher can work together to manage a variety of instructional grouping arrangements for reading in one classroom.

Following are some of the activities that teachers can implement to make small group instruction as effective as possible:

- Arrange your reading instruction schedule to allow for daily small group instruction for students who are behind in reading and several times a week for all other students.
- Provide flexible small group instruction that addresses the specific skills and instructional needs of students.
- Use student-led small groups to reteach or practice previously taught information, reread stories, develop and answer questions, and provide feedback on writing pieces.

One-to-One Instruction. One-to-one instruction occurs when a teacher works individually with a student. This instructional arrangement allows the teacher to provide intensive instruction, closely monitoring student progress and modifying and adapting procedures to match the student's learning patterns. The Fernald (VAKT) method of teaching word identification and Reading Recovery, discussed in Chapter 7, recommend a one-to-one instructional arrangement. At least some one-to-one instruction is recommended for students with learning and behavior problems, because it provides them with some time each day to ask questions and receive assistance from the teacher. The major drawback of one-to-one instruction is that while one student is working with the teacher, the other students need to be actively engaged in learning. To accomplish this, independent learning, collaborative learning, and peer tutoring are frequently used.

Independent Learning. Independent learning is one way to enable students to practice skills about which they have already received instruction and have acquired some proficiency in (Stephens, 1977; Wallace and Kauffman, 1986). We frequently associate independent learning with individual worksheets, but computer activities or various assignments such as listening to an audio book, writing a story, reading a library book, or making a map for a social studies unit can also be independent learning activities.

The key to effective use of independent learning is selecting activities that students can complete with minimal assistance. For example, when Miriam selects library books, Ms. Martino asks Miriam to read about 100 words to her, and then she asks Miriam several questions. If Miriam misses 5 or fewer words and can answer the questions easily, then Ms. Martino encourages her to read the book on her own. If Miriam misses 5 to 10 words, then Ms. Martino arranges for her to read the book using collaborative learning or peer tutoring. If Miriam misses more than 10 words and struggles to answer the questions, then Ms. Martino may encourage her to select another book. In fact, Ms. Martino has taught Miriam and the rest of the students in her self-contained classroom for students with behavior disorders the Five-Finger Rule: "If in reading the first couple of pages of a book, you know the words except for about five and you can ask yourself and answer five questions about what you have read, then this book is probably a good one for you to read."

Cooperative Learning. Cooperative learning occurs when students work together and use each other as a resource for learning. Four basic elements need to be included for small group learning to be cooperative: interdependence, individual accountability, collaborative skills, and group processing (Johnson, Johnson, and Holubec, 1993; Slavin, 1987, 1991). Interdependence is facilitated by creating a learning environment in which students perceive that the goal of the group is for all members to learn, that rewards are based on group performance, that all members of the group will receive the materials needed to complete the task, and that students have complementary roles that foster the division of labor. Collaborative skills are

required for a group to work together effectively. Teachers should teach collaborative skills explicitly by defining skills and their importance, modeling how the skills are used, allowing students to practice skills in cooperative groups, and providing students with corrective feedback (Putnam, 1998).

Progress Monitoring

Individual accountability ensures that each student is responsible for learning the required material and contributing to the group. Teacher evaluations (e.g., quizzes, individual products) can help to determine whether each student has learned the material. Students can also use progress monitoring forms to track their own behavior and progress. Progress monitoring forms might include questions such as How did I contribute to the learning of the group today? and In what way did I help or not help my group to complete our work? *Group processing* refers to giving the students the opportunity to discuss how well they are achieving their goals and working together (Johnson and Johnson, 1984a). Apply the Concept 4.1 provides additional guidelines for including students with disabilities in cooperative learning groups.

Apply the Concept 4.1

Guidelines for Including Students with Special Needs in Cooperative Learning Activities

When students with disabilities are included in a cooperative group lesson in the general education classroom, teachers may consider the following during planning (Johnson, Johnson, and Holubec, 1993; Stevens and Slavin, 1995):

- Adjust group size, and create heterogeneous groups of students who are likely to work well together. Would some students benefit from three students in a group instead of four or five?
- Consider each student's IEP goals and academic strengths and weaknesses when assigning roles. For example, modifications in materials may be necessary if a student with below-grade level

reading skills is assigned the role of reading directions.
- Arrange the room to ensure face-to-face interaction between students and to make groups easily accessible to the teacher. Round tables work well, but chairs clustered together or open floor areas can also be used.
- Inform students of criteria for both academic and interpersonal success. Some teachers hand out a grading rubric with an outline of specific criteria for grading in each area of evaluation (e.g., creativity, neatness, group work, correct information, quiz).
- Provide minilessons before and/or during the cooperative group activity to teach academic or cooperative skills. Students need to know what

group work "looks like," and many teachers conduct several lessons on how to work in cooperative groups before beginning the learning activities. Teachers can also provide small doses of instruction to individual groups during the activity as needed.
- Monitor and evaluate both individual achievement and group work. Many teachers carry a clipboard with students' names and lesson objectives so that they can record student progress as they monitor groups.
- Reflect on the cooperative learning activity and note changes for future lessons. Did the lesson go as well as you would have liked? Did students learn the required material?

Two basic formats for cooperative learning are often used in general or special education classrooms. In a *group project*, students pool their knowledge and skills to create a project or complete an assignment. All students in the group participate in the decisions and tasks that ensure completion of the project. Using the *jigsaw format*, each student in a group is assigned a task that must be completed for the group to reach its goal. For example, in completing a fact-finding sheet on fossils, each student might be assigned to read a different source to obtain information for the different facts required on the sheet.

Johnson and Johnson (1975) suggest the following guidelines for working cooperatively:

- Each group produces one product.
- Group members assist each other.
- Group members seek assistance from other group members.
- Group members change their ideas only when logically persuaded to do so by the other members.
- Group members take responsibility for the product.

Cooperative learning can be used to complete group projects in content area subjects, and teachers generally consider it to have positive outcomes for students with learning and behavior problems (Jenkins, Antil, Wayne, and Vadasy, 2003). However, teachers perceive that cooperative learning has greater benefits in terms of self-concept than academic gains. The process approach to teaching writing, discussed in Chapter 9, employs aspects of cooperative learning. For example, students might share their written pieces with each other to get ideas and feedback about their writing, and in some cases, they write pieces together. Cooperative Integrated Reading and Composition (Slavin, Stevens, and Madden, 1988) uses cooperative learning with a process approach for teaching composition and basal-related activities and direct instruction in reading comprehension. Slavin and his colleagues have also designed a mathematics curriculum using cooperative learning called Team-Assisted Individualization (Slavin, 1984). Using heterogeneous cooperative learning groups in general elementary classrooms, the researchers found that these types of programs paired with cooperative learning facilitate the learning of most mainstreamed special education and remedial students.

Opportunities to participate in cooperative learning experiences are particularly important for students with learning and behavior problems.

As well as supporting development of targeted academic skills, cooperative learning helps students experience positive interactions with peers and develop strategies for supporting others. These skills are particularly important when students with learning and behavior problems participate in general classrooms where cooperative learning is employed (Johnson and Johnson, 1984b, 1986; Nevin, 1998).

In orchestrating cooperative learning, it is important to provide students with sufficient directions that they understand the purpose of the activity and the general rules for working in groups. Initially, a teacher may want to participate as a collaborator, modeling such behaviors as asking what the other people think, not ridiculing other collaborators for what they think, and helping other collaborators and accepting help from others. As students become comfortable in collaborating, they can work cooperatively in teams without the teacher's input.

Peer Teaching. In this instructional arrangement, one student who has learned the targeted skills (the tutor) assists another student in learning those skills. This type of teaching takes place under a teacher's supervision. When using peer teaching, the teacher needs to plan the instruction and demonstrate the task to student pairs. The tutor then works with the learner, providing assistance and feedback. One advantage of peer teaching is that it increases opportunities for the student learning the skills to respond (Maheady, Harper, and Malette, 2001). Peer teaching achieves this by allowing peers to supervise their classmates' responses.

One important aspect of peer teaching is preparing the students to serve as peer tutors by teaching them specific instructional and feedback routines to ensure success (Fuchs, Fuchs, Mathes, and Simmons, 1997). Students benefit from learning basic instructional procedures for providing reinforcement and corrective feedback and for knowing when to ask the teacher for assistance.

Remember that poor readers show academic and social gains in both the tutor and tutee roles (Elbaum, Vaughn, Hughes, and Moody, 1999). Therefore, it is important to alternate roles so that students get the chance to benefit from serving as both the tutor and the tutee. Research focusing on peer tutoring with special education students has most frequently been used to teach or monitor basic skills such as oral reading, answering reading comprehension questions, and practicing spelling words, math facts, and new sight word vocabulary

(Fuchs, Fuchs, Hamlett, et al., 1997; Gerber and Kauffman, 1981; Scruggs and Richter, 1985). A recent review of the literature found that peer tutoring improved a broad array of social and academic outcomes for students with severe disabilities as well as increasing their access to the general education curriculum (Carter and Kennedy, 2006).

Another important type of peer teaching is cross-age tutoring, in which older students instruct younger ones. Cross-age tutoring has many advantages, including the fact that older students are supposed to know more than younger students, so there is less stigma about being tutored. Also, both the tutor and the tutee enjoy the opportunity to meet someone of a different age. Another aspect of cross-age tutoring that can be effective is allowing students with learning disabilities or behavior disorders to tutor younger students who also demonstrate learning or behavior disorders.

Classwide Peer Tutoring. Classwide peer tutoring is a structured technique for improving students' reading abilities. Students of different reading levels are paired (e.g., a high or average reader is paired with a low reader) and work together on a sequence of organized activities such as oral reading, story retelling, and summarization. The reading material can be a basal reader, a trade book or magazine, or other appropriate material. The criterion is that the lower reader in each pair be able to easily read the materials assigned to his or her dyad. Peer pairing can occur within class, across classes but within grade, and across grades. This teaching takes place under a teacher's supervision. Peer teaching increases the opportunities for a student to respond by allowing peers to supervise, to model reading, ask questions, and generally support their classmates' participation in reading. When using peer teaching, the teacher needs to plan the instruction and demonstrate the task to the pair. The tutor then works with the learner, providing assistance and feedback.

Extensive research on classwide peer tutoring (e.g., Heron, Welsch, and Goddard, 2003; Topping and Ely, 1998) and partner learning reveals that even students with disabilities as early as kindergarten (e.g., Fuchs, Fuchs, Thompson, et al., 2003), as well as secondary students (Calhoon and Fuchs, 2003), benefit when the procedure is implemented consistently (e.g., 30-minute sessions conducted three times per week for at least 16 weeks). Students of all ability levels demonstrate improved reading fluency and comprehension.

Partner learning is not limited to elementary school or only as a means to enhance reading fluency. Studies have demonstrated that partner learning can also improve students' outcomes in world history, reading, math, and across academic areas (Maheady, Harper, and Mallette, 2001; Mastropieri, Scruggs, Spencer, and Fontana, 2003).

Physical Arrangement

The physical layout of a room should be flexible enough to allow for different instructional arrangements. For example, the individual learning area can be reorganized into a large group instructional area by rearranging the desks. The small group instructional area can also be used for a cooperative learning project.

Following are eight ideas to keep in mind when developing the room arrangement:

1. To the extent possible, place the recreational and audiovisual/computer areas away from the teaching area. These areas will naturally be somewhat noisier than the other areas.
2. Place student materials in an area where students can easily get to the materials without bothering other students or the teacher.
3. Place your teaching materials directly behind where you teach so that you can reach materials without having to leave the instructional area.
4. If there is a time-out area, place it out of the direct line of traffic and use partitions that keep a student in the time-out area from having visual contact with other students. (See Chapter 2 for principles governing the use of time-out.)
5. Make the recreational area comfortable with a carpet, comfortable reading chairs, pillows, and a small game table if possible.
6. Place all the materials needed for a learning center in the learning center area. In this way, students will not be moving around the room to collect needed materials.
7. Instruct several students as to where materials and supplies are kept so that when students cannot find something, they do not ask you but ask other students.
8. Establish procedures and settings for students who have completed tasks and/or are waiting for the teacher.

Instructional Materials and Equipment

Selecting, developing, and organizing instructional materials and equipment are important aspects of getting a program organized. The instructional materials and the equipment used by a teacher have a major influence on what and how information and skills are taught (Wallace and Kauffman, 1986).

One decision a teacher has to make is whether to purchase materials that are already available or develop the materials. Some teachers tend to select published materials for their main instructional materials (e.g., sets of literature books based on different themes or units, several reading programs each representing a different approach to reading such as linguistic and phonic approaches), then develop instructional aids and games to supplement the program (e.g., flashcards, sentence strips, recordings of the stories, board games).

Whether selecting or developing materials, there are several factors to consider:

- What evidence is there that these materials or curricula have been effective with students with learning and behavior problems?
- What curricular areas (e.g., reading, English, math, social skills) will I be responsible for teaching?
- What are the academic levels of the students I will be teaching?
- In what instructional arrangement(s) do I plan to teach each curricular area?
- How can the materials be used across the stages of learning (i.e., acquisition, proficiency, maintenance, generalization, and application)?
- Will the materials provide a means for measuring learning?
- Are the materials designed for teacher-directed learning, student-to-student learning, or individual learning?

See Tech Tips 4.1 for materials to use to enhance socialization skills and to assist in monitoring and managing classroom behavior.

Selecting Published Materials

Besides considering the factors just mentioned, it is important to think of the cost, durability, consumability, and quality of published materials. Before materials are purchased, it is advantageous to evaluate them. Sample materials can generally be obtained from publishers or found at educational conferences or districtwide instructional centers. Teachers should read research reports that provide information about the effectiveness of materials. When research is not available, it is often useful to talk with other teachers who use materials to determine when and with whom they are effective. Sometimes it is possible to borrow the materials and have the students try them and evaluate them. Appendix 4.1 presents a form a teacher can use to evaluate published materials. It focuses not only on general information, but also on how the material will fit into the teacher's program. Appendix 4.2 presents a form the students can use to evaluate the materials.

Because most teachers have restricted budgets for purchasing instructional materials, it is helpful to prioritize them according to need. Before eliminating materials from the list of materials you select, determine whether they can be obtained without purchasing them. For example, school districts often have an instructional materials library that allows teachers to check out materials for a relatively long period of time. You may be able to borrow the materials from the library rather than purchase them. Librarians are often interested in additional materials to order; it might be possible to request that they order the materials for the school library. Publishers are often interested in how their materials work with low-achieving students and students with learning and behavior problems. They may be willing to provide a set of materials if the teacher is willing to evaluate the materials and provide feedback about how the materials work with actual students.

Selecting and Using Instructional Equipment

In addition to selecting instructional materials, teachers will want to choose equipment to facilitate learning. Along with various software programs, such equipment is becoming an increasingly important part of a teacher's toolkit. In addition to a computer in the classroom and/or the use of a computer lab in the school, other equipment can facilitate learning in your classroom.

Recorder. Tape recorders are relatively inexpensive and can be used in a variety of ways in the classroom. Headphones to accompany the tape recorder allow students to listen without disturbing others. Following are ten instructional applications for recorders:

1. A teacher can record reading books so that students can follow along during recreational reading or use for repeated reading. Apply the Concept 4.2 provides guidelines for recording books and stories.

2. One way to adapt textbooks is to record them.

3. It is helpful for some students to record what they want to write before they begin writing. They can record their ideas and then listen to them as they write their first drafts.

4. Students can record their reading every two to four weeks to hear their progress. After a student records his or her reading, it is important that the teacher and the student discuss the reading, identifying strengths and areas that need improvement. This recording can also be shared with parents to demonstrate progress and document continuing needs.

TECHTips

4.1 Using Technology to Enhance Socialization Skills

Teachers can use computers to enhance socialization skills by encouraging learners to work cooperatively with educational software. Programs that require learners to make decisions can foster appropriate social interactions within a structured game environment. *Oregon Train* and *Amazon Trail* from the Learning Company and *SimAnt* and *SimTown* from Maxis/EA are examples of simulation software that require players to make simulated real-life decisions and experience the consequences of those decisions. Also see the *Virtual Villagers* programs at www.bigfishgames.com. Problem-solving software like *The Factory* from Sunburst (www.sunburst.com) and *The Incredible Machine* (also *TIM: Even More Contraptions*) from Sierra (www.siera.com) require users to choose tools and parts and to sequence steps, building machines to match samples or create an animated contraption.

Another use of technology to aid socialization is for learners with behavior problems to graph data about their behaviors using any computer program that has graphing capabilities. As learners compare their behaviors from one day to the next, self-monitoring is facilitated.

Several types of computer programs can assist teachers in monitoring and managing classroom behavior. *PEGS—Practice in Effective Guidance Strategies* is an interactive classroom simulation that provides a variety of simulated classroom activities to help teachers promote appropriate participation with each learner. Teachers can learn how to apply specific behavioral strategies to match individual needs and observe the results of the interventions. *PEGS* has versions for preschool, elementary, and secondary classrooms and is available from: www.downloadlearning.com/teachers/pegs.html.

BOSR, an assessment tool that was mentioned in Tech Tips 1.1, is another useful behavior management program for teachers. It can be used to develop detailed intervention objectives divided into several subscales—personal, interpersonal, adaptive, self-management, communication, and task behaviors.

Programs available on the Internet to help with behavior management and behavior intervention plans include the following:

1. Center for Effective Collaboration and Practice: Functional Behavior Assessment
   http://cecp.air.org/fba/default.htm
2. Behavior Analysis Training System
   http://homepages.wmich.edu/~malott/rd/sm/layman1.html

Additionally, many Websites offer classroom management tips and suggestions for classroom teachers. As with other online advice, consider the source. Look for tips from recognized organizations, universities, and experts in the field. Following are some examples of such sites:

1. The Really Big List of Classroom Management Resources
   http://drwilliampmartin.tripod.com/classm.html
2. Classroom Management Links
   http://ss.uno.edu/ss/homepages/cmanage.html
3. Dr. Mac's Amazing Behavior Management Advice Site www.behavioradvisor.com

Screenshot of an Interactive Classroom Simulation from the PEGS Series

Source: Developmental Therapy Institute, Inc., www.developmentaltherapyinstitute.org.

5. Spelling tests can be recorded so that students can take them independently. The teacher first records the words to be tested, allowing time for the students to spell the words. After the test is recorded, the teacher spells each word so that the student can self-check.

6. When working on specific social or pragmatic language skills (e.g., answering the telephone, asking for directions, introducing someone), record the students so that they can listen to and evaluate themselves.

7. At the secondary level, class lectures can be recorded. Students can then listen to review the material and complete unfinished notes.

Progress Monitoring

8. Students can practice taking notes by listening to recordings of lectures. By using recordings, students can regulate the rate at which the material is presented.

9. Oral directions for independent learning activities can be recorded for students. This can be particularly helpful when a teacher is trying to conduct small group or one-to-one instruction while other students are working on independent learning activities.

10. Many instructional materials contain prerecorded resources.

Overhead or LCD Projector. These excellent teaching tools allow users to display the images from a transparency or PowerPoint slide on a screen or blank wall. Transparencies or PowerPoint slides are generally teacher-made, although some come with published instructional materials. Using a projector allows a teacher to model a skill and to highlight, write, color in, and/or point to important information. For example, a teacher may use a projector to demonstrate how to add quotation marks to a story, or a student may use it to demonstrate how he or she worked a long division problem. Using a projector can be easier than a chalkboard for presenting a lecture or leading a discussion because the overhead does not require a teacher to turn around to write.

The following are six suggestions for using an LCD or overhead projector:

1. Keep the amount of information presented relatively limited.
2. Use a different colored pen to highlight important points.
3. Have extra markers available.
4. Use the projector to develop language experience stories.
5. Use the projector to demonstrate editing and revisions in writing.
6. Use the projector along with a think-aloud procedure to demonstrate math procedures such as how to work long division.

Other Small Equipment. Several other pieces of small equipment should be considered in selecting equipment for either a resource room or a self-contained classroom.

A stopwatch can serve as an instructional tool and a motivator. For some tasks, it is important that students learn to respond at an automatic level (e.g., sight words, math facts). Students can use a stopwatch to time themselves or their classmates. These times can then be recorded on a time chart (see Figure 4.1). Using these charts, students can

FIGURE 4.1

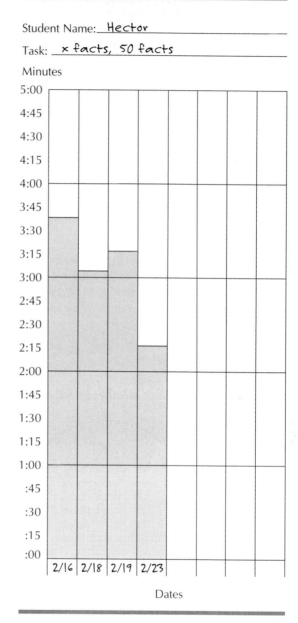

set goals, record their times, and try to improve on previous times.

An individual writing board is an excellent tool for obtaining individual written responses during small group and large group discussions. Mr. Howell uses these boards during review sessions in his resource high school history class. During the review sessions, he asks students questions, and they write their answers on the writing boards. He then asks them to display their boards. In this way, each student responds to each question in writing instead of one student orally responding to one question. Mr. Howell and the students believe that this is a better way to review because it requires them to think about and answer every question and to write the answers. Writing is important because it is generally required when the students take tests. Although small chalkboards can be used as individual writing boards, white boards and dry erase markers are now readily available.

Flannel boards and magnetic boards are particularly useful in elementary classrooms. These can be used in teaching and learning centers for such activities as depicting stories, spelling words, and working simple math problems. As we will discuss in Chapter 11, calculators are an invaluable tool for students when learning and for teachers when completing many of the routine activities associated with assessment and evaluation.

Developing Instructional Materials

In addition to purchasing published materials and equipment, most teachers find the need to develop their own instructional materials to supplement commercial materials. For example, some teachers make sentence strips containing the sentences from each story in a beginning reader. Many teachers develop materials to provide students with additional practice in skills they are learning. Developing self-correcting materials and/or materials in a game format can be advantageous.

Self-Correcting Materials. Self-correcting materials provide students with immediate feedback. Students with learning and behavior problems frequently have a history of failure and are reluctant

Progress Monitoring

to take risks when others are watching or listening. Self-correcting materials allow them to check themselves without sharing the information with others. Many computer programs and electronic learning games incorporate self-correction. Figure 4.2 presents an example of a self-correcting activity that teachers can easily make.

One key to self-correcting materials is immediate feedback (Mercer, Mercer, and Bott, 1984). The materials should be simple enough that students can learn to use them easily and check their answers quickly. The materials should be varied so that the interest and novelty level remain relatively high.

Another key to developing self-correcting materials is to make them durable so that they can be reused. Using heavy cardboard can increase the durability of materials. Laminating or covering the materials with clear Contact paper are good ways to make materials more durable. Special markers or grease pencils can then be used.

Instructional Games. Students with learning and behavior problems often need numerous opportunities to practice an academic skill. Instructional games can provide this practice in a format that is interesting to students.

The first step in designing an instructional game is to determine the purpose of the game. For example, the purpose might be to provide practice in the following:

- Forming word families (e.g., *-at: fat, sat, cat, rat*)
- Identifying sight words associated with a specific piece of reading material being used in the classroom
- Using semantic and syntactic clues by using the cloze procedure (e.g., For dessert Brian wanted an ice _____ cone.)
- Recalling multiplication facts
- Reviewing information (e.g., identifying the parts of a flower)

FIGURE 4.2

Self-Correcting Activity

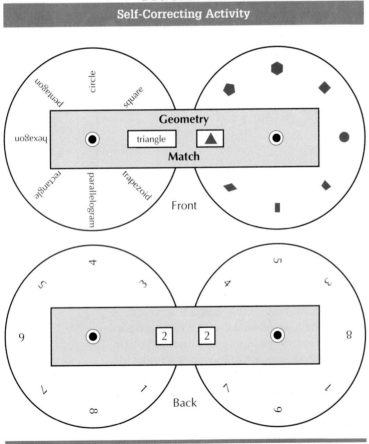

The second step is to select and adapt a game that can be used to practice a skill or review knowledge. For example, commercial games such as Monopoly, Chutes and Ladders, Candyland, Clue, Sorry, and Parcheesi can be adapted for classroom use. A generic game board can also be used (see Figure 4.3). Generic game boards can be purchased from some publishing companies. The key in selecting and adapting a game is to require the students to complete the instructional task as part of the turn-taking procedure. For example, when Candyland is adapted to practice sight words, students select a sight word card and a Candyland card. If they can correctly read the sight word, then they can use their Candyland card to move as indicated. When Monopoly is

FIGURE 4.3
Generic Board Game

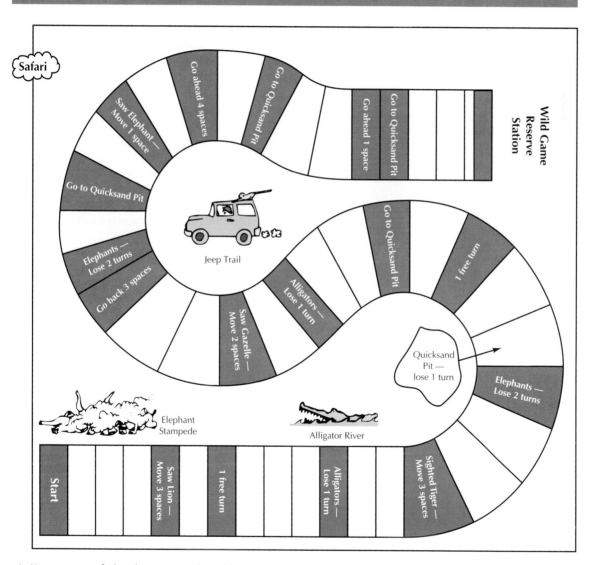

1. You are on a safari, trying to get to the Wild Game Reserve Station.
2. Begin at Start.
3. Each player rolls a die. The player with the highest number goes first.
4. Roll the die and draw a Game Card. If you answer the Game Card correctly, move the number shown on the die. If you do not answer the Game Card correctly, do not take a turn.
5. The first player to get to the Wild Game Reserve Station wins.

adapted for math facts, students first have to select and answer a math fact. If they answer it correctly, they earn the opportunity to throw the dice and take a turn.

When the same skills are being practiced by many students in a class, the teacher may want to develop a specific game for the skill. Math Marathon is a specific game in which students move forward on a game board, depicting a race, by answering math word problems. Different sets of math word problem game cards can be developed, depending on the students' problem-solving ability levels.

The third step is to write the directions and develop the materials. MacWilliams (1978) recommends making a rough draft of the game and testing it. Posterboard glued to cardboard makes a good game board, as does a manila folder. With a manila folder, the name of the game can be written on the tab, and the board can be stored so that the students can scan the tabs to find the game. The materials for the game can be kept in an envelope inside the folder. The directions for the game and a list of materials that should be found inside can be written on the envelope.

The fourth step is to demonstrate the game to the students so that they can learn to play it independently.

Organizing and Managing Materials

Selecting and developing materials is only one part of effective materials management. Classroom materials need to be organized in such a manner that the teacher and students have easy access to the materials without bothering other students.

Ms. Beyar coteaches in a language arts classroom for one hour each day, during which the class is divided into either mixed-ability or same-ability groups, depending on the lesson. Ms. Beyar has several suggestions regarding managing materials in the general education classroom:

> The first thing Ms. Casey [the general education teacher] and I did was expand the student library. We purchased books that represent a wider range of reading levels. We also began to purchase small sets of books to use in reading groups. Finally, we worked together to organize a closet and a file cabinet with adapted materials and manipulatives that we both use. I find that these materials are beneficial with children of all ability levels. I didn't realize that we would benefit so much from sharing materials!

Scheduling

When teachers talk about the most difficult aspects of their jobs, they often mention scheduling. Special education teachers generally work with between 5 and 10 general education teachers (though it can be as many as 25 teachers) to coordinate pull-out, in-class, and consultation services. Special education teachers also work closely with counselors and teachers at the secondary level to ensure that students are placed in classes that will help them reach the goals and objectives of the individual education program as well as meet graduation requirements. Even special education teachers who work in self-contained classrooms schedule students for integration into general education classroom activities for part of the day. It is essential that teachers work together to find time in the general education schedule that will be beneficial for the inclusion of students with more severe disabilities. In addition to adapting instruction, teachers need to consider whether students will have to be accompanied on their way to the general education classroom (by a student or a paraprofessional), and whether the classroom teacher or a paraprofessional will assist the students during the general education class.

When students spend most of their day in a self-contained classroom, special education teachers are responsible for their entire curriculum. Special education teachers make decisions about how to provide instruction in the various curricular areas (e.g., reading, math, writing, English, social studies, science, art, music) while still providing the students with adequate one-to-one and small group instruction so that the students can reach their educational goals in the academic areas of concern.

Scheduling within the Classroom

Whether teaching in an inclusion, resource, or self-contained classroom, it is important to use the time students spend in the classroom efficiently. There are no easy answers to scheduling problems. However, the following list presents some guidelines to use in developing a schedule:

• Schedule time to communicate with general education classroom teachers. The amount of time you schedule depends on the time your students spend in the general education classroom. Generally speaking, coteachers should schedule more time for this than resource teachers, and resource teachers should schedule more time than self-contained classroom teachers. While the frequency of such meetings will vary according to your students' needs, it is important that meeting times occur consistently. This time will prove invaluable in assisting students to be successful in regular classrooms.

• Schedule time to observe the classrooms in which your students are placed or are going to be placed. This alerts you to the class demands and schedules of the classroom and will help you in planning for your students' learning in that classroom.

• Schedule time to meet with other professionals (e.g., speech/language pathologist, school psychologist).

• Alternate instructional arrangements. For example, do not schedule a student to participate in independent learning activities for more than 30 minutes at a time.

• Plan for time to provide the students with advance organizers, feedback, and evaluation. In this way, students will know what is going to happen, and they will have the opportunity to think about what they have accomplished.

• Allow for explicit instruction. Sometimes we have students spend the majority of their time in independent learning activities, which results in little time for them to receive direct instruction from the teacher, aide, or tutor.

• Students who are included in general education classrooms still require specialized instruction. Organize time so that students with disabilities in general education classrooms receive the explicit instruction they need to be successful.

• Alternate preferred and less preferred activities, or make preferred activities contingent on the completion of less preferred activities.

• Let students know when the time for an activity is just about over. This gives them time to reach closure on this activity and get ready for the next activity or to ask for a time extension.

• Be consistent in scheduling yet flexible and ready for change.

• Schedule a session with each student in which you review his or her schedule in your room and in other teachers' classrooms. Be sure that students know what is expected of them.

• Plan time to meet and talk with members of your student's family, including parents.

Figures 4.4 and 4.5 present sample schedules for a resource room and a special education classroom. For the resource room, the schedule for one group of students is presented, whereas the entire day's schedule is presented for the special education program.

Developing an Overall Schedule for a Resource Consultant Program

Scheduling students' time while in the special education classroom is one issue, but the overall schedule for teaching in a resource or inclusion setting presents other issues and requires that the teacher work closely with other teachers and professionals in the school. Teachers who assume roles as resource teachers must first clarify and decide what their job responsibilities will be. Generally, these responsibilities can be divided into four general areas:

1. Providing direct instruction to the students, either in the general education classroom or in a separate classroom
2. Providing indirect instruction to the students by consulting with general classroom teachers and parents
3. Assessing current and referred students
4. Serving as an instructional resource for other teachers and professionals within the school

The time a teacher spends in each of these roles will directly influence the schedule he or she develops. For example, if the teacher's major roles are to provide instructional services indirectly to students, to assess current and referred students, and to serve as an instructional resource, then little time will be spent in scheduling groups of students in the resource room. Instead, the teacher will serve primarily as a consultant to others. A sample schedule for a teacher who provides direct and indirect support is presented in Figure 4.6.

By contrast, Ms. Beyar provides explicit instruction to most of the students she teaches for an average of 60 minutes per day, four days per week. Because she serves 22 students, she has developed a schedule that allows her some time to consult with general classroom teachers on a consistent basis, but she has also allocated time to teach and assess current and referred students. To facilitate her scheduling, she has grouped students according to grade level for the most part, with the older students attending in the morning and the younger students in the afternoon.

She explains her schedule as follows:

I have arranged for the older students to come in the morning because I feel that I can take over the responsibility for teaching these students reading and writing—the content that is usually taught in the morning in many general education classrooms.

FIGURE 4.4

Schedule for Fourth- through Sixth-Grade Students

Date: 4/15

Time	José	Amelia	Scott	Todd	Carmen	Frank
10:00	Small Group Instruction Reading ↓	Comprehension Computer Activity	Small Group Instruction Reading ↓	Social Studies Text Using Request Procedure with Carmen ↓	Social Studies Text Using Request Procedure with Todd ↓	Small Group Instruction Reading ↓
10:20	Inferential Comprehension Activity on Computer	Small Group Instruction Reading ↓	Social Studies Text with Self-Questioning	Small Group Instruction Reading ↓	Small Group Instruction Reading ↓	Word Drill Social Studies Text with Self-Questioning
10:40	Writing Process ↓	Writing Process ↓	Writing Process (Computer)	Writing Process ↓	Writing Process ↓	Writing Process (Computer)
	Spelling	Spelling	Spelling	Spelling	Spelling	Spelling
11:15	Practice Computer	Practice Game	Practice Game	Practice Tape Recorder Test	Practice Game	Practice Game

FIGURE 4.5

Sample Schedule for Intermediate-Level Special Education Program

	Activity			
Time	Group 1	Group 2	Group 3	Group 4
8:15	Writing Process Students working on reports			
9:15	Reading: Small group instruction (teacher)	Reading: Independent learning activities	Learning center: Map reading	Reading: Small group instruction (aide)
9:45	Reading: Independent learning activities	Reading: Small group instruction (aide)	Reading: Small group instruction (teacher)	Learning center: Map reading
10:15	Announcements			
10:20	Recess			
10:45	Math: Group instruction (teacher)		Computer lab for Math practice (aide)	
11:15	Computer lab (aide)		Group instruction (teacher)	
11:50	Lunch			
12:40	Recreational Reading/Writing			
1:00	Social Studies: Large group instruction			
1:45	Science: Cooperative learning activities			
2:15	Recess			
2:40	Health—Mon./Art—Tues./P.E.—Wed./Special Activity—Thurs., Fri. (Current: Producing a play)			
3:10	Earned "fun time" or time to complete work			
3:30	Dismissal			

FIGURE 4.6

Coteaching Teacher Schedule

Week of: ___April 15___

Time	Monday	Tuesday	Wednesday	Thursday	Friday
7:30	IEP Meeting	Instructional Review Meeting (2nd grade)	Child Study Team Meeting	IEP Meeting	Instructional Review Meeting (4th grade)
8:15	Work with 5th grade low reading group				→
9:00	Observe and assist LD/EH students in classroom (1st grade)	Assessment	Observe and assist (2nd grade, kindergarten)	3rd grade / 4th grade	5th grade / 6th grade
11:30	Meet with individual teachers	Planning and material development →		Meet with individual teachers	Planning and material development
12:30	Lunch				→
1:00	Work with 2nd grade low reading group				→
1:30	Conduct study skills class for selected 4th–6th graders	Conduct social skills class for group of EH students	Conduct study skills class	Conduct social skills class	Conduct study skills class
2:00	Work with Ms. Jones on implementing writing process →			Work with Mr. Peters on using semantic feature analysis for teaching vocabulary	Assessment
2:30	Provide direct instruction in reading to 5 students with learning disabilities			→	↓
3:30	Dismissal (check with teachers as needed)				→
3:45	End of day				

I have developed a strong program in teaching reading comprehension, and I am using a process approach to teaching writing. Currently I am using content area textbooks, trade books, and literature for teaching reading comprehension, and the students are working on writing reports, literature critiques, and short stories on topics of their choice. Because I am responsible for these students' reading and writing, I am accountable for grading the students in these areas. Using this schedule, these students for the most part are in the general education classroom for content area subjects and math. I feel that this is important. When they go to junior high, they will probably be taking general math, science, social studies, and other content area classes. If they have been missing these classes in the general education classroom during the fourth through sixth grades, they will really have trouble catching up. It's hard enough for these students—we want to give them every advantage possible.

I often provide their reading instruction in content areas such as social studies and science. Thus, while the emphasis is on reading rather than knowledge acquisition, I feel that I am extending their background knowledge of concepts they will be taught in social studies and science.

I have the younger students come after lunch, because I feel that many of these students need two doses of reading, writing, and math. These students get instruction in these areas in the morning in the general education classroom, and then I give them additional instruction in the afternoon. With this arrangement, it is important that I communicate with the general education classroom teachers so that we each know what the other is doing. We don't want to confuse the students by giving them conflicting information or approaches to reading.

I also have one day a week that I use for assessment, consulting with classroom teachers, checking on the students in the general education classroom, and meeting and planning with my teaching assistant. I feel that this time is very important. All of my students spend most of the school day in the regular classroom. If they are really struggling in those settings, I need to know so that I can provide additional support.

There are always some exceptions to the general guidelines I use for scheduling. I have three students whom I monitor only in the general classroom. These students see me as a group on my assessment/consulting day. We talk about how it is going and discuss what is working for them and what frustrates them. I feel that this time is critical for their successful inclusion. I also have 2 fifth-grade students who have good oral language skills but are reading on the first-grade level. They come for an additional 30 minutes late in the day, and we use the Fernald (VAKT) method to learn sight words.

I also developed a special schedule for my teachers' aide. She works directly with students to supplement and enhance skills they have initiated with me.

Coordinating Services for Students with Learning and Behavior Problems prior to Identification

If students with learning and behavior problems are to be successful in general education classrooms, making both academic and social progress, then special education and general education teachers need to work together. The strategies that follow can be incorporated into an instructional program whose objective is to

assist students in the general education classroom:

- Work closely with other teachers.
- Observe students in all of the settings in which they are learning to determine their academic and social demands.
- Assist teachers in adapting materials, instruction, and the instructional environment to facilitate the students' needs.
- Monitor the students once they are in general education classes.
- Meet regularly with the students to discuss progress and concerns.
- Communicate frequently with teachers to discuss progress and concerns.
- Suggest that classroom teachers use a buddy system in which a student with special needs is paired with a "veteran" to help the special needs student learn the rules, procedures, and routines of the classroom.
- Coteach to support the integration of students with special needs during instruction.

Special Considerations for Scheduling in Secondary Settings

Scheduling in resource and consultant programs in secondary settings generally is less flexible than in elementary-level programs. Teachers must work within the confines of the instructional periods and the curricular units that students must complete for high school graduation. One of the major responsibilities for resource/consultant teachers in secondary settings is to determine subject areas in which students need special classes and areas in which they can succeed in general education classes without instructional support. These decisions about scheduling must be made on an individual basis and should be made with the involvement and commitment of the student as well as the teachers involved.

With the greater use of learning and study strategies curriculums in secondary special education programs, secondary special education teachers may want to consider their role as that of learning specialists (Schumaker and Deshler, 1988). For the most part, they teach classes in learning and study strategies that provide students with the necessary skills and strategies to function in general content classes. These learning specialists may also spend part of their day consulting with the content area teachers/specialists and in some cases may coteach.

FOCUS
Question 2. How can teachers use classroom management and positive behavior support to promote prosocial behavior?

Classroom Management

When someone mentions classroom management, most teachers think of discipline and classroom management rules. In fact, many special education teachers most dread the part of their job that addresses students' behaviors, largely because teachers think of classroom management as what one does *after* a student has a behavior problem. Another way to think about classroom management is to consider what one can do to establish a classroom climate that promotes desirable behaviors and reduces inappropriate behaviors. Thus, the majority of a teacher's classroom management efforts take place *before* any behavior problems. Students are taught to have expectations for the behaviors and routines of the classroom.

It is important to establish processes and procedures early in the year that provide students with a clear understanding of the class routines and the behaviors that are acceptable within these routines. Organizing these acceptable practices as a group and establishing them early is a critical first step for successful classroom management (Rogers, 2002). One way to inform students of the classroom rules is to discuss the rules with them. The more specifically a teacher defines what he or she wants students to do and not do, the more likely the teacher is to see those behaviors. For example, teachers should consider providing clear expectations about the following:

- When it is acceptable to talk with peers and when it is not
- When it is acceptable to move around the classroom and when it is not
- How students are expected to move from the classroom to other settings in the school
- Behaviors expected during typical class routines such as group work, whole-class instruction, and individual study time
- When and how assignments should be submitted
- What students should do when they have a conflict with another student

As new children enter the class during the year, assigning a veteran student as a guide or mentor can help the new student to understand the rule system of the classroom.

The purpose of some classroom rules is to regulate student behaviors that are likely to disrupt learning and teacher activities or cause damage or injury to property or others. In addition to explicit conduct rules, most classrooms have a set of implicit rules under which they function (Erickson and Shultz, 1981). Sharing the explicit conduct rules and demonstrating the rewards of working within the rule system is particularly important for students with behavior problems. Making rewards contingent on full class participation can also assist a teacher because students will encourage each other to work within the rule system.

Ms. Schiller works with junior high students with emotional disorders in a self-contained setting. Establishing conduct rules early in the year and setting up a reward system for "good behavior" is an important part of her program. Ms. Schiller comments:

> As far as I know, all of the students in this class are here primarily because they cannot cope with the rule systems in regular classrooms. This happens for a variety of reasons, and as a part of our social skills program, we discuss some of the reasons and how to cope with them. But the majority of the day is focused on academic learning. To accomplish effective learning, we have a set of written and unwritten rules that the students and I are willing to operate under. We establish these rules at the beginning of the year during class meetings. In these meetings, we talk about how the school operates and the rules under which it operates, and then we decide what rules we want the classroom to function under. Usually it takes several days to establish these rules. The rules we generally decide on are these:
>
> - During discussions, one person talks at a time.
> - When a person is talking, it is the responsibility of the rest of us to listen.
> - Work quietly so you won't bother others.
> - No hitting, shoving, kicking, etc.
> - No screaming.
> - Do not take other people's possessions without asking.
> - Treat classmates and teachers with respect and consideration.
> - When outside the classroom, follow the rules of the school or those established by the supervisor.

Each day when we have a class meeting, we discuss the rules, our success with using these rules, and how the rules have operated. Sometimes we add new rules based on our discussions. I involve the students in this evaluation and decision making. Eventually, we begin to decide when the rules can be made more flexible. In this way, I hope that I am helping the students assume more responsibility for their own behavior while at the same time maintaining a learning environment that is conducive to academic as well as social growth.

I think there are three main reasons this rule system works in my classroom. First, the students feel like they own the system and have a responsibility to make it work. We have opportunities to discuss the system and to make changes. Second, we also establish a token system [see Chapter 2] for appropriate behavior and learning. Third, I communicate regularly with the parents, letting them know how their child is performing.

The classroom rules that a teacher establishes depend on the social context of the school and the classroom and the teaching–learning process as described in Chapter 1. Some guidelines to use in developing and implementing classroom rules and management systems follow:

- Have the students help in selecting rules for the classroom.
- Select the fewest number of rules possible.
- Check with the principal or appropriate administrative personnel to determine whether the rules are within the school guidelines.
- Select rules that are enforceable.
- Select rules that are reasonable.
- Determine consistent consequences for rule infractions.
- Have students evaluate their behavior in relation to the rules.
- Modify rules only when necessary.
- Have frequent group meetings in which students provide self-feedback as well as feedback to others about their behavior.
- Allow students to provide solutions to nagging class or school issues through problem solving.

Classroom Management and Student Behavior

Lisa Rosario is a first-year, middle school resource room teacher in a suburban school district. She is not happy with the behavior of the students who come to the resource room. She told an experienced special education teacher in her school, "I feel like I know what to teach and how to teach, but I just can't seem to get the students to behave so that they can learn. What can I do to make the students change?" The experienced teacher suggested that Ms. Rosario first look at her own behavior in order to change the behavior of the students in her classroom. Figure 4.7 provides a checklist for teachers to evaluate the effectiveness of their interventions.

Ms. Rosario is not alone. Teachers identify classroom management as a cause of stress and frequently cite it as the reason they leave the teaching profession (Cangelosi, 2004; Elam and Gallup, 1989). Following are some guidelines for Ms. Rosario to consider to assist in facilitating more appropriate behavior on the part of her students:

1. *Look for the positive behavior, and let students know you recognize it.* Most teachers indicate that they provide a lot of positive reinforcement to their students. However, observations in special and general education teachers' classes indicate relatively low levels of positive reinforcement (McIntosh et al., 1993). Teachers need to provide a lot more positive feedback than they think is necessary.

One of the fundamental rules about positive feedback is that it needs to be both specific and immediate. "Carla's homework is completed exactly the way I asked for it to be done. She has

FIGURE 4.7
Implementation Checklist

If your intervention is not working, consider the following:

- Have you adequately identified and defined the target behavior?
- Have you selected the right kind of reinforcer? (What you decided on may not be reinforcing to the student.)
- Are you providing reinforcement soon enough?
- Are you providing too much reinforcement?
- Are you giving too little reinforcement?
- Are you being consistent in your implementation of the intervention program?
- Have you made the intervention program more complicated than it needs to be?
- Are others involved following through (e.g., principal, parent, "buddy")?
- Is the social reinforcement by peers outweighing your contracted reinforcement?
- Did you fail to give reinforcers promised or earned?

Source: B. Larrivee, *Strategies for Effective Classroom Management: Creating a Collaborative Climate* (Boston: Allyn & Bacon, 1992). Reprinted with permission.

numbered the problems, left space between answers so that they are easy to read, and written the appropriate heading at the top of the paper." A second fundamental rule about positive feedback is that students need to be clear about what behaviors are desirable and undesirable.

A clear list of class rules and consequences is an important step in making classroom management expectations understandable. Rules and procedures form the structure of classroom management (Brophy, 1988; Cangelosi, 2004). Procedures that are part of the classroom routines need to be taught to students. Rules outline the behaviors that are acceptable and unacceptable. A teacher's criteria for what constitutes a behavior problem is the basis for classroom rules (Emmer, Evertson, Sanford, Clements, and Worsham, 1989). Think back to Lisa Rosario who indicated that she had difficulty with classroom management. In further discussion with the experienced teacher, Ms. Rosario realized she had difficulty establishing and enforcing classroom procedures. Once the experienced teacher observed in her classroom and assisted her in establishing routines, Ms. Rosario experienced significantly fewer difficulties with classroom management.

Positive reinforcement is more effective at the elementary level than in middle school, and least effective with high school students (Forness, 1973; Stallings, 1975). This does not mean that positive reinforcement should be avoided with older students, but merely that it should be handled in a different way. Elementary students find public recognition in front of the entire class more rewarding than do older students, who prefer to receive individual feedback.

2. *Reinforcers can be used to encourage positive behavior.* As we explained in Chapter 1, both positive reinforcement and negative reinforcement increase behavior. Most people think that negative reinforcement means something harmful or "negative," but that is not the case. As we described in Chapter 1, positive reinforcement is the presentation of a stimulus (verbal response, physical response such as touching, or a tangible response such as a reward) following the target behavior, intended to maintain or increase a target behavior. Figure 4.8 lists reinforcers that teachers may want to consider for use in their classrooms.

3. *Use a token economy.* A token economy is a structured plan for delivering reinforcers (tokens) following the display of target students behaviors and/or the absence of undesirable student behaviors. Token economies can be adapted for use in a variety of settings, and have been used

extensively in special education (Kazdin, 1989). For example, teachers can post in the classroom a list of desirable behaviors (e.g., raising a hand and waiting to be called on by the teacher before talking) as well as undesirable behaviors (e.g., hitting classmates). Posted along with the behaviors are the corresponding number of tokens (e.g., points, chips, tickets) that students can earn for exhibiting target behaviors and eliminating noxious behaviors. Teachers can award tokens as target behaviors occur and/or deliver tokens after a specific period of time has elapsed (e.g., Terrell receives one token at the start of each hour provided that he has not hit a peer during the previous 60 minutes). Teachers can award tokens to individuals as in the previous example, or award the entire class. Either way, the underlying principle is that students will be motivated to earn tokens that are collected and exchanged for previously determined privileges (e.g., a class pizza party or first choice of equipment at recess).

4. *Change inappropriate behavior.* Behaviors that are interfering are the ones that teachers can most easily identify. It is much easier for teachers to list the behaviors they would like to see reduced than to identify behaviors that they would like to see increased. Morgan and Reinhart (1991) identified the following guiding principles to assist in changing inappropriate behavior of students:

- Do not use threats. Consider carefully the consequences that you intend to use. Do not threaten students with a consequence that you are actually unwilling to use or that will force you to back down.
- Follow through consistently on the rules you make with the consequences you have predetermined.
- Do not establish so many rules that you spend too much time applying consequences. You will find yourself continually at war with the students.
- Do not establish consequences that are punishing to you. If you are stressed or inconvenienced by the consequence, you may eventually begin to resent the student, which would interfere with your relationship.
- Listen and talk to the student, but avoid disagreements or arguments. If you are tempted to argue, set another time to continue the discussion.
- Use logic, principles, and effective guidelines to make decisions. Avoid using your power to make students do something without connecting it to a logical principle.

FIGURE 4.8

Reinforcers Teachers Can Use to Increase Appropriate Behavior

Student Provides Self-Reinforcers
- Students give themselves points for behaving well.
- Students say positive things to themselves, "I'm working hard and doing well."
- Students monitor their own behavior.

Adult Approval
- Verbal recognition from the teacher that a student is behaving appropriately, "Juan you are following directions on this assignment."
- Physical recognition from the teacher that students are behaving appropriately. Teacher moves around the classroom and touches students on the shoulder who are behaving appropriately.
- Teacher informs family or other professionals of the appropriate behavior of a student. This can be accomplished with "good news notes" or verbally.

Peer Recognition
- Teacher informs other students of the appropriate behavior of a student. "The award for Student of the Day goes to the outstanding improvement in behavior demonstrated by [student's name]."
- Peers can put the names of students who have demonstrated appropriate behavior into a designated box. These names can be read at the end of the week.
- A designated period of time is allocated at the end of the class period (high school) or day (elementary school) to ask students to recognize their fellow classmates who have demonstrated outstanding behavior.

Privileges
- Students are awarded free time after displaying appropriate behavior.
- Students are allowed to serve in key classroom roles after demonstrating outstanding behavior.

- Students are awarded passes that they can trade in for a night without homework.

Activities
- Students can perform an activity they like (e.g., drawing) after they complete the desired activity (e.g., the activity during that class period).
- Students can perform their tasks on the computer.
- Students can perform their tasks with a partner they select.

Tokens
- Tokens are items (e.g., chips, play money, points) that can be exchanged for something of value.
- Use tokens to reward groups or teams who are behaving appropriately.
- Allow groups of individuals to accumulate tokens that they can "spend" on privileges such as no homework, or free time.

Tangibles
- Tangibles are rewards that are desirable objects to students but usually not objects that they can consume (e.g., toys, pencils, erasers, paper, crayons).
- Tokens can be exchanged for tangible reinforcers.
- Tangible reinforcers can be used to reward the class for meeting a class goal.
- Tangible reinforcers may be needed to maintain the behavior of a student with severe behavior problems.

Consumables
- Consumables are rewards that are desirable objects to students that they consume (e.g., raisins, pieces of cereal, candy).
- Tokens can be exchanged for consumable reinforcers.
- Consumable reinforcers can be used to reward the class for meeting a class goal.
- Consumable reinforcers may be needed to maintain the behavior of a student with severe behavior problems.

Source: Adapted from S. Vaughn, C. S. Bos, and J. S. Schumm, *Teaching Students Who Are Exceptional, Diverse, and at Risk* (Boston: Allyn & Bacon, 2007).

- Do not focus on minor or personal peeves. Focus on the problems that are the most interfering.
- Treat each student as an individual with unique problems and abilities. Avoid comparing students' behaviors or abilities, as this does not assist students in self-understanding or in better understanding the problems and abilities of others.
- Remember that students' problems belong to them. Although their problems may interfere with your work, they are not *your* problems. Students with behavior or emotional problems are often successful at transferring their problems to others. Students need to learn to resolve their own conflicts.

- Students often say or do things that are upsetting to teachers. Recognize your feelings, and do not let them control your behavior. Do not respond to the upsetting behavior of a student by striking back, humiliating, embarrassing, or berating the student.
- Solicit the assistance of families and students in putting any problem in writing to ensure that everyone agrees on what needs to be changed.
- Get student and family input on the behavior problem and suggestions for what might reduce it.
- Set up a plan that identifies the problem, consequence, and/or rewards for changes in

Family

FIGURE 4.9
Sample Behavior Contract

DATE: _____

Mr. Wangiri will give one point to Joleen when she exhibits any of the following in his classroom:

1. She raises her hand appropriately and waits for the teacher to call on her before responding to a question or seeking information.
2. She sits appropriately (in chair with all four legs on the ground).
3. When annoyed by other students, she ignores them or informs the teacher instead of yelling at and/or hitting others.

After Joleen has earned 10 points, she may select one of the following:

1. She may obtain a 20-minute coupon to be used at any time to work on the computer.
2. She may serve as the teacher's assistant for a day.
3. She may obtain a 15-minute coupon for free time.

4. She may have lunch with the teacher and brought by the teacher.

Joleen may continue to select awards for every 10 points earned. New awards may be decided upon by the teacher and Joleen, and added to the list. I, Joleen Moore, agree to the conditions stated above, and understand that I will not be allowed any of the rewards until I have earned 10 points following the above stated guidelines.

_____
(student's signature)

I, Mr. Wangiri, agree to the conditions stated above. I will give Joleen one of the aforementioned rewards only after she has earned 10 points.

_____
(teacher's signature)

---

behavior. See Figure 4.9 and Figure 4.10 for a sample behavioral contract and a self-management plan, respectively.

Positive Behavioral Support

In recent years, the principles of behavior management have been applied in various community settings (e.g., school, family) with supports to reduce problem behaviors and develop appropriate behaviors that lead to enhanced social relations. This modification of behavior management principles is called *positive behavioral support* (PBS). Many schools find that they are coping with increasing numbers of behavior problems, fighting, bullying, discontent among students, and general lack of discipline. This situation does not exist because teachers or administrators are not caring or lack concern about the issue. It occurs because a schoolwide adoption of a consistent and fluent model needs to occur. PBS is a proven model for establishing a positive schoolwide community (Sugai and Horner, 2001).

The focus of PBS is to develop individualized interventions that stress prevention of problem behaviors through effective educational programming to improve an individual's quality of life (Janney and Snell, 2000). Because behavior is a form of communication and is often related to the context, PBS involves careful observation of circumstances and the purpose of a problem behavior. A significant number of negative behaviors can be dealt with by modifying the environment (e.g., altering seating arrangements). PBS also

FIGURE 4.10
Self-Management Plan

Name: Kiernen Smathers

Target Behavior: Submit completed homework to the teacher on time or meet with teacher before the assignment is due to agree on an alternative date and time.

Where Behavior Occurs: Mathematics and Science

Goals:

1. Kiernen will use an assignment book and write down the assignments, guidelines, and due dates. The teacher will initial these to ensure that he understands them and has written them correctly.
2. Kiernen will interpret what he needs to do for each assignment and ask questions as needed.
3. Kiernen will discuss any assignments with the teacher ahead of time if he anticipates not having them ready on time.

Time Line: Meet each Friday to review progress and assignments. Revise plan as needed.

Reinforcer: Kiernen will receive 15 minutes of extra time to work on the computer each day his assignments are completed.

Evaluation: Kiernen will write a brief description of the program's success.

---

emphasizes teaching appropriate behaviors to replace the inappropriate behavior in a normalized setting (Janney and Snell, 2000).

Recall from Chapter 2 that applied behavior analysis is based primarily on operant learning principles. The application of these principles to change maladaptive behaviors is referred to as behavioral therapy. The three major components of applied behavior analysis are as follows:

1. *Target behaviors are defined operationally.* For example, a teacher described a behaviorally disturbed child in her classroom as "emotional." Although most of us know what *emotional* means, each of us probably imagines a somewhat different behavioral repertoire when we think of a student as behaving in an emotional way. In the same way, if asked to chart the emotional behavior of a student, it is unlikely that any two observers will offer the same observations. For this reason, teachers are asked to describe the behaviors that they observe when a student is acting emotional. *"When I ask her to turn in her work, she puts her head down on her desk, sighs, and then crumples her paper."* Identifying specific behaviors students exhibit assists teachers in clarifying what is disturbing them, and it also assists in the second step, measurement.

2. *Target behaviors are measured.* To determine a student's present level of functioning and to determine if a selected intervention is effective, target behaviors must be measured before and during intervention. Some behaviors are easy to identify and measure. For example, the number of times Val completes his arithmetic assignment is relatively easy to tabulate. However, behaviors such as "out of seat" and "off task" require more elaborate measurement procedures.

The three types of measurement procedures most frequently used are event, duration, and interval time sampling. *Event sampling* measures the number of times a behavior occurs in a designated amount of time. Sample behaviors include the number of times the bus driver reports a student's misconduct, the number of times a student is late for class, or the number of times a student does not turn in a homework assignment. *Duration sampling* measures the length of time a behavior occurs, for example the amount of time a student is out of seat, how long a student cries, or the amount of time a student is off task. It is possible to use event and duration samplings for the same behavior. The teacher might want to use both measurements or select the measurement procedure that will give the most information about the behavior. *Interval sampling* explores whether a behavior occurs during a specific interval of time. For example, a teacher may record whether a student is reported for fighting during recess periods. Interval sampling is used when it is difficult to tell when a behavior begins or ends and when a behavior occurs very frequently.

In addition to the measurement of the target behavior, it is helpful to identify the antecedents and consequences of the target behavior. Knowing what occurs before a problem behavior and what occurs immediately after gives important information that assists in developing an intervention. If every time a student cries, the teacher talks to the student for a few minutes, it could be the teacher's attention that is maintaining the behavior. Listing antecedents can provide information about the environment, events, or people who trigger the target behavior. An analysis of antecedents and consequences facilitates the establishment of a successful intervention procedure.

3. *Goals and treatment intervention are established.* On the basis of observation and measurement data and an analysis of antecedents and consequences, goals for changing behavior and intervention strategies are established. The purpose of establishing goals is to specify the desired frequency or duration of the behavior. Goal setting is most effective when the person exhibiting the target behavior is involved in establishing the goals. For example, Dukas is aware that he gets into too many fights and wants to reduce this behavior. After the target behavior has been identified and measured, the teacher and student examine the data and identify that the only time Dukas gets into fights is during the lunchtime recess. They set up a contract in which the teacher agrees to give Dukas 10 minutes of free time at the end of each day in which he does not get into a fight. The student agrees with the contract. The teacher continues to measure the student's behavior to determine whether the suggested treatment plan is effective.

There are many treatment strategies in behavior support that teachers can use to effect change. For example, teachers can use reinforcers to shape new behaviors, reinforce incompatible behaviors, or maintain or increase desired behavior. Teachers can use extinction, punishment, or time-out to eliminate undesired behaviors. Figure 4.11 presents guidelines for using time-out. Teachers may use contracts or token economies to change behavior. These strategies are discussed in the section on operant learning theory in Chapter 2. With these intervention strategies, consequences are controlled by another (e.g., the teacher). Self-management is a procedure in which the individual controls the consequences. Self-management is particularly effective with older children, adolescents, and adults because the control and responsibility for change are placed in their hands. With assistance from a teacher, counselor, or other influential adult, the adolescent implements a self-management program by following three steps:

1. Identify the behavior the person wants to change (e.g., being late for school).

2. Identify the antecedents and consequences associated with the behavior. For example, Kamala says, "When the alarm rings, I continue to lie in bed. I also wait until the last minute to run to the bus stop, and I frequently miss the bus."
3. Develop a plan that alters the antecedents and provides consequences that will maintain the desired behavior. For example, Kamala decides to get up as soon as the alarm rings and to leave for the bus stop without waiting until the last minute. She arranges with her parents to have the car on Friday nights if she has arrived at school on time every day that week.

An obvious disadvantage of a self-control model of behavior change is that it relies on the student's motivation for success. Students who are not interested in changing behaviors and who are not willing to analyze antecedents and consequences and develop potentially successful intervention strategies will be unsuccessful with self-determined behavior change plans.

Rick is a fourth-grade student who has a learning disability, poor social skills, and difficulty interacting with peers. He was seen hitting other students and is known to get into fights for no apparent reason. A careful observation of Rick's interactions with peers and his behaviors suggested that hitting was Rick's way of saying, "Get off my back." Rick was taught to say, "Get off my back" and walk away instead of hitting. All the teachers in the school reminded Rick to "use his words instead of his hands" to communicate. He was taught other specific skills necessary for successful social interactions such as joining a group and initiating and maintaining a conversation. Teachers tried to pair Rick with other students during classroom activities to provide him with opportunities to practice his new skills.

In this case, Rick's behavior and the environment in which target behaviors occurred were observed. Once the causes, circumstances, and purposes of the behaviors had been identified, the classroom teacher met with other teachers to discuss and enlist their help in providing Rick with the support he would need. The teachers also developed a list of specific social skills to teach Rick. Over time, Rick's problem behaviors decreased, his social skills improved, and he made friends with a few students.

Kasim is a first-grade student with behavior problems. He gets in trouble for taking materials from his neighbors without requesting their permission. His teacher moved Kasim's desk closer to the end of the row so that he would have only three neighbors. She also taught Kasim to think and

FIGURE 4.11

Time-Out: Guidelines for Effective Implementation

Using time-out can help reduce problem behaviors, but it can also be misused. What is time-out? Time-out is when students are informed of the negative behaviors for which they will be denied access to opportunities for positive reinforcement (Alberto and Troutman, 2006). Some examples of time-out practices outlined by Ryan, Sanders, Katsiyannis, and Yell (2007) include the following:

- *Planned Ignoring*—This occurs when the teacher allows the student to remain in the setting, however, all attention from the teacher and peers is removed for a designated period of time.
- *Withdrawal of Materials*—All materials related to the behavior are removed for a specified period of time. For example, if a student throws a ball at another student in an aggressive manner, he or she is not allowed access to the ball for a specified period of time.
- *Contingent Observation*—Students are removed from the setting but are able to observe. For example, on the playground a student who exhibits inappropriate behavior watches from the sidelines for a specified period of time.
- *Seclusion Time-Out*—The student is removed from the setting and placed in isolation for a specified period of time.

When using time-out practices, remember the following guidelines:

- Use time-out as a last resort.
- Discuss time-out procedures with school administrators and parents before implementation.
- Put time-out procedures in writing, and file them with school rules.
- Provide students with information in advance about what behaviors will result in time-out.
- Place students in time-out only for brief time periods (15–20 minutes).
- Before placing the student in time-out, specify the amount of time he or she will be in time-out.
- Tell the student to go to time-out. If the student does not comply, the teacher should unemotionally place the student in time-out.
- Use time-out *immediately* following the inappropriate behavior.
- Establish contingencies in advance for the student who fails to comply with time-out rules.
- Always monitor the time-out area.
- When the time specified for time-out is over, the student should join his or her classmates.
- Provide reinforcement for appropriate behavior after time-out.

take out all the materials he needed to do a particular assignment—for example, completing a worksheet requires the worksheet, pencil, and eraser. She even placed a small box labeled "materials needed" on his table so that Kasim could place all the materials he needed for a particular task in his box and not have to borrow from his neighbors. The teacher also taught Kasim appropriate ways of asking others to lend him their materials.

In this case, Kasim's target behaviors and the environment in which they occurred were observed, and then the causes, circumstances, and purposes of the behavior were determined. The teacher then decided to alter the physical environment (by moving Kasim's desk) to reduce the circumstances in which Kasim could intrude on his neighbors. She also taught him alternative behaviors (organizing his materials) to replace his inappropriate behaviors (taking materials from neighbors).

Schoolwide Positive Behavior Support Models.

What does a schoolwide PBS model look like? The first step is to establish a primary prevention model in which the focus is on preventing behavior problems schoolwide (Sugai, Horner, and Gresham, 2002). This requires ensuring that most school goals (80 percent or more) are stated in positive terms. The use of punishment is severely restricted only to emergency and very severe cases. This means that all school personnel know the positive rules that are established and that a concerted effort is made to ensure that all students are aware of positive school behavior and rules. School administrators are also actively involved in knowing and supporting implementation of the rules. This requires establishing contracts with students who have ongoing behavior problems to identify their needs and establish peer and adult support for changing their behaviors. Thus, ongoing progress monitoring is also an important feature. Though initially time-consuming to establish, PBS yields significant results over time, reduces behavior problems, and improves the school climate. For students with disabilities whose behavior problems are so profound that they interfere with their learning or that of their classmates, a functional behavioral assessment is required.

Considerable evidence shows that PBS can be taught to and used by parents/guardians very effectively (Lucyshyn, Dunlap, and Albin, 2002). Parents and other family members have successfully engaged students with severe problem behaviors in alternative behaviors and modified contexts that no longer support their behavior problems. How can this be done? Much like the procedures used by general and special education teachers with students with extreme behavior problems, family members can identify the behavior problems through assessment and then alter their feedback so that the child's behavior problems are no longer supported and thus become ineffective (Lucyshyn, Horner, Dunlap, Albin, and Ben, 2002). This yields more positive and constructive parent-child interactions.

FOCUS Question 3. What is the purpose of a functional behavioral assessment (FBA), and what are the procedures for developing an effective FBA?

Developing a Functional Behavioral Assessment

According to IDEA, students with disabilities who have significant behavior problems that interfere with their own learning or with the learning of other students must have a functional behavioral assessment (FBA). An FBA and a behavioral improvement plan (BIP) are designed to identify behavior problems of students and to develop an intervention plan to treat these behavior problems. The procedures and practices for developing an FBA are not nearly as well defined as are those for an IEP, and many school personnel still are unclear about how and when to design and use FBAs and BIPs. If a student's behavior is interfering with his or her learning, an FBA is required. Because it is much more likely that an FBA will assist a student than it will interfere, it is always a good idea to develop an FBA and a BIP.

According to Shippen, Simpson, and Crites (2003), there are several critical steps in designing an effective FBA:

1. Define the target behavior in behavioral terms. Clearly specify the behavior(s) you would like to see the student perform in observational terms that can be recorded and monitored.
2. Collect and monitor the target behaviors through ongoing data collection that considers frequency, intensity, and rate.
3. Record the events and behaviors that precede and follow the target behavior. In this way, the antecedent, behavior, and consequences are noted.
4. Develop a hypothesis of the conditions under which the target behavior occurs. This hypothesis guides the intervention plan.
5. Develop an intervention plan that considers the antecedents and reinforcers and is built to test the hypothesis.

Figure 4.12 provides an example of a functional behavioral assessment.

FIGURE 4.12

A Sample Functional Behavioral Assessment

Target Behavior I: _____

Baseline Assessment Method:
    parent interview
    teacher interview
    checklists
    systematic observation
    frequency counts of target behaviors
    sequence analysis (required)
    norm-referenced assessments

Baseline Frequency of Target Behavior:
_____
_____
_____
_____
_____
_____
_____

Target Behavior II: _____

Baseline Assessment Method:
    parent interview
    teacher interview
    checklists
    systematic observation
    frequency counts of target behaviors
    sequence analysis (required)
    norm-referenced assessments

Baseline Frequency of Target Behavior:
_____
_____
_____
_____
_____
_____
_____

Target Behavior III: _____

Baseline Assessment Method:
    parent interview
    teacher interview
    checklists
    systematic observation
    frequency counts of target behaviors
    sequence analysis (required)
    norm-referenced assessments

Baseline Frequency of Target Behavior:
_____
_____
_____
_____
_____
_____
_____

Purpose of Target Behavior I:

1. To obtain something?   yes   no   what? _____
2. To escape/avoid something?   yes   no   what? _____
3. Other factors?   yes   no   what? _____

Hypothesis: _____
Replacement Behavioral Goal: _____

Necessary Skills?   yes   no, needs additional instruction in _____

Purpose of Target Behavior II:

1. To obtain something?   yes   no   what? _____
2. To escape/avoid something?   yes   no   what? _____
3. Other factors?   yes   no   what? _____

Hypothesis: _____
Replacement Behavioral Goal: _____

Necessary Skills?   yes   no, needs additional instruction in _____

Purpose of Target Behavior III:

1. To obtain something?   yes   no   what? _____
2. To escape/avoid something?   yes   no   what? _____
3. Other factors?   yes   no   what? _____

Hypothesis: _____
Replacement Behavioral Goal: _____
Necessary Skills?   yes   no, needs additional instruction in _____

(continued)

FIGURE 4.12

Continued

Student Name: _____   School: _____   Meeting Date:_____

Submitting Teacher: _____   Beginning Date: _____   Review/End Date: _____

Functional Behavioral Assessment Worksheet
(Sequence Analysis)

Antecedent	Behavior of Concern	Consequence

I. Committee Determined Target Behaviors

1. _____

2. _____

3. _____

The following persons attended and participated in the FBA meeting:

Name:	Position:	Date:
_____	Parent	_____
_____	LEA Representative	_____
_____	Special Education Teacher	_____
_____	Student	_____
_____	General Education Teacher	_____
_____	_____	_____
_____	_____	_____

Method for Reporting Progress to Parent: **Frequency for Reporting Progress to Parent:**

☐ progress report   _____

☐ parent conference   _____

☐ other   _____

Response to Intervention and Classroom Behavioral Support

Many of the fundamental principles of response to intervention (RTI) have been used to support appropriate schoolwide behavior. For example, Sugai and colleagues (Fairbanks, Sugai, Guardino, and Lathrop, 2007; Sugai et al., 2000) emphasized graduated levels of social support as a means of improving schoolwide behavior as well as for addressing the social and behavioral problems of individual students. What does RTI mean with respect to social behavior issues?

- Tier I: As part of a schoolwide behavioral support program, a school might screen for behavior problems and introduce increasingly intensive interventions to meet school, teacher, and student needs. Schoolwide expectations establish appropriate consequences and procedures for reviewing progress toward schoolwide goals. Practices at the classroom level include opportunities for students to participate and be engaged in classroom activities; positive support for appropriate behavior; minimizing transition time between activities; and ongoing feedback and support for academics and social behavior.
- Tier II: In a behavioral support model, students who display similar behavior problems might be provided with an intervention that provides additional supports, prompts, feedback and acknowledgment to ensure that behavioral changes occur.
- Tier III: If the combination of a schoolwide behavioral support model and group interventions is not associated with improved behavioral outcomes, then more specific and intensive interventions focused at the student level are introduced and monitored.

| FOCUS |
| Question | 4. **What do we know about how students with behavior and learning difficulties feel about themselves, are perceived by others, and interact socially with others?**

Social Competence and Social Difficulties

Students with behavior problems often have social difficulties. More than 75 percent of students with behavior problems have problems significant enough for the students to be classified as in need of clinical intervention (Nelson, Babyak, Gonzalez,

and Benner, 2003). But what about students with learning disabilities?

Understanding the social difficulties of students with learning and behavior problems begins with an understanding of social competence and the characteristics associated with it. This section discusses the social characteristics of students with learning disabilities and describes the social problems associated with adolescents.

Definitions of Social Competence

We have all met people who seem to know what to say and do no matter whom they are with or what situation they are in. Sometimes we watch with envy as they move from person to person, from group to group—sometimes listening, sometimes talking, but always seemingly at ease. We often refer to these people as *socially competent*.

According to Foster and Ritchey (1979), *social competence* is defined as "those responses, which within a given situation, prove effective, or in other words, maximize the probability of producing, maintaining, or enhancing positive effects for the interactor" (p. 626) and, it should be added, without harm to others. Social skills are not a specific skill to be acquired, but rather a set of skills that allow one to adapt and respond to the expectations of society. Social competence is a process that begins at birth and continues throughout the life span. The process of developing social competence begins within one's immediate family and expands to include extended family, friends, neighbors, and social institutions.

Vaughn and Hogan (1990) have described a model of social competence that is analogous to intelligence in that it identifies social competence as a higher-order, global construct that is made up of many components. Their model of social competence includes the following four components:

1. *Positive relationships with others.* This includes the ability to form and maintain positive relationships with a range of people, including classmates, teachers, parents, and, at later ages, intimate partners. With students the focus is usually on relationships with peers, parents, and teachers.
2. *Accurate/age-appropriate social cognition.* This component includes how students think about themselves and others, as well as the extent to which they understand and interpret social situations. This component includes self-perceptions, social problem solving, attributions, locus of control, empathy, and social judgment.
3. *Absence of maladaptive behaviors.* This component focuses on the absence of behavior problems that interfere with social functioning,

such as disruptive behaviors, anxiety, attention problems, and lack of self-control.

4. *Effective social behaviors.* This includes the range of social behaviors that are often included in social skills intervention programs. These social behaviors include initiating contact with others, responding cooperatively to requests, and giving and receiving feedback.

The most discriminating characteristic of students with behavior problems is their lack of social competence. These students are referred for special education because of severe difficulty in adapting to society and interacting successfully with others. Among students who are in special education because of learning problems, social competence is also an issue—many students with learning disabilities are perceived by their peers and others as having social difficulties.

Behavior and social adjustment difficulties that teachers identify might be a function of the students' cultural and home backgrounds. It is useful for teachers to understand the expectations in the culture and home when they interpret the behavior and social skills of their students.

Perceptions of Students with Social Difficulties

The social interaction of students with behavior disorders is often described as having two dimensions: externalizing and internalizing (Cooper and Bilton, 2002). Externalizing behaviors are those that are extremely disturbing or intolerable to others (e.g., aggression, hyperactivity, delinquency). Conversely, internalizing behaviors are those that are more likely to adversely affect the student who displays them than other people (e.g., depression, immaturity, obsessive-compulsive behavior, shyness).

Students with behavior disorders who exhibit externalizing behaviors appear to be experts at identifying and performing the behaviors that are most disturbing to others. Donald, in the following example, is a student who exhibits externalizing behaviors.

When Mr. Kline discovered that Donald was to be placed in his fourth-grade class next year, his stomach did a flip-flop. "Any student but Donald," thought Mr. Kline, "he's the terror of the school." Every teacher who had had Donald in class had come to the teachers' lounge at the end of the day exhausted and discouraged. The real catastrophe was the effect Donald seemed to have on the rest of the class. Mild behavior problems in other students seemed to worsen with Donald's encouragement. Donald's hot temper and foul language left him continually fighting with other students.

This year, he had hit his teacher in the chest when she had tried to prevent him from running out of the classroom. While escaping, he shouted, "I'll sue you if you touch me." Mr. Kline had once seen Donald running at full speed down the hall, knocking over students along the way, and screeching as though he were putting on brakes as he swerved into his classroom. Mr. Kline knew that next year was going to be a difficult one.

Students like Donald are frequently avoided by more socially competent students in class and are disliked and feared by other class members. They are loners who move from one group to the next after alienating group members, or they develop friendships with other students whose behavior is also disturbing to others. These students present extremely difficult classroom management problems.

Students with behavior disorders who exhibit internalizing behaviors are often less disturbing to others but frequently create concern because of their bizarre behavior. Elisa, in the following example, is a student who exhibits internalizing behaviors.

Elisa, a fifth grader, had just moved to the area. Her mother brought Elisa to register for school but refused to speak with the school secretary. Instead, she demanded that she be allowed to register Elisa with the school principal. Elisa's mother told the school principal that Elisa would sometimes act "funny" to get attention and should be told to stop as soon as she tried it. The principal noted that Elisa had not said one word. In fact, she had sat in a chair next to her mother looking down and rocking gently. Elisa's mother said that Elisa had been receiving special education services during part of the day and was in a regular classroom most of the day. In the regular classroom, Elisa was a loner. She spoke to no one. When another student approached her, Elisa reared back and scratched into the air with her long fingernails, imitating a cat. If other children said something to her, Elisa would "hiss" at them. She would sit in the room, usually completing her assignments and, whenever possible, practicing writing elaborate cursive letters with her multicolored pen. She spent most of the day rocking. She even rocked while she worked.

Problems like Elisa's are usually thought of as being internal and resulting from a unique pathology. Other classmates, recognizing that these children are very different, may attempt to interact, but they are usually rebuffed. Students with internalizing behaviors are easy victims for students whose problem behaviors are more externalizing.

It is important to note that not all youngsters with behavior problems demonstrate either externalizing or internalizing problems. Many youngsters with behavior disorders display both externalizing and internalizing problems. This is not difficult to understand if one imagines a child who is often shy and withdrawn who, when frustrated or forced to interact with others, becomes aggressive and acts out.

Externalizing and internalizing behaviors are more frequently characteristics of students with behavior problems than of students with learning disabilities. Students with learning disabilities (LD) typically display less severe emotional and behavior difficulties. However, many students with LD have difficulties in making and maintaining positive interpersonal relationships with others. When compared with their peers without LD, students with learning disabilities are

- Inconsistent and less effective in displaying appropriate conversational skills, and exhibit difficulties in developing these skills (Hartas and Donahue, 1997; Westwood, 2003)
- Identified as being more poorly accepted by their peers even as early as kindergarten (Bryan 1976; Tur-Kaspa, 2004; Vaughn, Elbaum, and Schumm, 1996; Vaughn, McIntosh, and Spencer-Rowe, 1991; Wiener and Tardif, 2004)
- At greater risk for social alienation and rejection from teachers and classmates (Montague and Rinaldi, 2001; Seidel and Vaughn, 1991)
- More likely to be rejected, neglected, and unaccepted by peers (Kuhne and Wiener, 2000; Wiener, 2002)
- Perceived as having lower social status and social skills (Le Mare and de la Ronde, 2000; Stone and LaGreca, 1990)
- Less accepted by peers even before being identified as having LD (Vaughn, Hogan, Kouzekanani, and Shapiro, 1990)
- More willing to conform to peer pressure to engage in antisocial activities (Bryan, Pearl, and Fallon, 1989; Farmer, Pearl, and Van Acker, 1996)
- Less likely than other students to interact with teachers and classmates (Greenham, 1999; McIntosh et al., 1993)
- More likely to demonstrate higher levels of depression than general education students (Heath and Wiener, 1996; Howard and Tryon, 2002)
- More likely to report higher rates of loneliness and more concern and worry about their close personal relationships (Al-Yagon and Mikulincer, 2004)

Unfortunately, the lower social status of students with LD reflects not only the perceptions of peers but also of teachers. Teachers perceive these students as less socially competent and less desirable to have in the classroom (Juvonen and Bear, 1992; Vaughn, Schumm, Jallad, Slusher, and Saumell, 1996). However, findings indicate that teachers' perceptions of these students may be influenced by students' academic self-perceptions and that a cyclical relationship may exist between the two. Meltzer, Ranjini, Sales Pollica, Roditi, Sayer, and Theokas (2004) found that students with LD who exhibited positive academic self-perceptions were more likely to work hard and use strategies in their schoolwork than those who exhibited negative academic self-perceptions. Students with LD with positive academic self-perceptions were rated by their teachers as working as hard as, and academically performing similar to, their peers without LD. However, teachers rated students with LD with negative academic self-perceptions as achieving at below average level in comparison to their peers, and as making limited efforts.

One possible interpretation of the lower social status of students with LD is that it is a reflection of how the teacher feels about the students. The teacher's negative perception of a student with learning disabilities is conveyed to other students in the classroom, thus lowering the child's social status and how the child is perceived and responded to by peers. Some research suggests that this cannot completely explain the lower social status of students with LD because strangers, after viewing a few minutes of students' social interaction on videotapes, perceive students with learning disabilities more negatively than their peers without LD (Bryan, Bryan, and Sonnefeld, 1982; Bryan and Perlmutter, 1979; Bryan and Sherman, 1980). Additionally, as early as two months into their kindergarten year, students who are later identified as having learning disablities are already more often rejected and less frequently chosen as best friends than other students in the kindergarten class (Vaughn, Hogan, Kouzekanani, and Shapiro, 1990). Whereas teachers view students with learning disabilities more negatively than they view students without LD, teachers are more favorably disposed toward having students with LD in their classroom than they are students who are identified as emotionally or behaviorally disturbed, as having multiple disorders, or as mentally retarded (Cook, 2002; Moore and Fine, 1978). Teachers regard students with emotional disabilities as the most disruptive and the most difficult students to work with effectively within the regular classroom.

In general education classrooms where youngsters with learning disabilities are accepted by their teachers, they are also accepted by their peers (Vaughn, McIntosh, Schumm, Haager, and Callwood, 1993). In such classrooms, these students are as well accepted and have as many friends as other students. It can be speculated that teachers in inclusive settings spend more time with students with LD and therefore have different views toward these students. Wiener and Tardif (2004) found that children in more inclusive settings were better accepted by their peers and had fewer teacher-rated problem behaviors. Thus, an important role of special education teachers is to assist general education teachers in seeing the many positive outcomes of treating students with special needs as accepted members of the classroom.

The educational setting in which students are placed can affect the number of reciprocal friendships that students make and maintain. Reciprocal friends are two students who independently nominate each other as friends. For example, both Marta and Indira write down each other's names on a list of friends. Low-achieving students, average-achieving students, and those with learning disabilities demonstrated an increased number of reciprocal friendships in inclusive settings. In these settings, the special and general education teachers coplanned, and the special education teacher provided a range of services in the classroom, such as working individually or with small groups of students with learning disabilities and leading lessons and demonstrating adaptations. Students in classrooms where the special education teacher cotaught with the general education teacher for the entire day did not make similar gains (Vaughn, Elbaum, Schumm, and Hughes, 1998). However, a recent study found that although students in self-contained special education classes reported a similar number of friends as students in inclusive settings, these children also reported a lower quality of friendship and more loneliness than their peers in inclusive settings (Wiener and Tardif, 2004). These studies suggest that a classroom climate of high acceptance and expectations can enhance mutual regard and acceptance of students with learning disabilities and low-achieving students and may actually contribute to the quality of their friendships. Apply the Concept 4.2 describes a study examining the social

Apply the Concept 4.2

Does Inclusion Improve the Social and Emotional Functioning of Students with Learning Disabilities?

A primary rationale for placing students with learning disabilities (LD) in more inclusive settings is that these settings are expected to reduce students' social difficulties and promote peer acceptance and social adjustment. A recent study examined the social acceptance, number of friends, quality of relationships, self-concept, loneliness, and social skills of students with LD and their peers without LD across four educational settings related to the level of intensity of academic support required by the student (Wiener and Tardif, 2004):

High-Intensity Support of Student with LD

- Special education placement for at least 50 percent of the school day

- Inclusion in general education setting all day

Low-Intensity Support of Student with LD

- Resource room setting for part of the day
- Inclusion in general education setting all day with in-class support

Overall, the largest and greatest number of findings were differences in social functioning between students with LD and their classmates without LD, regardless of setting. Regardless of the type of program a student attended (resource, inclusion, self-contained), students with LD scored lower on all aspects of social functioning (e.g., social skills, loneliness, social acceptance, number of friends) than did their classmates without LD.

The social skills of students in more inclusive settings were better than those of students in resource or self-contained settings. For example, students with LD in inclusive classrooms perceived their classmates as better companions, and they were less lonely. Teachers also perceived these students' behavior as less problematic.

outcomes of students with learning disabilities in four different classroom types.

In discussing the social skills of students with learning disabilities and how others perceive them, it is important to realize that we are talking generally about students with learning disabilities. Not all students with learning disabilities have social difficulties. Many of them are socially competent, making and maintaining friends and struggling to please their teachers and parents. Many adults with learning disabilities who are participating in postsecondary education programs identify their social skills as their strengths.

An additional point to consider is that the findings on the social and behavioral functioning of youngsters with learning disabilities mostly reflect how they compare with their nondisabled peers. Studies that compare students with learning disabilities to their low-achieving classmates find few differences in social status or social or behavioral functioning (LeMare and de la Ronde, 2000; Vaughn, Haager, Hogan, and Kouzekanani, 1992; Vaughn, Zaragoza, Hogan, and Walker, 1993). Thus, low achievement may be a better indication of social difficulties than of learning disabilities per se. A synthesis of research confirms that children with learning disabilities as well as low achievers were at greater risk for social difficulties than were average- and high-achieving students (Nowicki, 2003).

Characteristics of Students with Social Disabilities

We expect students with behavior disorders to have difficulty in successfully interacting with others. Students with behavior disorders are identified and placed in special programs because their social problems are so interfering that these students are unable to function adequately with only the services provided by the regular classroom. Almost 75 percent (Kavale and Forness, 1996) of students with learning disabilities have difficulty developing and maintaining relationships with others. This may be because some students with learning disabilities display profiles of verbal difficulties that influence their academic and social performance, often referred to as a *verbal learning disability* (Rourke and Fuerst, 1992; Shapiro, Lipton, and Krivit, 1992) or an auditory processing disorder (APD; Matthews, 2003). Children with APD can typically hear information but have difficulty processing or interpreting it. Figure 4.13 provides suggestions for

FIGURE 4.13

Create a Learning Community That Celebrates Diversity

- Students are children or adolescents first. Look beyond the ways in which students differ, and respect their common needs and goals to be accepted, recognized, and valued members of the community. The classroom community is a primary source of students' perceptions of acceptance. Teachers' attitudes need to celebrate the diversity of students and at the same time recognize that students are more alike than they are different.
- Focus on abilities. Establish an environment in which teachers and students seek and use knowledge about the abilities and expertise of all class members. Myrna Rathkin, a sixth-grade teacher, framed a picture of each student in a decorated star and hung them from the classroom ceiling. Attached to each star were lists of self- and teacher-identified strengths or abilities. All students were encouraged to recognize the knowledge and skills of their fellow students and to discover new ways their fellow students were special. When they did so, they would add them to the list of attributes under the individual's star.
- Celebrate diversity. Teachers can view students' differences as something to be tolerated, mildly accepted, or celebrated.

Celebrating diversity means conveying to students the values added by having students as part of their learning community who have different learning styles, behavior profiles, physical abilities, languages, and cultural backgrounds. Sharon Andreaci, a sixth-grade teacher, was thrilled that many students she taught spoke Spanish and represented the cultural backgrounds of several Hispanic groups (e.g., Cuban, Nicaraguan, Colombian, Mexican). She often asked children about their backgrounds and encouraged them to share their knowledge and practices with others. She looked for ways to learn from others by asking such questions as, "Juan, how would you say that in Spanish? Anna, do you agree with Juan? Is there another way to say it in Spanish?"

Diversity

- Demonstrate high regard for all students. Demonstrating high regard for all students means treating each one of them as special and extraordinary in their own way. It means not having "favorites" even if you think you disguise it. Listen carefully to each student and find something meaningful in what each student says.

Source: Adapted from S. Vaughn, C. S. Bos, and J. S. Schumm, *Teaching Students Who Are Exceptional, Diverse, and at Risk* (Boston: Allyn & Bacon, 2007).

creating a learning community that celebrates student differences.

Social Interaction

The type and quality of interactions that students with learning disabilities engage in are different from those of their peers. Students with learning disabilities are more likely than students without LD to approach the teacher and ask questions (Dorval, McKinney, and Feagans, 1982; McKinney, McClure, and Feagans, 1982). Teachers report that questions from students with LD are inappropriate, as these students often ask questions when the answer to the question was just stated. Teachers interact almost four times as often with students with learning disabilities as with their peers; however, 63 percent of teachers' initiations toward students with LD involve managing their behavior (Dorval, McKinney, and Feagans, 1982). The interactions that students with learning disabilities have with their teachers are often inappropriate for the situation; these students impulsively attempt to display their knowledge, request more time to complete assignments, and request time to speak individually with the teacher to ask questions. Although classroom teachers spend more time with students with LD, the teachers do not view the nature of the involvement during that time positively (Siperstein and Goding, 1985). One teacher describes it this way: "When Carlos raises his hand, I dread it. He usually asks me what he is supposed to do. I find myself trying to reexplain a 30-minute lesson in 5 minutes. I'm sure he can tell I'm frustrated."

In one of the few studies that have been conducted to examine general education teachers' behavior toward middle and high school students with learning disabilities (McIntosh et al., 1993), the findings indicated that middle and high school teachers do not treat students with learning disabilities differently from other students in the classroom. There are, of course, positive and negative sides to this finding. From a positive perspective, teachers treated all students fairly and impartially, and although praise was given infrequently, it was given at the same rate both to students with learning disabilities and to students without learning disabilities. From a negative perspective, youngsters with learning disabilities interacted infrequently with the teacher, other students, and classroom activities, and teachers made few, if any, adaptations to increase the involvement or ensure the learning of these students.

However, students with learning disabilities can be taught specific behaviors to increase positive teacher and peer attention (Alber, Heward, and Hippler, 1999; Wolford, Heward, and Alber, 2001). In one study, students with learning disabilities were taught to show their work to the teacher and ask questions such as, "How am I doing?" The results indicated that students who asked questions received more positive teacher attention and instructional feedback. These students also completed their workbook assignments with increased accuracy (Alber et al., 1999). A second study found that when students with learning disabilities were taught how to recruit positive peer assistance, they were found to decrease the number of inappropriate recruiting responses, to decrease negative statements from peers and increase positive statements, and to increase their academic performance. Positive recruitment was done by training students on how and when to ask for help (Wolford et al., 2001). These studies suggest that although students with learning disabilities often play a passive role in the classroom, they can be taught specific behaviors to actively solicit positive teacher and peer attention. This is a simple but valuable tool that special education teachers can use to ensure that their students display behaviors in general education classrooms that increase their likelihood for teacher acceptance and feedback.

Communication Difficulties

Expressing one's ideas and feelings and understanding the ideas and feelings of others are integral parts of socialization. Adults and children who have good social skills can communicate effectively with others, whereas students with learning and behavior problems frequently have trouble in this area, known as *pragmatic communication*. Children with learning disabilities often have poor pragmatic skills, such as eye contact, turn-taking, initiative, interaction, sharing, requesting, and responding (Abudarham, 2002).

Torgeson (1982) describes the learning style of students with LD as inactive. An inactive learner is one who is passively involved in the learning process, does not attempt to integrate new information with previously learned information, and does not self-question or rehearse. Students with learning disabilities also demonstrate an inactive style during the communication process. While communicating with others, students with LD are less likely to make adaptations in their communication to accommodate the listener. When most of us speak with young children, we make modifications in how we speak to them, such as using simpler words and asking questions to be sure that they understand us. Many students with learning disabilities fail to make these modifications (Bryan and Pflaum, 1978; Soenksen, Flagg, and Schmits, 1981).

When discussing the reading difficulties of students with learning disabilities, we will talk about their difficulty in responding to ambiguous information in print. In much the same way, students with LD do not request more information when given ambiguous information through oral communication (Donahue, Pearl, and Bryan, 1980). They also have difficulty recognizing and interpreting the emotions expressed by their social partner and identifying deceptive statements (Jarvis and Justin, 1992; Most and Greenback, 2000; Pearl, Bryan, Fallon, and Herzog, 1991). For example, students were presented with stories that had sincere, deceptive, sarcastic, and neutral versions. Each story was followed by questions to determine the students' understanding of facts in the story, assessment of the speaker's belief and intent, and evidence used to determine the speaker's belief and intent. Students with learning disabilities were more likely to believe that the speaker was sincere but wrong, whereas peers without LD were more likely to believe that the speaker was insincere (Pearl et al., 1991). In Most and Greenback's study (2000), students were asked to identify six different emotions: happiness, anger, sadness, disgust, surprise, and fear. Each emotion was presented through three different modes: auditory, visual, and auditory-visual. Students with learning disabilities had greater difficulties than their peers without LD in perceiving the correct emotion.

The student with learning disabilities is often a difficult communication partner. For example, verbal disagreements during a learning task between students with mild intellectual disabilities and normal-achieving students were examined in one study (Okrainec and Hughes, 1996). Students with mild intellectual disabilities initiated conflicts less often, thus taking on a respondent/opposee role, and used higher-level conflict initiating strategies, such as justification, delay/distractions, and question/challenges, less often. Initiating conflicts less often can prevent the exchanges of ideas that promote intellectual development as well as moral development and social development for students with mild intellectual disabilities. In addition, justifications can be a useful verbal skill for averting conflicts that may result in aggressive or violent acts. It is interesting to note that familiarity with one's partner positively affects the performance on communication tasks of students with learning disabilities but has no impact for children without learning disabilities (Mathinos,

1987). Perhaps knowledge of one's partners serves as a motivator for students with learning disabilities to use the communication skills they have.

The communication style of students with learning disabilities appears to be egocentric. That is, they do not appear to be interested in the responses of their partner, and they demonstrate less shared responsibility for maintaining a social conversation (LaGreca, 1982). In a study of the friendship-making and conversation skills of boys with and without learning disabilities, LaGreca (1982) reports that the two groups of boys did not differ in how to handle social situations (positive and negative), nor did they differ in their knowledge of how to make friends. Naive observers identified the boys with learning disabilities as less adept in social situations, as more egocentric, and as lacking in reciprocity in their conversations. The impression is that many students with learning disabilities display communication styles that suggest that when listening, they are just waiting for the speaker to stop rather than being interested in what the speaker is saying.

Individuals with learning disabilities are less able to display interpersonal decentering (Horowitz, 1981) and less able to take on an alternative viewpoint (Wong and Wong, 1980). We know from the communication skills of populations with learning disabilities that they are less likely to make adjustments in their communication with others. It could be that their difficulty taking on the role of the "other" influences both their social relationships with others and their ability to communicate successfully with others. Because students with learning disabilities are frequently rejected by peers, it could be that this communication pattern is sufficiently frustrating to others that they find the student with learning disabilities an undesirable social partner.

Stone and LaGreca (1984) compared students with and without learning disabilities on their ability to comprehend nonverbal communication. Their findings indicated that when attention is controlled for with students with learning disabilities by reinforcing their attendance to the social cues given, they perform as well as their peers without LD. These authors suggest that the attention problems of students with learning disabilities often are manifested as poor social skills.

Problem Solving

Students with learning disabilities often demonstrate difficulties involving their ability to perceive, interpret, and process social information (Rudolph and Luckner, 1991), which in turn leads to inappropriate social responses and poor social problem-solving skills. For example, when students were presented with vignettes depicting an age-appropriate dilemma, students with learning disabilities performed below average in defining a problem and generating effective solutions (Shondrick, Serafica, Clark, and Miller, 1992). Tur-Kaspa and Bryan (1994) compared the social information-processing and social problem-solving skills of elementary and middle school students with learning disabilities with those of low-achieving and average-achieving students. Results indicated that students with learning disabilities demonstrated an increased tendency to select incompetent self-generated solutions to social situations. Similarly, adolescents with learning disabilities were found to experience difficulties in generating solutions to interpersonal problems (Hartas and Donahue, 1997). Asking students to generate solutions to problems and discussing the consequences of each of the solutions may help students in developing their own ideas about solutions to problems. Additionally, it may help students to choose more appropriate solutions for specific situations after taking into account the consequences of those solutions. All students will benefit from activities designed to help them to generate solutions to specific problems and connecting the effectiveness of the solutions to their consequences.

Aggression

Perhaps the behavior with which teachers are least able to cope is aggression (Hart, 2002). Aggressive behaviors include assaulting others, fighting, bullying, having temper tantrums, quarreling, ignoring the rights of others, using a negative tone of voice, threatening, and demanding immediate compliance. Many students with behavior problems display these types of aggressive behaviors.

In a study conducted by Lancelotta and Vaughn (1989), five types of aggressive behaviors and their relation to peer social acceptance were examined:

1. *Provoked physical aggression:* Attacks or fights back following provocation from another.
2. *Outburst aggression:* Has uncontrollable outbursts without apparent provocation that may or may not be directed at another person. An example is a student who gets angry and throws a fit for no apparent reason.

3. *Unprovoked physical aggression:* Attacks or acts aggressively toward another person without provocation. An example is a student who starts a fight for no reason.
4. *Verbal aggression:* Says aggressive things to another person to attack or intimidate them. An example is a student who threatens to beat up another.
5. *Indirect aggression:* Attacks or attempts to hurt another indirectly so that it is not likely to be obvious who did it. An example is a student who tells the teacher that another student does bad things.

The study demonstrated that girls are less tolerant of all types of aggression than are boys. Also, all types of aggression resulted in lower peer ratings by their fellow students, with the exception of provoked aggression for boys. This means that boys who fight back when they are attacked first by other boys are not any more likely to be poorly accepted. This, however, is not true for girls who fight back when they are attacked. All of the other subtypes of aggression are related to poor peer acceptance.

Aggression does not go away without treatment and is correlated with such negative outcomes as alcoholism, unpopularity, aggressive responses from others, academic failure, and adult antisocial behaviors. Specific skills for teaching students to deal more effectively with their aggressive responses are an important component of social skills programs for students with behavior disorders.

Following are some ways in which teachers can address aggression and bullying in the classroom:

- All students must understand what types of behaviors are considered "aggressive." Teachers can hold class discussions in which examples of aggressive behavior are identified and listed to ensure that all students know what is meant by *aggression.*
- Teachers can establish a no-tolerance rule regarding aggressive behavior and have a schoolwide plan for how every adult and child will handle aggression from others. *No tolerance* means that the school has a policy (other than expulsion) for responding to aggressive behavior.
- The teacher can inform students that they will be protected and demonstrate this (Shore, 2003).
- The teacher can provide preemptive techniques to prevent fights. This can include

stopping heated arguments and monitoring students who do not usually get along.

- The teacher and other school staff can stop fighting immediately and firmly (Shore, 2003).
- The teacher can identify when and where the student is aggressive and attempt to eliminate those situations.
- The teacher can teach students to resolve their own conflicts and mediate difficulties between other students.
- The teacher can ask students to describe what happened before and during an aggressive act (Shore, 2003).
- As a schoolwide model, the school staff can establish a caring and supportive environment for students and adults.

Apply the Concept 4.3 discusses the problem of bullying students with disabilities.

Appearance

Appearance may be a more important factor influencing the social status of students with learning difficulties than was previously thought. In a study evaluating the social status, academic ability, athletic ability, and appearance of students with learning disabilities (Siperstein, Bopp, and Bak, 1978), researchers found that whereas academic and athletic ability were significantly related to peer popularity, the correlation between physical appearance and peer popularity was twice as great as correlations with the other two.

Two children from a study by Vaughn, Lancelotta, and Minnis (1988) illustrate this point. Chris was a fourth-grade student with learning disabilities who worked as a model for children's clothing in a large department store. Her position gave her access to the latest children's fashions, and she was well recognized by both girls and boys in her class as attractive. When sociometric data asking peers to rate the extent to which they liked others in the classroom were analyzed, Chris ranked first. Her best friend, Carmen, who was also identified as having learning disabilities, ranked second from the bottom by her classmates on the same sociometric test. In looking at the tests of social skills administered to these students, there was little difference between the scores of Chris and Carmen.

In another study, 35 percent of junior high students with learning disabilities exhibited some problem in grooming, neatness of clothing, posture, and general attractiveness, compared with 6 percent of the junior high students without learning disabilities (Schumaker, Wildgen, and Sherman, 1982). Bickett and Milich (1987) found that boys with learning disabilities were rated as less attractive than were boys without learning disabilities. Because appearance is highly related to popularity, it could be helpful to give feedback and pointers to students who show problems with appearance. Many students with behavior disorders display atypical appearance as a means of demonstrating identification with a group or gang. These students may wear their hair or clothing in nonconforming ways to let others know their allegiance. This style may be highly accepted by a particular group and highly rejected by others.

Apply the Concept 4.3

Preventing Bullying and Teasing of Individuals with Disabilities

Have you ever worried about a school bully or excessive teasing? If you have, you are not alone. Schools and educators have reported that bullying and excessive teasing are a serious school problem, one that is exacerbated when students are perceived as "different." Thus, students with learning and behavior problems may be particularly susceptible to harassment and bullying. When students are isolated from their peers or do not participate in mainstream programs,

they are at increased risk for bullying (Hoover and Salk, 2003).

Following are some facts about bullying (Hoover and Stenhjem, 2003):

- Bullying is the most common form of aggression among youths.
- Many teachers (as many as 25 percent) do not perceive that bullying is wrong and therefore rarely intervene.
- Most students perceive that schools do little to respond to bullying.

- Physical bullying peaks in middle school.

Olweus (1993) has designed a schoolwide intervention program to prevent or reduce bullying. For information on implementing the model, visit the program Website at www.secondstep.org.

Attention Problems/Hyperactivity

Attention deficits and hyperactivity are characteristics that are often observed in students with learning and behavior disorders. Approximately one-third of all children with attention deficit hyperactivity disorder (ADHD) also have learning disabilities (National Institute of Mental Health, 1999). Families report that 3.7 percent of children have both ADHD and learning disabilities (Smith and Adams, 2006). Students with attention deficits frequently display a pattern of inattention, and students with hyperactivity often exhibit patterns of impulsivity; these patterns are evident in a variety of contexts, including home and school.

In the classroom, inattention is manifested in a failure to pay attention to details, careless mistakes, misplacing needed items, messy work, and difficulty in persisting with a task until completion (American Psychiatric Association, 1994; U.S. Department of Education, 2003). Hyperactivity may be exhibited through fidgetiness, inability to engage in quiet activities, difficulty staying seated, blurting out answers, flitting from one task to another, and excessive talking (American Psychiatric Association, 1994; U.S. Department of Education, 2003).

Students with attention deficits and/or hyperactivity can be treated with medication. Several stimulant medications (e.g., Dexedrine, Ritalin) are available that help students to focus by adjusting the parts of the brain that regulate attention, impulse control, and mood (Cooper and Bilton, 2002; Hallowell and Ratey, 1995). The Food and Drug Administration approved atomexetine, a new type of nonstimulant medication for the treatment of ADHD (U.S. Department of Education, 2003). As with any medication, unwanted side effects can occur. Some of the side effects of stimulant medications include facial tics, loss of appetite, headaches, and difficulty sleeping (Cooper and Bilton, 2002; Swanson et al., 1993). Some children experience unpleasant physical symptoms and are affected by the drugs in some settings but not in others. Most children who receive medication for hyperactivity are under the care of a physician whom they see infrequently. Thus, monitoring the effectiveness of the drug is often the responsibility of family members and teachers. Perhaps the most effective technique for monitoring the effects of drugs is observing the student's behavior and determining whether there have been significant changes, either positive or negative.

Similarly, educational evaluations can be used to assess the degree to which children's ADHD symptoms affect their academic performance. The teacher identifies and defines specific behaviors that are indicative of hyperactivity and then charts the occurrence of these behaviors (U.S. Department of Education, 2006). Whereas medication may be necessary for some children, even successful use of medication does not make the learning disability disappear (Routh, 1979; Silver and Hagin, 2002).

A learning characteristic that is frequently affected by hyperactivity is selective attention—the ability to attend to relevant information and ignore irrelevant information (Mason, Humphreys, and Kent, 2003; Pinel, 1993). This characteristic occurs in children with learning disabilities about two years later than in normal children (Tarver, Hallahan, Kauffman, and Ball, 1976). Delayed development of selective attention in children with learning disabilities may be related to a learning style that is more impulsive than reflective. A reflective learner is more likely to be successful in academic subjects such as reading and math, whereas an impulsive learner is more likely to have learning difficulties. One characteristic of impulsive responders is that they do not stop and think before responding (Goldstein, 1995; Merrell and Stein, 1992; Westwood, 2003).

When students demonstrate attention problems, teachers can do the following:

- Use clear ways of cueing students to obtain their attention (Shore, 2003). For example, say, "I'm counting backward to one, and then I want all eyes on me. Five, four, three, two, one." Some teachers use chimes or other instruments to obtain students' attention. Another idea is to tell students that you are going to clap a pattern and then you want them to "clap the same pattern and then look at me."
- Develop a signaling system with a student or selected students to cue them to pay attention. The signal could be a slight touch on the shoulder or passing the student a colored card to indicate that he or she is not paying attention.
- Look for times when students are attending and focusing, and establish a system for cueing them when they are doing well too.
- Consider where in the classroom and near whom students work, and make adjustments to promote better focus on assignments.
- Shorten the work periods and assignments. Focus on understanding and getting a few items right rather than completing all aspects of tasks.
- Provide clear and limited directions that are easier to follow.

- Assist students in making effective transitions.
- If a student is taking medication, monitor his or her behavior to note the effects of the medication and possible changes in behavior (Shore, 2003).
- Use computer-assisted learning (Westwood, 2003).

Self-Concept

How we view ourselves is highly related to our comparison group. Therefore, it is not surprising that students with learning and behavior difficulties often have poor self-concepts. When students perceive their disability in more positive terms, however, they also tend to report more positive global self-concepts (e.g., Rothman and Cosden, 1995). These students are aware of how their learning performance compares with that of others. Students with learning disabilities who also have reading difficulties view themselves more negatively than do students with learning disabilities and normal reading scores (Black, 1974), and older students with learning disabilities view themselves more negatively than do younger students with learning disabilities. In an attempt to interpret the sometimes conflicting results of studies, Morrison (1985) demonstrated that two factors significantly influence self-perception of students with learning disabilities: type of classroom placement (e.g., self-contained, general education classroom) and what aspect of self-perception is being evaluated (e.g., academic, social, behavioral, or anxiety-laden). When achievement is controlled, for example, there are no differences in self-perception measures between students with learning disabilities in resource rooms and self-contained settings (Yauman, 1980). When compared with classmates, the self-concept of students with learning disabilities is not significantly lower either before or after identification (Vaughn et al., 1992). This suggests that placement in a special education resource room had no negative effects on their self-concept.

The self-perceptions of students with learning disabilities can be surprisingly accurate. In general, they rate themselves as low on academic ability (Chapman and Boersman, 1980) and like other children on overall feelings of self-worth (Bear, Clever, and Proctor, 1991; Bryan, 1986). They identify reading and spelling as the academic areas in which they are lower than other children and yet perceive themselves as being relatively intelligent (Kloomok and Cosden, 1994; Renik, 1987). A longitudinal study of students with learning disabilities suggests that they may differ from low-achieving students in that they do not become more negative about themselves as they grow older (Kistner and Osborne, 1987).

What can teachers do to improve the self-concept of students with learning disabilities or behavior problems? A summary of research on self-concept and students with learning disabilities reveals that younger students do not benefit from counseling as an intervention, whereas middle and high school students do (Elbaum and Vaughn, 2001).

Students who excel in extracurricular activities such as sports or music demonstrate levels of self-concept similar to those of average-achieving students (Kloomok and Cosden, 1994). Teachers and parents can provide opportunities for students to demonstrate what they do well and provide encouragement in the areas of difficulty. One parent described it this way:

> The best thing that happened to my son is swimming. We knew from the time Kevin was an infant that he was different from our other two children. We were not surprised when he had difficulties in school and was later identified as learning-disabled. His visual/motor problems made it difficult for him to play ball sports, so we encouraged his interest in swimming. He joined a swim team when he was six, and all his friends know he has won many swimming awards. No matter how discouraged he feels about school, he has one area in which he is successful.

Locus of Control and Learned Helplessness

People who have an *internal locus of control* view events as controlled largely by their own efforts, whereas those with an *external locus of control* interpret the outcome of events as being due largely to luck, chance, fate, or other events outside of their own influence. Attributing success to external factors and failures to lack of personal ability fosters an external locus of control (Perry, 1999). Locus of control proceeds along a continuum, with learning- and behavior-disordered children frequently having a high external locus of control, unable to view the cause of events as related to their own behavior. For this reason, they are not motivated to change events that are undesirable to them because they feel that there is little they can do to improve the situation. Mrs. Mulkowsky, a junior high learning disabilities teacher, notes,

> My students act as though there is nothing they can do to improve their grades in their regular

classes. They feel that they are unable to succeed in most of these classes, and they give up. They come to my class, sit down, and expect me to tutor them in their regular classes. They act as though it is *my* responsibility. These students are actually the ones who are still working; others have given up entirely and expect little from themselves and little from me.

It could be that students with learning disabilities have difficulties in social situations because they fail to realize that successful interaction with others can be influenced by their behavior. To assist students in developing an internal locus of control, teachers need to show students the relationships between what they do and their actions' effects on others and reciprocally on themselves. Giving students ownership of their tasks and behavior and teaching them to set their own goals are first steps toward increasing their internal locus of control (Cohen, 1986). Teachers may also want to interview children to learn more about their locus of control orientation (Lewis and Lawrence-Patterson, 1989). Borkowski and colleagues (Borkowski, Weyhing, and Carr, 1988; Borkowski, Weyhing, and Turner, 1986) have used attributional training paired with specific strategy training (e.g., in the area of reading) to influence students' use and generalization of strategies. Attributional training helps students see the role of effort in academic success or strategy use. Reasons for not doing well that do not relate to controllable factors are discouraged. Students are encouraged to see the relationship between strategy use and success, "I tried hard, used the strategy, and did well" (Borkowski et al., 1988, p. 49).

Seligman (1975) introduced the concept of *learned helplessness* to explain the response animals and humans have when exposed to a number of trials in which they are unable to influence the outcome. When subjects learn that there is no relationship between what they do and their ability to affect the environment or reach their goal, they give up and respond passively. Although learned helplessness, or the perceived inability to influence a situation, may be situation-specific, it often generalizes to other learning situations. For example, when a student with learning disabilities and severe reading problems approaches a reading task, the student is often unable to reach his or her goal: being able to read the passage successfully. Students may initially be quite persistent in their attempts to read. However, students who meet with continued failure learn that their attempts are useless and there is nothing they can do to affect the situation; the students then respond as though they are helpless.

Learned helplessness leads to lowered self-concept, lethargy, reduction in persistence, and reduced levels of performance. There is a remarkable resemblance between the descriptions of learned helplessness and the observations of special education teachers about students with learning disabilities and behavior disorders. "Learning-disabled children have been portrayed as no longer able to believe that they can learn" (Thomas, 1979, p. 209).

Apply the Concept 4.4 describes what teachers may be able to do to affect learned helplessness and locus of control.

Social Difficulties That Are Prevalent during Adolescence

In addition to the characteristics of students with learning and behavior disorders that we discussed earlier, several difficulties are prevalent during adolescence that can affect students with special needs. These are the mental health issues of social alienation, suicide, anorexia nervosa, and alcohol and other drug abuse. Why might special education teachers need to consider these difficulties as well as other variables related to social adjustment in adolescents with learning and behavior problems? Perhaps the most important reason is that teachers are often the first to be aware of mental health problems and can be valuable resources for identification and support. The majority of youth and adolescents with self-reported mental health problems were provided special education services (Talbott and Fleming, 2003).

Social Alienation

Social alienation arises from the extent to which youngsters feel that they are part of or have an affinity for the school or the people in the school. Social alienation has been interpreted to refer to alienation from teachers or peers (Seidel and Vaughn, 1991). Not surprisingly, social alienation begins early in a youngster's school career but is most obvious during adolescence. In a study by Seidel and Vaughn (1991), students with learning disabilities who dropped out of school differed from those who did not when they rated how they felt about teachers and classmates. Not surprising, students with LD who drop out do not perceive their teachers as friends. Furthermore, these students are more likely to state, "The thing I hated most about school was my teachers." Students with learning disabilities who dropped out also felt that their classmates "would not have missed them if they moved away," and they did not look forward to seeing their friends at school. Interestingly, these students did not differ on their

Apply the Concept 4.4

How Teachers Can Affect Learned Helplessness and Locus of Control

To reduce the impact of learned helplessness and external locus of control on students' behavior, teachers may want to do the following:

1. Offer process-directed praise or criticism (Dweck and Kamins, 1999) such as, "This paper is clearly written" or, "You really concentrated and finished this biology assignment." Focus on the activity the students are engaged in, such as reading, writing, or art, and avoid person-directed praise or comments such as "You are good in biology." This will help reduce the amount of external reinforcement needed and instead reinforce student performance.
2. Reduce the amount of external reinforcement and focus on reinforcing student performance. Rather than saying, "Good work" or "Excellent job," focus on the behaviors, such as, "You really

concentrated and finished this biology assignment. You needed to ask for help, but you got it done. How do you feel about it?"

3. Link students' behaviors to outcomes. "You spent 10 minutes working hard on this worksheet, and you finished it."
4. Provide encouragement. Because they experience continued failure, many students are discouraged from attempting tasks they are capable of performing.
5. Discuss academic tasks and social activities in which the student experiences success.
6. Discuss your own failures or difficulties, and express what you do to cope with these. Be sure to provide examples of when you persist and examples of when you give up.
7. Encourage students to take responsibility for their successes. "You received a B on your biology test. How do you think you

got such a good grade?" Encourage students to describe what they did (e.g., how they studied). Discourage students from saying, "I was lucky" or "It was an easy test."

8. Encourage students to take responsibility for their failures. For example, in response to the question "Why do you think you are staying after school?" encourage students to take responsibility for what got them there. "Yes, I am sure Jason's behavior was hard to ignore. I am aware that you did some things to get you here. What did you do?"
9. Structure learning and social activities to reduce failure.
10. Teach students how to learn information and how to demonstrate their control of their learning task.
11. Teach students to use procedures and techniques to monitor their own gains in academic areas.

academic achievement scores but did differ on the extent to which they felt that they were socially accepted and liked by their teachers and classmates.

Different school environments trigger feelings of loneliness in students depending on the individual student's temperament. For example, Asher, Gabriel, and Hopmeyer (1993) found that aggressive students reported the highest levels of loneliness in classroom settings, whereas students described as withdrawn reported increased levels of loneliness in less structured contexts, such as the playground or lunch room (Asher et al., 1993). Thus, it is important for teachers to realize that students who are more withdrawn need additional support to be comfortable in less structured settings. It may be useful to rehearse with them what they can do or to assist them in establishing routines with which they are comfortable in these settings. Pavri and Monda-Amaya (2000) interviewed fourth- and fifth-grade students with learning disabilities to determine their experience with school-related loneliness, which coping

strategies the students used, and which intervention strategies the students perceived as useful. Students indicated self-initiated and peer-initiated strategies to be most helpful followed closely by teacher-initiated strategies.

To help students feel less socially alienated, teachers can do the following:

- Try for a small class size that encourages all students to participate.
- Set the tone in the class that all students are valuable and have something important to contribute.
- Take a moment between classes to ask about students and demonstrate that you care.
- Allow students to participate in decision making regarding class rules and management.
- Identify youngsters who are uninvolved and/or detached, and refer them to the counselor.
- Encourage students to participate in school-related extracurricular activities.

- Ask students who are lonely whether there is a person in the class they like, and seat them nearby.
- Try grouping students into small groups or pairing students during activities.
- Provide students with activities to engage in with peers (e.g., hide and go seek) during less structured times such as recess and lunch. Encourage students to play together.

Suicide

Two Leominster, Massachusetts, teenagers died in a shotgun suicide pact next to an empty bottle of champagne after writing farewell notes that included "I love to die I'd be happier I know it! So please let me go. No hard feelings" (*Boston Herald*, November 10, 1984, p. 1). Although the autopsy showed high levels of alcohol in the girls' bloodstreams, there were no indications that either girl was involved with other drugs or was pregnant. It appeared as though both girls willingly participated in the suicide act. In another note, one of the girls wrote, "I know it was for the best. I can't handle this sucky world any longer" (*Boston Herald*, November 10, 1984, p. 7). The cause of the suicide pact is unknown.

After being forbidden to see each other, a 14-year-old-boy and a 13-year-old-girl ran away. Shortly thereafter, they leaped into a river and drowned (*Miami Herald*, November 9, 1995, p. 10).

Any suicide is shocking, but the suicide of a child or adolescent is particularly tragic. Suicides between birth and the age of 15 are termed *childhood suicides*. Between ages 15 and 19, they are referred to as *adolescent suicides*. Many deaths of adolescents are viewed as accidents and not reported as suicide; therefore, the statistics on adolescent suicide are probably woefully underreported (Toolan, 1981). However, suicide is one of the top three causes of death for people under 24 years of age; 5,000 adolescents each year take their own lives in the United States. And there is agreement that the rate of adolescent suicide is on the rise (Cimbolic and Jobes, 1990; Henry, Stephenson, Hanson, and Hargett, 1993; Popenhagen and Qualley, 1998). Female attempts at suicide greatly outnumber those of males (Hawton, 1982); however, male attempts are more frequently successful.

Suicide attempts by adolescents are frequently made to accomplish one or more of the following four factors:

1. To escape stress or stressful situations
2. To demonstrate to others how desperate they are

3. To hurt or get back at others
4. To get others to change (Wicks-Nelson and Israel, 1984)

Suicide attempts most frequently occur after interpersonal problems with boyfriends or girlfriends, parents, or teachers (Wannan and Fombonne, 1998). Often, these relationships have had prolonged difficulties. Disturbed peer relationships are a significant contributing factor to suicide attempts. Adolescents feel unique, as if there are no solutions to their particular problems. In addition, adolescents often feel responsible for their problems and are unlikely to seek assistance, thus leaving them feeling isolated (Culp, Clyman, and Culp, 1995). "Life is a chronic problem. There appears no way out. Solutions previously tried have failed. To end the chronic problem, death appears to be the only way left" (Teicher, 1973, p. 137, in Sheras, 1983).

"Suicidal patients are often very difficult because they so frequently deny the seriousness of their attempts" (Toolan, 1981, p. 320). They often make comments such as "It was all a mistake. I am much better now." Even if they attempt to discount the attempt, it should be treated with extreme seriousness.

Early detection of students who are at risk for suicide can help in providing services and reducing that risk. Students who are contemplating suicide may provide subtle verbal clues such as "Don't bother grading my test, because by tomorrow it really won't matter what I got on it" (Guetzloe, 1989; Hicks, 1990; Kalafat, 1990; Popenhagen and Qualley, 1998). Hopelessness may be the best indicator of risk for suicide (Beck, Brown, and Steer, 1989). Other variables that are related to suicide include depression, flat affect, an emotion-laden event (e.g., parental divorce), and isolation. Teachers of students with learning and behavior problems should be particularly knowledgeable about these symptoms since these students, particularly those in special education classrooms, are considered by their counselors to be more at risk for depression (Howard and Tryon, 2002). Also, students with severe reading problems are significantly more likely to experience suicidal ideation or suicide attempts and also more likely to drop out of school (Daniel, Walsh, Goldston, Arnold, Reboussin, and Wood, 2007). Apply the Concept 4.5 presents some warning signs of suicide.

Sheras (1983) offers six general considerations for dealing with adolescent suicide attempts:

1. All suicide attempts must be taken seriously. Do not interpret the behavior as merely a

Apply the Concept 4.5

What Are Some of the Suicide Warning Signs?

These warning signs should be taken very seriously and never ignored. Teach adolescents and young adults these signs so that they can respond appropriately to their peers.

- Suicide Notes—If you find, read, or are told about a suicide note that has been written do not consider it silly or funny. Take it very seriously and report it.
- Threats—All threats to do harm to oneself should be taken very seriously.
- Previous Attempts—Pay particular attention to students who have attempted suicide in the past.
- Depression—When depression includes signs of helplessness or hopelessness be very concerned about risk for suicide.
- Final Arrangements—Consider efforts to make final arrangements

such as giving away valuable objects and preparing goodbyes as serious risk signs for suicide.
- Self-Injurious Behavior—Treat attempts at injuring oneself such as jumping out of a car and cutting as risk signs for suicide.
- Sudden Changes in Appearance, Personality, Friends, and Behavior—Observe dramatic changes in appearance (neat to sloppy), excessive changes in personality, and other significant changes as potential signs for risk of suicide.
- Death and Suicide Themes—Students may exhibit unusual and peculiar preoccupation with death themes that they demonstrate in their drawings and writings.

There are a variety of online resources that you can access for more information:

American Academy for Child and Adolescent Psychiatry
www.aacap.org

American Association of Suicidology
www.suicidology.org

Depression and Bipolar Support Alliance (DBSA)
www.dbsalliance.org

Light for Life Program
www.yellowribbon.org

National Institute of Mental Health Suicide Prevention Resources
www.nimh.nih.gov/suicideprevention/index.cfm

National Mental Health Association
www.nmha.org

U.S. Department of Health and Human Services, National Strategy on Suicide Prevention
www.mentalhealth.samhsa.gov/suicideprevention

Source: R. Lieberman and K. C. Cowan, *Save a Friend: Tips for Teens to Prevent Suicide* (Bethesda, MD: National Association of School Psychologists, 2006), www.nasponline.org.

plea for "attention." Do not try to decide whether the attempt is real. The National Mental Health Association (2003) indicates that four out of five suicidal adolescents provide clear signs that they are considering suicide, including the following:

- Direct and indirect threat
- Obsession with death
- Writing that refers to death
- Dramatic changes in appearance or personality (e.g., changes in eating and/or sleeping habits)
- Giving away possessions
- Change in school behavior

2. Develop or reestablish communication with the person. Suicide is a form of communication from a person who feels that he or she has no other way to communicate.

3. Reestablish emotional or interpersonal support. Suicide is an expression of alienation, and

the person needs to be reconnected with significant others.

4. Involve the adolescent in individual and/or family therapy. Often, the adolescent feels unable to establish communication with a significant person (e.g., a parent) and needs assistance from another to do so.

5. Work with the youngster to identify the problem or problems and to provide realistic practical solutions to the problems.

6. Devise a "no-kill" contract that requires a student to promise in writing not to inflict harm on himself or herself. Students who have agreed to such a contract tend to find it more difficult to follow through with plans of suicide (Pfeffer, 1986).

Rourke and colleagues (Rourke, Young, and Leenaars, 1989) have identified a specific subtype of learning disabilities that put students at risk for depression and suicide. This *nonverbal learning disability* subtype includes such characteristics as bilateral tactile-perceptual deficits, bilateral psychomotor coordination problems, severe difficulties in visual-spatial-organizational abilities, difficulty with nonverbal problem solving, good rote verbal capacities, and difficulty adapting to novel and complex situations. Fletcher (1989) urges that students with nonverbal learning disabilities be identified early and treated promptly. Because verbal skills are highly valued, particularly in school settings, it is likely that many students with nonverbal learning disabilities go unnoticed.

Eating Disorders

Eating disorders can take a variety of forms, and different definitions exist (Button, 1993; Tylka and Subich, 1999). Central to each definition, however, is the presence of abnormal patterns of behavior and thought related to eating (American Psychiatric Association, 1994). Levine (1987) indicates that these patterns include the following:

- The person's health and vigor are reduced or threatened by his or her eating habits.
- Obligations to self and others are affected by isolation and secretiveness related to eating problems.
- The person exhibits emotional instability and self-absorption associated with food and weight control.
- Dysfunctional eating habits persist despite warnings that they are affecting the person's health and functioning.

Eating disorders are not fundamentally about eating but are multidetermined and multidimensional reflections of the person's disturbance (Ashby, Kottman, and Shoen, 1998).

Eating disorders are much less prevalent among males; more than 90 percent of cases of bulimia or anorexia nervosa occur in females (American Psychiatric Association, 1994). The highest incidence is in females between the ages of 15 and 24, and these disorders occur most frequently at higher socioeconomic levels (Jones, Fox, Haroutun-Babigian, and Hutton, 1980). The National Center for Health Statistics (2002) estimates that 4.5 to 18 percent of women and 0.4 percent of men have a history of bulimia, and about 1 percent of females have a history of anorexia.

Characteristics associated with anorexia include the following:

- Loss of menstrual cycle
- Sensitivity to cold
- Sleep disturbance
- Depression

Characteristics associated with bulimia include the following:

- Loss of dental enamel
- Low self-esteem
- Anxiety
- Depression

Why someone would deliberately starve herself or himself is puzzling. In attempting to unravel the mystery of eating disorders, researchers have examined several factors that may contribute to the disease, including biological factors, such as malfunctioning of the hypothalamus, and psychodynamic factors, such as an enmeshed family, which makes it difficult for the adolescent to express individual identity; thus, the adolescent's refusal to eat becomes a form of rebellion. There is little doubt that a combination of these biological and psychological factors contributes to anorexia and bulimia.

Drug and Alcohol Abuse

Parents probably fear nothing more than the possibility that their child will abuse drugs. With the increase in availability and use of drugs in the early to mid-1960s, parents became aware of the numbers of adolescents who were using drugs. A great deal of media attention focuses on the consequences of drug use. Stories of youngsters from stereotypically "normal" families becoming addicted to drugs and committing crimes to maintain their habits are frequently featured in magazines, newspapers, and TV shows.

Parental concerns about the availability and use of drugs and alcohol among adolescents seem to have strong support. The 2002 Monitoring the Future study tracked drug and alcohol use nationwide of students in the eighth, tenth, and twelfth grades. Eighty-nine percent of high school seniors reported that marijuana was accessible; 76 percent and 47 percent of tenth and eighth graders, respectively, reported accessibility. Approximately 95 percent of seniors said the same thing about alcohol and 45 percent about cocaine. Inhalants were assumed to be universally available, while "club drugs" such as ecstasy showed a dramatic rise in seniors' perception of availability (Johnston, O'Malley, and Bachman, 2003). Availability of drugs is not the only concern. The study also found that 78 percent of high school students had consumed alcohol by the end of high school, more than half

(62 percent) of the seniors reporting having been drunk at least once. Among twelfth graders, 57 percent had tried cigarettes, and 27 percent reported being current smokers. In addition, 53 percent had tried an illicit drug by the time they finished high school, and 30 percent had used some illicit drug other than marijuana (Johnston et al., 2003).

Because of the prevalence of drug use, the pattern of drug and alcohol consumption is the most important issue. Typically, the pattern is conceptualized along five frequency points: nonusers, experimenters, recreational users, problem users, and addicts, with both the amount used and the types of substances used escalating as well (Kandel, 2002; Krug, 1983).

Because marijuana use is so much more widespread than that of any other illicit drug, teachers need to be familiar with some of the outcomes of marijuana use so that they can identify and counsel users. Users may suffer these adverse psychological and physical effects:

- Occasional anxiety and suspiciousness
- Impairment of immediate memory recall
- Long-term memory disorders
- Loss of goal-related drive
- Inability to think and speak clearly
- Lung damage
- Increased risk for certain types of cancer
- Flashbacks
- Possible suppression of the immune system

It is quite difficult to use characteristics from checklists to identify drug users. Many drug users are aware of the behavioral and physiological consequences of drug use and employ disguises such as eyedrops and sunglasses to hide their red eyes. They have also learned to control their behavior to avoid calling undue attention to themselves. Teachers most often rely on identifying drug abusers through the abusers' self-disclosures or disclosures by concerned others.

Understanding the difference between drug and alcohol use and abuse is difficult. Though not always easy to distinguish, substance use occurs when an individual actually uses a substance but it is infrequent and does not interfere with their life, whereas substance abuse relates to the maladaptive use of a substance. Many individuals who try illicit drugs do not go on to abuse them, thus providing another distinction between use and abuse (Sussman and Ames, 2001). In other words, behavior that would be considered drug abuse for one person is manageable use for another (Zinberg, 1984).

Teachers should be aware of drug and alcohol terminology, characteristics of users, and consequences (Maxwell and Liu, 1998). Familiarity with local referral agencies providing guidance and assistance to students who are involved with drugs and alcohol is important for all teachers.

Now that we understand social competence and how students with behavior and learning difficulties feel about themselves, are perceived by others, and interact socially with others, let us focus on intervention theory and specific programs and activities for teaching social skills.

Intervention Strategies

Understanding and using different interventions in attempting to affect the social skills of students with learning disabilities and behavior disorders is extremely important. There is a wide variety of social difficulties exhibited by students with learning and behavior disorders. Using a particular intervention may be effective with one student but considerably less effective with another student or another problem. By understanding many approaches, teachers increase the likelihood of success with all students. The real challenge is knowing when to use which approach with which child under which condition. The best way to determine whether an intervention is working is to target specific social skills and to measure their progress over time. Though immediate improvement is unlikely, there should be some improvement in four to six weeks; if there is no improvement, the teacher may consider trying another intervention.

There is a range of intervention strategies to assist in teaching appropriate social skills to students with learning disabilities and behavior disorders. The purpose of social skills training is to teach the students a complex response set that allows them to adapt to the numerous problems that occur in social situations. Common goals of social skills training programs include the ability to do the following:

- Solve problems and make decisions quickly
- Adapt to situations that are new or unexpected
- Use coping strategies for responding to emotional upsets
- Communicate effectively with others
- Make and maintain friends
- Reduce anxiety
- Reduce problem behaviors

Working with Families of Students with Social Difficulties

Children and adolescents who are connected with their parents and families are healthier than students who are not (Blum and Mann-Rinehart, 1997). Thus, working with families and engaging them in resolving social and behavioral issues at school and at home is an essential part of a successful intervention program. This is true regardless of the age of the student. Many teachers find it easier to engage families when they are teaching very young children. However, families of older students are critical links to effective social and behavioral outcomes for their children.

 Family

It is critical that children and youths with special needs have opportunities to share their hopes and dreams with key individuals such as family members and teachers. The National 4-H Council has identified eight "Keys for Kids" based on the work of Konopka (1973) and Pittman (1991).

1. *Security.* Children need to feel that they are emotionally and physically safe and comfortable in home, school, and community contexts.
2. *Belonging.* Students need to feel that they are part of the group at home, in school, and in the community. They need to feel that they have a place.
3. *Acceptance.* Students need to feel that their opinions and actions are accepted and valued. They need to develop self-worth through their actions and responses to their actions by important others.
4. *Independence.* Students need to discover that they can accomplish work and play on their own and be successful.
5. *Relationships.* Healthy and functional relationships at school, at home, and in the community are an essential feature of a healthy individual.
6. *Values.* Students need to hear the values of people at school and home and use them to build their own values.
7. *Achievement.* All individuals need to accomplish things and to have pride in what they do.
8. *Recognition.* Accomplishing things, even small things, warrants recognition and support from critical members of children's family, community, and school.

Interpersonal Problem Solving

Most people spend an extraordinary amount of time preventing and solving interpersonal problems.

Whether we are concerned about what to say to our neighbor whose dog barks loudly in the middle of the night, how to handle an irate customer at work, or our relationships with our parents and siblings, interpersonal problems are an ongoing part of life. Some people seem to acquire the skills necessary for interpersonal problem solving easily and with little or no direct instruction; others, particularly students with learning and behavior disorders, need more direct instruction in how to prevent and resolve difficulties with others.

The goal of interpersonal problem-solving training is to empower students with a wide range of strategies that allow them to develop and maintain positive relationships with others, cope effectively with others, solve their own problems, and resolve conflict with others. The problem-solving approach attempts to provide the student with a process for solving conflicts. Interpersonal problem solving has been used successfully with a wide range of populations, including adult psychiatric patients (Platt and Spivack, 1972), preschoolers (Ridley and Vaughn, 1982), kindergartners (Shure and Spivack, 1978), students identified as mentally retarded (Vaughn, Ridley, and Cox, 1983), students with learning disabilities (Vaughn, Levine, and Ridley, 1986), and aggressive children (Vaughn, Ridley, et al., 1984).

Four skills appear to be particularly important for successful problem resolution (Spivack, Platt, and Shure, 1976). First, the student must be able to identify and define the problem. Second, the student must be able to generate a variety of alternative solutions to any given problem. Third, the student must be able to identify and evaluate the possible consequences of each alternative. Finally, the student must be able to implement the solution. This may require rehearsal and modeling.

Whereas these four components are characteristic of most interpersonal problem-solving programs, programs often incorporate additional components and procedures. For example, a social problem-solving intervention was conducted with 50 students with serious emotional disturbances by Amish, Gesten, Smith, Clark, and Stark (1988). The intervention consisted of 15 structured lessons that occurred for 40 minutes once each week. The following problem-solving steps were taught:

1. Say what the problem is and how you feel.
2. Decide on a goal.
3. Stop and think before you decide what to do.
4. Think of many possible solutions to the problem.

5. Think about what will happen next after each possible solution.
6. When you find a good solution, try it.

The results of the intervention indicated that students with serious emotional disturbances who participated in the intervention improved their social problem-solving skills and were able to generate more alternatives to interviewing and role-playing measures.

The following sections describe several interpersonal problem-solving (IPS) programs that have been developed, implemented, and evaluated with students who have learning and behavior disorders.

FAST and SLAM

FAST is a strategy that is taught as part of an IPS program to second-, third-, and fourth-grade students with learning disabilities who have been identified as having social skills problems (Vaughn and Lancelotta, 1990; Vaughn, Lancelotta, et al., 1988; Vaughn et al., 1991). The purpose of FAST is to teach students to consider problems carefully before responding to them and to consider alternatives and their consequences. Figure 4.14 presents the FAST strategy. In step 1, Freeze and Think, students are taught to identify the problem. In step 2, Alternatives, students are taught to consider possible ways of solving the problem. In step 3, Solution Evaluation, students are asked to prepare a solution or course of action for solving the problem that is both safe and fair. The idea is to get students to consider solutions that will be effective in the long run. Step 4, Try It, asks students to rehearse and implement the solution. If they are unsuccessful at implementing the solution, students are taught to go back to alternatives.

FIGURE 4.14

FAST: An Interpersonal Problem-Solving Strategy

Freeze and think!
  What is the problem?

Alternatives?
  What are my possible solutions?

Solution evaluation
  Choose the best solution:
    safe?
    fair?

Try it!
  Slowly and carefully
  Does it work?

Students with learning disabilities practiced this strategy by using real problems generated by themselves and their peers.

CLASSROOM Applications

FAST

PROCEDURES:

1. In each classroom, ask peers to rate all same-sex classmates on the extent to which they would like to be friends with them. Students who receive few friendship votes and many no-friendship votes are identified as rejected. Students who receive many friendship votes and few no-friendship votes are identified as popular. See Coie, Dodge, and Coppotelli (1982) for exact procedures in assessing popular and rejected students.
2. A rejected student with learning disabilities is paired with a same-sex popular classmate, and the pair becomes the social skills trainers for the class and school. The school principal announces to the school and to parents through a newsletter who the social skills trainers are for the school.
3. Children who are selected as social skills trainers are removed from the classroom two to three times a week and are taught social skills strategies for approximately 30 minutes each session.
4. Social skills training includes learning the FAST strategy as well as other social skills, such as accepting negative feedback, receiving positive feedback, and making friendship overtures.
5. While the social skills trainers are learning social skills strategies, their classmates are recording problems they have at home and at school and placing their lists in the classroom problem-solving box. Trainers use these lists as they learn the strategies outside of class as well as for in-class discussion that occurs later and is led by the social skills trainers.
6. After the social skills trainers have learned a strategy, such as FAST, they teach it to the entire class with backup and support from the researcher and classroom teacher.
7. During subsequent weeks, social skills trainers leave the room for only one session per week and practice the FAST strategy as well as other strategies with classmates at least one time per week. These reviews include large group explanations and small group problem-solving exercises.

8. Students who are selected as social skills trainers are recognized by their teacher and administrator for their special skills. Other students are asked to consult the social skills trainer when they have difficulties

Apply the Concept 4.6 shows an activity sheet used as part of a homework assignment for students participating in the training.

COMMENTS: This approach to teaching social skills and increasing peer acceptance has been successfully applied in two studies with youngsters with learning disabilities (Vaughn, Lancelotta, et al., 1988; Vaughn et al., 1991) but has not been evaluated for behavior-disordered students or adolescents.

Based on principles similar to those of the FAST strategy, SLAM is a technique that can be used to assist students in accepting and assimilating negative feedback and comments from others (McIntosh, Vaughn, and Bennerson, 1995). The SLAM strategy is practiced in small groups and presented to the class. The components of the SLAM strategy are as follows:

1. *Stop*—Stop whatever you are doing.
2. *Look*—Look the person in the eye.

FIGURE 4.15

Lyrics to the SLAM Strategy Song

Accepting negative feedback, feedback, feedback.
Accepting negative feedback, feedback, feedback.
Stop what you're doing. Look them in the eye.
Fix your face. We'll tell you why.
Accepting negative feedback, feedback, feedback.
Accepting negative feedback, feedback, feedback.
Listen with your ears to what they say.
This is no time for you to play.
Accepting negative feedback, feedback, feedback.
Accepting negative feedback, feedback, feedback.
Ask a question if you don't understand.
Don't stand there in wonderland.
Accepting negative feedback, feedback, feedback.
Accepting negative feedback, feedback, feedback.
Make a response to their concerns.
Accepting negative feedback is the way to learn.

3. *Ask*—Ask the person a question to clarify what he or she means.
4. *Make*—Make an appropriate response to the person.

Figure 4.15 presents the lyrics to the SLAM Strategy Song.

Apply the Concept 4.6

Activity Sheet for FAST

This activity sheet can be used to give children written practice in using the FAST strategy.

You are in the cafeteria. Another student keeps bugging you. He hits you, pokes you, tries to steal your food, and will not stop bullying you. You start to get angry. What would you do? Use FAST to help you solve the problem.

1. *Freeze and think.* What is the problem?
   _____
   _____

2. *Alternatives.* What are your possible solutions?
   _____
   _____
   _____

3. *Solution evaluation.* Choose the best one. Remember: safe and fair; works in the long run.
   _____
   _____

4. *Try it.* Do you think this will work?
   _____
   _____

A friend of yours is upset. She is teased a lot, especially by a boy named Kenny. She told you that she wants to run away from school. What could you tell your friend to help her solve the problem? Use FAST to help you.

1. _____
   _____
   _____

2. _____
   _____
   _____
   _____

3. _____
   _____
   _____
   _____

4. _____
   _____
   _____
   _____

FIGURE 4.16
Living, Learning, and Working

Session 1
Developing group norms and learning about each other.

Session 2
Learning specific encouragement skills and behaviors.

Session 3
Learning cooperation skills for working in a group. Students learn that they will be helping younger students by learning specific strategies for reading, discussing, and role playing. The younger students are introduced and paired with the older students midway through the session.

Sessions 4–8
Each session follows a six-step format. Different books can be used for each session.

1. Read a developmentally appropriate story that involves diversity such as cognitive, physical, or social.
2. Process the story using story structure and the five *Ws* (*Who* were the main characters? *When* did the story take place? *What* were the main events? *What* were the main problems encountered in the story? *Where* did the story take place? *Why* did the characters have the problem?) and two *Hs* (*How* did the characters feel at the beginning, middle, and end of the story? *How* was the problem solved?).

3. Discuss similarities and differences between story characters and group members.
4. Brainstorm other ways to solve the problem introduced in the story.
5. Role-play various problem-solving solutions.
6. Provide feedback on role playing.

Session 9
Involve the whole group of older and younger students, and discuss ground rules for reading, discussing the story, and role playing.

Session 10
Have each pair of older and younger students read a story. Ask the older child to use a structured guide to discuss the story and role-play the solution to the problem identified in the story.

Session 11
Conduct a closure activity with the whole group.

Session 12
Bring both the older and younger groups of students together at the beginning of the session to discuss what the experience was like for them. Involve only the older students at the end of the session, and debrief them.

LLW: Living, Learning, and Working

Living, Learning, and Working (LLW) is a program that is designed to enhance listening, attending, empathy, social problem solving, and contributing skills among fourth and fifth graders (Brigman and Molina, 1999). This program can be implemented throughout a school with the cooperation of other teachers or a school counselor. The fourth and fifth graders work with a younger reading partner, and the pair read books that deal with specific issues, such as difficulty in making friends. This program is designed to be implemented in a group setting. The goals of the program are achieved in three phases: working together, learning together, and living together. Figure 4.16 presents the specific goals for each session. Bibliotherapy is a counseling strategy similar to LLW that can be used in the classroom to enhance the self-concept of students. Bibliotherapy also requires the use of age-appropriate books that focus on specific problems that the students are experiencing. Students discuss how they are like or unlike the characters in the book, discuss the characters' emotions, make predictions about events, and share similar life experiences with the class (Sridhar and Vaughn,

2000). Table 4.1 and Table 4.2 present lists of books along with their summaries to help teachers choose books.

ASSET: A Social Skills Program for Adolescents

The purpose of ASSET is to teach adolescents the social skills they need to interact successfully with peers and adults (Hazel, Schumaker, Sherman, and Sheldon, 1981). Eight social skills are considered fundamental to successful relationships:

1. *Giving positive feedback.* This skill teaches students how to thank someone and how to give a compliment.
2. *Giving negative feedback.* This skill teaches students to give correction and feedback in a way that is not threatening.
3. *Accepting negative feedback.* This skill teaches students the all-important ability to receive negative feedback without walking away, showing hostility, or other inappropriate emotional reactions.
4. *Resisting peer pressure.* This skill teaches students to refuse their friends who are trying to seduce them into some form of delinquent behavior.

TABLE 4.1
Books for Young Children

Topic	Book Citation	Summary
Accepting difference in people	Spier, P. (1980). *People*. New York: Doubleday.	Celebrating the variety of human beings, the book encourages acceptance and appreciation of all kinds of people with all kinds of eyes, noses, hair colors, languages, and so on.
Self-acceptance; tolerance of others	Cohen, M. (1985). *Liar, Liar, . Pants on Fire*. New York: Greenwillow.	Alex, a new boy in first grade, brags about his pony and rocket car. The other children consider him a liar and reject him. Their teacher gently explains that Alex really wants to be noticed and needs friends. So Alex is given another chance at making friends. The book focuses on being yourself and tolerating others.
Handling criticism; dealing with emotional hurt	Doleski, T. (1983). *The Hurt*. New York: Paulist.	Justin finds dealing with criticism particularly painful. Each criticism is shown as a hurt that grows larger and larger until it begins to crowd him out of his bedroom. His father suggests the hurt will go away if he stops thinking about it, and it never becomes big again. The book focuses on effectively dealing with criticism.
Reassuring late bloomers	Kraus, R. (1987). *Leo the Late Bloomer*. New York: Harper.	Leo the tiger cub is behind other animals in reading, writing, drawing, and eating neatly. Although his father is worried, his mother assures him that Leo will bloom with time, and he does. The book focuses on assuring late bloomers that children develop at different rates.
Friendship helps in difficult times	Dowell, F. O. (2004). *Where I'd Like to Be*. New York: Aladdin.	This is the story of an 11-year-old girl in a good children's home and her persistence to have a good life. Her friendship with other homeless children opens a door of imagination and inspires dreams of the future.
Self-acceptance; making friends	Wells, R. (1981). *Timothy Goes to School*. New York: Dial.	Timothy starts school with feelings of inadequacy that are made worse by Claude, who is condescending, critical, and annoyingly good at everything. Luckily, Violet, another animal child, is having similar problems and the two left-out animal children become happy friends. The book focuses on making friends and accepting different kinds of people.
Acceptance and usefulness of wearing glasses	Brown, M. (1979). *Arthur's Eyes*. Boston: Little, Brown.	Arthur is embarrassed about wearing glasses and often tries to lose them. One day a teacher whom he admires shows Arthur the usefulness of his glasses. Arthur's arithmetic and basketball improve, and his classmates also begin to want glasses. The book emphasizes the value of wearing glasses.
Acceptance of physical appearance	Brown, M. (1981). *Arthur's Nose*. New York: Avon.	Arthur is unhappy with his long nose and consults a "rhinologist" about changing it. He tries out several other noses such as an elephant's and a toucan's. Finally, he decides to keep his own, much to the relief of his friends. The book effectively deals with accepting physical differences.
We are all special; treating classmates kindly	Yashima, T. (1955). *Crow Boy*. New York: Viking.	Chibi has attended the village school for six years but has been too fearful to learn or make friends. Finally the beauty of his drawings and pictographs and the depth of his knowledge of nature, particularly crows, is recognized by a kind teacher. The book emphasizes individual uniqueness.

Diversity

Topic	Book Citation	Summary
We are all special	Leaf, M. (1977). *The Story of Ferdinand*. New York: Puffin.	A bull calf enjoys sitting quietly smelling the flowers instead of goring the matador in the bullring. He will not lose his temper even when tormented by *banderilleros* and *picadors*. The book focuses on the value of individuality.
Accepting people of various origins; accepting various handicaps; all children enjoy similar things	Brown, T. (1984). *Someone Special Just Like You*. New York: Holt.	Children of different origins with different handicaps all enjoy similar activities that normal children enjoy. The idea that children are more alike than different regardless of origin and disability is emphasized.
Inclusion of a blind child; accepting and understanding visual impairment	Cohen, M. (1983). *See You Tomorrow Charles*. New York: Greenwillow.	The inclusion of a blind first grader into a general education first-grade classroom is described. The class accepts the boy with friendliness, protectiveness, and interest.
Children with certain disabilities sometimes go to special schools; children with disabilities also have loving, caring families	Fassler, J. (1975). *Howie Helps Himself*. Chicago: Whitman.	A boy must go to a special school because his legs are weak. However, he learns the same things that all children learn, such as reading and counting. Although he learns many things, his greatest achievement is to wheel his wheel chair across the classroom to his father, who demonstrates love and caring.
People with disabilities may use different things but they are more similar than different from us	Hamm, D. (1987). *Grandmom Drives a Motor Bed*. Virginia Wright-Frierson. Niles, IL: Whitman.	A cheerful grandmother with paralyzed legs has to spend almost all her time in a motorized hospital bed. But she enjoys telephoning, visits from friends, watching television, and, most of all, seeing her grandson. The idea that she is like most grandmothers regardless of her paralyzed legs is emphasized.
Children with learning disabilities also enjoy doing the same things that other children do; children with learning disabilities have home lives similar to those of other children	Lasker, J. (1974). *He's My Brother*. Chicago: Albert Whitman.	Although Jamie has a learning disability, he enjoys activities that most children his age enjoy. His brother describes Jamie's problems, abilities, and likes at home and school.
Recognizing and appreciating individual differences	Bradman, T. (1995). *Michael*. New York: Macmillan.	Michael is not like the other students in class. He is usually late and frequently in trouble. However, Michael has special abilities that have not yet been recognized. His special abilities are indicated through the illustrations.
Having a sibling with mental retardation; managing conflicting emotions caused by individual differences	Wright, B. R. (1981). *My Sister Is Different*. Milwaukee: Raintree.	Carlo finds it difficult to accept his older sister Terry, who is mentally retarded. He finally realizes how special Terry is when he almost loses her.
Teasing can hurt	Hines, A. G. (1989). *They Really Like Me!* New York: Greenwillow.	Two mischievous older sisters tease their little brother who is left in their care. The little boy teaches them a lesson by hiding under the staircase after they pretend to abandon him in the woods. He finally reappears, and they promise to stop teasing him.
Communicating effectively and standing up for yourself	Drew, N. (2004). *The Kids' Guide to Working Out Conflicts! How to Keep Cool, Stay Safe, and Get Along*. Minneapolis, MN: Free Spirit.	It is tough to be a kid in today's world; it is hard at school and in some homes to choose a peaceful path instead of anger and violence. This upbeat and practical book is written specifically for kids with real-life examples of conflicts and how kids solved them, activities, self-tests, and action plans to bring the ideas into everyday life.

Source: Adapted from D. Sridhar and S. Vaughn (2000). Bibliotherapy for all: Enhancing reading comprehension, self-concept, and behavior. *Teaching Exceptional Children, 33* (2). Copyright 2000 by The Council for Exceptional Children. Reprinted by permission.

TABLE 4.2
Books for Second through Fourth Grades

Topic	Book Citation	Summary
What it is like to live with siblings with diabetes, asthma, and spina bifida	Rosenburg, M. B. (1988). *Finding a Way: Living with Exceptional Brothers and Sisters.* New York: Lothrop.	Children talk about how it is to live with siblings who have diabetes, asthma, and spina bifida. They talk about ways in which they help and about the mixed feelings they have about the siblings with medical conditions.
Children with disabilities also enjoy activities that other children enjoy	Rosenburg, M. B. (1983). *My Friend Leslie.* New York: Lothrop.	A bubbly, happy kindergartner with multiple handicaps is mainstreamed in a public school. She enjoys activities such as music, painting, exercise, and friendships, which most children enjoy. The book focuses on the normalcy of children with handicaps.
The value of a sibling	Zolotow, C. (1966). *If It Weren't for You.* New York: Harper & Row.	A little boy dreams about how much better life would be without his younger brother to share things such as cake, the bedroom, and Christmas presents. While dreaming, he suddenly realizes that he would then be alone with all the grownups and begins to see the value of having a little brother.
We are all unique and universal	Shan, E. L. (1972). *What Makes Me Feel This Way?* New York: Macmillan.	Feelings common to all children such as anger, fear, and shyness are treated as natural, and suggestions are made about understanding and expressing them acceptably.
Overcoming disabilities	White, E. B. (1970). *The Trumpet of the Swan.* New York: Harper.	Louis, a trumpeter swan, is born mute. However, he overcomes his handicap by learning to read, write, and play the trumpet. The book deals with the idea of overcoming disabilities.
Normality of children with handicaps	Wolf, B. (1988). *Don't Feel Sorry for Paul.* Philadelphia: Lippincott.	Paul is a young boy born with unfinished hands and feet and wears prostheses to substitute for his missing body parts. However, he rides in horse shows, wrestles with his sisters, and leads an active life. The normality of Paul's life is emphasized without ignoring his problems.

Source: D. Sridhar and S. Vaughn (2000). Bibliotherapy for all: Enhancing reading comprehension, self-concept, and behavior. *Teaching Exceptional Children, 33* (2). Copyright 2000 by The Council for Exceptional Children. Reprinted by permission.

5. *Problem solving.* This skill teaches students a process for solving their own interpersonal difficulties.
6. *Negotiation.* This skill teaches students to use their problem-solving skills with another person to come to a mutually acceptable resolution.
7. *Following instructions.* This skill teaches students to listen and respond to instructions.
8. *Conversation.* This skill teaches students to initiate and maintain a conversation.

The Leader's Guide (Hazel et al., 1981) that comes with the ASSET program provides instructions for running the groups and teaching the skills. Eight teaching sessions are provided on videotapes that demonstrate the skills. Program materials include skill sheets, home notes, and criterion checklists.

CLASSROOM Applications
ASSET—A Social Skills Program for Adolescents

PROCEDURES: Each lesson is taught to a small group of adolescents. There are nine basic steps to each lesson:

1. Review homework and previously learned social skills.
2. Explain the new skill for the day's lesson.
3. Explain why the skill is important and should be learned and practiced.
4. Give a realistic and specific example to illustrate the use of the skill.
5. Examine each of the skill steps that are necessary to carry out the new social skill.
6. Model the skill, and provide opportunities for students and others to demonstrate correct and incorrect use of the skills.
7. Use verbal rehearsal to familiarize the students with the sequence of steps in each social skill, and provide a procedure for students to be automatic with their knowledge of the skill steps.
8. Use behavioral rehearsal to allow each student to practice and demonstrate the skill steps until they reach criterion.
9. Assign homework that provides opportunities for the students to practice the skills in other settings.

These nine steps are followed for each of the eight specific social skills listed above.

COMMENTS: The ASSET program has been evaluated with eight students with learning disabilities (Hazel, Schumaker, Sherman, and Sheldon, 1982). That evaluation demonstrated that the students with learning disabilities involved in the intervention increased in the use of social skills in role play settings. The curriculum guide provides specific teaching procedures and is particularly relevant to teachers working with adolescents.

Mutual Interest Discovery

Rather than specifically teaching social skills, mutual interest discovery is an approach to increasing peer acceptance that has been used with students with learning disabilities (Fox, 1989). **Diversity** The rationale is that people are attracted to others with whom they share similar attitudes. The more we know about someone, the more likely it is that we will like that person. Structured activities are provided for students with and without learning disabilities to get to know each other with greater acceptance being the outcome.

CLASSROOM Applications
Mutual Interest Discovery

PROCEDURES: The overall goal of mutual interest discovery is to participate in structured activities with a partner (one partner with learning disabil-

ities and the other without) to identify things you have in common and to get to know your partner better.

1. All students in the class are paired; students with learning disabilities are paired with classmates without learning disabilities.
2. Students interact on preassigned topics for approximately 40 minutes once each week for several weeks. Preassigned topics include interviewing each other about such things as sports, entertainment preferences, hobbies, and other topics that are appropriate for the specific age group with which you are working.
3. After the structured activity, each member of the pair writes three things that he or she has in common with another person or three things that he or she learned about the other person.
4. Partners complete a brief art activity related to what they learned about their partner and place it in a mutual art book to which they contribute each week.
5. At the bottom of the art exercise, each partner writes two sentences about something new that he or she learned about his or her partner. If there is time, art activities and sentences are shared with members of the class.

COMMENTS: Partners who participated in the mutual interest discovery intervention demonstrated higher ratings of their partners over time than did a control group of students. This intervention is designed not to teach specific social skills but to increase the acceptance and likability of students with learning disabilities in the regular classroom. This intervention, paired with social skills training, appears to have promise for success with students with learning disabilities.

Circle of Friends

Circle of Friends is a friendship enhancement program that has been evaluated with 6- to 12-year-old students with emotional and behavioral disorders (Frederickson and Turner, 2003). The primary purpose of Circle of Friends is to establish a supportive meeting each week (for about one hour) to provide opportunities for peers to learn to interact and support their fellow students with emotional or behavior problems.

Open Circle Program

The Open Circle Program (Seigle, Lange, and Macklem, 1997) is designed to assist students in developing communication, self-control, and problem-solving skills. The lessons are designed to be used by teachers and can occur one to two times per week. The curriculum has 35 lessons. Although the program is implemented primarily by the teacher, other adults such as parents and school counselors may be involved. Open Circle provides an opportunity to:

- Discuss pressing issues
- Develop a supporting class environment
- Develop verbal and nonverbal ways of creating a respectful environment
- Teach students interpersonal problem solving
- Practice social skills, and
- Enhance self-esteem

The results of a study reveal that students who participated in the Open Circle Program for a full year were perceived by teachers as more socially skilled and less likely to exhibit behavior problems (Hennessey, 2007).

CLASSROOM Applications

Circle of Friends

PROCEDURES: Circles of Friends are run by the counselor or school psychologist with the classroom teacher as a participant. The focus child is a student whom the teacher has identified as having significant behavior problems and peer interaction difficulties that would improve if peers in the classroom provided the appropriate interactions and supports. An outside leader (usually school psychologist or counselor) conducts the Circle of Friends group. Students from the target student's class are included in the Circle of Friends. Typically, the target student is not present during the meetings.

Following are the main features in using Circle of Friends in the classroom:

1. During the first meeting, the leader explains to the group why the target student is not present and solicits the cooperation and support of the peers. Students who are participating are first asked to identify only the strengths and positive behaviors of the target student.
2. After the target student's positive behaviors have been identified, the leader asks students to identify the challenging behaviors that the target student exhibits. The leader makes links between the target student's difficult behaviors and the types of responses and supports that students could provide. Then the leader requests that six to eight students volunteer to serve as the Circle of Friends. The rest of the students are dismissed.
3. The Circle of Friends meet approximately eight times with the leader and the target student. During these meetings, students are reminded to follow the basic ground rules of confidentiality, seeking adult help if they are worried, and listening carefully to each person.
4. The leader and students identify a target behavior and roles that each of them will play to ensure that the student is able to maintain the target behavior. Students' role-play and set goals for the forthcoming week. Each week, they review and describe their success and establish new behavioral goals.

COMMENTS: Students with emotional and behavior disorders who participated in the Circle of Friends (Frederickson and Turner, 2003) were better accepted by their peers in the classroom after participation than were similar students who had not participated in such a program. Although the Circle of Friends did not influence students' overall perceptions of the climate of the classroom, it did (positively) influence their perceptions of the target student.

Structured Learning

Structured learning is a psychoeducational and behavioral approach to teaching prosocial skills to students both with and without disabilities (Goldstein, Sprafkin, Gerhsaw, and Klein, 1980). The procedure has four components and can be implemented by teachers, social workers, psychologists, or school counselors. A related program, the Stop and Think Social Skills Program (Knoff, 2003), provides a manual for teachers, a classroom set of materials for teacher and students, and specific lessons for all grade levels from kindergarten through eighth grade.

The first component, *modeling*, involves a verbal and behavioral description of the target skill as well as the steps that comprise the target skill. At this point, the teacher might role-play the steps in the skill, and other models may also role-play, exhibiting the target skill itself. During the second step, students are encouraged to enact role plays based on actual life experiences. These role plays are facilitated by coaching and cues from the teacher. Next, the teacher and other observers provide feedback. Specific attention is paid to elements of each role play that were effective and appropriate. Skills that were not role-played effectively are modeled by the teacher. In the final step, students are provided with opportunities to practice the steps and skills in the real world (e.g., outside the classroom).

The structured learning procedure for elementary students offers 60 prosocial skills and their constituent steps, arranged into five groups: classroom survival skills, friendship-making skills, skills for dealing with feelings, skill alternatives to aggression, and skills for dealing with stress. The structured learning procedure for adolescents also has 60 prosocial skills. It differs from the program for elementary students by including skills related to planning and decision making.

Social Life Program

The social life program developed by Griffiths (1991) for use with developmentally handicapped adults was modified and used successfully with 9- to 12-year-old students with learning disabilities (Wiener and Harris, 1997). The program is delivered through a board game similar in format to Monopoly that can be played by three to five students. Students take turns throwing the dice. After throwing the dice, the student moves to a colored square and must solve the social problem read by the teacher from a color-coded chart. Depending on the solution, the child receives or returns Monopoly money. The cards are designed specifically to encourage role playing, modeling of appropriate social behavior and problem solving, and performance feedback.

First Steps to Success: Helping Children Overcome Antisocial Behavior

The materials for this program contain information for students in prekindergarten through third grade. It has a home-to-school intervention component for young children. The materials include a guide, a homebase coach, a video, and materials to assist with implementation (Walker, Golly, Kavanagh, Stiller, Severson, and Feil, 2003).

Principles for Teaching Social Skills

There are a number of points that teachers need to consider, no matter what social skills program they utilize:

1. *Develop cooperative learning.* Classrooms can be structured so that there is a win–lose atmosphere in which children compete with each other for grades and teacher attention, or structured so that children work on their own with little interaction among classmates, or structured for cooperative learning so children work alone, with pairs, and with groups, helping each other master the assigned material. Cooperative learning techniques in the classroom result in increases in self-esteem, social skills, and learning (Johnson and Johnson, 1986). Teachers can structure learning activities so that they involve cooperative learning and teach students techniques for working with pairs or in a group. The following four elements need to be present for cooperative learning to occur in small groups (Johnson and Johnson, 1986):

a. Students must perceive that they cannot succeed at the required task unless all members of the group succeed. This may require appropriate division of labor and giving a single grade for the entire group's performance.

b. There must be individual accountability so that each member of the group is assessed and realizes that his or her performance is critical for group success.

c. Students must have the necessary collaborative skills to function effectively in a group. This may include managing conflicts, active listening, leadership skill, and problem solving.

d. Sufficient time for group process must be allowed, including discussing how well the group is performing, developing a plan of action, and identifying what needs to happen.

2. *Involve peers in the training program for low-social-status students.* An important function of social skills training is to alter the way in which peers perceive students who are identified as low in social status. Including popular peers in the social skills training program increases the likelihood that they will have opportunities to observe the changes in target students and to cue and reinforce appropriate behavior in the classroom. For example, a study conducted by Vaughn, McIntosh, and Spencer-Rowe (1991) found that popular students who were involved in the social skills training with low-social-status students were more likely to increase the social status ratings of the low-social-status students than were popular students who were not involved in the training.

Even when a social skills program is effective in producing the desired change in target students, it does not always alter the way in which these students are perceived by their peers (Bierman and Furman, 1984). Involving students with high social status with those with lower social status improves the way in which the low-social-status students are perceived by others (Frederickson and Turner, 2003).

Students benefit from working with peers in supportive and academically structured activities. A recent meta-analysis of the research literature (Ginsburg-Block, Rohrbeck, and Fantuzzo, 2006) revealed that students not only benefit academically when interventions focus on reading and math outcomes, but there is also a small effect for social, self-concept, and behavioral outcomes as well. Thus, there are benefits academically as well as socially.

3. *Use principles of effective instruction.* Many teachers claim that they do not know how to teach social skills. Considering the social skills difficulties of special education students, methods of teaching social skills to students may need to become part of teacher training programs.

Teaching social skills requires implementing principles of effective instruction. These are used and explained throughout this text and include obtaining student commitment, identifying target behavior, pretesting, teaching, modeling, rehearsing, role playing, providing feedback, practicing in controlled settings, practicing in other settings, posttesting, and follow-up. Following are social skills that learning- and behavior-disordered students frequently need to be taught:

- *Body language.* This includes how students walk, where they stand during a conversation, what their body language "says," gestures, eye contact, and appropriate facial reactions.
- *Greetings.* This may include expanding students' repertoire of greetings, selecting appropriate greetings for different people, and interpreting and responding to the greetings of others.
- *Initiating and maintaining a conversation.* This includes a wide range of behaviors such as knowing when to approach someone; knowing how to ask inviting, open questions; knowing how to respond to comments made by others; and maintaining a conversation with a range of people, including those who are too talkative and those who volunteer little conversation.
- *Giving positive feedback.* Knowing how and when to give sincere, genuine, positive feedback and comments.
- *Accepting positive feedback.* Knowing how to accept positive feedback from others.
- *Giving negative feedback.* Knowing how and when to give specific negative feedback.

- *Accepting negative feedback.* Knowing how to accept negative feedback from others.
- *Identifying feelings in self and others.* Being able to recognize feelings in both self and others is how students are able to predict how they will feel in a given situation and prepare for responding appropriately to one's own and others' feelings.
- *Problem solving and conflict resolution.* Knowing and using problem-solving skills to prevent and solve difficulties.

4. *Teach needed skills.* Many social skills training programs fail because youngsters are trained to do things that they already know how to do. For example, in a social skills training group with students with learning disabilities, the trainer was teaching the students to initiate conversations with others. Through role playing, the trainer soon learned that the students already knew how to initiate conversations but did not know how to sustain them. In addition to being taught appropriate skills, students need to learn when and with whom to use the skills. One student put it this way: "I would never try problem solving like this with my father, but I know it would work with my mom."

5. *Teach for transfer of learning.* Many programs for teaching social skills effectively increase students' performance in social areas during the skills training or within a particular context, but the skills do not generalize to other settings (Berler, Gross, and Drabman, 1982). For social skills to generalize to other settings, the program must require the rehearsal and implementation of target skills across settings. Social skills training programs need to ensure that learned skills are systematically demonstrated in the classroom, on the playground, and at home.

6. *Empower students.* Many students with learning difficulties feel discouraged and unable to influence their learning. They turn the responsibility for learning over to the teacher and become passive learners. How can we empower students?

- *Choice.* Students need to feel that they are actively involved in their learning.
- *Consequences.* Students will learn from the natural and logical consequences of their choices.
- *Documented progress.* In addition to teacher documentation of progress made, students need to learn procedures for monitoring and assessing their progress.
- *Control.* Students need to feel as though they can

Progress Monitoring

exercise control over what happens to them. Some students feel as though their learning is in someone else's hands and therefore is someone else's responsibility.

7. *Identify strengths.* When developing social skills interventions for students with special needs, be sure to consider their strengths as well as their needs. Because appearance and athletic ability relate to social acceptance, these areas need to be considered when determining the type of social intervention needed. For example, if a youngster's physical appearance is a strength, the teacher can compliment the student on his or her hair, what the student is wearing, or how neat and sharp the student looks. Also, knowing something about the students' areas of strength can be helpful in identifying social contexts that may be promising for promoting positive peer interactions (Vaughn and LaGreca, 1992). For example, a student with learning disabilities who is a particularly good swimmer and a member of a swim team may find it easier to make friends on the swim team than in the academic setting. Students with learning disabilities who acquire strengths in appearance and athletic activities may have areas of strength from which to build their social skills. However, many children with learning disabilities do not have the motor ability or eye–hand coordination to succeed in the athletic area. Other areas, such as hobbies or special interests, can be presented in the classroom so that the student with learning disabilities has an opportunity to be perceived as one who is knowledgeable.

In developing social skills interventions, it is important to consider the nature of children's friendships or social support outside of the school setting (Vaughn and LaGreca, 1992). Students with learning and behavior disorders who are not well accepted by their classmates may have friends in the neighborhood or within their families (e.g., cousins). Perhaps the most important point to remember is that if a child is not well accepted by peers at school, this does not necessarily mean that the child does not have effective social relationships outside of the school setting.

8. *Reciprocal friendships.* Reciprocal friendship is the mutual identification as "best friend" by two students; that is, a student who identifies another student as his or her best friend is also identified by that same youngster as a best friend. It has been hypothesized that reciprocal friendships play an important role in reducing the negative effects of low peer acceptance (Vaughn, McIntosh et al., 1993). From this perspective, it may be less important to increase the overall acceptance of a student in the classroom and more effective to concentrate on the development of a mutual best friend. Because it is quite unlikely that all students in the classroom are going to like all of the other youngsters equally, development of a reciprocal friendship is a more realistic goal for most youngsters with learning and behavior problems.

INSTRUCTIONAL ACTIVITIES

This section provides instructional activities related to developing socialization skills. Some of the activities teach new skills; others are best suited for practice and reinforcement of already acquired skills. For each activity, the objective, materials, and teaching procedures are described.

▶ Please Help

Objective: To teach students a process for asking for help when needed and yet continuing to work until assistance is given; to have a record-keeping system that allows the teacher to monitor how many times each day he or she assists each student.

Grades: Primary and intermediate

Materials: A six- to eight-inch card that states "Please Help _____ [student's name]" and provides a place to list the date and comments

PLEASE HELP JENNIFER		
DATE	TIME	COMMENTS

Teaching Procedures: Construct the Please Help card for each student, including a place to mark the date and comments. Give all the students a card, and inform them that they are to place the card on their desks when they need help. They are to continue working until the teacher or someone else is able to provide assistance.

When you or your assistant is able to provide help, mark the date and time on the card and any appropriate comments such as "We needed to review the rules for long division," or "She could not remember the difference between long and short vowels," or "He solved the problem himself before I arrived."

▶Problem Box

Objective: To give students an opportunity to identify problems they are having with others and to feel that their problems will be heard and attended to.

Grades: All grades

Materials: Shoebox decorated and labeled as "Problem Box"

Teaching Procedures: Show the students the box that is decorated and identified as the Problem Box. Place the box in a prominent location in the classroom. Tell the students that when they have problems with other students, teachers, or even at home, they can write the problems down and put them in the box. At the end of every day, you and the students will spend a designated amount of time (e.g., 15 minutes) reading problems and trying to solve them as a class. Be sure to tell students that they do not need to identify themselves or their notes.

During the designated time, open the Problem Box and read a selected note. Solicit assistance from the class in solving the note. Direct students' attention to identifying the problem, suggesting solutions, evaluating the consequences of the solutions, identifying a solution, and describing how it might be implemented.

▶A Date by Telephone

Objective: To give students structured skills for obtaining a date by telephone.

Grades: Secondary

Materials: Two nonworking telephones

Teaching Procedures: Discuss with the students why preplanning a telephone call with a prospective

date might be advantageous. Tell them that you are going to teach them some points to remember when calling to ask for a date. After you describe each of the following points, role-play them so that the students can observe their appropriate use:

1. Telephone at an *appropriate time.*
2. Use an *icebreaker,* such as recalling a mutually shared experience or a recent event in school.
3. *State what you would like to do and ask him or her to do it.* Ask the person whether he or she likes to go to the movies. When there is an initial lull in the conversation, mention a particular movie that you would like to take her or him to, and state when you would like to go. Then ask the person whether he or she would like to go with you.
4. If yes, *make appropriate arrangements* for day, time, and transportation. If no, ask whether you can call again.

Be sure that each student has an opportunity to role-play.

▶Making and Keeping Friends

Objective: To have students identify the characteristics of peers who are successful at making and keeping friends and, after identifying these characteristics, to evaluate themselves in how well they perform.

Grades: Intermediate and secondary

Materials: Writing materials

Teaching Procedures: Ask the students to think of children they know who are good at making and keeping friends. Brainstorm what these

---

How Good Are You at Making and Keeping Friends?

Next to each item, circle the face that best describes how well you do.

1. I tell friends the truth.

     ☺   😐   ☹

2. I call friends on the phone.

     ☺   😐   ☹

3. I share my favorite toys and games with friends.

     ☺   😐   ☹

children do that makes them successful at making and keeping friends. On an overhead projector or chalkboard, write the student-generated responses about the characteristics of children good at making and keeping friends. Then select the most agreed-on characteristics, and write them on a sheet of paper with smiley faces, neutral faces, and frowning faces so that students can circle the face that is most like them in response to that characteristic. Finally, ask students to identify one characteristic that they would like to target to improve their skills at making and maintaining friends.

▶Identifying Feelings

Objective: To identify the feelings of others and self and to respond better to those feelings.

Grades: Primary and intermediate

Materials: Cards with pictures of people in situations in which their feelings can be observed or deduced

Teaching Procedures: Select pictures that elicit feeling words such as *happy, angry, jealous, hurt,*

sad, and *mad.* Show the pictures to the students, and ask them to identify the feelings of the people in the pictures. Discuss what information in the picture cued them to the emotional states of the people. Then ask the students to draw a picture of a time when they felt as the person in the picture feels. Conclude by asking students to discuss their pictures.

▶I'm New Here (and Scared)

By Sandra Stroud*

Objective: To help students who are new to your community and school make a positive adjustment. For many students, moving to a new school can be an especially traumatic experience.

Grades: K–12

Materials: The *good will* of a group of socially competent student volunteers and their adult leader—a teacher, guidance counselor, or school administrator

Teaching Procedures: The adult in charge organizes a school service club whose purpose is to take new students under its wing and help them feel welcome at their school. Students in this organization can be given sensitivity training to help them understand how new students feel when they move to a new area of the country and enter a new school. The group can discuss and decide on the many strategies they can use to help new students feel at home. One of their functions could be to speak to whole classes about how it feels to be a new student at a school and to suggest how each student at this school can help new students when they arrive.

For a new student, nothing is quite as traumatic when entering a new school as having no friend or group with whom to sit when the students go to the cafeteria for lunch. Therefore, one of a new student's greatest needs is for someone to invite him or her to have lunch with them. This should be the number-one priority of the members of the welcoming club. New students may eventually become members of this club, joining in the effort of welcoming and helping the new students who follow them.

*Note: This instructional activity was written by a mother who would have been so grateful if her son's middle school had had such a program when he entered the eighth grade there. As it was, things were pretty rough for him until his band teacher realized that he was skipping lunch. She paved the way for him to begin eating lunch with a group of boys who became his best friends.

▶I'm in My Own Little House

By Sandra Stroud

Objective: To help young children acquire a sense of personal space as well as an understanding of other people's space. Many young children have not acquired an inner sense of space—of their own space and of space that belongs to others. As a result, the more active of these youngsters, usually little boys, tend to intrude on other children's space and, in the process, annoy the other children. As a result, they may not be well liked by their classmates. The problem is made worse by the fact that many primary school children sit at long tables where the space of one student often overlaps the space of others.

Grades: Primary

Materials: Individual student desks, and colored masking tape

Teaching Procedure: The teacher arranges the room so that each student desk sits in an area that is three feet square. The desks are just close enough to each other to make it possible for students to pass materials from one student to another without leaving their seats. On the floor around each desk, the teacher outlines the three-square-foot block with colored masking tape.

The teacher explains the taped areas, or blocks, by telling a story about a child who wanted a little house that was all her own where no one would bother her or her belongings. This was "her" house. Just as her house was hers, she knew that the other children needed their houses and that she shouldn't bother them or their houses either. (The teacher makes up the story according to his or her imagination or to fit the situation in the classroom.)

▶Introducing People

By Dheepa Sridhar

Objective: To teach students to introduce friends to one another appropriately.

Grades: Intermediate and secondary

Materials: None required

Teaching Procedures: Discuss the importance of introducing people. Allow students to share experiences such as when they were with a friend who was either good at or had difficulty in introducing them to his or her other friends. Tell students that you are going to teach them some points to remember when they introduce people to each other. After describing each of the following points, ask students to role-play to demonstrate their use:

- Provide additional information about the person being introduced such as "This is R. J.; he's new to our town" or "This is R. J.; he's good at baseball."
- Provide additional information about people in the group who have common interests with the new person such as "Steve plays basketball."
- Talk about those common interests.

▶Invitation to Play

By Dheepa Sridhar

Objective: To teach students to invite a classmate to play with them.

Grades: Primary

Materials: Toys

Teaching Procedures: Tell students that they should take the following steps when requesting a classmate to join them in play:

1. Decide what you want to play (e.g., jump rope, building with Legos).
2. Check to see whether you have the materials (rope or Legos).
3. Check to see what the person you want to play with is doing.
4. Wait for a lull in the activity that the person is engaging in.
5. Ask the person whether he or she would like to play (rope or Legos).
6. If the person refuses, ask what else he or she would like to play.
7. Have students role play and provide feedback.

▶In Your Shoes

By Dheepa Sridhar

Objective: To facilitate students in taking a different perspective.

Grades: Intermediate and high school

Materials: Cardboard cutouts of two pairs of shoes of different colors, masking tape, index cards with social problems written on them (e.g., "Jake was supposed to go to a baseball game with Ashraf over the weekend. He has been looking forward to this event all week. On Friday, Ashraf says that he would rather go to a movie instead of the game.")

Teaching Procedures: Discuss the importance of taking the other person's perspective. Tell the students this activity will help them see a different perspective.

1. Tape a line on the floor with the masking tape. Write the name of a character (e.g., Jake and Ashraf) on each pair of shoes. Place each pair of shoes on either side of the line.
2. Have two students volunteer to be Jake or Ashraf.
3. Ask one student to stand on Jake's shoes and the other student to stand on Ashraf's shoes.

4. Let them talk about the problem.
5. Ask the students to exchange places and discuss the problem.
6. Help the students to reach a solution that is acceptable to both parties.

This activity can also be used with students who are experiencing problems with each other instead of hypothetical situations. Although only two students can participate at a time, the rest of the class can help by generating solutions and discussing the consequences of those solutions.

SUMMARY for Chapter 4

This chapter described the social behaviors of students with learning and behavior disorders including practices for improving classroom management and techniques for using functional behavioral assessment (FBA). Students who are identified as behavior-disordered display behaviors that are inappropriate and/or harmful to self or others. Many behavior-disordered students have appropriate social skills but do not use them or do not know when and with whom to use them. Other students do not have the skills and need to be taught them.

Students with learning disabilities are frequently identified as having social difficulties. As a group, they are more frequently rejected by their peers and teachers. They have been characterized as having social interaction difficulties, communication difficulties, low role-taking skills, and low self-concepts.

Six interventions to increase appropriate social behavior and decrease inappropriate social behavior were presented: intervention by prescription, interpersonal problem solving, behavior therapy, Circle of Friends, positive behavioral support, and ASSET. Intervention by prescription is a model that focuses on the student's impulse management. Appropriate intervention procedures are applied according to the student's need for external control or ability to utilize internal control. Behavioral approaches are used when the student has low impulse control and needs external controls; more cognitively oriented interventions are used as the student demonstrates more internal impulse control. Interpersonal problem solving teaches students strategies for communicating effectively with others and solving and preventing interpersonal conflicts with others. Behavioral therapy is based on the principles of applied behavior analysis for increasing and decreasing behaviors.

Positive behavioral support is based on the principles of behavior therapy, but it focuses on improving the quality of life of students along with increasing positive behaviors. The goal of positive behavioral support is to provide individualized educational programs to prevent problem behaviors and enhance social relations of students.

A number of intervention approaches have been effectively implemented to increase appropriate social behaviors. Six of these approaches were discussed in this chapter and provide effective techniques for developing appropriate social behaviors.

FOCUS Answers

FOCUS Question 1. How should teachers arrange the physical and instructional environment of the inclusive classroom to promote prosocial behavior?

Answer: Special education teachers must pay attention to the physical space in which they teach. They should keep books and resources organized and clearly marked, and they should use a variety of instructional arrangements depending on student needs and learning activities.

FOCUS Question 2. How can teachers use classroom management and positive behavioral support to promote prosocial behavior?

Answer: The use of classroom management strategies is important because it creates an environment with structure and routine so that learning can occur. Teachers should develop procedures, rules, consequences, and reinforcers so that both they and the students know how to navigate the classroom and what to expect if something goes wrong. Teachers who implement effective classroom management recognize and reinforce positive behavior as well as identifying and changing inappropriate behaviors. Positive behavioral support (PBS) is a classroom management system that focuses on prevention of problem behaviors through attention to the learning environment. A functional behavioral assessment provides clear guidelines for determining students' problems and implementing a plan to improve behavior.

FOCUS Question 3. What is the purpose of a functional behavioral assessment (FBA), and what are the procedures for developing an effective FBA?

Answer: An FBA is designed to identify behavior problems of students, and a behavioral improvement plan (BIP) is used to develop an intervention plan to treat these behavior problems. An FBA is required if students' behavior is interfering with their learning.

FOCUS Question 4. What do we know about how students with behavior and learning difficulties feel about themselves, are perceived by others, and interact socially with others?

Answer: Students with behavior and learning difficulties often lack the social competence necessary to engage in effective interactions with others. Although students with behavior disorders by definition lack social competence and generally have severe emotional and behavioral difficulties, many individuals with learning disabilities also struggle to make and maintain positive interpersonal relationships with others. Individuals with learning disabilities often (but not always) have poor conversational skills; may have difficulty perceiving, interpreting, and processing social information; may exhibit aggressive behaviors or attention problems; and may display atypical appearance.

THINK and APPLY

- What is social competence?
- What are the characteristics of students with social disabilities?
- What are two types of social interventions that are used with students with learning and behavior problems? What are the procedures for implementing these social interventions?
- What are several principles for teaching social skills to students with learning and behavior problems?

- Why can the communication style of students with learning disabilities be called egocentric?
- How are student appearance and popularity related?
- Why do students whose behavior is aggressive require professional help?
- What advice would you give teachers and administrators who indicated that they had schoolwide problems with behavior?

APPLY the STANDARDS

 Council for Exceptional Children

1. Given the emotional and social characteristics of students with behavioral or learning problems (BD1K3, BD2K3, LD2K3) and your knowledge of strategies to improve behavior and social skills (BD1K5, BD4K2, BD4S2, BD5S1, BD4S1), (a) what important classroom features should be addressed to create a classroom environment that promotes prosocial behavior, and (b) what systems should be in place when students exhibit inappropriate behaviors?

   Standard BD1K3: Foundations and issues related to knowledge and practice in emotional/behavioral disorders.

   Standard BD2K3: Social characteristics of individuals with emotional/behavioral disorders.

   Standard LD2K3: Psychological, social, and emotional characteristics of individuals with learning disabilities.

   Standard BD1K5: Theory of reinforcement techniques in serving individuals with emotional/behavioral disorders.

   Standard BD4K2: Advantages and limitations of instructional strategies and practices for teaching individuals with emotional/behavioral disorders.

   Standard BD4S2: Use a variety of nonaversive techniques to control targeted behavior and maintain attention of individuals with emotional/behavioral disorders.

   Standard BD5S1: Establish a consistent classroom routine for individuals with emotional/behavioral disorders.

   Standard BD4S1: Use strategies from multiple theoretical approaches for individuals with emotional/behavioral disorders.

2. If you have access to a classroom setting, identify a student who exhibits behavior problems in class. Use the functional behavioral assessment (FBA) sample in this chapter to identify one problem behavior and to problem-solve possible solutions (BD4K4, BD4S2, BD7S2, BD8S2).

Standard BD4K4: Prevention and intervention strategies for individuals at risk of emotional/behavioral disorders.

Standard BD4S2: Use a variety of nonaversive techniques to control targeted behavior and maintain attention of individuals with emotional/behavioral disorders.

Standard BD7S2: Integrate academic instruction, affective education, and behavior management for individuals and groups with emotional/behavior disorders.

Standard BD8S2: Assess appropriate and problematic social behaviors of individuals with emotional/behavioral disorders.

WEBSITES as RESOURCES for Promoting Social Acceptance and Managing Behavior

The following Websites are extensive resources to expand your understanding of socialization and classroom management:

- LD Online www.ldonline.org
- Kristen Brooks Hope Center Website—National Hopeline www.hopeline.com
- Positive Behavioral Interventions and Supports www.pbis.org
- Institute on Violence and Destructive Behavior http://darkwing.uoregon.edu/~ivdb

PEARSON
myeducationlab
Where the Classroom Comes to Life

Video Homework Exercise Go to MyEducationLab and select the topic "CLASSROOM AND BEHAVIOR MANAGEMENT," then watch the video "Arranging Furniture and Materials" and complete the activity questions below.

In this video a first grade teacher discusses the choices she makes when she organizes the classroom, materials, and other procedures at the beginning of the school year.

1. What organizational features does the teacher in this video use and what rationale does she provide for each?
2. What additional organizational features are recommended in the chapter?
3. How can the arrangement of the classroom encourage student engagement and motivation?

Video Homework Exercise Go to MyEducationLab and select the topic "EMOTIONAL AND BEHAVIORAL DISORDERS," then watch the video "Teaching Respect" and complete the activity questions below.

In this video, first grade students watch a movie to learn about the importance of sharing and respecting each other's feelings. The teacher also discusses the importance of modeling respectful behavior for her students.

1. What are the children learning in this lesson? How will this information help them to respect students with behavioral and emotional disabilities in their classrooms?
2. List two additional activities that you could implement in your classroom to promote social competence for students with learning difficulties in general education classroom.

Appendix 4.1

Materials Evaluation Form

General Information

Name: <u>Schoolhouse: A Word Attack Skills Kit</u>
Author(s): <u>M. Clarke and F. Marsden</u>
Publisher: <u>Science Research Associates</u>

Copyright Date: <u>1973</u>
Cost: <u>$220</u>

Description of the Materials

Purpose of Materials: Provide practice with phonic and structural word analysis skills
Instructional Level(s) of Materials: first–third grades
Content of Materials: Plastic overlays and markers, 170 exercise cards (2 copies) and answer keys represent 10 color-coded areas (e.g., initial consonants, vowels), progress sheets
Target Age: Could be used with students ages 6–12
Theoretical Approach to Learning: Behavior approach in that it assumes skills can be taught in isolation
Type of Instructional Arrangement (Individual, Cooperative Learning, etc.): Individual
Teacher Involvement Requirements: Demonstrating mechanics of programs. Checking student understanding of directions and pictures. Spot checking of student self-checks. Evaluating progress.
Time Requirements: 10–15 minutes per exercise card.
Space Requirements: Materials come in 12"×12"×24" box.
Equipment Requirements: None

Evaluation	Poor	Fair	Good
1. *Is there any evidence that these materials are effective?*	1	②	3
2. *Materials sequentially organized*	1	2	③
Progress from easy to hard			
Use pictures in early exercises			
3. *Materials organized for easy retrieval*	1	2	③
Students should be able to find exercise card without assistance			
4. *Directions clear*	1	2	③
Yes and written with a low readability level			
5. *Provides adequate examples*	1	②	3
Most of the time			
6. *Provides for adequate practice*	①	2	3
Would like to see more cards covering each phonic or structural element			
7. *Conducive to providing feedback*	1	2	③
Student can self-check and could plot progress			
8. *Allows for checking/self-checking*	1	2	③
9. *Provides suggestions for adapting the materials*	①	2	3
No			
10. *Provides suggestions for generalization*	①	2	3
No, this is a major concern.			
11. *Interest level*	1	②	3
Although pictures are fairly easy to interpret, there is a limited number. Format repetitive.			

Description of Role in Instructional Program

How would this material fit into my instructional program?
Only as a reinforcement activity. Need to discuss with students how this practice will help them when they read (generalization).

Appendix 4.2 Student Materials Evaluation Form

Student Name: Jason

Date of Evaluation: March 15

Name of Materials: Criminal Justice (textbook)

Evaluation	Poor	Fair	Good
1. *Directions are clear.*	1	2	③
I understand the activities at the end of the chapter.			
2. *Materials are interesting.*	1	2	③
Yes. I like the personal stories.			
3. *There are enough examples so that I know what to do.*	1	②	3
Pretty much			
4. *I get enough practice so that I learn the information or the skill.*	1	②	3
Only if we discuss it in class			
5. *It is easy to determine if I am doing the tasks correctly.*	①	2	3
Not really			
6. *I like using these materials.*	1	2	③

7. *I think that these materials teach:*
   About how our government works

8. *The thing(s) I like best about these materials is:*
   They're interesting

9. *The thing(s) I don't like about these materials is:*
   Sometimes it doesn't tell enough and I have to read other places

10. *I would recommend using these materials for:*
   Government classes

Communicating, Collaborating, and Coteaching: Working with Professionals and Families

As you read the chapter, watch for these questions to help you focus your learning:

1. **What are some of the challenges of working in an inclusive classroom and working with general education teachers?**

2. **What are three major models for consultation and collaboration?**

3. **What are the principles of communication, when are they likely to be used, and how can teachers of individuals with learning and behavior problems develop the interview skills needed to effectively communicate with families and professionals?**

4. **What is the teacher's role in addressing the needs of the entire family, assisting families with activities that occur outside of school, and coordinating family involvement in school?**

5. **What is the role of the special education teacher as a consultant to general education teachers, and what are the considerations and barriers for successful inclusion?**

Mrs. Tupa works in a hospital emergency room, so she is accustomed to talking to people who are grieving. Mrs. Tupa states:

I often speak to parents about the recovery of their children. Fortunately, most of the children have injuries or illnesses from which they will recover completely. I've been trained in the importance of telling the parents as quickly and completely as possible all we know about their child's condition. The only reason I'm telling you this is that I want you to understand that I am accustomed to dealing with difficulties. But I was unprepared for the inconsistent information I would receive about our son.

When our third child, Chad, was born, my husband and I couldn't have been happier. Our first two children were girls, whom we enjoy immensely, but both of us were hoping for a boy. Chad walked and talked later than the girls, but I knew that boys are often developmentally slower than girls, so we were not concerned. Even when he was a preschooler, we knew Chad was different. He often had difficulty thinking of the right word for an object, and he was clumsier than other children his age. When we spoke with his pediatrician, the doctor informed us that this was not uncommon.

When Chad entered kindergarten, he did not know all of his colors and showed little ability to remember the names of the letters in the alphabet. His kindergarten teacher said that she had seen a number of students like Chad, often boys, and suggested that we keep Chad in kindergarten another year. Our neighbor, who is a teacher, thought this might not be a good idea, since Chad was already large for his age. We spoke with the principal, who seemed very busy and thought we should take the advice of the kindergarten teacher. We retained Chad. Spending another year in kindergarten seemed to do little good, however. Chad was still unable to identify letters, though he was very popular because of his size and knowledge of the kindergarten routine.

First grade was worse yet. Chad showed no signs of reading and was confusing letters. His writing resembled that of a much younger child. By now, we were very concerned and made several appointments with his first-grade teacher. She was very responsive and suggested that we have Chad tutored during the summer. The tutor said that Chad had an attention problem and was having trouble with letter and word reversals. She suggested that we have him tested for learning disabilities. The school psychologist agreed to do the testing, and it was late in the fall before we were called and given the results.

Though both my husband and I are professionals, we felt somewhat intimidated by the number of school personnel at the meeting. On our way home, as we tried to reconstruct what we heard, we realized that we had misunderstood and missed a lot of information. I heard the school personnel say Chad's intelligence was normal, but my husband thought that it couldn't be normal because his verbal intelligence was low. We decided to make a list of questions to ask at our next meeting. We felt that we had made a major stride forward, since Chad would now be receiving special instruction for one hour each day from a learning disabilities specialist; however, we still felt we understood very little about his problems. I only wish we had been told more completely and quickly about Chad's problem.

Many parents have had similar experiences. They have noticed that their child is different in some areas from other children the child's age. These parents seek advice from friends, medical professionals, and school professionals and often feel confused and frustrated. When the child is identified as having learning disabilities or emotional disorders many parents at first feel relieved, hoping that this identification will lead to solutions that will eliminate the child's learning or behavior problem. The difficult adjustments are that the child will probably always have learning or behavior problems and that the special education teacher will be unable to provide any magic cures and certainly no quick solutions.

Learning disabilities and emotional disorders are complex phenomena, and knowledge of all the factors that they involve is incomplete. Special education teachers must be sensitive to parental concerns about identification and intervention yet speak honestly about what they know and do not know. Teachers must provide families with encouragement without giving false hopes. Families need to know what educators' best knowledge of their child's learning and behavior problem is and to be informed of what educators are less sure of.

This chapter focuses on the teacher as an effective communicator. Communication occurs between teachers and family members and between special education teachers and other school-related professionals. Effective communication skills are the basis for working effectively with family members and other professionals. In the same way that management and communication are the cornerstones of business, they are the cornerstones of effective teaching. Whether working in a coteaching setting, as a consultant, as a resource, or as a self-contained teacher, the special education teacher makes thousands of management decisions each day regarding the teaching–learning process and the instructional cycle. A teacher's abilities to develop a teaching–learning context that facilitates communication and learning; to set learning and instructional goals and market those goals to others, including students; and to establish sound classroom and instructional policies, routines, and procedures are what make the difference between success and failure. Management and communication are central to the task of teaching (Doyle, 1979, 1986). This chapter deals with the issue of the special education teacher as a manager, communicator, and collaborator.

FOCUS Question 1. What are some of the challenges of working in an inclusive classroom and working with general education teachers?

Challenges to Successful Inclusion and Coteaching

There has probably never been a time in history when educators faced greater challenges and opportunities than those we face in the United States today. Classroom teachers are required to provide instruction for increasingly diverse student populations and are still held accountable for covering the prescribed curriculum in a manner that ensures most students learn that content. Classroom teachers sometimes feel that they must choose between covering the full content of the curriculum or spending sufficient instructional time on curriculum components to ensure that their slower students learn what they are supposed to learn. Many teachers make the choice to "go on," even when students with disabilities and other low-achieving students have not learned very much. Research has shown, however, that high-achieving students *want* teachers to take extra time and to try different instructional approaches that help ensure that the lower-achieving students also learn the content (Vaughn et al., 1991). Teachers doubt that their curriculum supervisors, fellow teachers, and the parents of the high achievers are as flexible about content coverage.

Many special education students need more time to master new concepts and skills, and they master those concepts and skills only if instruction is presented to them in a manner that enables them to grasp the new material. Unfortunately, an instructional strategy that works for one student may not work for another. Therefore, teachers must know and use a variety of instructional strategies to ensure that all students have an opportunity to learn. This takes time and planning. The first priority must be to ensure that students succeed in learning the content that is covered.

In general, teachers at the middle and high school levels indicate that it is often not feasible for them to plan specifically for students with special needs (Schumm and Vaughn, 1992a, 1992b; Schumm, Vaughn, Haager, McDowell, Rothlein, and Saumell, 1995). Furthermore, when coteaching has been compared to other models such as resource room settings, the findings for students are mixed (Zigmond and Magiera, 2002). This suggests that the model of service delivery may not be the issue; rather, the quality of instruction provided to students is what makes the difference (Zigmond, 2003). General education teachers are willing to work with special education professionals to make accommodations for students with special needs as they teach—particularly when those accommodations are useful to other learners in the classroom. There are many opportunities for special and general education teachers to align their knowledge and skills and improve outcomes for students with disabilities.

Challenges to Special Education Teachers

Two special education teachers at different schools had very different points of view about their experiences working as coteachers with general education teachers to improve learning for students with disabilities. One teacher said, "It was the best year of my teaching career. Ms. Walberg was terrific and taught me so much about what to expect from regular education. I think all of the students benefited because we worked so well together and shared so much of the teaching." Another teacher at a different school said, "This year was enough to get me to leave education. I never really felt like I was an equal partner in the classroom. I always felt like I was the teaching assistant. Furthermore, it was so painful to watch how practices were implemented for students who needed help and weren't getting it. Yet I never really felt anyone was listening to me."

Ms. Peres describes her strategy for coteaching as follows:

I am convinced that these students need to be in general education classrooms if at all possible. However, I have learned that we need to prepare them both socially and academically. Much of what we do in special education classrooms does not prepare them for general education. They are used to individual and small group instruction, receiving lots of feedback and lots of reinforcement, and being relatively free to ask for and receive assistance. This does not reflect what

happens in the general education classrooms in this school. Although the teachers are great, they have 28 to 32 students in each class. Large group instruction and cooperative and independent learning are the most frequently used instructional arrangements.

The first key to making inclusion work is to cooperate with the general classroom teacher and to observe that classroom to determine the learning and social demands.

The second key is to gain a commitment from the student. He or she has to want to work toward the goal. I always describe the classroom demands to the student, and sometimes he or she goes to observe. Then we plan how we're going to get ready for "going to Mrs. Fereira's class for math."

The third key is to begin simulating those learning and social demands in my classroom. I start gradually. Usually, I begin by decreasing the feedback and reinforcement. Next I focus on the academic demands. I get the lessons and textbooks from the classroom teacher, and I begin to assign the lessons. At first, the rate of learning is matched to the student's learning rate. But once the student is succeeding with the assignments, I begin to increase the rate until it matches that of the general education classroom. As this procedure continues, I gradually reduce the amount of reinforcement and feedback and work with the student to become a more independent learner.

The fourth key is to monitor the student and to continue to work with the classroom teacher to modify and adapt materials, methods, and the teaching–learning environment as needed.

I have developed this strategy through experience. Many times, I have found that my test scores, informal assessments, and student progress data indicate that the student is reading at grade level. In the past, I would jump to the conclusion that the student was ready to perform without assistance in the general education classroom. Yet too often I would find the student in difficulties within three weeks. I was really setting the students up for failure. I had attended only to their reading level, not to the social and academic demands.

I've been very successful with this strategy. I have all but 4 of my 14 students included for most of the school day.

Ms. Peres's discussion of how she provides effective instruction and behavioral support for her students in the general education classroom demonstrates that she has a philosophy that places importance on communication, collaboration, and consultation with the general education classroom teachers.

Understanding the Challenges of General Education Classrooms

Special education teachers need to understand what students with special needs can reasonably expect in general education classrooms so that they can provide the support and skills necessary for success. Although expectations vary considerably between elementary and secondary teachers (Salend, Gordon, and Lopez-Vona, 2002; Schumm and Vaughn, 1992a, 1992b) and obviously from teacher to teacher, there are some common expectations:

• General education teachers are willing to make adaptations and accommodations that require little preplanning. These adaptations and accommodations are more likely to occur if they can be done during the instructional process. See Apply the Concept 5.1 for a list of feasible adaptations.

• Teachers treat students with special needs in much the same way that they treat other students (McIntosh et al., 1993). This is, of course, both good and bad news. Teachers treat students with special needs with the same respect and consideration they give to other students. However, they provide few accommodations (particularly at the middle and high school level) to meet the students' individual learning needs.

• Students with special needs participate infrequently in class activities, ask fewer questions than other students do, and rarely respond to teachers' questions (McIntosh et al., 1993). Students with special needs display a passive learning style that does little to increase the likelihood that general education teachers will meet their learning needs.

• Whole-class activity is by far the primary mode of instruction at the middle and high school level and for social studies and science at the elementary level (McIntosh et al., 1993; Schumm et al., 1995). Thus, students with special needs who are accustomed to working in small groups and receiving extensive teacher direction are unlikely to receive these same considerations in the general education classroom.

• Undifferentiated large group instruction is representative of what occurs in general education classrooms (Baker and Zigmond, 1990; McIntosh et al., 1993). Teachers largely follow the sequence of activities provided in the teacher's manual and do not consider the learning needs of groups or individual students.

Students' Perceptions of Teachers' Adaptations

Students' perceptions of general education teachers' adaptations are particularly significant because those perceptions are likely to influence teachers' behavior, and teachers are unlikely to make adaptations for students with special needs that they feel would take away from nondisabled students. A recent series of studies has investigated students' perceptions of general classroom teachers' adaptations to meet the needs of students with special needs

Apply the Concept 5.1

Adaptations General Education Teachers Are Willing to Make

Teachers identified the following as *highly* feasible to implement:

1. Provide reinforcement and encouragement to assist students with learning.
2. Establish a personal relationship with included students.
3. Involve included students in whole-class activities.
4. Establish routines that are appropriate for included students.
5. Establish expectations for learning and behavior.

Teachers identified the following as *not* likely to be implemented:

1. Adapt long-range plans to meet the needs of included students.
2. Adjust the physical arrangement of the room to meet the needs of included students.
3. Use alternative materials or adapt current materials for students with special needs.
4. Adapt scoring and grading criteria for students with special needs.
5. Provide individualizing instruction to meet students' special needs.

Source: Adapted from J. S. Schumm and S. Vaughn (1991). Making adaptations for mainstreamed students: General classroom teachers' perspectives. *Remedial and Special Education, 12* (4), pp. 18–27.

(Vaughn, Schumm, and Kouzekanani, 1993; Vaughn, Schumm, Niarhos, and Daugherty, 1993; Vaughn, Schumm, Niarhos, and Gordon, 1993). A summary of the findings and their implications for instruction follow:

• Elementary, middle, and high school students overwhelmingly prefer teachers who make adaptations to meet the special needs of students, with three exceptions: adaptations in tests, homework, and textbooks. Consistent findings show that all students appreciate using the same textbooks and having the same homework. Interviews with students reveal that having the same homework is particularly important because homework serves as the rationale for multiple telephone calls or instant messages to friends after school. Students who do not have the same homework run the risk of being left out of the social circle.

• Across all grade groupings, high-achieving students are more likely to prefer teachers who make adaptations than are low-achieving students. This seems surprising at first glance because high-achieving students would seem to have the least to gain from adaptations that teachers make. Their interest in adaptations thus seems altruistic.

• Students with special needs who were placed in general education classrooms for more than half of the school day had perceptions of teachers similar to those of the high-achieving students, with two exceptions: The students with special needs did not demonstrate significant preferences for no adaptations in tests and textbooks. Because students with special needs are accustomed to having tests and textbooks modified, they did not find these procedures unusual on the part of the regular classroom teacher.

• All students want to be taught learning strategies to assist them in acquiring information on their own (Vaughn, Schumm, Klingner, and Saumell, 1995).

FOCUS Question 2. **What are three major models for consultation and collaboration?**

Consultation and Collaboration

Although both terms—*consultation* and *collaboration*—are often used to describe the role of many special education teachers, teachers prefer the term *collaboration* (Arguelles, Vaughn, and

Schumm, 1996; Morrison, Walker, Wakefield, and Solberg, 1994). Why? Teachers indicate that they prefer collaborative modes of working on student problems rather than handing over problems to experts or working on them independently (Morrison et al., 1994). Teachers perceive that the term *collaboration* more accurately describes the nature of their relationships. As one special education teacher noted, "We actually work together to solve problems. It's not like I have all of the answers or she has all of the problems. We really help each other come up with ideas that work." We have found that general education teachers feel much the same way.

What is collaboration? Collaboration refers to the interaction that occurs between two professionals, often between special education teachers and general education teachers, and to the roles that they play as equal partners in problem-solving endeavors. Pugach and Johnson (1995) identified the following characteristics of collaborative teachers:

• They recognize and value the benefits of working collaboratively, and believe that in order for schools to meet the diverse needs of all students, everyone's efforts are necessary.
• They enjoy the social aspect of problem solving and the process of generating potential solutions.
• They recognize the creativity that emerges during the problem-solving process. The probems that schools face are often complex; collaborative teachers acknowledge that working together often yields more effective and creative solutions.
• They continually reflect on their own practice instructionally and in the collaborative process and are willing to change their practices when necessary.

What are some of the ways in which special education teachers might expect to collaborate with other professionals? A significant part of their role is to collaborate with parents and any other specialist who is associated with the special needs students with whom the teacher works. Whether working as a resource room teacher, a self-contained special education teacher, or a coteacher, special education teachers also have considerable opportunities to collaborate with general education teachers. They may also work in a program in which most of the workday involves collaboration with other teachers. At the elementary, middle, and secondary school levels, teachers are increasingly working in more collaborative ways with other professionals (Idol, Nevin, and Paolucci-Whitcomb, 2000; Pugach and Johnson, 1995).

One important way in which special education teachers collaborate with general education professionals is in developing ways to make curricula more accessible to students with special needs (Dettmer, Dyck, and Thurston, 1999; Warger and Pugach, 1996). Curriculum planning can address such important issues as identifying changes in curriculum that are forecasted by national boards and professional groups, identifying the ways in which these new trends will affect the curriculum and students with special needs, examining the scope and sequence of the present curriculum and determining where changes best fit, identifying new goals and discussing the prerequisite skills needed for students with special needs, and identifying areas of mismatch or in which new curriculum is inappropriate for target students.

Additional ways in which special education teachers collaborate with general education teachers include:

- *Coteaching*—Working with classroom teachers to provide instruction together in general education classrooms
- *Consultant teaching*—Working with classroom teachers to solve problems for students with disabilities who will be included in general education classrooms. Special education teachers may observe, assess, and help to plan for instruction but do not provide direct instruction in the general education classroom.
- *Coordination of paraprofessionals*—Working with classroom teachers to coordinate and support the activities of paraprofessionals who assist students with disabilities in the general education classroom
- *Teacher assistance teams*—Participating in school-based teams of support professionals, classroom teachers, and administrators that assist classroom teachers in meeting the instructional and behavior needs of individual students

Procedures for Collaboration

In working collaboratively with other professionals, it is helpful to have a list of common procedures to follow to resolve dilemmas and solve problems. Most procedures for peer collaboration include the following five steps:

1. *Initiator and facilitator.* Usually, one member of the team has a problem or issue that needs to be resolved. That person is referred to as the initiator. The person who is assisting with the problem is referred to as the facilitator. There

may be more than one facilitator. Facilitators serve as guides to assist in resolving the issue.
2. *Clarifying questions.* The initiator describes the problem or dilemma. The facilitator attempts to clarify the problem by asking questions.
3. *Summarization.* The problem is summarized by the team. The following format can be used to assist in summarizing the problem: (a) establish the pattern of behavior, (b) acknowledge the teacher's feelings about the problem, and (c) identify aspects of classroom and school environments that the teacher can modify (Pugach and Johnson, 1995).
4. *Interventions and predictions.* The team generates at least three interventions that address the problem. They consider the likely outcomes of each of the interventions identified.
5. *Evaluation.* The team develops an evaluation plan that includes strategies for keeping track of the intervention, recording the student's progress, and meeting again to review progress.

Resources Needed for Collaboration

No resource impedes successful collaboration more than time. Special and general education teachers confirm the difficulties of finding adequate time to effectively collaborate during the work day (Friend, 2000; Voltz, Elliott, and Cobb, 1994). If time is not built into teachers' schedules, collaboration is unlikely to occur on a regular basis. Furthermore, if it is not part of the schedule, then teachers come to resent having to collaborate because it means taking time from their personal schedules. Another critical aspect of time management for special education teachers is finding mutually available time when they can collaborate with the many teachers with whom they work. Time management is especially challenging at the secondary level. Following are some ways in which collaborative time can be arranged (Vaughn, Bos, and Schumm, 1997):

- Administrators designate a common time for collaborating professionals to work together (e.g., all fifth-grade team members).
- School boards pay professionals for one extra time period each week that can be used to collaborate or meet with families.
- School districts provide early dismissal for students one day a week so that team members have a common planning time.
- Teachers meet for brief but focused planning periods on a regularly scheduled basis.

- Resources such as administrators, families, volunteers, and university students are used to help cover classes. For example, short planning sessions may be scheduled during recess when larger groups of students can be monitored by a teacher and a volunteer.

Space for meeting is another necessary resource. Special education teachers are often fortunate because they have an office or a small classroom for their materials. But finding a quiet place to meet is particularly challenging in schools where overcrowding is the norm.

Additionally, participants in collaborative models need to be familiar with procedures for successful collaboration. An orientation that addresses basic questions about their roles and responsibilities is helpful to all personnel who are involved in collaboration. Administrative support can be crucial to ensuring that teachers are given appropriate time, space, and knowledge of procedures to implement an effective collaborative model.

School Collaboration

The purposes of collaborative consultation are to prevent learning and behavior problems, to provide appropriate instruction for students with learning and behavior problems, and to coordinate instructional programs (West et al., 1989). Collaboration in the schools (West, Idol, and Cannon, 1989) is one of a number of consultation models that focus on special education teachers who work directly with classroom teachers to assist them in the successful inclusion of students with learning and behavior problems. This model grew out of a need to provide more effective and coordinated services for students with special needs. This consultation model is based on the concept of collaborative consultation, which Idol and West and their colleagues define as

> an interactive process that enables people with diverse expertise to generate creative solutions to mutually defined problems. . . . The major outcome of collaborative consultation is to provide comprehensive and effective programs for students with special needs within the most appropriate context, thereby enabling them to achieve maximum constructive interaction with their nonhandicapped peers. (Idol, Paolucci-Whitcomb, and Nevin, 1986, p. 1)

West and Idol (1990) cite three reasons for using collaborative consultation models. One reason is the expense of assessing and placing students with learning and behavior problems in special

education. They suggest that collaborative problem solving can serve as a preventative model. The second reason is evidence from research on effective schools (see Purkey and Smith, 1985, for a review), which indicates that collaborative planning and collegial relationships are two key process variables that are present in effective schools. A third reason is based on a professional development needs survey of the members of the Council for Exceptional Children, the major professional organization for special educators, which ranked collaboration, communication, and consultation between special and general educators as the top three concerns.

CLASSROOM Applications

School Collaboration

PROCEDURES: The model is based on a six-stage collaborative consultation process completed by a collaborative team:

1. *Goal/entry.* Roles, objectives, responsibilities, and expectations are negotiated.
2. *Problem identification.* Nature and parameters of the presenting problem are defined.
3. *Intervention of recommendations.* Potential interventions are generated and effects predicted. Recommendations are prioritized and selected. Objectives are developed to specify the intervention details, the procedures, and the means for determining if the problem has been solved.
4. *Implementation of recommendations.* Procedures and plan of action are implemented.
5. *Evaluation.* The intervention is evaluated, including its impact on the student, the consultant and consultee, and the system or context in which the intervention is occurring.
6. *Redesign.* Intervention is continued, redesigned, or discontinued based on the evaluation (West and Idol, 1990).

Collaborative consultation may occur at varying levels of teacher and school involvement. For example, special and general education teachers in middle schools or high schools may use collaborative consultation to assist students with learning disabilities who are included in general education English classes. Or, an intermediate special education teacher and the speech/language pathologist may work with the intermediate teachers in an elementary school to develop strategies for facilitating concept and language development in the content areas. Or, an elementary school may adopt collaborative consultation at the building level with the consultation used in the prereferral process as well as for a means of coordinating the special and general education programs for students with special needs.

COMMENTS: Collaborative consultation has been used in a number of schools and districts throughout the United States and Canada. West and Idol (1990) suggest that a number of factors need to be considered in implementing collaborative consultation, including systematic and ongoing staff development, administrative support, and scheduling.

Like other educational approaches, consultation and collaboration models have the potential for benefit as well as misuse and misunderstanding. Apply the Concept 5.2 describes potential benefits and misuses.

Collaboration Issues and Dilemmas

All special education teachers work collaboratively with general education teachers and many special education teachers work with general education teachers at least 50 percent of the time.

Consequently, special education teachers need to recognize several issues and dilemmas in order to perform their job effectively.

1. *Student ownership.* Traditionally, special education students have been the responsibility of the special education teacher, even if they were placed in a general education classroom for part of the day. This perspective is no longer feasible or desirable. The new perspective is one of shared ownership whereby all educators feel responsible for the success of the student with special needs.

2. *Individual versus class focus.* A year-long case study of the planning and adaptations for students with special needs by 12 effective general education teachers (four elementary, four middle school, and four high school; Schumm, Vaughn, Haager, McDowell, Rothlein, and Saumell, 1995) found that the teachers did not plan or make adaptations for individual students but considered the class as a whole. This focus contrasts with that of special education teachers, whose planning and instruction is aimed at the needs of individual students. Neither of these perspectives is inherently better than the other (Glatthorn, 1990), but differing perspectives often promote conflict. Mrs. Vermillion put it this way: "I am a special education teacher and so the direction of my interest is

Apply the Concept 5.2

Benefits and Misuses of Consultation and Collaboration

Consultation and collaboration models have several potential benefits and misuses (Huefner, 1988; Zigmond, 2003).

Potential Benefits

1. Reduction of stigma
2. Better understanding across education disciplines
3. On-the-job training for general education teachers in skills for effectively meeting the needs of special education students
4. Reduced mislabeling of students as disabled
5. Suitability in meeting the needs of secondary school students
6. Spillover benefits to general education students from working cooperatively with special education teacher

Potential Misuses/Problems

1. Excessive caseload management for special education teachers
2. Unrealistic expectations from viewing the consulting model as a panacea and/or under-training and overloading the special education teacher
3. Inadequate support and cooperation from classroom teachers
4. Converting the model to a tutoring or aide approach
5. Providing inadequate funding
6. Faulty assumptions about cost savings

7. Faulty assumptions about program effectiveness
8. Unrealistic expectations for changes in academic success and social acceptance
9. Inadequate preparation for vocational experiences after school
10. Inadequate time to plan, communicate, and effectively instruct target students

Overall, the most important question to address is whether students with learning and behavior problems are having their needs met through a consultation and collaborative model. The model may be highly effective for some students and less so for others.

always with the individual student and how the educational setting can be altered to meet his or her needs. During the last few years I realize that I've needed to adjust my perspective if I am to work effectively with classroom teachers. When they think about planning for students, they think about the class as a whole."

3. *Content versus accommodation.* When classroom teachers discuss their planning and instruction, one of the most consistent themes is content coverage (Schumm et al., 1995; Vaughn and Schumm, 1994). Classroom teachers feel that guidelines at the state, local, and school levels pressure them to cover more content and these requirements often conflict with knowledge acquisition. A representative comment from a ninth-grade science teacher is, "Waiting until the students understand would result in lack of adequate coverage of material" (Vaughn and Schumm, 1994).

This notion of content coverage as the horse leading the instructional wagon is a consistent and pervasive problem in general education and now directly influences the instruction of students with special needs. There is some consensus that "less is more" and that a reduced focus on content coverage would enhance the quality of instruction for all learners.

You can imagine the difficulty for classroom teachers who feel pressured to cover extensive amounts of content when special education teachers make suggestions that slow down the pace or require them to make adaptations for students' special learning needs. This issue is not insolvable. One year-long research project designed to improve the planning and adaptations of classroom teachers (social studies and science) found that teachers are willing to make adaptations and accommodations they believe will help students and do not require extensive amounts of preparation (Schumm and Vaughn, 1992a).

4. *New roles for special education teachers.* Perhaps one of the greatest challenges for teachers who are learning to work collaboratively with other teachers is that they assume different roles than those they previously had. These roles can include supporting special education students in the general education classroom; teaching with another teacher in a content area in which they have little or no background knowledge, particularly at the secondary level; helping students with assignments; and engaging in disciplining and classroom management of a range of students (Weiss and Lloyd, 2002). A veteran special education teacher tells of the changing roles and responsibilities of moving from her own classroom to coteaching

with other teachers. She discusses this role shift with the kind of nostalgia that shows that she misses many of the comforts of her own classroom and routines yet realizes that many students are benefiting from her engagement in the general education classroom (Klingner and Vaughn, 2002).

5. *Real world versus the student's world.* Another dichotomy between general and special education teachers is the purpose of education. Classroom teachers feel that they are preparing students for the "real world." From their perspective, people in the real world do not make accommodations for different learning styles. Fundamentally, they view the real world as expecting the same thing from everybody and therefore, to best prepare youngsters, their role as teachers is to expect the same thing from every student. This position is more common among middle and high school teachers, who feel increased pressures to prepare students for the real world, than among elementary teachers (Schumm and Vaughn, 1992b).

Ms. McDowell, a secondary special education teacher, handles the problem this way: "When classroom teachers talk to me about the real world, I'm prepared. First, I present them with the idea that students are never going to be successful in the real world if they do not have an opportunity to learn and experience success in their present world. Their present world is that teacher's classroom. Second, I present them with the fact that employers are required by law to make reasonable accommodations for individuals with disabilities. Also, I never ask general education teachers to make adaptations or accommodations that aren't useful to most students in the classroom." In fact, instructional interventions that are used to improve learning for students with disabilities are at least as effective—and sometimes more effective—for students without disabilities (Vaughn, Gersten, and Chard, 2000).

Teacher Assistance and School-Based Teams

The teacher assistance teams model (Chalfant and Pysh, 1989, 1992; Chalfant, Pysh, and Moultrie, 1979) is a within-building problem-solving approach designed to provide a teacher support system for classroom teachers. Chalfant and Pysh identified five reasons schools may struggle with meeting the needs of all students when students with disabilities are included in the general education classroom. First, with more students with special needs remaining in the classroom and the increasing number of at-risk students in the general school population, the demands on classroom teachers have increased. Second, sufficient funds are not available to provide direct supportive services to all the children who need individualized assistance within our schools. Third, classroom teachers may lack the time or background to plan and individualize instruction for these students. Fourth, because of the necessary assessment and placement safeguards built into the special education support system, this system is often not responsive to the immediate needs of teachers. Fifth, in some cases, the teachers' perceived need for help has led to the overreferral of students for special education assessment and placement (Chalfant, 1987, 1989; Chalfant et al., 1979).

The teacher assistance team (TAT) is a school-based problem-solving unit that assists teachers in generating intervention strategies. The TAT model provides a forum wherein classroom teachers can engage in a collaborative problem-solving process. The model is based on four assumptions related to teacher empowerment:

1. Considerable knowledge and talent exist among classroom teachers.
2. Classroom teachers can and do help many students with learning and behavior problems. Every effort should be made in the general classroom before a referral for special education services is made.
3. Teachers can resolve more problems by working together than by working alone.
4. Teachers learn best by doing; the best way to increase teachers' knowledge and skills is by helping them solve immediate classroom problems (Chalfant and Pysh, 1989; Chalfant et al., 1979).

Under the TAT approach, a team of professionals works cooperatively with classroom teachers to develop successful programs and strategies in the general education classroom for students with learning and behavior problems. Often, these teams are established to eliminate unnecessary testing and referral for special education. Whereas the original purpose was to work with students who have learning and behavior problems who were not currently placed in special education, it is possible to establish teams that focus on students already identified as special needs students.

Who serves on the team? Members can include the building principal, two regular classroom teachers, the teacher who is seeking assistance, and other people as needed, such as a parent/guardian, the student, or a member of the special education staff. Team members can be selected by the staff or appointed by the principal.

How is the team contacted for assistance? When a classroom teacher seeks assistance in solving a student's learning or behavior problems in the classroom, the teacher seeks help from the school-based assistance team. Chalfant and Pysh (1983) suggest that assistance be requested by answering four questions:

1. What do you want the student to do that he or she is not currently doing?
2. What does the student do (assets) and not do (deficits)?
3. What have you done to help the student cope with his or her problem?
4. What other background information and/or test data are relevant to the problem?

The team often responds to a problem identified by the classroom teacher. Frequently, the teacher identifies the problem and selects a member of the team to observe the student and/or the teacher. In addition, informal assessment may be conducted. The team generates instructional alternatives and may assist in the implementation of these alternatives. It also establishes policies for monitoring progress and providing feedback.

School-based assistance teams have successfully decreased the number of referrals for special education. They also provide the support that classroom teachers need to cope effectively with students who have learning and behavior disorders.

CLASSROOM Applications

Teacher Assistance Team (TAT)

PROCEDURES: The core team in the TAT model is generally composed of three elected members (primarily classroom teachers rather than special education teachers) with the requesting teacher also participating as a team member. The team may ask other teachers, specialists, or the principal to join the team as they deem necessary or to serve as permanent members. One person serves as coordinator and is charged with such responsibilities as alerting the team members to the time and place of the meetings and distributing information so that the members are briefed before coming to the problem-solving meeting.

When teachers refer classroom problems to the team, they complete a request for assistance in which they address four areas:

1. Describing what they would like students *to be able to do* that they do not currently do
2. Describing what students *do* (assets) and what they *do not do* (deficits)
3. Describing what they have done to help students cope with their problems
4. Providing background information and/or previous assessment data that are relevant to the problem (Chalfant and Pysh, 1981; Chalfant et al., 1979)

When a request for assistance is received, the team member responsible for that case reviews the information provided in the request, observes in the classroom if necessary, interviews the teacher to clarify information, and constructs a problem–interaction diagram that visually represents and summarizes the concerns (Chalfant and Pysh, 1993). This information is distributed to the team members before the meeting.

At the TAT meeting, team members complete a 30-minute problem-solving process for each request. The process consists of the following steps:

1. Reviewing the summary information, providing the opportunity for the teacher to clarify or provide additional information, and reaching consensus on what the problem is
2. Identifying the primary concern and establishing an objective for solving the problem
3. Brainstorming ideas for solving the problem and reaching the objective
4. Having the teacher requesting assistance select intervention strategies, which the teacher and team refine into a classroom intervention plan
5. Developing a means of measuring the success of the intervention plan
6. Establishing a date and time for a 15-minute follow-up meeting

Using this format, a teacher assistance team generally handles two new requests, or one new request and two follow-ups, during a one-hour meeting.

COMMENTS: The TAT model has been used widely throughout the United States and Canada. It has been shown to be effective in helping teachers cope with the learning and behavior problems of students in the general school population. It is also particularly effective in reducing the number of students who are inappropriately referred for special education (Schrag and Henderson, 1996). Due to its success in reducing the number of inappropriate referrals to special education, the TAT model is identified in the literature as a prereferral

intervention. However, the original intent of the process was to serve as a resource for all students at a school. This process has also been used with students previously identified as having special needs, with the children's special education and general education teachers serving as team members and participating in the problem-solving process.

Several factors seem particularly relevant to the success of this model within a school. First, it is important that the school administration support such a program by providing teachers with time for meetings and some type of incentive for serving as team members. Second, schoolwide staff training in effective and efficient problem-solving strategies and the TAT process facilitates the success of the model (Bay, Bryan, and O'Connor, 1994; Chalfant and Pysh, 1989).

How can a school maintain a continuum of services (inclusion, pull-out, or a combination)? Keeping in mind that a range of services is necessary (e.g., Council for Exceptional Children, 1993; Fuchs and Fuchs, 1995; Kauffman, 1995; Roberts and Mather, 1995), TAT decisions should be based on what is best for the students who are being served and should be made on a case-by-case basis. What works for one student will not necessarily work for another. It is recommended that teachers and administrators work with their districts to develop a plan that can effectively use resources (e.g., time, funding, staff) to implement appropriate services in their school's student population (Idol, 1997). See Apply the Concept 5.3 for a description of one school's TAT, the inclusion assistance team.

Coteaching

Coteaching, or cooperative teaching, occurs when general and special education teachers coordinate their efforts and jointly teach special and general education students (Bauwens, Hourcade, and Friend, 1989). Although there is some debate over the effectiveness of coteaching as a way to meet the needs of students with disabilities (Zigmond, 2001), limited data indicate that coteaching can have a positive impact on student achievement (Murawski and Swanson, 2001). Of course, the effectiveness of coteaching is related to what students need to learn and whether they can learn it well within a coteaching setting.

How Coteaching Works

When coteaching, special and general education teachers plan broad, overall goals and desired out-

Apply the Concept 5.3

The Inclusion Assistance Team

Because consultation is increasingly used in schools and districts throughout the United States, Fuchs and colleagues (Bahr, Fuchs, and Fuchs, 1999; Fuchs, Fuchs, and Bahr, 1990; Fuchs, Fuchs, Harris, and Roberts, 1996) designed a prescriptive approach to problem solving in which a specialist (e.g., the special education teacher or school psychologist) serves in the role of the consultant

and the classroom teacher serves as the consultee. The inclusion assistance team follows four common problem-solving steps:

1. Problem identification
2. Problem analysis
3. Plan implementation
4. Problem evaluation

One of the unique aspects of the inclusion assistance team is that the

team uses a list of preidentified potential interventions to facilitate the process, assist on generating ideas, and save time. Research indicates that both special education and general education teachers were satisfied with the idea, the process, and the outcomes from implementing the program.

---

comes for the class as a whole as well as for specific students in the class. Both special and general classroom teachers lead instruction during the same instructional period. Although one teacher may provide some instruction to the group as a whole, most of the instructional time involves both teachers working with small groups or with individual students. Because students are frequently grouped heterogeneously, the special education teacher works with many students, including those who are identified as benefiting from special education. Complementary instruction and supportive learning activities are part of the teachers' coplanning and instruction.

Apply the Concept 5.4 provides guidelines for effective coteaching in middle school classes for students with learning and behavior problems.

Coteaching Models

Coteaching involves much more than just putting a special and a general education teacher in the same classroom. For example, Weiss and Lloyd (2002, 2003) found that in coteaching situations, it was often difficult for special education teachers to provide the type of focused, explicit instruction that they used in special education classrooms. Therefore, to be successful, both teachers must carefully plan what role each will take and the type of instruction they will each provide.

Teachers can implement a variety of coteaching models. Many teachers select a coteaching model based both on overall instructional goals and the individual needs of students in the classroom. Before choosing a coteaching model, the general and special education teachers need to decide what

lesson or unit will be taught, being careful to consider general education curriculum requirements as well as the individual needs of students with disabilities specified on their IEP. Most teachers find that they use more than one model during a week and even during a day. Following are several coteaching models that teachers have found useful (Vaughn, Schumm, and Arguelles, 1997).

Model A: One Group. One Lead Teacher, One Teacher "Teaching on Purpose": Many teachers in coteaching situations end up spending their time grazing, that is, going from student to student to make sure they are following along but without a specific plan or goal in mind. "Teaching on purpose" is a method of checking for understanding and providing short installments of explicit instruction that are related to key ideas, concepts, or vocabulary from the main lesson. When teaching on purpose, one of the teachers gives short lessons to individuals, pairs, or small groups of students during or as a follow-up to whole-group instruction. In one or two minutes, the teacher who is teaching on purpose might approach a student after instruction to follow up on key ideas and concepts, encourage participation, answer questions, or review directions. In about five minutes, the teacher can review concepts and vocabulary or check for understanding. If further instruction is needed, the teacher can take a bit longer to provide a minilesson that is related to the main lesson (e.g., how to find the main idea). When coteaching is used effectively, the teacher has a specific objective in mind and targets particular students to ensure that they are learning specified material.

Apply the Concept 5.4

Guidelines for Effective Coteaching

Effective coteaching involves the following:

1. *Voluntary participants.* Teachers should choose to work together and should not be forced into a collaborative teaching situation (Vaughn, 1995). Ms. Andrews is a special education teacher who has been coteaching in 3 fourth-grade classrooms for several years. She began collaborating after attending a workshop on coteaching with the fourth-grade team from her school. She says the reason she and her team are successful is because "we enjoy working together, have compatible teaching styles, and feel comfortable discussing differences."

2. *Shared responsibility.* Teachers combine their knowledge and resources to plan instruction.

Therefore, they also share the accountability for the outcomes of those decisions.

3. *Reciprocity of ideas.* While the amount and nature of input will vary by teacher, both teachers must accept each other's contributions as integral to the collaborative process.

4. *Problem solving.* Not only must teachers collaborate to identify and find solutions to meet student needs, they also must accept that problems will arise when two professionals work together to coordinate instruction. Dealing with problems that arise during collaboration is not so different from finding solutions to student problems. To solve a problem it is helpful to identify concerns, share

information regarding the problem, brainstorm possible solutions, evaluate the ideas and create a solution plan, try the solution, and evaluate its success (Snell and Janney, 2000).

5. *Interactive communication.* Effective communication occurs when teachers trust each other and are not afraid to voice either their agreement or disagreement, when they communicate accurately and directly, and when they remain sensitive to differences (Snell and Janney, 2000).

6. *Conflict resolution.* Disagreements and even arguments are inevitable in any collaborative process. Implementing a plan to resolve conflicts can lead to better solutions than if the problem had been ignored (Idol et al., 2000).

Model B: Two Mixed-Ability Groups. Two Teachers Teach the Same Content: In Model B, the class is divided into two mixed-ability groups, and each teacher instructs one group. The purpose of this coteaching model is to reduce the group size so as to increase the number of opportunities for students to participate and interact with one another and to have their responses and knowledge monitored by a teacher. This format is often used when difficult new content is introduced or when smaller groups are beneficial for certain instructional activities, such as discussion. For example, the coteachers may divide the class into two heterogeneous groups during the discussion of a book that has been read as a whole group. At the end of the lesson, the two groups come together to summarize what they learned and to integrate information between groups.

Model C: Two Same-Ability Groups. Teachers Teach Different Content: Students are divided into two groups on the basis of their skill level in the topic area. One teacher reteaches while the other teacher provides alternative information or extension activities to the second group. For

example, during a unit on fractions, one teacher can lead a reteaching activity on dividing the parts of a whole, while the other teacher facilitates an activity on creating story problems using fractions. In effective coteaching, the general education teacher does not always assume the role of lead teacher, nor does the special education teacher always reteach. Teachers share responsibilities and alter roles from one lesson to the next.

Model D: Multiple Groups. Teachers Monitor/Teach: Model D is often used during cooperative learning activities and in reading groups and learning centers. One option for Model D is to have several heterogeneous groups and one or two homogeneous groups based on skill level. One or both teachers work with individual groups for the entire period. Another possibility is to have students move in small groups through four or five centers. Two centers are teacher-assisted, and the remaining centers have activities that can be done independently by groups. Students might also work in cooperative groups or pairs while both teachers provide minilessons and monitor progress.

Model E: Whole Class. Two Teachers Teach Together: In this model, teachers work cooperatively to teach a lesson. One teacher may lead the whole class lesson while the other teacher interjects to clarify the material. Often the general education teacher provides curriculum material, and the special education teacher adds strategies to help students with disabilities remember key ideas and organize information. For example, teachers might spend 10 minutes modeling problem-solving techniques and explaining directions for a science lesson on observation in which students will work cooperatively to record observations and make predictions about a "mystery matter." One teacher lists the steps of the activity, while the other points to a flowchart indicating the correct sequence to follow.

Coplanning

Special education teachers often coplan with general education teachers for the students with special needs who are in their classrooms. Sometimes special education teachers also coteach in those classrooms; at other times, they assist the teacher in planning and making adaptations for students with special needs to lessons that will be taught without their assistance.

In long-range coplanning, special education and general education teachers plan broad overall goals and outcomes for a class and the specific students with disabilities who are in that class. This coplanning of broad goals occurs quarterly or more frequently as needed, and accommodates the IEPs of students with disabilities.

Special education and general education teachers may also coplan specific lessons and outcomes for a unit of study or for a designated period of time (e.g., weekly). The planning pyramid (Schumm, Vaughn, and Harris, 1997; Schumm, Vaughn, and Leavell, 1994) provides a process for coplanning by special and general education teachers to meet the needs of students with disabilities in general education classrooms. As can be seen in Figure 5.1, a form for unit planning, and in Figures 5.2 and 5.3, forms for lesson planning, forms can be used to facilitate the process. Working together, teachers complete the forms to identify their objectives, materials needed, and their roles and responsibilities in delivering the instruction. While planning, the special education teacher can provide ideas for adaptations, clarification, scaffolding, and use of materials to facilitate learning. Essential to the success of the planning pyramid is the identification of core ideas, concepts, vocabulary, and/or principles that the teachers determine to be essential for all students to learn. This information is entered at the base of the pyramid. Information that the teacher deems important for most students to learn is written in the middle of the pyramid. Information for a few students to learn is written at the top of the pyramid. Teachers who implement the planning pyramid find that it not only facilitates the

FIGURE 5.1
Unit-Planning Form

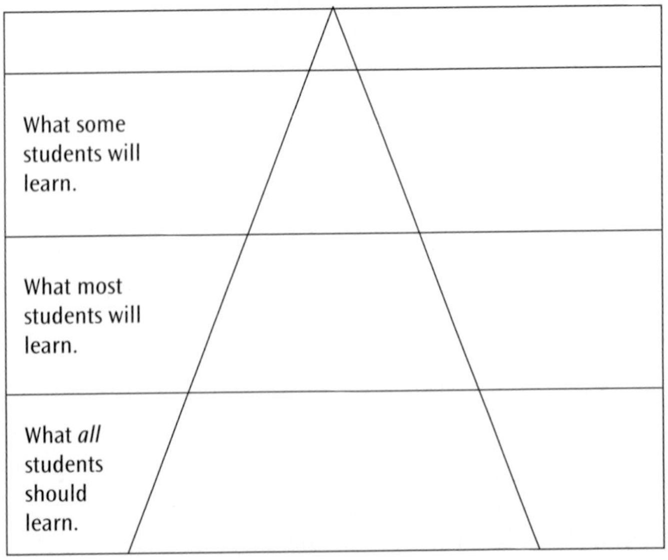

Date: ____________ Class Period: ____________

Unit Title: ____________

Materials/Resources:

____

Instructional Strategies/Adaptations:

____

Evaluation/Products:

____

FIGURE 5.2

Weekly Coplanning Form

Time Period: _____   Week Of: _____   Content Area: _____

Goals: GE   SE

_____   _____

Activities: GE   SE

Monday   _____   _____

Tuesday   _____   _____

Wednesday _____   _____

Thursday _____   _____

Friday   _____   _____

Material(s):   GE   SE

Monday   _____   _____

Tuesday   _____   _____

Wednesday _____   _____

Thursday _____   _____

Friday   _____   _____

Groups/Students: GE   SE

Monday   _____   _____

Tuesday   _____   _____

Wednesday _____   _____

Thursday _____   _____

Friday   _____   _____

Evaluation: **Other:**

_____   _____

organization of the material they intend to teach, but also provides guidelines for instruction (Schumm et al., 1997).

Successful Coteaching

Joyce Duryea is an elementary special education teacher who has worked as a resource room teacher for nine years (Klingner and Vaughn, 2002, provide a case study of Joyce if you would like to read more about her). She was asked to work collaboratively with three general education teachers who had approximately five students with disabilities in each of their classrooms. Joyce said, "When I was preparing to be a special education teacher it never occurred to me that I would need to know how to coteach in a general education classroom. I always thought I would have my group of students with special needs and that is the way it would be." However, she has found her new role exciting and challenging. Joyce puts it this way: "I think I'm a better teacher now, and I definitely have a much better understanding of what goes on in the general education classroom and what kinds of expectations I need to have for my students."

On the basis of extended observations and interviews with more than 70 general education–special education teacher teams, several core issues

FIGURE 5.3

Example Elementary Coteaching Lesson Plan

General Educator ___Ms. Marco___   Special Educator ___Ms. Sanders___   Grade ___5___

Date	Coteaching Technique	Specific Teacher Tasks	Materials	Evaluation	Individual Student Needs
2/8	Model B: Two mixed-ability groups	Literary Discussion: Both teachers lead discussions on the class reading of *The Cay*. In each group, teacher and students write comprehension questions. Students call on volunteers to respond to their questions. Teacher interjects throughout the discussion, making sure all students have a chance to ask and answer questions.	Student copies of *The Cay* Discussion journals	Evaluate discussion journals Monitor participation	Assist Roger in formulating a response to share with class; remind Sam to pause first to organize thoughts before responding; Joe completes journal on computer
2/9	Model D: Five same-ability groups	Literacy Groups: Teachers each work with one of the two lower groups to provide explicit instruction in word analysis. The other three student groups work independently to complete reading and literacy assignments.	Student books Reading log	Chart number of words decoded correctly Evaluate reading logs	Ms. M: Minilesson on *r* controlled vowels Ms. S: Reteach syllabication strategy for decoding
2/10	Model D: Six mixed-ability groups	Survival Centers: Ms. S works at the Vocabulary center with Roger's group. She then follows his group to the Survival Word Game station and provides a word building minilesson. Ms. S remains at the Word Building station and provides a building words minilesson to Sandy's group. Ms. M monitors the remaining groups.	Center activities	Monitor group work Evaluate student work in word building	Roger works in a pair instead of in a foursome; Sandy brings behavior contract to stations
2/11	Model A: One group: Teaching on purpose	Research Reports: Ms. S gives directions for research report. Ms. M monitors work while Ms. S sees three small skill level groups (10–12 minutes each) to work on fluency/decoding.	Step-by-step research planners	Record fluency progress on student charts Evaluate planners	Roger uses modified research planner; Joe and Pedro complete work on computer
2/12	Model C: Two groups: One reteach	Research Reports: Ms. S works with students who are ready to begin research while Ms. M reteaches students who need assistance to develop a plan for their individual research projects.	Step-by-step research planners Research materials	Evaluate planners	Julie and Sam paraphrase steps before writing; Joe and Pedro complete work on computer

---

must be addressed if coteaching partnerships are likely to be successful (Vaughn and Schumm, 1996):

• *Who gives grades, and how do we grade?* Perhaps the issue that warrants the most discussion before coteaching is grading. Special education teachers are accustomed to grading based on the effort, motivation, and abilities of their students. General education teachers consider grades from the perspective of a uniform set of expectations. Communicating about grading procedures for in-class assignments, tests, and homework will reduce the friction that is frequently associated with grading students with disabilities in the general education classroom.

• *Whose classroom management rules do we use, and who enforces them?* Most general and special education teachers know the types of academic and social behaviors they find acceptable and unacceptable. Rarely is there disagreement between teachers about the more extreme behaviors; however, the subtle classroom management issues that are part of the ongoing routines of running a classroom can cause concerns for teachers. It is beneficial for teachers to discuss their classroom management styles and their expectations for each other in maintaining a smoothly running classroom. Critical to success is determining when and with whom the special education teacher should intervene for discipline purposes.

• *What space do I get?* When a special education teacher spends part of his or her day instructing in another teacher's classroom, it is extremely useful to have a designated area for the special education teacher to keep materials. Special education teachers who coteach for part of the school day in another teacher's classroom feel more at home and are better accepted by the students when they have a legitimate claim on space, including a designated desk and chair.

• *What do we tell the students?* Teachers often wonder whether students should be told that they have two teachers or whether they should reveal that one of the teachers is a special education teacher. We think that it is a good idea to inform the students that they will be having two teachers and to introduce the special teacher as a "learning abilities" specialist. Students both accept and like the idea of having two teachers. In interviews with elementary students who had two teachers (special education and general education), the students revealed that they very much liked having two teachers in the classroom (Klingner, Vaughn, and Schumm, 1998). Similarly, early in the school year, inform parents that their child will have two teachers and that both will be responsible for their child's learning.

• *How can we find time to coplan and coordinate?* The most pervasive concern of both general and special education teachers who coteach is finding enough time during the school day to plan and discuss their instruction and the learning of their students. This is of particular concern for special education teachers who are working with more than one general education teacher. Teachers need a minimum of 45 minutes of uninterrupted planning time each week if they are to have a successful coteaching experience. One suggestion that has been made by several of the teacher teams with whom we have worked is to designate a day or a half-day every six to eight weeks when teachers meet exclusively to plan and discuss the progress of students as well as changes in their instructional practices.

• *How do we know if it's working?* Many teachers work so hard to make coteaching work that they overlook the most important goal: ensuring that students learn. Teachers must collect and evaluate student data to determine whether instruction is effective. A general rule to follow if students are not making adequate progress is to increase the intensity of instruction and decrease the teacher–student ratio. In addition to student learning, it is important that coteachers take time to evaluate the coteaching process. Dieker (2001) found that effective coteachers discussed their roles and responsibilities on an ongoing basis and made adjustments as needed.

Collaboration with Families and Paraprofessionals

In addition to working closely with general educators, special education teachers must also collaborate frequently with students' families and various paraprofessionals. While some of the same principles for collaborating with general educators apply when collaborating with families and/or paraprofessionals, it is important to keep in mind that the differences in roles and expertise between you and the families and paraprofessionals will influence how you communicate and collaborate. However, you all should share a common goal: student success.

Collaborating with Families

Family involvement and collaboration is fundamental to implementation of the legal requirements of IDEA 2004, based on the idea that family involvement will be beneficial to the student through increased school-to-home continuity (Shea and Bauer, 1991). However, relationships between family members and schools often are not collaborative (Rochelle, 2001). This may be due to the fact that family members are overwhelmed by the amount of information and jargon used at IEP meetings. In addition, family members may still be coming to terms with the fact that their child has a disability. Cultural and linguistic differences between the family and school personnel may also interfere with genuine collaboration.

What can you do to help increase family and school collaboration? Dettmer and colleagues (2005) provided some key ideas:

• Place the focus of any discussion on the needs and wants of the family and the students and not on their values.

• Accept the family and the student as they are. Stop wishing that they were different.

- Remember that most family members are not trying to provide poor parenting. Rather, they are often doing the best they can in their given circumstances.
- Respect the family's right to have different values than you do. That does not make them poor parents.

In addition, remember that family members are often experts on their child. In most circumstances, they know their child much better than you do. Approach them with this knowledge in mind. Do your best not to talk down to parents; treat them as you would like to be treated if your roles were reversed. By establishing a collaborative relationship with parents, you may obtain insights about your students that you would not be able to get in any other manner.

When working with families from diverse cultural and linguistic backgrounds, it is important to learn as much as you can about your students' backgrounds. A minimal, but

Diversity

important step is to learn the correct pronunciation of the family's name and a few words in their native language. Enlist the support of a translator, if possible. Ideally, the translator should be trained in special education as well as have translation skills.

Matuszny, Banda, and Coleman (2007) developed a four-step plan for collaborating with culturally and linguistically diverse families. The plan is designed to aid teachers in better understanding a particular family's needs as well as to strengthen the trust between the family and the teacher. The first phase is *initiation*. During this phase, which preferably occurs prior to start of the school year, the family members and teacher get to know each other. This contact should be informal and fun. True collaboration is difficult if the relationship between a family and teacher remains impersonal and/or uncomfortable. During *building the foundation*, the second phase, teachers establish trust with families by providing them with choices (such as how they would like to be involved in the classroom or how they would like to receive information from the teacher) and asking for input on certain classroom routines or behavioral procedures. The third phase, *maintenance and support*, involves positive communication, which is delivered according to the families' preferences about how they would like to be contacted and in a culturally appropriate way. *Wrap-up and reflection* is the last phase of collaboration. In this phase, the teacher and the family reflect on what worked and did not work in terms of their collaboration. This information can be used to plan for the next year or passed on to the next teacher.

Collaborating with Paraprofessionals

Schools often rely on paraprofessionals to provide support to general and special education teachers and students. Often, the special education teacher is in charge of supervising paraprofessionals. Many exceptional education specialists work closely with paraprofessional teaching assistants. Although teaching assistants never have complete responsibility for planning, implementing, or evaluating a student's program, they often participate in all of these areas. It is important that paraprofessionals not be assigned to students whom the teacher then spends little time seeing. Paraprofessionals need to have their teaching responsibilities rotated among many students so that the teacher spends frequent intervals teaching and evaluating all students. Because paraprofessionals are often responsible for implementing class rules, they need to be completely familiar with class and school rules and their consequences. Many paraprofessionals comment that they are successful in their roles when they have confidence that they understand what is expected of them. Suggestions for working with paraprofessionals are provided in Apply the Concept 5.5.

What skills are important in working with paraprofessionals? Wallace and her colleagues (2001) found several competencies that administrators, teachers, and paraprofessionals identified as important for teachers to have when working with paraprofessionals.

- *Open communication.* Teachers should share student-related information as well as explain the role of the paraprofessional to the paraprofessional as well as to all other personnel.
- *Planning and scheduling.* Coordinating the paraprofessionals' schedules is the responsibility of the special education teacher at most schools.
- *Instructional support.* Teachers should provide regular feedback to paraprofessionals about their instruction.
- *Modeling for paraprofessionals.* Modeling instructional strategies and a professional manner of interacting with students are part of a teacher's responsibility when supervising paraprofessionals.
- *Training.* Special education teachers are often responsible for providing on-the-job training for paraprofessionals.

Apply the Concept 5.5

Working with Paraprofessionals

Jamie DeFraites is a first-grade teacher in New Orleans. Her multicultural classroom of 22 students includes 11 Vietnamese children and 2 Hispanic students who are English language learners. Jamie explains, "I love my class and was actually asked to loop to second grade—so I'll have the same students next year!"

Jamie is fortunate enough to work with two paraprofessionals, who join her classroom at different times during the day. Here are Jamie's tips for working with paraprofessionals:

1. It's important to have mutual respect and trust. I let the paraprofessionals know how fortunate I feel to have additional adults in the classroom and how important their job is in helping all students learn. I also thank them every chance I get—in the presence of the principal, parents, and students.

2. At the beginning of the year, I talk with the paraprofessionals individually about their interests and skills and try to match their duties with their strengths. Both paraprofessionals are bilingual (one in Vietnamese and one in Spanish), so assisting me with parent communication is very important. One of the paraprofessionals is very creative and helps me design learning centers. The other is very interested in math and helps me with review and extra practice for students with challenges in that area.

3. Each of the paraprofessionals is eager to learn new skills and strategies. It is worth my time to explain instructional strategies to them so that they can do more than grade papers—they can actually interact with children in small groups or individually. It took me a long time to learn to teach—I'm still learning. I don't assume that the paraprofessionals automatically know how to teach. If I can share some of my training, the payoff is big for my students.

4. At the beginning of the year, we also clarify roles, responsibilities, classroom routines, and expectations for student learning and behavior. Spending that time in planning and communicating is time well spent. We're on the same page.

5. The paraprofessionals both work with several other teachers, so their time in my class is very limited. We have to make each minute count. Their tasks have to be well defined. I also plan a backup—what to do when there is nothing to do.

6. Finally, I encourage the paraprofessionals to get additional professional training. I let them know about workshops and other opportunities to learn. The more they learn, the more my students benefit!

Jamie admits that she would like to have a regular planning time with the paraprofessionals. As she says, "Often, we have to plan on the run." Also, her school district does not require periodic feedback or performance review sessions. This is something Jamie definitely recommends. "Fortunately, I have not run into problems with either paraprofessional, but if I did, it would be a good idea to have a system for giving feedback in a systematic way."

Source: Sharon Vaughn, Candace S. Bos, and Jeanne Shay Schumm, *Teaching Exceptional, Diverse, and At-Risk Students in the General Education Classroom,* 3rd ed. (Boston: Allyn & Bacon, 2003). Copyright © by Pearson Education. Reprinted by permission of the publisher.

- *Management.* Teachers need to maintain regular and positive interactions with paraprofessionals and support their skill improvements.

Collaboration in a Response to Intervention Model

Collaboration among the various personnel involved in a school's RTI model is essential for a number of reasons. First, remember that using an RTI framework can help a school identify what supplemental instruction or intervention students may need to "catch up" to their grade-level peers. In order to ensure that a student is receiving appropriate intervention, communication among the classroom teacher, intervention provider, and other school personnel (such as the reading coach, special education teacher, or school psychologist) needs to be consistent and frequent. Many schools implementing RTI set aside regular weekly or monthly meeting times and space for teachers and specialists to discuss student data and make instructional changes, if necessary.

Collaboration between professionals also helps schools address what several administrators have identified as the number-one challenge to successful implementation of RTI: scheduling. By having teachers work collaboratively in creating schedules conducive to providing interventions, schools are better able to offer interventions on a consistent basis. Mrs. Middlestock, an elementary special education teacher, works with teachers at each grade level prior to the beginning of the school year to help teachers identify a common time across grade levels when students can be pulled out for interventions. By working collaboratively with her colleagues to identify intervention times, Mrs. Middlestock feels that she achieves greater teacher buy-in in terms of support for RTI and that teachers are more likely not to forget to send their students to her for Tier II interventions.

In some schools, particularly at the middle school level, Tier II interventions are used to preteach or reteach concepts from the general education curriculum. Therefore, it is crucial that classroom teachers and intervention teachers collaborate on pacing and content so that students are pretaught vocabulary and concepts and/or given additional practice on concepts or skills in a timely and appropriate manner. In addition, collaboration can be used to ensure that intervention teachers are delivering interventions with fidelity. In schools using RTI to identify students with learning disabilities, it is necessary to ensure that the interventions the students receive are delivered as they were designed to be taught. Mrs. Middlestock collaborates frequently with the other intervention providers and when possible observes them to make certain that all of the interventions are being delivered with fidelity.

> **FOCUS Question** 3. What are the principles of communication, when are they likely to be used, and how can teachers of individuals with learning and behavior problems develop the interview skills needed to effectively communicate with parents and professionals?

Communication Skills

In addition to assessment, intervention, curriculum development, and classroom management, a major role for the teacher of students with learning and behavior problems is communication. Effective special education teachers communicate regularly with families, other special and regular education teachers, school administrators, and other educational and psychological professionals such as the school psychologist, speech/language therapist, and so on. Ability to communicate effectively is a skill that significantly affects an educator's job success. Despite the importance of this skill, most teachers finish school with no formal training in communication.

Principles of Communication

Having parents as partners in the educational process is important to achieving success in education. Many researchers found that the amount and quality of teacher communication influence parental involvement and the success of the partnerships (RMC Research Corp., 1995; Watkins, 1997). In other words, the degree to which parents/guardians become involved is based on communications they receive from their children's teachers.

Some teachers communicate effectively with families and other teachers with little effort. They seem to be naturally good at making other people feel at ease and willing to disclose information. However, most teachers can benefit from specific skills training in effective communication. The following section outlines some basic principles designed to facilitate the communication process with parents, teachers, and other professionals.

Mutual Respect and Trust

Building mutual respect and trust is essential for successful communication (RMC Research Corp., 1995). Several researchers have been interested in studying ways of building mutual respect and trust. Simpson (1990) suggested that parents trust professionals when they feel professionals advocate for their children. Also, he emphasized a positive outlook, sensitivity to needs, and honesty. Stewart (1986) mentioned the importance of safe sharing situations. He suggested that being able to express feeling of anger or frustration facilitates trust and effective communication. In summary, both families and professionals need to perceive that they have a cooperative relationship (Berry and Hardman, 1998).

Acceptance

People know if you do not accept them or do not value what they have to say. Parents/guardians are aware when teachers do not really want to see them during conferences but are merely fulfilling a responsibility. Lack of acceptance interferes with parental and professional participation in a child's program. Some teachers seem to know how to extend and project their acceptance and interest. Ms. Skruggs has been teaching special education for 12 years. She has worked with a range of parents and professionals during her career, some easier to work with than others. Despite expected frustrations and disappointments, she communicates her care and concern to the parents and professionals with whom she interacts and always manages to find the few minutes necessary to meet with them. Ms. Skruggs says, "Parents have a great deal to teach me. They have spent a lot of time with their child and have seen patterns of behavior that can assist me in teaching."

Pointers for communicating acceptance include the following:

- Demonstrate respect for the families' knowledge and understanding of their child.
- Demonstrate respect for the diverse languages and cultures that families and their children represent.
- Introduce families to other members of the education team in a way that sets the tone for acceptance.
- Give families an opportunity to speak and be heard.
- Represent the families to other professionals, and ensure that a language of acceptance is used by all professionals and families.

Listening

Effective listening is more than waiting politely for the person to finish. It requires hearing the message the person is sending. Often this requires restating the message to ensure understanding. Effective listeners listen for the real content of the message as well as for the feelings in the message. Without using phony or overused statements or parroting what was said, they restate the message (though not after every statement) and allow the speaker an opportunity to confirm and/or correct.

Mrs. Garcia, the mother of 12-year-old Felipe, telephoned his special education resource room teacher, Mr. Sanchez.

Mrs. Garcia: Felipe has been complaining for the past couple of weeks that he has too much work to do in his biology and math classes and that he is falling behind. He says he is flunking biology.

Mr. Sanchez: How much would you say he is studying each night?

Mrs. Garcia: It's hard to say. He stays out with his friends until dinner, and then after dinner, he starts talking about all his homework. Sometimes he sits in front of the TV with his books, and sometimes he goes to his room.

Mr. Sanchez: He has mentioned in my class how much work he has to do. I wonder if he is feeling a lot of pressure from different teachers, including me?

Mrs. Garcia: Well, he has said he thinks you are working him too hard. I know sometimes he is lazy, but maybe you could talk to him.

Mr. Sanchez: Felipe works very hard in my class, and I expect a great deal from him. I will talk with him after school and arrange a meeting with his other teachers as well.

Mrs. Garcia: Thank you, and please do not tell Felipe I called. He would be very upset with me.

Plain Language

Teachers often use academic language or jargon when they communicate with families, which intimidates many parents/guardians (Skinner, 1991). Plain, straightforward talk by teachers is most effective with families. *Plain language* is language that expresses information in a straightforward, simple manner so as to make communication efficient and quick (RMC Research Corp., 1995). Using plain language helps families better understand information, reduces intimidation, and helps parents/guardians whose native language is not English (RMC Research Corp., 1995).

Questioning

Knowing what type of questions to ask can help individuals to obtain the information they need. Questions can be open or closed. An *open question* is a question that allows the respondent a full range of responses and discourages short, yes-or-no answers. Open questions begin with *how, what, tell me about*, and similar phrases. Following are several open questions:

- What do you think might be happening?
- What do you know about _____?
- How do you interpret it?
- What do you suggest?
- How might you describe it?
- How does this relate to his behavior at home?
- Tell me your opinion about _____.

Mrs. Lishenko suspected that Matt, one of her students, was staying up very late at night, because he was coming to school very tired and seemed to drag all day. He was also resting his head on his desk in the afternoon. She decided to call Matt's father to discuss the problem. She started the conversation by giving Matt's father some information about a meeting of family members that was going to be held in the school district that she thought would be of particular interest to him. She then proceeded to describe Matt's behavior in class. Finally, Mrs. Lishenko asked, "What do you think might be happening?" Matt's father began to confide that he was not paying much attention to Matt's bedtime and that Matt was staying up late watching movies on the new DVD player. Mrs. Lishenko's question gave Matt's father the opportunity to explain what he thought was happening. Rather than posing several possibilities or telling Matt's father that Matt was staying up too late at night, Mrs. Lishenko asked an open question, which allowed Matt's father to interpret the situation. Matt's father suggested that he would establish a firm bedtime. In this situation, asking an open question allowed

Matt's father both to indicate how he felt and to offer a solution.

Involving people in identifying problems increases the likelihood that they will not feel threatened and that they will be willing to make necessary changes. Apply the Concept 5.6 provides recommendations for communication between parents and teachers.

Encouragement

Begin and end with something positive but genuine. With every student, even ones who have serious learning and behavior problems, teachers can find something positive to say. Perhaps the child is improving in some area, perhaps he or she contributed some interesting information to a class discussion, perhaps he or she said or did something that was humorous. In addition to hearing positive reports about their children, families and professionals need

Apply the Concept 5.6

Recommendations for Active Communication between Teachers and Families about Homework

General and Special Educators

- Attend IEP meetings and all other conferences between schools and families.
- Require students to keep a daily assignment book, and remind them of due dates.
- Provide families with a list of suggestions about assisting with homework, and a list of major assignments at the beginning of the school year.
- Mail important information about homework procedures to the home.

Families

- Monitor their child's homework daily.
- Attend family–teacher conferences.
- Sign a daily assignment book.
- Inform teachers of their telephone numbers and reachable time.
- Share their expectations about home–school communication with teachers.

Schools

- Provide teachers with release time to engage in regular communication with families.
- Encourage frequent written communication about homework with families.
- Schedule family–teacher conference in the evenings.
- Provide incentives for teachers engaging in specific activities to improve home–school communication.
- Assign one person in the school for communication with families about the homework.
- Provide families with teachers' telephone numbers and reachable times.
- Establish telephone homework hotlines to allow families to call about homework.
- Provide families with computerized student progress reports.
- Establish systems that enable teachers to place homework assignments on audiotapes so that families can access them by phone.

- Use answering machines so that families can leave messages at any time.
- Provide mail services so that teachers can send assignments home electronically.
- Schedule after-school sessions for students to get help on their homework.
- Provide peer tutoring programs.
- Use community volunteers to assist with homework assignment.
- Provide sufficient study hall time during school hours.

Students

- Keep a daily assignment book.
- Make sure they understand what the assignment is.
- Learn how to manage their time effectively.
- Attend family–teacher conferences.

Source: Adapted from W. D. Bursuck, M. K. Harniss, M. H. Epstein, E. A. Polloway, M. Jayanthi, and L. M. Wissinger (1999). Solving communication problems about homework: Recommendations of special education teachers. *Learning Disabilities Research and Practice,* *14* (3), pp. 149–158. Reprinted by permission.

encouragement about what they are doing. Because special education teachers often have meetings with families and professionals to discuss problems, it is important to begin and end these meetings on a positive note. If possible, give genuine positive feedback to the families and professionals with whom you work.

Staying Directed

Follow the lead of families and professionals whenever they are talking about a student. A skillful consultant is able to respond to others and still keep the discussion focused. It is not uncommon for families to mention other related home factors that may be influencing their child's progress in school, such as marital difficulties, financial problems, or other personal problems. When families or students begin discussing serious problems that are beyond our reach as educators, teachers need to assist them in finding other resources to help them with their problems.

Listening to, summarizing, and responding to the dialogue of families and professionals often means teachers receive information in confidence. Teachers need to decide quickly whether the information they receive is within their bounds as educators or whether to refer the family or professional to someone else. Figure 5.4 provides a list of tips for effective communication with families and professionals.

Developing a Working Alliance

It is important that, in every way possible, teachers, families, and professionals all share a common goal: developing the best program for the child. Teachers should demonstrate genuine interest in the student. Families are exceedingly appreciative when professionals acknowledge the challenges that they have at home as well (Fox, Vaughn, Wyatte, and Dunlap, 2002). Whenever possible, teachers should share information about changes in a child that would be of interest. Teachers should also let families know when a student is making exceptional progress and let other professionals know when their interventions are paying off. There should be a team spirit in which all members feel that they are working together to enhance the student's education and social development.

A recent study (Blue-Banning, Summers, Frankland, Nelson, and Beegle, 2004) with adult

FIGURE 5.4

Facilitating Effective Communication with Families and Professionals

1. Indicate respect for the family's knowledge and understanding of their child.
2. Demonstrate respect for the diverse languages and cultures families and their children represent.
3. Introduce the family to other members of the education team in a way that sets the tone for acceptance.
4. Give family members an opportunity to speak and be heard.
5. Represent the family to other professionals and ensure that a language of acceptance is used by all professionals and family members.
6. Even when you are busy, take the time to let families and professionals know that you value them, and that you are just unable to meet with them at this time.
7. Avoid giving advice unless it is requested. This does not mean that you can never give suggestions; however, the suggestions should be given with the expectation that the person may or may not choose to implement them.
8. Avoid providing false reassurances to colleagues or families. Reassurances may make them and you feel better in the short run but in the long run are harmful. When things do not work out as you predicted, everyone can become disappointed and potentially lose trust.
9. Ask specific questions. Using unfocused questions makes it difficult to conduct a consistent, purposeful conversation.
10. Avoid changing topics too often; this requires that you monitor the topic and direct others to return to the topic.
11. Avoid interrupting others or being interrupted, which disturbs the conversation and makes effective collaboration difficult.
12. Avoid using clichés. A cliché as a response to a problem situation makes the other person feel as though you are trivializing the problem.
13. Respond to colleagues and family members in ways that attend to both the content of their message and their feelings.
14. Avoid jumping too quickly to a solution. Listening carefully and fully to the message will help you get at the root of the problem.

Source: S. Vaughn, C. S. Bos, and J. S. Schumm, *Teaching Students Who Are Exceptional, Diverse, and At-Risk in the General Education Classroom* (Boston: Allyn & Bacon, 1997). Reprinted with permission.

family members of individuals with disabilities and their service providers, as well as individual interviews with non-English-speaking parents and their service providers, provides valuable information about what they value and consider as indicators of positive collaboration and communication. The following factors indicate a positive collaboration between the providers (schools) and families:

- *Effective communication that suggests that there is honest, open, and respectful dialogue between key stakeholders.* This includes being resourceful and tactful with families as well as respecting their knowledge and experiences.
- *Commitment to the successful implementation of the goals and objectives established by the family.* This includes viewing the partnership as more than a job and realizing that it is a long-standing and engaged commitment.
- *Equity of power and influence in the decision making and directions for the target student.* This includes validating parents' points of view and recognizing when there is disagreement about the goals.
- *Trust in the partnership.* This includes a family's feeling that their child is safe and that services will be of dependably high quality.
- *Demonstration of high esteem for and by members of the team.* This includes giving each other feedback about what is going well and what needs adjustment, obvious valuing of the child, and nonjudgmental responses.

Developing Interviewing Skills

Interviews are the key to open communication and effective intervention. Special education teachers often work as consultants to regular classroom teachers, to other educational and psychological specialists, and to families. Consultants need interviewing skills to identify problems fully and to implement appropriate interventions. These interviewing skills help to meet the need to ask questions that inform and to follow up appropriately on information provided. There are five steps to good interviewing:

1. *Ask open questions.* As we discussed in the previous section, an open question permits respondents a full range of answers, allowing them to bring up a topic or problem they have on their mind. Open questions are generally followed by questions that require more specificity. Mr. Schwab, the special education resource room teacher, began his interview with Mrs. Francosa, the fourth-grade teacher, by asking an open question: "How is Yusuf's behavior lately?"

2. *Obtain specificity.* This requires asking questions or making restatements that identify or document the problem. After Mrs. Francosa describes Yusuf's behavior in the regular classroom, Mr. Schwab attempts to identify key points and to obtain specificity in describing the behavior: "You said Yusuf's behavior is better in the classroom but worse on the playground. Can you identify which behaviors in the classroom are better and which behaviors on the playground are worse?" Without drilling the interviewee, an attempt is made to identify the problem and provide documentation for its occurrence so that an appropriate intervention can be constructed.

3. *Identify the problem.* Problem identification can be based on information obtained, or it can be decided by the person being interviewed, often in the process of answering questions: "It seems like there is good progress in terms of completing classroom work. Let's figure out a way of reinforcing that behavior. There's a problem with Yusuf's responding to teasing on the playground. His response has been to fight, which is getting him in more trouble. Any thoughts about how we might change that behavior?"

After listening to suggestions from the teacher, Mr. Schwab might add, "Let me provide some suggestions that have been effective in the past with other students."

4. *Problem solve.* Suggestions for solving identified problems and implementing the solutions are generated. Both the professional being interviewed and the consultant contribute suggestions to solving the problem. Often, other professionals are included in the suggestions: "Perhaps we could discuss Yusuf's problem with his counselor and ask her to teach him some strategies for coping with teasing. We could also identify the students who are teasing him and reinforce them for not teasing."

The tone for problem solving should be one of flexibility. There are often many possible solutions but only a few that will work with a particular student. The goal is to find a solution the teacher is willing to implement that is effective for the student.

5. *Summarize and give feedback.* Summarize the problem and the plan of action. Be sure to indicate who is responsible for what. Whenever possible, establish a timeline for completing the tasks: "You will send home notes to Yusuf's parents, informing them of his progress in seatwork in the classroom. I will meet with the counselor about his problem on the playground, and you will talk with his peers and arrange a system for reinforcing them for not teasing. I'll check back with you during lunch this

FIGURE 5.5

Steps to a Successful Interview

Step 1:   Ask open questions:
"Tell me about Yusuf's behavior."

Step 2:   Obtain specificity:
"How do the other children respond when Yusuf gets angry?"

Step 3:   Identify the problem:
"Sounds like fighting is occurring during noon recess most frequently after Yusuf is teased."

Step 4:   Problem solve:
"Let's start by seeing how Yusuf perceives the problem and developing an intervention that includes his peers. What might be reinforcing to Yusuf and/or his peers?"

Step 5:   Summarize and give feedback:
"You'll meet with Yusuf and his peers tomorrow. I'll speak with the counselor and we'll schedule a team meeting for Wednesday."

week to see how things are going. I'm very pleased with this progress, and I am sure much of it is due to your hard work and follow-up." Figure 5.5 provides a summary of the interview process.

Effective consultants listen openly without taking a defensive posture. They stay focused and remember the needs of students. They note that solutions effective with previous students and teachers may not be effective in current cases. They look for alternatives that can be implemented and they seek the advice of other professionals. When plans for solving problems are developed, they determine who is responsible for what tasks and provide feedback on performance.

Three Forms of Communication between Teachers and Families

Three forms of communication are commonly used by schools: in-person contact, phone calls, and written information. Each form is important and has a different purpose. In-person contact involves scheduled parent–teacher conferences, informal school meetings, home visits, or family information/training seminars. Phone calls can be used to provide families regular reports on the progress of their children, follow up after a conference, or deal with an immediate crisis. Written information includes progress reports, daily interactive journals, or notification of events using multiple communication methods such as email (Berry and Hardman, 1998).

FOCUS Question | **4.** What is the teacher's role in addressing the needs of the entire family, assisting families with activities that occur outside of school, and coordinating family involvement in school?

Working with Families

This section of the chapter highlights teachers' interaction with families. Family adjustment to a child with learning and behavior problems is discussed first. Within this section, family adjustment, sibling adjustment, and the problems of constructing an effective summer program are described. We also explore families' involvement with the schools and their role in the planning of the child's educational program.

Family Adjustment

A great deal has been written about family response to having a child with disabilities (Ferguson, 2002). Most of what is written focuses on families of children with mental retardation and physical handicaps. This literature may provide little insight into the adjustment of families whose children the schools have identified as learning- or behavior-disordered. Most families of children with learning and behavior problems do not receive a "diagnosis" until the child is in school. Though they may have recognized that the child's behavior was different from that of their other children and peers, most families are unsure of what the problem is. Often, they seek advice from their family physician, who either makes referrals to other professionals or suggests that they wait until the child enters school. Although many families are aware that their child has learning or behavior problems long before diagnosis, they continue to hope that their observations are incorrect and that the child will outgrow the problem.

The family is an important force in a child's learning and development. From a systems perspective, many mental health professionals recommend an integrated approach to working with students with learning disabilities and behavior disorders. This integrated approach typically involves all or part of the family in the program, including an initial meeting with the entire family, involvement of selected family members, or ongoing clinical help that involves the family at certain times. Not all families who have children with learning and behavior problems need therapeutic assistance. For example, a family-centered approach to positive behavioral supports has been heralded for families of children with severe behavior and emotional difficulties (Carr et al., 2002).

Because of concern for their child, mothers of children with learning disabilities often expect less of them than the children expect of themselves (Margalit, Raviv, and Ankonina, 1992). Teachers need to realize when families are expecting too little of their children and assist them in readjusting their expectations. The misconceptions about children under which many families and teachers function often tell children that they are unable, and as a result, many children act as though they are unable to learn. Many students with learning disabilities leave school unprepared for work, postsecondary education, and life expectations. Often they leave school with fewer skills than children with mental retardation (Cummings and Maddux, 1985). Teachers can help families by reminding them to communicate the importance of education to their child—for example, sharing their successes and failures when they were in school, and emphasizing that even when they did not do well they continued to do the best they could.

Simpson (1982) suggests that the needs of families of children with learning and behavior problems fall into five general categories:

1. *Information exchange.* Families need conferences, program and classroom information, progress reports, interpretations of their child's academic and social needs, and informal feedback about their child.

2. *Consumer and advocacy training.* Families need information about their rights and responsibilities, procedures for interacting during conferences, resources available through the school and community, and assertiveness training.

3. *Home/community program implementation.* Families need procedures for assisting their child academically and behaviorally at home, including procedures for tutoring and behavior management.

4. *Counseling, therapy, and consultation.* Families need support groups, consultation, referrals for conflict resolution, problem solving, and therapy.

5. *Family-coordinated service programs.* Families need to be in a position to provide services to and receive services from other parents through advisory councils, parent-to-parent participation, advocacy, and other options.

In a study reported by Simpson (1988), the most widely requested services by families of children with learning and behavior problems were program information and informal feedback.

Adjusting to a child with learning and behavior disorders is difficult (Simeonsson and Simeonsson, 1993). Understanding how families adjust and interact with the child on the basis of their interpretation of the child's needs is an important role for the special education teacher. However, several key findings about families of children with disabilities have positive implications in working with these families (Ferguson, 2002):

- Overall patterns of adjustment and well-being are similar across families with children with and without disabilities. Thus, families who have a child with a disability are probably more like other families than they are different.
- Significant numbers of parents and siblings report that there are perceived benefits and positive outcomes from having a child or sibling with disabilities. This does not suggest that all aspects are easy but that many aspects are viewed positively.
- Having a family member with disabilities is stressful to all members of the family, but engaging the family in meaningful and functional ways is beneficial.

Siblings

In addition to how parents respond to a child with learning or behavior problems, the responses of other siblings is important. Having a brother or sister with disabilities provides special experiences (Lian and Aloia, 1994). On the positive side, siblings develop greater empathy, understanding, and tolerance of individual differences (McLoughlin and Senn, 1994). Many siblings also report many positive aspects of having a brother or sister with disabilities. On the negative side, they may develop inappropriate behaviors, emotional problems related to the experience (e.g., resentment, jealousy, guilt, fear, shame, embarrassment), or damaged self-esteem (McLoughlin and Senn, 1994). Lardieri, Blacher, and Swanson (2000) conducted a study to determine whether the presence of a child with learning disabilities, with or without reported behavior problems, affects the psychological well-being and self-concept of the child's siblings. Although sibling relationships in families of children with and without learning disabilities differed in their perception of the quality of their sibling relationships and self-reports of their own behavior, the difference was not significant enough to render a clinical diagnosis of sibling maladjustment. Not surprisingly, some siblings appear to be affected very little, whereas others are affected more seriously.

Many families are concerned because their child with learning disabilities or behavior disorders takes more of their time and consideration than do the other children in the family. Siblings may feel as though the child with special needs is getting all of the family's attention and special privileges. It is important for parents/guardians to develop schedules in which they assign special time for each of their children. A sibling of a child with learning disabilities commented:

> Everything always seems to center around Scott. He always seems to be the focus of the conversation and whom my parents are concerned about. I do pretty well in school and don't seem to have many problems, so sometimes I feel left out. It really meant a lot to me when my mother and father both scheduled time during the week for me to be alone with them. Usually my dad and I would go to the park, and sometimes we would go on an errand. Often my mom and I would work together in the kitchen, making my favorite dessert, chocolate chip cookies. The best part was that it was just me and them. I really think it helped me be more understanding of Scott. Somehow, I just didn't resent him so much anymore.

Powell and Ogle (1985) suggested strategies for parents to respond to siblings, including the following:

- Be open and honest.
- Value each child individually.
- Limit siblings' caregiving responsibilities.
- Use respite care and other supportive services.
- Be fair.
- Accept the disability.
- Put together a library of children's books on disabilities.
- Schedule special time with each sibling.
- Let siblings settle their own differences.
- Praise siblings.
- Listen to siblings.
- Involve the siblings.
- Provide opportunities for the child with a disability to be as independent as possible.
- Recognize each child's unique qualities and family contribution.

- Encourage the development of special sibling programs.
- Help to establish a sibling support group.
- Recognize special stress times for siblings, and plan to minimize negative effects.

Family-Centered Practice

Because family-centered practice is so integral to effective special education, it is important to ensure that there is a common understanding of what is meant by *family-centered practice*. "Family-centered service delivery, across disciplines and settings, views the family as the unit of attention. This model organizes assistance in a collaborative fashion and in accordance with each individual family's wishes, strengths, and needs" (Allen and Petr, 1996, p. 64).

What does this mean to a teacher? How could the teacher design each student's program with consideration of the family's strengths and needs? There are two essential things for teachers to keep in mind: The family should be viewed as the director of the service delivery process and as the ultimate decision maker; and teachers should focus on a family's strengths, not its deficiencies. Important components of family-centered practice include:

- The concept of family as the unit of attention or concern
- The importance of a collaboration between families and professionals
- An understanding of family needs and its strengths or capabilities
- Family choice or decision making and the uniqueness or culture of families
- The provision of specific types of services
- Maintenance of children in their own homes
- Empowerment of families

It may be useful to consider that schools perceive that they are more "family-centered" than they actually are. In addition, family-centered practices are more likely to occur at the preschool level and then occur less frequently as students move through the grades (Dunst, 2002).

Figure 5.6 shows a worksheet to use in gathering feedback from families in family-centered practice.

Wrap-Around Services

As society has become more aware of individuals with disabilities, many professionals have sought to improve services for them. Wrap-around services are a result of new ways of thinking about individualized services. The term

FIGURE 5.6

Parent–Teacher Collaboration Review and Reflection Worksheet

Directions: Please answer the following questions. Where you see the word *Other*, if desired, please write in any information that you want to add.

1. What helped you feel more comfortable working with your child's teacher? (Check the events/activities that you believe were most helpful to you):

____ The beginning of the year celebration that gave parents and teachers the chance to meet each other as people first (event held before school started)

____ Being asked about what I needed and how I wanted to receive information (The Parent Needs and Preferences Information Worksheet)

____ The information that was provided

____ The way information was provided (Tell how info. was provided: _____)

____ The frequency with which I received information (How often? _____)

____ Adjusting meeting times to meet my schedule

____ Other: _____

2. What was *not* helpful in making you feel more comfortable working with your child's teacher? (Check the events/activities that you believe were not helpful to you):

____ The beginning of the year celebration that gave parents and teachers the chance to meet each other as people first (event held before school started)

____ Being asked about what I needed and how I wanted to receive information (such as The Parent Needs and Preferences Information Worksheet that you may have completed earlier this year)

____ The information that was provided

____ The way information was provided (Tell how info. was provided: _____)

____ The frequency with which I received information (How often? _____)

____ Adjusting meeting times to meet my schedule

____ Other: _____

3. Please write down any supports that you want to see more of and any additional ideas you have for how the school/teacher can help you maintain your connection and comfort in working collaboratively with them in the upcoming year. If more space is needed, please feel free to use the back of this page to provide your thoughts and ideas.

Source: Adapted from R. M. Matuszny, D. R. Banda, and T. J. Coleman (2007). A progressive plan for building collaborative relationships with parents from diverse backgrounds. *Teaching Exceptional Children,* (Mar./Apr.), pp. 24–31. Copyright 2007 by the Council for Exceptional Children. Reprinted with permission.

wrap-around services refers to adding or deleting any services and supports in tailoring a program to meet a child's or family's specific needs and achieve specific goals (Karp, 1996; Katz-Leavy, Lourie, Stroul, and Ziegler-Dendy, 1992). Components of wrap-around services include the following:

- Community-based and unconditional services that never reject a child or family from appropriate services, and make changes based on the needs of the child or family

- Coordinated, custom-made services in three or more life domains of a child and family (family life, residential, social, educational, medical, recreational, etc.)

- Services developed by a team of interdisciplinary service providers, including the family, an advocate, systems' representatives, and other people who are important in the child's and family's life (Karp, 1996; Katz-Leavy et al., 1992)

Eligibility criteria for individualized and wrap-around services include: (1) having a serious emotional or behavior disorder; (2) having functional impairments; (3) needing multiagency services; (4) being placed, or at risk for placement, in a restrictive residential treatment setting; and (5) having difficult and complex needs that are not being met within the framework of the existing service system (Katz-Leavy et al., 1992).

Summers

Summers seem to be particularly difficult for children with learning and behavior problems, who may face too much unstructured time and too many opportunities to find trouble. If the summer represents an extended period of time without exposure to structured learning experiences, what was accomplished during the school year can be undone. Families often have a very difficult time with the additional pressure to find an appropriate educational or social experience during summer vacations. Billy's mother describes it this way:

> My son, Billy, needs a special summer program so he can learn to play with other kids. . . . My ex-husband, Arthur, thinks I bug Billy too much and that we should leave him alone. That's what happened last summer, and it didn't work. I don't know how to convince him or where to begin to find a good camp. I'm exhausted. I'm doing all I can manage. Last week, the school people reminded me that it was time to plan for the summer. And then they told me how much trouble Billy was having playing with the other children. Maybe I misinterpreted it, but I felt they were saying I should be helping him even more. (*Exceptional Parent*, 1984, p. 43)

Teachers can assist families during the summer by developing a list of community resources that provide structured programs for children and adolescents. Each community has a range of such programs, some of which include the following:

- *Public library.* The public library offers many programs that focus on literacy, including authors reading their books, books on tapes and records, and other special programs.
- *Children's museums.* Many towns and cities have children's museums that offer a range of special programs for children.
- *Theater groups.* Often, local theater groups offer summer programs on acting, cinema, and stage design.
- *Museums.* Local art museums, historic museums, and science museums may offer programs for children or adolescents during the summer.
- *Parks and recreation.* Parks offer arts and crafts as well as organized recreational activities during the summer that are often free or very inexpensive.

- *YMCA/YWCA.* These organizations offer many special summer programs, including day camps, swimming lessons, and arts-and-crafts classes.
- *Universities, colleges, and community colleges.* Often, these organizations offer special programs for children in the summer.

Preparing a list of activities that are available in the community as well as a list of tutors available during the summer helps parents and children to make a smooth transition from school to summer and can help teachers the following fall with the transition from summer to school. Perhaps the most important thing is to provide a structured activity each day without demanding that the entire day be structured (see Apply the Concept 5.7 for additional ways to encourage summer reading).

Family Members as Tutors

It is the responsibility of the family to "insure that the home is a relaxed and pleasant place, a source of strength to the child" (Kronik, 1977, p. 327). Often families want so much to help that they get overly involved in the child's homework or tutoring. Although spending time with their children in relaxing activities such as reading, going for walks, sitting and talking, and going to the zoo are recommended by all educational and psychological specialists, few recommend direct instructional tutoring in the home. Home tutoring by family members usually creates more problems than it solves. Often students need help with homework assignments; this is not the equivalent of home tutoring. Home tutoring is the supplementing of the student's educational program by the family member in the home. If family members insist on home tutoring, ask them to comply with the following suggestions adapted from Cummings and Maddux (1985):

- Develop specific, realistic goals with the special education or classroom teacher.
- Begin and end each tutoring session with a fun activity in which the child is successful.
- Keep the tutoring session brief—not more than 15 minutes for children up to grade 6 and not more than 30 minutes for older students.
- Work on small segments of material at a time.
- Use creative and novel ways of reviewing and teaching new material.
- Prevent the student from making mistakes. If the student does not know the answer, give it.
- Keep a tutoring log in which you record a couple of sentences about what you did and how the child performed.
- Provide encouragement and support.

Apply the Concept 5.7

Tips for Families about Summer Reading

Summer should not mean taking a break from learning. For reading, this is even more true. Many students lose reading skills over the summer break. At the same time, students also need fun time in the summer. So summer reading should be fun. The following is a list of tips for summer reading:

- Read aloud with your children. Do not make this activity formal. Make it fun.
- Show your children your own enjoyment of reading. Keep lots of reading materials in the house.
- Let your children choose the books they want to read.
- Provide your children with books on tapes. Listen to books often.
- Connect daily events to reading (e.g., let your children read sentences on the items at the grocery, let them read traffic signs, play books on tape while in the car).
- Let your children join in summer reading club activities.
- Encourage your children to become pen pals with their friends over summer vacation.
- Encourage your children to make a summer scrapbook in which they can put pictures, postcards, or photos. They can also write notes under these cards, or on the back.

Source: Adapted from Coordinated Campaign for Learning Disabilities (1999). Summer reading tips for parents. *LDA Newsbriefs, 34* (4), pp. 1–24.

- Practice the activities in ways that reduce boredom.
- Ensure that the work is challenging but not too difficult.
- Tutor at the same time and in the same place so that the child has an expectation for what will happen.
- If you are getting frustrated or your interactions with your child are strained or stressful during the tutoring, stop the session. Your relationship with your child is much more important than what you can teach him or her during the tutoring session.

Homework is a significant problem for many families and even more so for families of children with disabilities. Following are things teachers can do to make sure homework is appropriate:

- Design homework assignments that are meaningful. If students with disabilities are receiving homework from other teachers, guide the teachers in how to adjust assignments so that they are meaningful for the students.
- Communicate clearly what the homework assignment is and when it is due. If possible, check to be sure that students understand what they are supposed to do and have written the assignment down.
- Provide families with a general idea of homework assignments (e.g., students should be expected to do 30 minutes of homework Monday through Thursday).
- Grade homework in a timely fashion and provide feedback to students.
- Consider designing a homework Website on which homework assignments can be posted with clear specifications to families and students about what is expected, due dates, and so on. These homework Websites can be particularly helpful to families and tutors who are working to assist students with disabilities with successful homework completion. Salend, Duhaney, Anderson, and Gottschalk (2004) provide an overview of how to design and use a homework Website to communicate with families.

Apply the Concept 5.8 provides an overview of a study that examined family involvement in literacy development.

Family Members as Service Providers

Many significant developments in the field of special education have been accomplished by family members rather than professionals (Turnbull and Turnbull, 1990). Families of students with disabilities organized with other families on local and state levels to obtain appropriate services for their children. Some families conducted fund-raising campaigns; others even started their own schools. The efforts resulted in national organizations that today play multiple roles related to appropriate services for their children with disabilities, including advocacy, political lobbying, raising funds, and providing services (Alper et al., 1994; Roos, 1985).

Apply the Concept 5.8

Family Involvement in Reading and Writing Instruction for Their Children

Hughes, Schumm, and Vaughn (1999) conducted a study of Hispanic families of children with learning disabilities to determine the type of involvement they value in their child's reading and writing acquisition. Families were asked to provide information on the types of reading and writing activities that they practiced in the home and the extent to which they thought various reading and writing activities were feasible to implement.

Hispanic families who participated in the study reported that a wide variety of reading and writing activities were used in the home. Reading to each other was the activity that was most frequently reported. Families implemented reading activities more frequently than writing activities. Families identified the following activities as helpful:

- More communication with teacher about reading and writing activities they could do at home
- Further information about how to do the reading and writing activities with their children because the children had difficulties with reading and writing
- More information about appropriate home reading activities in the family's language (Spanish)

Family Involvement with Schools

By the time children reach school, families have already spent five years observing them. Many families are aware from the day their child enters school that the child is different from other children. Often the child spends two to three difficult years in school before being referred for learning disabilities or behavior disorders. During this time, many families have spent hours communicating with school counselors, psychologists, and teachers. In a study in which families of students with learning disabilities were interviewed after their child's initial placement, families reported having had an average of six contacts with the school before their child was identified (Vaughn, Bos, Harrell, and Laskey, 1988). Some of these contacts were initiated by the family members. Often, family members feel frustrated and alone. They are unsure what to do, and because of the complexity of their child's condition, professionals are often unable to provide the precise answers parents need. Apply the Concept 5.9 describes what families generally want from professionals. See Tech Tips 5.1 for ideas about using technology to build partnerships.

Apply the Concept 5.9

What Families of Students with Learning Disabilities Want from Professionals

In a survey of over 200 families of children with learning disabilities, families indicated what they really wanted from professionals (Dembinski and Mauser, 1977). A summary of the findings follows:

1. Families want professionals to communicate without the use of jargon. When technical terms are necessary, they would like to have the terms explained so that they can understand.
2. Whenever possible, they would like conferences to be held so that all family members can attend.
3. They would like to receive written materials which provide information that will assist them in understanding their child's problem.
4. They would like to receive a copy of a written report about their child.
5. They would like specific advice on how to manage specific behavior problems of their child or how to teach needed skills.
6. They would like information on their child's social as well as academic behavior.

TECHTips

5.1 Using Technology to Enhance Communication

Technology can facilitate both collaboration and communication. For communicating with parents and families, one solution is a classroom email list. An advantage of this option is that you no longer need to depend upon printed notes actually making it home! Of course, a big disadvantage is that some families may not have access to email. An additional technique is a class Website. A class Website could have semi-permanent content—daily schedules, reading lists, study tips—and weekly information such as spelling and vocabulary lists, homework assignments, and suggested Websites to complement current instructional units. The key to making a class Website successful is to keep the material up to date. For an example, see the image of a sample class Website.

Instant messaging is an ideal tool for collaboration with colleagues. Where once we had to walk to another part of a building, hoping to find a colleague free, now we can check instantly and schedule quick meetings at any time. Within a closed system, such as a school building where the computers are networked, it is an easy task to set up instant messaging for quick meetings and consultations with colleagues. Instant messaging can work on local networks as well as over the Internet.

Take the instant messaging idea one step further: video conferencing. Video conferencing is like instant messaging with a camera! As the cost of Web cameras drops while quality improves, educators should consider the benefits of communicating and collaborating via video conferencing. Impromptu meetings with colleagues can be easy.

A Sample Class Website

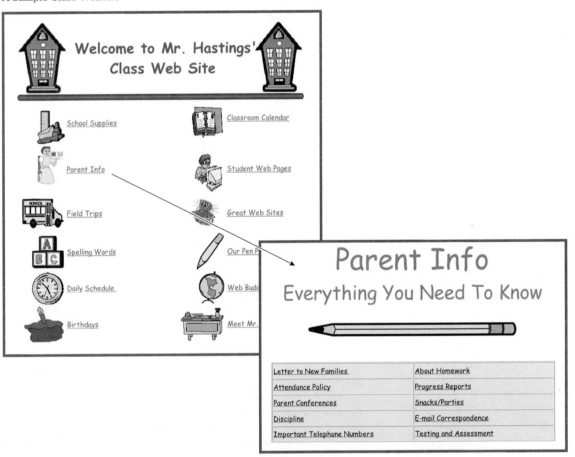

Family Involvement in Planning and Placement Conferences

Turnbull, Turnbull, and Wheat (1982) consider the provisions of PL 94-142 radical because of the extent of family participation it mandates. Families provide consent for evaluation, participate in the program and educational plan, and are kept involved in all decisions regarding a child's educational program.

The rationale for extensive family involvement is twofold. First, it ensures cooperation between home and school. Families can provide information about the child to which the schools may not have access, and family members can follow up on educational goals in the home. Second, it ensures that families will have access to information about student evaluations and records and can better monitor appropriate placement and programming by the school. One area that holds significant potential benefits is involving family members in the planning and placement conference for the child. The information that is obtained about the child's learning and behavior problems can increase family members' understanding, which in turn can lead to changes in family behavior toward the child. In addition, family members learn about the focus of the child's school program and can reinforce those learning and behavior efforts in the home. Unfortunately, this is more the ideal than a description of the real world. Despite the best intentions of school personnel and parents, cooperative and extensive family involvement in the placement and planning process is minimal.

There are many explanations for lack of family involvement in educational planning. One is that school personnel do not have adequate time to meet with families and fully explain the child's program or do not know how to take advantage of family members' knowledge and preferences (Harry, 1992; Harry et al., 1995). Often families can attend meetings only early in the morning before going to work or in the evening on their way home. These times usually conflict with the schedules of school personnel and require them to meet with families outside of their required work time. Because of their dedication and interest in children, professionals are often willing to meet at these times, but they are not motivated to meet for extended periods of time.

A second explanation is that many families feel that professionals will make the decisions in their child's best interest and do not want to be co-participants in the educational program. Rather than a lack of interest in the child's program, this may actually indicate less confidence in their own ability to participate effectively.

To assume that all families want to be actively involved in planning their child's educational program may not be accurate. Winton and Turnbull (1981) found that when they interviewed parents of preschool children with disabilities, 65 percent of the parents identified informal contact with teachers as the activity they most preferred, followed by 13 percent who chose parent training opportunities, and 10 percent who identified opportunities to help others understand the child. A common theme in studies evaluating family satisfaction with the placement and IEP conference is that parents state that they feel satisfied with the conference even though data indicate that the parents played relatively passive roles (Lynch and Stein, 1982; Vaughn, Bos, et al., 1988). Some 25 percent of the parents of students with learning disabilities who participated in placement and planning conferences did not recall the IEP document itself; of those who did recall it, few had any knowledge of its content (McKinney and Hocutt, 1982).

It could be that families would like to be more involved but feel intimidated by the number of professionals and the uncommon terminology.

> No matter how well we might know our own children, we are not prepared to talk to teachers, principals, psychologists, or counselors, much less participate in the educational decision making process. Although parents do have a lot of information, it is not the "right" kind. When we go to speak to administrators at school we hear about IEP's, MA's, criteria, auditory processing, regulations, and sometimes, due process. At first, there seems to be no correspondence between what we know and what the people in schools are talking about. (*Exceptional Parent*, 1984, p. 41)

During conferences, special education teachers need to be sensitive to family members' feelings and needs. They can serve as advocates for the parents, asking questions of the classroom teacher or other professionals that he or she feels the family member may have wanted to ask but did not.

 # Spotlight on Diversity

Practices for Families Who Are Culturally Diverse

Because the focus of much of the advice for families of children with disabilities focuses on the disability and what parents/guardians can do at home, very little advice considers the cultural and linguistic diversity of families. This discrepancy prevents many families from fully participating and engaging with the schools and professionals, because the advice and suggestions they receive seem so out of touch with their own family practices. According to Harry (2002), there are several key principles for the professional provision of culturally appropriate services:

- Families from different cultural and linguistic backgrounds may perceive a disability very differently.
- Stress may be handled and viewed differently.
- Educational professionals may subtly and not so subtly communicate dissatisfaction in family involvement with little consideration of the cultural factors that may influence this involvement.
- Dissonance may exist between a family's values and the values of the educational program.

Apply the Concept 5.10 provides considerations for working with parents from culturally and linguistically diverse groups.

Conferences with Family Members: Planned and Unplanned

Planned conferences with family members occur frequently and include multidisciplinary team meetings, annual parent–student meetings, or regularly scheduled meetings to report on academic and behavioral progress. Conferences provide teachers with the opportunity to do the following:

- Review the student's materials, grades, and work progress
- Meet with other professionals to provide an overall review and report on student progress
- Review the student's portfolio, assessment information, and progress reports
- Provide samples of the student's most recent work
- Establish and review goals and criteria for academic and behavioral work

Sometimes conferences with families are unplanned (Turnbull and Turnbull, 1990). Family members may phone, stop by the school, or schedule a conference with little notice. When this occurs, there are several procedures for the teacher to remember: Listen carefully until the family members have expressed the purpose of their visit, paraphrase what you understand to be their question or issues, and respond to the question and issue as completely as possible. Often family members stop by with a simple question or concern that is a disguise for a larger issue; that is why it is important to listen carefully and wait until family members are finished.

Individuals with Disabilities Education Act and Family Involvement

The Individuals with Disabilities Education Act (IDEA) was passed in 1990 and was most recently amended in 2004. This law ensures that all

Apply the Concept 5.10

Considerations for Families Who Are Linguistically Diverse

1. Assume that families want to help their children.
2. Provide materials in a range of formats including orally, in writing (family's language), through videotape, and through formal and informal presentations.
3. Provide opportunities for families to learn the skills and activities the students are learning so they can reinforce them in the home.
4. Provide opportunities for families to influence their children's educational program.

5. Provide workshops that include role playing and rehearsing situations between families and school personnel to increase families' confidence in working with school personnel.
6. Involve families from the community who are familiar with the culture and speak the home language of the children's families in work at the school.
7. Provide an informal meeting with families so they can exchange experiences and learn tips from each other.

8. Invite families to school and ask them to share their backgrounds or activities with other students and families.

 Diversity

Source: Adapted from T. W. Sileo, A. P. Sileo, and M. A. Prater (1996). Parent and professional partnerships in special education: Multicultural considerations, *Intervention in School and Clinic, 31* (3), pp. 145–153; and A. Misra, Partnership with Multicultural Families, in S. K. Alper, P. J. Schloss, and C. N. Schloss, *Families of Students with Disabilities* (Boston: Allyn & Bacon, 1994), pp. 143–176.

youngsters with disabilities receive a free, appropriate public education, which emphasizes special education and related services designed to meet their unique needs. All students between the ages of 3 and 21 are eligible for a program of special education and related services under Part B of the IDEA; children with disabilities from birth through age three are eligible for special education and related services under Part C. Part C, which is a subchapter of the IDEA, is about infants and toddlers with disabilities.

The law provides for early intervention services that meet the developmental needs of children and their families, including physical development, cognition, language, social, and self-help skills. Parents and families play an important role, and an individualized program plan must be designed to meet their needs. This program plan, called the Individualized Family Service Plan (IFSP), should provide a coordinated array of services, including the following:

- Screening and assessment
- Psychological assessment and intervention
- Occupational and physical therapy
- Speech, language, and audiology
- Family involvement, training, and home visits
- Specialized instruction for parents and the target student
- Case management
- Health services that may be needed to allow the student to benefit from the intervention service

See Apply the Concept 5.11 for an overview of family involvement in special education.

Apply the Concept 5.11

Family Involvement in the Special Education Process

The chart presents an overview of the special education process for families. It covers issues from the time a child is referred for evaluation through the development of the IEP for the child. It shows how to share information between schools and families or how families can participate in the process.

Family

```
┌──────────────────────────────────────────────────────────┐
│ Families or school district staff or others request an   │
│ evaluation: In this stage, written consent from parents  │
│ or guardians is needed.                                   │
└──────────────────────────────────────────────────────────┘
                            ↓
┌──────────────────────────────────────────────────────────┐         ┌──────────────┐
│ Evaluation and eligibility decision: Families are        │    →    │ Not eligible │
│ introduced to the team process at this point. It is      │         └──────────────┘
│ important to provide evaluation information thoroughly    │
│ because this information is the basis for developing      │
│ the IEP.                                                  │
└──────────────────────────────────────────────────────────┘
                            ↓
              ┌────────────────────────────────┐
              │ Eligible for special education │
              └────────────────────────────────┘
                            ↓
┌──────────────────────────────────────────────────────────┐         ┌──────────────────┐
│ IEP is developed and placement is determined: Not only   │    →    │ Parents/guardians│
│ recommendations by professionals but also the family's   │         │ disagree         │
│ willingness are important in this process. Parents/      │         └──────────────────┘
│ guardians have a right to attend IEP meetings and        │
│ participate in the development of the IEP. Their          │
│ agreement is needed.                                      │
└──────────────────────────────────────────────────────────┘
                            ↓
              ┌────────────────────────────────┐
              │ Parents/guardians agree        │
              └────────────────────────────────┘
                            ↓
┌──────────────────────────────────────────────────────────┐
│ Annual IEP meeting: Families and professionals need to   │
│ meet regularly to share information about progress.      │
│ There is an annual IEP meeting to examine the process    │
│ and revise the IEP if necessary. Families may require    │
│ certain services.                                         │
└──────────────────────────────────────────────────────────┘
```

Criteria for Establishing an IFSP

The IFSP is a family-oriented approach to designing an effective management plan for the student with disabilities. The IFSP must be developed by a multidisciplinary team and should include the following elements:

- A description of the student's level of functioning across the developmental areas: physical, cognitive, communication, social or emotional, and adaptive
- An assessment of the family, including a description of the family's strengths and needs as they relate to enhancing the development of the child with disabilities
- A description of the major goals or outcomes expected for the child with disabilities and the family (as they relate to providing opportunities for the student)
- Procedures for measuring progress, including a timeline, objectives, and evaluation procedures
- A description of natural environments in which the early intervention services will be provided
- A description of the early intervention services needed to provide appropriate help for the child and family
- Specifically when the specialized intervention will begin and how long it will last
- A designated case manager
- A specific transition plan from the birth-to-three program into the preschool program

Family Education Programs

In a review of family involvement programs for families of children with learning disabilities, the two types of programs that were most frequently provided for families were counseling and tutoring (Shapero and Forbes, 1981). Overall findings indicated that family involvement programs can have positive effects on the academic performance of students with learning disabilities. Providing organized family programs may help some families of children with learning and behavior problems, when these programs are interactive and take advantage of the knowledge and needs of the participants.

One simple procedure that involves families in their child's education is described in Apply the Concept 5.12.

A number of variables influence the success of adults with learning disabilities, including parental factors. The educational and economic levels of the parents significantly influence the likelihood that children with learning disabilities will have good jobs that pay well (O'Connor and Spreen, 1988).

Waggoner and Wilgosh (1990) interviewed eight different families about their experiences and concerns regarding having a child with learning disabilities. The results of these interviews elucidated several common themes, including parental involvement in the child's education, parents' relationship with the school, support for the parents, social concerns for the child, concerns about the child's future, emotional strains of parenting, and the effects on the family. The interviews indicated that parents needed to be willing to help the child at home with schoolwork and to interact frequently with the school to serve as an advocate for their child. Although all of the parents reported at least one positive experience with teachers and the schools, seven out of eight of the parents also reported negative experiences. These negative experiences revolved around teachers feeling not

Apply the Concept 5.12

Pairing Teacher Praise Notes with Family Praise

Imber, Imber, and Rothstein (1979) found that pairing teacher praise notes with family praise regarding the note was effective in producing improvement in their children's academic performance. After praise notes from the teacher were sent home, families were asked to do the following:

1. Read the note and praise the child as soon as possible.
2. Praise the child in front of others in the family.
3. Place the note where others can see it.
4. Express to the child the hope that the child will receive another such note.

only that the child did not have a "real" problem, but also that the child was just not performing as well as he or she could.

Response to Intervention and Family Involvement

Families have an important role to play when schools implement response to intervention (RTI). This model provides new challenges and opportunities for engaging and communicating with families about their children's progress. Technically, most of what occurs within an RTI model occurs within general education, so questions can arise about when and how to communicate effectively with families.

First, many families may neither know what RTI is nor understand why their child is being screened for learning difficulties. Second, families value knowing if their child is receiving secondary or tertiary interventions and having access to the findings from progress monitoring. Third, teachers can assist families by providing them with a list of sample questions they might want to ask about RTI. An excellent source of information for parents about RTI is the National Center for Learning Disabilities (www.LD.org).

Response-to-Intervention: Ten Questions Parents Should Ask

As states and school districts work to implement an RTI process that provides early help to struggling students, families need to understand the components essential to the appropriate implementation of RTI. Here are ten questions to ask about RTI to help guide you through the process.

1. Is the school district currently using an RTI process to provide additional support to struggling students? If not, do they plan to?
2. What screening procedures are used to identify students in need of intervention?
3. What are the interventions and instructional programs being used? What research supports their effectiveness?
4. What process is used to determine the intervention that will be provided?
5. What length of time is allowed for an intervention before determining if the student is making adequate progress?
6. What strategy is being used to monitor student progress? What are the types of data that will be collected and how will student progress be conveyed to parents?
7. Is a written intervention plan provided to parents as part of the RTI process?
8. Is the teacher or other person responsible for providing the interventions trained in using them?
9. When and how will information about a student's performance and progress be provided?
10. At what point in the RTI process are students who are suspected of having a learning disability referred for formal evaluation?

FOCUS Question 5. What is the role of the special education teacher as a consultant to general education teachers, and what are the considerations and barriers for successful inclusion?

Working with Other Professionals

Consulting and communicating with professionals is an important task for teachers of students with learning and behavior problems. Teachers need to develop and maintain contact with the school psychologist, counselor, speech/language therapist, physical therapist, occupational therapist, principal, and other related professionals. Because 90 percent of all students with learning and behavior disorders are included for all or part of the day, a positive, cooperative working relationship with general classroom teachers may be most important of all.

Communication with General Education Teachers

Peters and Austin (1985) describe the characteristics of a leader and a nonleader. Many of these characteristics are important for special education teachers, as they often serve as team leaders who are working to develop the best programs for students with special needs. Table 5.1 lists these characteristics.

When a student with a learning or behavior problem is placed in the regular classroom, there are several steps the special education teacher can take to communicate effectively with the general education teacher:

1. Describe the type of learning or behavior problem the child has and some general guidelines for how to deal with it in the regular classroom.

TABLE 5.1

Characteristics of Leaders and Nonleaders	
Leaders	**Nonleaders**
Appeal to the best in each person	Give orders to staff—expect them to be carried out
Think of ways to make people more successful; look for ways to reinforce them	Think of personal rewards or how they look to others
Schedule frequent, short meetings to touch base	Meet infrequently with coworkers
Good listeners	Good talkers
Notice what's going well and improving	Only notice what's going wrong
Available	Hard to reach
Persistent	Give up
Give credit to others	Take credit
Consistent and credible	Unpredictable
Never divulge a confidence	Cannot be trusted with confidences
Make tough decisions	Avoid difficult decisions
Treat teachers and students with respect	Treat others as if they don't matter

Source: Adapted from T. Peters and N. Austin, *A Passion for Excellence* (New York: Random House, 1985).

2. Provide a copy of the child's IEP to the classroom teacher, and discuss the goals, objectives, special materials, and procedures needed.
3. Describe the progress reports you will be providing to the home and putting in your files.
4. Develop a schedule for regular meetings, and discuss other times that both the classroom teacher and special teacher are available for meetings.
5. Ask the classroom teacher how you can help, and describe the special accommodations that are needed.

In addition to communicating with teachers, there are a number of other services that the special education teacher can provide to facilitate inclusion. These services include providing inservice education on special education procedures or methods, bringing in guest speakers to discuss relevant topics, writing newsletters, and developing teacher assistance teams. Even when special education teachers develop and maintain an effective communication program with general education teachers, there are still a number of potential barriers to successful inclusion:

1. *The general education teacher may feel unable to meet the needs of the included student with disabilities.* Ms. Huang has been teaching second grade for two years. When she was informed that Omar,

a student who has been identified as having an emotional disorder, was going to be included in her general education classroom for several hours each morning, she panicked. She explained to the principal that she had not taken any coursework in special education and did not feel able to meet the needs of the new student. The special education teacher met with Ms. Huang to describe Omar's behavior and explain the progress he was making. She assured Ms. Huang that Omar would be carefully monitored and that she would check with Omar and Ms. Huang daily at first and then less frequently as he adapted to the new setting and schedule. She asked Ms. Huang to explain what types of activities usually occurred during the time Omar would be in her room, and she identified ways for Ms. Huang to be successful with Omar. The special education teacher took careful notes and asked many questions about Ms. Huang's expectations so that she could prepare Omar before his transition to the regular classroom. In this situation, communication that provided specific information about the student's learning problems and what the classroom teacher could do to ensure a successful learning environment proved most helpful. In addition, the special education teacher obtained expectations about the general education classroom so that she could best prepare the student for the transition.

2. *The general education classroom teacher may not want to work with the included student with disabilities.* Mr. Caruffe, a seventh-grade science teacher, expected all students to perform the same work at the same time, with no exceptions. He was particularly opposed to having special education students in his classroom because he felt that they required modifications to his core program. His philosophy was "If students need modifications, they don't belong in the general education classroom, they belong in special education." Dealing with teachers like Mr. Caruffe can be particularly challenging for special education teachers. Despite continuous attempts to work out a collaborative effort, educational philosophies can be sufficiently different that special education teachers feel it is hopeless to attempt inclusion in certain classrooms. Problems arise when alternative classrooms are not available without reducing the content areas available to special students. If there are multiple teachers for each content area, students may be included into classes where teachers are more accepting. Principals can help by setting a school policy that rewards teachers for working appropriately with pupils who have learning and behavior problems.

In a survey of elementary, middle, and high school teachers (Schumm and Vaughn, 1992a, 1992b), the majority of teachers indicated that they felt unprepared to meet the needs of special education students but were willing to have them in their classrooms. This suggests that special education teachers need to work closely with other teachers to improve their knowledge, skills, and confidence.

3. *Finding time to meet regularly with all classroom teachers is difficult.* At the elementary level, special education teachers meet regularly with all classroom teachers who have students included for all or part of the day. This consultation includes discussing students' progress, planning students' programs, adapting instruction in the general classroom, and solving immediate academic and social problems with students. It is better to meet weekly with classroom teachers for a short period of time (10 to 15 minutes) than to meet less often for longer periods of time. When classroom teachers and their students perceive the special education room as a resource rather than a closed room for special students, they have positive perceptions of the teacher and of the students who attend (Vaughn and Bos, 1987).

At the secondary level, continued involvement with all classroom teachers is a challenge. In large schools, the exceptional students' general education classroom teachers vary within content area and by year. It is possible for special education teachers to have over 25 teachers with whom they consult. Special education teachers manage this by meeting with teachers in small groups. Sometimes they organize these groups by content area to discuss successful adaptations made within a common content. Sometimes meetings are organized to focus on the needs of a particular student, and all teachers who work with this student meet at the same time. Finding time and maintaining contact with general education teachers requires creativity and persistence.

4. *Students may not be accepted socially by peers in the general education classroom.* This problem occurs not just with students who have behavior problems, but also with students who have learning disabilities. Placing students in classrooms where their peers are displaying appropriate social behaviors does not mean that students with learning and behavior disorders will internalize and display these appropriate behaviors (Gresham, 1982). According to both general education and special classroom teachers, the skills most essential to success in the general education classroom are interacting positively with others, following class rules, and exhibiting proper work habits (Salend and Lutz, 1984). Following is a list of behaviors that are considered important by both general education and special educators for success in the general education classrooms:

- Follows directions
- Asks for help when appropriate
- Begins an assignment after the teacher gives the assignment to the class
- Demonstrates adequate attention
- Obeys class rules
- Tries to complete a task before giving up
- Doesn't speak when others are talking
- Works well with others
- Respects the feelings of others
- Refrains from cursing and swearing
- Avoids getting in fights with other students
- Plays cooperatively with others
- Respects the property of others
- Shares materials and property with others
- Refrains from stealing the property of others
- Tells the truth

Special education teachers may want to focus on teaching these behaviors before and during their transition to inclusion.

Working with Administrators

The principal is the instructional and administrative leader of the school. The principal's perceptions of and actions regarding special education will be conveyed to classroom teachers and will be reflected in the procedures that are established to handle students with learning and behavior problems. A supportive principal is the key to a supportive staff. When building principals view special education as nothing but a headache or additional paperwork, they convey this message to the staff. When principals view special education as an opportunity to provide necessary services to students with special needs, they convey this message. An effective relationship between the principal and the special education teacher promotes better programs for students and overall job satisfaction (Cheek and Lindsey, 1986).

Often, the principal serves as the leader and coordinator of services between general and special education. There are five activities that principals can perform to facilitate the role of special education in the school (Chalfant and Pysh, 1979, 1986).

1. *Set the tone.* The principal sets a tone that establishes the importance of developing effective and responsive programs for students with learning and behavior problems. Too few teachers view administrators as support personnel. Many special education teachers feel that they have to do as much as they can for students with little administrative support. In fact, many teachers state that they just wish administrators wouldn't get in the way; they have long since given up on getting support. Many special education teachers have found that a positive tone about special education can be obtained from building principals through informing and involving principals in special education achievements, not just problems; providing feedback about how special education is achieving child gains; soliciting family and community support; and developing good intervention programs that get school and district recognition.

2. *Reinforce teachers for developing programs that respond to the individual needs of students.* Principals can be effective agents for encouraging classroom teachers to develop programs that respond to the individual needs of the special students in their classrooms.

3. *Provide consultation time.* Principals can arrange staff schedules to provide programs for students with learning and behavior problems. The school psychologist, speech/language therapist, physical therapist, counselor, special education teacher, and other support staff can serve as consultants to regular classroom teachers.

4. *Provide inservice activities to staff.* Workshops, consultation, or lectures that focus on the needs of staff can enhance services to students with learning and behavior disorders.

5. *Organize school-based assistance teams.* School-based assistance teams can assist classroom teachers with all students who have learning and behavior problems, not just students identified to receive special education services. In fact, the school-based assistance teams (Chalfant and Pysh, 1993) were originally developed to assist in reducing unnecessary referrals for special education.

SUMMARY for Chapter 5

Effective and efficient management and communication are key aspects of good teaching, particularly in designing and implementing educational programs for students with learning and behavior problems. This chapter provided information about the management and communication responsibilities of special education teachers.

We also addressed issues related to collaborating with other professionals. Collaboration involves shared decision making among coequals who have a common interest. Because working collaboratively takes time, issues arise related to planning time and resources, and developing skills. These skills are needed not just by the special education teacher, but by other professionals in the school as well. This chapter provided suggestions and considerations to make coteaching and relationships with families and paraprofessionals more successful.

Because management and communication vary depending on the setting, we encourage you to visit several special education programs and speak with the teachers to familiarize yourself with different programs and settings for students with learning and behavior problems. This should help you envision how the information presented in this chapter can be used in school settings.

One of the most important roles for the special education teacher is communicating with families and professionals. Although most of the chapters in this book discuss strategies for improving teachers' skills in working directly with students who have learning and behavior disorders, this chapter focused on communicating effectively with the key people who interact with the student: families and professionals.

We presented several communication skills that teachers can use to facilitate effective interactions with families and professionals, such as mutual respect, trust, acceptance, effective listening, plain language, effective questioning, providing encouragement, keeping the focus of the conversation directed, and developing working alliances. Because teachers often work as consultants, they will also want to become skilled in interviewing. Effective interviewing skills include asking open questions, obtaining specifics, identifying problems, solving problems, and providing feedback.

We also identified practices for effectively communicating with families by better understanding their needs. Families play a critical role in the successful delivery of services to students with special needs. Although families may be aware that their child is different from peers, they often receive the identification of the learning or behavior disorder only from the school and are still unsure of what the actual problem is. In communicating with families, special education teachers play many critical roles. They disseminate knowledge about the disorder and communicate assessment and educational planning information to family members. They also communicate most frequently with family members about daily progress. Special education teachers assist families in readjusting the academic expectations they have for their child. In addition, special education teachers need to be aware of how families are adjusting to and interacting with their child. In this manner, these professionals can facilitate family adjustment as well as procedures for facilitating family member involvement in the placement and programming of their student.

The special education teacher's role in working with other professionals facilitates the success of students with disabilities in general education settings. Because the special education teacher serves as the primary consultant for the general education classroom teacher, effective two-way communication is necessary. Ways to facilitate useful communication in the inclusion process and barriers that may interfere with successful inclusion were discussed. In addition, special education teachers must establish effective working relationships with the school principal. This is especially important because the school principal often sets the tone in the building for the acceptance of students with special needs.

The role the special education teacher plays in facilitating effective communication with families and professionals is critical. Although teachers may be effective in providing the academic and social instruction their students require, unless they are equally effective in communicating with families and professionals, they will not be successful. The special education teacher spends relatively little time with the student in comparison to the time the student spends with others. A student's progress is ensured only when all people who interact with the student are working cooperatively to advance educational and social goals.

FOCUS Answers

FOCUS Question 1. What are some of the challenges of working in an inclusive classroom and working with general education teachers?

Answer: General education teachers have different levels of experience in working with other teachers and students with learning and behavioral problems. Furthermore, many students are not prepared for general education classrooms. Potential problems can be avoided if general education teachers know and use a variety of instructional strategies. This effort takes time and planning, and it can result in less content coverage within a given time frame. Special education teachers can facilitate inclusion by working closely with general education teachers; observing general education classrooms; simulating the academic and social demands of general education classrooms in the special education classroom; and assisting classroom teachers in adapting materials, instruction, and the instructional environment.

FOCUS Question 2. What are three major models for consultation and collaboration?

Answer: Special education teachers work with other professionals to develop systems that meet the needs of students with learning and behavioral problems within an individual school setting. Coteaching occurs when special education and classroom teachers provide instruction together in the general education classroom. Consultant teaching occurs when the special educator works with the classroom teacher to solve problems for students with disabilities in the general education classroom. Special education teachers also coordinate paraprofessionals who assist students with disabilities in the general education classroom. Teacher assistance teams (TAT) are school-based teams (including support professionals, classroom teachers, and administrators) that assist the classroom teacher in meeting individual students' instructional and behavior needs.

FOCUS Question 3. **What are the principles of communication, when are they likely to be used, and how can teachers of individuals with learning and behavior problems develop the interview skills needed to effectively communicate with parents and professionals?**

Answer: Teachers should take the time to build mutual trust, to accept others' points of view, to really listen to what families and other professionals say, to provide encouragement to family members and personnel who work with students with special needs, and to use straightforward language to explain information. In addition, teachers can learn more from personal communication by asking open-ended questions that solicit thorough responses. Teachers must also balance listening and responding to others with focusing the conversation or meeting. In this way, teachers develop a working alliance in which all members of the group have a common goal of developing an appropriate program for the student.

FOCUS Question 4. **What is the teacher's role in addressing the needs of the entire family, assisting families with activities that occur outside of school, and coordinating family involvement in school?**

Answer: Families have different issues and concerns; identifying and addressing the needs of the entire family is essential to assisting a student. Teachers can also assist families by attending to students even when they are not in school, such as providing resources for summer activities, guidelines for assisting students with homework or academic skills, and accessing support systems with other parents or organizations. Furthermore, teachers must be familiar with the laws regarding parent involvement in planning and placement conferences (IEP) for school-age children or in coordinating family services in an Individualized Family Service Plan (IFSP) for children from birth to age three. By valuing the parents' role in their child's education and by using the knowledge parents have about their child, teachers and families can work together to develop an appropriate educational program. Response to intervention practices provide a unique opportunity for schools and families to communicate and collaborate prior to referral, during screening and assessment, when secondary interventions are provided, and through examining data collected.

FOCUS Question 5. **What is the role of the special education teacher as a consultant to general education teachers, and what are the considerations and barriers for successful inclusion?**

Answer: Most students with behavior and learning problems are included in general education classes for some or all of the school day. Positive and cooperative working relationships between special education and general education teachers are essential to the success of students with special needs. Special educators provide information to classroom teachers regarding students' disabilities, academic and social functioning, goals, and progress toward goals. In addition, they schedule regular meeting times to consult with general education teachers. Finally, preteaching and supporting the use of skills associated with positive peer interactions can assist students with socialization when they are in general education classrooms.

THINKand APPLY

- Why are effective management and communication important for success as a special education teacher?
- Compare and contrast the TAT and collaboration in the schools models.
- What is collaboration, and what are some ways in which professionals can collaborate effectively?
- What are some of the resources professionals need to collaborate? How might these be obtained?
- What are some of the issues and dilemmas that occur when teachers coteach? How might they be resolved?
- How is collaborating with families and/or paraprofessionals similar to collaborating with general education teachers? How is it different?

- What are some reasons it is important for professionals to collaborate in an RTI model?
- What are the principles of communication that facilitate the communication process with families, teachers, and other professionals?
- What are the steps for conducting an effective interview?
- What are some of the needs of families of children with learning disabilities and behavior problems? How can you meet these needs?

APPLY the STANDARDS

 Council for Exceptional Children

1. Use the ideas presented in Chapter Five—such as consultation models, grouping arrangements, and scheduling—and your knowledge of the relevant CEC standards (BD4K2, BD10K3, LD4K2, LD7K2, LD10K1) to describe how you might overcome the potential challenges of inclusion and coteaching to benefit students with disabilities and those with emotional/behavioral disorders in various settings.

   Standard BD4K2: Advantages and limitations of instructional strategies and practices for teaching individuals with emotional/behavioral disorders.

   Standard BD10K3: Collaborative and consultative roles of the special education teacher in the reintegration of individuals with emotional/behavioral disorders.

   Standard LD4K2: Methods for ensuring individual academic success in one-to-one, small group, and large group settings.

   Standard LD7K2: Sources of specialized curricula, materials, and resources for individuals with learning disabilities.

   Standard LD10K1: Coplanning and coteaching methods to strengthen content acquisition of individuals with learning disabilities.

2. How can effective communication with parents and professionals assist you in identifying the needs of, planning for, providing appropriate interventions for, and assessing students with learning or behavior problems (BD4K4, LD4S1, LD7K3, CC878)?

   Standard BD4K4: Prevention and intervention strategies for individuals at risk of emotional/behavioral disorders.

   Standard LD4S1: Use research-supported methods for academic and nonacademic instruction of individuals with learning disabilities.

   Standard LD7K3: Interventions and services for children who may be at risk for learning disabilities.

   Standard CC878: Evaluate instruction and monitor progress of individuals with exceptional learning needs.

WEBSITES as RESOURCES to Assist in Facilitating Communication and Collaboration with Families and Other Professionals

The following Websites are extensive resources to expand your understanding of facilitating communication with families and professionals:

- Targeting Home-School Collaboration for Students with ADHD www.ldonline.org/ld_indepth/add_adhd/tec_home_school_collab.html
- What You Need to Know About Special Education http://specialed.about.com/education/specialed/library/weekly/blswchwaub2.htm?terms=collaboration
- Helping Children Succeed in School www.urbanext.uiuc.edu/succeed/09-communication.html
- Parental Involvement www.ed.gov/legislation/ESEA/Title_I/parinv.html
- The ABCDEs of Co-Teaching www.ldonline.org/ld_indepth/teaching_techniques/tec_coteaching.html
- Thinking about Inclusion and Learning Disabilities: A Teachers Guide www.ldonline.org/ld_indepth/teaching_techniques/dld_ecologies.html
- Caring Community: Collaborative Teams www.ualberta.ca/~jpdasddc/index.html
- OnWEAC: Special Education Inclusion www.weac.org/resource/june96/speced.htm
- Project Choices www.projectchoices.org/faq.aspx

Where the Classroom Comes to Life

Article Homework Exercise Go to MyEducationLab and select the following topic: "INCLUSIVE PRACTICES." Then read the article "Making Inclusive Education Work" and complete the activity questions below.

This article describes how to make inclusion successful using both systems-level support and classroom-level strategies.

1. What are the challenges of working in an inclusive classroom?
2. Describe several ideas from the chapter and the article that you see as pertinent to making inclusion and co-teaching effective.

Video Homework Exercise Go to MyEducationLab and select the topic "COLLABORATION, CONSULTATION, AND CO-TEACHING," then watch the video "The Inclusive Classroom," and complete the activity questions below.

Special education teacher Penny Brandenburg teaches language arts collaboratively with the regular education teacher to a class that includes some students with special needs. In this video clip we see Penny providing assistance to students in the general education classroom. After the lesson, she meets with her mentor and the regular education teacher to discuss the lesson.

1. Describe the roles of the general education and the special education teacher in the video. How can these roles benefit students?
2. How does the special education teacher provide assistance to students with special needs in this classroom?

Video Homework Exercise Go to MyEducationLab and select the topic "COLLABORATION, CONSULTATION, AND CO-TEACHING," then watch the video "The Collaborative Process," and complete the activity questions below.

A classroom teacher works with the special needs teacher to provide help for students who need it. They provide a good example of collaboration.

1. Describe the effective principals of communication outlined in the chapter that are demonstrated in this video.
2. In what ways do the students in this video benefit from having these two teachers plan the lesson together?

Video Homework Exercise Go to MyEducationLab and select the following topic: "PARENTS AND FAMILIES." Then watch the video "Parents as Child Advocates" and complete the activity questions below.

This video demonstrates the importance of parents as advocates for their students with disabilities. Parents are able to help teachers get to know their child both as a student and as a member of their family.

1. What can teachers and the IEP team gain from involving families in the education of their students with special needs?
2. What recommendations would you give to parents to increase their participation in their children's education planning?

Article Homework Exercise Go to MyEducationLab and select the topic "COLLABORATION, CON-SULTATION, and CO-TEACHING," then read the article "Common Space, Common Time, Common Work," and complete the activity questions below.

Teachers at a rural high school found collegial interaction to be the most valued means of support. This article describes how the school used every day structures to increase interaction and planning among teachers.

1. Describe how common space, common time, and common tasks supported collaboration in the article.

2. Identify several areas in which special education teachers and other professionals can benefit from successful collaboration.

Chapter 6

Assessing and Teaching
Oral Language

As you read the chapter, watch for these questions to help you focus your learning:

1. What are the two main areas of language delays, and how do they manifest themselves in the development of content, form, and use of language?

2. What are some examples of strategies that can be used to teach oral language, content, form, and use, and how would each strategy support language development?

3. What are the strategies and considerations on which teachers should focus when teaching culturally and linguistically diverse learners?

4. What is metalinguistics, and how can teachers use it to promote language development?

5. How can special education teachers work with language specialists to implement RTI?

6. Why is it important to work with families to develop students' language skills, and what are some examples of activities in which families can engage with their children?

Malik is a second grader who is good at sports. He seems bright until he talks. Whether he is having a conversation or trying to read, he has difficulty thinking of the right words. Yesterday he was trying to describe the work that he and his dad had done on his go-cart. He could not think of the words *screwdriver, hammer, sandpaper, wheels, axle, steering wheel,* and *engine.* Sometimes he tried to describe what he wanted to say; for example, when he could not think of *screwdriver,* he said, "It's the thing you use to put in things that are kind of like nails." Sometimes he can only think of a word that is similar to the word he is trying to say; for example, he said, "I was using the hitter to hit some nails." Malik also has trouble remembering words when he reads. He does not remember simple sight words and consequently has to resort to attempting to sound out the words. Often, the words he cannot remember are not phonetic (e.g., *come, are, was, very*), so his strategy is only somewhat useful. Malik is in a second-grade classroom, but he receives speech and language therapy for his language problems, and in addition to his core reading program, he receives tutoring support for his reading difficulties.

Monica is in fifth grade. If you just listen to her, you would not necessarily recognize that she has a language problem. Her vocabulary is adequate for a student her age, and she uses fairly sophisticated sentences. But Monica's language frequently seems to get her in trouble. Monica is growing up in a tough neighborhood, but she goes to school in a middle-class neighborhood across town. She has difficulty switching her language style to match the new context of the school. She continues to use the language she uses with friends, resulting in the interpretation that she is both arrogant and disrespectful to teachers. Monica also has other problems using language effectively. She has difficulty determining when a listener is not understanding what she is trying to explain. Instead of restating her point in another way, she continues with her description or explanation. When the listener asks her to clarify a point, Monica implies that the listener is stupid. She also does not take turns easily during conversations. She either monopolizes the conversation or expects the other person to do all the talking while she gives little feedback to indicate that she is listening. Consequently, Monica is perceived as a student with behavior problems, although there is no indication of any serious emotional problems. She sees her counselor once a week. However, this is really not enough. She has difficulty with reading and writing, and this influences her learning in social studies and science as well. In the last several months, the speech/language pathologist has been consulting with the counselor and Monica's teachers. They are working with Monica to help her use language more effectively and to vary it across contexts. Perhaps with all professionals working together, they will be able to eliminate some of the learning and behavior problems Monica is currently experiencing.

Antoine is a third grader with language delays. He started talking at age three and a half, and his language now seems more like that of a first grader. He began receiving speech and language therapy at age four. Although he is currently in a class for students with mild to moderate disabilities, he receives speech and language therapy for 30 minutes, four days a week. Antoine is delayed in all aspects of language. His vocabulary is limited, he uses simple sentence patterns, and he uses language primarily to obtain information and attention and to inform others of his needs. He rarely initiates a conversation, but he will carry on a conversation if the other person takes the lead. Mrs. Borman, his teacher, works closely with the speech/language pathologist to help ensure that Antoine is receiving the structured language programming he needs throughout the school day. One of Mrs. Borman's roles in this programming is to provide Antoine with many opportunities to practice and receive feedback on the skills he is learning in speech/language therapy.

As teachers, we will undoubtedly work with students like Malik, Monica, and Antoine. To assist these students in developing effective language and communication skills, we need to understand the *content of language instruction* and *strategies for teaching language.*

FOCUS Question | 1. What are the two main areas of language delays, and how do they manifest themselves in the development of content, form, and use of language?

Content of Language Instruction

Language is a vehicle for communicating our ideas, beliefs, and needs. It is "a code whereby ideas about the world are represented through a conventional system of arbitrary signals for communication" (Bloom and Lahey, 1978, p. 4). Language allows us to share our knowledge with others and organize the knowledge in our long-term memory so that we can retrieve it and use it to communicate.

The major purpose of language is communication. Both in school and in our society, language is a powerful resource. We use language to do the following:

- Maintain contact with others
- Facilitate learning to read
- Gain information
- Give information
- Persuade
- Accomplish goals
- Monitor our own behavior when we talk to ourselves

Language functions as an integral part of the communication process because it allows us to represent ideas by using a conventional code.

A person's ability to understand what is being communicated is referred to as *comprehension* or *receptive language,* whereas a person's ability to convey an intended message is referred to as *production* or *expressive language.* It is assumed that for the communication process to be effective a speaker and a listener will use the same code and know the same rules of language. You have probably had the experience of trying to explain a need to someone who speaks a different language. You probably found yourself using many more gestures than usual. This is because although your listener could not understand your verbal communication code, he or she could understand your nonverbal code (gestures).

Some students with learning or language problems also experience developmental delays in comprehension or receptive language. They frequently ask for information to be repeated or clarified. In school, these students have difficulties with the following:

- Following directions
- Hearing the sounds in words (phonemes)
- Blending and segmenting the sounds in words
- Understanding the meaning of concepts (particularly temporal and spatial concepts and technical or abstract concepts)
- Seeing relationships among concepts
- Understanding humor and figurative language
- Understanding multiple meanings
- Understanding questions (particularly "how" and "why" questions)
- Understanding less common and irregular verb tenses
- Understanding compound and complex sentences
- Realizing that they are not understanding what is being said

Students with language problems may also have delays in production or expressive language. Sometimes these students choose not to communicate as frequently as other students. Students

with delays in expressive language have difficulty with the following:

- Using correct grammar
- Using compound and complex sentences
- Thinking of the right word to convey the concept (word finding)
- Discussing abstract, temporal, or spatial concepts
- Changing the communication style to fit various social contexts
- Providing enough information to the listener (e.g., starting a conversation with "He took it to the fair," when *he* and *it* have not been previously identified)
- Maintaining the topic during a conversation
- Retelling narratives and past events
- Repairing communication breakdowns

Although some students with learning or language problems have difficulty with both receptive and expressive language, other students experience difficulty primarily with expressive language. Students who have only expressive language difficulties generally understand much more than they are able to communicate.

Relationship of Oral and Written Communication

We use language when we read, write, and communicate orally. In written communication, the writer is similar to the speaker in that the writer is responsible for sending a message. The reader is similar to a listener, whose job it is to interpret or construct the message. The relationship of speaking and listening to writing and reading is presented in Figure 6.1. Because both oral and written communication are language based, a student who is having difficulty in oral communication (e.g., understanding figurative language) will also have difficulty in written communication. For example, research consistently tells us that vocabulary knowledge is one of the best predictors of reading achievement (Bartlett, Brzustowicz, Flax, Hirsch, Realpe-Bonilla, and Tallal, 2003; Catts and Kamhi, 1999; Nagy, Berninger, Abbott, Vaughan, and Bermeulen, 2003). Furthermore, youngsters who have oral language difficulties in general or difficulties with grammatical knowledge are also at risk for reading disabilities (Catts, Fey, Tomblin, and Zhang, 2002). However, there are important differences between oral and written communication (Bunce, 1993). For example, in oral communication there is a dynamic shifting between the roles of speaker and listener. A

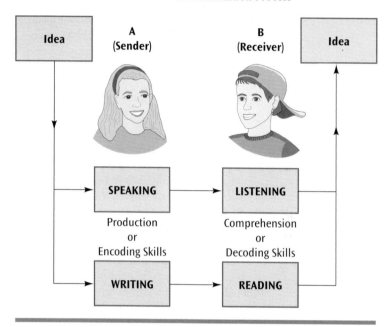

FIGURE 6.1

Relationship of Oral and Written Communication

A Model of the Communication Process

Source: Adapted from J. Lerner, *Learning Disabilities: Theories, Diagnosis, and Teaching Strategies*, 8th ed. (Boston: Houghton Mifflin, 2000), p. 344.

speaker can obtain immediate feedback from a listener. Consequently, the speaker can adjust the way in which a message is expressed (e.g., lower the vocabulary level, reexplain, or restate) more easily than the author can. This chapter presents methods for teaching students who have difficulty with oral communication; the next three chapters describe methods for teaching students who have difficulty with written communication (reading and writing). Some of the instructional ideas will be similar because of the underlying language base of both oral and written communication. In some instances, an instructional strategy that is suggested as a reading comprehension strategy can also be used as a listening or writing strategy (e.g., teaching students to ask themselves the questions Who? What? When? Where? Why? and How? as they read, write, speak, or listen). We encourage you to keep in mind the close relationship of oral and written communication as you read the next four chapters.

Components of Language

The content of language instruction for students with learning or language problems focuses on teaching the language code, the rules of the code, and how to use the code to communicate. To help us understand language so that we can more effectively plan the content of language instruction, we will consider several components of language.

Content

Content, also called *semantics*, refers to the ideas or concepts we are communicating. Keiko can communicate her desire for two chocolate-chip cookies in numerous ways. For example, she can say, "I want two chocolate-chip cookies" or "Me want choc-chip cookies" (while pointing to the cookie jar and then holding up two fingers). In both cases, the content or ideas are the same.

When we teach content, we are teaching concepts and helping students to learn the labels (vocabulary) for those concepts. When a young child asks such questions as What's that? or What are you doing? we often respond by giving the label for the object (e.g., spoon, blanket, shirt) or the action (i.e., stirring, making the bed, ironing). In this way, we are teaching the labels for the ideas or concepts.

We are also teaching content when we help students see the relationships among the ideas or concepts. The semantic network diagram of the concept of "bird," depicted in Figure 2.9 (on page 59) is one way to demonstrate how ideas are related. In that case, we used a network that represented the concept of "bird" in terms of its class, properties, and examples. Much of education, whether teaching about fruits and vegetables in primary grades or the characteristics of capitalism and communism in high school, centers on teaching about ideas, the relationships among the ideas, and the vocabulary that labels the ideas (Anders and Bos, 1986; Beck, McKeown, and Kucan, 2002; Bunce, 1993; Lenz and Bulgren, 1995; Reyes and Bos, 1998).

Form

Form refers to the structure and sound of language. In the example of Keiko wanting two chocolate-chip cookies, two different forms were presented for the underlying meaning of the message. Form is usually further divided into phonology, morphology, and syntax.

Phonology. Phonemes are the actual sounds produced by speakers. Phonemes are the smallest linguistic units of sound that can signal a meaning difference. In the English language, there are approximately 45 phonemes or speech sounds that are classified as either vowels or consonants (e.g., /a/, /k/, /ch/). Learning speech sounds and their relationships to the written letters can help students to identify unknown words when they read and

spell (Blachman, 2000; Catts and Kamhi, 1999; Wagner, Torgesen, and Rashotte, 1994). More information about speech sounds and letter–sound correspondence is provided in Chapter 7. Phonology refers to the rules for combining and patterning phonemes within the language. Phonology also includes the control of vocal features (timing, frequency, duration) that influence the meaning we express when talking. Without changing any words, we can vary the underlying meaning of a sentence simply by the way we change our voice (e.g., intonation, pitch, and stress). For example, try saying, "I like that?" and "I like that." Depending on the intonation, stress, and pitch, the first statement can mean "I don't like that," and the second one can mean "I do like that."

Morphology. Whereas phonology focuses on sounds, morphology focuses on the rule system that governs the structure of words and word forms. Whereas phonemes are the smallest sound units, morphemes are the smallest unit of language that conveys meaning. There are two different kinds of morphemes: root words or words that can stand alone (e.g., *cat, run, pretty, small, form*), and affixes (prefixes, suffixes, and inflectional endings) that are added to words that change the meaning of the words (e.g., *cats, rerun, smallest, transformation*).

Helping elementary and secondary students learn the various affixes and their meanings can assist them in decoding words, determining the meaning of words, and spelling. For example, students who do not recognize or know the meaning of the word *predetermination* can break it into the root word *determine* (to decide), the prefix *pre-* (before), and the suffix *-tion* (denoting action in a noun). Then the students can decode or spell the word and generate the meaning of *predetermination* as a decision made in advance.

Developmentally, inflectional endings are the easiest to learn, followed by suffixes and then prefixes (Owens, 2005; Rubin, 1988). Inflectional endings can be taught through conversational milieu; suffixes and prefixes usually require more formal instruction in both oral and written form (Moats, 1995). The most frequently used prefixes in American English are *un-, in-, dis-,* and *non-*. Table 6.1 presents some common prefixes, suffixes, and inflectional endings, along with their meanings and several examples. As you can see from the table, definitions of prefixes and suffixes are sometimes vague. Although only one or two definitions are provided in the table, some affixes have four or more definitions (Gunning, 2001). Teaching this information (or a simplified list for

TABLE 6.1

Common Inflectional Endings, Prefixes, and Suffixes

Common Forms	Meanings	Examples
Inflectional Endings		
-ed	notes past tense on verbs	helped, studied
-ing	notes present progressive on verbs	helping, studying
-s/-es	notes third person singular on verbs	he helps, she studies
-s/-es	notes plurals on nouns	cats, parties
-'s	notes possessive	Juan's, cat's
Prefixes		
ante-	before, front	antecedent, anterior
anti-	against	antifreeze, antitoxin
bi-	two	bicycle, bisect
co-	with, together	coworker, cooperate
de-	down, remove, reduce, do the opposite	descent, dethrone, devalue, deactivate
dis-	opposite	distrust, distaste
en-	to cover, to cause to be	encompass, enslave
ex-	former, from	expatriate, explain
hyper-	above, more, excessive	hyperactive, hyperventilate
hypo-	below, less	hypoactive, hypodermic
il-	not	illogical
im-	not, in, into	impatient
in-	not, in, into	incomplete, inclusion
inter-	between, together	interact, intervene
ir-	not, into	irreversible
mis-	wrong	miscalculate
non-	not	nonstop
out-	beyond, exceeds	outlast, outside
pre-	before, in front of	preface, precaution
pro-	before, in front of, in favor of	proceed, proactive
re-	again, backward motion	repeat, rewind
semi-	half	semifinalist
sub-	under, less than	subordinate, subtitle
super-	above, superior	superordinate
trans-	across, beyond	transportation
un-	not	unlucky, unclear
Suffixes		
-able	capable of, tendency to	dependable
-age	result of action or place	breakage, orphanage
-al	pertaining to	personal
-ance	changing an action to a state	hindrance
-ation	changing an action to a state	determination
-ant	one who (occupation)	accountant, attendant
-en	noting action from an adjective	harden, loosen
-ence	changing an action to a state	dependence, reference
-er/or	notes occupation or type of person	lawyer, writer, sculptor
-er	notes comparative (between two)	larger, younger

(continued)

TABLE 6.1

Common Inflectional Endings, Prefixes, and Suffixes   (continued)

Common Forms	Meanings	Examples
-est	notes superlative (among more than two)	largest, youngest
-ful	full of	bountiful, joyful
-fy	to make	magnify, identify
-ible	capable of, tendency to	credible, collectible
-ion/-tion	changing an action to a state	confusion, transformation
-ish	belonging to, characteristic of	Finnish, greenish
-ist	one who (occupation)	artist, biologist
-ive	changes action to characteristic or tendency	creative, active
-less	unable to, without	harmless, thoughtless
-ly	denotes adverbs	loudly, friendly
-ment	result of an action (noun)	entertainment, excitement
-ness	quality, state of being	happiness, deafness
-ous	full of, having	victorious, harmonious
-some	quality or state	handsome, bothersome
-ward	turning to	homeward, wayward
-y	characterized by, inclined to	dirty, sleepy

elementary-age students) can assist students in understanding and learning new vocabulary and in decoding unknown words. To give students a sense of the meanings, provide experiences with several examples. More ideas for teaching affixes are provided in Chapter 4.

Syntax. Syntax refers to the order of words in sentences and the rules for determining that order. Just as phonemes combine to form words, words combine to form phrases and sentences. In the same way that rules determine how phonemes can be combined, rules also determine how words can be combined. The basic syntactical structure for English is subject + verb + object (e.g., "Mike eats cereal").

The rules for combining words vary across languages. For example, in English, adjectives almost always precede the noun they modify (e.g., a delicious apple), whereas in Spanish, adjectives generally follow the noun they modify (e.g., *una manzana deliciosa*—"an apple delicious").

Use

Language use or pragmatics grows significantly during the school years (Nippold, 1998; Owens, 2005). *Pragmatics* refers to the purposes or functions of communication or how we use language to communicate (Roberts and Crais, 1989). During the school years, students become quite adept at using communication for a variety of functions. During the later school years, students use language proficiently with multiple meanings, employing figurative language, sarcasm, and jokes (Bernstein, 1986; Schultz, 1974). Students also learn to vary their communication style or *register* on the basis of a listener's characteristics and knowledge concerning the topic (Eckert, 1990; Nippold, 1998). By the age of 13, students can switch from peer register to adult register depending on the person with whom they are talking and from formal register to an informal register depending on the setting and circumstances (McKinley and Larson, 1991; Owens, 2005). Pragmatics for students in middle school is an important aspect of functioning within the classroom, because pragmatic skills are critical to academic progress and in building peer relationships (Brice and Montgomery, 1996).

The way a speaker uses language will also be influenced by the knowledge the speaker thinks the listener has about the topic being discussed. If you are describing how to hang a picture on a wall, the language you use will depend on whether you think the listener is familiar with a plastic anchor and screw. The manner in which a topic is introduced, maintained, and changes, as well as how we reference topics, is governed by rules of pragmatics. Students who are learning English as a second language and bilingual students with communication disorders may need explicit instruction in pragmatics.

FIGURE 6.2

Components of Language from a Functionalist Perspective

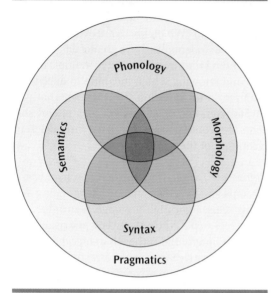

Formalist views of language have assumed that language is a composite of various rule systems consisting of semantics, phonology, morphology, syntax, and pragmatics. However, more recent views of language and language intervention have highlighted language as a social tool; in this view, pragmatics is viewed as the overall organizing aspect of language (Owens, 2005; Prutting, 1982). This model (see Figure 6.2) has direct implications for language intervention in terms of both targets for intervention and methods of intervention. An approach in which pragmatics is the overall organizing aspect calls for an interactive, conversational approach to teaching and one that mirrors the environment in which the language is to be used (Owens, 2005). This has been referred to as a *functional* or *holistic approach* to language intervention (Muma, 1986).

School-Age Language Development and Difficulties

Knowing how language develops during the school years and what difficulties students with learning or language problems demonstrate during these years will help us make decisions concerning the content and focus of language instruction.

Much of the research in language development has focused on the preschool child. Between the ages of birth to five, most children become amazingly facile with their language and communication (Brown, 1973; de Villiers and de Villiers,

1978; Owens, 2005). Because of the quantity and quality of development that occurs during this period, the preschool child has been the center of focus for most language researchers. However, the last 20 years has seen growing interest in the language development that takes place during the school years (Merritt and Culatta, 1998; Nippold, 1998; Wallach and Miller, 1988) and in the difficulties that students encounter with language in school settings (Bashir and Scavuzzo, 1992; Bunce, 1993; Johnson et al., 1999; Wiig, 1992). Bashir and Scavuzzo (1992) summarized the longitudinal research on school-aged children who have language disorders in the preschool years and noted that these children show changes in the type and severity of their language problems during the school-age years; the acquisition of language forms is the same as for nondisordered children but occurs more slowly; language problems persist for many of these children throughout childhood and adolescence; and additional language problems may develop in middle school when children are required to understand or produce more complex language, develop and understand narratives and expository text structures, and use language for higher-order thinking skills such as persuasion and interpretation.

Knowing about school-age language development is particularly important for teachers of students who have reading problems. There is growing evidence to suggest that many of these students have mild to moderate language problems (Gerber, 1993; Johnson et al., 1999; Nelson, 1998; Rubin, Patterson, and Kantor, 1991; Sanger, Maag, and Shapera, 1994; Wiig and Wilson, 1994). The largest subgroup of students with learning disabilities are those who experience language difficulties (Simon, 1985; Wiig and Secord, 1998).

Although more research would be valuable to support a comprehensive scope and sequence for school-age language development, there is enough information to assist us in planning the content of language instruction. Let's examine the development of content, form, and use at the school-age level and the difficulties that students with learning or language problems demonstrate.

Content

During the school years, children increase the size of their vocabularies and their ability to understand and talk about abstract concepts.

Vocabulary Growth. During the school years, one of the areas in which students demonstrate the greatest amount of growth is vocabulary. When students enter school, their estimated speaking vocabulary is about 2,500 words (Owens, 2005). In comparison, when technical words are not counted, average adult speakers converse in everyday conversation using about 10,000 words, and the average high school graduate knows and uses an estimated 60,000 to 80,000 words (Carroll, 1964). School provides students with opportunities to listen, read, and learn, thus increasing their vocabularies. Even math, which is often considered less language-based than social studies and science, contains a significant number of concepts and words to learn (e.g., *subtract, estimate, rational number, trapezoid*).

There is also an increase in the breadth and specificity of meanings. For example, for a pre-schooler, the word *bird* may refer to any animal that flies. However, most children later learn a whole set of specific vocabulary that defines different types of birds and their characteristics. The semantic network that was depicted in Figure 2.9 (page 59) becomes increasingly complex and more interrelated as a student's knowledge of birds increases.

During the school years, students' abilities to understand and organize abstract concepts improve significantly (Anglin, 1970; Nippold, 1998). This results in the ability to group words by such abstract features as animate or inanimate, spatial (location) or temporal (time) relationships, and real or imaginary. For example, in learning about fossils, students learn to simultaneously classify different types of fossils (e.g., trilobites, crinoids, brachiopods) according to plant/animal, extinct/not extinct, and location (e.g., sea, lake, or land).

Multiple meanings of many common words are acquired during the school years (Menyuk, 1971; Nippold, 1998). For example, the word *bank* has several meanings and can function as a noun or a verb:

> Lou sat on the *bank* fishing.
> You can *bank* on him to be there.
> Put your money in the *bank* for now.

Students with language problems generally have vocabularies that are more limited than average, and their word meanings are generally more concrete and less flexible (Gerber, 1993; Wiig and Secord, 1998). For example, fifth-grade students with reading disabilities sometimes had difficulty considering three different characteristics of fossils simultaneously (Bos and Anders, 1990a). Questions such as "Which fossils are extinct sea animals?" required the students to juggle too much information. In comparison, they could easily answer questions for which they had to deal with only one characteristic at a time, for example, "Which fossils live in the sea?" "Which fossils are animals?" and "Which fossils are extinct?"

These students also have greater difficulty understanding that words can have multiple meanings and knowing which meaning to apply. For example, in the question "Was the *fare* that you paid for your taxi ride to the *fair* a *fair* price?" students are required to know and use three different meanings for the word *fair/fare*.

Figurative Language. During the school years, students also develop greater understanding and ability to use figurative language. Figurative language represents abstract concepts and usually requires an inferential rather than literal interpretation. Figurative language allows students to use language in truly creative ways (Owens, 2005). The primary types of figurative language include the following:

- Idioms (e.g., "It's raining cats and dogs.")
- Metaphors (e.g., "She had her eagle-eye watching for him.")
- Similes (e.g., "He ran like a frightened rabbit.")
- Proverbs (e.g., "The early bird catches the worm.")

Students with language disorders and other disabilities and students who are from other cultures or who have English as their second language tend to have difficulty with figurative language. Yet figurative language, particularly idioms, is used frequently in the classroom. Classroom research has shown that teachers use idioms in approximately 11 percent of their utterances and that third- to eighth-grade reading programs contain idioms in approximately 6.7 percent of their sentences (Lazar, Warr-Leeper, Nicholson, and Johnson, 1989). Table 6.2 presents some common American English idioms. Discussing and using these idioms and adding to the list can assist students with language disorders and second language learners in improving their understanding and use of the English language.

Word Retrieval. Some students with learning or language problems also experience difficulties with word retrieval or word finding (German, 1987, 1992; McGregor and Leonard, 1989; Nippold, 1998). A word retrieval problem is like having the word on the tip of your tongue but not quite being able to think of it. The following dialogue presents

TABLE 6.2
Common American English Idioms

Animals

a bull in a china shop
as stubborn as a mule
going to the dogs
playing possum
a fly in the ointment
clinging like a leech
grinning like a Cheshire cat

Body Parts

on the tip of my tongue
raised eyebrows
turn the other cheek
put your best foot forward
turn heads

Clothing

dressed to kill
hot under the collar
wear the pants in the family
fit like a glove
straitlaced

Colors

grey area
once in a blue moon
tickled pink
has a yellow streak

red-letter day
true blue

Games and Sports

ace up my sleeve
cards are stacked against me
got lost in the shuffle
keep your head above water
paddle your own canoe
ballpark figure
get to first base
keep the ball rolling
on the rebound
jockey for position

Foods

eat crow
humble pie
that takes the cake
a finger in every pie
in a jam

Plants

heard it through the grapevine
resting on his laurels
shrinking violet
no bed of roses
shaking like a leaf
withered on the vine

Tools and Work

bury the hatchet
has an axe to grind
hit the nail on the head
throw a monkey wrench
    into it
doctor the books
has a screw loose
hit the roof
nursing his wounds
sober as a judge

Vehicles

fix your wagon
like ships passing in the night
on the wagon
don't rock the boat
missed the boat
take a back seat

Weather

calm before the storm
haven't the foggiest
steal her thunder
come rain or shine
right as rain
throw caution to the wind

Source: R. E. Owens, Jr., *Language Disorders: A Functional Approach to Assessment and Intervention*, 2nd ed. (Boston: Allyn & Bacon, 1995), p. 347. Copyright © 1995 by Allyn and Bacon. Reprinted with permission. Compiled from Boatner, Gates, and Makkai (1975); Clark (1990); Gibbs (1987); Gulland and Hinds-Howell (1986); Kirkpatrick and Schwarz (1982); Palmatier and Ray (1989).

a conversation between 2 third-grade students—one with normal language and the other with word retrieval problems.

Setting: Third-grade classroom
Topic: Discussion about how to make an Easter basket

Susan: Are you going to make, uh, make, uh . . . one of these things [pointing to the Easter basket on the bookshelf]?
Cori: Oh, you mean an Easter basket?
Susan: Yeah, an Easter basket.
Cori: Sure, I'd like to, but I'm not sure how to do it. Can you help me?
Susan: Yeah, first you'll need some, uh, some, uh, the things you cut with, you know . . .
Cori: Scissors.
Susan: Yeah, and some paper and the thing you use to stick things together with.
Cori: Tape?
Susan: No, uh, uh, sticky stuff.
Cori: Oh, well let's get the stuff we need.
Susan: Let's go to, uh, uh, the shelf, uh, where you get, you know, the stuff to cut up.
Cori: Yeah, the paper, and let's also get the glue.

It is obvious from the conversation that both students were frustrated by the communication process. Susan's language is filled with indefinite words (*thing, stuff*), circumlocutions ("The things you cut with"), and fillers ("Let's go to, uh, the shelf, um, where you get, you know, the stuff to cut up"). At first, students like Susan may seem very talkative because of their overuse of descriptions, circumlocutions, and fillers (Swafford and Reed, 1986); however, after one listens to them for a while, their language seems empty of information.

Word retrieval or word-finding problems can result from two possible sources (Kail and Leonard, 1986). One source is with the storage, in that the student's understanding is not elaborate; in other words, the semantic network is not well developed, and the meaning is shallow (German, 1992). For example, when a student's semantic network for the concept "bird" (see Figure 2.9, page 59) is well developed, it will be easier to retrieve the word than if the semantic network is limited and the word has been learned in isolation. Therefore, in assisting students, it is important to help them develop more elaborate understandings of concepts. A second source of word-finding problems is with the retrieval or search and recovery of the word. In this case, teaching and providing cues (e.g., it's something you ride; peanut butter and _____; it's a type of bird) can assist in retrieval (Nippold,

1992, 1998; Wiig and Semel, 1984). Students with learning or language problems may have difficulty with word storage problems, word retrieval problems, or both (German, 1992; Johnson et al., 1999).

Form

During the school years, students continue to grow in their ability to use more complex sentence structures (Nippold, 1993, 1998; Scott and Stokes, 1995). Although by age five most students understand and generate basic sentences, first graders produce sentences that are neither completely grammatical ("He'll might go to jail") nor reflect the syntactical complexities of the English language. Table 6.3 presents the sequence for selected syntactical structures. Some of the most difficult structures require the use of complex sentences and cohesive devices such as causals (*because*), conditionals (*if*), and enabling relationships (*so that*).

TABLE 6.3

Developmental Sequence for Comprehension of Sentence Types

Syntactic Structure	Sentence	Age of Comprehension By 75%		By 90%
Simple imperative	Go!	4–6*	to	6–0 years
Negative imperative	Don't cross!	5–6	to	7–0+ years
Active declarative				
Regular noun and present progressive	The girl is jumping.	3–0	to	3–0 years
Irregular noun and present progressive	The sheep is eating.	6–6	to	7–0 years
Past tense	The man painted the house.	5–6	to	7–0+ years
Past participle	The lion has eaten.	6–0	to	7–0+ years
Future	He will hit the ball.	7–0	to	7–0+ years
Reversible	The car bumps the train.	6–6	to	7–0+ years
Perfective	The man has been cutting trees.	7–0+	to	7–0+ years
Interrogative				
Who . . .	Who is by the table?	3–0	to	3–0 years
What . . .	What do we eat?	3–6	to	5–0 years
When . . .	When do you sleep?	3–6	to	5–6 years
Negation				
Explicit	The girl isn't running.	5–6	to	7–0+ years
Inherent	These two are different.	6–6	to	7–0+ years
Reversible passive	The boy is chased by the dog.	5–6	to	6–0 years
Conjunction				
If . . .	If you're the teacher, point to the dog; if not, point to the bear.	7–0+	to	7–0+ years
. . . then	Look at the third picture; then point to the baby of his animal.	7–0+	to	7–0+ years
neither . . . nor	Find the one that is neither the ball nor the table.	7–0+	to	7–0+ years

*4–6 = 4 years, 6 months

Source: E. H. Wiig and E. Semel, *Language Assessment & Intervention for the Learning Disabled*, 2nd ed. (Columbus, OH: C. E. Merrill, 1984). Reprinted with permission of the senior author, Elizabeth H. Wiig, Ph.D., Knowledge Research Institute, Inc.

Another later-developing sentence structure involves passive construction ("The boy is chased by the dog"), which is usually not established until ages five to seven (Chomsky, 1969; Owens, 2005). What makes older students' language different from that of younger students in terms of form is the new arrangements and increasingly complex combinations of basic forms (Scott and Stokes, 1995).

As sentence complexity increases, so does the average length of sentences. Yet it is important to know that mature language still has some grammatical errors, false starts, hesitations, and revisions. Table 6.4 demonstrates the growth in the number of words per sentence or communication unit. As is evident in Table 6.4, spoken sentence length matches chronological age (i.e., an eight-year-old student's sentences are, on the average, eight words long) until the age of approximately nine years, when the growth curve begins to slow. By high school, adolescents' conversational utterances average 10 to 12 words (Nelson, 1998; Scott and Stokes, 1995). Average sentence length, however, is consistently shorter in conversational discourse than in narrative discourse (Leadholm and Miller, 1992).

Children also continue to increase in their ability to use inflectional endings, suffixes, prefixes,

TABLE 6.4

Average Number of Words per Communication Unit (mean)

Grade	High Group	Random Group	Low Group
1	7.91	6.88	5.91
2	8.10	7.56	6.65
3	8.38	7.62	7.08
4	9.28	9.00	7.55
5	9.59	8.82	7.90
6	10.32	9.82	8.57
7	11.14	9.75	9.01
8	11.59	10.71	9.52
9	11.73	10.96	9.26
10	12.34	10.68	9.41
11	13.00	11.17	10.18
12	12.84	11.70	10.65

Source: W. Loban, *Language Development: Kindergarten through Grade Twelve*, Res. Report #18 (Urbana, IL: National Council of Teachers of English, 1976), p. 27. Reprinted by permission of the publisher.

and irregular verbs. Table 6.5 presents the order of and age ranges for the acquisition of selected features. Students with language problems are slower

TABLE 6.5

Development of Word Formation Rules and Irregular Verbs

Word Formation Rules and Irregular Verbs	Age Range (in Years–Months)
Regular noun plurals (balls, chairs)	3–6 to 7–0+
Present progressive tense (running)	3–0 to 3–6
Present progressive tense (going)	3–6 to 5–6
Adjective forms	
Comparative (smaller, taller)	4–0 to 5–0
Superlative (shortest, tallest)	3–0 to 3–6
Noun derivation	
-er (hitter, painter, farmer)	3–6 to 6–6
-man (fisherman)	5–6 to 6–0
-ist (artist, bicyclist)	6–6 to 7–0+
Adverbial derivation (easily, gently)	7–0+
Irregular verbs	
went	4–6 to 5–0
broke, fell, took, came, made, sat, threw	5–0 to 6–0
bit, cut, drive, fed, ran, wrote, read, rode	6–0 to 7–0
drank, drew, hid, rang, slept, swam	7–0 to 8–0
caught, hung, left, built, sent, shook	8–0 to 9–0

Source: Adapted from E. Carrow, *Test of Auditory Comprehension of Language* (Austin, TX: Urban Research Group, 1973); K. Shipley, M. Maddox, and J. Driver (1991). Children's development of irregular past tense verb forms. *Language, Speech, and Hearing Services in Schools, 22*, pp. 115–112; E. H. Wiig and E. Semel, *Language Assessment and Intervention for the Learning Disabled*, 2nd ed. (Columbus, OH: C. E. Merrill, 1984).

to develop advanced syntactic structures; these delays are most evident in the elementary grades (Owens, 2005).

Use

The area of most important linguistic growth during the school years is language use or pragmatics, as discussed earlier in this chapter. Throughout the school years, students become more empathetic toward the listener and able to understand a variety of perspectives. Older children can vary their communication style or register, as we discussed earlier.

According to White (1975), young school-age children use language to do the following:

- Gain and hold adult attention in a socially acceptable manner.
- Use others, when appropriate, as resources for assistance or information.
- Express affection or hostility and anger appropriately.
- Direct and follow peers.
- Compete with peers in storytelling and boasts.
- Express pride in themselves and in personal accomplishments.
- Role-play.

By adolescence, students reflect communicative competence (Fujiki, Brinton, and Todd, 1996; Owens, 2005; Wiig and Semel, 1984) in that they can do the following:

- Express positive and negative feelings and reactions to others.
- Present, understand, and respond to information in spoken messages related to persons, objects, events, or processes that are not immediately visible.
- Take the role of another person.
- Understand and present complex messages.
- Adapt messages to the needs of others.
- On the basis of prior experience, approach verbal interactions with expectations of what to say and how to say it.
- Select different forms for their messages on the basis of the age, status, and reactions of the listeners.
- Use sarcasm and double meanings.
- Make deliberate use of metaphors.

Some students with learning or language problems also experience difficulties with language *use* or pragmatics (Brinton, Fujiki, and McKee, 1998; Owens, 2005). The following dialogue demonstrates how Brice, an adolescent with behavior disorders and subsequent learning problems,

has difficulty using language effectively in a conversation with a peer. He tends to switch topics (lack of topic maintenance), does not provide enough context for his listener, does not provide adequate referents for his pronouns, and does not respond to his listener's requests for clarification. In addition, Brice is unaware of his failure to communicate effectively and blames his conversational partner for communication breakdowns.

Setting: Computer lab
Topic: Brice is explaining to Reid how to play a computer game.

Brice: Did you get in trouble for last night?
Reid: What do you mean for last night?
Brice: You know, for what you did.
Reid: I'm not sure what you're talking about.
Brice: Want to learn how to play Chopperlifter?
Reid: Yeah, I guess, but what about last night?
Brice: Well, one thing you do is put it in the slot and turn on the computer.
Reid: What thing? Do you mean the CD?
Brice: Sure I do. Now watch. *Brice boots the CD and selects Chopperlifter from a game menu.* You got to take it and go pick up the men.
Reid: You mean the helicopter?
Brice: Yeah, aren't you listening?
Reid: Yeah, but you're not telling me enough about the game.
Brice: Yes I am. You're just like my brother, you don't listen.
Reid: I'm not going to put up with this. I'll see you around.

Although this is not reflected in the language sample, Brice also has difficulty varying his language for different audiences. Like other students with pragmatic language problems (Kuder, 1997; Nelson, 1998; Sanger, Maag, and Shapera, 1994), he sometimes sounds disrespectful to adults because he does not vary his language to suit different speakers or contexts. Finally, Brice and other students with pragmatic language difficulties, including students with behavior disorders, tend to misinterpret emotions or meanings indicated by nonverbal communication, including facial expressions and body language, more frequently than their normal peers do (Brinton and Fujiki, 1999; Fujiki et al., 1996; Giddan, Bade, Rickenberg, and Ryley, 1995; McDonough, 1989).

However, it is important to remember that content, form, and use are related. Sometimes students who appear to have difficulties with language use have them because of limited content and form. For these students, it is important to focus instruction in the areas of content and form and find out whether language use automatically improves.

Wrap-Up

Even though students enter school with numerous language skills already mastered, there are still numerous skills that develop during the school years. Students' vocabulary grows significantly in breadth, size, and abstractness. They learn to use and control more difficult sentence structures, such as compound, complex, and passive sentences, and they learn to use more complex figurative language, prefixes, suffixes, and inflectional endings. Students' uses for language expand, and their ability to communicate increases as they become more aware of listeners and their needs in the communication process. In short, language development in the areas of content, form, and use increases measurably during the school years. This process happens almost automatically for most students because of the opportunities that school and expanding environments afford for learning language. Students with learning or language problems, however, are often delayed in this development and require more explicit instruction. We will now focus on the procedures for language instruction.

| FOCUS |
| Question | 2. **What are some examples of strategies that can be used to teach oral language, content, form, and use, and how would each strategy support language development?**

Guidelines for Teaching Language

In teaching students with learning or language problems, teachers have traditionally focused on teaching academic skills and have placed less emphasis on the development of oral language skills. However, it is clear that language continues to develop during the school years and that students with reading problems show difficulties in oral language that affect oral as well as written communication (Cooper, Roth, Schatschneider, and Speece, 2002). Let's look at some general principles and

procedures for teaching oral language skills to these students.

General Guidelines for Teaching Oral Language

Opportunities for teaching oral language abound in the school setting. When we teach students new concepts and vocabulary in content area subjects, we are teaching oral language. When students learn how to give oral reports or retell a story, how to introduce themselves, or how to use irregular verbs, they are learning language. A list of general procedures or guidelines for teaching language to students with learning problems is presented in Figure 6.3 and discussed in this section. The principles can serve as guidelines for teaching. The speech/language pathologist is a good source for additional guidelines, techniques, and teaching ideas.

Teach Language in Purposeful Contexts

Whether a teacher is teaching a student to use causal relationships (form), to categorize fossils (content), or how to use the telephone to request information (use), it is important to teach language in context. It is difficult to imagine teaching someone how to use a hammer, drill, or saw without using nails, boards, and probably the goal of making a simple wood project. The same should apply in teaching students to use language. Rote practice of sentence structures or rehearsal of word definitions will teach the student little unless this is paired with how to use language.

FIGURE 6.3

General Principles for Teaching Language

- Teach language in purposeful contexts.
- In most cases, follow the sequence of normal language development.
- Teach comprehension and production.
- Use conversations to promote language development.
- Adjust pacing, chunk information, and check for understanding to promote comprehension.
- Increase wait time to promote production.
- Use effective teaching strategies when presenting a new concept or skill.
- Use self-talk and parallel talk to describe what you and others are doing or thinking.
- Use modeling to demonstrate language.
- Use expansion and elaboration.
- Use structured language programs to provide intensive practice and feedback.
- Use language as an intrinsic motivator.
- Systematically plan and instruct for generalization.

To foster teaching language in context, the teacher should plan activities that highlight the language skill being taught. For example, Mr. Cardoni used the contexts of following a recipe for chocolate-chip cookies and of building bird feeders to teach the vocabulary related to fractions (e.g., half, one-quarter, two-thirds, part, whole, fraction). During the activities, the students measured and compared the different fractional parts (e.g., determining what fraction one teaspoon is of one tablespoon). This allowed Mr. Cardoni and his students to talk about the concepts of fractions in a situation in which fractions played an important role in the project and to demonstrate with concrete examples the differences between fractions.

In Most Cases, Follow the Sequence of Normal Language Development

Determining the content of instruction is a major part of the teaching–learning process, whether it be in language, academics, content areas, or social areas. Although the developmental sequence of language skills for students with learning disabilities is not well documented, there is some evidence to suggest that these students develop language knowledge and skills in the same sequence as students who are normal achievers, but at a slower rate (Kamhi, 1999; Nelson, 1998; Nippold, 1998; Wiig and Semel, 1984). They may also have more difficulty in one component of language—content, form, or use. For example, Susan, the third grader with word-finding problems (see page 203) has difficulty primarily in the area of content. On the other hand, Brice (see page 206) appears to have adequate content and form in his language but has difficulty with use. Therefore, in planning a language program, begin by determining what knowledge and skills a student has already acquired in the areas of content, form, and use, and then target the subsequent areas in the development process. For instance, if the student is already using past tense ("The boy ate the cake"), you might next focus on past participle ("The boy has eaten the cake") (see Table 6.3). A speech/language pathologist can be an excellent resource for helping to determine what to teach next.

Teach Comprehension and Production

Be sure to give students opportunities to develop both their understanding (comprehension) and their ability to express (production) the new knowledge or skill you are teaching. For example, when teaching students to comprehend the past participle, a teacher should label examples of

FIGURE 6.4

Sequence Cards to Help Students Comprehend and Produce Tenses

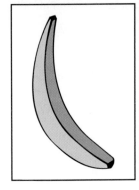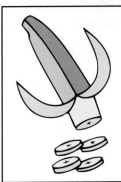

events that have already happened (e.g., "Juan has sharpened his pencil" or "Kim has finished her math assignment"). When providing intensive practice and feedback, the teacher could show the students picture-sequence cards (see Figure 6.4) and have the students identify the picture that demonstrates that something "has happened." To teach production, have the students explain what has happened by using the past participle form. For example, the teacher could ask, "What have you just done?" When teaching the concepts and vocabulary associated with a new unit or piece of literature, the teacher should provide students with opportunities not only to listen to explanations but also to discuss their knowledge of the concepts. Using the pause procedure (Di Vesta and Smith, 1979; Ruhl, Hughes, and Gajar, 1990) provides such opportunities. The teacher pauses at logical breaks in the lecture or discussion and lets students discuss what they are learning with a partner or in a small group.

Use Conversations to Promote Language Development

Students with language problems need opportunities to engage in conversations. Observational research has shown that teachers, in general, are not as responsive to students with language problems as they are to average- and high-achieving students (Pecyna-Rhyner, Lehr, and Pudlas, 1990). Plan opportunities for students to engage in conversations with you and other students as they work, think, and play. Using discussion groups rather than a question–answer format for reviewing a book or current event is an example of how conversations can be integrated into the classroom. During conversations, let the students

Apply the Concept 6.1

Promoting Language through Conversations

- Talk about things in which the child is interested.
- Follow the child's lead. Reply to the child's initiations and comments. Share the child's excitement.
- Don't ask too many questions. If you must, use questions such as *how did/do . . . , why did/do . . . ,* and *what happened . . .* that result in longer explanatory answers.
- Encourage the child to ask questions. Respond openly and honestly.
- Use a pleasant tone of voice. You can be light and humorous.

- Children love it when adults are a little silly.
- Don't be judgmental or make fun of a child's language. If you try to catch and correct all errors, the child will stop talking to you.
- Allow enough time for the child to respond.
- Treat the child with courtesy by not interrupting when the child is talking.
- Provide opportunities for the child to use language and to have that language work to accomplish his or her goals.

- Include the child in family and classroom discussions. Encourage participation and listen to his/her ideas.
- Be accepting of the child and of the child's language. Hugs and acceptance go a long way.

Family

Source: Adapted from R. E. Owens, Jr., *Language Disorders: A Functional Approach to Assessment and Intervention,* 2nd ed. (Boston: Allyn & Bacon, 1995), p. 416.

direct the topics of the conversations. These conversations need not be long, and in secondary settings, they can be accomplished as students enter the room. Apply the Concept 6.1 provides more ideas that you can use and share with parents about how to promote language through the use of conversations.

Adjust Pacing, Chunk Information, and Check for Understanding to Promote Comprehension

Second language learners and students with language problems often have difficulty comprehending what is being said during class, particularly in content area classes. To promote language comprehension, adjust your pacing so that these students have time to process the language input. The flow of instruction need not suffer, but when you are discussing new or difficult concepts or ideas, slow the pace and highlight the key ideas by writing them, demonstrating their meaning, and/or repeating them. It is not unusual for teachers to privately identify several students whom they use to gauge the pacing of their instruction and determine when to move on. Be sure to include the students with language and learning problems in this group.

It is also helpful if the amount of information that is provided in each segment is reduced. Consequently, information can be chunked or segmented into smaller amounts. For example, observing his students in Mr. Hunt's fifth-grade

science class, Mr. Fong noticed that his students usually listened to Mr. Hunt present the first 5 of 15 vocabulary words for a new chapter and recorded about 3 of the words in their science notebooks. After Mr. Fong shared this information with Mr. Hunt, Mr. Hunt decided to chunk the vocabulary into groups of 3 to 5 words and introduce each group only when they were needed rather than all of them at the beginning of a new chapter.

Checking for understanding is also important for facilitating language comprehension. Having a student repeat directions or tell another student what was just discussed are ways to check for understanding other than asking questions.

Increase Wait Time to Promote Production

When Sharon Kutok, a speech/language pathologist, talks about the most important principles for teachers to use when teaching students with language and learning problems, the first one she mentions is wait time. Some students need time to understand what has just been said and to construct a response. These students may have particular difficulty with form (e.g., syntax) and need the extra time to think about the form they should use in constructing their response. Therefore, when a response is required from these students, a teacher should give students extra time to formulate their answer before giving an additional prompt or calling on another student. For students with problems in the area of content, they may have difficulty with word retrieval or word finding (German, 1992).

Use Effective Teaching Strategies in Presenting a New Concept or Skill

Critical to new content or concepts is the use of effective teaching strategies. Students' knowledge of concepts grows exponentially during the school years, as we discussed in the section on vocabulary development. A teacher's use of effective teaching strategies will assist students with language difficulties to gain the concepts and content that they need for success in content area classes. Based on the teaching–learning process, there are a number of effective teaching strategies that should be incorporated into language instruction. Figure 6.5 lists key strategies that can be used in teaching a new concept.

Use Self-Talk and Parallel Talk to Describe What You and Others Are Doing or Thinking

Using self-talk and parallel talk demonstrates how language is connected to activities. Self-talk describes what the teacher is doing or thinking; parallel talk describes what the student(s) is doing or thinking. Ms. Baraka, a special education teacher who is coteaching in a first-grade classroom, uses

FIGURE 6.5

Effective Teaching Strategies for Presenting a New Concept or Skill

When teaching new language concepts or patterns, keep the following strategies in mind:

- Gear the activities to the students' interests and cognitive level.
- Get the students' attention before engaging in communication activities.
- Bombard the student with the concept or skill frequently throughout the day in a functional manner.
- When speaking, place stress on the target concept or language pattern.
- Pause between phrases or sentences so that the student has time to process the new concept or language pattern.
- Decrease the rate of presentation when first introducing the concept or language pattern.
- When introducing a new concept or language pattern, use familiar, concrete vocabulary and simple sentence patterns.
- If possible, present the new concept or language pattern by using more than one input mode (e.g., auditory, visual, kinesthetic). Gestures and facial expressions that are paired with a specific language pattern often assist students in understanding the form. For example, giving a look of puzzlement or wonder when asking a question can serve as a cue to the students.
- Pair written symbols with oral language. For instance, demonstrating morphological endings such as *s* (plurals) and *ed* (past tense) can be done in writing. The students can then be cued to listen for what they see.

parallel talk and self-talk when she joins the students at the different learning centers. She explains, "When I join a center, I try to sit down and join in the activities rather than asking students questions. I describe what I am doing and what other students in the group are doing. For example, I might say, 'Voytek is making a clay animal. It's blue, and right now he is putting a ferocious snarl on the animal's face. I wonder what kind of animal it is. I think I'll ask Voytek.'" In this way, the students get to hear how words can describe what someone is doing and thinking, and it focuses the attention on the student and the ongoing activities.

Use Modeling to Demonstrate Language

Modeling plays an important role in learning language. Whether for learning a new sentence structure, new vocabulary, or a new function or use for language, modeling is a powerful tool. For example, Ms. Simons and her eighth-grade students in resource English class were working on improving discussion skills during literature discussion groups. Ms. Simon was concerned about the number of students who did not clarify what they were saying when it was obvious that other students were not understanding.

To teach clarification skills, Ms. Simons initiated a discussion about clarifying ideas and then modeled how not clarifying ideas and not asking for clarification can lead to confusion. She exaggerated the examples, and the students seemed to enjoy this. Next, Ms. Simons modeled clarification skills as she participated with the students in their literature discussions. As individual students used effective clarifying skills, she commented on this, so that peers were also serving as models. Use of computers with speech recognition and synthetic speech capability also provides for language models and systematic practice (see Tech Tips 6.1).

Use Expansion and Elaboration

Language expansion is a technique that is used to facilitate the development of more complex language form and content. By repeating what students say in a slightly more complex manner, the teacher demonstrates how their thoughts can be more fully expressed. For example, Ms. Lee, an elementary teacher, is working to get Rob to connect his ideas and to use adverbs to describe his actions. As he finished several math problems, Rob reported, "I got the first one easy. The second one was hard." Ms. Lee replied, "Oh, you got the first one easily, but the second one was hard." The teacher does not want to imply that she is correcting the student; she is simply showing him a more

TECHTips

6.1 Using Software to Improve Oral Language Skills

Laureate Learning Systems (www.laureatelearning.com) is a software company that markets research-based language development software for infants and preschoolers; learners with developmental disabilities, autism, and visual impairments; adolescents and adults with developmental disabilities, aphasia, and traumatic brain injury; and instructional programs for elementary reading and English as a second language. Laureate describes seven stages of language functioning that include interpreted communication, intentional communication, single words, word combinations, early syntax, syntax mastery, and complete generative grammar. The language acquisition ages described with the stages range from 0–4 months to 5 years and up.

Talk Time with Tucker and *Tiger's Tale* are software programs requiring the learner to speak to the computer, thus encouraging expressive language and stimulating speech. In *Talk Time with Tucker*, a voice-activated program, Tucker, an animated character, talks and moves with the learner's vocalizations. Clear articulation is not required. In *Tiger's Tale* an animated tiger has lost his voice. The learners speak to help the tiger and can play back the completed movie, listening to their own recorded voices speaking for the tiger.

Additional software programs from Laureate Learning Systems that help to teach critical oral language skills are *Following Directions*, *First Categories*, *Twenty Categories*, and *Micro-LADS*. These programs teach learners to follow instructions, categorize objects, and learn language syntax.

The *Thinkology* series from Heartsoft, Inc. (www.heartsoft.com) is another useful

software option for oral language improvement. This series offers carefully crafted instruction in *Volume I: Clarity, Volume II: Accuracy*, and *Volume III: Logic* and is appropriate for learners from kindergarten through grade 4. These titles track learners' progress and provide superb handouts and worksheets to help orient learners to the material as well as paper-and-pencil follow-up to the computer instruction.

Two additional programs are available from Tool Factory (www.toolfactory.com). *Sound Beginnings—Making Sounds* is a set of voice-activated games designed for students who are at the early stages of acquiring spoken language. *Idiom Track* is a program using fun graphics that illustrate the literal and real meanings of idiomatic phrases. Activities gradually build up the learners' understanding and confidence in the social skills of communication.

A Screenshot from *Thinkology*
(*Thinkology* is a registered trademark of KidSmart, LLC, publisher of Heartshot Educational Software. Screenshot used with permission.)

I WANT IT: Activity 6

---

complex way of expressing the thought. Also, the teacher should expand only one or two elements at once, or the expansion will be too complex for the student to profit from it.

Language elaboration is used to build on the content of a student's language and provide additional information on the topic. For example, Chris, a fourth-grade student with language disabilities, was explaining that snakes have smooth skin. Mr. Anderson elaborated on Chris's idea by

commenting, "Snakes have smooth skin and so do lizards. Are there other animals in the desert that have smooth skin?"

Use Structured Language Programs to Provide Intensive Practice and Feedback

Teaching in context is critical for learning and generalization. However, sometimes by teaching in context, we do not provide the students with adequate opportunities to practice a new skill. Students who have learning problems need the practice and feedback provided in many language programs and activities to gain mastery of the skill. For example, Language for Learning (Englemann and Osborn, 1999), DISTAR Language (Engelmann and Osborn, 1987), and Figurative Language: A Comprehensive Program (Gorman-Gard, 1992) provide intensive practice in different language content and forms. However, these programs should not serve as the students' entire language program. Although they provide practice and feedback, they generally do not teach the skill within the relevant contexts that are needed for purposeful learning and generalization.

Use Language as an Intrinsic Motivator

Because language is such an enabling tool, it carries a great deal of intrinsic reinforcement for most children. Rather than using praise ("I like the way you said that" or "Good talking"), we can capitalize on the naturally reinforcing nature of language. For example, during a cooking activity, Mr. Shapiro asks the students, "How can we figure out how much two-thirds of a cup plus three-fourths of a cup of flour is?" After Nikki explains, Mr. Shapiro comments, "Now we know how to figure that out. Shall we give it a try?" Later, the teacher asks how to sift flour. After Rona explains, Mr. Shapiro says, "I've got it. Do you think we can sift it just the way Rona explained to us?" Rather than commenting on how "good" their language was and disrupting the flow of communication, Mr. Shapiro complimented Nikki and Rona by letting them know how useful the information was. When a student's purposes and intents are fulfilled because of the language the student uses, those language behaviors are naturally reinforced. The student learns that appropriate language use is a powerful tool in controlling the environment (Nelson, 1998; Owens, 2005).

Systematically Plan and Instruct for Generalization

As is the case in teaching other skills, language instruction must incorporate into the instructional sequence a variety of contexts, settings, and people with which students interact if they are to generalize the language skills (Beck et al., 2002).

Because language is a tool that is used across so many contexts, it is relatively easy to incorporate generalization into language instruction. Ms. McDonald, a special education resource teacher; Mrs. Kim, the second-grade teacher; and Ms. Cortez, the speech/language pathologist, are working with Julie, a second-grade child with learning disabilities, on sequencing events and using sequence markers (e.g., first, second, next, last). When Julie goes to language and resource classes, Mrs. Kim sends a note that lists, in order, the activities Julie has participated in so far during the day. When Julie returns from language and resource class, Ms. Cortez sends back a note that lists her language activities. Each teacher then converses with Julie about what she did in the other teachers' classes, emphasizing sequence and sequence markers. Other activities also build generalization for Julie. Whenever the teachers or Julie's mother reads Julie a story, Julie retells the story and is asked sequence questions. During the weekly cooking activity, Julie and the other students tell the steps in making the food for the day, and these steps are written on large chart paper with numbers listed beside them. Julie also arranges picture sequence cards and is then asked to describe them. With these activities, Julie receives numerous opportunities to generalize this language skill to a variety of contexts, persons, and settings.

Teaching Content

We teach language content throughout the day. For example, one of the major goals in teaching a new unit in social studies and science is for the students to understand and use the new vocabulary. What are some of the basic vocabulary categories that we may want to teach? Table 6.6 lists some general categories of words and word relationships. Let us look at some strategies for teaching content or vocabulary, whether it be the more general vocabulary listed in Table 6.6 or the specific vocabulary found in content area instruction.

Emphasize the Distinguishing and Critical Features of the Concepts Being Taught

When teaching new concepts, emphasize the features that are important to the meaning. For example, in teaching the concepts of "mountains" and "hills," the distinguishing or critical features to emphasize are "size" and "height." In comparison, the "texture of the land" is not important, since it is not a feature that usually helps us to distinguish between hills and mountains. Comparing and contrasting two concepts using a Venn diagram can help students to see the important characteristics (see Figure 6.6). Students remember vocabulary better if they think about how they can use it.

TABLE 6.6
Categories of Words and Word Relationships

Categories	School-Related Examples
Existence/nouns	science, math, reading, vowels, consonants, sentences, paragraphs
Actions/verbs	verbs often used in instruction—draw, write, circle, underline, discuss, compare, critique, defend
Attributes/adjectives	words that describe such attributes as size, shape, texture, weight, position (high/low, first/last), color, age, speed, affect, attractiveness
Attributes/adverbs	words that describe actions, such as easily, hurriedly, busily, willingly
Prepositions	locative (in, on, under, beside, in front of, ahead of, behind), directional (off, out of, away from, toward, around, through), temporal (before, after, between), for, from, at, of, to, with, without

Personal pronouns	*Subjective*	*Objective*	*Possessive*
	I	me	my, mine
	you	you	your
	she, he, it	her, him, it	her, his, its
	we	us	our
	they	them	their

Categories	School-Related Examples
Demonstrative pronouns	this, that, these, those
Indefinite and negative pronouns	a/an, someone, somebody, something, somewhere, anyone, anybody, anything, anywhere, no one, nobody, nothing, nowhere, the
Antonyms	full/empty, boiling/freezing, easy/hard, soft/hard
Synonyms	pants/slacks/trousers/britches laugh/giggle/chuckle happy/glad/pleased/elated/tickled pink
Homonyms	sail/sale, bear/bare
Multiple-meaning words	run fast, run in your stockings, go for a run, in the long run
Comparative relationships	taller than, shorter than
Spatial relationships	*see* Prepositions
Temporal-sequential relationships	words connoting measurement, time (days of the week, minutes, seasons), temporal prepositions (first, last, next, then)
Conditional relationships	if . . . then
Causal relationships	because, therefore, since
Conjunctive relationships	and
Disjunctive relationships	either . . . or
Contrastive relationships	but, although
Enabling relationships	in order that, so that
Figurative language	*Idioms:* catch a plane; hit the road *Metaphors:* her eagle eye *Similes:* her eyes twinkled like stars; busy as a beaver *Proverbs:* The early bird catches the worm.

Figure 6.7 presents one way in which students can think about a concept in multiple ways.

Concepts Should Be Introduced in a Number of Different Ways

When teaching the concept of "precipitation," for instance, the teacher may present pictures of different types of precipitation (e.g., snow, rain, sleet, hail, and mist) and have the students tell about a time when they remember each type of precipitation. The class can discuss what is happening to the water in the atmosphere when it is precipitating and what the weather is like when precipitation is present.

FIGURE 6.6

Venn Diagram for Comparing Concepts

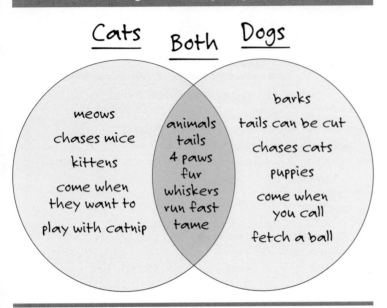

Present Examples and Nonexamples of the Concept

For example, in learning about cacti, students may generate two lists of plants: one that represents examples of cacti and one that represents nonexamples. Then students can talk about and list the features that make the cacti different from the nonexamples.

Categorize New Concepts So That Students Understand How the Concept Relates to Other Concepts

If the concept of "melancholy" is being taught, the students should learn that this is an example of a feeling or emotion. Other feelings are "gladness," "relief," and "hurt." Characteristics of people who are melancholy are "not happy," "quiet," "not talkative," and "somber." These ideas can be depicted in a visual diagram, such as a semantic map, which shows how the different concepts relate to one another (see Figure 6.8).

Present New Vocabulary in Simple Sentences or Phrases

It is harder to learn a new concept or idea if the teacher is using difficult language to explain what it means. The rule of thumb is to use simple sentences or phrases to introduce new concepts (i.e., four- to seven-word sentences and two- to four-word phrases).

Use Games and Other Activities to Reinforce Newly Introduced Concepts

For example, Twenty Questions is a good game to use to get students to think about the characteristics of a concept and the categories in which the concept falls.

Name That Category is a game that can be played similarly to Name That Tune, except that the object of the game is to earn points by naming the category when examples of a category are given. The sooner the category is named, the more points the player receives.

Oral or written *cloze* passages, like that shown in Figure 6.9, can be used to highlight a particular set of concepts being taught.

Idioms, metaphors, similes, and proverbs can be used when playing Charades, with the students acting out the literal meanings of the phrases (e.g., *catch a plane, blow your stack*).

Additional ideas for teaching new concepts and the relationships among those concepts, particularly as they relate to teaching content area subjects (i.e., science, social studies, vocational areas), are discussed in Chapter 10. A number of language materials and programs are available for teaching concepts to school-age students. Appendix 6.1 presents the names and short descriptions of several of these programs and materials.

Increase Word-Finding Ability

Another difficulty that some students with learning disabilities encounter involves word finding. These students know words but are unable to recall them automatically. Most frequently, these words are nouns. Several techniques can be used to assist students in increasing their ability to recall words, thereby increasing the accuracy and fluency of their expressive language (Casby, 1992; Clark and Klecan-Aker, 1992; German, 1992; Lahey and Edwards, 1999; Nippold, 1998).

Teach Students to Classify and Categorize Words. Teaching students to classify and categorize words should improve their long-term memory and thus help them to recall and retrieve specific words. When learning new concepts, students should be encouraged to name the category and then rapidly name the vocabulary in the category. Pictures, written words, and graphic representations such as a semantic map (see Figure 6.8) may help with this activity. When students are having difficulty retrieving a word, providing the category helps them to retrieve the word (Halperin, 1974).

FIGURE 6.7
Thinking about a Concept in Multiple Ways

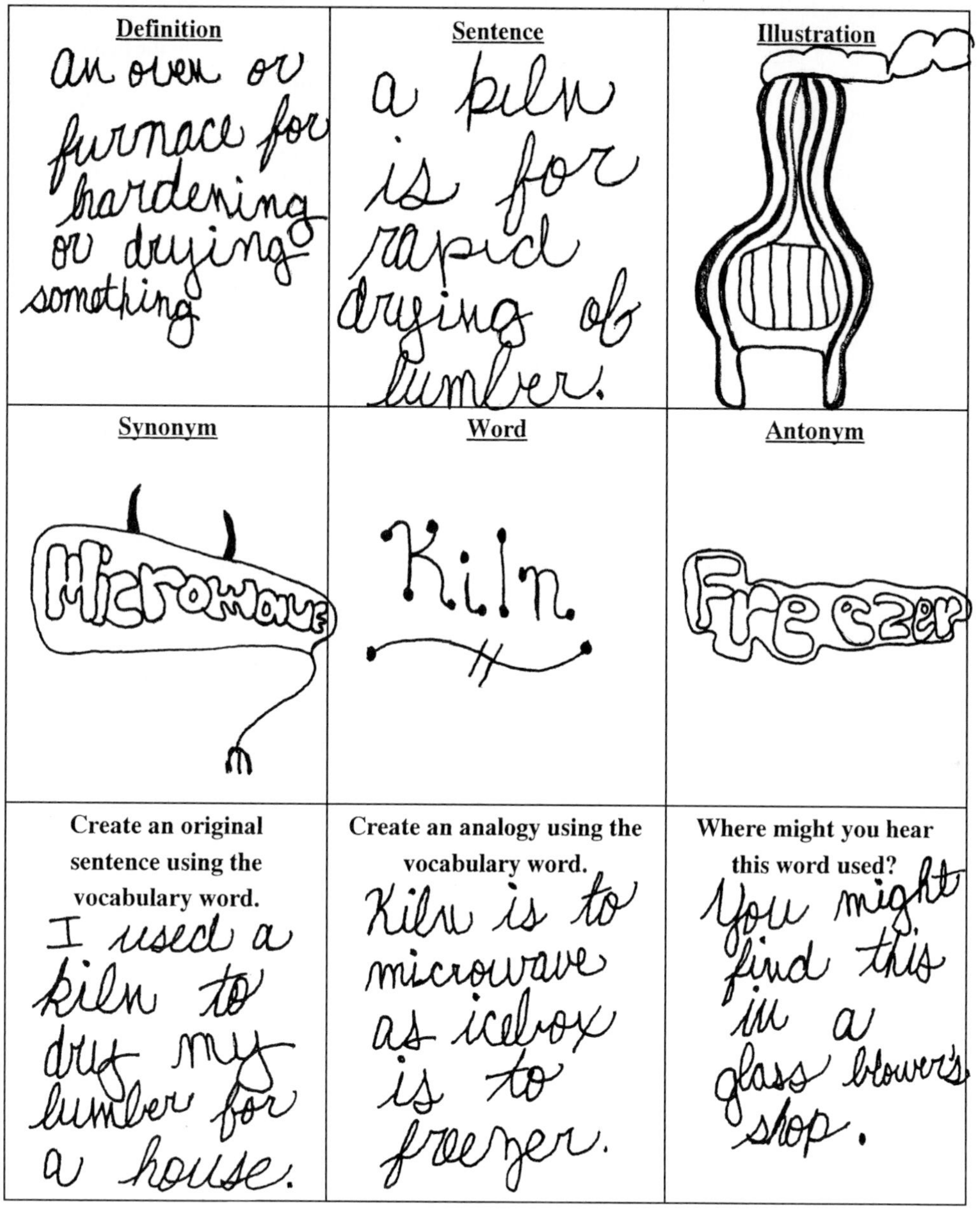

Definition	**Sentence**	**Illustration**
An oven or furnace for hardening or drying something	a kiln is for rapid drying of lumber.	
Synonym	**Word**	**Antonym**
Microwave	Kiln	Freezer
Create an original sentence using the vocabulary word.	**Create an analogy using the vocabulary word.**	**Where might you hear this word used?**
I used a kiln to dry my lumber for a house.	Kiln is to microwave as icebox is to freezer.	You might find this in a glass blower's shop.

Teach Students to Use Visual Imagery. Getting students to "see" in their minds the objects they are trying to retrieve can sometimes help them think of words. To help students develop these mental images, encourage them to picture new words in their minds. For example, when students are trying to learn the parts of a flower, have them picture a flower in their minds, with the labels for the parts written on the different parts. Have them talk about the kind of flower they pictured, discussing the parts as they describe the flower.

Teach Students to Use Word Association Clues to Help in Retrieving Words. Activities in which students learn and practice word associations (e.g., peanut butter and _____; red, white, and _____) can facilitate word retrieval. These activities may be as broad as asking students to name as many things as they can think of in a given amount of time. But generally, the teacher will want to focus the associations. Figure 6.10 presents a variety of association tasks that are more focused. In using these

FIGURE 6.8
Semantic Map of the Concept of "Melancholy"

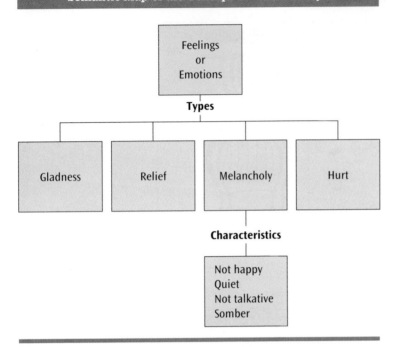

focused activities, keep the pace rapid and the total time for the activity short (one to three minutes). If students have established strong word associations, then when they cannot think of the

FIGURE 6.9
Sample Cloze Emphasizing Prepositions

Cloze passages can be used either as an oral or written activity, or combined with the oral activity reinforcing the written.

More than anything else, Robert wanted _____ climb _____ the top

_____ the mountain. Every day _____ his way home _____ school he

looked up _____ the mountain. It was so high that the few trees _____

the top looked very small. He had heard that it would take a day _____ climb

_____ the summit, and a day to get back _____ the mountain. One

evening when he was looking _____ his window, he saw a campfire burning

_____ the top of the mountain. He knew _____ only he practiced hiking,

he could make it.

Well, this spring he would start practicing. He and his friend Jim could join the

Young Hikers' Club and _____ early summer they would be ready _____

the climb. Robert could hardly wait _____ spring _____ come.

correct word, providing an associative clue can assist them in retrieving the correct word.

Teach Students to Use Synonyms and Antonyms. When students cannot recall the precise word they want, an alternative word can be used. Students may be taught to state that the desired word "is the opposite of _____" or "is almost like _____." For example, when struggling to find the word *joyful*, a student can be encouraged to say, "It's when you're really happy" or "It's the opposite of feeling sad."

Use Sound, Semantic, or Multiple-Choice Cues to Assist Students in Recalling Words. Providing students with cues can assist them in retrieving words. For example, teachers might cue, "It starts with a /k/" (sound cue), "It's not a peach, it's a _____" (semantic cue), or "It's either a banana, a cat, or a bowl" (multiple-choice cue).

Increase Elaboration in Language

Some students with learning disabilities use language that is not very elaborate. When asked to retell stories or events or to give descriptions, these students provide only the most basic information.

To teach language elaboration, Wiig and Semel (1984) suggest that the teachers use a sequence of three steps: first for an object or pictured object, then for an event or pictured event, and finally for an event sequence or pictured event sequence. Their three steps for an object or pictured object are as follows:

1. *Model elaboration by introducing familiar objects or pictured objects and by demonstrating verbal descriptions of their attributes and functions.* In this step, the teacher describes the object, noting its attributes and functions. In some instances, the teacher may want to contrast it to similar or related objects—for example, describing a cactus and comparing it to a rosebush.

2. *Have students elaborate in response to direct questions.* After modeling, the teacher asks students direct questions about the object that require them to focus on its attributes and functions. For example, the teacher may ask, "What kind of stem does a cactus have? Why does it have such a chunky stem?"

3. *Have students spontaneously describe the object or pictured object.* The teacher asks students to describe the object, using such cues as "Tell me about the cactus. What else can you tell me about

FIGURE 6.10

Associative Tasks for Improving Word Retrieval and Developing Vocabulary

Free Association Tasks

Name as many things as you can in a specified amount of time (usually one to three minutes).

Controlled Association Tasks

Name as many foods, animals, things you take hiking, kinds of fish, etc., as you can think of in a specified amount of time (usually one to three minutes).

Antonym Association Tasks

Listen to each word and tell me the word that means the exact opposite.

girl
man
hot
inside
happy

Synonym Association Tasks

Listen to each word and tell me the word that means about the same thing.

small
giggle
mad
rapid

Categorization Tasks

Listen to these words and tell me what they are.

dog, cat, fish, alligator
bread, fruit, vegetables, chicken
robin, sparrow, eagle

Temporal Relationship Tasks

Listen to each word and tell me what you think of.

winter	(ice skating, skiing, sledding)
evening	(watching TV, supper, homework)
Christmas	(gifts, Santa Claus, carols)

Agent–Action Relationship Tasks

Listen to the names of these animals and objects. Each of them goes with a special action. Tell me what special thing each one of these does.

plane	(flies)
lion	(roars)
doorbell	(rings)

Action–Object Relationship Tasks

Listen to these actions. Each one goes with special objects. Tell me what the objects are.

fly	(planes, helicopters, kites)
run	(animals, insects)
button	(shirts, jackets)

Source: E. H. Wiig and E. Semel, *Language Assessment & Intervention for the Learning Disabled,* 2nd ed. (Columbus, OH: C. E. Merrill, 1984). Reprinted with permission of the senior author, Elizabeth H. Wiig, Ph.D., Knowledge Research Institute, Inc.

it? Are there any other things about it that are important? In what way is a cactus like a rosebush?"

The sequence for teaching events and event sequences would be the same.

Teaching Form

Form refers to the structure of language. Tables 6.3 and 6.5 (pages 204 and 205, repectively) present syntactical and morphological forms that are relevant in teaching school-age students with language and learning problems. This section presents some procedures and activities for teaching these language forms:

Teach New Sentence Structures or Prefixes, Suffixes, and Inflectional Endings According to Developmental Sequences or the Order of Difficulty

Tables 6.3 and 6.5, as well as language programs and activities designed to teach form (see Appendix 6.1), can assist teachers in deciding the order in which to teach the various sentence and morphological forms.

When Teaching a New Structure or Form, Use Familiar, Concrete Examples and Vocabulary

For example, Mrs. Ogbu wants to have her students work on passive sentences. She begins by having her students act out simple events (e.g., Julio tagged Maria during a relay race). Then she asks the students to tell her a sentence about the event. She writes it on the board ("Julio tagged Maria"). Next she shows the students how she can say what had happened in a different way ("Maria was tagged by Julio"). Then the students act out other events and give sentences in the passive voice. In this way, Mrs. Ogbu starts with concrete experiences and uses familiar, simple vocabulary to teach the new sentence structure.

Use Simple Sentences When Teaching a New Sentence or Morphological Form

When Mrs. Ogbu initially taught her students passive voice sentences, she used very simple sentences. She could have said, "Julio chased Maria while playing tag," but this sentence would have been much more difficult for the students to put in the passive voice.

Once the Students Have Learned the New Form, Have Them Extend It to Situations That Need More Elaborated and Complex Sentences and Less Familiar Vocabulary

For example, when teaching the morphological ending *-er*, move from familiar vocabulary such as *teacher*, *reader*, and *writer* to less familiar vocabulary such as *painter*, *plumber*, *framer*, and *landscaper* in the context of house construction and to the exceptions in this area, such as *mason* and *electrician*.

Use Actual Objects and Events or Pictures of Them When Initially Teaching a New Structure or Form and Pair Oral Communication with Written Communication

Mrs. Ogbu uses the event of playing tag to teach passive voice sentences. She also pairs the oral sentences with the written sentences by writing them on the board. Word and sentence boundaries are clarified by written language, and pictures or actual experiences can assist the students in focusing on the target language pattern. Figure 6.11 demonstrates how pictures and written words can demonstrate possessives.

FIGURE 6.11

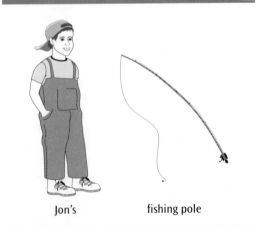

Visual Representation Depicting Possessive Marker

Jon's   fishing pole

TABLE 6.7

Comparison Chart

Item	Long	Longer	Longest
red pencils	Susan	Kim	Danny
blue pencils	Susan	Cori	Ken
yellow pencils	Kim	Danny	Ken
white shoelaces	Kim	Danny	Ken
black shoelaces	Cori	Susan	Kim
brown hair	Cori	Kim	Susan
blond hair	Danny	Ken	Stefan

New Sentence or Word Forms Should Be Introduced in a Variety of Ways

For example, when teaching comparative and superlative forms of adjectives during a measuring activity, Ms. Kamulu has the students determine who has the "long/longer/longest" pencils, pens, scissors, shoelaces, hair, and so on. Numerous comparisons can be made by using items found in a classroom, and the various comparisons may be depicted on a chart such as the one shown in Table 6.7. Students can then use the examples and the chart to discuss the comparisons and to practice the targeted language skills.

Teaching Use

Instruction in language use is often one of the most important areas for students with learning disabilities. One method to organize pragmatic language instruction is based on five ways in which language is used (Wells, 1973): ritualizing, informing, controlling, feeling, and imagining. Examples of ritualizing include greetings and farewells, introductions, requests to repeat and requests to clarify, and initiating and responding to telephone calls. Informing examples include asking for and telling information, asking for and telling about objects and events, asking for and telling about conditions and states, and asking for and telling about preferences. Some examples of controlling are asking for and telling about wants and needs; asking for and offering favors, help, or assistance; giving and responding to warnings; asking for and giving permission; asking for and telling about intentions; and making and responding to complaints. Examples in the area of feeling include expressing and responding to affection, expressing and responding to expressions of appreciation and approval, asking for and telling about feelings, apologizing and responding to apologies, and expressing and responding to agreements and disagreements. Imagining includes understanding and telling a story and understanding and telling a joke. These skills are drawn from *Let's Talk for Children* (Wiig and Bray, 1983), a language program designed to assist preschool and early elementary–level children to acquire, use, maintain, and generalize communication functions, and *Let's Talk: Developing Prosocial Communication Skills* (Wiig, 1982), a language program designed for preadolescents, adolescents, and young adults.

Other pragmatic skills that can be taught include the following:

- Varying language to match the person to whom one is talking (e.g., speak differently to a young child, a peer, and an adult)
- Varying language to match the context in which the language is occurring (e.g., the school, playground)
- Maintaining a topic during a conversation
- Taking turns during a conversation
- Recognizing when the listener is not understanding and take clarifying actions to assist the listener
- Being a considerate speaker and listener (i.e., attend to the other person's cognitive, affective, and language needs)

Several guidelines can be used in teaching the various skills associated with language use.

Use Role Playing to Simulate Different Situations in Which the Targeted Pragmatic Skills Are Required

Ms. Peterson uses role playing in her class so that students will have some idea what it will feel like when they are in a situation that requires them to communicate in a certain way or for a specific purpose. Last week, the students had to ask each other for directions to their houses during pretend telephone conversations. This week students are practicing how to ask questions during a simulated science lesson.

Use Pictures or Simulations to Represent Feelings

Some students have difficulty discriminating different nonverbal and verbal communication that accompanies various feelings. By using pantomime or pictures, students can determine what feelings are being expressed and can discuss the cues that helped them determine the feelings. Encourage students to attend to other students' feelings by using such statements as "You look like you're feeling . . ." or "I bet you feel really . . ." or "I can't tell how you're feeling."

Use Conversations as a Framework for Teaching Functional Language

Conversations about topics that are familiar to the students or about common experiences can serve as ideal situations for building students' pragmatic skills (Hoskins, 1990; Merritt and Culatta, 1998). Teachers can serve as facilitators by assisting students in using the following conversational skills (Hoskins, 1987):

- Introducing a topic
- Maintaining a topic
- Introducing a topic in an elaborated form
- Extending a topic
- Changing a topic
- Requesting clarification
- Responding to requests for clarification

FOCUS Question 3. What are the strategies and considerations on which teachers should focus when teaching culturally and linguistically diverse learners?

Planning Instruction for Students Who Are Culturally and Linguistically Diverse

Diversity

As a teacher, you will have students from many different cultures and students who are in the process of acquiring English as a second language or second dialect. You may or may not be familiar with the culture and language of these students. Still, it will be important for these students to feel comfortable in your class.

Francisco is a good example of such a student. He immigrated from Costa Rica to New Mexico at the age of four with his parents and siblings. Having lived in a rural community in Costa Rica, his parents spoke only Spanish when they arrived. Francisco and his family now live in a Spanish-speaking community within an urban setting. Although he has some exposure to English and his father is taking a night course to learn English, Francisco entered school at age five with Spanish as his first language and only limited knowledge of English. This situation is common for children who immigrate from countries in Central and South America, Asia and the Pacific Islands, and Eastern Europe. A growing number of students who enter school in the

United States are learning English as a second language while in school. Teachers' knowledge of second language acquisition and general instructional guidelines can help to make school a success for students like Francisco. Students must know that their home language and culture are viewed as assets rather than obstacles to learning (Altwerger and Ivener, 1994; Echevarria and Graves, 1998).

To promote learning, teachers should incorporate the students' first language and culture into the curriculum, demonstrate that they value their students' culture and language, have high expectations for these students, and make accommodations so that students can learn successfully. Research on the characteristics of effective teachers of students with cultural and linguistic diversities (Garcia, 1991; Ladson-Billings, 1995; O'Shea, Williams, and Sattler, 1999; Tikunoff, 1983) indicates that effective teachers do the following:

- Have high expectations of their students and believe that all students are capable of academic success
- See themselves as members of the community and see teaching as a way to give back to the community
- Believe in diversity, meeting individual student needs, and interacting with other teachers to support shared decision making
- Display a sense of confidence in their ability to be successful with students who are culturally and linguistically diverse

FIGURE 6.12

Iceberg Analogy of Language Proficiency

Source: Adapted from J. Cummins, *Bilingualism and Minority Language Children* (Ontario: Ontario Institute for Studies in Education, 1980). Reprinted with permission of University of Toronto Press.

- Honor the languages of the students in their class by recognizing these languages as valuable and acquiring even a few words from each language
- Communicate directions clearly, pace lessons appropriately, involve the students in decisions, monitor students' progress, and provide feedback

Second Language Acquisition

When students are acquiring a second language, an important variable is the degree of acquisition or proficiency in the first language. Cummins (1991) in a review of research concluded that the better developed the students' first language proficiency and conceptual foundation, the more likely they were to develop similarly high levels of proficiency and conceptual ability in the second language. He has referred to this as the *common underlying proficiency* and has used the analogy of an iceberg (see Figure 6.12) to explain the relationship between first and second language acquisition, and why proficiency in the first language complements proficiency in the second language (Cummins, 1981).

As can be seen in Figure 6.12, both languages have separate surface features, represented by two different icebergs. However, less visible below the surface is the underlying proficiency that is common to both languages. For example, Table 6.8 compares the phonological, morphological, and syntactical features in Spanish and English, and Table 6.9 highlights some of the grammatical contrasts in African American Vernacular English and Standard American English. Regardless of the language a person is using, the thoughts that accompany the talking, reading, writing, and listening come from the same language core. One implication of this analogy is that individuals who are *balanced bilinguals* have an advantage over monolingual individuals in that they have greater cognitive flexibility and a greater understanding of language (Galambos and Goldin-Meadow, 1990; Skutnabb-Kangas, 1981).

Important to the learning process is the developmental nature of the second language. Cummins (1984) suggested that, in general, students acquire competency in the *basic interpersonal communication skills* (BICS) before they acquire competency in *cognitive academic language proficiency* (CALP). The BICS refer to the conversational competencies that we develop with a second language. They are the greetings and the small talk between peers that do

TABLE 6.8
Comparison of Spanish and English Languages

Phonological	Morphological	Syntactical
Fewer vowel sounds: no short *a* (hat), short *i* (fish), short *u* (up), short double *o* (took), or schwa (sofa)	*de* (of) used to show possession: *Joe's pen* becomes *the pen of Joe*	use of *no* for *not:* He no do his homework.
Fewer consonant sounds: no /j/ (jump), /v/ (vase), /z/ (zipper), /sh/ (shoe), /ŋ/ (sing), /hw/ (when), /zh/ (beige)	*más* (more) used to show comparison: *faster* becomes *more fast*	no auxiliary verbs: She no play soccer.
Some possible confusions:		adjectives after nouns: the car blue
/b/ pronounced /p/: *cab* becomes *cap*		agreement of adjectives: the elephants bigs
/j/ pronounced /y/: *jet* becomes *yet*		no inversion of question: Anna is here?
/ŋ/ pronounced as /n/: *thing* becomes *thin*		articles with professional titles: I went to the Dr. Rodriguez.
/v/ pronounced as /b/: *vote* becomes *boat*		
/y/ pronounced as /j/: *yes* becomes *jes*		
/sk/, /sp/, /st/ pronounced as /esk/, /esp/, /est/: *speak* becomes *espeak*		
/a/ pronounced as /e/: *bat* becomes *bet*		
/i/ pronounced as /ē/: *hit* becomes *heat*		
/ē/ pronounced as /i/: *heal* becomes *hill*		
/u/ pronounced as /o/: *hut* becomes *hot*		
/o͞o/ pronounced as /o͞o/: *look* becomes *Luke*		

Diversity

Source: Adapted from C. A. O'Brien, *Teaching the Language-Different Child to Read* (Columbus, OH: C. E. Merrill, 1973).

TABLE 6.9
Grammatical Contrasts between African American English and Standard American English

African American English Grammatical Structure	SAE Grammatical Structure
Possessive -'s	
Nonobligatory word where word position expresses possession	Obligatory regardless of position
Get *mother* coat.	Get *mother's* coat
It be mother's.	It's mother's.
Plural -s	
Nonobligatory with numerical quantifier	Obligatory regardless of numerical quantifier
He got ten *dollar*.	He has ten *dollars*.
Look at the cat.	Look at the cats.
Regular past -ed	
Nonobligatory; reduced as consonant cluster	Obligatory
Yesterday, I *walk* to school.	Yesterday, I *walked* to school.
Irregular past	
Case by case, some verbs inflected, others not	All irregular verbs inflected
I *see* him last week.	I *saw* him last week.
Regular present tense third person singular -s	
Nonobligatory	Obligatory
She *eat* too much.	She *eats* too much.

Diversity

(continued)

TABLE 6.9

Grammatical Contrasts between African American English and Standard American English   (continued)

African American English Grammatical Structure	SAE Grammatical Structure
Irregular present tense third person singular -s	
Nonobligatory	Obligatory
He *do* my job.	He *does* my job.
Indefinite an	
Use of indefinite a	Use of *an* before nouns beginning with a vowel
He ride in a airplane.	He rode in *an* airplane.
Pronouns	
Pronominal apposition: pronoun immediately follows noun	Pronoun used elsewhere in sentence or in other sentence; not in apposition
Momma *she* mad. She . . .	Momma is mad. *She* . . .
Future tense	
More frequent use of *be going to* (gonna)	More frequent use of *will*
I *be going to* dance tonight.	I *will* dance tonight.
I *gonna* dance tonight.	I *am going to* dance tonight.
Omit *will* preceding *be*	Obligatory use of *will*
I *be* home later.	I *will* (I'll) *be* home later.
Negation	
Triple negative	Absence of triple negative
Nobody don't never like me.	*No* one ever likes me.
Use of *ain't.*	*Ain't* is unacceptable form
I *ain't* going.	*I'm not* going.
Modals	
Double modals for such forms as *might, could,* and *should*	Single modal use
I *might could* go.	I *might be able to* go.
Questions	
Same form for direct and indirect	Different forms for direct and indirect
What *it is*?	What *is it*?
Do you know what *it is*?	*Do you* know what *it is*?
Relative pronouns	
Nonobligatory in most cases	Nonobligatory with *that* only
He the one stole it.	He's the one *who* stole it.
It the one you like.	It's the one (that) you like.
Conditional if	
Use of *do* for conditional *if*	Use of *if*
I ask *did* she go.	I asked *if* she went.
Perfect construction	
Been used for action in the distant past	*Been* not used
He *been* gone.	He left a long time ago.
Copula	
Nonobligatory when contractible	Obligatory in contractible and noncontractible forms
He sick.	He's sick.
Habitual or *general state*	
Marked with uninflected *be*	Nonuse of *be*; verb inflected
She *be* workin'.	She's *working* now.

not require much cognitive effort or social problem solving. The CALP, on the other hand, refers to the more cognitively demanding language skills that are required for new learning that is characteristic of school settings. In general, BICS develop in a second language before CALP does. Cummins (1981) suggested that it takes from one to two years to develop BICS, whereas it takes five to seven years to develop CALP.

Although these generalizations are influenced by situational factors, linguistic input, and the learner's characteristics, they do have implications for teaching. Teachers may assume that students who can converse easily in their second language are ready to learn new concepts, strategies, and skills in that language, but this is not necessarily the case. The process of second language acquisition varies substantially with each individual (Ovander and Collier, 1998). This is related to the interactions among sociocultural processes, language development, academic development, and cognitive development.

For example, when Jong Hoon entered Ms. Dembrow's third-grade class, she immediately noticed that he conversed easily with the other students in the class and with her. Jong Hoon had immigrated from Korea two years earlier and had begun learning English through the school's ESL program. His parents are also studying English in a night course and feel that learning English is important for their economic and personal success in America. Still, Korean is the language that the family speaks primarily in the home. Jong Hoon's language acquisition experiences illustrate the four components described by Ovander and Collier (1998).

These components have strong implications for the classroom teacher. As Ms. Dembrow became familiar with Jong Hoon, she realized that while his conversational skills made him a comfortable member of the classroom community (*language development*), he was not proficient in academic tasks such as reading and writing in English (*academic development*). She also found that in social studies and science, it was important for her to provide lots of context for teaching new concepts (*cognitive development*). When Ms. Dembrow referred Jong Hoon for possible special education services because of his difficulty with academics, she was not aware of typical patterns of second language acquisition difficulties. But in problem-solving discussions with the bilingual speech/language pathologist and ESL teacher, she learned that different timelines for developing academic knowledge and skills are to be expected and

should not be confused with reading disabilities (*sociocultural processes*) (Duran, 1989; Hamayan and Damico, 1991; Langdon, 1992; Ovander and Collier, 1998; Willig and Ortiz, 1991).

Strategies for Teaching Culturally and Linguistically Diverse Learners

Diversity

In planning for second language learners who may or may not also have learning disabilities, it is important to incorporate the first language and culture. Culturally and linguistically responsive teaching results in lesson modifications and adaptations that are culturally relevant for students (Graves, 1995). For example, in preparing for a thematic unit on California, Ms. Dembrow worked with the ESL teacher and incorporated an extended segment on farming communities in the unit because Jong Hoon and other students came from Asian and Mexican farming communities. For Jong Hoon and the other students, she checked out books and magazines from the school and public libraries about farming and rural life in China, Vietnam, Korea, Mexico, and Central America. The students also had the opportunity to visit not only a California market, but also Asian and Mexican food markets. They compared the foods from the three markets and learned how the foods had been grown. For Jong Hoon and the other students who came from other cultures and who were in the process of acquiring English as a second language, providing the link to their cultures helped to give them a context in which they could build both their language and cognitive skills. This is an example of the context-embedded communication and instruction that Cummins (1981) and others (Chamot and O'Malley, 1994a, 1994b; Echevarria and Graves, 1998) recommend to facilitate second language learning.

Other teaching strategies and accommodations include the following:

- Simplify your language.
- Repeat important phrases and emphasize key vocabulary.
- Demonstrate concepts; use manipulatives.
- Make use of all senses.
- Adapt the materials, don't water down the content.
- Include both language development and content vocabulary development.
- Brainstorm with the whole group.
- Provide direct experiences (e.g., read sources, watch videos).

- Increase wait time.
- Respond to the *message*, not to the correctness of the pronunciation or grammar.
- Don't force reluctant students to speak.
- Pair or group native speakers together.
- Use cooperative learning and peer group strategies.
- Learn as much as you can about your students' language and culture.
- Build on the students' prior knowledge.
- Bring the students' home languages and cultures into the classroom and curriculum (Bos and Reyes, 1996; Echevarria and Graves, 1998; Gersten and Baker, 2000; Sullivan, 1992; Towell and Wink, 1993).

Second language acquisition can be facilitated by using a good English language development program (Gersten and Baker, 2000). Components of such a program that could complement second language acquisition are a focus on development and proficiency in English; teaching phonological, morphological, and grammatical aspects of the use of English; and learning new academic content in English.

Many educators suggest that students should be encouraged to continue to develop proficiency in their first language even if it is not formally supported through bilingual education (e.g., Baker, 1993; Cummins, 1989; Tharp et al., 1999). To promote this, teachers can do the following:

- Encourage students to use the first language around the school.
- Provide opportunities for students from the same language group to communicate with one another in their first language where possible (e.g., in cooperative learning groups, during informal conversations throughout the school).
- Learn some common words and phrases in the student's native language.
- Recruit people who can tutor students in the first language.
- Provide books written in the various languages in both the classrooms and school library.
- Incorporate greetings and information in the various languages in newsletters and other official school communications (Cummins, 1989).

At some time, most teachers will work with students who are culturally and linguistically diverse. Making accommodations and using strategies that promote second language acquisition while fostering an understanding of the students' first languages and cultures will assist the students in becoming successful learners.

> **FOCUS Question 4. What is metalinguistics, and how can teachers use it to promote language development?**

Metalinguistics

When students use metalinguistics, they think about, analyze, and reflect on language as an object in much the same way one describes a table or friend (Wallach and Miller, 1988). *Metalinguistics* refers to the awareness that learners develop about language, and it requires that the learner shift attention from the meaning of language to its form, thereby seeing language as an entity separate from its function (Nelson, 1998).

Young children learn to use language without really understanding how it operates and functions. They use the linguistic rules that govern language, but if you asked them to tell you about or explain the rules, they would have great difficulty. As children mature, however, they become more sophisticated language learners. For example, when preschool children say that *care* and *bear* rhyme and that *little* and *lucky* start with the same sound or when they can clap the number of words in a sentence, they are using metalinguistics. Starting about age two, children begin to develop metalinguistic knowledge and skills. Wallach and Miller (1988) have arranged information on the development of metalinguistic skills to correspond in rough approximations to Piaget's stages of cognitive development (see Figure 6.13). It is evident from this figure that during the second stage, children develop metalinguistic knowledge and skills that are important for the development of early literacy.

Teaching students with learning disabilities to understand how language operates is important for their success as language users. For example, understanding that words can have multiple meanings, that figurative language does not use literal meanings, and that language style or register can be manipulated to fit the audience and context allows students to become highly sophisticated users of language. Labeling and explaining such language concepts are critical to the development of metalinguistic knowledge and skills.

FIGURE 6.13

Stages of Children's Metalinguistic Development

Stage One (Ages 1½ to 2)

- Distinguishes print from nonprint
- Knows how to interact with books: right side up, page turning from left to right
- Recognizes some printed symbols, e.g., TV character's name, brand names, signs

Stage Two (Ages 2 to 5½ or 6)

- Ascertains word boundaries in spoken sentences
- Ascertains word boundaries in printed sequences
- Engages in word substitution play
- Plays with the sounds of language
- Begins to talk about language parts and about talking (speech acts)
- Corrects own speech/language to help the listener understand the message (spontaneously or in response to listener request)
- Self-monitors own speech and makes changes to more closely approximate the adult model; phonological first; lexical and semantic speech style last
- Believes that a word is an integral part of the object to which it refers (word realism)
- Able to separate words into syllables
- Unable to consider that one word could have two different meanings

Stage Three (Ages 6 to 10)

- Begins to take listener perspective and use language form to match

- Understands verbal humor involving linguistic ambiguity, e.g., riddles
- Able to resolve ambiguity: lexical first, as in homophones; deep structures next, as in ambiguous phrases ("Will you join me in a bowl of soup?"); phonological or morphemic next (Q: "What do you have if you put three ducks in a box?" A: "A box of quackers.")
- Able to understand that words can have two meanings, one literal and the other nonconventional or idiomatic, e.g., adjectives used to describe personality characteristics such as *hard, sweet, bitter*
- Able to resequence language elements, as in pig Latin
- Able to segment syllables into phonemes
- Finds it difficult to appreciate figurative forms other than idioms

Stage Four (Ages 10+)

- Able to extend language meaning into hypothetical realms, e.g., to understand figurative language such as metaphors, similes, parodies, analogies, etc.
- Able to manipulate various speech styles to fit a variety of contexts and listeners

Source: G. P. Wallach and L. Miller, *Language Intervention and Academic Success* (San Diego: College Hill, 1998), p. 33. Reprinted with permission.

Examples of language concepts that can be taught include the following:

- Phoneme, syllable, and word boundaries
- Figurative language and multiple meanings
- The structure of stories (e.g., setting, problem, episodes with attempts to solve the problem and outcomes from the attempts, final resolution, and ending)
- How to manipulate speech style to fit the audience and context

As you read the next three chapters on teaching reading and written expression, think about how written language and print support the development of metalinguistic knowledge and skills.

> **FOCUS Question** 5. How can special education teachers work with language specialists to implement RTI?

Response to Intervention: Working with the Speech/Language Teacher

The role of the school-based speech/language teacher has changed significantly in the past decades because of legislative changes in special education. Traditionally, the speech/language teacher has used a clinical/medical model of assessment and intervention, treating students individually or in small groups in a separate resource room. However, educational reforms have increased participation of students with disabilities in the general education classroom. In particular, response to intervention (RTI) has provided opportunities for increasing interaction among classroom teachers, special education teachers, and speech/language personnel.

Response to intervention models have provided many speech/language teachers opportunities to work closely with other school professionals and parents in a team model, using a combination of direct and indirect service methods to promote language development and assist students with communication disorders. In addition to providing individual or group therapy, these teachers may also collaborate with classroom teachers to develop modifications and strategies for students within the classroom. The role of the speech/language teacher may vary owing to differences in caseload, state or district regulations, and staffing needs (American Speech-Language-Hearing Association, 2000).

The American Speech-Language-Hearing Association (2006) recognizes that response to intervention provides interesting and valuable new roles and responsibilities for the speech/language educator and also new challenges. With respect to **Progress Monitoring** assessment, as districts move from more formal models of assessment to ongoing assessments, speech language therapists will need to shift their assessment procedures as well so that they think about assessment as it contributes to decision making about student progress. This will require that more instructionally relevant assessments are administered more frequently.

Speech/language therapists may also engage in expanded roles related to prevention and intervention. For example, they may assist in schoolwide screening to identify students with early literacy and oralcy problems, may assist in developing and/or delivering appropriate prevention practices schoolwide, and may provide interventions to students with communication difficulties.

There are a variety of ways in which speech/language teachers may help students with language difficulties within the school setting. For students with literacy and language difficulties, they may:

- Collaborate with classroom teachers to implement developmentally appropriate language arts and literacy programs.
- Assist in modifying and selecting language and instructional strategies that integrate oral and written communication skills.
- Provide information and training to school personnel regarding the linguistic bases of reading and writing.

- Provide information and support for parents of at-risk children regarding language and literacy activities in the home environment.
- Collaborate with reading professionals and classroom teachers to augment the success of students with language and reading impairments.

For students with difficulties with social-emotional communication skills, they may:

- Provide information regarding the link between social-emotional problems and social communication skills (pragmatics).
- Assist in training school staff to use effective verbal and nonverbal communication strategies in conflict resolution.
- Demonstrate lessons to enhance pragmatic communication skills (problem solving, social communication).

Ehren, Montgomer, Rudenbsch, and Whitmire (2006) provide suggestions to speech/language therapists about how they might expand their role to facilitate RTI in the schools. They indicate that with respect to program design, speech/language therapists can:

- Explain the role of language in curriculum and instruction.
- Provide research-based knowledge on language screening and assessment.
- Provide research-based knowledge on effective language interventions.
- Assist in identifying screening measures.
- Provide professional development on language.
- Interpret the school level progress in addressing intervention needs of students.
- Participate in the development and implementation of progress monitoring.
- Consult with teachers on issues related to RTI and intervention.
- Help families understand the language basis of literacy and learning.

Involving speech/language therapists in the RTI model implemented schoolwide involves communication and collaboration, but the benefits for teachers, students, and parents are significant.

Assessment

Although much of the assessment that occurs related to oral language and communication is likely to be conducted or directed by the speech/language therapist, **Progress Monitoring** teachers have a variety of tools for assessing language development at their disposal. There are several tests of comprehensive language that may provide useful information to special education teachers:

- Test of Language Development—Primary (TOLD—P:3; Newcomer and Hammill, 1997). This test was designed for students who range in age from four to eight and is individually administered in approximately one hour. The test provides information on vocabulary, meaningful use of spoken words, grammatic understanding, word articulation, and word discrimination.
- Test of Language Development—Intermediate (TOLD—I:3; Hammill and Newcomer, 1997). This test was designed for students who range in age from 8 to 12 and is individually administered in about 40 minutes. The test provides information on spoken language, malapropisms, picture vocabulary, sentence combining, and grammatic comprehension.
- Test for Auditory Comprehension of Language (TACL—3; Carrow-Woolfolk, 1999). This test was designed for students who range in age from 3 to 10 and is individually administered in 15 to 25 minutes. The test measures receptive spoken vocabulary, grammar, and syntax.
- Test of Narrative Language (TNL; Gillam and Pearson, 2004). This test is appropriate for students ranging in ages from 5 through 11 and is individually administered in 15 to 20 minutes. The assessment provides information on language impairments, understanding of literal and inferential comprehension questions, and use of narrative discourse.
- Comprehensive Assessment of Spoken Language (CASL; Carrow-Woolfolk, 1999). Designed for students ages 3 to 21 and individually administered in 30 to 45 minutes, this measure was developed to provide an assessment of language-processing skills and structural knowledge across the age range. Information is provided that addresses lexical/semantic, syntactic, supralinguistic, and pragmatic knowledge and use.
- Adolescent Language Screening Test (ALST; Morgan and Guilford, 1984). This screening instrument is designed to provide professionals with a quick (less than 15 minutes) yet complete approach to individually screening adolescents ages 11 to 17 for speech and language problems.

FOCUS Question 6. Why is it important to work with families to develop students' language skills, and what are some examples of activities in which families can engage with their children?

Working with Families to Extend Language Concepts

Children are more likely to learn new vocabulary and language structures when they are active participants in their learning and can practice new concepts in different contexts (home and school). Keep all language activities short and fun so that parents/guardians do not view communication as homework. In planning language activities, it is also important to be aware of cultural and linguistic differences in the home. If a family does not speak English, encourage the student to complete these activities in the language used at home. The following are some suggestions for using newly learned language concepts in a variety of environments:

- Send home a short description or picture of a recent classroom activity or field trip. Encourage parents/guardians to ask open-ended rather than closed questions about the activity. For example, a parent might say, "I understand that you made a papier-mâché vase today. How did you do that?"
- Inform parents/guardians of new vocabulary that children are learning. Have children write a note to their families about what they learned. A child might say, "I learned the word *notorious* today."
- Have children bring new words to class that they have heard at home. Create a word "treasure chest" and encourage the children to be vocabulary "hunters."
- Inform parents of new social language concepts that their children have practiced in class. Have children describe the concept to their families. For instance, a child might say, "I learned what to say if someone is bullying me." Encourage families to practice similar role plays with the child at home.
- When possible, have students ask their parents questions about topics that they are learning in class. For example, if the class is

discussing the food pyramid, have the children ask their families about favorite foods, and set aside a time for them to report back to the class on their findings.

- To practice figurative language, have children tell jokes or word puns to their families at home.
- To practice asking questions and listening skills, have students ask their families about hypothetical situations discussed in class. Themes may come from journal topics such as "What would you do if you had a million dollars?"
- Encourage families to discuss books that they read with their children. Send home some tips to encourage discussion around a book (e.g., talk about the pictures, relate the story to the child's own experiences).

INSTRUCTIONAL ACTIVITIES

This section provides instructional activities related to oral language. Some of the activities teach new skills; others are best suited for practice and reinforcement of already acquired skills. For each activity, the objective, materials, and teaching procedures are described. When possible, use these activities to reinforce the oral language within the curriculum content (current vocabulary or class topic).

▶Partner Talk

Objective: To provide students with opportunities to produce and orally share ideas and thoughts about a topic (including responses to comprehension questions).

Grades: Primary

Materials: Two or three questions prepared beforehand by the teacher for discussion. These may be comprehension questions (literal and interpretive) or any type of questions for discussion.

Teaching Procedures: Have all students find a partner and sit knee to knee, facing each other. Tell the students you would like them to respond to the question you are going to ask. Ask the question, then allow two to three minutes for students to think of their individual responses. Instruct each member of the pair to take a turn responding to the question, and then to discuss their responses together. For example, if using story comprehension questions, students might discuss what each

thinks will happen next in the story, what each thinks is the story problem, or what each might have done differently if he or she were the main character. After three to five minutes, ask students to return to the larger group, and invite them to share their responses.

Adaptations: This activity can be adapted for older students by having them write responses or new endings to stories together.

▶Chef for a Day

Objective: To provide students with opportunities to provide a detailed explanation while using ordinal words (*first, second, next,* etc.).

Grades: Primary

Materials: 8" × 11" card stock, about five sheets per student

Teaching Procedures: Tell students that they will be explaining to their classmates how to make their favorite meal or snack. Students should draw pictures of the ingredients and steps in the process on separate sheets of card stock (ingredients on one sheet, each step in the process on a separate, additional sheet) and should number their sheets of paper to correspond with the order of steps in the process. Students then share their recipes with their classmates.

Younger students may only provide two or three steps in the process, whereas older students may have more than five steps. Monitor student progress, and suggest adding or combining steps on the sheets of paper as needed. Encourage the students to use specific vocabulary (e.g., *mix, stir, pour, combine,* and *spread*) rather than general vocabulary (e.g., *put*) in their explanations. The recipes should not be too simple (with too few steps to adequately create the snack) or too complicated (so many details that the process is not well understood).

Adaptations: Have students work in pairs or groups to create the recipe. Have students write some or all of the words in their recipe (this is a good activity for practicing the command form of verbs). If more than one student chooses the same snack, have them compare their recipes to notice similarities and differences in the ways each makes the same snack. Try to make the food item following one of the student's directions.

▶Creature from Outer Space

Objective: To provide students with opportunities for elaboration in response to "wh-" questions regarding concrete, everyday objects and actions (not in response to a story).

Grades: 2–5

Materials: Everyday classroom objects

Teaching Procedures: Tell the class that you are a space creature who has just landed on planet Earth. You are trying to gather information about life on Earth to take back to share with scientists on your planet. Then ask about anything in the room, and follow up student responses with additional questions that require further elaboration or definition. For example:

> Teacher: "What is this?"
> Student: "It's a pair of scissors."
> Teacher: "What are scissors?"
> Student: "You use them to cut paper."
> Teacher: "What is paper?"
> Student: "It's something you write on."
> Teacher: "What is writing?"
> Student: "It's making words on paper."
> Teacher: "Why do you make words on paper?"

At some point (before students become frustrated) you can tell them you understand and then move on to the next object (or continue the next day).

Adaptations: For younger children, use a puppet to represent the alien creature. This activity can be made more difficult by asking more "how" and "why" questions and by selecting things in the classroom that will require higher levels of thought and explanation (e.g., asking about a poem on the wall or about a science experiment). This is also a great activity to check understanding of new vocabulary.

▶ What Did You Say?

Objective: To provide students with opportunities to practice saying things in different ways for different purposes.

Grades: 1–5

Materials: None

Teaching Procedures: This activity helps students understand how the same thing can be said in very different ways (intonation and wording), depending on the context of the situation and the person being spoken to. Have students say the following words, phrases, and sentences using different intonations, given the contexts that follow each:

> *"Hello"*

- To the principal
- To their best friend

- To a baby
- To a person they don't like
- When answering the phone

> *"Good-bye"*

- To their best friend at the end of the day
- To their teacher
- To a friend who is moving away
- To their mom on the phone
- To someone they don't know on the phone

> *"How are you?"*

- As if they were a teacher asking a student at the beginning of the day
- To a friend who is sick
- To a classmate who seems sad
- To someone they just met

Adaptations: Have students think of different words or expressions they could use instead of the words in quotations above. For example, a student may say "Hi!" or "Hey!" to his or her best friend instead of "Hello." Use simple puppets (e.g., pictures on Popsicle sticks) to assist the students in adopting different roles. For older students, have them practice more complex language tasks in different contexts (making requests, asking for advice, describing a past event).

▶ Which One Doesn't Belong?

Objective: To have students identify specific relationships among vocabulary words that they have learned.

Grades: 1–5

Materials: Weekly vocabulary words as a foundation for a list of four words, of which three of the four words are related according to a specific dimension, and one is not. (They do not necessarily need to be written for students.) You may need to use other, related words in the activity to provide relationships to your target vocabulary words. This will vary according to the idea or concept and the students' ability level.

Teaching Procedures: Tell students that you are going to play a game that will help them think about the main idea you are stressing, for example, colors, animal groups, or important events in state history. You will tell them four words or phrases, and they are to tell you which one of the four does not belong with the others and why. Tell the students the four items. Then have the students tell you which are related and why. Then have them tell you why the fourth is not related to the other three. For example, if one of the weekly vocabulary words is *valley*, the teacher may write *valley*, *mountain*, *river*, and *desert* on the board. Students explain why *valley*, *mountain*, and *desert* are similar and why *river* is different. You may also ask them to generate other words in the same category.

Adaptations: Have younger students choose from items that can be visualized, such as colors, animals, or objects. The difficulty of the task can be mediated by having the actual objects or pictures of the objects for the students to see or by having the students visualize the objects. Older students can choose more successfully from the idea and concept level, although visuals to trigger knowledge may be helpful.

▶It's for Sale!

Objective: To have students use language to elaborate and persuade.

Grades: 3–6 or above (maybe grade 2 at a much simpler level)

Materials: Slips of paper with various products on each one, either written or as pictures from a magazine (e.g., camera, soccer ball, car, perfume or makeup, specific shoes, etc.)

Teaching Procedures: This can be done in small or large group format on one day or with a few students a day across many days. Students should be familiar with skills used in persuasion before undertaking this activity.

Ask students to draw a slip of paper or item from a jar or hat. Allow them a short but sufficient amount of time to gather their initial thoughts about the item, then give each student five minutes to try to "sell" their product to the class or small group. The goal is for students to convince their classmates that they really need or want this product.

After the student is finished, allow classmates five minutes to ask him or her questions about the product; the "salesperson" will have to come up with answers to support his or her case and/or further descriptions of the product (these, of course, may be invented).

Adaptations: Students can be given extra points for including recent idioms or vocabulary in their presentation. After students ask questions of the "salesperson," have them raise their hands to show whether they would want to buy the product. Whoever "sells" the most wins. Students can also work in groups rather than individually to present the product. Have older students try to sell an idea rather than a product. For example, if you have been studying the food pyramid and nutrition, you could write on a piece of paper: "It's important to eat vegetables." The student who draws this paper has to give a persuasive argument to eat vegetables.

▶Scavenger Hunt

Objective: To provide students with opportunities to consider and state relationships between two objects.

Grades: K–2 (see the "Adaptations" section for similar activity for students in grades 3–5)

Materials: Different items from around the classroom or ones typically found in a house (e.g., envelope, ruler, paintbrush, book, spatula, sponge, cookie cutter)

Teaching Procedure: Prepare a list of pairs of seemingly unrelated items in advance (e.g., book and paintbrush). Tell each student the pair of items they are to find (or have pictures of the items for younger students; for older students, write the names of the objects). Direct students to look for the items. When they find them, have students talk about the two objects—how they are alike, how they are different, how they are used, and how they might go together. In the example of book and paintbrush, a child might be able to relate the two objects by saying that the illustrator used a paintbrush to make the pictures in the book. For an example such as pencil and paintbrush, they are alike because both are used to write or draw, but they are different because a paintbrush also needs paint in order to write or draw. For kindergarten students, the comparisons will need to be simpler and more concrete than for older students.

Adaptations: Adapt this game for students in grades 3–5 by having them compare two nouns (or any other types of words or parts of grammar that are being studied). Prepare 30–40 word cards with nouns on them (this is great for reviewing and practicing new vocabulary). Divide the class into two groups. Give the first two students in each group a word card each. Direct the two students from each group to work together to create a sentence comparing the two nouns; the first pair to create a sentence wins a point for their team. Continue until one of the teams reaches a predetermined goal and wins the game.

▶Daydream Chair

Objective: To provide students with opportunities to generate ideas about and elaborate on concepts or future story events.

Grades: 1–4

Materials: A special chair in the classroom (e.g., a rocking chair or a director's chair)

Teaching Procedures: Ask a few students each day to take turns sitting in the "Daydream Chair," describing what each would do if he or she were a certain person or object (or, for older students, in a certain situation).

Adaptations: For younger students, ask them what they would do if they were a famous person, a tree, a book, a paintbrush, or a similar object. Vary the object or person by student so that each is describing something different. This can also be done in relation to occupations, by having students discuss what people in different occupations do as part of their jobs. To assist the students in portraying their character, have them hold a picture of the person or object in front of them as they are speaking in the first person (e.g., "I am an astronaut . . ."). Older students can be asked similar questions about what they would do, would have done, or might do in the future if they were a particular character from a story. Vary characters by student.

▶Find the Way

Objective: To provide students with practice in giving and interpreting directions.

Grades: All grades

Materials: (1) Maps of different areas. For example, use a map of the school for younger students, and use a map of the local area, the state, or the area you are studying in social studies for older students. The map should be labeled. (2) Put the names of places on the map and on small cards so that the cards can be drawn during the game.

Teaching Procedures: One student is designated as "It." This student is given a map and draws a card that gives the name of the place he or she is to find. The student draws the route on his or her map. The other students are given the same map, but they do not know the destination or the route. Without showing the map to the other students, the student who is "It" must describe, by using words only, how to get to the destination. The other students are allowed to ask three questions to help clarify the directions.

To modify this exercise into a game format, each student can receive a point for each time he or she is successful in directing the other students to the location. After a student has finished, discuss how he or she was effective in giving directions, and make recommendations to improve his or her language abilities.

Adaptations: A similar format can be used with one student directing the other students on a treasure hunt.

▶Many Meanings

Objective: To give students practice with using homonyms and words with multiple meanings.

Grades: Intermediate and secondary

Materials: (1) Any generic game board with a die or spinner and pieces to serve as players. (2) A variety of meaning cards and homonyms or words that have multiple meanings (e.g., *heal/heel, meet/meat*) written on one side.

Teaching Procedures: Have the students set up the game and clarify the rules. For each turn, a student rolls the die or spins the spinner. The student then picks a card and uses each homonym in a separate sentence to show the difference between the meanings of the words or the multiple meanings. If the student's sentences reflect correct meanings, he or she moves the marker the number of spaces shown on the die or spinner. If the student is unable to make a sentence, other students may help him or her, but the student cannot move the marker. The first student to reach the finish line wins.

Adaptations: Have the students work in teams, or have the students give definitions of the words rather than using them in sentences.

▶Surprise Pouches

Objective: To give students practice in describing objects.

Grades: Primary

Materials: (1) A cloth pouch with a drawstring. (2) Small objects that will fit in the pouch.

Teaching Procedures: Place a small object in the pouch, and have one student in the group feel the object without looking in the pouch. The student cannot give the name of the object but must describe it. The student describes what he or she feels while the rest of the students in the group try to guess what is in the pouch. When the student who is feeling the object thinks the other students have guessed correctly, he or she takes the object out to see whether the students are right. Have the students discuss how the descriptive words helped them guess the object. For example, "Smooth and round made me think it was a ball."

Put a new object in the pouch, and have another student describe the object. Each student should get several turns at describing the objects.

▶I Spy

Objective: To provide students with opportunities to practice and develop descriptive vocabulary.

Grades: Elementary

Materials: Objects in the surrounding environment or vocabulary words

Teaching Procedures: Locate an object in the environment. Provide the students with clues that describe the object using the stem "I spy...." For example, "I spy something that has green, narrow leaves." "I spy something that has rough bark." After each clue, the students try to guess what you are spying. The first person to identify the object becomes the next person to select an object and describe it.

Adaptations: For some students, you may need to assist in picking an object and giving "I spy" clues. If your weekly vocabulary list includes adjectives, give the students extra points for using those words in their descriptions. For older children, place a written list of vocabulary words on the board and ask them to describe words from that list in the game.

▶The Add-On Game

Objective: To provide students with practice in listening to each other while categorizing and making associations between words within a topic.

Grades: Primary

Materials: Starter phrases that allow students to develop a list. For example:

- I went to the desert and I saw . . .
- I went up in space and I saw . . .
- I went back in time and I saw . . .

Teaching Procedures: The students and teacher sit in a circle. Use a topic from social studies, language arts, or science to start your discussion. For example, if you have been studying animals in the rain forest, a student can begin the game by saying, "I went to the rain forest and saw. . . ." This student names one thing that he or she might see in the rain forest. The next student in the circle then repeats the sentence, listing the first item and adding another item. The next student repeats both items and adds a third, and so on. This game can be played in two ways. To play competitively, the student is eliminated from the game when he or she cannot list all the items. The last student to remain in the game wins. To play cooperatively, the object of the game is for the group to beat the number of items remembered in previous games. To keep all students in the game, each student may be allowed two assists from a friend during the game (students are not "out" when incorrect). If a student has already used the two assists, then the number of items the group has correctly remembered is determined and compared to see whether the group beat previous scores.

Adaptations: This can be adapted to current events or holidays (e.g., gifts for Christmas or treats you got for Halloween).

▶Round-Robin Stories

Objective: To provide students with opportunities to develop story grammar.

Grades: Elementary

Materials: None required, though a picture of a scene or setting may help students to start the story.

Teaching Procedures: To get students ready to start round-robin stories, tell them that they are going to be telling a story as a group and that each student is to build on the story. Using a picture (if available and needed), tell what the story is going to be about. For example, "This story is about a group of friends who want to earn money to buy something." Have the students identify basic components of the story (names of the characters, setting) and begin telling the story. After several sentences, start a sentence, and have one student in the group finish the sentence. Model a variety of sentence starters. For example:

Subordinate Clauses
- When Jimmy went into the store, he . . .
- After Rita saw the dog in the window, she . . .

Direct Quotations
- Then the father said, ". . ."
- Suddenly, Raul screamed, ". . ."

Causal and Conditional Complex Sentences
- She didn't want to buy the brown dog because . . .
- He felt sad because . . .
- If she spent all of her money, she . . .

On the basis of their ending, start another sentence, and have another student finish it. As students become accustomed to this storytelling process, they should be able to build directly on each other's sentences without your having to start each sentence.

Adaptations: Use the same procedure, but use wordless picture books to guide students in telling the story.

▶Barrier Game

Objective: To provide students with practice in describing how to make something and to provide practice in listening to directions.

Grades: Elementary

Materials: (1) Colored blocks for building objects or crayons for drawing objects. (2) Some type of barrier to block the view between the two students or the student and the teacher.

Teaching Procedures: Divide class into pairs, and explain the directions to the students. Have the students sit so that the barrier is between them. One student draws a simple picture or builds a simple block design. During or after the building or drawing, the student describes to the other student how to make the design. The other student attempts to duplicate the work and can ask questions to get help. When the second student has finished, remove the barrier and have the students compare their work.

Adaptations: After the students become successful at the activity, the number of questions that can be asked can be limited.

▶Category Sort

Objective: To provide students with practice in sorting objects or word cards by categories.

Grades: Primary

Materials: (1) Objects or word cards that can be sorted by one or more categories (e.g., colored bears, colored blocks, colored buttons, colored marbles, types of animals, types of food). (2) Word cards that represent categories. (3) Sorting boxes (i.e., small boxes in which the students can sort objects or cards).

Teaching Procedures: Put a category word card next to each box. Demonstrate how to name each object or word card, and then put all the like objects or cards in the same box. Once the student has sorted the objects or cards, he or she names each category and the objects or cards in each category. The student then talks about what is alike about all the objects or cards in one category. Give older students vocabulary or spelling words to sort. Model how to sort the words in different ways (by meaning, spelling, part of speech, etc.)

▶Create a Comic

Objective: To provide students with practice in using dialogue and telling stories.

Grades: Intermediate and junior high

Materials: Familiar comic strips or sequences in comic books. Blank out the words in the balloons.

Teaching Procedures: Present the comic strip to the students, and discuss with them what they know about the comic strip characters, what is happening, and what could be written in each of the balloons. Have the students write in the different balloons. Take turns reading the comic strip with different students reading what different characters say. The different comic strips can be put into a comic book that can be shared with other students.

Adaptations: After students are comfortable with this activity, they can illustrate and dictate their own comic strips.

▶Play the Part

Objective: To provide students with practice in using language during simulations of typical interactions.

Grades: Intermediate and secondary

Materials: Simulation cards. Each card should describe the situation, the characters, and the goal of the language interaction. Some examples are given below.

Situation 1: Two friends meet a third person who is an old friend and known to only one of them.

Characters: New friend, old friend, person making the introductions. *Goal:* Introduce new friend to old friend and get a conversation started among the three of you.

Situation 2: One person approaches another asking how to find a store about 10 blocks away. *Characters:* Stranger, person giving directions. *Goal:* Give directions that will allow the stranger to find the store.

Situation 3: Two friends are in a store. One tells the other that he or she intends to steal a small item from the store. *Characters:* Friend, person persuading. *Goal:* Convince the friend not to shoplift.

Teaching Procedures: Explain that each person is to assume the described role and participate as if this were a real situation.

Have the students assume the various characters and discuss what they are going to say in their roles. The students then carry out the role play. Have the students discuss how effective each person was in using language to accomplish the goal.

▶ Fun with Figurative Language

Objective: To provide students with opportunities to enhance proverb and/or idiom understanding.

Grades: Intermediate and junior high

Materials: Text from class that contains proverbs (e.g., "The early bird catches the worm.") or idioms (e.g., "Keep your head above water.")

Teaching Procedures: Select a proverb or idiom that is easily explained (e.g., "One rotten apple spoils the barrel"), and model how to interpret the meaning. First, examine the literal meaning, and draw a rough picture if necessary. Then examine the context of the proverb, and consider the character's motivations and feelings. Divide students into small groups. Each group may discuss one or two proverbs within the story using the modeled techniques. In addition, relate the proverb to students' lives and experiences. Discuss when and why a person may use a particular proverb or idiom.

SUMMARY for Chapter 6

Language is a vehicle for communicating our ideas, beliefs, and needs. Although most children enter school with many language skills already mastered, language continues to develop throughout the school years. However, some students with learning disabilities experience considerable difficulty in the development of language skills during the school-age years. Some of these students may have problems primarily focused in one of the three components of language (content, form, and use), but because of the interactive nature of these components, such students generally have difficulty in all three areas and require more explicit instruction.

Some general guidelines for teaching oral language include teaching language in purposeful contexts; following the sequence of normal development; teaching comprehension and production; using conversations to promote language development; adjusting pacing, chunking information, and checking for understanding to promote comprehension; increasing wait time to promote production; using effective teaching strategies when presenting new concepts or skills; using self-talk and parallel talk to describe what the teacher is doing; using modeling to demonstrate language; using expansion and elaboration; using structured language programs to provide intensive practice and feedback; using

language as an intrinsic motivator; and systematically planning and instructing for generalization.

In addition, strategies for teaching content or vocabulary can be implemented, including emphasizing critical features of concepts being taught, introducing concepts in a number of ways, presenting both examples and nonexamples of the concept, categorizing new concepts, presenting new vocabulary in simple sentences, and using games to reinforce newly introduced concepts. Methods for increasing word-finding ability and elaboration can be used.

Several useful strategies for teaching form or the structure of language include teaching new sentence structures according to developmental sequences or order of difficulty; using familiar, concrete examples when teaching new structures; using simple sentences when teaching a new sentence form; having students extend learned forms to situations that need elaborated sentences; using actual objects and events when initially teaching a new structure form; and introducing new sentences in a variety of ways. Helpful strategies for teaching use or pragmatics include the use of role play to simulate situations in which the targeted pragmatic skills are required, the use of pictures to represent feelings, and the use of conversations as frameworks for teaching functional language.

Given the complexity of language at the school-age level and the need to teach language in context, providing language instruction for students with learning problems is a challenge. We encourage teachers of such students to work with a speech/language pathologist. This specialist is generally willing to participate in collaborative language programs for students. Such efforts will help to make the teacher's instruction consistent and integrative. Finally, we encourage all teachers to accept the challenge of teaching language. Providing students with the language skills to be effective communicators in school and other life settings may be one of the most important tasks we undertake as teachers.

FOCUS Answers

FOCUS Question 1. **What are the two main areas of language delays, and how do they manifest themselves in the development of content, form, and use of language?**

Answer: Language delays occur either in receptive language (e.g., following directions) or in expressive language (e.g., word finding). Difficulties in either area commonly influence the production and understanding of the *content* aspect of language, which may lead to difficulty with creative aspects of language, such as understanding and using figurative language. The *form* of language refers to its structure and sound, so for students with language delays, sentences are often shorter and do not progress to contain the same complexity as do the sentences of their peers. *Use*, or pragmatics, is perhaps the most important aspect of language growth. Some students with language difficulties tend to misinterpret meanings and emotions expressed by others and may not be able to express themselves effectively.

FOCUS Question 2. **What are some examples of strategies that can be used to teach oral language, content, form, and use, and how would each strategy support language development?**

Answer: One strategy that promotes *oral* language development includes providing opportunities for students to engage in meaningful conversations. *Content* teaching involves vocabulary development and understanding and applying new concepts. Teaching *form* requires teaching and practicing specific language structures such as prefixes and suffixes. To develop pragmatics, use role plays or pictures to simulate situations such as greetings, question asking, and expressing emotions.

FOCUS Question 3. **What are the strategies and considerations on which teachers should focus when teaching culturally and linguistically diverse learners?**

Answer: Effective instruction for culturally and linguistically diverse learners incorporates two key components. Teachers must both develop the student's English language acquisition and incorporate the student's first language and culture into learning experiences.

FOCUS Question 4. **What is metalinguistics, and how can teachers use it to promote language development?**

Answer: Metalinguistics refers to knowing and awareness of language and its form. Teachers can use metalinguistic practices to promote language development by asking students to count the number of syllables in a word, the number of words in a sentence, and the number of sounds or phonemes in a word. Teaching students the structure of stories and that word and language can have multiple meanings is also a way to promote metalinguistic awareness.

FOCUS Question 5. **How can special education teachers work with language specialists to implement RTI?**

Answer: Within RTI frameworks, special education teachers can work with language specialists to promote language and literacy development with at-risk students as well as students with special needs by (a) collaborating and coteaching with the general education teacher to promote appropriate language and literacy activities including modifying and adjusting typical instruction, (b) provide professional development to school personnel regarding the linguistic bases of reading and writing, (c) provide information and support for parents of at-risk children regarding language and literacy activities in the home environment, and (d) demonstrate lessons that promote language and literacy outcomes for at-risk students and students with disabilities.

FOCUS Question 6. **Why is it important to work with families to develop students' language skills, and what are some examples of activities in which families can engage with their children?**

Answer: Children are more likely to learn new vocabulary and language structures when they can practice new concepts in different contexts (home and school). Examples of home activities include informing families of the vocabulary that is being learned at school and encouraging them to discuss these new words with their children; having families ask open-ended questions about field trips, books that they are reading at home, or current events; and inviting families and children to play with language by telling jokes or making puns.

THINKand APPLY

- What are the major components of oral language? Listen to a conversation between two students, and think about how the components function.
- What three general teaching strategies can you easily employ when building oral language skills? Converse with a child, and use these strategies.
- Name at least five different functions for which we use language. Observe students as they play, and note the different ways in which they use language.
- Using several of the principles recommended for teaching content, plan how to teach students to categorize ideas about a topic.

- What is word-finding difficulty? Describe several strategies you could use to help a student who has word-finding difficulty.
- When planning instruction for students whose first language is not English, what considerations should you keep in mind?
- Choose a lesson plan, and adapt it to demonstrate sensitivity to students who are culturally and linguistically diverse.

APPLYthe STANDARDS

Council for Exceptional Children

1. Select five principles for teaching language (see Figure 6.3). For each principle, (1) describe a classroom example and (2) provide a rationale for how this example supports language development for students with learning and behavior problems who exhibit difficulties with oral language (BD4K4, BD4S1, LD6K1, LD6K2, LD7K3, LD9S2).

   Standard BD4K4: Prevention and intervention strategies for individuals at risk of emotional/behavioral disorders.

   Standard BD4S1: Use strategies from multiple theoretical approaches for individuals with emotional/behavioral disorders.

Standard LD6K1: Typical language development and how that may differ for individuals with learning disabilities.

Standard LD6K2: Impact of language development and listening comprehension on academic and nonacademic learning of individuals with learning disabilities.

Standard LD7K3: Interventions and services for children who may be at risk for learning disabilities.

Standard LD9S2: Use research findings and theories to guide practice.

WEBSITESas RESOURCES | to Assist in Teaching Oral Language and English as a Second Language

The following Websites are extensive resources to expand your understanding of teaching oral language and English as a second language:

- Net Connections for Communication Disorders and Sciences www.mnsu.edu/dept/comdis/kuster2/welcome.html
- Learning Disabilities Association of America www.ldanatl.org
- Interesting Things for ESL Students www.manythings.org
- Dave's ESL Café www.eslcafe.com/index.html
- The Internet Teachers of English as a Second Language Journal http://iteslj.org
- Word-Finding Difficulties www.wordfinding.com
- Jim Cummins' Second Language Learning and Literacy Development Web www.iteachilearn.com/cummins

Where the Classroom Comes to Life

Video Homework Exercise Go to MyEducationLab and select the topic "COMMUNICATION DISOR-DERS," then watch the video "Diana's Language Sample" and complete the activity questions below.

This video demonstrates a language assessment given by a speech pathologist to a student, Diana, in a stimulating interactive play environment.

1. How do the areas assessed in the video connect to the content of language instruction described in the chapter?
2. What are some of Diana's strengths and needs in the areas of receptive and expressive language?

Video Homework Exercise Go to MyEducationLab and select the topic "COMMUNICATION DISOR-DERS," then watch the video "Who is George?" and complete the activity questions below.

In this video clip a resource teacher and a general education teacher discuss the goals and progress of George, a first grader who has received support in the area of communication.

1. List several areas of development mentioned by the teachers in the video.
2. Create two language goals for George. Then use the information provided in the chapter to give an example of two instructional strategies that you could use to help George work towards these goals.

Appendix 6.1   Selected Materials for Teaching Language

Programs and Games for Global Language Development

HELP 3 (1988), *HELP 4* (1989), and *HELP 5* (1991) by Andrea M. Lazzari and Patricia M. Peters. East Moline, IL: LinguiSystems, Inc.

Each book targets a different set of linguistic concepts. *HELP 3* is aimed at increasing ability to integrate conceptual thinking skills with language concepts. Activities include practice on linguistic concepts, paraphrasing activities, thinking and problem-solving tasks, and pragmatic skills. *HELP 4* targets language in daily life. Exercises include tasks in defining and describing activities, linguistic concepts, and use of humor and riddles. *HELP 5* has exercises for processing information, comparing and contrasting words, understanding math language, and activities using words to express opinions and feelings. Contains IEP goals.

Language Lessons in the Classroom (1993) by Susan Diamond. Phoenix, AZ: ECL Publications.

Aimed at providing activities for the classroom consultant, this can also be used by regular educators to develop language skills. Intended for students in grades K–5.

Peabody Language Development Kits (Rev. Ed. 1981) by L. M. Dunn, J. O. Smith, K. B. Horton, and D. D. Smith. Circle Pines, MN: American Guidance Service.

This program consists of two kits: one for kindergarten and one for first grade. Each kit consists of lesson manuals, picture cards grouped by categories, puppets to demonstrate concepts, posters depicting scenes and stories, sound books of sound and song activities, and colored chips for manipulation activities such as counting, sequencing, and grouping.

Programs for Auditory Processing

HELP for Auditory Processing (1994) by Andrea M. Lazzari and Patricia M. Peters. East Moline, IL: LinguiSystems, Inc.

This sourcebook includes exercises for processing information in word classes, following directions, identifying relevant details, making inferences, asking and answering questions, sequencing information, and listening to sounds in words. It includes IEP goals and is designed for ages six to adult.

50 Quick-Play Listening Games (2005) by Kelly Malone, Karen Stontz, and Paul F. Johnson. East Moline, IL: LinguiSystems, Inc.

This book contains ready-to-copy games that reflect classroom listening demands, including phonological awareness, identifying the main idea and details, and following directions. The games are easy to play and may be used individually or in small groups. Intended for grades K–5.

100% Listening 2-Book Set (2002) by LinguiSystems, Inc. East Moline, IL: LinguiSystems, Inc.

This two book set targets classroom listening skills necessary at both the primary and intermediate levels. Skills are presented sequentially and mirror daily classroom situations. The books are also sold separately. Targets grades K–5.

Programs and Games for Vocabulary Development and Word Retrieval

HELP for Word Finding (1995) by Andrea M. Lazzari and Patricia Peters. East Moline, IL: LinguiSystems, Inc.

Exercises to enhance word-finding strategies and increase vocabulary. Includes exercises for automatic associations, thematic groupings, definitions, answering questions, parts of speech, and use of contextual cues. Intended for ages 6 to adult, the program includes an answer key and IEP goals.

50 Quick-Play Vocabulary Games (2004) by Paul F. Johnson and Patti Halfman. East Moline, IL: LinguiSystems, Inc.

The games included in this resource target thematic vocabulary (such as animals, transportation, and space) and vocabulary skills (such as figurative language, context clues, and abbreviations). The path and card games will help engage your students target vocabulary needs. Intended for grades 1–6.

125 Vocabulary Builders (2000) by Linda Bowers, Rosemary Huisingh, Carolyn LoGiudice, Jane Orman, and Paul F. Johnson. East Moline, IL: LinguiSystems, Inc.

A book of paper-and-pencil tasks for students ages 10–15. These tasks are designed to provide practice with newly acquired vocabulary words.

HELP for Vocabulary (1999) by Andrea M. Lazzari. East Moline, IL: LinguiSystems, Inc.

Part of the HELP series by LinguiSystems. As with all books in the HELP series, each page is a mini-lesson with IEP goals listed. Targets ages 8 to adult.

10 Quick-Play Folder Games: Associations (2005) by Lauri Whiskeyman and Barb Truman. East Moline, IL: LinguiSystems, Inc.

One in a series of folder games (targeting skills such as categories, rhyming, and concepts) this kit contains five double-sided game boards that are ready to play. Targeted skills included describing functions, assigning categories, and reviewing words with multiple meanings. Also available in Spanish. Intended for grades PreK–4.

Rocky's Mountain: A Word-Finding Game (1999) by Gina V. Williamson and Susan S. Shields. East Moline, IL: LinguiSystems, Inc.

A board game that assists children ages 4–9 with acquiring one of four word-finding strategies. The four strategies are visual imagery, word association, sound/letter cuing, and categorization.

WordBURST (1997) by Gina V. Williamson and Susan S. Shields. East Moline, IL: LinguiSystems, Inc.

A word-recall board game for students ages 8 to adult. The word retrieval strategies are the same as *Rocky's Mountain;* this is similar but designed with the older student in mind.

It's on the Tip of My Tongue (2001) by Diane J. German. Chicago, IL: Word Finding Materials, Inc.

This program provides activities to help students ages 2½–10 increase memory/word retrieval skills and vocabulary.

10 Quick-Play Folder Games: Vocabulary (2007) by LinguiSystems. East Moline, IL: LinguiSystems, Inc.

The games in the set address many skills necessary for vocabulary acquisition. Stimulus items are presented in both Spanish and English. Intended for ages 9–13.

Programs and Games for Grammar

HELP for Grammar (1995) by Andrea M. Lazzari. East Moline, IL: LinguiSystems, Inc.

In-depth grammar practice of cumulative grammatical exercises. Activities include applications for nouns, pronouns, adverbs, and adjectives, and contextual usages. For ages 8 to adult, it includes answer key and IEP goals.

Teaching Morphology Developmentally (Revised) (1989) by Kenneth G. Shipley and Carolyn J. Banis. Tucson, AZ: Communication Skill Builders.

This program is designed for students ages 2½ to 10. Activities for teaching bound morphemes include present progressive, plurals, possessives, past tenses, third person singulars, and superlatives. Includes 552 stimulus cards, a manual, and a reproducible worksheet manual.

Grammar Scramble: A Grammar and Sentence-Building Game (1998) by Rick and Linda Bowers. East Moline, IL: LinguiSystems, Inc.

A board game with a crossword puzzle format in which students have to intersect sentences. Appropriate for students ages 8 to adult, this program is useful for developing carryover skills for grammar.

100% Grammar (1997) by Mike and Carolyn LoGiudice. East Moline, IL: LinguiSystems, Inc.

A series of paper-and-pencil activities designed to teach essential grammar components for students ages 9–14. The program includes pretests and post-tests for each concept, making it helpful for charting progress. Also available in a LITE edition with practice items that have fewer contextual demands than the items in the regular edition.

Scissors, Glue, and Grammar, Too! (1996) by Susan Boegler and Debbie Abruzzini. East Moline, IL: LinguiSystems, Inc.

Cut-and-paste activities for students ages 4–9. Engaging activities to reinforce regular and irregular verbs, comparatives and superlatives, possessive pronouns, "wh-" questions, and more.

Gram's Cracker: A Grammar Game (2000) by Julie Cole. East Moline, IL: LinguiSystems, Inc.

Students "help" the mouse get to his hole by practicing grammar concepts such as use of pronouns, possessives, past tense verbs, comparatives, superlatives, copulas, present progressive verbs, and negatives. This game has four levels of difficulty (identification, multiple choice, sentence completion, and sentence formulation). It is designed for students ages 4–9.

Programs for Pragmatics

Ready-to-Use Social Skills Lessons and Activities for Grades 1–3 (1995) edited by Ruth Weltmann Begun. West Nyack, NY: Center for Applied Research.

Develop positive social communication with these systematic reproducible lessons. Students obtain instruction in social uses of communication.

Room 14 (1993) by Carolyn Wilson. East Moline, IL: LinguiSystems, Inc.

Uses stories, comprehension activities, and organized lessons to teach social skills. Skills targeted include how to make and keep friends, fitting in at school, handling feelings, self-control, and

responsibility. Program includes instructor's manual, activity book, and picture book, and is intended for students ages 6–10.

Friendzee: A Social Skills Game (1992) by Diane Figula. East Moline, IL: LinguiSystems, Inc.

Teaches students ages 7–11 social skills such as body language, tone of voice, polite forms, giving information, listening, asking questions, and problem solving in a board game format. Themes include home, school, and community.

Conversations: A Framework for Language Intervention (1996) by Barbara Hoskins. Eau Claire, WI: Thinking Publications.

Offers professionals a framework for facilitating conversational interaction with individuals, who are having difficulty with communication skills, ages nine and up. This resource provides the facilitator with plans for helping groups of individuals work together to become more effective conversational partners. Conversations provide many specific activities and suggestions. Professionals may also use them to generate, adapt, and develop other productive ways of working with these varying age groups.

Who? What? When? . . . And More (1999) by Pro-Ed, Inc. Austin, TX: Pro-Ed, Inc.

This board game requires players to answer a mix of wh- questions. Intended for ages 6–12.

Publishing Companies That Produce a Large Number of Materials for Improving Speech and Language

Academic Communication Associates
www.acadcom.com
888-758-9558

Cognitive Concepts
www.earobics.com
888-328-8199

Great Ideas for Teaching
www.gift-inc.com
800-839-8339

LinguiSystems
www.linguisystems.com
800-776-4332

Chapter **7**

Assessing and Teaching Reading: Phonological Awareness, Phonics, and Word Recognition

As you read the chapter, watch for these questions to help you focus your learning:

1. What are the two overarching concepts that should guide reading instruction, and how do teachers decide where to focus instruction?

2. What are the definitions of phonological awareness, letter–sound correspondence, and phonics, and what are some examples of activities that can be used to teach them?

3. What are the definitions of the six main decoding strategies, and how does each contribute to successful word identification?

4. How can the use of explicit and implicit code instruction be compared?

Special education teachers teach many students who have difficulties in learning to read. Whether working as a coteacher with a kindergarten or first-grade teacher; working with a group of students and providing intensive, small group instruction in an elementary school; or teaching English and reading in a middle or high school, special education teachers spend a great deal of their time teaching reading. Why is this the case? First, reading is often considered to be the most important area of education (National Reading Panel, 2000; Snow, Burns, and Griffin, 1998). Skill at reading is a prerequisite for many of the learning activities in content-area classes such as social studies, science, and vocational education and for successful employment. Second, students with learning and behavior disabilities have reading targeted as an area of need and have IEP goals related to reading more than any other academic area. Third, longitudinal research indicates that if students with learning and behavior problems do not learn to read by the end of third grade, their chances of having reading difficulties throughout their schooling and into adulthood are about 50 percent (Lyon, 1998). Therefore, it is critical that students learn to read and accomplish this task early in their schooling.

Students have a variety of strengths and needs in the area of reading. Let's look at two students and see what effective instruction might be for these students. Kyle is a second grader who is receiving special education services for his learning disability in the area of reading. He reads at a beginning level and can recognize only about 30 words. When he comes to a word he does not recognize, he sometimes attempts to sound out the word. However, he has difficulty remembering common letter–sound correspondences. This means that when he sees letters, he does not automatically know the sound that letter makes. He also struggles with blending the sounds so that he can generate a word that is close enough to the correct word that he can figure it out. For Kyle, reading instruction will focus primarily on building phonological awareness, letter–sound correspondences, decoding strategies, and fluent word identification. The methods for teaching these components of reading that are presented in this chapter could assist in developing the automatic word recognition that would allow him to focus more of his attention on understanding what he reads. However, though the emphasis is placed on these more basic skills, his instructional program should also include repeated reading of independent and instructional-level decodable books (i.e., books that primarily use words that reflect the phonic and word patterns he has already learned) to build fluency. It should also include the listening, supported reading, and discussion of a wide variety of literature and content area materials to support his development of vocabulary and comprehension. Strategies for teaching these components (fluency, vocabulary development, and reading comprehension) are discussed in Chapters 8 and 10. Finally, it will be important for Kyle to pair reading and writing activities so that as he builds reading decoding skills, he can work simultaneously on spelling. Similarly, as he develops his understanding of different types of text and genres (e.g., narratives such as folktales, adventure stories, and mysteries; expositions such as descriptions, comparisons/contrasts, persuasions), he can build skills at writing (see Chapter 9).

Manuel, the other student, is an eighth grader who is reading at approximately the fourth-grade level. He entered school speaking both Spanish and English. He struggled with learning to read in Spanish because of his limited vocabulary knowledge and comprehension skills (e.g., getting the main idea, comprehension monitoring). He began reading in English during second grade and continued to struggle with vocabulary knowledge and comprehension and also had difficulty with decoding in English, because its letter–sound relationships are not as regular as those in Spanish. As an eighth grader, he is taking English/language arts from Ms. Gonzalez, the special education teacher. Ms. Gonzalez described Manuel's instructional reading program as follows:

> Manuel and the other students in his group are working on building their vocabulary, comprehension, and advanced decoding skills. Currently, they are learning to decode multisyllabic words (e.g., construction, renovation, reconsider) in which they learn to identify and separate the prefixes, suffixes, and endings. Then if they don't recognize the root word, they use the information they know about open and closed syllables to decode the root word. One of the benefits of this strategy is that the students learn the meanings of the prefixes and suffixes, so it really helps them in learning what the word means. They also use the context by rereading the sentence or the surrounding sentences. For Manuel, this helps him build his decoding skills and vocabulary knowledge at the same time. We also take the time to learn related words. For example, if the word is *construction*, we make a "struct" web with words such as *destruction, construct, reconstruction,* and *deconstruct.* For teaching comprehension, Manuel and his classmates are learning to use collaborative strategic reading. It teaches the comprehension strategies previewing, questioning, summarizing, clarifying, and comprehension monitoring. The students work in collaborative learning groups, and we have been focusing on the eighth-grade social studies content, since Manuel and his fellow students are in general education social studies classes. Next semester, the social studies teacher and I are planning to coteach, and we'll use collaborative strategic reading two to three days a week to build comprehension skills while learning social studies content knowledge.

Like Kyle's, Manuel's reading program contains various components of reading depending on his needs: word identification (this chapter), vocabulary development (Chapter 10), and comprehension (Chapter 8).

In this chapter, we present specific methods, techniques, and approaches for teaching phonological awareness, letter–sound relationships, and the alphabetic principle as well as strategies for teaching word identification and word study. In Chapter 8, we discuss instructional strategies for assisting students to become fluent readers and active comprehenders. In Chapter 10, we discuss teaching concepts and vocabulary within the context of content area reading.

Although we have divided our discussion of reading and writing instruction into four chapters (Chapters 7 through 10), we stress the importance of the relationships between reading and writing. Critical to successful reading instruction for students with learning and behavior problems are opportunities for them to spell the words they are learning to read, write about what they are reading, and write stories and essays using structures and conventions similar to the ones they are reading. As you read the next four chapters, think about how reading and writing are reciprocal processes and how they can be taught in such a way that each complements and supports the other. Also think about how the strategies and instructional techniques that were discussed in Chapter 6 on oral language are related to reading and writing and could be incorporated into your teaching.

FOCUS Question | 1. What are the two overarching concepts that should guide reading instruction, and how do teachers decide where to focus instruction?

Reading and Reading Instruction

The goal of reading instruction is to give students the skills, strategies, and knowledge to read fluently and understand various texts for purposes of enjoyment and learning, whether reading a book, magazine, sign, pamphlet, email message, or Internet site. To accomplish this goal, it is important to think about two overarching concepts.

1. *Reading is a skilled and strategic process in which learning to decode and read words accurately and rapidly is essential.* The average student entering school has a broad command of oral language. However, reading requires students to be able to distinguish the individual sounds that make up words and understand that letters represent sounds in language. Reading entails using the attentional, perceptual, memory, and retrieval processes necessary to automatically identify or decode words. Remember how in Chapter 2, you had no difficulty reading THE CAT (p. 57) even though the *H* and *A* were exactly the same? You used selective attention, feature analysis, your knowledge of the letter–sound relationships, and context to help you automatically recognize the words. This process of recognizing words is called *decoding* or *word recognition.* As students become proficient readers, they recognize most words with little effort. But as students are learning to read or when readers encounter an unknown word, they use decoding to segment and then blend the word by sounds and patterns (e.g., individual sounds, spelling patterns such as -at, -ight, prefixes, suffixes, syllables) and use syntax and context (e.g., semantics) to assist in decoding. In developing decoding skills, students develop metalinguistics, that is, knowledge and skills focused on how language operates.

Knowing and demonstrating how to blend and segment words into sounds or phonemes is a key phonological or metalinguistic skill for decoding and one for which students with learning/reading disabilities have particular difficulty (e.g., Lyon, 1998; Torgesen, 2000). When decoding is fluent, effort can be focused on comprehension.

Thus, a goal of reading and reading instruction is to decode effortlessly so that attention is on comprehension.

As emergent readers encounter print in their environment, they ask questions and learn about how language is represented in its written form. They engage in the following:

- Pretending to read favorite print (e.g., books, poems, songs, chants)
- Reading what they have drawn or written, even when no one else can
- Pointing to just one word, the first word in a sentence, one letter, the first letter in the word, the longest word, etc.
- Recognizing some concrete words (e.g., their names, friends' names, words in the environment such as McDonald's)
- Recognizing and generating rhyming words
- Naming many letters and telling you words that begin with the common initial sound (Allington, 1994; Cunningham and Elster, 1994; Sulzby and Teale, 1991)

As beginning readers proceed with learning to read they learn to:

- Identify letters by name
- Say the common sounds of letters
- Blend the sounds represented by letters into decodable words
- Read irregular words
- Read words, then sentences, and then longer text

2. *Reading entails understanding the text and depends on active engagement and interpretation by the reader.* Understanding is influenced by both the text and the readers' prior knowledge (Anderson and Pearson, 1984). When readers read, the author does not simply convey ideas to the readers but stimulates readers to actively engage in such strategies as *predicting* to make hypotheses about the meaning, *summarizing* to put in their own words the major points in the text, *questioning* to promote and check for understanding, and *clarifying* when concepts are not clear. Effective readers regularly monitor their comprehension to determine whether they understand what they are reading. When they are not sure, they may decide to employ fix-up strategies such as rereading or reading on for further clarification, or they may decide not to worry about the confusion depending on the purpose for reading. Knowing about these strategies and in which situations to apply

different strategies is called *metacognition* (see Chapter 2).

Students who have reading difficulties tend to have difficulty with metacognitive skills, including efficient memory processing for words (Ashbaker and Swanson, 1996; Bauer, 1987; Mann 1991) and comprehension monitoring (Billingsley and Wildman, 1990; Bos and Filip, 1984; Palincsar and Brown, 1987; Wong, 1979, 1987). Research in the area of memory processing indicates that these students do not effectively use elaborative encoding strategies, such as rehearsal, categorization, and association, when trying to remember words or word lists. Studies with good and poor readers suggest that the poor readers do not automatically monitor their comprehension or engage in strategic behavior to restore meaning when there is a comprehension breakdown.

These two overarching concepts can assist in organizing reading instruction into components or areas as depicted in Figure 7.1. These components and their integration are important in learning how to read effectively and in using reading as a vehicle for learning and entertainment. Because it is important to emphasize certain components or

FIGURE 7.1
Components of Reading and Reading Instruction

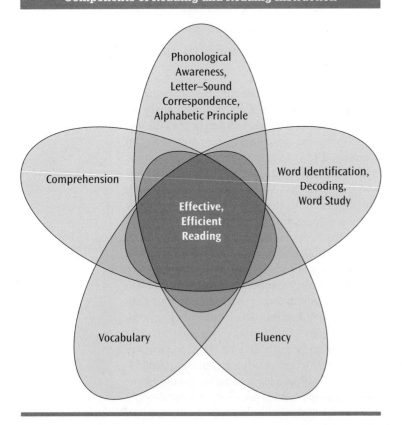

aspects of reading based on the student's level of development and needs, particularly for students with learning/reading disabilities, instruction should integrate these components. For example, while Kyle's reading program emphasized developing phonological awareness, letter–sound correspondences, and word recognition skills, he also engaged in activities to promote fluency and listening/reading comprehension. In contrast, Manuel's reading program focused on advanced decoding skills, fluency, and comprehension. In this chapter, we turn our attention to the first two components of reading and reading instruction.

FOCUS Question 2. What are the definitions of phonological awareness, letter–sound correspondence, and phonics, and what are some examples of activities that can be used to teach them?

Phonological Awareness, Letter–Sound Correspondence, and Phonics

What is phonological awareness? Simply stated, *phonological awareness* is knowing and demonstrating that spoken language can be broken down into smaller units (words, syllables, phonemes), which can be manipulated within an alphabetic system or orthography (Podhajski, 1999). Phonological awareness encompasses the discrimination, counting, rhyming, alliteration, blending, segmentation, and manipulating of syllables, onset-rimes, and phonemes. Examples of activities that support these skills are presented in Figure 7.2.

Phonemic awareness is the most complex part of a phonological awareness continuum that includes rhyming and segmenting words and sentences. Phonemic awareness is the ability to recognize the smallest sound units of spoken language and how these units of sound, or *phonemes*, can be separated (pulled apart or segmented), blended (put back together), and manipulated (added, deleted, and substituted). The phoneme is the smallest sound in spoken language that makes a difference in words. For instructional purposes related to reading, a phoneme is a single sound that maps to print—sometimes to one letter and sometimes to more than one letter.

FIGURE 7.2
Phonological Skills and Example Activities

- *Discrimination:* students listen to determine whether two words begin or end with the same sound
- *Counting:* students clap the number word in a sentence, syllables in a word (e.g., *cowboy, carrot*), sounds in a word (e.g., *me, jump*)
- *Rhyming:* students create word families with rhyming words (e.g., *all, call, fall, ball*)
- *Alliteration:* students create tongue twisters (e.g., Sally's silly shoe sank slowly in the slime.)
- *Blending:* students say the sounds in a word and then say them fast while the teacher pushes blocks or letters together to demonstrate blending
- *Segmenting:* students say the word and then clap and say each syllable or sound (e.g., *running* is /run/ /ing/ is /r/ /u/ /n/ /i/ /ng/)

- *Manipulating:* deleting, adding, substituting, and transposing

  Deleting: students listen to words and say them without the first sound (e.g., *bat* becomes *at*)

  Adding: students listen to words and add syllables (e.g., *run* becomes *running, come* becomes *coming*)

  Substituting: students listen and change sounds (e.g., change /r/ in *run* to /b/ and make *bun*)

  Transposing: students reverse the sounds (e.g., *nat* becomes *tan*)

Phonological awareness engages students in oral language activities. However, before students can apply these skills to reading, they need to understand phonics. *Phonics* is the way in which the sounds of our language (not the letters) map to print. It is knowing how letter names and sounds relate to each other (i.e., *letter–sound correspondence*). Let's see how a teacher applies these concepts.

Ms. Hernandez, the special education teacher, works for 30 minutes, three times a week in Ms. Harry's kindergarten class. She works with a small group of students who have the most difficulty learning to make letter–sound correspondences and who have difficulty separating words into their individual phonemes and blending and segmenting phonemes. With these kindergartners, Ms. Hernandez reinforces the key words that Ms. Harry is teaching with each letter–sound, (e.g., *b, ball,* /b/), and has students participate in listening activities in which they have to count the number of syllables in words and sounds in simple words (e.g., *me* and *sit*) and create word families (e.g., *it, sit, mit, bit, fit, hit*). At first, she has the students listen when working on these activities. Then she uses letters to demonstrate how the syllables and sounds are related to print.

Ms. Hernandez also works with a small group of six students in Ms. Yu's first-grade class who have difficulty learning to read. Ms. Hernandez engages these students in such activities as listening and clapping the number of sounds in words to help them segment the sounds; saying each sound in a word slowly and then saying them fast to practice blending. When writing the sound, she has

them say the word, then say the sounds, then say the first sound and write it, then say the first two sounds and write the second sound, and so on until they have written the word. She consistently pairs speech and print.

Ms. Hernandez is directly teaching phonological awareness, letter–sound relationships, and phonics, all of which are associated with successful reading and spelling. Evidence from research provides consistent support for the important role that phonological awareness and processing play in learning to read (Adams, 1990; Blachman, 2000; McCardle and Chahabra, 2004; National Reading Panel, 2000; Snow et al., 1998). The skills associated with phonological processing, particularly blending and segmenting individual phonemes, have been one of the most consistent predictors of difficulties in learning to read. Children who lack this metalinguistic insight are likely to be among the poorest readers and, because of their poor reading, to be identified as having a learning or reading disability (e.g., Blachman, 1997; Bradley and Bryant, 1983; Foorman, Fletcher, Francis, and Schatschneider, 1998; Juel, 1994; Torgesen and Burgess, 1998; Vellutino et al., 1996). Hence, Ms. Hernandez is working with students in kindergarten and first grade to help prevent or lessen later reading disabilities.

Development of Phonological Awareness and Phonics

In general, children's awareness of the phonological structure of the English language develops

TABLE 7.1

Phonological Awareness Continuum

Later Developing

Skill	Example
Phoneme blending, segmentation, and manipulations	Blending phonemes into words, segmenting words into individual phonemes, and manipulating phonemes (e.g., deleting, adding, substituting, transposing) in spoken words
Onset-rime blending and segmentation	Blending/segmenting the initial consonant or consonant cluster (onset) from the vowel and consonant sounds spoken after it (rime)
Syllable blending and segmentation	Blending syllables to say words or segmenting spoken words into syllables
Sentence segmentation	Segmenting sentences into spoken words
Rhyme/alliteration	Matching the ending sounds of words/producing groups of words that begin with the same initial sound

Early Developing

Source: Adapted from *First Grade Teacher Reading Academy* (Austin: University of Texas, Texas Center for Reading and Language Arts, 2000).

from larger units of sounds (e.g., words in a sentence, syllables in a word) to smaller units (e.g., onset-rimes, phonemes). Skills such as rhyming and alliteration develop earlier, and skills such as sound blending, segmenting, and manipulation of phonemes develop later. Table 7.1 presents a continuum for the development of phonological awareness with definitions. While phonological awareness encompasses the entire continuum, activities that focus on individual sounds in words describe *phonemic awareness.*

The more advanced skills of phoneme blending, segmenting, and manipulation are most related to success in learning to read (Goswami and Bryant, 1990; Stanovich, 1992; Torgesen, Wagner, and Rashotte, 1994). This is an important point for teachers to remember because it should guide their instruction. The primary focus of phonemic awareness with young children is not rhyming; rather, the focus should be on increasing their awareness of the individual sounds in language and how each of these sounds can be represented by a letter or combination of letters. Learning to manipulate these sounds through blending and segmenting is the most important goal of phonemic awareness and is associated with improved reading performance (Cavanaugh, Kim, Wanzek, and Vaughn, 2004). Remember, linking sounds to print is the most immediate goal.

In general, using a developmental sequence is helpful for planning instruction. For example, on the basis of the developmental sequence, the teacher would teach segmenting and blending words and syllables before teaching segmenting and blending onset-rimes and phonemes. However, some children vary in the acquisition of these skills. For example, although some children can learn to blend, segment, and manipulate sounds, they continue to have difficulty with rhyming. Therefore, instruction at the phoneme level should never be delayed until students understand rhyme or any other phonological awareness skill on the continuum.

Teaching Phonological Awareness and Phonics

The majority of students at risk for reading difficulties, and who are later identified as having a learning or reading disability, have poor phonological awareness and can profit from explicit instruction in phonological awareness, particularly blending, segmenting, and manipulating sounds (Foorman et al., 1998; Muter and Snowling, 1998; Torgesen, 1999) and mapping these sounds to letters as quickly as possible. As students learn the letter–sound correspondences, phonological tasks such as oral blending and segmenting of onset-rimes and phonemes can be paired with graphemes (letters), thereby explicitly teaching the relationship of speech to print—the alphabetic principle (Goswami, 1998; Greaney, Tunmer, and Chapman, 1997).

Teaching phonological awareness includes such activities as the following:

- Listening for words that begin with the same sound (e.g., having all the students whose name begins with /b/ line up)

- Clapping the number of words in a sentence, syllables in words, and phonemes in words
- Blending and segmenting words by syllables and sounds
- Segmenting and manipulating sounds and syllables

To build blending and segmenting skills, a frequently used technique that assists students in learning to separate and blend sounds is the use of the Elkonin procedure, often referred to as Elkonin boxes (Elkonin, 1973). As a phonological task, students listen to a word and push a marker, block, or other small object into a printed square for each sound they hear (see Figure 7.3). As students gain knowledge about the letter–sound relationships, they can push or write letters in the boxes. It is one way in which an oral language activity can be made more visible and kinesthetic. Other ways are tapping one finger to the thumb for each sound or watching your mouth in a mirror and feeling the facial movements by placing your fingers on your cheeks and concentrating on how your mouth changes when different sounds are made (Lindamood and Lindamood, 1998).

In teaching phonological awareness to students who are having difficulty learning to read, it is important to determine the tasks that are difficult for the student and then to focus instruction according to the students' level of development and needs. For example, Emilia is a second-semester first grader who can segment and blend syllables and onset-rimes (e.g., s-it, f-at, r-un) but has great difficulty segmenting and blending individual phonemes. She has been using manipulatives and counting on her fingers to assist herself, but she is still having difficulty hearing the individual sounds. One activity might be to build on her ability to segment and blend onset-rimes and demonstrate how

the rime is further divided into individual sounds. Emilia could also watch and feel her mouth as she says each sound to see how it changes as when saying the /a/ and then /t/, the sounds in the word *at*. For Emilia, who has learned the letter–sound correspondences for about six consonant sounds and the short vowel /a/, using letters in the boxes can help her understand how speech maps to print.

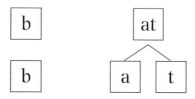

Students may also need assistance in learning how to blend sounds. Figure 7.4 presents a simple procedure for teaching sound blending. The same procedure can be used for teaching how

FIGURE 7.4
Procedure for Teaching Sound Blending

To train a child in sound blending, use the following procedure.

Teacher: Say *shoe.*
Child: Shoe.
Teacher: Now, what am I saying? **/sh-sh-sh/oo-oo-oo/**. [Say it with prolonged sounds, but no break between the sounds.] If the child responds correctly, say: Good. Now what am I saying? [Give a little break between the sounds.] **/Sh/oe/**. [Then say it with the child.] Shoe. Now what am I saying? [Give a quarter-second break between the sounds.] **/Sh/oe/**.
Child: Shoe.
Teacher: Shoe. Good What am I saying now? [with a half-second break between the sounds] **/Sh/oe/**.
Child: Shoe.
Teacher: Now what am I saying? [Give a one-second break between the sounds.] **/Sh/oe/**.

At each step, if the child does not respond with "shoe," repeat the previous step and then again stretch out the sounds, confirming or prompting at each step. Proceed by increasing the duration until the child can say "shoe" in response to the sounds with approximately one second between them.

Repeat this experience with the word *me.*

The main task for the teacher is to give a word with two sounds, increasing the duration of time between them until the child gets the idea of putting the sounds together. Then the child is presented with three-sound words such as **/f/a/t/**, and then with four-sound words such as **/s/a/n/d/**. It is important to recognize that the number of sounds in a word may not correspond to the number of letters in a word. For example, the word *shoe* has four letters, but only two sounds. The teacher must be careful to present the sounds correctly and use the correct timing.

Source: S. A. Kirk, W. D. Kirk, and E. H. Minskoff, *Phonic Remedial Reading Lessons* (Novato, CA: Academic Therapy Publications, 1985), pp. 12–13. Reprinted by permission.

FIGURE 7.3
Using the Elkonin Procedure to Support Phonemic Awareness

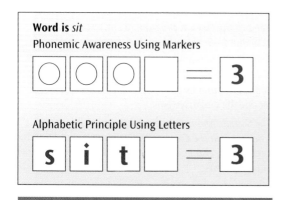

to segment words, except that the teacher would begin with the sounds separated and then gradually present them closer together until they are blended into a word.

General guidelines for teaching phonological awareness activities include the following:

- Consider the students' levels of development and tasks that need to be mastered.
- Model each activity.
- Use manipulatives and movement to make auditory or oral tasks more visible.
- Move from easier to more difficult tasks considering level of development (syllables, onset-rimes, phonemes), phoneme position (initial, final, medial), number of sounds in a word (*cat* is easier than *split*), and phonological features of the words (e.g., continuants consonants /m/, /n/, /s/ are easier than stops or clipped sounds /t/, /b/, /d/).
- Provide feedback and opportunities for practice and review.
- Make learning fun.

A number of programs and resources are available for teaching phonological awareness and phonics (see Figure 7.5 for a selected list), and a number of sources provide lists of children's books focused on different aspects of phonological awareness (Coldwell, 1997; Opitz, 1998; Perfect, 2000; Yopp, 1992). Tech Tips 7.1 highlights information about using computer software to teach phonological awareness skills.

Response to Intervention and Progress Monitoring: Phonological Awareness and Phonics

Successfully preventing reading disabilities and appropriately serving students with reading disabilities requires an understanding of how response to intervention (RTI) and progress monitoring can be coordinated at the early grades to address phonological awareness and phonics.

Response to Intervention

How do we know if students are responding to instruction in phonemic awareness and phonics? The answers to several questions can provide valuable information for determining students' responses to instruction.

- Have students received scientifically based reading instruction in phonemic awareness and phonics from their classroom teacher?
- Have students received adequate opportunities to respond, obtain feedback, and see modeling to scaffold their learning?
- How does the performance of students with low response compare to the performance of other students in the class?
- Have students with low phonemic awareness received instructional opportunities in small groups to acquire phonemic awareness and phonics?
- Is progress monitoring data available to show the scope of the student's progress?

FIGURE 7.5

Selected Programs and Resources for Teaching Phonological Awareness

A Basic Guide to Understanding, Assessing, and Teaching Phonological Awareness by Torgesen, J. K., and Mathes, P. G., 2000, Austin, TX: PRO-ED.

Interventions for Reading Success by Haager, D., Domino, J. A., and Windmueller, M. P., 2006, Baltimore: Brookes.

Ladders to Literacy: A Kindergarten Activity Book, 2nd ed., by O'Connor, R. E., Notari-Syverson, A., & Vadasy, P. F., 2005, Baltimore: Brookes.

The Lindamood Phoneme Sequencing Program for Reading, Spelling, and Speech by Lindamood, P. A., and Lindamood, P., 1998, Austin, TX: PRO-ED.

Phonemic Awareness in Young Children: A Classroom Curriculum by Adams, M. J., Foorman, B. G., Lundberg, I., and Beeler, T., 1998, Baltimore: Brookes.

Phonological Awareness and Primary Phonics by Gunning, T. G., 2000, Boston: Allyn & Bacon.

Phonological Awareness Assessment and Instruction: A Sound Beginning by Lane, H. B., and Pullen, P. C., 2004, Boston: Allyn & Bacon.

The Phonological Awareness Book by Robertson, C., and Salter, W., 1995, East Moline, IL: LinguiSystems.

Phonological Awareness Training for Reading by Torgesen, J. K., and Bryant, B. R., 1994, Austin, TX: PRO-ED.

Road to the Code: A Program of Early Literacy Activities to Develop Phonological Awareness by Blachman, B. A., Ball, E. W., Black, R., and Tangel, D. M., 2000, Baltimore: Brookes.

Sounds Abound by Catts, H., and Olsen, T., 1993, East Moline, IL: LinguiSystems.

The Sounds Abound Program: Teaching Phonological Awareness in the Classroom (formerly *Sounds Start*) by Lechner, O., and Podhajski, B., 1998, East Moline, IL: LinguiSystems.

TECHTips

7.1 Using Technology to Build Phonological Awareness and Word Recognition

Its multimedia capabilities make the computer an ideal tool for building phonological awareness and word recognition—tirelessly repeating sounds, words, and phrases for students who need reinforcement of these concepts.

Don Johnston Incorporated (www.donjohnston .com) offers *Simon S. I. O.*, a program that can help students to learn sounds, build words, and learn word families. They can read words aloud into a microphone and hear them repeated back. The software reinforces correct responses and keeps an accurate accounting of learner progress. It also encourages comprehension in addition to pronunciation.

The *Earobics* series is another software offering from Don Johnston, Inc. In *Earobics Step 1*, *Earobics Step 2*, and *Earobics for Adolescents and Adults*, learners can practice sound blending, rhyming, and sound discrimination. These programs concentrate on phonological awareness skills for learners who are struggling to improve reading and spelling skills. Other tutorial software from this publisher that provide structured literacy activities includes *WordMaker* and *All My Words*.

Balanced Literacy, from IntelliTools, Inc. (www.intellitools.com), provides a full year reading program for beginning readers. Using sequential presentation of skills, the program includes guided reading, comprehension, phonics instruction, and beginning writing. Also from IntelliTools, Inc.,

are *Phonemic Awareness Activities*, which are add-ons to the *Classroom Suite* software.

Word Munchers from The Learning Company (www.learningcompany.com) is an arcade-like game in which the learner must "munch" words with specific vowel sounds. Unlike the previous software that were tutorials, this game is obviously reinforced practice—learners are practicing skills taught prior to playing the game. *Word Muncher Deluxe* includes games using vocabulary, sentence structure, and grammar, in addition to vowel sounds.

A Screenshot from *Simon S.I.O.*
(Copyright © 2005 Don Johnston Incorporated)

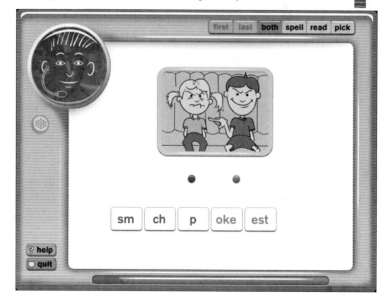

Answering these questions can help us determine whether students have received adequate instruction and thus whether their low response is a function of exceptional needs in the target area. Knowing the opportunities students have to learn helps us discern the severity of the problem.

How do we know when students are responding adequately to instruction in phonics and word study? If students are receiving scientifically based reading instruction in phonics and word study, we can determine whether they are low- or high-responders based on two essential criteria: (1) how do they respond relative to others in their class and others in the same grade in other classes in the school, and (2) what is the slope of their progress based on progress monitoring measures acquired at

least every two weeks. If a student's progress is significantly below other students in the class and/or their slope for their progress based on progress monitoring of phonics and word study is lower than expected, then the student may not be responding adequately to phonics and word study instruction.

Progress Monitoring

Determining students' performance in any academic area is an essential first step in designing an effective intervention program, for several reasons. First, when a teacher assesses students, the teacher can determine what the students know and what they need to know. This information

Progress Monitoring

allows the teacher to design an instructional program that is targeted to the needs of the students. Assessments that tell the teacher specifically how a student is performing and what else the student needs to know are referred to as *diagnostic assessments*. Second, by using appropriate assessments, the teacher can determine how the student's performance compares with those of other students of that same age or in that grade. This gives the teacher some idea of what students need to know to achieve grade-level performance. These assessments are referred to as *norm-based assessments*. Third, appropriate assessments allow the teacher to monitor the progress of students and determine whether their progress is on track and appropriate or whether the teacher needs to alter instruction to improve their performance. These assessments are referred to as *progress monitoring assessment* or *curriculum-based measures*. In all of the academic chapters, we will discuss the assessments and progress monitoring that teachers require to determine the progress of their students.

Progress monitoring of students' knowledge and skills in phonological awareness and the alphabetic principle provides teachers with necessary data to inform decision making about grouping and instruction. An effective progress monitoring system informs teachers about what to teach, including which phonemes students know or need to know. A good progress monitoring system will also allow teachers to determine whether any of the three important aspects of phonemic awareness are problematic: deletion, segmenting, and/or blending.

Progress monitoring in phonemic awareness assists teachers in identifying students who are at risk for failing to acquire phonemic awareness skills, and in monitoring the progress that students make in response to phonemic awareness instruction. There are two important aspects of phonemic progress-monitoring measures: They should be predictive of later reading ability, and they need to guide instruction. The following brief descriptions of tests and progress-monitoring measures may be useful for teachers as they make decisions about what methods they will use to monitor students' progress in phonemic awareness:

• *STAR: Early Literacy (SEL)*. SEL is a computer-adaptive procedure that provides for ongoing assessment of early literacy skills including general readiness to read, graphophonemic knowledge, phonemic awareness, phonics, comprehension, structural analysis, and vocabulary. The test takes approximately 10 minutes and can be used with students in grades K through 3. The program is available through Renaissance Learning (www.renlearn.com).

• *AIMSweb Systems*. These systems offer progress monitoring tools for letter naming fluency, letter–sound fluency, phoneme segmentation fluency, and nonsense word fluency. There are 23–33 alternative forms available for each grade and ongoing technical support is provided. The program is available from Edformation, Inc. (www.aimsweb.com).

• *Yopp-Singer Test of Phoneme Segmentation*. Students are asked to segment each phoneme separately in a list of 22 presented words. Students receive credit if they say all of the sounds in the word correctly. For example, if students are asked to identify the phonemes in *fit*, they would receive no credit for getting the first phoneme correct if they missed the following two phonemes. Students also receive feedback after each response. For responses that are correct, students are told that they were right. For responses that are incorrect, students are told the correct response by the test administrator. Like most phonemic awareness measures, this one is administered individually to children (Yopp, 1995).

• *Phoneme Segmentation Fluency*. There are 20 forms of this measure with 20 words for each form. All forms have two to five phonemes for each of the 20 words. This measure is also individually administered; however, unlike the Yopp-Singer Test of Phoneme Segmentation, this measure is timed. Students are given 60 seconds to get as many phonemes correct as possible. Students receive points for each phoneme (word part) correct even if the entire word is not correct. Also, students are not provided corrective feedback for errors (Kaminski and Good, 1996).

• *Comprehensive Test of Phonological Processing (CTOPP)*. The CTOPP is administered individually to students to determine their skill in phonological awareness and to guide the teacher in designing appropriate instruction. The test is designed for individuals between the ages of 5 and 24 and assesses three areas: phonological awareness, phonological memory, and rapid naming ability. If teachers are interested in assessing more specific areas of phonological awareness, additional subtests are available.

When selecting good screening measures for their students, teachers should consider the following important characteristics:

• Does it allow them to accurately predict which students will have later difficulties in reading?

- Does it allow them to differentiate current high, average, and low performers?
- Does it tell them which phonemic awareness skills they need to teach?
- Does it have multiple forms, or is it designed so that you can administer it more than one time per year?

If the teacher can answer yes to all of the above, the measure will serve well.

Teaching Letter–Sound Correspondences

As students learn letter–sound correspondences and move to higher phonological awareness skills such as blending, segmenting, and manipulating sounds, it is important that they associate speech with print (Chard and Dickson, 1999; Simmons, Kame'enui, Stoolmiller, Coyne, and Harn, 2003; Torgesen, 1999), thereby teaching the alphabetic principle or understanding that the sequence of letters in written words represents the sequence of sounds in spoken words. In Figure 7.3, while the task in the first row involves asking the students to segment words into sounds by moving a counter into a box for each sound (phonemic awareness), in the second row the students pair the sounds with letters by writing the letters in the boxes (alphabetic principle). Sometimes a phoneme is represented by more than one letter (e.g., consonant digraphs such as /sh/, /ch/, /ph/). One way to note this is by using a dotted line between the letters in the digraphs.

Knowledge of individual speech sounds is not particularly important when using oral language to converse. However, in learning to read and write and in developing a second language, this knowledge can be quite valuable and is accentuated by these tasks. Expert estimates of the number of speech sounds or phonemes in English vary from 40 to 52. For purposes of teaching students, most estimates are about 44 (Fromkin and Rodman, 1998; Owens, 2001). In learning to read and write, students learn more than 100 spellings (graphemes) for these phonemes.

The largest division of phonemes is consonants (C) or vowels (V). Table 7.2 presents the 25 consonant sounds with their typical spellings and representative words that use these sounds. The table groups the sounds according to the manner in which they are articulated and highlights how the sounds are related. For example, there are eight sound pairs in which the only difference between the two sounds in each pair is whether the sounds are produced with a resonance in the throat (voiced) or without resonance (voiceless):

Voiced	Voiceless
/b/ bat	/p/ pat
/d/ dig	/t/ tack
/g/ gate	/k/ kite
/v/ vase	/f/ fit
/th/ this	/th/ think
/z/ zip	/s/ sat
/zh/ buzz	/sh/ ship
/j/ jump	/ch/ chip

For students who consistently confuse voiced or voiceless sounds, it is helpful to teach whether the sounds are voiced or unvoiced. They can distinguish the difference by placing their fingers on their throat to feel the vibrations in their larynxes or by covering both their ears and listening as they say the sound pairs. Having students check whether they can feel the sound can help them to decode or spell a word (Clark and Uhry, 1995).

Consonant sounds can also be distinguished by the flow of air as stops or continuants. Stops are aptly named because they are of short duration and the airflow is stopped completely for a short time (Moats, 2000). Stops (or clipped sounds) include /b/, /d/, /g/, /j/, /k/, /p/, /t/, and /ch/. In contrast, continuant sounds can be blended smoothly with the next sound without a break in the air flow (e.g., /f/, /s/, /v/, /w/, /z/, /sh/, /zh/, and /th/). The following are important points to remember when teaching consonants:

- CVC words that begin with continuants and end with stops are generally the easiest for blending the sounds (e.g., *fat*, *sap*).
- In some programs, when blending stops it is suggested to "bounce the stop sounds," such as /b-b-b-b-a-t-t-t/ for *bat* (Slavin, Madden, Karweit, Dolan, and Wasik, 1992), so that students do not attach a schwa sound to the stop consonants (e.g., /buh/ and /tuh/).
- Nasal sounds are difficult to hear, sound different in the middle of words (e.g., *wet* or *went*), and are often omitted or substituted by emergent readers and writers (Read, 1975). One strategy that students can use to check for a nasal is to gently touch their noses while

TABLE 7.2
Consonant Sounds, Typical Spellings, and Manner of Articulation

Consonant Sounds	Typical Spellings	Initial	Middle, Final	Manner of Articulation
/p/	p	pot, pick	stop	voiceless stop @ lips
/b/	b	bat, barn	cab, robe	voiced stop @ lips
/t/	t, -ed	time, tap	pot, messed	voiceless stop @ tongue behind teeth
/d/	d, -ed	deer, dinner	bad, ride, cried	voiced stop @ tongue behind teeth
/k/	c, k, ck, qu	kiss, can, quick	back, critique	voiceless stop @ back of mouth
/g/	g	gate, girl	rag	voiced stop @ back of mouth
/f/	f, ph	first, fit	graph, off, rough	voiceless fricative @ lip/teeth
/v/	v	very, vase	love	voiced fricative @ lip/teeth
/th/	th	think, thin	mother, either	voiceless fricative @ tongue between teeth
/th/	th	the, then	both, ether	voiced fricative @ tongue between teeth
/s/	s, c	sap, cent, psychology	less, piece	voiceless fricative @ tongue behind teeth
/z/	z, -es, -s, x	zip, xerox	has, dogs, messes, lazy	voiced fricative @ tongue behind teeth
/sh/	sh	ship, sure, chef	push, mission, ration	voiceless fricative @ roof of mouth
/zh/	z, s		azure, measure, beige	voiced fricative @ roof of mouth
/ch/	ch, tch	chip, chase	much, hatch	voiceless affricate @ roof of mouth
/j/	j, g	jump, gist	judge, soldier	voiced affricate @ roof of mouth
/m/	m	me, mom	him, autumn, comb	nasal @ lips
/n/	n, kn, gn, pn, mn	now, know, gnat, pneumonia, mnemonics	pan, sign	nasal @ tongue behind teeth
/ng/	ng		sing, English	nasal @ back of mouth
/y/	y	you, use	feud	voiced glide @ roof of mouth
/wh/	wh	where, whale		voiceless glide @ back of mouth with rounding of lips
/w/	w	we, witch	sewer	voiced glide @ back of mouth with rounding of lips
/h/	h	happy, who		voiceless glide @ throat
/l/	l	lady, lion	mail, babble	liquid @ tongue behind teeth
/r/	r	ride, write		liquid @ tongue behind teeth

Source: Adapted from V. Fromkin and R. Rodman, *Introduction to Language*, 4th ed. (Orlando, FL: Harcourt Brace, 1993); and L. C. Moats, *Spelling: Development, Disability and Instruction* (Baltimore: York Press, 1995).

saying the word and feel whether the nose vibrates.

- Students may have problems hearing the difference between /wh/ and /w/ because many Americans pronounce them in the same manner—for example, *witch* and *which* (Moats, 2000).
- The sounds /r/ and /l/ can be difficult for some students because they are some of the last sounds that students learn to articulate and

because their pronunciation varies considerably across languages (e.g., in Spanish, they may be trilled or rolled; in Japanese and Cantonese, the sounds of these two phonemes are not differentiated).

This information about consonant sounds is helpful when teachers analyze students' oral reading and spelling. Students who know the letter–sound correspondences are more likely to substitute similar sounds. For example, it is more likely that students would substitute /n/ or /m/ for /ng/ than other sounds because they are nasals. Similarly, substitutions of /d/ for /b/ and /p/ for /b/ could well be related to the similar manner in which the sounds are articulated (i.e., /d/ and /b/—similar formation of the mouth; /p/ and /b/—same formation of mouth but voiceless and voiced) rather then to visual processing.

The English language also makes use of consonant digraphs and consonant blends. A *consonant digraph* is two consonants that represent one sound (*ph* for /f/). A *consonant blend* combines the sounds of two or more consonants so that they are clustered together. Table 7.3 provides a listing of the consonant digraphs and blends. When students omit a letter in a cluster, such as reading *fog* for *frog*, ask questions that lead them to see that the second sound in the blend is missing (e.g., "Listen, what sound do you hear after the /f/ in *frog*, /f-r-o-g/?" "What two sounds does the word *frog* begin with?"). It may also be helpful to have the students compare the words in written form or use boxes to assist students in seeing the missing letter.

f		o	g

TABLE 7.3
Common Consonant Digraphs and Clusters

Common Consonant Digraphs

Correspondence	Examples
ch = /ch/	chair, church
gh = /f/	rough, tough
kn = /n/	knot, knob
ng = /ŋ/	thing, sing
ph = /f/	phone, photograph
sc = /s/	scissors, scientist
sh = /sh/	shoe, shop
th = /th/	there, them
th = /th/	thumb, thunder
wh = /w/	wheel, where
wr = /r/	wrench, wrestle

Common Initial Consonant Clusters

With l	Example Words	With s	Example Words
bl	blanket, black	*sc*	score, scale
cl	clock, clothes	*sch*	school, schedule
fl	flag, fly	*scr*	scream, scrub
gl	glove, glue	*sk*	sky, skin
pl	plum, place	*sl*	sled, sleep
sl	slide, show	*sm*	smoke, smile
		sn	snake, sneakers
With r	**Example Words**	*sp*	spider, spot
br	broom, bread	*st*	star, stop
cr	crow, crash	*str*	street, stream
dr	dress, drink	*sw*	sweater, swim
fr	frog, from		
gr	green, ground		
pr	prince, prepare		

Common Final Consonant Clusters

With n	Example Words	With l	Example Words
nce	prince, chance	*ld*	field, old
nch	lunch, bunch	*lf*	wolf, self
nd	hand, wind	*lk*	milk, silk
nk	tank, wink	*lm*	film
nt	tent, sent	*lp*	help
		lt	salt, belt
Other	**Example Words**	*lve*	twelve, solve
ct	fact, effect		
mp	jump, camp		
sp	wasp, grasp		
st	nest, best		

Source: Adapted from T. G. Gunning, *Creating Literacy Instruction for All Students*, 6th ed. (Boston: Allyn & Bacon, 2008).

FIGURE 7.6

Vowel Spellings by Mouth Position Using Phonic Symbols

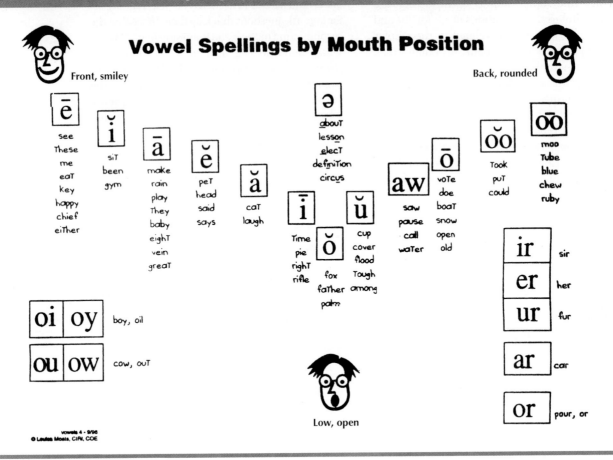

Source: L. C. Moats, *Speech to Print: Language Essentials for Teachers* (Baltimore: Brookes, 2000), p. 94. Copyright © 2000 by Paul H. Brookes Publishing Co. Inc. Reprinted with permission. (www.brookespublishing.com/store/books/moats-3874/index.htm.)

The second category of sounds is vowels. In general, there must be a vowel in every English syllable, and consonants are formed around the vowel. Vowel sounds can be ordered on the basis of the open or closed position of the mouth, as shown in the vowel circle in Figure 7.6. Say each of the vowels in the vowel circle, and note how your mouth moves from a closed, smiling position (e) to an open position (oo).

As with the consonants, we can analyze students' oral reading and spelling to learn about their knowledge of vowels sounds. For example, substituting an /e/ for /a/ would be more likely than substituting an /e/ for /o/ because of the closeness of the sounds. It is also obvious why students often confuse /ir/, /er/, and /ur/ in spelling, since these three spellings represent the same sound. Thus, *bird* can be spelled *bird*, *burd*, and *berd*, and the student must use visual memory to remember that it is *bird*. The vowel sounds have different spelling patterns as demonstrated in Table 7.4. Sometimes the same spelling pattern

has different sounds (e.g., the "ea" in *beat* and *bread* or the "ou" in *soup, could,* and *shout*). For students with severe difficulties in decoding, it may be helpful to systematically teach the frequency of the sounds for a vowel combination so that when decoding an unknown word, they can try the various sounds in a systematic manner and use syntax and semantics (i.e., context of the text) to determine the word. Vowel combinations with order of frequency for the different sounds (Herzog, 1998) are as follows:

Vowel	Order of Frequency Combination for Different Sounds
ea	/e/ as in *eat,* /e/ as in *bread,* /a/ as in *great*
ei	/e/ as in *ceiling,* /a/ as in *vein*
ey	/e/ as in *key,* /a/ as in *grey*
ie	/e/ as in *piece,* /i/ as in *pie*
oo	/oo/ as in *moon,* /oo/ as in *book*
ou	/ou/ as in *house,* /oo/ as in *soup*
ow	/ou/ as in *owl,* /o/ as in *snow*

TABLE 7.4
Vowel Spellings

	Vowel Sound	Major Spellings
Short Vowels	/a/	*rag, happen*
	/e/	*get, letter, thread*
	/i/	*wig, middle, event*
	/o/	*fox, problem, father*
	/u/	*bus*
Long Vowels	/ā/	*name, favor, say, sail*
	/ē/	*he, even, eat, seed, bean, key, these, either, funny, serious*
	/ī/	*hide, tiny, high, lie, sky*
	/ō/	*vote, open, coat, bowl, old, though*
	/ū/	*use, human, few*
Other Vowels	/aw/	*daughter, law, walk, off, bought*
	/oi/	*noise, toy*
	/o͝o/	*wood, should, push*
	/o͞o/	*soon, new, prove, group, two, fruit, truth*
	/ow/	*tower, south*
	/ə/	*above, operation, similar, opinion, suppose*
r Vowels	/ar/	*far, large, heart*
	/air/	*hair, care, where, stair, bear*
	/i(ə)r/	*dear, steer, here*
	/ər/	*her, sir, fur, earth*
	/or/	*horse, door, tour, more*

Source: Adapted from T. G. Gunning, *Creating Literacy Instruction for All Students,* 6th ed. (Boston: Allyn & Bacon, 2008).

Schwa is the vowel sound that is often found in unaccented syllables (e.g., *suppose, familiar, sofa, mission*) and is the most frequently occurring vowel sound (Wilde, 1997). As you can see, schwa has many different spellings.

Diversity

Students who are acquiring English and speak another language may not have developed fluency in all the English sounds. This is because different languages use different speech sounds, and students are most comfortable using the speech sounds of their native language. Table 6.8 on page 221 provides a comparison of the phonological as well as the morphological and syntactical features of Spanish and English. Common phonological confusions include the following:

/b/ pronounced as /p/
/v/ pronounced as /b/
/ch/ pronounced as /sh/
/j/ pronounced as /h/
/l/ pronounced as /y/
A number of differences in vowel pronunciations

Consequently, students may have difficulty not only pronouncing these sounds but also hearing

them. Do not be surprised if *chin* is read and spelled as *shin* or *vase* is read and spelled as *base.*

Guidelines for Teaching Letter–Sound Correspondences

Students use letter–sound correspondences to decode words. Therefore, it is important to teach these correspondences and how to blend and segment sounds to struggling readers so that they can decode and spell words. A number of programs have been developed using systematic approaches to introduce the letter–sound relationships and how to decode words to struggling readers (e.g., *Word Detectives: Benchmark Word Identification Program for Beginning Readers* [Gaskins, Cress, O'Hara, and Donnelly, 1998]; *Corrective Reading* [Engelmann, Meyer, Carnine, Becker, Eisele, and Johnson, 1999]; *Lindamood Phoneme Sequencing Program for Reading, Spelling, and Speech* [Lindamood and Lindamood, 1998]; *Phonic Remedial Reading Lessons* [Kirk, Kirk, and Minskoff, 1985]; *Alphabet Phonics* [Cox, 1992]; *Kindergarten Peer Assisted Learning,* or *KPALS* [Mathes, Torgeson, and Howard, 2001]). These

FIGURE 7.7

Words Using 11 Common Letter–Sound Correspondences

i, t, p, n, s, a, d, l, f, h, g

1. it	16. sin	31. tan	46. tap	61. slat	76. lint	91. pass	106. pits
2. if	17. fin	32. pan	47. nap	62. flat	77. hint	92. lass	107. sits
3. in	18. lid	33. Dan	48. sap	63. flap	78. past	93. glass	108. fits
4. tip	19. did	34. fan	49. lap	64. flag	79. fast	94. pill	109. hits
5. nip	20. hid	35. pad	50. gap	65. span	80. last	95. hill	110. pats
6. sip	21. dig	36. sad	51. gas	66. snap	81. list	96. gill	111. hats
7. pip	22. fig	37. dad	52. snip	67. plan	82. lisp	97. still	112. taps
8. lip	23. pig	38. lad	53. slip	68. glad	83. gasp	98. stiff	113. naps
9. pit	24. gig	39. fad	54. spit	69. snag	84. stand	99. sniff	114. gaps
10. sit	25. at	40. had	55. slit	70. and	85. gland	100. staff	115. slips
11. fit	26. an	41. tag	56. flit	71. sand	86. plant	101. add	116. slits
12. lit	27. pat	42. nag	57. tilt	72. hand	87. slant	102. tips	117. flips
13. hit	28. sat	43. lag	58. flip	73. land	88. split	103. nips	118. flaps
14. tin	29. fat	44. sag	59. spin	74. sift	89. splat	104. sips	119. snaps
15. pin	30. hat	45. pal	60. slid	75. lift	90. splint	105. lips	120. lifts

Source: Neuhas Education Center, Bellaire, Texas. Based on A. R. Cox, *Foundations for Literacy: Structures and Techniques for Multisensory Teaching of Written English Skills* (Cambridge, MA: Educators Publishing Services, 1992).

programs have similar features of instruction that include:

- Teaching a core set of frequently used consonants and short vowel sounds that represent clear sounds and nonreversible letter forms (e.g., /a/, /i/, /d/, /f/, /g/, /h/, /l/, /n/, /p/, /s/, and /t/). (See Figure 7.7 for a list of 120 words that can be made using these 11 letter–sound correspondences.)
- Beginning immediately to blend and segment the sounds to read and spell the words and read the words in decodable text (i.e., text in which most of the words are composed of letter–sound correspondences that have been taught)
- Separating the introduction of letter sounds with similar auditory or visual features (e.g., /e/ and /i/, /m/ and /n/, /b and /d/)
- Using a consistent key word to assist students in hearing and remembering the sound (e.g., *a apple* /a/, *b boy* /b/)
- Teaching that some letters can represent more than one sound. For each letter, first teach the most frequent sound, and then teach other sounds (e.g., in English, /c/ in *cat* then /s/ in *city* and /g/ in *gate* then /j/ in *Jim*; in Spanish, /g/ in *gato* (cat) then /h/ in *gemelo* (twin).
- Teaching that different letters can make the same sound, such as the /s/ in *sit* and *city*
- Teaching that sounds can be represented by a single letter or a combination of letters (e.g., /e/ in *me* and *meet*)

- Adding a kinesthetic component by having students trace or write the letter as they say the sound
- Having students use mirrors and feel their mouths to see and feel how sounds are different.
- Color-coding consonant and vowel so that the two categories of sounds are highlighted

Knowing letter–sound correspondences is a key element in understanding the alphabetic principle and learning to decode and spell unknown words. However, programs that focus too heavily on teaching letter–sound relationships and not on putting them to use are likely to be ineffective. Through modeling and discussion, students need to understand that the purpose for learning these relationships is to apply them to their reading and writing activities (National Reading Panel, 2000). Hence, it is critical to apply knowledge in phonological awareness, letter–sound relationships, and the alphabetic principle to word identification and decoding as discussed in the sections that follow.

Family Participation in Beginning Reading

Parents/guardians are very interested in having information that will allow them to provide the best support possible to their children as they acquire the important early skills related to reading. Teachers can use many sources of information to inform families. Consider sending for copies of these materials so that you can share them with families. It may be fun to demonstrate some of the activities that family members can do at home and encourage them to engage children in fun and meaningful activities that are associated with improved outcomes in reading. The following are some inexpensive or free materials available to families:

- *A Child Becomes a Reader: Birth to Preschool* (2002). This 31-page guide is written for parents/guardians and provides excellent ideas to build early language and sound awareness skills in young children. The first section of the guide is designed for parents who have infants and toddlers (birth through age two) and provides activities related to language and literacy development. The second section is designed for parents who have preschoolers between ages three and four. This section provides excellent information on what children should be able to do by age four, what parents can do at home to help, and what to look for in day care centers and preschools. The end of the book provides definitions of relevant terms. To order copies of this booklet, contact the National Institute for Literacy at EdPubs, P.O. Box 1398, Jessup, MD 20794–1398. Call 800-228-8813, or email edpuborders@edpubs.org.

- *A Child Becomes a Reader: Kindergarten to Grade 3* (2002). This 63-page guide is written for parents/guardians and provides valuable and exciting ideas and activities that parents can use at home to enhance reading outcomes for their children in kindergarten through third grade.

　　The first section of the book provides an overview of the building blocks of reading and writing. Each subsequent section provides for each grade level (kindergarten, first, second, and third) a description of what children should be able to do by the end of the grade level, what parents can do at home to help, and what to look for in each grade level. At the end of the book a list of terms and their definitions is provided.

　　To order copies of this booklet, contact the National Institute for Literacy at EdPubs, P.O. Box 1398, Jessup, MD 20794-1398. Call 800-228-8813, or email edpuborders@edpubs.org.

Many Websites also contain valuable information for parents on how to teach young children to read. Some useful sites include the following:

- The Partnership for Reading (www.nifl.gov/partnershipforreading)

- National Institute for Literacy (NIFL) (www.nifl.gov)
- No Child Left Behind Especially for Parents (www.nochildleftbehind.gov/parents)

FOCUS Question | 3. **What are the definitions of the six main decoding strategies, and how does each contribute to successful word identification?**

Word Identification, Decoding, and Word Study

Being able to quickly and easily recognize words is the key to successful reading (Ehri, 1998; Gough, 1996; Shaywitz, 2003). Successful readers identify words fluently and, if a word is unknown, have effective decoding strategies to decipher the word. Therefore, it is important that students develop a sight word vocabulary (i.e., words that students recognize without conscious effort) and decoding strategies to support them when they encounter an unknown word (Ehri, 2004; National Reading Panel, 2000; Snow et al., 1998).

What Is a Sight Word?

A *sight word* is a word for which students can recognize the pronunciation and meaning automatically. When reading words by sight, the words are accessed from information in memory, that is, from one's storehouse of words. For emergent readers, visual cues assist in recognizing familiar words when they are highly contextualized (e.g., a child recognizes *McDonald's* when it is presented with the golden arches but not when the word is presented without that context). Knowledge of letter–sound relationships serves as a powerful system that ties the written forms of specific words to their pronunciations and allows children to recognize words (e.g., *McDonald's* as an individual word; Ehri, 1998). In addition, students are able to more efficiently store words in memory when they group or consolidate words by multiletter units such as onset-rimes, syllables, suffixes, prefixes, and base words. For example, if readers know -*tion*, *in*-, and -*ing* as multiletter units, then learning longer sight words such as *questioning* and *interesting* is easier. Thus, teaching key spelling patterns, prefixes and suffixes, and major syllable types can assist students in learning to automatically recognize words and read more fluently (Juel, 1983).

You can tell when readers are reading words by sight because they read the words as whole units, with no pauses between smaller units (syllables, sounds), and they read the words within one second of seeing them (Ehri and Wilce, 1983). To experience how powerful automatic word recognition is, look at Figure 7.8. Say the name of each picture as quickly as you can, and ignore the words printed on the pictures. Was it almost impossible to ignore the words? This occurs because you are processing the words automatically, in this case despite your intention to ignore them. It is particularly important that readers have multiple opportunities to practice reading and spelling words until they become automatic and have word identification or decoding strategies to assist them in decoding a word when it is not automatically recognized.

Decoding Strategies for Identifying Words

What decoding or word identification strategies do readers employ to decode words they do not know automatically? Research on teaching struggling readers, including those with specific reading disabilities, would suggest that seven strategies are helpful in teaching these students to decode words (see Figure 7.9).

Phonic Analysis

Identify and Blend Letter–Sound Correspondences into Words. This is referred to as *phonic analysis* or *phonics.* This strategy builds on the alphabetic principle and assumes that the students have basic levels of phonological awareness and knowledge of some letter–sound correspondences. It entails the process of converting letters into sounds, blending the sounds to form a word, and searching memory to find a known word that resembles those blended sounds. Teachers use many cues to assist students in using phonic analysis to decode words:

- Cue the students to say each sound, and then have them say it fast.
- Demonstrate and have the students point to each letter sound as they say the sound, and then have the students sweep their fingers under the word when they say it fast.
- Place letters apart when saying the sounds, and then push the letters together when you say it fast.

FIGURE 7.8

Picture-Naming Task Demonstrating How Words Are Processed Automatically

Source: Adapted from L. Ehri (1987). Learning to read and spell words. *Journal of Reading Behavior, 19,* pp. 5–11.

FIGURE 7.9

Strategies for Decoding Unknown Words

- *Phonic Analysis:* Identify and blend letter–sound correspondences into words
- *Onset-Rime:* Use common spelling patterns (onset-rimes) to decode words by blending the initials sound(s) with the spelling pattern or by using analogy
- *Structural Analysis:* Use knowledge of word structures such as compound word, root words, suffixes, prefixes, and inflectional endings to decode words and assist with meaning
- *Syllabication:* Use common syllable types to decode multisyllabic words
- *Automatic Word Recognition:* Recognize high-frequency and less predictable words and practice to automaticity
- *Syntax and Context:* Use knowledge of word order (syntax) and context (semantics) to support pronunciation and confirm word meaning
- *Use Other Resources:* Use other resources such as asking someone or using a dictionary

---

- Begin with simple familiar VC (*in*) and CVC (*him*) words and then move to more complex sound patterns (e.g., CCVC (*slim*), CVCC (*duck*), CVCe (*make*)).

Appendix 7.1 provides a scope and sequence for teaching phonics.

Onset-Rime

Use Common Spelling Patterns to Decode Words by Blending. One salient feature of the English language is the use of spelling patterns, **Diversity** also referred to as onset-rimes, phonograms, or word families. When using spelling patterns to decode an unknown word, students can segment the word between the onset (/bl/ in the word *blend*) and the rime (end) and then blend the onset and rime to make the word (*blend*). Figure 7.10 presents a list of 37 common rimes that make almost 500 words (Wylie and Durrell, 1970) and a more complete list of rimes is presented in Appendix 7.2. Guidelines for teaching onset-rimes follow the same guidelines as those suggested for teaching phonic analysis except that the word is segmented at the level of onset-rime rather than at the phoneme level. In contrast, Spanish does not use onset-rime to the extent that English does and, consequently, it is generally not taught. However, words that contain rhyming syllables can form

FIGURE 7.10

Thirty-Seven Common Rime Patterns from Primary-Grade Texts				
-ack	-ail	-ain	-ake	-ale
-ame	-an	-ank	-ap	-ash
-at	-ate	-aw	-ay	
	-ell	-est		
-eat				
-ice	-ick	-ide	-ight	-ill
-in	-ine	-ing	-ink	-ip
-ir				
-ock	-oke	-op	-ore	-or
-uck	-ug	-ump	-unk	

word families, such as /sa/ in *masa* (flour), *tasa* (cup), and *casa* (home).

Teaching word analysis by having students learn individual letter–sound correspondences or rime patterns and then blending the sounds together to make the word is referred to as a *synthetic method* for teaching word analysis. For example, if the word is *pan*, then the students would say each sound individually (/p/ /a/ /n/) or the onset-rime (/p/ /an/) and then blend them together to make the word *pan*. Using this method, the students are saying the individual sounds or onset-rime and then *synthesizing* or combining them to make the word.

Teachers can also use an *analogy method* for teaching word analysis, thereby providing students with a means of decoding a word other than sounding it out or blending the sounds into a word. When teaching onset-rime, teachers would cue the students to look at the unknown word to determine the spelling pattern (e.g., /an/). Then they think of the key word (e.g., *pan*) or other words with the same spelling pattern (*ran, than, tan*). The students then substitute the initial sound(s) of the unknown word for the initial sound(s) of the key word (*fat*). Cues that students can use to promote decoding by analogy are as follows:

"What words do I know that look the same?"

"What words do I know that end (or begin) with the same letters?"

Structural Analysis

Use Knowledge of Word Structures Such as Compound Words, Root Words, Suffixes, Prefixes, and Inflectional Endings to Decode Words and Assist with Meaning. Between the third and seventh grades, children learn from 3,000 to

26,000 words. Most of these words are encountered through reading, and only a limited number are taught directly (Wysocki and Jenkins, 1987). Teach students to analyze words for compound words, root words, prefixes, suffixes, and inflectional endings for the following reasons:

- It provides students with ways to segment longer, multisyllabic words into decodable (and meaningful) parts (Henry, 1997).
- It assists students in determining the meaning of words.

For example, the word *unbelievable* can be segmented into three parts, un-believe-able. Not only does chunking make the word easier to decode, it also tells us about the meaning. In the case of *unbelievable*, un- means "not," and *-able* means "is or can be." Hence, *unbelievable* means "something that is not to be believed."

Teaching students to divide words into meaning parts (morphemes) is often first begun by analyzing compound words. Then high-frequency prefixes (e.g., *dis-*, *re-*, *in-*, *un-*), suffixes (e.g., *-er/-or*, *-ly*, *-tion/-ion*, *-ness*), and inflectional endings (e.g., *-s*, *-es*, *-ing*, *-ed*) can be taught. See Apply the Concept 7.1 to learn more about what prefixes and suffixes to teach. Table 6.1 on page 199 provides a list of common prefixes, suffixes, and inflectional endings and their meanings.

Ideas and guidelines for teaching and reinforcing structural analysis include the following:

- Teach meanings along with recognition of the meaning parts.
- Explain and demonstrate how many big words are just smaller words with prefixes, suffixes, and endings.
- Write words on word cards, and cut the cards by meaning parts. Have students say each

part and then put the word together and blend the parts together to say the word. Discuss the meaning of each part.
- Ask students to sort or generate words by meaning parts. Following is an example:

Pre- (before)	In (not)	Re- (again)	Super- (superior)
precaution	incomplete	replace	supermarket
prevent	incompatible	return	superintendent
precede	insignificant	redo	superman

- Present words that have the same prefix or suffix but in which the prefix or suffix has different meanings. Ask students to sort words by their meanings. Following is an example:

People Who Do	Things That Do	More	Words That Have -er
reporter	computer	fatter	cover
geographer	heater	greater	master
runner	dishwasher	shorter	never

If students are sorting, leave space so that they can add more words.
- Ask students to decode words they do not know by covering all but one part of the word and having them identify it, then uncovering the next part and identifying it, and so on. Then have them blend the parts together to read the word.
- Make a class or student dictionary that has each word part, its meaning, and several example words.

Apply the Concept 7.1

Which Prefixes, Suffixes, and Inflectional Endings Should You Teach?

How many prefixes do you need to teach? Four prefixes, *un-*, *re-*, *in-* (and *im-*, *ir-*, *il-* meaning *not*), and *dis-* account for 58 percent of all prefixed words. If you add 14 more prefixes (*en-/em-*, *non-*, *in-/im-* (meaning *in*), *mis-*, *sub-*, *pre-*, *inter-*, *fore-*, *de-*, *trans-*, *super-*, *semi-*, *anti-*, and *mid-*)

you will have accounted for about 95 percent of words with prefixes (White, Sowell, and Yanagihara, 1989). The inflectional endings of *-s/-es*, *-ed*, and *-ing* account for about 65 percent of words that have inflectional endings and suffixes. If you add the suffixes *-ly*, *-er/or*, *-ion/-tion*,

-ible/-able, *-al*, *-y*, *-ness*, *-ity*, and *-ment*, you have accounted for over 85 percent. Other suffixes that are used frequently include *-er/est* (comparative), *-ic*, *-ous*, *-en*, *-ive*, *-ful*, and *-less* (White et al., 1989). Remember, it is important to teach the meanings along with how to decode them.

- Develop word webs or maps that demonstrate how one root word can make a cadre of related words (see Figure 7.11).

Syllabication

Use Common Syllable Types. Many students with reading disabilities have particular difficulty decoding multisyllabic words. This skill becomes critical by about third grade. Six basic syllable configurations or types can be identified in English spelling; these are presented in Table 7.5. The syllable types are useful because they encourage students to look for and recognize similar chunks of print across words.

In teaching about syllable types, it is important that students learn that each syllable has one vowel sound. However, the vowel sound may be represented by one or more letters (e.g., CVCe, vowel team). Ideas for teaching include dialogues that promote discovering the generalization, word sorts by syllable types, and games to provide practice. For example, in teaching the CVCe, the following dialogue encourages students to induce the generalization:

Teacher: How many vowel sounds do you hear in each of these words? [Say, "five, rope, cape, cube, kite, these."]
Students: One.
Teacher: [Write, "five, rope, cape, cube, kite, these."] How many vowels do you see?
Students: Two.
Teacher: Which vowel sound do you hear? Tell me what is happening with the *e*?
Students: The first vowel is long, and you do not hear the *e*.

FIGURE 7.11
Root Word Map of *Friend*

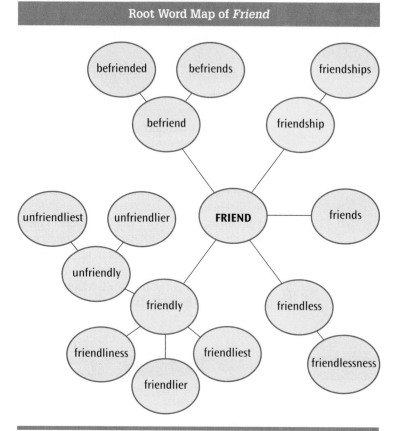

Source: Adapted from C. S. Bos, N. Mather, H. Silver-Pacuilla, and R. Friedmann Narr (2000). Learning to teach early literacy skills—collaboratively. *Teaching Exceptional Children, 32* (5), pp. 38–45.

Demonstrate how adding the *e* to the end of CVC words makes the short vowel change to a long sound (*cap* becomes *cape*, *kit* becomes *kite).* For younger students, teachers may want to generate

TABLE 7.5
Six Syllable Types

Type	Description/Examples
Closed (CVC)	Ends in at least one consonant; vowel is short: *bed, lost,* and *magnet,* dap- in *dapple,* hos- in *hostel*
Open (CV)	Ends in one vowel; vowel is long: *me,* mo- in *moment,* ti- in *tiger,* ta- in *table*
Vowel-Consonant-e (CVCe)	Ends in one vowel, one consonant, and a final *e;* vowel is long, the final *e* is silent: *name, slope, five,* -pite in *despite,* -pete in *compete*
Vowel Team (CVVC)	Uses two adjacent vowels; sounds of vowel teams vary: *rain, sweet,* -geal in *congeal,* train- in *trainer,* bea- in *beagle*
R-controlled (CV+r)	Vowel is followed by /r/ and vowel pronunciation is affected by /r/: *fern, burn, car, forge, charter*
Consonant-le (-C+le)	Unaccented final syllable with a consonant plus /l/ and silent *e:* -dle in *candle,* -tle in *little,* -zle in *puzzle*

a story about how the *e* bosses the vowel and makes it a long vowel sound—hence, "The Bossy E." Books such as *Market Day for Mrs. Wordy* also demonstrate the concept.

Automatic Word Recognition

Automatically Recognize High-Frequency and Less Phonetically Regular Words. Regardless of their letter–sound predictability, words need to be taught so that they are automatically recognized. Furthermore, it is not practical to teach students to analyze all words in the English language because the patterns they follow may not occur frequently enough to teach. Figure 7.12 presents a list of 200 high-frequency words in order of their frequency of occurance. This list is drawn from a compilation of words that occur in books and other materials read by school children and make up about 60 percent of the words found in these texts (Zeno, Ivens, Millard, and Duvvuri, 1995).

For example, the most frequently occurring word, *the*, makes up about 2 percent of words.

Two factors should be considered in deciding what words to teach as high-frequency words: utility and ease of learning (Gunning, 2006). The biggest payoff for students will be learning words that occur most frequently. The words *the, of, and, a, to, in, is, you, that,* and *it* account for more than 20 percent of the words that students will encounter. In considering the ease of learning, nouns and words with a distinctive shape are generally easier to learn. With struggling readers, teachers should first teach the words that the students will encounter most frequently.

The following guidelines can be used for teaching less predictable words (Cunningham, 2000; Gunning, 2006):

- Teach the most frequently occurring words.
- Check to make sure that students understand word meaning, particularly if they have limited

FIGURE 7.12

High-Frequency Words

1. the	30. had	59. would	88. find	117. same	146. different	175. am
2. of	31. but	60. other	89. use	118. right	147. numbers	176. us
3. and	32. what	61. into	90. water	119. look	148. away	177. left
4. a	33. all	62. has	91. little	120. think	149. again	178. end
5. to	34. were	63. more	92. long	121. also	150. off	179. along
6. in	35. when	64. two	93. very	122. around	151. went	180. while
7. as	36. we	65. her	94. after	123. another	152. tell	181. sound
8. you	37. there	66. like	95. word	124. came	153. men	182. house
9. that	38. can	67. him	96. called	125. three	154. say	183. might
10. it	39. an	68. time	97. just	126. word	155. small	184. next
11. he	40. your	69. see	98. new	127. come	156. every	185. below
12. for	41. which	70. no	99. where	128. work	157. found	186. saw
13. was	42. their	71. could	100. most	129. must	158. still	187. something
14. on	43. said	72. make	101. know	130. part	159. big	188. thought
15. are	44. if	73. than	102. get	131. because	160. between	189. both
16. as	45. will	74. first	103. through	132. does	161. name	190. few
17. with	46. do	75. been	104. back	133. even	162. should	191. those
18. his	47. each	76. its	105. much	134. place	163. home	192. school
19. they	48. about	77. who	106. good	135. old	164. give	193. show
20. at	49. how	78. now	107. before	136. well	165. air	194. always
21. be	50. up	79. people	108. go	137. such	166. line	195. looked
22. this	51. our	80. my	109. man	138. here	167. mother	196. large
23. from	52. then	81. made	110. our	139. take	168. set	197. often
24. I	53. them	82. over	111. write	140. why	169. world	198. together
25. have	54. she	83. did	112. sat	141. things	170. own	199. ask
26. not	55. many	84. down	113. me	142. great	171. under	200. turn
27. or	56. some	85. way	114. day	143. help	172. last	
28. by	57. so	86. only	115. too	144. put	173. read	
29. one	58. these	87. may	116. any	145. years	174. never	

Source: Thomas G. Gunning, *Creating Literacy Instruction for All Children,* 3rd ed. (Boston: Allyn & Bacon, 2000). Copyright © 2000 by Pearson Education. Reprinted by permission of the publisher. Adapted from S. M. Zeno, S. H. Ivens, R. T. Millard, and R. Duvvuri, *The Educator's Word Frequency Guide* (Brewster, NY: Touchstone Applied Science Associates, 1995).

language, a specific language disability, or are English language learners.

- Introduce new words before students encounter them in text.
- Limit the number of words that are introduced in a single lesson.
- Reinforce associations by adding a kinesthetic component such as tracing, copying, and writing from memory.
- Introduce visually similar words (e.g., *where* and *were*, *was* and *saw*) in separate lessons to avoid confusion.
- Ask students to compare visually similar words (e.g., *what* with *when*) and highlight the differences between the two words.
- Provide multiple opportunities for students to read words in text and as single words until they automatically recognize the words.
- Review words that have been taught previously, particularly if the students miscall them when reading text.
- Provide opportunities for students to get automatic at recognizing words, such as with games that require quick word recognition or power writing (i.e., writing the words multiple times in a short length of time).

Syntax and Semantics

Use Knowledge of Word Order (Syntax) and Context (Semantics) to Support Pronunciation and Confirm Word Meaning. Although students with reading difficulties often rely too heavily on syntax and context to decode unknown words (Briggs, Austin, and Underwood, 1984), good readers use syntax and context to cross-check their pronunciation and monitor comprehension (Share and Stanovich, 1995; Torgesen, 1999). Key questions that students can ask are as follows:

"Does that sound right here?"
"Does that make sense?"

Students should first be taught to decode unknown words using phonics, structural analysis, and syllabication. Then teach them to cross-check pronunciation by asking whether words "make sense."

In looking at these seven word-decoding strategies, it is clear that instruction for students who are having difficulty learning to read should include systematic instruction in letter–sound correspondences, phonic and structural analysis, and syllabication because they are the powerful strategies for reading text in alphabetic writing systems. In addition, reading instruction should provide numerous and varied opportunities to read and write so that students can employ semantic and syntactic clues and so that the recognition of words becomes automatic. This frees most of the reader's attention to focus on comprehension.

FOCUS Question 4. How can the use of explicit and implicit code instruction be compared?

Teaching Phonics, Word Recognition, and Word Study

Diversity

Jamal, a third grader, has the lowest reading level in his class, and he is not making progress in reading. When he reads first-grade level texts out loud, the teacher assists him in pronouncing about 30 percent of the words. He reads slowly and cannot remember previously known words. He knows fewer than 30 sight words, and he applies inconsistent strategies to decode words. Sometimes he attempts to sound out a word letter by letter, but he has difficulty with the letter–sound relationships beyond the first several letters, particularly the vowel sounds, as well as difficulty in accurately blending the sounds together. Hence, this strategy rarely results in his pronouncing the words correctly. Even though Jamal struggles in decoding the individual words, he can generally get the gist when reading these simple texts. He has good oral language skills, and his life experiences result in his being familiar with much of the content of what he reads. His math skills are at a third-grade level, although he has not yet learned his math facts to the automatic level.

Lupita, another third grader, is also struggling to learn to read. Like Jamal, she is reading at the first-grade level, and she has a sight vocabulary of about 40 words in Spanish and 25 in English. When she entered kindergarten, she had limited oral language proficiency in both Spanish and English. She is in a bilingual program that initially taught reading in Spanish but began transitioning her to English in second grade. This year, much of the reading instruction is in English. Like Jamal, she has difficulty remembering words automatically, and her reading, even of very easy text, is slow and laborious. Her decoding strategies rely primarily on sounding out words, but she does not know many of the letter–sound correspondences and has difficulty blending. When she does not recognize a word, her most consistent strategy is to look to the teacher for assistance. Lupita's oral language in both Spanish and English continues to be somewhat limited as measured on language assessments. Although she communicates with her friends, she is shy about responding in class and appears to have limited background experiences to assist her understanding what she is reading or learning. Lupita does well in basic math but has difficulty with word problems.

In beginning to work with students who have limited sight words and word identification strategies, like Jamal and Lupita, it is helpful not only to determine the students' current strategies, but also to determine what approaches have been used previously, how consistently, for how long, and with what success. It is also helpful to use the intervention research to inform the teacher's decision making.

Beginning reading approaches that emphasize explicit, direct teaching of phonological awareness and word identification strategies that rely on using phonics, onset-rime, and structural analysis result in greater gains in word recognition and comprehension than approaches in which phonological awareness and phonics are more implicitly taught (National Reading Panel, 2000; Swanson, 1999b). Consequently, explicit code instruction approaches should be a part of a balanced reading approach for most students with special needs.

The rest of the chapter focuses on teaching approaches and techniques that build word recognition and word identification strategies. The first section presents several explicit code instruction approaches and the next section focuses on implicit code instruction approaches or approaches in which teaching phonic and structural analysis is not emphasized or less direct. The third section presents several techniques that provide students with repeated opportunities to practice identifying words until automatically recognized. It is important to remember that this is just one aspect of a reading program, although it is a very important one for students with reading problems. A reading program should also incorporate multiple opportunities to teach listening and reading comprehension and to read for learning and enjoyment. In addition, it should provide opportunities for students to write about what they are reading.

Explicit Code Instruction

Explicit code approaches teach phonological awareness, letter–sound correspondences, the alphabetic principle, and the use of phonic analysis, structural analysis, and syllabication to decode unknown words. They emphasize three instructional features:

1. Systematic instruction of letter–sound correspondences and teaching students to blend the sounds to make words and segment sounds to spell words
2. Scaffolded instruction so that modeling, guidance, and positive and corrective feedback are integral features of instruction
3. Multiple opportunities for practice and review in various contexts (e.g., games with words cards, constructing sentences, reading texts)

Typically, the beginning reading materials that are associated with these approaches are controlled for the phonic and structural patterns they use; hence, they are referred to as *decodable text*. See Apply the Concept 7.2 for information about different text types and their purposes related to teaching students beginning reading.

Linguistic Approach: Onset-Rime and Word Families

The linguistic approach uses controlled text and word families (onset-rimes, phonograms, or spelling patterns) such as *-at*, *-ight*, and *-ent* to teach word recognition. This approach was introduced by the linguists Bloomfield and Barnhart (1961) and Fries (1963). It gained popularity in the late 1960s and early 1970s. Recent research has highlighted the effectiveness of teaching onset-rime (Ehri, 1998; Goswami, 1998), particularly for students who experience difficulties learning to read (see the discussion of onset-rime on page 259 in the section entitled "Decoding Strategies for Identifying Words").

Beck (2006) describes word building sequences in which word types are organized into four categories.

• The A category addresses CVC words and short vowels with blends and digraphs. Students learn to read simple word combinations with a minimal number of variations in letter–sound combinations and then increasingly more complex. Words like *sat, lit, sand.*

• The B category addresses instruction in CVCe words. Words like *rate, bike, tone.* The words are organized based on the complexity of their patterns and thus teachers can readily determine where students are having difficulty and what to reteach.

• The C category addresses instruction in long-vowel digraphs and vowel pairs that have the same vowel phoneme (e.g., *pail, day*).

• The D category focuses on r-controlled vowels such as *car, turn,* and *fern.*

Apply the Concept 7.2

Text Types and How They Facilitate Learning to Read

For students with learning and behavior problems who are learning to read, as well as other students, it is important to match the type of text with the goals and purposes of reading instruction. When the text type matches the level and purpose for instruction, it can provide a scaffold that supports students as they learn to read as well as provide them with opportunities to practice what they are learning (Brown, 1999/2000; Mesmer, 1999). Beginning text can be classified into five general categories, each of which serves a different but complementary purpose for teaching students to read.

Type of Text and Characteristics

Predictable/Pattern Language

- Repeated language patterns with accompanying pictures that make it easy to predict what the rest of the text says
- Control of language pattern, rhyme, rhythm, sentence structure with difficulty increasing gradually across levels of text
- Example of text: "I have a soccer ball (picture of soccer ball). I have a basketball (picture). I have a baseball (picture). I have a kick ball (picture). I like to play ball."

Types:

- Patterned text with picture/text match
- Cumulative pattern with information added on each page (e.g., I ate an apple. I ate an apple and some grapes. I ate an apple, some grapes, and three bananas. I have a stomachache.)
- Familiar poems and songs

Support for Beginning Reading

Emphasizes student use of:

- Memory
- Context and picture clues
- Repeating language patterns
- Repeating reading of text

Emphasizes teacher use of:

- Modeling the concept that print has meaning
- Modeling how books work (e.g., concept of a sentence, word; directionality)
- Developing oral reading fluency and expression

Decodable Text

- Text that introduces sound–symbol relationships, onset-rimes, and sight words in a controlled sequence so that difficulty level increases across levels
- Text that provides opportunities to apply the alphabetic principle and begin reading using the letter–sound correspondences and onset-rimes that have been taught
- Control for words, sound–symbol relationships, onset-rimes, sentence structure
- Example: "Peg had a pet pup. The pup was sad. The pup wanted to get fed, but Peg was in bed. The pup ran to Peg's bed."

Types:

- Emphasizes onset-rimes such as "The fat cat sat on the hat." Sometimes called *linguistic readers.*
- Emphasizes systematic introduction of sound/symbol relationships usually starting with a few consonants and short vowels in CVC words. Sometimes called *phonic readers.*

Emphasizes student use of:

- Blending sounds and sounding out words to decode them
- Using onset-rimes to make words and using analogy to decode words (e.g., "If I know *pit*, then this word must be *lit*")
- Learning to recognize less predictable words by sight as whole words (e.g., *was, come*)

Emphasizes teacher use of:

- Modeling how to blend and segment sounds and providing independent practice in these skills
- Developing students' letter–sound and simple spelling pattern knowledge
- Sounding out words when unknown
- Using onset-rime or word chunks to decode words
- Developing independent, fluent reading of words, sentences, and connected text

(continued)

Apply the Concept 7.2

Text Types and How They Facilitate Learning to Read   (continued)

Transitional Text

- Integrates predictable and decodable text so that across levels predictability decreases and decodability increases
- Example: "So she said to Grandpa, 'Can you rock Nick for a little while? Maybe you can get him to stop.' 'Sure,' Grandpa said. 'Now I can try.' But Grandpa had no luck. So he said to me. 'Can you play with Nick for a little while? Maybe you can get him to stop.' 'Sure,' I said. 'I will pick him up. It's my turn to try!'" (*Pick Up Nick* by Kate McGroven, pp. 10–14).

Emphasizes student use of:

- Diminishing use of memory and context clues to identify words
- Increasing use of blending sounds, sounding out words, and onset-rime to decode unknown words
- Learning to recognize less predictable words by sight

Emphasizes teacher use of:

- Modeling how to blend and segment sounds
- Modeling how to sound out and use onset-rime to decode unknown words
- Developing independent, fluent reading of words, sentences, and connected text

---

Easy Reader Text

- Series of books that gradually increase in difficulty across levels but are less controlled than predictable, decodable, or transitional texts
- Less control of words with more difficult high-frequency words, more polysyllabic words, and more complex sentences
- More complex plot and information and more text per page
- Some use of short chapters
- Example: "'And it means that we can begin a whole new year together, Toad. Think of it,' said Frog. 'We will skip through the meadows and run through the woods and swim in the river . . .'" (*Frog and Toad Are Friends* by Arnold Lobel, p. 8).

Emphasizes student use of:

- Using simple syllabication, prefixes/suffixes, and chunking with polysyllabic words (e.g., unprepared) and using more complex spelling patterns (e.g., fright)
- Using sight word knowledge and working on automaticity and fluency

Emphasizes teacher use of:

- Modeling more complex decoding strategies using more difficult words
- Developing student's oral reading fluency and expression
- Modeling comprehension strategies while reading aloud

Authentic Literature and Nonfiction

- Text that is written with limited regard for word or sentence difficulty and provides more complex plots and information
- Varies widely in style and genre

Examples:

- *Peter Rabbit* by Beatrix Potter
- *Owl Moon* by Jane Yolen
- *Bearman: Exploring the World of Black Bears* by Laurence Pringle

Emphasizes student use of:

- Listening and reading comprehension strategies
- Developing knowledge of different writing styles and genres
- Applying advanced decoding strategies in less controlled texts

Emphasizes teacher use of:

- Reading for enjoyment and model fluency when reading aloud
- Motivating students and creating interest in reading
- Discussing literature and teaching listening/reading/comprehension strategies

CLASSROOM Applications

Linguistic Approach—Onset-Rime and Word Families

PROCEDURES: The linguistic approach is built on a salient feature of the English language, that is, onset-rime. Figure 7.10 (page 259) presents a list of 37 common rimes and an even more complete list is found in Appendix 7.2. In teaching onset-rime, words are segmented and blended at the onset-rime level rather than the phoneme level, and words are taught in related groups that are often referred to as *word families* (e.g., at: *cat, fat, bat, sat, rat;* ight: *right, might, fight*). Sight or less phonetically regular words are kept to a minimum. Figure 7.13 provides an example of a beginning text from a typical linguistic reader. These readers give the students extensive practice with the word families and systematically introduce onset-rime patterns. Figure 7.14 presents a list of selected linguistic reading programs and linguistic readers.

When students cannot identify a word-family word, one strategy is to use a synthetic method of decoding by having them segment the word at the onset-rime level (e.g., for the word *flat*, cover the /fl/ and have the student read the /at/, then cover the /at/ and have the student give the sound /fl/, and then expose the whole word and have the student blend the two segments together to make the word *flat*). Another strategy is to use an analogy method in which the students think of another word, or the key word, they know with the same rime pattern (e.g., *cat*) and then substitute the initial sound(s) to make the word *flat*. Activities such as word sorts in which students sort words by word families, constructing word walls using onset-rime patterns, making word family houses (see Figure 7.15), and playing games such as Word Family Concentration and Can You Write a Word That Rimes With are all ways of reinforcing onset-rime patterns.

FIGURE 7.14
Selected Linguistic Reading Programs and Readers

The Basic Reading Series, Rasmussen, D., and Goldberg, L., 2000, Columbus, OH: SRA/McGraw-Hill.
Foundations, 2004, Bothell, WA: The Wright Group/McGraw-Hill.
Let's Read: A Linguistic Reading Program, Bloomfield, L., and Barnhart, R. K., 1965, 1994–1997, Cambridge, MA: Educators Publishing Service.
Merrill Reading Program, Bertin, P., et al., 1999, Columbus, OH: SRA/McGraw-Hill.
Preventing Academic Failure, Bertin, P., and Perlman, E., 1999, Columbus, OH: SRA/McGraw-Hill.
Ready Readers, 2004, Parsippany, NJ: Modern Curriculum Press/Pearson.
Sullivan's Programmed Reading (3rd ed.), Buchanan, C., 1988, Honesdale, PA: Phoenix Learning Resources.
Sundance Phonic Letters, Sounds, Readers, 1998–1999, Northborough, MA: Sundance.

FIGURE 7.13
Sample Linguistic Reading Story

Nat and the Rat

Nat is a cat.

She is a fat cat.

She likes to sit on her mat.

Dad likes to pat Nat.

One day Nat sat on Dad's lap for a pat.

Nat saw a rat.

She jumped off Dad's lap and ran after the rat.

That made Nat tired.

So Nat sat on her mat.

FIGURE 7.15
Word Family House

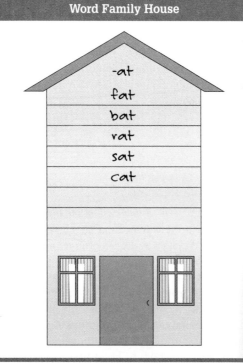

COMMENTS: Teaching students about onset-rime and word families gives them another context for understanding the alphabetic principle and how English sounds map to print. It also reinforces the phonological awareness skill of rhyming. The use of a linguistic approach and linguistic readers provides struggling readers with multiple opportunities to learn and practice onset-rime patterns. Because of the highly controlled vocabulary, students are frequently able to experience success in comparison to learning to read whole words (Goswami, 1998; Levy and Lysynchuk, 1997; O'Shaughnessy and Swanson, 2000). It is unclear from research, however, whether decoding at the phoneme level (e.g., /c-a-t/) versus the onset-rime level (e.g., /c-at/) is more advantageous and for which students. Recent research suggests that students should develop facility with decoding at the phoneme level before instruction in onset-rime decoding begins. Students with reading problems who are instructed in both these decoding methods make the greatest gains in reading (Lovett, Lacerenza, Borden, Frijters, Steinbach, and De Palma, 2000). Several cautions should be mentioned in regard to this approach. First, like other explicit code instruction, the texts often provide limited opportunities for the development of comprehension. Therefore, the use of children's narrative and expository literature should be incorporated into the reading program to develop listening comprehension. To demonstrate this point, reread the text given in Figure 7.13, and then try to generate five comprehension questions. Second, some words that are introduced in a family may represent unfamiliar or abstract concepts. For example, when learning the -og family, a student may be asked to read about "the fog in the bog."

Reading Mastery and Corrective Reading

Reading Mastery: Rainbow Edition (Engelmann, Bruner, Hanner, Osborn, Osborn, and Zoref, 1995) and *Corrective Reading* (Engelmann et al., 1999) are highly structured, systematic reading programs that use a direct instruction model for teaching (Carnine, Silbert, and Kame'enui, 1997) and a synthetic method for teaching phonics and structural analysis. These programs directly teach individual sound–symbol relationships, blending of sounds, and how to build these sounds into

words. The programs include components in decoding and comprehension, with comprehension focusing on the systematic development of logical reasoning skills and the use of questioning to promote comprehension. Whereas *Reading Mastery* is designed for elementary-level students, *Corrective Reading* is designed for students in grades 4 through 12 who have not mastered decoding and comprehension skills. Both programs are best taught in small- to medium-sized groups.

CLASSROOM Applications
Reading Mastery and Corrective Reading

PROCEDURES: *Reading Mastery* and *Corrective Reading* are built on principles of direct instruction (Carnine et al., 1997), which for reading include the following:

- Design instruction to maximize the amount of time students are engaged (e.g., students work in small groups with teacher; students give responses in unison after adequate wait time so that all students have time to think).
- Teach students to rely on strategies rather than require them to memorize information (e.g., teach several letter sounds such as /m/, /t/, /s/, /f/, /a/, and /i/ and the sounding-out strategy to decode words).
- Teach procedures to generalize knowledge (e.g., have students apply the sounding-out strategy to new sounds to build additional words).
- Use a teaching format that includes an introduction stage, followed by guided practice, independent practice, and review.
- Teach to mastery (specific criterion level).
- Teach one skill or strategy at a time.
- Systematically teach skills and strategies in a cumulative manner.

  - Prerequisite knowledge or skills are taught first (e.g., sounds of letters before words).
  - Instances that are consistent with the strategy are introduced before exceptions (e.g., teach consistent CVCe words such as *gave* and *made* before exceptions such as *have*).
  - High-utility knowledge is introduced before less useful knowledge (e.g., teach

frequent irregular words such as *of* and *was* before less frequent ones such as *heir* and *neon*).

- Easy skills are taught before more difficult ones.
- Information and strategies that are likely to be confused are introduced separately (e.g., letters *b* and *d* and words *were* and *where*).
- Systematic review and practice are provided.

- Monitor student performance and provide corrective feedback.
- Use a reinforcement system that promotes student engagement and learning.

In both programs, students are taught a consistent method of responding to sounds and sounding out words. Using the guide in Figure 7.16, teachers touch the first ball of the arrow and cue as follows:

"Say it with me or sound it out. Get ready."

They touch quickly under each sound, saying each sound: /rrreeed/. They repeat until students are consistent and then cue as follows:

"Say it fast. What sound or what word?"

They repeat until students consistently respond with the sound or word.

In both programs, the teacher is given specific procedures to follow, including scripted lessons. These scripted lessons specify what the teacher is to say and include hand signals. Part of an early lesson from *Corrective Reading: Word Attack Basics—Decoding A* is presented in Figure 7.17. Each lesson contains multiple exercises that focus on word attack skills such as sound identification, pronunciations, say the sounds, word reading, sentence reading, story reading, and spelling from dictation. Lessons are designed to last from 30 to 50 minutes with time provided for direct teaching, group reading, individual reading practice, and monitoring of progress with feedback. Both programs have placement tests.

FIGURE 7.16

Guide for Sounding Out a Word

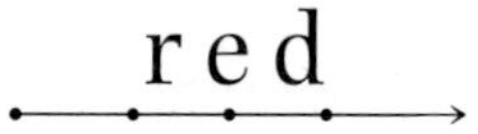

r e d

Whereas *Corrective Reading* uses standard print, the initial levels of *Reading Mastery* employ modified print that includes marking the long vowel sounds and reducing the size of silent letters (see Figure 7.18). Both programs provide for reading of decodable text; though *Corrective Reading* emphasizes reading expository texts.

Corrective Reading teaches skills in word identification including word attack, decoding strategies, and skill application and skills in comprehension including thinking basics, comprehension skills, and concept applications. The program provides daily feedback and has a built-in reinforcement system.

COMMENTS: Research has demonstrated that these programs are effective for improving the reading skills of students with reading difficulties and students from disadvantaged backgrounds (Becker, 1977; Gersten, Carnine, and Woodward, 1987; Gregory, Hackney, and Gregory, 1982; Grossen, 1999; Kame'enui et al., 1998; Polloway, Epstein, Polloway, Patton, and Ball, 1986; Thorne, 1978; Vitale, Medland, Romance, and Weaver, 1993). Much of the teaching of phonic analysis skills is conducted in an explicit manner, which has been demonstrated to be advantageous for students with learning and behavior problems (Swanson, 1999b). Several cautions should be noted. First, these programs rely heavily on oral presentation by the teacher and oral responses and reading by the students. Second, the programs are highly scripted, making modifications difficult. Third, the nonstandard print used with Levels I and II of *Reading Mastery* may limit some students' access to other decodable books. Although other books with the nonstandard print are available, the number is limited.

Phonic Remedial Reading Lessons

The *Phonic Remedial Reading Lessons* (Kirk et al., 1985) were developed in the 1930s to teach phonic analysis skills to students who had mild mental retardation. The lessons follow principles of systematic direct instruction in that they utilize such principles as minimal change, one response to one symbol, progress from easy to hard, frequent review and overlearning, corrective feedback, verbal mediation, and multisensory learning. The lessons are designed as an intensive phonics program to be used individually or in groups of no more than two or three students. They are not recommended as a

FIGURE 7.17

Portion of an Early Lesson from Corrective Reading

EXERCISE 2
PRONUNCIATIONS

Note: Do not write the words on the board. This is an oral exercise.

Task A

1. Listen. He was mad. [Pause.] **Mad.** Say it. [Signal.] *Mad.*
2. Next word. Listen. They wrestled on a mat. [Pause.] **Mat.** Say it. [Signal.] *Mat.*
3. Next word: **ram.** Say it. [Signal.] *Ram.*
4. [Repeat step 3 for *sat, reem, seem.*]
5. [Repeat all the words until firm.]

Task B Sit, rim, fin

1. I'll say words that have the sound iii. What sound? [Signal.] *iii.* Yes, *iii.*
2. [Repeat step 1 until firm.]
3. Listen: **sit, rim, fin.** Your turn: **sit.** Say it. [Signal.] *Sit.* Yes, *sit.*
4. Next word: **rim.** Say it. [Signal.] *Rim.* Yes, *rim.*
5. Next word: **fin.** Say it. [Signal.] *Fin.* Yes, *fin.*
6. [Repeat steps 3–5 until firm.]
7. What's the middle sound in the word rrriiimmm? [Signal.] *iii.* Yes, *iii.*
8. [Repeat step 7 until firm.]

EXERCISE 3
SAY THE SOUNDS

Note: Do not write the words on the board. This is an oral exercise.

1. First you're going to say a word slowly without stopping between the sounds. Then you're going to say the word fast.
2. Listen: *ssseee.* [Hold up a finger for each sound.]
3. Say the sounds in [pause] ssseee. Get ready. [Hold up a finger for each sound.] *ssseee.* [Repeat until the students say the sounds without stopping.]
4. Say it fast. [Signal.] *See.*
5. What word? [Signal.] *See.* Yes, *see.*
6. [Repeat steps 2–5 for *sad, mad, mat, me, seed, in, if, sat, ran, rat.*]

EXERCISE 4
SOUND INTRODUCTION

1. [Point to *i.*] One sound this letter makes is *iii.* What sound? [Touch.] *iii.*
2. [Point to *d.*] This letter makes the sound *d.* What sound? [Touch.] *d.*
3. Say each sound when I touch it.
4. [Point to 1.] What sound? [Touch under] i. *iii.*
5. [Repeat step 4 for d, e, d, r, t, s, ă, m.]

   To correct:
   a. [Say the sound loudly as soon as you hear an error.]
   b. [Point to the sound.] This sound is _____. What sound? [Touch.]

c. [Repeat the series of letters until all the students can correctly identify all the sounds in order.]

6. [Point to the circled letters.] The sound for one of these letters is the same as the letter name. That's the name you say when you say the alphabet.
7. [Point to *i.*] Listen: iii. Is that a letter name? [Signal.] *No.* Right, it isn't.
8. [Point to *a.*] Listen: **ăăă.** Is that a letter name? [Signal.] *No.* Right, it isn't.
9. [Point to *e.*] Listen: **eee.** Is that a letter name? [Signal.] *Yes.* Yes, it is. Remember, the sound you're learning for eee is the same as the letter name.

Individual Test

I'll call on different students to say all the sounds. If everybody I call on can say all the sounds without making a mistake, we'll go on to the next exercise. [Call on two or three students. Touch under each sound. Each student says all the sounds.]

EXERCISE 6
WORD READING

Task A Sat

1. Say each sound when I touch it
   [Point to *a.*] What sound?
   [Touch under *s.*] sss.
   [Point to *a.*] What sound?
   [Touch under *a*] **ăăă.**
   [Point to *t.*] What sound?
   [Touch under *t.*] *t.*
2. [Touch the ball of the arrow for *sat.*]
   Now I'm going to sound out the word. I won't stop between the sounds.
   [Touch under *s, a, t* as you say.] **sssăăăt.**
   [Point to *t.*] What sound?
3. [Touch the ball of the arrow.] Do it with me. Sound it out. Get ready.
   [Touch under *s, a, t.*] **sssaaat.** [Repeat until the students say the sounds without pausing]
4. Again. Sound it out. Get ready. [Touch under *s, a, t.*] **sssaaat.** [Repeat until firm.]
5. All by yourselves. Sound it out. Get ready. [Touch under *s, a, t.*] **sssaaat.** [Repeat until firm.]
6. [Touch the ball of the arrow.] Say it fast. [Slash right, along the arrow. *Sat.*] Yes, you read the word *sat.*

s a t

Source: S. Engelmann, L. Carnine, and G. Johnson, *Corrective Reading: Word-Attack Basics, Teacher Presentation Book I—Decoding A* (Columbus, OH: SRA/McGraw-Hill, 1999), pp. 26–29. Reprinted by permission of the McGraw-Hill Companies.

FIGURE 7.18

Sample from a Story from *Reading Mastery: Rainbow Edition*

thē fat man and his dog had →

a car. thē car did not run. →

Source: S. Engelmann and E. C. Bruner, *Reading Mastery I: Rainbow Edition—Storybook I* (Columbus, OH: SRA/McGraw-Hill, 1995), pp. 53–54. Reprinted by permission of the McGraw-Hill Companies.

general technique for teaching beginning reading; rather, they are a technique to use with students who have not yet learned an efficient method of identifying unknown words (Kirk et al., 1985).

CLASSROOM Applications

Phonemic Remedial Reading Lessons

PROCEDURES: The program begins by developing the readiness level for the lessons. Readiness skills include auditory discrimination and auditory sound blending. Figure 7.4 (p. 247) presented a simple procedure for teaching sound blending. Developing readiness also includes learning the sound–symbol associations for the short *a* sound and eleven consonant sounds (i.e., /c/, /d/, /f/, /g/, /h/, /l/, /m/, /p/, /s/, /t/, /w/).

Once these skills have been learned, the first lesson is introduced (see Figure 7.19). For each lesson, students sound out each word in each line, one letter at a time, and then give the complete word. Each lesson is organized into four parts and is based on the principle of minimal change. In the first part, only the initial consonant changes in each sequence; in the second part, only the final consonant changes; in the third part, both the initial and final consonants change; in the fourth part, the space between letters in a word is normal.

In addition to these drill lessons, high-frequency sight words are introduced and highly controlled stories are interspersed throughout the program. Frequent review lessons are also provided.

COMMENTS: This program provides a systematic and intensive approach to teaching phonic analysis skills to beginning readers. However, the approach

FIGURE 7.19

First Lesson from Phonic Remedial Reading Lessons

a

at	sat	ma t	ha t	fat
am	ham	Sam	Pam	tam
sad	mad	had	lad	dad
wag	sag	tag	lag	hag

sat	sap	Sam	sad
map	mam	mad	mat
hag	ham	hat	had
cat	cap	cad	cam

sat	am	sad	pat	ma d
had	mat	tag	fat	ham
lag	ham	wag	hat	sap
sad	tap	cap	dad	at

map	hag	cat	sat	ham	tap
sap	map	hat	sad	tag	am
Pam	mat	had	tap	hat	dad
fat	mad	at	wag	cap	sag

Source: S. A. Kirk, W. D. Kirk, and E. H. Minskoff, *Phonic Remedial Reading Lessons* (Novato, CA: Academic Therapy Publications, 1985), p. 22. Reprinted by permission.

places little emphasis on comprehension and reading for meaning and incorporates limited practice in connected text. The authors suggest using other books to give students the opportunity to practice their word identification and comprehension skills with other reading materials.

 SpotlightonDiversity

English Language Learners and Reading Difficulties

To what extent are the practices identified for phonological awareness and phonics appropriate for students who are English language learners (ELLs)? If they are appropriate, how can teachers facilitate their acquisition of these skills in English? Teachers should ask these questions and continue to acquire relevant knowledge as the number of students with special needs who are ELLs increases. Educational decisions that are informed by the language backgrounds and needs of special education students who are ELLs are particularly necessary when their primary education needs are in language-demanding areas such as reading. For most students with learning disabilities—as many as 80 percent (Lyon et al., 2001)—their primary educational needs are related to their reading difficulties. Therefore, the need to better understand and identify appropriate interventions for ELLs with reading difficulties is high.

Unfortunately, we know substantially more about teaching students with reading difficulties who are monolingual English students than about teaching students who are ELLs. However, there is a growing knowledge base to inform our instruction in early reading with ELLs (Denton, Anthony, Parker, and Hasbrouck, 2004; Gunn, Biglan, Smolkowski, and Ary, 2000; Linan-Thompson, Vaughn, Hickman-Davis, and Kouzekanani, 2003; Stuart, 1999; Vaughn, Cirino et al., 2006). A summary of findings reveals:

- English language learners who were given direct instruction in early reading in English benefited in the number of words read correctly per minute (Gunn et al., 2000).
- Bilingual students with significant reading problems who participated in 22 tutoring sessions in a systematic and explicit approach to phonics and word and sentence reading significantly improved on word identification when compared with controls (Denton et al., 2004).

- Moderate to high effect sizes were reported for word attack, passage comprehension, phoneme segmentation, and oral reading fluency among second-grade ELLs at risk for reading disabilities participating in 58 sessions (35 minutes each) of supplemental intervention in group sizes of one to three students (Linan-Thompson et al., 2003). Only three students made less than six months' growth during the three-month intervention.
- In a study with young children with problems learning to read in English but who spoke Sylheti (a dialect from Bangladesh), students who participated in Jolly Phonics rather than Big Books made significant gains on phonics recognition and recall and writing sounds, as well as on reading words and reading nonwords (Stuart, 1999). Findings indicate that a more structured, systematic approach that includes phonics resulted in better outcomes for ELLs than interventions without these elements.
- Young bilingual students (Spanish/English) with low literacy and oralcy skills taught to read in English made considerable gains over their first-grade year and maintained these advantages into second grade (Vaughn, Cirino, et al., 2006; Vaughn, Mathes, et al., 2006). Similarly, young bilingual students (Spanish/English) with low literacy and oralcy skills taught to read in Spanish also made considerable gains and outperformed comparison students and maintained these gains into second grade (Vaughn, Cirino, et al., 2006; Vaughn, Linan-Thompson, et al., 2006).

In summary, good readers—whether they are monolingual English or English language learners—rely primarily on decoding words (understanding the sound to print correspondence or alphabetic principle). They do not rely primarily on context or pictures to identify words. When they use context it is to confirm word reading or to better understand text meaning. Well-developed phonics instruction helps ELLs develop the skills and strategies they need to effectively and efficiently establish a map for making sense of how English language works in print. As with monolingual students, phonics instruction is a piece of the reading instruction, not the entire program. Good phonics instruction is well integrated into language activities, story time, and small group support to create a balanced reading program. Learning to read in languages in which the print is less consistently connected to sounds (like English) takes longer than learning to read in languages that have more consistent orthographies such as Spanish (Seymour, 2006).

Multisensory Structured Language Instruction

Multisensory structured language programs combine systematic explicit teaching of phonemic awareness, the alphabetic principle, phonics and structural analysis, syllabication, and decoding with activities that incorporate the visual, auditory, tactile (touch), and kinesthetic (movement) (VAKT) modalities. Multisensory structured language instruction was developed in the 1930s by Samuel Orton, a neuropathologist, and Anne Gillingham, a school psychologist. They developed reading remediation methods that built associations between the modalities such as "having the child trace [the letter] over a pattern drawn by the teacher, at the same time giving its sound or phonetic equivalent" (Orton, 1937, p. 159) or teaching spelling through analysis and writing of the sequence of sounds in words. The content of multisensory structured language programs includes teaching phonology and phonological awareness; sound–symbol associations that must be mastered in two directions: visual to auditory and auditory to visual; syllable instruction; morphology syntax; and semantics. These programs use the following instructional features or principles (McIntyre and Pickering, 1995):

- Simultaneous, multisensory presentation of visual, auditory, and kinesthetic-tactile (VAKT) modalities are used simultaneously to enhance memory and learning.
- Systematic and cumulative progression that follows the logical order of the language, moves from easy to difficult, and provides systematic review to strengthen memory
- Direct instruction that entails the explicit teaching of all concepts, skills, and strategies
- Systematic practice of decoding and spelling skills at the word, sentence, and text levels in controlled, decodable text
- Diagnostic teaching that requires teachers to be adept at individualizing instruction on the basis of careful and continual assessment of students' learning
- Instruction that incorporates synthetic methods (teaching the parts and how they work together to make a whole) and analytic methods (teaching the whole and how it can be broken down into its component parts)

FIGURE 7.20
Selected Phonics Reading Programs

Alphabetic Phonics and Foundations for Literacy, Cox, A. R., Cambridge, MA: Educators Publishing Service.

Fundations: Wilson Language Basics for K–3, Wilson, B. A., 2005, Millbury, MA: Wilson Language Training Corporation.

The Herman Method for Reversing Reading Failure, Herman, R. D., 1993, Sherman Oaks, CA: Herman Method Institute.

Language: A Curriculum for At-Risk and ESL Students, Greene, J. F., 1995, Longmont, CO: Sopris West.

Lindamood Phoneme Sequencing Program for Reading, Spelling, and Speech: The LiPS Program, Lindamood, P., and Lindamood, P., Austin, TX: PRO-ED.

Project Read, Enfield, M. L., and Greene, V., 2006, Bloomington, MN: Language Circle Enterprise.

Read Well, Sprick, M., Longmont, CO: Sopris West.

Recipe for Reading: A Structured Approach to Linguistics, Traub, N., Bloom, F., et al., 2000, Cambridge, MA: Educators Publishing Service.

Wilson Reading System, Wilson, B. A., 2004, Millbury, MA: Wilson Language Training Corporation.

The Writing Road to Reading, 5th ed., Spalding, R. B. and North, M.E., 2003, Phoenix, AZ: Spalding Educational International.

These programs are designed for students with dyslexia or those who are experiencing substantial difficulty learning to read. Examples of multisensory structured language programs are presented in Figure 7.20. The Gillingham-Stillman method (Gillingham and Stillman, 1973) is described in more detail. It is designed for third- through sixth-grade students of average or above average ability and normal sensory acuity who are having difficulty learning to read. With some adaptations, it can be modified to work with both older and younger students.

CLASSROOM Applications
Teaching Phonic Generalizations

PROCEDURES: This method teaches students how to identify words by teaching phonic generalizations and how to apply these generalizations in reading and spelling. It is designed to be used as the exclusive method for teaching reading, spelling, and penmanship for a two-year period at minimum. Initially, students who use this method should read only materials that are designed to conform with the method. Other written information, such as content area textbooks, should be read to the students.

The method is introduced by discussing the importance of reading and writing, how some children have difficulty learning to read and spell using whole-word methods, and how this method has helped other students. Thereafter, a sequence of lessons is completed, beginning with learning the names of the letters and the letter sounds, learning words through blending sounds, and reading sentences and stories.

Teaching Letters and Sounds. The teaching of letter names and letter sounds employs associations between visual, auditory, and kinesthetic inputs. Each new sound–symbol relationship or phonogram is taught by having the students make three associations:

1. *Association I (reading).* Students learn to associate the written letter with the letter name and then with the letter sound. The teacher shows the students the letter. The students repeat the name. The letter sound is learned by using the same procedure.

2. *Association II (oral spelling).* Students learn to associate the oral sound with the name of the letter. To do this, the teacher says the sound and asks the students to give its corresponding letter.

3. *Association III (written spelling).* The students learn to write the letter through the teacher modeling, tracing, copying, and writing the letter from memory. The students then associate the letter sound with the written letter by the teacher directing them to write the letter that has the _____ sound.

The following six features are important to note in teaching these associations:

1. Cursive writing is preferred and suggested over manuscript.
2. Letters are always introduced by a key word.
3. Vowels and consonants are differentiated by different-colored drill cards (i.e., white for consonants, salmon for vowels).
4. The first letters introduced (i.e., *a, b, f, h, i, j, k, m, p,* and *t*) represent clear sounds and nonreversible letter forms.
5. Drill cards are used to introduce each letter and to provide practice in sound and letter identification.
6. The writing procedure is applied to learning all new letters. The procedure for writing is as follows:
   a. The teacher makes the letter.
   b. The students trace the letter.
   c. The students copy it.
   d. The students write it from memory.

Teaching Words. After the first 10 letters and sounds have been learned by using the associations, students begin blending them together into words. Words that can be made from the 10 letters are written on yellow word cards and are kept in student word boxes (jewel cases). Students are taught to read and spell words.

To teach blending and reading, the letter drill cards that form a word (e.g., *b—a—t*) are laid out on the table or put in a pocket chart. The students are asked to give the sounds of the letters in succession, repeating the series of sounds again and again with increasing speed and smoothness until they are saying the word. This procedure is used to learn new words. Timed activities are used to give the students practice reading the words.

To teach spelling, the analysis of words into their component sounds should begin a few days after blending is started. To teach this method of spelling, the teacher pronounces a word the students can read, first quickly and then slowly. The teacher then asks the students, "What sound did you hear first?" and then asks, "What letter says /b/?" The students then find the *b* card. When all cards have been found, the students write the word. Gillingham and Stillman (1973) stress the importance of using this procedure for spelling. After the teacher pronounces /bat/:

1. Students repeat.
2. Students name letters *b-a-t.*
3. Student write, naming each letter while forming it /b-a-t/.
4. Students read *bat.*

This procedure is referred to as simultaneous oral spelling, or SOS. Gillingham and Stillman comment that after a few days of practice in blending and SOS, it should be an almost invariable routine to have students check their own errors. When a word is read wrong, students should be asked to spell what they have just said and match it against the original word. When a word is misspelled orally, the teacher may write the offered spelling and say, "Read this (e.g., *bit*)." The students would respond, "Bit." The teacher would say, "Correct, but I dictated the word /bat/."

As the students continue to learn and practice new words, they also continue to learn new sound–symbol associations or phonograms. As new phonograms are introduced, more and more words are practiced and added to the word boxes. An example of a daily lesson might be the following:

1. Practice Association I with learned phonograms.
2. Practice Association II with learned phonograms.

3. Practice Association III with learned phonograms.
4. Practice timed word reading for automaticity and accuracy.
5. Practice time spelling and writing words for automaticity and accuracy.

Sentences and Stories. When students can read and write three-lettered phonetic words, sentence and story reading is begun. This begins with reading simple, highly structured stories called "Little Stories." These stories are first practiced silently until the students think they can read them perfectly. Students may ask the teacher for assistance. The teacher pronounces nonphonetic words and cues the student to sound out phonetically regular words. Then the students read the sentence or story orally. The story is to be read perfectly with proper inflection. Later, the stories are dictated to the students. An example of a story is as follows:

Sam hit Ann.
Then Ann hit Sam.
Sam ran and Ann ran.
Ann had a tan mitten.
This is Ann's tan mitten.
Ann lost it.
Sam got the mitten.
Sam sent the mitten to Ann.

CLASSROOM Applications
Multisensory Structured Language Instruction

COMMENTS: For the most part, multisensory structured language programs have been designed and used as remedial programs for students who have not learned to read successfully. Much of the original research that supports their use was clinical case studies and summarized in a review by McIntyre and Pickering (1995) and more recently analyzed by Ritchey and Goeke (2006). Studies of older students with reading disabilities, although limited, do indicate that these students make substantial gains when the principles and content of multisensory structure language are employed (Greene, 1996; Torgesen, Wagner, and Rashotte, 1997; Torgesen, Wagner, Rashotte, Alexander, and Conway, 1997). Several considerations are worth keeping in mind when deciding to use structured language programs. First, they are best employed by teachers who have been trained in multisensory procedures. A list of institutions and organizations that offer training can be obtained from the International Dyslexia Association (800-222-3123), Academic Language Therapy Association (972-907-3924), Academy of Orton-Gillingham Practitioners and Educators (914-373-8919), and International Multisensory Structured Language Education Council (972-774-1772). Second, in general, these programs emphasize decoding skills and strategies and use text with such controlled vocabulary and it can be difficult to build comprehension skills. Hence, a number of the programs suggest simultaneously building listening comprehension until students are able to read more conventional text. Finally, there is limited research to support that the addition of the tactile-kinesthetic component facilitates learning (Moats, 1999).

Word Study: Making Words, Word Building, and Word Walls

Both reading and special educators have stressed the importance of word study as a way of learning the relationships between speech sounds and print, of building word recognition and spelling skills, and of developing vocabulary (Bear, Invernizzi, Templeton, and Johnston, 2000; Cunningham, 2000; Gunning, 2006; Henry, 1997). For students with learning and behavior problems, opportunities to construct words using magnetic letters, letter tiles, or laminated letters provide experience in manipulating sounds to find out how the words are affected. For example, the teacher might start with the sounds /s/, /t/, /r/, /n/, and /a/ and ask, "What two sounds make the word *at*?" The teacher would then ask the students to add a letter sound to the beginning to make the word *sat*. Then the sudents would be directed to remove the /s/. The teacher would then say, "What sound would you add to the beginning to make the word *rat*? Now listen. We're going to make a three-letter word. Take off the /t/ sound at the end of the word. Now add the sound that will make the word *ran*."

CLASSROOM Applications
Word Study

PROCEDURES: There are many activities that can be developed around word sorts, building words, and word walls. A number of resource books are available, including the following:

- *Building Words: A Resource Manual for Teaching Word Analysis and Spelling Strategies* (2001) by T. Gunning, Boston: Allyn and Bacon.

- *Making Words* (1994a) and *Making Big Words* (1994b) by P. Cunningham and D. Hall, Parsippany, NJ: Good Apple.
- *Patterns for Success in Reading and Spelling: A Multisensory Approach to Teaching Phonics and Word Analysis* (1996) by M. Henry, Austin, TX: Pro-Ed.
- *Phonics They Use: Words for Reading and Writing* (3rd ed.) (2000), by P. Cunningham, New York: Longman.
- *Word Journeys: Assessment-Guided Phonics, Spelling, and Vocabulary Instruction* (2000) by K. Ganske, New York: Guilford Press.
- *Words Their Way: Word Study for Phonics, Vocabulary, and Spelling Instruction* (2000) by D. Bear, M. Invernizzi, S. Templeton, and F. Johnston, Upper Saddle River, NJ: Merrill.

Making Words (Cunningham and Hall, 1994a) is one method that has been used and adapted for students with learning and behavior problems (Schumm and Vaughn, 1995). Using a specific set of letters (e.g., *a, c, h, r, s, t*), students make approximately 15 words beginning with two-letter words (e.g., *at*) and progressing to three-, four-, and five-letter words (e.g., *tar, cart, star, cash*) until the final "mystery word" is made (e.g., *scratch*). To use *Making Words*, each student needs a set of letters, and the teacher needs a large set of letters and a sentence strip chart to hold the cards and words that are constructed. Before the lesson, the teacher puts the letters the students will need during the lesson in plastic bags and gives a bag to each student. The three steps in the activity are as follows:

1. *Making words.* After the students have identified their letters, the teacher writes the numeral on the board for the number of letters the students are to put in their words. Next, the teacher cues the students to make different two-letter words. For example, with the word *scratch*, the teacher might ask the students to construct the word *at*. When working with a class of students, after each word has been constructed, the teacher selects one student who was correct to use the set of large letters and the chart to spell the word for the other students to check their work. Then the teacher might ask the students to add /c/ to the word *at* to make *cat* or to make the word *art* and then rearrange the letters to make the word *tar.* The teacher continues to guide students through the lesson by directing them to make words with their letters. The last word includes all the letters a student has been given for the lesson.

2. *Word sorting.* The teacher puts up on the sentence strip chart all the words the students have constructed. The teacher then asks the students how some of the words are alike, and students sort the words by spelling patterns. For example, the teacher would take the word *car* and have the students find the other words that begin with c—*cars, cash, cart;* or the teacher would take the word *art* and have the students find the other art words—*cart, chart.* Other students hypothesize why the words are alike, which assists the students in seeing the spelling patterns.

3. *Making words quickly.* Students write as many words as they can using the day's letters, writing the words in a Making Words Log. Students first write the letters from the lesson, and when the teacher says, "Go," they write words for two minutes.

COMMENTS: Both special education and general education teachers have found this practice an effective and efficient way to organize word identification instruction. Students report that they enjoy the activity and manipulating the letters (Cunningham, 1991; Schumm and Vaughn, 1995). However, Schumm and Vaughn (1995) found it necessary to develop simpler lessons and to focus more on teaching word families with less able readers.

Implicit Code Instruction

In comparison to explicit code instruction approaches, implicit code instruction in general does the following:

- Places more emphasis on using context clues, including picture clues, in decoding unknown words
- Begins by teaching an initial set of sight words
- Uses known words to discover word patterns and phonic generalizations
- Teaches onset-rime and phonic and structural analysis within the context of meaningful stories and books
- Puts less emphasis on systematically controlling the introduction of letter–sound relationships and spelling patterns
- Uses text in which the language patterns are at the sentence level (e.g., "I see a dog," "I see a cat," "I see a bear") rather than the word family or phoneme level (e.g., "The fat cat sat on a mat").

This section presents two implicit code instruction approaches that have been used with students who experience difficulties in developing fluent word recognition and effective word identification strategies: Modified Language Experience and the Fernald (VAKT) Method.

Modified Language Experience Approach

This approach to teaching early reading facilitates the transfer from oral language to written language by capitalizing on children's linguistic, cognitive, social, and cultural knowledge and abilities (Stauffer, 1970). Language experience approaches are congruent with principles based on Vygotsky's theory of cognitive development, and on learning frameworks such as whole language and process writing (Veatch, 1991). These approaches use the students' own language, repeated reading, visual configuration, and context clues to identify words. Language experience approaches are often considered language arts approaches, since they integrate oral language, writing, and reading (Allen, 1976; Nelson and Linek, 1999). Several methods for teaching language experience approaches have been developed: Allen's Language Experience Approach in Communication (Allen, 1976; Allen and Allen, 1966–68, 1982); Ashton-Warner's Organic Reading (Ashton-Warner, 1958, 1963, 1972); and Stauffer's Language-Experience Approach (Stauffer, 1970). The modified language experience approach that we describe is designed for students who have limited experience or success with reading and little or no sight vocabularies. The six objectives are as follows:

1. To teach the concept that text is talk written down
2. To teach the metalinguistic skills of sentence and word segmentation
3. To teach left-to-right progression
4. To teach use of semantic and syntactic clues
5. To teach recognition of words both within the context of the experience story and in isolation
6. To teach phonic and structural analysis by discovering patterns in known words

The approach is built on the idea that oral and written language are interdependent and that oral language can serve as the base for the development of written language.

CLASSROOM Applications

Modified Language Experience Approach

PROCEDURES: The procedures for this modified language experience approach are similar to those suggested by Stauffer (1970). However, more structure and practice have been incorporated into

FIGURE 7.21
Dictated Language Experience Story

Woody Woodpecker was driving a jet to outer space and saw some aliens. And he got on his jet and went to Jupiter and saw some people from outer space and they were driving jets, too.

this modification to provide for the needs of students who experience difficulties in learning to read. It is designed to be used individually or with groups of two to five students. At the heart of this approach is the language experience story, a story the students write about events, persons, or things of their choice (see Figure 7.21).

First day: For the first day of instruction, guidelines for developing a language experience story are:

1. *Provide or select an experience.* Provide or have the students select an experience that is of interest to them. Sometimes a picture can help to stimulate ideas, but be sure the students have experiences related to the picture. Remember—you are relying on the students' memory of the experience and their memory for the language used to describe the experience.

2. *Explain the procedure to the students.* Explain that the students are going to be dictating a story about the selected experience. This story will then become their reading text or book.

3. *Discuss the experience.* Discuss the experience with students so that they can begin to think about what they want to put in the dictated story. Students with learning and behavior problems sometimes have difficulty organizing their thoughts. The discussion can serve as time for the students to plan what they want to say. To facilitate the planning process, you may want to write notes or construct a map or web.

4. *Write the dictated story.* Have the students tell the story while you write it. Students should watch as you write or type it. If you are working with several students you may want to write the story on large chart paper. Have each of the students contribute to the story. If you are working with an individual, sit next to the student so that he or she can see what you write. Encourage the students to use natural voices. The language experience story presented in Figure 7.21 was dictated by Sam, a third grader reading at the primer level.

5. *Read the story to the students.* Ask the students to listen to the story to determine whether they want to make any changes. Make changes accordingly.

6. *Have students read the story.* First have the students read the story together with you (choral reading) until they seem comfortable with the story. When you are choral reading, point to the words so that the students focus on the text as they read. Next have the students read individually and pronounce words that they cannot identify. In some cases, a student may give you a lengthy story, yet his or her memory for text is limited. When this occurs, you may work on the story in parts, beginning with only the first several sentences or first paragraph.

7. *Encourage the students to read the story to others.* This is often a very intrinsically reinforcing activity.

8. *Type the story.* If the story has not already been typed, type it and make one copy for each student. Also make a second copy for each student to keep and use for record keeping.

Second day: For the second day of instruction, guidelines for reading the story are as follows:

1. *Practice reading the story.* Have the students practice reading the story using choral reading, individual reading, and reading to one another. When the students are reading individually and they come to a word they do not recognize, encourage them to look at the word and think of what word would make sense. Having the students read to the end of the sentence can also help them to think of a word that makes sense. If students cannot recall the word, pronounce it.

2. *Focus on individual words and sentences.* Have the students match, locate, and read individual sentences and words in the story. Discuss what markers are used to denote sentences and words. Finally, have the students read the story to themselves and underline the words they think they know.

3. *Check on known words.* Have each student read the story orally. On your copy of the story, record the words the student knows.

4. *Type the words from the story on word cards.* Type the words each student knows from the story on word cards.

Third day: Guidelines for the third day are as follows:

1. *Practice reading the story.* Repeat the type of activities described in step 1 of the second day.

2. *Focus on individual sentences and words.* Repeat the type of activities described in step 2 of the second day.

3. *Check on known words.* With the word cards in the *same order* as the words in the text, have each student read the word cards, and record the words the student knows.

4. *Practice reading the story.* Repeat the type of activities described in step 1 of the second day.

5. *Focus on sentences and words.* Repeat the type of activities described in step 2 of the second day.

6. *Check on known words.* With the cards in *random order*, have each student read the words, and record the words each student knows.

Fourth day: Guidelines for the fourth day are as follows:

1. *Check on known words.* Repeat step 3 from the third day, using only the words the student knows from the previous day.

2. *Enter known words in word bank.* Each student should make word cards (3 × 5 index cards or scraps of posterboard work well) for the words that he or she can identify in step 1. These words should be filed by the student in his or her word bank (index card box). Words that the student cannot identify should not be included.

3. *Read, illustrate, and publish the story.* Have the students read the story and decide whether they want to illustrate it and/or put it into a language experience book. Books can be developed for individual students, or one book can be made for the group. Students can then share these books with each other and with other interested people and place them in the library.

Once the students have completed at least one story and have developed 15 to 20 words in their word banks, they can begin to use the banks for a variety of activities, such as generating new sentences, locating words with similar parts (i.e., inflectional endings, beginning sounds, shapes), and

FIGURE 7.22

Suggested Activities for Word Bank Cards

1. Alphabetize words in word banks.
2. Match the word with the same word as it occurs in newspapers, magazines, etc.
3. Make a poster of the words known.
4. Complete sentences using word banks. Provide students with a stem or incomplete sentences and have students fill slot with as many different words as possible. Example:

    He ran to the _____. The _____ and _____ ran into the park.

5. Find or categorize words in word banks:

naming words	science words
action words	color words
descriptive words	animal words
words with more than one meaning	names of people
words with the same meaning	interesting words
opposites	funny words
people words	exciting words

6. Locate words beginning the same, ending the same, or meaning the same.
7. Locate words with various endings.
8. Match sentences in stories with words from word bank.
9. Use word bank cards for matching-card games, such as grab and bingo.
10. Organize words into a story. Students might need to borrow words for this use and may wish to illustrate or make a permanent record of it.
11. Delete words from a story. Have students use words from their word banks to complete the story.
12. Scramble the sentences in the story or words in a sentence.
13. Establish class word banks for different classroom centers, such as science words, number words, weather words, house words, family words.

Source: Adapted from R. J. Tierney, J. E. Readence, and E. K. Dishner, *Reading Strategies and Practices: Guide for Improving Instruction* (Boston: Allyn & Bacon, 1980), pp. 285–287.

categorizing words by use (e.g., action words, naming words, describing words).

As the number of sight words continues to increase, students can write their own stories, using the words from the word bank to assist them. More suggestions for developing activities based on the word bank are given in Figure 7.22.

COMMENTS: The modified language experience approach provides a method for teaching children initial skills in reading, including the recognition of sight words. The approach utilizes the students' memory, oral language, and background experiences (Robertson, 1999), as well as visual configuration and context clues. Once the initial sight vocabulary has been built to between 30 and 100 words, students should be encouraged to read other books and stories. This approach also provides a way to monitor students' reading development, including word recognition and fluency (Stokes, 1989). Having students record their stories during initial reading and reading on the fourth day allows the teacher to monitor growth.

This approach lends itself to the use of computer technology (Duling, 1999), particularly with the use of word processing, desktop publishing, and multimedia software that incorporates voice and graphics, such as Children's Writing and Publishing Center (Learning Company), *Kidwriter II* (Davidson and Associates), and *Kid Pix* (Broderbund), or language experience-based software programs such as *Writing to Read* (Martin and Friedburg, 1986). For example, Stratton, Grindler, and Postell (1992) integrated word processing and photography into a language experience for middle school students.

Activities are incorporated into the approach to encourage the development of the metalinguistic skills of sentence and word segmentation. However, this approach does not present a systematic method for teaching phonic and structural analysis. For students who have difficulty with these skills, a more structured method of teaching phonic and structural analysis may be needed after they have developed an initial sight vocabulary. This approach may not provide some students with enough drill and practice to develop a sight vocabulary. In those cases, it will be necessary to supplement this approach with activities presented in the section on techniques for building sight words. For a research review of language experience approaches to teaching beginning reading, see Stahl and Miller (1989).

Fernald (VAKT) Method

The Fernald method (Fernald, 1943, 1988) uses a multisensory or visual-auditory-kinesthetic-tactile (VAKT) approach to teach students to read and write words. This method was used by Grace Fernald and her associates in the clinic school at the University of California at Los Angeles in the 1920s. It is designed for students who have severe difficulties learning and remembering words when reading, who have a limited sight vocabulary, and for whom other methods have not been successful. It is usually taught on an individual basis.

CLASSROOM Applications

Fernald Method (VAKT)

PROCEDURES: The Fernald method consists of four stages through which students progress as they learn to identify unknown words more effectively. The first stage, which is the most laborious, requires a multisensory approach and utilizes a language experience format. By the final stage, students are reading books and are able to identify unknown words from the context and their similarity to words or word parts already learned. At this stage, the students are no longer tracing or writing a word to learn it.

Stage One: Guidelines for Stage One are as follows:

1. *Solicit the student's commitment to learn.* Tell the student that you are going to be showing him or her a technique for learning to read unknown words that has been successful with many students who have not learned in other ways. Inform the student that this method will take concentration and effort on his or her part, but it should be successful.

2. *Select a word to learn.* Have the student select a word (regardless of length) that he or she cannot read but would like to learn to read. Discuss the meaning of the word, and listen for the number of syllables.

3. *Write the word.* Sit beside the student, and have him or her watch and listen while you:

    a. Say the word.

    b. Using a broad-tipped marker on a piece of unlined paper approximately 4" × 11", write the word in blackboard-size script, or in print if the student does not write in cursive. Say the word as you write it.

FIGURE 7.23

Sample Word Using Fernald Technique

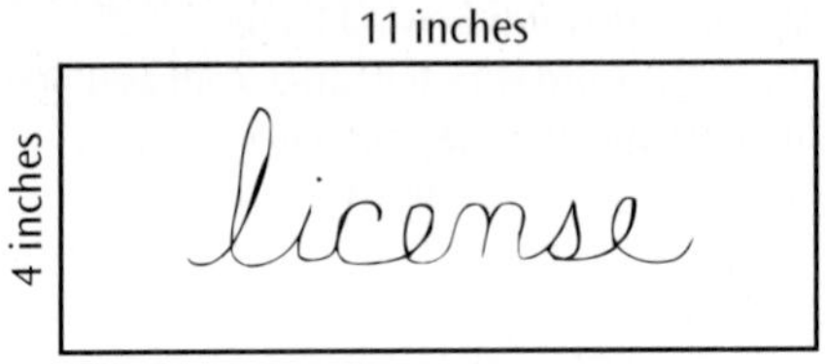

11 inches

4 inches

license

    c. Say the word again as you smoothly move your finger underneath the word. See Figure 7.23 for a model.

4. *Model tracing the word.* Model how the student is to trace the word so that he or she might learn it. Do not explain the process, but simply say to the student, "Watch what I do and listen to what I say."

    a. Say the word.

    b. Trace the word using one or two fingers. The fingers should touch the paper in order to receive the tactile stimulation. As you trace the word, say the word. Fernald (1943) stresses that the student must say each part of the word as he or she traces it. This is necessary to establish the connection between the sound of the word and its form so that the student will eventually recognize the word from the visual stimulus alone. It is important that this vocalization of the word be natural; that is, it should be a repetition of the word as it actually sounds—not stilted or distorted sounding—out of letters or syllables in such a way that the word is lost in the process. The sound for each letter is never given separately or overemphasized. In a longer word, such as *important*, the student says *im* while tracing the first syllable, *por* while tracing the second syllable, and *tant* as he or she traces the last syllable.

    c. Say the word again while moving the tracing finger(s) underneath the word in a sweeping motion.

Model this process several times, and then have the student practice the process. If the student does not complete the process correctly, stop the student when he or she makes an error and cue, "Not quite. Watch me do it again." Continue this procedure until the student is completing the three-stage process correctly.

5. *Trace until learned.* Have the student continue tracing the word until the student thinks that he or she can write the word from memory.

6. *Write from memory.* When the student feels ready, remove the model, and have the student write the word from memory, saying the word as he or she writes. Fernald (1943) stresses that the student should always write the word without looking at the copy. She comments:

> When the child copies the word, looking back and forth from the word he is writing to the copy, he breaks the word up into small and meaningless units. The flow of the hand in writing the word is interrupted and the eye movements are back and forth from the word to the copy instead of those which the eye would make in adjusting to the word as it is being written. This writing of the word without the copy is important at all stages of learning to write and spell. The copying of words is a most serious block to learning to write them correctly and to recognize them after they have been written (pp. 37–39).

It is also important that the student write the word as a unit. If the student makes an error in writing the word or hesitates unduly between letters, stop the student immediately, cross out the word, and have the student again practice tracing the large model. The word is never erased and rewritten. Fernald states, "The reason for this procedure is that the various movements of erasing, correcting single letters or syllables, and so forth, break the word up into a meaningless total which does not represent a word" (p. 39). It also can interfere with the student's motor memory for the word. The student should write the word from memory correctly at least three consecutive times.

7. *File the word.* After the word has been written three times correctly, the student should place it in his or her word bank.

8. *Type the word.* Within an interval of 24 hours, the student should type and read each word learned by using this process. This helps to establish the link between the written and typed word.

The number of words learned per session using this VAKT process depends on the number of tracings a student needs to learn a new word. This number varies greatly among students. We have worked with students who need fewer than five tracings to learn a new word, whereas other students required over 50 tracings when first beginning this approach.

Fernald (1943) reports, "As soon as a child has discovered that he can learn to write words, we let him start 'story writing' " (p. 33). As the student writes a story and comes to a word he or she cannot spell, the tracing process is repeated. These stories should be typed within 24 hours so that the student can read the newly learned words in typed form within the context of the story.

Fernald suggests that no arbitrary limit be set for the length of the tracing period (Stage One). The student stops tracing when he or she is able to learn without it. This is usually a gradual process, with the student sometimes feeling the need to trace a word and sometimes thinking that the word does not need to be traced.

Stage Two: When the student no longer needs to trace words to learn them, he or she moves to Stage Two. In this stage, the teacher writes the requested word in cursive (or manuscript) for the student. The student then simply looks at the word, saying it while looking at it, and then writes it without looking at the copy, saying each part of the word as he or she writes it from memory. As with Stage One, words to be learned are obtained from words the student requests while writing stories. The word bank continues to function as a resource for the student, but a smaller word box can be used, since the teacher is writing the words in ordinary script size.

Stage Three: The student progresses to the third stage when he or she is able to learn directly from the printed word without having it written. In this stage, the student looks at the unknown printed word, and the teacher pronounces it. The student then says the word while looking at it and then writes it from memory. Fernald reports that during this stage, students still read poorly but are able to recognize quite difficult words almost without exception after having written them.

During this stage, the student is encouraged to read as much as and whatever he or she wants. Unknown words are pronounced, and when the passage is finished, the unknown words are learned by using the technique described in the preceding paragraph.

Stage Four: The student is able to recognize new words from their similarity to words or parts of words he or she has already learned. At first, a student may need to pronounce the word and write it on a scrap of paper to assist in remembering it, but later this becomes unnecessary. The student continues to read books that interest him or her. When reading scientific or other difficult material, the student is encouraged to scan the paragraph and lightly underline each word he or she does not know. These words are then discussed for recognition and meaning before reading.

COMMENTS: Empirical evidence lends support to this approach for teaching word identification to students with severe reading disabilities (Berres and Eyer, 1970; Coterell, 1972; Fernald, 1943; Kress and Johnson, 1970; Thorpe and Borden, 1985). Although this approach tends to be successful with such readers, the first several stages are very time-consuming for both the teacher and the student. Consequently, it should be used only if other approaches have not been successful.

Techniques for Building Sight Words

Students who read fluently recognize individual words automatically or when they are reading text (see sections "What Is a Sight Word?" on page 257, and "Automatic Word Recognition" on page 262). Students with reading disabilities struggle with automatic word recognition, which is important not only for words that are decodable (e.g., *and, then, it*), but especially for high-frequency words that are less phonetically regular (e.g., *the, you, was, have*). See Figure 7.12 (p. 262) for a list of high-frequency words. This section presents several techniques that teachers can use to assist students in remembering words. In addition, a number of games and computer programs can be used to provide students with practice in recognizing words presented individually and in text. These techniques can be incorporated into a reading program for the purpose of building automatic word recognition and can be used with either explicit or implicit code instruction.

Sight Word Association Procedure

The sight word association procedure (SWAP; Bradley, 1975) uses corrective feedback and drill and practice to assist students in associating spoken words with written form. The procedure is appropriate to use with students who are beginning to learn to identify words across various contexts or texts or with students who require more practice

of new words than their current reading program provides. It is designed to be used individually or with small groups.

CLASSROOM Applications

Sight Word Association Procedure

PROCEDURES: Begin by selecting words from the text that the students consistently miscall or do not identify at an automatic level. Write each word on a word card. The procedure for teaching these words (usually three to seven words at a time) is as follows:

1. Discuss the words with students to ensure that they understand the meanings of the words as the words are being used in the text.

2. Present the words to the students one word at a time. Each word is exposed for five seconds, and the teacher says the word twice.

3. Shuffle the cards, and ask students to identify the word on each card. Provide corrective feedback by verifying the correctly identified words, giving the correct word for any word that is miscalled, and saying the word if students do not respond in five seconds.

4. Present all the words again, using the format given in step 2.

5. Have students identify each word, using the format given in step 3. Repeat this step at least two more times or until they can automatically recognize all the words.

If students continue to have difficulty recognizing a word after the seventh exposure to the word, switch from a recall task to a recognition task. To do this, place several word cards on the table, and have the learners point to each word as you say it. If the students still continue to have difficulty learning the words, use a different technique to teach the words, such as picture association techniques, sentence/word association techniques, or a cloze procedure. A record sheet for keeping track of individual student responses is presented in Figure 7.24.

After teaching the words on the initial day, the words should be reviewed for several days to determine whether the words are being retained; reteach if necessary.

COMMENTS: This procedure provides a technique for systematically practicing unknown words. It utilizes principles of corrective feedback and mass and distributed practice to teach words. However, there are several important cautions regarding

FIGURE 7.24

Sight Word Association Procedure (SWAP) Record Sheet

Words	Initial Teaching					Retention			Comments
	1	2	3	4	5	1	2	3	

✓ Correct
0 Incorrect

sight word association. First, it needs to be used in conjunction with an approach to reading that stresses reading text and utilizing other decoding strategies. Second, students should understand the meanings of the words being taught. Third, in addition to the isolated word practice provided by this technique, students should be given ample opportunity to read these words in context.

Picture Association Technique

Using a key picture to aid in identifying a word can be beneficial (Mastropieri and Scruggs, 1998). This method allows the readers to associate the word with a visual image. It is on this premise that picture association techniques use key pictures to help students associate a spoken word with its written form.

CLASSROOM Applications

Picture Association Technique

PROCEDURES: Select words that the students are having difficulty identifying when reading. At first, choose words that are easily imaged, such as nouns, verbs, and adjectives. Write each word on a card (usually three to seven words). On a separate card, draw a simple picture, or find a picture and attach it to the card. In some cases, the students may want to draw their own pictures. Use the following procedure to teach the picture–word association:

1. Place each picture in front of the students, labeling each one as you present it. Have the students practice repeating the names of the pictures.

2. Place next to each picture the word it represents, again saying the name of the word. Have students practice saying the names of the words.

3. Have students match the words to the pictures and say the name of the word while matching it. Repeat this process until students easily match the pictures and words.

4. Place the words in front of the students, and have them identify the words as you say them. If they cannot identify the correct word, have them think of the picture to aid in their recognition. If they still cannot point to the word, show them the picture that goes with the word.

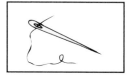

needle

5. Have students recall the words by showing the word cards one at a time. Again, if students cannot recall a word, have them think of the picture. If they still cannot think of the word, tell them to look at the picture that goes with the word.

6. Continue this procedure until the students can identify all the words at an automatic level. The same record sheet as the one used for SWAP (Figure 7.24) can be used for this procedure.

7. Have students review the words on subsequent days and, most important, give them plenty of opportunities to read the words in text. When a student is reading and cannot identify a word, encourage the student to think of the picture.

COMMENTS: This picture association technique assists students in forming visual images that facilitate their identification of words. As with the sight word association procedure, this procedure should be used only as a supplemental technique, and students should be given ample opportunities to read the words in text.

Picture associations have been used in beginning reading programs such as the *Peabody Rebus Reading Program* (Woodcock, Clark, and Davies, 1969) and word processing programs such as *Kid Writer Deluxe* (Davidson). Students learn to read these symbols and then transfer their skills to traditional print by making picture–word associations.

Sentence–Word Association Technique

The sentence–word association technique encourages students to associate an unknown word with a familiar spoken word, phrase, or sentence to aid in remembering the word when reading.

CLASSROOM Applications

Sentence–Word Association Technique

PROCEDURES: Select three to seven words that students are consistently having difficulty recognizing. Discuss these words with the students, and ask them to find the words in the text and read them in a sentence. Tell the students to decide on a key word, phrase, or sentence that will help them to remember the word. For example, for the word *was* a sentence might be "Today he is, yesterday he _____." For the word *there* the sentence might be "Are you _____?" Put the words to be taught on word cards, and put the associated word, phrase, or sentence on separate cards. Teach the associations between the key word, phrase, or sentence and the unknown word, using the same procedures as were described for the picture association technique. After teaching, when a student is reading and comes to one of the new words and cannot remember it, have the student think of the associated clue. If the student cannot think of the associated clue orally, tell him or her the clue.

INSTRUCTIONAL ACTIVITIES

This section provides instructional activities that are related to phonological awareness, phonics, and word identification. Some of the activities teach new skills; others are best suited for practice and reinforcement of already acquired skills. For each activity, the objective, materials, and teaching procedures are described.

▶ Grocery Store

Objective: To increase students' awareness of print in the environment and to provide practice in matching words.

Grades: Primary

Materials: (1) An area that is set up as a grocery store. (2) Commonly used packaged and canned goods with labels left on (e.g., instant pudding, toothpaste, cornflakes, chicken noodle soup). Remove the contents of packaged goods and re-close the box. (3) Cards with names of items written on them. (4) Baskets and/or bags that students can use when shopping.

Teaching Procedures: This center can be used in a variety of ways. Word cards can be placed by each food item. When students are shopping and select a food item, they also pick up the card, read it, and match it to the label on the box. When students go through checkout, they can read each card and hand the cashier the item that goes with it, or the teacher and students can decide which items students want to buy. The teacher gives those word cards to the students, who shop for those items by matching the cards to the items on the shelves.

Students can serve as stockers by reshelving the items the other students have purchased. When stockers reshelve an item, they can find the card that matches the item and then place the card next to the item.

▶ My Sound Book

Objective: To provide students with practice in finding pictures that start with a specific consonant or vowel sound.

Grades: Primary

Materials: (1) A three-ring binder or folder into which "Sound Pages" can be inserted. (2) Magazines, old books, or workbooks that can be cut up. (3) Stickers, scissors, and glue.

Teaching Procedures: Explain to the students that each of them will be making a book where they can collect and keep pictures and stickers that start with various sounds. Select one sound that the students are learning, and have them write the letter representing the sound on the top of the page. Then have them look through magazines, old books, and workbooks to find pictures starting with the sound.

Once they have selected the pictures, have them say the names to you so that you both can determine whether the pictures represent the designated sound. Then have students glue the pictures on the sound pages, leaving room to add other pictures they find while looking for pictures representing other sounds. Have students put the sound page in the notebook and share their pictures with other students. Continue until the book is complete. As students collect stickers, you may want to encourage them to put them in the sound book.

▶Vowel Match

Objective: To provide students with practice in decoding words that have various vowels sounds.

Grades: Primary and intermediate

Materials: (1) One file folder that is divided into two playing areas that consist of 10 boxes for each player. In each box, paste a picture that illustrates a vowel sound. (2) Thirty to 40 playing cards with pictures illustrating vowel sounds.

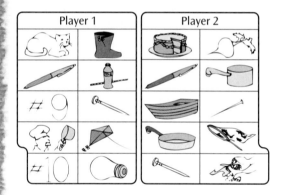

Teaching Procedures: Explain the game to the students. Shuffle the cards and place them face down near the players. Each student draws a card and checks to see whether the vowel sound illustrated on the card matches one of the pictures on his or her side of the game folder. If it does, the player places the card over the picture on the game folder. If the picture does not match, the card is discarded. The player to cover all the boxes first wins the game.

Adaptations: This game is easily adapted to teaching rhyming words and other sounds such as consonant digraphs or blends.

▶Sight Word Bingo

Objective: To provide students with practice in recognizing words.

Grades: Primary and intermediate

Materials: (1) Posterboard cut into 10" × 8" pieces to use for bingo cards. (2) A list of new words students have encountered in their reading. Such lists can be found in the back of basal readers or in books of lists such as *The New Reading Teacher's Book of Lists* (Fry, Fountoukidis, and Polk, 1985). To make the bingo cards, randomly select words from the list, and write them on the card as illustrated. (3) Colored markers.

Word Bingo			
happen	should	night	enough
below	never	complete	thought
grow	where	while	building
every	through	include	were
country	even	important	between

Teaching Procedures: One student (or the teacher) is designated as the caller. Each of the remaining students gets a bingo card. The caller randomly selects a word from the list and says the word. The students place a colored marker on the square in which the word is written. The first person to cover all the squares in a horizontal, vertical, or diagonal row calls, "Bingo." The caller and the student then verify the words. If they are verified, that student wins.

Adaptations: Bingo is a generic game that can be adapted to provide practice for a variety of skills. Following are some examples:

- *Consonant bingo:* Put pictures of objects that start with initial consonants, blends, or digraphs on the bingo cards. The caller says the letters, and the students mark the pictures that have the same consonant, blend, or digraph. This can also be adapted for final consonants.
- *Prefix bingo:* Write prefixes on the bingo cards. The caller says a word with a prefix or gives the definition of a prefix, and the students mark the prefix on their cards.
- *Math fact bingo:* Write the answers to math facts on the bingo cards. The caller says a math fact, and the students mark the answer.

▶Compound Concentration

Objective: To give students practice in identifying compound words and to illustrate how words may be combined to form compound words.

Grades: Intermediate and secondary

Materials: Thirty-six index cards (3" × 5") on which the two parts of 18 compound words have been written. Make sure that each part can only be joined with one other part.

Teaching Procedure: Explain the game. Have a student shuffle the cards and place the cards face down in six rows with six cards each. Each player takes a turn at turning over two cards. The student then decides whether the two words make a compound word. If the words do not make a compound word, then the cards are again turned face down, and the next player takes a turn. If the words make a compound word, then the player gets those two cards and turns over two more cards. The student continues playing until two cards are turned over that do not make a compound word. The game is over when all the cards are matched. The winner is the player with the most cards.

Adaptations: Concentration can be adapted for many skills. Students can match synonyms, antonyms, prefixes, suffixes, initial or final consonants, categories, and math facts.

▶Go Fish for Rimes

Objective: To give the students practice in identifying and reading words with rimes.

Grades: Intermediate and secondary

Materials: Twenty to 30 index cards (3" × 5") on which words with a particular rime pattern (e.g., -ake, -ail, -ime, -ight, etc.) are written. Make sure that each word is written on two cards so that students can match them.

Teaching Procedures: Explain the game. Have a student shuffle the cards and deal five cards to each player. The rest of the cards are placed face down in a pile on the table. Each player reads his or her own cards. Any player who has two cards that contain the same word reads the word and places the pair of cards face up in front of himself or herself (provide assistance as necessary). After everyone has laid out their pairs, the first student asks one other student whether he or she has a specific word (e.g., "Do you have *rake?*"). The student who was asked looks at his or her cards. If that student has the card, he or she reads the card and hands it to the first student. That student puts the pair face up in front of him or her and takes another turn. If the student who is being asked for a card does not have the card, he or she says, "Go fish," the first student takes a card from the pile, and the next student takes his or her turn. When a student has laid down all of his or her cards, the game is over. The person with the most pairs wins.

Adaptations: Go Fish can be adapted for many skills. Students can match synonyms, antonyms, prefixes, suffixes, or compound words.

SUMMARY for Chapter 7

Reading is one of the most important areas of education, and special education teachers who work with students with learning and behavior problems spend more time teaching reading than any other area. Reading is a skilled and strategic process in which learning to decode and read words accurately and rapidly is essential. It entails understanding a text and is dependent on active engagement and interpretation by the reader. Therefore, the goal of reading instruction is to provide students with the skills, strategies, and knowledge to read fluently and understand a text for purposes of enjoyment and learning.

Many students with learning or reading disabilities experience significant difficulties in developing phonemic awareness, letter–sound correspondence, and the understanding of how speech maps to print. Systematically teaching this knowledge and related skills will be crucial to these

students' success in learning to read. The skills of blending, segmenting, and manipulating phonemes are particularly important.

In developing strategies for decoding words, students can rely on phonic analysis, using onset-rimes or spelling patterns, structural analysis (e.g., affixes and inflectional endings), syllabication, syntax, and semantics. Ideas for teaching these various decoding strategies are presented in this chapter.

Although some words lend themselves to using decoding strategies such as phonic analysis, structural analysis, and syllabication, other words may be more effectively learned as whole units because they are less predictable phonetically. For these words, a number of strategies for teaching sight words are presented including the sight word association, picture association, and cloze.

FOCUS
Answers

FOCUS Question 1. **What are the two overarching concepts that should guide reading instruction, and how do teachers decide where to focus instruction?**

Answer: Reading instruction involves teaching the basic skills necessary to read words accurately and rapidly. Reading instruction also incorporates strategies to assist readers in understanding what they read by expanding vocabulary and using comprehension strategies. There is a general progression of skills, and instruction should be organized into the essential components, the focus of which is based on individual student needs.

FOCUS Question 2. **What are the definitions of phonological awareness, letter–sound correspondence, and phonics, and what are some examples of activities that can be used to teach them?**

Answer: Phonological awareness is knowing and demonstrating that spoken language can be broken down into smaller units (words, syllables, phonemes). Activities in phonological awareness are conducted orally. For example, a teacher says the word *that*, and students clap the number of sounds they hear (three claps). Letter–sound correspondence is knowing how letter names and sounds relate to each other. Phonics is the idea that words are composed of letters that represent sounds, that those sounds are related to each other (letter–sound correspondence), and that they can be used to pronounce or spell words. Activities involving phonics relate sounds to print and may involve direct teaching of letter sounds, phonemes, and activities to practice the letter–sound relationships. For example, a teacher gives students the phoneme *at*, and students add letters to make additional words (e.g., *cat, that, mat, splat*).

FOCUS Question 3. **What are the definitions of the six main decoding strategies, and how does each contribute to successful word identification?**

Answer:

1. Phonics analysis involves identifying and blending letter–sound correspondences into words. Practice in blending sounds into words increases ease of decoding and fluency. To avoid an overreliance on any one method of decoding, students should be taught to use a variety of strategies and the appropriate situations in which to apply them.
2. Onset-rime consists of using common spelling patterns to decode words by blending either individual sounds/patterns or using an analogy method to think of a word with similar sounds/patterns. Knowledge of common rimes assists readers in recognizing a large number of words that contain the core patterns.
3. Structural analysis involves analyzing words to assist with decoding and determining the meanings of words. Structural analysis is particularly effective for decoding longer, multisyllabic words.
4. Knowledge of syllabication assists readers in recognizing similar chunks of print across words.
5. Automatic word recognition is knowing a word without having to decode it. Because certain words are repeated so often (e.g., the), reading is made easier when one can automatically recognize high-frequency words that are less phonetically regular.
6. A knowledge of syntax (word order) and semantics (word meaning) can assist readers in cross-checking pronunciation and monitoring comprehension.

FOCUS Question 4. **How can the use of explicit and implicit code instruction be compared?**

Answer: Explicit code instruction is used to teach phonological awareness; letter–sound correspondence; phonics; and the use of phonic analysis, structural analysis, and syllabication to decode unknown words. Reading materials associated with this technique generally use decodable texts that highlight specific phonic or structural patterns. Implicit code instruction emphasizes the use of context clues, including picture cues, to decode unknown words. Texts are chosen that will be meaningful to readers and not for particular letter–sound relationships or spelling patterns. Implicit code instruction is often used with emergent readers who have had difficulties developing sight vocabulary and word analysis skills.

THINK and APPLY

- What are the components of reading instruction?
- What are the characteristics of phonological awareness, and how can a teacher recognize students who are struggling with phonological awareness?
- Why are phonological awareness, phonics and letter–sound correspondences so vital to later reading success?
- Observe a kindergarten classroom for evidence of each of the phonological awareness skills in the continuum of development.
- Think about how phonological awareness and phonics are interrelated. How can these skills be utilized and expanded on to develop word reading and spelling skills?

- Develop several games for promoting letter–sound correspondences.
- What are some different ways in which you can teach phonological awareness to one student, a small group of students, and a whole class of students?
- What are the characteristics of a phonics-based method for reading instruction?
- What are the key features of direct and explicit instruction? Why are these features so vital for the instruction of students with learning or reading disabilities?

- Compare and contrast explicit and implicit code instruction. Describe what type of learner might profit from each.
- Review several early reading programs or basal readers, and describe how they sequence phonics instruction.
- Develop several games for building sight words.

APPLY the STANDARDS

 Council for Exceptional Children

1. How might the assessment procedures and activities described in this chapter be integrated into reading instruction in a general education classroom to develop basic skills in reading before referral and identification of learning disabilities in young children (LD4S1, LD4S2, LD7K3, LD9S2, CC8S2)?

Standard LD4S1: Use research-supported methods for academic and nonacademic instruction of individuals with learning disabilities.

Standard LD4S2: Use specialized methods for teaching basic skills.

Standard LD7K3: Interventions and services for children who may be at risk for learning disabilities.

Standard LD9S2: Use research findings and theories to guide practice.

Standard CC8S2: Administer nonbiased formal and informal assessments.

2. To prepare for meeting the needs of students who range in reading ability, use your knowledge of the CEC standards (LD4S8) to plan a reading lesson that incorporates at least one reading skill (e.g., phonological awareness, decoding) and is differentiated to meet the unique needs of students with learning disabilities and emotional or behavioral disorders who struggle with reading. Include the grade level, skill, and the differentiated activity within that skill for students at various levels.

Standard LD4S8: Use reading methods appropriate to the individual with learning disabilities.

WEBSITES as RESOURCES | to Assist in Teaching Reading

The following Websites are extensive resources to expand your understanding of teaching reading:

- National Reading Panel www.nationalreadingpanel.org
- International Dyslexia Association www.interdys.org
- International Reading Association www.reading.org
- Vaughn Gross Center for Reading at the University of Texas www.texasreading.org
- Florida Center for Reading at the Florida State University www.fcrr.org
- LD Online www.ldonline.org
- Reading Rockets www.readingrockets.org

Where the Classroom Comes to Life

Video Homework Exercise Go to MyEducationLab and select the topic "READING INSTRUCTION," then watch the video "Word Chunking" and complete the activity questions below.

In this video, a teacher works with a first grader on word recognition and chunking.

1. What strategy discussed in the chapter is the teacher using in this clip?
2. What skills is she developing with this student?

Video Homework Exercise Go to MyEducationLab and select the topic "READING INSTRUCTION," then watch the video "Phonics" and complete the activity questions below.

In this video a teacher teaches phonics to a small group of students.

1. Teaching phonics in isolation is not a recommended practice. What does the teacher in this video do to contextualize the phonics instruction she provides?
2. How does this instructional episode connect to the two overarching concepts that guide reading instruction discussed in the chapter?

 **Scope and Sequence for Teaching Phonics**

Level	Categories	Correspondence	Model Word	Correspondence	Model Word
Preparatory	Letter names, phonemic awareness, rhyming, segmentation, perception of initial consonants				
1	High-frequency initial consonants	$s = /s/$	sea	$r = /r/$	rug
		$f = /f/$	fish	$l = /l/$	lamp
		$m = /m/$	men	$g = /g/$	game
		$t = /t/$	toy	$n = /n/$	nine
		$d = /d/$	dog	$h = /h/$	hit
	Long vowels: word-ending single-letter vowels and digraphs	$e = /e^-/$	he, me	$ee = /e^-/$	bee, see
		$o = /o^-/$	no, so		
	Lower-frequency initial consonants and x	$c = /k/$	can	$c = /s/$	city
		$b = /b/$	boy	$g = /j/$	gym
		$v = /v/$	vase	$y = /y/$	yo-yo
		$j = /j/$	jacket	$z = /z/$	zebra
		$p = /p/$	pot	$x = /ks/$	box
		$w = /w/$	wagon	$x = /gs/$	example
		$k = /k/$	kite		

Level	Categories	Correspondence	Model Word	Correspondence	Model Word
	High-frequency initial consonant digraphs	*ch* = /ch/	church	*th* = /th/	thumb
		sh = /sh/	ship	*wh* = /wh/	wheel
		th = /th/	this		
	Short vowels	*a* = /a/	hat	*u* = /u/	pup
		i = /i/	fish	*o* = /o/	pot
		e = /e/	net		
2	Initial consonant clusters	*st* = /st/	stop	*fr* = /fr/	free
		pl = /pl/	play	*fl* = /fl/	flood
		pr = /pr/	print	*str* = /str/	street
		gr = /gr/	green	*cr* = /kr/	cry
		tr = /tr/	tree	*sm* = /sm/	small
		cl = /kl/	clean	*sp* = /sp/	speak
		br = /br/	bring	*bl* = /bl/	blur
		dr = /dr/	drive		
	Final consonant clusters	*ld* = /ld/	cold	*mp* = /mp	lamp
		lf = /lf/	shelf	*nd* = /nd/	hand
		sk = /sk/	mask	*nt* = /nt/	ant
		st = /st/	best	*nk* = /dk/	think
	Less frequent digraphs and other consonant elements	*ck* = /k/	lock	*ng* = /ng/	hang
		dge = /j/	bridge		
	Long vowels: final *e* marker	*a-e* = /a&/	save	*e-e* = /e&/	these
/o&/	*i-e* = /&&/ hope	five	*u-e* = /u&/	use	*o-e* =
	Digraphs and trigraphs	*ee* = /e&/	green	*ow* = /o&/	show
/o&/	*ai/ay* = /a&/ boat	aim, play	*igh* = /&&/	light	*oa* =
/e&/	bean	*ea* = /e&/	bread		*ea* =
	Other vowels	*ou/ow* = /ow/	out, owl	*oo* = /oo&/	book
/aw/	*oi/oy* = /oi/ author, paw	oil, toy	*oo* = /oo&&/	tool	*au/aw* =
	r vowels	*ar* = /ar/	car	*are* = /air/	care
/&r/	*er* = /&r/ sir	her	*air* = /air/	hair	*ir* =
/&r/	*ear* = /i(&)r/ burn	fear			*ur* =
	for	*eer* = /i(&)r/	steer		*or* = /or/
3	Consonants mission	*ti* = /sh/	action		*ssi* =
/sh/		*t, ti* = /ch/	future question		
	Consonant digraphs	*ch* = /k/	choir	*kn* = /n/	knee
	ch = /sh/ ghost	chef	*wr* = /r/	wrap	*gh* =/g/
		ph = /f/	photo		
	Vowels	*y* = /e&/	city	*o* = /aw/	off
	y = /&&/ gym	why	*al* = /aw/	ball	*y* = /i/
	father	*ew* = /u&/	few		*a* = /o/
		e = /i/	remain		

Source: Thomas G. Gunning, *Creating Literacy Instruction for All Students,* 3rd ed. (Boston: Allyn & Bacon, 2000), pp. 182–183. Copyright © 2000 by Pearson Education. Reprinted by permission of the publisher.

Appendix **7.2**   Common Rime/ Spelling Patterns

	Vowel Sound	Major Spellings	Model Word
Short Vowels	/a/	rag, happen, have	cat
	/e/	get, letter, thread	bed
	/i/	wig, middle, event	fish
	/o/	fox, problem, father	mop
	/u/	bus	cup
Long Vowels	/ā/	name, favor, say, sail	rake
	/ē/	he, even, eat, seed, bean, key, these, either, funny, serious	wheel
	/ī/	hide, tiny, high, lie, sky	nine
	/ō/	vote, open, coat, bowl, old, though	nose
	/ū/	use, human	cube
Other Vowels	/aw/	daughter, law, walk, off, bought	saw
	/oi/	noise, toy	boy
	/o͝o/	wood, should, push	foot
	/o͞o/	soon, new, prove, group, two, fruit, truth	school
	/ow/	tower, south	cow
	/ə/	above, operation, similar, opinion, suppose	banana
r Vowels	/ar/	far, large, heart	car
	/air/	hair, care, where, stair, bear	chair
	/i(ə)r/	dear, steer, here	deer
	/ər/	her, sir, fur, earth	bird
	/i(ə)r/	fire, wire	tire
	/or/	horse, door, tour, more	four

Source: Thomas G. Gunning, *Creating Literacy Instruction for All Students*, 3rd ed. (Boston: Allyn & Bacon, 2000), p. 161. Copyright © 2000 by Pearson Education. Reprinted by permission of the publisher.

Chapter 8

Assessing and Teaching Reading: Fluency and Comprehension

As you read the chapter, watch for these questions to help you focus your learning:

1. **What is reading fluency, and how is progress in fluency monitored?**

2. **What are the instructional practices for increasing reading fluency?**

3. **What is the purpose of comprehension instruction?**

4. **What assessments and instructional components should be present in a reading comprehension program?**

Although Jeff can recognize most of the words in his second-grade reader, he continues to sound out many words. Consequently, his reading, whether oral or silent, is very slow. He expends so much effort on identifying words that he frequently misses the main points of the story. He concentrates his effort on unlocking a word rather than on reading the word automatically.

Shoshanna, a fourth grader, had great difficulty learning to read. After several years of failure, she finally learned to identify words by multisensory structured language instruction. However, Shoshanna's reading rate is slow, which interferes with her understanding. When asked to define reading, she places emphasis on reading words correctly rather than on understanding what she reads. Though Jeff and Shoshanna have developed systems for identifying words, they are having difficulties reading fluently—that is, quickly and easily with accuracy and expression.

Why is poor fluency performance a problem? Research indicates that students with significant reading disabilities have difficulty developing fluency and continue to be slow readers into adolescence and adulthood (Chard, Vaughn, and Tyler, 2002; Shaywitz and Shaywitz, 1996; Stanovitch, 1986; Torgesen et al., 1994). Their ability to listen to text and understand the information usually exceeds their ability to gain understanding when reading text (Mosberg and Johns, 1994). Fluency instruction is one means of improving their ability to recognize words automatically and to allocate more effort to constructing meaning from what they are reading.

Chapter 7 addressed the building blocks of reading: foundational skills such as phonemic awareness, phonics, and word recognition, that serve as a necessary base for acquiring more proficiency in reading. Subsequently, this chapter addresses issues related to improving the speed and accuracy (fluency) and comprehension of students with learning problems. Research indicates that one key to becoming a good reader is to engage in reading for learning and enjoyment. Yet students with reading difficulties often do not have as many opportunities to engage in reading during school and do not choose reading as a leisure-time activity.

Teachers can assist students in becoming fluent readers and provide them with a wide choice of literature and other materials to read and discuss so that reading becomes a source of learning, enjoyment, and satisfaction. To reach this goal, it is important to plan instruction that focuses not only on word recognition and decoding as discussed in Chapter 7 but also on strategies for building fluency and promoting active reading comprehension as presented in this chapter.

FOCUS
Question | 1.   What is reading fluency,
and how is progress in fluency monitored?

Assessing Fluency and Monitoring Student Progress

Fluency is the ability to read a text quickly, accurately, and with expression. We often refer to *fluent readers* as individuals who read with automaticity. By *automaticity* we mean the quick, effortless, and accurate reading of words. It is important to note that although there is emphasis on speed of reading, we do not mean that students should race through what they read without enjoyment or without monitoring their understanding. We are referring to a rate of reading that occurs with little focus or emphasis on decoding individual words.

Of all of the elements of reading (e.g., phonemic awareness, phonics, word study, comprehension),

Progress Monitoring

fluency is the one that is most readily assessed and monitored. That is because in relatively little time, teachers can determine whether students are making adequate progress in fluency and how their progress compares to other students in the same grade at that time of year. Fluency has three parts: rate of reading, accuracy of word reading, and

prosody or the expression used while reading. We typically assess rate and accuracy of reading to determine progress in fluency because prosody is not a particularly strong predictor of reading fluency or comprehension, whereas rate and accuracy of word reading are very good predictors of fluency and comprehension (Stahl and Kuhn, 2002).

Remember that the goal of improving children's rate of reading is not that they read faster, but that they read with such automaticity that they can free up their thinking to understand and enjoy text. With the increased emphasis on oral reading fluency as a progress monitoring measure, there is concern that some teachers may loose touch with the most important aspect of reading, "eyes on print"—opportunities to read to learn and enjoy.

Monitoring Student Progress in Fluency

Fluency is most frequently measured by the number of words correct per minute (WCPM) and through observations of phrasing, smoothness, and pace. An important reference for teachers to know is the number of words read correctly per minute in a specified grade-level passage. For example, Michael reads 50 words per minute in mid-first-grade-level passages. Because Michael is a third-grade-level student, his fluency indicates that he is considerably behind expectations. Table 8.1 provides an overview of fluency norms and rates by grade level.

TABLE 8.1

Reading Fluency Guidelines for Grades 2–5 (Medians)				
Grade	Student Percentile	Fall WCPM*	Winter WCPM	Spring WCPM
2	75	82	106	124
	50	53	78	94
	25	23	46	65
3	75	107	123	142
	50	79	93	114
	25	65	70	87
4	75	125	133	143
	50	99	112	118
	25	72	89	92
5	75	126	143	151
	50	105	118	128
	25	77	93	100

*Words correct per minute.

Source: Adapted from J. E. Hasbrouck and G. Tindal (1992). Curriculum-based oral reading fluency norms for students in grades 2 through 5. *Teaching Exceptional Children, 24* (3), pp. 41–44.

How do you measure WCPM? To use this measure to assess progress in fluency, a teacher selects two to three passages that are unfamiliar to a student and are at a student's instructional or independent word recognition levels (i.e., word recognition from 90 to 100 percent). After selecting the passages, the teacher makes two copies of each passage of text to be used with the targeted student: one for recording errors and one for the student to read. A stopwatch can be used for timing, and it is often helpful to tape record the student's reading on a monthly basis so that the student can hear as well as see his or her progress. The teacher tells the student, "When I say 'Begin,' start reading aloud at the top of the page. Do your best reading. If you come to a word that you don't know, I'll tell it to you." If a student does not read a word within three seconds, the teacher pronounces the word. The student reads for one minute. Following along as the student reads, the teacher marks his or her own copy by putting a slash (/) through words that were read incorrectly. This includes mispronunciations, substitutions, omissions, words pronounced after hesitations of more than three seconds, and reversals. Insertions, self-corrections, and repetitions should not be counted. The teacher should also note whether the student is having difficulty with phrasing; is ignoring punctuation; is reading slowly, word by word, or laboriously; and/or has frequent extended pauses, false starts, sound-outs, and repetitions. The teacher notes the last word the student read when the one minute is up. If the student is in the middle of a sentence when the time is up, the teacher should have the student finish the sentence but count only the words the student read up to the stop point. If using WCPM infrequently (once every 10 weeks), the teacher should use two passages to ensure accuracy.

The following formula is used to calculate fluency:

$$\frac{\text{Number of words read}}{\text{correctly in one minute}} - \text{Number of errors}$$

For example, if a student reads 83 words during a one-minute sample and makes 6 errors, then the WCPM would be 83 minus 6, which equals 77. The scores are averaged across at least two passages to get a mean rate. For example, if on the second reading of a different passage at the same grade level, the student read 84 words correctly but made 11 errors, the WCPM would be 73. The average of 73 and 77 is 75, so during this period, the student's WCPM is recorded as 75.

Guidelines for fluency rates for grades 2 through 5 were presented in Table 8.1. They are based on the performance of 9,000 students in grades 2 to 5 between 1981 and 1990 in five Midwestern and Western states (Hasbrouck and Tindal, 1992). Rates are given for students reading at the 25th, 50th, and 75th percentiles during the fall, winter, and spring of each year. For example, if Maria, a fourth grader, was reading fourth-grade-level materials at 90 WCPM during the winter, then she would be reading similarly to other students at the 25th percentile.

Teachers should consider several critical points when assessing reading fluency:

- Text passages that are used for assessment should be comparably leveled each time so that when a student's performance is compared over time, the test is at an appropriate level to compare performance. More difficult texts reduce the rate and accuracy of reading, making comparisons with previous fluency checks invalid.
- Words that are pronounced correctly within the context of a passage are considered read correctly (Shinn, 1989). If a student repeats a word or phrase, it is counted as correct. When students make an error but correct themselves within three seconds, it is also counted as correct.
- Words that are read incorrectly are counted as errors. Errors include mispronunciations, substitutions, and omissions.
- When students pause for more than three seconds, you should tell them the word and then mark it as an error.

Apply the Concept 8.1 offers commercial fluency measures that provide leveled passages.

Using Oral Reading Fluency Scores to Establish Fluency Goals

Fluency information can be plotted in graphs such as the one shown in Figure 8.1. Having students record their own progress serves as a motivation for reading, provides immediate feedback, and allows the students to set goals and see concrete evidence of their progress. Generally, for students with fluency problems, the goal is to add one or two more WCPM per week, with fluency increasing more quickly in the earlier grades (Fuchs, Fuchs, Hamlett, Walz, and Germann, 1993). Audiotape recordings of readings allow students not only to graph their progress but also to hear their progress over time. Generally, these reading samples are collected every one to two months and can be kept across the year.

Apply the Concept 8.1

Published Fluency Assessments

Teachers can use several sources of passages to compare students' fluency rates over time. Each year there are additional companies and individuals who publish fluency assessments. Following is a brief description of some of the more frequently used fluency measures.

Diversity

Dynamic Indicators of Basic Early Literacy Skills (DIBELS, Sixth Edition—Good and Kaminski, 2003). DIBELS has leveled reading passages for assessing fluency for kindergarten through sixth grade. The fluency assessment passages are also available for kindergarten through third grade in Spanish (*Indicadores dinámicos del éxito en la lectura*—Good, Bank, and Watson, 2004). DIBELS is administered to individual students and takes about two to three minutes per student.

Dynamic Measurement Group, Inc.
http://dibels.uoregon.edu
http://sopriswest.com

The Test of Oral Reading Fluency (TORF; Children's Educational Services, 1987). Like DIBELS, TORF is administered individually and takes about two to three minutes per student. Eighteen different passages at each level provide plenty of text for monitoring students' progress.

Children's Educational Services, Inc. and WebEdCo
www.edcheckup.com
Phone: 952-229-1440

AIMSweb. This group provides multiple passages at each grade level to provide extensive text for monitoring students' progress. They also provide professional development and training as needed.

Edformation
www.aimsweb.com
Phone: 1-888-944-1882

Test of Silent Word Reading Fluency (TOSWRF). This group-administered measure is designed to determine whether students can recognize printed words accurately and efficiently and can be administered to students in first grade and above.

PRO-ED
www.proedinc.com
Phone: 1-800-897-3202

Jeff's fluency instruction and progress as shown in Figure 8.1 was measured weekly by using beginning second-grade instructional-level reading materials. He was making consistent progress and increased substantially from the third to the fourth week (three words), when he began to rely less on sounding out words and to attempt to read the words automatically. This also resulted in better phrasing and reading with more expression.

Teachers and students can establish baseline fluency scores and then target acceptable rates of growth in fluency on a bimonthly basis. For example, a student in third grade who reads 50 words per minute in a second-grade passage is below grade level in both accuracy (the text is below grade level) and speed (the student is reading too slowly). The teacher and student may decide to establish one word per week as the improvement goal. These goals can motivate to students and provide excellent reporting data to parents. Using fluency data can assist teachers in making instructional decisions (University of Texas Center for Reading and Language Arts, 2002), as seen in Table 8.2.

Response to Intervention (RTI) and Fluency

Oral reading fluency is frequently used in lower grades to monitor students' progress in reading. For this reason, it is also used as means for determining how students with reading difficulties may be responding to interventions. For example, many schools screen students in first, second, and third grade using oral reading fluency to determine students who are "at risk" for reading problems. They then provide a standardized intervention to these students, four to five times per week for 20–40 minutes per day over an 8- to 12-week period. During this intervention, students typically receive an oral reading fluency test every week or two so that the "slope" of their progress can be determined. Thus, based on students' overall progress and the extent to which they are "closing the gap" between their oral reading fluency prior to intervention and during intervention, a decision is made about participation in subsequent interventions. To illustrate, Jeanine, a second grader, was making adequate progress in

FIGURE 8.1
Fluency Monitoring

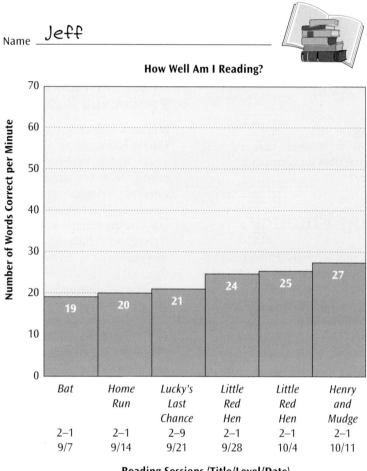

Name _Jeff_

How Well Am I Reading?

Reading Sessions (Title/Level/Date):

Title	Level	Date	Words Correct per Minute
Bat	2–1	9/7	19
Home Run	2–1	9/14	20
Lucky's Last Chance	2–9	9/21	21
Little Red Hen	2–1	9/28	24
Little Red Hen	2–1	10/4	25
Henry and Mudge	2–1	10/11	27

reading after she was placed in an intervention (more than two words correct per week gain on average) and appeared to be very close to meeting expected reading performance. Her teachers decided that it would be in her best interest to continue in the intervention for another 10 weeks. Max displayed a different pattern of learning. His overall progress was very low (less than one word correct per week on average) and teachers were concerned that he needed even more intensive intervention.

TABLE 8.2
Using Fluency Data

Student Data Show	Instructional Decisions
Student is making steady progress.	Continue in the same level of text.
Student meets goals on first reading.	Move to higher level of text or raise goal.
Student has difficulty achieving goals.	Alter fluency instruction; move to lower level text or lower fluency goal.

Source: University of Texas Center for Reading and Language Arts (2002). Reprinted by permission.

They adjusted his instruction both in the classroom and in the intervention and provided one-on-one support to determine his response to intervention over time.

Oral reading fluency provides an important data source for decision making related to response to intervention. Unfortunately, we know considerably less about the role of oral reading fluency and its application within RTI models with older readers.

> **FOCUS Question 2.** What are the instructional practices for increasing reading fluency?

Teaching Fluency

Fluency instruction is designed to increase automatic word recognition, or the smoothness of the reading; rate, or the pace of reading; and prosody, or expression, appropriate phrasing, and attention to punctuation (Richards, 2000; Zutell and Rasinski, 1991). According to the theory of automaticity (LaBerge and Samuels, 1974; Samuels, 1997), fluent readers automatically process information at the visual and phonological levels and are therefore able to focus most of their attention on the meaning of the text, integrating this information into their existing knowledge. The fluent reader's multitask functioning is made possible by the reduced demands on cognitive resources: The reader no longer has to focus on word recognition and other reading processes, thus freeing cognitive resources for comprehension (National Reading Panel, 2000; Stahl and Kuhn, 2002). Because poor readers take much longer and require more exposures to automatically recognize and rapidly recall words than do normally reading students (Ehri and Wilce, 1983), it is important that fluency instruction provide multiple opportunities for practice.

However, it is important to note that fluency may be much more important with beginning readers (students who are reading at the first- and second-grade levels) than it is when students become more mature readers. In the beginning stages of reading, being able to read words automatically and effortlessly is associated with comprehension. As students read better (more than 70 WCPM) fluency may be less important (Stahl, 2004).

Fluency instruction and guided practice reading are important parts of any reading program, particularly for students with learning and behavior problems. Good fluency instruction provides students with repeated practice of reading materials at the student's independent or instructional reading level. In the following section, we will examine several proven practices for assisting students in developing fluency in their reading as well as ideas for making difficult text more accessible.

Reading Aloud and Previewing Books

Students develop the concept of fluent reading through listening to and watching others read aloud, through previewing books, and through practice reading materials that are at their instructional to independent word–recognition levels (word recognition from 90 to 100 percent). There is a growing emphasis on the importance of reading aloud to children and previewing a book as ways not only to develop an enjoyment of literature and books but also to model and build fluent reading (Gunning, 2006; Whitehurst and Lonigan, 2001)

Guided oral reading is recommended practice for enhancing students' fluency (National Reading Panel, 2000). What is guided reading? Guided reading refers to many related approaches of providing support to improve students' fluency. These approaches include reading aloud, modeling fluent reading while students read along, providing opportunities for better readers to serve as models for other students, listening to text read aloud on a tape recorder and then reading aloud, and reading poems and other genres after they have been read aloud by the teacher. Guided oral reading promotes the development of reading fluency in a number of ways. First, it allows a teacher to model fluent reading. In reading aloud to a group of students who are just learning to read, the use of big books can be helpful because it allows the teacher to make more visible the literacy act and creates interest in the story. If a teacher, family member, or volunteer is reading aloud to one child, then sitting close to the child makes it easy for the child to interact with the print and the teacher. When reading aloud, the teacher or volunteer should read with expression, pointing to the words while reading or sweeping the fingers underneath them.

Second, modeling fluent reading by reading aloud provides background knowledge for students so that they can read a book by themselves, with a partner, or while listening to an audio recording. Reading aloud gives the teacher the opportunity to preview difficult words and unfamiliar concepts. Once students have listened to and previewed a

Apply the Concept 8.2

Guidelines for Implementing Previewing for Promoting Fluency

1. *Decide on an appropriate book or text* (i.e., one that is of interest to the students and at their independent to instructional reading levels). For longer books, preview only a section of the book at a time. Have student copies of the book or text.

2. *Introduce the book or text* using the title and looking through the text or section. With the students, make predictions about the content. Introduce words that may be difficult for the stu-

dents to automatically recognize or for which the meaning may be unfamiliar. Students may write these words in a personal dictionary or on word cards.

3. *Have students follow along as you read the book or text orally* at a relatively slow conversational rate (approximately 130 words per minute).

4. After you have read a section, *have students partner and take turns reading* the same section. Have the stronger partner read

first, and as one student reads, have the other student provide support by pronouncing words the student does not know.

5. *Have the students review the difficult words* using techniques for building sight words discussed in Chapter 7.

6. On a regular basis, *monitor students' reading fluency* by using the procedures discussed in the section on monitoring student progress.

---

book, they have a wealth of knowledge about the book to assist them in reading. In addition, once children have listened to a book, they are more likely to select it as a book they want to read. In a study of kindergartners, Martinez and Teale (1988) found that children chose familiar books (i.e., those read repeatedly by the teacher) to read during free time three times more frequently than they chose unfamiliar books (books the teacher had not read). Rose (1984) compared the effects of teacher-directed previewing and not previewing texts with six students with learning disabilities and found that previewing substantially increased oral reading rates. Other studies have investigated the effects of taped previewing (Rose and Beattie, 1986) and peer previewing (Salend and Nowak, 1988). These procedures also increased fluency of the text but not to the degree that teacher-directed previewing did. Apply the Concept 8.2 presents a procedure for teacher-directed previewing.

Third, modeling fluent reading aloud for students exposes them to books that may be too difficult for them to read. Many students with learning and behavior problems have listening comprehension that is several years more advanced than their reading comprehension. Reading a book aloud affords students the opportunity to talk about literature that is at a more advanced level.

Fourth, reading aloud can be orchestrated so that older, less adept readers can read books to young children and serve as cross-age tutors. This gives the older students the opportunity to read aloud and to model the role of a good reader, an

opportunity that is not often available in the regular or resource classroom.

Jim Trelease, author of *The Read-Aloud Handbook* (2001), suggests that reading aloud has the following benefits:

- It provides a positive reading role model.
- It furnishes new information.
- It demonstrates the pleasures of reading.
- It develops vocabulary.
- It provides examples of good sentences and good story grammar.
- It enables students to be exposed to a book to which they might not otherwise be exposed.
- It provides opportunity for discussions concerning the content of the book.

Repeated Reading

Have you noticed how young children thoroughly enjoy having the same story read to them over and over again? As the adult sits with the child and reads a familiar book, the child automatically begins to read along. At first, the child joins in on some of the words and phrases. Eventually, the child is reading along for most of the book. With repeated reading of a story, children become so familiar with the text that their memory becomes a great aid to them. Repeated reading as a means of enhancing fluency is based on the idea that as students repeatedly read text, they become fluent and confident in their reading (Samuels, 1979, 1997). And because they are exposed to the same story several times, they have the opportunity to practice identifying unknown words while relying on their memory of the language flow to assist them.

Repeated reading is an empirically based practice that has improved rate of reading in elementary students with reading difficulties. What about the use of repeated reading with secondary students? There are considerably fewer studies examining the effectiveness of repeated reading with older students with disabilities and the studies we have reveal low effects (see Wexler et al., in press). Another question that teachers may have about repeated reading is whether there are special considerations for students who are English language learners. According to a recent report on effective instruction for English language learners (Francis, Rivera, Rivera, Lesaux, and Kieffer, 2006), successful repeated reading includes:

 Diversity

- Oral reading providing opportunities for students to attend to words and opportunities to practice speaking and reading with expression
- Corrective feedback from adults drawing students' attention to miscues and pronunciation
- Discussions and questioning about the text read
- Increased exposure to print
- Increased engagement and motivation to read

CLASSROOM Applications

Repeated Reading

PROCEDURES: Repeated reading consists of rereading short, meaningful passages several times until a satisfactory level of fluency is reached. The procedure is then repeated with a new passage. Generally, the student repeatedly reads passages that range from 50 to 200 words in length, until he or she reaches a more fluent reading rate (see Table 8.1) and an adequate word recognition level (e.g., 90 to 100 percent word recognition). When a student reads under the direct supervision of a teacher, the words a student does not recognize are pronounced by the teacher. To foster comprehension, discussion of the passage follows reading.

A number of researchers have investigated the use of tape-recorded books for this procedure (Carbo, 1978, 1997; Chomsky, 1976; Conte and Humphreys, 1989; Dowhower, 1987; Hasbrouck, Ihnot, and Rogers, 1999; Rasinski, 1990a,

1990b). Using audio books, students listen to the stories and read and/or follow along with the written text. They listen to and read the same story until they can read the book by themselves. The teacher then listens to students individually read the story and discusses the story with the students. Guidelines for using recorded books, keeping records of students' reading, and using computers are presented in Apply the Concept 8.3.

COMMENTS: Students reading below grade level who have used repeated reading have consistently demonstrated gains in both fluency and reading comprehension (for reviews, see Dowhower, 1994; Mastropieri, Leinart, and Scruggs, 1999; Meyer and Felton, 1999; National Reading Panel, 2000; Strecker, Roser, and Martinez, 1998). From these reviews of research, several instructional guidelines for using repeated reading can be generated (Chard, Vaughn, and Tyler, 2002; Meyer and Felton, 1999):

- Consistently using repeated reading with poor readers increases reading speed, accuracy, expression, and comprehension.
- Text materials should be at the students' independent to instructional level (90 to 100 percent word recognition).
- Passages should be read three to five times.
- Multiple reading of phrases may improve fluency.
- Specific strategies should take into account individual student's characteristics. For more impaired readers, provide more adult guidance during reading, use more decodable texts as reading materials, practice on words and phrases from the text before reading the text, practice reading shorter passages, and model expressive reading.
- Short, frequent sessions of fluency practice (generally 10 to 15 minutes) should be used.
- Transfer of fluency is increased when the overlap of words across passages is substantial (Rashotte and Torgesen, 1985).
- Having a way for students to set goals and record their progress should be provided.

Using tape-recorded stories, Carbo (1987) found that rereading small segments of text can be helpful. When Shany and Biemiller (1995) compared teacher assistance during repeated reading with students listening to taped readings on a speed-controlled recorder, they found that reading rates and reading comprehension increased in both cases. Students who used taped readings, however, read twice the amount and had higher listening

Apply the Concept 8.3

Using Tapes and eBooks for Repeated Reading

Selecting Books and Passages

Diversity

Select books and passages that are of interest to the students and for which the students' word recognition is from 85 to 95 percent. For more impaired readers select more decodable texts (see Chapter 7). Pattern language books (see Chapter 7) can be another good source of books because they provide students with frequent repetition of language patterns and words. For older readers, high-interest, low-vocabulary stories provide another source.

Tape-Recording the Books

Use a good quality recording tape and recorder. Audiotape a book speaking at a conversational rate and with expression. Use appropriate phrasing. Provide the students with cues to assist them in keeping their place in the text while listening to the recording.

- Allow 10 seconds of blank tape before recording.
- Remind students of any strategies you want them to use (e.g., "Remember to use your finger or a marker as a guide.").
- Use a signal to cue turning the page.
- For a new page announce each page number.
- Direct students to put their finger on the first word on the page.

Family

Record about 10 minutes of reading on each side of tape so that it will be easy for students to find their place. Label each side of the tape with the title of the book and the page numbers covered. You can instruct parent volunteers to record books. Kirk (1986) suggests forming student committees to select, practice, and record the books. You can also purchase prerecorded taped books, but be aware that they may not provide the same level of cueing.

Store the books with their tapes in clear plastic bags. Inside the bag, place the book and tape. If you have multiple copies of the book with a tape, they can be stored together.

Keeping Student Records

Have each student make a reading folder. Staple forms inside the folder on which the student can record the name of the book, the author, the date, how he or she read the book, and with whom he or she discussed the book. In this way, both the teacher and the student have a record of the student's reading.

Computer-Based Reading Practice

Computer software provides another avenue for children to repeatedly read books using the computer. For example, *Living Book Series* (Discus Books) and *Wiggleworks* (Scholastic) both provide opportunities for students to listen to books being read, to read along with the computer, and, in the case of *Wiggleworks*, to record their own reading of the book. Reading software provides flexibility; the text can be read in sentences or phrases, or the students can highlight individual words and have them pronounced. Many of these programs easily switch languages (most commonly between English and Spanish) and have built-in record-keeping systems so that teachers know the number of times students read the books and the type of assistance they use.

Research suggests that computer reading programs help students with learning disabilities to build word recognition and reading comprehension (Leong, 1995; Lundberg, 1995; Torgesen and Barker, 1995).

Using Taped Books at Home to Support English Language Learners

Taped books can also be integrated into a home reading component. In the *Dog Gone Good Reading Project,* first-grade teachers provided additional opportunities for linguistically diverse students to repeatedly read books by audiotaping books and having students listen to them and read along at home (Koskinen, Blum, Bisson, Phillips, Creamer, and Baker, 1999). In preparing the tapes, the books were read twice, first at a slow but expressive read-along rate and second at a faster rate, more typical of fluent oral reading. Cues for turning pages and using a finger to point were inserted. Simple tape recorders were also provided. Students were taught how to use the taped books, and notes went home with the audiotaped books reminding the children and their parents to read the books two or three times every day. This technique promoted literacy for all students but was particularly helpful for students who were learning to read in English but had limited access to English role models and books in English.

Using Voicemail to Support Summer Reading

Elementary-aged students with learning and behavior problems usually do not choose reading as a recreational activity during the summer. Ann Willman, a reading specialist, used her school's voicemail to promote summer reading (Willman, 1999). She sent home books with the students along with directions on how to use the school voicemail. The students practiced reading a book until they were comfortable. Then she asked the students, with the assistance of their parents, to call her voicemail and read the book to her for three minutes or to summarize the book. She called backed to compliment the students. Ann also invited parents to leave a message about how the process was going. Parents noted that they liked the summer school connection that made their "sometimes reluctant reader more amenable to reading during vacation" (p. 788).

(continued)

Apply the Concept 8.3

Using Tapes and eBooks for Repeated Reading   (continued)

Name of Book	Author	Dates	Read with				Discussed with	
			Self	Tape	Student	Teacher	Student	Teacher

comprehension scores. Dowhower (1987) compared the effects of independent repeated reading versus reading along with tape-recorded books with below-average second-grade readers (reading rate less than 50 words per minute). Although students in both methods improved in reading fluency, students using the tapes improved more in their ability to read meaningful phrases. Dowhower also noted that students who read between 25 and 45 words per minute were less frustrated in the read-along condition, while students who read more than 45 words per minute appeared more able to practice reading independently.

Choral Repeated Reading

Choral repeated reading is a technique that combines ideas and procedures from repeated reading and choral reading. It was developed by one of the authors (Bos, 1982) because of her concern that fluency-building strategies for less-adept readers tend to ignore the teaching of either word identification skills or comprehension (e.g., neurological impress). We have used the approach with students who have significant reading difficulties in word identification and reading rate.

CLASSROOM Applications

Choral Repeated Reading

PROCEDURES: Choral repeated reading is designed for students who can comprehend material that is read to them but, because of difficulties in word identification and reading rate, are unable to read material commensurate with their listening comprehension level. Students should have a sight vocabulary of at least 25 words. We suggest the following procedure:

1. Explain the technique to the student.
2. With the student, select a book of interest that is at a challenging reading level (85 to 90 percent word recognition) and that has frequent repetition of words and decodable text.
3. Establish a purpose for reading by introducing the book and making predictions. Read the book with the student, using the following three-step process:
   a. *Teacher reads:* Start at the beginning of the book, and read a piece of text to the student, ranging from several sentences to a paragraph. (The length of each section should be short enough that the student can rely on his or her short-term memory as an aid for reading.) Read at a normal rate, and move your finger smoothly along underneath the words as the student watches, making sure that your reading matches your movement from word to word.
   b. *Teacher and student read:* Read the same section together aloud with the student. Continue to point to the words. The two of you may read the section once or several times, rereading until the student feels comfortable reading the section independently.
   c. *Student reads:* Have the student read the section independently. Pronounce any unknown words, and note words that the student consistently has difficulty recognizing.
4. After reading each section, discuss how it related to your predictions and what you have learned. New predictions and purposes for reading can be set.
5. Repeat the three-step process throughout the book. The length of each section usually increases as the book is read, and the number of times you and the student read together

usually decreases. For some students, the first step is discontinued.

6. Write on word cards the words that the student consistently has difficulty identifying automatically. Use a variety of activities to give the student more experience with these words. For example, discuss the word meanings or locate the words in the text and reread the sentences.

7. Have the student keep records of his or her progress (see Figure 8.1 on p. 297). Check the student's progress at least every third day when initially using the procedure.

In this method, reading sessions usually last 10 to 15 minutes, most of the time being focused on oral reading. As the student becomes more confident in reading ability, use repeated readings with tape-recorded books or stories as independent reading activities. Spelling words can be selected from words in the books, and words can be organized to teach phonic and structural analysis skills (see Chapter 7).

COMMENTS: We have used this procedure with a number of students who have severe word identification and/or fluency problems. Choral repeated reading allows the teacher and student to attend to word identification skills and comprehension as well as fluency. Using the three-step process also allows the student to read more difficult books. We have found this particularly rewarding for older nonreaders in that the technique quickly gives them success in reading books. Others have noted that choral reading is valuable not only for increasing fluency but also for helping students learn English as a second language (McCauley and McCauley, 1992; Van Wagenen, Williams, and McLaughlin, 1994).

Peer-Supported Reading

One concern for students with learning and behavior problems is that they read substantially less than high-achieving readers and spend less time engaged in academic behaviors (Allington, 1983a, 1983b; Greenwood et al., 1989). How can the amount of time devoted to text reading be increased? One strategy is to use peers to support each other when reading for the purpose of building fluency as well as supporting word recognition and comprehension. Techniques such as *assisted reading* (Hoskisson and Krohm, 1974), *classwide peer tutoring* or *partner reading* (e.g., Fuchs, Fuchs, and Burish, 2000; Fuchs et al., 1997; Simmons, Fuchs, Fuchs, Hodge, and Mathes, 1994), and *dyad reading* (Eldredge and

Quinn, 1988) provide opportunities for students to work in pairs and provide support for each other while reading. For the most part, these techniques have been used in general education classrooms to provide more opportunities for students to actively engage in reading. It is important to note that peer-supported reading is an opportunity for supportive practice and not an alternative to instruction provided by teachers. Research suggests that adult instruction to promote fluency is quite important (Kuhn and Stahl, 2003).

CLASSROOM Applications
Peer-Supported Reading

PROCEDURES: How to successfully pair students and how to select appropriate reading materials are important considerations in planning for peer-supported reading. It is advantageous to pair a stronger reader with a weaker reader. However, students' reading levels should not be so different as to make the reading irrelevant for the better reader. One way to pair students is to rank order the class on the basis of reading fluency and reading level. Then split the class in half, and pair the top-ranked high-performing student with the top-ranked low-performing student, the second-ranked high-performing student with the second-ranked low-performing student, and so on. It is important to check whether there are partners who will not work well together socially, and adjust accordingly. Maintain the pairings for three to four weeks. Reading materials should be at the lower-performing student's independent to instructional reading levels. If peer-supported reading is used three to four times per week, have enough materials selected so that students can work on two new passages per week. As in other fluency techniques, such as repeated reading and repeated choral reading, the reading materials will vary according to the students' needs. At first, it may be advantageous to use short passages or books as students learn the procedures, but high-interest–low-vocabulary chapter books can also be a good source of reading materials. (See Figure 8.2 for a selected list of publishers and Websites.)

Teach students how to be both tutors/listeners and tutees/readers, and provide role-play practice and feedback. Give the tutors guidelines for how to correct errors during oral reading (e.g., point out the word, pronounce the word, and have the tutee say the word) and the questions they should ask when the tutee has finished reading (e.g., "What is the story about? What is happening in the story now?

FIGURE 8.2

| **Selected List of Publishers of High Interest Texts with Controlled Reading Levels** ||

Publishers	Contact Information
Academic Communication Associates	www.acadcom.com 888-758-9558
Capstone Press	www.capstone-press.com 888-747-4992
Curriculum Associates	800-225-0248
Globe Fearon	800-872-8893
High Noon Books	www.academictherapy.com 800-422-7249
Incentives for Learning	www.incentivesforlearning.com 888-444-1773
Modern Curriculum Press	www.pearsonlearning.com 800-321-3106
National Reading Styles Institute	www.nrsi.com 800-331-3117
New Readers Press	www.newreaderspress.com 800-448-8878
Perfection Learning	www.perfectionlearning.com 800-831-4190
Phoenix Learning Resources	www.phoenixlr.com 800-526-6581
Remedia	www.rempub.com 800-826-4740
Rigby	www.rigby.com 800-822-8661
Saddleback Educational	www.sdlback.com 888-735-2225
Scholastic (Includes Book Clubs & Software Club)	www.scholastic.com 888-246-2986
Steck-Vaughn	www.steck-vaughn.com 800-531-5015
Sundance	www.sundancepub.com 800-343-8204
Wright Group	www.wrightgroup.com 800-523-2371
National Geographic	www.nationalgeographic.com 800-647-5463
National Wildlife Federation	www.nwf.com 800-822-9919
Smithsonian Institute	www.siedu.com 800-766-2149

What do you think will happen next?"). Also assist the students in giving positive feedback.

When the students work with their partners, first the stronger reader reads aloud to serve as a model, and then the other reader reads. The teacher should refer to them as *reader one* and *reader two*. Because the lower-performing students read what has just been read by the higher-performing students, the lower-performing students are more likely to read fluently and comfortably (Fuchs et al., 1997). How much material is read before the students switch roles depends on the material and the readers; it usually ranges from a sentence to a page, or each student reads a specified amount of time (e.g., five minutes). Partners can take turns reading a book or passage several times, thus adding a repeated reading component (Koskinen and Blum, 1984; Mathes and Fuchs, 1994; Simmons et al., 1994). Copies of guidelines for the tutor and reader can be posted, and each pair can rate themselves on their effort (see Figure 8.3).

COMMENTS: Research consistently indicates that peer-supported reading has positive outcomes for

FIGURE 8.3

Guidelines for Peer-Supported Reading

Partner Reading Procedures
- First reader reads.
- Second reader reads.
- Students discuss reading with one student asking questions and other student answering.
- Repeat until story is complete.

Tutoring Rules
- Talk only to your partner.
- Talk only about partner reading.
- Be cooperative.

Kinds of Errors
- Saying the word wrong.
- Leaving out a word.
- Adding a word.
- Waiting longer than 4 seconds.

Feedback about Words
- Stop. You missed this word (point to it). Can you figure it out?
- That word is _____. What word? (Reader says word). Good! Read the sentence again.

the reading fluency and comprehension of students with learning and behavior problems (see Mastropieri et al., 1999 for a review) even in first-grade classrooms (Mathes, Grek, Howard, Babyak, and Allen, 1999; Mathes et al., 2001). Such features as adding a repeated reading component (Simmons et al., 1994) or phonological awareness instruction (Mathes et al., 2001) did not differentially affect students' progress. The research results suggest that the strength of the intervention may be related to the additional instructional time and student reading involvement afforded by peer-supported reading.

Reading Performance

Although Ms. Sadlowski, the special education teacher, and Ms. Martinez, the fifth-grade teacher, were pleased with the progress students with learning and behavior problems were making in fluency through specific fluency-building activities, they wanted the students to have the opportunity to practice reading for purposes other than to build fluency. They decided to use readers' theater and buddy reading as techniques in which students practice reading a selection until they are fluent and then perform the reading, sometimes referred to as *reading performance* (Worthy and Broaddus, 2002).

CLASSROOM Applications
Reading Performance

PROCEDURES: In *readers' theater*, students perform a play or a book adapted to script form by reading it aloud to an audience. Because the focus is on reading fluently, students are not expected to memorize the text, and props are minimal. Students with different reading skills can use the same text, since the different parts often vary widely in reading level. Once parts have been chosen, students practice reading their parts with a teacher, tutor, and/or other students who are taking part in the performance. Finally, the group practices rehearsing the entire performance. Performances may be given to a variety of audiences, including other groups of students in the class, other classes, and parents. Even simple texts can be adapted to a script form, as Figure 8.4 illustrates.

Buddy reading consists of the students practicing and reading texts to younger students. This provides opportunities for students with learning and behavior problems to practice reading texts that are not at their grade level but are at their independent reading level without the stigma of reading "easy" books. In using buddy reading, it is important to choose books that the students can read easily and that are appropriate for and interesting to younger children.

COMMENTS: Although techniques such as readers' theater and buddy reading do not provide the level of explicit instruction and support that are used with techniques such as repeated choral reading and peer-supported reading, they do give students who have learning and behavior problems opportunities to transfer their reading fluency to tasks other than practicing fluency. Furthermore, they lend themselves to implementation in general education classrooms.

FIGURE 8.4
Example of Adapting a Simple Text to Script Format for Readers' Theater

Original Text

One day Mrs. Duck went to the pond. It was hot and she wanted a cool drink. Mr. Fox was sitting by the side of the pond. He told Mrs. Duck that she could not get a drink because he was in a bad mood and did not want anyone near his pond. Mrs. Bird heard Mr. Fox say this and she called down sweetly from her branch. . . .

Scripted Text

Mrs. Duck:	I have been working so hard and now I am so thirsty. I need to go to the pond for a nice, cool drink.
Mr. Fox:	Hello, Mrs. Duck. I am in a very bad mood. No one can drink from my pond today.
Mrs. Bird:	This is not your pond. It belongs to everyone.

Source: Adapted from Texas Center for Reading and Language Arts, *Professional Development Guide: Reading Fluency: Principles of Instruction and Progress Monitoring* (Austin: Texas Center for Reading and Language Arts, University of Texas–Austin, 2000).

Making Easy Books Acceptable and Difficult Books Accessible

One key to becoming a fluent reader is to read. Yet students with learning and behavior problems who have difficulty reading generally are not given as many opportunities to read books in school and do not select reading books as a leisure-time activity (Anderson, Wilson, and Fielding, 1988; Spear-Swerling and Sternberg, 1996). Stanovitch (1986) has referred to this as the *Matthew effect*, in which students who read well read more and improve their reading abilities, while those who read poorly read less, increasingly falling further behind in developing proficiency. (This term is a reference to the Bible passage Matthew 25, "To those who have much, more will be given.") Two reasons why these students may choose not to read are because they perceive easy books as unacceptable and embarrassing and because when they try to read books that they perceive as interesting, the books are too difficult. Fielding and Roller (1992) discuss instructional practices that teachers can use to make easy books more acceptable or legitimate, including the following:

- *Model your own use and enjoyment of easy books.* In adult life, most pleasure reading is easy reading.
- *Alter the purposes for easy reading.* Have students read easy books for the purpose of reading to younger students or children in preschool.
- *Have students make tape recordings of their reading.* Students will often choose easier books and reread them several times so that they sound good on the tape recording.
- *Broaden the definition of acceptable reading.* Poems, songs, raps, jump-rope chants, and cheers often are easier to read because of the predictable language and repetition. Some examples are Joanna Cole's (1989) collection of popular jump-rope chants in *Anna Banana* and Joanna Cole and Stephanie Calmenson's (1990) collection of children's street rhymes in *Miss Mary Mack.*
- *Make simple nonfiction books available.* Simple books that contain new information about a topic of student interest are often not perceived by the student as easy or boring.

Fielding and Roller (1992) and Worthy (1996) discuss several strategies for making difficult books more accessible to older readers with disabilities. These strategies include the following:

- Using tape-recorded books and books on CD-ROM, DVD, or eBooks for the computer (see Apply the Concept 8.2)

- Reading aloud to the students
- Using partner reading, in which less able and more able readers are paired
- Preceding difficult books with easier books about the same topic or genre (e.g., books about comets, the solar system, or ghosts; fairy tales; mystery books), thereby familiarizing the child with the vocabulary and text structure in books that are easier to read
- Using series books to increase students' comfort level. Reading books in a series provides benefits that are similar to those of repeated reading of the same text because of the consistent use of characters, language, and content. Examples are Bridwell's *Clifford the Big Red Dog,* Rylant's *Henry and Mudge,* Park's *Junie B. Jones,* Scieska's *Time Warp Trio,* and Applegate's science fiction, *Animorphs.*

Integrating Fluency Building into a Reading Program

Fluency building is an integral part of a reading program for students who have reading difficulties, and generally represents 15–25 minutes of time approximately three times per week. Figure 8.5 describes several programs that have been developed specifically to build fluency. In teaching fluency, strategies for improving word identification skills and comprehension should also be instructional goals. As we mentioned in the discussions of previewing and repeated choral reading, word recognition and word extension activities can be developed naturally from the text. For example, the same activities that we recommended for the word cards generated from language experience stories (see Chapter 7) can be used with word cards generated from these fluency techniques. Although improving fluency can allow students to allocate more attention to comprehension, not all students will automatically acquire the skills associated with effective comprehension. For some students, methods of teaching comprehension may be required.

Helping Families Improve Their Children's Reading Fluency

Perhaps one of the most necessary tools for improving reading outcomes for children with special needs is wide reading. *Wide reading* refers to both the amount and type of reading in which children are engaged. When students read widely, they read often—at least 20 minutes a day—and they read across many genres. This means that

FIGURE 8.5

Selected List of Fluency-Building Programs

Peer-Assisted Learning Strategies—Reading (PALS)
(Classwide Peer Tutoring)

PALS Reading was developed for students in kindergarten through high school. It is designed primarily for general education classrooms and as supplements to a teacher's more comprehensive reading program. PALS programs target key reading skills including fluency and, because students work with students on these skills, PALS provides students with intensive practice. Evaluative studies indicate that on average PALS accelerates the reading achievement of students with LD, low-achieving students, and average- and high-achieving students. PALS Math uses a similar format but focuses on math.

Contact: PALS Outreach
Vanderbilt University
Peabody Box 328
230 Appleton Place
Nashville, TN 37203-5701
615-343-4782
email: PALS@vanderbilt.edu

Read Naturally

Students read along while listening to a tape of leveled, recorded high-interest passages and practice until they can read them at a predetermined rate. Students graph WCPM before and after practicing. Comprehension questions provided.

Contact: Read Naturally
750 S. Plaza Dr. #100
Saint Paul, MN 55120
800-788-4085
Website: www.readnaturally.com
email: info@readnaturally.com

Great Leaps

Great Leaps addresses fluency at three levels: Phonics—students identify sounds and decode simple word patterns; Sight Phrases—students read phrases with sight words; Reading Fluency—students read stories. Students graph progress.

Contact: Diarmuid, Inc.
Box 357580
Gainesville, FL 32635
877-GRL-EAPS
Website: www.greatleaps.com
email: info@greatleaps.com

Carbo Reading Styles Program

The Carbo reading method has children listen to and repeatedly read along with audiotapes of books that have been recorded at a slow pace but with proper phrasing and intonation until they can read fluently. Books can be recorded by the teacher or can be purchased from the National Reading Styles Institute.

Contact: National Reading Styles Institute, Inc.
Box 737
Syosset, NY 11791
800-331-3117
Website: www.nrsi.com
email: readingstyle@nrsi.com

First Grade PALS (Peer-Assisted Literacy Strategies)

This program contains 48 lessons, enough for teachers to use three times a week for 16 weeks as a supplement to their reading program. The emphasis is on peer-interacted learning that addresses phonemic awareness and fluency tasks. The goal is to improve accuracy through repeated practice.

Contact: Sopris West
4093 Specialty Place
Longwood, CO 80504-5400
800-547-6747
Website: www.sopriswest.com
email: customerservice@sopriswest.com

The Six-Minute Solution: A Reading Fluency Program

This program has high-interest nonfiction practice passages (approximately 20 for each of the eight levels). The materials include assessment records, charts, word lists, and differentiated instruction through multiple reading levels.

Contact: Sopris West
4093 Specialty Place
Longwood, CO 80504-5400
800-547-6747
Website: www.sopriswest.com
email: customerservice@sopriswest.com

QuickReads

This series of program books and materials features short, high-interest nonfiction texts at second- through fourth-grade levels. The materials are designed to improve students' fluency, comprehension, and background knowledge. Each grade level sequentially builds across three books and includes increasingly more difficult high-frequency words and phonics elements. The program includes a pre- and posttest for placement, 12 copies each of the three leveled student books per grade level, a teacher's resource manual, and three read-along audio CDs per grade level. Additional comprehension strategies and extension lessons can be used to support ESL/ELL students (Hiebert, 2002).

Contact: Modern Curriculum Press
299 Jefferson Road
Parsippany, NJ 07054
800-321-3106
Website: www.pearsonlearning.com
email: technical.support@pearson.com

they read different types of books, not just narrative or information books but biographies, history, and technical books. How can teachers increase the wide reading of the students they teach? The best way may be to engage family members in supporting wide reading.

The following are some ideas that teachers can share with families to promote wide reading with their children:

- Establish a time each evening when you read with your child. For beginning readers, this may mean that you take turns reading from a book on his or her level. If your child is a more advanced reader, you may each read different books, but you sit near each other and are engaged in the reading process.
- Determine many ways to access books and print materials. Libraries, bookstores, and online activities are excellent resources to access a wide range of books and print materials. Take advantage of every opportunity to examine and discuss books and other print materials.
- Share what you are reading. Discuss the books and materials that you are reading with your child. If your child is an able reader, share materials or sections of your reading so that the child can access the same information and knowledge that you have.
- Ask questions about what your child is reading. The types of questions you ask about what your child is reading can promote continued reading. Children are likely to engage in and extend reading when family members show interest in what children are reading.
- Read different types of print materials and share them with your child. Sources that adults read include recipes, newspapers, magazines, reference books, and leisure books. Share these types of reading materials with your child, and engage your child in reading different sources of text. Remember wide reading is associated with overall improved vocabulary and knowledge.

Spotlight on Diversity

Instructing English Language Learners Who Are at Risk for Reading Problems

What instructional practices should teachers consider when providing reading instruction to students with reading difficulties who are also English language learners (ELLs)? Teachers might consider the following seven best practices for instruction:

1. *Consider the commonalities between reading instruction in English and the reading instruction that is provided in the student's native language.* These commonalities can be used to build bridges between languages and apply what is known in one language to the other. Many commonalities exist between reading instruction practices in different languages, even though features of the instructional practices may differ (Gersten and Geva, 2003; Linan-Thompson and Vaughn, 2007). For example, oral language instruction, fluency, and reading comprehension are important aspects of learning to read for learners of all languages (Scarborough, 2001).

2. *Identify procedures for instructing students in all of the critical elements of beginning reading (phonemic awareness, spelling, phonics, vocabulary, language development, fluency, and comprehension).* The following are six instructional practices in reading that are effective for beginning ELLs (Gersten and Geva, 2003; Linan-Thompson and Vaughn, 2007):

   a. Explicit teaching
   b. Promotion of English language learning
   c. Phonemic awareness and decoding
   d. Vocabulary development
   e. Interactive teaching that maximizes student engagement
   f. Instruction that produces opportunities for accurate responses, which scaffolds feedback for struggling learners

The foundation skills of phonemic awareness and phonics are more critical in the very beginning stages of reading and less important as students become readers of connected text. Improving vocabulary and word knowledge is an important part of reading and all content learning all along. Improving listening comprehension is initially important, and then transferring these comprehension skills to text understanding becomes important.

3. *Recognize that English is the most difficult language of all alphabetic languages to learn to read, and therefore, many of the foundation skills such as spelling and phonics require more explicit and systematic instruction than they might in other alphabetic languages.* A study across 12 alphabetic languages revealed that many of the foundation skills of reading take

English than in other alphabetic languages such as Spanish (Seymour, Aro, and Erskine, 2003). Thus, students who know another alphabetic language such as Spanish or Italian will require more time to learn foundation skills such as phonics and spelling to develop fluency and comprehension.

4. *Make connections between the home language and the language of instruction in school.* There are many benefits when teachers make connections between the home language and English. First, it provides students with a ready connection between what they know and what they need to know. Second, it helps students learn more quickly because much of what they know can be used as a foundation for learning a new literacy. Third, it honors the students' home language and background, building language concepts and self-esteem.

5. *Capitalize on every opportunity to use and promote language development during instruction, and give opportunities for students to engage in higher-order questions.* ELLs often have limited opportunities to use oral language during instruction and few opportunities to address challenging or higher-order questions. Because students' language development may still be growing, teachers often ask these students questions that allow for one- or two-word responses. These students may have difficulty providing more complex answers, but with structured conversation and opportunities to use academic language, their skills will improve. For example, oral participation can be facilitated by providing scaffolding in the form of sentence stems that offer students a structure for orally responding to challenging questions. To assist students in addressing higher-order questions, teachers may initially model more complex syntactic structures and fade support as students become more proficient in English. Planned discussions can be promoted to encourage academic language, providing small group or paired cooperative learning activities and development of prior knowledge (O'Malley and Chamot, 1999).

6. *Promote all opportunities to teach and engage in vocabulary and concept building.* Vocabulary development is an essential feature of reading, comprehension, and content learning for ELLs. To fully appreciate and interpret what they are reading, students will be required to learn new words to understand expository and narrative texts (e.g., *civil, equity, molecule*) as

well as to learn the meaning of descriptive words (e.g., *worried, marvelous, eagerly*). Teachers will add to students' vocabulary knowledge by providing highly organized, focused, and repeated opportunities to learn core words well enough to both understand their meaning in context and to apply them in their own language use. Ulanoff and Pucci (1999) suggest that students benefit from previewing important concepts and vocabulary in their primary language before listening to stories read in English and reviewing key concepts in both languages after the reading.

7. *Peer pairing and cooperative groups can be used to enhance learning.* Peer pairing and structured group activities are effective practices for improving oral language, acquisition of higher-level comprehension skills, and interaction for ELLs (Klingner and Vaughn, 1996, 2000; Saenz, Fuchs, and Fuchs, 2005). Peer pairing or cooperative grouping provides intensive individualized instruction for students from varied literacy backgrounds by increasing the amount of time spent in academic engagement and providing immediate feedback (e.g., reading errors, pacing, etc.) from peers (Fuchs et al., 1997). Cooperative grouping may be particularly beneficial for ELLs by presenting opportunities for them to take greater risks in using language for both academic and social purposes (Larsen-Freeman, 2001).

FOCUS Question | 3. What is the purpose of comprehension instruction?

Assessing Comprehension and Monitoring Progress in Reading Comprehension

Reading comprehension is the most difficult aspect of reading to assess. Perhaps this is because understanding and interacting with text occurs largely as thinking and cannot be observed by the teacher. The only access teachers have to knowing whether and how students understand text is

Progress Monitoring

to ask them to describe what they have read or to ask them questions about it. Both of these ways to assess students' comprehension have difficulties. Figure 8.6 lists 12 tests that can assist teachers in making decisions about their students' reading comprehension. These tests can be combined to assess students' comprehension more accurately and completely.

Teachers must consider several critical aspects of a comprehension test before selecting one. First, what is the purpose of the test? Does the teacher want to screen, monitor, diagnose, or evaluate students? Second, what type of information about the students' comprehension is the teacher seeking? Does the teacher want to know whether they can recall what is in the text? Is the teacher interested in whether the students can tell the main idea or make inferences? Third, does the test require a short or long amount of time, is it difficult or easy to score, and will it provide the type of information that will inform instruction?

When children are at the beginning stages of reading (first- or second-grade-level readers) and read fewer than 80 words correct per minute, it is possible for teachers to monitor their reading comprehension by monitoring the students' fluency. For early readers, fluency is an excellent predictor of reading comprehension—though not a perfect one—for classroom teachers because it provides a reasonable and feasible means for determining whether students understand what they read and whether they are likely to pass high-stakes reading comprehension tests. However, as students develop more mature reading skills, other practices for monitoring their reading comprehension are needed.

One way to monitor students' comprehension is to ask them to retell the most important parts of a text that they have just read. Story retelling provides an alternative to traditional questioning techniques for evaluating students' reading comprehension because it involves the integration of many skills that are necessary for reading comprehension. It requires students to sequence and reconstruct key information presented in text. It also requires students to rely on their memory for factual details and to relate them in an organized meaningful pattern. One advantage to story retelling is that the teacher can learn a great deal about what students understand and can determine what additional comprehension skills need to be taught.

For the purposes of monitoring the progress of comprehension, story retelling is administered individually. The following procedures can be applied:

1. Select brief passages (one to two minutes) that are at the students' reading level.

2. Ask younger students to read their passage aloud. Ask older students to read their passage silently.
3. Tell the students, "Start at the beginning, and you tell me the story" (Lipson, Mosenthal, and Mekkelson, 1999).
4. Score the story retelling on the basis of the depth of information provided. Teachers may want to consider whether students mentioned characters, the story problem, events, problem resolutions, and story quality.

Another way to monitor students' comprehension is by using maze passages. Maze passages provide text written at a range of grade levels and provide students with opportunities to select words from several options that fulfill the meaning of the text where words have been deleted. Sources of maze passages for progress monitoring can be obtained from the National Center on Student Progress Monitoring (www.studentprogress.org).

What about monitoring and assessing the understanding of students who are English language learners for whom we may have fewer measures for determining their **Diversity** reading comprehension? There are also informal ways to determine how much students understand about what they read.

- Listen to students talk about what they are reading. Ask questions to determine how well they are connecting with text and learning.
- Ask students to develop questions about what they read.
- Ask students implicit and explicit questions about their understanding of text. Listen carefully and probe to learn more.
- Confer with students before and after reading to determine how much they know about the text and what they have learned.
- Examine written work samples that reflect what students are reading.

Response to Intervention and Reading Comprehension

Earlier in this chapter, we identified oral reading fluency as an important progress monitoring measure for determining response to intervention (RTI) with younger readers (first, second, and third graders). How can teachers use reading comprehension practices to determine RTI? Particularly for older students, isn't it important to determine how well they understand text as we monitor their response to intervention? Knowing students' comprehension of

FIGURE 8.6

Title	Ages/Grade Levels	Estimated Testing Time	Key Elements and Strategies	Administration
Clay Observational Survey (Clay, 2002)	Grades K–3	15 minutes	• Oral reading • Reading vocabulary (i.e., words known in reading)	Individual
Comprehensive Reading Assessment Battery (Fuchs, Fuchs, and Hamlett, 1989)	Grades K–6	30–40 minutes	• Fluency • Oral comprehension • Sentence completion	Individual
Gates-MacGinitie Reading Tests (MacGinitie et al., 2000)	Grades K–12 and adult	55–75 minutes	• Word meanings (levels 1 and 2) • Comprehension (short passages of 1–3 sentences for levels 1 and 2; paragraphs for levels 3 and up)	Group
Gray Diagnostic Reading Tests (Bryant, Wiederholt, and Bryant, 2004)	Ages 6–13	45–60 minutes	• Letter/word identification • Phonetic analysis • Reading vocabulary • Meaningful reading	Individual
Gray Oral Reading Test 4 (Wiederholt and Bryant, 2001)	Ages 6–19	15–45 minutes	• Comprehension (14 separate stories, each followed by 5 multiple-choice questions)	Individual
Gray Silent Reading Test (Wiederholt and Blalock, 2000)	Ages 7–26	15–30 minutes	• Comprehension (13 passages with 5 questions each)	Individual, small groups, or entire class
Qualitative Reading Inventory (Leslie and Caldwell, 2001)	Emergent to high school	30–40 minutes	• Comprehension • Oral reading • Silent reading • Listening	
Test of Early Reading Ability 3 (Reid et al., 2001)	Preschool–second grade	20 minutes	• Comprehension of words, sentences, and paragraphs • Vocabulary • Understanding of sentence construction • Paraphrasing	Individual
Test of Reading Comprehension (Brown et al., 1995)	Ages 7–18	30–90 minutes	• General vocabulary • Understanding syntactic similarities • Paragraph reading (6 paragraphs with 5 questions each) • Sentence sequencing (5 randomly ordered sentences that need reordering) • Diagnostic supplement: content area vocabulary in math, social studies, and science • Reading directions	Individual, small groups, or entire class
Standardized Reading Inventory 2 (Newcomer, 1999)	Ages 6–14-and-a-half	30–90 minutes	• Vocabulary in context • Passage comprehension	Individual
Woodcock Reading Mastery (Woodcock, 1998)	Ages 5–75	10–30 minutes	• Word comprehension (i.e., antonyms, synonyms, analogies)	Individual
Woodcock-Johnson III Diagnostic Reading Battery (Woodcock, Mather, and Schrank, 2006)	Ages 2–90	5–10 minutes	• Phonemic awareness • Phonics • Fluency • Vocabulary • Reading comprehension	Individual

Source: S. Vaughn and S. Linan-Thompson, *Research-Based Methods of Reading Instruction, Grades K–3* (Alexandria, VA: Association for Supervision and Curriculum Development, 2004), pp. 102–103. Reprinted by permission.

text is the single most important outcome of interest when determining their response to intervention. There are several progress monitoring measures that attempt to tap comprehension. For example, the "maze" test provides a means for determining whether students can identify the syntactically and semantically correct word that fits in a passage providing some information about text understanding. However, the most accurate way of learning more about what students' learn from text is to be able to score their oral retelling of the passage. Oral "retells" are often difficult and time-consuming to score and may not lend themselves to progress monitoring. It is likely that in the next few years more reliable and valid means of determining students' understanding of text will be available.

| FOCUS Question | 4. What assessments and instructional components should be present in a reading comprehension program? |

Teaching Comprehension

Comprehension is the essence of reading and the ultimate goal of reading instruction. Reading comprehension is the process of constructing meaning by integrating the information provided by an author with a reader's background knowledge. It consists of three elements: the reader, the text, and the purpose for reading (RAND Reading Study Group, 2002). It involves complex cognitive skills and strategies with which the reader interacts with the text to construct meaning. There are many reasons why students may have difficulty comprehending what they read.

As a fourth grader reading at second-grade level, Amanda would probably better comprehend what she reads if she did not have to allocate so much attention to word identification. On the other hand, Scott is a word caller. He thinks that reading is "reading the words correctly." Even though he is able to read fluently, he does not attend to the meaning of passages. He frequently has difficulty recalling both the gist and details of a story. Sofia has been diagnosed as having language disabilities, with difficulties in syntax and semantics. These low oral-language skills affect her comprehension of what she reads.

Sam can remember what he reads but does not relate it to what he already knows about the topic (schema). Therefore, he has particular difficulty answering questions that require him to use his background knowledge. Paolo, on the other hand, relies too heavily on his background knowledge. This is adversely affecting his reading comprehension.

Kim fails to monitor her comprehension as she reads. She often reports that everything makes sense. Yet when her teacher asks questions, it becomes obvious that Kim has achieved limited comprehension.

All these students are struggling with reading comprehension, although their problems are very different. For students such as Amanda, word identification difficulties get in the way of comprehension. Focusing on building word identification skills is probably appropriate for her. However, comprehension skills should not be ignored. This may mean building listening comprehension at her current grade level as well as extending her knowledge of word meanings. For Amanda, it is making sure that reading is perceived as understanding and interacting with the text to construct meaning, not just reading the words correctly. Although word identification skill development will be important, it needs to be coupled with teaching comprehension.

For Scott, a considerable amount of emphasis in his reading program should be on comprehension. He requires assistance in changing his definition of the reading process. Helping Scott to set comprehension-oriented purposes for reading and teaching him how to ask questions as he reads should assist him in changing his definition of reading.

Sofia's difficulties relate to a language problem that affects her reading comprehension as well as her receptive language. For students such as Sofia, instruction in reading comprehension often parallels instruction in receptive language. Both reading and listening comprehension can be improved simultaneously. For example, when Sofia either listens to or reads a story, she needs to learn to ask and answer such questions as Who is the story about? Where did it happen? What was the problem in the story? What happened to solve the problem? How did the story end?

Some students fail to relate what they are reading to what they already know about a topic. This is the case with Sam. Other students have limited background knowledge to bring to the reading process. Research in schema theory has shown that the knowledge one brings to the reading task affects comprehension, particularly inferential comprehension (Anderson, Reynolds, Schallert, and Goetz, 1977; Carr and Thompson, 1996; Hansen and Pearson, 1983; McKeown, Beck, Sinatra, and Loxterman, 1992; Williams, 1998). Teaching strategies that encourage students to activate their knowledge or activities that provide opportunities for students to enrich their backgrounds before reading can facilitate comprehension.

Although some students do not rely enough on background knowledge, other students rely too much on background knowledge, as is the case with Paolo. Often, these are the same students who tend to overrely on context clues when identifying unknown words. When these students begin reading informational and technical texts that require accurate recall of information, comprehension problems become more evident. Comprehension strategies that encourage self-questioning can encourage such students to pay closer attention to the information presented in the text.

Kim, like many other students with learning disabilities, has difficulty with the metacognitive skill of comprehension monitoring (Bos and Filip, 1984; Ellis, 1996; Palincsar and Brown, 1987; Pressley, 1998; Wong, 1987, 1996). Strategies that teach students to ask questions about their comprehension and that require them to paraphrase and summarize what they read should help them to develop metacognitive skills (Graves, 1986; Mastropieri, Scruggs, Bakken, and Whedon, 1996; Wong and Jones, 1982).

Increasing emphasis is being placed on reading comprehension and teaching comprehension strategies for improving reading comprehension (e.g., Gattney and Anderson, 2000; National Reading Panel, 2000; Pearson and Camperell, 1994; Pressley, 2000; RAND Reading Study Group, 2002). First, we will look at a framework for reading comprehension to better understand the scope of comprehension. Then we will focus on instructional strategies for improving reading comprehension. Finally, we will discuss approaches used for teaching reading and reading comprehension.

A Framework for Reading Comprehension

One way of guiding reading comprehension instruction is to determine the different reasoning and information-processing skills that are required by readers to construct meaning from what they read. Read the passage in Apply the Concept 8.4. Now answer each of the following questions, and think about the processes that were needed for you to arrive at an answer.

1. What did Pat do first to get help?
2. Where did you find the information to answer the question?

The answer, of course, is in the text. If information is found in the text, then we say that the information is *textually explicit* or *literal* (i.e., taken directly from the text) or that we are *reading the lines* (Dale, 1966).

3. What time of day was it in the story?
4. Where did you find that information?

You may have automatically answered question 3 as "early in the morning" or "in the morning" without looking back at the text. If you did this, go back and read to find out whether that

Apply the Concept 8.4

Thinking about Reading Comprehension

The Drive to Big Lake

Pat and her father were driving to Big Lake in the Blue Mountains. They were going to Big Lake to go fishing. As they drove Pat watched her father talk on the C.B. radio and watched the sun come up over the mountains.

When Pat and her father were near Big Lake it became very foggy. Pat's father drove slowly but did not see a sharp bend in the road. The car ran off the road and into a ditch. Pat

was OK, but she knew that she needed to get help for her father.

She climbed out of the car and went to the road. She thought maybe a car would come by, but none did.

She walked down the road. She was looking for a house. As she walked, she yelled for help.

Then she remembered the C.B. radio that was in the car. She ran back to the car. She had never used the C.B., but she tried to call for help on it. A fisherman at Big Lake was

listening to his C.B. Pat told him where she and her father were. Fifteen minutes later help came.

By this time Pat's father had opened his eyes and was OK. The police helped Pat and her father get the car out of the ditch and back on the road. Everyone was proud of Pat.

Source: C. S. Bos, Inferential Operations in the Reading Comprehension of Educable Mentally Retarded and Average Students. Doctoral dissertation. (Tucson: University of Arizona, 1979), p. 164.

information is in the text. It is not. Instead, you will find in the first paragraph that Pat "watched the sun come up over the mountains." You may have automatically integrated that information with your background knowledge to conclude that it was in the morning. When information is not in the text but requires you to integrate your background knowledge with text information to generate the answer, then we say the information is *implicit* or *inferential* (e.g., not stated directly in the text). Can we be more specific about this kind of implicit information? Pearson and Johnson (1978) refer to this kind of relationship between the question and the answer as *scriptually implicit*. It requires the reader to use a schema or *script* about "morning" to generate the answer. Dale (1966) has referred to this as *reading beyond the lines*.

5. Was Pat successful in using the C.B. radio?
6. Where did you find that information?

It was in the text, but not nearly as clearly as was the case for the first question. In this case, you had to read several sentences and piece the information together. The information was *implicit* in that it was not directly stated in the text, but it did not require you to use your background knowledge in the same way that question 4 did. Pearson and Johnson (1978) refer to this kind of implicit information as *textually implicit*. The relationship between the question and the answer required you to get the information from the text, but the relationship is not directly, or *explicitly*, stated. You had to use your knowledge about language and how ideas related to answer the question. Dale (1966) has referred to this relationship as *reading between the lines*.

Therefore, when teaching reading comprehension, we can divide comprehension into types of reasoning according to how readers have to activate their background knowledge to construct the meaning. These three arbitrary categories are as follows:

1. *Textually explicit:* Information is derived directly from the text with minimal input from the readers' background knowledge.
2. *Textually implicit:* Information is derived from the text, but readers are required to use their background knowledge to put together the ideas presented in the text.
3. *Scriptually implicit:* Information is not stated in the text. Readers have to activate and use their background knowledge to obtain the information.

We can also categorize comprehension by the type of information or relationship it represents. For example, the first question, "What did Pat do first to get help?" requires the reader to focus on the sequence of the events in the story. Therefore, it requires a sequencing or temporal relationship. The question "Why was everyone proud of Pat?" requires understanding of a causal relationship. Barrett (1976) has identified a number of types of information or relationships that can be represented in text (e.g., main ideas, details, sequence, cause and effect) as part of his taxonomy of reading. We can combine types of information with processes required (i.e., textually explicit, textually implicit, and scriptually implicit) to form a matrix for reading comprehension (Figure 8.7).

This matrix can be used in planning comprehension instruction, such as planning activities that will encourage students to engage in all the different facets of comprehension (cells in the matrix). For example, to work on sequencing of ideas, students could retell a story by having each student in the group tell one episode from the story, copy a story onto sentence strips and discuss how to arrange the sentences in a logical order, read an explanation of how to do something and write a list of the steps in order, ask each other sequence questions about a description of how to make something, and write a description of how to make something and then have the other students in the group read the description and make the object. Whereas all of these activities focus on sequencing, both explicit and implicit comprehension are required to complete the various activities.

A matrix rather than a taxonomy is used to depict the various aspects of comprehension because comprehension should not be thought of as a set of hierarchical skills. The comprehension process entails ongoing transactions between a text, the reader, and the author and the active use of comprehension strategies such as predicting, activating background knowledge, asking questions, clarifying, and checking for understanding (Klingner, Vaughn, and Boardman, 2007; National Reading Panel, 2000).

But comprehension goes further than this. We also read to reflect on and judge the quality of the information. Thus, we engage in *critical reading* including such skills as the following:

- Recognizing the author's purpose
- Distinguishing between facts and opinions
- Identifying words that signal opinions
- Verifying factual statements
- Detecting assumptions
- Judging sources
- Identifying persuasive language
- Detecting propaganda
- Drawing logical conclusions

FIGURE 8.7

Matrix for Reading Comprehension

Type of Information or Relationship	Type of Reasoning Based on Background Knowledge		
	Textually Explicit	Textually Implicit	Scriptually Implicit
Main idea/summary	X	X	X
Detail	X	X	X
Sequence	X	X	X
Comparative relationship	X	X	X
Cause/effect relationship	X	X	X
Conditional relationship	X	X	X
Vocabulary definition	X	X	X
Vocabulary application	X	X	X
Figurative language definition	X	X	X
Figurative language application	X	X	X
Conclusion	X	X	X
Application		X	X
Analysis		X	X
Synthesis		X	X
Evaluation			X

Critical reading involves both affective and cognitive skills. To read critically, students must be able to suspend judgment, consider other viewpoints, and draw logical conclusions.

In *aesthetic reading,* a reader's attention is centered on the literacy style of a piece and the feelings that are engendered by reading the piece (Rosenblatt, 1978). Reading aesthetically results in a deeper level of involvement, with the reader identifying with the characters and picturing the story in his or her mind (Cox and Many, 1992).

Both critical and aesthetic reading involve thinking about the text in relation to the readers' beliefs. For example, when Ms. Andretti, the intermediate-level inclusion teacher, was working on critical and aesthetic reading in a third-grade classroom, she had the students read the passage about Pat and her father (Apply the Concept 8.4). After reading, she asked the students, "Have you ever had an experience that made you feel like Pat?" Figure 8.8 lists sample areas of critical and aesthetic reading and sample comments teachers might use to encourage critical and aesthetic reading.

Guidelines for Teaching Reading Comprehension

If comprehension is the essence of reading, how do teachers go about teaching students with learning and behavior problems to be effective comprehenders? Twenty-eight years ago, observational research indicated that teachers spent little time teaching

FIGURE 8.8

Critical and Aesthetic Reading

Critical Reading

Critical reading: The reader reflects on and makes judgments about the content or information in the piece.

Sample Areas of Reflection or Judgment	Sample Comments
Reality or Fantasy	I don't think the author expected us to think this could really happen.
Fact or Opinion	You really get the idea they are pushing their point of view.
Adequacy and Validity	Some of this information just isn't right.
Worth	This piece really helped me write my report. I think this article could hurt his political campaign.

Aesthetic Reading

Aesthetic reading: The reader reflects on and makes judgments about the literary style of a piece.

Sample Areas of Reflection or Judgment	Sample Comments
Plot	I like the way the author always kept me interested in what was happening.
Characters	I didn't know enough about the witch to really understand why she did it.
Imagery	I could just picture myself being there.
Language	When the author said, "That was one frightened man," I felt a chill in my body.

children how to comprehend (Duffy, Lanier, and Roehler, 1980; Durkin, 1978–79). For example, in Durkin's observational studies of reading instruction in fourth-grade classrooms, only 20 minutes of comprehension instruction was observed in more than 4,000 minutes of reading instruction. Much of what teachers did to "teach" comprehension was ask questions, have students respond, and provide feedback. Furthermore, they provided a steady diet of literal or textually explicit comprehension questions, a ratio of 4:1 literal to inferential, with lower reading groups getting asked even more literal questions than higher-level groups (Guszak, 1972).

Since then, instructional research and practice have focused on how to teach reading comprehension. Even when students have reading comprehension problems, it is important to first determine the factors that may be contributing to these reading difficulties. Before focusing solely on reading comprehension instruction, teachers should answer the following questions:

- Do students have adequate decoding and phonics skills so that they can read words?
- Do students read within the expected rate of reading for their grade level?
- Do students have adequate knowledge of the meaning of words?
- Does students' background knowledge adequately prepare them to understand the text?

For any student who does not meet these criteria, a complete reading comprehension program will require additional emphasis on decoding, fluency, vocabulary, and building background knowledge. It is unlikely that comprehension strategies alone will be sufficient for any student with reading difficulties. Apply the Concept 8.5 looks at comprehension issues with students who are ELLs.

One of the keys to teaching reading comprehension, particularly for students with learning and behavior problems, is to teach them to use comprehension and comprehension-monitoring strategies (Klingner et al., 2007; Mastropieri and Scruggs, 1997; National Reading Panel, 2000; RAND Reading Study Group, 2002). This includes such strategies as the following:

- *Activating background knowledge:* Thinking about what one already knows about the topic and how one's knowledge relates to what one is reading
- *Preteaching critical vocabulary and concepts:* Teaching students to prepare to read a text by preteaching essential vocabulary and concepts that facilitate learning and understanding
- *Generating questions:* Asking relevant questions that promote understanding such as who, what, when, where, why, and how questions
- *Monitoring comprehension:* Checking for understanding and using fix-up strategies (e.g.,

Apply the Concept 8.5

Understanding Reading Comprehension with Students Who Are English Language Learners

For each of the questions below, ask yourself whether you implement the practice: never (1), some of the time, but not enough (2), whenever needed (3). Then, choose several instructional practices that you rated 1 or 2 and begin to implement them more frequently.

Do you

- ask students to make predictions about what they are going to read by using such features of the text as title, pictures, and key words?
- provide students with opportunities to integrate their background knowledge with the critical concepts in the text?
- identify the language demands of the text they are reading and

preteach related vocabulary and concepts?

- request that students monitor the words and concepts they do not understand while they're reading, make note of them and then follow up with them?
- ask students questions they can answer and then scaffold responses to meet language needs?
- model and provide opportunities for students to construct mental images that represent text, so they can better remember and understand what they read?
- provide opportunities for students to seek clarification about confusing aspects of what they read?
- plan language-related activities that link with comprehending text

and then make these explicit to students?

- give students adequate opportunities to develop questions about what they have read and pose these questions to fellow students?
- give students adequate time and practice responding orally?
- provide practice in summarizing and integrating information from text?

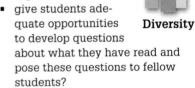

Diversity

Source: S. Linan-Thompson, and S. Vaughn. *Research-Based Methods of Reading Instruction for English Language Learners.* (Alexandria, VA: ASCD, 2007). Reprinted with permission.

rereading, clarifying a concept) to facilitate comprehension
- *Clarifying:* Clarifying unclear concepts or vocabulary
- *Using graphic organizers:* Using visual aids that illustrate concepts and relationships among concepts in a text while reading the text
- *Finding main ideas:* Determining the most important information and explaining this information in one's own words
- *Summarizing:* Identifying the main ideas, connecting the main ideas, eliminating redundant information, and putting this information in one's own words
- *Using text structure:* Using knowledge of different text structures (e.g., narrative, expositive) as a framework for comprehension

In other words, teachers need to teach cognitive strategies that will give students with learning and behavior problems the tools for understanding and constructing meaning from what they are reading.

Intervention research has provided not only information on the importance of teaching comprehension and comprehension monitoring strategies, but also evidence of how to teach these strategies. As is the case with higher-level academic learning, this is particularly challenging because comprehension involves thinking processes that are not nearly as visible as they are in other skills, such as spelling and math calculations. Therefore, instruction in reading comprehension should incorporate many of the aspects of cognitive behavior principles and should scaffold instruction (see Chapter 2) as well as include explicit instruction in the following:

- Providing rationales and evidence for the effectiveness of its use
- Describing and modeling the strategy using thinking-aloud
- Providing supported practice and feedback
- Providing independent practice
- Teaching for generalization (i.e., when and where strategies apply) and maintenance

This instruction can be accomplished through more direct explanations and mental modeling associated with cognitive strategy instruction and exemplified in the strategies intervention model (Deshler and Schumaker, 1986) in Chapter 2 or through more interactive dialogues that are based on a sociocultural theory of cognitive development. This instruction engages students and teachers in instructional conversations and demonstrations about how the strategies work as is exemplified in the Early Literacy Project (Englert et al., 1994) described in Chapter 2 and the Benchmark School Reading Program

(Gaskins, Anderson, Pressley, Cunicelli, and Satlow, 1993; Pressley et al., 1992). Using scaffolded instruction, the teacher's instruction is guided as much out of the analysis of the learner's understanding as it is from the analysis of the text (Dole, Brown, and Trathen, 1996; Pearson and Fielding, 1991; Pressley et al., 1995).

Based on ideas from information-processing and schema theories, our instruction assists students in activating their prior knowledge about a topic before they read so that they can apply this knowledge both during and after reading. Students also learn the importance of predicting and questioning as they read. In this way, comprehension is the association of new information with prior knowledge or experience (Perez and Torres-Guzman, 1992; Pressley, 2000).

Comprehension instruction should encourage students to engage actively not only in discussions related to the content of the text, but also in instructional conversations about the reading process. These discussions can be prompted by the following steps:

1. *Before reading,* the teacher activates the students' background knowledge for the selected passage and/or provides experiences to enrich their backgrounds. The teacher assists students in thinking about how this text may be related to other texts in terms of content, story line, and text structure. The teacher helps students to set purposes for reading by predicting and asking questions about what they are going to read. It is important that teacher support and scaffolding are used to prevent students from "guessing" without consideration of relevant text cues. It is also valuable for teachers to preteach proper nouns and to give students key ideas about the text prior to reading.

2. *During reading,* the teacher encourages students to self-question and monitor their comprehension as they read.

3. *After reading,* the teacher uses follow-up activities such as:
- Discussions that focus on the content of the reading as well as evaluation of the content and the writing style
- Discussions that encourage students to generate more questions and ideas for further reading and investigation
- Retellings that assist students in summarizing and organizing what they have read

Explicit instruction in comprehension strategies yields positive learner outcomes, especially for students with reading difficulties (Klingner et al., 2007; RAND Reading Study Group, 2002). The

TECHTips

8.1 Using Software to Develop Fluency and Comprehension

Commercially available computer software programs can help learners with reading fluency and comprehension. For example, story software that highlights text as it is read allows the reader to follow along. Any of the Living Books series of interactive storybooks by Riverdeep Interactive Learning Limited (http://riverdeep .net) can provide supplemental reading activities for young readers to help develop reading fluency.

Another example of such reading software is the *Start-to-Finish* books series (Don Johnston, Incorporated) that includes history, myths and legends, classic adventure, classic literature, short stories, science and nature, mysteries, and sports. The Gold and Blue series, readability levels of Grades 2–3 and Grades 4–5, respectively, provide audiotape, print, and CD-ROM versions of the books. In addition

to the literature titles, there is a newer core content series. See the Website (www.donjohnston.com) for lists of currently available titles, as they frequently add new programs. The computer programs include comprehension quizzes, word meanings quizzes, and fluency practice. Teachers can customize the programs' options to meet the individual needs of learners.

Other categories of computer software for fluency and comprehension are programs that scan print text and digitize it—for example, *CAST eReader* by CAST, Inc. (www.cast.org), *WYNN Reader* by Freedom Scientific (freedomscientific.com), and *Kurzweil 3000* from Kurzweil Education Systems (www.kurzweiledu .com). With programs such as these, textbooks can be turned into computer text that can be read aloud to the learner, but also allow the student to read along.

Sample Page and Quiz from *20,000 Leagues Under the Sea,* One of the Classic Adventures from the Start-To-Finish Gold Series (Copyright © 2004 Don Johnston Incorporated)

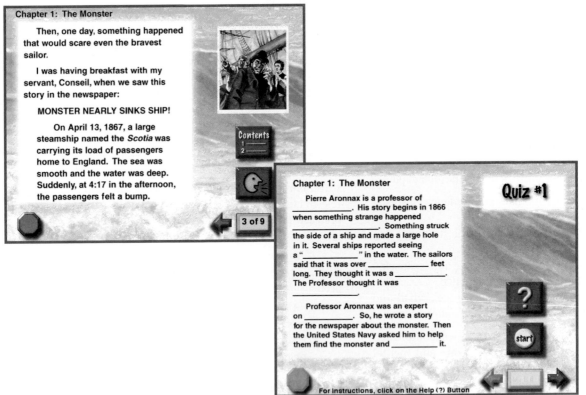

idea behind explicit instruction of comprehension is that comprehension can be improved by teaching students to use specific cognitive strategies or to reason strategically when they encounter barriers to comprehension while reading. The goal is to

achieve competent and self-regulated reading (National Reading Panel, 2000). Tech Tips 8.1 describes how text enhancements and speech feedback provided by a computer can support self-regulated reading.

Whether reading narrative or expository texts, comprehension strategy instruction should focus on previewing, predicting, and activating background knowledge; questioning to promote understanding, clarifying, and monitoring comprehension; and summarizing information. The next three sections highlight specific teaching strategies associated with these three goals.

Previewing, Predicting, and Developing Prior Knowledge

Reading comprehension instruction occurs before reading through previewing, predicting, and activating/developing background knowledge. Prereading activities help students prepare to understand and learn from what they read. Taking time to prepare students before they read can pay big dividends in terms of their understanding and finding reading an enjoyable experience (Graves, Juel, and Graves, 2001). Graves and his colleagues suggest that prereading activities should do the following:

- Set purposes for reading
- Motivate students to read
- Activate and build background knowledge
- Build knowledge of the text features
- Relate reading to students' lives
- Preteach vocabulary and concepts
- Provide opportunities for prequestioning, predicting, and direction setting

What instructional techniques can a teacher use that will help students with learning and behavior problems to activate relevant background knowledge (schema), bridge what they know to what they are reading, motivate them to read, assist them in making predictions about what they are going to be reading, preview the reading, and assist them in becoming familiar with difficult vocabulary? Four such techniques are brainstorming, the PreReading Plan (Langer, 1981), Text Preview (Graves et al., 2001), and K-W-L (Ogle, 1986).

Activating prior knowledge is particularly important for students with learning and behavior problems. It is also important for second language learners or students from culturally diverse backgrounds, for they bring unique real-world knowledge to learning situations (Bos and Reyes, 1996; Echevarria and Graves, 1998; Jiménez and Gersten, 1999). As with all learners, their prior knowledge is crucial to the successful

Diversity

construction of meaning. Apply the Concept 8.6 presents ideas for facilitating and teaching comprehension with these students. Although the strategies in this section may be used as specific activities, they should also be integrated into reading lessons and discussions about the literature and literacy.

Brainstorming

Brainstorming is a teaching strategy that activates the students' relevant prior knowledge, aids the teacher in determining the extent of the students' prior knowledge, and stimulates interest in the topic.

CLASSROOM Applications

Brainstorming

PROCEDURES: Brainstorming works best with groups of students who are reading the same or related selections. Before beginning the activity, determine the major topic or concept presented in the selection(s). Next decide what to use as a stimulus to represent that topic. It might be a single word or phrase, a picture, a poem, or a short excerpt from the reading passage. Before reading, conduct the brainstorming session:

1. Present the stimulus to the students.
2. Ask the students to list as many words or phrases as they can associate with the stimulus. Encourage them to think about everything they know about the topic or concept. Allow several minutes for the students to think and get ready to report their ideas. (If appropriate, have students write their ideas.)
3. Record the students' associations on the board. Ask for other associations, and add them to the list. While writing ideas on the board, assist students in making connections among these ideas by talking about how they are related.
4. With the students, categorize the associations. Clarify the ideas and discuss what titles to use for the categories.

You may also want to organize the ideas into a map. Strategies for organizing story maps are discussed later in this chapter, and strategies for developing content maps are discussed in Chapter 10.

Although the brainstorming activity usually ends before reading begins, we recommend encouraging students to continue to add to their list of associations as they read and after they read. After the reading, review the list, and add new associations.

Apply the Concept 8.6

Strategies for Promoting Reading Comprehension for Students Who Are Culturally Diverse and/or English Language Learners

Diversity

For students from culturally and linguistically diverse backgrounds and for English language learners, a number of strategies can be used to promote reading comprehension.

Making Input More Comprehensible

- Begin teaching new concepts by working from the students' prior knowledge and incorporating the funds of knowledge from the students' communities.
- Use demonstrations and gesture to augment oral and written communication.
- Discuss connections between the concepts being read and the students' home cultures.
- Encourage students to share the new vocabulary in the first lan-

guage and incorporate the first language into instruction.
- If students share a common first language, pair more-proficient English language learners with less-proficient peers, and encourage students to discuss what they are reading.
- Provide opportunities for students to learn to read and to read in their first language.
- Highlight key words and phrases in text and incorporate them into semantic maps.
- Teach text structures and use visual representations of text structures.
- When asking questions or discussing new ideas or vocabulary, slow the pace.
- Repeat key ideas and write them.

- Use think-alouds to make comprehension strategies more explicit.

Incorporating Multicultural Literature into the Reading Program

- Select literature that reflects various cultures.
- Study authors from various cultures.
- Read literature that incorporates various dialects.
- Select genres that are typical of different cultures.
- Use book lists, directories, Websites, and textbooks on multicultural education as resources for multicultural literature.
- In the classroom and school libraries, have literature written in the students' first languages available to the students.

COMMENTS: Brainstorming is a quick and simple way to activate background knowledge. It usually takes 5 to 10 minutes to complete. However, for some students and topic combinations, simple associations without further discussion may not provide enough input to activate and build on students' prior knowledge. The next procedure provides additional activities for further activating relevant schemas.

PreReading Plan

The PreReading Plan (PReP) is a three-phase instructional–assessment strategy that builds on the activity of brainstorming. Designed by Langer (1981), it assists students in accessing knowledge related to the major concepts presented in a reading selection.

CLASSROOM Applications

PreReading Plan

PROCEDURES: Before beginning the activity, provide a phrase or picture to stimulate group discussion about a key concept in the text. For

example, if a science selection is about the types and characteristics of mammals, *mammals* might serve as the stimulus word. After introducing the topic, conduct the following three-phase process:

1. *Initial association with the concept.* Cue students by saying something like, "Say what you think are attributes of mammals." Have the students generate a list of ideas, words, and associations. Record the key ideas on the board, noting the student's name by each association.

2. *Reflections on initial associations.* Now ask the students, "What made you think . . . [the responses given by each of the students during phase 1]?" This phase requires the students to bring to the conscious level their prior knowledge and how it relates to the key concept. It also allows the students to listen to each other's responses. Langer (1981) states, "Through this procedure they [students] gain the insight which permits them to evaluate the utility of these ideas in the reading experience" (p. 154).

3. *Reformation of knowledge.* After students have had an opportunity to think and tell about what triggered their ideas, ask, "On the basis of our discussion, do you have any new ideas about

FIGURE 8.9

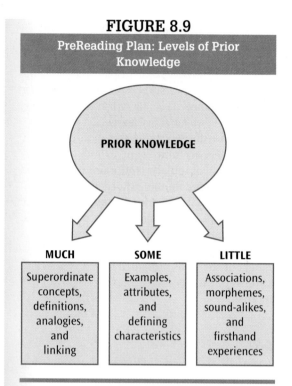

PreReading Plan: Levels of Prior Knowledge

PRIOR KNOWLEDGE

MUCH	SOME	LITTLE
Superordinate concepts, definitions, analogies, and linking	Examples, attributes, and defining characteristics	Associations, morphemes, sound-alikes, and firsthand experiences

Source: J. A. Langer, Facilitating test processing: The elaboration of prior knowledge, in J. A. Langer and M. T. Smith-Burke (Eds.), *Reader Meets Author/Bridging the Gap* (Newark, DE: International Reading Association, 1982), p. 156. Reprinted by permission of Judith A. Langer and the International Reading Association.

mammals?" This question gives the students the opportunity to discuss how they have elaborated or changed their ideas on the basis of the previous discussion. Because the students have had the opportunity to listen to other students, new links between prior knowledge and the key concept are also formed.

On the basis of the information gathered during this three-phase procedure, Langer presents a means of assessing prior knowledge into levels to determine whether further concept building will need to be completed before reading (see Figure 8.9). Langer found this assessment method a better predictor of reading comprehension for a particular passage than either IQ or standardized reading scores (Langer and Nicholich, 1981). The three levels and their instructional implications are as follows:

1. *Much knowledge.* Students whose free associations reflect superordinate concepts, definitions, analogies, or a linking of the key concept to other relevant concepts demonstrate *much* integration of the key concept with concepts that are already in accessible memory. Comprehension for these students should be adequate.

2. *Some knowledge.* Students whose free associations are primarily examples, attributes, or defining characteristics have *some* knowledge about the concepts being taught. Comprehension should be adequate, but some instructional activities that assist the students in making the critical links between existing and new knowledge may be necessary.

3. *Little knowledge.* Students whose free associations reflect morphemes (prefixes, suffixes, root words), rhyming words, or unelaborated or unrelated firsthand experiences demonstrate *little* knowledge of the concept. These students need concept instruction before reading commences, with the reported firsthand experiences serving as a reference point for starting instruction.

COMMENTS: The PreReading Plan provides a direct means of activating the students' background knowledge. The authors have frequently used both brainstorming and PReP, particularly with upper-elementary and secondary students with learning and behavior problems. We find that taking the extra time to conduct PReP is worthwhile, since it requires students to bring to the conscious level why they made their associations, and it gives them the opportunity to reflect on what they have learned through the discussion. It is a good idea to have students add to and adjust their lists during reading and after they read.

Text Preview

Text previews are designed to increase students' prior knowledge, motivate students to read, and provide a scaffold for text comprehension (Graves et al., 2001). Text previews can be used with students at varying reading and grade levels and with both narrative and expository texts.

CLASSROOM Applications

Text Preview

PROCEDURES: The two major steps in using text previews are preparing the preview and then using it with the students.

1. *Preparation and construction of text previews.* A text preview is a synopsis of a text which is written in an organized framework that enhances student comprehension of the text by bridging it to their real-world experiences. It has three sections: one that piques student interest, a brief discussion of the text's theme (e.g., for stories this could include the setting, character descriptions, and essential story organization), and questions or directions that guide student reading.

FIGURE 8.10
Connections Chart about Dolphins

Connection to Dolphins

Connections to Our Experiences	Connections to World Knowledge
Reneé, Maria, Jon, Marcos petted the dolphins at Sea World	Skin is soft and smooth
Peter saw dolphins swim under boat when his family was sailing in Florida	Seem to communicate with one another
	Bottlenose dolphin
Everyone has seen dolphins on TV	Have to come to surface to breathe

2. *Presentation of text previews.* The following steps are suggested for implementing the text preview and should take no longer than 5 to 10 minutes:

- Cue students about the new reading.
- Discuss an interesting aspect of the story or content that will pique motivation.
- Make connections to the students' lives and world knowledge.
- Present the questions or directions that should guide student reading.
- Have students read the text.

Discussing an interesting aspect of the story or content helps students to delve into reading materials, knowing that there will be new knowledge, discoveries, and/or excitement. These motivational activities often involve hands-on experiences and intrigue that are then tied to the story that is being read. For example, a teacher might say, "Feel these fabrics, and tell me what it makes you think about and how it makes you feel. In the story, Robbie has a special blanket made out of these fabrics—satin and flannel. As you read the story think about what is special about this blanket and how it feels." Making connections to the students' lives and their world knowledge also activates background knowledge and creates motivation. Using a connections chart such as the one in Figure 8.10 helps students think about connections they can make to their own lives and to world knowledge they have about a topic. For example, in reading about dolphins, students can list experiences they have had with dolphins as well as facts they know about dolphins before they read and then add to the list after they read.

COMMENTS: Although text previews take time to prepare, students report that previews enable them to understand texts to a fuller extent (Chen and Graves, 1996; Dole, Valencia, Greer, and Wardrop, 1991). Text previews can be especially beneficial for students who have learning or behavior problems and with English language learners.

When using text previews with expository text, the teacher may want to include important points, vocabulary, and more implicit and experience-based thinking (Readence, Bean, and Baldwin, 1995). Additionally, teachers can use text previews as potential writing assignments. Students can be assigned to develop text previews for other students' guided reading. Critical thinking about the ideas presented in a text selection will ensue as students create text previews for one another.

K-W-L

K-W-L is a strategy that is designed to activate students' background knowledge and to assist students in setting purposes for reading expository text (Bryant, 1998; Ogle, 1986, 1989). This strategy is based on research that highlights the importance of background knowledge in constructing meaning (e.g., Anderson et al., 1977).

CLASSROOM Applications
K-W-L

PROCEDURES: The K-W-L strategy consists of three basic steps representative of the cognitive/metacognitive steps that students employ as they use the strategy:

1. Accessing what I <u>K</u>now
2. Determining what I <u>W</u>ant to learn
3. Recalling what I <u>L</u>earned

To assist the students in using the strategy, Ogle (1986, 1989) developed a simple worksheet for the students to complete during the reading–thinking process (see Figure 8.11).

During the *Know* step, the teacher and students engage in a discussion that is designed to assist students in thinking about what they already know about the topic of the text. For this step, the teacher starts by using a brainstorming procedure (see the section on brainstorming). As in the PreReading Plan, students are encouraged to discuss where or how they learned the information so as to provide information about the source and substantiveness of their ideas. After brainstorming,

FIGURE 8.11

K-W-L-Q Chart for Pond and Pond Life

What I Know	What I Want to Learn	What I Learned	More Questions I Have
Contains water	How does the pond get its water?	Underground springs and rain	Why do ponds die?
Smaller than a lake	Why are ponds green and muddy?	Algae and other plants make it green	What happens to a pond in winter?
Fish			
Ducks	Does the temperature change?	Like the air but temperature is less affected the deeper you go	How does algae help or hurt a pond?
Frogs			
Muddy	What fish live in the pond?	Blue gill, trout, bass, catfish	
Algae	What insects live in the pond?	Dragonflies, mosquitoes, water fleas	
Insect on top	What plants live in the pond?	Algae, cattails, water lilies	
Birds eat insects			

Source: Adapted from P. R. Schmidt (1999). KWLQ: Inquiry and literacy learning in science. *The Reading Teachers,* 52, pp. 789–792.

the teachers and students discuss the general categories of information that are likely to be encountered when they read, and how their brainstormed ideas could help them determine the categories. "For example, a teacher might say 'I see three different pieces of information about how turtles look. Description of looks is certainly one category of information I would expect this article to include'" (Ogle, 1986, p. 566).

During the *Want to Learn* step, the teacher and students discuss what they want to learn from reading the text. Although most of this step utilizes group discussion, before students begin to read, each student writes down the specific questions in which he or she is most interested.

During the *Learned* step, the students write what they learned from reading. They should also check the questions that they generated in the previous step to find out whether they were addressed in the text.

COMMENTS: K-W-L is a strategy for helping students to actively engage in the reading process and for assisting teachers in teaching reading using an interactive model of reading. Informal evaluation of the strategy indicates that students recalled more information in articles when they used K-W-L and that they enjoyed using the strategy and used it independently (Ogle, 1986). Carr and Ogle (1987) added mapping and summarizing activities to K-W-L to gain the advantage of these powerful comprehension tools. Ogle (1989) added a fourth column "what we still want to learn" and referred to this adaptation as K-W-L Plus. Bryant (1998) referred to it as K-W-W-L to assist students in gener-

ating questions and designing scientific experiments, and Schmidt (1999) referred to it as K-W-L-Q, with the Q representing more questions. This addition encourages further research and reading.

Questioning Strategies

Asking questions is a major vehicle that teachers use to foster understanding and retention and to check for comprehension. When questions are asked about information in text, that information is remembered better. Asking higher-level questions that require integration of background and text knowledge (see Figure 8.7) will promote deeper processing and therefore more learning (Sundbye, 1987). Even asking "Why?" and "How?" can significantly increase retention of information (Menke and Pressley, 1994; Pressley, 1998).

However, simply asking questions does not ensure that students will develop questioning strategies. Students' answers to questions can give limited insight into their understanding of text. As has already been demonstrated, teacher and student questioning before reading helps to activate prior knowledge and to set purposes for reading. Self-questioning during reading (e.g., Does this make sense? Am I understanding what I am reading? How does this relate to what I already know? What will happen next?) assists students in comprehension and monitoring comprehension (one of the metacognitive activities discussed in Chapter 2). Encouraging students to engage in ongoing questioning before, during, and after reading is a valuable practice.

The section that follows presents teaching questioning strategies. These techniques require teachers to model comprehension questions and comprehension-monitoring questions, teach students to recognize types of questions, and encourage students to self-question before, during, and after they read.

ReQuest or Reciprocal Questioning

The ReQuest procedure is a reciprocal questioning technique that is designed to assist students in formulating their own questions about what they read. The procedure was developed by Manzo (1969; Manzo and Manzo, 1993), who stressed the importance of students' setting their own purposes for reading and asking their own questions as they read.

CLASSROOM Applications

ReQuest or Reciprocal Questioning

PROCEDURES: This technique relies heavily on modeling, which is a major premise of cognitive strategy instruction. To use ReQuest, select materials at the students' instructional to independent reading levels. You and the students read a sentence or section of the passage and then take turns asking each other questions. Your role is to model good questioning and to provide feedback to students about their questions. In modeling, include higher-level questions that require you to use scripturally and textually implicit information and that require critical and aesthetic reading. Also include monitoring questions (e.g., Does this make sense?).

Manzo suggests that this procedure first be introduced on an individual basis and then used in small groups. The following explanation can be used to introduce ReQuest:

> The purpose of this lesson is to improve your understanding of what you read. We will each read silently the first sentence [section]. Then we will take turns asking questions about the sentence [section] and what it means. You will ask questions first, then I will ask questions. Try to ask the kinds of questions a teacher might ask in the way a teacher might ask them.
>
> You may ask me as many questions as you wish. When you are asking me questions, I will close my book (or pass the book to you if there is only one between us). When I ask questions, you close your book (Manzo, 1969, p. 124).

The rules are that the answer "I don't know" is not allowed, unclear questions are to be restated, and uncertain answers are to be justified by reference to the text or other source material if necessary. In addition, you and the students may need to discuss unfamiliar vocabulary.

The procedure itself consists of the following steps:

1. *Silent reading.* You and the students read the sentence or section.
2. *Student questioning.* Close your book while the students ask questions. Model appropriate answers, and reinforce appropriate questioning behavior. The students ask as many questions as possible.
3. *Teacher questioning.* The students close their books, and you ask questions modeling a variety of question types (see Figure 8.7).
4. *Integration of the text.* After completing the procedure with the first sentence or section, repeat the process with subsequent sentences or sections. Integrate the new section with previous sections by asking questions that relate to new and old sections.
5. *Predictive questioning.* When the students have read enough to make a prediction about the rest of the passage, ask predictive questions (e.g., What do you think will happen? Why do you think so?). If the predictions and verification are reasonable, you and the students move to the next step.
6. *Reading.* You and the students read to the end of the passage to verify and discuss your predictions.

COMMENTS: One important aspect of this strategy is the questions that the teacher models. Manzo and Manzo (1990, 1993) suggest that teachers use a variety of questions including these:

- *Predictable questions:* The typical who, what, when, where, why, and how questions
- *Mind-opening questions:* Questions that are designed to help the students understand how written and oral language are used to communicate ideas
- *Introspective questions:* Metacognitive questions that are oriented toward self-monitoring and self-evaluation
- *Ponderable questions:* Questions that stimulate discussion and for which no right or wrong answer is apparent
- *Elaborative knowledge questions:* Questions that require students to integrate their background knowledge with the information given in the text

The ReQuest procedure assists students in developing appropriate questions. We have used several variations of these procedures. For instance, we have introduced the ReQuest procedure as a game. The students and teacher take turns asking questions and keeping score of appropriate answers. We also recommend that the text be read in longer, more natural segments rather than individual sentences. Legenza (1974) has adapted this procedure by having kindergartners ask questions about a picture rather than a text. Some students benefit from having question starters to help them initiate questions. These question starters could be things like: Why did he . . . ? Why do you think the ending . . . ? What would happen if . . . ?

Question–Answer Relationships Strategy

The question–answer relationships strategy (QARs; Raphael, 1982, 1984, 1986) is designed to assist students in labeling the type of questions that are asked and to use this information to help guide them as they develop answers. QARs was developed by Raphael and Pearson (1982) to facilitate correct responses to questions. The strategy is based on question–answer relationships developed by Pearson and Johnson (1978) discussed earlier in this chapter (e.g., textually explicit, textually implicit, and scriptually implicit). It helps students to realize they need to consider both the text and their prior knowledge when answering questions and to use strategic behavior to adjust the use of each of these sources.

CLASSROOM Applications

Question–Answer Relationships Strategy

PROCEDURES: QARs was originally taught by Raphael (1984), using the three categories of information suggested in the matrix for reading comprehension (Figure 8.7). The three categories were renamed for use with students:

1. *Right There:* Words used to create the question and words used for the answer are in the same sentence (textually explicit).
2. *Think and Search:* The answer is in the text, but words used to create the question and those used for an appropriate answer would not be in the same sentence (textually implicit).
3. *On My Own:* The answer is not found in the text but in one's head (scriptually implicit).

On the basis of input from teachers, Raphael (1986) modified these categories to include two major categories—*In the Book* and *In My Head*—and then further divided these categories, as shown in Figure 8.12.

Raphael suggests the following procedure for introducing QARs: The first day, introduce the students to the concept of question–answer relationships (QARs), using the two major categories. Use several short passages (from two to five sentences) to demonstrate the relationships. Provide practice by asking students to identify the type of QAR, the answer to the question, and the strategy they used for finding the answer. The progression for teaching should be from highly supportive to independent:

1. Provide the text, questions, answers, QAR label for each question, and reason why the label was appropriate.
2. Provide the text, questions, answers, and QAR label for each question. Have the students supply the reason for the label.
3. Provide the text, questions, and answers, and have the students supply the QAR labels and reasons for the labels.
4. Provide the text and questions, and have the students supply the answers, QAR labels, and reasons for the labels.

When the students have a clear picture of the difference between *In My Head* and *In the Book*, teach the next level of differentiation for each one of the major categories. First, work on *In the Book*, then go to *In My Head*. The key distinction between the two subcategories under *In My Head* (i.e., *Author and You* and *On My Own*) is "whether or not the reader needs to read the text for the questions to make sense" (Raphael, 1986, p. 519). When the information must come from the reader but in connection with the information presented by the author, then the QAR is *Author and You*. For example, in the story about Pat and her father (Apply the Concept 8.4), the question "How did the fisherman alert the police?" requires the reader to use his or her background knowledge but relate it to the information in the text. In comparison, the question "What would you have done if you were in Pat's shoes?" is an example of an *On My Own* QAR.

Once the students are effectively using the QARs strategy in short passages, gradually increase the length of the passages and the variety of reading materials. Review the strategy, and model its use on the first question. Have the students then use the strategy to complete the rest of the questions.

COMMENTS: After teaching this strategy using the original three categories, Raphael (1984)

FIGURE 8.12

Cue Card for Question–Answer Relationships (QARs)

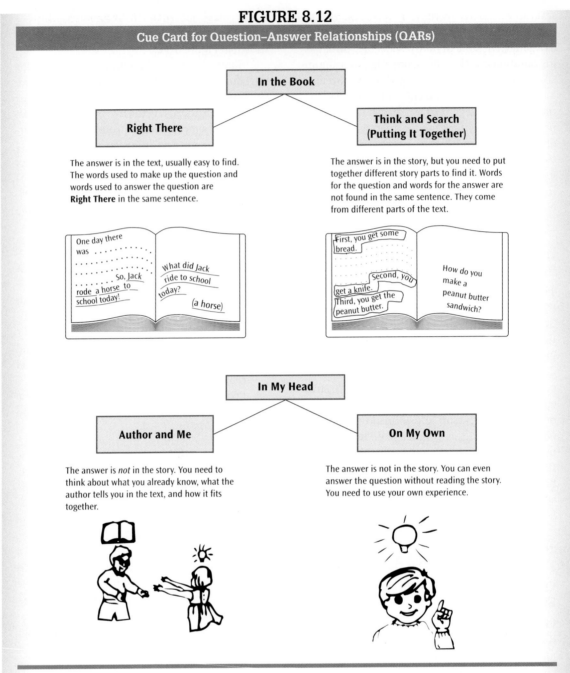

Source: Adapted from T. E. Raphael (1986). Teaching question–answer relationships, revisited. *The Reading Teacher, 39* (6), pp. 516–523.

found that groups of low-, average-, and high-achieving fourth-grade students had higher performance on a comprehension test and gave evidence that the question–answer relationships strategy transferred to reading improvement in the content areas. This strategy helped lower-achieving students to answer all three types of questions, particularly their performance on textually explicit and implicit questions. Simmons

(1992) taught 24 special education teachers to implement either QARs or selected traditional methods of reading comprehension instruction, including the skills of answering literal questions (recall of factual information and main ideas), locating supportive details, and drawing conclusions. Using a lesson sequence similar to the one just described, they found that students who participated in QARs instruction performed better than other students on tests of comprehension over the social studies text they read. Labeling the types of questions and then using that information to assist in answering questions appear to constitute an effective strategy for students and one that encourages active involvement in the comprehension process.

Self-Questioning Strategies

Self-questioning strategies are a good example of how metacognition assists students in reading. These questions typically have the student focus on activating prior knowledge and setting purposes for reading, asking questions to assist the comprehension process, checking understanding during reading, and reviewing after reading to determine understanding. For example, Alvermann and her colleagues (1989) suggest the following self-questions to foster comprehension:

Think Ahead

- What is this section about?
- What do I already know about the topic?
- What do I want to find out?
- What is my goal?
- How should I go about reading to meet my goal?

Think while Reading

- What have I read about so far?
- Do I understand it?
- If not, what should I do?
- What is the author saying, and what did I think about it?

Think Back

- Have I learned what I wanted to learn?
- How can I use what I read?

One strategy focuses primarily on questions related to the main idea (Wong, 1979; Wong and Jones, 1982). When investigating the reading comprehension skills of upper-elementary students with learning disabilities, Wong (1979) found that in text without inserted questions, the students had poorer recall of the thematically important ideas than average readers did. She hypothesized that the students do not self-question when they read. To demonstrate this point, she inserted questions in the text for a second group of students with learning disabilities and average students, and she no longer found significant differences between the recall of the two types of

readers. Whereas the inserted questions resulted in significantly better recall for the students with learning disabilities, no such effect was evident for average readers, indicating that the students with learning disabilities were not as effective at self-questioning. On the basis of this research, Wong and Jones (1982) developed a self-questioning technique to determine whether junior high students with learning disabilities could be taught to self-question as they read.

CLASSROOM Applications
Self-Questioning Strategies

PROCEDURES: First, teach the students the concept of a main idea. During this stage, teach them how to identify the main idea(s) in paragraphs. For Wong and her colleagues, this took up to 3 one-hour sessions.

During the next stage, teach the students the steps in self-questioning strategy:

1. What are you studying this passage for? (So that you can answer some questions you will be given later.)
2. Find the main idea(s) in the paragraph, and underline it (them).
3. Think of a question about the main idea you have underlined. Remember what a good question should be like. ("Good questions" are those that directly focus on important textual elements. Write the question in the margin.)
4. Learn the answer to your question. (Write the answer in the margin.)
5. Always look back at the previous questions and answers to see how each successive question and answer provides you with more information.

In teaching, model the strategy, and then have the students study the steps in the strategy. Next, have the students practice using this strategy on individual paragraphs, and provide them with immediate corrective feedback. Have the students use a cue card like the one in Figure 8.13 to assist them in remembering the steps in the strategy. When the students are successful, switch to multiple-paragraph passages, and gradually fade the use of the cue cards. Give feedback at the end of each passage. At the end of each lesson, discuss the students' progress and the usefulness of the self-questioning strategy.

COMMENTS: Results from the Wong and Jones (1982) study indicate that students with learning disabilities who learned the self-questioning strategy

FIGURE 8.13

Frame for Answering Wh- and How Questions

Student Name: _____

Title: _____

Pages: _____

Date: _____

Who?

What?

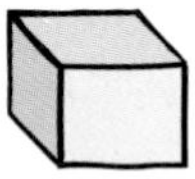

Where?

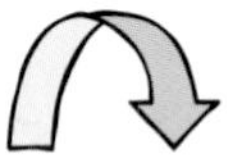

When?

Why?

How?

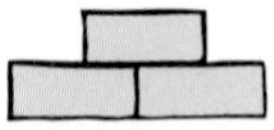

performed significantly higher on comprehension tests than did students who were not taught the strategy.

Another self-questioning strategy, the KU-CRL self-questioning strategy, was developed at the Kansas University Center for Research on Learning (Clark, Deshler, Shumaker, Alley, and Warner, 1984). This strategy was used to assist secondary-level students with learning disabilities in comprehending and remembering the important information presented in content area textbooks. The KU-CRL self-questioning strategy focuses on teaching students how to generate questions about important information in a passage, predict the answers, search for the answers while reading, and talk to themselves about the answers by using a mnemonic "ASK IT." The ASK IT steps are as follows:

Step 1: Attend to the clues as you read
Step 2: Say some questions
Step 3: Keep predictions in mind
Step 4: Identify the answer
Step 5: Talk about the answers

For self-questioning strategies to be effective for students with reading difficulties, it is important that teachers provide modeling, direct coaching, prompting, and guidance (Chan, 1991; Gersten, Williams, Fuchs, and Baker, in press; Mastropieri, Scruggs, Hamilton, Wolfe, Whedon, and Canevaro, 1996). Teaching students to stop and question themselves before, during, and/or after reading is another key element of success (Edmonds, Vaughn, et al., in press; Mastropieri and Scruggs, 1997).

Questioning the Author

Though not technically a practice designed to teach students to ask themselves questions, Questioning the Author (Beck and McKeown, 2006) provides students with well-scaffolded instruction that supports their interactions with texts and eventually with each other as though the "author" were available for comment and conversation. The idea is to have students actively engage with a text. With Questioning the Author, the teacher has given distinct goals and several queries that assist students in reaching those goals. First, students and teachers require coherent texts so that understanding and engaging in discussion is a possible enterprise. Second, students need to have some background knowledge of the topic so that they can adequately discuss what they are reading; and third, teachers and students require a logical set of questions to better understand text.

CLASSROOM Applications

Questioning the Author

PROCEDURES: First, select text that is coherent. The text type selected may be either narrative or expository. Be sure to consider the background knowledge that students require to understand the text. To the extent possible, identify key ideas and concepts and preteach them to students prior to reading the text.

Second, students are taught to "grapple" with ideas while they are reading and to consider what the author means and the extent to which the author may not have communicated very well. In this way, meaning is built "as they read" rather than at the end of the reading. In this way, students share and discuss while reading, enhancing background knowledge and understanding and increasing understanding of text as they continue reading. The focus is not on the discussion per se but on the understanding of what they are reading.

Third, teachers and students use queries to promote understanding and to place responsibility for understanding text onto the students; for example, What is the author trying to tell us? and Why do you think the author is saying this?

Fourth, the teacher establishes the fallibility of the author with the students so that they learn that a text is simply one person's ideas written down and that these ideas should be considered in light of other knowledge and their own experience. This provides students with an engagement with text and the author that is typically not available.

COMMENTS: Several studies document the effectiveness of Questioning the Author in classwide implementation in general education classrooms with at-risk students (for a review, see Beck and McKeown, 2006). Findings have not been conducted separately for students with learning disabilities. Also, studies have been conducted with fourth-grade students. Consequently, Questioning the Author may be a very valuable way to engage students with learning disabilities—particularly older students.

According to McKeown and Beck (2004), "the development of meaning in [Questioning the Author] focuses on readers' interactions with text as it is being read, situates reader-text interactions in whole-class discussion, and encourages explanatory, evidence based responses to questions about text" (p. 393). Evidence from their studies in many classrooms suggest that teachers and students who adopted this Questioning the Author perspective also became increasingly engaged with text. In addition, interactions in the classroom changed from the traditional question-and-answer routines, which appear to be much like test questions and answers, to more collaborative discussions that involved both teacher and students in questioning and the development and elaboration of new ideas.

Text Structure and Summarization Strategies

Text structure refers to the organizational features of text that can serve as a frame or pattern (Englert and Thomas, 1987). According to Simmons and Kame'enui (1998), there is a strong relationship between a reader's awareness of text structure and his or her reading comprehension. However, many students with learning and behavior problems are insensitive to text structures (Williams, 1998). Therefore, teaching text structures can be helpful for students, particularly those with reading difficulties or dyslexia, to facilitate reading comprehension (Mastropieri and Scruggs, 1997; Swanson, 1999a, 1999b). Often, teachers divide text into two major types: narrative and expository. *Narrative texts* tell a story and can be organized into components such as setting, problem statement, goals, event sequences or episodes, and ending. This component analysis has been referred to as *story grammar* and is a set of rules designed to show how the parts of a story are interrelated (Mandler and Johnson, 1977; Stein and Glenn, 1979). Generally, stories are easier for students to comprehend than expository text is because the story structure is more consistent and has a linear orientation, making it more predictable. Carnine et al. (1997) suggest that teachers use the following four story grammar questions:

1. Who is the story about?
2. What is she or he trying to do?
3. What happens when she or he tries to do it?
4. What happens in the end?

Typical questions that focus on story grammar include:

- Where does the story take place (setting)?
- When does the story take place (setting)?
- Who are the main people in the story (characters)?
- What problems does the main character face (problem)?
- What are the main character's goals (goal)?
- What does the main character want to do to solve the problem (goal)?

- What are the main things that happened in the story to solve the problem (plot)?
- How did each thing work out (plot)?
- Is the problem finally resolved? If so, how (outcome/ending)?

Expository texts are designed to explain phenomena or provide information. These are the informational texts that students encounter not only in school content area subjects such as social studies, science, math, and vocational education, but also in newspapers and magazines and on the Internet. Expository texts can be more difficult to comprehend because there is more variation in their organization (e.g., describing an object, comparing and contrasting two ideas, explaining a cause–effect relationship), the content may be less familiar, and there may be a high proportion of technical terms. Teaching types of expository texts can help students with comprehension problems to understand the more complex scientific style of thinking that is evident in expository text. Figure 8.14 presents six types of expository texts with signal words and cohesive ties which note the relationships and sample

frameworks that depict the relationships. These text structures can also guide the types of questions that promote comprehension. For example, here are some questions that can be asked to help students understand the process of rusting (cause–effect structure) and how it relates to their lives (Muth, 1987):

- What causes rusting?
- What are some of the effects of rusting?
- What conditions cause rusting?
- What kinds of things rust in your home and why?
- What can be done around your home to prevent rusting? Why would these things work?

The type of text may vary within an expository passage or paragraph, and thinking about the specific type can facilitate comprehension. In this section, we first discuss strategies for using story grammar to facilitate comprehension and then discuss strategies that focus on expository text. More techniques related to expository texts are presented in Chapter 10 in the discussion of content area learning.

FIGURE 8.14
Types of Expository Texts

Text Type	Cohesive Ties and Signal Words	Sample Frameworks
Descriptive or Enumerative Describes the characteristics, attributes, examples, or a series of facts about a topic	for example, for instance in addition besides to illustrate characteristics are can be described as moreover such as in other words	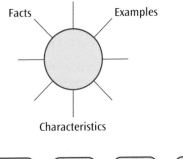
Sequential or How To Tell how to do something or a series of events presented in order	first, second, third next last, finally before, after in the past, in the future currently	
Compare–Contrast Two or more topics are compared according to the their likenesses and differences	different from same as, alike however in contrast in comparison, compared to instead of on the other hand whereas similarly	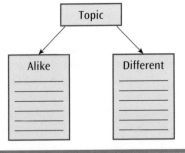

Story-Mapping and Story-Retelling Strategies

Story-retelling strategies provide students with a framework for retelling the key points of narrative texts. The strategies can be combined with story maps, which provide students with a visual guide to understanding and retelling stories. Figure 8.15 shows a visual framework for a simple story.

Teachers have taught students with reading problems how to use story maps and story strategies to aid in comprehending and retelling stories (Bos, 1999; Cain, 1996; Gurney, Gersten, Dimino, and Carnine, 1990; Idol, 1987a, 1987b; Williams, 1998; Williams, Brown, Silverstein, and deCani, 1994). For example, Idol (1987a, 1987b) used a model-lead-test paradigm (Carnine et al., 1997) to teach story mapping to five intermediate-grade students with learning disabilities. Bos (1987) used a story-retelling strategy to assist intermediate students with learning and language disabilities in retelling stories. Whereas these two strategies focus on the components of the story, Williams (1998) has developed an instructional lesson to assist students with severe learning disabilities to identify the themes of stories and relate them to their lives.

CLASSROOM Applications

Story Mapping

PROCEDURES: Idol (1987b) used the visual in Figure 8.15 and the following procedure to teach story mapping:

1. During the *model* phase, model how to use the story map by reading the story aloud, stopping at points where information pertaining to one of the story components is presented. Ask the students to label the part, and then demonstrate how to write the information on the story map. Have the students copy the information on their own maps. If the information is implicit in the story, model how to generate the inference.

2. During the *lead* phase, have students read the story independently and complete their maps, prompting when necessary. Encourage the

Text Type	Cohesive Ties and Signal Words	Sample Frameworks
Cause–Effect Explanation of the reason(s) for something or why something happened and the resulting effect(s)	cause because therefore thus as a result of if . . . then consequently for this reason	
Problem–Solution Statement of a problem and possible solutions, sometimes with resulting effects	problem is possible solutions are one, two, next, last, etc., solutions as a result	
Argument or Persuasion Statement of a position on an issue with justification	the point is first, second, next, last reasons major reason consequently therefore	

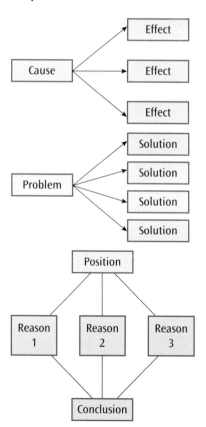

FIGURE 8.15

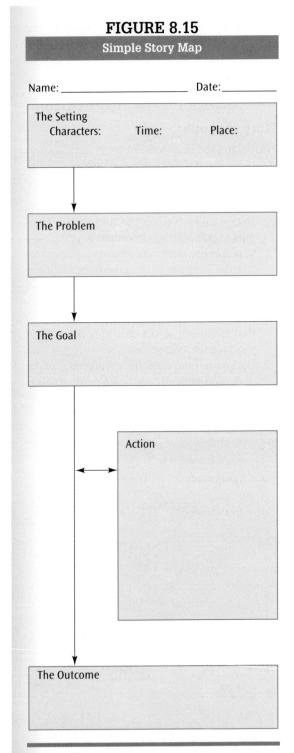

Simple Story Map

Name: _____ Date: _____

The Setting
Characters: Time: Place:

The Problem

The Goal

Action

The Outcome

Source: L. Idol (1987). Group story mapping: A comprehension strategy for both skilled and unskilled readers. *Journal of Learning Disabilities, 20,* p. 199. Reprinted by permission.

students to review their maps after completing the story, adding details that may have been omitted.

3. During the *test* phase, ask students to read a story, generate their map, and then answer

questions such as, Who were the characters? Where did the story take place? and What was the main character trying to accomplish?

Bos (1987) used principles based on cognitive strategy instruction to teach a story-retelling strategy. The procedures are as follows:

1. Motivate the students to learn the strategy by demonstrating how it will help them remember what they have read.
2. Describe the components in a story and the steps used to identify and remember the different components:

    STORE the Story
    *S*etting: Who, what, when, where
    *T*rouble: What is the trouble that the main character(s) needs to solve?
    *O*rder of action: What action(s) does the main character(s) take to solve the problem?
    *R*esolution: What was the outcome (resolution) for each action? How does the main character(s) react and feel?
    *E*nd: What happened in the end?

    Explain how answering these questions will help the students STORE, or remember, the important parts of the story.
3. Practice together reading stories, labeling the components, and retelling the stories. The students can retell their stories to the teacher, retell them to each other, tape record their retellings, or answer questions about the stories.
4. Have the students independently read stories and retell them by using the STORE the Story strategy.

Williams (1998) developed an instructional program to assist students with learning disabilities to generate themes for stories and relate them to the students' lives. The lesson was organized around a single story and had five parts, as demonstrated for the story "Kate Shelly and the Midnight Limited." This story is about how Kate braved great danger to warn the stationmaster that a railroad bridge had collapsed and thereby averted the wreck of the Midnight Limited. The procedure was as follows:

1. *Prereading discussion about lesson purpose and story topic.* This includes discussion of the importance of identifying and understanding the theme.
2. *Story reading.* The students listen to and/or read the story and discuss the story grammar components and the story (e.g., What do you

think will happen next? Do you think Kate was brave? Why?).

3. *Discussion to generate theme.* The teacher and students discuss five questions designed to help generate the theme:
   - Who is the main character? (Kate Shelly)
   - What did he or she do? (She ran more than a mile in a terrible storm to warn the stationmaster about a collapsed railroad bridge; she persevered.)
   - What happened? (She reached the station in time to save the train and the passengers.)
   - Was this good or bad? (Good.)
   - Why was this good or bad? (It was good that Kate persevered because she saved lives.)

4. *Writing the theme.* The teachers and students write the theme using the format "Kate should have persevered. We should persevere."

5. *Generalization to real-life experiences.* Discussion is focused around the following two questions: To whom would this theme apply? When would it apply? In what situations?

Williams compared this theme discussion framework to more traditional discussions about stories.

COMMENTS: Results from the Idol (1987b) and Bos (1999) studies indicate that students were able to recall substantially more relevant information after learning each strategy. They were also able to answer more explicit and implicit comprehension questions about the stories. Students were also more likely to label the parts of the story in their retellings, thereby providing the listener with a framework for listening. Results from the Williams (1998) study indicate that students were able to generate and apply qualitatively better themes. These same strategies have also been adapted and used to help students plan and write stories.

One aspect that is particularly challenging for students to comprehend is different characters' perspectives and internal reactions as the story progresses (Emery, 1996; Shannon, Kame'enui, and Baumann, 1988). Emery (1996) suggests using story guides in which the story events are outlined in one column and different characters' perspectives are listed in subsequent columns. This assists the students in seeing how different characters react to different events in the story. Using "why" questions about the characters during discussions (e.g., Why did the characters act that way? Why did the characters feel that way?) also promotes comprehension.

Paraphrasing Strategy

Getting the main idea(s), paraphrasing, and/or summarizing when reading expository materials are important skills, particularly in content area subjects such as science and social studies. The paraphrasing strategy, developed and validated at Kansas University Center for Research on Learning (Schumaker et al., 1993), instructs students in recalling the main ideas and specific facts of materials they read.

CLASSROOM Applications

Paraphrasing Strategy

PROCEDURES: To teach the strategy, you would use the strategy intervention model presented in Chapter 2. The steps in the strategy that the students learn are as follows:

1. *Read a paragraph.* As you silently read, think about what the words mean.

2. *Ask yourself, "What were the main ideas and details of this paragraph?"* This question helps you to think about what you just read. To help you, you may need to look quickly back over the paragraph and find the main idea and the details that are related to the main idea.

3. *Put the main idea and details in your own words.* When you put the information into your own words, it helps you to remember the information. Try to give at least two details related to the main idea.

The acronym for the steps in the strategy is RAP. (Paraphrasing is like rapping or talking to yourself.) Students are also given the following two rules for finding the main idea:

1. Look for it in the first sentence of the paragraph.
2. Look for repetitions of the same word or words in the whole paragraph (Schumaker et al., 1993).

The criteria that are used in generating a paraphrase are that it (1) must contain a complete thought and have a subject and a verb; (2) must be accurate; (3) must make sense; (4) must contain useful information; (5) must be in one's own words; and (6) must have one general statement per paragraph (Schumaker et al., 1993). Specifics for teaching the strategy, including a scripted lesson, cue cards for learning and generalizing the strategy, record and worksheets, and suggested materials for practicing the strategy, are presented in the instructors' guide, *The Paraphrasing Strategy*

(*Learning Strategies Curriculum*) (Schumaker et al., 1993).

COMMENTS: Students with learning disabilities who learned and used the paraphrasing strategy increased their ability to answer comprehension questions about materials written at their grade level from 48 percent to 84 percent (Schumaker et al., 1993). This strategy provides an example of how metacognitive skills can be taught to students. Although the research was conducted with high school students, we have used the strategy with upper-elementary students and have found it successful.

When using this strategy, students orally repeat the paraphrases into a tape recorder rather than write them. This approach seems particularly advantageous for students with learning and behavior problems, since many of them also experience writing problems. However, once students have mastered the skill, it may be helpful for them to write their paraphrases. Students can then use the paraphrases as an overview to integrate the information across the entire passage.

We have had students put their paraphrases for each paragraph or section on sticky notes so that they can then arrange the notes to make a summary of the whole reading selection. You and the students may also want to vary the size of the unit that the students paraphrase. For example, for some books, it may work better to paraphrase each section or subsection rather than each paragraph.

Summarization Strategies

Summarization also requires students to generate the main idea and important details from a text. On the basis of analyses of informational or expository texts, Brown and Day (1983) generated five rules for writing summaries:

1. Delete irrelevant or trivial information.
2. Delete redundant information.
3. Select topic sentences.
4. Substitute a superordinate term or event for a list of terms or actions.
5. Invent topic sentences when the author has not provided any.

Gajria and Salvia (1992) used these rules to teach sixth- through ninth-grade students with learning disabilities how to summarize expository passages. They employed many of the principles of cognitive strategy instruction, including explicit explanation of the rules, modeling of the strategy,

guided practice in controlled materials, monitoring with corrective feedback, independent practice, and teaching each rule to criterion (see Chapter 6).

CLASSROOM Applications

Summarization Strategy

PROCEDURES: To teach the summarization strategy, use sets of short paragraphs, each set highlighting a different rule. In this way, the rules can be explained, modeled, and practiced individually. Then apply the rules to informational passages. Gajria and Salvia (1992) adapted passages from the *Timed Reading Series* (Spargo, Williston, and Browning, 1980). As the students learn the rules and their application, give the students more responsibility for practicing the rules and checking that each rule has been applied. Figure 8.16 presents a checklist that students can use to judge the quality of their summaries and teachers can use to monitor student progress.

COMMENTS: When Gajria and Salvia (1992) taught the summarization strategy to 15 students with learning disabilities, they found that at the end of instruction (ranging from 6.5 to 11 hours), the students in the trained group performed significantly better than an untrained control group of students with learning disabilities on main idea and inference questions and factual questions, better than a group of average-achieving students on main idea and inference questions, and similarly to the average-achieving group on factual questions. Students who participated in the strategy instruction also generalized these skills, as demonstrated by improved performance on a reading test.

Malone and Mastropieri (1992) taught middle school students with learning disabilities how to summarize and self-question using two questions:

1. Who or what is the passage about?
2. What is happening (to them)?

Using principles of direct instruction and explicit teaching of the summarization and self-questioning, they found that these middle school students outperformed students who had received traditional comprehension instruction on recall of the passage content and that the students could generalize the strategy to new texts.

FIGURE 8.16

Student Checklist for Monitoring Summaries

How Good Is That Summary?

Student: _____   Date: _____

Title: _____

Pages: _____

Summary:

_____

_____

_____

Rating: 3 = Clear, Concise Summary

2 = Somewhat Clear, Concise Summary

1 = Several Sentences That Do Not Accurately Summarize Information

0 = Not Completed

_____   Does the summary state the **main idea**?

_____   Is the **main idea** stated first?

_____   Does the summary give *only* **the most important information**?

_____   Is the summary brief with **unimportant and redundant information** deleted?

_____   Is the summary written well and clear?

Using Multicomponent Cognitive Strategy Instruction to Teach Comprehension

So far, we have discussed techniques to facilitate the use of specific comprehension skills such as activating prior knowledge, predicting, asking and answering questions, getting the main idea, and summarizing the text. Students with learning and behavior problems often have difficulty with a number of these skills. For example, even when Shamika, an eighth-grade student with decoding and reading comprehension problems, is reading text that is easy for her to decode (about fifth-grade level), she still has difficulty understanding what she reads. Her approach to reading comprehension is to "just begin reading and read to the end." She reads quickly and, when finished, can answer detailed questions about what she has read if the information is provided in the text. If she is not sure about an idea, Shamika reports, "I usually just skip it." She has difficulty generating a summary and reports that she does not make predictions during reading and does not think about how what she is reading relates to what she already knows. For students like Shamika, who have several comprehension skills that need attention, research would suggest that it is more efficient and

effective to teach a multicomponent strategy that includes several robust strategies such as predicting, questioning, and summarizing than to teach individual strategies (National Reading Panel, 2000; RAND Reading Study Group, 2002; Swanson, 1999b). This section discusses one such multicomponent approach to teaching comprehension—reciprocal teaching (Palincsar and Brown, 1984, 1986; see Rosenshine and Meister, 1994, for a review)—and two adaptations of reciprocal teaching: collaborative strategic reading (CSR; Klingner and Vaughn, 1996; Vaughn and Klingner, 1999) and POSSE (Englert and Mariage, 1991).

All three are built on ideas associated with metacognition, schema theory, and the sociocultural theory of learning. From metacognition comes the strong emphasis on comprehension monitoring (e.g., checking to determine whether understanding is adequate, given the purposes for reading). From schema theory, these approaches incorporate activities that encourage students to activate and use relevant background knowledge. From sociocultural theory comes scaffolded instruction in which the teacher and students take turns assuming the leader role.

These instructional techniques build on the idea that successful comprehension and learning are based on six activities:

1. Clarifying the purpose of reading (i.e., understanding the task demands, both explicit and implicit)
2. Activating relevant background knowledge
3. Allocating attention to the major content at the expense of trivia
4. Evaluating content for internal consistency and compatibility with prior knowledge and common sense
5. Monitoring ongoing activities to determine whether comprehension is occurring by engaging in such activities as periodic review and self-questioning
6. Drawing and testing inferences including interpretations, predictions, and conclusions (Brown, Palincsar, and Armbruster, 1984)

Although all three approaches build on these activities, reciprocal teaching was developed first; CSR and POSSE further elaborate on reciprocal teaching.

Reciprocal Teaching

In the initial research on reciprocal teaching, Palincsar and Brown (Palincsar, 1982; Palincsar and Brown, 1984) chose four comprehension strategies to teach seventh-grade students who had average decoding skills but had significant difficulty with comprehension. The four strategies were as follows:

1. Predicting
2. Clarifying
3. Questioning
4. Summarizing

They used an interactive mode of teaching that emphasized modeling, feedback, and scaffolded instruction.

CLASSROOM Applications

Reciprocal Teaching

PROCEDURES: The procedure used to teach the four strategies was *reciprocal teaching*, a technique in which the teacher and students took turns leading a dialogue that covered sections of the text. The procedure is similar to, but more extensive than, the reciprocal questioning used in the ReQuest procedure (Manzo and Manzo, 1969, 1993), discussed earlier in the section on questioning. Palincsar and Brown (1984) described the teaching procedure as follows:

> The basic procedure was that an adult teacher, working individually with a seventh-grade poor reader, assigned a segment of the passage to be read and either indicated that it was her turn to be the teacher or assigned the student to teach the segment. The adult teacher and the student then read the assigned segment. After reading the text, the teacher (student or adult) for that segment asked a question that a teacher or test might ask on the segment, summarized the content, discussed and clarified any difficulties, and finally made a prediction about future content. All of these activities were embedded in as natural a dialogue as possible, with the teacher and student giving feedback to each other. (Palincsar and Brown, 1984, pp. 124–125)

The teacher initially modeled the leader role, and as the students assumed the role, the teacher provided feedback by using the following sequence:

1. *Modeling.* "A question I would have asked would be . . ."
2. *Prompting.* "What question do you think might be on a test?"
3. *Instruction.* "Remember, a summary is a short version—it doesn't include details."
4. *Modifying the activity.* "If you can't think of a question right now, go ahead and summarize, and then see if you can think of one."
5. *Praise.* "That was a clear question, because I knew what you wanted." "Excellent prediction—let's see if you're right."
6. *Corrective feedback.* "That was interesting information. It was information I would call a detail. Can you find the most important information?"

Palincsar (1988) suggests that to introduce reciprocal teaching, it is logical to start with a discussion about why text may be difficult to understand, why it is important to have a strategic approach to reading and studying, and how reciprocal teaching will help students understand and monitor their understanding. Students are given an overall description emphasizing the use of interactive dialogues or discussions and of a rotating leader. To ensure a level of competency, each strategy is introduced individually and in a functional manner (e.g., summarize a television show or movie), and opportunities are provided for the students to practice using the strategy. Palincsar (1988) provides a number of suggestions for teaching each comprehension strategy.

Predicting

- Begin a new passage by having students predict on the basis of the title.

- Encourage students to share information they already know about the topic.
- Refer to, and interweave the text with, their predictions and background knowledge as you read.
- Use headings to help students make predictions.
- Use other opportunities to predict, such as when the author asks questions or gives information about what will be covered next.
- Use predictions in an opportunistic and flexible manner.

Questioning
- Encourage students to ask teacherlike questions.
- Fill-in-the-blank questions should be discouraged.
- If the students cannot think of a question, have the students summarize first.
- Provide prompts if needed (e.g., identify the topic, provide a question word).

Summarizing
- Encourage students to identify the main idea and an example of supportive information.
- Encourage students to attempt their summaries without looking at the passage.
- Remind students of the rules for generating summaries:

  Look for a topic sentence.

  Make up a topic sentence if one is not available.

  Give a name to a list of items.

  Delete what is unimportant or redundant.

Clarifying
- Opportunities for clarifying generally occur when referents (e.g., *you, he, it*) are unclear; difficult or unfamiliar vocabulary is presented; text is disorganized or the information is incomplete; or unusual, idiomatic, or metaphorical expressions are used.
- Clarifying will not always be necessary.
- It may be helpful if students are asked to point out something that may be unclear to a younger student.

COMMENTS: Palincsar and Brown studied the effectiveness of reciprocal teaching with poorly comprehending seventh-grade students who were taught individually or in groups of four to seven students (Brown, Palincsar, and Armbruster, 1984; Palincsar, 1986; Palincsar and Brown,

1984). They found the effects of this instruction to be substantial, reliable, durable over time, and generalizable to classroom settings. Even substantial improvements in standardized reading comprehension scores were reported. Lovett and her colleagues (1996) found that reciprocal teaching resulted in significant improvements in the comprehension skills of seventh- and eighth-grade students with reading disabilities compared to control students. Like Palincsar and Brown (1984), they also found that reciprocal teaching transferred to new texts. Lederer (2000) found that reciprocal teaching improved the ability of fourth through sixth graders with learning disabilities to compose summaries of what they read but not their ability to answer comprehension questions. When three student teachers used reciprocal teaching, the teachers reported that "once they got started, there were two specific trouble spots: teaching the clarification and question-generating strategies and bridging the transition from teacher to students' control" (Speece, MacDonald, Kilsheimer, and Krist, 1997, p. 186). They reported that marking children's copies of the text with cue pictures, implementing a reward system to maintain focus, and selecting interesting and challenging literature were important for student success.

In addition, reciprocal teaching is effective with a wide range of students: middle school ELLs with learning disabilities, including low decoders (Klingner and Vaughn, 1996; Vaughn and Klingner, 2004); high school students in remedial classes (Alfassi, 1998); average and above-average readers at various grade levels (Rosenshine and Meister, 1994); fourth graders (Lysynchuk, Pressley, and Vye, 1990); and fifth graders (King and Parent Johnson, 1999).

Collaborative Strategic Reading

Collaborative strategic reading (CSR) borrows ideas from a multicomponent strategy, reciprocal teaching, established by Palincsar and colleagues but elaborates on its use by focusing on expository text, specifying use of strategies, engaging students in pairs or cooperative groups, and teaching students to record what they are learning through learning (Klingner et al., 2007; Klingner, Vaughn, and Schumm, 1998; Vaughn, Klingner, and Schumm, 1996). This approach uses cooperative learning in diverse classrooms to help students read content area materials more efficiently and effectively and provides materials for teacher implementation (Klingner and Vaughn, 1998, 1999a, 1999b, 2000; Klingner, Vaughn, Dimino, Schumm, and Bryant, 2001).

CLASSROOM Applications

Collaborative Strategic Reading

PROCEDURES: As with reciprocal teaching, students learn four strategies: Preview (i.e., brainstorming and predicting), Click and Clunk (i.e., comprehension monitoring and clarifying), Get the Gist (i.e., summarization), and Wrap-Up (i.e., self-questioning and summarization). Preview is used before reading, and Wrap-Up after reading the entire text.

Previewing

The goals of previewing are for students to learn as much about the passage as they can in two to three minutes, activate their background knowledge about the topic, make predictions about what they will read, and pique their interest in the topic to foster active reading. Using the analogy of a movie preview is a good way to teach previewing. In previewing, students are taught to check out the headings, key words, pictures, tables, graphs, and other key information to identify what they know about the topic and to make predictions. Ms. Royal, who teaches a fifth-grade class that includes a number of students with learning and behavior problems, gives her students 1.5 minutes to write down everything they already know about the topic, 1 minute to share with the group, 1.5 minutes to write down predictions, and 1 minute to share (Klingner and Vaughn, 1998). Figure 8.17 presents the four strategies for CSR with key questions the students can ask as they complete the process.

Click and Clunk

Students "click and clunk" while reading each section of the text. *Clicks* are the portions of the text that make sense, and *clunks* are the portions that aren't clear (e.g., students do not know the meaning of a word). The clicking and clunking strategy is designed to assist students in monitoring their comprehension and to employ fix-up strategies to clarify their understanding. Ms. Royal places the fix-up strategies on clunk cards so that the cooperative groups can use them during reading:

- Reread the sentence and look for ideas that help you to understand the word.
- Reread the sentence leaving out the clunk. What word makes sense?

- Reread the sentences before and after the sentence with the clunk.
- Look for prefixes or suffixes in the word.
- Break the word apart and look for smaller words you know.

Getting the Gist

Students learn to get the gist by reading each section and then asking themselves the following questions:

- Who or what is it about?
- What is most important about the who or what?

The goal is to teach the students to restate in their own words the most important point as a way of making sure they understand what they read (Klingner and Vaughn, 1998). Students are taught that a "good" gist does the following:

- Answers the two questions: Who or what is it about? and What is most important about the who or what?
- Is paraphrased in your own words
- Contains 10 words or fewer (Fuchs et al., 1997)

In teaching how to get the gist, we have used the analogy of a sand sieve to demonstrate that the sand (i.e., details) goes through, and all that is left are the rocks (i.e., the main details that answer the two questions). Using the gists from several students or groups to discuss and construct a "best" gist is another technique that can assist students in understanding how to get the gist or main idea. Students repeat the second and third strategies (Clink and Clunk and Getting the Gist) for each paragraph or section of the passage. Having students keep a CSR learning log such as the one in Figure 8.18 can help them to identify information that will assist them in completing the last strategy: Wrap-Up.

Wrap-Up

In the Wrap-Up step, students formulate questions and answers about the key ideas from the entire passage and discuss what they have learned. The goal is to improve their knowledge, understanding, and memory of what they read (Klingner and Vaughn, 1998). For students with learning and language disabilities, it may be necessary to explicitly teach them to ask questions using "what," "where," "who," "when," "why," and "how." As in reciprocal teaching, students are to think about questions that a teacher might ask. To assist students in generating higher-level questions, it is important to model question stems

FIGURE 8.17

Plan for Collaborative Strategic Reading (CSR)

During Reading

Before Reading

Preview

1. Brainstorm

What do we already know about the topic?

2. Predict

What do we think we will learn about the topic when we read the passages?

Find the clues in the title, headings, pictures, key words.

Click & Clunk

1. Monitor

Were there any parts or words that were hard to understand (clunks)?

2. Fix Up

How can we fix the clunks? Use fix-up strategies:

(a) Reread the sentence and look for key ideas to help you understand the word.

(b) Reread the sentences leaving out the "clunk." What word makes sense?

(c) Reread the sentence before and after the clunk looking for clues.

(d) Look for a prefix or suffix in the word.

(e) Break the word apart and look for smaller words.

After Reading

Wrap-Up

1. Ask questions

What questions would help us check to see whether we understand the most important information in the passage? Can we answer the questions?

2. Review

What did we learn?

Get the Gist

1. Ask questions

(a) What is the most important person, place, or thing?

(b) What is the most important idea about the person, place, or thing?

2. Paraphrase

Answer the questions in 10 words or less.

Source: Adapted from J. K. Klingner and S. Vaughn (1999). Promoting reading comprehension, content learning, and English acquisition through collaborative strategic reading (CSR). *The Reading Teacher, 52,* pp. 738–747.

such as, What do you think would happen if . . . ? How were _____ and _____ the same? How were they different? and Why do you think . . . ? Students can use the gists they have generated for the different sections to think about the most important information in the whole passage.

Cooperative Learning Groups

Once they have developed proficiency in applying the comprehension strategies through teacher-led activities, the students learn to use CSR in peer-led cooperative learning groups of about four or five students. Typical roles that are used during CSR include the following:

FIGURE 8.18

Example of CSR Learning Log

CSR Learning Log

Name: _____

Title: _____   Date: _____

Pages: _____

Preview

What I already know about the topic: _____

_____

What I predict I will learn: _____

_____

Clicks and Clunks

List your clunks and what they mean.

Getting the Gist

Write/tell the gists for the sections you read.

Wrap-Up

What was the most important thing the entire passage was about? _____

_____

Write questions you may have for your classmates. _____

_____

What I learned. _____

_____

- *Leader:* Leads group by saying what to read and what strategy to use next
- *Clunk expert:* Reminds students to use clunk strategies to figure out a difficult word or concept
- *Announcer:* Calls on different members to read and share ideas
- *Encourager:* Watches the group and gives encouragement and feedback
- *Reporter:* During the whole-class wrap-up, reports to class the important ideas learned and favorite questions
- *Timekeeper:* Keeps time and lets the group know when it is time to move on

Students should change roles on a regular basis. After wrapping up in their cooperative groups, a whole-class wrap-up is completed to give the teacher and groups the opportunity to report and to discuss the content.

COMMENTS: Collaborative strategic reading has been used by a number of classroom teachers who have students with learning and behavior problems and English language learners included in their classrooms (Klingner et al., 1998; Klingner and Vaughn, 1996, 2000). For example, seventh- and eighth-grade ELLs with learning disabilities were taught to apply CSR while working on social studies content (Klingner and Vaughn, 1996). Students' reading comprehension scores for the passages they read as well as their scores on standardized tests improved significantly. It has also been a successful practice with upper-elementary and middle school students with reading problems (Bryant, Vaughn, Linan-Thompson, Ugel, Hamff, and Hougen, 2000; Klingner et al., 1998; Klingner, Vaughn, Arguelles, Hughes, and Ahwee, 2003). CSR has also been used through technology with middle and high school students with reading difficulties or disabilities (Kim, 2002; Kim et al., 2003). The computer program Computer-Assisted Collaborative Strategic Reading is designed to provide systematic instruction in comprehension strategies of CSR along with ample practices to apply those strategies. Students' ability to find main ideas and generate comprehension questions improved significantly, and their scores on standardized comprehension tests also improved to a moderate extent (Kim et al., 2003). Overall, the results demonstrate the effectiveness of explicit instruction of cognitive strategy training and comprehension monitoring in improving a range of reading comprehension skills.

POSSE (Predict, Organize, Search, Summarize, Evaluate)

Englert and Mariage (1990, 1991) combined reciprocal teaching and the teaching of expository text structure to develop a strategy called POSSE (Predict, Organize, Search, Summarize, and Evaluate).

CLASSROOM Applications
POSSE

PROCEDURES: In the POSSE process, two of the strategies (predict and organize) were presented before reading and were led by the teacher. The other three strategies (search, summarize, and evaluate) were used during reading and students took turns leading the discussion. The Predict step included having the students brainstorm and preview the text, similar to the procedure in CSR. In the Organize step, students categorized and labeled their ideas from the Predict process and generated a semantic map (see Figure 8.19). This map was then reviewed to help students identify unknown information and set the purpose for learning. During the Summarize step, the group leader began the dialogue by giving the

main idea for the section and then discussing it with the students. When they agreed, it was recorded on the map. The group leader then asked questions to help the group generate supporting details about the main idea that were also recorded on the map. This was completed for each section until a semantic map was generated for the article. The Evaluate step included three reading strategies to further guide the group's discussion: compare, clarify, and predict. First, the students compared the map they generated before reading with the map they generated during reading. Second, the students asked questions to clarify unfamiliar vocabulary and unclear information. Third, the students predicted what the next section would be about. Finally, after reading the entire selection, they reviewed the Prediction and Search/Summarize maps to compare their prior knowledge with what they read and to find out whether their prior concepts were confirmed or disconfirmed by the text.

To facilitate the students' use of the strategy in their discussions about the text, they emphasized the following cues through the use of a cue card:

- Predict
  I predict that . . .
  I'm remembering . . .
- Organize
  I think one category might be . . .
- Search/Summarize
  I think the main idea is . . .
  My question about the main idea is . . .
- Evaluate
  I think we did (did not) predict this main idea
  Are there any clarifications?
  I predict the next part will be about . . .

COMMENTS: Englert and Mariage (1991) taught fourth through sixth graders with learning disabilities to use POSSE during a two-month period. They found that students who learned the strategy recalled significantly more information from the expository texts than did students who read the texts using usual classroom reading and discussion. However, they also noted that the teacher had an effect on how well the students learned the POSSE strategy. In reviewing videos of the discussions during POSSE, they found that one of the keys to success was the teachers' ability to transfer control for completing the steps in the strategy to the students and fade reliance on the POSSE strategy sheet as the students became successful at implementing the POSSE process.

FIGURE 8.19

POSSE Strategy Sheet for an Article on the Bermuda Triangle

POSSE

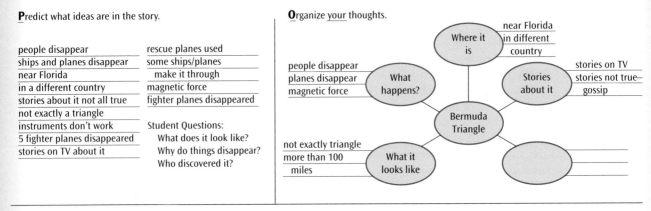

Predict what ideas are in the story.

people disappear	rescue planes used
ships and planes disappear	some ships/planes
near Florida	make it through
in a different country	magnetic force
stories about it not all true	fighter planes disappeared
not exactly a triangle	
instruments don't work	Student Questions:
5 fighter planes disappeared	What does it look like?
stories on TV about it	Why do things disappear?
	Who discovered it?

Organize your thoughts.

Search for the structure.

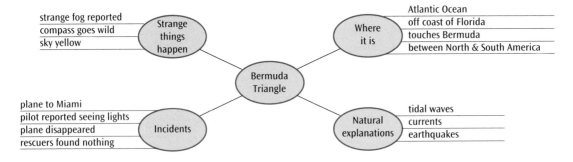

Summarize. Summarize the main idea in your own words. Ask a "teacher" question about the main idea.

Evaluate. Compare. Clarify. Predict.

Source: C. S. Englert and T. V. Mariage (1991). Making students partners in the comprehension process: Organizing the reading POSSE. *Learning Disabilities Quarterly, 14,* p. 129. Reprinted by permission of Council for Learning Disabilities.

Adapting Approaches to Teaching Reading in Inclusive Classrooms

This chapter and Chapter 7 have addressed a number of techniques and strategies that can be used to teach students with learning and behavior problems how to read. These have included strategies for building phonological awareness, knowledge of letter–sound correspondence, and phonics; techniques for teaching word recognition, decoding strategies, and word study; techniques for building reading fluency; and strategies for teaching reading comprehension. In this section, we discuss three lesson frameworks or approaches to teaching reading that are often used in general education elementary classrooms and found in basal reading programs. These are approaches that many students with learning and behavior problems encounter; therefore, practices for adapting them for effective instruction of these students are presented. They include aspects of all the areas of reading we have discussed (e.g., word recognition, fluency, comprehension).

The first approach, the Directed Reading Activity (Betts, 1946), has been a standard framework used for organizing the reading lesson in basal readers. The Directed Reading–Thinking Activity (Stauffer, 1969, 1970) is an adaptation of this framework that encourages more active participation on the part of the reader. Literature-based reading (Cullinan, 1992; Holdaway, 1979) and whole language (Goodman, 1986, 1996) emphasize the use of literature as the major medium for teaching reading. The approaches advocate for integrating reading, writing, speaking, and listening, and focus on reading comprehension and implicit code instruction for teaching word recognition. Each of these three approaches is summarized, and modifications for students with reading difficulties are discussed. For more comprehensive discussions of these approaches, see textbooks on methods for teaching reading in elementary schools (e.g., Graves et al., 2001; Gunning, 2000).

Directed Reading Activity

The Directed Reading Activity (DRA), developed by Betts (1946), is the general framework or lesson plan used in many basal readers (Gunning, 2000; Wilkinson and Anderson, 1995). The DRA is a systematic method for providing instruction in reading, including procedures for teaching word identification as well as comprehension.

CLASSROOM Applications

Directed Reading Activity (DRA)

PROCEDURES: This general method for teaching reading is designed to be used with students reading at any level who are reading the same selection. The following outline presents the stages that are usually found in a DRA (Betts, 1946):

1. Readiness
   a. Developing conceptual background
   b. Creating interest
   c. Introducing new vocabulary
   d. Establishing purposes for reading
2. Directed silent reading
   a. Constructing meaning
   b. Monitoring comprehension
3. Discussion and comprehension check
   a. Revisiting purposes for reading
   b. Clarifying concepts and vocabulary
   c. Correcting difficulties in applying word identification and comprehension strategies
   d. Evaluating student performance
4. Rereading
   a. Clarifying information
   b. Obtaining additional information
   c. Enhancing appreciation and understanding
   d. Providing opportunities for purposeful oral reading

5. Follow-up activities
   a. Extending skill development
   b. Enriching and generalizing

COMMENTS: Although the DRA is suggested as a framework for teaching in basal readers, modifications are necessary for students who experience reading difficulties. For example, in both the earlier and later elementary grades, many of these students need more systematic, explicit instruction in phonics and decoding strategies than are usually provided. Incorporating fluency building through repeated and partner reading will also assist in providing the needed practice required of these students. The PreReading Plan and previewing could be added to the readiness stage of the DRA to activate and build on prior knowledge. Explicit instruction of comprehension and comprehension-monitoring strategies such as self-questioning and summarizing would also support students with reading difficulties. Finally, it is important that reading materials that are used within a DRA framework be at the students' instructional level.

One concern about the DRA is that it is teacher-dominated and therefore may not facilitate the development of independent reading skills. Encouraging the students to set their own purposes for reading, to self-question as they read, and to generate their own questions and follow-up activities is emphasized in the next framework: the Directed Reading–Thinking Activity.

Directed Reading–Thinking Activity (DR–TA)

Stauffer (1969, 1970, 1976) developed the Directed Reading–Thinking Activity (DR–TA) as a framework for teaching reading that stresses students' abilities to read reflectively and to use prediction and preview strategies to set their own purposes for reading (Gunning, 2000). The purpose of the DR–TA is to provide readers with the ability to do the following:

- Determine purposes for reading
- Extract, comprehend, and assimilate information
- Use prediction while reading
- Suspend judgments
- Make decisions based on evidence gained from reading

DR–TA is based on the notion that reading is a thinking process that requires students to relate their own experiences to the author's ideas and thereby construct meaning from the text.

In using this approach, the construction of meaning starts with setting purposes for reading and generating hypotheses about meaning. Constructing meaning from text continues as students acquire more information, confirm or disconfirm hypotheses, and establish new hypotheses. It ends when the hypotheses have been confirmed and the purposes for reading have been met.

Stauffer (1969) describes seven distinguishing features about group DR–TA activities:

1. Students of approximately the same reading level are grouped together.
2. The group size ranges from 2 to 10 students to promote interaction and participation.
3. All students in a group read the same material at the same time. This permits each student to compare and contrast predictions, justifications for answers, and evaluations with those of his or her peers.
4. Purposes for reading are declared by students; students ask questions to become active readers and thinkers.
5. Answers to questions are validated. Proof is found and tested, and the group judges whether the offered proof is trustworthy.
6. Immediate feedback helps develop integrity and a regard for authenticity.
7. The teacher serves as a facilitator or moderator and asks provocative questions that require the students to interpret and make inferences from what they have read.

The DR–TA can be used with reading materials written at any level and with either narrative or expository texts. Stauffer (1969) suggests that primer and preprimer materials that have limited plots will not lend themselves to this procedure.

CLASSROOM Applications

DR–TA

PROCEDURES: Adapt the following procedures in using a DR–TA:

1. After each student receives a copy of the material, direct the students to identify a purpose for reading by studying the title, subtitles, pictures, and other elements, to develop a hypothesis about what the passage is about. Following are two questions you might ask to stimulate hypotheses: What do you think a story with this title might be about? What do you think might happen in this story? Have students share these hypotheses, discussing how they arrived at them. Have students use information from their prior knowledge to substantiate their predictions.

2. Once each student has stated his or her hypothesis, encourage the students to adjust their rate of silent reading to their purpose for reading.

3. Teach the students or remind them of the strategies they can use when they come to a word they cannot identify, such as sounding out the word parts and thinking what makes sense and asking for assistance.

4. Select a logical segment of the passage, and direct the students to read it to themselves to check on their predictions. Be responsible for ensuring that students read for meaning by observing reading performance and helping those who request help with words.

5. When the students have finished reading, have them discuss their predictions. Two target questions to ask are as follows: Were you correct? What do you think now? Have students reread orally the sections of the text that confirm or contradict their hypotheses. Assist the students in determining whether other source materials may be necessary to clarify meaning, and have the students discuss concepts and vocabulary that are critical to the comprehension process.

6. Repeat the procedure (hypothesis setting, silent reading to validate, oral reading to prove, and discussion) with subsequent segments of the text.

7. Once the passage has been completed, use skill activities to teach skill training (Stauffer, 1969). This entails rereading the story, and reexamining selected words, phrases, pictures, and/or diagrams for the purpose of concurrently developing the students' reading–thinking abilities with the other reading-related skills (Tierney and Readence, 2000). These might include word attack skills and concept clarification and development.

The processing involved in a DR–TA is summarized as follows:

1. Pupil actions
   a. Predict (set purposes)
   b. Read (process ideas)
   c. Prove (test answers)
2. Teacher actions
   a. What do you think? (activate thought)
   b. Why do you think so? (agitate thought)
   c. Prove it! (require evidence) (Stauffer, 1969)

Stauffer (1969) suggests that once the students are comfortable with the DR–TA process, they should be encouraged to use an individualized

FIGURE 8.20

Directed Reading–Thinking Activity Individual Prediction Sheet

Name: _____

Passage/Book _____

Pages	*Prediction*	*Outcome*

Summary _____

_____

DR–TA. In other words, students should use this systematic, predictive process as they read individually. Figure 8.20 presents a sample worksheet that students may use to guide them as they complete individual DR–TAs.

COMMENTS: The DR–TA provides teachers with a procedure for teaching students to become active thinkers as they read. This is particularly relevant for students with learning and behavior problems, since it requires that students assume responsibility for the reading–learning process. Dixon and Nessel (1992) present strategies for using the DR–TA with second language learners. In comparison to the DRA, in which the teacher sets the purpose for reading and preteaches vocabulary, the DR–TA encourages the students to set their own purposes and decide which vocabulary warrants further development.

Widomski (1983) suggests incorporating DR–TA with semantic mapping, thereby enabling students to construct a visual representation on which to test their predictions in much the same way that the predictions are tested by the students in POSSE, presented earlier.

Two cautions, however, seem relevant to the DR–TA. First, it requires a great deal of self-directiveness on the part of the students, particularly when they use the individualized DR–TA. For students with learning and behavior problems, teachers will need to scaffold instruction so that there is a systematic movement from teacher modeling and control to student control. Second, there is little or no emphasis on teaching word decoding and word identification or fluency-building skills in a direct or systematic manner. Like DRA, providing direct instruction in these areas and having students work in instructional-level materials will be important modifications to make in inclusive classes.

Literature-Based Reading and Whole Language

Literature-based reading and the whole-language philosophy of reading and learning are based on the assumption that students will learn to read by having multiple opportunities to engage in listening, talking about, reading, and writing about interesting and engaging literature. This orientation is reflected in basal reading programs that include literature anthologies and patterned language books (for early readers) and the wide use of children's literature as core reading materials for instruction. Whole language and, to a varying degree, literature-based reading are derived from a more student-centered, sociolinguistic model of teaching and learning and from a psycholinguistic model of reading as articulated by Goodman (1984, 1986, 1996). The philosophy is evident in the following statements:

> A "psycholinguistic approach" to reading would be the very antithesis of a set of instructional materials. . . . The child learning to read seems to need the opportunity to examine a large sample of language, to generate hypotheses about the regularity underlying it, and to test and modify these hypotheses on the basis of feedback that is appropriate to the unspoken rules that he happens to be testing. (Smith and Goodman, 1971, pp. 179–180)

> In this method there are no prereading skills, no formalizing reading readiness. Instead, learning is expected to progress *from whole to part*, from general to specific, from familiar to unfamiliar, from vague to precise, from gross to fine, from highly contextualized to more abstract. Children are expected to read, first, familiar meaningful wholes—easily predictable materials that draw on concepts and experiences they already have. These may be signs, cereal boxes, or books. . . . By carefully building on what children already know, we assure their readiness. (Goodman and Goodman, 1982, p. 127)

Literature-based programs and whole language emphasize that language be treated as a whole, children use language in ways that relate to their lives and cultures, and strategies for reading be taught within the context of meaningful activities and texts (Baumann, Hooten, and White, 1999; Freppon and Dahl, 1998; Weaver, 1998).

CLASSROOM Applications

Literature-Based Reading and Whole Language

PROCEDURES: The focal points of whole-language and literature-based reading programs center on involving students in lots of reading and writing, creating an environment that accepts and encourages risk taking, and maintaining a focus on meaning (Goodman, 1986, 1996; Weaver, 1990).

In literature-based or whole-language classrooms, the curriculum is often organized around themes and units that integrate oral language, reading, and writing. With the focus on meaning, phonics and word recognition skills are generally not taught in isolation but within the context of connected text, when children are writing during writer's workshop, and according to the the students' needs (Dahl and Scharer, 2000; Dahl, Scharer, Lawson, and Grogan, 1999; Stahl, Pagnucco, and Suttles, 1996). Strategies for comprehension are taught within the context of books; teachers and students discuss not only the content but also the processes that are used in constructing meaning from text (Goodman, Watson, and Burke, 1996; Jewell and Pratt, 1999). Literature circles, literature discussion groups, book clubs, and reader response journals are techniques that have been used to structure discussions about books and to promote critical reading.

Literature circles are often used to structure discussions about books (Short, 1997; Short and Harste, with Burke, 1995). Literature circles facilitate literacy by providing opportunities for students to explore ideas about the content and craft of literacy and to think critically and deeply about what they read. In literature circles, a teacher initially introduces several books for which there are multiple copies, and the group decides which book to read. Students read the book or, if it is too long, chapters or smaller segments of the book, and then meet in the literature circle to discuss the book. The first day the discussion starts with a broad focus (e.g., What was the story about?). In the discussion, the teacher listens to what the students highlight as interesting or challenging and leads the students to talk about the outstanding characteristics of the book (e.g., character development, plot development, use of dialogue). As the discussions progress across several meetings, the teacher models and guides the students in making connections between the book they read and their personal experiences and other literature they have read or written (Bos, 1991; Martinez-Roldain and López-Robertson, 2000; Raphael, 2000). Apply the Concept 8.7 presents a list of sample questions that foster discussion and understanding of literature both from the reader's and author's perspectives. The questions focus on character development, authenticity, mood, voice, writing style and genre, text structure, comparison across literature, and tying reader to author. At the end of each discussion, the group decides what they want to discuss the next time. They prepare for the next discussion by rereading sections of the book or related literature. Students also keep notes about the discussion and their reading in literature logs (Atwell, 1984).

Apply the Concept 8.7

Discussion Questions to Foster Understanding of Reading and Writing

- Is the story like any other story you have heard, read, or watched? How are they alike? (comparisons across literature)
- What questions would you ask if the author were here? How might the author answer these? (tying reader to author)
- Who are the main characters of the story? What kind of people are they? How does the author let you know? (character development)
- Do the characters change during the story? How do they change? What changes them? Do the changes seem believable? (character development)
- How does the author make the story seem possible? (authenticity)

- Does the language used in the story seem real for the character? (authenticity)
- Did you notice any natural breaks in the book where it seemed like a good place to stop? (text structure)
- Think of a different ending or beginning to the story. How would the rest of the story have to change to have the different ending or beginning work? (text structure)
- Are there any signs or clues that the author gives you to help you with the break? If so, what are they? (writing style and genre)
- Does the story create a specific feeling or mood? What words does

the author use to create the mood? (mood)
- Is there anything unique about this author's style? If so, what? (writing style)
- What does the author do to help you feel like you are part of the story? (writing style)
- Who is the teller or narrator of the story? How would the story change if the narrator were someone different? (voice)

Source: Adapted from G. D. Sloan, *The Child as Critic,* 2nd ed. (New York: Teachers College Press, 1984); and K. Vandergrift, *Child and Story* (New York: Neal-Schuman, 1980).

In literature-based and whole-language classrooms, writing is reciprocally tied to reading so that the students have opportunities to work in the roles of both reader and author. Process writing (see Chapter 9) and conferencing about books and written pieces allow the teacher to facilitate the students' understanding of the processes associated with language learning.

Literature for reading and topics for writing are often self-selected, giving the students the opportunity to explore topics of interest to them. Students also learn about the authors and illustrators of the books they are reading. With this approach, librarians, annotated bibliographies of children's literature, and teacher resource books are important tools for teaching.

COMMENTS: Using literature-based reading programs and whole language emphasizes the purposeful reading, writing, discussion, and analyzing of literature in learning to read, critically analyze, and appreciate literature. These approaches are student-oriented, and the social nature of activities such as literature circles fits well with the sociocultural theory of learning and teaching (see Chapter 2). Research investigating the use of literature-based programs and whole language,

primarily using case studies, indicates that there is some evidence that such approaches facilitate reading and positive attitudes toward reading by students with learning and behavior problems (e.g., Allen, Michalove, Shockley, and West, 1991; Mills, O'Keefe, and Stephens, 1992; Morrow, 1992; Stires, 1991). However, there is substantial evidence that students with learning and behavior problems need more direct and intensive instruction than is usually associated with these approaches (National Reading Panel, 2000; Snow et al., 1998; Swanson, 1999b).

What kinds of modifications might be helpful for students with reading problems? For Jesse, a second-grade student who was struggling with learning to read, explicitly teaching sound–symbol relationships and word patterns (e.g., *-ight, -ate*) and how to segment and blend the sounds and patterns to decode the words assisted him. Providing ample opportunities to read the words using word sorts and word games and simple decodable books allowed Jesse to practice the relationships and patterns he was learning. Benjamin, a fourth grader with learning disabilities, was having particular difficulty finding the main idea and summarizing what he had read, in both reading and social studies. Ms. Lin, his resource special education teacher, supported him by teaching him how to use paraphrasing strategy as part of his instruction in the resource room. Because several students with learning disabilities or difficulties similar to Benjamin's were in Mr. Brown's fourth-grade class, Ms. Lin and Mr. Brown cotaught social studies so that they could teach the entire class how to use collaborative strategic reading (see Chapter 5 for information on coteaching). In both cases, the adaptations that were provided used teaching strategies that emphasized explicit teaching of skills and strategies using modeling, cueing, guided and independent practice, corrective feedback, and progress monitoring as would be suggested by research (Mastropieri and Scruggs, 1997; Pressley and Rankin, 1994; Swanson, 1999a).

INSTRUCTIONAL ACTIVITIES

This section provides instructional activities that are related to reading comprehension and fluency. Some of the activities teach new skills; others are best suited for practice and reinforcement of already acquired skills. For each activity, the objective, materials, and teaching procedures are described.

▶ Choral Reading

Objective: To provide students with opportunities to practice reading aloud rapidly, accurately, and expressly with the teacher

Grades: Kindergarten through primary

Materials: Reading passages

Teaching Procedures:
1. Provide each student with a copy of the reading passage.
2. Model fluent reading of the passage by reading aloud. The teacher reads the passage accurately with prosody and sets the pace.
3. Students read along with the teacher the second time the passage is read. This strategy can be implemented individually, in whole groups, or in small groups.

Source: Adapted from University of Texas Center for Reading and Language Arts (2003b).

▶ Partner Reading

Objective: To improve students' reading accuracy and rate

Grades: Elementary through secondary

Materials: Reading passages, graph paper, colored pencils, timer for the teacher

Teaching Procedures:
1. Pair students, using the following procedure: (1) Rank the students according to reading ability, (2) split the list in half, (3) pair the top-ranked student in the higher-performing half (partner 1) with the top-ranked student in the lower-performing half (partner 2) and so forth.
2. Give each pair two copies of the reading passage at the instructional level of the less fluent student. (Instructional reading level means that the reader is able to decode about 90 percent of the words correctly.)
3. Remind students of the procedures for partner reading: (1) read for four minutes each; (2) correct errors (omission/addition of words, stopping more than three seconds, etc.); (3) do the best one-minute reading (while timed); (4) calculate the fluency rate; and (5) graph the fluency rate.
4. Have partner 1 model fluent reading for four minutes while partner 2 follows along and identifies and corrects errors. Partner 2 should use the following procedure for error correction:
   a. Say, "Sound it out."
   b. Wait 4 seconds.
   c. If the partner figures out the word, say, "Good. Now reread the sentence."
   d. If the partner doesn't figure out the word, say, "That word is ____. What word?" Wait for the partner to respond. Say, "Good. Now reread the sentence."
5. Have the students reread the passage for one minute (best reading), with partner 1 reading first. Partner 2 follows along, marks errors, and marks the last word read at the one-minute mark.
6. Have the students calculate their fluency during the one-minute best reading using words correct per minute (WCPM). This is found by subtracting the number of errors from the total number of words read: (Total − errors = fluency).

7. Have the students graph their fluency using colored pencils and graph paper, as shown in Figure 8.21.

▶Phrase Card Reading

Objective: To help students improve their reading rate and accuracy

Grades: Elementary through intermediate

Materials: Reading passages, index cards, pens

Teaching Procedures:
1. Pair students, using the procedure described in "Partner Reading."
2. Give each pair two copies of the reading passage at the instructional level of the less fluent student.
3. Have each pair highlight phrases from the passage that include difficult words.
4. Have each pair write these phrases on index cards.
5. Have the more fluent reader in each pair read the phrases from the cards first.
6. Then have the less fluent reader in each pair read the same phrases from the cards. While the less fluent reader reads the phrases, the fluent reader identifies and corrects errors, if any.

Source: Adapted from University of Texas Center for Reading and Language Arts (2002).

▶Tape-Assisted Reading

Objective: To help students improve their reading rate and accuracy

Grades: Elementary through secondary

Materials: Reading passages, tape recorder, blank tapes

Teaching Procedures:
1. Before the instruction, select a reading passage at each student's instructional or independent reading level. Record the passage. While recording, read with appropriate rate, accuracy, and expression.
2. Tell the students to listen to the passage on tape and to follow along by running their fingers under the line of the print. (*Note:* Students should not point to each word.)
3. Have the students read the passage aloud three times along with the tape.

FIGURE 8.21

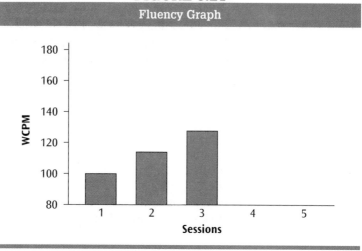

Source: Adapted from University of Texas Center for Reading and Language Arts (2001a). Reprinted by permission.

4. Have the students read the passage aloud along with the tape while you listen to identify and correct errors.
5. Have the students read the passage aloud without listening to the tape for one minute.
6. Have the students calculate fluency rate and graph fluency rate (using the procedure described in "Partner Reading").

Source: Adapted from University of Texas Center for Reading and Language Arts (2002).

▶Chunk Reading

Objective: To help students improve their reading accuracy and rate while reading phrases

Grades: Elementary

Materials: Reading passages, graph paper, colored pencils, timer for the teacher

Teaching Procedures:
1. Before the instruction, select a reading passage at an instructional level that is appropriate for the less fluent students. Place slash marks between chunks (i.e., phrases) to mark two- to five-word sentence segments and prepositional phrases in each passage.
2. Pair students using the procedure described in "Partner Reading."
3. Give each pair two copies of the reading passages with chunking marks.
4. Tell the students that connected text is divided into meaningful phrases and that

paying attention to these phrases while reading will enhance their fluency and comprehension.

5. Tell the students to pause briefly between phrases, exactly as marked. No pauses should be made except at slash marks.

6. Remind students of the procedure for partner reading: (1) four-minute reading for each, (2) one-minute best reading for each, (3) calculating fluency, and (4) graphing.

7. Have partner 1 model fluent reading while partner 2 follows along. Partner 1 emphasizes chunking phrases together for meaning. For instance, read the sentence "One day last week my sister and I drove to the lake" like this: "One day last week / my sister and I / drove to the lake." (A slash indicates a pause.) Then partner 2 reads the passage while partner 1 follows along.

8. Tell the students to reread the passage for one minute (best reading), with partner 1 reading first. While partner 1 reads, partner 2 follows along, marks errors, and marks the last word read at the one-minute mark.

9. Ask the students to calculate the fluency using WCPM (see the procedures in "Partner Reading") and to graph their fluency on the graph paper with colored pencils.

Source: Adapted from University of Texas Center for Reading and Language Arts (2001a).

▶Dramatic Reading

Objective: To help students improve their reading fluency

Grades: Elementary through secondary

Materials: Copies of a play for each student

Teaching Procedures:

1. Make groups of four, consisting of two more fluent readers and two less fluent readers.

2. Give a copy of the play to each student, and assign each student a role.

3. Tell students that they will practice the play with other group members and will put on the play for the class.

4. Set a performance day and time.

5. Instruct students to practice the play in their group. Have each student practice reading his or her lines while the other group members listen and provide feedback.

6. Next, have students work together to read their parts as if in a play. Encourage students to provide feedback to each other.

7. On the performance day, have each group put on their play for the class.

Source: Adapted from University of Texas Center for Reading and Language Arts (2002).

▶Critiquing Oral Reading

Objective: To provide students with opportunities to critique their oral reading

Grades: Primary and intermediate

Materials: Reading passages, tape recorder, a blank tape for each student labeled with the student's name

Teaching Procedures:

1. Explain that the purpose of the activity is to give the students an opportunity to listen to how they read.

2. Let the students know that they are to listen for things they do well and things they want to improve.

3. Model the process by practicing, recording, listening, and critiquing a passage you read.

4. Before the students read into the tape recorder, have them practice the segment. Each student should practice and then read and record a passage of about 100 to 500 words.

5. After the students record, they should listen to their tapes and finish writing the following statements:

   When I read orally, I do a really good job of _____.

   One thing I could do better when I read out loud is _____.

6. Listen to and discuss each tape, and then ask the students to critique each presentation. Have the students record their oral reading every three to six weeks so that they can compare and hear how they are improving.

Adaptations: Each student can record two passages: one that has been practiced and one that is unpracticed.

▶Previewing

Objective: To help students activate their prior knowledge and make predictions about what they are going to learn from the passage

Grades: Elementary through secondary

Materials: Expository reading passage, copies of a preview log (see Figure 8.22)

FIGURE 8.22

Preview Log

Topic:

What do I already know about the topic?

How does this topic relate to previous lessons?

Key vocabulary and definitions

1. _____ : _____
2. _____ : _____
3. _____ : _____

Predictions

By looking at the   ☐ title   ☐ headings   ☐ pictures   ☐ others: _____
I think that I am going to learn about . . .

By looking at the   ☐ title   ☐ headings   ☐ pictures   ☐ others: _____
I think that I am going to learn about . . .

Teaching Procedures:

1. Pass out a preview log to each student.
2. Introduce the topic of the lesson, and ask students to record it at the top of their preview logs.
3. Divide the class into small groups.
4. Give each group two minutes to brainstorm what they already know about the topic, and ask them to record their ideas in their preview logs along with how this topic relates to previous lessons.
5. Ask several groups to share their brainstorming ideas.
6. Introduce and discuss three key vocabulary words. Have students record the words along with the definition in their preview logs.
7. Pass out a reading passage to each student.
8. Ask the students to scan the passage, looking for clues or physical features, such as the title, subtitle, headings, subheadings, bolded words, graphics, and/or pictures, which could be used to make predictions about the passage.
9. Ask each group to make two predictions about what they think they are going to learn from the passage. Have students record their predictions in their preview logs.
10. Ask several groups to share their predictions.

11. After the lesson, discuss and check students' predictions to see how close their predictions were to what they actually learned from the text.

Source: Adapted from University of Texas Center for Reading and Language Arts (2001a).

▶ Getting the Gist

Objective: To help students identify the main idea of a paragraph

Grades: Elementary through secondary

Materials: Expository reading passage, copies of a gist log (see Figure 8.23)

Teaching Procedures:

1. Pass out a reading passage and a gist log to each student.
2. Explain to students that a gist statement represents the main idea of a paragraph. The main idea is the most important information in a paragraph.
3. Tell students that there are three steps to getting the gist: (1) naming the who or what the paragraph is mostly about, (2) telling the most important information about the who or

FIGURE 8.23

Gist Log

1. Who or what is the paragraph mostly about?

2. What is the most important information about the who or what?

(Use this information to develop the gist statement.)

3. Write a gist of 10 words or less in a complete sentence.

---

what, and (3) writing a complete sentence about the gist in 10 words or less.

4. Pair the students, and have them take turns reading with a partner.
5. After each paragraph, each pair identifies who or what the paragraph is mostly about.
6. Next, each pair identifies the most important information about the who or what.
7. Then each pair puts the two pieces of information together in a complete sentence of 10 words or less.
8. After all pairs complete getting the gist statements, call on several pairs to share their statements with others.

Source: Adapted from Klingner, Vaughn, Dimino, Schumm, and Bryant (2001).

▶Self-Monitoring

Objective: To help students monitor their understanding

Grades: Secondary

Materials: Two different triple-spaced reading passages, two transparencies of both passages, copies of a monitoring symbol cue card, overhead projector, marker

Monitoring Symbol Cue Card

✓	= Got it!
?	= What Does This Mean?
MBI	= Must Be Important
RR	= Reread
DW	= Difficult Word
LG	= Look at Graphs

Teaching Procedures:

1. Introduce monitoring symbols, and tell students that the use of the symbols will help them to monitor their understanding
2. Present and describe each symbol.
3. Pass out the first triple-spaced passage.
4. Place the first passage on the overhead projector, and model how to use the symbols while reading.
5. Read the passage aloud, and insert the symbols where appropriate to mirror your self-monitoring strategies. Tell why you insert the symbols.
6. Pass out the second reading passage and a monitoring symbol cue card to each student.
7. Ask the students to insert monitoring symbols as they read.
8. Circulate around the class, and provide additional support if necessary.
9. After the students finish the second passage, place the second passage on the overhead projector. Call on several students to share which symbols they used and why.
10. Answer any questions about the passage or difficult words.

Adaptations: This instructional activity can be used with a "click and clunk" activity, which is described in Chapter 11. A teacher can ask students to use the "click and clunk" strategy when they come across difficult words.

Source: Adapted from University of Texas Center for Reading and Language Arts (2002).

▶Generating Questions

Objective: To help students generate questions about important information after reading

Grades: Elementary through secondary

Materials: Two different reading passages, overhead projector, marker, transparency

Teaching Procedures:

1. Pass out the first reading passage to each student.
2. Explain to students that there are three types of questions: "right there" questions (the answer to the question is right in the text), "think and search" questions (the answer to the question is in the text, but students have to read the text and to compose the answer themselves based on what they have read), and "on my own" questions (the answer to the question is not in the text, and students have to integrate their own previous experiences with what they have learned from the text).
3. Read the entire reading passage aloud.
4. Model how to generate questions about the important information by using the key words *how, who, what, when, where,* and *why.*
5. Pass out the second reading passage to each student.
6. Remind students that there are three types of questions.
7. Pair the students, and have them take turns reading with a partner.
8. After reading the entire passage, have each pair generate at least one question for each type.
9. Monitor the students to make sure that they all properly generate questions.
10. After all pairs have finished generating the questions, call on several pairs to share their questions with others.

Source: Adapted from Klingner et al. (2001).

▶Directed Reading–Thinking Activity (DR–TA)

Objective: To help students make and check predictions before, during, and after reading

Grades: Elementary through secondary

Materials: Reading passage in which a teacher marks several stop points, copies of a DR–TA organizer (see Figure 8.24)

Teaching Procedures:

1. Pass out a reading passage and a DR–TA organizer to each student.
2. Before reading, discuss the topic.
3. Show pictures, graphs, headings, or bolded text in the passage, and ask students what they think the passage topic could be.
4. Call on several students to share their predictions about the passage topic. Discuss with students how to generate the best predictions, and record the predictions on the DR–TA organizer. Have students write predictions on their DR–TA organizers.
5. Have students take turns reading the first part of the passage (before the first stop point).
6. Ask the students to think back about predictions they generated and what evidence is presented to either confirm or disprove their predictions.
7. Ask the students to revise or make new predictions if necessary.
8. Call on several students to share their revised and/or new predictions. Discuss with students how to generate the best predictions, and record the predictions on the DR–TA organizer.

FIGURE 8.24

DR-TA Organizer

Title: _____

Predictions based on the topic:

Predictions based on skimming information such as the title, pictures, etc.:

Predictions after reading the first part of the text: Pages _____ to _____

Predictions after reading the second part of the text: Pages _____ to _____

Predictions after reading the third part of the text: Pages _____ to _____

FIGURE 8.25

Expository Comprehension Cards

Concept or Definition

1. What topic or concept is described? _____

2. What are some of its characteristics? _____

3. What is its function? _____

4. To what category does it belong? _____

5. What are some related ideas or words? _____

6. What are some examples? _____

7. What do you think is the most unusual or memorable characteristic? _____

Cause and Effect

1. What happens? _____

2. What causes it to happen? _____

3. What are the important elements or factors that caused it to happen? _____

4. Will the result always happen this way? Why or why not? _____

5. How can elements or factors change? _____

Compare and Contrast

1. What is being compared and contrasted? _____

2. How are things similar? _____

3. How are they different? _____

4. What are the most important qualities that make them the same or different? _____

5. What conclusions can we make? _____

6. How can the things be classified? _____

Position Statement or Support

1. What is the opinion, hypothesis, theory, or argument? _____

2. Are valid reasons given to accept it? _____

3. Do you agree with the viewpoint, theory, hypothesis presented? Why? Why not? _____

4. What credible evidence and data are presented? _____

Have the students write the predictions on their DR–TA organizers.

9. Repeat the same procedure until the entire passage is read.

10. After finishing the entire passage, ask the students to reflect on their predictions.

11. Call on several students to share their reflections.

Source: Adapted from Blachowicz and Ogle (2001).

▶Expository Text Question Cards

Objective: To teach students to identify different types of expository text structure and to ask comprehension questions appropriate to each text structure while reading text

Grades: Secondary

Materials: Expository reading passages (two different passages for each text structure type), expository comprehension cards (one card set for each text structure type; see Figure 8.25)

Teaching Procedures:

1. Hand out a passage with a concept/definition type to each student.

2. Tell students that the text is the concept/definition type.

3. Provide the students with the card set for the concept/definition type.

4. Model how the students can use the sample questions on the card to ask and answer specific questions about the content.

5. Hand out another passage with the concept/definition type to each student.

6. Have the students take turns reading.

7. During reading, periodically stop the students from reading, and ask several students to use the sample questions on the card to ask and answer specific questions about the content.

8. Use the same procedure for expository reading passages with other text structure types (e.g., cause and effect, compare and contrast).

Source: Adapted from University of Texas Center for Reading and Language Arts (2003a).

▶Using Narrative Comprehension Cards

Objective: To teach students to use narrative comprehension cards while reading text

Grades: Elementary

Materials: Narrative reading passage, narrative comprehension cards (see Figure 8.26), pocket chart

Teaching Procedures: Before the instruction, set narrative comprehension cards on the left side of the pocket chart in the correct order (1 to 15)

1. Hand out a reading passage to each student.
2. Introduce narrative comprehension cards. Explain to students that each card is color-coded. Tell them that green cards are used *before reading,* yellow cards are used *during reading,* and red cards are used *after reading.*
3. Before reading, read the first green card question (card 1) aloud.
4. Call on several students to answer the question. As the first green card question is answered, move the card to the right side of the pocket chart to indicate that the question has been answered.
5. Repeat the same procedure until all green card questions have been answered.
6. Have the students take turns reading.
7. During reading, periodically stop the students from reading, and ask several students to answer the first yellow card question (card 4).
8. As each yellow card question is answered, move the card to the right side of the pocket chart.
9. Repeat the same procedure until all of the yellow card questions have been answered.
10. After reading, ask the students the first red card question.
11. As each red card question is answered, move the card to the right side of the pocket chart.
12. Repeat the same procedure until all red card questions have been answered.

Source: Adapted from University of Texas, Center for Reading and Language Arts (2000a, 2000b).

▶Story Jumble

Objective: To provide students practice in sequencing a story

Grades: Primary and intermediate

Materials: Short stories that have been cut into story parts (e.g., setting, episodes, endings), paragraphs, or sentences; index cards with the segments of the story mounted onto them

Teaching Procedures:
1. Present the cards to the students, and have the students read each part and arrange the cards so that the story makes sense.

FIGURE 8.26
Narrative Cards

Green Cards—Use before Reading

Card 1: What does the title tell me about this story?

Card 2: What do the pictures tell me?

Card 3: What do I already know about?

Yellow Cards—Use during Reading

Card 4: Who? (Tell who the story is about, or name the characters.)

Card 5: What? (State the problem.)

Card 6: When? (Tell the time the story takes place.)

Card 7: Where? (Tell the place of the story.)

Card 8: Why? (Explain why something happened.)

Card 9: How? (Tell how the problem was solved.)

Card 10: What do I think will happen next? (Make predictions.)

Red Cards—Use after Reading

Card 11: Who were the characters?

Card 12: What was the setting? (when and where)

Card 13: What was the problem?

Card 14: How was the problem solved?

Card 15: Why did . . . ? (Elaborate on why something happened.)

2. Have students read the story again to determine whether it makes sense. If students disagree about the order, have them explain why they prefer a certain order.

Adaptations: Students can work on this activity in groups of two or three or individually.

▶Predict the Plot

Objective: To provide students with practice in predicting the events and plots in stories

Grades: Intermediate and secondary

Materials: Cartoon strips such as *Peanuts, Broom-Hilda,* or *Beetle Bailey.*

Teaching Procedures:
1. Select a cartoon strip, and expose one frame at a time for the students to read.
2. Have students predict the plot by asking such questions as these:
   - What do you think is going to be pictured in the next frame? Why?
   - Of the ideas we have generated, which one do you like best? Why?
   - How do you think the cartoonist will end this story? Why?

3. Read the next frame, discussing the previous predictions and making predictions about the next frame.
4. After the story is completed, have students draw and write their own cartoons, using the characters presented in the strip or creating new characters.
5. Have students share their cartoons with others.

Adaptations: Mystery and adventure stories also lend themselves to this type of plot prediction. Segments of the story could be read, and then predictions could be made. Students could also finish this activity by writing a mystery or adventure story.

▶WH Game

Objective: To provide students with practice in answering "who," "what," "when," "where," "why," and "how" questions

Grades: Elementary through secondary

Materials: Generic gameboard, spinner or die, and markers; WH cards, which are small cards with "WH Game" written on one side and one of the following words written on the other side: Who, What, When, Where, Why, How; sets of Story and Article Cards, which are copies of short

stories and articles mounted on cards. There should be one copy for each player. Select topics of interest for the age level of students.

Teaching Procedures:
1. Explain the game to the students.
2. Have students select a set of Story or Article Cards.
3. Have all students read the story or article and place their cards face down.
4. Have students take a turn by throwing the die or spinning and selecting a WH Card.
5. Have the student make up a question using the "Wh-" word indicated on the card and answer it correctly in order to move his or her marker.
6. If another player questions the validity of a player's question or answer, the players may look at the story or article card. Otherwise, these cards should remain face down during play.
7. After questions have been asked using one Story or Article Card, another set is selected. The students read this card, and then the game continues.
8. The first player to arrive at the finish wins.

Adaptations: Students may also work in pairs, with one person on the team making up the question and the other person answering it.

SUMMARYfor Chapter 8

Many students with learning and behavior problems struggle with learning word identification skills. Special education teachers spend a considerable amount of their instructional time focusing on these skills, assuming that fluency and comprehension will follow. What we have found is that these students also experience difficulties in reading fluently and comprehending what they read even when they have learned how to decode the words. Consequently, after determining that students can read words correctly, teachers need systematically to plan and implement fluency and comprehension instruction.

The first step in determining how a student is progressing in fluency is to measure the number of words read correctly per minute (WCPM). This statistic allows teachers to determine how a student's reading fluency compares with norms and whether a student is making adequate progress. Strategies for fluency instruction first focus on providing students frequent opportunities to listen to literature being read

aloud and model reading by the teacher. Giving students structured opportunities to read and reread text is valuable. The techniques of repeated reading, repeated choral reading, and peer-supported reading are stressed because they provide students with additional instructional support while they are developing fluent reading patterns.

Much of what teachers refer to as instruction in reading comprehension is, in fact, better described as an assessment of students' comprehension after they have read. This means that teachers often ask students questions after they read as the sole or primary means of teaching reading comprehension. To draw attention away from teacher questioning, this chapter presents a framework for reading comprehension that is not tied to the level of reading comprehension questions. Instead, it is tied to the reasoning processes that are required (i.e., textually explicit, textually implicit, or scriptually implicit) and the types of information or relationships that are represented. We can use this matrix in planning instruction to implement techniques and strategies that will ensure that many different facets of comprehension are tapped.

In discussing methods for teaching reading comprehension, emphasis is placed on the importance of planning activities before the students read that will help them preview the text and activate their background knowledge or schemas. Techniques such as brainstorming, the PreReading Plan, Text Preview, and K-W-L can facilitate this process. In the area of questioning, emphasis is placed on helping students learn to predict and ask their own questions rather than just respond to the questions of the teacher.

Teaching students to paraphrase, summarize, monitor their comprehension, and use fix-up strategies when there are problems are also critical skills for effective reading. Rather than

a steady diet of teacher questions, what is needed is explicit, cognitive strategy instruction in these comprehension strategies. Using multicomponent strategies such as reciprocal teaching, collaborative strategic reading, and POSSE can be both effective and efficient for students with reading problems.

Most students with learning and behavior problems receive reading instruction using such frameworks as directed reading activities, directed reading–thinking activities, and literature-based reading and whole language. Adapting these frameworks to make instruction more explicit with greater opportunities for modeling, practice, and feedback is important if these students are to be successful readers.

FOCUS Answers

FOCUS Question 1. What is reading fluency, and how is progress in fluency monitored?

Answer: Fluency is the ability to read a text quickly, accurately, and with expression. For assessing fluency, the progress monitoring practice most frequently used and the one highly associated with comprehension is oral reading fluency. Oral reading fluency can be addressed by determining the number of words read correctly per minute using a grade-level appropriate text.

FOCUS Question 2. What are the instructional practices for increasing reading fluency?

Answer: The following techniques have been identified as effective for increasing reading fluency for struggling readers:
- Reading aloud and modeling fluent reading while students read along
- Repeated reading of a text
- Choral repeated reading
- Peer-assisted reading
- Reading performance

FOCUS Question 3. What is the purpose of comprehension instruction?

Answer: Comprehension instruction should encourage students to engage actively in discussions related to the content of the text and about how to read for meaning. The components of reading comprehension instruction include preview techniques, questioning strategies and comprehension monitoring, and text structure and summarizing strategies.

FOCUS Question 4. What assessments and instructional components should be present in a reading comprehension program?

Answer: Comprehension is a difficult task to measure quickly (in less than 5 minutes) although maze or cloze procedures are used to assess reading comprehension for progress monitoring purposes. There are several standardized and norm-referenced measures that take between 25 and 45 minutes to administer (some group administered and some individually administered) that provide reliable and valid information on students' reading comprehension.

THINKand APPLY

- Describe several reasons why a student might have difficulty with fluency or reading comprehension.
- Define fluency, and write down the formula that is used to calculate fluency.
- Compare repeated reading with peer-supported reading. Note their similarities and differences.
- Why is it important to measure students' fluency frequently?

- Describe activities that teachers can use to help students become more fluent readers.
- Select an informational text that you plan or might plan to read with students. Describe how you would use brainstorming, PreReading Plan, Text Preview, or K-W-L to assist students in activating background knowledge.
- Describe how a think-aloud would be used with a paraphrasing or retelling strategy. Select a passage and a

strategy (e.g., RAP, STORE), and do a think-aloud by describing what you are thinking as you carry out the steps in the strategy.

- Identify the four comprehension and comprehension-monitoring strategies that are taught in reciprocal teaching and collaborative strategic reading and explain why they are used.

- Describe how you would adapt the directed reading activity, the directed reading–thinking activity, and literature-based reading and whole language to support students with reading problems.

APPLYthe STANDARDS

Council for Exceptional Children

1. Describe how instruction and practice in fluency can help students who struggle in this area become better readers (LD4S2, LD4S6, LD7K1, LD7K3, LD4S11).

   Standard LD4S2: Use specialized methods for teaching basic skills.

   Standard LD4S6: Use responses and errors to guide instructional decisions and provide feedback to learners.

   Standard LD7K1: Relationships among reading instruction methods and learning disabilities.

   Standard LD7K3: Interventions and services for children who may be at risk for learning disabilities.

   Standard LD4S11: Implement systematic instruction to teach accuracy, fluency, and comprehension in content area reading and written language.

2. Given your knowledge of the CEC standards related to reading comprehension (LD4S5, LD4S7, LD4S8, LD4S9, LD4S1, LD4S11), describe why instruction in reading comprehension is particularly important for students with learning disabilities and behavior problems. How can instruction in reading comprehension strategies support individuals in accessing the general education curriculum?

   Standard LD4S5: Use instructional methods to strengthen and compensate for deficits in perception, comprehension, memory, and retrieval.

   Standard LD4S7: Identify and teach essential concepts, vocabulary, and content across the general curriculum.

   Standard LD4S8: Use reading methods appropriate to the individual with learning disabilities.

   Standard LD4S9: Implement systematic instruction in teaching reading comprehension and monitoring strategies.

   Standard LD4S1: Use research-supported methods for academic and nonacademic instruction of individuals with learning disabilities.

   Standard LD4S11: Implement systematic instruction to teach accuracy, fluency, and comprehension in content area reading and written language.

WEBSITESas RESOURCES | to Assist in Teaching Reading

The following Websites are extensive resources to expand your understanding of teaching reading (see also the Chapter 7 Websites):

- LDOnline, Reading Fluency www.ldonline.org/ld_indepth/reading/reading_fluency.html
- Big Ideas in Beginning Reading http://reading.uoregon.edu
- Reading Fluency www.ves.wpsb.org/focus/fluency.html
- Reading Quest http://curry.edschool.virginia.edu/go/readquest/strat
- Reading Rockets www.readingrockets.org

Case Study Homework Exercise Go to MyEducationLab and select the topic "READING INSTRUC-TION," then read the case study "Fluency and Word Identification" and complete the activity questions below.

Several case studies provide examples of students who struggle with fluency and word identification. Strategies to support students are provided on Star sheets.

1. Select a case involving a student who struggles reading fluently and study the associated Star sheets.

2. Based on this case, what recommendations from the chapter or the Star sheets would use to develop this student's fluency?

3. Describe several assessment procedures described in the chapter that would be appropriate to use for this case student.

Video Homework Exercise Go to MyEducationLab and select the topic "READING INSTRUCTION," then watch the video "Defining Reading Comprehension" and complete the activity questions below.

Reading comprehension is the ultimate goal of reading, and should be addressed at every stage of reading. At the beginning stage, students often focus on the elements of the reading process without understanding what they are reading.

1. How does the teacher in this clip assess the student's reading comprehension?

2. How does the assessment in the video differ from re-telling methods described in the chapter?

Module Homework Exercise Go to MyEducationLab and select the topic "INSTRUCTIONAL PRACTICES AND LEARNING STRATEGIES," then read the module "Using Learning Strategies: Instruction to Enhance Student Learning" and complete the activity questions below.

This module features the Self-Regulated Strategy Development (SRSD) model, which outlines the six steps required to effectively implement any instructional strategy and emphasizes the time and effort required to do so.

1. Briefly summarize the Self-Regulated Strategy Development model.

2. There are many learning strategies outlined in the chapter and in this module. Select one learning strategy that you would like to try and provide a rationale for why you chose it.

Chapter 9

Assessing and Teaching
Writing and Spelling

Mike York, a high school teacher of students with learning disabilities reports, "The adolescents in my program do not want to write. They do not even want to answer questions in writing. Writing a theme for a class is torture." He goes on to describe the students in his class. "You should see the handwriting of the majority of students in my class. It is awful. They print poorly and slowly. So even when they are motivated to write it is painfully difficult for them. Furthermore, most of them have little experience writing before they get to secondary school. Many were identified as learning disabled in the early elementary grades and then were provided with writing assistance as they went through school. Fortunately, some of the students were provided with instruction in how to use a keyboard and this helps with their writing production. However, production is not the only problem. Quality of writing is also extremely poor. This poor writing influences their success in content area classes. For example, several of my students are very interested in science and work hard to understand and participate in the general education classroom. They also know a lot more about science that they can talk about than that they are able to write about. Unfortunately, almost all assessments in the classroom require students to write their answers. Since my students have writing challenges, they frequently write brief and incomplete answers which give an inaccurate portrait of what they really know. I am now working closely with my students to improve their writing production and quality so that they can be more successful in both general education classrooms as well as the world of work."

Most young children love to scribble. They enjoy writing and drawing on paper, sidewalks, chalkboards, and, unfortunately, even walls. On the first day of school, when first graders are asked whether they know how to write, most of them say yes. What happens to the interest and joy in writing from age 3 to age 13?

Many researchers in the field believe that students do not spend enough time on writing as a craft and are given too little choice about what they write. Writing has many negative associations for students because it is often used as a form of punishment, and when their writing is returned to them, it is covered with corrections. Even when good instruction supports writing, there is little question that writing is one of the most difficult tasks that students must perform in school (Bereiter, 1980; Isaacson, 1988).

The good news is that we have made considerable progress on how to effectively teach writing to students with disabilities (Graham and Harris, 2005; Vaughn et al., 2000). We have also made progress with bilingual students with disabilities (Echevarria and Graves, 1998; Graves, Valles, and Rueda, 2000). When teachers implement effective intervention approaches that use both the conventions of teaching writing (e.g., capitalization, punctuation, sentence structure) and strategies for improving written expression (e.g., planning, composing the results), the results are quite positive (Gersten and Baker, 2001). Using instructional time to improve writing for students with reading difficulties is an important task (Dixon, Isaacson, and Stein, 2002). This chapter is about what happens in writing when students are given choices in topics and the time and encouragement to write. The chapter presents background and instructional procedures for using writing strategies and effectively using the writing process approach. Getting started in writing, the writing process, and establishing a writing community are discussed. In addition, this chapter presents approaches to teaching spelling, handwriting, and keyboarding to students who have learning difficulties and provides a table showing the pros and cons of teaching cursive versus manuscript.

> **FOCUS Question** **1.** What assessment and instructional practices should teachers attend to when implementing the writing process with students with learning and behavior problems?

Assessing and Teaching the Writing Process

Several years ago, Marynell Schlegel, a resource room teacher who works with students who have learning and emotional disabilities, decided that she disliked teaching writing almost as much as the students hated learning it. Questioning her students about the characteristics of good writing revealed that they perceived good writing as spelling words correctly, writing correct sentences, and having good handwriting—the very skills that these students often have the most difficulty developing. None of the students included a purpose for writing in their description of good writing. Her students did not perceive writing as a means of conveying a message, which experts consider to be the most important element in writing (Murray, 1984, 1985).

During the summer, Ms. Schlegel decided to read about writing and to change her writing instruction. She decided to implement the writing process approach to written expression as part of her overall writing program (Graves, 1983; MacArthur et al., 1995).

The Writing Process for Students with Learning and Behavior Problems

After spending the summer preparing for the changes in her instructional approach to writing, Ms. Schlegel decided that she was ready to begin. (See Apply the Concept 9.1.) She arranged for students with writing difficulties including students with LD to be in the same classroom so that she could coteach with a general education teacher for three 40-minute periods a week. During this time, students were to write and participate in skills groups. Initially, instruction included selecting topics of the student's choice, focusing first on the message and then on the mechanics of writing within each written piece. Skills such as organizing ideas and editing for capitalization, punctuation, and spelling would be taught on the basis of the students' individual needs both within the context of their written pieces and through outside models and examples.

Apply the Concept 9.1

Knowledge of Writing Strategies

Students who have been identified as learning disabled differ from low-achieving and high-achieving students in their knowledge of strategies related to writing. They are less aware of steps in the writing process and ideas and procedures for organizing their written text. Students with learning disabilities are also more dependent on external cues, such as how much to write, teacher feedback, and mechanical presentation of the paper. They demonstrate significant difficulties in planning, writing, and revising text (Englert, Raphael, Fear, and Anderson, 1988).

Ms. Schlegel initiated the writing process approach but also retained many of the elements of her old writing program that were effective, such as recognizing the scope and sequence of writer development and teaching writing conventions. She knew that to implement the writing process approach in her instruction, she would need to consider setting, scheduling and preparing materials, teaching skills, and the teacher's role as a writer. Furthermore, she was aware that there were many strategic approaches to enhance writing that she wanted to include in her instruction.

Setting

According to Graves (1983), the setting should create a working atmosphere similar to that of a studio, one that promotes independence but in which students can easily interact. Figure 9.1 depicts how Ms. Schlegel and the classroom teacher arranged the room to create such an atmosphere. Materials and supplies for writing, and the students' individual writing folders were stored in specific locations in the room. Students knew where materials could be found, so they did not have to rely on the teacher to get them started at the beginning of the writing period. The room arrangement facilitated conferencing between small groups of students, teacher and student, and student and student.

Scheduling and Preparing Materials

Ms. Schlegel set up individual writing folders. In the daily writing folders, illustrated in Figure 9.2, students kept all their unfinished writing, a list of possible writing topics, a list of all writing pieces they had completed, a list of writing skills they had mastered, a list of skills and topics in which they had expertise, and dates when conferences with the teacher were held. Students also kept mnemonic cues to assist them in practicing writing strategies that they were learning. A list of the words an individual student was learning to spell, along with a procedure for learning the words and measuring mastery, were also included in the folder (see Figure 9.3). In addition to this daily writing folder, students had access to their permanent writing folder, which included all of the writing they had completed.

Ms. Zaragoza is an elementary teacher who uses the writing process with all learners in her classroom. She organized skill lessons, 5 to 20 minutes each day, for small groups of students and individual skill lessons for students who had specific difficulties. She also addressed a writing difficulty that most of the students in the class were

FIGURE 9.1
Setting the Stage

1. Create a working atmosphere that is similar to a studio.
2. Create an atmosphere in which students can interact easily.
3. Create an atmosphere that encourages independence.

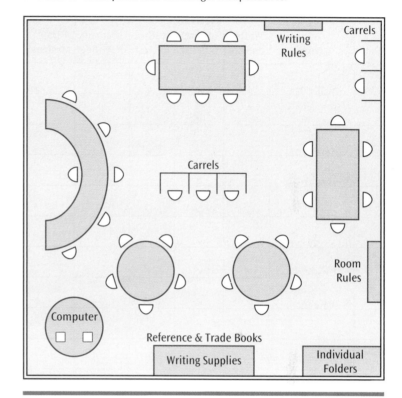

FIGURE 9.2
Individual Writing Folder

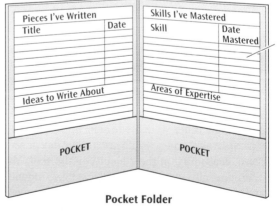

Pocket Folder

FIGURE 9.3

Sample Spelling Form for the Individual Spelling Folder

Student: _____

Words I'm Learning to Spell

Date	Word	Written on Card	Practiced Using Strategy	Learned for Test	Learned in Writing	Date Mastered
3/12	1. mystery	✓	✓	✓		
	2. chasing	✓	✓	✓		
	3. haunted	✓	✓	✓		
	4. wouldn't	✓	✓			
	5. elsewhere	✓	✓	✓		
	6. whatever	✓	✓	✓		
	7. their	✓	✓	✓		
	8. there	✓	✓	✓		
	9.					
	10.					

demonstrating by providing approximately 20 minutes of whole-class instruction two to three times per week. When she noticed that several students were having difficulty with a particular skill (e.g., quotation marks) or thought that several students were ready to learn a more advanced writing procedure (e.g., the difference between first and third person when writing), she would organize a skill group. She taught approximately one skill group a day and advertised the skill group by writing the name of it on the board as well as the time it would occur. She would write the names of the students who she believed would benefit from the skill group on the board but would also allow other students to sign up for the skill group. A skill group would last for one day or several, depending on the difficulty of the skill. Ms. Zaragoza also taught daily skill lessons to individual students. Sometimes these skill lessons were responses to a teachable moment—for example, a student might ask how to develop an ending for a story—and at other times were planned and scheduled. Ms. Zaragoza's viewpoint was that practice in writing is essential to enhancing writing skills, but practice alone is insufficient, and skill groups are an essential way to keep students moving and learning as writers.

Teaching Writing Conventions

Students with learning disabilities display a wide range of abilities in writing (Berninger, Abbott, Witaker, Sylvester, and Nolen, 1995). They are also very different in terms of the writing skills they need to acquire and the ways in which they respond to instruction (Berninger et al., 1995). In designing effective writing skills programs for students with learning problems, variables such as motivation and attitude must be considered, as well as writing conventions.

Therefore, Ms. Schlegel taught the skills (e.g., spelling, capitalization, and punctuation) during each writing period, and then Ms. Schlegel looked for these skills in students' writing. Much of the time was devoted to small group instruction and individual writing and conferences with classmates and the teacher. Time for sharing ideas and drafts was often scheduled near the end of the period.

Ms. Schlegel conducted short (5- to 15-minute) skill lessons with individuals or small groups of students. The topics and groupings for these lessons were based on the students' needs. Skill lessons were decided on the basis of observations of student writing, requests for help, and data collected from conferences. Students were selected to participate in the skill lessons contingent on their abilities and needs. The same topic with different activities was usually covered for four lessons to help provide sufficient practice. To help promote generalization, Ms. Schlegel and her students would use conferences to discuss how the skill functioned in the writing process. She would maintain records on each skill area so that she could carefully monitor students' progress. Ms. Schlegel realized that teaching the elements of writing as well as teaching writing conventions provided her students with the tools they needed to make progress in their writing.

Remember the following critical points about teaching conventions (Fearn and Farnan, 1998):

- Attention to conventions does not disrupt the flow of writing but is part of the discipline of writing.
- Focus on the conventions of writing does not inhibit growth in writing but facilitates it.
- Teach even young children writing and spelling conventions (see Figure 9.4).

- Provide about 20 percent of the instructional time of students with learning and behavior problems in writing conventions.

Perhaps the most important thing to remember about teaching writing to students with learning and behavior problems is that they require adequate time to write—to practice the craft. However, they also require explicit and systematic instruction in the critical elements and skills necessary for effective writing.

Using the Writing Process in General Education Classrooms

Ms. Zaragoza conducts workshops for other teachers on the use of the writing process. She is frequently asked whether students who are at risk for learning problems or identified as learning disabled can successfully use this approach. She conducted three year-long case studies involving students who had been identified as gifted, low-achieving, and learning disabled in which she examined their progress in writing and writing-related skills (e.g., capitalization, spelling, punctuation; Zaragoza and Vaughn, 1992). For the first two months, one student with learning disabilities was very hesitant about writing. He asked for constant teacher assistance and would not write unless a teacher worked closely with him. He wrote slowly and neatly even on first drafts. His first piece of writing was untitled and incomplete. He was insecure about working with other students and never volunteered to share his writing. His piece, entitled "Disneyworld," demonstrated an understanding that you can write down what you really think.

FIGURE 9.4

Instructional Timeline: Awareness to Mastery									
Instructional Concept	**K**	**1**	**2**	**3**	**4**	**5**	**6**	**7**	**8**
End Punctuation	*	*	*						
Commas in Dates	*	*	*						
Commas in Series	*	*	*	*					
Commas in Addresses	*	*	*	*					
Apostrophes in Contractions		*	*	*	*				
Periods in Abbreviations		*	*	*	*				
Commas in Compound Sentences			*	*	*				
Punctuation in Dialogue			*	*	*	*			
Apostrophes in Possessives			*	*	*	*			
Commas in Complex Sentences				*	*	*			
Quotation Marks and Underlining in Published Titles				*	*	*			
Commas in Series of Adjectives				*	*	*			
Commas to Set Off Appositives				*	*	*	*		
Commas after Introductory Words				*	*	*	*		
Commas after Introductory Phrases				*	*	*	*		
Commas in Compound-Complex Sentences					*	*	*	*	
Commas to Set Off Parenthetical Expressions					*	*	*		
Dashes and Parentheses to Set Off Parenthetical Expressions					*	*	*	*	
Colons in Sentences					*	*	*	*	
Semicolons in Sentences					*	*	*	*	
Capital Letters to Begin Sentences	*	*	*						
Capital Letters in Names	*	*	*						
Capitalizing	*	*	*						
Capital Letters in Days and Months	*	*	*	*					
Capital Letters in Place Names	*	*	*	*					
Capital Letters in Person's Title		*	*	*	*				
Capital Letters in Published Titles		*	*	*	*				
Capital Letters to Show Nationality, Ethnicity, and Language		*	*	*	*				
Capital Letters in Trade Names, Commercial Products, and Company Names		*	*	*	*				
Capital Letters in Names of Institutions, Associations, and Events		*	*	*	*				

Source: L. Fearn and N. Farnan, *Writing Effectively: Helping Children Master the Conventions of Writing* (Boston: Allyn & Bacon, 1998). Copyright © 1998 by Allyn & Bacon. Reprinted by permission.

He included his own dog in a Disney World theme ("Goofy is a dog I like to play with but Goofy is not better than my dog."). The other students loved this story and asked him to read it over and over again. After this, he volunteered frequently to share his writing in front of the class. He had a flair for good endings and became the class expert on developing endings. For example, in "The Spooky Halloween," he ended with this sentence, "Halloween is nothing to play with." "Freddy Is In My Room" ended with the sentence, "Give it up." The ending that was most appreciated by all was from "Part 4." This story was about a child who, because he did not get a Christmas present, wanted to die. He went to the graveyard and started to lie down but then said, "Holy macaroni not this dead." Ms. Zaragoza's case studies reveal that students across achievement groups benefit from participating in the writing process. The students demonstrated gains on standardized writing measures as well

as increased confidence and skills in their daily writing. Apply the Concept 9.2 discusses using the writing process approach.

Monitoring Student Progress

How does a teacher monitor students' progress in writing? When teachers monitor students' progress on critical elements regularly (at least every two weeks), students make improved progress (Gunning, 1998). Teachers record students' progress so that they, the students, and parents can see progress, such as the number of words written for younger children and developing a checklist of story elements and their quality for older students.

Teachers monitor students' progress by noting the following:

- Whether students can complete the written project

Apply the Concept 9.2

Can the Writing Process Approach Meet the Needs of All Students in a Heterogeneous Classroom?

A study that demonstrated the practicality and effectiveness of the writing process approach for meeting the diverse writing skill needs of students in a heterogeneous classroom was conducted by Zaragoza and Vaughn (1992). For six months, they studied 3 second graders in a regular classroom setting as the writing process approach was implemented with their class.

One of the three youngsters in this study was a girl who had previously been identified as low-achieving. The second was a boy who had been diagnosed as having a learning disability in the areas of reading and written language and who had problems with distractibility and behavior as well. The third was a gifted child from India; she had lived in the United States from the age of three and was highly verbal, cooperative, and self-motivated.

When the writing process approach was initiated, the writing

skills of the low achiever and those of the student with learning disabilities were so underdeveloped that it was difficult to read anything that either of them wrote. In addition, they had difficulty thinking about what they might write and were reluctant to put any words on paper. The gifted learner spelled imperfectly, but she enjoyed writing and had no difficulty expressing her thoughts in writing.

Progress was initially slow for both the low achiever and the student with learning disabilities. However, as they witnessed their peers busily discussing and writing their ideas and as their teacher worked with them to develop their own ideas for writing, they grew increasingly comfortable and confident in expressing those ideas in writing. Realizing that errors in spelling, punctuation, capitalization, and language were not the priority in the initial stages of their writing

encouraged the children to take risks. Mistakes could wait to be corrected during the final stages of the writing process.

All three children made gains in written expression, spelling, punctuation, usage (grammar), proofing (identifying errors), and dictation (writing correctly from dictation). In addition, a writing-attitude scale administered at the conclusion of the study showed that all three students developed positive attitudes toward writing. Their positive attitudes were further demonstrated by the fact that all three children continued to write during the summer following the six-month period of study.

Source: Adapted from N. Zaragoza and S. Vaughn (1992). The effects of process writing instruction on three second-grade students with different achievement needs. *Learning Disabilities Research and Practice, 7,* pp. 184–193.

- How proficient they are at each element of the writing process (e.g., planning, spelling, handwriting, composing)
- Whether they can apply the skills and knowledge to other contexts (e.g., at other times during the day)
- How they explain the process they are using

See Figure 9.5 for questions concerning progress monitoring.

For example, as students write, the teacher would notice what strategies they use to compose text (e.g., outline, notes, key words), reflect on the appropriateness of the task and teaching presentation, and keep written records to document student progress, such as notes, checklists, and samples of students' work. Monitoring students' progress in writing involves evaluating written products and observing the writing process. Teachers can observe students as they write and use conference times to assess and record their progress. By observing and examining writing processes and products, teachers can plan instruction to meet individual needs. Many teachers keep anecdotal records by creating a record sheet to quickly document students' progress on writing projects. They include a summary of what they observe, the date, and context, and they list skills and writing strategies that need to be taught. Collections of students' written work help teachers, families, and students document growth and development over the school year. Journals and writing folders also provide insight into writing growth. Teachers may periodically review and select representative pieces to show writing development and use progress monitoring to establish writing goals for students.

Perhaps the most important activity is to determine how the teacher will measure writing progress for each student. For example, for young students, the teacher may monitor the number of words written, number of words spelled correctly, and use of capital letters and punctuation. As students mature in their writing, the teacher may decide to monitor use of adjectives and vivid verbs, facility in editing and revising, and overall quality of the writing. It is important to focus on only one or two things at a time. After students demonstrate progress in the target areas, the teacher can add other elements of writing. This way, progress is recorded, but students are not overwhelmed by the number of writing conventions that they need to monitor.

Elements of the Writing Process

The elements of the writing process include prewriting or planning, composing, revising, editing, and publishing. When students learn to write they do not proceed through the process in a linear fashion. In fact, many authors circle back through previous elements and jump ahead to later ones when they are writing their drafts. Also, not all writing leads to publishing. For

---

FIGURE 9.5

Questions to Consider in Monitoring Student Progress

Assessing Progress

How does the student respond during the activity?

- Can the student complete the task?
- How comfortably and proficiently is the task completed?
- Can the student explain the process used to complete the task?
- Can the student apply the skills and knowledge to other contexts?
- Are there aspects of the task that are causing difficulties?

Adjusting Instruction

Will a different approach, materials, or setting improve student progress?

Different approaches
- Simplify tasks into small steps
- Do more modeling or demonstration
- Provide more review
- Give more guidance

Progress Monitoring

Different materials
- Decrease difficulty of the material
- Use different types of writing genres
- Provide checklists or cue card

Different setting
- Use peers to assist
- Change time of day of instruction
- Change location of task

Sources: Adapted from I. C. Fountas and G. S. Pinnell, *Guided Reading: Good First Teaching for All Children* (Portsmouth, NH: Heinemann, 1996); T. G. Gunning, *Assessing and Correcting Reading and Writing Difficulties* (Boston: Allyn & Bacon, 1998); and B. Rosenshine, Advances in research on instruction, in J. W. Lloyd, E. J. Kame'enui, and D. Chard (Eds.), *Issues in Educating Students with Disabilities* (Mahwah, NJ: Erlbaum, 1997), pp. 197–220.

example, Steven realized after he read his draft to his friend Jacob that he needed to have more information about what submarines look like on the inside. He returned to the prewriting stage and checked out several books on submarines so that he could complete his story. Furthermore, students must learn to master these elements in a variety of writing styles, including reports, letters, notes, and stories.

In prewriting, students collect information about a topic through observing, remembering, interviewing, and reading. When composing, students attempt to get ideas on paper in the form of a draft. This process tells students what they know and do not know. During revising, points are explored further, ideas are elaborated, and further connections are made. When students are satisfied with the content, they edit the piece, reviewing it line by line to determine that each word is necessary. Punctuation, spelling, and other mechanical processes are checked. The final element is publication. If the piece is a good one for the student, it is published. Obviously, not all pieces are published.

Students with disabilities differ from other students in the degree to which elements of the writing process are difficult for them (Englert and Raphael, 1988; Graham, 1990; Thomas, Englert, and Gregg, 1987). Many students with learning disabilities experience significant problems in editing and writing final copies because they have difficulty with mechanical skills such as spelling, punctuation, and handwriting. These students often produce well-developed stories that are hard to read because of mechanical errors. Other students with learning disabilities have difficulty organizing their first drafts and need to rethink sequencing and order during their revisions.

Graham, Harris, and their colleagues (Graham and Harris, 2005; Sexton, Harris, and Graham, 1998; Troia et al., 1999) have successfully taught students with learning disabilities to use the following strategy with subsequent improvement in their composition:

1. Think: who will read this, and why am I writing it?
2. Plan what to say using TREE (note Topic sentence, note Reasons, Examine reasons, note Ending).
3. Write and say more.

Prewriting: Getting Started

The first hurdle in starting the writing process approach with students is topic selection. "The most important thing children can learn is what they know and how they know it" (Graves, 1985, p. 39). This is the essence of topic choice. Once students can identify what they know and talk about it, they have completed the first step in topic selection.

Give students a piece of paper. Say to them, "You know lots of things about yourself, about your family, and about your friends. You have hobbies and activities that you like to do. You have stories about things that have happened to you and/or to others you know. You have lots of things to share with others. I want you to make a list of things you would like to share with others through writing. Do not put them in any specific order—just write them as you think of them. You will not have to write about all of these topics. The purpose of this exercise is to think of as many topics as you can. I will give you about 10 minutes. Begin." Model the process for the students by writing as many topics as you can think of during the assigned time. When time is up, tell the students to pick a partner and share their topics with him or her. They may add any new topics they think of at this time. When they finish sharing their topics with their partner, share your list with the entire group, and comment on topics you are looking forward to writing about as well as the topics you think you may never write about. Ask for volunteer students to read their topic lists to the entire group. Now ask the students to select the three topics they are most interested in writing about, to write them at the top of their lists, and then to place their topic lists in their writing folders. Explain that these lists can be consulted later for possible topics. Also tell the students that if they think of new topics they want to write about, they may add them to their lists. Finally, ask the students to select a topic and begin writing. Throughout the day, consider what you are reading, discussing, and doing, and make opportunities for students to identify additional topics for writing. After they become more comfortable writing and more expert in their use of writing conventions, you can work with students to identify, select, and write about an increasing range of genres including information pieces, reports, persuasive writing, and poetry.

Problems in Topic Selection. There are two common problems in topic selection: difficulty in finding a topic and persistence in writing about the same topic.

Maintaining a supply of writing topics is difficult for some students and rarely a problem for others. When students tell you stories, ask them whether the story generates a topic they want to write about. When students are reading or you are reading to them, ask whether the reading has given them ideas for their own writing. If they were going to write the ending of this story, how would they do it? If they were going to continue this story, what would happen? If they were going to add characters to the story, what types of characters would they add? Would they change the setting?

Teachers can also facilitate topic selection by presenting a range of writing styles including stories, factual descriptions, mysteries, persuasive writing, writing that involves comparing and contrasting, reporting on topics, and observing. Students often begin writing by telling personal experiences. Through the writing of other authors, students can be introduced to a wide range of categories that can provide exposure to other genres. Figure 9.6 presents a list of suggestions for students when they are stuck about a topic for writing. One of those suggestions, asking a friend to help, is discussed in Apply the Concept 9.3.

FIGURE 9.6

Up in the Air for a Topic?

- Check your folder and reread your idea list.
- Ask a friend to help you brainstorm ideas.
- Listen to others' ideas.
- Write about what you know: your experiences.
- Write a make-believe story.
- Write about a special interest or hobby.
- Write about how to do something.
- Think about how you got your last idea.

Apply the Concept 9.3

A Friend Helps with Topic Selection

Ruth Ann returned with a piece of blank paper, which she handed to Cary. Cary wrote Ruth Ann's name on the paper and underlined it. Then she conducted a rather sophisticated interview.

"Think of three ideas. Want to write about your first day of school?"

"I can't remember. That was five years ago," answered Ruth Ann.

"How about the first day in the learning lab?" continued Cary.

"I don't remember that either. It was over a year ago."

Looking at her idea sheet, Cary commented, "I'm writing about a talking dishwasher. Do you want to write about that?"

"Not really," replied Ruth Ann.

"Where do you go on vacations?" asked Cary.

"To Iowa, but I've already written about that."

"Well, have you ever been to a circus?" Cary pursued.

"No."

"How about a zoo?"

"The Los Angeles Zoo," Ruth Ann answered.

"Do you want to write about that?" asked Cary.

"Yeah," remarked Ruth Ann, "that's a good idea."

Cary wrote the number 1 on the paper she had labeled with Ruth Ann's name, and wrote, "las angels zoo" beside it. She remarked, "I don't know how to spell Los Angeles."

"Don't worry," Ruth Ann commented. "I can find that out when I start writing about it."

"OK, let's think up another idea. Have you ever ridden a horse?" asked Cary as she continued the interview.

"No," replied Ruth Ann.

"Do you have any pets?" asked Cary.

"Yeah, I have a cat named Pierre."

"Do you want to write about him?" continued Cary.

"Yes, I could do that," replied Ruth Ann enthusiastically.

Cary wrote the number 2 on the paper and beside it wrote, "writing about your cat."

The conversation continued, with Cary explaining that it is helpful to think up three ideas so that you have some choice when you decide what to write about. After more questioning, Ruth Ann decided that it would be okay to write about a talking shoe, so Cary wrote down Ruth Ann's third idea. Then Cary helped Ruth Ann decide that she was first going to write about her cat. Cary wrote this idea at the bottom of the page and starred it to note that Ruth Ann had selected this topic. Cary ended the interview by saying, "Put this paper in your writing folder so that the next time you have to select a topic, we'll already have two ideas thought up."

In addition to difficulty in thinking of a topic, immature writers often repeat the same topic. Many children with learning and behavior problems find security in repeating the same topic or theme in their writing. They like the control they have over the language, spelling, and content. The teacher should look carefully at their work and determine whether the stories are changing through vocabulary development, concept development, story development, or character development. It could be that the student is learning a great deal about writing even though the story content is changing very little. The teacher can provide specific examples of other genres and instructional procedures for how to write in these genres.

Some teachers may become concerned when a student selects a topic and other students copy the idea. For example, Taro wrote a story about a talking dictionary that was stolen and how Taro endangered his own life to recover the dictionary. The idea had special meaning for him, because he generally misspelled about 50 percent of the words he used in his writing. Once the story was shared with his classmates, over half of the other children wrote about talking objects, including dishwashers, brooms, and shoes. The stories written by other students that repeated Taro's theme served as the vehicle for several students to write better-developed stories than they had written previously and for one rather good storyteller to expand the story format into a traditional murder mystery for her next story. Of course, when she shared her story, many students followed by copying the mystery theme. Thus, rather than being problematic, imitation of a classmate's story is a natural way for students to improve their writing.

Prewriting Strategies. Many students with learning and behavior problems begin writing without much planning about what they are going to write. They find that when they read their drafts aloud, others have difficulty understanding the story or following the sequence. Students with learning disabilities often have limited text organization skills because they have difficulty categorizing ideas related to a specific topic, providing advanced organizers for the topic, and relating and extending ideas about the topic (Englert and Raphael, 1988). Consequently, we need to teach students prewriting skills so that the writing and rewriting stages will be easier.

In teaching the organization that goes into writing a piece, teachers can model their thinking as they move from topic selection to writing a first draft. Some teachers find it helpful to teach this thinking process by writing their ideas in an organized structure (Bos, 1991; Thomkins and Friend, 1986) and by asking students to set goals, brainstorm ideas, and sequence their ideas while they are writing (Troia et al., 1999). Some teachers use graphic organizers across curriculum areas to organize writing for both narrative and expository texts (Fuchs, Mathes, and Fuchs, 1994).

Graphic organizers that are used to assist in writing are referred to as *brainstorm sheets* or *structured organizers* (Pehrsson and Robinson, 1985), *semantic maps* (Pearson and Johnson, 1978), and *story frames or maps* (Fowler and Davis, 1985). Although these visual organization devices have been used as aids to reading comprehension, they also serve to facilitate the writing process (Pehrsson and Robinson, 1985). Ms. Turk, a resource teacher who works with Ms. Schlegel, used a think-aloud technique to model how to use the brainstorm sheet presented in Apply the Concept 9.4. She drew a large brainstorm sheet on the

Apply the Concept 9.4

Sample Brainstorm Sheet

Name: Mrs. Turk

Date: 2/7

Working Title: Horseback Ride

Setting:

Where: Mt. Graham
start at trash dump

When: When I was ten years old

Who: Dad and I, also mom and brother

Dad and I were riding on trail.
Trail got bad.

Action: Dad's horse stumbled on rock. Dad fell off + hurt his arm. Finally he got on horse. I helped. Rode to top of mt. Mom met us. So did brother. Went to hospital.

Ending: Dad was OK.

board and then introduced the brainstorming technique to the students.

Ms. Turk began, "I want to write a story about a time when I was really scared. So I decided to write about the time when I was about 10 years old and my dad and I went for a horseback ride. He got hurt, and I wasn't sure we'd get back to the car. There is so much to remember about this story that I am going to jot down a few ideas so that when I begin to write my story, I can remember them all and put them in order. To help me organize my ideas, I'm going to use a brainstorm sheet."

At this point, Ms. Turk explained the brainstorm sheet and the parts of a story. Through class discussion, the students identified a story they had written recently and each part in their story.

Ms. Turk continued modeling, using the brainstorm sheet. "I am going to call my story 'Horseback Ride' for now. I may want to change the name later, since it's easier for me to think of a title after I write the story. Well, it happened when we were on a trip to Mount Graham. So I'm going to write 'Mt. Graham' by 'Where.' I'm not sure how to spell Mt. Graham, but it doesn't matter that I spell it correctly now. I can find out later. Also, since the brainstorm sheet is for me, I don't have to write sentences—just ideas that will help

me remember when I'm writing my first draft of the story." Ms. Turk continued to think aloud as she completed the sheet.

Ms. Turk demonstrated that the students did not have to fill in the brainstorm sheet in a linear fashion. Sometimes it is easier to fill out the ending first. She also demonstrated how, after she listed all the ideas under the action section, she could go back and number them in the order that made the most sense.

In subsequent lessons, Ms. Turk demonstrated how to write a story from the brainstorm sheet. She also worked individually with students to complete brainstorm sheets and to use them in their writing.

During the year, several different brainstorm sheets were used in Ms. Turk's classroom. Figure 9.7 shows a brainstorm sheet that was developed for expository writing (writing that describes the facts or information about a subject area; often associated with social studies and science). However, the students also used this brainstorm sheet for stories. They wrote the title in the center circle, and information related to the setting, problem, action, and ending in the four other circles and their accompanying lines. Students also developed their own brainstorming sheets. For example, Cary combined topic selection and brainstorming and developed the brainstorm

FIGURE 9.7

Brainstorm Sheet

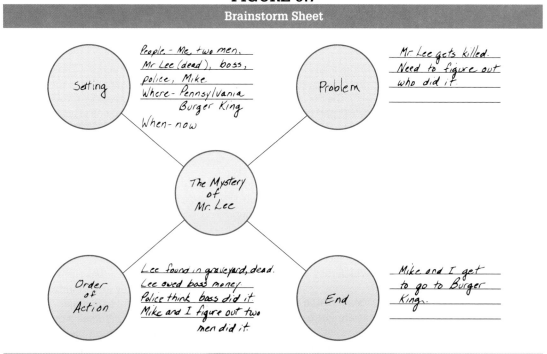

FIGURE 9.8

Cary's Brainstorm Sheet

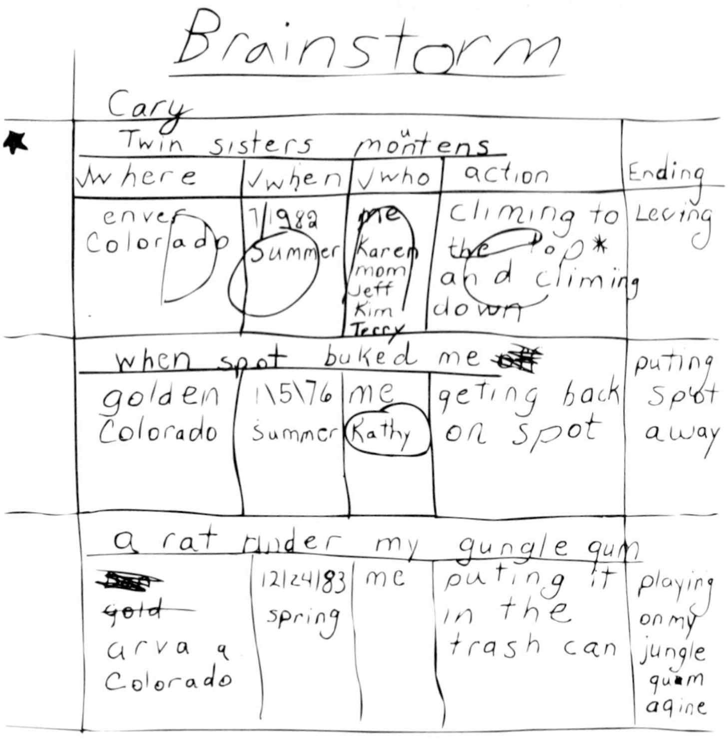

sheet in Figure 9.8. Graphic organizers can assist students in organizing the key ideas in their writing, remembering the steps in completing a well-written piece, and remembering writing strategies that they need to use.

Teaching students to think about what they are going to say before they write is generally a helpful technique. However, completing a visual representation before writing may not facilitate writing for all students (see Apply the Concept 9.5).

Composing

Many students with learning and behavior problems begin the writing process here. They think of a topic and, without much planning, begin to write. They write ideas as they think of them, and each idea they write serves as a stimulus for the next idea (Graham, Harris, et al., 1995). Therefore, another important instructional goal is to guide students to be more reflective as they write (Graham, Harris, et al., 1995).

Some authors suggest using cue cards to assist students in writing better-developed stories or essays (De La Paz, 1999). A cue card, used by Montague and Leavell (1994), asks students to consider the following elements when composing: where and when, character (have them think and feel just like real people), problem and plan, and story ending.

Apply the Concept 9.5

The Big Picture

"The most difficult thing for me to teach my students," said Ms. Zaragoza, "is to think about the ideas in their writing and to be willing to revise. My students thought good writing and good spelling were the same thing."

A common problem with poor writers is that the surface structure of their writing—the spelling, grammar, and punctuation—prevents them from expressing their ideas in writing. Many students with learning problems do not focus on thinking about their story. Their stories are often poorly organized, and their ideas are disconnected and/or missing. These same students can *tell* you about the story but have a hard time

getting all of the ideas about the story in writing.

Following is the description of a procedure developed by Kucer (1986) to help poor writers focus on the "big picture" of writing:

1. Give students notecards, and allow them to write possible topics on the cards (one topic per card). Students then share ideas about topics and make additions on their topic cards.
2. Students select a writing topic about which they would like to write.
3. Major ideas related to the writing topic are written on notecards. The major ideas may come

from the student's knowledge and experience or, if the writing is in a content area, the student may need to seek the assistance of class notes, books, and magazines. Major ideas are written as key concepts or thoughts rather than as complete sentences.
4. Students share their major ideas about the topics with each other. They make any additions or comments about the ideas they feel will be helpful in writing about the topics.
5. Once major ideas have been selected, they are organized in a meaningful sequence.
6. With their cards as a guide, students write their pieces.

Englert and her colleagues (Englert et al., 1991) developed think sheets to assist students in first planning and then organizing their ideas before writing. Figure 9.9 presents the plan think sheet, and Figure 9.10 presents the organization think sheet for the text structure associated with explanations.

FIGURE 9.9
Plan Think Sheet

PLAN

Name ________________ Date ________________

TOPIC: ____________________

WHO: Who am I writing for?

____

____

WHY: Why am I writing this?

____

____

WHAT: What do I know? (Brainstorm)

1. ____________________________________
2. ____________________________________
3. ____________________________________
4. ____________________________________
5. ____________________________________
6. ____________________________________
7. ____________________________________
8. ____________________________________

HOW: How can I group my ideas?

[ ] [ ]

________________ ________________

________________ ________________

[ ] [ ]

________________ ________________

________________ ________________

How will I organize my ideas?

___ Compare/Contrast ___ Problem/Solution
___ Explanation ___ Other

Source: C. S. Englert, T. E. Raphael, and L. M. Anderson, *Cognitive Strategy Instruction in Writing Project* (East Lansing, MI: Institute for Research on Teaching, 1989). Reprinted by permission.

Once children begin composing, sharing their work with others plays an important role in the writing process. Children need time to read and discuss their pieces with individual students, small groups of students, and the teacher. The author's chair (Graves and Hansen, 1983) is one way to provide a formal opportunity to share writing. Leila, a fifth grader with behavior problems, signed up for the author's chair early in the week. She thought that her story about a dog that could fly was pretty good, and she looked forward to reading it to the entire class. During author's chair, Leila enjoyed the attention from the group while she read her story to them. After the reading, she asked them whether they had any comments or questions. She called on several students who commented on sections of the story they liked and other students who asked questions. Chitra wanted to know more about what the wings on the dog looked like. Rhonda wondered why the story ended the way it did. Leila answered the questions with the ownership of a professional author and made some decisions about parts she would change and how she would add more description about what the dog looked like.

Teachers often need to set rules about students' behavior when a classmate is sharing work in the author's chair. These rules may include raising one's hand, asking a question or making a positive comment, and giving feedback when asked.

One of the skills that students must acquire is how to write sentences that are effective and then to organize these effective sentences into meaningful paragraphs. There are several critical elements that students with learning and behavior problems must be taught explicitly: how to add vivid words and lively verbs, how to combine short and choppy sentences to make more productive sentences, how to reduce long and run-on sentences, and how to read and revise to add meaning. These skills can be taught and practiced separately and then monitored and supported when students write texts. Instructional principles and examples include:

- Teach students to paint a picture with words by using adjectives and adverbs to show readers what they mean. For example, rather than "I ate lunch," the student can write, "I ate my lunch quickly, shoving large bites into my mouth."
- Teach students to avoid using common verbs such as *was, were,* and *said* and instead use more interesting verbs such as *avoided, clamored, quipped, barked, existed,* and *repeated.* In fact, teachers can make lists of words to substitute for more common words and post the lists in the room as a resource. Students can expand the lists themselves by adding more interesting words.
- Teach students to list ideas and then to sequence them (Troia and Graham, 2002).

FIGURE 9.10

Organization Think Sheet for Explanation of Text Structure

Explanation Organization Form

What is being explained?

[ ]

Materials/things you need?

[ ]

Setting?

[ ]

What are the steps?

First,

[ ]

Next,

[ ]

Third,

[ ]

Then,

[ ]

Last,

[ ]

Source: C. S. Englert, T. E. Raphael, and L. M. Anderson, *Cognitive Strategy Instruction in Writing Project* (East Lansing, MI: Institute for Research on Teaching, 1989). Reprinted by permission.

Spotlight on Diversity

Guidelines for Teaching Writing to Students Who Are English Language Learners

When teaching writing to English language learners (ELLs), it is important to know that their writing is influenced by several factors: their knowledge of the English language, English vocabulary development, understanding of word use, and knowledge of the conventions of writing such as noun–verb agreement. For this reason, teachers should be familiar with what these learners know about English and should expect that the development of their writing will reflect this knowledge. For example, teachers should not expect the same level of grammatical accuracy from ELLs as from most native English speakers. However, it is important to provide ELLs with many opportunities to use written expression and to promote and support their acquisition of writing skills. Many of the approaches to writing that are discussed in this chapter are highly appropriate for ELLs. Teachers should ask themselves the following questions when planning writing instruction for ELLs (Haley and Austin, 2004):

- Do they know what they want to write about?
- Do they feel comfortable using their personal, family, and other relevant experiences in their writing?
- Do they use what they know to support their writing?
- What ways are helpful to get them to start thinking about their composition?
- Do they try to use new words in their writing?
- Do they get suggestions for their writing from family and friends?
- Do they use procedures for deciding what is important and not important in their writing?
- Do they choose different ways to express their ideas and feelings in their writing?
- Do they increasingly use more appropriate and effective language in their writing?

Revising

Revising is a difficult task for all authors and especially for students with learning problems. Getting the entire message down on paper the first time is difficult enough; making changes so the piece is at its best and can be understood by others is a most formidable task. Many authors need to go back to prewriting and obtain more information, or they spend time conferring with others to find out what parts of their sentences or ideas require additional work. It is also at this stage that some authors abandon the piece. They believe it can never be really good, and so they start again with a new idea.

Most students with learning and behavior problems have difficulty revising. They approach revision as a "housekeeping" task, making few or no substantive changes (MacArthur, Graham, and Schwartz, 1991). Many would like to move straight to publication, with little or no revision. Ms. Takamura suggests modeling and patience.

She finds that students will revise their pieces if teachers show them how through the work of other students or the work of professional authors.

At first, their writing is more like a journal—a chance to write about how they feel and what is happening in their relationships. It is an intimate exchange between them and the teacher, eventually between them and selected students, and finally between them and a larger audience. This progression does not happen quickly nor necessarily in this order.

Students with learning disabilities, particularly adolescents (Wong, Butler, Ficzere, and Kuperis, 1997), can learn procedures such as diagnosing, comparing, and operating to assist them during the revision process (De La Paz, Swanson, and Graham, 1998). When teachers model, demonstrate, and provide feedback using the following procedure, students' revisions and writing improve.

Compare and Diagnose. Read your writing and consider the following:

- It ignores the obvious point against my idea.
- There are too few ideas.
- Part of the essay doesn't belong with the rest.
- Part of the essay is not in the right order.

Tactic Operations. The listed problems can be fixed by doing the following:

- Rewrite
- Delete
- Add
- Move

Compare. Reread the paper, and highlight problems.

Diagnose and Operate. Read your writing and determine whether any of the following apply:

- This doesn't sound right.
- This isn't what I intended to say.
- This is an incomplete idea.
- This part is not clear.
- The problem is _____.

Teachers can show students how to use a "box and explode" strategy as a means for selecting the one sentence in their writing that is the most important but may not be adequately expanded (Block, 1997; Gersten and Baker, 2001; Strickland, Ganske, and Monroe, 2002). Students learn to put this sentence in a box and then to use it as a focus for extending the idea and clarifying story events. Students are taught to "explode" the main idea in the box. For example, suppose a student wrote the following paragraph:

> Julia went to her aunt's house on Sunday. After she got there she saw that her aunt's door was open. She walked in the house and saw her uncle on the floor. She didn't know what to do.

Students would be taught to put a box around the sentence "She walked in the house and saw her uncle on the floor." Then they would work to "explode" that sentence so that the reader would learn more about what happened.

Editing

In addition to editing their own work, students serve as editors for the work of their peers. This can work in several ways. One way is to have students edit their own work first and then ask a friend to edit it. Another possibility is to establish a class editor. The responsibility of the class editor is to read the material and search for mechanical errors. The role of the class editor could rotate so that every student has an opportunity to serve in that capacity.

Whereas revision focuses mainly on content, editing focuses mainly on mechanics. After the student and teacher are happy with the content, it is time to make corrections for spelling, capitalizing, punctuation, and language. Students are expected to circle words they are unsure how to spell, put boxes in places where they are unsure of the punctuation, and underline the sentences about which they feel the language may not be correct. Students are not expected to correct all errors but are expected to correct known errors. Figure 9.11 provides a poster that can be used in a classroom to remind students of the editing rules. Figure 9.12 depicts a form that can be included inside the students' folders to remind them of editing skills they know how to use. Figure 9.13 provides guidelines for how teachers and peers might respond to writing.

Although many spelling, punctuation, and language modifications are made during writing

FIGURE 9.11
Editing Rules

Ⓒircle misspelled words.

Put a box around punctuation.

Underline writing that doesn't sound so good.

Add a ^ to insert a word or phrase.

Add a ⓪̂ with a number to insert a sentence.

FIGURE 9.12
Editing Skills I Know

Spelling

1. done
2. was
3. from
4. come
5. girl
6. because
7. what
8. where
9. children
10. playground

Punctuation

1. Put a period at the end of a sentence.
2. Put a question mark at the end of an asking sentence.

Capitalization

1. Capitalize the first letter of a sentence.
2. Capitalize the first letter of a person's name.
3. Capitalize the name of a town.

FIGURE 9.13
Ways for Teachers and Peers to Respond to Writing

Suggestions to Compliment Writing

- I like the way your paper began because . . .
- I like the part where . . .
- I like the way you explained . . .
- I like the order you used in your paper because . . .
- I like the details you used to describe . . .
- I like the way you used dialogue to make your story sound real.
- I like the words you used in your writing, such as . . .
- I like the facts you used like . . .
- I like the way the paper ended because . . .
- I like the mood of your writing because it made me feel . . .

Questions and Suggestions to Improve Writing

- I got confused in the part about . . .
- Could you add an example to the part about . . .
- Could you add more to this _____ part because . . .
- Do you think your order would make more sense if you . . .
- Do you think you could leave this part out because . . .
- Could you use a different word for _____ because . . .
- Is this _____ paragraph on one topic?
- Could you write a beginning sentence to "grab" your readers?

and revising, when students edit, they focus solely on mechanical errors. Often, they need to read the text for each type of error. First, they read the text looking for spelling difficulties; next, they read the text looking for punctuation and capitalization difficulties; and finally, they read the text looking for language problems such as noun–verb agreement. Young students may not know what noun–verb agreement is, so they should simply look for sentences that do not "sound right" when they read them aloud.

The following suggestions are designed to assist students in removing the mechanical errors from their writing (Isaacson and Gleason, 1997):

- Have students dictate their story to improve the flow of their writing.
- Provide students with a list of key words and words that are hard to spell to assist with writing and editing.
- Teach students to use a word book.
- Promote peer collaboration in editing.
- Teach students to use technology to support editing and writing.
- Hold students accountable for using the rules of writing they know, such as punctuation, spelling, and other writing conventions that they have been taught.

Publishing

Not all writing is published; often, only one in five or six pieces is published. What does it mean to have a piece published? A piece is prepared in some way that it can be read and shared by others. For younger students this may be in the form of books that have cardboard binding decorated with contact paper, scraps of wallpaper, or clip art. Sometimes these books include a picture of the author, a description of the author, and a list of books published by the author.

Older students who spend more time composing and revising are more likely to "publish" or "publicly share" work that is the result of many weeks of effort and several revisions. Why publish? Publishing is a way of confirming a student's hard work and sharing the piece with others. Writing requires an audience, and periodically we need to share what we write. It is important for all students to publish—not just the best authors. Publishing is a way of involving others in the school and home with the students' writing.

What Can Families Do to Promote Children's Writing?

Encourage parents/guardians to play with their children and adolescents using words. Ask them to be sure that the writing they promote and do with their children is fun, interesting, and encourages learning. As children get older, encourage them to use writing as a means of communicating with grandparents or other family members. Suggest that parents/guardians leave notes for their children on their pillows, by their plates, and in other places where the children are likely to find them. Encourage the children to leave notes for family members.

Following are some fun and simple activities that children (and their families) will love. Families can make the activities easier or more challenging depending the children's ability.

For beginning or reluctant writers:

- Spell with letter blocks or magnetic letters, or write the alphabet on small pieces of paper and store it in an envelope. Give children four or five letters, and ask them to spell simple words. Ask the child to find the letters that spell *bed, bad, bat,* and *bet.* This is writing without actually having to "write."
- Help children make labels for their room. Use colorful markers and paper to write *chair, desk, bed, window, curtains, computer, fish, floor, closet,* and so on. Tape the labels on the objects.
- Go on a word walk. Go outside with a pad or clipboard. Look in one direction, and write everything you see. Compare notes with the children. Or write down only things that are green, moving, in the sky, or on the ground, and so on.
- Make a list. Children love to help with grocery lists, lists of errands, wish lists, chores, things to do on a rainy Saturday, and so on.
- Make a word collage. Have children cut words out of the newspaper or old magazines and glue them on paper to make a word collage. Help children read the words they found.

For more competent writers:

- Play the "What am I?" game: Take turns writing or giving a description and trying to guess what it is. *You can sit on me. I like to be near tables. I am sometimes made of wood. What am I?* Answer: *A chair.*
- Do a sentence switcheroo. Start by writing a simple sentence. For example, "The man walked down the street." Take turns changing or adding words. The sentence might become "The friendly old man ran up the gigantic mountain."
- Write alliterative sentences with words that start with the same letter. For example, "Six slimy snakes slithered into my salami sandwich."
- Write a letter to a friend or relative, and send it in the mail or use email.

- Write questions. Children have lots of questions. Write them down. For example, "Do dogs dream? What do ladybugs eat? Why can't I eat candy for breakfast?" Help children find answers to their questions at the library or on the Internet.

Tech Tips 9.1 provides ideas for using computer software to help young writers.

Promoting Writing

Writing conferences in which teachers use time with students to promote and improve their writing are a critical aspect of promoting successful writing. The writing conference and establishing a writing community are discussed in the next sections.

The Writing Conference

Conferring is the heart of the writing process. Students come to the writing conference prepared to read their piece, to describe problem areas, and to be asked questions. When students confer with the teacher, they know they will be listened to and responded to. The teacher's nonverbal and verbal interactions communicate to students that he or she wants to listen and help.

Students also know that they will be asked challenging questions about their work. Questions are not asked in a rapid-fire sequence with little time for the student to formulate answers. Instead, questions are carefully selected, and enough time is allowed for the student to respond. Conferences focus on specific areas and are not designed to address all elements of the writing process. During the conference with the author of "My Best Football Game" (see Apply the Concept 9.6), the teacher realized that the piece of writing had many problems. She was aware of grammatical, spelling, and punctuation errors. She was also aware that the story rambled, lacked sufficient details, and did not reflect the author's voice. However, she was ecstatic that this 14-year-old student with severe emotional problems had produced a piece of writing that he was excited about. Apply the Concept 9.7 presents the conference the teacher had with the student.

Some key points about conferring with students are as follows:

- Do not attempt to get the writer to write about a topic because it is of interest to you or to write the story the way you would write it.
- Ask the student what steps in the writing process were used to develop this piece.
- Ask questions that teach. (Apply the Concept 9.8 illustrates a conference in which the teacher asks questions that teach.)

9.1 Using Technology to Develop Written Expression

Computer programs can help learners with written expression in many ways. First, there are the basic utilities that most of us use at one time or another—word processors, spelling checkers, and grammar checkers. Word processing programs with spelling and grammar checkers built in can be configured different ways through software preferences or formatting options. There are also freestanding spelling and grammar programs for use with email or other text entry software without built-in checkers.

Another type of program called word prediction software can help learners who are poor spellers or poor typists. When the user types an initial letter, the software brings up a list of words beginning with that letter. If the desired word is in the list, the user can select it several different ways. If it is not in the list, the learner types the second letter. The list changes to reflect the letters typed by the learner. *Co:Writer*™ *SE* from Don Johnston Incorporated (www.donjohnston.com) is used in conjunction with any word processor or text entry program to reduce the keystrokes necessary to enter text, providing spelling help along the way.

Talking word processors are another tool for learners who have difficulty with writing. Word processors such as *IntelliTalk 3* from IntelliTools, Inc. (www.intellitools.com) or *Write:OutLoud*™ from Don Johnston Incorporated can read any text aloud. Although these programs may have fewer features than typical word processors, the speech features offer functionality such as speaking letters as they are typed and speaking words, sentences, and paragraphs. Other speech features include speaking any selected text and changing voice and speed.

Programs that teach writing are another useful option. First, a great program for teaching beginning spelling is *Show Me Spelling* from IntelliTools, Inc. From the

same company, *ReadyMade Primary Writing* provides standards-aligned activities, graduated in units of increasing difficulty to reinforce growing literacy skills. *The Secret Writer's Society* from 99V Smart Kids Software (www.smartkidssoftware.com) for grades three and up has six levels (missions) teaching topics such as capitalization, end punctuation, sentence writing, paragraph writing, planning and ordering sentences, and revision and editing. A final level guides the learner through the five-step writing process. *Draft:Builder*™ from Don Johnston Incorporated guides learners through three key steps in creating a first draft—organizing ideas, taking notes, and writing the draft, while displaying a visual representation of the steps as the learner progresses.

Don Johnston Incorporated has packaged *Co:Writer*™, *Write:OutLoud*™, *Draft:Builder*™, and a newly added title *Read:OutLoud*™ into a single integrated package called *SOLO*™ that helps learners build skills and utilize strategies as they use guided supports for reading comprehension and structured models for writing.

Using *Co:Writer*™ to Write a Fishing Story

My grandfather will take me fishing on Saturday. We are going to Summit Lake.

CoWriter - sample

I hope that I will ca

1: call
2: care
3: catch
4: carry
5: camp

6: cash
7: cause
8: calm
9: cancel

- Agree on the steps the student will take to improve the paper, and establish a procedure for checking that these activities occur.
- Conferences should be frequent and brief. Although conferences can range from 30 seconds to 10 minutes, most of them last only 2 to 3 minutes.

Establishing a Writing Community

Writing requires trust. For students to write well within their classroom, an environment of mutual

trust and respect is essential. Establishing a writing community requires that you take the following steps:

1. *Write every day for at least 30 minutes.* Students need time to think, write, discuss, rewrite, confer, revise, talk, read, and write some more. Good writing takes time.

2. *Encourage students to develop areas of expertise.* Younger students write about what they know. However, with encouragement, both

Apply the Concept 9.6

Sample Student Writing

"My best football game"

Football is my favorite game I like to play it even when I was little I played for a good team the bandits and one game we played against Macarther school and it started off with us 0 and them 7 and then the game was tied 7 to 7 and then it was time for me to sit on the bench and the score was 7-14 we was winning soon they told me to go back into the game it was getting close to the end and we wanted to win they said it was my turn to run a play and so I ran fast down the feild after the ball was Mike and I look back and see the ball coming right at me and I thought I was going to miss it but I kept looking at it and after I watched it I reached up and pulled the ball down and I kept on running and we won the game 7 to 21.

younger and older students can become experts in a particular area, subject, or writing form. This expertise takes time and inducement but provides students with confidence and experience in writing.

3. *Keep students' writing in folders.* Folders should include writing as documentation of what each student knows and has accomplished. This means that students' work stays with them during the year. Students can refer to their work to illustrate their progress, to indicate skills learned, and to demonstrate range of topic. Students should keep selected pieces from the year for the next year.

4. *Monitor students' progress, establish writing goals, and hold students accountable for learning and practicing what they know.* Together, identify the expected goals for each student, discuss what aspects of these goals are achieved and represented in their writing, and guide rewriting and skills lessons to ensure that these goals are met.

5. *Share writing.* Conclude writing time with an opportunity for students to read their writing to others and exchange comments and questions.

6. *Expand the writing community outside of the classroom.* Place published books by your students

Apply the Concept 9.7

Conferencing with the Author of "My Best Football Game"

Teacher: "Mark, this football game was a special one for you. I bet you have a lot of feelings about this game. What are some of your feelings about this game?"

Mark: "I felt good."

Teacher: "Did you feel good like when you remember your homework or was it stronger than that?"

Mark: "It was stronger. I felt great. Like I was a hero or something."

Teacher: "Like a hero?"

Mark: "Yeah, like in the movies. I really saved the game.

Well, I guess not really saved the game because we were already winning. But it was, like, 'cause I made the last touchdown it really said something."

Teacher: "What do you think it said?"

Mark: "It said, hey, watch out 'cause I'm good. Also, that we won and I scored the final points. It was great."

Teacher: "What could you do so the reader of your piece would know all of the things you just told me?"

Mark: "I guess I could include more about how I felt and all."

Teacher: "How could you do that? Where would it go?"

The teacher decided it was too early to focus on mechanical errors such as spelling and punctuation. Besides being discouraging to Mark, focusing too early on mechanical errors would sidetrack this writer from the story. After the author's story is complete, then work on mechanical errors can begin.

Apply the Concept 9.8

Conferencing: Following the Lead of the Student

During conferences, the teacher listens to what students say, follows the lead of the students, and asks questions that teach.

Teacher: "How's it going, Karin?"
Karin: "Not very good. I don't know what to write about."
Teacher: "You are having trouble with a topic?"
Karin: "I was going to write about how I want to go and live with my real mom again

but I don't know what to say. All I do is write that I want to live with my real mom and then the story is over."
Teacher: "It's hard to think of what else might go in the story?"
Karin: "Well, yeah. I guess I could tell why, but I don't know why, I just want to."
Teacher: "Would it be any easier to get started if you told the

story as though it were about someone else?"
Karin: "Like I could tell about a kid who wanted to go and live with her real mom. Then I could tell it like a story."
Teacher: "What are some of the things you might write if you told the story this way?"

in the library for use by other students, and allow students to share their writing with other classes. Encourage authors from other classrooms to visit and read their writings.

7. *Develop children's capacity to evaluate their own work.* Students need to develop their own goals and document their progress toward them. By conferring with the teacher, they will learn methods for evaluating their own work.

8. *Facilitate spelling during writing.* Teachers and students can provide instructional feedback to support students in spelling correctly during the writing process. (See Figure 9.14 for suggestions.)

9. *Assist students who are culturally and linguistically diverse.* Students from diverse cultures and whose first language is other than English often have specific needs in writing. With a few adjustments, teachers can create classroom communities that promote their success and learning. See Apply the Concept 9.9 for suggestions.

10. Remember to *teach students specific strategies for writing purposefully* such as compare and contrast, reports, persuasive writing, and interviews.

The writing process approach to instruction of children who have special needs requires time—time to follow the progress of students, confer with students, and teach skills. Most important, it requires time each day for the students to write. (See Apply the Concept 9.10.) Ms. deSouza, a teacher of emotionally disturbed adolescents who used the writing process approach

for the first time, commented, "Yes, it takes a great deal of time, but it's worth it. The students want to write. They have even started their own school newsletter. Best of all, they are seeing the connection between reading and writing. I feel it is worth the time."

Using Computers to Facilitate Writing

The use of spell checkers and speech synthesizers to facilitate writing effectiveness for students with learning disabilities has been well documented (Graham and Perin, 2007; MacArthur, 1988; McNaughton, Hughes, and Ofiesh, 1997; Morocco, Dalton, and Tivnan, 1992). These tools can be used to assist students whose writing or motor skills interfere with their ability to develop independent writing skills. Displaying writing on a computer monitor facilitates discussion between students and teachers and allows for immediate and easy editing (Zorfass, Corley, and Remz, 1994). When a computer-based speech recognition program was provided to college students with learning disabilities, the students performed significantly better on tasks of written expression than did students without the speech recognition program and as well as those who had an assistant (Higgins and Raskind, 1995).

Computers facilitate writing for students with learning problems because they do the following:

- Make revising and editing easier
- Increase the amount and quality of revision completed
- Provide spell-checking features

FIGURE 9.14

Providing Instructional Feedback to Facilitate Spelling Correctly

Prompts to Help Students Notice Errors

- Check to see if that looks/sounds right.
- There is a tricky word on this line.
- You are nearly right.
- Try that again.
- Try it another way.
- You have almost got that. See if you can find what is wrong.

Prompts to Help Students Find Errors

- Find the part that is not right.
- Look carefully to see what's wrong.
- You noticed something was wrong.
- Where is the part that is not right?
- What made you stop?
- Can you find the problem spot?

Prompts to Help Students Fix Errors

- What do you hear first? Next? Last?
- What word starts with those letters?
- Do you think it looks/sounds like _____?
- What does an *e* do at the end of a word?
- What do you know that might help?
- What could you try?
- You have only one letter to change.
- That sounds right, but does it look right?
- One more letter will make it right.
- It starts like that. Now check the last part.
- Did you write all the sounds you hear?
- Did you write a vowel for each syllable?
- It starts (ends) like _____.
- There is a silent letter in that word.
- You wrote all the sounds you hear. Now look at what you wrote—think!

Prompts of Encouragement

- I like the way you worked that out.
- The results are worth all your hard work.
- You have come a long way with this one.
- That was some quick thinking.
- That looks like an impressive piece of work.
- You are right on target.
- You are on the right track now.
- Now you have figured it out.
- That is quite an improvement.
- That is quite an accomplishment.
- That is coming along.

- You are really settling down to work.
- You have shown a lot of patience with this.
- You have been paying close attention.
- You have put in a full day today.
- I knew you could finish it.
- You make it look so easy.
- You have really tackled that assignment.
- This shows you have been thinking/working.
- It looks like you have put a lot of work into this.

Sources: Adapted from I. C. Fountas and G. S. Pinnell, *Guided Reading: Good First Teaching for All Children* (Portsmouth, NH: Heinemann, 1996); I. C. Fountas and G. S. Pinnell, *Word Matters: Teaching Phonics and Spelling in the Reading/Writing Classroom* (Portsmouth, NH: Heinemann, 1998); and E. B. Fry, J. E. Kress, and D. L. Fountoukidis, *The Reading Teacher's Book of Lists* (New York: Center for Applied Research in Education, 1993).

- Produce neat printed copies that enhance readability
- Allow for easy error correction (MacArthur et al., 1995)

Response to Intervention and Writing

Response to intervention can be used with writing, as described in previous chapters addressing writing and in the subsequent chapter on math. How might response to intervention be used for students with writing difficulties? Students with extreme writing challenges might be provided extra time each day (20 minutes) and extra instruction to determine if their writing improved. Specific research-based strategies like those identified in Graham and Harris (2005) might be implemented. Teachers can

maintain copies of students' writing to determine if adequate progress in writing has occurred.

Writing with Older Students

Most of the practices described above are designed to be used with a broad range of learners. However, the crises in the overall poor quality of students' writing has provided a push for improving writing with older students. Recently, the Carnegie Corporation of New York (Graham and Perin, 2007) issued a report on effective writing practices for older students (grades 4–12). They suggest the following research-based practices:

- Teach students writing strategies that include planning, revising, and editing their compositions. Many of the writing strategies

Apply the Concept 9.9

Considerations for Students Who Are Culturally and Linguistically Diverse

Creating a learning community in the classroom that provides opportunities for all students to succeed is essential to promoting effective written expression. A few guidelines follow.

- Have high expectations for all students. Teachers demonstrate respect and provide opportunities when they treat each student as an able writer and provide the support necessary to ensure their success.
- Allow students to write about topics they know and have experienced. Students with diverse backgrounds and experiences should be viewed as having a rich source of material for writing. Students benefit when they are encouraged to tap into their backgrounds and experiences and to share them with others.
- Allow students to teach all of us about their backgrounds and expe-

riences through their writing. Students' writing can be viewed as an opportunity for them to better inform us about themselves, their families and communities, and their interpretations of them. Students will want to write when they perceive that their writing has a purpose and is instructive to others.

- Encourage family involvement in writing. Parents and/or family members often have a rich bank of stories and experiences that they are willing to share with the class if encouraged to do so. These experiences and stories can provide background for students' writing or can be used to prompt stories and ideas.
- Create a classroom setting that is culturally compatible. The social organization of the classroom can facilitate or impair the written expression of students from diverse

cultures. Whole-class instructional formats with high expectations for students to volunteer to answer questions may not be compatible with their cultural backgrounds. Read and ask questions about the cultures of the students in your classroom so that you can establish a writing lab that is responsive to their learning styles.

Diversity

Family

- Use materials, stories, and books that are culturally relevant. Read stories about a range of cultures to students. Encourage students to exchange stories that are culturally familiar. Provide examples of cultures that are similar and different from the ones represented in your classroom.

---

discussed previously were developed to meet this recommendation.

- Help students combine sentences to achieve more complex sentence types and to summarize texts.
- Provide opportunities for students to work together in pairs and groups toward cooperative written products to facilitate quality of composition.
- Establish goals for students' writing to improve outcomes.
- Give students access to and instruction in word processing to facilitate writing.
- Assist students in developing prewriting practices that help generate or organize ideas for writing.
- Use inquiry activities to analyze data related to writing reports.
- Use writing process approaches that provide extended time for writing and revision.
- Provide students with good models of writing to study and to compare with their own writing.
- Use writing as a tool to enhance content knowledge.

FOCUS Question 2. **What are the critical features of spelling assessment and instruction for students with learning and behavior problems?**

Assessing and Teaching Spelling

Most students with learning and behavior disorders need specific instruction in spelling and handwriting. This is in part because students with spelling difficulties do not have visual memory problems (Lennox and Siegel, 1996) but have poor phonological processing skills (Lennox and Siegel, 1998). In other words, the core phonological deficit, discussed in the reading chapter as causing reading problems, also causes spelling difficulties.

Manuel hates spelling and finds it the most frustrating part of writing. He is an eighth-grade student who is adjusting to the transition from a self-contained classroom for emotionally disturbed

Apply the Concept 9.10

Ten Pointers for Teaching Writing to Students with Special Learning Needs

1. *Allocate adequate time for writing.* Adequate time is a necessary but not sufficient criterion for improving the writing skills of special learners. Students who merely spend 10 to 15 minutes a day practicing the craft of writing are not spending adequate time to improve their skills. Students need a minimum of 30 minutes of time for writing every day.

2. *Provide a range of writing tasks.* Writing about what students know best—self-selected topic— is the first step in writing. After students' skills improve, the range of writing tasks should broaden to include problem solving, writing games, and a variety of writing tasks.

3. *Create a social climate that promotes and encourages writing.* Teachers set the tone through an accepting, encouraging manner. Conferences between students, students and teachers, and students and other persons in the school are conducted to provide constructive feedback on their writing and to provide an audience to share what is written.

4. *Integrate writing with other academic subjects.* Writing can be integrated with almost every subject that is taught. This includes using writing as a means of expression in content area subjects such as social studies and science as well as part of an instructional activity with reading and language arts.

5. *Focus on the processes central to writing.* These processes include prewriting activities, writing, and rewriting activities.

6. *During the writing phase, focus on the higher-order task of composing, and attend to the basic elements of spelling and punctuation after the writing is complete.* Some students' mechanics of writing are so poor that they interfere with the students' ability to get ideas down on paper successfully. With these students, focus first on some of the basic elements so that the writing process can be facilitated.

7. *Teach explicit knowledge about characteristics of good writing.* The implicit knowledge about writing needs to be made explicit. For example, different genres and their characteristics need to be discussed and practiced.

8. *Teach skills that aid higher-level composing.* These skills include conferencing with teachers and peers, and strategy instruction. Strategy instruction may provide guidelines for brainstorming, sentence composition, or evaluating the effectiveness of the written piece.

9. *Ask students to identify goals for improving their writing.* Students can set realistic goals regarding their progress in writing. These goals can focus on prewriting, writing, and/or rewriting. Both the students and the teacher can provide feedback as to how successful the students have been in realizing their goals.

10. *Do not use instructional practices that are not associated with improved writing for students.* Several examples of instructional practice not associated with improved writing are grammar instruction, diagramming sentences, and overemphasis on students' errors.

Source: Adapted from S. Graham and K. R. Harris (1988). Instructional recommendations for teaching writing to exceptional students. *Exceptional Children, 54* (6), pp. 506–512.

students to a resource room in a junior high setting. He has been involved in the writing process approach for the past two years and has learned to use writing to express his feelings, convey information, and create stories. Manuel is proud of the way his writing has improved, and he often shares his stories with others. But he has difficulty with spelling. Manuel has learned to use inventive spelling (spelling words the way they sound or the way he thinks they are spelled) to aid in getting his ideas on paper, but he has difficulty editing because he is unable to detect or correct most of his spelling errors. Like many students with learning and behavior disorders, Manuel

needs specialized instruction in spelling to be a successful writer.

Spelling is an important tool in our society. Many people measure one's intelligence or education by the ability to spell. Spelling is particularly difficult in the English language because there is not a one-to-one correspondence between the individual sounds of spoken words and the letters of the written words. We learn to spell many words by remembering the unique combination or order of letters that produce the correct spelling of that word. Spelling facilitates the writing process by freeing the writer to concentrate on content. Although most students with learning disabilities have spelling difficulties (Johnson and Myklebust, 1967), spelling is often difficult even for those without a learning disability. Most beginning writers identify spelling as the key problem they need to solve in writing (Graves, 1983). Many good readers are poor spellers, and almost all poor readers are poor spellers (Carpenter and Miller, 1982, Frith, 1980).

Students who have a very difficult time learning to read perform poorly when compared with average readers on tasks of phonological awareness (e.g., Vellutino and Scanlon, 1987). Ehri (1989) suggests that they have phonological difficulties because they have not learned to read and spell.

This section will focus on teaching spelling to students who have learning difficulties. Techniques for analyzing students' spelling errors will be discussed first, followed by a discussion of principles to be applied in developing spelling programs, approaches to teaching spelling, and what the research says about teaching spelling.

Error Analysis

The first step in developing an appropriate spelling program is to determine the type and pattern of the students' spelling errors. After completion of an error analysis, a spelling approach based on students' needs can be implemented.

Error analysis should be done by using both dictated spelling tests and a student's written work. Random errors do not occur in the spelling of most students with learning disabilities. They are consistent in the types of misspellings to which they are prone (DeMaster, Crossland, and Hasselbring, 1986).

When Manuel and his teacher, Laurie Redwing, attempted to develop Manuel's spelling program, they began by selecting samples of his written work, which included writing he had created and work written from dictation. Ms. Redwing examined these pieces to determine whether there was a pattern to his spelling errors. Ms. Redwing asked herself the following questions about Manuel's spelling:

- Is he applying mistaken rules?
- Is he applying rules that assist him in remembering spellings?
- Is he making careless errors on words he knows how to spell?
- Is he spelling words correctly in isolation but not in context?
- Are there frequently used words that he is consistently misspelling?

After examining the written work and answering these questions, Ms. Redwing discovered the following:

- Manuel did not apply the "-ing" rule appropriately. For example, *run* became *runing*.
- Manuel did not use the spelling rule "*i* before *e* except after *c*." For example, he spelled *believe* as *beleive* and *piece* as *peice*.
- He was inconsistent in spelling words. He would spell them correctly in one piece of written work but not in another.
- He spelled several words correctly on spelling tests but not in context.
- He misspelled many frequently used words, such as *there, was, because, somewhere, very,* and *would.*

After answering the questions, Ms. Redwing examined Manuel's work to look for the following error patterns:

- Additions of unneeded letters (e.g., *boxxes*)
- Omissions of letters (e.g., *som*)
- Reflections of mispronunciations (e.g., *ruf* for *roof*)
- Reflections of dialect (e.g., *sodar* for *soda*)
- Reversals of whole words (e.g., *eno* for *one*)
- Reversals of consonant order (e.g., *cobm* for *comb*)
- Reversals of consonant or vowel directionality (e.g., *Thrusday* for *Thursday*)
- Phonetic spellings of nonphonetic word parts (e.g., *site* for *sight*)
- Neographisms, which are spellings that don't resemble the word (e.g., *sumfin* for *something*)
- Combinations of error patterns

In addition to examining Manuel's work, Ms. Redwing interviewed and observed Manuel to determine what strategies he used when he was unable to spell a word and whether he used any corrective or proofreading strategies after he wrote. Ms. Redwing observed Manuel's writing and then asked him the following two questions:

1. *When you finish writing a piece, what do you do?* (Ms. Redwing was attempting to determine whether Manuel rereads for spelling errors.)
2. *If you are writing and do not know how to spell a word, what do you do?* (Ms. Redwing was attempting to determine what, if any, strategies he used. Did he use invented spelling to facilitate the writing process and underline the word so that he could check the spelling later? Did he stop and try to visualize the word or look for how it was spelled in another location? Did he continue writing and go back later to check the spelling?)

Ms. Redwing discovered that Manuel used few strategies to check or recall spelling when he was writing. In addition to teaching and rehearsing spelling rules, Manuel needed to learn and apply strategies for improving his spelling. After error analysis, intervention included discussing with Manuel the types of errors he was making, teaching him proofreading skills, teaching him techniques for remembering the correct spelling of words, and teaching him one of the spelling approaches discussed in the following subsections. Before looking at specialized approaches to teaching spelling to students with learning and behavior disorders, we will first examine traditional approaches to spelling instruction.

Traditional Spelling Instruction

Spelling is taught in most classrooms through an integrated reading and writing approach or the use of spelling basal programs. Typical spelling basals include a prescribed list of weekly words to be mastered by all students. In the usual procedure, a pretest occurs on Monday, followed on Tuesday by a description of the spelling theme (e.g., long *e* words, homophones, *au* words). Wednesday and Thursday typically involve assignments from the text that students work on independently. These assignments usually include dictionary activities; sentence or paragraph writing using the spelling words; writing the words a designated number of times; and using the words in sentences, stories, or crossword puzzles. Friday is usually designated for the posttest in spelling. Although variations on this format occur, such as when the teacher attempts to individualize the spelling program, most classrooms follow a procedure similar to this.

How effective is this procedure for teaching spelling to students with learning disabilities? What other procedures might need to be considered in developing effective spelling strategies for these students? The spelling practices used in most classrooms are based more on tradition than on research (Gettinger, 1984; Gordon, Vaughn, and Schumm, 1993; Graham, 1999). For most students with learning difficulties, the introduction of all the words at once, often words that are not in the students' reading vocabularies, and the lack of systematic practice and specific feedback make spelling difficult if not impossible. Before discussing specific strategies for teaching spelling to students with learning disabilities, in the following section we discuss the role of phonics rules in teaching spelling.

Phonics Rules for Spelling

How much emphasis should be placed on teaching phonics rules to improve spelling? There is probably no area of the language arts curriculum that has been more carefully reviewed, researched, and debated than spelling. At the heart of many of the debates is the efficacy of using a phonics approach to teaching spelling. Some researchers suggest that a phonics approach improves spelling ability (Baker, 1977; Gold, 1976; Thompson, 1977), others argue that students learn the rules without direct instruction in phonics (Schwartz and Doehring, 1977), and still others insist that intensive phonics instruction is not necessary (Grottenthaler, 1970; Personkee and Yee, 1971; Warren, 1970). Recent evidence suggests that students who are taught spelling alongside code-based (phonics) reading instruction improve in both spelling and word reading (O'Connor and Jenkins, 1995; Snow, Burns, and Griffin, 1998). At least for young children, a code-based approach to reading and spelling is likely to be both necessary and helpful. Students with learning problems require systematic and explicit instruction in phonics rules and how these rules relate to writing words. Thus, students need to be taught the clear connection between phonics rules in reading and spelling.

Because there is a lack of consistency in phonics rules, primary emphasis should be given to basic spelling vocabulary with supplemented instruction in basic phonics rules (Graham and Miller, 1979). According to Graham and Miller (1979), the phonetic skills that should be taught include base words, prefixes, suffixes, consonants, consonant blends, digraphs, and vowel sound–symbol associations. The important relationship between rhyming and spelling is illustrated in Apply the Concept 9.11.

Principles for Teaching Spelling to Students with Learning Difficulties

Several principles should be included in any spelling approach that is used in teaching students who have learning problems.

Teach in Small Units

Teach 3 words a day rather than 4 or 5 (or 15 at the beginning of the week). In a study (Bryant, Drabin, and Gettinger, 1981) in which the number of spelling words allocated each day to students with learning disabilities was controlled, higher performance, less distractibility, and less variance in overall performance were obtained from the group with learning disabilities assigned 3 words a day, when compared with groups assigned 4 and 5 words a day.

Apply the Concept 9.11

Relationship between Rhyming and Spelling

Rhyming and alliteration are positively and significantly related to progress in spelling (Bradley and Bryant, 1983). A possible explanation is that rhyming teaches students to identify phonological segments and it demonstrates how words can be grouped together according to common sounds. Students' participation at an early age, before they start school, in rhyming games and activities may be an important prerequisite to spelling success.

Teach Spelling Patterns

If the spelling lists each week are based on spelling patterns (Bloodgood, 1991; Carrekar, 1999), students have a better chance of learning and remembering them. Several sample word lists based on patterned spelling follow:

List 1	List 2	List 3
cat	am	aim
bat	slam	claim
rat	clam	chain
fat	tram	rain
sat	tam	train
can	Pam	gain
fan	same	regain
ran	fame	brain
man	tame	pain
tan	blame	afraid
	flame	braid
	frame	

Zutell (1993) and Graham, Harris, and Loynachan (1996) recommend the use of contrast words to assist in identifying and teaching spelling patterns. Thus, the spelling patterns that are taught in the sample word lists 1–3 would be supplemented with several words that do not fit the pattern. Students would then be encouraged to identify the pattern and sort the words that do not fit.

Provide Sufficient Practice and Feedback

Give students opportunities to practice the words each day and provide feedback. Many teachers do this by having students work with spelling partners who ask them their words and provide immediate feedback. The following method can be used for self-correction and practice. Fold a paper into five columns. Write the correctly spelled words in the first column. The student studies one word, folds the column back, and writes the word in the second column. The student then checks his or her spelling with the correctly spelled word in the first column. After folding the column back, the student writes the word in the third column. The student continues writing the word until it has been spelled correctly three times. The student then moves to the next word and continues until the word is spelled correctly three times in a row. This procedure should not be confused with spelling assignments that require the student to write the assigned spelling words a designated number of times. Those procedures are often ineffective because the student does not attend to the details of the spelling word as a whole, often writes the word in segments, and usually copies rather than writing from memory. The student also fails to check words after each writing, sometimes resulting in words being practiced incorrectly. Adding peer tutoring can help to alleviate these problems (see Apply the Concept 9.12).

Select Appropriate Words

The most important strategy for teaching spelling is that the students already should be able to read the word and know its meaning. Spelling should not focus on teaching the students to read and know the meaning of words. Selection of spelling words should be based on the students' reading and meaning vocabularies. Ideally, high-frequency words should be used (Graham and Voth, 1990).

Teach Spelling through Direct Instruction

Incidental learning in spelling is reserved primarily for good spellers. Spelling words can be selected from the students' reading or written words or can be part of a programmed text, such as lists provided in basal readers. Direct instruction includes mastery of specific words each day, individualized instruction, and continual review.

Apply the Concept 9.12

Peer Tutoring and Spelling

Use of peer tutors to teach spelling can be helpful in improving spelling for the tutors and the tutees. When a peer tutoring system was used with a mainstreamed student with learning disabilities and a good speller from the classroom, the spelling performance of the student with learning disabilities improved and both students rated the peer tutoring system favorably (Mandoli, Mandoli, and McLaughlin, 1982). To increase effectiveness, peer tutors should be trained to implement the spelling approach that is most suitable for the target student.

Use Instructional Language

The language of instruction, or the dialogue between teachers and students, is critical to success in spelling, particularly for youngsters with learning and behavior problems. Gerber and Hall (1989) indicate that a teacher's language provides a structure that calls attention to critical relationships within and between words and also isolates critical letter sequences. For example, "You wrote 'nife'; however, the word *knife* starts with a silent letter. It is very unusual, and you just have to remember that it is there. Think about the letter *k* as looking like an open jackknife, and remember that the word *knife* starts with a *k*."

Maintain Previously Learned Words

Maintenance of spelling words requires that previously learned words be assigned as review words, and interspersed with the learning of new spelling words. Previously learned words need to be reviewed frequently to be maintained. Gettinger, Bryant, and Fayne (1982) conducted a study of students with learning disabilities to determine the efficacy of a spelling procedure that was designed to practice the principles of teaching smaller units, sufficient and distributed practice, and maintenance of words learned. Students were able to reach an 80 percent criterion on more of the spelling words and were able to spell 75 percent of the transfer words when compared with a control group that was involved in a spelling program that did not emphasize these principles. After spelling words have been mastered, provide opportunities for students to see and use spelling words in context.

Motivate Students to Spell Correctly

Using games and activities, selecting meaningful words, and providing examples of the use and need for correct spelling are strategies that help to motivate students and give them a positive attitude about spelling (Graham and Miller, 1979).

Include Dictionary Training

As part of the spelling program, dictionary training should be developed, which includes alphabetizing, identifying target words, and locating the correct definition when several are provided. Some students can develop a personal spelling dictionary to assist with their writing (Scheuremann, Jacobs, McCall, and Knies, 1994).

Spelling Approaches

There are many approaches to teaching spelling. No one approach has been proven to be superior to others for all students with learning disabilities. Some students learn effectively with a multisensory approach, such as the Fernald method; others learn best with a combination of several approaches. A recent synthesis of spelling interventions (Wanzek, Vaughn, Wexler, Swanson, and Edmonds, 2006) indicated that spelling practices which provide students with spelling strategies or systematic study and word practice methods yield the highest rates of spelling improvement. Other approaches, including sensorimotor activities and technology supports for spelling, resulted in a slight advantage for students over students in comparison conditions. Following are several approaches to teaching spelling, all of which make use of the principles discussed in the previous section.

Test-Study-Test Method

This method of learning spelling words is superior to the study-test method (Fitzsimmons and Loomer, 1978; Yee, 1969). In using the test-study-test method, students are first tested on a list of words and then instructed to study the missed words. Strategies are taught for recalling the correct spelling of these words. These strategies often include verbal mediation—saying the word while writing it or spelling it aloud to a partner. After instruction and study, students are then

FIGURE 9.15

Effective Word Study Procedures

Kinesthetic Method (Graham and Freeman, 1986)

1. Say the word.
2. Write and say the word.
3. Check the word and correct if needed.
4. Trace and say the word.
5. Write the word from memory, check it, and correct if needed.
6. Repeat steps one through five.

Copy-Cover-Compare (Murphy et al., 1990)

1. Examine the spelling of the word closely.
2. Copy the word.
3. Cover the word and write from memory.
4. Check the word and correct if needed.
5. If spelled correctly, go to next word.
6. If spelled incorrectly, repeat steps one through four.

Connections Approach (Berninger et al., 1998)

1. Teacher says word, points to each letter, and names it.
2. Child names word and letters.
3. Child shown a copy of the word with the onset and rime printed in different colors.

4. Teacher says the sound and simultaneously points to the onset and rime in order.
5. Child looks at, points to, and says the sound of the onset and rime in order.

Simultaneous Oral Spelling (Bradley, 1981)

1. Teacher reads the word.
2. Child reads the word.
3. Child writes the word saying the name of each letter.
4. Child says word again.
5. Teacher examines correctness of written response; child corrects if needed.
6. Repeat steps one through five two times.

Visual Imagery (Berninger et al., 1995)

1. Look at word and say its name.
2. Close your eyes and imagine the word in your mind's eye.
3. Name letters with your inside voice.
4. Open eyes and write word.
5. Check spelling and repeat steps one through four if the word is not spelled correctly.

Source: S. Graham (1999). Handwriting and spelling instruction for students with learning disabilities: A review. *Learning Disability Quarterly, 22* (2), pp. 78–98. Reprinted with permission.

retested. Using this process, students then correct their own spelling test, which is an important factor in learning to spell.

Several word study techniques that can be applied in using the test-study-test method are presented in Figure 9.15.

Visualization Approach

This approach to spelling teaches students to visualize the correct spelling as a means to recall. The visualization approach uses the following procedures:

1. On the board or on a piece of paper, the teacher writes a word that the children can read but cannot spell.
2. Students read the word aloud.
3. Students read the letters in the word.
4. Students write the word on paper.
5. The teacher asks the students to look at the word and "take a picture of it" as if the students' eyes were a camera.
6. The teacher asks the students to close their eyes and spell the word aloud, visualizing the letters while spelling it.
7. The teacher asks the students to write the word and check the model for accuracy.

The Five-Step Word Study Strategy

This strategy requires students to learn and rehearse the following five steps and practice them with the teacher and then alone. The steps are as follows:

1. Say the word.
2. Write and say the word.
3. Check the word.
4. Trace and say the word.
5. Write the word from memory and check.
6. Repeat the first five steps.

When students learn this technique the teacher models the procedure, then the students practice the procedure with assistance from the teacher, and finally the students demonstrate proficiency in the application of the procedure without teacher assistance. This procedure has been effectively used with elementary students with learning disabilities (Graham and Freeman, 1986).

Johnson and Myklebust Technique

Johnson and Myklebust (1967) suggest working from recognition to partial recall to total recall when teaching new spelling words. Recognition can be taught by showing students a word and then writing the word with several unrelated words, asking the students to circle the word they previously saw. The task can gradually be made more difficult by writing distracting words that more closely resemble the target word. In teaching partial recall, the correct word can be written with missing spaces for completing the spelling under it. For example,

with

w ___ th

wit ___

___ ith

wi ___ ___

w ___ ___ ___

___ ___ ___ ___

Total recall requires the students to write the word after it is pronounced by another or write the word in a sentence. This approach gives repeated practice and focuses students on the relevant details of the word. Johnson and Myklebust (1967) also suggest that when initial spelling tests are given, the teacher may need to say the word very slowly, emphasizing each syllable. As students learn to spell the words correctly, the test is given in a normal voice and at a normal rate.

Cloze Spelling Approach

This is referred to as the cloze spelling approach because students need to supply missing letters systematically in much the same way that students supply words in the cloze reading procedure. The cloze spelling approach uses a four-step process for teaching students to spell words.

1. *Look-study.* Students are shown the word on a card. Students look at the word and study the letters and their order.
2. *Write missing vowels.* Students are shown the same word on a card with blanks where the vowels usually appear. Students write the entire word, supplying the missing vowel(s).
3. *Write missing consonants.* Students are shown the word with blanks where the consonants usually appear. Students write the entire word, supplying the missing consonant(s).
4. *Write the word.* Students write the word without the model.

Fernald Method

Fernald (1943) believed that most spelling approaches were useful for the extremely visual student but not for students who need auditory and kinesthetic input for learning. Because poor spellers are characterized as having poor visual imagery, many may need to be taught through multisensory approaches such as the Fernald method.

According to Fernald (1943), specific school techniques that tend to produce poor spellers include the following:

- Formal spelling periods in which children move through a series of practice lessons, writing, and taking dictation with little time to think about how the word is spelled before writing it
- A focus on misspellings and spelling errors, which builds a negative attitude toward spelling

A brief description of the Fernald approach to teaching spelling includes the following procedures:

1. The teacher writes the word to be learned on the chalkboard or paper. The word can be selected from the spelling book or by the children.
2. The teacher pronounces the word clearly. The students repeat the pronunciation of the word while looking at the word. This is done several times for each word.
3. The teacher allows time for students to study the word for later recall. If a student is a kinesthetic learner, the teacher writes the word in crayon and has the student trace the letters of the word with his or her finger. Fernald found that tracing is necessary in learning to spell only when the spelling difficulty is coupled with a reading disability.
4. The teacher removes the word and has the students write it from memory.
5. The students turn the paper over and write the word a second time.
6. The teacher creates opportunities for students to use the word in their writing.
7. The teacher gives written, not oral, spelling drills.

In contrast with Fernald's approach, which recommends not focusing on the student's errors and suggests blocking out errors immediately, other researchers have found some support for a spelling strategy that emphasizes imitation of students' errors plus modeling (Kauffman, Hallahan, Haas, Brame, and Boren, 1978; Nulman and Gerber, 1984). Using the imitation plus modeling strategy, the teacher erases the misspelled word and imitates the child's error by writing it on the board. The teacher then writes it correctly with the student and asks the student to compare what he or she wrote with the correct spelling of the word.

Gillingham and Stillman Approach

According to Gillingham and Stillman (1973), "spelling is the translation of sounds into letter names (oral spelling) or into letter forms (written spelling)" (p. 52). Spelling is taught by using the following procedures:

1. The teacher says the word very slowly and distinctly, and students repeat the word after the teacher. This is referred to as *echo speech.*
2. Students are asked what sound is heard first. This process continues with all of the letters in the words. This is referred to as *oral spelling.*
3. The students are asked to locate the letter card with the first letter of the word on it and then to write the letter. Students continue with this process until the card for each letter is found, placed in order, and written. This is referred to as *written spelling.*
4. Students read the word.

When writing the word, students orally spell the word letter by letter. This establishes visual-auditory-kinesthetic association.

Correctional procedures in the Gillingham and Stillman approach include the following:

1. Students check their own written words and find errors.
2. If a word is read incorrectly, the students should spell what they said and match it with the original word.
3. If a word is misspelled orally, the teacher writes what the students spelled and asks them to read it, or the teacher may repeat the pronunciation of the original word.

Constant Time Delay Procedure

The time delay procedure is designed to reduce errors in instruction. Stevens and Schuster (1987) applied the procedure this way:

1. The verbal cue "Spell _____ (target word)" is immediately followed with a printed model of the target word to be copied by students.
2. After several trials in which there is no time delay between asking students to spell a word and providing a model of the word, a five-second delay is introduced. This allows children to write the word, or part of the word, if they know it but does not require them to wait very long if they are unable to correctly write the word.
3. The amount of time between the request to spell the word and the presentation of the model can be increased after several more trials.

The time delay procedure has been effective with students with learning disabilities and has several advantages as a spelling instructional method. It is a simple procedure that is easy to implement. Also, it is fun for students because it provides for nearly errorless instruction.

Self-Questioning Strategy for Teaching Spelling

Wong (1986) has developed the following self-questioning strategy for teaching spelling.

1. Do I know this word?
2. How many syllables do I hear in this word?
3. Write the word the way I think it is spelled.
4. Do I have the right number of syllables?
5. Underline any part of the word that I am not sure how to spell.
6. Check to see whether it is correct. If it is not correct, underline the part of the word that is not correct, and write it again.
7. When I have finished, tell myself I have been a good worker.

Morphographic Spelling

Developed by Dixon (1976, 1991), morphographic spelling provides a highly structured and sequenced approach to teaching remedial spelling to fourth graders through adulthood. This teacher-directed approach assumes that students have some spelling skills and begins with teaching small units of meaningful writing (morphographs). Students are taught to spell morphographs in isolation, then to combine them to make words.

Instructional Practices in Spelling

Most students with learning disabilities have problems with spelling. Yet students with learning disabilities have been the focus of relatively few research studies on spelling acquisition. In a search for empirically based instructional practices for improving the spelling skills of students with learning disabilities, Gordon et al. (1993) reviewed 15 studies on spelling acquisition, dating from 1978 with the results recently updated in a synthesis of spelling interventions (Wanzek et al., 2006) in which students with learning disabilities were the focus of the research. Findings from the studies can be grouped into eight areas of instructional practice:

1. *Providing a weekly list of words.* Students benefit when teachers provide a weekly list of words that are taught to accuracy. This procedure

allows students to practice words throughout the week. Monitoring correct use of these words in writing and then following up on accuracy in spelling with these words is valuable.

2. *Error imitation and modeling.* Students with learning disabilities need to compare each of their incorrectly spelled words with the correct spellings. The teacher imitates the students' incorrect spelling and, beside it, writes the word correctly. The teacher then calls attention to features in the word that will help students remember the correct spelling.

3. *Unit size.* Students with learning disabilities tend to become overloaded and to experience interference when they are required to study several words at once. Students with learning disabilities can learn to spell if the unit size of their assigned list is reduced to only three words per day and if effective instruction is offered for those three words.

4. *Modality.* It has long been thought that students with learning disabilities learn to spell most easily when their modality preferences are considered. An investigation of the usefulness of a spelling study by writing the words, arranging and tracing letter shapes or tiles, and typing the words at a computer revealed that students with learning disabilities learned equally well when studying words by any of these procedures. Of significance, however, was the fact that most of the students preferred to practice their spelling words at a computer. Because students' preferences are likely to affect their motivation to practice, teachers are wise to consider students' personal preferences.

5. *Computer-assisted instruction.* Computer-assisted instruction (CAI) has been shown to be effective in improving the spelling skills of students with learning disabilities. CAI software programs for spelling improvement often incorporate procedures that emphasize awareness of word structure and spelling strategies, and make use of time delay, voice simulation, and sound effects. Such capabilities make the computer an instructional tool with much potential to aid and motivate students with learning disabilities in learning to spell.

6. *Peer tutoring.* A teacher's individual help is preferable, but the realities of the classroom frequently make individualized instruction difficult to offer. Structured peer tutoring can be a viable alternative. In a study conducted by Harper, Mallete, and Moore (1991), peer tutoring was extended to a classwide setting and incorporated a team game format into daily peer tutoring sessions. The students with learning disabilities who were tutored by their peers for the game achieved 100 percent mastery of their weekly spelling words.

7. *Study techniques.* Study techniques help students with learning disabilities to organize their spelling study by providing a format for that study. As the students approach the study of a new word, they know exactly how to go about their study. This is in contrast to the haphazard, unproductive study used by students who follow no such strategy.

8. *Explicit and systematic instruction in spelling.* Interventions in spelling that systematically and explicitly taught students common patterns and strategies for spelling words were associated with the highest outcomes in spelling.

Most of the research investigating the effectiveness of spelling interventions for students with learning and behavior problems has involved the use of teaching single words from lists rather than spelling in context (Fulk and Stormont-Spurgin, 1995). Nevertheless, spelling instruction for students with learning problems is best conducted explicitly and directly rather than through indirect methods that are often part of whole-language approaches (Graham and Harris, 1994; Wanzek et al., 2006).

> **FOCUS Question** | **3.** What are the characteristics of students with handwriting problems, and what components should be included in an effective handwriting and keyboarding program?

Teaching Handwriting and Keyboarding

Often described as the most poorly taught subject in elementary curriculum, handwriting is usually thought of as the least important. However, handwriting difficulties create barriers to efficient work production and influence grades received from teachers (Briggs, 1970; Markham, 1976). Many students dislike the entire writing process because they find the motor skill involved in handwriting so laborious.

Despite the use of word processors, handheld computers, and other devices that can facilitate the writing process, handwriting remains an important skill. Taking notes in class, filling out forms, and success on the job often require legible, fluent writing.

Handwriting Problems

Students with dysgraphia have severe problems learning to write. Hamstra-Bletz and Blote (1993) define *dysgraphia* as follows:

> Dysgraphia is a written-language disorder that concerns the mechanical writing skill. It manifests itself in poor writing performance in children of at least average intelligence who do not have a distinct neurological disability and/or an overt perceptual-motor handicap. . . . Furthermore, dysgraphia is regarded as a disability that can or cannot occur in the presence of other disabilities, like dyslexia or dyscalculia. (p. 60)

Students with dysgraphia may exhibit any or all of the following characteristics:

- Poor letter formation
- Letters that are too large, too small, or inconsistent in size
- Incorrect use of capital and lowercase letters
- Letters that are crowded and cramped
- Inconsistent spacing between letters
- Incorrect alignment (letters do not rest on a base line)
- Incorrect or inconsistent slant of cursive letters
- Lack of fluency in writing
- Slow writing even when asked to write as quickly as possible (Weintraub and Graham, 1998)

TABLE 9.1

Manuscript versus Cursive

Manuscript	Cursive
1. It more closely resembles print and facilitates learning to read.	1. Many students want to learn to write cursive.
2. It is easier for young children to learn.	2. Many students write cursive faster.
3. Manuscript is more legible than cursive.	3. Many adults object to students using manuscript beyond the primary grades.
4. Many students write manuscript at the same rate as cursive and this rate can be significantly influenced through direct instruction.	
5. It is better for students with learning disabilities to learn one writing process well than to attempt to learn two.	

Fortunately, with direct instruction and specific practice, many of these problems can be alleviated. It is important to alleviate handwriting problems for several reasons: They are associated with reduced interest in writing and thus influence written expression, and students with handwriting difficulties spell worse than those without handwriting problems even when spelling interventions are provided (Berninger et al., 1995).

Manuscript and Cursive Writing

Traditionally, most students learn manuscript writing first and then, generally in second or third grade, make the transition to cursive writing. Although this procedure seems to be effective for most students, many students with learning disabilities have difficulty transitioning from one writing form to another. Many learning disability specialists advocate the use of instruction in only one form of handwriting, either manuscript or cursive. Some argue that manuscript is easier to learn, is more like book print, is more legible, requires less difficulty in making movement (Johnson and Myklebust, 1967), and should be the only writing form that is taught. Others believe that cursive is faster, is continuous and connected, makes it more difficult to reverse letters, teaches students to perceive whole words, and is easier to write. They believe that cursive should be taught first as the only writing form. (See Table 9.1 for a summary of arguments for manuscript versus cursive.) Some critics maintain that time could be better spent in teaching students to use a keyboard. Students should be able to use one form (print or cursive) to communicate effectively and there are some advantages to learning early and well to print since it corresponds more obviously with the print students read (Spear-Swerling, 2006).

The bulk of evidence appears to support teaching students with learning disabilities to use manuscript effectively and neatly, with the exception of learning to write their name in cursive. For most students with learning disabilities and handwriting difficulties, manuscript should be taught in the early years and maintained throughout the educational program. Some students with learning disabilities can and want to make the transition to cursive and benefit from its instruction. On some occasions, students who have struggled with manuscript writing feel that learning cursive is "grown up" and therefore respond well to the introduction of a new writing form.

Reversals

When five-year-old Abe signed his name on notes to his grandmother, he often reversed the direction of the *b* in his name. He would often write other letters backward or upside down. His mother worried that this might be an indication that Abe was dyslexic or having reading problems. Many parents/guardians are concerned when their children make reversals, and often their alarmed response frightens their children. Most children, ages five and younger, make reversals when writing letters and numbers. Reversals made by students before the age of six or seven are not an indication that the student has learning disabilities or is dyslexic and are rarely cause for concern.

Teachers should recognize the following:

- Reversals are common before the age of six or seven. Teachers should provide correctional procedures for school-age students who are reversing letters and numbers but should not become overly concerned.
- A few students continue to reverse numbers and letters after the age of seven and may need direct intervention techniques.

For students who persist in reversing letters and numbers, the following two direct instructional techniques may be helpful:

1. The teacher traces the letter and talks aloud about the characteristics of the letter, asking the students to model the teacher's procedure. For example, while tracing the letter *d*, the teacher says, "First I make a stick starting at the top of the page and going down, and then I put a ball in front of the stick." Students are asked to follow the same procedure and to talk aloud while tracing the letter. Next, the students are asked to do the same procedure, this time drawing the letter. Finally, the students are asked to draw the letter and say the process to themselves.

Tracing letters is a frequently used method of improving legibility; however, there is little research to suggest that tracing is an effective method of teaching letter formation. Hirsch and Niedermeyer (1973) found that copying is a more effective technique for teaching letter formation than tracing.

2. The teacher and students can develop a mnemonic picture device that helps the students recall the direction of the letter. For example, with a student who is reversing the direction of the letter *p*, the teacher might say, "What letter does the word *pie* begin with? That's right, *pie* begins with the letter *p*. Now watch me draw *p*." Drawing the straight line, the teacher says, "This is my straight line before I eat pie, then after I eat pie my stomach swells in front of me. Whenever you make *p* you can think of pie and how your stomach gets big after you eat it, and that will help you make a *p* the right way." This procedure can be repeated several times, with the student drawing the letter and talking through the mnemonic device. Different mnemonic devices can be developed to correspond with the specific letter or number reversal(s) of the child.

The next section focuses on teaching handwriting, including discussions on posture, pencil grip, position of the paper, and legibility and fluency in writing. Specific instructional techniques such as the Hanover approach and Hagin's Write Right-or-Left are also discussed.

Components of Handwriting

Teaching handwriting requires the teacher to assess, model, and teach letter formation, spacing, and fluency as well as posture, pencil grip, and position of the paper. A brief description of these important components of an effective handwriting program follows.

Legibility

Legibility is the most important goal of handwriting instruction, and incorrect letter formation is the most frequent interference.

The following six letters account for many of the errors (48 percent) that students make when forming letters: *q, j, z, u, n,* and *k* (Graham, Berninger, and Weintraub, 1998). Spacing between letters, words, and margins; connecting lines; and closing and crossing of letters (e.g., *t, x*) also influence legibility (Kirk and Chalfant, 1984).

Graham and Miller (1980) have suggested the following remedial procedures for teaching letter formation:

1. Modeling
2. Noting critical attributes (comparing and contrasting letters)
3. Physical prompts and cues (physically moving the student's hand or using cues such as arrows or colored dots)
4. Reinforcement (providing specific reinforcement for letters or parts of letters that are formed correctly and corrective feedback for letters that need work)
5. Self-verbalization (saying aloud the letter formation and then verbalizing it to oneself while writing)
6. Writing from memory
7. Repetition

Fluent Writing

What is fluency as it relates to handwriting? Just as not knowing how to read words fluently impairs reading comprehension, inadequate fluency in writing letters and words impairs written expression and the quality of written responses (Spear-Swerling, 2006). Nine-year-old Nguyen's handwriting has improved considerably during the past year. She and her teacher have identified letters that were not formed correctly, and Nguyen has learned to write these letters so that they are legible. Now that her handwriting is easier to read, the teacher realizes that Nguyen has another handwriting problem. In the regular classroom, Nguyen has difficulty taking notes and writing down assignments that are given orally, because she is a very slow writer. She needs to learn writing fluency, which is the ability to write quickly and with ease without undue attention to letter formation.

Nguyen's teacher decides to teach fluency by gradually increasing expectations about the speed at which letter formation occurs. Nguyen selects two paragraphs and is told to write them as quickly as she can while still maintaining good letter formation. The teacher times her in this procedure. They decide to keep a graph of Nguyen's progress by indicating the time it takes her each day to write the two paragraphs legibly. Nguyen finds that graphing her progress is very reinforcing (see Figure 9.16 and Apply the Concept 9.13). Because Nguyen's fluency problems were not just for copying but also for writing from dictation, her teacher implemented the same program, this time requiring Nguyen to time herself on oral dictations. Nguyen's time for completion of the passage decreased considerably over a three-week period.

FIGURE 9.16

Nguyen's Fluency

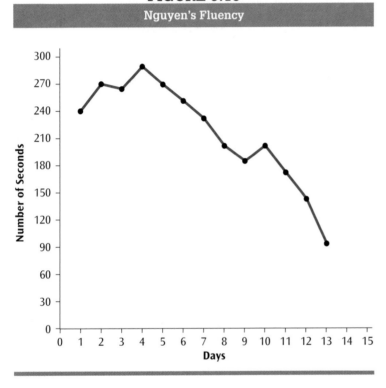

Posture, Pencil Grip, and Position of the Paper

Many students have handwriting problems because they do not correctly perform three important components of the handwriting process:

1. *Posture.* The lower back should touch the back of the chair, and the feet should rest on the floor. The torso leans forward slightly, in a straight line, with both forearms resting on the desk and elbows slightly extended.

Apply the Concept 9.13

Obtaining a Fluency Sample

The following procedures can be used to obtain a fluency sample:

1. Have the student become familiar with the test sentence.
2. The teacher tells the student to write the test sentence a designated number of times at his or her usual rate (two- to three-minute sample).
3. After relaxing, have the student write the sentence as well and as neatly as he or she can.
4. After relaxing, have the student write the sentence as quickly and as many times as he or she can in three minutes.
5. After relaxing, the student and the teacher repeat this process with the same sentence.

2. *Pencil grip.* The pencil should be held lightly between the thumb and first two fingers, about one inch above the point. The first finger rests on top of the pencil. The back of the pencil points in the direction of the shoulder and rests near the large knuckle of the middle finger.

3. *Position of the paper.* When the student is writing manuscript, the paper should be in front of him or her. For a right-hander, the left hand holds the paper in place, moving it when necessary. In writing cursive, the paper is slanted counterclockwise for a right-hander and clockwise for a left-hander.

Instructional Principles

The following instructional principles are suggested for any effective handwriting program:

- Teach handwriting explicitly including letter formation.
- Provide modeling and feedback to ensure correct letter formation. It may be necessary to guide the stroke of the pencil by providing manual assistance.
- Initially focus on the motor pattern and then increasingly focus on legibility.
- Teach handwriting frequently, several times a week.
- In addition to separate minilessons on handwriting and letter formation, provide short handwriting lessons in the context of the students' writing assignment.
- Handwriting skills should be overlearned in isolation, then applied in context and periodically checked.
- Ask students to evaluate their own handwriting and, when appropriate, the handwriting of others.
- The teacher's handwriting should be a model for the students to follow.
- In the beginning stages of letter formation, teachers can integrate letter writing with letter naming, letter sounds, or spelling words.
- After students acquire proficiency in letter formation, provide opportunities for them to improve fluency through speed and accuracy of letter writing.

Self-instructional strategies can be taught to students to improve their handwriting (Graham, 1983; Kosiewicz, Hallahan, Lloyd, and Graves, 1982). The self-instructional procedure that was used in the Graham (1983) study was based on a cognitive-behavioral model. The six-step procedure is as follows:

1. The teacher models the writing of the target letter and describes the formation of the letter. Students then describe the formation of the letter. This step is repeated three times.

2. The teacher writes the letter while describing the process. This continues until the students can recite the process for writing the letter.

3. Students trace the letter, and the teacher and students recite the process of the letter formation together.

4. The teacher writes the letter, traces it, and then verbally discusses the process, including corrections (e.g., "My letter is too slanted"), then provides self-reinforcement (e.g., "Now, that looks a lot better"). The procedure continues with and without errors until the students can model the process.

5. The teacher writes the letter, and the students copy it while defining the process and providing self-correction. Students need to complete this process successfully three times before moving to step 6.

6. Students write the letter from memory.

Following are two methods that have been devised for teaching students who have handwriting difficulties.

Write Right-or-Left

Hagin (1983) suggests a process for teaching cursive that is based on manuscript and the vertical stroke learned in manuscript. In Hagin's Write Right-or-Left approach, the students learn cursive writing using the following procedure:

1. Students learn motifs that form the foundation for later letter formation. These motifs are taught and practiced on the chalkboard. See Figure 9.17 for an illustration of the motifs and the letters that correspond with them.

2. After learning the motifs at the chalkboard, students learn and practice the letters associated with each of the motifs at the chalkboard.

3. At their desk, students trace the letters while the teacher gives verbal cues as to letter direction and formation.

4. Students write the letters without a model.

5. Through matching, students compare the model with the product produced in step 4. Both the teacher and students give feedback and determine whether additional practice is needed before the next step.

6. Students write a permanent record of the letters they have mastered.

FIGURE 9.17

Write Right-or-Left: Learning Motifs

Ferry boats

Teaches smooth movements across the page.

Waves

Foundation for the letters *a, c, d, g,* and *q*

Pearls

Foundation for the letters *e, i, h, j, m, n, u, y,* and *z*

Wheels

Foundation for the letters *o, v, b, w,* and *x*

Arrows

Foundation for the letters *k, l, t, r,* and *f*

Source: Adapted from R. H. Hagin (1983). Write right or left: A practical approach to handwriting. *Journal of Learning Disabilities, 16* (5), pp. 266–271.

Hanover Method

Hanover's (1983) method of teaching cursive writing is founded on a single principle: the grouping of letters based on similar strokes into letter families. The letter families include the following:

e, l, h, f, b, k	This is the *e* family and is taught first.
b, o, v, w	This family has a handle to which the next letter is attached.
n, s, y	This family is grouped together to emphasize the correct formation of hump-shaped letters.
c, a, d, o, q, g	This is the *c* family.
n, m, v, y, x	This is the hump family.
f, q	This family has tails in the back.
g, p, y, z	This family has tails in the front.

Some letters are included in more than one group. This approach is based on the idea that cursive letters are learned faster and more easily when they are taught in their grouped families because of the similar strokes within the groups.

Teaching Handwriting at the High School Level

Handwriting often becomes important later in school because of the emphasis on taking notes and submitting written assignments. Many students have found that although the content of their assignment is correct, they have lost points or were given a lower grade because their handwriting was difficult to read. Teaching handwriting to older students is difficult because the immediate needs of most older students are content-related, and it is often difficult for teachers to justify instructional time for handwriting. Also, most materials for handwriting instruction were developed for younger students and can seem insulting to older students. Teachers need to carefully evaluate students' handwriting problems to determine whether handwriting instruction could be helpful in a relatively short period of time or the students should learn compensatory methods, such as typing. The two most important criteria for evaluating handwriting of older students are legibility and fluency.

In selecting a curriculum for older students, specific attention should be given to the students' letter formation and fluency within context. Corrective feedback, short trace and copy exercises, and content exercises that require little thinking and allow the students to concentrate on letter formation and fluency should be emphasized in teaching handwriting to older students (Ruedy, 1983).

Teaching Keyboarding

Since many students with learning disabilities exhibit difficulties in handwriting, what additional options are there for improving their communication through writing? The most obvious solution is one that students will be expected to know in almost any job situation, familiar and fluent use of the computer keyboard. How and when can students learn keyboarding skills? Most students are at least somewhat familiar with keyboards as early as kindergarten and first grade, and they are able to enter their first name into the computer to log onto programs. Keyboarding skills continue to improve as students proceed through early elementary grades, however formal instruction in keyboarding usually begins in third or fourth grade. As many teachers and employers note, the "hunt-and-peck" method of keyboarding is no longer acceptable and students who are keyboard familiar are better advantaged in both school and work settings.

One of the first things that students should learn is correct hand position on the keys and how to develop the motor memory skills for using the keyboard while reading or writing a report. In other words, effective keyboarding skills require not looking at the keys. Following are some tips for improving keyboarding skills in students:

- Be sure students are using the correct hand position on the keys.
- Give students opportunities to practice their technique by keyboarding their own writing or assignments so that there is personal benefit from acquiring keyboarding skills.
- Provide students with ample opportunities to practice.
- Assure students that even though they are slow when first learning to keyboard without looking at the keys, they will ultimately become much faster and successful.
- Provide demonstrations to students so that they can observe good technique and facile keyboard use.
- Initially, emphasize proper form and not speed.
- Students should have their fingers on the key and their thumbs on the space bar.
- As students' technique improves then increasing speed is a reasonable goal.
- Develop procedures in school so that all teachers encourage and support keyboarding.
- Involve families in reinforcing good form and keyboarding at home.

Keyboarding is an important skill that will improve students' success as writers and also make writing a less laborious process. Further benefits are that students can use a printer to demonstrate what they've written in ways that are easily read and reviewed making revision and editing more successful. There is much to be gained by teaching students to keyboard.

INSTRUCTIONAL ACTIVITIES

This section provides instructional activities that are related to written expression, including spelling and handwriting. Some of the activities teach new skills; others are best suited for practice and reinforcement of already acquired skills. For each activity, the objective, materials, and teaching procedures are described.

▶ Cubing

Objective: To help students develop preliminary ideas about the topic during the prewriting phase

Grades: Elementary through secondary

Materials: A cube-shaped outline, glue, scissors

Teaching Procedures:
1. Explain to students that the topic is like a cube that contains different information on each side. Topics can be explored from different angles.
2. Introduce six different ways in which the topic can be explored.

   a. *Describe:* What does it look like?
   b. *Compare:* What is it similar to? What is it different from?
   c. *Associate:* What does it remind you of?
   d. *Analyze:* What are the parts?
   e. *Apply:* What can you do with it?
   f. *Argue for or against:* Take a stand about your topic. Why is it good or why is it not good?

3. Pass out a cube-shaped outline to each student.
4. Have students write their ideas down on the cube-shaped outline. Students work through each side of the cube: describe, compare, associate, analyze, apply, and argue for or against the topic. (Depending on the topic, questions for each dimension will need to be adjusted.)
5. Have the students cut out the outline and glue it together to make a cube.

Extended Activity: The cube can be used as a resource in writing the essay.

Source: Adapted from University of Texas Center for Reading and Language Arts (2000a, 2000b).

▶ Writing Warm-Up

Objective: To help students, especially reluctant writers, gain writing experiences

Materials: Graph paper, colored pencils, timer for the teacher

Grades: Elementary through secondary

Teaching Procedures:

1. Explain to students that writing is like exercising. Tell them that writing practice can help them improve their writing and make the writing easier.
2. Choose a topic that will be easy for students to write about. Have students do writing warm-up once or twice a week.
3. Introduce the day's topic (e.g., homework).
4. Ask students to write as much as they can about the topic for three minutes. Tell the students that they do not need to worry about spelling, grammar, or punctuation.
5. Set a timer for three minutes. When time is up, have the students put their pencils down and count the number of words they have written.
6. Have students graph the number of words they have written, using colored pencils and graph paper.
7. When students feel comfortable writing their ideas about the topic, introduce the next writing process (e.g, organizing their ideas, revising, editing).

Source: Adapted from University of Texas Center for Reading and Language Arts (2000a, 2000b).

▶Writing Reports

Objective: To help students prepare for a research report by providing guidelines for gathering information necessary for writing a research report

Grades: Secondary

Materials: Report planning sheet (see Figure 9.18)

Teaching Procedures:

1. Explain to students that a report planning sheet will help them to prepare for writing a research report. After filling out the planning sheet, they can use the information on the planning sheet to write their report.
2. Introduce the day's topic (e.g., volcanoes).
3. Pass out a planning sheet to each student.
4. Have students brainstorm a list of everything they know about the topic and write it down in the first column (i.e., What I Know).
5. Have the students examine their brainstorming ideas carefully to identify the areas in need of further research. For instance, if a student knows names of active volcanoes but not much about how a volcano is formed, the student may want to study that. Have students identify what they want to study and write that down in the second column.
6. In the third column, have students write down why they want to study the subtopic they selected.
7. Have students think about a variety of sources where they can find information (e.g., science textbook, Websites, etc.) on the subtopic and list those sources in the fourth column.
8. Have students conduct their research and write down what they learn in the fifth column.
9. After the students have completed the planning sheet, have them use that information to write the report.

Source: Adapted from Macrorie (1980) and Ogle (1986).

▶The Use of Graphic Organizers for Writing

Objective: To help students organize their ideas when writing first drafts

FIGURE 9.18

Report Planning Sheet				

Topic: _____

What I Know	What I Want to Find Out	Why I Want to Find Out	How I Will Find Out	What I Learned

FIGURE 9.19
Graphic Organizer

Topic: _____

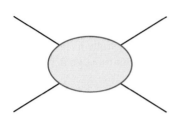

Sentence describing the topic:

1. _____

2. _____

3. _____

Grades: Elementary through secondary

Materials: Copies of a graphic organizer (see Figure 9.19)

Teaching Procedures:
1. Explain to students that graphic organizers can help them write their draft. (*Note:* Different types of graphic organizers are used depending on type of text.)
2. Model how to use graphic organizers. For instance, write the topic in the center and supporting details on the branches on the graphic organizer. Then create sentences describing the topic by using ideas written on the graphic.
3. Introduce the topic, and pass out copies of a graphic organizer to each student.
4. Have students use the graphic organizer as they write their draft with a partner, in a small group, or independently.
5. After students finish filling out the graphic organizer and creating sentences, call on several students to share their drafts. Provide feedback on their drafts.

Source: Adapted from Nancy and Dill (1997).

▶Peer Editing

Objective: To provide students with opportunities to edit a revised draft as one part of the editing process

Grades: Elementary

Materials: Student-generated revised draft, peer editing checklist (see Figure 9.20)

Teaching Procedures:
1. Explain to students that editing focuses on correcting technical aspects of writing.
2. Introduce each of the five editing points on the checklist:
   a. End punctuation
   b. Beginning capitalization
   c. Complete sentences
   d. Indented paragraphs
   e. Spelling check
3. Pair students, making sure that each pair consists of a good writer and a poor writer.

FIGURE 9.20
Peer Editing Checklist

	Yes	No	Edits Made
1. Does each sentence end with a period, question mark, or exclamation point?			
2. Does each sentence start with a capital letter?			
3. Is each sentence a complete sentence?			
4. Is the first sentence of each paragraph indented?			
5. Did my partner check my spelling (by using dictionary and/or thesaurus)?			

4. Pass out peer editing checklists to each pair, and ask students in pairs to exchange their revised drafts.

5. Have the good writer in each pair edit his or her partner's draft by following editing steps, which are outlined on the peer editing checklist. If a step is followed, a check mark should be placed in the Yes column after that step. If a step is not followed, then a check should be placed in the No column.

6. While the student is completing the checklist, have his or her partner correct errors, if any, and record what corrections were made in the Edits Made column.

7. Repeat the procedure, this time with the poor writer editing his or her partner's draft by following editing steps.

Source: Adapted from University of Texas Center for Reading and Language Arts (2001b).

▶Peer Revision

Objective: To give students an opportunity to work together in pairs to elaborate on their writing as one part of the revision process

Grades: Elementary through secondary

Materials: Student-generated rough draft, sticky notes

Teaching Procedures:

1. Explain to students that good writers get help from their friends and colleagues to improve their writing. One way to do this is to get ideas for elaborating or expanding on what you have already written. Each student needs a rough draft that is ready to be revised (and is neat enough to be read by another student and checked by the teacher).

2. Students work in pairs to complete the following revision steps:
   a. Have a student read his or her rough draft out loud to his or her partner. While the student is reading, he or she may catch a few mistakes. Encourage the student to correct them.
   b. Have the partner read through the rough draft, focusing on the content. The partner makes three sticky note comments and puts them on the rough draft. One comment is positive (e.g., I really liked the part where . . .). The other two comments are helpful (e.g., Tell me more about . . . and I don't understand the part where . . .).
   c. Repeat the process with the second partner.

d. Have each student work individually to elaborate on his or her draft by addressing the peer sticky note comments.

▶Acrostic Writing in the Content Areas

Objective: To help students improve their understanding of content through acrostic writing

Grades: Secondary

Materials: Content area textbook

Teaching Procedures:

1. Explain to students that they will write a poem about what they have read (e.g., the unit on Native Americans in social studies).

2. Review important information on the previously studied unit (e.g., Native Americans), and create a semantic map by writing the word "the name of the tribe they read about (e.g., Apache)" on the blackboard, asking the students to share what they have read about this tribe (prompt the students if necessary), and recording the students' responses on the blackboard.

3. Have students write a poem to describe important characteristics of the Apache by using each letter in it to create one sentence. For instance,

   <u>A</u>mazing hunters who once enjoyed a nomadic style of life
   <u>P</u>owerful nation of warriors
   <u>A</u>daptable people who learned to tend fields of maize, beans, pumpkins, and watermelons when buffalo became scarce
   <u>C</u>ourageous Indians known for their resistance to the U.S. government
   <u>H</u>ut building, farming, trading, and horse riding were necessary for survival of this proud nation
   <u>E</u>pidemics of smallpox and other European diseases almost decimated the once large tribe

4. Call on several students to share their poems. Provide feedback on their poems in terms of the writing styles and the content.

Source: Adapted from Bromley (1999).

▶Proofreading with SCOPE

Objective: To teach students a mnemonic strategy (SCOPE) to help with proofreading their writing

Grades: Upper elementary through secondary

Materials: Student-generated writing piece that needs to be edited

Teaching Procedures:

1. Discuss with students how they can get into difficulty if they are not sufficiently skilled at proofreading their papers before they submit them and therefore get low grades because their papers have many errors.
2. Teach the students SCOPE, a mnemonic strategy that will assist them in proofreading their work before they submit it:

    Spelling: Is the spelling correct?

    Capitalization: Are the first words of sentences, proper names, and proper nouns capitalized?

    Order of words: Is the syntax correct?

    Punctuation: Are there appropriate marks for punctuation where necessary?

    Express complete thought: Does the sentence contain a noun and a verb, or is it only a phrase?
3. Next, demonstrate using SCOPE with a sample piece of writing on an overhead projector.
4. Give the students ample practice and opportunity to apply SCOPE to their own work.

▶Interview a Classmate

Objective: To give students practice in developing and using questions to obtain more information for the piece they are writing

Grades: Upper elementary through secondary

Materials: Writing materials and a writing topic, a list of possible questions, a tape recorder (optional)

Teaching Procedures:

1. Using the format of a radio or television interview, demonstrate and role-play mock interviews with sports, movie, music, and political celebrities. (*Note:* Give students opportunities to play both roles.)
2. Discuss what types of questions allow the interviewee to give elaborate responses (e.g., open questions) and what types of questions do not allow the interviewee to give an expanded answer (e.g., closed questions). Practice asking open questions.
3. Use a piece that you are writing as an example, and discuss whom you might interview to obtain more information. For example, "In writing a piece about what it might have been like to go to the New York World's Fair in 1964, I might interview my grandfather, who was there, to obtain more information."
4. Ask students to select an appropriate person to interview for their writing piece and write possible questions.
5. In pairs, have students refine their questions for the actual interview.
6. Have students then conduct interviews and later discuss how information from the interview assisted them in writing their piece.

▶What Would You Do If . . . ?

By Alison Gould Boardman

Objective: To give students experience developing ideas for narrative writing and following simple story structure

Grades: Upper elementary and middle school

Materials: Pencil, drawing paper, writing paper

Teaching Procedures:

1. Have students fold a piece of drawing paper so that there are four squares.
2. Ask students what they would do if they were invisible for 24 hours. Share ideas, and probe students to add details (e.g., "You would go to the moon. Great, how would you get there? Would you take anyone with you?"). Tell students that now that they have some ideas, they are going to make a rough drawing of four possible things they would do if they were invisible for 24 hours.
3. Students should use pencil or one color to draw pictures of their ideas, one in each box. Pictures can be rough drawings or sketches. The purpose of the drawings is to help students generate interest in and remember what they want to write about without the pressure of having to write it down.
4. Begin with the introduction. Students write about how they become invisible. For the body of the story, students choose three of their four ideas to expand on. They use their pictures and build from there. The ending of the story details what happens when they become visible again and concludes their invisible day.

Adaptations: This assignment can be repeated with topics (from the teacher or students) such as, What would you do if you could fly, run 50 miles an hour, drive a car, etc.? Depending on students' skill levels, the length and content requirements can be adjusted.

▶Step-by-Step Cartoon Writing

By Alison Gould Boardman

Objective: To give beginning or reluctant writers experience sequencing steps, using transition words, and writing a paragraph

Grades: Elementary

Materials: Index cards without lines, colored pencils, tape, writing materials

Teaching Procedures:

1. Discuss as a group the types of things students do to get ready for school in the morning.
2. Tell students that they will be drawing a comic strip about what they do when they get up in the morning.
3. Have students draw one event on each index card (e.g., waking up, getting dressed, eating breakfast). Encourage the students to add de-

tail to their pictures to help them remember exactly what happens.

4. Have students put their ideas in order and tape the cards together like a comic strip.
5. Before the students begin writing, have them use their comic strip as a guide to help them tell the story out loud. Encourage students to use transition words such as *first, next, later,* and *finally.* Teachers can post a list of transition words for students to use while telling and writing their paragraphs.
6. Have students write one descriptive sentence about each frame of their comic strip to form a paragraph.
7. Attach the final copy of the paragraph to the comic strip and display in the classroom.

Adaptations: Students can use this procedure to write any sequenced or how-to paragraph, such as how to bake a cake, make a peanut butter and jelly sandwich, play checkers, or make a bed.

SUMMARYfor Chapter 9

Students start school feeling confident that they know how to write. It is not uncommon to see young children writing notes to grandparents and other significant people, making up letters and words as they go along, sure that they are able to communicate in print. Most of these same students later find expressing themselves in writing one of the most difficult tasks required of them in school. This chapter described several specific practices to enhance writing, particularly for students with writing difficulties. This chapter also presented practices for how to teach spelling and handwriting skills as aids to written expression. The assumption underlying the writing process approach presented in this chapter is that all children benefit from opportunities to practice writing and systematic instruction and feedback before, during, and after they write. This approach has potential with students who have learning and behavior problems, as it focuses on writing from their own experiences and feelings, giving them a systematic process for interacting with peers and teachers and providing consistent opportunities to write and receive feedback.

This chapter presented procedures for starting the writing process approach, including a description of materials needed, skills taught through the process approach, and the teacher as writer, modeling through writing and sharing with students. The elements of the writing process approach, which include prewriting, composing, revising, editing, and publishing, were defined, and examples were presented to show how they can be taught and integrated into the writing process approach with students who have learning and behavior problems. Guidelines for conducting effective writing conferences, the key to successful writing, were described, and examples of students conferring with each other as well as with the teacher were provided.

In addition to describing the writing process as an approach to written expression, this chapter discussed how to teach spelling and handwriting skills to students with learning and behavior problems. Students with learning or behavior problems need direct instruction in spelling and handwriting, and this chapter provided specific instructional techniques that have been successful. Because effective spelling instruction begins with understanding the types of spelling errors the student makes, how to conduct an error analysis in spelling was presented. Principles for teaching spelling to students with learning difficulties were discussed, and spelling approaches were presented.

The handwriting section of the chapter discussed the advantages and disadvantages of teaching manuscript and/or cursive, as well as information all teachers should know about reversals. Approaches to teaching handwriting were also presented.

FOCUS Answers

FOCUS Question 1. **What assessment and instructional practices should teachers attend to when implementing the writing process with students with learning and behavior problems?**

Answer: For many students with learning and behavior problems, writing is a chore that focuses on skills they have not mastered well, such as spelling and handwriting. Teachers need to consider these negative associations when they set up a writing program that encourages students to explore and expand their writing ability while practicing the writing conventions that students will need to express themselves effectively. Assessment practices that include ongoing progress monitoring of the accuracy of letter formation, speed of writing, and quality of writing provide important feedback to teachers as they alter their writing instruction. The physical environment, or setting, is an important feature that sets the tone for writing. Scheduling and materials are also essential. Finally, teachers must be organized so that they can monitor progress regularly.

FOCUS Question 2. **What are the critical features of spelling assessment and instruction for students with learning and behavior problems?**

Answer: Many students with learning and behavior problems do not benefit from traditional approaches to spelling (e.g., weekly word lists) and need instruction in phonics rules and how these rules relate to writing words. The first step is to conduct a spelling error analysis to identify which spelling patterns students understand and which are misunderstood. Through ongoing instruction in these spelling patterns and

progress monitoring to determine learning, teachers can integrate assessment and instruction for improving spelling outcomes for their students. Teachers should teach in small units, and cluster new words according to spelling patterns. They should allow time for students to practice new words, provide feedback, and maintain previously learned words through frequent reviews. Finally, they can motivate students by making spelling fun.

FOCUS Question 3. **What are the characteristics of students with handwriting problems, and what components should be included in an effective handwriting and keyboarding program?**

Answer: Handwriting difficulties often result in low motivation to write as well as spelling difficulties that can affect work production and grades. Weaknesses in handwriting can be assessed by examining legibility, fluency, and hand position and can usually be remediated with direct instruction and specific practice. Principles of instruction include using a variety of techniques to provide direct instruction that is specific to a student's individual handwriting needs. Provide short, frequent instruction in handwriting skills and many opportunities to practice. Skills should be thoroughly learned in isolation and then applied in the context of the student's writing assignment. Students should evaluate their own handwriting and use the teacher as a model. Handwriting should also be taught as a combined visual–motor task. For each student, teachers must assess, model, and teach the needed skills as well as provide opportunities for practice and feedback.

THINKand APPLY

- Think about the elements of the writing process approach to instruction. How can you integrate them into your instruction? What is a writing conference, and how can it be used with students with learning and behavior problems?

- What are several critical aspects to establishing a writing program for students with learning and behavior problems?
- In what ways can you monitor the writing progress of students with learning problems?

- In what ways can computers facilitate writing for students with learning problems?
- How do you conduct and apply error analysis to the spelling errors of students with learning problems? What are the key principles for teaching spelling to students with learning problems?
- Can you describe several methods of teaching spelling to students with learning and behavior problems?
- Can you describe several methods of teaching handwriting to students with learning and behavior problems?
- What instructional principles are suggested for an effective spelling program?

- What key findings should you consider when increasing the spelling performance of students with learning disabilities?
- "Rhyming and alliteration are positively and significantly related to progress in spelling" (Bradley and Bryant, 1983). What is a possible explanation of this phenomenon?
- What instructional principles are suggested for an effective handwriting program?

APPLYthe STANDARDS

 Council for Exceptional Children

1. Describe the writing process approach to instruction and explain how its features are aligned with the CEC standards for written expression (BD4K5, LD4K5, LD4S5, LD4S6, LD4S10, LD4S11, LD5S1, LDS4).

Standard BD4K5: Strategies for integrating student-initiated learning experiences into ongoing instruction for individuals with emotional/behavior disorders.

Standard LD4K5: Methods for guiding individuals in identifying and organizing critical content.

Standard LD4S5: Use instructional methods to strengthen and compensate for deficits in perception, comprehension, memory, and retrieval.

Standard LD4S6: Use responses and errors to guide instructional decisions and provide feedback to learners.

Standard LD4S10: Teach strategies for organizing and composing written products.

Standard LD4S11: Implement systematic instruction to teach accuracy, fluency, and comprehension in content area reading and written language.

Standard LD5S1: Teach individuals with learning disabilities to give and receive meaningful feedback from peers and adults.

Standard LDS4: Teach individuals with learning disabilities to monitor for errors in oral and written communications.

WEBSITESas RESOURCES | to Assist in Teaching Writing and Spelling

The following Websites are extensive resources for expanding your understanding of teaching written expression:

- LD Online www.ldonline.org
- Teaching Writing to Students with LD www.readingrockets.org
- Edbydesign.com www.edbydesign.com/parentres.html
- Website for the National Council of Teachers of English www.ncte.org
- International Reading Association and National Council of Teachers of English www.readwritethink.org
- Kids' Space www.kids-space.org

Where the Classroom Comes to Life

Article Homework Exercise Go to MyEducationLab and select the topic "INSTRUCTIONAL PRAC-TICES AND LEARNING STRATEGIES," then read the article "Writing; Article 2: Helping Writers Find Power" and complete the activity questions below.

Teachers and parents often focus on errors in writing. The author describes methods to demonstrate that you value students writing while supporting the development of writing skills and concepts.

1. What three essential processes are described in the article to help students find power in their writing?

2. How could you apply the methods in the article while using the writing process described in the chapter?

Case Study Homework Exercise Go to MyEducationLab and select the topic "INSTRUCTIONAL PRACTICES AND LEARNING STRATEGIES," then read the case study "A Broken Arm" and complete the activity questions below.

Spelling was impossible for Jim despite the accommodations made by his resource teacher.

1. What are the issues in this case and how can effective collaboration practices support Jim more effectively?

2. What modifications did Mary make for Jim? Were the modifications successful?

3. What other strategies are described in the chapter that could support Jim in the classroom?

Artifact Homework Exercise Go to MyEducationLab and select the topic "TECHNOLOGY USE IN THE CLASSROOM," then look at the artifact "Dear Thomas Jefferson (Social Studies 3–5)" and complete the activity question below.

This is a writing sample of a letter written with a word processor by a student with dysgraphia.

1. How might the use of word processing software help a student who has impaired fine motor skills?

Chapter 10

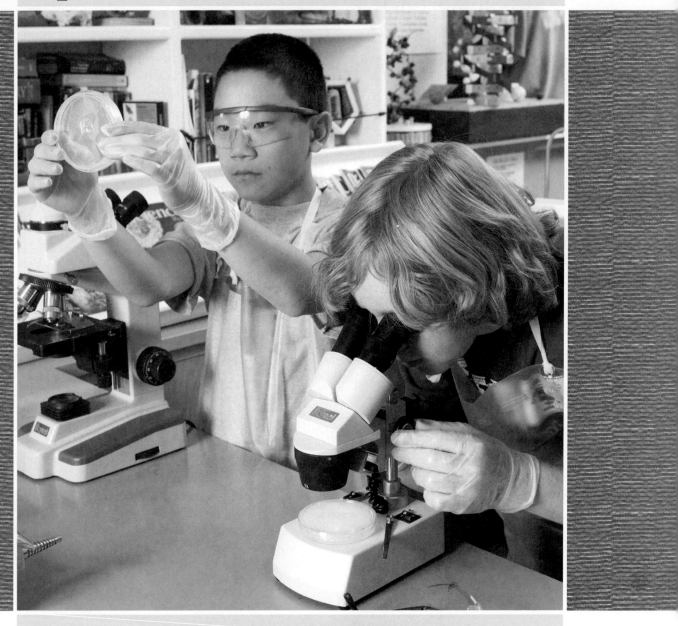

Assessing and Teaching Content Area Learning and Vocabulary Instruction

As you read the chapter, watch for these questions to help you focus your learning:

1. How can teachers use specific word instruction and word-learning strategies to teach vocabulary?

2. What is content enhancement, and how can teachers use it to teach content area reading?

3. How do teachers adapt textbooks, lectures, assignments, homework, and tests to meet the needs of students with learning and behavior problems?

4. What are the three types of study skills, and why are they important to learning?

When Ms. Cho moved from her elementary resource room job to a high school resource position, her experience and education in teaching learning strategies and the writing process served her well for part of the school day. However, in addition to the two English periods she teaches daily, she is expected to teach sections of American history and American government to students with learning and behavior problems. Although she minored in political science and history in college, she feels that her content knowledge is rusty in these areas and that her techniques for teaching content information are limited. She has also been asked to teach a section of general science; she has chosen to team-teach the class with a science teacher because of her limited content knowledge and her desire to integrate the special education students into general education classes.

Juan, a fourth grader with a reading disability, moved to the United States from Mexico when he was in the first grade. With the help of his special education teacher, Juan has made considerable progress in reading and understanding texts that have stories. Since entering fourth grade, however, he has been challenged by vocabulary words in expository texts (his math and social studies texts). The vocabulary words that he is encountering in these texts are more complex and abstract than the words in narrative texts, for example, *exponent, ecosystem, matriculate, fibrosis.* As a result, Juan is having significant difficulty understanding what he reads in his math and social studies classes and he is failing to learn the content from these texts.

When Desmond entered Bailey Middle School, he had been receiving help in a special education resource room since second grade. During that time, Ms. Jackson, the resource room teacher, had been working with Desmond on word identification and basic comprehension skills as well as spelling and writing compositions. In elementary school, Desmond went to the resource room for 45 minutes every afternoon. He consistently missed either social studies or science in the general education classroom while he was receiving special assistance in the resource room.

Desmond made many changes when he transitioned to middle school. He attends resource English and reading, but he has social studies, science, and home economics classes in general education classes. All of these classes require him to listen to lectures in class and take notes, read textbooks and answer the questions at the end of each section, take timed tests, write reports, and keep track of assignments and turn them in on time. Textbooks for these classes are information-driven and contain unfamiliar technical vocabulary. It is challenging for Desmond to learn from textbooks because he does not know the meaning of many of the vocabulary words that are crucial to understanding the content. By the end of the first nine weeks, Desmond has received failing slips in all three classes. He is frustrated by his classes and is becoming disruptive.

Doreen worked hard in high school and, despite her reading and writing disabilities, graduated with a high enough grade point average to enter college. However, as a freshman at a large university, she is feeling overwhelmed by the demands of her classes. She is barely passing freshman English and classical literature and is even struggling in her math and science courses—areas that were her strengths in high school. Doreen can't seem to get organized. She has difficulty estimating how long it will take her to complete an assignment, and she is unable to keep up with the reading assignments in literature class. Doreen is a bright student with good potential to succeed as an architect or engineer, but she may never get through the basic liberal arts courses required for her degree.

Both Desmond and Doreen need strategies to assist them in being more effective learners. They need skills in managing time, organizing notebooks, taking notes, studying for tests, taking tests, reading textbooks, learning new vocabulary, and writing reports and essays. Desmond and Doreen have mastered many of the basics of reading and writing, but they are having difficulty applying them in content area classes.

Both Juan and Desmond need systematic vocabulary instruction that introduces important vocabulary words and word building strategies. Preteaching specific vocabulary words that are crucial to understanding the texts should improve their comprehension. Also, word building strategies they can apply to figure out the meanings of a variety of words would help improve their vocabulary acquisition.

Ms. Cho, Juan, Desmond, and Doreen are experiencing difficulties functioning in the upper-elementary, secondary, postsecondary school, and professional environments. In these environments, the task demands for teachers and students change dramatically. Special education teachers often coteach, teach content subjects, or need to provide content area teachers with learning and teaching strategies to support students so that they can access the general education curriculum. Students are asked to apply learning strategies and study skills as well as skills in listening, reading, writing, and math to learn content area subjects such as biology, American history, art history, welding, computer programming, and home economics (Putnam, Deshler, and Schumaker, 1993; Tralli, Colombo, Deshler, and Schumaker, 1996; Vaughn et al., 2007).

This chapter focuses on strategies for teaching vocabulary and content area information, *making adaptations*, and teaching learning strategies and study skills. The chapter is divided into four sections. First, we will look at teaching strategies to assist students with learning and behavior problems learn vocabulary and content area information. These strategies are useful to special education teachers whether they are directly teaching the content or collaborating with content area teachers (Bos and Duffy, 1991; Bulgren and Scanlon, 1997; Deshler et al., 1996; Larkin and Ellis, 1998; Schloss, Smith, and Schloss, 2001; Tindal and Nolet, 1996). Next, we will discuss what general education teachers and their students think about teachers making adaptations. We will also present some general strategies for making adaptations for textbooks, lectures, assignments, and tests. Finally, we will examine methods of teaching students to be more effective and efficient learners. Many of the reading comprehension and writing strategies highlighted in Chapters 8 and 9 are effective in promoting content area learning and effective studying and learning. In addition, the strategies intervention model in the section on cognitive behavior modification presented in Chapter 2 can be used to teach many of the study skills and learning strategies suggested in this chapter.

FOCUS Question | **1. How can teachers use specific word instruction and word-learning strategies to teach vocabulary?**

Teaching Content Area Information and Vocabulary

Vocabulary knowledge plays an important role in the development of reading skills (Bauman and Kame'enui, 2004; National Reading Panel,

2000). According to Rupley, Logan, and Nichols (1998), "vocabulary is the glue that holds stories, ideas, and content together . . . making comprehension accessible for children" (p. 339). Limited vocabulary has been viewed as both a cause and an effect of poor reading achievements (Gunning, 1998). Not only do students with limited vocabulary know fewer words, but their knowledge of the words may also lack depth (Shand, 1993). After third grade, when content area texts contain more unfamiliar technical and abstract vocabulary words than primary-grade-level texts do, the cumulative vocabulary differences between these two groups of students gets larger. In fact, good readers know about twice as many words as do poor readers in the first grade, and as these students go through the grades, the gap widens. Stanovich (1986) described this phenomenon as the Matthew Effect—the rich get richer and the poor get poorer. By the end of high school, good readers know four times as many words as do their counterparts with limited reading skills (Smith, 1941). This growing gap means that when students with a rich vocabulary read or hear new words, they are more likely to figure out the meaning of unknown words on the basis of words they already know. Students with limited vocabulary are more likely to miss the opportunities to learn unknown words. Closing the gap is challenging; however, systematic, explicit vocabulary instruction holds promise.

Types of Vocabulary and Vocabulary Instruction

In general, there are two types of vocabulary: oral and reading. *Oral vocabulary* refers to words that a reader recognizes in listening and uses in speaking. *Reading vocabulary* refers to words that a reader recognizes or uses in print (National Reading Panel, 2000). If the word is in a reader's oral vocabulary, the reader can understand what the word means as long as he or she can decode it. However, if the word is not in the reader's oral vocabulary, the reader must learn its meaning. As students read more complex content area texts, they usually encounter more unfamiliar words that are not part of their oral vocabulary. This relationship between oral and reading vocabulary provides insight into vocabulary learning and instruction. Figure 10.1 presents different kinds of word learning and instruction that is appropriate to each kind.

The scientific research on vocabulary instruction reveals two main approaches to teaching vocabulary: the indirect approach and the direct approach (National Reading Panel, 2000). Students can learn vocabulary words indirectly when they hear and see words through conversations with other people, especially adults; through listening to adults read aloud; and through reading extensively on their own. Because not all the words in a text can be taught directly, it is important that teachers promote students' indirect learning of vocabulary.

Many students with learning and behavior problems are less likely to learn words indirectly than are their average-achieving peers. Because of this, direct instruction is recommended as an effective approach to improve vocabulary knowledge for poor readers or at-risk students (Baumann and

Kame'enui, 1991). In the direct approach to vocabulary instruction, students learn difficult words that are not usually part of their everyday experiences through systematic, explicit instruction of individual words and word-learning strategies. Direct instruction provides opportunities to learn vocabulary words that students, especially those with reading difficulties, may not pick up incidentally. Vocabulary instruction for students with learning disabilities should combine a variety of instructional strategies (such as oral language and morphemic analysis) to enhance word learning (Bryant, Goodwin, Bryant, and Higgins, 2003).

Families and Vocabulary Acquisition

To support their children's efforts to build vocabulary, families should have fun with words during reading at home and throughout the day. Activities that develop vocabulary (or other school-like skills) should be a positive experience for children at home. If they do not enjoy an activity, families should try something else.

Teachers can suggest the following activities to do while waiting in line, driving in the car, having dinner, or taking a walk:

* Play with words by rhyming, finding synonyms and antonyms, or categorizing words (things that are *hot*, different ways to say *good*).
* Select a family word of the day—a difficult word that you or your child chooses. Define the word, and see how many times you and your child can use the new word during the day. At the end of the day, discuss how and when you used the word.
* Read and discuss the vocabulary you see in the community on billboards, signs, at the

FIGURE 10.1

Word Learning and Instruction	
Kind of Word Learning	**Instruction**
Knows a word when hears it but does not recognize its meaning	Teach the word in printed form
Knows the concept but does not know the particular word for that concept	Teach the word and relate it to the concept that the reader knows
Recognizes the word but does not know the concept	Develop the concept
Does not know the word and the concept	Develop the word and the concept

Source: Adapted from National Reading Panel (2000); Ruddell (1994).

grocery store, and so on. For example, when you are at the Department of Motor Vehicles renewing your driver's license, talk about what you are doing using relevant words such as *application, license, examination* and *renew.*

Teachers can also suggest ways to improve reading at home through the following activities:

- Choose books that your child is interested in reading. You may want to select a short passage or read just a few pages each day depending on the length of the book.
- Before reading a story aloud or listening to your child read, select a few difficult words and give simple definitions using familiar language. Write down the words and definitions (for example, *flee: to run away*).
- During reading, tell your child to listen for the vocabulary words, and encourage the child to use clues in the story to find out what they mean.
- After reading, ask questions to help your child *explain* and *describe* what has been read. Listen for use of one or more of the vocabulary words in your child's retelling of the story (Hickman, Pollard-Durodola, and Vaughn, 2004; Report of the National Reading Panel, 2000).

Games that encourage vocabulary development can also be played at home. For example, word games such as Scrabble, Scattegories, Balderdash, and Taboo expose children to new words and encourage them to use a wide range of vocabulary.

Teaching Vocabulary through Specific Word Instruction

Specific word instruction, or teaching individual words, helps students to build in-depth understanding of concepts or words. We introduce two types of specific word instruction here. For both types, instruction starts with teachers' careful selection of a few vocabulary words (about 7 to 10 per week) that are critical for understanding the text and difficult for students. Students should have multiple interactions with selected vocabulary words. Beck and colleagues (1985) suggest that students need approximately 12 exposures to a word before they will be able to use the word to aid their comprehension. Exposures should allow students to interact with the words in a variety of formats, such as classroom discussions, multiple texts, and writing exercises.

Using Oral Language

For young students, a teacher can teach words from texts that are read aloud to students (Beck, McKeown, and Kucan, 2003; Hickman et al., 2004). Regular read-alouds provide students with opportunities to be exposed to new words that may be difficult for them to read. Remember, it is valuable to select text that is slightly above the level of students so that new information, concepts, and vocabulary can be acquired. The teacher identifies about three key vocabulary words in a reading passage for direct teaching. Consider selecting words that have high utility and that many students would not know. High utility words are words that students will encounter in a variety of contexts as well as are necessary for understanding the main idea of a particular text. After a story is read aloud to students, the teacher discusses the passage with students to provide a context in which to begin the vocabulary instruction. Then the teacher provides systematic vocabulary instruction:

1. Contextualize the word in the story. (Teacher: "In the story, the leaders of the Cherokee Nation were *amazed* by characters developed by Sequoyah.")
2. Ask students to repeat the word (e.g., *amazed*) so that they know how to pronounce it. (Teacher: "Say the word with me.")
3. Provide a simple definition so that students can easily understand its meaning. (Teacher: "When people are *amazed*, they are very surprised.")
4. Provide other examples to further facilitate students' understanding of word meaning. (Teacher: "Someone might be *amazed* by the number of stars in our galaxy, or someone might be *amazed* by how big a bear is.")
5. Ask students to use their own examples to promote their active involvement. (Teacher: "Tell about something you would be *amazed* by. Try to use *amazed* when you tell about it. You could say 'I would be *amazed* _____.'")

Using Preteaching before Reading

Preteaching vocabulary before reading is an effective strategy to enhance students' knowledge of word meanings (National Reading Panel, 2000). Preteaching vocabulary is especially helpful for students with learning problems because it provides them with background knowledge on the text that they will be reading. To increase the effectiveness of preteaching vocabulary, it is important for teachers to appropriately select words that are critical to understanding the passage and are challenging for their students. Teachers may need to prioritize words by their importance and select the words that are most crucial to understanding the text.

Preteaching key words and concepts is effective for older readers as well and is effective when teaching reading, social studies, science, and math. Preteaching such key words as *freedom, abolitionist, advocate, decimal, galaxy,* and *incubate* helps all readers prepare to read and read with meaning. These words can be considered as high-utility words as students may encounter them in a variety of contexts.

Using synonyms, examples, and/or definitions can be an effective way to enhance students' understanding of a word's meaning when preteaching (Carnine et al., 1997; National Reading Panel, 2000). First, when students know synonyms of the new word, using synonyms may be a good way to teach the new word. Second, teachers can provide examples when few words are available to appropriately define the concept (e.g., *feeling*). Third, teachers can use definitions when introducing new words that are complex. As students progress through the grades and words become more complex, teachers may increasingly use definitions to introduce new words. It is important to note that for young students, teachers should provide student-friendly definitions consisting of words that students know:

- Introduce a vocabulary word (e.g., *immigrant*), and ask students to repeat the word so that they know how to pronounce the word.
- Discuss the meaning of the word using synonyms, examples, and/or definitions (e.g., *immigrant* means "someone who comes from abroad to live permanently in another country").
- Test students on their understanding of the word by asking students to figure out positive or incorrect examples and to explain why. (Positive example of the word *immigrant*: "Tom's grandparents came to the United States from England in 1912. They lived in the United States until they passed away." Ask the students, "Are Tom's grandparents immigrants? Why or why not?" An example of an incorrect use of the word *immigrant*: "Recently, many international students came to the United States to study." Ask the students, "Are the international students immigrants? Why or why not?")

Teaching Vocabulary through Word-Learning Strategies

In addition to specific word instruction, it is critical to teach students word-learning strategies that they can use independently while reading, because teachers cannot teach every individual word that the students do not know. Word-learning strategies that are supported by research include using contextual analysis, morphemic analysis, and dictionaries and other reference aids.

Using Contextual Analysis

Contextual analysis involves using the context or text that surrounds an unknown word as clues to reveal its meaning (Blachowicz and Ogle, 2001; Stahl, 1999). Contextual analysis may be a useful word building strategy for students to use during their independent reading. Writers often provide the definition, synonym, description, or examples of the word that may be difficult for the reader in text (Carnine et al., 1997). Writers provide several types of context clues in their text:

- *Definition.* The word is defined in the sentence. (Example: The *surplus*—that is, an amount left over—was so great that the office was full and desks and chairs were lying on the floor.)
- *Synonym.* The word is compared to another word with a similar meaning. (Example: When Tom went to the parking garage and his car was not there, he was *furious. Tom was very mad.*)
- *Description.* The word is described by the context. (Example: After taking a spill on her bike, she was able to stand up, get back on the bike, and pedal away on her own *volition.*)
- *Contrast.* The word is compared with some other word like an antonym. (Example: Kim was *lethargic,* yet her sister was very energetic.)
- *Comparison.* The word is compared with some other word or phrase to illustrate the similarities between them. (Example: John was exhausted after the *interview,* which was more work than mowing grass all day in the neighborhood.)

Regardless of types of context clues, the first step in teaching contextual analysis is to provide explicit modeling in looking at the words surrounding an unknown word and finding possible clues that may help students figure out its meaning. Then a teacher gives students ample opportunities to practice how to use contextual analysis and engage them in lively discussions. Teachers should introduce a few types of context clues (about two) at one time and sequence types of context clues from easy (e.g., definition) to difficult (e.g., comparison).

The following activity helps students understand the supporting role of context in understanding word meanings:

1. Prepare a series of passages in which context is used to define a difficult word.
2. Present the difficult word in isolation.
3. Ask students for the definition of the word.
4. Present the difficult word in context, and point out the word.
5. Have students reread the sentence before, with, and after the one with the difficult word to look for context clues.
6. Ask students for the definition of the word and how the definition is derived.
7. Have students compare the definition of the word from context with that of the word in isolation.
8. Present other vocabulary words in context. Pair students, and ask them to analyze the context to figure out the meaning of each vocabulary word and record the definition for each word.
9. Have students look up the definitions for the vocabulary words in a dictionary (University of Texas Center for Reading and Language Arts, 2002).

It is valuable to prepare students for text that does not provide sufficient information to help them understand words and concepts. They will undoubtedly encounter text in content areas as well as narrative that provides little information or perhaps even misleading information about words and concepts. It is necessary to help students distinguish words that are not defined in text and how to use other resources to gain meaning.

Using Morphemic Analysis

Morphemic analysis in vocabulary instruction involves breaking a word into morphemes, the smallest linguistic units that have meaning, and using their meanings to figure out the meaning of the whole word (Carnine et al., 1997). There are two types of morphemes: free, which can stand alone (e.g., *some*), and bound, which must be linked to words or other morphemes (i.e., prefixes and suffixes). Because Greek and Latin morphemes are found commonly in content area textbooks, teaching morphemes and their meanings helps students to independently figure out the meanings of the words. Figure 10.2 provides common Greek and Latin roots and their meanings. Having students break words into small parts based on meaning can help them to figure out the meaning of words on the basis of what they know about the meanings of the smaller parts (Stahl and Shiel, 1992). For instance, a student can break the word *unchangeable* into the word parts *un*, *change*, and *able*. If the student knows the meanings of these word parts (*un* meaning "not," *change*, and *able* meaning "able to"), the student can determine that *unchangeable* means "not able to change." Figure 10.3 presents common prefixes and suffixes and their meanings.

Learning prefixes is relatively easy in comparison to learning suffixes (National Reading Panel, 2000). Prefixes generally have clearer meanings and are spelled more regularly than suffixes. For instance, the prefixes *un-* and *re-* have clear meanings of "not" and "again," respectively, and are spelled as *un* and *re* all the time. In contrast, the suffixes *-tion* and *-ness* have more abstract meanings of "the act or process of" and "the state or condition of," respectively. Some suffixes can also be spelled differently depending on the base words (e.g., *-tion*, *-ion*, *-sion*). However, not all suffixes have abstract meanings (e.g., *-less* meaning "without" and *-ful* meaning "full of").

Morphemic analysis instruction involves presenting new morphemes and their meanings in several specific steps:

1. Introduce a new morpheme and its meaning.
2. Introduce words containing that morpheme.
3. Provide practice for determining the meaning of words that contain that morpheme.
4. Test students on the meaning of several words that contain that morpheme.
5. Provide practice for the meaning of the new morpheme and previously taught morphemes.

FIGURE 10.2

Common Greek and Latin Roots

Root	Meaning	Sample Words
astro	star	astrology, astronaut, asteroid
aud	hear	auditorium, audition
bio	life	biography, biology
dict	speak	dictate, dictator
geo	earth	geography, geology
meter	measure	thermometer
mit, mis	send	transmit, mission, missile
ped	foot	pedal, pedestrian
phon	sound	microphone, phonograph
port	carry	portable, transport
scrib, script	write	manuscript, scribble
spect	see	inspect, spectator
struct	build	construction, destruction

Source: Adapted from University of Texas Center for Reading and Language Arts (2002). Reprinted by permission.

FIGURE 10.3

Common Prefixes and Suffixes

Prefix	Meaning	Sample Words		Suffix	Meaning/Function	Sample Words
ante-	before, front	antechamber		-able, -ible	can be done	comfortable, changeable
anti-	against	antislavery, antisocial		-al, -ial	characteristic of	natural, remedial
bi-	two	bicycle		-ance, -ence	state of	importance
co-	with, together	coworker		-ation, -ition, -tion, -ion, -sion	act, process	tension, attention, imagination
de-	opposite of, down, remove, reduce	deactivate, devalue, dethrone		-ant	person connected with	accountant
dis-	not, opposite of	dishonest, disagree		-en	noting action from an adjective made of	harden, loosen, wooden
en-, em-	cause to	enable, embrace				
ex-	out, out of	exterior, exhaust, expose		-er, -or	person connected with	painter, director
fore-	before	foreground		-ful	full of	fearful, beautiful, hopeful
in-	in or into	inside, interior		-fy	make	clarify
in-, im-, ir-, il-	not	inactive, immature, irregular, illegal		-ic	having of	poetic
				-ish	characteristic of	greenish
inter-	between	international, intersection		-ity, -ty	state of	necessity, honesty
				-ive, -ative, -itive	noting action from an adjective	active, affirmative
intra-	inside	intrastate				
mid-	middle	midnight		-less	without	fearless, tireless, hopeless
mis-	wrongly	misbehave, mispronounce		-ly	characteristic of	gladly, happily
				-ment	result of an action	entertainment, excitement
non-	not	nonfiction		-ness	state of, condition of	kindness, happiness
over-	too much	overdue, oversleep		-ous, -eous, -ious	having of	joyous, gracious
pre-	before	preheat, preschool				
re-	again	reread, redo		-y	characterized by	rainy
semi-	half	semicircle				
sub-	under	submarine, subway				
super-	above	supernatural				
trans-	across	transport				
tri-	three	tricycle				
un-	not, opposite of	unable, unchangeable				
under-	too little	underpaid				

Source: Adapted from University of Texas Center for Reading and Language Arts (2002). Reprinted by permission.

Although morphemic analysis can help students build their vocabulary, several cautions should be considered when planning morphemic analysis instruction. First, this strategy works with a limited set of words; therefore, morphemic analysis instruction should not be too long. Second, only one or two prefixes or suffixes should be introduced at a time with an emphasis on their applications to unfamiliar words. Teachers can utilize small groups to promote student discussion of the meanings of word parts and the new words. Third, to avoid confusion, any similar prefixes or suffixes should not be taught too closely to each other (Carnine et al., 1997; Stahl and Shiel, 1992; White, Power, and White, 1989).

Using Dictionaries and Other Reference Aids

It is important for students to learn how to use dictionaries, glossaries, and thesauruses to help broaden and deepen their word knowledge (National Institute for Literacy, 2001). Using dictionaries and other reference aids can be a difficult task for young students for several reasons

(Carnine et al., 1997). First, dictionary definitions often contain words that students do not understand. Therefore, when possible, teachers should select dictionaries that are written at the appropriate reading level. Young students or students who struggle with reading may benefit from picture dictionaries and other resources that include sentences which provide clear examples of word meanings or student-friendly definitions.

Second, many words have more than one definition listed in the dictionary (e.g., the word *parcel* can mean something wrapped up or packaged or a portion or plot of land). Teachers should teach students how to decide on the most appropriate meaning based on the word's use in context. For example, a teacher may present a word having several meanings in sentences. The teacher then asks students to look up the word, examine the definitions listed in the dictionary, read the sentence substituting each definition in the dictionary to see whether it makes sense, and select the definition that is most appropriate for the sentence. Although using dictionaries and other reference aids is an important word building strategy students can use while reading, students should not look up every unknown word. Teachers should encourage students to use contextual analysis and morphemic analysis to assist in determining word meanings. Also, teachers should encourage students to decide whether a word is important to understanding the passage. When students fail to figure out the meaning of important words through contextual analysis and morphemic analysis, they can look up the word in a dictionary or other reference aid.

Assessing Vocabulary

Vocabulary is perhaps one of the most difficult areas of reading and content learning to assess. It is difficult to determine what words students actually know of the many words that they need to understand and learn from texts. Vocabulary is also difficult to assess because there are many different levels of knowing what a word means. We can recognize the word when we see or hear it, we can know what the word means when someone else uses it, and/or we can use the word adeptly in conversation and writing. For the purposes of instruction, teachers can monitor the words and concepts related to understanding text or learning from their content area instruction.

Progress Monitoring

What can teachers do to monitor their students' vocabulary and concept learning? The first step is to identify the words and concepts that students most need to know and understand for the text or unit to make sense to them. Although it is tempting to select a lot of words for instruction, the most important goal is to select words that have high impact on learning and comprehension. For example, Mr. O'Malley, a middle school social studies teacher, was concerned that many of his students would not understand many of the most important words in his unit on how money works. He realized that he couldn't teach every word at a deep enough level that students would be able to use them orally and in their writing. He selected eight words for the first week of his unit. He decided to teach two new words each day for the first four days and then briefly review the words that he had previously taught. He monitored the progress of students' understanding of these words in two ways. First, he did daily checks with selected students to determine whether they knew what the words meant. Second, he asked students to document in their notebook if they saw or heard any of the key words either during the day at school or at home. Third, he provided a paper-and-pencil assessment of all eight words at the end of the week so that he would know which words required further review during the second week of the unit.

> **FOCUS Question** 2. What is content enhancement, and how can teachers use it to teach content area reading?

Teaching Content Area Reading through Content Enhancement

To teach content area information in any subject, a teacher must teach the important concepts and vocabulary and their relationships (Bos and Anders, 1990c; Readence, Bean, and Baldwin, 1998; Vacca and Vacca, 1999). The goal is to enhance the content and teach related vocabulary so that the "critical features of the content are selected, organized, manipulated, and complemented in a manner that promotes effective and efficient information processing" (Lenz, Bulgren, and Hudson, 1990, p. 132).

Content enhancements are techniques to help students identify, organize, and comprehend important content information (Lenz and Bulgren, 1995; Lenz et al., 1990). In addition, content enhancements inform students of the purpose of instruction and increase student motivations (Mastropieri and Scruggs, 2000). Several types of content enhancements have been developed and recommended: advance organizers, concept diagrams, comparison tables, semantic feature analysis, or semantic maps.

Concepts are general ideas that are associated with smaller but related ideas (Anders and Bos, 1984; Vacca and Vacca, 1999). The following concept might be used in a science course:

> Bacteria are a class of microscopic plants that help people, other animals, and plants; however, bacteria also do things that hurt people, other animals, and plants.

Several related ideas that elaborate on the concept of bacteria are as follows:

> Bacteria are small; you use a microscope to see them; bacteria multiply; bacteria live in soil, water, organic matter, plants, or animals; bacteria can make you ill; bacteria can spoil food.

The vocabulary associated with the general concept and its related concepts is the *conceptual vocabulary.* These are the words that are necessary for understanding the general idea and are associated with it. Examples of the conceptual vocabulary for a unit on bacteria in a science text are *bacteria, microscope, colony, multiply, reproduce,* and *decay.* These words and their meanings facilitate understanding of the general concept.

According to Bulgren and colleagues (2007), content enhancement routines ensure that students possess the prerequisite background knowledge or provide scaffolded instruction so students can obtain this knowledge; assist students in working with related concepts; and give students the skills to predict, problem solve, infer, and synthesize information in a variety of settings. A six-step process or teaching routine can be used to teach concepts and their labels through content enhancement (Anders, Bos, and Filip, 1984; Lenz and Bulgren, 1995). This process is presented in Figure 10.4 and discussed in more detail in the following sections.

Step One: Selecting Concepts and Related Vocabulary

The first step in getting ready to teach content information is selecting the major concepts and related vocabulary to be taught and generating a framework for facilitating understanding of the ideas to be learned. Selecting the major concepts and related vocabulary to be taught in a unit, a chapter, a section of a book, or a lecture is best completed before students interact with the material (Bos and Anders, 1990b; Readence et al., 1998). A teacher needs to determine the conceptual framework for the unit so that the information can be presented in an organized fashion on the basis of this framework. During this step, the teacher should focus on what the critical information or knowledge all students need to understand about a particular unit (Bulgren, Deschler, and Lenz, 2007).

The process that a teacher uses for determining the major concepts depends on his or her expertise and knowledge in the content area, knowledge of the structure of the textbook information, and knowledge about the students' background for the content and their study/reading skills (Bulgren and Lenz, 1996; Reyes and Bos, 1998). A teacher who has specialized in a given content area can probably generate concepts from expert knowledge and experiences and use the assigned textbook along with key resource books and Websites as the primary resources for verifying the appropriateness of those concepts. A teacher with limited background knowledge could use a variety of resources, such as the assigned textbooks, trade books, state or local curriculum guides, Websites and other computer-based resources, and other teachers or experts in the field. Some texts—especially those written for students with reading problems—tend to provide too much detail and fail to explain the overall concept or to relate the concepts (Armbruster and Anderson, 1988; Scanlon and Anders, 1988).

After articulating the major concepts to be learned, the teacher next generates and organizes the related vocabulary. To do this, the teacher studies the assigned text and instructional materials and compiles a list of relevant related words and phrases. In doing this, the teacher might

FIGURE 10.4

Process for Teaching Concepts

A six-step process can be used to teach concepts and their labels:

1. Decide what concepts and related conceptual vocabulary to teach.
2. Evaluate the instructional materials to be used for reader-friendliness or considerateness.
3. Assess the students on their background knowledge for the concepts and related vocabulary.
4. Use prelearning or prereading activities to facilitate and support learning.
5. Conduct the learning or reading activity.
6. Provide postlearning activities that further reinforce and extend the concepts and information learned.

realize that some important vocabulary is missing from the text; if so, it can be added to the list.

To organize the vocabulary list, a teacher can group words that are related and then create a semantic or content map to visually represent the relationships among these terms (Scanlon, Duran, Reyes, and Gallego, 1992). Figure 10.5 depicts a map that was developed with the conceptual vocabulary a teacher generated from a chapter in a biology text. The map highlights the critical vocabulary and the organization and relationships of the concepts (Anders and Bos, 1984; Lenz and Bulgren, 1995). The map helps to solve an all too common problem that confronts content area teachers: deciding what concepts and related vocabulary to teach in a content lesson.

Step Two: Evaluating Instructional Materials

Before teaching concepts and related vocabulary, teachers need to evaluate the instructional materials they intend to use in teaching the unit. Whether teachers are teaching the content themselves or collaborating with content teachers, this evaluation is critical to support students with learning and behavior problems and to know how to make adaptations so that students can access the content. Although the breadth of instructional materials has increased with the use of the Internet and other media, textbooks still continue to predominate as the medium of instruction (Ciborowski, 1992; O'Brien, Stewart, and Moje, 1995; Vacca and Vacca, 1999). In terms of the general education curriculum, textbooks structure from 65 to 90 percent of secondary classroom instruction (Woodward and Elliott, 1990). How concepts are presented in a text, whether it is the class textbook, a resource book, or on the Internet, will affect how easily the students comprehend and learn the concepts (McKeown et al., 1992). The manner in which the text is organized (e.g., use of headings and subheadings, highlighted words, marginal notes) will also affect the comprehensibility of the text.

FIGURE 10.5

Content Map of a Biology Chapter on Mollusks

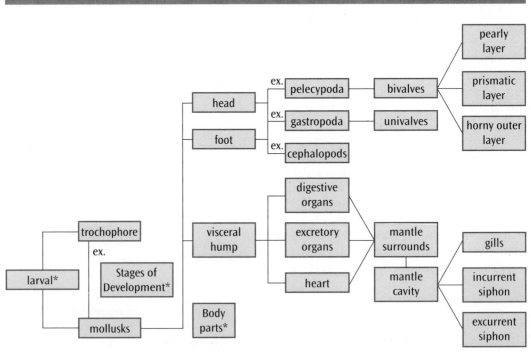

*Note: There seem to be two concepts being developed (apologies to the biologists among us):

1. When classifying animals biologists look for relationships between animals during the various stages of development from birth to adulthood.

2. Biologists describe the body parts of animals and the functions of each part.

Source: P. L. Anders and C. S. Bos (1984). In the beginning: Vocabulary instruction in content classes. *Topics in Learning and Learning Disabilities 3* (4), p. 56. Reprinted with permission of PRO-ED.

Readability

Traditionally, evaluations of content area texts emphasized readability as determined by readability formulas (e.g., Dale and Chall, 1948; Fry, 1977). Most readability formulas, including the Fry readability formula presented in Figure 10.6, are based on two factors: sentence complexity as measured by sentence length and word difficulty as indexed by word length or frequency. One of the most frequently used procedures for determining the reading level of text is by assessing the lexile level of the text (www.lexile.com).

Readability formulas should be used cautiously and as only one aspect of evaluating a text for

FIGURE 10.6

Fry Readability Graph for Estimating Readability—Extended

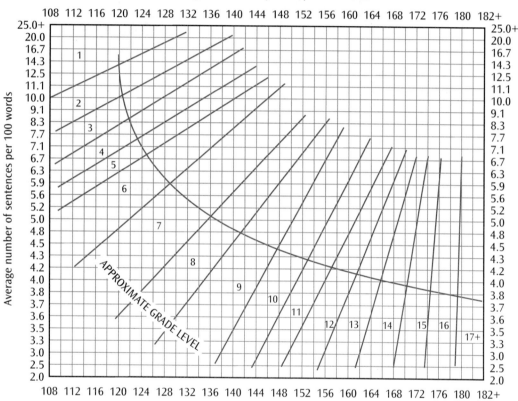

1. Randomly select three text samples of exactly 100 words, beginning with the beginning of a sentence. Count proper nouns, numerals, and initializations as words.

2. Count the number of sentences in each 100-word sample, estimating the length of the last sentence to the nearest one-tenth.

3. Count the total number of syllables in each 100-word sample. Count one syllable for each numeral or initial or symbol; for example, 1990 is one word and four syllables, LD is one word and two syllables, and "&" is one word and one syllable.

4. Average the number of sentences and number of syllables across the three samples.

5. Enter the average sentence length and average number of syllables on the graph. Put a dot where the two lines intersect. The area in which the dot is plotted will give you an approximate estimated readability.

6. If there is a great deal of variability in the syllable or sentence count across the three samples, more samples can be added.

Source: E. Fry (1977). Fry's readability graph: Clarifications, validity, and extension to level 17. *Journal of Reading, 21*, pp. 242–252.

several reasons (Alvermann and Phelps, 1998; Anders and Guzzetti, 1996). First, the typical standard error of measurement for readability formulas is plus or minus approximately 1.5 grade levels (Singer and Donlan, 1989). Consequently, a text whose readability formula is predicted to be 7.5 can range by chance from 6.0 to 9.0. Second, readability formulas do not take into account many characteristics of text that are important in comprehension and learning. For example, to reduce the reading level or difficulty as measured by readability formulas, textbooks—particularly adapted textbooks that are designed for students with learning and behavior problems—are written in short sentences. Often this means that important relational words such as *and, or, because,* and *if . . . then* have been eliminated to shorten the length of the sentences and thus lower the readability level as predicted by the formula. However, it is these relational words that signal the reader about the relationships among the concepts (Davison, 1984). Consequently, although the readability level according to the formula may be lower, the text is actually more difficult to understand. Third, students' prior knowledge of the content and the concepts and technical vocabulary associated with the content can dramatically affect how easy a text is to comprehend. Fourth, readability formulas neglect to consider other reader characteristics that affect comprehension, such as interest, purpose, and perseverance.

Considerate or User-Friendly Text

What characteristics should be considered in evaluating how considerate or user-friendly a text is? Armbruster and Anderson (1988) conducted a program of research to develop salient criteria for determining the considerate text. Their criteria fall into three broad categories:

1. *Structure* refers to the manner in which a text is organized and how the text signals its structure. Use of titles, headings, subheadings, introductions, and summary statements; informative and relevant pictures, charts, and graphs; highlighted key concepts; marginal notes; and signaling words (e.g., *first, second, then, therefore*) can facilitate comprehension. In evaluating a text, it is important to check not only whether such structural features are used, but also whether they match the content. For example, sometimes headings will not relate well to the text that follows the headings. In this case, the structural features may serve more as a source of confusion than as an aid. Also, the teacher should check whether the highlighted words in the text represent the important concepts or simply the words that are difficult to decode.

The teacher should also consider whether the format and the table of contents help readers to draw relationships between the various chapters by using such devices as sections and subsections. Do introductions to each section or chapter encourage readers to make connections between previous ideas and concepts already discussed and the new ideas to be presented? Some key features to consider in assessing text structure include:

- The introduction is clearly identified.
- The introduction provides purpose, relevance, and overview.
- Titles, headings, and subheadings reflect main ideas of content.
- Key vocabulary words are highlighted and reflect important concepts.
- Definitions of key terms are provided.
- Signal words or headings are provided.
- Margin notes provide summaries or expand on information.
- Illustrations and pictures enhance important information.
- The summary is clearly identified.
- The summary reviews goals and the most important concepts.
- Review questions require students to think about key concepts and ideas.
- The questions have good balance among main concepts, fact/detail, and critical thinking (application, analysis, reactions).

2. *Coherence* refers to how well the ideas in a text "stick together" (Armbruster and Anderson, 1988). With coherent text, the relationships among concepts are clear. For example, when Herman, Anderson, Pearson, and Nagy (1987) rewrote a text about the circulatory system and made explicit the connections between motive and action, form and function, and cause and effect, student learning improved. Coherence is also facilitated by using different kinds of *cohesive ties—*linguistic forms that help to convey meaning across phrase, clause, and sentence boundaries (Anders and Guzzetti, 1996). Examples of cohesive ties are *conjunctions* and *connectives, pronoun referents* (using a pronoun to refer to a previously mentioned noun), and *substitutions* (using a word to replace a previously used noun or verb phrase).

3. *Audience appropriateness* refers to how well a textbook is suited to the readers' content knowledge, reading, and study skills. The text needs to provide enough explanation, attributes, examples, and analogies to give readers adequate information to relate to their background knowledge. Superficial mentions of new topics about which the reader has limited background knowledge do

little to build understanding. On the other hand, too many or too few technical supporting details can obscure the important concepts.

Another area to consider in relation to the audience is the explicitness of main ideas. As we discussed in Chapter 8, many students with learning and behavior problems have difficulty identifying and comprehending the main ideas of a text. Therefore, text in which the main ideas are explicit and are regularly placed at the beginning of paragraphs and sections should facilitate learning. However, in examining social studies textbooks designed for the second, fourth, sixth, and eighth grades, Baumann and Serra (1984) found that only 27 percent of the short passages contained explicitly stated main ideas, only 44 percent of the paragraphs contained them, and only 27 percent of the paragraphs began with them.

Part of the process of preparing to teach content knowledge is evaluating instructional materials for readability and friendliness. By considering the structure, cohesion, and audience appropriateness when evaluating text or other types of instructional materials (e.g., films, lectures, demonstrations), teachers develop a good idea of how considerate or user-friendly the materials are. Based on this evaluation, teachers may decide to modify, augment, or adapt the instructional materials (see the section on adapting textbooks later in this chapter).

The ultimate judge of the readability and friendliness of a textbook is the reader. The FLIP chart strategy helps students learn to evaluate text on their own (Schumm and Mangrum, 1991). FLIP stands for Friendliness, Language, Interest, and Prior knowledge. By filling out charts like the one shown in Figure 10.7, students learn what is comfortable for them individually as readers. After students have completed the FLIP chart, you can learn (through class discussions and individual conferences) what is difficult for them in terms of text friendliness, language, interest, and prior knowledge. Students with reading and learning problems especially need to learn how to talk about the textbook and any problems they have with it. Classroom discussions based on the FLIP chart strategy also help students to think as a group about effective strategies for coping with text they find difficult.

Step Three: Assessing Students' Prior Knowledge

Before content area teachers assign a specific chapter or text to read or present a lecture on a topic, they need to assess the students' background knowledge for the concepts and related vocabulary to be covered. Prior knowledge plays a critical role in determining how effectively students will comprehend and retain the information and vocabulary to be presented. One technique for assessing prior knowledge is using the PreReading Plan (PReP) discussed in Chapter 8. This plan not only assesses students' knowledge, but also serves to activate their knowledge, thus facilitating comprehension.

A second procedure that can be used to assess and activate students' background knowledge is semantic mapping (Johnson, Pittelman, and Heimlich, 1986; Pearson and Johnson, 1978; Scanlon et al., 1992). Like PReP, this technique uses brainstorming ideas about the topic to generate a list of words and phrases related to the key concept. The teacher and students take the ideas given by the students and relate them to the key concept, developing a network that notes the various relationships (e.g., categories, subcategories, definition, class, examples, properties, or characteristics). A semantic map for the concept of "desert" was developed by a group of fifth-grade students with learning disabilities who were preparing to study deserts. The map, shown in Figure 10.8, indicates that the students could give examples and characteristics of a desert. However, the students did not produce a superordinate class (landform) or a definition ("What is it?"). Additionally, the property and example relations that were generated lacked technical vocabulary, despite further probing on the part of the teacher. The semantic map in Figure 10.8 serves not only as a visual representation of the students' current understanding of the concept of deserts, but also as an initial blueprint for teaching (Bos and Anders, 1992; Reyes and Bos, 1998).

Using activities such as semantic mapping and PReP not only provides teachers with valuable information about their students' knowledge, but also activates their knowledge. This is particularly important for English language learners and culturally diverse learners with learning and behavior problems who may have limited knowledge of more formalized content. We have found that promoting discussions during these activities and encouraging students to relate first-hand experiences helps both students and teachers make connections (Reyes and Bos, 1998). Having English language learners clarify concepts in their home language can also facilitate activation of background knowledge and understanding of key concepts (Bos and Reyes, 1996; Echevarria and Graves, 1998; Reyes, Duran, and Bos, 1989).

On the basis of assessment information from such procedures as PReP or semantic mapping,

Diversity

FIGURE 10.7
The FLIP Chart

Title of assignment _____

Number of pages _____

General directions: Rate each of the four FLIP categories on a 1–5 scale (5 = high). Then determine your purpose for reading and appropriate reading rate, and budget your reading/study time.

Friendliness: How friendly is my reading assignment?

Directions: Examine your assignment to see if it includes the friendly elements listed below.

Friendly text features

Table of contents	Index	Glossary
Chapter introductions	Headings	Subheadings
Margin notes	Study questions	Chapter summary
Key terms highlighted	Graphs	Charts
Pictures	Signal words	Lists of key facts

1 ——————————— 2 ——————————— 3 ——————————— 4 ——————————— 5
No friendly text features   Some friendly text features   Many friendly text features

Friendliness rating _____

Language: How difficult is the language in my reading assignment?

Directions: Skim the chapter quickly to determine the number of new terms. Read 3 random paragraphs to get a feel for the vocabulary level and number of long, complicated sentences.

1 ——————————— 2 ——————————— 3 ——————————— 4 ——————————— 5
Many new words;   Some new words: No new words;
complicated sentences   somewhat complicated sentences   clear sentences

Language rating _____

Interest: How interesting is my reading assignment?

Directions: Read the title, introduction, headings/subheadings, and summary. Examine the pictures and graphics included.

1 ——————————— 2 ——————————— 3 ——————————— 4 ——————————— 5
Boring   Somewhat interesting   Very interesting

Interest rating _____

Prior knowledge: What do I already know about the material covered in my reading assignment?

Directions: Think about the title, introduction, headings/subheadings, and summary.

1 ——————————— 2 ——————————— 3 ——————————— 4 ——————————— 5
Mostly new information   Some new information   Mostly familiar information

Prior knowledge rating _____

Overall, this reading assignment appears to be at:

❏ a comfortable reading level for me
❏ a somewhat comfortable reading level for me
❏ an uncomfortable reading level for me

Source: J. S. Schumm and C. T. Magnum (1991). FLIP: A framework for textbook thinking. *Journal of Reading, 35,* pp. 120–124. Copyright by the International Reading Association.

teachers can make decisions as to the need and type of further prelearning activities to provide.

Step Four: Using Prelearning Activities

Limited background knowledge signals the teacher that students need more instruction to learn the information that will be presented in a text or lecture. Teachers can present any number of prelearning activities—such as advance organizers, semantic feature analysis, semantic mapping, and concept diagrams—that students can use before reading an assigned text or listening to a lecture. All these activities enhance the content and have been referred to as *content enhancement devices* (Bulgren, Schumaker, and Deshler, 1988; Walther-Thomas and Brownell, 2000). Teachers

FIGURE 10.8

Concept Map of Fifth-Grade Students' Knowledge of Deserts

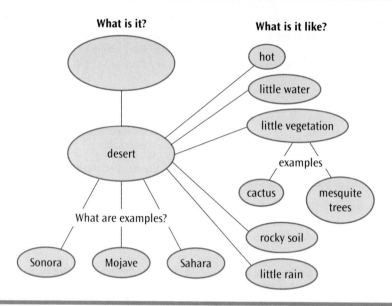

can also use other learning experiences such as field trips, experiments, computer simulations, Internet investigations, and films.

Advance Organizers

Advance organizers are activities that orient students to the material before reading or class presentation (Slavin, 2000). They provide students with an overview or preview of the content they will be learning (Keel, Dangle, and Owens, 1995). Use of advance organizers is based on schema theory and the notion that students profit from having a framework for the material to be learned to help them assimilate the new information into their current schemas or cognitive structure. Advance organizers should inform students of the purpose of instruction, identify topics and subtopics, supply background information, introduce new vocabulary, provide an organizational structure, and state the intended student outcomes. Reviews of studies that have explored the effectiveness of advance organizers on learning have drawn the following conclusions (Corkill, 1992; Mayer, 1979):

- Groups that are given advance organizers consistently perform better than control groups that do not receive them. This advantage diminishes when the material is familiar, when the learners have an extensive background of knowledge about the area, when the learners have high IQs, and when tests fail to measure the breadth of transfer ability.

- Advance organizers particularly aid students of lower ability and/or limited background knowledge.
- Advance organizers are more effective when presented before a learning task than when presented after the task.

Using this information, Lenz (1983; Lenz, Alley, and Schumaker, 1987) demonstrated that both the quality and quantity of learning for adolescents with learning disabilities could be significantly improved by using advance organizers. He also found that regular content area teachers are able to implement advance organizers.

CLASSROOM Applications

Advance Organizers

PROCEDURES: Lenz (1983) identified 10 steps to use an advance organizer (see Figure 10.9). The resource teacher trained the students in the resource classroom to use advance organizers by giving the students a worksheet with each of the 10 steps as headings. The students then practiced listening to advance organizers given by the resource teacher and completing the worksheets. Next, the students used the advance organizer worksheet in inclusive content area classes, and the resource teacher and students met afterward to discuss the success of the worksheets. They discussed how the advance organizer information

FIGURE 10.9

Steps in Using an Advance Organizer

1. Inform the students of advance organizers.
   a. Announce the advance organizer.
   b. State the benefits of the advance organizer.
   c. Suggest that students take notes on the advance organizer.

2. Clarify the action to be taken.
   a. State the teacher's actions.
   b. State the students' actions.

3. Identify the topics or tasks.
   a. Identify major topics or activities.
   b. Identify subtopics or component activities.

4. Provide background information.
   a. Relate the topic to the course or previous lesson.
   b. Relate the topic to new information.

5. State the concepts to be learned.
   a. State specific concepts/ideas from the lesson.
   b. State general concepts/ideas that are broader than the lesson's content.

6. Clarify the concepts to be learned.
   a. Clarify by examples or analogies.
   b. Clarify by nonexamples.
   c. Caution students of possible misunderstandings.

7. Motivate the students to learn.
   a. Point out the relevance to students.
   b. Be specific, short-term, personalized, and believable.

8. Introduce vocabulary.
   a. Identify the new terms and define them.
   b. Repeat difficult terms and define them.

9. Provide an organizational framework.
   a. Present an outline, list, or narrative of the lesson's content.

10. State the general outcome desired.
    a. State the objectives of the instruction/learning.
    b. Relate the outcomes to test performance.

Source: Adapted from B. K. Lenz (1983). Promoting active learning through effective instruction. *Pointer, 27* (2), p. 12.

could be used to organize notes and how the worksheet could be modified to assist the students to cue in on the most common organizing principles used by particular teachers.

In giving an advance organizer, the teacher provides an organizational framework for the information to be learned (see step 3 in Figure 10.9). This framework might be an outline, a diagram in which the parts are labeled, or a picture semantic map, as discussed earlier. Townsend and Clarihew (1989) found that a pictorial component in a verbal advance organizer was necessary to improve the comprehension of eight-year-old students with limited background knowledge. The use of visual representations or pictures is particularly salient for students with learning and behavior problems (Schwartz, Ellsworth, Graham, and Knight, 1998).

COMMENTS: Lenz and his colleagues (1987) found that regular content area teachers are able to implement advance organizers with minimal teacher training (45 minutes). Teachers who used advance organizers expressed satisfaction with the students' response to the instruction as well as the improvement in the overall quality of their own instruction. However, Lenz did find that teacher use of an advance organizer alone was not enough to facilitate student learning. "Learning disabled students had to be made aware that advance organizers were being presented and then had to be trained in the types of information presented in the advance organizer and ways in which that information could be made useful" (Lenz, 1983, p. 12).

Concept Diagrams and Comparison Tables

The concept diagram as part of the *Concept Mastery Routine* (Bulgren et al., 1988, 1996) is a content enhancement tool that can be used to assist students in understanding important key concepts in the reading or lecture; it also works well as a prelearning activity. Research revealed that the Concept Mastery Routine led to gains in students' knowledge in concept and expression of information. In addition, teachers easily learned the routine (Bulgren et al., 1988; Bulgren, Deshler, Schumaker, and Lenz, 2000). The concept diagram is a visual tool that supports students as they delineate a concept by doing the following:

- Exploring their prior knowledge of the concept
- Understanding the relationship of the concept to the overall concept class to which it belongs
- Classifying characteristics of the concept
- Generating examples and nonexamples
- Constructing a content-related definition of the concept

CLASSROOM Applications

Concept Diagrams and Comparison Tables

PROCEDURES: In using a concept diagram (see Figure 10.10), the first step is to prepare the diagram. The teacher identifies major and related concepts of which the students need a deeper or more technical understanding. In a science chapter on fossils, Mr. Bello felt that it was important that the students develop a more technical understanding of the concept of fossils, so this became the concept to diagram. Second, Mr. Bello used the instructional materials and his knowledge to list important characteristics of fossils. He also thought about whether each characteristic is "always present," "sometimes present," or "never present." Third, he located examples and nonexamples of the concepts in the instructional materials. In reviewing the chapter he found that nonexamples were not provided, so he decided to show the students fossils and nonfossils to help them to start thinking about examples and nonexamples. Finally, Mr. Bello constructed a definition. Lenz and Bulgren (1995) specify a concept definition as the "naming of the superordinate concept which includes the concept under consideration,

FIGURE 10.10

Concept Diagram

CONCEPT DIAGRAM

Concept	fossils

Overall Concept	past geologic age

Classifying Characteristics

Always Present	Sometimes Present	Never Present
remains or prints	frozen in ice	still alive
plants or animals	trapped in tar	still decaying
thousands of years old	crushed by water	
preserved in the earth	in volcanic ash	

Example:	Nonexample:
tigers in La Brea tar pits	your pet cat
Siberian mammoth	elephant in Africa today
petrified forest in Arizona	tree limbs and leaves in your yard
fish skeleton in limestone layers	fish in supermarket

Definition:	Fossils are remains or prints of plants or animals who lived thousands of years ago that have been preserved in the earth.

a listing of the characteristics which must always be present in the concept, and a specification of the relationships among those characteristics" (p. 33).

After preparing the concept diagram, the next step is using it with the students to develop their understanding of the concept. After giving an advance organizer to explain its purpose, how the diagram works, and the expectations, the teacher can use what Bulgren and her colleagues refer to as the linking steps to teach the concept:

Convey the concept name and why it is the focus of study.

Offer the overall or overarching concept.

Note the key words by having the students brainstorm words related to the concept.

Classify the characteristics by using the key words and other ideas to generate characteristics that are always, sometimes, and never present.

Explore and list examples and nonexamples.

Practice with the examples by having students discuss how the examples relate to the characteristics.

Tie down a definition by generating a content-related definition that includes the concept, the overall concepts, and the characteristics that are always present.

The acronym CONCEPT can be used to help remember the teaching routine. The routine should employ interactive discussion that encourages the students to fine-tune and deepen their understanding of the concept being studied (Bulgren et al., 1988).

COMMENTS: When Bulgren and her colleagues (1988) worked with content area high school teachers in whose classes students with learning disabilities were included, they found that when the teachers used the concept diagrams and the CONCEPT teaching routine, the learning performance of all the students in the class, including those with learning disabilities, improved. Bulgren and her colleagues have extended the idea of concept diagrams to allow students to visually represent the comparison of two concepts (Bulgren, Lenz, Deshler, and Schumaker, 1995). Figure 10.11 presents a sample comparison table and includes the steps that are used in generating the table (see the steps in the upper right-hand corner, which use the acronym COMPARING). An important part of this table and the steps in generating it is outlining the similar and dissimilar characteristics.

Bulgren and her colleagues note that both the concept diagram and the comparison table as shown in Figures 10.10 and 10.11 are "instructional tools developed and researched at the University of Kansas Center for Research on Learning. They represent a number of organizing and teaching devices designed for teachers to use as they teach content information to classes containing diverse student populations. They are data-based teaching instruments that have been found effective when used in instructional routines that combine cues about the instruction, specialized delivery of the content, involvement of the students in the cognitive processes, and a review of the learning process and content materials (Bulgren, Lenz, et al., 1995). They have not been shown to be effective tools if they are simply distributed to students" (J. Bulgren, personal communication, November 20, 2000).

Semantic Feature Analysis/Relationship Charts

Like an advance organizer, semantic feature analysis (SFA) is a prelearning activity that serves to organize the major concepts and related vocabulary to be taught in a unit, chapter, or lecture. Whereas the concept diagram can be used to clarify a concept that is difficult for the students, this activity helps students to see the relationships between the major concepts, the related vocabulary, and their current knowledge of the topic.

The theoretical foundations for the SFA teaching strategy are schema theory (Rumelhart, 1980), concept attainment theory (Klausmeier and Sipple, 1980), and a Vygotskian perspective of cognitive development (Vygotsky, 1978; see Chapter 2). These theories suggest that knowledge is hierarchically organized, that relating the new concepts to students' prior knowledge will help students learn these new concepts, that teaching attributes of a concept as well as teaching examples and nonexamples are important to concept learning, and that principles of scaffolded instruction and interactive dialogues will promote learning.

CLASSROOM Applications

Semantic Feature Analysis and Relationship Charts

PROCEDURES: The first step in preparing for an SFA activity is to develop a relationship chart. This chart is based on the idea that ideas or concepts are related to one another in terms of a hierarchy of abstractness. The most inclusive or abstract ideas are called *superordinate concepts*; the most concrete or narrow ideas are identified as *subordinate concepts*. Ideas or concepts that fall in between the superordinate and subordinate

FIGURE 10.11

Comparison Table for the Concepts of Decimals and Fractions

COMPARISON TABLE

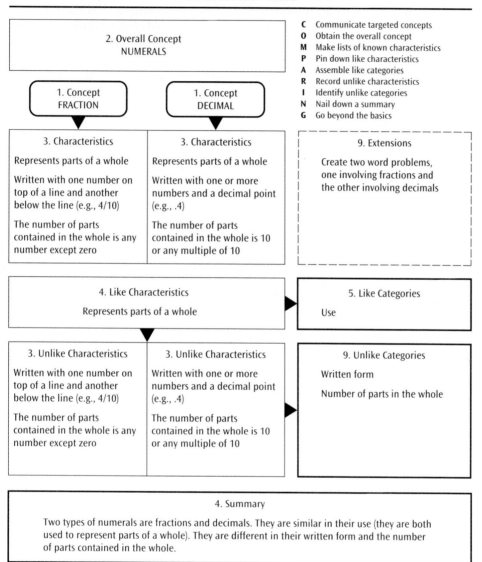

2. Overall Concept
NUMERALS

C   Communicate targeted concepts
O   Obtain the overall concept
M   Make lists of known characteristics
P   Pin down like characteristics
A   Assemble like categories
R   Record unlike characteristics
I   Identify unlike categories
N   Nail down a summary
G   Go beyond the basics

1. Concept
FRACTION

1. Concept
DECIMAL

3. Characteristics

Represents parts of a whole

Written with one number on top of a line and another below the line (e.g., 4/10)

The number of parts contained in the whole is any number except zero

3. Characteristics

Represents parts of a whole

Written with one or more numbers and a decimal point (e.g., .4)

The number of parts contained in the whole is 10 or any multiple of 10

9. Extensions

Create two word problems, one involving fractions and the other involving decimals

4. Like Characteristics

Represents parts of a whole

5. Like Categories

Use

3. Unlike Characteristics

Written with one number on top of a line and another below the line (e.g., 4/10)

The number of parts contained in the whole is any number except zero

3. Unlike Characteristics

Written with one or more numbers and a decimal point (e.g., .4)

The number of parts contained in the whole is 10 or any multiple of 10

9. Unlike Categories

Written form

Number of parts in the whole

4. Summary

Two types of numerals are fractions and decimals. They are similar in their use (they are both used to represent parts of a whole). They are different in their written form and the number of parts contained in the whole.

Source: J. A. Bulgren, B. Lenz, D. D. Deshler, and J. B. Schumaker, *The Concept Comparison Routine* (Lawrence, KS: Edge Enterprises, Inc., 1995), p. 55. Reprinted with permission.

concepts are referred to as *coordinate concepts* (Frayer, Frederick, and Klausmeier, 1969). These ideas are then organized into a relationship chart, and the students and teacher discuss the relationship between the various levels of concepts and their own background knowledge. This SFA activity was originally developed for use in teaching a specific concept, such as is used with concept diagrams (Johnson and Pearson, 1984). In their interactive teaching research, Bos and her colleagues have adapted this strategy to text

(Anders and Bos, 1986; Bos and Anders, 1992; Reyes and Bos, 1998).

When Ms. Cho, the teacher described at the beginning of the chapter, used this technique in her American government class, she first read the assigned American government chapter on contracts. As she read, she listed the important concepts or vocabulary and then arranged them according to superordinate, coordinate, and subordinate concepts. She used words as well as relevant phrases:

Contract
Promise
Contracting parties
Buyer
Seller
Written contracts
Verbal contracts
Contractual offer

Counteroffer
Holding good
Conditions
Acceptance
Consideration
Statute of frauds
Legal obligation
Legal action

Next, she organized the vocabulary into a relationship chart (see Figure 10.12). The superordinate concept "Contracts" is used as the name for the chart. The five coordinate concepts (main ideas in the text) serve as the column headings and are listed as the important or major ideas. The related vocabulary or subordinate concepts are listed down the side of the chart. Notice that Ms. Cho left blank spaces for adding important ideas and important vocabulary. She encourages students to add relevant information from their background knowledge.

The relationship chart became Ms. Cho's instructional tool. She made a copy for each student and a transparency so that the class could complete the chart as a group. To do this, she introduced the topic (superordinate concept) of the assignment.

The students then discussed what they already knew about contracts. Next, she introduced each coordinate concept (important idea) by assisting the students in generating meanings. During this introduction and throughout the activity, she encouraged students to add their personal experiences or understandings of the terms. For example, when Ms. Cho presented the major idea of "contract," Joe inquired whether a contract had to be written to be legal. This led to Anya's conveying a firsthand experience of her father's making a verbal contract and having the contract honored in court even though it was not written. The discussion ended with one of the purposes for reading being the clarification of what was needed for a verbal contract to be considered legal.

Following the discussion of the coordinate concepts, Ms. Cho introduced each subordinate concept. Again Ms. Cho and her students predicted what the meanings would be in relation to the topic of "contracts." For the more technical vocabulary (e.g., *contractual offer, statute of frauds*), Ms. Cho sometimes provided the meaning, or the students decided to read to clarify the concept. After introducing each concept, she and the students discussed

FIGURE 10.12

Relationship Chart: Contracts

CONTRACTS

Name _____

Period _____

Important Ideas

Important Vocabulary	Contract	Promise	Written Contracts	Verbal Contracts	Conditions	
Legal action						
Consideration						
Legal obligation						
Holding good						
Contractual offer						
Counteroffer						
Acceptance						
Statute of frauds						
Contracting parties						

+ = positive relationship
− = negative relationship
0 = no relationship
? = unknown relationship

the relationship between each coordinate concept or phrase and each subordinate term or phrase. They used a plus sign (+) to represent a positive relationship, a minus sign (−) to represent a negative relationship, a zero (0) to signify no relationship, and a question mark (?) to indicate that no consensus could be reached without further information.

Ms. Cho found that student involvement during the discussion was important to the success of the SFA strategy. One key to a fruitful discussion was encouraging students to ask each other why they had reached a certain relationship rating. This seemed to encourage students to use their prior knowledge about the topic and seemed to encourage other students to activate what they already knew about the vocabulary.

After completing the relationship chart, Ms. Cho guided the students in setting purposes for reading. These purposes, for the most part, focused on the chart, reading to confirm their predictions and to determine the relationships between the terms for which no agreement could be reached. After completing the reading, Ms. Cho and the students reviewed the relationship chart. They discussed changes to any of the relationships if necessary and reached consensus on those that were previously unknown.

Sometimes when Ms. Cho and her students used a relationship chart, they found that some information was still unclear after reading the text. Then they checked other sources, such as experts in the field, technical and trade books, the Internet, and other media. Ms. Cho also taught the students how to use the relationship chart to study for chapter tests by asking each other questions based on the meanings of the concepts and vocabulary and on their relationships (e.g., What is a contractual offer? What are the conditions necessary to have a contract?). She also taught how the chart could be used to write a report about the concepts.

COMMENTS: Bos and colleagues conducted a series of intervention studies using the SFA teaching strategy with upper-elementary and secondary students who have learning disabilities. Whether comparing it to the more traditional activity of looking the words up in the dictionary (Anders et al., 1984; Bos and Anders, 1990a, 1990b, 1990c, 1992; Bos, Anders, Jaffe, and Filip, 1985, 1989) or to the direct instruction of word meanings (Anders, Bos, Jaffe, and Filip, 1986; Bos, Allen, and Scanlon, 1989), they found that when teachers and researchers used this strategy, students consistently learned more vocabulary and had better comprehension of the chapters they read. Findings from a synthesis on graphic organizers (Kim, Vaughn, Wanzek, and Wei, 2004)

also confirmed that semantic feature analysis was consistently associated with gains in comprehension. One of the most important questions that is asked during discussion is, Why? (e.g., Why is *evidence* positively related to *evidence in court?*). Students need to justify their reasoning. By answering "why" questions, students think through concepts, reaching a deeper understanding and more effectively relating new information to old.

Semantic Maps

Semantic maps (Klingner et al., 2007; Scanlon et al., 1992;) are ways of visually representing the concepts and important vocabulary to be taught (see Figure 10.8 on p. 421). These content enhancement devices can be used as prelearning activities that assist students in activating their prior knowledge and in seeing the relationships between new concepts and related vocabulary.

CLASSROOM Applications
Semantic Maps

PROCEDURES: In using semantic maps, the teacher can begin by putting the major concept for a lecture or text on the board and then ask students to generate a list of related vocabulary from their background knowledge, as described in the section on brainstorming (see Chapter 8). However, when presenting more technical vocabulary, the teacher could begin by writing on the board the list of important vocabulary he or she generated in reviewing the text chapter or developing the lecture. After the words have been listed, the teacher discusses the meanings of the words, using a procedure similar to the one just presented in the section on semantic feature analysis. Next, the teacher arranges and rearranges the vocabulary with the students until the class has a map that shows the relationships that exist among the ideas.

For example, when presenting the following words for a chapter on fossils, the students and teacher first grouped the animals together.

Trilobites	Small horses
Crinoids	Winged insects
Ferns	Geography of the present
Dinosaurs	Land masses
Lakes	Brachiopods
Bodies of water	Saber-tooth tigers
Animals	Guide fossils
Geography	Rivers of the past
Trees	Plants
Oceans	Continents

Next, they grouped the plants together. In the case of guide fossils and several other types of fossils with which the students were not familiar (e.g., crinoids, trilobites), they decided to wait until they had read before placing the concepts on the map. Finally, they grouped together the geography terms.

After the map is completed, the teacher instructs the students to refer to the map while reading and/or listening to the lecture. Like the relationship chart, the semantic map can provide a framework for setting purposes for reading. The students read to confirm and clarify their understanding in relation to the map and make changes to it during discussions held as they read or after completing a chapter. The map can also serve as a blueprint for studying and for writing reports.

COMMENTS: A number of researchers have investigated the use of semantic mapping with students who are low achievers or have learning disabilities (see for review, Kim et al., 2004). In some cases, the students generated the maps as described above (Bos et al., 1989; Bos and Anders, 1990a; Boyle, 1996; Scanlon, Deshler, and Schumaker, 1996); in other studies, the framework for the map was already generated, and the students filled in the information (Horton, Lovitt, and Bergerud, 1990; Idol, 1987a, 1987b; Lovitt and Horton, 1994). In still other studies, the map or visual spatial display (see Figure 10.13) was presented to the students in completed form, and systematic direct instruction (Carnine, 1989) was used to assist the students in learning the information contained in the display (Bergerud, Lovitt, and Horton, 1988; Darch and Carnine, 1986). The research has been consistently encouraging in this area: The use of semantic maps or visual representations of information improves the learning performance of students with learning and behavior problems.

FIGURE 10.13
Visual Spatial Display

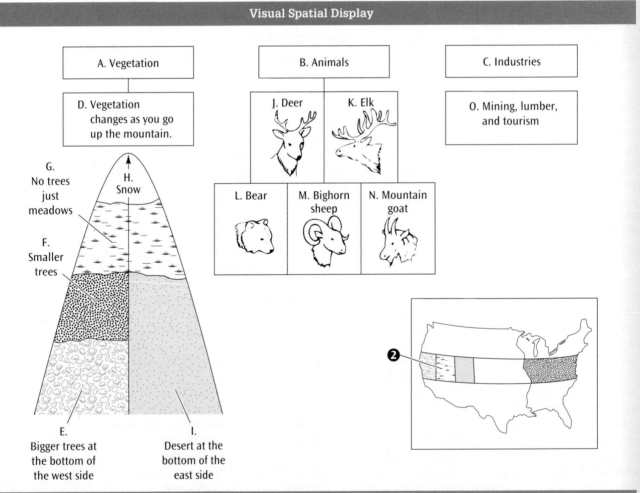

Source: C. Darch and D. Carmine (1986). Teaching content area material to learning disabled students. *Exceptional Children,* 53, p. 243. Copyright © 1986 by the Council for Exceptional Children. Reprinted with permission.

Apply the Concept 10.1

Teaching Content to English Language Learners

English language readers who also have learning disabilities have specific difficulties with vocabulary, syntax, and background knowledge when learning to read English. The Cognitive Academic Language Learning Approach (CALLA; Chamot and O'Malley, 1994b) is an interactive content-based approach to content learning that makes use of interactive teaching and metacognitive strategies that improve English language learners' general reading skills (Chamot, 1998; Chamot and O'Malley, 1994b). Some of these strategies are elaboration and active use of prior knowledge, planning or setting a purpose for learning, monitoring for comprehension with questions, and self-evaluation.

Metacognition is more prevalent in the last two of these strategies. In monitoring comprehension with questions, teachers can teach students to make inferences or self-question for clarification, by explicitly modeling either or both techniques. Self-evaluation allows students to reflect on what they have learned, read, or discussed. Self-ratings and learning logs can be used at all grade levels (Echevarria and Graves, 1998). The benefits of having students think about their learning can be transferred to their becoming more successful both in the content and in the use of English.

Diversity

Progress Monitoring

Steps Five and Six: Reinforcing Concept Learning during and after Learning

In a typical "learning from reading" or "learning from lecturing" assignment, the teacher has three opportunities to enhance the learning of concepts and the related vocabulary: *before* the reading or listening, *during* the actual reading or lecture, and *after* the assignment has been read or heard. Here, we discuss the second and third opportunities.

Whether using an advance organizer, semantic feature analysis, semantic map, concept diagram, or comparison table, these frameworks can be used to guide students as they read a text or listen to a lecture and as they react to their learning. For example, a semantic map can be used before, during, and after a lesson—students can add new vocabulary to the existing map during the lesson and can revise the map after the lesson. Also, the list of major ideas that is obtained from the advance organizer can serve as the framework in which students can take notes when listening to a lecture. After the lecture, students can meet in small groups and share their notes to create one overview that can serve as a study guide for the test. Students can be instructed on how to develop questions based on a concept diagram or semantic map. These questions can serve as self-questions to be asked when reading and when studying for a test.

Students generally require considerable practice in using these content enhancement devices. Additionally, devices that are used for one content area may not transfer to other areas automatically (Scanlon et al., 1996; Swanson, 1999a, 1999b). Therefore, numerous applications of each strategy may need to be taught explicitly (Bulgren and Lenz, 1996; Hudson, Lignugaris-Kraft, and Miller, 1993; Pressley, 1998). Second language learners who have learning disabilities are sometimes referred to as *doubly challenged* when learning content information. Apply the Concept 10.1 presents ideas for promoting content learning for these students.

> **FOCUS Question 3.** How do teachers adapt textbooks, lectures, assignments, homework, and tests to meet the needs of students with learning and behavior problems?

Making Adaptations

Special and general education teachers understand the need to make adaptations for those students in their classrooms who have special learning needs, and they express the desire to make those modifications. In actuality, however, research indicates most content area teachers seldom implement many adaptations (Moody, Vaughn, and Schumm, 1997; Schumm, Moody, and Vaughn, 2000; Schumm and Vaughn,

1992a; Schumm, Vaughn, and Saumell, 1992; Vaughn, Schumm et al., 1996).

Why do classroom teachers make relatively few instructional adaptations for students with disabilities? First, adapting instructional materials takes time, and teachers' time for planning and preparing for instruction is already limited. Second, adaptations often slow down instruction, and teachers cannot cover as much material as they would like. Third, some teachers think that making adaptations for the few students who need them is not fair to the higher-achieving students who are ready to work at a faster pace. When asked to make specific modifications for a student with learning disabilities in her high school French class, a teacher commented, "I have a number of students in my class who would benefit from the modifications you are asking me to make for Mia. I'm not sure it would be fair to the other students for me to do these things for Mia and not offer the other students the same opportunities."

We have investigated how students respond when teachers make adaptations for individual students within the regular classroom and the kinds of adaptations that students view as acceptable and unacceptable. Some of our findings surprised us and should put to rest some of the concerns teachers have about taking the time to make adaptations (Elbaum, Schumm, and Vaughn, 1997; Klingner and Vaughn, 1999a, 1999b; Klingner, Vaughn, Schumm, Cohen, and Forgan, 1998; Vaughn, Schumm, and Kouzekanani, 1993; Vaughn, Schumm, Niarhos, and Daugherty, 1993).

What do students think about adaptations? Both elementary and secondary students overwhelmingly preferred teachers who made adaptations for students who needed more help. They liked teachers who used flexible grouping for learning, who met with and assisted students with individual needs, and who varied instruction to meet those needs. They liked mixed-ability grouping and working in pairs with mixed ability. They also preferred teachers who gave all students the same homework assignments. Elementary students did not mind if some students were given different tests as long as the tests were the same length and took the same amount of time. Secondary students, however, preferred teachers who gave all students the same tests and textbooks because they were concerned that they would be embarrassed if friends recognized that they took different tests or read different textbooks. Similarly, some low-achieving students preferred a teacher who made no adaptations for students with special needs. Two

possible reasons that they felt negatively about teacher adaptations were because they were concerned about fitting in socially and did not wish to have their deficiencies revealed to their peers.

An especially interesting finding was that high-achieving students not only were aware that certain students in their classrooms needed extra help, but also preferred a teacher who made adaptations to help all the students learn. No high-achieving student in these studies expressed concern that instructional time would be taken away from him or her if the teacher took the time to give extra help to those who needed it. The following comment by one high-achieving high school student illustrates the altruism that was typical: "Even though I am smart enough to deal with any method of teaching, I realize not everyone else is. I like to see a diversified method of teaching in which the individual needs of students are met. Often students who do not perform as well are overlooked as ignorant and stupid, unable to learn. But these students are the ones that must be concentrated on so that they can develop better" (Vaughn, Schumm, Niarhos, and Daugherty, 1993). These nonreaders were the ones for whom same-ability grouping was perceived as advantageous (Elbaum et al., 1997).

Adapting Textbooks

Despite the concerns about making adaptations described previously, research indicates that students at all achievement levels feel that they need textbook adaptations and are not getting the adaptations they need (Schumm et al., 1992). Text adaptation is a technique that involves making changes to or adding to an existing text to make it more comprehensible for students with and without special needs. Apply the Concept 10.2 lists textbook adaptations that teachers may consider, three of which are discussed here in greater depth.

Study Guides

Study guides are tools teachers can use to lead students through a reading assignment. A typical study guide is a series of questions or activities that emphasize important content information. Study guide formats include short-answer questions, framed outlines, and matching (Bergerud et al., 1988; Lovitt, Rudsit, Jenkins, Pious, and Benedetti, 1985, 1986). Students complete study guides while they read a selection. Study guides help direct students to the key points to be learned. The study guide also provides an organizational

Apply the Concept 10.2

Guidelines for Adapting Content Area Textbooks

Substitute the textbook for students who have severe word recognition problems:

- Audiotape textbook content.
- Read textbook aloud to students.
- Pair students to master textbook content.
- Use direct experiences, films, videotapes, tape recorders, and computer programs as substitutes for textbook reading.
- Work with students individually or in small groups to master textbook material.

Simplify the textbook for students whose reading level is far below that of the textbook used in class:

- Construct abridged versions of the textbook content, or use the publisher's abridged version.
- Provide students with chapter outlines or summaries.
- Use a multilevel, multimaterial approach.

Highlight key concepts for students who have difficulty comprehending textbook material:

- Preview reading assignments with students to orient them to the topic and provide guidelines for budgeting reading and study time.
- Provide students with a purpose for reading.
- Provide an overview of an assignment before reading.
- Structure opportunities for students to activate prior knowledge before starting a reading assignment.
- Introduce key vocabulary before assigning reading.
- Develop a study guide to direct learning.
- Summarize or reduce textbook information to guide classroom discussions and independent reading.
- Color-code or highlight textbooks.
- Reduce the length of assignments.
- Slow down the pace of reading assignments.
- Provide assistance in answering text-based questions.
- Demonstrate or model effective reading strategies.

- Place students in cooperative learning groups to master textbook content.
- Teach comprehension-monitoring techniques to improve ongoing understanding of text material.
- Teach students to use graphic aids to understand textbook information.

Increase idea retention for students who have difficulty with long-term memory:

- Structure postreading activities to improve retention of content.
- Teach reading strategies to improve retention.
- Teach students to record key concepts and terms for study purposes.
- Teach memory strategies to improve retention of text material.

Source: Adapted from J. S. Schumm and K. Strickler (1991). Guidelines for adapting content area textbooks: Keeping teachers and students content. *Intervention in School and Clinic, 27* (2), pp. 79–84.

structure for students to reflect about what they are reading and to engage in higher-order thinking. In short, study guides help to "tutor" a student through a chapter.

Commercially prepared study guides can be purchased or obtained through the Internet as supplements to some textbooks. The advantage of commercial study guides is that they are already prepared, so they are real time-savers. The disadvantage is that the publisher does not know a given teacher's style of teaching, emphasis, or school district's requirements. Moreover, the publisher does not know the students. For these reasons, many teachers construct their own study guides.

Many types of study guides exist. Some are designed to help students activate prior knowledge, others to help students understand literal or inferential information in the textbook, others to foster peer interaction and discussion, and still others to help students recognize meaning patterns in text (e.g., cause and effect, compare and contrast). Following are some general suggestions for developing study guides (Wood, Lapp, and Flood, 1992):

- *Decide whether a guide is needed.* Is textbook information particularly dense? Are there few considerate features? Will students with special needs require support and guidance to get through the chapter and to grasp the most important ideas?
- *Analyze the chapter.* Can some parts be omitted? Are some parts easier to understand than others? What skills will students need to read and understand this material?

- *Decide how you want to structure your study guide.* Create one that includes the suggested components.

In general, all study guides should also include the following components (Hudson, Ormsbee, and Myles, 1994; Readence et al., 1998):

- Specific information about the reading assignment (page numbers, title)
- Learning objectives of the assignment
- Purpose statement for the assignment
- Introduction of key terms or vocabulary
- Activities for students to complete
- Questions for students to answer as they read

Text Highlighting

Students with comprehension problems have difficulty sifting out important information. Underlining or highlighting key points in textbooks can help students attend to the most salient information (Echevarria and Graves, 1998). Teachers can highlight the information in a textbook that they think is most important. Then students or adult volunteers can use this book as a guide to highlight the same information in books for students with reading and learning disabilities. Keep in mind that the teacher will also want to teach students this and other textbook study skills (see the section on teaching study skills).

Using Alternative Reading Materials

For students with very low reading skills who are able to learn by listening, the teacher can do the following:

- *Audiotape textbook chapters.* Some publishers provide cassettes or CDs with their textbooks. If the textbook you are using is not accompanied by an audio version, adult and/or student volunteers can read the chapters on audiotape. Students can then listen to the tapes at home or in their resource classes. Tech Tips 10.1 provides ideas for using technology to aid in content area learning.
- *Read text aloud to students.* Encourage students to follow along, reading silently. Pause frequently to assess student learning from the reading.
- *Pair a good reader with a poor reader.* The good reader reads the textbook material aloud and, together, the two students learn the content. Both students should use self-monitoring comprehension strategies to ensure that both readers comprehend the text.

Sometimes teachers find it necessary to use alternative materials that present similar content, such as films, videotapes, and trade books. Computer software programs in which the text can be read by the computer, such as encyclopedias on CD-ROM, are other resources.

Teachers may also supplement textbooks with informational trade books (both fiction and nonfiction) and other reading materials (such as magazines and journals). By providing additional reading material that covers similar content to the textbook, teachers enable students who cannot read the textbook to access the content. Informational picture books have been found to be effective in teaching content to English language learners (Hadaway and Mundy, 1999) and struggling readers (Cassady, 1998).

People today discuss software programs in terms of their user-friendliness. Is the program easy to understand? Does the program use familiar language or at least define unfamiliar terms? Does the program give the user cue words or icons to signal the important ideas and processes? If the user does not understand something, does the program allow the user to ask questions? Does the program have more than one way to explain a difficult concept or process? If the program has these features, then one might consider it user-friendly.

Now take a minute to reread the previous paragraph, but substitute the word *lecture* for the word *program* and the word *listener* for the word *user.* Just as using "considerate" or "user-friendly" text assists students in learning the critical information, a well-organized lecture makes the students' work easier in that it assists them in seeing relationships among concepts and distinguishing important from supplementary information. It also helps them relate new information to old. Well-designed lectures seem particularly beneficial for students with learning or language disabilities, English language learners, and listeners with relatively limited language skills and/or little prior knowledge of the content.

Diversity

As teachers plan their teaching, the following guidelines can make lectures "listener-friendly":

- Use advance organizers.
- Preteach important vocabulary.
- Use cue words or phrases to let students know what information is important (e.g., "It is important that you know . . . ," "The key information to remember is . . . ," "In summary . . . ").
- Repeat important information.
- Write important information on the board, a transparency, and/or a handout.

TECHTips

10.1 Using Assistive Technology to Develop Content Area Learning

Learners with difficulties in reading and comprehending written text often experience failure in content classes such as science and social studies. Although learners may receive support with their reading and writing skills, they also need support for their content area classes. Computer software that can read a textbook aloud can remove some of the frustration and difficulties learners encounter when attempting to comprehend content area books.

Learners who have difficulty taking notes because of handwriting difficulties may find note-taking easier using the smart keyboard, AlphaSmart 3000 (and Neo) by AlphaSmart, Inc. (www.alphasmart.com). The light, portable keyboard runs on AA batteries and can connect to a computer to download notes into a word processor or directly to a printer. A newer model from AlphaSmart, Inc., is the Dana (and Dana Wireless), the traditional AlphaSmart keyboard but running a Palm operating system and having a slightly larger screen. All versions of AlphaSmart keyboards can also run a version of *Co:Writer*™ called *Co:Writer*™ *Smart Applet*, creating an ideal portable environment for learners to produce text.

Another kind of software to help struggling students is reference software—digital versions of more traditional reference materials such as a dictionary, thesaurus, and encyclopedia. Some of these programs are available for purchase; others are available free on the Internet.

Learners with special needs can encounter overwhelming difficulties in laboratory settings. Tasks such as reading chemical labels and measurement marks on containers, handling potentially dangerous chemicals, assembling physics experiments, and performing dissections in biology can be difficult or even impossible for many students who are otherwise capable of mastering the content. An alternative or supplement for "live" lab experiments are virtual labs or computer-based lab simulations. Each year brings better and more realistic computer simulations of science lab experiments. Materials range from free online sites to full semesters of work in a single software package to install on local computers. Here are a few to sample: interactive physics simulations (www.myphysicslab.com), chemistry (www.chemistryteaching.com/chemsim.htm), and general math and science for grades 6–8 (www.explorelearning.com).

An Alpha Smart 3000 Keyboard

- Stress key points by varying the tone and quality of your voice.
- Number ideas or points (e.g., first, second, next, then, finally).
- Write technical words or words that are difficult to spell.
- Use a study guide that lists the major concepts, with space for students to add other information.
- Use pictures, concept diagrams, and content maps to show relationships among ideas.

- Provide examples and nonexamples of the concepts you are discussing.
- Ask questions and encourage discussion that requires students to relate the new information to ideas they already know (from their own background or your previous lectures).
- Stop frequently and have students discuss what they have learned with partners.
- Allow time at the end of a lecture for students to look over their notes, summarize, and ask questions.

TABLE 10.1

Cues to Listen and Watch for in Lectures

Type of Cue	Examples
Organizational cues	Today, we will be discussing . . .
	The topic I want to cover today . . .
	There are [number] points I want you to be sure to learn . . .
	The important relationship is . . .
	The main point of this discussion is . . .
	Any statement that signals a number or position (e.g., first, last, next, then).
	To review/summarize/recap . . .
Emphasis cues	
Verbal	You need to know/understand/remember . . .
	This is important/key/basic/critical . . .
	Let me repeat this . . .
	Let me check, now do you understand . . .
	Any statement is repeated.
	Words or terms are emphasized.
	Teacher speaks more slowly, more loudly, or with more emphasis.
	Teacher stresses certain words.
	Teacher spells words.
	Teacher asks rhetorical question.
Nonverbal	Information written on overhead/board.
	Information handed out in study guide.
	Teacher emphasizes the point using gestures.

Source: Adapted from S. K. Suritsky and C. A. Hughes, Notetaking strategy instruction, in D. D. Deshler, E. S. Ellis, and B. K. Lenz, *Teaching Adolescents with Learning Disabilities*, 2nd ed. (Denver: Love, 1996), p. 275.

Table 10.1 provides cues that can assist students in "seeing" the key information. By using these guidelines, teachers will naturally incorporate cues that indicate what information is important.

One technique that has been effective for students with learning and behavior problems in enhancing their understanding and recall of information presented through lectures is the pause procedure (e.g., Ruhl, 1996; Ruhl et al., 1990; Ruhl, Hughes, and Schloss, 1987). This procedure consists of pausing during natural breaks in lectures and having students work as partners for about two minutes to discuss what they are learning and review their notes. At the end of the two minutes, the teacher asks students whether they have any questions or concepts that need further discussion or clarification. The teacher then resumes lecturing. Using this procedure, college students with and without learning

disabilities performed better than listening to the lectures without the pauses for discussion both on multiple-choice tests and on free recalls of the information presented (Ruhl et al., 1990).

Adapting Class Assignments and Homework

One area in which students with learning and behavior problems often struggle is the completion of assignments and homework. In a survey of students with and without learning disabilities in grades 6–8, the students with learning disabilities had greater difficulty completing homework assignments because of problems with attention, motivation, and study skills (Gajria and Salend, 1995). Furthermore, students with special learning needs spend more time completing homework assignments than average-achieving students (Harniss, Epstein, Bursuck, Nelson, and Jayanthi, 2001). At the same time, homework has become a significant part of schooling. In the 1996 National Assessment of Educational Progress in math and science, more than half of all 8th and 12th graders and nearly half of the 4th graders reported having at least one hour of homework every night (Bursuck et al., 1999), accounting for more than 20 percent of the time students spend on academic tasks (Cooper and Nye, 1994). In one survey, middle school students indicated that they preferred adaptations in which assignments are finished at school, extra credit is allowed, assignments are graded according to effort, and assignments are begun and checked for understanding in class (Nelson, Epstein, Bursuck, Jayanthi, and Sawyer, 1998). These same students were least supportive of adaptations in which shorter or different assignments were given to students with learning problems or these students' assignments were graded more easily.

After conducting a comprehensive review of the literature, Cooper and Nye (1994) concluded that homework assignments for students with disabilities should be brief, focused on reinforcement rather than new material, monitored carefully, and supported through parental involvement. The most important aspect of making assignments is to give complete information. Teachers need to let students know why an assignment is important, when it is due, what support they will have for completing the task, and the steps necessary for getting the job done. Having complete information helps to motivate students, as does giving them real-life assignments (i.e., assignments that connect homework to events or activities in the home)

FIGURE 10.14

Tips for Giving Assignments

1. Explain the purpose of the assignment. Stress what you expect students to learn and why learning the skill or concept is important. Connect the skill or concept to real-life applications.
2. Explain in detail the procedures for completing the assignment. To check for understanding, ask one or two students to summarize the procedures.
3. Get students started by modeling one or two problems or by providing an example.
4. Describe the equipment and materials needed to complete the assignment.
5. Anticipate trouble spots, and ask students how they might tackle difficult parts in the assignment.
6. Explain when the assignment is due.
7. Explain how the assignment will be graded and how it will affect students' grades.
8. Describe appropriate ways to get help or support in completing the assignment.
9. For an in-class assignment, explain your expectations for student behavior while they complete the assignment and what students who finish early should do.
10. Address students' questions.

plus reinforcement, using homework planners, and graphing homework completion (Bryan and Sullivan-Burstein, 1998). The tips in Figure 10.14 can help teachers to provide students with a complete set of directions.

Class assignments and homework can be adapted for special learners so that they can experience success without undue attention being brought to their learning difficulties. The key to success is to make assignments appropriate in content, length, time required to complete, and skill level needed to accomplish the task. It is also important to explain the assignments, model several problems if appropriate, and check for understanding (Sawyer, Nelson, Jayanthi, Bursuck, and Epstein, 1996). Students should know how and where to get help if they get stuck.

Constructing and Adapting Tests

The best way to discover what students have learned is to construct student-friendly tests, adapt test administration and scoring as necessary, consider alternatives to testing (such as assessment portfolios), and teach test-taking skills. Student-friendly tests are considerate to the test-taker in both content and format. The content has been covered in class or assigned readings, and students have been told explicitly that they are responsible for learning it. The format is clear and easy to understand.

Progress Monitoring

To construct student-friendly tests, a teacher must first decide what skills and concepts to include. In the test format, directions should be clear and unambiguous, and items should be legible and properly spaced. Students should have sufficient room to place their answers and specific guidelines if answers are to be written on a separate sheet (Salend, 1995, 2000). Attention to format is important for all students, but particularly for those who have difficulty reading and taking tests and who are overly anxious about taking tests.

Even with student-friendly tests, students with learning and behavior problems may have difficulty reading tests, working within time constraints, or resisting distractions during a test. Poor or laborious writing can cause them to tire easily and inhibit performance on a test. Figure 10.15 suggests accommodations for test administration and scoring. Nelson, Jayanthi, Epstein, and Bursuck (2000) examined student preferences for test adaptations in general education classrooms. Results revealed that the most preferred test adaptations involved providing assistive materials during a test (e.g., open-notes tests, open-book tests, dictionaries and calculators, extra answer space). In contrast, the least-preferred test adaptations involved differential assistance for students with special needs (e.g., teacher reading of questions to students, tests with fewer questions, tests covering less materials). This finding is supported by other research that reveals students do not prefer adaptations that overtly differentiate them from others (Vaughn, Schumm, Niarhos, and Daugherty, 1993). More important, as teachers decide which, if any, adaptations to use, they should consider the material to be covered by the test, the test's task requirements (e.g., reading, taking dictation), and the particular needs of special learners.

In addition to or instead of tests, teachers may use portfolios as an assessment tool. Apply the Concept 10.3 presents ideas for developing and using portfolios.

FIGURE 10.15

Testing Accommodations

- Teach students test-taking skills.
- Give frequent quizzes rather than only exams.
- Give take-home tests.
- Test on less content than the rest of the class.
- Change types of questions (e.g., from essay to multiple-choice).
- Give extended time to finish tests.
- Read test questions to students.
- Use tests with enlarged print.
- Highlight key words in questions.
- Provide extra space on tests for answering.
- Simplify wording of test questions.
- Allow students to answer fewer questions.
- Give extra help in preparing for tests.

- Give practice questions as a study guide.
- Give open-book and note tests.
- Give tests to small groups.
- Allow the use of learning aids during tests (e.g., calculators).
- Give individual help with directions during tests.
- Allow oral instead of written answers (e.g., tape recorders).
- Allow answers in outline format.
- Allow word processors.
- Grade for content, not for spelling and writing mechanics.
- Give feedback to individual students during tests.

Source: Adapted from M. Jayanthi, M. H. Epstein, E. A. Polloway, and W. D. Bursuck (1981). Testing adaptations: A national survey of the testing practices of general education teachers. *Journal of Special Education, 30,* pp. 99–115.

Apply the Concept 10.3

Using Portfolios to Monitor Student Progress

Assessment portfolios are collections of work samples that document a student's progress in a content area. You can use portfolios to provide tangible evidence of student performance over a period of time. Portfolios can include writing samples of all stages of the writing process in all genres. Suggestions for developing assessment portfolios include the following:

- Develop a portfolio plan that is consistent with your purposes for the assignment.
- Clarify what work will go into portfolios.
- Start with only a couple of different kinds of entries, and expand gradually.
- Compare notes with other teachers as you experiment with portfolios.
- Make it a long-term goal to include a variety of assessments that address content, process, and attitude goals across the curriculum.
- Make portfolios accessible in the classroom. Students and teachers

should be able to add to the collection quickly and easily.
- Develop summary sheets or graphs that help to describe a body of information (e.g., "I can do" lists, lists of books read, or pieces of writing completed). Let students record these data when possible.
- Work with students to choose a few representative samples that demonstrate the student's progress.
- Review portfolios with students periodically (at least four times during the school year). The review should be a time to celebrate progress and to set future goals.
- Encourage students to review portfolios with a classmate before reviewing with the teacher. Students should help to make decisions about what to keep.
- In preparation for a family conference, have students develop a table of contents for the portfolio (Radencich, Beers, and Schumm, 1993, pp. 119–120).

Examples of items that can be included in a portfolio are as follows:

Progress Monitoring

- Student assignments and work samples
- Student interviews
- Self-assessments
- Audiotapes
- Videotapes
- Diagnostic tests
- Achievement tests
- Teacher-made tests
- Pages from writing journals
- Awards
- Personal reading and writing records
- Interest and attitude inventories
- Photographs
- Copies of passages read fluently
- Contributions from parents
- Report cards
- List of accomplishments
- Observation checklists

FOCUS
Question 4. What are the three types of study skills, and why are they important to learning?

Study Skills and Learning Strategies

Even when teachers plan user-friendly lectures and make adaptations, students will still need to develop study skills and learning strategies. Particularly as students move into secondary and postsecondary settings, their tasks increasingly require time management, self-monitoring and feedback, listening and note-taking, studying from textbooks, and test-taking skills (Brinckerhoff, Shaw, and McGuire, 1992). Surveys and observational studies conducted in secondary settings show a heavy reliance on written products as a means of evaluating performance, the need to listen to lectures containing few advance organizers and limited opportunities for interactions, and a limited amount of individual help and teacher feedback (Putnam, 1992a, 1992b; Schumaker, Wildgen et al., 1982; Schumm et al., 1995a). In order for students with disabilities to succeed in these settings, they need to learn specific strategies and study skills that enable them to meet classroom demands.

Study skills are the competencies associated with acquiring, recording, organizing, synthesizing, remembering, and using information and ideas (Pauk, 2001). Study skills are the key to independent learning, and they help students gain and use information effectively. Students with effective study skills can be characterized as executive learners (Schumm and Post, 1997) in that they:

- Are knowledgeable about personal learning strengths and challenges
- Have a clear understanding about tasks to be accomplished
- Have a repertoire of learning strategies that can be applied in independent learning situations
- Have developed a set of help-seeking behaviors to activate when additional assistance is needed

Study skills can be divided into three areas:

1. *Personal development skills:* personal discipline, management and organizational skills, self-monitoring and reinforcement, and positive attitudes toward studying
2. *Process skills:* technical methods of studying such as note-taking, outlining, learning in-formation from a text, and library reference skills
3. *Expression skills:* retrieval skills, test-taking skills, and using oral and/or written expression to demonstrate understanding

As one would expect, these are the very skills and strategies that students with learning and behavior problems have difficulty developing. One reason for this may be that most study skills are not directly and systematically taught in the manner that reading and math skills are taught (Larkin and Ellis, 1998).

Personal Development Skills

Personal development skills include personal discipline, goal setting, management and organizational skills, self-monitoring and reinforcement, and positive attitudes toward studying. Many of the personal development skills related to school focus on time management, scheduling, organization, self-monitoring, and reinforcement.

Time Management and Scheduling

Jon's mother is concerned because Jon, who has learning disabilities, falls asleep while trying to finish book reports the night before they are due. Even if she gets him up early in the morning, there is little chance that he will have time to finish. Even though he knows about the assignments in advance, he waits until they are due to start reading, despite his mom's queries about homework. Granted, it takes Jon longer than the other students to complete assignments, but his teacher gives him the assignments early. He has the skills to get a B or a C if he would just start working on assignments earlier.

Many families and teachers can identify with this scenario. Jon has the skills to complete assignments successfully, but he lacks personal management skills, particularly time management. Teaching a unit on time management at the beginning of the year and then reinforcing students during the year for the effective use of time can be well worth the effort.

Building a Rationale. The first step in getting students to schedule and manage their time is to build a rationale for its importance to success in school and later life. Discuss the following ideas with your students to build a rationale for effective time management:

- Parents/guardians will get off your back when they see that you are getting your work done on time.

- If you write down what you have to do, you don't have to try to remember everything.
- If you set a time to begin, it is easier to get started and not procrastinate.
- When you set a time frame to complete an assignment, it helps you work for a goal and concentrate.
- When you have a schedule, you're less likely to let a short break become a long break.
- Being in control of time makes you feel that you have more control of your life.
- When you get assignments and jobs done on time, then you can really enjoy your free time.
- Scheduling your time helps you to get jobs done and have more time for fun and your friends.

Determining How the Time Is Spent. Before students can decide how to schedule their time, they need to determine how they are currently spending it. Using a schedule, have students keep track of their activities for one or two weeks. Also have them list the school assignments they have for the time period and whether they have "too little," "enough," or "too much" time to complete them.

Estimating Time. As part of the time management process, have students determine how long it takes them to complete regularly scheduled tasks such as meals, going to and from school, reading assignments in their various textbooks, writing a paragraph on a topic, and completing a 10-problem math assignment. Although there will probably be considerable variability in the time taken to complete a task, most students with learning and behavior problems underestimate the time it takes. Having students get an idea of the time required can be helpful in planning a schedule. This step will also help students identify and prioritize tasks that need to be completed.

Scheduling. If students feel that they do not have enough time to get their tasks completed or if they do not have regular times for studying, encourage them to set up a schedule. Some suggestions that students might want to use when setting up their schedules are as follows:

1. Plan regular study times.
2. Plan at least one-hour blocks of time in which to study.
3. Plan which assignments you are going to work on during study time.
4. Take the first five minutes of each study activity to review what you have done already and

what you have learned and to plan what you are going to accomplish today. This helps to promote long-term learning and a sense of accomplishment.
5. When studying longer than one hour, plan breaks and stick to the time allowed for the breaks.
6. Use daytime or early evening for study if possible. Most people work less efficiently at night.
7. Work on your most difficult subjects when you are most alert.
8. Distribute your studying for a test over several days rather than cramming the night before the test.
9. Balance your time between studying and other activities. Allow time for recreational activities.
10. Reward yourself by marking through your schedule each time you meet a scheduled commitment and by crossing off items you complete on your to-do list.

Not only should regular times for studying be listed on the schedule, but due dates for assignments and dates for other events should also be noted so that the schedule serves as a calendar. Students should be encouraged to set aside some time they can use as they please if they accomplish their tasks on schedule during the day or week. This type of self-determined reinforcer can serve as an extra motivation for some students.

Monitoring and Using a To-Do List. Setting up a schedule does little good unless students follow and monitor their schedules. Teachers can have students fill in the activities they feel are important to monitor on a weekly schedule. Figure 10.16 presents a schedule and to-do list for Jon. His study time, time spent working out, time spent at his after-school job, and TV time were the most important tasks for him to monitor, so he scheduled them in each week. He also noted when the next book report was due and used his to-do list to schedule daily reading, crossing off tasks as they were accomplished.

Jon developed a contract with himself. If he studied at least 80 percent of the time he had scheduled during the week, then he could work out at the gym or goof off two extra hours on Saturday. In this way, Jon was not only monitoring his schedule, but also setting goals and providing rewards for meeting his goals. After two weeks, Jon's teacher encouraged him to review his deadlines and adjust his schedule based on how he had done over the past two weeks. While Jon had met his goal of studying 80 percent of the scheduled time, he still did not complete all his tasks. He had to adjust his goal in order to complete all of this work on time. Although Jon realized that schedules need to be flexible, he found that planning, even when plans change, helped him to get more work accomplished in a timely manner.

Self-Monitoring and Reinforcement

There is much evidence to support the hypothesis that students with learning and behavior problems have difficulty setting goals and self-monitoring, whether it be in the areas of attention and memory, reading comprehension, or personal and management skills (Bos and Filip, 1984; Larkin and Ellis, 1998; Schunk, 1996; Wilson and David, 1994). Van Reusen and Bos (1990) developed a strategy that students can use to assist them in setting goals and keeping track of their progress. The strategy uses the acronym MARKER (it gives students a *mark* to work toward and is a *marker* of their progress) and includes the following steps:

Make a list of goals, set the order, set the date.
Arrange a plan for each goal and predict your success.
Run your plan for each goal and adjust if necessary.
Keep records of your progress.
Evaluate your progress toward each goal.
Reward yourself when you reach a goal, and set a new goal.

For each goal, students use a goal-planning sheet (see Figure 10.17) to answer the following questions:

- Can I describe my goal?
- What is the reason or purpose for the goal?
- What am I going to do first, second, and third to complete this goal?
- How much time do I have to complete the goal?
- What materials do I need to complete the goal?
- Can I divide the goal into steps or parts? If so, in what order should I complete each step or part?
- How am I going to keep records of my progress?
- How will I reward myself for reaching my goal?

The teacher can use the steps in the strategies intervention model (see Chapter 2) to teach the students the marker strategy. After learning the strategy, students usually work on one to three goals at a time, keeping progress data on each goal.

When Van Reusen and Bos (1992) used this strategy with middle and high school students with learning disabilities and behavior disorders, they found that students accomplished more

FIGURE 10.16
Jon's Weekly Schedule and To-Do List

NAME: Jon

WEEK OF: Oct 14

	MON.	TUES.	WEDS.	THURS.	FRI.	SAT.	SUN.	
6:00 a.m.	get up	and eat →						6:00 a.m.
7:00	ride →					sleep	sleep	7:00
8:00	bus							8:00
9:00	History					house		9:00
10:00	English	same	every day			yard	go to	10:00
11:00	PE					chores	church	11:00
12:00	Welding						eat	12:00
1:00 p.m.	Lunch					eat	read	1:00 p.m.
2:00	Algebra					go	for fun	2:00
3:00	General Science					to gym	goof	3:00
4:00	ride bus						off and	4:00
5:00	recreational	activity		study	eat	eat and	eat	5:00
6:00	eat →				have fun	have fun		6:00
7:00	study	study	study	study			study	7:00
8:00	↓	↓	↓	↓			↓	8:00
9:00	↓	↓	↓	↓			↓	9:00
10:00	sleep →						sleep	10:00
11:00	↓				sleep →		↓	11:00

TO-DO LIST

history paper due math assign finish book	math assign	math assign book report due	math assign welding project due	science test math test	chores mow grass pull weeds fix cooler	start English paper

FIGURE 10.17

Goal-Planning and -Monitoring Sheet

Name: _____   Class: _____   Date: _____

1. Goal: _____

2. Reason(s) for working on goal: _____

3. Goal will be worked on at: _____

4. Date to reach goal (due date): _____

5. Materials needed: _____

_____

6. Steps used to reach the goal:

_____

_____

7. Progress toward the goal: Record in each box the date and progress rating.

   3—Goal reached   2—Good progress made   1—Some progress made   0—No progress made

Date / Rating					

8. Reward for reaching goal: _____

Source: Adapted from A. K. Van Reusen and C. S. Bos, *Use of the Goal-Regulation Strategy to Improve the Goal Attainment of Students with Learning Disabilities* (Final Report) (Tucson: University of Arizona, 1992).

goals and gained a more informed perspective of their educational and personal goals.

Hughes and his colleagues (Hughes, Ruhl, Deshler, and Schumaker, 1995) developed an assignment completion strategy for the Strategies Intervention Model that is similar. The steps in this learning strategy are as follows:

Psych up. Prepare your assignment-monitoring form and your mind.

Record and ask. Record the assignment, think about it, and ask questions.

Organize. Break the assignment into parts, estimate and schedule the number of study sessions, and organize your materials.

Jump to it. Survey the assignment, and set goals and a reward.

Engage in the work. Follow the instructions, note questions, and get help if you need it.

Check the work. Check for requirements and quality, store the assignment, and reward yourself.

Turn it in. Take it to class, turn it in, record the date, and praise yourself.

Set your course. Record your grade, evaluate your assignment, and think about future assignments.

Classroom Participation

Students who actively participate in class tend to be more successful academically than their quieter, less attentive peers (Ellis, 1991; Larkin and Ellis, 1998). Students with learning and behavior problems may benefit from specific strategies to enhance their classroom participation. The SLANT strategy is part of the strategies intervention model (see Chapter 2) and was designed to increase active participation in class. The acronym SLANT stands for the following:

Sit up.
Lean forward.
Activate your thinking.
Name key information.
Track the talker.

Examples of activating your thinking include asking yourself questions (What is this about? What do I need to remember?), answering your questions (This is about _____. I need to remember _____.), and asking the teacher a question when you do not understand. Examples of naming key information include answering the teacher's questions, sharing your ideas, and additions to other's comments (Ellis, 1991). This general set of activities can be used in any learning situation to improve students' active participation.

An important part of assignment completion and class participation in inclusive classrooms is recruiting positive teacher attention. Students with learning and behavior problems often get the teacher's attention for their negative behaviors rather than their positive behaviors in class. Using instruction, role play, and reinforcement, one special education teacher taught four middle school students with learning disabilities to recruit positive teacher attention in their general education classrooms (Alber et al., 1999). Students were taught to raise their hands and wait quietly or at an appropriate time to ask such questions as "How am I doing?" or "I don't understand" or "Would you please look at my work?" Observations in the general education classrooms demonstrated that students increased their amount of positive teacher recruiting and teachers increased their rate of student praise. Teaching students strategies for self-monitoring, self-reinforcement, and classroom participation is an important part of the special education curriculum in that these skills, like study skills, support student success in the general education classroom and curriculum.

Process Skills

Process skills include the technical methods of studying such as note-taking, outlining, learning information from text, and research and library skills.

Listening and Taking Notes

In school, students spend more time listening than reading, speaking, or writing. On the average, teachers in secondary settings spend at least half of their class time presenting information through lectures (Putnam et al., 1993). Furthermore, teachers rely on information presented in class discussion and lectures as the basis for a significant number of items on tests (Putnam et al., 1993). Note-taking is one of the most efficient ways to record this information and retrieve it in one's own words. It has several important functions:

- Note-taking increases students' attention.
- Note-taking, as opposed to simply listening, requires a deeper level of cognitive processing in that students must make sense of the information to write the ideas.
- Because the information has been processed more deeply, note-taking helps students learn and remember the information more easily.

These three statements are supported by research which demonstrates that note-taking gives students an advantage over simply listening (Anderson and Armbruster, 1986; Kiewra, 1985). Even if students do not go back and review their notes, just the act of taking notes results in greater recall of information on tests.

Students with learning and behavior problems often have difficulties with listening and note-taking. For some students with severe writing disabilities, it will be important that they have a note-taker. Lightweight laptop computers or devices designed specifically for taking notes, such as the AlphaSmart (see Tech Tips 10.1 on p. 433), are also very beneficial if students are instructed in how to use them. Students with learning disabilities may have difficulty with the following:

- Paying attention
- Writing fast and legibly
- Deciding what information to write
- Spelling
- Making sense of notes after the lecture

They also have limited use of abbreviations and limited use of a comprehensive note-taking system (Suritsky and Hughes, 1996). Given the importance of taking notes and the difficulty some students encounter with this skill, teachers will want to teach students how to take notes and consider using listener-friendly lectures to make note-taking easier.

Teaching Students to Take Notes. Note-taking is a procedure that requires students to listen, interpret, organize, and record information. Therefore, students with limited reading and study skills often feel overwhelmed when they must take notes. Numerous formats for note-taking have been suggested (Bragstad and Stumpf, 1982; Langan, 1982; Pauk, 2001; Roberts, 1999). One aspect that these systems have in common is the focus on making note-taking and reviewing an interactive learning process (Schumm and Post, 1997). To facilitate this interactive process, two- or three-column note-taking systems have been developed. Figure 10.18 gives an example of each system. Students take class notes in the far right-hand column in both systems, using only the front side of the paper. Modified outlining is the format that is most often suggested for taking these notes. In the two-column system, students note the key concepts in the left-hand column, sometimes referred to as *triggers*, since they are meant to trigger the ideas noted in the other column. Later, in reviewing, students should be able to cover the

FIGURE 10.18

Formats for Note-Taking

Sample Two-Column System

Topic: _____   Date: _____

Triggers or Key Concepts	Class Notes

Sample Three-Column System

Topic: _____   Date: _____

Triggers or Key Concepts	Class Notes	Text Notes

right column and use their personal triggers to help them remember the ideas covered in the class notes. In three-column systems, the additional column generally serves as a space to write textbook notes so that they can be integrated with class notes. This is most helpful when the teacher's lectures make frequent, direct ties to the textbook. It is also important to teach some students note-taking subskills such as using abbreviations, diagrams to related ideas, or visual markers and editing notes.

The following list gives several hints for helping students to develop efficient note-taking skills:

- Take notes using a two- or three-column system.
- Take notes on only one side of the paper.
- Date and label the topic of the notes.
- Generally use a modified outline format, indenting subordinate ideas and numbering ideas when possible.
- Skip lines to note changes in ideas.
- Don't worry about punctuation or grammar.
- Write ideas or key phrases, not complete sentences.
- Don't write down every word the teacher says.
- Use pictures and diagrams to relate ideas.
- Use consistent abbreviations (e.g., w/ = with, & = and).
- Put question marks by any points you don't understand. Check them later with the teacher.

- Underline or asterisk information that the lecturer stresses as important.
- Write down information that the lecturer writes on the board or transparency.
- If you miss an idea you want to include, draw a blank _____ so that you can go back and fill it in.
- If you cannot automatically remember how to spell a word, spell it the way it sounds or the way you think it looks.
- If possible, review the previous sessions' notes right before the lecture.
- If the lecture is about an assigned reading topic, read the information before listening to the lecture.
- As soon as possible after the lecture, go over your notes, filling in the key concept column and listing any questions you still have.
- After going over your notes, try to summarize the major points presented during the lecture.
- Listen actively. In other words, think about what you already know about the topic being presented and how it relates.
- Review your notes before a test.

Direct Instruction in Note-Taking. Regardless of the note-taking format chosen, a teacher should provide direct instruction in note-taking. Direct instruction should include explicit demonstrations of the note-taking process and ample opportunities for students to practice with guidance and feedback. For many students with learning and behavior problems, telling them how to take notes is insufficient; note-taking practice is key. Teachers may want to develop and conduct a unit on listening and note-taking. The following is a list of teaching ideas for developing such a unit:

1. *Have students evaluate the effectiveness of their current note-taking skills and determine whether they will profit from instruction.* Generally, this can be assessed in two ways. First, have students bring to class current examples of notes, and have them evaluate the notes for completeness, format, ease of use for review, and legibility. Figure 10.19 presents one way that students can evaluate their own notes. Second, present a simulated 10- to 15-minute lecture or a videotape of a lecture, and ask the students to take notes. Give a test covering the information on the following day. Have the students again evaluate their notes and their test results.

2. *Use videotaped lectures when teaching students to listen effectively and to take notes.* The use of videotaped lectures is particularly helpful because it allows the students to replay the tape so that

FIGURE 10.19
Note-Taking Inventory

From time to time, it's smart to check the quality of your notes to see how you're doing. Then you'll know if you need to make any changes or improvements. Use this Note-Taking Inventory whenever you feel the need. Simply check it against that day's class notes.

You'll need a piece of paper and something to write with. Number the paper from 1–10. Give yourself one point for each item you find in your notes.

1. Date of lecture
2. Title of lecture
3. Writing neat enough for you to read (that's all that counts)
4. No more than one idea per line
5. Plenty of blank space to add extra ideas later
6. All main ideas brought up during class
7. All important details mentioned during class
8. All key terms and definitions given during class
9. Abbreviations used where necessary
10. No unnecessary words

Scoring: Add up your points.
9–10 points: You're a great note-taker!
7–8 points: You're a good note-taker!
5–6 points: You need to take better notes.
4 points or less: Make a note of this—practice, practice, practice.

Source: Schumm, J. S. (2001). *School Power: Study Skill Strategies for Succeeding in School.* Minneapolis, MN: Free Spirit Publishing, Inc.

they can watch or listen for main ideas. For example, you may be teaching students to watch and listen for cues the lecturer gives to note the important information. After listening to a short segment of videotape, have the students list the cues and then discuss why they are important. Then replay the segment so that students can verify their list of cues and add other cues.

3. *Control the difficulty of the lectures.* When first introducing new listening or note-taking skills such as listening for cues or using a two-column system, begin with short, well-organized lectures with ample use of advance organizers and visual aids, covering fairly simple, relatively familiar materials. As students reach proficiency, gradually increase the length of the lectures, reduce the use of organizers and visual aids, and increase the difficulty and novelty levels of the materials.

4. *Have students learn how to review their notes for tests.* Although students may learn to take more effective notes, they may fail to use the notes to study for tests. Teach students how to review their notes and ask themselves questions, using the Triggers column to develop questions about the material in the Notes column.

5. *Have students monitor the use and effectiveness of note-taking in other classes.* To increase the probability that students will generalize the note-taking skills to other classes, have them discuss in which classes the skills would be helpful and then have them monitor and discuss their effectiveness in those classes.

6. *Have students determine the effects that note-taking has on learning.* Students need to know that there is a payoff for their increased effort. Have students rate how well they feel they have taken notes over a unit or lecture, and have them monitor their performance on tests of the material. This will aid them determine whether better note-taking leads to better learning.

Learning from Text

Probably the best-known technique for learning information from text is SQ3R, developed by Robinson (1946). This acronym stands for the five steps in this study skill: Survey, Question, Read, Recite, Review. The purpose of this technique is to provide students with a systematic approach to studying text. The following is a brief description of each one of the five steps in the process.

Survey. Read through the headings quickly to learn what is to be studied.
Question. Change each heading into a question (to have in mind what is to be learned from the reading).
Read. Read to answer the question.
Recite. At the end of each heading, either write brief notes about the highlights of the reading or engage in self-recitation.
Review. After completing the above steps on the entire selection, review the main points of the notes by self-recitation. Check to see if the information is correct. (Robinson, 1946)

Although SQ3R seems well based in information-processing theory, research has yet to support its effectiveness (Adams, Carnine, and Gersten, 1982; McCormick and Cooper, 1991). One of the major difficulties associated with the SQ3R method is the complexity of the process, particularly for students who are experiencing reading problems. In content area classes, these students are often attempting to read and learn information from textbooks that are written above their instructional reading levels.

Multipass. Schumaker, Deshler, et al. (1982) developed a strategy based on SQ3R that incorporates the learning acquisition and generalization stages from the strategy intervention model (see Chapter 2) for students who experience problems learning information from textbooks. This strategy is referred to as Multipass because students make three passes through a text while carrying out the process. Each pass through the text (i.e., Survey, Size-Up, and Sort-Out) entails the use of a different substrategy. Because each substrategy represents a fairly complex set of behaviors, each of the substrategies is taught as a unit, with students reaching proficiency in the first substrategy before learning the next substrategy. Prerequisite skills include the ability to paraphrase and a reading level of fourth grade or above. Research conducted with eight high school students with learning disabilities indicated that the students were able to master the strategy in instructional-level materials and were able to use the strategy in grade-level materials without further training or practice. The students' grade on content tests improved—from barely passing to a grade of C or better.

CLASSROOM Applications

Multipass

PROCEDURES: During the Survey Pass, students become familiar with the main ideas and organization of the chapter (Deshler, Schumaker, and McKnight, 1997). In completing the Survey Pass, students complete the following steps:

1. *Title.* Read the chapter title. Think about how it fits with what you have already studied. Predict what the chapter will be about.
2. *Introduction.* Read the introduction, and make a statement about the main idea of the chapter. If there is no introduction, read the first paragraph, which is usually the introduction.
3. *Summary.* Turn to the last page of the chapter, read the summary, and make a summary statement. If there is no summary, check the last paragraph to see whether it is a summary. If it is not a summary, make a mental note so that you can summarize later.
4. *Organization.* Look through the chapter to see how the chapter is organized. Use the major headings to make a written outline. Paraphrase each heading.

5. *Pictures, maps, charts.* Look at the illustrations. Think about why they might have been included.
6. *Table of Contents.* Determine how this chapter fits in with the other information in the book by perusing the table of contents. Decide what relationships this chapter has with the others, especially the chapters immediately preceding and following it. For example, in a history book, chapters are often related because of chronological sequence. Chapters might also have a causal relationship (e.g., perhaps Chapter 6 talks about the causes of the Depression, and Chapter 7 talks about its effects). Other types of frequently occurring relationships include general/specific, compare/contrast, and related concepts.

After completing this process, close the book, and think about what the chapter is going to be about and what you already know about the topic.

Using the strategies intervention model, the teacher first describes and then models this survey process. Students should practice with guidance and feedback in materials at their reading instructional level until they are effective and efficient at surveying a chapter.

During the Size-Up Pass, students gain more specific information from the chapter without reading the chapter from beginning to end. Whereas the Survey Pass provides a general framework for the chapter, the Size-Up Pass allows the students to look for the information that fits into that general framework using textual cues. In learning the Size-Up Pass, students complete the following steps:

1. *Illustrations.* Again look over the pictures, maps, and charts, and read the captions. Think about why they are included.
2. *Questions.* Read the questions, including those found at the beginning or interspersed in the chapter. If you can already answer a study question, put a check mark by it.
3. *Words.* Read over the vocabulary words, including any vocabulary list and words highlighted in the chapter.
4. *Headings.* Read a heading. Ask yourself a question that you think will be answered in the section. Scan for the answer. When you find the answer, paraphrase it orally, or state something that you have learned from the information under the heading. Note on your outline what information you have learned from the section.

As with the Survey Pass, the teacher needs to describe the Size-Up process, and the students should practice in instructional-level material until they are proficient.

During this third and final pass, the Sort-Out Pass, students test themselves on the material in the chapter. This pass assists them in determining what they have learned and on what information they should still concentrate. In the final pass, the students read and answer each question at the end of the chapter, using the following process.

1. *Read.* Read the study question at the end of the chapter or each question provided by the teacher.
2. *Answer.* Answer the question if you can.
3. *Mark.* If you can answer a question, put a check by it; if you cannot answer it, put a box in front of it. If you do not know the answer, scan the headings on your outline to determine in which section it most likely will be answered. When you find the likely section, look for the answer. If you find the answer, paraphrase it and check the box. If you do not find the answer, scan the headings a second time for another likely place to find the answer. Again, look for the answer, and paraphrase it if you find it. If you do not find the answer after trying twice, circle the box so that you know you need to come back to it later and possibly get help.

As in the other two steps, the students should practice with materials at their instructional level until they are effective and efficient at answering questions over the material presented in the chapter.

COMMENTS: From the description of Multipass, it should be clear that when students use this strategy, they do not have to read a text in its entirety. Instead, they study the text to determine the main ideas, its overall framework, and related details and to answer the study questions. In this way, students can use this strategy with textbooks that are written above their instructional level. However, several cautionary notes are in order. First, remember to have the students reach proficiency on each substrategy before they begin learning the next substrategy. Second, when the difference between the students' instructional reading level and reading level of the textbook is greater than one to two years, students may have difficulty moving from instructional-level materials to grade-level materials. Teachers will generally need to provide graduated instructional

materials. (For example, Hector's instructional reading level is fifth grade, and he is a ninth grader. Hector will probably need to practice using the strategy in seventh-grade material as an intermediary step.) Third, do not expect students with learning and behavior problems to transfer this study strategy automatically to various content area textbooks. You will need to instruct for generalization.

Expression Skills

Expression skills include memory, retrieval, and test-taking skills, as well as other oral and/or written expression skills that are used to demonstrate understanding and application of knowledge.

Remembering Information

Have you ever arrived at the grocery store without your grocery list? What strategies do you use to help you remember what was on the list? Maybe you know how many items were on the list, and now you just need to find out how many of them you can recall. Or maybe you read the list over several times, almost rehearsing it, so it was easier to recall. Or you might use association by thinking of the meals that you were planning for the next few days and trying to associate the needed items with the meals. Or you might visualize your kitchen and quickly think about the refrigerator and each cabinet and the items needed for each. Finally, you might categorize the items on the basis of the sections in the grocery store (e.g., produce, cereal, dairy products, frozen foods). Clearly, there are many strategies for remembering information.

In many ways, remembering information for a test is similar to remembering the items on a grocery list. Often we are asked to remember a list of things (e.g., the major exports of the United Kingdom, the different kinds of flour and their uses, the names of the cranial nerves). During tests, we may be asked to take this information and apply it to specific situations (e.g., to explain why the U.K. economy is struggling), but we still need to remember the basic information.

Students with disabilities often have difficulty memorizing information, whether it be for tests, presentations, or written work (Ashbaker and Swanson, 1996). Sometimes the students do not understand the information to be learned, but in other cases poor performance may be due to difficulties with retrieval of the information (Swanson and Cooney, 1991), failure to use deliberate memory strategies (Ceci, 1985), and/or poor motivation for school tasks (Licht, 1983). Research suggests that these students also have difficulty with metamemory (i.e., awareness of memory strategies and the ability to use and monitor these strategies) in that they have trouble with one or more of the following:

- Knowing, selecting, and using appropriate strategies
- Estimating their own memory capacity for specific tasks
- Predicting accuracy on a memory task
- Allotting appropriate time to study
- Deciding when they have studied enough (Hughes, 1996)

Consequently, it is important to teach students memory strategies and tricks for remembering. Because teachers regularly ask students to remember information (e.g., for tests, class discussions), it is relatively easy to incorporate teaching memory strategies into the content curriculum. Incorporating the general teaching principles presented in Apply the Concept 10.4 makes the information more memorable and encourages learning and remembering the information.

Many content area learning strategies such as semantic mapping, advance organizers, and semantic feature analysis can be thought of as teaching procedures that facilitate memory. In addition to these kinds of activities, a number of formal strategies have been deliberately designed to improve memory. These are often referred to as *mnemonics*.

Mnemonics are strategies for improving memorization. The word *mnemonics* literally means "aids memory." Mnemonics aid memory and retrieval by forming associations that do not exist naturally in the content (Eggen and Kauchak, 1992). To use mnemonics, the information needs to be distilled so that the students are learning conceptual lists or frameworks. The students then operate on this information by using mnemonics. Mnemonic strategies can be grouped into three types: organization and association, visualization or mental imagery, and rehearsal.

Organization and Association. Organizing and associating information refers to arranging the information or associating it with other information in such a way that it is easier to remember. Study the following list of terms in order to remember them:

Democracy	Mammals
Socket wrench	Judiciary
Biology	Anatomy
Photosynthesis	Drill press
Lathe	Blowtorch
Freedom of speech	Constitution

Chances are that you categorized the words according to three superordinate categories, possibly labeled *tools, science concepts,* and *social studies concepts.* Now, instead of learning 12 unrelated words, you are learning three sets of 4 related words. Research shows that the second task is considerably easier. Research and practice have also demonstrated that students experiencing learning problems do not tend to make these associations spontaneously (Howe, O'Sullivan, Brainerd, and Kingman, 1989). Therefore, one mnemonic to

Apply the Concept 10.4

General Teaching Principles for Increasing Students' Memory of Information

- Orient student attention before presenting information, and emphasize important vocabulary and concepts when they occur.
- Activate prior knowledge, and help students to make connections between old and new knowledge.
- Use visual aids such as graphic organizers to highlight the important information and make it more memorable.
- Control the amount of information presented; group related ideas.
- Control the rate at which the information is presented.
- Provide time to review, rehearse, and elaborate on the information.
- Teach the students how to use and apply memory strategies and devices.
- Provide time and guidance in developing associations and mnemonics such as acronyms and acrostics.
- Provide opportunities for distributed review of information, and encourage mastery.

teach students when they are trying to remember lists of information is to associate or categorize related ideas.

Another type of association is the use of acrostics and acronyms. *Acrostics* are sentences made of words that begin with the first letters of a series of words.

Do you remember learning the names of the spaces on the musical staff as the word *FACE* and the names of the lines as *"Every Good Boy Does Fine"*? *Acronyms* are words that are created by joining the first letters of a series of words. Examples are *radar* (radio detecting and ranging), *scuba* (self-contained underwater breathing apparatus), and *laser* (light amplification by stimulated emission of radiation). If needed, extra letters can be inserted, or the letters can be rearranged. This technique has been used extensively in the development of learning strategies for students with learning and behavior problems (Deshler et al., 1996). By teaching students to construct acronyms and acrostics, sharing them in class, and then cueing students to use them when they study and take tests, you help them to learn and retrieve information.

The FIRST-letter mnemonic strategy (Nagel et al., 1994) is one way to help students construct lists of information to memorize and develop an acronym or acrostic for learning and remembering the information. The strategy includes an overall strategy (LISTS) and a substrategy for making the mnemonic device (FIRST). The steps in the overall strategy include the following:

Look for clues. In the class notes and textbooks, look for lists of information that are important to learn. Name or give a heading to each list.

Investigate the items. Decide which items should be included in the list.

Select a mnemonic device, using FIRST. Use the FIRST substrategy, explained next, to construct a mnemonic.

Transfer the information to a card. Write the mnemonic and the list on one side of a card and the name of the list on the other side of the card.

Self-test. Study by looking at the heading using the mnemonic to recall the list.

To complete the Select step, students use the FIRST strategy to design an acronym or acrostic:

Form a word. Using uppercase letters, write the first letter of each word in the list; see whether an acronym—a recognizable word or nonsense word—can be made.

Insert a letter(s). Insert one or more letters to see whether a word can be made. (Be sure to use lowercase letters so that you know they do not represent an item on the list—BACk, for example.)

Rearrange the letters. Rearrange the letters to see whether a word can be made.

Shape a sentence. Using the first letter of each word in the list, try to construct a sentence (an acrostic).

Try combinations. Try combinations of these steps to generate the mnemonic.

This strategy is taught by using the strategies intervention model presented in Chapter 2. It can be used with most content but is particularly effective with science and social studies in which lists of information are to be learned. The strategy provides a systematic method for students to review text and class notes, construct lists, and develop acronyms and acrostics that help them to remember and retrieve information.

Visualization and Key Word Method. Another strategy that is helpful in remembering information is visualization. Visualization is making a mental image of what you want to remember. Sometimes the visual image is simply the information that needs to be remembered. For example, it is not unusual to notice students closing their eyes when they are trying to remember how to spell a word. They may be using visualization to recall "what the word looks like."

If the information is complex, however, it may be helpful for the students to change the image of what they want to remember into a picture that will trigger or cue the information. One strategy used to do this is the *key word method* (e.g., Mastropieri and Scruggs, 1998; Mastropieri, Sweda, and Scruggs, 2000). Using this visualization strategy, students construct a picture that represents an interactive relationship between a concept and its definition. Figure 10.20 shows a key word picture generated for the concept of *allegro* and its definition (i.e., to move quickly). This picture is used to link the vocabulary word with the definition using a key word(s) that sounds like the vocabulary word. In Figure 10.20, *leg* and *row* are the key words used to construct a picture that triggers the definition of *allegro*.

The following steps are suggested for creating the key word picture (King-Sears, Mercer, and Sindelar, 1992) and use the acronym IT FITS:

Identify the word or term.

Tell the definition or answer information.

Find a key word that sounds like the new word or the word you need to remember.

FIGURE 10.20

Key Word Picture Generated for the Concept "Allegro"

Source: C. A. Hughes, Memory and test-taking strategies, in D. D. Deshler, E. S. Ellis, and B. K. Lenz, *Teaching Adolescents with Learning Disabilities*, 2nd ed. (Denver: Love, 1996), p. 223. Reprinted with permission.

Imagine an interaction, that is, something that the key word and the answer information can do together. If you draw a sketch of the interaction, you may review it later for improved memory.

Think about the key word and the interaction.

Study your vocabulary and the information using your key word to help you remember. Review by asking for each item: What was my key word for [word]? What was happening in my picture [or image]? What is the information I am supposed to remember?

The key word method is most effective in increasing the recall of information by students with learning disabilities when the key word relationships are presented to the students rather than having individual students generate them (Fulk, Mastropieri, and Scruggs, 1992; Mastropieri and Scruggs, 1989; Scruggs and Mastropieri, 1989a, 1989b). Students should have ample opportunities to create key word associations as a class or in cooperative groups before having students work individually.

Verbal Rehearsal. Repeating the information aloud or to yourself can help to facilitate memory. Verbal rehearsal is the major cognitive strategy that is used to enhance short-term memory (Hughes, 1996). Rehearsal is most effective if there is limited interference between the time of the rehearsal and the time of recall, the number of items to be remembered is limited, and the information is clustered or chunked.

General Memory Strategies. Often several mnemonics are used simultaneously. For example, after you have categorized the words in a list, you can use acronyms within each category to help you remember the specific words and then use rehearsal to practice, review, and test your memory. Teaching students with learning and behavior problems which strategies to use for which types of information and how to combine strategies is generally necessary. In addition to teaching students how to use the various memory strategies, it is also important to teach students to use periodic review to minimize forgetting.

Studying and Taking Tests

Studying and taking tests are important aspects of secondary schools. Tests are the primary means that teachers use to determine whether students have learned new concepts and can apply them. For example, Putnam (1992a) surveyed 120 English, science, social studies, or mathematics teachers of grades 7 to 12 to determine how frequently they used tests. In a nine-week grading period, students were expected to take an average of 11 tests in each content area. On the average, teachers used scores on tests to determine approximately half of a grade for a course. Although a great deal of effort is placed on tests to measure learning, only 25 percent of the teachers surveyed indicated that they taught strategies for taking tests. Yet research on students with disabilities and at-risk students indicates that they have limited study and test-taking strategies to employ (Hughes and Schumaker, 1991; Scruggs and Mastropieri, 1988). For example, the only strategy college students with learning disabilities regularly reported using when taking objective tests was skipping over difficult or unknown items. For essay questions, only half the students reported rereading questions or proofreading their responses.

Studying for Tests. Studying for tests means that students should be reviewing information on a regular basis so they are not left cramming the day before the test. To help promote positive study habits, Teri Martinez, a middle school resource social studies teacher, taught the following guidelines for studying:

1. *Manage your study time.* Keep up with assignments, and do daily and weekly reviews. Ms. Martinez planned five minutes each day at the end of her social studies class for students to review the material. On Monday, she took an extra five minutes and had the students review the previous week's work. She used individual, small group, and whole-class discussion to review.

2. *Create study aids.* Create a semantic map or other graphic organizer to help students remember key information. Ms. Martinez often used an ongoing map during review sessions, and the students added to the map each day. Ms. Martinez also taught the students how to create and use flashcards for key concepts and vocabulary. She taught the students the following procedures.

- When learning vocabulary, put the word on one side and the definition and an example on the other side.
- When learning other information, put the question on one side and the answer on the other side.
- When learning a formula, put the formula on one side and examples of how it is used on the other side.
- Review the flashcards in random order or after sorting the cards into categories or making a semantic map.
- Keep index cards in notebooks and on desks during class.
- Make a card when learning about a key concept or idea.

3. *Learn about the test.* The more information students learn about the format, type, and time allotted for the test, the more effectively they can prepare for it. Rather than telling the students about the test, Ms. Martinez would start the discussion by saying, "Let's talk about the test. What do you want to ask me?" She used the following checklist to guide the students' questioning:

- Format of test, types of questions
- How much test is worth
- Date of test
- Time allotted for test
- Whether books or notes are allowed
- Information covered
- Teacher recommendations for how to study
- Teacher recommendations for what to study

4. *Predict questions.* Ms. Martinez also demonstrated how the students can predict the questions that will be asked. The students can use what they know about the teacher's testing style, their class notes, their maps, and other study aids to predict questions. Two days before a test, Ms. Martinez had the students work in cooperative groups and write what they thought would be the most important questions on the test and then answer them.

5. *Think positive.* An important part of doing well on a test is having a positive attitude and believing that one is going to do well. Ms. Martinez finds that she enjoys working with the students on having positive attitudes. Each day during their review, she asks the students about the following:

- What they learned today
- How it relates to what they already know
- What they will be working on tomorrow
- How well they have learned the information

She also has them rate how well they think they will do on the test and think about what they could do to improve their ratings. Just before a test, Ms. Martinez takes several minutes to review test-taking strategies and to have the students visualize themselves being successful as they take the test.

Test-Taking Strategies. In a 2005 study, Carter and colleagues taught 38 high school students with disabilities the following test-taking strategies in a series of six lessons:

- Bubble sheet completion and pacing
- Sorting problems: identifying which items are the easiest and solving those problems first
- Estimating: solving math problems by rounding
- Substitution and backsolving: substituting the given answers into the question to find the correct answer
- Recopying problems: rewriting problems in a more familiar form
- Underlining and reading all answers
- Elimination of redundant or off-the-wall answers

While students in the study did demonstrate small increases in their test scores after learning the strategies, Carter et al. (2005) feel that in order to see larger gains, students with disabilities need to learn test-taking strategies within the content instruction. In other words, in order to best prepare students with disabilities to take multiple-choice tests, you should integrate test-taking instruction into content instruction on a regular basis.

Other test-taking strategies and hints that can help students perform better on tests include:

- Survey the test.
- Read the directions carefully. Underline key words in the directions that tell you what to do.
- Be sure you understand the scoring system (e.g., is guessing penalized?).
- If you have memorized specific outlines, formulas, mnemonics, and the like, write down that information before you forget it.
- When answering questions, place a mark in the margin for those questions about which you are unsure and/or want to review.
- Place the questions in the context of what has been discussed in class and what you have read.
- Avoid changing answers arbitrarily.
- Review your answers.

Taking Objective Tests. For students with learning and behavior problems, it may be beneficial to teach specific test-taking strategies. The PIRATES strategy can be used for taking objective tests (Hughes et al., 1988) and uses the strategies intervention model described in Chapter 2. Research indicates that students with learning disabilities can increase their performance by 20–40 percentage points by learning and applying this strategy. The steps in the strategy are as follows:

Prepare to succeed.
- Put your name and PIRATES on the test.
- Allot time and order the sections.
- Say affirmations.
- Start within two minutes.

Inspect the instructions.
- Read instructions carefully.
- Underline what to do and where to respond.
- Notice special requirements.

Read, remember, reduce.
- Read the whole question.
- Remember what you studied.
- Reduce your choices.

Answer or abandon.
- Answer the question.
- Abandon the question for the moment.

Turn back.

Estimate your answer.
- Avoid absolutes.
- Choose the longest or most detailed choice.
- Eliminate similar choices.

Survey.
- Survey to ensure that all questions have been answered.
- Switch an answer only if you are sure.

When using this strategy, a student repeats, for each section of the test, the second, third, and fourth steps (i.e., inspect the instructions; read, remember, reduce; answer or abandon).

In addition to this strategy, there are a number of hints for taking objective tests. Apply the Concept 10.5 presents information that is helpful in answering objective questions (e.g., true-false, multiple-choice, matching, and completion).

Taking Essay Tests. Essays tests are not used as frequently as objective tests (Putnam, 1992b), but when essay questions are incorporated into a test, they make up a sizable portion of the test grade (Hughes, 1996). This type of test can be particularly difficult for students with disabilities. Not only do the test-takers have to recall information, they have to write clearly in terms of organization, legibility, spelling, and grammar. Students with difficulties in written expression may be able to orally express the answer to the question, but their writing skills may make it difficult for them to communicate that knowledge. You may want to record the student's answers on audiotape. For some students, it may be advantageous to teach a strategy for answering essay questions so that the students organize the information and communicate it effectively. One strategy that has been developed to assist students in organizing better responses to essay questions is called ANSWER (Hughes, Schumaker, and Deshler, 2001). The steps include the following:

Analyze the situation.
- Read the question carefully.
- Underline key words.
- Gauge the time you need.

Notice requirements.
- Scan for and mark the parts of the question.
- Ask and say what is required.
- Tell yourself that you will write a high-quality answer.

Set up an outline.
- Set up the main ideas.
- Assess whether they match the question.
- Make changes if necessary.

Work in details.
- Remember what you learned.
- Add details to the main ideas using abbreviations.
- Indicate the order.
- Decide whether you are ready to write.

Apply the Concept 10.5

Tips for Answering Objective Questions

True-False Questions

- Remember, *everything* in a true statement must be true. One false detail makes it false.
- Look for qualifying words that tend to make statements false, such as *all, always, everyone, everybody, never, no, none, no one, only.*
- Look for qualifying words that tend to make statements true, such as *generally, most, often, probably, some, sometimes, usually.*
- Simplify questions that contain double negatives by crossing out both negatives and then determining whether the statement is true or false.
- Don't change an answer unless you have a good reason to. Usually, your first impression is correct.

Matching Questions

- Read directions carefully. Determine whether each column contains an equal number of items and whether items can be used more than once.
- Read both columns before you start matching, to get a sense of the items.
- Focus on each item in one column and look for its match in the other column.

- If you can use items only once, cross out each item as you use it.

Multiple-Choice Questions

- Determine whether you are penalized for guessing.
- Answer the questions you know, putting a check mark in the margin next to items you want to return to later.
- Read all possible options, even when you are pretty sure of the right answer.
- See whether multiple options are available (e.g., c. A and B; d. All of the above).
- Minimize the risk of guessing by reading the stem with each option to see which option is most logical.
- Use a process of elimination, crossing out options you know are wrong.
- When you do not know the answer and you are not penalized for guessing, use the following signals to help you select the right option:
  - The longest option is often correct.
  - The most complete answer is often correct.
  - The first time the option "all of the above" or "none of the

above" is used, it is usually correct.
- The option in the middle, particularly if it is the longest, is often correct.
- Answers with qualifiers such as *generally, probably, sometimes,* and *usually* are frequently correct.

Completion Questions

- Determine whether more than one word can be put in one blank.
- If blanks are of different lengths, use length as a clue for the length of the answer.
- Read the question to yourself so that you can hear what is being asked.
- If more than one answer comes to mind, write them down; then reread the question with each answer to see which one fits best.
- Make sure that the answer you provide fits grammatically and logically.

Source: Selected ideas adapted from J. Langan, *Reading and Study Skills,* 2nd ed. (New York: McGraw-Hill, 1982).

Engineer your answer.
- Write an introductory paragraph.
- Refer to your outline.
- Include topic sentences.
- Tell about details for each topic sentence.
- Use examples.

Review your answer.
- Look to see whether you answered all parts of the question.
- Inspect to see whether you included all main ideas and details.
- Touch up your answer.

In her social studies class, Ms. Martinez taught the ANSWER strategy because essay questions were one format she used in her tests. She also gave students a list of direction words for essay questions (see Figure 10.21). She demonstrated how taking one concept such as "democracy" and using different direction words would change the response. In her daily reviews, she frequently discussed one of the cue words in relation to the content that had been covered that day. She provided examples of how to write an answer to a question using that cue word.

FIGURE 10.21

Direction Words for Answering Essay Questions

Cue	Meaning	Cue	Meaning
Analyze	Break into parts, and examine each part.	Interpret	Explain, and share your own judgment.
Apply	Discuss how the principles would apply to a situation.	Justify	Provide reasons for your statements or conclusion.
Compare	Discuss differences and similarities.	List	Provide a numbered list of items or points.
Contrast	Discuss differences and similarities, stressing the differences.	Outline	Organize your answer into main points and supporting details. If appropriate, use outline format.
Critique	Analyze and evaluate, using criteria.		
Define	Provide a clear, concise statement that explains the concept.	Prove	Provide factual evidence to support your logic or position.
Describe	Give a detailed account, listing characteristics, qualities, and components as appropriate.	Relate	Show the connection among ideas.
		Review	Provide a critical summary in which you summarize and present your comments.
Diagram	Provide a drawing.	State	Explain precisely.
Discuss	Provide an in-depth explanation. Be analytical.	Summarize	Provide a synopsis that does not include your comments.
Explain	Give a logical development that discusses reasons or causes.	Trace	Describe the development or progress of the idea.
Illustrate	Use examples or, when appropriate, provide a diagram or picture.		

Add your own direction words and definitions!

Spotlight on Diversity

Families and Vocabulary Acquisition for English Language Learners

Children of all ages love to be read to by both their teacher and family members. Not only is it fun, but reading out loud to English language learners is an important way to increase vocabulary development and to assist them in accessing texts that would be too difficult for them to read on their own. When children are read to, they have the opportunity to hear and discuss authentic and relevant stories, and they are also exposed to challenging and stimulating vocabulary that is critical to their understanding of and engagement with texts. Storybook Reading (Hickman et al., 2004) is a read-aloud activity that can be used to promote vocabulary development for English language learners.

Adults can make a read-aloud book a fun and language-enhancing time by using the following procedure:

1. Help your child to select a book that is interesting and at a level that he or she understands. It should be difficult enough that there are a few new words to learn but not so difficult that the child has trouble maintaining interest and understanding the book. Instead of reading the whole book all at once, you may want to break the book into short passages (one or two pages). It may take several days to read one story.

2. Choose two or three new words, and give simple definitions for them (e.g., *surplus: more than what is needed; extra*). Write down the words and their definitions.

3. Tell your child to listen for the new words while you read. Ask the child to hold up a finger or gently squeeze your arm when he or she hears one of the new words. Briefly discuss the word in the context of the story.

4. Read the passage, and then discuss what has been read. If the child has a question, stop and answer it.

5. After reading, ask your child to tell you what happened in the story. Ask probing questions (*who, what, where, when,* and *why* questions) to encourage your child to expand on

his or her explanation. Try to let your child do most of the talking.

6. If your child seems ready, ask him or her to use the vocabulary words during the story retelling.

Remember, if adults are doing this activity at home, it can be conducted in the language in which both the adult and the child are most comfortable.

INSTRUCTIONAL ACTIVITIES

This section provides instructional activities that are related to content area learning and study skills. Some of the activities teach new skills; others are best suited for practice and reinforcement of already acquired skills. For each activity, the objective, materials, and teaching procedures are described.

▶Word Association Map

Objectives: To teach students a strategy for learning vocabulary words

Grades: Secondary

Materials: Textbook chapter, word association map worksheet (see Figure 10.22)

Teaching Procedures:
1. Introduce a key vocabulary word (e.g., *wicked*), and write it on the map.
2. Ask students to brainstorm what the word means.
3. With student input, come up with a "good" definition, and write it on the map. If necessary, provide examples to help students understand the meaning of the word.
4. Test students on several examples and nonexamples (e.g., example: "The witch in the children's story is mean for no reason and is wicked"; nonexample: "Diana is a considerate boss who is always willing to listen").
5. Ask the students to identify synonyms and antonyms of the word and write them on their word maps (e.g., synonyms: *unkind, bad*; antonyms: *good, considerate*).
6. Finally, ask the students to create their own personal sentences with the word.

Source: Adapted from University of Texas Center for Reading and Language Arts (2001a).

▶Add-a-Part: Prefixes and Suffixes

Objective: To give students practice in creating words with prefixes and suffixes

Grades: Fourth through secondary

Materials: Cards with prefixes (e.g., *dis-*), cards with suffixes (e.g., *-able*), cards with root words (e.g., *honest, comfort*) that can be combined with these prefixes and suffixes, two plastic bags

Teaching Procedures:
1. Have students sit in a circle.
2. Place the plastic bag of cards with prefixes and suffixes and the other bag with root words in the middle of the circle within reach of everyone.
3. Model playing the "add-a-part" game by drawing one card out of each bag, saying the affix (e.g., *-less*) and the root word (e.g., *care*) on the cards, and creating a new word with the affix (e.g., *careless*). Say the new word and its meaning, and tell whether the word is real or not.
4. Have the students take turns playing the game.

Source: Adapted from University of Texas Center for Reading and Language Arts (2001b).

▶VOCAB

Objective: To teach students the VOCAB strategy and enhance their vocabulary

Grades: Secondary

Materials: A list of vocabulary terms that are generally related (e.g., federal government, legislative

FIGURE 10.22

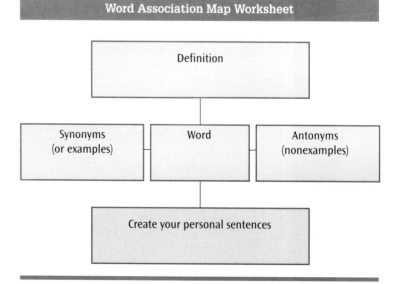

Word Association Map Worksheet

Definition

Synonyms (or examples) — Word — Antonyms (nonexamples)

Create your personal sentences

branch, executive branch, judicial branch); index cards or pieces of paper

Teaching Procedures:

1. Discuss the components of the VOCAB strategy, and introduce the strategy step by step:

   Verify the key vocabulary terms and concepts to be learned, and put them on individual vocabulary cards or pieces of paper.

   Organize the vocabulary word cards into a diagram that shows the relationship of the words to each other as you understand them in the context of what is being learned.

   Communicate your reasoning, and share your diagram with a partner and vice versa.

   Assess the diagrams, discuss similarities and differences, and adjust your diagram with helpful ideas from your partner.

   Build your understanding with self-testing.

2. Identify and provide for students a list of vocabulary words.

3. Have the students write one of the words on each of the index cards or pieces of paper.

4. Ask the students to organize the words in any way that they think shows the correct relationships among the words.

5. Have the students explain how and why they organized the words the way they did.

6. On the basis of the discussion, have the students reorganize their words if they think they have a different understanding of the meaning of the words.

7. Circulate among the pairs, and monitor students' discussions to make sure that they are building their understanding of the words through self-testing.

8. As a whole class, have several pairs of students share how and why they arranged their words.

Source: Adapted from University of Texas Center for Reading and Language Arts (1999).

▶Click and Clunk

Objective: To help students monitor their understanding as they read and apply fix-up strategies to determine the meanings of unfamiliar words

Grades: Elementary through secondary

Materials: Reading passage, clunk card, paper

Teaching Procedures:

1. Introduce clunk cards. Explain to students that "click" means words or ideas they understand and "clunk" means the words or ideas that they do not know. The students continue to read until they have a clunk. Tell the students that they can use the clunk cards when they have a clunk to figure out the meaning of a word.

2. Model each of the fix-up strategies on the clunk cue cards.

3. Provide opportunities for guided practice, followed by independent practice in which students apply these strategies as they read.

4. Pair students, and ask them to read each paragraph of the passage.

5. After reading each paragraph, have the students find clunks and write them on the paper. Then, have the students use the fix-up strategies on the clunk cards to figure out what the clunks mean. Provide supports if necessary.

6. Have the students record the definition of the clunk on the paper.

7. Repeat the same procedure until the entire selection has been read.

8. When the entire selection has been read, have several pairs of students share their clunks and the fix-up strategies they used to help them determine meaning.

Source: Adapted from Klingner et al., (2001).

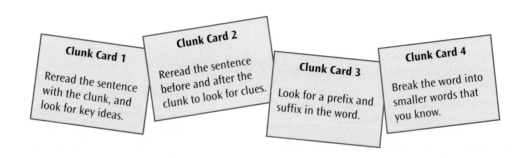

Clunk Card 1

Reread the sentence with the clunk, and look for key ideas.

Clunk Card 2

Reread the sentence before and after the clunk to look for clues.

Clunk Card 3

Look for a prefix and suffix in the word.

Clunk Card 4

Break the word into smaller words that you know.

►Contextual Searching

Objective: To help students use various context clues to identify the meaning of the words

Grades: Secondary

Materials: Ten vocabulary words; contextual sentences for each vocabulary word using the five types of context clues (i.e., definition, description, contrast, comparison, synonym); sentence strips; list of possible definitions; dictionary

Teaching Procedures:

Before the instruction,

1. Identify 10 vocabulary words.
2. Develop one context clue for each word. Be sure to use different types of context clues.
3. Write a sentence with a vocabulary word containing one context clue type (definition, description, contrast, comparison, or synonym) on each sentence strip.

During the instruction,

4. Present the first five vocabulary words in isolation (e.g., *cilia, volition, lethargic, inquisition,* and *literally*).
5. Ask the students for definitions of the words.
6. Write the words and the students' definitions on the chalkboard or overhead.
7. Present the vocabulary words in context.
8. Model how to use the type of context clue to figure out the meaning of the unfamiliar words. (See Figure 10.23.)
9. Have the students compare the definitions from context to their definitions in isolation.
10. Present the other five vocabulary words in isolation.

11. Ask the students for definitions of the words.
12. Write the words and the students' definitions on the chalkboard or overhead.
13. Present the vocabulary words in context.
14. Pair students, and ask them to analyze the context to figure out the meaning of each vocabulary word and record their definitions for each word.
15. Ask the students to identify which type of context clue they used for each vocabulary word.
16. Ask the students to compare their definitions from context clues to their definitions in isolation.
17. Have students look up the definitions for the vocabulary words in the dictionary.
18. Call on several pairs of students to share how the dictionary definition fits with their definition from context clues.

Source: Adapted from University of Texas Center for Reading and Language Arts (2002).

►Jeopardy!

Objective: To give students practice in using reference and trade books to obtain information and to generate questions

Grades: Secondary

Materials: Reference and trade books, Jeopardy! board with four categories and five answers per category, index cards to fit in the Jeopardy! board

Teaching Procedures:

1. Divide the students into three teams of two to four students. Explain that each team is going to make a Jeopardy!-style game for the other students to play.

FIGURE 10.23

Using Context Clues

Context Clue Type	Example
Definition: The word is defined in the sentence.	If disease reaches your bronchial tubes, *cilia*—tiny hairlike structures—are another barrier to prevent infection.
Description: The word is described by the context.	After taking a spill on her bike, she was able to stand up, get back on the bike, and pedal away on her own *volition*.
Contrast: The word is compared with some other word as an antonym.	Kim was *lethargic,* yet her sister was very energetic.
Comparison: The word is compared with some other word or phrase to illustrate the similarities between them.	Birgit was exhausted after the *inquisition,* which was like being in a boat on rough seas.
Synonym: The word is compared to another word with a similar meaning.	Tom interpreted the message *literally;* that is, he believed the message as though every word were real.

JEOPARDY!

Pop Music	Presidents	Football	Southwest
20	20	20	20
40	40	40	40
60	60	60	60
80	80	80	80
100	100	100	100

2. To make the game, each team needs to select four categories. Then have the students use reference books, trade books, and other sources to generate five questions and answers for each category that other students could possibly answer. Have them write the questions and answers on separate index cards and order the questions and answers from easy to difficult.

3. Each team then takes a turn directing its Jeopardy! game. First, the team inserts their category names and answer cards into the Jeopardy! board. Then they direct the game as the two other teams compete against each other. To direct the game, one student should serve as master of ceremonies, another as timekeeper, and the rest as judges.

4. To play, each team takes a turn selecting a category and a level underneath the category. The answer is then exposed, and the team members have 15 seconds to give the question. If the question is correct, they get the number of points indicated and are allowed to make another selection. If the answer is incorrect, the other team has 15 seconds to give an answer.

▶Study Groups

Objective: To provide students with the opportunity to work in groups when studying a textbook for a test

Grades: Secondary

Materials: Content area textbook chapter or sections on which the students are going to be tested, index cards

Teaching Procedures:

1. Have students who are studying for tests that cover the same material work in groups of two to three students. (*Note:* When students first do this activity, the teacher will generally need to demonstrate and guide the students through the process.)

2. Have the students read the assigned materials together, stopping at the end of each paragraph or section to discuss the main ideas and the important vocabulary. Each main idea and important vocabulary for each section should be written on an index card.

3. After the students finish reading the assignment using this technique, they should take all the main idea cards and arrange them in logical groupings or in a logical order.

4. Have the students take each important vocabulary card and write a simple definition that makes sense according to the text. Then have them arrange the important vocabulary next to the related main idea.

5. Next, have each student copy onto paper the arrangement that was organized for the main ideas and vocabulary (with definitions).

6. Finally, the students should study the paper and then take turns quizzing each other on the information.

▶Learn Those Words!

Objective: To teach students a simple strategy for memorizing vocabulary words—either English words or those of a foreign language

Grades: Fifth through secondary

Materials: Index cards used whole or cut in half or in thirds, a pen, a paper cutter or scissors

Teaching Procedures:

1. Have students write a word on one side of an index card and its definition or translation on the reverse side.

2. Have students study the words and then test themselves. Have them form two piles of cards as they work: a pile for the words they know and another for those they do not know. Students continue to study the words they don't know until there are no more cards in the unknown pile.

3. Tell the students that they should always keep a set of words with them. While they are waiting in line or waiting for class to begin, they can test themselves on their words.

4. Have students make new sets of words and continuously review the old sets.

SUMMARYfor Chapter 10

As students with learning and behavior problems progress through grades, many are challenged by curriculum demands, such as learning a number of new vocabulary words, understanding complex concepts presented in textbooks, and being able to study independently. Therefore, teacher effectiveness in building students' vocabulary, content area reading, and study skills are critical for students with learning and behavior problems to succeed in schools. This chapter focused on those topics as well as adaptations, capitalizing on the relationship between the teacher and the learner.

To build students' vocabulary, teachers can provide specific word instruction and/or can teach word-learning strategies. Specific word instruction can be effectively coordinated with other content area subjects because teachers can preteach several important vocabulary words before the lesson. For young students who may not acquire adequate decoding skills or English language learners, teachers can build students' vocabulary by reading text aloud to students and discussing new vocabulary words. In addition to specific word instruction, teachers should teach students word-learning strategies that they can use independently while reading. These strategies include contextual analysis, morphemic analysis, and use of dictionaries and other aids.

For successful content area reading, students need to select, organize, manipulate, and complement content information in a manner that promotes effective and efficient information processing. Content enhancements are techniques to help students identify, organize, and comprehend important content information. Several types of content enhancements have been developed; advance organizers, concept diagrams, comparison tables, semantic feature analysis, or semantic maps are content enhancements that have proved effective.

At the same time, teachers can work with students to teach them effective methods of studying. This includes time management and organization skills, strategies for learning from lectures and texts, strategies for remembering and retrieving information, and strategies for taking tests.

If teachers can provide students with sound vocabulary and content area instruction while teaching study skills, then teachers have facilitated students' success in school settings and in later life.

FOCUS Answers

FOCUS Question 1. How can teachers use specific word instruction and word-learning strategies to teach vocabulary?

Answer: In specific word instruction, teachers select a few vocabulary words that are critical for understanding a text and are difficult for students. Words can be selected from a text that the teacher will read aloud or from a text that students will read themselves. Teachers can highlight selected words after reading or preteach the vocabulary words. Students also need word-learning strategies that they can use indepedently while reading. Effective word-learning strategies include using contextual analysis, morphemic analysis, and reference aids.

FOCUS Question 2. What is content enhancement, and how can teachers use it to teach content area reading?

Answer: Content enhancement is used to help students identify, organize, and comprehend important content. First, teachers select important concepts and related vocabulary. Next, teachers evaluate materials. Reviewing texts before reading helps teachers to identify the difficulty of the ideas or concepts. Teachers then assess students' prior knowledge through the use of activities. Next, teachers can implement appropriate prelearning activities that students can use before reading an assigned text or listening to a lecture. Finally, the semantic map, concept diagram, or other activity becomes a learning tool that can be used as a guide during and after reading.

FOCUS Question 3. How do teachers adapt textbooks, lectures, assignments, homework, and tests to meet the needs of students with learning and behavior problems?

Answer: Text adaptation involves changing an existing text to make it more comprehensible for students. Methods for adapting textbooks include using study guides, highlighting important points, or using alternatives to reading such as audiotaping text chapters or reading aloud. Lectures can be adapted by making their organization and key points clear to students through aids such as advance organizers, vocal cues, or visual aids. Teachers who are aware of students' abilities and needs construct assignments and homework that are appropriate in content, length, time required to complete, and skill level. Teachers should always communicate why an assignment is important, when it is due, what support is available, and what steps are involved. Tests are an extension of assignments because they monitor the attainment of important information and skills. Teachers should tell students explicitly what they will be responsible for knowing, should design tests that are clear and easy to understand, and should provide acommodations during testing situations.

FOCUS Question 4. **What are the three types of study skills, and why are they important to learning?**

Answer: Personal development skills, process skills, and expression skills are three types of study skills. They are important because they help students to manage their time; use strategies to organize, synthesize, and remember new information; and communicate what they have learned to others. Study skills are critical to independent and efficient learning.

THINKand APPLY

- Explain two types of vocabulary, and describe how teachers can enhance each type of vocabulary knowledge of their students.
- Compare indirect vocabulary and direct vocabulary. Explain why students with reading difficulties or dyslexia benefit from direct instruction more so than average-achieving students.
- What considerations should teachers use in selecting vocabulary words for specific word instruction?
- List three word building strategies, and describe the teaching procedure for each strategy.
- Why is it difficult for students with learning problems to succeed in content area classes in secondary schools?
- What is "considerate" text? Using the ideas in the section entitled "Considerate or User-Friendly Text," select a text and evaluate it for considerateness and appropriateness for your students.

- Explain the difference between a concept diagram, a content map, and a relationship chart. Select a chapter from a book that students use, and develop each of these instructional aids for the chapter. Compare the differences and similarities.
- What should teachers keep in mind when they adapt a textbook? Select a chapter from a text, and adapt it for students with learning and behavior problems.
- What should you include in a unit on self-management? Plan such a unit for a group of students with learning and behavior problems.
- What are the characteristics of listener-friendly lectures? Plan a lecture that is listener-friendly.
- Conduct a content analysis of a chapter you selected previously, and then develop key word mnemonics to teach hard-to-learn technical vocabulary.

APPLY the STANDARDS

 Council for Exceptional Children

1. Describe why teaching vocabulary and key concepts is important for students with learning and behavior problems, and give several examples of ways in which to integrate vocabulary and concept instruction into content area teaching (LDS1, LD4S7, LD4S5, LD4S1).

   Standard LDS1: Use research-supported methods for academic and nonacademic instruction of individuals with learning disabilities.

   Standard LD4S7: Identify and teach essential concepts, vocabulary, and content across the general curriculum.

   Standard LD4S5: Use instructional methods to strengthen and compensate for deficits in perception, comprehension, memory, and retrieval.

   Standard LD4S1: Use research-supported methods for academic and nonacademic instruction of individuals with learning disabilities.

2. What factors should teachers consider when designing or adapting tests for individuals with learning and behavior problems (LD4K1, LD8S1, LD4K5)?

   Standard LD4K1: Strategies to prepare for and take tests.

   Standard LD8S1: Choose and administer assessment instruments appropriate to the individual with learning disabilities.

   Standard LD4K5: Methods for guiding individuals in identifying and organizing critical content.

WEBSITESas RESOURCES | for Teaching Content Area Learning and Study Skills

The following Websites are extensive resources to expand your understanding of teaching content area learning and study skills:

- NSTA Website www.nsta.org
- National Council for the Social Studies www.socialstudies.org
- Strategic Instruction Model www.ku-crl.org
- NIFL Vocabulary Instruction www.nifl.gov/partnershipforreading/publications/reading_first1vocab.html
- Study Skills Help Page www.mtsu.edu/studskl

Where the Classroom Comes to Life

Video Homework Exercise Go to MyEducationLab and select the topic "CONTENT AREA TEACHING," then watch the video "Vocabulary Strategies" and complete the activity questions below.

In this video clip, students use several vocabulary strategies while reading content area texts.

1. What is a vocabulary strategy and why is it important in school and in life?
2. List five vocabulary strategies demonstrated in the video or described in the chapter.

Lesson Plan Homework Exercise Go to MyEducationLab and select the topic "INSTRUCTIONAL PRACTICES AND LEARNING STRATEGIES," then read the lesson plan "Semantic Maps" and complete the activity questions below.

This lesson plan describes how to use a semantic map to activate prior knowledge and guide the preview of a new text.

1. In what ways can creating a semantic map prior to reading benefit students?
2. In this lesson, a semantic map is used as part of a previewing activity. What other ways can a semantic or concept map be used as part of content enhancement?

Video Homework Exercise Go to MyEducationLab and select the topic "INSTRUCTIONAL PRACTICES AND LEARNING STRATEGIES," then watch the video "Reading a Textbook" and complete the activity questions below.

In this video clip, a middle school teacher discusses with her students the difficulties of reading a science text.

1. How is textbook reading different than other types of reading?
2. Describe two adaptations outlined in the chapter that you could use to support students who struggle to read textbooks?

Chapter **11**

Assessing and Teaching Mathematics

1. What characteristics are common to students who exhibit deficits in math skills, how can these characteristics influence math ability, and what should teachers consider when planning instruction for these students?

2. How is assessment used in mathematics, and what is CBM? What are some examples of several types of assessment techniques that can be used to determine number sense in young children?

3. What are the prenumber skills students need to progress in arithmetic?

4. What are several numeration concepts?

5. What factors contribute to difficulties with problem solving, and how can teachers assist students in learning problem-solving strategies?

6. What are the three types of math interventions, and how can they be used to improve math performance?

anjay, a third-grade student who has behavior disorders, spends most of his day in the general education third-grade classroom. He is in the top math group and is proud of this achievement. His special education teacher is pleased that he is fulfilling his behavior contract and has not had any serious disturbances since he has been included in the general education classroom.

Claudia, a seventh-grade student who spends part of her day in a classroom for students with learning disabilities, is not nearly as successful in math. In fact, when asked what her favorite academic time is during the day, she says, "I love to write. In fact, I think I will be an author. I have already written several books for the classroom, and one was even selected for the library." When asked what she thinks of math, she looks away and says, "No way! Don't even mention it. I can't do math. We don't get along."

Claudia has had difficulty with mathematics since she was in the primary grades. Her first-grade teacher thought that she simply was not interested in math and suggested that her parents obtain special tutoring help during the following summer. Her parents found that the special help did little good, and when Claudia continued to have serious difficulty with math in second grade, the teacher referred her for assessment for possible learning disabilities. The assessment results suggested that she had difficulty with spatial relations and using memory to recall rote math facts. She has received special help in math for the past four years, and though she seems to have made progress, her math skills are still her weakest academic area.

Some students with learning and behavior problems have difficulty with language arts (reading, writing, and spelling), some have difficulty with mathematics, and some have difficulty with both. Compared with students who only have math problems, students who have both math and reading problems are far more likely to continue to have math problems in later grades (Jordan and Hanich, 2003). However, despite the number of students who have math problems, by far the skill that has received the most attention from researchers, writers, and even clinicians is reading. Reading is often viewed as an essential skill for survival in our society, whereas math is often considered less important. With an increased need for students to understand problem solving for success in the workplace, the inferior status of mathematics instruction may need to change.

This chapter will increase your understanding of how to assess and teach mathematics to students who have difficulty learning. The chapter begins with factors and characteristics that interfere with math performance and then presents teaching perspectives that provide general guidelines for teaching math. This presentation is followed by teaching suggestions for prenumber skills, numbers and place value, computation, fractions, and measurement. The chapter concludes with a discussion of strategies for teaching problem solving and approaches to increasing math performance.

FOCUS Question 1. What characteristics are common to students who exhibit deficits in math skills, how can these characteristics influence math ability, and what should teachers consider when planning instruction for these students?

Factors Influencing Math Ability

Kosc (1981) identified four variables that are significant influences on mathematics ability:

1. *Psychological factors* such as intelligence/cognitive ability, distractibility, and cognitive learning strategies
2. *Education factors* such as the quality and amount of instructional intervention across the range of areas of mathematics (e.g., computation, measurement, time, and problem solving)
3. *Personality factors* such as persistence, self-concept, and attitudes toward mathematics
4. *Neuropsychological patterns* such as perception and neurological trauma

Considering these four factors, it is not surprising that many students with learning and behavior problems have difficulty in math. Interestingly, though students with learning disabilities demonstrate significant difficulties with math, they do not report lower self-perceptions of their math skills than those of average-achieving students (Montague and van Garderen, 2003). Because much of their educational intervention has focused on computation, they often have limited exposure to other elements of math, including measurement, time, and practical problem solving. Many students with learning and behavior problems struggle with applying computation skills to everyday math problems. Persistence and motivation to succeed are associated with good math performance and many students with learning and behavior problems lack these qualities. The fourth factor that was identified, unique neuropsychological patterns, characterizes many students with learning and behavior problems.

The following six difficulties may interfere with the mathematics performance of a student with learning disabilities (Ginsburg, 1997):

1. *Perceptual skills.* Students with learning disabilities often have difficulties with spatial relationships, distances, size relationships, and sequencing, which interfere with such math skills as measurement, estimation, problem solving, and geometry. Students with weak perceptual skills will need practice in estimating size and distance and then in verifying estimates with direct measurement.

2. *Perseveration.* Some students may have difficulty in mentally shifting from one task or operation to the next. This can interfere with their performance on problems that require multiple operations or on applied mathematics problems that generally require several steps. Teachers can provide cues to illustrate the number of steps that are involved in each operation. After the students have mastered the skills for two operations (e.g., addition and subtraction), teachers can provide opportunities to practice both types of problems.

3. *Language.* Students may have difficulty understanding such mathematical concepts as first, last, next, greater than, and less than. In teaching arithmetic, a teacher's instructions should be precise. Presenting unnecessary concepts and rules can confuse students and distract them from concentrating on the concept being presented. Demonstrating how to perform problems and guiding students in completing the work independently are effective instructional practices. Give plenty of examples, and allow students to provide examples to demonstrate their understanding of the concepts.

4. *Reasoning.* Reasoning is often difficult because it requires a great deal of abstract thinking. Teachers should use concrete materials and real-life application whenever possible. After students understand a mathematical concept at an automatic level, the teacher can introduce tasks that ask students to think through the process, explain the rationale, and apply reason. Some students acquire "bugs" (Ginsburg, 1997) in their thinking that have led them to develop faulty ideas about how practices in mathematics work. These bugs need to be "reprogrammed" so that the students can understand the correct operation.

5. *Memory.* Many students with learning and behavior problems have difficulty remembering information. Teachers can assist students who have memory problems by reducing the amount of new information they are required to learn, increasing the number of exposures to new material, and giving the students opportunities to verbalize and demonstrate their ability with new material.

6. *Symbolism difficulty.* Many students with learning disabilities have a difficult time understanding mathematics symbols, sometimes even

gaining the vaguest idea of what the symbols mean. These students may know the rote behavior for what they are supposed to do but cannot tell you the meaning or use of such symbols as equals, subtract, and multiply.

Johnson and Myklebust (1967) referred to students with dyscalculia—poor skills in numerical calculating—as demonstrating such social difficulties as disorientation, deficiencies in self-help skills, and poor organization. Rourke's (1993) research supports the finding that social deficits are associated with individuals who have good reading and poor math skills. Recently, Barnes, Wilkinson, Khemani, Boudousquie, Dennis, and Fletcher (2006) reported that students with math disabilities are likely to have problems with both math facts and math procedures.

In a study by Badian and Ghublikian (1983), students with significantly lower math than reading skills (low math) were compared with two other groups, students with significantly higher math skills than reading skills and students who had similar math and reading skills. The results indicated that the low math group demonstrated lower scores overall on the following abilities:

- Paying sustained attention
- Working in a careful and organized manner
- Accepting responsibility

These findings partially explain why students with learning and behavior problems have difficulty with mathematics. Students with learning disabilities often have difficulty applying learning strategies and are frequently characterized as having perceptual and neurological complications. Students with emotional disturbances may have greater difficulties with mathematics than with other subjects because it requires persistence and concentration. Students with mild mental retardation have more difficulty with mathematics than students with learning disabilities do (Parmar, Cawley, and Miller, 1994). Furthermore, adolescents with learning disabilities perform in many areas of mathematics, such as multiplication, in ways that are similar to those of much younger non-learning-disabled students (Barrouillet, Fayol, and Lathuliere, 1997).

In summary, students with math disabilities are less at risk than are students with both math and reading disabilities. Students with math disabilities often have other related difficulties, such as problems with memory, difficulty in considering math problems from a "reasonable" perspective, poor calculation skills, number reversals, and difficulty understanding operation signs (Bryant, Bryant, and Hammill, 2000; Bryant, Hartman, and Kim, 2003).

Teaching Considerations

Teachers need to consider a number of factors when developing math programs for students with special needs, regardless of the age or program.

Comprehensive Programming

Mr. Noppe was not happy with his math program. He taught students in special education at an elementary school, and 90 percent of his math program consisted of teaching math computation. In discussing his math program with a coteacher, he said, "I know I need to include more than just computation, but I'm not sure what else I should be teaching. I guess I should ask the students to apply some of their math computation. Next year, I want to concentrate on my math program and make it more comprehensive."

Students need to be taught and be involved in a full range of mathematics skills, including basic facts, operations, word problems, mathematical reasoning, time, measurement, fractions, and math application. Teachers should not focus their entire mathematics program on math facts and the four basic operations of addition, subtraction, multiplication, and division. The National Council of Teachers of Mathematics (NCTM) has issued standards for a comprehensive mathematics program. Many special education teachers of students with learning and behavior problems report that they have very little knowledge of the NCTM standards (Maccini and Gagnon, 2002). These standards (listed in Apply the Concept 11.1) can be useful to teachers as they design curriculum and instruction for students with special needs.

Remember that a relevant feature of a comprehensive math program is to teach concepts and vocabulary—to make sure that students understand the language of mathematics. Students with disabilities are less likely to know the relevant concepts related to mathematics learning. Thus, when they are participating in problem solving in real-life contexts, they may not understand key words such as *perimeter* or *diameter*; younger students may not understand words like *minus, half,* or *percentage.*

Individualization

Sanjay and Claudia, the two students described at the beginning of this chapter, have very different

Apply the Concept 11.1

NCTM Standards 2000

Instructional programs from prekindergarten through grade 12 in the following areas should enable all students to use the following concepts:

1. Number and operations
   - Understand numbers, ways of representing numbers, relationships among numbers, and number systems
   - Understand meanings of operations and how they relate to one another
   - Compute fluently and make reasonable estimates

2. Algebra
   - Understand patterns, relations, and functions
   - Represent and analyze mathematical solutions and structures using algebraic symbols
   - Use mathematical models to represent and understand quantitative relationships
   - Analyze change in various contexts

3. Geometry
   - Analyze characteristics and properties of two- and three-dimensional geometric shapes, and develop mathematical arguments about geometric relationships
   - Specify locations and describe spatial relationships using coordinate geometry and other representational systems
   - Apply transformations and use symmetry to analyze mathematical situations
   - Use visualization, spatial reasoning, and geometric modeling to solve problems

4. Measurement
   - Understand measurable attributes of objects and the units, systems, and processes of measurement
   - Apply appropriate techniques, tools, and formulas to determine measurements

5. Data analysis and probability
   - Formulate questions that can be addressed with data, and collect, organize, and display relevant data to answer them
   - Select and use appropriate statistical methods to analyze data
   - Develop and evaluate inferences and predictions that are based on data
   - Understand and apply basic concepts of probability

6. Problem solving
   - Build new mathematical knowledge through problem solving
   - Solve problems that arise in mathematics and in other contexts
   - Apply and adapt a variety of appropriate strategies to solve problems
   - Monitor and reflect on the process of mathematical problem solving

7. Reasoning and proof
   - Recognize reasoning and proof as fundamental aspects of mathematics
   - Make and investigate mathematical conjectures
   - Develop and evaluate mathematical arguments and proofs
   - Select and use various types of reasoning and methods of proof

8. Communication
   - Organize and consolidate their mathematical thinking through communication
   - Communicate their mathematical thinking coherently and clearly to peers, teachers, and others
   - Analyze and evaluate the mathematical thinking and strategies of others
   - Use the language of mathematics to express mathematical ideas precisely

9. Connections
   - Recognize and use connections among mathematical ideas
   - Understand how mathematical ideas interconnect and build on one another to produce a coherent whole
   - Recognize and apply mathematics in contexts outside of mathematics

10. Representation
    - Create and use representations to organize, record, and communicate mathematical ideas
    - Select, apply, and translate among mathematical representations to solve problems
    - Use representations to model and interpret physical, social, and mathematical phenomena

Source: National Council of Teachers of Mathematics, *Principles and Standards for School Mathematics* (2000). Available online at www.nctm.org/standards.

needs in math. Individualization in math programming refers not just to the task but also to the way in which the task is learned (Carnine, 1991). Some students learn math facts through rote drill, whereas other students learn math facts by associating them with known facts. We often assume that an individualized program means that a student works alone; but individualization actually means that the program is designed to meet the individual needs of the student. It is often beneficial for the students to work in small groups to learn new skills and rehearse and practice problems. In addition, small groups that focus on solving the same problem can include students of different abilities, particularly when the teacher creates a cooperative environment for solving the problems and allowing the students to learn from each other.

Correction and Feedback

Receiving immediate feedback about performance is particularly important in math. If students are performing an operation incorrectly, they should be told which parts are correct and which parts are incorrect. Showing students patterns in their errors is an important source of feedback. Students also need to learn to check their own work and monitor their errors. Remember, feedback includes pointing out improvements as well as needed changes.

Students in Ms. Wong's math class were given a worksheet to practice their new skill of using dollar signs and decimal points in their subtraction problems. Ms. Wong told the students to do only the first problem. After they completed the problem, they were to check it and make any necessary changes. If they thought that their answer to the problem was correct, they were to write a small *c* next to their answer; if not, they were to write a small *i* for incorrect next to the answer. They were also to indicate with a check mark where they thought they had made a mistake. Ms. Wong moved quickly from student to student, checking their work. Students who had the first problem correct were given encouragement and directions for the rest of the problems. "Good for you. You got the first problem correct, and you had the confidence, after checking it, to call it correct. I see you remembered to use both a decimal point and a dollar sign. After you finish the first row, including checking your problems, meet with another student to see how your answers compare. Do you know what to do if there is a discrepancy in your answers? That's right. You'll need to check each other's problem to locate the error." When a student solved the problem incorrectly, Ms. Wong said, "Tell aloud how you did this. Start from the beginning, and as you think of what you're doing, say it aloud so I can follow." Ms. Wong finds that students often notice their own errors, or she will identify some faulty thinking by the students that keeps them from correctly solving the problem.

Alternative Approaches to Instruction

If a student is not succeeding with one approach or program, the teacher should not hesitate to make a change. Despite years of research, no single method of mathematics instruction has been proven to be significantly better than others. This includes using a range of formats such as textbooks, workbooks, math stations, and manipulatives.

Applied Mathematics

Concrete materials and real-life applications of math problems make math relevant and increase the likelihood that students will transfer skills to applied settings such as home and work. Students continue to make progress in math throughout their school years. Emphasis needs to be on problem solving rather than on rote drill and practice activities (Cawley and Miller, 1989).

The term *situated cognition* refers to the principle that students will learn complex ideas and concepts in the contexts in which they occur in day-to-day life. Students need many opportunities to practice what they learn in the ways in which they will eventually use what they learn. This is a critical way to promote the generalization of mathematical skills. For example, when teaching measurement, a teacher can give students opportunities to measure rooms for carpet, determine the mileage to specific locations, and so on.

When Ms. Wong's students were able to successfully use dollar signs and decimals in subtraction, she gave each of them a mock checkbook, which included checks and a ledger for keeping their balance. In each of their checkbooks she wrote the amount of $100.00. During math class for the rest of the month, she gave students "money" for their checkbook when their assignments were completed and their behavior was appropriate. She asked them to write her checks when they wanted supplies (pencils, erasers, chalk) or privileges (going to the bathroom, free time, meeting briefly with a friend). Students were asked to maintain their balance in their checkbooks. Students were penalized $5.00 for each mistake the "bank" located in the checkbook ledgers at the end of the week.

Generalization

Generalization, or transfer of learning, needs to be taught. As most experienced teachers know, students often can perform skills in the special education room but are unable to perform them in a regular classroom. To facilitate the transfer of learning between settings, teachers must provide opportunities to practice skills by using a wide range of materials such as textbooks, workbooks, manipulatives (e.g., blocks, rods, tokens), and word problems. Teachers also need to systematically reduce the amount of help they provide students in solving problems. When students are first learning a math concept or operation, teachers provide a lot of assistance in performing it correctly. As students become more skillful, they need less assistance.

When Ms. Wong's students were able to correctly apply subtraction with dollars and decimals in their checkbooks, she asked students to perform similar problems for homework. Ms. Wong realized that before she could be satisfied that the students had mastered the skill, they needed to perform it outside of her classroom and without her assistance.

Participation in Goal Selection

Allowing students to participate in setting their own goals for mathematics is likely to increase their commitment to achieving goals. Students who selected their own math goals improved their performance on math tasks over time more than did those students whose math goals were assigned to them by a teacher (Fuchs, Bahr, and Rieth, 1989). Even very young children can participate in selecting their overall math goals and can keep progress charts on how well they are performing.

Discovery versus Didactic Instruction

Many teachers wonder whether and how they should use more discovery-oriented approaches to teaching mathematics. On the basis of the available literature (Dixon, Carnine, Lee, Wallin, and Chard, 1998), very little evidence favors discovery learning for mathematics unless it is in the application of already known principles. Students are more likely to be successful if teachers use a guided discovery mode or didactic mode.

The National Research Council (NRC) has examined U.S. mathematics education from kindergarten through graduate study (National Research Council, 1989). This study was conducted jointly with the Mathematical Sciences Education Board, Board on Mathematical Sciences, Committee on the Mathematical Sciences in the Year 2000. Their extensive report not only outlines problems in mathematics education but also charts a course for remedying them. The suggestions that relate to students with learning and behavior problems include:

- Do not alter curricular goals to differentiate students; instead, change the type and speed of instruction.

- Make mathematics education student-centered, not an authoritarian model that is teacher-focused.
- Encourage students to explore, verbalize ideas, and understand that mathematics is part of their life.
- Provide daily opportunities for students to apply mathematics and to work problems that are related to their daily lives. Instill in students the importance and need for mathematics.
- Teach mathematics so that students understand when an exact answer is necessary and when an estimate is sufficient.
- Teach problem solving, computer application, and use of calculators to all students.
- Teach students to understand probability, data analysis, and statistics as they relate to daily decision making, model building, operations research, and applications of computers.
- Shift from performing primarily paper-and-pencil activities to use of calculators, computers, and other applied materials.

The NRC (2001) indicates that "mathematical proficiency" is the essential goal of instruction. What is "mathematical proficiency"? It is what any student needs in order to acquire mathematical understanding. The NRC describes five interwoven strands that comprise proficiency. Consider how you are integrating these strands into your instruction. Also consider how you might determine whether the students you teach are making progress along each of these strands.

1. *Conceptual understanding* refers to understanding mathematic concepts and operations.
2. *Procedural fluency* is being able to accurately and efficiently conduct operations and mathematics practices.
3. *Strategic competence* is the ability to formulate and conduct mathematical problems.
4. *Adaptive reasoning* refers to thinking about, explaining, and justifying mathematical work.
5. *Productive disposition* is appreciating the useful and positive influences of understanding mathematics and how ones disposition toward mathematics influences success.

See Apply the Concept 11.2 for suggested instructional practices.

It is particularly important for teachers to design mathematics programs that enhance learning for all students, especially those with diverse cultural or linguistic backgrounds. See Spotlight on Diversity for suggestions on how to do this.

Apply the Concept 11.2

Instructional Practices for Mathematics

On the basis of several recent syntheses of mathematics instruction for students with learning and behavior problems (Baker, Gersten, and Lee, 2002; Cawley, Parmar, Yan, and Miller, 1998; Dixon et al., 1998; Rivera, Smith, Goodwin, and Bryant, 1998; Xin and Jitendra, 1999), we recommend the following 10 instructional practices:

1. *Use data to make decisions about instruction and progress.* Teachers and/or students should use data to determine if instructional changes are needed. The links to changes in instruction are central to the use of data-based decision making.
2. *Involve peers* in working together to practice computation and word problems. In addition to practice, peers can provide support by correcting answers and charting data for progress monitoring.
3. *Inform parents* about students' progress and success in math so that they can enhance interest

and practice in mathematics at home. Provide parents with information about students success in mathematics so that they can recognize those accomplishments at home.

4. *Instructional routines* that focus on cognitive behavioral techniques benefit students with learning and behavior problems and engage them in the learning process.
5. *Instructional design features* are effective ways to teach students to differentiate problem types, use a wide range of examples, separate confusing elements, and provide opportunities for students to reach performance levels before introducing more new principles.
6. *Teach students the principles of mathematics to mastery* and then move to more advanced principles. Many students with special needs are given the same instructional math curriculum (e.g., subtraction with regroup-

ing) from second through ninth grades.

7. *Establish realistic goals* for progress in mathematics with students by providing information to students about their present performance and what they need to learn.
8. *Monitor progress* on a weekly basis through graphing or visual display so that students can chart and see how they are performing. Make adjustments in teaching, materials, grouping, or other features of instruction if students are not making adequate progress.
9. *Provide evidence* that hard work and effort yield good outcomes and progress. Students can also learn to reinforce themselves for setting and meeting goals in mathematics.
10. *Computer-assisted instruction* can provide an effective way to learn arithmetic computation and mathematical problem solving.

Spotlight on Diversity

Considerations for Students Who Are Culturally and Linguistically Diverse: Enhancing Skills in Mathematics

An essential part of a successful mathematics program is providing instructional practices and assignments that facilitate learning in mathematics for all students. To do so, you must consider the needs of students from diverse cultures and language backgrounds. Here are some suggestions to consider:

- Continually consider ways to infuse the various cultures of students in your classroom

and the cultures of students not represented in your mathematics curriculum. Students will appreciate, feel accepted, and learn a great deal about other cultures when cultural diversity is a part of their daily learning routines.

- Develop story problems that reflect events from diverse cultures. Encourage students to design story problems that are reflective of the happenings of other cultures.
- Read books about families from other cultures. Use the stories and data from these books to design story problems.
- In designing mathematical problems, use data from newspapers or magazines that provide information about individuals or events representing other cultures.
- Design mathematical studies that address real problems of individuals or groups who

are not from the mainstream culture. Assign these studies to individuals, students in pairs, or small groups.

- Ensure that goals are challenging for all students and provide adequate support for their participation and effort. These challenges should provide opportunities for success, with infrequent failure.

- Model an enthusiastic and positive attitude about appreciating and learning more about the cultures and languages of other groups.

- Link students' accomplishments to their hard work and effort. Remind students that they performed a task well because they worked hard, persisted, reread, rethought, revisualized, modeled, and so forth (Mercer and Mercer, 2005).

- Use manipulatives to concretely explore the meaning of mathematical symbols and problems. Manipulatives enhance learning and provide an easy means of crossing potential language barriers.

- Use culturally relevant materials as a springboard for mathematics learning. The ways in which mathematics are practiced in various cultures, mathematical games that are played, and the use of mathematics cross-culturally can be embedded into mathematics instruction.

- Use the languages of the students throughout the instruction. Ask students to provide the word that means the same as "_____" and then use both words when referring to the term. Encourage all of the students in the room to use and apply multiple terms that represent the languages of the students in the class. Communicate to students that you value their home language.

- Use technology to enhance learning and understanding of mathematical principles (Woodward, 1995). Computers provide a language that should be available to all students. Encourage expertise on the computer and provide multiple opportunities to practice math skills on the computer.

FOCUS Question **2.** How is assessment used in mathematics, and what is CBM? What are some examples of several types of assessment techniques that can be used to determine number sense in young children?

Assessing and Progress Monitoring Mathematics Performance

Progress Monitoring

Mr. Sebeny is a first-year special education teacher. He is fortunate to work in a middle school with three other special education teachers who have been at the school for several years and are used to team teaching. They've asked Mr. Sebeny whether he would be comfortable teaching all of the special education students mathematics. Because he is good at mathematics, Mr. Sebeny thought that this arrangement would give him an opportunity to learn to teach one content area very well. He quickly realized that his first task would be to determine the mathematics performance level of all of his students. Mr. Sebeny knows that he needs to select a measure that will tell him what students know and don't know and how they compare with other students in their grade.

There are many ways in which Mr. Sebeny could obtain the information he needs to develop instructional programs for his students. One of the first questions Mr. Sebeny needs to address is whether he has the time to use an individually administered assessment or whether he needs to use a group-administered measure. For students with special needs, individually administered measures yield the most information for teachers. Second, Mr. Sebeny needs to determine whether the measure is designed for students in the age range of the students he is teaching. Figure 11.1 provides a list of mathematics measures, states whether they are group or individually administered, and lists the age range for which they are appropriate. Figure 11.2 provides a list of progress monitoring measures for math.

How can teachers best make decisions about whether students are learning mathematics effectively? How can teachers monitor the progress of their students so that they can document the rate and progress they are making in mathematics? Bryant and Rivera (1997) have stated that "one would be hard-pressed to find a more effective technique than curriculum-based measurement (CBM) for directing, monitoring, and redirecting remedial efforts" (p. 63). There is considerable and growing evidence that when teachers use CBM to monitor their students' progress and to adjust their instruction accordingly, students

FIGURE 11.1

Measures to Assess Mathematics Performance

Test Name	How Administered	Age/Grade Appropriate	Other Information
Comprehensive Math Assessment	Group	Grades 2–8	Based largely on the National Council of Teachers of Mathematics' critical elements in mathematics instruction
Diagnostic Achievement Battery	Individual	Most grade levels	Provides normative data on student performance but not specific information for designing strengths and weaknesses
Wide Range Achievement Test	Individual or group	Most grade levels	Provides normative data on student performance but difficult to identify students' needs for instruction
Woodcock Johnson III Tests of Achievement	Individual	Most grade levels	Provides normative data on student performance but may not provide adequate information for designing instruction
Test of Early Mathematics Ability	Individual	Ages 3–9	Provides information to assist with designing and monitoring instruction
BRIGANCE Diagnostic Comprehensive Inventory of Basic Skills—Revised	Individual	Prekindergarten–grade 9	Provides information to assist with designing and monitoring instruction
Comprehensive Mathematical Ability Test	Individual	Grades 1–12	Provides information to assist with designing instruction
Key Math—Revised	Individual	Grades 1–12	Provides information to assist with designing instruction
Test of Mathematical Abilities	Individual	Grades 3–12	Provides information to assist with designing instruction
Math—Level Indicator: A Quick Group Math Placement Test	Group	Grades 4–12	Takes approximately 30 minutes, and because it is group administered, it quickly determines the performance levels of a large group of students. The problems are based on the NCTM standards.

Progress Monitoring

make gains at much more rapid rates than when CBM is not used.

What is CBM for math? Simply stated, it is a way of documenting the extent to which the student is learning the critical elements in the curriculum that you have targeted. To illustrate, let's consider the case of Ricky, a fifth-grade boy with learning and attention problems, who has been struggling with math. His goals for the next 10 weeks are to know all subtraction facts up to 100 automatically and quickly, to be able to do addition with regrouping word problems, and to be able to appropriately use basic measurement terms such as *inches, feet,* and *yards.* Here is how Ricky and his teacher use CBM.

Ricky's teacher pretested on all 100 subtraction facts in random order, timing him while he completed the worksheet. She then showed Ricky how to graph his performance in two ways: by graphing how long it took him to complete the worksheet and by graphing the number of correct problems. Together, they agreed that Ricky would take a version of this test once every week to determine whether he could decrease the amount of time he needed to complete the test and increase the number of problems he got correct. Together, they established a schedule of work assignments and practice sessions. Figure 11.3 shows the graph that Ricky kept.

Ricky's teacher followed a similar procedure with measurement and problem solving to determine what Ricky knew and what he needed to know. Then the teacher established a simple graph that Ricky could complete to monitor his progress. Ricky and his teacher frequently discussed Ricky's progress and modified assignments and instruction to facilitate his learning.

FIGURE 11.2

Progress Monitoring Measures for Math

Test Name	Concepts Addressed	Grade	Websites	Forms
Monitoring Basic	Math computation	Grade 1 and above	www.proedinc.com	30 forms per grade
Skills Progress	Math concepts			
PASeries Math	Numbers Operations Geometry Algebra Data analysis Measurement	Grades 3–12	www.paseries.com	6 forms per grade
Star Math	Computation Application Concepts	Grades 1–12	www.renlearn.com	Unlimited forms
Yearly ProgressPro	Curriculum-based measurement	Grade 1 and above	Mhdigitallearning.com	13 forms per grade
AIMSweb Systems	Oral counting Number identification Quantity discrimination Missing number Basic skill areas	Grades K–8	www.aimsweb.com	33–50 forms for each construct

Teachers may want to consider using a computerized application of CBM procedures. These are available for mathematics as well as spelling and reading (Fuchs, Hamlett, and Fuchs, 1990).

One promising practice for monitoring the progress of young children in mathematics and determining children who have mathematics difficulties or disabilities is by assessing their number sense. *Number sense* refers to whether a student's understanding of a number and of its use and meaning is flexible and fully developed. One definition of number sense is "a child's fluidity and flexibility with numbers, the sense of what numbers mean, and an ability to perform mental mathematics and to look at the world and make comparisons" (Gersten and Chard, 1999, p. 19). In terms of assessment, number sense is particularly important because it assists teachers in determining which students currently have mathematical difficulty and even serves as a predictor for students who may have learning difficulties in the future.

Several counting measures can be used as effective screening tools for students with mathematical difficulties or to monitor students' progress in this area (Clarke and Shinn, 2004):

1. *Count to 20.* This is a beginning-level skill requiring students to count to 20 while the teacher records which numbers were known in the correct sequence and which ones were not.
2. *Count by 3 and 6.* This skill requires students to count from a predetermined number, such as 5, in increments of 3 or 6. The teacher records the accuracy and speed with which the students perform this task.
3. *Count by 2, 5, or 10.* This skill requires student to count by the designated number—2, 5, or 10—in increments up to a specified number, such as 20 for 2s, 30 for 5s, or 100 for 10s. The teacher records the accuracy with which students perform this task.

Clarke and Shinn (2004) and Fuchs and colleagues (2007) describe measures that can be used

FIGURE 11.3

Ricky's Progress-Monitoring Chart

Ricky's teacher developed three versions of a subtraction fact sheet that had 30 problems representing the 100 subtraction facts he was learning. Once a week, Ricky was timed on one version of the test and the number of problems correct were counted. Ricky kept the following two charts to demonstrate his progress.

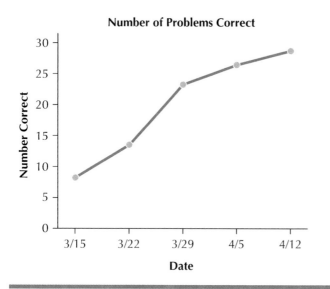

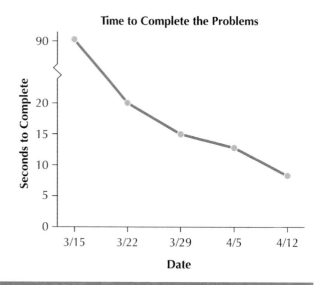

to determine students' understanding of number. These include the following five:

1. *Number identification.* In this task, students must orally identify numbers between 0 and 20 when these are presented randomly on a piece of paper.
2. *Number writing.* Students are asked to write the number when given a number orally between 1 and 20.
3. *Quantity discrimination.* This task requires students to name which of two numbers is the larger (or smaller).
4. *Missing number.* Students are provided with a string of numbers and are asked to identify which number is missing.
5. *Computation.* Students are asked to complete computations that are representative of their grade level. Students have two minutes to complete as many problems as possible.

How Effective Are Test Accommodations in Mathematics for Students with Disabilities?

The idea behind test accommodations is that individuals with disabilities profit more from them than individuals without disabilities—thus, the test accommodations are more responsive to their individual needs. Elbaum (2007) reports that when mathematics tests are read aloud to students with disabilities and their performance on these tests are compared with students without disabilities, the read-aloud condition is more helpful to elementary students with disabilities than elementary students without disabilities. However, the reverse is true for secondary students with disabilities whose improved performance with accommodations is overall lower than for students without disabilities.

Response to Intervention (RTI) and Math

Response to Intervention (RTI) has been applied most frequently to the academic area of early reading. However, there are currently schools and districts using RTI in mathematics as well. How can RTI be used in math? Many of the same principles that apply to the use of RTI in reading also apply to math. These include:

- *Screening.* Students can be screened to determine if they have math problems in numeracy, math calculations, and/or problem solving.

- *Evidence-based math.* Schools and districts can ensure that math instruction for all students is based on the best research available.
- *Interventions.* When students have difficulties that are not adequately addressed through the evidence-based math program in the classroom, additional instruction through short-term interventions (10–20 weeks) can be implemented.
- *Progress monitoring.* Students' progress in the classroom and in interventions can be documented to ensure that they are staying on track and meeting curriculum benchmarks.

In summary, assessment is an important part of the instructional routine. Teachers use assessment to assist them in determining what students know and what they need to know. Assessments can also tell teachers how students compare to others at their same age or grade level. Finally, appropriate assessments allow teachers to monitor students' progress and to make effective instructional decisions that will improve the students' performance.

FOCUS Question 3. What are the prenumber skills students need to progress in arithmetic?

Prenumber Skills

Many students come to school with few experiences that allow them to develop important prenumber skills, such as one-to-one correspondence, classification, and seriation. This section focuses on these important skills.

One-to-One Correspondence

Matching one object with another is a core skill in any mathematics curriculum. It eventually leads the student to a better understanding of numeration and representation. Ancient humans used one-to-one correspondence when they kept track of how many bags of grain they borrowed from a neighbor by placing a rock in a pile to represent each one. One-to-one correspondence is used today when we set a table, one place setting for each person; go to the theater, one ticket and seat for each person; and distribute paper in the classroom, one piece for each student. Activities for teaching one-to-one correspondence include the following:

- Use every opportunity to teach students the relationship between number words (e.g., *one*,

two, three, four) and objects. For example, "Here are two paintbrushes: one for you and one for Madju." "There are five students in our group, and we need one chair for each student."
- Use familiar objects such as toy cars or blocks, and give a designated number (e.g., three) to each student. Pointing to the objects, ask students to place one block next to each of the objects. "You have one block here, and you placed one block next to it. You have a second block here, and you placed a block next to it. And you have a third block here, and you placed a block next to it."
- Give the student a set of cards with numbers that the student recognizes. Ask the student to put the correct number of blocks on top of each number card. Reverse the task by giving objects to students and asking them to put the correct number card next to the objects.

Classification

Classification is the ability to group or sort objects on the basis of one or more common properties. For example, classification can be done by size, color, shape, texture, or design. Classification is an important prenumber skill because it focuses on common properties of objects and requires students to reduce large numbers of objects to smaller groups. Most students are naturally interested in sorting, ordering, and classifying. A sample of activities for teaching classification includes the following:

- Ask students to sort articles into groups. Ask them which rule they used for sorting their articles.
- Give each student an empty egg carton and a box of small articles. Ask the students to sort the articles according to one property (e.g., color). Now ask them to think of another way in which they can sort the articles (e.g., size, texture).
- Using an assortment of articles, ask a student to classify several of the articles into one group. Other students then try to guess the property that qualifies the articles for the group.
- Students can use pictures for sorting tasks. Animals, foods, plants, toys, and people can all be sorted by different properties.
- Board games and bingo games can be played by sorting or classifying shapes, colors, or pictures.

Seriation

Seriation is similar to classification in that it depends on the recognition of common attributes of objects. With seriation, ordering depends on the degree to which the object possesses the attribute. For example, seriation can occur by length, height, color, or weight. A sample of activities for teaching seriation might include the following:

- Give students some objects of varied length, and ask the students to put the objects in order from shortest to longest.
- Ask students to stack their books from largest to smallest.
- Using a peg with varied sizes of rings, ask students to put the rings on the peg from largest to smallest.
- Fill jars of the same size with varied amounts of sand or water, and ask students to put them in order.

FOCUS Question **4.** What are several numeration concepts?

Math Concepts and Computation

Numeration and Place Value

Teachers and parents often assume that children understand numerals because they can count or name them. Understanding numerals is an essential basic concept; many children who have trouble with computation and word problems are missing numeral concepts. For example, Nadia's beginning experiences with math were positive. She had learned to read and write numerals and even to perform basic addition and subtraction facts. However, when Nadia was asked to perform problems that involved addition with regrouping, she demonstrated that she had very little knowledge of numerals and their meaning (as shown here) and thus quickly fell behind her peers in math.

$$\begin{array}{ccc} 48 & 37 & 68 \\ +26 & +55 & +17 \\ \hline 614 & 812 & 715 \end{array}$$

Understanding numeration and place value is necessary in the following areas:

- *Progress in computation.* Like Nadia, many students fail to make adequate progress in math

because they lack understanding of numerals and place value.
- *Estimation* (e.g., "number sense"). Many students with learning difficulties in math do not have a sense of how much $1.00 is, what it means to have 35 eggs, or "about" how much 24 and 35 equals. They cannot check their answers by looking at problems and determining which answers could not be correct because the answer doesn't make "sense."
- *Reducing conceptual errors.* Students who understand the meaning of the numerals 43 and 25 would be less likely to make the following error:

$$\begin{array}{c} 43 \\ -25 \\ \hline 22 \end{array}$$

- *Understanding place value.* Students who know the meaning of the numeral 28 are going to have far less difficulty understanding the value of the 2 and the 8. Students need to understand that the 2 in 28 represents two 10s and the 8 represents eight 1s.
- *Understanding regrouping.* Regrouping errors, such as those below, are less likely to occur if a student understands numeration.

$$\begin{array}{ccc} 39 & 56 & 41 \\ +27 & -18 & -24 \\ \hline 516 & 42 & 23 \end{array}$$

- *Application of math computation to everyday problems.* Students who do not understand the real meaning of numerals have difficulty applying computation to everyday problems.
- *Understanding zero.* Students need to understand that 0 (zero) has more meaning than just "nothing." For example, in the number 40, they need to understand the meaning of the 0 as a place holder.

Readiness for Numeration: Seventeen Concepts

Engelhardt, Ashlock, and Wiebe (1984) identified 17 numeration readiness concepts that can be assessed through paper-and-pencil assessment and interview. A list of the behaviors that correspond to each concept, along with examples of how each concept can be assessed, follows.

Concept 1: Cardinality. The face value of each of the 10 digits 0 through 9 tells how many.

1. Identify sets with like numerousness (1 through 9). Circle the groups with the same number of *x*s.

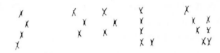

2. Identify, write, and name the numeral that corresponds to the numerousness of a set (1 through 9). Circle the numeral showing how many mice there are.

How many mice are there?

3   2   6   4   9

3. Construct sets with a given numerousness (1 through 9). "Draw five dots."
4. Recognize sets of one to five without counting. Place from one to five objects behind a book. Say to the students, "As soon as I move this book, I want you to tell me how many objects there are." Without counting, the students should tell you how many objects are in the group.
5. Represent and name the numerousness of the empty set (zero). "The box has 2 hats in it. Make 0 hats in the circle."

Concept 2: Grouping Pattern. When representing quantity, objects are grouped into sets of a specified size (base) and sets of sets.

1. Form sets of 10 from a random set of objects or marks. Circle the *x*s to make as many groups of 10 as possible.

xxxxxxxxxxxxx   xxxxx   xxxxxxx

xxxxxxxxxxxxx   xxxxx   xxxxxxx

2. Construct appropriate groups to show how many. Give students about 125 Popsicle sticks and rubber bands. Say, "Bundle these sticks so that it will be easy to tell how many there are."

Concept 3: Place Value. The position of a digit in a multidigit numeral determines its value (places are assigned values).

1. Given two multidigit numerals with the same digits but in different orders, identify the position of the digits as distinguishing the two numerals. How are 145 and 154 alike? How are they different?
2. Explain that the value of a digit in a multidigit number is dependent on its position. Using the number 5, place it in each column and ask, "How does the number change? How much is it worth?"

100s	10s	1s

Concept 4: Place Value (Base 10). A power of 10 is assigned to each position or place (the place values).

1. Identify, name, and show the values for each place in a multidigit numeral. Show the number 1,829 and say, "What is the name of the place the number 8 is in?"
2. Select the place having a given value. Show the number 6,243 and say, "Circle or point to the number in the thousands place."

Concept 5: One Digit per Place. Only one digit is written in a position or place.

1. Identify and name which numerals (digits) can be assigned to a place. Say to the students, "Tell me the numbers that can be written in the tens place."
2. State that no more than one digit should be written in a place or position. Then ask, "What's wrong with these problems?"

85	27	13
+39	+35	+48
1114	512	511

3. Rewrite or restate a nonstandard multidigit numeral (or its representation) as a numeral with only one digit in each place or position. Say to the students, "Write the number for this:"

10s	1s
5	4

Concept 6: Places—Linear/Ordered. The places (and their values) in a multidigit (whole-number) numeral are linearly arranged and ordered from right to left.

1. Identify the smaller-to-larger ordering of place values in a multidigit numeral. Show the number 6,666 to the students and say, "Underline the 6 that is worth the most, and put an *x* through the 6 that is worth the least."
2. Describe how the place values are ordered. Show the number 8,888 to the students, and ask, "How can you tell which 8 is worth more?"
3. State or demonstrate that the places in a multidigit numeral are linearly arranged. Say to the students, "Rewrite this problem correctly."

```
    7   1
        2   4
    6   3   8
+       0
```

Concept 7: Decimal Point. The decimal point in a decimal fraction indicates the location of the units (ones) and tenths places.

1. Given a decimal fraction, identify the digit in the units (ones) place. Show the number 29.04 to the students, and say, "Circle the number in the ones place."
2. Given juxtaposed digits and a digit's value, identify and place the decimal point to show the appropriate multidigit numeral. Show the number 284 to the students, and say, "Place the decimal in the correct place to show 4 tenths, 2 tens, and 8 ones."
3. State the meaning (function) of the decimal point.

Concept 8: Place Relation/Regrouping. Each place in a multidigit numeral has a value 10 times greater than that of the place to its right and one-tenth the value of the place to its left (place relationships and regrouping).

1. Describe the relationships between the values of two adjacent places in a multidigit number. Show the number 222 to the students, and say, "How does the first 2 in the number compare with the second 2?"
2. Express the value of a multidigit numeral in several ways. Give the following problem to the students: 1 hundred, 8 tens, and 6 ones can also be expressed as _____ tens and _____ ones.

Concept 9: Implied Zeros. All numerals have an infinite number of juxtaposed places, each occupied by an expressed or implied digit. In places to

the left of nonzero digits in numerals for whole numbers, zeros are understood; in places to the right of nonzero digits and the decimal point in decimal fractions, zeros are understood.

1. Name the digit in any given place for any multidigit numeral. Tell the students to rewrite each numeral and show a digit in each place.

	1000s	100s	10s	1s
683				
27				
79				

2. Rewrite a given numeral with as few digits as needed. Tell the students to cross out the zeros that are not needed.

0301　　004
1010　　105

3. State a rule for writing zeros in a multidigit numeral. Ask the students, "When do we need to write zeros in a number?"

Concept 10: Face Times Place. The value of any digit in a multidigit numeral is determined by the product of its face and place values (implied multiplication).

1. Show, name, and identify the value of a specified digit within a multidigit numeral. Show the number 1,468 to the students, and ask, "How much is the 6 worth: 0, 6, 10, 60, or 16?"
2. Name and identify the operation that is used to determine the value of a digit in a multidigit numeral. Ask the students, "In 1,468 do we find 6 is worth 60 when we add, subtract, multiply, or divide?"
3. State a rule for finding the value of a specified digit in a multidigit numeral. Ask the students, "How do you know that 6 is worth 60 in the number 1,468?"

Concept 11: Implied Addition. The value of a multidigit numeral is determined by the sum of the values of each digit (implied addition).

1. Express any multidigit numeral as the sum of the values of each digit.

294 = __ ones + __ tens + __ hundreds

2. Express the sum of digit values as a multidigit numeral.

$$4 \text{ ones } + 3 \text{ tens } + 6 \text{ hundreds } = \underline{}$$

3. Identify the operation that is used to determine the value of a multidigit numeral. Ask the students, "To know the value of 287, do we add, subtract, multiply, or divide the value of each numeral?"

Concept 12: Order. Multidigit numerals are ordered.

1. Order multidigit numerals. Say to the students, "Put these numbers in the correct order from smallest to largest: 1689, 1001, 421, 1421."
2. Describe a procedure for determining which of two unequal multidigit numerals is larger. Show the numbers 984 and 849 to the students and ask, "How do you know which is larger?"

Concept 13: Verbal Names (0 through 9). In English, the verbal names for the numbers 0 through 9 are unique.

1. Identify the oral/written names of the 10 digits. Ask the students to write the name next to each digit:

    0 ____   4 ____   7 ____
    1 ____   5 ____   8 ____
    2 ____   6 ____   9 ____
    3 ____

2. State the name for the 10 digits.

Concept 14: Verbal Names with Places. In English, the verbal names for multidigit numbers (except 10 through 12) are closely associated with the written numerals (i.e., combining face and place names).

1. Give a multidigit numeral, identify the verbal name for one of the digits that includes both a face and place name. Show the number 2,847 and ask the students, "How is the 8 read?"

    a. eight   c. eighty
    b. eighty hundred   d. eighteen

2. Identify the digit in a multidigit numeral that is stated first in giving the verbal name. Say to the students, "Write the number that is said first in reading the number."

    44 _____   6,186 _____
    284 _____   37 _____

3. Select two-digit numerals whose naming pattern is different from most. Ask the students to circle the numbers that when read aloud are different from the others: 17, 43, 126, 11, 281.

Concept 15: Periods and Names. Beginning with the ones place, clusters of three (whole numbers) adjacent places are called *periods* and are named by the place value of the rightmost member of the number triad (e.g., ones, thousands, millions).

1. Given a multidigit numeral, insert commas to form periods. Ask the students to put commas in the correct places: 28146   682   7810   192642
2. Name the periods of a given multidigit numeral. Ask the students, "Which number represents the periods?"

    284,000,163 _____

    ones, tens, hundreds, thousands, millions

Concept 16: Naming in the Ones Period. Numerals in the ones period are named by stating, from left to right, each digit's name (except zero) followed by its place name (ones being omitted). Special rules exist for naming tens.

1. Name three-digit numerals (tens digit not 1). Tell the students to write the name for 683.
2. Name three-digit numerals (tens digit of 1). Tell the students to write the name for 718.

Concept 17: Naming Multidigit Numerals. In naming a multidigit numeral, the digits in each period are read as if they were in the ones period, followed by the period name (ones period name being omitted).

1. Name multidigit numerals up to six digits. Tell the students to write the name for 284,163.
2. Name multidigit numerals over six digits. Ask the students to read the following numbers:

    1,846,283   27,219,143
    103,600,101   3,078,420

Teaching Place Value

Place value is directly related to the students' understanding of numeration. Students need to be able to do the following:

• *Group by ones and tens.* Using manipulatives, pictures, and then numerals, students need practice and instruction in grouping by ones and tens.

Students can sort manipulatives such as buttons or sticks in groups of 10. Students can also use a table grid to record their answers.

Tens	Ones	Numerals
2	3	23
6	2	62
4	7	47

Source: J. M. Engelhardt, R. B. Ashlock, and J. H. G. Wiebe, *Helping Children Understand and Use Numerals* (Boston: Allyn & Bacon, 1984), pp. 89–149. Copyright 1984 by Allyn & Bacon. Adapted by permission.

Use "tens blocks" and "single blocks" to represent numerals. For example, 24 can be represented as follows:

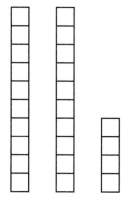

Flannel boards can also be used to group tens and ones.

• *Naming tens.* Teach students to identify numerals by the number of tens. For example, 6 tens is 60, 4 tens is 40, 8 tens is 80, and so on. Give students opportunities to count by tens and then name the number. For example, "Count by tens 3 times." "Ten, twenty, thirty." "Count by tens 7 times." "Ten, twenty, thirty, forty, fifty, sixty, seventy." Also give students opportunities to draw picture diagrams that represent the place values of tens and ones and to identify the number from diagrams.

• *Place value beyond two digits.* Once students can accurately group and identify numbers at the two-digit level, introduce them to three- and four-digit numbers. It is a good idea to be certain students have mastered the concept of two-digit place value before the teacher introduces numerals and place values greater than two digits. Many of the principles that students have learned in terms of two-digit place value will generalize to three digits and beyond. Give students plenty of opportunity to group, orally name, and sequence three- and four-digit place values.

• *Place value with older students.* Because place value is a concept that is taught during the primary grades, students who have not adequately learned the skill will likely have problems with computation and word problems. Students need opportunities to learn place value. Many of the games and activities that have been designed to teach place value focus on young children and are less appropriate for older students. Following are five sources of numbers that may be useful for teaching place value to older students:

1. An odometer
2. Numbers from students' science or social studies texts
3. Numbers from the population of your school (e.g., number of freshmen, sophomores, juniors, seniors)
4. Population data from your town, county, state, or country
5. The financial data page from a newspaper

Addition, Subtraction, Multiplication, and Division

Most of students' time in math instruction is spent on computation. Memorizing facts and practicing addition, subtraction, multiplication, and division problems are the primary components of many math programs. Students spend lots of time completing math sheets, workbook pages, and problems copied from books that require the continued practice and application of math computation principles. It is probably for this reason that many students find math boring and do not its applicability to everyday life.

Teachers can help to make computation exercises and fact learning more engaging by using computer-assisted instruction, which is equally effective for teaching basic arithmetic facts as the conventional drill and practice (Okolo, 1992). Students are likely to be more persistent in solving math problems and have a better attitude toward math when they participate in computer-assisted instruction (Cawley, Foley, and Doan, 2003).

Teachers can also improve students' understanding of computation as they improve students' conceptual knowledge and understanding of mathematics. One intervention for third-grade students with math disabilities addressed conceptual knowledge (Kaufmann, Handl, and Thony, 2003). Students were taught counting principles, the use of arithmetic symbols, memorization of numerals that equaled 10, strategies for memorizing facts, complex multistep calculations, and procedural language for using memorized facts. Students who participated in the intervention made significant gains.

Computing math problems is much easier for students if they understand numeration and place value and if they are given frequent practical application of the math problems. When students are having difficulty performing math computation, it may be for the following three reasons:

1. They do not have an understanding of numeration and/or place value.
2. They do not understand the operation they are performing.
3. They do not know basic math facts and their application to more complicated computation.

Students with attention deficit disorder often demonstrate difficulty in computation because they fail to automatize computational skills at an appropriate age (Ackerman, Anhalt, and Dykman, 1986). By *automatize*, we mean learning computational facts so that they are automatic. Students with attention deficit disorder require time for computation.

Understanding the Operation

Students should be able to demonstrate their understanding of an operation by drawing picture diagrams and illustrating with manipulatives. For example, Sara was able to write the correct answer to the multiplication fact $3 \times 2 = 6$. However, when asked to draw a picture to represent the problem, she drew three flowers and two flowers. She seemed totally undisturbed that the number of flowers she drew was different from the answer she wrote. When asked why she had drawn the number of flowers she did, Sara said, "I drew three flowers for the 3 and two flowers for the 2." When the teacher questioned her further, she discovered that Sara had no understanding of multiplication. By rote, she had memorized the answers to some of the elementary multiplication facts. The teacher used manipulatives such as chips and buttons to illustrate multiplication.

The following activities can be helpful in teaching students to understand mathematical operations:

- The following drawing illustrates how chips in rows can be used to illustrate multiplication. For example, ask, "How many 4s make 20? Fours are placed on the board _____ times."

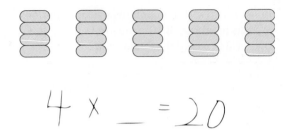

- Have students talk aloud about what is involved in solving a problem. Do not let them merely *read* the problem; ask them to *explain* what it means. For example, "$63 - 27$ means that someone had 63 jelly beans and gave 27 of them to a friend."
- Have students explain the process to another student by using block manipulatives. For example, "$24 + 31$ is the same as adding 4 one-block pieces to 1 one-block piece and 2 ten-block pieces to 3 ten-block pieces."
- Have students close their eyes and use noises to illustrate operations. For example, to illustrate multiplication, the teacher can tap in groups of six and ask, "How many times did I tap a group of 6?"

  tap-tap-tap-tap-tap-tap
  tap-tap-tap-tap-tap-tap
  tap-tap-tap-tap-tap-tap

"Yes, I tapped a group of 6 three times. Now I am going to tap a group of 6 three times again and I want you to tell me how many taps there are altogether. Yes, when you tap a group of 6 three times there are 18 total taps." This same process can be used for addition and subtraction (Bley and Thornton, 1981).

Knowing Basic Math Facts

Two of the reasons students may have difficulty with computation have been discussed: They do not understand numeration and/or place value, and they do not understand the computation process. A third reason students may have difficulty with computation is they do not know basic math facts. A common instructional misconception is that if students learn basic arithmetic facts they will no longer have difficulties with other arithmetic operations and problems. Arithmetic facts do not help students in analyzing or understanding the application of arithmetic operations; however, they do aid in the acquisition and speed of performing arithmetic operations. Students who do not know basic math facts are going to be considerably slower and less accurate in math computation. It is difficult for students to understand the math process because so much of their attention is focused on computing one small segment of problems.

Using thinking strategies assists in the acquisition and retention of basic math facts (Thornton and Toohey, 1985). Without direct instruction, students with learning disabilities often do not discover and use these strategies and relationships for learning and retaining math facts (Thornton, 1978). Some thinking strategies that are used by students who are successful at solving basic math facts (Thornton and Toohey, 1985; Thornton, Tucker, Dossey, and Bazik, 1983) can be taught to students who are having difficulties:

- *Using doubles.* Students can learn to use doubles to solve basic math facts. If a student knows $6 + 6 = 12$, then the student can easily compute $6 + 7$.
- *Counting-on.* Students do not need to resort to counting from one to solve math facts. They can learn to count on from the largest numeral in an addition fact. For example:

$$7 + 2 = \underline{\quad}$$

The student counts on two more from 7: "seven, eight, nine." Students can use this same principle when subtracting, only they count backwards. For example:

$$7 - 2 = \underline{\quad}$$

The student counts backwards two from 7: "seven, six, five." Students can be taught counting-on before operations, and then they will only need to learn to apply the principle.

- *Using the commutative idea.* The commutative property means that adding or multiplying any two numbers always yields the same answer regardless of their order. Students can be taught that with addition and multiplication, if they know it one way they know it the other. For example:

$$3 + 5 = 8$$
$$5 + 3 = 8$$
$$2 \times 9 = 18$$
$$9 \times 2 = 18$$

- *Thinking one more or less than a known fact.* Rasheed knew several basic math facts but had trouble with the more difficult ones. When his teacher taught him how to use the math facts he knew to solve the more difficult ones, his math performance improved. For example, Rasheed knew $5 + 5 = 10$, but when he was presented with $5 + 6$, he began count-

ing on his fingers. His teacher taught him to think of $5 + 6$ as one more than $5 + 5$, and $5 + 4$ as one less than $5 + 5$. Pictures such as the following can help to illustrate the principle:

$$5 + 5 = 10$$

$$5 + 6 = $$

$$5 + 4 = $$

- *Using tens.* Students can learn that 10 + any single-digit number merely changes the 0 in the 10 to the number they are adding to it.
- *Using nines.* There are two strategies that students can apply to addition facts that involve nines. First, they can think of the 9 as a 10 and then subtract 1 from the answer. As illustrated here, the student is taught to think of the 9 as a 10.

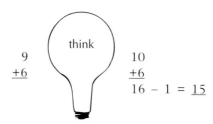

- *Counting by twos, threes, and fours.* Being able to count by multiples helps in addition, multiplication, and division. Multiplication facts can be taught by interpreting 3×4 as counting by threes 4 times. Division facts, such as $8 \div 2$, can be interpreted as, "How many times do you count by twos before you reach 8?"
- *Relationships between addition and subtraction, between multiplication and division.* After students learn addition facts, you can show them the relationship between the addition fact and subtraction. For example, if students know $7 + 6 = 13$, they can learn the relationships between the known addition fact and the subtraction fact, $13 - 7 = \underline{\quad}$. Whenever possible, reinforce this principle as students are working, "You know $8 + 4 = 12$, so $12 - 4 =$ must be $\underline{\quad}$." Give students known addition facts and ask them to form subtraction

FIGURE 11.4

Relationships between Addition and Subtraction; Multiplication and Division

Known Addition Facts	Made-Up Subtraction Facts
5 + 5 = 10	$10 - 5 = 5$
3 + 2 = 5	_____
8 + 8 = 16	_____
6 + 4 = 10	_____

Known Multiplication Facts	Made-Up Division Facts
7 × 4 = 28	$28 \div 4 = 7$
8 × 8 = 64	_____
5 × 9 = 45	_____
5 × 10 = 50	_____

problems. These sample relationships can be used to teach multiplication and division facts (see Figure 11.4).

Van Luit and Naglieri (1999) have been successful in teaching students to compute multiplication and division by ensuring that they learn the following six concepts:

1. Multiplication is repeated addition.
2. Reversibility means that 4 × 7 is the same as 7 × 4.
3. The need to memorize the basic multiplication facts below 100.
4. Division is repeated subtraction.
5. The need to memorize the basic division facts below 100.
6. Ways to apply multiplication and division in real-life problems.

If you think these strategies for assisting students in learning math facts seem logical and automatic, you are right. For most students, they are. However, students with learning difficulties in math do not automatically use these strategies, and this prevents them from acquiring the math facts they need for accurate and speedy computation.

When these strategies are taught directly, students' math performance improves. When Ms. Pappas taught math strategies to students who were having difficulty in math, she used the math strategies summarized in Apply the Concept 11.3, and she enlisted the help of other students who were performing the math skill accurately. She interviewed students who knew how to perform the skill and asked them to talk aloud while they solved the problems so that she could learn what strategies they used. She then taught these strategies to students who were having problems.

Peer-Assisted Instructional Practices. Perhaps one of the most effective procedures for teaching math facts to students with learning and behavior problems is the use of cross-age tutors. Cross-age tutors are older students, often students who do not have learning or behavior problems, who serve as tutors for younger students with learning difficulties. Cross-age tutors are particularly effective in teaching math facts because the skills they need to be effective can be acquired quickly, in as little as two 45-minute periods. In a study that successfully used cross-age tutors to teach addition facts to students with learning disabilities (Beirne-Smith, 1991), tutors were trained to do the following:

- Use contingent reinforcement
- Use task and error correction procedures
- Use procedures for counting-on
- Use procedures for rote memorization of facts
- Repeat skills and instruction till mastery

Cooperative learning groups, usually small groups of students (three to five per group), can be used to have students work together to solve problems. Maheady, Harper, and Sacca (1988) conducted a cooperative learning math instruction program for 9th- and 10th-grade students with mild disabilities. Students who participated in the cooperative teams performed better in mathematics and received higher grades than those who did not.

Constant Time Delay Procedure. Constant time delay is a procedure for teaching math facts that provides for systematic assistance from the teacher through near errorless control of the prompt to ensure the successful performance of the student (Gast, Ault, Wolery, Doyle, and Belanger, 1988; Schuster, Stevens, and Doak, 1990; Stevens and Schuster, 1988; Wolery, Cybriwsky, Gast, and Boyle-Gast, 1991). Students are presented with a math problem and are allowed a specific amount of time to give the correct answer. If students do not respond within the allotted time, a controlling prompt, typically the teacher modeling the correct response, is provided. Students then repeat the model. Correct responses before and after the prompt are reinforced; however, only correct responses that are provided before the prompt are counted toward criterion.

Math Computation Errors

How could students make the errors in Figure 11.5? It appears as though all the students did was

Apply the Concept 11.3

Strategies for Teaching Addition Facts

Addition Facts Groups by Strategy for Recall

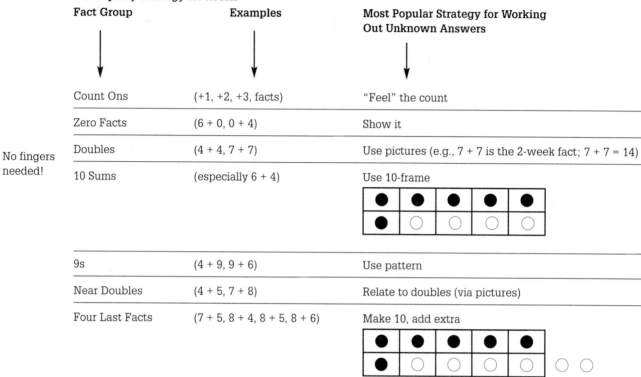

	Fact Group	Examples	Most Popular Strategy for Working Out Unknown Answers
	Count Ons	(+1, +2, +3, facts)	"Feel" the count
	Zero Facts	(6 + 0, 0 + 4)	Show it
No fingers needed!	Doubles	(4 + 4, 7 + 7)	Use pictures (e.g., 7 + 7 is the 2-week fact; 7 + 7 = 14)
	10 Sums	(especially 6 + 4)	Use 10-frame
	9s	(4 + 9, 9 + 6)	Use pattern
	Near Doubles	(4 + 5, 7 + 8)	Relate to doubles (via pictures)
	Four Last Facts	(7 + 5, 8 + 4, 8 + 5, 8 + 6)	Make 10, add extra

Note: Turnarounds (commutatives of facts within each group) would be learned before moving to a different group of facts.

Verbal Prompts Used in the Addition Program

Fact Group	Sample	Facts	Sentence Patterns (Verbal Prompts)
Count Ons	8 + 2	3 + 7	Start BIG and count on.
Zeros	6 + 0	0 + 3	Plus zero stays the same.
Doubles	5 + 5	7 + 7	Think of the picture.
Near Doubles	5 + 6	7 + 8	Think doubles to help.
9s	4 + 9	9 + 7	What's the pattern?
Near 10s	7 + 5	6 + 8	Use 10 to help.

Source: C. A. Thornton and M. A. Toohey (1985). Basic math facts: Guidelines for teaching and learning. *Learning Disabilities Focus, 1* (1), pp. 50, 51. Reprinted with permission of the Division for Learning Disabilities.

FIGURE 11.5

Math Computational Errors

```
(A)      15    (B)      15    (C)      63
        - 7          + 23          × 23
        ----         ----         -----
         65           45          2412


         (D)    37    (E)    13
                27          +4
                17          ----
               ----         53
                72
```

guess. Yet each of the students who computed the problems can tell you what he or she did to get the answer. Most errors that students make are rule-governed. Although the rule they are applying is not always obvious, the students are using some rule to tell them how to compute a problem. In problem A in Figure 11.5, Erika said, "I took 1 away from 7 to get 6 and took 0 away from 5 to get 5." In problem B, Jeff added across, adding the 3 and 1 to get 4 and adding the 2 and 3 to get 5. In problem C, Yolanda said, "I knew this wasn't right, but it was the best I knew how to do. I multiplied 3 × 4 to get 12, and then 6 × 4 to get 24." In problem D, Shawn knew that 7 plus 7 plus 7 was 21, but he was operating under the faulty rule that you always carry the smaller number, so he wrote the 2 in the ones column and carried the 1. In problem E, Jae said, "I added 4 plus 1 because it was easier than adding 4 plus 3." When given several similar problems, she had no concerns about placing the number in the ones or tens column depending on where it was easier for her to add. All of these students applied faulty rules as they performed math computations. Once the teacher discovered the faulty rules they were applying, she was able to teach them the underlying concepts and the correct rule for completing computations.

Teachers can learn a great deal about students' thinking in mathematics through an oral diagnostic interview (Lankford, 1974). Such an interview will provide information about what each student is doing and why he or she is doing it that way. For the diagnostic interview to yield accurate, helpful information, the teacher must ask the student questions about math computation in a nonthreatening way. For example, "I am interested in learning what you say to yourself while you do this problem. Say aloud what you are thinking." It is often most effective to use a problem that is different from the one the student has performed incorrectly. The assumption behind this interview is that there is an underlying reason behind the mistakes, and understanding why a student is making errors provides valuable diagnostic information that leads directly to instruction. Roberts (1968) identified four common failure strategies in computation, which are summarized in Apply the Concept 11.4.

Apply the Concept 11.4

Errors in Computation

1. *Wrong operation.* The student attempts to solve the problem by using the wrong process. In this example the student subtracted instead of adding.

```
    24
  + 11
  ----
    13
```

2. *Computational error.* The student uses the correct operation but makes an error recalling a basic number fact.

```
    24
  + 11
  ----
    58
```

3. *Defective algorithm.* The student attempts to use the correct operation but uses a wrong procedure for solving the problem. The error is not due to computation.

```
    24
  - 17
  ----
    13
```

4. *Random response.* The student has little or no idea how to solve the problem, and writes numbers randomly.

```
    304
  - 196
  -----
    396
```

Source: Adapted from G. H. Roberts (1968). The failure strategies of third-grade arithmetic pupils. *The Arithmetic Teacher, 15*, pp. 442–446.

Students with learning problems are slower but not necessarily less accurate when it comes to doing computation and learning math facts. When teaching mathematics in your classroom, teachers should consider that students with learning problems may need additional practice to learn math facts and more time to perform mathematics computations because they often lack the skill in automatization to perform math computation effectively and efficiently.

Language of Math Computation

"What do you mean by 'find the difference'?" a student might ask. "Am I supposed to add or subtract? Why don't you just say it in plain English?" Many students with learning and behavior problems have difficulty with the language of computation. However, understanding the vocabulary is important for success in the regular classroom, application to math story problems, and communication with others. Understanding the terminology of the four basic operations as well as the symbols associated with the processes is important. Students also need to understand the vocabulary that is associated with the answer derived from each of these processes. Table 11.1 illustrates the relationship between the process, symbol, answer, and problem.

After teaching the information on the chart, the teacher can use the following three activities:

1. Cover one column (e.g., the symbols), and ask the student to write the answer.
2. Place each of the symbols, answers, and problems on a separate index card, and ask the student to sort them by process.
3. Play concentration with two columns. Two columns of index cards (e.g., the symbol cards and answer cards) are laid answer down, and the students take turns searching for matching pairs by selecting two cards. When a student picks up a corresponding pair, he or she keeps the pair and takes another turn.

TABLE 11.1

Relationship of Process, Symbol, Answer, and Problem

Process	Symbol	Answer	Problem
Addition	+	Sum	6 + 4 =
Subtraction	−	Difference	5 − 3 =
Multiplication	×	Product	8 × 5 =
Division	÷	Quotient	12 ÷ 6 =

Use of Calculators

Many students with learning and behavior problems let computation interfere with their ability to learn problem solving. They spend so much time learning to compute the problem accurately that they miss the more important aspects of mathematics, such as concept development and practical application.

Many teachers do not use calculators because they believe that the use of calculators threatens the acquisition of basic skills. Mr. Coffland, a third-grade teacher, put it this way: "If I let my students use calculators to solve problems, they will not have adequate practice in basic skills. They will become too dependent on using the calculator." Research suggests that Mr. Coffland has little to fear. The results of a summary of 79 studies (Hembree, 1986) on the use of calculators suggest the following:

- The use of calculators does not interfere with basic mathematics skill acquisition. In fact, calculator use can improve skill acquisition.
- Only in fourth grade does sustained calculator use interfere with skill development.
- The use of calculators in testing situations results in much higher achievement scores, particularly when students are low in problem-solving ability.
- Using calculators improves students' attitudes toward mathematics.
- Calculators can be introduced at the same time that paper-and-pencil practice exercises are introduced.
- Students can use calculators to solve complex problems that they construct. This also provides support for improved self-concept with math skills.

In summary, as long as students get basic skills instruction, the use of calculators is a positive aid to mathematics instruction. There are several ways in which students who are having difficulty with mathematics instruction can use calculators:

1. *To develop a positive attitude.* Using a calculator removes the drudgery associated with solving computations and makes problem solving fun.
2. *To improve self-concept.* Being able to compute extremely complex problems on a calculator gives students confidence in their mathematics abilities.
3. *To improve practice in problem solving.* Students are willing to tackle difficult problem-solving

tasks when they have a calculator to help solve the problem. Students still have to decide what numbers are used, what operation is involved, and whether additional operations are necessary. Using a calculator can free students from the burden of computation and allow more focus on thinking about the problem.

4. *To develop their own problems.* Using a calculator lets students develop their own problems. They can then exchange their problems with each other and use their calculators to solve them.

Fractions

The concept of fractions is one of the most difficult math concepts to teach. Because of the availability of calculators, teachers now place less emphasis on being able to compute fractions and more emphasis on understanding the meaning and use of fractions.

The concept of a fraction can be introduced before the actual fractions are even discussed. For example, Figure 11.6 shows the relationship between common fractional terminology and represented units.

Children as young as three, four, and five are introduced to the concept of fractions as they help to cook. "We use one cup of milk and one-half cup of flour." "You'll need to share the cookie with your brother. You each may have half of the cookie." Teachers often use cooking activities to enhance students' understanding of fractions. Many manipulative aids can be used to teach frac-

tions: colored rods, cardboard strips and squares, blocks, fractional circle wheels, cooking utensils such as measuring cups, and any unit dividers such as egg cartons and muffin pans.

Teaching fractions, like teaching most concepts, proceeds from concrete to abstract. Apply the Concept 11.5 demonstrates the teaching sequence.

However, the use of intuitive procedures for the acquisition of knowledge in fractions is unlikely to be successful with low achievers (Kelly, Gersten, and Carnine, 1990). Success in understanding fractions is likely to occur when the following three variables are presented (Kelly et al., 1990):

1. *Systematic practice in discriminating among different problem types.* Students with learning and behavior problems often confuse algorithms when computing fractions. For example, they learn to compute denominators and then use this procedure when adding, subtracting, multiplying, and dividing.

2. *Separation of confusing elements and terminology.* Much of the language of learning fractions is unfamiliar and confusing to youngsters. If the language is well explained and the concepts are well illustrated, students are more likely to be successful in learning fractions.

3. *Use a wide range of examples to illustrate each concept.* Students have a difficult time generalizing beyond the number of examples provided by the teacher; a wide range and large number of examples facilitate understanding.

FIGURE 11.6

Unit Representation of Fractions

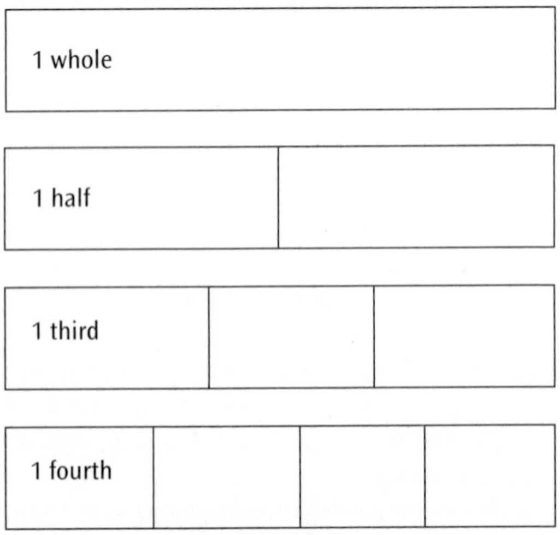

Measurement

Measurement includes weight, distance, quantity, length, money, and time. Measurement can be taught almost entirely with applied problems. For example, students learn time by using the clock in the classroom or by manipulating a toy clock; they learn money by making purchases with real or toy money; and they learn measures such as pint, liter, and teaspoon through following recipes. With each measurement unit that is taught (e.g., weight, distance, money), students need to learn the vocabulary and concepts for that unit. Only after students understand the terminology and concepts and have had experience applying the concepts in real measurement problems should they be exposed to measurement instruction through the use of less applied procedures such as textbooks and worksheets.

Apply the Concept 11.5

Sequence for Teaching Fractional Concepts

The student

1. Manipulates concrete models (e.g., manipulating fractional blocks and pegs)
2. Matches fractional models (e.g., matching halves, thirds, fourths)
3. Points to fractional model when name is stated by another (e.g., the teacher says "half" and the student selects a model of "half" from several distractors)
4. Names fractional units when selected by another (e.g., the teacher points to a fractional unit such as a "fourth" and the student names it)
5. Draws diagrams or uses manipulatives to represent fractional units (e.g., the teacher says or writes fractional units such as "whole," "half," and "third," and the student uses manipulatives or drawings to represent these units)
6. Writes fraction names when given fractional drawings (e.g., next to ▬▬ the student writes "half")
7. Uses fractions to solve problems (e.g., place $1\frac{1}{2}$ cups of sugar in a bowl)

Time

Even before coming to school, most children can tell time by the hour or know when the clock says that it is time to go to bed or time for dinner. The following teaching sequence assists students in understanding time:

1. *Teach students to sequence events.* Younger students can sequence the normal routine of the school day. For instance, "First we have a group story, then reading, then we go to recess." Additional practice in sequencing events can occur with story cards, events that occur at home, field trips, and so on.
2. *Ask students to identify which events take longer.* Name two events (e.g., math time and lining up for recess), and ask students to identify which event takes longer. Name several events, and ask students to put them in order from the event that takes the longest to the one that is quickest to complete.

1:25

one twenty-five

A scope and sequence list of skills for teaching time is presented in Figure 11.7.

FIGURE 11.7

Time—Scope and Sequence of Skills

- Tells time to the hour
- Tells time to the half hour
- Knows the days of the week
- Knows the names of the months
- Tells time to the quarter hour
- Knows the number of days in a week
- Knows the number of months in a year
- Can use a calendar to answer questions about the date, the day, and the month
- Writes time to the hour
- Writes time to the half hour
- Writes time using five-minute increments
- Can solve simple story problems using time

Money

Students with learning disabilities often have difficulty applying money concepts because they have not mastered many of the earlier concepts, such as the value of coins, how coins compare (e.g., a quarter is more than two times as much as a dime), and how the value of the coins relates to what can be purchased. One parent reported that her child was frequently taken advantage of because he would trade coins of high value for coins of less value. Students with learning difficulties often do not know the price of common goods. Although they may not need to know the exact price of a loaf of bread or a television set, they should be able to estimate what these items cost.

When initially teaching students to identify money, start with real coins. After they learn to recognize real coins, switch to play money and then to representations of money on workbook pages. The following sequence is useful in teaching money identification:

1. *Teach students to match the same coins.* Give students several different coins, and ask them to place all of the same coins in the same group.
2. *Ask students to point to the coin when you name it.* Depending on the students' skill level, you may want to start with two coins (e.g., a penny and a nickel) and then progress to three and four. At this point, students do not need to be able to tell the name of the coin; they merely need to be able to locate it when it is named.
3. *Students name the coin.* At this level, the students tell the name of the coin.

When students can accurately identify the name of the coins, the value of the coins is discussed. Coins and dollars are discussed in terms of both their purchase power and how they relate to each other. Activities and problems that require students to use money and make change assure students that they can apply what they have learned about money. For example, students can learn to keep and balance a checkbook and to give change when role-playing a clerk in a store.

A scope and sequence list for teaching money is presented in Figure 11.8.

FIGURE 11.8

Money—Scope and Sequence of Skills

- Correctly identifies penny, nickel, and dime
- Knows how many cents are in a penny, nickel, and dime
- When shown combinations of pennies, nickels, and dimes, can add to the correct amount
- Can describe items that can be purchased with combinations of pennies, nickels, and dimes
- Can solve simple word math problems involving pennies, nickels, and dimes
- Correctly identifies quarter, dollar, 5 dollars, 10 dollars, and 20 dollars
- Knows the value of combination of quarters and dollars
- Can solve verbal math problems with quarters and dollars

FOCUS Question 5. **What factors contribute to difficulties with problem solving, and how can teachers assist students in learning problem-solving strategies?**

Problem Solving

"I can read the arithmetic all right; I just can't read the writing" (Barney, 1973, p. 57). Many students with learning problems have trouble with traditional story problems in mathematics because their difficulty in reading makes understanding the math problem almost impossible. In addition, students with learning problems often have difficulty with logical reasoning, which is the basis of many story problems. It is also common that their mathematics education has focused primarily on operations and not on understanding the reasons for operations or even a thorough understanding of the numbers that are involved in operations. Because of their difficulties with reading and logical reasoning and perhaps because of insufficient instruction in mathematics, students with learning problems often find problem solving the most difficult aspect of mathematics.

Despite its difficulties, problem solving may be the most important skill we teach students who have learning and behavior problems. Whereas most other students are able to apply the operations they learn to real-life problems with little direct instruction, students with learning problems will be less able to apply these skills without instruction, rehearsal, and practice. Students with learning disabilities lack metacognitive knowledge about strategies for math problem solving. Poor math performance is not solely a function of math computation difficulties (Montague and Bos, 1990). Students who are taught strategies for problem solving are more likely to be successful than are students who are taught the sequence for solving problems (Wilson and Sindelar, 1991).

Students need to know when and how to add, subtract, multiply, and divide. Knowing *when* involves understanding the operation and applying it in the appropriate situation. Knowing *how* is the accurate performance of the operation. Most students are better at *how* than at *when;* problem solving gives students practice at these skills.

Factors Affecting Successful Verbal Problem Solving

Teachers need to consider the factors that affect successful story problem solving (Carnine, 1997;

Goodstein, 1981; Jitendra, Hoff, and Beck, 1999) when writing and selecting story problems and instructing students. Use the following strategies:

• *Teach big ideas.* When students understand the big idea or principle, all of the subordinate concepts around that big idea make more sense and are easier to learn and remember (Carnine, 1997). An example of a big idea is volume. You can teach students the principle of volume and then provide examples of real-life problems that students can solve by applying the big-idea principles they learn about volume.

• *Sameness analysis.* Carnine and colleagues determined the importance of sameness in mathematical problem solving through a series of research investigations (Engelmann, Carnine, and Steely, 1991). The idea is to connect math concepts so that students see the ways in which aspects of mathematical problem solving are the same. Identify types of word problems, and then explicitly teach students the ways in which these word problems are alike.

• *Cue words.* The presence or absence of cue words can significantly affect students' abilities to solve verbal word problems. The cue word *altogether* is illustrated in the following example: Maria has four erasers. Joe has seven erasers. How many erasers do they have *altogether?* The cue word *left* is illustrated in the following example: Jasmine has nine pieces of candy. She gave three pieces to Lin. How many does she have *left?* Students need to be taught to look for cue words that will guide them in solving problems.

• *Reasoning.* Ask students to think about the idea behind the story problem. Does it appear that the person in the problem will get more or less? Why? What operation will help to solve this? What numbers in the story do we have to use? Are there numbers that we do not have and need to compute? Ask students to explain the way in which they set up and calculated the problem so that they can justify what they've done and why they've done it that way.

• *Syntactic complexity.* The sentence structure within the story problem needs to be kept simple. Learner performance can be significantly impaired when the sentence contains a complex interrogative sentence structure (Larsen, Parker, and Trenholme, 1978). The sentence length and vocabulary can also affect verbal problem solving.

• *Extraneous information.* Extraneous information in word problems causes difficulties because the majority of students attempt to use all of the information in solving the problem. For example: Mary's mother baked 10 cookies. Mary's sister baked 8 cookies. Mary's brother baked 3 cupcakes. How many *cookies* were baked? The information regarding Mary's brother baking three cupcakes is extraneous, yet many students will use the information in attempting to solve the problem. Extraneous information in story problems is associated with decreases in accuracy and computation speed with students. Blankenship and Lovitt (1976) explain students' difficulties with extraneous information by suggesting that the difficulties are based not on reading the entire story problem but merely on knowing which numbers are needed to solve the problem. Students will construct the problem using the numbers available in the story problem, disregarding the question and the content available in the story problem. When students are able to complete story problems successfully without extraneous information, teach them to complete story problems with extraneous information.

• *Content load.* The content load refers to the number of ideas contained within a story problem. The story problem should not be overloaded with concepts (West, 1978). Students need to be taught to discriminate between relevant and irrelevant concepts.

• *Suitable content.* Story problems should contain content that is interesting and appealing to students and relevant to the types of real problems that students have or are likely to encounter.

• *Monitor progress.* Use weekly tests of word problem solving to monitor study progress on each type of word problem students have mastered and/or are learning. Reteach when necessary.

• *Provide guided practice.* Use diagrams to demonstrate how to solve the problem, and guide students through the development and use of these diagrams. As students demonstrate increasing proficiency with independent use of diagrams and strategies for effective problem solving, reduce the amount of support provided.

• *Use computer-assisted instruction.* Computer-assisted instruction gives students opportunities to practice computation and problem solving independently and provides correction and feedback. Many students prefer to do mathematics with the computer. *My Math* (Cawley, 2002) is an example of a computer software program that incorporates three mathematical components: computation problems, arithmetic word problems, and arithmetic story problems. See Tech Tips 11.1 for additional information about using software to enhance mathematics instruction.

TECHTips

11.1   Using Software to Assist Mathematics Instruction

Educational software designed to enhance mathematics instruction can fit in several different software categories. As a tool or utility, programs that offer a better calculator or simple spreadsheet can speed up basic calculations and predictions, enabling the learner to focus on the broader concepts. *Big:Calc,* a talking calculator from Don Johnston Incorporated (www.donjohnston.com), provides auditory cues that can assist learners who reverse numerals; it offers six different screen layouts to adjust to an individual's preferred learning style. Programs such as *MathPad* and *MathPad Plus* from IntelliTools, Inc., (www.intellitools.com) enable learners to do arithmetic directly on the computer. These programs are ideal for learners who need help organizing or navigating through math problems or who have difficulty with math using pencil and paper.

Additionally, a plethora of mathematics programs providing reinforced practice for concepts previously taught; many of the programs are in game format. For example, a learner must answer questions and solve problems in order to advance a character along an adventurous journey. These programs provide another avenue for learners to practice newly learned skills. In choosing a math game, be sure the learner has been taught the skills necessary to complete the game successfully.

Tutorial programs actually teach math concepts. *Number Concepts 1* (Grades K–2) and *Number Concepts 2* (Grades 3–5) from IntelliTools, Inc., provide exploration modes along with instruction. The earlier program teaches counting (1–20), greater than, less than, equals, and beginning addition and subtraction. The second level teaches

hundreds, place value, skip counting, and factoring. With both of these programs teachers can select number ranges and choose a level for auditory support.

Another category of mathematics software offers activity authoring to teachers and students. *IntelliMathics 3,* part of *Classroom Suite* from IntelliTools, Inc., offers activities using virtual mathematics manipulatives for grades prekindergarten to grade 8. Manipulatives include base ten blocks, fraction bars, decimal grids, sorting bins, tangrams, geoboards, and coins, dice, and spinners for probability. Teachers and students can create activities from scratch, modify activities from provided templates, or download activities and activity templates along with easy tutorials from the IntelliTools Website. Teacher features include answer tracking and performance assessment.

A Beginning Addition Activity from *IntelliMathics 3* (Used with permission of IntelliTools, Inc.)

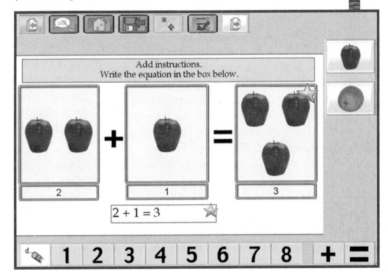

Methods of Teaching Story Problem Solving

There are three important considerations in preparing students for success in solving story problems: (1) providing anchored instruction that relates to a real-life problem the students might encounter (Goldman, Hasselbring, and the Cognition and Technology Group at Vanderbilt, 1997); (2) providing story problems in an appropriate sequence; and (3) making students aware of common types of errors. Students also need to learn

specific strategies that will assist them in using a successful process for mastering story problems in class and applying those principles to the mathematics of everyday life.

A step-by-step strategy for teaching sixth-grade students to solve story problems is illustrated in Apply the Concept 11.6 (Smith and Alley, 1981). Students first need to learn the strategies, then practice them with support from a teacher, and finally practice them independently until they can apply the principles with success. After continued success, students make adaptations in or

Apply the Concept 11.6

Steps for Teaching Students to Solve Story Problems

Story Problem: Mark had $1.47 to spend. He spent $0.34 on gum. How much money does he have left?

I. Read the Problem
    A. Find unknown words
    B. Find "cue words" (e.g., *left*)

II. Reread the Problem
    A. Identify what is given
       1. Is renaming needed?
       2. Are there unit changes?

B. Decide what is asked for
    1. What process is needed?
    2. What unit or category is asked for? (e.g., seconds, pounds, money)

III. Use Objects to Show the Problem
    A. Decide what operation to use

IV. Write the Problem

V. Work the Problem

---

condense the steps they use. The section on cognitive behavior modification in Chapter 2 discusses how to teach students learning strategies.

Fleischner, Nuzum, and Marzola (1987, p. 216) devised the following instructional program to teach arithmetic problem solving to students with learning disabilities:

READ	What is the question?
REREAD	What is the necessary information?
THINK	Putting together = addition
	Taking apart = subtraction
	Do I need all the information?
	Is it a two-step problem?
SOLVE	Write the equation
CHECK	Recalculate
	Label
	Compare

Montague and Bos (1986a, 1986b) demonstrated the efficacy of the learning-strategy approach, described in Apply the Concept 11.7, with high school adolescents with learning disabilities.

In summary, when teaching story problems to students with learning and behavior problems, teachers should keep the following guidelines in mind:

- Be certain the students can perform the arithmetic computation before introducing the computation in story problems.
- Develop a range of story problems that contain the type of problem you want the student to learn to solve.

- Instruct with one type of problem until mastery is attained.
- Teach the students to read through a word problem and visualize the situation. Ask them to read the story aloud and tell what it is about.
- Ask the students to reread the story—this time to get the facts.
- Identify the key question. In the beginning stages of problem solving, the students should write the key question so that they can refer to it when the computation is complete.
- Identify extraneous information.
- Reread the story problem, and attempt to state the situation in a mathematical sentence. The teacher plays an important role in this step by asking the students questions and guiding them in formulating the arithmetic problem.
- Tell the students to write the arithmetic problem and compute the answer. (Students can compute some problems in their heads without completing this step.)
- Tell the students to reread the key question and be sure that they have completed the problem correctly.
- Ask the students whether their answer is likely, based on their estimate.

Teaching math story problems does not have to be limited to the content area of math. Cawley (1984) discusses how story problems can be integrated with instruction in reading so that reading level does not interfere with understanding the math problems. At the same time, story problems can enhance and support what the student is doing

Apply the Concept 11.7

Teaching Adolescents to Solve Story Problems

The eight steps in the verbal math problem-solving strategy are described below:

1. *Read the problem aloud.* Ask the teacher to pronounce or define any word you do not know. (The teacher will pronounce and provide meanings for any words if the student asks.)

   Example: In a high school there are 2,878 male and 1,943 female students enrolled. By how many students must the enrollment increase to make the enrollment 5,000?

2. *Paraphrase the problem aloud.* State important information giving close attention to the numbers in the problem. Repeat the question part aloud. A self-questioning technique such as What is asked? or What am I looking for? is used to provide focus on the outcome.

   Example: Altogether there are a certain number of kids in high school. There are 2,878 boys and 1,943 girls. The question is by how many students must the enrollment increase to make the total enrollment 5,000. What is asked? How many more students are needed to total 5,000 in the school?

3. *Visualize.* Graphically display the information. Draw a representation of the problem.

4. *State the problem.* Complete the following statements aloud. I have . . . I want to find. . . . Underline the important information in the problem.

   Example: I have the number of boys and the number of girls who go to the school now. I want to find how many more kids are needed to total 5,000.

5. *Hypothesize.* Complete the following statements aloud. If I . . . then . . . how many steps will I use to find the answer? Write the operation signs.

   Example: If I add 2,878 boys and 1,943 girls, I'll get the number of kids now. Then I must subtract that number from 5,000 to find out how many more must enroll. First add, then subtract. + − This is a two-step problem.

6. *Estimate.* Write the estimate. My answer should be around . . . or about . . . (The skills of rounding and estimating answers should be reinforced at this step.) Underline the estimate.

   Example: 2,800 and 2,000 are 4,800. 4,800 from 5,000 is 200. My answer should be around 200.

7. *Calculate.* Show the calculation and label the answer. Circle the answer. Use a self-questioning technique such as, Is this answer in the correct form? (Change from cent sign to dollar sign and decimal point should be reinforced when solving money problems.) Correct labels for the problems should be reinforced.

   Example:
   $$\begin{array}{cc} 2{,}878 & 5{,}000 \\ +1{,}943 & -4{,}821 \\ \hline 4{,}821 & 179 \text{ students} \end{array}$$

8. *Self-check.* Refer to the problem and check every step to determine accuracy of operation(s) selected and correctness of response and solution. Check computation for accuracy. (Checking skills will be reinforced at this step.) Use the self-questioning technique by asking whether the answer makes sense.

Source: M. Montague and C. S. Bos (1986a). The effect of cognitive strategy training on verbal math problems solving performance of learning disabled adolescents. *Journal of Learning Disabilities, 19,* pp. 26–33. Copyright © 1986 by PRO-ED, Inc. Reprinted by permission.

in reading. For example, a story about a mother duck and her babies was part of a student's reading lesson. During mathematics, the teacher made minor changes in the story and used it for instruction in story problems in mathematics (see Figure 11.9).

This same procedure can be used with junior high and high school students' content area textbooks. Math story problems can be taken from social studies and science tests; Cawley and Miller (1986) refer to these as knowledge-based problems. Usually, these problems require specific knowledge in the content area. Cawley (1984) identifies the integration of math into other content areas as an important means of promoting generalization of math concepts.

Pictures can be used to facilitate processing information in solving mathematic word problems. For example, using Figure 11.10, a teacher could say, "The small monkeys have four bananas, and the large monkeys have six bananas. How many bananas would they have if they put them all together?"

FIGURE 11.9

Example of Teacher-Altered Story for Use in Story Problem Instruction

The Mother duck went to the pond with her *eight* babies. They looked for their new friend. *Two* more baby ducks joined them. How many baby ducks were there?

FIGURE 11.10

Pictures Help to Solve Math Story Problems

Instructional manipulatives can also be used to assist students with learning problems in solving mathematical word problems. Cuisenaire rods can be used to represent the numerical values in the problem and assist students in better understanding and solving mathematical word problems (Marsh and Cooke, 1996).

Helping Families Help Their Children with Mathematics

Many families are interested in knowing how to help their children with mathematics. If mathematics came easily to them, family members may be confused about why their children have such difficulty. Some family members get easily frustrated and concerned with their children's performance in mathematics. Other relatives had difficulty with mathematics too.

Family

They may be sympathetic to their children's difficulties in mathematics but may think that their own math skills are not good enough to help. Teachers can provide some general guidelines to families to assist them in providing mathematics support to their children:

• Families can engage their children in issues relating mathematics and math problem solving to everyday events. For example, with young children, talk about the cost of items at the store, and allow the children to determine which items cost more or less. As children get older, engage them in mathematical problem solving around issues related to the mileage between home and a driving destination or the amount they could accumulate in a month if they saved their allowance every week.

• Families can discuss activities related to mathematics that they and other family members engage in that make knowing math useful. For example, they should explain that they have to make a budget each week or month. The budget requires them to add up all of their expenses and then consider all of their income. When they subtract their expenses from their income, it tells them how much they have for other purchases.

• Families can involve children in saving for desired items. For example, even young children can learn early that when they have a financial goal, they can reach that goal by saving money. Older children may want to purchase clothing or electronics, and parents can engage them in saving to reach those goals.

• Discuss the use of mathematics in jobs. For example, discuss the many ways in which mathematics might be used in careers such as pharmacy, teaching, law, food service, and medicine.

FOCUS Question 6. What are the three types of math interventions, and how can they be used to improve math performance?

Improving Math Performance

There are three types of interventions for mathematics instruction for individuals with learning disabilities (for review, see Mastropieri, Scruggs, and Shiah, 1991; Parmar and Cawley, 1997). One type of intervention is cognitive, one is behavioral, and the third is alternative instructional delivery systems, which includes cooperative learning, computer-assisted instruction, and interactive video disks. Mastropieri, Scruggs, and Shiah (1991) reflect that a broad array of interventions are effective, including strategy instruction, worksheets, computers, peer-assisted instruction, and direct measurement.

Cognitive Approaches

Cognitive behavior modification (CBM) can be used with instructional procedures in mathematics. CBM often takes the form of self-instruction, which relies on using internalized language to facilitate the problem-solving process. Based largely on the work of Meichenbaum (1977, 1985), CBM is receiving attention as an alternative strategy for teaching arithmetic to students with learning difficulties. When verbalizations are added to the arithmetic process, either by naming the sign before proceeding (Parsons, 1972) or verbalizing the steps in the arithmetic process while solving the problem (Grimm, Bijou, and Parsons, 1973), there is a significant improvement in performance.

Leon and Pepe (1983) taught a five-step self-instructional sequence to special education teachers. Students receiving arithmetic instruction from these teachers who were trained in the sequence improved greatly both in arithmetic computation and in generalizing the skills they acquired. Second-grade students with learning disabilities became more proficient at learning addition through strategy instruction than through drill and practice. This study demonstrated that even very young children with learning disabilities can benefit from cognitive approaches to math instruction (Tournaki, 2003). The following sequence for using self-instruction in mathematics is a modification of the approach used by Leon and Pepe (1983):

1. *Modeling.* The teacher demonstrates how to compute a problem by using overt self-instruction. This overt self-instruction, or talking aloud of the process, assists students who have learning problems in knowing what they should say to themselves and what questions they should ask to keep them focused on the process.
2. *Coparticipation.* The teacher and students compute the problem together by using overt self-instruction. This step helps the students to put the procedure in their own words yet supplies the support of the teacher while the students are still learning the process.

3. *Student demonstration.* The students compute the problem alone by using overt self-instruction, and the teacher monitors the students' performance. The students are more independent in this step; however, the teacher is still available to give correction and feedback.
4. *Fading overt self-instruction.* The students continue to demonstrate the computation of the problem with internal self-instruction. Often students have a check sheet of symbols or key words to cue them to the key points.
5. *Feedback.* The students complete the problem independently by using covert self-instruction and providing self-reinforcement for a job well done.

Behavioral Approaches

Behavioral techniques are also available to improve students' math performance. As you know, stimulus cues precede responses and often control or provide information to control responses. In arithmetic instruction, teachers need to identify relevant cues and determine whether the students are aware of these cues and are using them appropriately. In Figure 11.11, three different problems are presented; there are many different cues that a student must understand and attend to before accurately performing these problems. For example, in problem 1 of Figure 11.11, the student must know what "+" means, what the numbers represent, and what procedure to follow to perform the problem. In problem 2, the student must know what the picture represents, the difference between the short and long hands of the clock, and what each of the numbers represents. Problem 3 requires the student to understand the cue *long* and to know what type of tool is needed to address the problem. Math provides many stimulus cues, and teachers need to be certain that students recognize and understand the cues and attend to them.

FIGURE 11.11

Math Problems Enlisting Various Cues

(1)
```
   37
   24
 + 89
```

(2)

What time is it?_____

(3) How long is this line?_____

Teachers can also provide cues to assist students in learning new skills. For example, the following list illustrates cues a teacher provided when students were first learning long division:

÷ (divide) $6\overline{)478}$ $8\overline{)521}$
× (multiply)
− (subtract)
↓ (bring down)

Providing corrective feedback reinforces student performance. Corrective feedback involves telling the students what they are doing well, including procedures, accuracy of responses, and work style. It also involves identifying areas in which a student needs further assistance. Corrective feedback should be given frequently. Teachers should not wait until students have completed tasks but should give feedback while they are working on the task. Feedback should also be precise. Rather than saying, "You are doing a good job," a teacher should say, "You remembered to carry. All of the answers in the first row are correct. Good job."

Task analysis is a process of specifying the behaviors needed for a particular task that can help to shape student responses. Students are taught behaviors from the simple to the more complex until they can perform the target behavior. For example, a teacher's goal may be for a student to complete two-place addition with carrying by solving a verbal math problem. The student's present level of performance is knowledge of math facts when adding numbers between 0 and 9. Through task analysis, the teacher identifies the many problem-solving skills that need to be shaped

through instruction and practice before the student is performing the target behavior, in this case a verbal math problem with two-place addition:

- Number concepts for 0–9
- Number concepts for 10–100
- Place value
- Simple oral word problems, requiring addition knowledge for 0–9
- Simple written word problems, requiring addition knowledge for 0–9
- Two-place addition problems
- Oral addition word problems requiring knowledge of two-place addition
- Written addition word problems requiring knowledge of two-place addition

The teacher decided that it would take approximately three months to reach the goal. He knew that his mathematics program would focus on other skills during that period (e.g., time, measurements, and graphs). Apply the Concept 11.8 lists several things teachers can do to improve their students' math performance.

Focus on Real-World Mathematics

Many students with learning and behavior problems manage to graduate despite having only a minimal understanding of mathematics skills. Many, relieved to escape formal education in mathematics, have the unfortunate misconception that they are finished with mathematics. Unfortunately, they are sadly mistaken, and they

Apply the Concept 11.8

Ways to Improve Math Performance

Baker, Gersten, and Lee (2002) conducted a synthesis of all of the empirical research on teaching mathematics to students with math difficulties. They reported several themes from these studies that teachers should consider in their instructional routines:

- Use ongoing progress-monitoring data in mathematics. These data allow teachers to determine how students are progressing, adjust

instruction, and give feedback to students on their performance.

- Use peer-assisted learning to provide support for mathematical learning. When peers work together on organized practices of computing and problem solving, both peers benefit.
- Use explicit and systematic instruction in the elements of mathematics, which is associated with improved outcomes in math for students. This type of instruction

guides students through problems and calculations rather than relying on students to figure it out independently.

Progress Monitoring

- Provide families with information on how their students are performing, and engage families as the supporters and motivators for their children's progress in mathematics.

Family

FIGURE 11.12

Mathematical Concepts for the Everyday World

More and more science and technology are permeating our society, and with this, the need for more mathematics to understand the scientific and technological concepts is increasing. The new level of mathematical competencies, skills, and attitudes toward mathematics required of modern citizenry is much higher than what was expected 25 years ago. The following represent the skills and competencies considered necessary for adults to participate effectively in contemporary society:

1. Numbers and numerals
   - Express a rational number using a decimal notation.
   - List the first ten multiples of 2 through 12.
   - Use the whole numbers (four basic operations) in problem solving.
   - Recognize the digit, its place value, and the number represented through billions.
   - Describe a given positive rational number using decimal, percent, or fractional notation.
   - Convert to Roman numerals from decimal numerals and conversely (e.g., data translation).
   - Represent very large and very small numbers using scientific notation.

2. Operations and properties
   - Write equivalent fractions for given fractions such as $\frac{1}{2}$, $\frac{2}{3}$, $\frac{3}{4}$, and $\frac{7}{8}$.
   - Use the standard algorithms for the operations of arithmetic of positive rational numbers.
   - Solve addition, subtraction, multiplication, and division problems involving fractions.
   - Solve problems involving percent.
   - Perform arithmetic operations with measures.
   - Estimate results.
   - Judge the reasonableness of answers to computational problems.

3. Mathematical sentences
   - Construct a mathematical sentence from a given verbal problem.
   - Solve simple equations.

4. Geometry and measurement
   - Recognize horizontal lines, vertical lines, parallel lines, perpendicular lines, and intersecting lines.
   - Recognize different shapes.
   - Compute areas, surfaces, volumes, densities.
   - Understand similarities and congruence.
   - Use measurement devices.

5. Relations and functions
   - Interpret information from a graphical representation.
   - Understand and apply ratio and proportion.
   - Construct scales.

6. Probability and statistics
   - Determine mean, average, mode, median.
   - Understand simple probability.

7. Mathematical reasoning
   - Produce counter examples to test invalidity of a statement.
   - Detect and describe flaws and fallacies in advertising and propaganda where statistical data and inferences are employed.
   - Gather and present data to support an inference or argument.

8. General skills
   - Maintain personal bank records.
   - Plan a budget and keep personal records.
   - Apply simple interest formula to calculate interest.
   - Estimate the real cost of an item.
   - Compute taxes and investment returns.
   - Appraise insurance and retirement benefits.

Source: M. C. Sharma, "Mathematics in the Real World" in J. F. Cawley (Ed.) *Developmental Teaching of Mathematics for Learning Disabled* (Austin, TX: PRO-ED, 1984), pp. 224–225. Reprinted with permission of PRO-ED, Inc.

soon find that functioning as an adult requires applying mathematic concepts. Managing money, checkbooks, interest on loans, and credit cards is only the beginning. Adults must file taxes, complete employment forms for deductions, and use basic math skills in their jobs. Figure 11.12 lists the mathematics skills all students need to acquire because they are essential for survival in the real world. To function adequately in society, all students should be able to demonstrate applied knowledge and understanding of these skills.

Mathematics instruction for students with learning disabilities needs to focus on teaching functional skills necessary for independent living (Patton, Cronin, Bassett, and Koppel, 1997). Many of the skills that are most important for students with learning disabilities are not part of general mathematics curricula because they do not need to be taught through direct instruction to non-learning-disabled students. Halpern (1981) suggests that students with learning disabilities learn the realistic prices of products, how to estimate, and how to tell time and estimate time intervals. According to Halpern (1981), most arithmetic that is done in the real world is done orally, yet arithmetic done in classrooms is largely

FIGURE 11.13

Content for Teaching Functional Math

Consumer Skills

Making change
Determining cost of sale items utilizing percentages
    (e.g., "25% off")
Determining tax amounts
Doing cost comparisons
Buying on "time"
Balancing a checkbook
Determining total cost of purchases

Homemaking Skills

Measuring ingredients
Budgeting for household expenses
Calculating length of cooking and baking time when there are
    options (e.g., for a cake using two 9" round pans vs. two 8"
    round pans)
Measuring material for clothing construction
Doing cost comparisons

Health Care

Weighing oneself and others
Calculating caloric intake
Determining when to take medication

Auto Care

Calculating cost of auto parts
Measuring spark plug gaps
Determining if tire pressure is correct
Figuring gas mileage

Home Care

Determining amount of supplies (paint, rug shampoo) to buy
Determining time needed to do projects

Measuring rods and drapes
Finding cost of supplies
Finding cost of repairs

Vocational Needs

Calculating payroll deductions
Determining money owed
Knowing when to be at work
Doing actual math for various jobs

Leisure Activities

Comparing travel expenses
Magazine and newspaper costs
Membership fees
Entertainment: movies, video rentals, sporting and artistic
    events

Home Management

Determining where to live
Moving expenses
Move-in expenses
Utilities
Insurance
Furniture
Additional expense

Transportation

Public or automobile
Maintenance
Insurance

Source: Adapted from J. R. Patton, M. E. Cronin, D. S. Bassett, and A. E. Koppel (1997). A life skills approach to mathematics instruction: Preparing students with learning disabilities for the real-life demands of adulthood. *Journal of Learning Disabilities, 30* (2), pp. 178–187; and S. E. Schwartz and D. Budd (1981). Mathematics for handicapped learners: A functional approach for adolescents. *Focus on Exceptional Children, 13* (7), pp. 7–8. Reproduced by permission of Love Publishing Company.

done with pencil and paper. More attention to oral practice in the classroom is needed.

Math instruction for students with disabilities requires teachers to consider the functional math skills that students need. Figure 11.13 presents an outline of content for teaching functional math.

Schwartz and Budd (1981) recommend an eight-step sequence for teaching a functional math curriculum. This approach appears to be particularly useful with junior high and high school students.

1. *Become motivated.* Students need to feel that there is a valid reason for learning to solve mathematics problems. This may include identifying how math is used at home and on the job. Students can interview their parents to determine all of the ways in which they use functional math. Former students or speakers can be invited to discuss the need for math when they joined the work world.

2. *Choose the operation.* When students are able to identify the question being asked, they find it much easier to identify the appropriate operation for

resolving the question. Students must understand how an operation is performed before they use the operation in functional mathematics.

3. *Understand the problem.* Students need to understand the type of question being asked in verbal problem solving. They need to understand such terms as *fewer, greater, more, altogether,* and *in addition to* in order to be successful in doing functional math. The teacher should present realistic problem situations and discuss the questions being asked. The teacher then asks students to focus on key words and discuss their meaning and assists students in identifying unnecessary information.

4. *Estimate the answer.* This step encourages students to check to determine whether their selected operation is reasonable. For example, a teacher may give the following problem: After Lee lends half of his total savings of $8.40 to his sister, how much money will he have left? A student selects multiplication as the operation for solving the problem. The student estimates the answer and has a second opportunity to check whether the correct operation was chosen. Questions such as the following should be asked of the student: After multiplying, will Lee have more money or less? When we lend money to people, do we usually have more money or less? Is multiplying the correct operation?

5. *Do the operation.* Students should be able to perform the operation, but a review of skills may be necessary.

6. *Check the answer.* Students check to be sure that numbers were copied correctly and the problem was performed correctly. Students are encouraged to answer the question, Is this a reasonable answer to the problem?

7. *Understand the answer.* After determining the answer, students should be able to interpret it. The teacher may ask additional questions that allow students to demonstrate more fully that they understand the answer and the problem.

8. *Apply the skill.* The application of the first seven steps is discussed in relation to problems generated by the students and the teacher.

Curriculum and Materials

Traditional math curricula have provided problems for students with learning disabilities. These problems have been summarized by Blankenship (1984):

- The reading vocabulary is difficult, and the reading level is too high.

- The sequencing of material presented is poor, multiple concepts are introduced, and focus skips from one concept to another.
- There is an insufficient number of problems covering each concept.
- There are insufficient opportunities and problems focusing on application.
- There is too much variance in the formatting of the pages.
- Students often do not have the prerequisite skills that the text assumes they possess.

Teachers who attempt to use traditional curricula with students who have learning difficulties will need to control for these factors in their teaching.

A number of curricula have been developed that focus on teaching math skills to students with learning difficulties. Some of these curricula are described in Apply the Concept 11.9.

INSTRUCTIONAL ACTIVITIES

This section provides instructional activities related to mathematics. Some of the activities teach new skills; others are best suited for practice and reinforcement of already acquired skills. For each activity, the objective, materials, and teaching procedures are described.

▶ Two-Digit Numbers: Focus on Reversals

Objective: To help students understand and use two-digit numbers successfully (for use with students who write 23 for 32, 41 for 14, etc.)

Grades: Primary

Materials: Objects that can be grouped by tens (e.g., pencils, paper, chips, sticks)

Teaching Procedures: Four steps are recommended: First, tell the students to group objects such as Popsicle sticks or chips in tens and then to tell the number of tens and the number of ones left

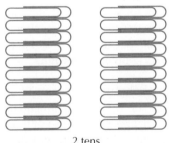

2 tens

3 ones

Apply the Concept 11.9

Sources of Curriculum and Materials

- *Connecting Math Concepts* (Bernadette, Carnine, Engelmann, and Engelmann, 2003) is designed to provide explicit instruction and explanations of basic math concepts and the relationships between concepts for students in grades K–8. Mastered concepts are then used to build problem-solving skills. The lessons proceed in small, incremental steps with continuous review. Materials include teacher's guides, student textbooks and workbooks, and fact and independent worksheets for additional practice. All lessons are scripted for teachers and provide systematic instruction in story problems.
- *Math Exploration and Applications*, developed by Bereiter, Hilton, Rubinstein, and Willoughby (1998), provides instruction, games, and manipulatives for building fluency in math skills. It is also available in Spanish.
- The *Corrective Mathematics Program*, by Englemann, Carnine,

and Steely (2005), provides remedial basic math for students in grades 3 through 12 addressing seven areas: addition, subtraction, multiplication, division, basic fractions, decimals and percents, and rations and equations.
- *Structural Arithmetic*, by Stern, Stern, and Gould (1998), involves students in prekindergarten through third grade in making, discovering, and learning math concepts and facts. Colorful blocks are used to assist students in discovering math concepts.
- Cuisenaire rods, developed by M. Georges Cuisenaire, help impart conceptual knowledge of the basic structure of mathematics.
- *Real-Life Math* (Ellen McPeek Glisam) provides an imaginary town (Willow, USA) where students learn math by learning to live on a paycheck. Students learn to budget money and pay expenses. Activity book and materials are available from PRO-ED publishers (www.proedinc.com).

- *Key Math Teach and Practice*, by Connolly (1988), was developed to provide diagnosis of math difficulties and remedial practice. Materials include a teacher's guide, student progress charts, and sequence charts. Activities and worksheets are also provided.
- *Saxon Math* for kindergarten through secondary grades was developed to provide math instruction that continuously builds on previous instruction while increasing the complexity to learn math concepts in depth. Math concepts, problem solving, and applications are sequential.
- *Progress in Math*, developed by William H. Sadlier (Sadlier Oxford, 2006) for students in kindergarten through sixth grade, teaches math concepts with an emphasis on strategies for solving math problems. Step-by-step problem-solving strategies are taught, and the use of specific strategies is scaffolded throughout the lessons.

---

over. Next, the students count orally by tens and use objects to show the count (e.g., 2 tens is 20, 6 tens is 60, and so on). When multiples of ten are established, extra ones are included (e.g., 2 tens and 3 is 23). Because of naming irregularities, teens are dealt with last.

The students then group objects by tens and write to describe the grouping. The tens–ones labels, used in early stages, are gradually eliminated. On separate sheets of paper, the students write the number that corresponds with the grouping. The children use objects (tens and ones) to help compare and sequence numbers.

▶ Two Up

Objective: To practice multiplication facts by rehearsing counting by twos, threes, fours, and so on.

Grades: Primary through intermediate

Prerequisite Behaviors: Counting by twos, threes, and so on

Materials: A set of 48 cards made by printing the multiples of 2 from 1 to 12, using a different color of pen for each set (e.g., 2, 4, . . . , 12 in red, blue, green, and brown)

Teaching Procedures: Directions for playing the game are as follows: The cards are shuffled and dealt, giving an equal number of cards to each player. The player who has the red 2 starts the game by placing the red 2 in the middle of the table. The next player must place a red 4 on top of the red 2 or pass. Next a red 6 is needed, and so on. Each of the players plays in a similar manner. A player can play only one card each turn.

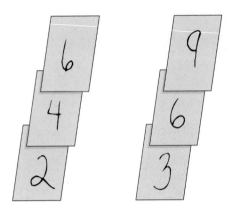

The object of the game is to play the cards from 2 on up. The first player to play all of his or her cards is the winner.

Adaptations: This game can be played with decks of threes, fours, sixes, and so on, called "Three Up," "Four Up," and so on. A different deck of cards must be made for each multiple.

▶ Clock-Reading Bingo

Objective: To give students practice in associating the time on a clock face to its written and spoken form

Grades: Primary

three o'clock	seven o'clock	fifteen minutes after four	twenty minutes after twelve
fifteen minutes after six	twenty minutes after twelve	twenty minutes to eleven	twenty minutes after eleven
five minutes after five	fifteen minutes after ten	twenty-five minutes after one	twenty-five minutes to eleven
nine thirty	five minutes to seven	twenty-five minutes after twelve	ten o'clock

Materials: Cards that show times on a standard clock, large game boards with 16 squares and with times written at the bottom of each square, 16 "clock" chips (made by placing gummed labels on cardboard chips and drawing a clock on the face of the label), markers

Teaching Procedures: A caller holds up a clock face. The players must decide whether the time shown by that clock is on their game board. If it is, the player places a marker in the square that contains the written form. The winner is the first person who correctly completes a row in any direction and reads the time in each winning square.

▶ Coin Concentration

Objective: To practice reading money amounts in four different notations and to reinforce coin recognition

Grades: Primary, intermediate to high school (see adaptation for older students)

Prerequisite Behaviors: Coin value, value placement, coin recognition of dollars and cents

Materials: Money picture card, money word card, money decimal card, money cents card

Teaching Procedures: The game of Coin Concentration can be played at several levels of difficulty, with varying skill emphasis depending on specific classroom needs. At the simplest level, use only one kind of money card. (Make two copies of the card, and cut it apart on the solid lines so students play with a total of 20 cards.) Decide on the number and type of cards to be used, and place them face down on the table.

The first player turns over two cards, one at a time, trying to match values. If the cards match, the player keeps them. If not, the player turns them back over on the table in their original location. Then the next player tries to make a match by turning over two more cards and so on, until all the cards are matched with their pair.

The winner is the player with the most matched cards. For variety, ask the students to add the total value of their cards and the player with the highest value wins. To add variety and increase difficulty, put different type cards down, and players can match 4¢ to $.04 or to *four cents.*

Adaptations: This activity can be used with older students by increasing the difficulty of the coin values represented and by adding a fifth card. On the fifth card is the name of an object that costs the corresponding amount. For example, if the money value is $329.00, the fifth card may have "Videocassette Recorder" written on it.

▶Shopping Spree

Objective: To give students practice using money and understanding the concept of addition and subtraction with money

Grades: Elementary-age students who are having difficulty with the money concepts (see adaptations for use with older students)

Materials: Coins (and dollar bills when teaching the more advanced concepts), pictures of items

Teaching Procedures: Cut out magazine pictures of things children would like to buy, and put a price on each picture. Start with easy amounts, such as 5¢, 10¢, 25¢; then in future lessons, increase the complexity of the amounts to such things as 63¢ and 51¢. For higher grades, use dollar amounts. Have the class divide into two groups, with half the students serving as store clerks and the other half as shoppers. The shoppers buy picture items from the clerks. The shoppers are responsible for giving the correct amount of money. The clerks are responsible for giving the correct change. Then have students trade roles.

At a later date, distribute specific amounts of money and ask students to select several items without going over their designated amount.

Or, ask students to show two or three different items and tell which item they can afford with their amount of money.

Adaptations: For older students, you can distribute pretend checkbooks. Each student gets a specified amount in his or her checkbook and must make appropriate deductions as he or she makes purchases.

▶99

Objective: To generalize and practice adding numbers in one's head or on paper

Grades: Intermediate to high school

Materials: Playing cards, paper, and pencils

Teaching Procedures: Explain that the objective of this game is to add cards up to a score of 99. Establish the following rules:

> Jacks and queens = 10
> Kings = 99
> Nines = free-turn pass—to be used anytime
> Fours = pass
> Aces = 1
> Other cards = face value

Each player is dealt three cards. The rest of the cards go face down on a draw pile. The players take turns discarding one card from their hand face up on a discard pile and drawing one card from the draw pile to put back in their hand. As a player discards his or her card, the player must add the number from the card to any previous score acquired up to that point in the game and say the new score out loud. Note the exceptions: If a player plays a nine, he or she receives a free-turn pass. If a player plays a four, he or she has to pass a turn with no score. The first player to score higher than 99 loses the game.

▶Shopping

Objective: To provide practice in addition, subtraction, and comparing prices (problem solving)

Grades: Junior high

Materials: Supermarket sale ads that include the price per item (optionally mounted individually on cardboard and covered with clear plastic), made-up shopping lists to hand out to the class, pencil, and paper

Teaching Procedures: Divide the class into small groups. Tell the students that their shopping list

contains the items that they will need this week. Assign each group a designated amount for groceries (e.g., $30.00). The object is to buy everything on the list while spending the least amount of money. Place on each desk the supermarket sale ads, each with the name of its store. After students buy an item, they record its price and the store where they bought it. (It's easier if one student in each group buys the meats, one buys the dairy products, and so on.) When the students have bought all the items on the list, tell them to total their bills and be ready to present the results.

▶ Cake for Four—No, Make That Six!

By Sandra Stroud

Objective: Developing students' concept of fractions by having them partition an object into equal parts

Grades: Second through fourth grades (possibly higher)

Materials: For each student, a six-inch paper circle; five strips construction paper, one inch wide by eight inches long, in a color contrasting to that of the paper circle; eight small cookies, placed in a small sandwich bag

Teaching Procedures: Students move desks together so that each student has a partner with whom to compare his or her work. Materials are distributed. The teacher introduces the lesson by telling the students that they are going to take part in a "Let's Pretend" activity that will help them to learn that when they eat a piece of cake that has been divided into equal parts, they are actually eating a fraction of that cake.

The students are asked to imagine that they have just helped to bake a cake. It is their favorite kind of cake, and because there are four people in their pretend family, they are planning to divide it into four equal pieces. They are asked to think of the paper circle on their desk as the top of the cake and to show the teacher—and their partners—how they would use the strips of paper to divide the cake into four equal parts. When each child has successfully demonstrated this first partitioning task, they are asked what fraction of the whole cake each piece is and how that fraction is written.

Next, they are asked to imagine that their grandmother and grandfather have arrived unexpectedly and that the grandparents have accepted the family's invitation to stay for supper. The family certainly wants to share the cake with their grandparents, so into how many pieces will they now divide their cake? The teacher makes sure that each student shows six equal portions and that they understand that each piece of cake is now 1/6 of the whole—just enough for the six people at the dinner table. However, before that cake is served, Uncle Bob and Aunt Doris arrive! Now the cake will be divided into how many equal pieces? Finally, the time comes to decorate the cake with the cookies and to cut and serve the cake. (As a reward for all their good thinking, the students now get to eat the decorations—1/8 at a time!)

Students enjoy the story associated with this activity, and they enjoy comparing their partitioned cakes with those of their peers. This is a good example of cooperative learning. Students especially enjoy eating their cookies at the end of this activity.

▶ The Values of Coins

By Ae-Hwa Kim

Objective: To help students learn the relative values of coins (for example, students will determine that a quarter is worth 25 times as much as one cent)

Grades: Primary

Materials: Models with real coins for each step

Teaching Procedures: For the initial instruction, the teacher shows all models and coins and addresses the objective of the lesson. During the lesson, the teacher models and verbally explains each step, provides students with guided and independent practice, and gives them feedback.

1. Show students proportionate models to represent the values of coins.

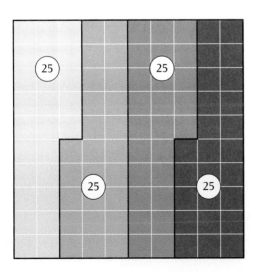

1	1	1	1	1	1	1	1	1	1
1	1	1	1	1	1	1	1	1	1
1	1	1	1	1	1	1	1	1	1
1	1	1	1	1	1	1	1	1	1
1	1	1	1	1	1	1	1	1	1
1	1	1	1	1	1	1	1	1	1
1	1	1	1	1	1	1	1	1	1
1	1	1	1	1	1	1	1	1	1
1	1	1	1	1	1	1	1	1	1
1	1	1	1	1	1	1	1	1	1

2. Teach the values of coins and their relative values with models, which visually represent the values of coins and their relative worth. For example, one nickel is worth five pennies and so takes up the space of five pennies.

3. Teach the value of a set of coins with models, which visually represent the value of a set of coins.
4. Teach the students to compare the values of sets of coins with models.
5. Teach the students to use models to create a set of coins with a given value. Allow the students to use different combinations of coins to make the given value.
6. Teach the students to create a set of coins with a given value by using the fewest coins with models.

Source: Based on an activity by R. L. Drum and W. G. Petty (1997). Teaching the value of coins. *Teaching Children Mathematics*, 5 (5), pp. 264–268.

▶Learning Addition

By Ae-Hwa Kim

Objective: To help students understand how to do addition with three-digit numbers and provide practice in addition through activities

Grades: Primary

Materials: Pictures of three different types of animals; three lengths of bricks (short, medium, and long); scratch paper

Teaching Procedures:
1. Seat three volunteer "animals" (e.g., zebra, giraffe, and deer) on chairs side by side in front of a chalkboard. Hang a sign with a picture of each animal around the neck of the student who acts as that animal. The sign on the right (deer) also has the word *ones* or *1s*, signifying the units place of the number. The middle sign (giraffe) shows the word *tens* or *10s*, signifying the tens place of the number. The sign on the left (zebra) has the word *hundreds* or *100s*, signifying the hundreds place of the number. Throughout the activity, the place-value words are visible.
2. Give each animal a supply of bricks. Long bricks signify hundreds; medium bricks signify tens; and short bricks signify single units. Give two long bricks to the hundreds zebra, five medium bricks to the tens giraffe, and eight short bricks to the ones deer. (First number = 258.)
3. Ask each animal to tell what he or she has been given as the teacher writes the combined number on the chalkboard.

4. Teach students the rules to this activity:
   - All business exchanges begin with the ones deer, then the tens giraffe, and finally the hundreds zebra. The animals receive their shipments in turn and take inventory of their bricks as they are received.
   - The inventory process ensures that the ones deer never has 10 ones bricks (short), the tens giraffe never has 10 tens bricks (medium), and the hundreds zebra never has 10 hundreds bricks (i.e., each animal's total is nine or less). If any animal has more than 10 bricks, he or she must trade 10 bricks for 1 brick of the next greater value.
5. The brick suppliers will arrive to deliver more bricks to each animal. For example, the supplier may bring 4 hundreds bricks, 7 tens bricks, and 3 ones bricks. (Second number = 473.)
6. When the ones deer inventories 11 bricks, a teacher reminds him or her of the rules and establishes that the ones deer must deliver a stack of 10 short bricks back to the supplier in exchange for 1 medium brick, which must then be given to the tens giraffe. The single short brick that remains is recorded on the chalkboard. When the 7 newly delivered medium bricks are added to the original 5 medium bricks and the medium brick passed from the ones deer, the tens giraffe then has 13 medium bricks. Therefore, he or she delivers one set of 10 bricks to the supplier in exchange for 1 long brick, which is then given to the hundreds zebra. The tens giraffe then reports an inventory of 3 medium bricks remaining. Our hundreds zebra then reports a total inventory of 7 long bricks, or hundreds. (Final answer: 258 + 473 = 731.)

Source: Based on an activity by M. M. Bartek (1997). Hands-on addition and subtraction with the Three Pigs. *Teaching Children Mathematics, 4* (2), pp. 68–71.

▶ Addition and America

By Ae-Hwa Kim

Objective: To motivate students to solve addition problems as well as to increase their accuracy of solving problems

Grades: Second through fourth grades (possibly higher)

Materials: Map of the United States, tickets made of cards on which math addition facts are printed

Teaching Procedures:
1. Show students the map of the United States to get their attention.
2. Explain the rules of game:
   - The students try to move from their home state to another state across the nation.
   - Students have to have their ticket to travel from state to state.
   - Students must solve the addition problem printed on the ticket and read the name of the state. (The name of the state will be printed on the map, so students just need to read the word.)
   - Only when students get the right answer are they allowed to move to the next state. If students miss the problem, they have to stay in their current state until their next trial time.
3. Let the students play a game. During the game, the teacher assists them and also records the speed and accuracy of their answers.

Note: This game can be extended to subtraction, multiplication, and division.

Source: Based on an activity by D. E. Miller (1997). Math across America. *Teaching Exceptional Children, 24* (2), pp. 47–49.

▶ The Value of Numbers

By Ae-Hwa Kim

Objective: To help students understand the value of numbers (ones value, tens value, and hundreds value)

Grades: Primary

Materials: Popsicle sticks; rubber bands to group the Popsicle sticks; a sign; number cards; three boxes to hold ones, tens, and hundreds of Popsicle sticks

Teaching Procedures:

Practice

1. Count the number of Popsicle sticks.
2. Model putting a rubber band around a group of 10 sticks; then ask students to put a rubber band around each new group of 10 sticks.
3. Model putting 1s in the ones box, 10s in the tens box, and so on. Ask students to put 1s in the ones box, 10s in the tens box, and so on.

Activity

4. Show the students a sign that says "Thank you for the _____ Popsicle sticks" (e.g., 157).

5. Model putting that number of Popsicle sticks in the boxes; then ask students to put the number of Popsicle sticks in the boxes.
6. Change the numbers on the sign repeatedly, and allow students to practice grouping Popsicle sticks according to the sign.

Source: Based on an activity by C. Paddock (1997). Ice cream stick math. *Teaching Exceptional Children, 24* (2), pp. 50–51.

SUMMARY for Chapter 11

Developing appropriate mathematics instruction for students with learning and behavior problems involves comprehensive programming with an emphasis on applying math to daily living skills. Special attention is given to factors that might influence the math learning abilities of special students. Psychological factors, educational factors, neuropsychological factors, perceptual skills, language skills, and reasoning need to be considered in developing a student's instructional program.

There has been increasing interest in early identification of students who are at risk for mathematical problems or with mathematical disabilities. For this reason, it is important to assess and monitor the progress of students in mathematics. Measures for determining students' knowledge and application of mathematics are useful tools for teachers. Universal screening in math can identify students at risk for math problems. Applying a response to intervention (RTI) model, students receive math interventions and have their progress documented.

In developing comprehensive programming, it is necessary to consider all facets of math instruction, including numeration, place value, facts, computation, time, money, fractions, and verbal problem solving. Success in teaching math is directly related to students' ability to apply the concepts to math problems that occur in daily living.

Traditional math curricula have provided problems for students with learning and behavior problems. Often the reading level is difficult, the material is not sequenced, and there are not enough problems covering each concept that mastery can be ensured before the next concept is introduced. These students need math problems to be directly linked to real-world applications.

Teaching math to students with learning and behavior problems is a challenge—potentially, a very rewarding challenge. Students with learning difficulties have shown greater gains in math through appropriate instruction than in most other content areas. Although students have access to computers and calculators, which can assist them in solving math problems they understand, they must know what problems they want to solve, which operation is needed, and the procedures necessary for computing the answers before they can fully use these instruments. Because of the increased need to use mathematics in the workplace, students need to understand mathematics now more than ever before.

FOCUS Answers

FOCUS Question 1. What characteristics are common to students who exhibit deficits in math skills, how can these characteristics influence math ability, and what should teachers consider when planning instruction for these students?

Answer: Deficits in math skills are commonly seen in perceptual skills, such as spatial relationships and sequencing; perseveration, making it difficult to shift from one task to another; language ability, impacting understanding of math concepts and vocabulary; reasoning, or dealing with abstract concepts that prevail in math; poor memory, making it difficult to remember new concepts; and symbolism difficulties, interfering with learning what symbols refer to. Many students with learning disabilities and behavior problems also have difficulty in paying and sustaining attention, working carefully, and accepting responsibility. Furthermore, because of their difficulty with math, many of these students have received an overabundance of instruction in basic skills but have not been exposed to essential math concepts and problem-solving strategies. In planning curricula for these students, teachers should consider such factors as comprehensive yet individualized programming, providing correction and feedback, generalizing examples to real-life situations, allowing students to participate in goal selection, and using discovery instead of didactic instruction.

FOCUS Question 2. **How is assessment used in mathematics, and what is CBM? What are some examples of several types of assessment techniques that can be used to determine number sense in young children?**

Answer: Assessment helps teachers determine what students know and need to know as well as how students compare to others of the same age or grade level. In addition, appropriate assessments allow teachers to monitor students' progress and make effective instructional decisions based on the information they have gathered. When curriculum-based measurement is used to monitor students' progress and adjust instruction accordingly, students make gains at much more rapid rates. Assessments that measure number sense include counting measures, number identification measures, and number writing.

FOCUS Question 3. **What are the prenumber skills students need to progress in arithmetic?**

Answer: Prenumber skills that facilitate students' growth in math include one-to-one correspondence, classification, and seriation.

FOCUS Question 4. **What are several numeration concepts?**

Answer: Numeration concepts include: cardinality; grouping patterns; place value; one digit per place; linear order; decimal point; place relation; implied zones; implied addition; order; name of numbers; periods and names; and understanding "zero."

FOCUS Question 5. **What factors contribute to difficulties with problem solving, and how can teachers assist students in learning problem-solving strategies?**

Answer: Reading problems, poorly developed logical reasoning skills, and instruction that focuses primarily on computation contribute to difficulty with mathematical problem solving. Teachers can increase students' problem-solving abilities by teaching big ideas, using sameness analysis, teaching cue words, teaching reasoning strategies, simplifying the sentence structure of word problems, eliminating extraneous information, and monitoring the number of concepts presented as well as the interest level. Computer-assisted instruction is a motivational way to provide practice in problem solving and feedback on performance.

FOCUS Question 6. **What are the three types of math interventions, and how can they be used to improve math performance?**

Answer: Cognitive approaches to math instruction rely on verbalizing or making explicit steps or strategies in solving math problems. Behavioral approaches use the idea of stimulus-response learning to focus on the cues that students need to know in order to be successful in math. Alternative ways to deliver math instruction include cooperative learning, computer-assisted instruction, and interactive video. The best approach to teaching math is one that combines a variety of techniques that are appropriate for the student and the skills that need to be developed. New curricula have been developed specifically for teaching math skills to students with learning and behavior problems.

THINKand APPLY

- What factors and learning difficulties might interfere with mathematics learning for students with learning and behavior problems?
- What are three important teaching perspectives that should be considered in designing a math intervention program for students with learning and behavior disorders?
- How might teachers monitor the progress of students with difficulties in mathematics?
- What mathematical skills need to be taught so that students will have adequate knowledge of numeration and place value?
- What strategies can be taught to students who are having difficulty with basic math facts?

- How would you convince a fellow teacher that using calculators can be helpful when learning mathematics?
- What factors affect successful problem solving, and what problem-solving strategy might be effective to help students become better math problem solvers?
- Why is it so important that special education teachers make use of concrete materials and stress the real-life application of math problems?
- Why are traditional math curricula and materials often inadequate for meeting the needs of students with learning disabilities?

APPLYthe STANDARDS

 Council for Exceptional Children

1. A new student who is struggling to succeed in math has entered your class. Using the information from Chapter Eleven and your knowledge of the relevant CEC standards (LD4K3, LD4S6, LD7K3, LD8S1), describe how you could use curriculum-based measurement to identify learning needs and to monitor progress.

Standard LD4K3: Interventions and services for children who may be at risk for learning disabilities.

Standard LD4S6: Use responses and errors to guide instruction and feedback.

Standard LD7K3: Methods for increasing accuracy and proficiency in math calculations and applications.

Standard LD8S1: Choosing and administering assessment instruments appropriate to the individual with learning disabilities.

WEBSITESas RESOURCES | to Assist in Teaching Mathematics

The following Websites are extensive resources to expand your understanding of teaching mathematics:

- Helping Your Child Learn Math www.ed.gov/pubs/parents/Math/index.html
- Super Kids Math Worksheet Creator www.superkids.com/aweb/tools/math
- Aplusmath.com Worksheets www.aplusmath.com/Worksheets/index.html
- Awesome Library Website www.awesomelibrary.org/Classroom/Mathematics/Mathematics.html
- Schwab Learning.org Website www.schwablearning.org/articles.asp?r=446

myeducationlab
Where the Classroom Comes to Life

Case Study Homework Exercise Go to MyEducationLab and select the topic "INSTRUCTIONAL PRACTICES AND LEARNING STRATEGIES," then read the case study "Applying Learning Strategies to Beginning Algebra" and complete the activity questions below.

This case study unit outlines some of the common problems students face when beginning to learn more advanced math subjects, such as algebra. It also provides strategies for teaching algebra using math vocabulary, the Concrete-Representational-Abstract method, graphic organizers, and mnemonic devices.

To answer the following questions, read one of the case studies provided in this case study unit.

1. Read the Star (Strategies and Resources) sheets recommended for the case you selected. Briefly summarize each strategy and describe the ways in which it could assist you in meeting the needs of the student outlined in the case study.

2. Connect these strategies to the teaching perspectives outlined in the chapter to support students who struggle in math. Which perspectives are supported for the case you selected?

Video Homework Exercise Go to MyEducationLab and select the topic "INSTRUCTIONAL PRACTICES AND LEARNING STRATEGIES," then watch the video "Real World Math Methods" and complete the activity questions below.

Math concepts are interrelated. In this video, the students use real-world examples to connect to the math concepts, make sense of math, and understand its importance.

1. What is the teacher's goal in this lesson?

2. What are some of the benefits described in the chapter and in the video of using real-world examples to solve math problems?

Chapter 12

Transition Planning Process

by James R. Patton, Ed.D.
University of Texas–Austin

As you read the chapter, watch for these questions to help you focus your learning:

1. When do transitions occur, and what are three features that can facilitate effective transitions for individuals with disabilities?

2. What is transition education, and what different options are available for offering transition education to students?

3. What are the purpose and the key features of the transition planning process?

Eileen is a 16-year-old student who has experienced numerous learning-related problems in school. Through the years, she has had multiple diagnoses: a learning disability, dyslexia, and attention deficit hyperactivity disorder. Her school experience thus far has been difficult and full of inconsistencies and frustration. Some of her teachers have interpreted her behavior as laziness and noncompliance; others feel her performance reflects carelessness.

Eileen would like to attend college in a different city from where she currently lives. She is very interested in living in a dorm and experiencing the typical college lifestyle. College is a realistic goal for her—she is bright enough to handle the content and she has taken the coursework required for entry into college. Her parents did not go to college, so the whole process of selecting and applying to colleges is a new experience for the family.

Eileen does not have any serious difficulties in the area of daily living skills. She has the skills needed to perform everyday duties around the house. However, she does have some problems with money management. She has a driver's license and will have a car when she graduates high school.

Reading is particularly challenging for Eileen. She has to devote extra time to reading narrative and expository text, because she has to use various strategies to extract key meaning from these types of materials. Her problems with reading exceed her writing difficulties, but her writing skills are not strong. She has trouble organizing her thoughts and ideas when she has to write a paper about a theme or an issue. She is much better at writing short, more fact-based, technical types of assignments.

Eileen also has problems with various academic support skills such as test-taking, time-management, and organizational skills. Foreign-language studies were extremely difficult for her in high school. These factors have contributed to self-devaluation during the latter years of high school.

Eileen has superb verbal skills; she does well in any setting that involves verbal interaction. It is clear, based on the elaborate coping strategies she has developed to deal with situations that are problematic for her, that she is quite creative. She has discovered a talent in the area of drama, which has given her confidence. Through drama, she has been able to develop her verbal skills and sense of self-worth.

Fundamental Issues Related to Transition

Most people have a general sense of what *transition* means—often associating transition with a period in time when change occurs. Specifically, transition relates to the processes associated with movement from one situation or setting to another. Many different transitions are part of the daily lives of all individuals. In Eileen's case, transition refers to a process that will consider various features of her current strengths and needs in the context of her future adult life. In this case, the actual act of transition planning is a coordinated set of activities that assist in preparing Eileen, and her family, for the transition from high school to life as a young adult that is going to take place.

Important transitions occur throughout everyone's life. Some are predictable (vertical); others are specific to the individual and occur at unpredictable points in time (horizontal). Figure 12.1 highlights both types of transitions. As the figure indicates, the life span–related (i.e., vertical) transitions are associated with predictable life events, such as beginning school, leaving elementary

FIGURE 12.1

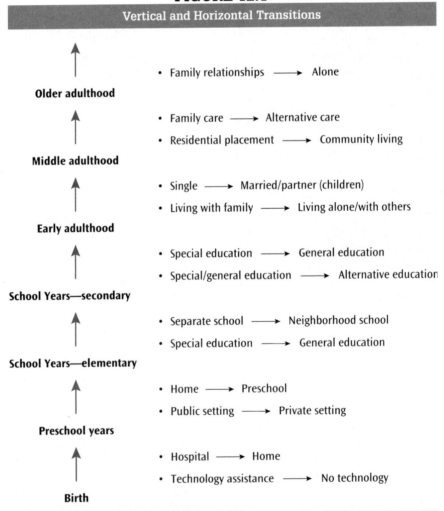

Vertical and Horizontal Transitions

Source: Adapted from G. Blalock and J. R. Patton (1996). Transition and students with learning disabilities: Creating sound futures. *Journal of Learning Disabilities, 29*(1), p. 8. Copyright 1996 by PRO-ED, Inc. Adapted with permission.

school, and growing older. Coordinated planning for key vertical transitions (e.g., transition from elementary to secondary school) can minimize the anxiety that may arise and can make such transitions smoother. But in reality, little comprehensive planning occurs in the lives of most individuals.

Horizontal transitions refer to movement from one person-specific situation or setting to another. One of the most important and frequently discussed horizontal transitions is the movement from segregated settings to more inclusive ones. This is an example of a transition that is not age specific, as opportunities for such movement are available throughout the life span to people with disabilities.

As important as transition planning might seem for a variety of situations in which change occurs, specific transition planning activities are mandated for only two of the many possible transitions depicted in Figure 12.1. The first mandated transition involves very young children (toddlers and their families) who are receiving services under Part C of the Individualized with Disabilities Education Act (IDEA) and who are approaching three years of age. As required by law, an Individualized Family Service Plan (IFSP) has been developed for each of these young children. One component of the IFSP serves to smooth the movement of these young children from the early intervention services to any number of other settings (e.g., being at home, early childhood special education, other preschool programs).

The second mandated transition affects students like Eileen who are preparing to exit the school system. Currently, transition planning activities must be initiated by age 16 for all youths who receive special and related services under IDEA. We will discuss transition planning later in this chapter. The remainder of this chapter will focus on this second mandated transition.

Key Elements of Successful Transitions

A few key provisions allow students to navigate the many transitions they face throughout their lives. These factors are of two types: student-related factors and system-related factors. Most transitions can be accomplished more smoothly if the following two sets of elements are in place:

Student-Related Factors
- Student involvement
- Commitment to personal goals
- Motivation

System-Related Factors
- Comprehensive planning (needs assessment and individual planning)
- Implementation of a plan of action
- Coordination, cooperation, communication, and collaboration

Student-Related Factors

The transition process, especially the one for students who are preparing to move from school to living in the community, is enhanced in a number of ways when students are more fully engaged in the process. Student involvement implies that students not only are invited to participate but also are provided the knowledge and skills to do so competently. What should never be lost in this process is that it is the student's life that is being considered, discussed, and acted on. As such, ensuring that students are actively involved in choosing and setting their own personal goals is critical. The third factor, motivation, contributes greatly to how driven students are to pursue the goals that they have set and how much work the students put into the process.

System-Related Factors

The initial critical element of system-related factors is comprehensive planning, which includes two related subcomponents. First, the special education teacher or transition specialist must conduct some type of needs assessment. This involves collecting information to determine a student's strengths, preferences, interests, and needs in relation to life after high school. Techniques for obtaining this information include the use of informal and formal instruments and certainly should involve talking with the student who is getting ready to transition and with his or her family members. It is essential to explore the possible settings, such as the workplace or postsecondary education (e.g., technical school, community college, university), into which the student will be transitioning. In other words, the more school-based professionals know about the setting into which the student is transitioning (i.e., what is required to be successful, what kinds of supports, services, or accommodations are available if needed) along with the student's existing competencies (strengths and needs), the better the chances are for an effective transition. In Eileen's case, the results of an initial needs assessment indicate certain areas to which attention must be directed before she leaves school as well as later on when she is in college. Eileen's personal transition strengths and needs must be considered in relation to the demands of the college environment that she will encounter when she graduates from high school.

The other subcomponent, individual planning, entails developing a "plan of action" based on the strengths/needs assessment. The overriding consideration is that the plan of action balance the student's and the family's current values, preferences for the future, and personal interests with the realistic demands of postschool settings that are being considered. Some sample transition goals that need to be developed for Eileen are provided later in the chapter. It is interesting to note that individualized planning must be formalized in a written document such as the IEP; nevertheless, for most of the transitions listed in Figure 12.1, ideas are discussed but a written document is not generated.

The second element is implementing the plan of action. Of course, needs assessments and individualized plans are useless if the plan of action is not implemented effectively. Far too often, good plans are not put into effect. Whether the transition involves transitioning a young child with severe language or learning disabilities from a preschool program to an inclusive kindergarten with special education support or transitioning an adolescent with emotional or behavioral disabilities from a residential treatment facility to a public school setting, certain actions must occur to achieve the desired results. Implementation of transitions frequently suffers from three potential threats:

1. Certain key aspects of the plan are not carried out because the needs assessment and/or the planning phase were completed inadequately or inappropriately.
2. The plan is simply not executed as it was designed.
3. The person or people who are assigned responsibility for carrying out some portion of the plan of action do not fulfill their commitments.

The last key element of a successful transition involves *coordination* and *cooperation* with the various people at the various settings or agencies involved in the transition itself (i.e., receiving settings). Such coordination and cooperation require ongoing *communication* at a minimum and *collaboration* as the most desirable relationship. For example, Eileen's transition from high school to college will be facilitated by coordination between a school-based transition specialist and key individuals at the college, such as admissions officers, academic advisors, and professionals associated with the office that works with students with disabilities.

When the key elements highlighted above are absent, transitions from one setting to another are likely to result only in physical relocation and not the more meaningful outcomes that are associated with favorable transitions.

Definitional Perspectives of Transition Services

The transition planning process has been and can be defined in various ways. In a general sense, transition services suggest an assortment of activities that lead to the successful movement of a student from school to living in the community. The key factor is that this assortment of activities is not haphazard; rather, it is a systematic (i.e., coordinated) set of actions that provides a framework for school-based personnel. The specific pieces of the transition planning process will be discussed later in the chapter; in the interim, it is important to recognize two definitional perspectives of transition. The first is the definition provided in the most current reauthorization of IDEA 2004, and the other definition comes from the major professional organization dedicated to the topic of transition.

Federal Definition of Transition

IDEA provides the guiding framework with regard to transitions for youth with disabilities. The IDEA mandate requires that the individualized education program (IEP) include a statement of needed transition services beginning no later than the first IEP in effect when the child is 16 and that the IEP be updated annually (focusing on needed services, linkages, and interagency responsibilities). The 2004 amendments of IDEA define *transition services* as follows:

> A coordinated set of activities for a child with a disability that (1) is designed to be within a results-oriented process, that is focused on improving the academic and functional achievement of the child with a disability to facilitate the child's movement from school to post-school activities, including post-secondary education, vocational education, integrated employment (including supported employment), continuing and adult education, adult services, independent living, or community participation; (2) is based on the individual child's needs, taking into account the child's strengths, preferences, and interests; and (3) includes instruction, related

services, community experiences, the development of employment and other post-school adult living objectives, and when appropriate, acquisition of daily living skills and functional vocational evaluation. (IDEA 2004, Section 602(34) [A-C])

The 2004 amendments included some notable changes from IDEA 1997, including:

- Changing the term *outcomes-oriented process* to *results-oriented process*
- Using the phrasing "academic and functional achievement"
- Including the phrase "taking into account the child's strengths"

Professional Perspective

Another definitional perspective of transition is provided by the Division on Career Development and Transition (DCDT) of the Council for Exceptional Children. Their definition reflects contemporary thinking and underscores the realities associated with students leaving school and assuming a variety of adult roles in the community. It also stresses the proactive nature of transition education and the importance of actively involving students in this process whenever possible.

> *Transition* refers to a change in status from behaving primarily as a student to assuming emergent adult roles in the community. These roles include employment, participating in post-secondary education, maintaining a home, becoming appropriately involved in the community, and experiencing satisfactory personal and social relationships. The process of enhancing transitions involves the participation and coordination of school programs, adult agency services, and natural supports within the community. The foundations for transition should be laid during the elementary and middle school years, guided by the broad concept of career development. . . . Students should be encouraged, to the full extent of their capabilities, to assume a maximum amount of responsibility for such planning. (Halpern, 1994, p. 117)

Rationale for Providing Transition Services

The adult status of many individuals has been a driving force behind the need for transition services. The fact that special education had been mandated for all students with disabilities since 1975 highlighted the need to examine what impact this special education was ultimately having on students when they departed formal schooling. Follow-up studies conducted in various parts of the country in the 1980s and early 1990s pointed to a less-than-positive scenario of unemployment and underemployment, restricted living options, and few social interactions/activities (Sitlington, Frank, and Carson, 1993).

The most comprehensive study, conducted in the late 1980s and published in the early 1990s, was the National Longitudinal Transition Study (Wagner, Blackorby, Cameto, Habbeler, and Newman, 1993). The overall results of this study corroborated the findings of other studies. The results of a second recently conducted, comprehensive study, the National Longitudinal Transition Study-2 (NLTS2), indicate that the adult outcomes of students formerly served in special education have improved in many areas. Nevertheless, much more work needs to be done. (Results that have been made available can be found on www.nlts2.org.)

IDEA 2004 stressed the importance of functional achievement. This means that students leaving school need to possess competence in a range of everyday, functional areas. One area that the NLTS-2 examined was the functional skills. Table 12.1 shows the results of interviews of parents in regard to how they perceived the functional skills of their adult children after they left school. What is dramatic about the findings is the significant percentage of adults across disability categories who were not rated "high" by parents on:

- Functional cognitive skills (e.g., making change)
- Social skills
- Communicating with no trouble

A source of data on adult outcomes is the U.S. Census Bureau. The following statistics, based on the 2000 census and available online at the Census Bureau's Website, provide additional information with regard to the outcomes of persons with disabilities:

- Number of people age 5 and over in the civilian, noninstitutionalized population with at least one disability: 49.7 million
- Percentage of people with disabilities who report more than one disability: 46 percent
- Percentage of working-age men with disabilities who are employed: 60 percent (10.4 million)

TABLE 12.1

Functional Skills of Out-of-School Youth by Disability Category

	Learning Disability	Speech/ Language Impair- ment	Mental Retar- dation	Emo- tional Distur- bance	Hearing Impair- ment	Visual Impair- ment	Ortho- pedic Impair- ment	Other Health Impair- ment	Autism	Trau- matic Brain Injury	Multiple Disabili- ties
Percentage rated by parents "high" on:											
Self-care skills	98.5	96.1	84.2	97.7	99.3	90.6	67.8	89.4	66.0	73.5	56.3
	(1.3)	(3.0)	(5.7)	(1.6)	(1.2)	(5.6)	(7.1)	(3.4)	(9.1)	(9.2)	(9.5)
Functional cognitive skills	80.4	84.5	42.3	83.6	84.1	63.9	82.8	84.8	72.2	74.5	44.5
	(4.5)	(5.7)	(7.8)	(4.2)	(5.2)	(9.3)	(6.3)	(4.0)	(8.8)	(9.3)	(9.6)
Percentage with social skills rated:[a]											
High	19.1	14.1	7.3	5.4	32.6	36.5	24.3	16.2	3.1	9.9	17.7
	(4.7)	(5.8)	(4.3)	(2.6)	(7.0)	(9.5)	(7.2)	(4.2)	(3.8)	(6.6)	(8.5)
Low	17.4	16.5	26.0	45.8	9.7	10.6	17.1	22.5	28.1	30.0	25.9
	(4.5)	(6.2)	(7.2)	(5.8)	(4.4)	(6.1)	(6.3)	(4.8)	(9.8)	(10.1)	(9.8)
Percentage communicating with no trouble	83.3	61.3	55.2	80.4	41.1	92.7	77.2	81.8	65.4	62.1	54.5
	(4.1)	(7.5)	(7.7)	(4.3)	(6.8)	(4.9)	(6.8)	(4.2)	(9.2)	(10.2)	(9.6)
Percentage with health reported to be:[b]											
Excellent	41.2	50.7	30.4	36.0	40.8	50.7	28.1	40.5	47.0	21.1	27.3
	(5.5)	(7.7)	(7.1)	(5.2)	(6.8)	(9.4)	(7.3)	(5.4)	(9.6)	(8.5)	(8.4)
Fair or poor	8.1	6.6	12.1	13.5	10.4	7.1	19.3	13.6	5.9	32.0	18.5
	(3.0)	(3.8)	(5.0)	(3.7)	(4.2)	(4.9)	(6.4)	(3.8)	(4.5)	(9.7)	(7.4)

Source: NLTS2 (2005) Wave 2 parent/youth interviews.
[a]The category "medium" is omitted from the exhibit.
[b]The categories "very good" and "good" are omitted from the exhibit.
Standard errors are in parentheses.

- Percentage of working-age women with disabilities who are employed: 51 percent (8.2 million)
- Median 1999 earnings of the 12 million year-round, full-time workers (in six disability areas): $28,803 (median income of workers without disabilities: $33,970)
- Percentage of individuals with disabilities ages 18 to 34 of all individuals enrolled in school: 12 percent (1.9 million individuals)

Overriding Themes of Transition

Certain critical themes should guide the transition process for all youths with disabilities, whether transition planning results from mandate (IDEA) or is part of an ongoing set of services provided to all students in a school (career counseling and guidance). The following 10 themes reflect best and promising practices (Patton and Dunn, 1998):

1. Transition education efforts should start early. Transition education can begin at the preschool level; however, without question more formalized activities should begin at the middle school level.

2. Transition planning must be comprehensive. Transition assessment and planning must look at the demands of adulthood across a broad spectrum of adult functioning (i.e., beyond an employment-only focus).

3. Transition needs assessment should capitalize on a student's strengths in addition to the obvious focus on areas of transition need. A strength-based approach is both good practice, and it is also mandated by IDEA 2004.

4. Student participation is crucial. This means more than inviting the student to attend critical meetings at which transition topics will be discussed; it also involves preparing the student to engage in the process to the fullest degree possible.

5. Family involvement is not only desired but essential. Families typically will remain key players in the lives of young adults. The roles of family members change but their impact, importance, and influence remains.

6. Transition activities must be sensitive and responsive to cultural, family, community, and gender issues. The importance of recognizing individual difference is essential in this process; at its core, it is about the individual and his or her family.

7. The use of supports—particularly natural supports—is desirable and a part of everyday life. All of us use supports in our lives (e.g., babysitters, neighbors, take-out restaurants). Teaching students how to use a variety of natural and specialized supports is warranted.

8. Timing is critical in achieving a seamless transition to certain services. Transition planning cannot be done quickly or at the last minute. It involves a sequence of key activities that require time.

9. It may be necessary to prioritize transition needs, if there are many to address and there is limited time to do so. Often, upon the completion of a comprehensive transition needs assessment, a lengthy list of areas is generated that require planning and action. Sometimes, given the complexity of a student's transition needs or the constraints of time, a decision has to be made as to which transition goals should be addressed first.

10. Transition planning and services are good for *all* students, not just those who qualify under IDEA. Some school systems (e.g., in Michigan) require that all students have an "Educational Development Plan" that documents an ongoing process of career planning.

These themes provide a backdrop for the delivery of high-quality transition services to youths with disabilities. To date, too few transition programs have demonstrated all of these themes, and as a result, too many students are not well served. A study published by the National Council on Disability (2000) confirmed this point. The study found significant shortcomings in certain transition practices (notice to parents, statements of needed services, and meeting participants) across the United States.

> **FOCUS Question 2.** What is transition education, and what different options are available for offering transition education to students?

Transition Education

In the previous section, the importance of beginning the transition process early was stressed. What is notable about transition planning is that it tends to be mostly a *reactive* process. That is, transition strengths and needs are identified at a later point in a student's school career (e.g., at age 16), and then attempts are made to do something about the situation late in the student's school career. A better approach would be a more *proactive* process in addressing the topics associated with successful adult functioning, one that started in the elementary years and covered important real-life topics. Transition education (i.e., real-life skills coverage), when considered broadly, accomplishes this goal.

The term *life skills instruction* is problematic. Often it is interpreted to mean the program of study provided to students with developmental disabilities, especially those who might have intellectual deficits. Although a curricular focus that is particularly life skills–oriented might indeed be provided to these students, the notion of life skills instruction, as promoted in this chapter, is much more expansive. The notion of transition education, or real-life skills coverage, includes a broad array of real-world topics that are likely to be meaningful to all students with disabilities. In fact, real-life skills are important to all students, with or without disabilities. A strong argument can be made that more than a few students who are identified as gifted are deficient in some everyday living skills (e.g., doing laundry).

The term *transition education*, although not widely used in schools, is a refreshing way to refer to real-life skill topics in the context of transition practices. In this chapter, the term *transition education* refers to all education-related activities, particularly in the areas of curriculum and instruction, that correspond to and prepare students for the demands of adulthood. The term implies that many transition-related activities can occur

12.1 Technology Tools for Transition Help

TECHTips

Computer software can play an important role in helping to prepare students for transition. Programs that reinforce life skills such as budgeting, balancing a checkbook, making change with money, and shopping can give learners beginning practice in a controlled setting. However, for the skills to be learned successfully, this practice must continue beyond the school environment.

Two devices can be especially useful for transition students. First, a voice-activated cell phone helps a student stay in closer contact with parents, teachers, and other support persons. When a student says something like "call mom" into the phone, it will dial the preprogrammed number. Another useful device is a personal digital assistant (PDA); there are many brands and models such as a Palm or Sony. Using a PDA, a student can store addresses and phone numbers, maintain a to-do list, keep a calendar, make memos, and set an alarm to prompt a particular time or event. PDAs also have a built-in calculator and clock. These features are standard with all models, and they can help students to stay organized. In addition, the user can add software for increasing functionality such as a dictionary, games for leisure time, and all sorts of productivity software.

The Internet can be especially useful for transitional students. Sending eCards to friends, paying bills online, locating public transportation, and reading local newspapers are all recommended activities. Students can also do comparative shopping and practice figuring taxes and shipping charges. As with younger students, transition students should be warned about talking with strangers on the Internet or revealing any personal information online.

before the mandated transition process that formally begins by age 16. See Tech Tips 12.1 for technology resources to support students preparing for transitions.

Demands of Adulthood

A number of conceptual models can be used as a framework for identifying and organizing the real-life content that can be addressed from a curricular and instructional perspective before beginning the transition planning process. Two models serve as good examples of the adult domains that teachers should keep in mind when considering coverage of real-life content: the Life-Centered Career Education (LCCE) model (Brolin, 1997) and the Major Life Demands model (Cronin, Patton, and Wood, 2007). The general features of these two models are presented in Table 12.2.

As noted earlier, adults need to have at least a minimal degree of competence and independence across a range of adult functioning areas. The two models highlighted in Table 12.2 afford teachers a framework for recognizing these areas. The LCCE model provides a useful framework for organizing areas of adult competence. It focuses on three major curricular areas (daily living skills, personal-social skills, and occupational guidance and preparation), under which 22 competencies and 97 subcompetencies are organized. The Major Life Demands model includes six major adult domains, along with the 23 subdomains. Organized

under these subdomains are 147 major life demands that serve as a organizational framework from which one can identify important real-life content.

Relationship of Real-Life Topics to Academic or Social Skills Development

Reading, writing, conversing, computing, and solving problems are skills that educators strive to instill in students before they leave school. Parents and school professionals consider these skills along with other skills and knowledge obtained in areas such as science, social skills, study skills, and learning strategies (discussed in Chapters 4 and Chapters 6–11) to be the primary exit skills for all students, and their incorporation into instructional programs is critical. Figure 12.2 illustrates how critical everyday skills relate to key academic and social skills development at the secondary level.

Integrating a transition education perspective into curriculum and instruction provides a rational method for applying relevant real-life situations to important skill areas associated with the general education curriculum. The sample activities presented in the matrix (Figure 12.2) are only a sampling of everyday functional applications; many others exist. (See Cronin et al., 2007, for elementary level examples as well.) Furthermore, each situation and community setting may demand slightly different types of real-life activities,

TABLE 12.2
Models of Adult Functioning

Model	Adult Domain/Curriculum Area	Subdomains/Competency Areas
Life-Centered Career Education (Brolin, 1997)	Daily Living Skills	Managing Personal Finances
		Selecting and Managing a Household
		Caring for Personal Needs
		Raising Children and Meeting Marriage Responsibilities
		Buying, Preparing, and Consuming Food
		Buying and Caring for Clothing
		Exhibiting Responsible Citizenship
		Utilizing Recreational Facilities and Engaging in Leisure
		Getting Around the Community
	Personal-Social Skills	Achieving Self-Awareness
		Acquiring Self-Confidence
		Achieving Socially Responsible Behavior
		Maintaining Good Interpersonal Skills
		Achieving Independence
		Making Adequate Decisions
		Communicating with Others
	Occupational Guidance and Preparation	Knowing and Exploring Occupational Possibilities
		Selecting and Planning Occupational Choices
		Exhibiting Appropriate Work Habits and Behavior
		Seeking, Securing, and Maintaining Employment
		Exhibiting Sufficient Physical-Manual Skills
		Obtaining Specific Occupational Skills
Domains of Adulthood	Employment/Education	General Job Skills
		General Education/Training Considerations
		Employment Setting
		Career Refinement and Reevaluation
	Home and Family	Home Management
		Financial Management
		Family Life
		Child Rearing
	Leisure Pursuits	Indoor Activities
		Outdoor Activities
		Community/Neighborhood Activities
		Travel
		Entertainment
	Community Involvement	Citizenship
		Community Awareness
		Services/Resources
	Physical/Emotional Health	Physical Health
		Emotional Health
	Personal Responsibility and Relationships	Personal Confidence/Understanding
		Goal Setting
		Self-Improvement
		Relationships
		Personal Expression

Source: J. R. Patton, M. E. Cronin, and S. Wood, *Infusing Real-Life Topics into Curricula at the Elementary, Middle, and High School Levels: Recommended Procedures and Instructional Examples* (Austin, TX: PRO-ED, 1999), p. 3. Reprinted with permission.

FIGURE 12.2

	Employment/ Education	Home and Family	Leisure Pursuits	Community Involvement	Emotional/ Physical Health	Personal Responsibility/ Relationships
Reading	Read classified ads for jobs.	Interpret bills.	Locate and understand movie information in newspaper.	Follow directions on tax forms.	Comprehend directions on medication.	Read letters from friends.
Writing	Write a letter of application for a job.	Write checks.	Write for information on a city to visit.	Fill in a voter registration form.	Fill in your medical history on forms.	Send thank-you notes.
Listening	Understand oral directions of a procedure change.	Comprehend oral directions for making dinner.	Listen to a weather forecast to plan outdoor activity.	Understand campaign ads.	Attend lectures on stress.	Take turns in a conversation.
Speaking	Ask your boss for a raise.	Discuss morning routines with your family.	Inquire about tickets for a concert.	State your opinion at the school board meeting.	Describe symptoms to a doctor.	Give feedback to a friend about the purchase of a CD or DVD.
Math Applications	Understand the difference between net and gross pay.	Compute the cost of doing laundry in a laundromat versus at home.	Calculate the cost of a dinner out versus eating at home.	Obtain information for a building permit.	Use a thermometer.	Plan the costs of a date.
Problem Solving	Settle a dispute with a coworker.	Decide how much to budget for rent.	Role-play appropriate behaviors for various places.	Know what to do if you are the victim of fraud.	Select a doctor.	Decide how to ask someone for a date.
Survival Skills	Use a prepared career planning packet.	List emergency phone numbers.	Use a shopping center directory.	Mark a calendar for important dates (e.g., recycling, garbage collection).	Use a system to remember to take vitamins.	Develop a system to remember birthdays.
Personal/ Social	Apply appropriate interview skills.	Help a child with homework.	Know the rules of a neighborhood pool.	Locate self-improvement classes.	Get a yearly physical exam.	Discuss how to negotiate a price at a flea market.

Secondary Matrix: Relationship of Scholastic and Social Skills to Adult Domains

depending on the expectations for adult success in that community.

Although most secondary-level students with learning and behavior problems are taking general education classes, they may still require basic skills instruction in reading or mathematics. However, this necessity does not have to preclude the teaching of important real-life concepts. Integrating real-life situations into instruction often becomes a motivating factor for success in learning the basic skills. For example, mathematical instruction should incorporate activities that relate to the student's current experiences.

Relationship of Real-Life Topics to Standards-Based Education

The emphasis on standards and testing to see whether students are meeting these standards has become a major theme in general education in recent years, especially since the implementation of No Child Left Behind (NCLB). Students with special needs have been affected by this standards-based movement because of the heavy emphasis given to making sure that these students have access to the general education curriculum in the reauthorization of IDEA in 2004.

Bassett and Kochhar-Bryant (2006) highlight one of the key differences between standards-based education (SBE) and special education services.

> In contrast to the assumption of common performance standards, special education services are guided by the principle that students with disabilities be provided with a free and appropriate education and that school systems be responsible to accommodate their individual needs (McDonnell et al., 1997). Individualized education relies on a private process . . . . The special education framework for students with disabilities encompasses a broader range of educational outcomes for students. (p. 4)

At first glance, it seems that real-life topics and content and performance standards are not a good match. However, real-life topics can fit well within a standards-based world. In a review of standards taken from a variety of states, Patton and Trainor (2002) concluded that most standards do relate to real-life topics and coverage of these topics could be worked into lessons designed to meet state standards. The critical dimension for ensuring that functional content is addressed, however, is that teachers must make the effort to relate course content that has to be covered (i.e., explicit curriculum) to life skills–related topics. Specific ways for accomplishing this task will be provided in the next section.

Programmatic Options

Various ways exist to cover real-life topics. For students with disabilities who are included in general education classes, finding significant blocks of instructional time to cover these topics can be difficult. However, with careful coordination between general and special educators and the use of co-teaching, as discussed in Chapter 5, instructional activities that use real-life topics can be provided to students, regardless of their educational placement. A number of sources (Cronin et al., 2007; Patton, Cronin, and Jarrells, 1997) present techniques for showing how students' real-life skills needs can be addressed through various types of transition education–oriented coursework or through the integration of real-life topics into existing content.

Real-Life Coursework

One option for covering real-life topics is through the development of courses. This comprehensive approach to covering real-life topics would include a series or set of specific life skills courses, with titles such as "Personal Finance," "Health and Hygiene," and "Practical Communications," available to all students. This particular option is most likely to occur when there is significant curricular freedom. The second option usually results in the creation of a single course that covers a wide variety of real-life topics. Such a course might be called "Life 101," "Skills for Life," or "Introduction to Adulthood" and could be offered to all students in the school as an elective. The last option usually entails the development of a single course that focuses on a single subject area such as "Teen Skills" or "Consumer Math" or one of the courses in the comprehensive curriculum just described (e.g., "Personal Finance"). These courses vary according to local educational and community needs. One example is the "Science for Living" course developed by the Dubuque Iowa Community Schools (Helmke, Havekost, Patton, and Polloway, 1994).

Integration of Real-Life Topics into Existing Curricular Content

Another method of covering life skills topics is to integrate real-life topics into the content of existing courses. Two major ways of accomplishing this are recommended: dedicating a portion of an existing course to relevant topics (augmentation) and infusing real-life topics and activities into the scope and sequence of existing courses.

The first integration technique, *augmentation,* requires that additional instructional time be available to focus on real-life topics. If thoughtfully planned, such allocation of instructional time can be accomplished without sacrificing time needed to cover the content that is explicitly stated in the course sequence (Cronin et al., 2007; Patton et al., 1997). For example, it might be appropriate to augment a consumer math course by including additional lessons that address the real-life topics associated with moving into an apartment or how to budget for dating. Knowing how to accomplish these real-life tasks when they exit school is particularly important for students such as Eileen, and it is one that is not typically covered in existing secondary-level instructional materials.

The second integration technique, *infusion*, uses existing course content or class opportunities as the basis for exploring real-life topics. The primary goal is to infuse real-life topics directly into information being covered.

FIGURE 12.3
Infusing Real-Life Topics into Existing Curricula

The children did not like to hear arguing. The boys asked Jenny, "What is wrong? Why are Mom and Dad fighting?"

Jenny could not answer the question. She hugged Ian and Bruce. Then Mom and Dad came into the room. They looked very unhappy. Bruce, Ian, and Jenny did not laugh. They all felt very sad, and they were scared. Everyone in the family was worried.

Source: S. P. Quigley, C. M. King, P. L. McAnally, and S. Rose, *Reading Milestones: An Alternative Reading Program*, Level 5, Brown Reader 1, 2nd ed. (Austin, TX: PRO-ED, 1991), p. 22. Copyright © 1991 by PRO-ED, Inc. Reprinted by permission.

In reality, two types of infusion options exist. The first technique is "spontaneous" infusion whereby the teacher capitalizes on a "teachable moment" to infuse real-world topics into instruction for a particular day. Rossman (1983) provides a great science example of spontaneous infusion. The other infusion technique is "planned" infusion. With this approach, the course content is closely examined to determine where important real-life topics relate and how they can be woven into instruction.

Using the planned infusion approach, the teacher would become very familiar with the content of a book or other instructional material before the lesson occurs. Then, the teacher would identify specific content in the material that in some way relates to various real-life topics. The teacher may need to relate this real-life content to standards as well. Some planning would need to occur to prepare for covering the real-life topics, as the teacher needs to decide which real-life topics to infuse into the lesson. Some time might be needed as well to acquire any needed materials. The amount of time devoted to such coverage does not have to be substantial—often a quick "hit" or "infusion burst" (Patton, Cronin, and Wood, 1999) is all the time that is possible or all that is needed. On other occasions, more time might be devoted to a particularly important topic.

For example, real-life skills related to personal relationships could be integrated into a reading lesson in which the topic of the story is a family dealing with the realities of divorce (see Figure 12.3). In this case, a discussion could be started using the following prompts: Describe how it makes you feel when two people in your family argue; identify some ways that you could convey your feelings and concerns; and so on. The discussion would not have to be long or very detailed but would provide an opportunity to address a topic that affects many children directly and other students indirectly.

This infusion approach provides relevance to course content that is taught on a daily basis in addition to covering important real-life skills topics, no matter what the course is or what the nature of the class might be. This method works well within a standards-based system that emphasizes mastery of content and skills acquisition so that students can perform well on the high-stakes assessments they will face in the latter part of the school year. Moreover, this approach may be the only one available when students are in inclusive settings and the real-life skills coursework option is not available or does not exist. A valuable point

TABLE 12.3

Augmentation and Infusion Examples

Source	Topic Covered	A/I	Sample Activities
Practical math textbook (Secondary level)	"Budgeting for Recreation"	A	Add coverage on the "economics" of dating
		I	Identify best time and cost for going to a movie
	"Credit Card Math"	A	Add coverage of how to get the best deal on a credit card (e.g., low APR, no annual fee)
		I	Present ways to get lower APR or waiver of annual fee
	"Maintaining a Vehicle"	A	Add coverage of the realities of being involved in an accident and what one needs to do
		I	Discuss the importance of keeping tires inflated at the proper levels
Basal math textbook (Elementary level)	"Using Decimals: Adding and Subtracting Money" —buying a sleeping bag	A	Add coverage of costs of purchasing or renting camping gear
		I	Discuss where one can buy or rent a sleeping bag
	"Using Tables to Solve Problems"	A	Add coverage on how to use the weather map from the newspaper
		I	Identify other tables that have numbers

Note: A = augmentation; I = infusion

Source: J. R. Patton, M. E. Cronin, D. S. Bassett, and A. E. Koppel (1997). A life skills approach to mathematics instruction: Preparing students with learning disabilities for the real-life math demands of instruction. *Journal of Learning Disabilities, 30*, p. 185. Reprinted by permission.

from a pure pedagogical perspective is that this technique embeds meaning into the content being taught not only to students identified as having a disability, but also to all other students in the same instructional setting.

Additional examples of the techniques of augmentation and infusion for integrating real-life topics into existing curricular materials are illustrated in Table 12.3. The table shows examples of both augmentation and infusion ideas for a variety of math topics at both the elementary and secondary levels.

FOCUS Question 3. What are the purpose and the key features of the transition planning process?

The Transition Planning Process

The actual process of planning for the transition of students from school to life after school is complex. To be done effectively, it requires that key people are actively involved, certain critical elements of the process are implemented, and specific activities are carried out, as was highlighted at the beginning of the chapter. An understanding has to be reached whereby all players involved in the transition process share responsibility for ensuring that it transpires successfully. What this means is that responsibility for undertaking the varied activities of transition planning is not the sole responsibility of the school.

The primary objectives of this process are a seamless transition to postschool settings and being able to function successfully in adult life (i.e., dealing reasonably well with the demands of adulthood)—knowing that all of us struggle at times with the realities of everyday life. The vehicle for documenting that this will happen to the best extent possible is the individualized education plan (IEP). In this section of the chapter, we identify best and recommended practices that contribute to this primary objective and that comply with federal mandates.

Key Elements of the Transition Planning Process

The key elements of the transition planning process are illustrated in Figure 12.4. The first box, identified as "Proactive Transition Education,"

FIGURE 12.4

Transition Planning Process

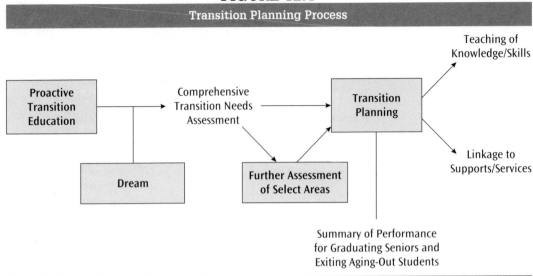

Source: Adapted from Patton and Dunn (1998).

refers to the real-life topics that were discussed in the previous section of the chapter. Essentially, it refers to coverage of adult-referenced topics across all levels of schooling beginning in the early grades. Early on, it is essential that students receive opportunities to "dream" about what they want to be, where they want to live, and how they want to live when they grow up.

The formal phase of the transition planning process begins with the comprehensive assessment of a student's transition needs. The general areas in which a transition needs assessment should focus include a range of transition domains. The key transition areas that are identified by different states vary greatly; some of the more common transition planning areas are as follows:

- Community participation
- Daily living
- Employment
- Financial and income management
- Health
- Independent living (includes living arrangements)
- Leisure and recreation
- Postsecondary education
- Relationships and social skills
- Transportation and mobility
- Vocational training

It is important that a comprehensive transition needs assessment consider all of these areas. If a needs assessment is conducted effectively, the results should lead to the development of transition-related goals. In some cases, the results will lead to the recognition that more in-depth information is needed.

The actual transition planning phase comprises goal development and should illuminate two different types of goals and a number of activities that are needed to accomplish the goals. One type of goal is *instructional,* in that it focuses on knowledge and skill needs in academic, social, behavioral, and other functional areas. Goals that are instructional should be written into a student's IEP. The other type of goal emphasizes *linkage* to needed services and supports. These goals may be quick action items (e.g., a phone call to place one's name on a waiting list), or they may be more elaborate activities (e.g., going through the process of selecting an appropriate postschool training program). For most students, it is unlikely that both types of goals will be required for every transition area that is assessed.

In the case study that was introduced at the beginning of this chapter, we can see that Eileen's transition needs will involve both types of goals. Clearly, she has instructional needs in a variety of areas such as writing and study skills. Eileen's transition needs also indicate that she has linkage needs, related to the demands of the college she is likely to attend.

The reauthorization of IDEA in 2004 introduced a new component to the transition process. IDEA regulations state:

> For a child whose eligibility terminates under circumstances described in paragraph (e)(2) of this section, a public agency must provide the child

Apply the Concept 12.1

Guiding Principles for the Transition Planning Process

- The more that is known about the receiving settings and about the student's levels of competence to deal with these settings, the more likely a seamless transition can be achieved.
- The more comprehensive the transition needs assessment is, the

easier it is to develop useful and meaningful transition plans.
- Effective transition assessment and plans can be achieved only when school-based transition personnel know the students or have ways to acquire this information.

- Student involvement in the transition-planning process is not only highly desirable but also required by law (i.e., based on the student's preferences and interests).

with a summary of the child's academic achievement and functional performance, which shall include recommendations on how to assist the child in meeting the child's postsecondary goals. (Section 300.305(e)(3))

This new feature is designed to provide students, and their families, with a document that should be useful in a variety of adult settings (workplace, postsecondary education). The key features of the summary of performance document include generation of information on both academic and functional levels; a revisiting of "measurable" postsecondary goals; and a list of recommendations that will be helpful in settings related to the goals.

Aside from the implications that are stated in the federal definition of transition services, certain principles should guide the transition planning process. Apply the Concept 12.1 highlights the four key guiding principles, the first two of which are adapted from Patton and Dunn (1998, p. 21).

Assessing Transition Needs

The collection of information about a student's transition needs requires a methodology that school-based personnel who have transition responsibilities find acceptable. In other words, they want techniques that are neither complicated nor time-consuming, and deliver useful information for generating transition plans.

A variety of assessment techniques, along with a number of existing sources of information, are available for generating a comprehensive picture of a student's transition needs. Four useful professional resources that provide information on transition assessment are *Assess for Success: A Practitioner's Handbook on Transition Assessment*, 2nd

edition (Sitlington, Neubert, Begun, Lombard, and Leconte, 2007), *Transition Assessment: Planning Transition and IEP Development for Youth with Mild to Moderate Disabilities* (Miller, Lombard, & Corbey, 2007), *Assessment for Transitions Planning*, 2nd edition (Clark, 2007), and *Transition Assessment: Wise Practices for Quality Lives* (Sax and Thoma, 2002).

A number of informal and formal techniques for obtaining transition-related information exist. Sitlington and colleagues (2007) have identified some of the most frequently used procedures:

- Analysis of background information
- Interviews
- Person-centered planning
- Standardized tests
- Curriculum-based assessment techniques (criterion-referenced testing, domain-referenced testing, curriculum-based measurement, portfolio assessment)
- Performance samples
- Behavioral observation techniques
- Situational assessment

A sampling of select commercially available resources for acquiring transition-related information is presented in Table 12.4. A thorough description of these instruments and a detailed discussion of other nonstandardized procedures can be found in Clark (2007).

Transition personnel need a systematic way to obtain comprehensive transition-related information on students. Whichever system is ultimately chosen, it must be one that has the following features:

- Gathers information effectively, efficiently, and on students who are not known well by the school-based transition person

TABLE 12.4

Commercially Available Tests and Procedures for Assessing Transition Needs

General Category	Selected Types of Measures	Specific Example(s)
Nonspecific to transition	Achievement tests	*Adult Basic Learning Examination—Second Edition* (Karlsen and Gardner, 1986)
	Adaptive behavior measures	*AAMR Adaptive Behavior Scales—School, Second Edition* (Lambert, Nihira, and Leland, 1993)
	Aptitude tests	*Differential Aptitude Test, Fifth Edition* (Bennett, Seashore, and Wesman, 1990)
	Communication tests	*Communicative Abilities in Daily Living* (Holland, 1980)
	Learning styles	*Learning Styles Inventory* (Dunn, Dunn, and Price, 1985)
	Manual dexterity	*Crawford Small Parts Dexterity Test* (Crawford, 1981)
	Occupational interest	*Occupational Aptitude Survey and Interest Schedule—2* (Parker, 1991)
	Personality/social skills	*Basic Personality Inventory* (Jackson, 1995)
Specific to transition	Needs assessment	*Transition Planning Inventory* (Clark and Patton, 1997)
		Enderle—Severson Transition Rating Scale—Revised (Brolin, 1992)
	Life skills	*BRIGANCE Life Skills Inventory* (Brigance, 1995)
		LCCE Knowledge and Performance Battery (Brolin, 1992)
		Tests for Everyday Living (Halpern, Irvin, and Landman, 1979)
	Self-determination	*Arc's Self-Determination Scale*
	Quality of life	*Quality of Life Questionnaire* (Schalock and Keith, 1993)
		Quality of Student Life Questionnaire (Keith and Schalock, 1995)
	Work-related behavior	*Transition Behavior Scale* (2nd ed.) (McCarney, 2000)
	Social	*Social and Prevocational Information Battery—Revised* (Halpern, Irvin, and Munkres, 1986)

Source: Adapted from J. R. Patton and C. Dunn, *Transition from School to Young Adulthood: Basic Concepts and Recommended Practices* (Austin, TX: PRO-ED, 1998), p. 24. Reprinted with permission.

- Leads logically and quickly to the planning phase
- Can be used with large numbers of students

Eileen's situation, described at the beginning of the chapter, serves as a good example of how a transition-needs assessment works. Eileen was administered the *Transition Planning Inventory* (TPI; Clark and Patton, 1997), one of the instruments listed in Table 12.5. The TPI requests information from three sources (student, parents, and school-based personnel) about 46 competencies (organized along nine transition planning areas). Although the TPI administration identified a number of areas for which transition planning should be done, we will focus only on one: success in postsecondary education.

As is noted in Figure 12.5, all three sources (the transition coordinator at school, Eileen's parents, and Eileen herself) rated Eileen low on item 10, "Can succeed in a postsecondary program." In essence, the three sources perceived Eileen as being likely to have certain problems at the college level, but more detailed information was needed. As a result, another part of the TPI, *Informal Assessments in Transition* (Clark, Patton, and Moulton, 2001), was used to provide a more in-depth analysis of the "succeeding in college"

TABLE 12.5

Present Levels of Performance and Selected Goals for Eileen

	PLEP	Instructional Goal	Linkage Goal
Employment	Eileen is knowledgeable about finding and maintaining employment. She has difficulty identifying job requirements in the field of her choosing, drama.	Eileen will use key career exploration references and identify three positions of interest in the field of drama/entertainment.	Eileen will shadow a member of the local actor's guild.
Postsecondary Education/ Training	Eileen is highly motivated to attend college. She needs to develop key study skills in the areas of organization and time management.	Eileen will demonstrate that she can use a specific organizational system to keep appointments and make deadlines.	Eileen will enroll in a study skills elective while in high school.
Communication	Eileen's verbal communication skills are excellent. Eileen's written communication skills are very basic and a source of embarrassment for her.	Eileen will demonstrate skill in using a minimum of three learning strategies in the area of reading and writing.	

Source: A. Trainor, J. Patton, and G. Clark, *Case Studies in Assessment for Transition Planning* (Austin, TX: PRO-ED, 2005), pp. 52–53. Reprinted with permission.

concern. Figure 12.6 shows the results of this additional assessment, indicating the areas for which goals need to be written.

Another informal instrument, the *Study Skills Inventory* (Hoover and Patton, 2007) was completed to further specify the nature of Eileen's study skills difficulties. The results of this assessment yielded the following information: "Most [study skill] areas need attention—particular emphasis needs to be given to note taking, test taking, and time management." A discussion of the transition goals that will need to be developed on the basis of these results is presented in the next section.

Developing Transition Goals

A thorough assessment of a student's transition needs should be useful in determining present levels of academic achievement and functional performance and developing sound transition goals that will serve as a guide for the student, the family, and the school in terms of preparing the student for postschool life. As is noted in Figure 12.4 and as was discussed previously, two types of goal statements can emerge from a transition needs assessment: those related to instructional activities and those related to linkage activities.

Instructional goals relate to knowledge and skills needs and should be written in the IEP as academic or social goals. Linkage goals—the types of goals that are typically associated with transition planning—focus on making connections to the

supports and services that will be needed in postschool situations and are written in the section of the IEP that deals with transition services.

In the past, some states required another document, an individual transition plan (ITP), which was a separate document from the IEP, as the principal vehicle for guiding transition activities. Most states simply included transition goals as part of the existing IEP under a section typically called "Statement of Transition Services." Historically, the focus of transition planning was primarily on linkage-type goals. The emerging practice is to include all transition planning information on the IEP. The critical issue, as discussed in this chapter, is the importance of considering both instructional and linkage goal statements for areas of need.

The components of good instructional goals have been discussed elsewhere in this book. Useful linkage-type goal statements should include the following four components, all of which contribute to development of an effective plan of action:

1. Present level of performance
2. Specific activities to be performed to accomplish the goal
3. Anticipated date of completion of activities
4. Person(s) responsible

Eileen's situation provides a clear-cut example of why two different types of goals often need to be developed. As evident from Figure 12.6 and the results of the *Study Skills Inventory*, certain

FIGURE 12.5

Portion of Eileen's Transition Planning Inventory

Section V. Profile

Planning Areas / Goals	School Rating (Strongly Disagree · Strongly Agree)	Home Rating (Strongly Disagree · Strongly Agree)	Student Rating (Strongly Disagree · Strongly Agree)	Knowledge/Skills Goals	Linkage
Employment					
1. Knows job requirements and demands	NA 0 1 2 ③ 4 5 DK	NA 0 1 2 3 ④ 5 DK	NA 0 1 ② 3 4 5 DK		
2. Makes informed choices	NA 0 1 2 ③ 4 5 DK	NA 0 1 2 ③ 4 5 DK	NA 0 1 2 3 ④ 5 DK		
3. Knows how to get a job	NA 0 1 2 3 ④ 5 DK	NA 0 1 2 ③ 4 5 DK	NA 0 1 2 3 ④ 5 DK		
4. Demonstrates general job skills and work attitude	NA 0 1 2 ③ 4 5 DK	NA 0 1 2 3 ④ 5 DK	NA 0 1 2 3 4 ⑤ DK		
5. Has specific job skills	ⓃA 0 1 2 3 4 5 DK	NA 0 1 2 3 4 5 ⒹⓀ	ⓃA 0 1 2 3 4 5 DK		
Further Education/Training					
6. Knows how to gain entry into community employment training	ⓃA 0 1 2 3 4 5 DK	ⓃA 0 1 2 3 4 5 DK	ⓃA 0 1 2 3 4 5 DK		
7. Knows how to gain entry into GED program	ⓃA 0 1 2 3 4 5 DK	ⓃA 0 1 2 3 4 5 DK	ⓃA 0 1 2 3 4 5 DK		
8. Knows how to gain entry into vocational/technical school	ⓃA 0 1 2 3 4 5 DK	ⓃA 0 1 2 3 4 5 DK	ⓃA 0 1 2 3 4 5 DK		
9. Knows how to gain entry into college or university	NA 0 1 2 3 ④ 5 DK	NA 0 1 ② 3 4 5 DK	NA 0 1 2 ③ 4 5 DK		
10. Can succeed in a postsecondary program	NA 0 ① 2 3 4 5 DK	NA 0 1 ② 3 4 5 DK	NA 0 ① 2 3 4 5 DK		

Source: G. M. Clark, J. R. Patton, and R. Moulton. *Informal Assessments in Transition Planning* (Austin, TX: PRO-ED, 2001), p. 156. Reprinted with permission.

FIGURE 12.6

Goals/Objectives Needed	Further Assessments Needed	Further Education/Training	Notes
☑	☑	10. Can succeed in an appropriate postsecondary program	_____
☐	☐	Can use the academic support skills (e.g., organizational skills, time management, and other study skills) necessary to succeed in a given postsecondary setting	_Study Skills Inventory_____
☑	☐	Can perform reading skills required in the program	_____
☐	☐	Can perform writing skills required in the program	_____
☐	☐	Can perform math skills required in the program	_____
☐	☐	Can analyze information and draw conclusions	_____
☐	☐	Can manage finances	_____
☑	☐	Knows how to balance priorities between classes, work, home duties, and leisure time	_____
☐	☐	Knows how to use disability support services	_____
☐	☐	Knows how to develop a social support system	_____
☐	☐	Knows how to assess (with others) what types of support/modifications are needed	_____
☐	☐	Knows how to appropriately meet with instructor (or professor) to discuss and advocate for reasonable accommodations (e.g., manner of presentation, timeliness, knowledge of necessary reasonable accommodations)	_____
☐	☐	Knows how to develop and implement a plan and a time line for completion of postsecondary training program	_____

Source: G. M. Clark, J. R. Patton, and R. Moulton, *Informal Assessments in Transition Planning* (Austin, TX: PRO-ED, 2001), p. 156. Reprinted with permission.

areas were identified as needing attention. The following goals need to be written for Eileen in relation only to item 10 from the TPI assessment:

Instructional Goals (Knowledge/Skills Goals)
- Develop strategies to assist with demands of comprehending textual material.
- Improve note-taking skills.
- Improve test-taking skills.
- Develop time management skills.
- Improve various types of writing skills needed in college courses.

Linkage Goals (Transition Services Goals)
- Make Eileen aware of the Services for Students with Disabilities Office, its services, and how to qualify.
- Identify resources that may be needed to obtain a comprehensive evaluation to document that Eileen has a learning disability if she chooses to disclose this and use specialized services.
- Make Eileen aware of the general services (courses, workshops, personal assistance) provided to all students at the college to improve study skills.
- Connect Eileen with a contact person at the college to whom she can go if she runs into problems with academics, managing time, and so on.
- Compile a list of names and phone numbers of private tutors whom Eileen can contact to assist with study skill needs.

Table 12.5 shows present levels of performance and goals for certain critical transition areas based on Eileen's needs as determined by the assessment process.

Key Considerations

Three important issues that relate to the transition-planning process are worthy of special attention. All three are intricately involved with preparing students and their families to better engage in the transition planning process on their own terms. The first issue involves the active and meaningful participation of students in their own transition process. The second issue concerns sensitivity to family and cultural values. The third issue centers on the need to prepare students for the assessment phase by discussing transition-related topics before commencement of the formal transition process.

Student Involvement

Most professionals and researchers who are interested in transition issues and practice place student involvement and self-determination high on the list of critical topics (Bassett and Lehman, 2002; Flexar, Baer, Luft, and Simmons, 2008). The idea of getting students actively involved in their own transition planning makes sense because it is their lives about which key decisions are being made. However, one cannot assume that students will know how to participate or will feel comfortable being actively involved in transition planning.

Many students, especially those with disabilities for whom decision making, self-determination, and communication (refer to Table 12.1) are areas of significant challenge, need to develop skills to be actively involved at an early age. Bassett and Lehman (2002) stress that students should be taught skills necessary for a variety of student-directed roles during the elementary school years. They provide step-by-step techniques for teaching students how to participate in three different types of meetings (see Table 12.6). Other curricular materials are also available to teach students with disabilities how they can direct their own IEP meetings and transition planning process. Table 12.7 describes several commercially available programs that have demonstrated effectiveness with students who have learning and behavior problems.

Family and Cultural Diversity

As teachers work with students and their families on their current and postsecondary transition-related

TABLE 12.6

Types of Meetings to Encourage Self-Determination

Characteristic	Student-Led Conference	Student-Centered Planning	Student-Directed Meeting
Purpose	Student shares academic and classroom work with family and teacher(s); normally uses portfolio or some other information-gathering system	Student is at the center of planning for school, community, and future	Student leads or is active facilitator in IEP or transition planning
Grade level	Elementary grades through graduation	Elementary grades through graduation and beyond	Middle grades through graduation and beyond
Who is involved?	Student, family members, teacher(s)	Student, family members, friends, relevant professionals	Students, family members, relevant professionals
How often does the meeting occur?	Each time a school-based conference is held (e.g., every quarter, every semester, annually)	Depends, could be once, annually, or multiple times	Annually or upon need of student, family, or school personnel
Average length of meeting	30 minutes–1 hour	1–3 hours	1–3 hours
Outcomes of the meeting	Student learns to assess value of work, selects appropriate artifacts, articulates progress and needs for improvement	Student is central to capacity-based discussion on strengths and needs, vision for the future, and development of an action plan to achieve goals	Student provides self-assessment, current and future goals, and ways to achieve them

Source: D. S. Bassett and J. Lehmann, *Student Focused Conference and Planning* (Austin, TX: PRO-ED, 2002), p. 11. Copyright © 2002 by PRO-ED, Inc. Reprinted with permission.

TABLE 12.7

Student-Directed IEP Programs

Program	Description
ChoiceMaker Self-Determination Transition Curriculum (Martin and Marshall, 1995)	Teaches self-determination through student self-management of the IEP process and includes three components: choosing goals, expressing goals, and taking action. Students lead their IEP meetings to the greatest extent possible, based on their strengths.
Whose Future Is It Anyway? (Wehmeyer and Kelchner, 1995)	Introduces the student to the concept of transition planning and teaches them to take an active role in the planning process by focusing on the constructs involved in self-determination. *A Coach's Guide* (Wehmeyer and Lawrence, 1995) is available to assist the person that the student has identified as the coach.
Next S.T.E.P.: Student Transition and Education Planning (Halpern, Herr, Doren, and Wolf, 2000)	Teaches and engages students in the skills involved in successful transition planning through four instructional modules (getting started, self-exploration and self-evaluation, developing goals and activities, and putting a plan into place). Videos and printed materials for teachers, students, and their families are included.
Self-Advocacy Strategy for Education and Transition Planning (Van Reusen, Bos, Schumaker, and Deshler, 1994)	Teaches both student-directed transition planning and self-advocacy skills. The program emphasizes the importance of self-advocacy in increasing student motivation and empowerment using the I-PLAN strategy (inventory your strengths, needs, goals, and needed accommodations; provide your inventory information; listen and respond; ask questions; and name your goals).
TAKE CHARGE for the Future (Powers, 1996)	Promotes student involvement in education and transition planning through: skill facilitation (i.e., achievement, partnership, and coping skills), mentoring with same-gender adults who have had similar experiences, peer support activities, and parent support in promoting their child's active involvement. The model was adapted from a validated approach (TAKE CHARGE) used to increase self-determination skills in students both with and without disabilities.

Source: Adapted from M. L. Wehmeyer, M. Agran, and C. Hughes, *Teaching Self-Determined Students with Disabilites: Basic Skills for Successful Transition* (Baltimore: Paul H. Brookes, 1998); and R. W. Flexer, T. J. Simmons, P. Luft, and R. M. Baer, *Transition Planning for Secondary Students with Disabilities* (Upper Saddle River, NJ: Merrill/Prentice Hall, 2001).

needs, it is important to understand that everyone who engages in this process has a cultural identity that informs his or her values and beliefs in regard to the transition between adolescence and adulthood. For example, the idea that certain individuals should be encouraged and prepared to live independently, apart from immediate family members, may be considered inappropriate or unappealing by some students and families. Whereas living independently in a dormitory or an apartment once a student has graduated from high school is acceptable to some people, others may prefer more interdependence, in which unmarried children live at home with immediate family members until they begin their own families. Our values and beliefs, determined in part by our cultural identities, help us to form our perceptions about other concepts that impact transition planning such as disability, self-determination, and independence (deFur and Williams, 2002).

Family

Diversity

Teachers have the challenging task of helping students and their families plan for the future while maintaining awareness of and sensitivity to the impact culture has on the planning process, use of services, and desired outcomes of the people they serve (Trainor and Patton, 2008).

Teachers must understand how their personal biases and preferences affect their own participation in the transition planning process. This initial task, recognizing one's own cultural values and beliefs, can be as difficult as seeing the proverbial forest for the trees. Teachers, many of whom share a certain cultural identity (European American, middle-class, college-educated, female), may mistakenly think that their own beliefs and values are universal. For example, teachers may value the idea of self-determination and equate this concept with autonomy. Therefore, they may encourage or expect their young adult students to make their own decisions about their futures. Some students, however, may be members of families that expect children to defer to their parents and/or significant elders in their family or community. Other families may allow gender to inform their preferences regarding self-determination. During transition planning, it is essential to consider both one's own values and how they influence the guidance one gives to students as well as the biases that students and their families bring to the process.

Preassessment Preparation

The third important issue that must be addressed results from the fact that when students are actually involved in their own transition planning, they may not know how to respond to many of the adult issues with which they are being confronted. The stereotypic adolescent response of "I don't know"—and, in some cases, "I don't care"—may well be a valid answer when the student is confronted with transition topics that have never been raised before.

Giving students the opportunity to think about and discuss the many topics on which their transition planning will be based and about which we would like to have their input makes perfect sense. How to do this is not so readily apparent. Now that middle and high school personnel are involved with the transition planning process in ways that they were not before, it is important to allow opportunities for students to discuss these topics as early as possible. Some instructional time should be dedicated to introducing students to the topics for which transition goals will be developed (e.g., employment, further education, living arrangements). Many school districts have wonderful career development programs that are provided through the counseling and guidance staff. However, most of these excellent programs do not address all of the areas associated with comprehensive transition planning.

Innovative techniques are needed that address transition topics before asking students formally for their opinions. Commercial materials, such as the *Next S.T.E.P.* program (Halpern, Herr, Doren, and Wolf, 2000), provide a systematic and planned way of accomplishing this task. This type of material provides a curricular sequence that exposes students to an array of lessons that help them take charge of their own transition planning process. At the very least, it is critical to develop activities or lessons related to a set of major transition areas. Other programs, such as the *Self-Directed IEP* (part of the *ChoiceMaker* materials), offer school personnel effective ways of teaching students how to lead their transition planning meetings.

Recommendations

The transition planning process requires that certain key elements—assessment, individual planning, follow-through, and coordination—be implemented effectively and efficiently. As mentioned earlier in this chapter, this process requires the active involvement of several key players: the student; the family, who in many situations will become the service coordinator for their adult child; a variety of adult service providers; and a combination of school-based personnel whose duties include transition services. Apply the Concept 12.2

Apply the Concept 12.2

How Different Entities Can Contribute to the Transition Planning Process

How Students Can Contribute to the Transition Effort

- Identify their own preferences and interests.
- Take an interest in this process.
- Participate as a contributing member of their transition team.
- Follow through on designated activities.
- Know where and how to access support and services.

How Families Can Ensure Successful Transition

- Become informed about the demands of adulthood and the transition planning process.
- Participate actively in the transition process.

- Follow through on designated linkage activities.
- Seek assistance when needed.
- Advocate for their children.

How Adult Service Providers Can Facilitate Successful Transition

- Identify the demands and requisite skills needed in their particular settings or programs.
- Provide information about their settings or programs to school-based personnel.
- Participate in the transition process when feasible.
- Offer accessibility and assistance to families.

How Schools Can Best Prepare Students for Adulthood

- Address proactively the important life skills within the curriculum.
- Develop self-determination and self-advocacy skills in students.
- Assess and plan comprehensively for transitional needs.
- Provide community-based experiences.
- Assist families in dealing with the adult service arena.

Source: J. R. Patton and C. Dunn, *Transition from School to Young Adulthood: Basic Concepts and Recommended Practices* (Austin, TX: PRO-ED, 1998), pp. 59–60. Reprinted with permission.

presents the four key entities that can best contribute to the transition planning process as identified originally by a group of professionals connected to the *Hawaii Transition Project* (1987) and restated by Patton and Dunn (1998).

SUMMARYfor Chapter 12

This chapter focused on the topic of transition services. The overriding theme of the chapter is that the transition process should begin during the elementary years and culminate in a series of sound practices that lead to a seamless transition from school to any number and types of postschool settings.

The first major section of the chapter highlighted the fact that all of us move through a relatively large number of transitions throughout our lives. Some of these transitions are predictable and common to all, and others are idiosyncratic. IDEA 2004 requires that certain activities occur for two of the transitions through which children and youths with disabilities move. The discussion stressed how important it is to have certain elements in place to ensure successful transitions. Attention was also directed to a set of principles or themes that should guide transition practices.

The second section of the chapter focused primarily on how it is possible to teach real-life topics to students with special needs. The concept of transition education was introduced as a way of thinking about the instruction of real-life skills to all students with disabilities. Major life demands were identified, and the relationship of important real-life skills to academic and social skills was established. Recognition that real-life topics can relate to standards was also made. Two approaches, augmentation and infusion, for integrating real-life content into existing curricular content were presented.

The last section of the chapter described the key elements of the more formal transition planning process. Emphasis was given to ways to assess transition strengths and needs and to develop transition goals. The final part of the chapter discussed the importance of student involvement in this process, explained the need to be responsive to diversity concerns, and identified critical preassessment issues that must be considered to achieve effective transition planning.

FOCUS Answers

FOCUS Question 1. When do transitions occur, and what are three features that can facilitate effective transitions for individuals with disabilities?

Answer: Some transitions occur naturally throughout life (vertical transitions), such as beginning school, moving from middle school to high school, and growing older. Other transitions are person-specific, do not occur at definite times, and may involve moving from a more restrictive to a more inclusive educational setting or changing jobs. Three essential features that can facilitate the transition process are comprehensive planning, implementation of a transition plan, and coordination and cooperation among the people who are in contact with the individual as well as ongoing communication and collaboration.

FOCUS Question 2. What is transition education, and what different options are available for offering transition education to students?

Answer: The term *transition education* refers to teaching life skill–related issues. It can occur as a separate academic course, covering a range of real-life topics or focusing on one area such as consumer math. Another option is to augment the existing curriculum by infusing real-life topics into current course content.

FOCUS Question 3. What are the purpose and the key features of the transition planning process?

Answer: The primary objective of the transition planning process is a seamless transition to postschool settings and everyday living, characterized by being able to deal successfully with the demands of adulthood. The IEP is used to document the transition plan. The transition planning process has three key components: The individual participates in his or her own transition planning; teachers maintain sensitivity to family and cultural diversity; and students often need preparation for the assessment phase.

THINK and APPLY

- Is going to college a realistic goal for Eileen?
- Other than those shown in Figure 12.1, what are some horizontal transitions that students with disabilities might experience?
- What themes should guide the preparation of students with disabilities for postschool life?
- How do diversity issues affect the transition planning process?
- What are some other ways in which the domains of adulthood could be organized?

- What titles could you give to possible life skills courses other than the ones suggested in this chapter?
- What are the differences between instructional goals and linkage goals as discussed in this chapter?
- What basic components should be part of any individual transition plan?
- Why should the transition process be considered a shared set of activities?
- Why are transition services valuable for all students in school?

APPLY the STANDARDS

 Council for Exceptional Children

Use the information presented in this chapter and your knowledge of the relevant CEC standards (BD4K3, BD4K5, LD4S1, LD7K2, LD10K2) to describe the role of the special education teacher in coordinating the various aspects of transition services for students with emotional/behavior disorders or learning disabilities.

Standard BD4K3: Resources and techniques used to transition individuals with emotional/behavioral disorders into and out of school and postschool environments.

Standard BD4K5: Strategies for integrating student-initiated learning experiences into ongoing instruction for individuals with emotional/behavioral disorders.

Standard LD4S1: Use research-supported methods for academic and nonacademic instruction of individuals with learning disabilities.

Standard LD7K2: Sources of specialized curricula, materials, and resources for individuals with learning disabilities.

LD10K2: Service, networks, and organizations that provide support across the life span for individuals with learning disabilities.

WEBSITES as RESOURCES for Transition Planning and Transition Education

The following Websites provide extensive resources to expand your understanding of the transition planning process:

- NICHCY Publications www.nichcy.org/pubs/transum/ts7.pdf
- Life Skills Classroom Projects www.aafcs.org/resources
- Job Accommodation Network http://janweb.icdi.wvu.edu
- Secretary's Commission on Achieving Necessary Skills (SCANS) http://wdr.doleta.gov/SCANS
- Association on Higher Education and Disability www.ahead.org

Where the Classroom Comes to Life

Article Homework Exercise Go to MyEducationLab and select the topic "TRANSITION PLANNING," then read the article "College Opportunities for Students with Learning Disabilities" and complete the activity questions below.

This brief includes information about college for students with learning disabilities. Topics include challenges, characteristics for success in college, transition planning for college, and selecting a college.

Consider opening scenario of this chapter and the case of Eileen as you read the brief and answer the questions.

1. What information about college and students with learning disabilities is relevant to Eileen's situation?
2. How can the transition process support Eileen in her transition from high school to college?

Article Homework Exercise Go to MyEducationLab and select the topic "TRANSITION PLANNING," then read the article "Self Determination: Supporting Successful Transition," and complete the activity questions below.

This article describes the concept of self-determination theory and how this concept is relevant to students with disabilities.

1. In what ways could self-determination be incorporated into transition education?
2. How are these ideas applicable to instruction in general education classrooms?

Article Homework Exercise Go to MyEducationLab and select the topic "TRANSITION PLANNING," then read the article "Preparing Students for Life After High School," and complete the activity questions below.

This article describes how high schools should prepare all students for the transition to adulthood by engaging them in significant, meaningful experiences in a variety of settings outside of school.

1. Why is the transition process important for all students?
2. What specific challenges might students with disabilities face that makes the transition process especially important for them?

Appendix 12.1   Individual Transition Plan

Student's Name			
	Eileen	J.	Smith
	First	M.I.	Last

Birth date	3/17/93	School	Valley High School
Student's ID No.	0213	ITP Conference Date	10/7/08

Participants

Name	Position
Eileen	student
Linda	mother
John	father
Scott	transition coordinator
Erica	diagnostician

(continued)

I. Career and Economic Self-Sufficiency	
1. Employment Goal	
Level of present performance	
Steps needed to accomplish goal	
Date of completion	
Person(s) responsible for implementation	
2. Vocational Education/Training Goal	
Level of present performance	
Steps needed to accomplish goal	
Date of completion	
Person(s) responsible for implementation	
3. Postsecondary Education Goal #1	*Eileen needs to apply to college for Fall 2009 admission.*
Level of present performance	*Eileen and her parents know procedures and have appropriate forms.*
Steps needed to accomplish this goal	*Complete forms* *Send by due date.*
Date of completion	*April 1, 2009*
Person(s) responsible for implementation	*Eileen* *parents*
Postsecondary Education Goal #2	*Make Eileen aware of the Services for Students with Disabilities Office.*
Level of present performance	*Eileen and her parents are not aware of this office.*
Steps needed to accomplish this goal	*Provide documents on services.* *Provide name and contact information of office.*

Date of completion	December 1, 2008
Person(s) responsible for implementation	transition coordinator
Postsecondary Education Goal #3	Identify resources that may be needed to obtain a comprehensive evaluation.
Level of present performance	Eileen and her parents do not have any information.
Steps needed to accomplish this goal	Provide a list of professionals who provide evaluations. Obtain recommendations from college staff.
Date of completion	April 1, 2009
Person(s) responsible for implementation	transition coordinator
Postsecondary Education Goal #4	Make Eileen aware of general support services available at the college.
Level of present performance	Eileen and her parents are not aware of these services (i.e., Learning Assistance Center).
Steps needed to accomplish this goal	Obtain documents from college. Obtain name and contact information for Learning Assistance Center.
Date of completion	December 1, 2008
Person(s) responsible for implementation	Eileen parents
Postsecondary Education Goal #5	Connect Eileen with a contact person at college.
Level of present performance	Eileen and her parents do not know any faculty or staff at college.
Steps needed to accomplish this goal	Provide name of a faculty member (Prof. Miller). Contact Prof. Miller to alert that she may be contacted.
Date of completion	April 1, 2009

Person(s) responsible for implementation	*transition coordinator*
Postsecondary Education Goal #6	*Develop a list of private tutors.*
Level of present performance	*Eileen and her parents do not have this information.*
Steps needed to accomplish this goal	*Contact staff at college.* *Combine with current list.* *Provide list to Eileen/parents.*
Date of completion	*April 1, 2009*
Person(s) responsible for implementation	*transition coordinator*

Source: Adapted from P. Wehman, *Individual Transition Plans: The Teacher's Curriculum Guide for Helping Youth with Special Needs* (Austin, TX: PRO-ED, 1995). Copyright © 1995 by PRO-ED, Inc.

CEC Knowledge and Skill Base for All Beginning Special Education Teachers of Students with Learning Disabilities

Standard 1: Foundations

Common Core

Knowledge

CC1K1	Models, theories, and philosophies that form the basis for special education practice.
CC1K2	Laws, policies, and ethical principles regarding behavior management planning and implementation.
CC1K3	Relationship of special education to the organization and function of educational agencies.
CC1K4	Rights and responsibilities of students, parents, teachers, and other professionals, and schools related to exceptional learning needs.
CC1K5	Issues in definition and identification of individuals with exceptional learning needs, including those from culturally and linguistically diverse backgrounds.
CC1K6	Issues, assurances, and due process rights related to assessment, eligibility, and placement within a continuum of services.
CC1K7	Family systems and the role of families in the educational process.
CC1K8	Historical points of view and contribution of culturally diverse groups.
CC1K9	Impact of the dominant culture on shaping schools and the individuals who study and work in them.
CC1K10	Potential impact of differences in values, languages, and customs that can exist between the home and school.

Skills

CC1S1	Articulate personal philosophy of special education.

Learning Disabilities

Knowledge

LD1K1	Historical foundations, classical studies, and major contributors in the field of learning disabilities.
LD1K2	Philosophies, theories, models, and issues related to individuals with learning disabilities.
LD1K3	Impact of legislation on the education of individuals with learning disabilities.
LD1K4	Laws and policies regarding pre-referral, referral, and placement procedures for individuals who may have learning disabilities.
LD1K5	Current definitions and issues related to the identification of individuals with learning disabilities.

Skills	*None in addition to Common Core*

Standard 2: Development and Characteristics of Learners

Common Core

Knowledge

CC2K1	Typical and atypical human growth and development.
CC2K2	Educational implications of characteristics of various exceptionalities.
CC2K3	Characteristics and effects of the cultural and environmental milieu of the individual with exceptional learning needs and the family.
CC2K4	Family systems and the role of families in supporting development.
CC2K5	Similarities and differences of individuals with and without exceptional learning needs.
CC2K6	Similarities and differences among individuals with exceptional learning needs.
CC2K7	Effects of various medications on individuals with exceptional learning needs.

Learning Disabilities

Knowledge

LD2K1	Etiologies of learning disabilities.
LD2K2	Neurobiological and medical factors that may impact the learning of individuals with learning disabilities.
LD2K3	Psychological, social, and emotional characteristics of individuals with learning disabilities.

Skills   *None in addition to Common Core*

Standard 3: Individual Learning Differences

Common Core

Knowledge

CC3K1	Effects an exceptional condition(s) can have on an individual's life.
CC3K2	Impact of learners' academic and social abilities, attitudes, interests, and values on instruction and career development.
CC3K3	Variations in beliefs, traditions, and values across and within cultures and their effects on relationships among individuals with exceptional learning needs, family, and schooling.
CC3K4	Cultural perspectives influencing the relationships among families, schools, and communities as related to instruction.
CC3K5	Differing ways of learning of individuals with exceptional learning needs including those from culturally diverse backgrounds and strategies for addressing these differences.

Learning Disabilities

Knowledge

LD3K1	Impact of co-existing conditions and exceptionalities on individuals with learning disabilities.
LD3K2	Effects of phonological awareness on the reading abilities of individuals with learning disabilities.
LD3K3	Impact learning disabilities may have on auditory and information processing skills.

Skills   *None in addition to Common Core*

Standard 4: Instructional Strategies

Common Core

Skills

CC4S1	Use strategies to facilitate integration into various settings.
CC4S2	Teach individuals to use self-assessment, problem solving, and other cognitive strategies to meet their needs.
CC4S3	Select, adapt, and use instructional strategies and materials according to characteristics of the individual with exceptional learning needs.
CC4S4	Use strategies to facilitate maintenance and generalization of skills across learning environments.
CC4S5	Use procedures to increase the individual's self-awareness, self-management, self-control, self-reliance, and self-esteem.
CC4S6	Use strategies that promote successful transitions for individuals with exceptional learning needs.

Learning Disabilities

Knowledge

LD4K1	Strategies to prepare for and take tests.
LD4K2	Methods for ensuring individual academic success in one-to-one, small-group, and large-group settings.
LD4K3	Methods for increasing accuracy and proficiency in math calculations and applications.
LD4K4	Methods for teaching individuals to independently use cognitive processing to solve problems.
LD4K5	Methods for guiding individuals in identifying and organizing critical content.

Skills

LD4S1	Use research-supported methods for academic and nonacademic instruction of individuals with learning disabilities.
LD4S2	Use specialized methods for teaching basic skills.
LD4S3	Modify the pace of instruction and provide organizational cues.
LD4S4	Identify and teach basic structures and relationships within and across curricula.
LD4S5	Use instructional methods to strengthen and compensate for deficits in perception, comprehension, memory, and retrieval.
LD4S6	Use responses and errors to guide instructional decisions and provide feedback to learners.
LD4S7	Identify and teach essential concepts, vocabulary, and content across the general curriculum.
LD4S8	Use reading methods appropriate to the individual with learning disabilities.
LD4S9	Implement systematic instruction in teaching reading comprehension and monitoring strategies.
LD4S10	Teach strategies for organizing and composing written products.
LD4S11	Implement systematic instruction to teach accuracy, fluency, and comprehension in content area reading and written language.
LD4S12	Use methods to teach mathematics appropriate to the individual with learning disabilities.
LD4S13	Teach learning strategies and study skills to acquire academic content.

Standard 5: Learning Environments and Social Interactions

Common Core

Knowledge

CC5K1	Demands of learning environments.
CC5K2	Basic classroom management theories and strategies for individuals with exceptional learning needs.
CC5K3	Effective management of teaching and learning.
CC5K4	Teacher attitudes and behaviors that influence behavior of individuals with exceptional learning needs.
CC5K5	Social skills needed for educational and other environments.
CC5K6	Strategies for crisis prevention and intervention.
CC5K7	Strategies for preparing individuals to live harmoniously and productively in a culturally diverse world.
CC5K8	Ways to create learning environments that allow individuals to retain and appreciate their own and each others' respective language and cultural heritage.
CC5K9	Ways specific cultures are negatively stereotyped.
CC5K10	Strategies used by diverse populations to cope with a legacy of former and continuing racism.

Skills

CC5S1	Create a safe, equitable, positive, and supportive learning environment in which diversities are valued.
CC5S2	Identify realistic expectations for personal and social behavior in various settings.
CC5S3	Identify supports needed for integration into various program placements.
CC5S4	Design learning environments that encourage active participation in individual and group activities.
CC5S5	Modify the learning environment to manage behaviors.
CC5S6	Use performance data and information from all stakeholders to make or suggest modifications in learning environments.
CC5S7	Establish and maintain rapport with individuals with and without exceptional learning needs.
CC5S8	Teach self-advocacy.
CC5S9	Create an environment that encourages self-advocacy and increased independence.
CC5S10	Use effective and varied behavior management strategies.
CC5S11	Use the least intensive behavior management strategy consistent with the needs of the individual with exceptional learning needs.
CC5S12	Design and manage daily routines.
CC5S13	Organize, develop, and sustain learning environments that support positive intracultural and intercultural experiences.
CC5S14	Mediate controversial intercultural issues among students within the learning environment in ways that enhance any culture, group, or person.
CC5S15	Structure, direct, and support the activities of paraeducators, volunteers, and tutors.
CC5S16	Use universal precautions.

Learning Disabilities

Knowledge   *None in addition to Common Core*

Skills

LD5S1	Teach individuals with learning disabilities to give and receive meaningful feedback from peers and adults.

Standard 6: Language

Common Core

Knowledge

CC6K1	Effects of cultural and linguistic differences on growth and development.
CC6K2	Characteristics of one's own culture and use of language and the ways in which these can differ from other cultures and uses of languages.
CC6K3	Ways of behaving and communicating among cultures that can lead to misinterpretation and misunderstanding.
CC6K4	Augmentative and assistive communication strategies.

Skills

CC6S1	Use strategies to support and enhance communication skills of individuals with exceptional learning needs.
CC6S2	Use communication strategies and resources to facilitate understanding of subject matter for students whose primary language is not the dominant language.

Learning Disabilities

Knowledge

LD6K1	Typical language development and how that may differ for individuals with learning disabilities.
LD6K2	Impact of language development and listening comprehension on academic and nonacademic learning of individuals with learning disabilities.

Skills

LD6S1	Enhance vocabulary development.
LD6S2	Teach strategies for spelling accuracy and generalization.
LD6S3	Teach methods and strategies for producing legible documents.
LD6S4	Teach individuals with learning disabilities to monitor for errors in oral and written communications.

Standard 7: Instructional Planning

Common Core

Knowledge

CC7K1	Theories and research that form the basis of curriculum development and instructional practice.
CC7K2	Scope and sequences of general and special curricula.
CC7K3	National, state or provincial, and local curricula standards.
CC7K4	Technology for planning and managing the teaching and learning environment.
CC7K5	Roles and responsibilities of the paraeducator related to instruction, intervention, and direct service.

Skills

CC7S1	Identify and prioritize areas of the general curriculum and accommodations for individuals with exceptional learning needs.
CC7S2	Develop and implement comprehensive, longitudinal individualized programs in collaboration with team members.
CC7S3	Involve the individual and family in setting instructional goals and monitoring progress.
CC7S4	Use functional assessments to develop intervention plans.
CC7S5	Use task analysis.

CC7S6	Sequence, implement, and evaluate individualized learning objectives.
CC7S7	Integrate affective, social, and life skills with academic curricula.
CC7S8	Develop and select instructional content, resources, and strategies that respond to cultural, linguistic, and gender differences.
CC7S9	Incorporate and implement instructional and assistive technology into the educational program.
CC7S10	Prepare lesson plans.
CC7S11	Prepare and organize materials to implement daily lesson plans.
CC7S12	Use instructional time effectively.
CC7S13	Make responsive adjustments to instruction based on continual observations.
CC7S14	Prepare individuals to exhibit self-enhancing behavior in response to societal attitudes and actions.

Learning Disabilities

Knowledge

LD7K1	Relationships among reading instruction methods and learning disabilities.
LD7K2	Sources of specialized curricula, materials, and resources for individuals with learning disabilities.
LD7K3	Interventions and services for children who may be at risk for learning disabilities.

Skills   *None in addition to Common Core*

Standard 8: Assessment

Common Core

Knowledge

CC8K1	Basic terminology used in assessment.
CC8K2	Legal provisions and ethical principles regarding assessment of individuals.
CC8K3	Screening, pre-referral, referral, and classification procedures.
CC8K4	Use and limitations of assessment instruments.
CC8K5	National, state or provincial, and local accommodations and modifications.

Skills

CC8S1	Gather relevant background information.
CC8S2	Administer nonbiased formal and informal assessments.
CC8S3	Use technology to conduct assessments.
CC8S4	Develop or modify individualized assessment strategies.
CC8S5	Interpret information from formal and informal assessments.
CC8S6	Use assessment information in making eligibility, program, and placement decisions for individuals with exceptional learning needs, including those from culturally and/or linguistically diverse backgrounds.
CC8S7	Report assessment results to all stakeholders using effective communication skills.
CC8S8	Evaluate instruction and monitor progress of individuals with exceptional learning needs.
CC8S9	Develop or modify individualized assessment strategies.
CC8S10	Create and maintain records.

Learning Disabilities

Knowledge

LD8K1	Terminology and procedures used in the assessment of individuals with learning disabilities.
LD8K2	Factors that could lead to misidentification of individuals as having learning disabilities.
LD8K3	Procedures to identify young children who may be at risk for learning disabilities.

Skills

LD8S1   Choose and administer assessment instruments appropriate to the individual with learning disabilities.

Standard 9: Professional and Ethical Practice

Common Core

Knowledge

CC9K1   Personal cultural biases and differences that affect one's teaching.

CC9K2   Importance of the teacher serving as a model for individuals with exceptional learning needs.

CC9K3   Continuum of lifelong professional development.

CC9K4   Methods to remain current regarding research-validated practice.

Skills

CC9S1   Practice within the CEC Code of Ethics and other standards of the profession.

CC9S2   Uphold high standards of competence and integrity and exercise sound judgment in the practice of the professional.

CC9S3   Act ethically in advocating for appropriate services.

CC9S4   Conduct professional activities in compliance with applicable laws and policies.

CC9S5   Demonstrate commitment to developing the highest education and quality-of-life potential of individuals with exceptional learning needs.

CC9S6   Demonstrate sensitivity for the culture, language, religion, gender, disability, socio-economic status, and sexual orientation of individuals.

CC9S7   Practice within one's skill limit and obtain assistance as needed.

CC9S8   Use verbal, nonverbal, and written language effectively.

CC9S9   Conduct self-evaluation of instruction.

CC9S10   Access information on exceptionalities.

CC9S11   Reflect on one's practice to improve instruction and guide professional growth.

CC9S12   Engage in professional activities that benefit individuals with exceptional learning needs, their families, and one's colleagues.

Learning Disabilities

Knowledge

LD9K1   Ethical responsibility to advocate for appropriate services for individuals with learning disabilities.

LD9K2   Professional organizations and sources of information relevant to the field of learning disabilities.

Skills

LD9S1   Participate in activities of professional organizations relevant to the field of learning disabilities.

LD9S2   Use research findings and theories to guide practice.

Standard 10: Collaboration

Common Core

Knowledge

CC10K1   Models and strategies of consultation and collaboration.

CC10K2   Roles of individuals with exceptional learning needs, families, and school and community personnel in planning of an individualized program.

CC10K3	Concerns of families of individuals with exceptional learning needs and strategies to help address these concerns.
CC10K4	Culturally responsive factors that promote effective communication and collaboration with individuals with exceptional learning needs, families, school personnel, and community members.

Skills

CC10S1	Maintain confidential communication about individuals with exceptional learning needs.
CC10S2	Collaborate with families and others in assessment of individuals with exceptional learning needs.
CC10S3	Foster respectful and beneficial relationships between families and professionals.
CC10S4	Assist individuals with exceptional learning needs and their families in becoming active participants in the educational team.
CC10S5	Plan and conduct collaborative conferences with individuals with exceptional learning needs and their families.
CC10S6	Collaborate with school personnel and community members in integrating individuals with exceptional learning needs into various settings.
CC10S7	Use group problem solving skills to develop, implement, and evaluate collaborative activities.
CC10S8	Model techniques and coach others in the use of instructional methods and accommodations.
CC10S9	Communicate with school personnel about the characteristics and needs of individuals with exceptional learning needs.
CC10S10	Communicate effectively with families of individuals with exceptional learning needs from diverse backgrounds.
CC10S11	Observe, evaluate, and provide feedback to paraeducators.

Learning Disabilities

Knowledge

LD10K1	Co-planning and coteaching methods to strengthen content acquisition of individuals with learning disabilities.
LD10K2	Services, networks, and organizations that provide support across the life span for individuals with learning disabilities.

Skills	*None in addition to Common Core*

Notes:

1. "Individual with exceptional learning needs" is used throughout to include individuals with disabilities and individuals with exceptional gifts and talents.
2. "Exceptional condition" is used throughout to include both single and co-existing conditions. These may be two or more disabling conditions or exceptional gifts or talents co-existing with one or more disabling conditions.
3. "Special curricula" is used throughout to denote curricular areas not routinely emphasized or addressed in general curricula; e.g., social, communication, motor, independence, self-advocacy.

Source: Council for Exceptional children. (2003). *What Every Special Educator Must Know: The International Standards for the Preparation and Certification of Special Education Teachers* (5th ed.). Copyright © 2003 by the Council for Exceptional Children.

CEC Knowledge and Skill Base for All Beginning Special Education Teachers of Students with Emotional and Behavioral Disorders

Standard 1: Foundations

Common Core

Knowledge

CC1K1	Models, theories, and philosophies that form the basis for special education practice.
CC1K2	Laws, policies, and ethical principles regarding behavior management planning and implementation.
CC1K3	Relationship of special education to the organization and function of educational agencies.
CC1K4	Rights and responsibilities of students, parents, teachers, and other professionals, and schools related to exceptional learning needs.
CC1K5	Issues in definition and identification of individuals with exceptional learning needs, including those from culturally and linguistically diverse backgrounds.
CC1K6	Issues, assurances, and due process rights related to assessment, eligibility, and placement within a continuum of services.
CC1K7	Family systems and the role of families in the educational process.
CC1K8	Historical points of view and contribution of culturally diverse groups.
CC1K9	Impact of the dominant culture on shaping schools and the individuals who study and work in them.
CC1K10	Potential impact of differences in values, languages, and customs that can exist between the home and school.

Skills

CC1S1	Articulate personal philosophy of special education.

Emotional/Behavioral Disorders

Knowledge

BD1K1	Educational terminology and definitions of individuals with emotional/behavioral disorders.
BD1K2	Models that describe deviance.
BD1K3	Foundations and issues related to knowledge and practice in emotional/behavioral disorders.
BD1K4	The legal, judicial, and educational systems serving individuals with emotional/behavioral disorders.
BD1K5	Theory of reinforcement techniques in serving individuals with emotional/behavioral disorders.
BD1K6	Principles of normalization and concept of least restrictive environment for individuals with emotional/behavioral disorders in programs.

Skills   *None in addition to Common Core*

Standard 2: Development and Characteristics of Learners

Common Core

Knowledge

CC2K1	Typical and atypical human growth and development.
CC2K2	Educational implications of characteristics of various exceptionalities.
CC2K3	Characteristics and effects of the cultural and environmental milieu of the individual with exceptional learning needs and the family.
CC2K4	Family systems and the role of families in supporting development.
CC2K5	Similarities and differences of individuals with and without exceptional learning needs.
CC2K6	Similarities and differences among individuals with exceptional learning needs.
CC2K7	Effects of various medications on individuals with exceptional learning needs.

Emotional/Behavioral Disorders

Knowledge

BD2K1	Etiology and diagnosis related to various theoretical approaches in the field of emotional/behavioral disorders.
BD2K2	Physical development, disability, and health impairments related to individuals with emotional/behavioral disorders.
BD2K3	Social characteristics of individuals with emotional/behavioral disorders.
BD2K4	Factors that influence overrepresentation of diverse individuals in programs for individuals with emotional/behavior disorders.

Skills   *None in addition to Common Core*

Standard 3: Individual Learning Differences

Common Core

Knowledge

CC3K1	Effects an exceptional condition(s) can have on an individual's life.
CC3K2	Impact of learners' academic and social abilities, attitudes, interests, and values on instruction and career development.
CC3K3	Variations in beliefs, traditions, and values across and within cultures and their effects on relationships among individuals with exceptional learning needs, family, and schooling.
CC3K4	Cultural perspectives influencing the relationships among families, schools, and communities as related to instruction.
CC3K5	Differing ways of learning of individuals with exceptional learning needs including those from culturally diverse backgrounds and strategies for addressing these differences.

Emotional/Behavioral Disorders

Knowledge   *None in addition to Common Core*

Skills   *None in addition to Common Core*

Standard 4: Instructional Strategies

Common Core

Skills

CC4S1	Use strategies to facilitate integration into various settings.
CC4S2	Teach individuals to use self-assessment, problem solving, and other cognitive strategies to meet their needs.

CC4S3	Select, adapt, and use instructional strategies and materials according to characteristics of the individual with exceptional learning needs.
CC4S4	Use strategies to facilitate maintenance and generalization of skills across learning environments.
CC4S5	Use procedures to increase the individual's self-awareness, self-management, self-control, self-reliance, and self-esteem.
CC4S6	Use strategies that promote successful transitions for individuals with exceptional learning needs.

Emotional/Behavioral Disorders

Knowledge

BD4K1	Sources of specialized materials for individuals with emotional/behavioral disorders.
BD4K2	Advantages and limitations of instructional strategies and practices for teaching individuals with emotional/behavioral disorders.
BD4K3	Resources and techniques used to transition individuals with emotional/behavioral disorders into and out of school and postschool environments.
BD4K4	Prevention and intervention strategies for individuals at risk of emotional/behavioral disorders.
BD4K5	Strategies for integrating student initiated learning experiences into ongoing instruction for individuals with emotional/behavioral disorders.

Skills

BD4S1	Use strategies from multiple theoretical approaches for individuals with emotional/behavioral disorders.
BD4S2	Use a variety of nonaversive techniques to control targeted behavior and maintain attention of individuals with emotional/behavioral disorders.

Standard 5: Learning Environments and Social Interactions

Common Core

Knowledge

CC5K1	Demands of learning environments.
CC5K2	Basic classroom management theories and strategies for individuals with exceptional learning needs.
CC5K3	Effective management of teaching and learning.
CC5K4	Teacher attitudes and behaviors that influence behavior of individuals with exceptional learning needs.
CC5K5	Social skills needed for educational and other environments.
CC5K6	Strategies for crisis prevention and intervention.
CC5K7	Strategies for preparing individuals to live harmoniously and productively in a culturally diverse world.
CC5K8	Ways to create learning environments that allow individuals to retain and appreciate their own and each others' respective language and cultural heritage.
CC5K9	Ways specific cultures are negatively stereotyped.
CC5K10	Strategies used by diverse populations to cope with a legacy of former and continuing racism.

Skills

CC5S1	Create a safe, equitable, positive, and supportive learning environment in which diversities are valued.
CC5S2	Identify realistic expectations for personal and social behavior in various settings.

CC5S3	Identify supports needed for integration into various program placements.
CC5S4	Design learning environments that encourage active participation in individual and group activities.
CC5S5	Modify the learning environment to manage behaviors.
CC5S6	Use performance data and information from all stakeholders to make or suggest modifications in learning environments.
CC5S7	Establish and maintain rapport with individuals with and without exceptional learning needs.
CC5S8	Teach self-advocacy.
CC5S9	Create an environment that encourages self-advocacy and increased independence.
CC5S10	Use effective and varied behavior management strategies.
CC5S11	Use the least intensive behavior management strategy consistent with the needs of the individual with exceptional learning needs.
CC5S12	Design and manage daily routines.
CC5S13	Organize, develop, and sustain learning environments that support positive intracultural and intercultural experiences.
CC5S14	Mediate controversial intercultural issues among students within the learning environment in ways that enhance any culture, group, or person.
CC5S15	Structure, direct, and support the activities of paraeducators, volunteers, and tutors.
CC5S16	Use universal precautions.

Emotional/Behavioral Disorders

Knowledge

BD5K1	Advantages and disadvantages of placement options and the continuum of services for individuals with emotional/behavioral disorders.
BD5K2	Functional classroom designs for individuals with emotional/behavioral disorders.

Skills

BD5S1	Establish a consistent classroom routine for individuals with emotional/behavioral disorders.
BD5S2	Use skills in problem solving and conflict resolution.

Standard 6: Language

Common Core

Knowledge

CC6K1	Effects of cultural and linguistic differences on growth and development.
CC6K2	Characteristics of one's own culture and use of language and the ways in which these can differ from other cultures and uses of languages.
CC6K3	Ways of behaving and communicating among cultures that can lead to misinterpretation and misunderstanding.
CC6K4	Augmentative and assistive communication strategies.

Skills

CC6S1	Use strategies to support and enhance communication skills of individuals with exceptional learning needs.
CC6S2	Use communication strategies and resources to facilitate understanding of subject matter for students whose primary language is not the dominant language.

Emotional/Behavioral Disorders

Knowledge   None in addition to Common Core

Skills   None in addition to Common Core

Standard 7: Instructional Planning

Common Core

Knowledge

CC7K1	Theories and research that form the basis of curriculum development and instructional practice.
CC7K2	Scope and sequences of general and special curricula.
CC7K3	National, state or provincial, and local curricula standards.
CC7K4	Technology for planning and managing the teaching and learning environment.
CC7K5	Roles and responsibilities of the paraeducator related to instruction, intervention, and direct service.

Skills

CC7S1	Identify and prioritize areas of the general curriculum and accommodations for individuals with exceptional learning needs.
CC7S2	Develop and implement comprehensive, longitudinal individualized programs in collaboration with team members.
CC7S3	Involve the individual and family in setting instructional goals and monitoring progress.
CC7S4	Use functional assessments to develop intervention plans.
CC7S5	Use task analysis.
CC7S6	Sequence, implement, and evaluate individualized learning objectives.
CC7S7	Integrate affective, social, and life skills with academic curricula.
CC7S8	Develop and select instructional content, resources, and strategies that respond to cultural, linguistic, and gender differences.
CC7S9	Incorporate and implement instructional and assistive technology into the educational program.
CC7S10	Prepare lesson plans.
CC7S11	Prepare and organize materials to implement daily lesson plans.
CC7S12	Use instructional time effectively.
CC7S13	Make responsive adjustments to instruction based on continual observations.
CC7S14	Prepare individuals to exhibit self-enhancing behavior in response to societal attitudes and actions.

Emotional/Behavioral Disorders

Knowledge

BD7K1	Model programs that have been effective for individuals with emotional/behavioral disorders across the age range.

Skills

BD7S1	Plan and implement individualized reinforcement systems and environmental modifications at levels equal to the intensity of the behavior.
BD7S2	Integrate academic instruction, affective education, and behavior management for individuals and groups with emotional/behavioral disorders.

Standard 8: Assessment

Common Core

Knowledge

CC8K1	Basic terminology used in assessment.
CC8K2	Legal provisions and ethical principles regarding assessment of individuals.
CC8K3	Screening, prereferral, referral, and classification procedures.
CC8K4	Use and limitations of assessment instruments.
CC8K5	National, state or provincial, and local accommodations and modifications.

Skills

CC8S1	Gather relevant background information.
CC8S2	Administer nonbiased formal and informal assessments.
CC8S3	Use technology to conduct assessments.
CC8S4	Develop or modify individualized assessment strategies.
CC8S5	Interpret information from formal and informal assessments.
CC8S6	Use assessment information in making eligibility, program, and placement decisions for individuals with exceptional learning needs, including those from culturally and/or linguistically diverse backgrounds.
CC8S7	Report assessment results to all stakeholders using effective communication skills.
CC8S8	Evaluate instruction and monitor progress of individuals with exceptional learning needs.
CC8S9	Develop or modify individualized assessment strategies.
CC9S10	Create and maintain records.

Emotional/Behavioral Disorders

Knowledge

BD8K1	Characteristics of behavioral rating scales.
BD8K2	Policies and procedures involved in the screening, diagnosis, and placement of individuals with emotional/behavioral disorders including academic and social behaviors.
BD8K3	Types and importance of information concerning individuals with emotional/behavioral disorders available from families and public agencies.

Skills

BD8S1	Prepare assessment reports on individuals with emotional/behavioral disorders based on behavioral-ecological information.
BD8S2	Assess appropriate and problematic social behaviors of individuals with emotional/behavioral disorders.
BD8S3	Monitor intragroup behavior changes from subject to subject and activity to activity applicable to individuals with emotional/behavior disorders.

Standard 9: Professional and Ethical Practice

Common Core

Knowledge

CC9K1	Personal cultural biases and differences that affect one's teaching.
CC9K2	Importance of the teacher serving as a model for individuals with exceptional learning needs.
CC9K3	Continuum of lifelong professional development.
CC9K4	Methods to remain current regarding research-validated practice.

Skills

CC9S1	Practice within the CEC Code of Ethics and other standards of the profession.
CC9S2	Uphold high standards of competence and integrity and exercise sound judgment in the practice of the professional.
CC9S3	Act ethically in advocating for appropriate services.
CC9S4	Conduct professional activities in compliance with applicable laws and policies.
CC9S5	Demonstrate commitment to developing the highest education and quality-of-life potential of individuals with exceptional learning needs.
CC9S6	Demonstrate sensitivity for the culture, language, religion, gender, disability, socio-economic status, and sexual orientation of individuals.
CC9S7	Practice within one's skill limit and obtain assistance as needed.
CC9S8	Use verbal, nonverbal, and written language effectively.
CC9S9	Conduct self-evaluation of instruction.
CC9S10	Access information on exceptionalities.
CC9S11	Reflect on one's practice to improve instruction and guide professional growth.
CC9S12	Engage in professional activities that benefit individuals with exceptional learning needs, their families, and one's colleagues.

Emotional/Behavioral Disorders

Knowledge

BD9K1	Organizations and publications relevant to the field of emotional/behavioral disorders.

Skills

BD9S1	Participate in activities of professional organizations relevant to the field of emotional/behavioral disorders.

Standard 10: Collaboration

Common Core

Knowledge

CC10K1	Models and strategies of consultation and collaboration.
CC10K2	Roles of individuals with exceptional learning needs, families, and school and community personnel in planning of an individualized program.
CC10K3	Concerns of families of individuals with exceptional learning needs and strategies to help address these concerns.
CC10K4	Culturally responsive factors that promote effective communication and collaboration with individuals with exceptional learning needs, families, school personnel, and community members.

Skills

CC10S1	Maintain confidential communication about individuals with exceptional learning needs.
CC10S2	Collaborate with families and others in assessment of individuals with exceptional learning needs.
CC10S3	Foster respectful and beneficial relationships between families and professionals.
CC10S4	Assist individuals with exceptional learning needs and their families in becoming active participants in the educational team.
CC10S5	Plan and conduct collaborative conferences with individuals with exceptional learning needs and their families.
CC10S6	Collaborate with school personnel and community members in integrating individuals with exceptional learning needs into various settings.

CC10S7   Use group problem solving skills to develop, implement, and evaluate collaborative activities.

CC10S8   Model techniques and coach others in the use of instructional methods and accommodations.

CC10S9   Communicate with school personnel about the characteristics and needs of individuals with exceptional learning needs.

CC10S10   Communicate effectively with families of individuals with exceptional learning needs from diverse backgrounds.

CC10S11   Observe, evaluate, and provide feedback to paraeducators.

Emotional/Behavioral Disorders

Knowledge

BD10K1   Services, networks, and organizations for individuals with emotional/behavioral disorders.

BD10K2   Parent education programs and behavior management guides that address severe behavioral problems and facilitate communication for individuals with emotional/behavioral disorders.

BD10K3   Collaborative and consultative roles of the special education teacher in the reintegration of individuals with emotional/behavioral disorders.

BD10K4   Role of professional groups and referral agencies in identifying, assessing, and providing services to individuals with emotional/behavioral disorders.

Skills

BD10S1   Teach parents to use appropriate behavior management and counseling techniques.

Notes:

1. "Individual with exceptional learning needs" is used throughout to include individuals with disabilities and individuals with exceptional gifts and talents.

2. "Exceptional condition" is used throughout to include both single and co-existing conditions. These may be two or more disabling conditions or exceptional gifts or talents co-existing with one or more disabling conditions.

3. "Special curricula" is used throughout to denote curricular areas not routinely emphasized or addressed in general curricula; e.g., social, communication, motor, independence, self-advocacy.

Source: Council for Exceptional Children. (2003). *What Every Special Educator Must Know: The International Standards for the Preparation and Certification of Special Education Teachers* (5th ed.). Copyright © 2003 by the Council for Exceptional Children.

References

Abudarham, S. (2002). Assessment and appraisal of communication needs. In S. Abudarham and A. Hurd (Eds.), *Management of communication needs in people with learning disability* (pp. 33–81). London: Whurr.

Ackerman, P. T., Anhalt, J. M., and Dykman, R. A. (1986). Arithmetic automatization failure in children with attention and reading disorders: Associations and sequelae. *Journal of Learning Disabilities, 19*, 222–232.

Adams, A., Carnine, D., and Gersten, R. (1982). Instructional strategies for studying context area texts in the intermediate grades. *Reading Research Quarterly, 18*(1), 27–55.

Adams, M. J. (1990). *Beginning to read: Thinking and learning about print.* Cambridge, MA: MIT Press.

Adelman, H., and Taylor, L. *Guidance notes: The relationship of response to intervention and systems of learning supports.* Los Angeles: UCLA Center for Mental Health in Schools. Retrieved December 14, 2007, from http://smhp.psych.ucla.edu/dbsimple.aspx?Primary=2311&Number=9904.

Ahlberg, J., and Ahlberg, A. (1979). *Each peach pear plum: An "I Spy" story.* New York: Viking.

Al Otaiba, S., and Fuchs, D. (2006). Who are the young children for whom best practices in reading are ineffective? *Journal of Learning Disabilities, 39*, 414–431.

Alber, S. R., Heward, W. L., and Hippler, B. J. (1999). Teaching middle school students with learning disabilities to recruit positive teacher attention. *Exceptional Children, 65*, 253–270.

Alberto, P. A., and Troutman, A. C. (2006). *Applied behavior analysis for teachers.* Upper Saddle River, NJ: Merrill/Prentice Hall.

Alfassi, M. (1998). Reading for meaning: The efficacy of reciprocal teaching in fostering reading comprehension in high school students in remedial classes. *American Educational Research Journal, 35*(2), 309–332.

Allen, J., Michalove, B., Shockley, B., and West, M. (1991). I'm really worried about Joseph: Reducing the risks of literacy learning. *The Reading Teacher, 44*, 458–472.

Allen, R. I., and Petr, C. G. (1996). Toward developing standards and measurements for family-centered practice in family support programs. In G. H. S. Singer, L. E. Powers, and A. L. Olson (Eds.), *Redefining family support* (pp. 57–86). Baltimore: Brookes.

Allen, R. V. (1976). *Language experiences in communication.* Boston: Houghton Mifflin.

Allen, R. V., and Allen, C. (1966–68). *Language experiences in reading* (Levels I, II, and III). Chicago: Encyclopedia Britannica.

Allen, R. V., and Allen, C. (1982). *Language experience activities* (2nd ed.). Boston: Houghton Mifflin.

Alley, G. R., and Deshler, D. D. (1979). *Teaching the learning disabled adolescent: Strategies and methods.* Denver: Love.

Allington, R. L. (1983a). Fluency: The neglected reading goal. *The Reading Teacher, 36*, 556–561.

Allington, R. L. (1983b). The reading instruction provided readers of differing reading abilities. *The Elementary School Journal, 83*, 548–559.

Alper, S. K., Schloss, P. J., and Schloss, C. N. (1994). *Families of students with disabilities.* Boston: Allyn & Bacon.

Altwerger, B., and Ivener, B. L. (1994). Self-esteem: Access to literacy in multicultural and multilingual classrooms. In K. Spangenberg-Urbschat and R. Pritchard (Eds.), *Kids come in all languages: Reading instruction for ESL students* (pp. 65–81). Newark, DE: International Reading Association.

Alvermann, D. E., and Phelps, S. (1998). *Content reading and literacy: Succeeding in today's diverse classrooms.* Boston: Allyn & Bacon.

Alvermann, D., Bridge, C., Schmidt, R., Seafoss, L., Winograd, P., Paris, S., Priestly, C., and Santeusanio, N. (1989). *Health reading.* Lexington, MA: D. C. Heath.

Al-Yagon, M., and Mikulincer, M. (2004). Patterns of close relationships and socioemotional and academic adjustment among school-age children with learning disabilities. *Learning Disabilities Research and Practice, 19*(1), 12–19.

American Psychiatric Association. (1994). *Diagnostic and statistical manual of mental disorders* (4th ed.). Washington, DC: Author.

American Speech-Language-Hearing Association. (2000). *Guidelines for the roles and responsibilities of the school-based speech-language pathologist.* Rockville, MD: Author.

Amish, P. L., Gesten, E. L., Smith, J. K., Clark, H. B., and Stark, C. (1988). Social problem-solving training for severely emotionally and behaviorally disturbed children. *Behavioral Disorders, 13*(3), 175–186.

Anders, P. L., and Bos, C. S. (1984). In the beginning: Vocabulary instruction in content classroom. *Topics in Learning and Learning Disabilities, 3*(4), 53–65.

Anders, P. L., and Bos, C. S. (1986). Semantic feature analysis: An interactive strategy for vocabulary development and text comprehension. *Journal of Reading, 29*(7), 610–616.

Anders, P. L., and Guzzetti, B. J. (1996). *Literacy instruction in the content areas.* Fort Worth, TX: Harcourt Brace College.

Anders, P. L., Bos, C. S., and Filip, D. (1984). The effect of semantic feature analysis on the reading comprehension of learning disabled students. In J. A. Niles and L. A. Harris (Eds.), *Changing perspectives on reading/language processing and instruction* (pp. 162–166). Rochester, NY: National Reading Conference.

Anderson, J. R. (1990). *Cognitive psychology and its implications* (2nd ed.). San Francisco: W. H. Freeman.

Anderson, J. R. (1995). *Cognitive psychology and its implications* (3rd ed.). San Francisco: Freeman & Company.

Anderson, L. M., Raphael, T. E., Englert, C. S., and Stevens, D. D. (April 1991). *Teaching writing with a new instructional model: Variations in teachers' practices and student performance.* Paper presented at the annual meeting of the American Education Research Association, Chicago.

Anderson, R. C., and Pearson, P. D. (1984). A schema-theoretic view of basic processes in reading. In P. D. Pearson (Ed.), *Handbook of reading research* (pp. 255–292). New York: Longman.

Anderson, R. C., Reynolds, R. E., Schallert, D. L., and Goetz, E. T. (1977). Frameworks for comprehending discourse. *American Educational Research Journal, 14*, 367–382.

Anderson, R. C., Wilson, P. T., and Fielding, L. G. (1988). Growth in reading and how children spend their time outside school. *Reading Research Quarterly, 23*, 285–303.

Anderson, T. H., and Armbruster, B. B. (1986). *The value of taking notes during lectures* (Report No. 374). Cambridge, Massachusetts: Bolt, Beranek and Newman and Center for the Study of Reading, Urbana, Illinois (ERIC Document Reproduction Service No. ED277996).

Anglin, J. (1970). *The growth of meaning.* Cambridge, MA: MIT Press.

Archer, A., and Edgar, E. (1976). Teaching academic skills to mildly handicapped children. In S. Lowenbraun and J. Q. Affect (Eds.), *Teaching mildly handicapped children in regular classes.* Columbus, OH: Merrill.

Arguelles, M. E., Vaughn, S., and Schumm, J. S. (1996). *Executive summaries of 69 schools throughout the state of Florida participating in the ESE/FEFP 1995–1996 pilot program.*

Armbruster, B. B., and Anderson, T. H. (1988). On selecting "considerate" content area textbooks. *Remedial and Special Education, 9*(1), 47–52.

Arndt, S. A., Konrad, M., and Test, D. W. (2006). Effects of the self-directed IEP on student participation in planning meetings. *Remedial and Special Education, 27*(4), 194–207.

Ashbaker, M. H., and Swanson, H. L. (1996). Short-term memory and working memory operations and their contribution to reading in adolescents with and without learning disabilities. *Learning Disabilities Research and Practice, 11*, 206–213.

Ashby, J. S., Kottman, T., and Schoen, E. (1998). Perfectionism and eating disorders. *Journal of Mental Health Counseling, 20*(3), 261–271.

Asher, S. R., Gabriel, S. W., and Hopmeyer, A. (1993, April). *Children's loneliness in different school contexts.* Paper presented at the biennial meeting of the Society for Research in Child Development, New Orleans, LA.

Ashton-Warner, S. (1958). *Spinster.* New York: Simon and Schuster.

Ashton-Warner, S. (1963). *Teacher.* New York: Simon and Schuster.

Ashton-Warner, S. (1972). *Spearpoint.* New York: Knopf.

Atkinson, J. W., and Shiffrin, R. M. (1968). Human memory: A proposed system and its control processes. In K. W. Spence and J. T. Spence (Eds.), *The psychology of learning and motivation: Advances in research and theory* (Vol. 2). New York: Academic Press.

Atwell, N. (1984). Writing and reading literature from the inside out. *Language Arts, 61,* 240–252.

Atwell, N. (1987). *In the middle: Writing, reading, and learning with adolescents.* Portsmouth, NH: Heinemann.

August, D., and Shanahan, T. (2006). *Developing literacy in second-language learners: Report of the National Literacy Panel on language-minority children and youth.* Mahwah, NJ: Erlbaum.

Axelrod, S. (1998). *How to use group contingencies.* Austin, TX: PRO-ED.

Badian, N. A., and Ghublikian, M. (1983). The personal-social characteristics of children with poor mathematical computation skills. *Journal of Learning Disabilities, 16*(3), 154–157.

Bahr, M. W., Fuchs, D., and Fuchs, L. S. (1999). Mainstream Assistance Teams: A consultation-based approach to pre-referral intervention. In S. Graham and K. Harris (Eds.), *Working together* (pp. 87–116). Cambridge, MA: Brookline Books.

Baker, C. (1993). *Foundations of bilingual education and bilingualism.* Clevedon, England: Multilingual Matters.

Baker, G. A. (1977). *A comparison of traditional spelling with phonemic spelling of fifth and sixth grade students.* Unpublished doctoral dissertation, Wayne State University, Detroit.

Baker, J. M., and Zigmond, N. (1990). Are regular education classes equipped to accommodate students with learning disabilities? *Exceptional Children, 56,* 515–526.

Baker, S., Gersten, R., and Lee, D. (2002). A synthesis of empirical research on teaching mathematics to low-achieving students. *The Elementary School Journal, 103*(1), 51–73.

Bandura, A. (1977). *Social learning theory.* Englewood Cliffs, NJ: Prentice Hall.

Bandura, A. (1986). *Social foundations of thought and action: A social cognitive theory.* Englewood Cliffs, NJ: Prentice Hall.

Barkley, R. A. (1997). Behavioral inhibition, sustained attention, and executive functions: Constructing a unifying theory of ADHD. *Psychological Bulletin, 121,* 65–94.

Barnes, M. A., Wilkinson, M., Khemani, E., Boudousquie, A., Dennis, M., and Fletcher, J. M. (2006). Arithmetic processing in children with spina bifida: Calculation accuracy, strategy use, and fact retrieval fluency. *Journal of Learning Disabilities, 39,* 174–187.

Barney, L. (1973). The first and third R's. *Today's Education, 62,* 57–58.

Barrett, T. (1976). Taxonomy of reading comprehension. In R. Smith and T. Barrett (Eds.), *Teaching reading in the middle grades.* Reading, MA: Addison-Wesley.

Barrouillet, P., Fayol, M., and Lathuliere, E. (1997). Selecting between competitors in multiplication tasks: An explanation of the errors produced by adolescents with learning difficulties. *International Journal of Behavioral Development, 21*(2), 253–275.

Bartlett, C. W., Brzustowicz, L. M., Flax, J. F., Hirsch, L. S., Realpe-Bonilla, T., and Tallal, P. (2003). Specific language impairment in families: Evidence for co-occurrence with reading impairments. *Journal of Speech, Language, and Hearing Research, 46,* 530–543.

Bashir, A. S., and Scavuzzo, A. (1992). Children with language disorders: Natural history and academic success. *Journal of Learning Disabilities, 25,* 53–65.

Bassett, D. S., and Kochhar-Bryant, C. A. (2006). Strategies for aligning standards-based education and transition. *Focus on Exceptional Children, 39*(2), 1–19.

Bassett, D. S., and Lehmann, J. (2002). *Student involvement.* Austin, TX: PRO-ED.

Bateman, B. (1965). Learning disabilities: An overview. *Journal of School Psychology, 3*(3), 1–12.

Batsche, G., Elliott J., Graden, J. L., Grimes, J., Kovaleski. J. F., Prasse, D., Reschly, D. J., Schrag, J., and Tilly, W. D. (2005). *Response to intervention: Policy considerations and implementation.* Alexandria, VA: National Association of State Directors of Special Education.

Battle, J., and Blowers, T. (1982). A longitudinal comparative study of the self-esteem of students in regular and special education classes. *Journal of Learning Disabilities, 15*(2), 100–102.

Bauer, R. H. (1987). Control processes as a way of understanding, diagnosing, and remediating learning disabilities. In H. L. Swanson (Ed.), *Advances in learning and behavioral disabilities* (Supplement 2, pp. 41–81). Greenwich, CT: JAI Press.

Baumann, J. F., and Kame'enui, E. J. (1991). Research on vocabulary instruction: Ode to Voltaire. In J. Flood, J. M. Jensen, D. Lapp, and J. R. Squire (Eds.), *Handbook of research on teaching the English language arts* (pp. 604–632). New York: Macmillan.

Baumann, J. F., and Kame'enui, E. J. (2004). *Vocabulary instruction: Research to practice.* New York: Guilford.

Baumann, J. F., and Serra, J. K. (1984). The frequency and placement of main ideas in children's social studies textbooks: A modified replication of Braddock's research on topic sentences. *Journal of Reading Behavior, 16,* 27–40.

Baumann, J. F., Hooten, H., and White, P. (1999). Teaching comprehension through literature: A teacher-research project to develop fifth graders' reading strategies and motivation. *The Reading Teacher, 53,* 38–51.

Bauwens, J., Hourcade, J. J., and Friend, M. (1989). Cooperative teaching: A model for general and special education integration. *Remedial and Special Education, 10*(2), 17–22.

Bay, M., Bryan, T., and O'Connor, R. (1994). Teachers assisting teachers: A prereferral model for urban educators. *Teacher Education and Special Education, 17*(1), 10–21.

Bear, D. R., Invernizzi, M., Templeton, S., and Johnston, F. (2000). *Words their way: Word study for phonics, vocabulary, and spelling instruction* (2nd ed.). Columbus, OH: Merrill.

Bear, G. C., Clever, A., and Proctor, W. A. (1991). Self-perceptions of nonhandicapped children and children with learning disabilities in integrated classes. *Journal of Special Education, 24,* 409–426.

Beck, A. T., Brown, G., and Steer, S. A. (1989). Sex differences on the revised Beck Depression Inventory for outpatients with affective disorders. *Journal of Personality Assessment, 53,* 693–702.

Beck, I. L. (2006). *Making sense of phonics.* New York: Guilford.

Beck, I. L., and Juel, C. (1995). The role of decoding in learning to read. *American Educator, 19*(2), 8, 21–25, 39–42.

Beck, I. L., and McKeown, M. G. (1981). Developing questions that promote comprehension: The story map. *Language Arts, 58,* 913–918.

Beck, I. L., and McKeown, M. G. (2006). *Improving comprehension with questioning the author.* New York: Scholastic.

Beck, I. L., McKeown, M. G., and Kucan, L. (2002). *Bringing words to life: Robust vocabulary instruction.* New York: Guilford.

Beck, I. L., McKeown, M. G., and Kucan, L. (2003). Using oral language to build young children's vocabularies. *American Educator, 27*(1), 36–46.

Becker, W. C. (1977). Teaching reading and language to the disadvantaged: What we have learned from field research. *Harvard Educational Review, 44*(4), 518–543.

Bedard, A. C., Ickowicz, A., Logan, G. D., Hogg-Johnson, S., Schachar, R., and Tannock, R. (2003). Selective inhibition in children with attention-deficit hyperactivity disorder off and on stimulant medication. *Journal of Abnormal Child Psychology, 31*(3), 315–327.

Beirne-Smith, M. (1991). Peer tutoring in arithmetic for children with learning disabilities. *Exceptional Children, 57,* 330–337.

Bereiter, C. (1980). Development in writing. In L. W. Gregg and E. R. Steinberg (Eds.), *Cognitive processes in writing* (pp. 73–96). Hillsdale, NJ: Erlbaum.

Bereiter, C., Hilton, P., Rubinstein, J., and Willoughby, S. (1998). *Math exploration and applications.* Chicago: Science Research Associates.

Bergerud, D., Lovitt, T. C., and Horton, S. (1988). The effectiveness of textbook adaptations in life science for high school students with learning disabilities. *Journal of Learning Disabilities, 21,* 70–76.

Berler, E. S., Gross, A. M., and Drabman, R. S. (1982). Social skills training with children: Proceed with caution. *Journal of Applied Behavior Analysis, 15,* 41–53.

Berliner, D. C. (1983a). The executive functions of teaching. *Instructor, 93*(2), 28–33, 36, 38, 40.

Berliner, D. C. (1983b). *If teachers were thought of as executives: Implications for teacher preparation and certification.* Washington, DC: Dingle

Associates, Inc. (ERIC Document Reproduction Service No. ED245357).

Bernadette, K., Carnine, D., Engelmann, S., and Engelmann, O. (2003). *Connecting math concepts.* Chicago: Science Research Associates.

Berninger, V. W., Abbott, R. D., Whitaker, D., Sylvester, L., and Nolen, S. B. (1995). Integrating low- and high-level skills in instructional protocols for writing disabilities. *Learning Disability Quarterly, 18,* 293–310.

Bernstein, D. K. (1986). The development of humor: Implications for assessment and intervention. *Topics in Language Disorders, 6*(4), 65–71.

Berres, F., and Eyer, J. T. (1970). In A. J. Harris (Ed.), *Casebook on reading disability* (pp. 25–47). New York: David McKay.

Berry, J. O., and Hardman, M. L. (1998). *Life-span perspectives on the family and disability.* Boston: Allyn & Bacon.

Betts, E. A. (1946). *Foundations of reading instruction.* New York: American Book.

Bickett, L. G., and Milich, R. (April 1987). *First impressions of learning disabled and attention deficit disordered boys.* Paper presented at the Biennial Meeting of the Society for Research in Child Development, Baltimore, MD.

Bierman, K. L., and Furman, W. (1984). The effects of social skills training and peer involvement on the social adjustment of preadolescents. *Child Development, 55,* 151–162.

Billingsley, B. S., and Wildman, T. M. (1990). Facilitating reading comprehension in learning disabled students: Metacognitive goals and instructional strategies. *Remedial and Special Education, 11*(2), 18–31.

Blachman, B. A. (2000). Phonological awareness. In M. L. Kamil, P. B. Mosenthal, P. D. Pearson, and R. Barr (Eds.), *Handbook of reading research* (pp. 251–284). Mahwah, NJ: Erlbaum.

Blachman, B. A. (Ed.). (1997). *Foundations of reading acquisition and dyslexia implications for early intervention.* Mahwah, NJ: Erlbaum.

Blachowicz, C., and Ogle, D. (2001). *Reading comprehension: Strategies for independent learners.* New York: Guilford.

Black, F. (1974). Self-concept as related to achievement and age in learning disabled children. *Child Development, 45,* 1137–1140.

Blair, K. S. (1996). *Context-based functional assessment and intervention for preschool age children with problem behaviors in childcare.* Unpublished dissertation, University of Arizona, Tucson.

Blankenship, C. S. (1984). Curriculum and instruction: An examination of models in special and regular education. In J. F. Cawley (Ed.), *Developmental teaching of mathematics for the learning disabled.* Rockville, MD: Aspen.

Blankenship, C. S., and Lovitt, T. C. (1976). Story problems: Merely confusing or downright befuddling. *Journal for Research in Mathematics Education, 7,* 290–298.

Bley, N. S., and Thornton, C. A. (1981). *Teaching mathematics to the learning disabled.* Rockville, MD: Aspen.

Bliss, L. S. (1993). *Pragmatic language intervention.* Eau Claire, WI: Thinking Publications.

Block, C. C. (1997). *Literacy difficulties: Diagnosis and instruction.* Orlando, FL: Harcourt Brace.

Bloodgood, J. (1991). A new approach to spelling instruction in language arts programs. *Elementary School Journal, 92,* 203–211.

Bloom, L., and Lahey, M. (1978). *Language development and language disorders.* New York: Wiley.

Bloomfield, L., and Barnhart, C. L. (1961). *Let's read: A linguistic approach.* Detroit: Wayne State University Press.

Blue-Banning, M., Summers, J. A., Frankland, M. C., Nelson, L. L., and Beegle, G. (2004). Dimensions of family and professional partnerships: Constructive guidelines for collaboration. *Exceptional Children, 70,* 167–184.

Blum, R. W., and Mann-Rinehart, P. (1997). *Reducing the risk: Connections that make a difference in the lives of youth.* Bethesda, MD: National Institute on Alcohol Abuse and Alcoholism. (ERIC Document Reproduction Service No. ED412459).

Boatner, M. T., Gates, J. E., and Makkai, A. (1975). *A dictionary of American idioms* (rev. ed.). Woodbury, NJ: Barron's.

Boegler, S., and Abruzzini, D. (1996). *Scissors, glue, and grammar too!* East Moline, IL: LinguiSystems.

Borkowski, J. G., Weyhing, R. S., and Carr, M. (1988). Effects of attributional retraining on strategy-based reading comprehension in learning-disabled students. *Journal of Educational Psychology, 80*(1), 46–53.

Borkowski, J. G., Weyhing, R. S., and Turner, L. A. (1986). Attributional retraining and the teaching of strategies. *Exceptional Children, 53*(2), 130–137.

Bos, C. S. (1982). Getting past decoding: Using modeled and repeated readings as a remedial method for learning disabled students. *Topics in Learning and Learning Disabilities, 1,* 51–57.

Bos, C. S. (1987, October). *Promoting story comprehension using a story retelling strategy.* Paper presented at the Teachers Applying Whole Language Conference, Tucson, AZ.

Bos, C. S. (1991). *Strategies for teaching students with learning and behavior problems* (2nd ed.). Boston: Allyn & Bacon.

Bos, C. S. (1999). Informed, flexible teaching: Promoting student advocacy and action. In P. Westwood and W. Scott (Eds.), *Learning Disabilities: Advocacy and action* (pp. 9–19). Melbourne: Australian Resource Educators Association.

Bos, C. S., Allen, A. A., and Scanlon, D. J. (1989). Vocabulary instruction and reading comprehension with bilingual learning disabled students. In S. McCormick and J. Zutell (Eds.), *Cognitive and social perspectives for literacy research and instruction* (Thirty-eighth yearbook, pp. 173–180). Chicago: National Reading Conference.

Bos, C. S., and Anders, P. L. (1990a). Effects of interactive vocabulary instruction on the vocabulary learning and reading comprehension of junior-high learning disabled students. *Learning Disability Quarterly, 13,* 31–42.

Bos, C. S., and Anders, P. L. (1990b). Toward an interactive model: Teaching text-based concepts to learning disabled students. In H. L. Swanson and B. Keogh (Eds.), *Learning disabilities: Theoretical and research issues* (pp. 247–261). Hillsdale, NJ: Erlbaum.

Bos, C. S., and Anders, P. L. (1990c). Interactive teaching and learning: Instructional practices for teaching content and strategic knowledge. In T. E. Scruggs and B. Y. L. Wong (Eds.), *Intervention research in learning disabilities* (pp. 166–185). New York: Springer-Verlag.

Bos, C. S., and Anders, P. L. (1992). A theory-driven interactive instructional model for text comprehension and content learning. In B. Y.

L. Wong (Ed.), *Contemporary intervention research in learning disabilities: An international perspective* (pp. 81–95). New York: Springer-Verlag.

Bos, C. S., Anders, P. L., Jaffe, L. E., and Filip, D. (1985). Semantic feature analysis and long-term learning. In J. A. Niles (Ed.), *Issues in literacy: A research perspective* (Thirty-fourth yearbook, pp. 42–46). Rochester, NY: National Reading Conference.

Bos, C. S., and Duffy, M. L. (1991). Facilitating content learning and text comprehension for students with learning disabilities. *Exceptionality Education Canada, 1*(3), 1–13.

Bos, C. S., and Filip, D. (1984). Comprehension monitoring in learning disabled and average students. *Journal of Learning Disabilities, 17*(4), 229–233.

Bos, C. S., and Reyes, E. I. (1996). Conversations with a Latina teacher about education for language-minority students with special needs. *Elementary School Journal, 96,* 343–352.

Bos, C. S., and Van Reusen, A. K. (1986). *Effects of teaching a strategy for facilitating student and parent participation in the IEP process* (Partner Project Final Report G008400643). Tucson: University of Arizona, Department of Special Education.

Bowers, L., Huisingh, R., LoGiudice, C., Orman, J., and Johnson, P. F. (2000). *125 vocabulary builders.* East Moline, IL: LinguiSystems.

Bowers, R., and Bowers, L. (1998). *Grammar scramble: A grammar and sentence-building game.* East Moline, IL: LinguiSystems.

Boyle, J. R. (1996). The effects of a cognitive mapping strategy on the literal and inferential comprehension of students with mild disabilities. *Learning Disability Quarterly, 19,* 86–98.

Bradley, J. M. (1975). *Sight word association procedure.* Unpublished manuscript, College of Education, University of Arizona, Tucson.

Bradley, L. (1981). The organization of motor patterns for spelling: An effective remedial strategy for backward readers. *Developmental Medicine and Child Neurology, 23,* 83–91.

Bradley, L., and Bryant, P. (1983). Categorizing sounds and learning to read: A causal connection. *Nature, 39,* 419–421.

Bradley, R., Danielson, L., and Doolittle, J. (2005). Response to intervention. *Journal of Learning Disabilities, 38,* 485–486.

Bradley, R., Danielson, L., and Doolittle, J. (2007). Responsiveness to intervention: 1997–2007. *Teaching Exceptional Children, 39*(5), 8–12.

Bradley, R., Danielson, L., and Hallahan, D. P. (2002). *Identification of learning disabilities: Research to practice.* Mahwah, NJ: Erlbaum.

Bragstad, B. J., and Stumpf, S. M. (1982). *A guidebook for teaching: Study skills and motivation.* Boston: Allyn & Bacon.

Brainerd, C. J., and Reyna, V. F. (1991). Acquisition and forgetting processes in normal and learning-disabled children: A disintegration/reintegration theory. In J. E. Obrzut and G. W. Hynd (Eds.), *Neuropsychological foundations of learning disabilities* (pp. 147–178). San Diego, CA: Academic Press.

Bransford, J. D., and Johnson, M. D. (1972). Contextual prerequisites for understanding: Some investigations of comprehension and recall. *Journal of Verbal Learning and Verbal Behavior, 11,* 717–726.

Brice, A., and Montgomery, J. (1996). Adolescent pragmatic skills: A comparison of Latino students in English as a second language and speech and language programs. *Language, Speech, and Hearing Services in Schools, 27,* 68–81.

Briggs, A., Austin, R., and Underwood, G. (1984). Phonological coding in good and poor readers. *Reading Research Quarterly, 20,* 54–66.

Briggs, D. (1970). The influence of handwriting on assessment. *Educational Research, 13*(1), 50–55.

Brigman, G., and Molina, B. (1999). Developing social interest and enhancing school success skills: A service learning approach. *Journal of Individual Psychology, 55*(3), 342–354.

Brinckerhoff, L. C., Shaw, S. F., and McGuire, J. M. (1992). Promoting access, accommodations, and independence for college students with learning disabilities. *Journal of Learning Disabilities, 25,* 417–429.

Brinton, B., and Fujiki, M. (1999). Social interactional behaviors of children with specific language impairment. *Topics in Language Disorders, 18*(2), 49–69.

Brinton, B., Fujiki, M., and McKee, L. (1998). Negotiation skills of children with specific language impairment. *Journal of Speech, Language, and Hearing Research, 41,* 927–940.

Brolin, D. E. (1997). *Life centered career education: A competency-based approach* (5th ed.). Reston, VA: Council for Exceptional Children.

Bromley, K. (1999). Key components of sound writing instruction. In L. B. Gambrell, L. M. Morrow, S. B. Neuman, and M. Pressley (Eds.), *Best practices in literacy instruction* (pp. 152–174). New York: Guilford.

Brophy, J. (1988). Educating teachers about managing classrooms and students. *Teacher and Teacher Education, 4,* 1–18.

Brown, A. L. (1980). Metacognitive development and reading. In R. J. Spiro, B. C. Bruce, and W. F. Brewer (Eds.), *Theoretical issues in reading comprehension* (pp. 453–482). Hillsdale, NJ: Erlbaum.

Brown, A. L., and Day, J. D. (1983). Macrorules for summarizing texts: The development of expertise. *Journal of Verbal Learning and Verbal Behavior, 22,* 1–14.

Brown, A. L., and Palincsar, A. S. (1982). Including strategic learning from texts by means of informed, self-control training. *Topics in Learning and Learning Disabilities, 2*(1), 1–17.

Brown, A. L., Palincsar, A. S., and Armbruster, B. B. (1984). Instructing comprehension-fostering activities in interactive learning situations. In H. Mandl, N. L. Stein, and T. Trabasso (Eds.), *Learning and comprehension of text* (pp. 255–286). Hillsdale, NJ: Erlbaum.

Brown, K. J. (1999/2000). What kind of text—For whom and when? Textual scaffolding for beginning readers. *The Reading Teacher, 53*(4), 292–307.

Brown, R. (1973). *A first language: The early stages.* Cambridge, MA: Harvard University Press.

Brown, V. L., Cronin, M., and McEntire, E. (1994). *Test of Mathematical Abilities-Second Edition.* Austin, TX: PRO-ED.

Bruck, M., and Treiman, R. (1992). Learning to pronounce words: The limitations of analogies. *Reading Research Quarterly, 27,* 375–388.

Bryan, J. H., and Perlmutter, B. (1979). Immediate impressions of LD children by female adults. *Learning Disability Quarterly, 2,* 80–88.

Bryan, J. H., and Sherman, R. (1980). Immediate impressions of nonverbal ingratiation attempts by learning disabled boys. *Learning Disabilities Quarterly, 3,* 19–29.

Bryan, J. H., Bryan, T. H., and Sonnefeld, L. J. (1982). Being known by the company we keep! The contagion of first impressions. *Learning Disability Quarterly, 5*(3), 228–293.

Bryan, T. H. (1986). Self-concept and attributions of the learning disabled. *Learning Disabilities Focus, 1*(2), 82–89.

Bryan, T. H., and Pflaum, S. (1978). Social interactions of learning disability children: A linguistic, social, and cognitive analysis. *Learning Disability Quarterly, 1,* 70–78.

Bryan, T., Pearl, R., and Fallon, P. (1989). Conformity to peer pressure by students with learning disabilities: A replication. *Journal of Learning Disabilities, 22*(7), 458–459.

Bryant, B. R., and Rivera, D. P. (1997). Educational assessment of mathematics skills and abilities. *Journal of Learning Disabilities, 30*(1), 57–68.

Bryant, D. P., Bryant, B., and Hammill, D. (2000). Characteristic behaviors of students with LD who have teacher-identified math weaknesses. *Journal of Learning Disabilities, 33,* 168–177, 199.

Bryant, D. P., Goodwin, M., Bryant, B. R., and Higgins, K. (2003). Vocabulary instruction for students with learning disabilities: A review of the research. *Learning Disability Quarterly, 26,* 117–128.

Bryant, D. P., Hartman, P., and Kim, S. A. (2003). Using explicit and systematic instruction to teach division skills to students with learning disabilities. *Exceptionality, 11*(3), 151–164.

Bryant, D., Vaughn S., Linan-Thompson, S., Ugel, N., Hamff, A., and Hougen, M. (2000). Reading outcomes for students with and without reading disabilities in general education middle school content area classes. *Learning Disability Quarterly, 23,* 238–252.

Bryant, J. (1998). K-W-W-L: Questioning the known. *The Reading Teacher, 51,* 618–620.

Bryant, N. D., Drabin, I. R., and Gettinger, M. (1981). Effects of varying unit size on spelling achievement in learning disabled children. *Journal of Learning Disabilities, 14*(4), 200–203.

Bulgren, J., Deshler, D. D., and Lenz, B. K. (2007). Engaging adolescents with LD in higher order thinking about history concepts using integrated content enhancement routines. *Journal of Learning Disabilities, 40*(2), 121–133.

Bulgren, J., and Lenz, B. K. (1996). Strategic instruction in the content areas. In D. D. Deshler, E. S. Ellis, and B. K. Lenz, *Teaching adolescents with learning disabilities: Strategies and methods* (2nd ed., pp. 409–473). Denver: Love.

Bulgren, J. A., and Scanlon, D. (1997). Instructional routines and learning strategies that promote understanding of content area concepts. *Journal of Adolescent and Adult Literacy, 41,* 292–302.

Bulgren, J. A., Deshler, D. D., Schumaker, J. B., and Lenz, B. K. (2000). The use and effectiveness of analogical instruction in diverse secondary content classrooms. *Journal of Educational Psychology, 92*(3), 426–441.

Bulgren, J. A., Hock, M. F., Schumaker, J. B., and Deshler, D. D. (1995). The effects of instruction in a paired associates strategy on the information mastery performance of students with learning disabilities. *Learning Disabilities Research and Practice, 10*(1), 22–37.

Bulgren, J. A., Lenz, B. K., Schumaker, J. B., and Deshler, D. D. (1995). *The content enhancement series: The concept comparison routine.* Lawrence, KS: Edge Enterprises.

Bulgren, J., Schumaker, J. B., and Deshler, D. D. (1988). Effectiveness of a concept teaching routine in enhancing the performance of LD students in secondary-level mainstream classes. *Learning Disability Quarterly, 11,* 3–17.

Bulgren, J., Schumaker, J. B., and Deshler, D. D. (1996). *The content enhancement series: The concept mastery routine.* Lawrence, KS: Edge Enterprises.

Bunce, B. H. (1993). Language of the classroom. In A. Gerber (Ed.), *Language related learning disabilities: Their nature and treatment* (pp. 135–159). Baltimore: Brookes.

Burdette, P. (2007). *Response to intervention as it relates to early intervening services: Recommendations.* Alexandra, VA: National Association of State Directors of Special Education.

Burns, M. K., and Ysseldyke, J. E. (2005). Questions about response-to-intervention implementations: Seeking answers from existing models. *California School Psychologist, 10,* 9–20.

Bursuck, W. D., Harniss, M. K., Epstein, M. H., Polloway, E. A., Jayanthi, M., and Wissinger, L. M. (1999). Solving communication problems about homework: Recommendations of special education teachers. *Learning Disabilities Research and Practice, 14*(3), 149–158.

Button, E. (1993). *Eating disorders: Personal construct therapy and change.* New York: Wiley.

Byrnes, J. P. (1996). *Cognitive development and learning in instructional contexts.* Boston: Allyn and Bacon.

Cain, K. (1996). Story knowledge and comprehension skill. In C. Cornoldi and J. Oakhill (Eds.), *Reading comprehension difficulties* (pp. 167–192). Hillsdale, NJ: Erlbaum.

Calhoon, M. B., and Fuchs, L. S. (2003). The effects of peer-assisted learning strategies and curriculum-based measurement on the mathematics performance of secondary students with disabilities. *Remedial and Special Education, 24*(4), 235–245.

Callins, T. (2007). Culturally responsive literacy instruction. *Teaching Exceptional Children, 39*(2), 62–65.

Cambourne, B., and Turnbill, J. (1987). *Coping with chaos.* Portsmouth, NH: Heinemann.

Camp, B. W., Blom, G. E., Herbert, F., and Van Doorninck, W. J. (1977). "Think around": A program for developing self-control in young aggressive boys. *Journal of Abnormal Child Psychology, 5,* 157–169.

Cangelosi, J. S. (2004). *Classroom management strategies: Gaining and maintaining students' cooperation.* Hoboken, NJ: Wiley.

Canter, A. (2006). Problem solving and RTI: New roles for school psychologists. NASP *Communiqué, 34*(5). Retrieved December 14, 2007, from www.nasponline.org/publications/cq/cq345rti.aspx.

Carbo, M. (1978). Teaching reading with talking books. *The Reading Teacher, 32,* 267–273.

Carbo, M. (1987). Deprogramming reading failure: Giving unequal learners an equal chance. *Phi Delta Kappan, 69*(3), 197–202.

Carbo, M. (1997). *Continuum of modeling methods: Release your students' learning power.* Syosset, NY: National Reading Styles Institute.

Carnine, D. (1989). Teaching complex content to learning disabled students: The role of technology. *Exceptional Children, 55,* 524–533.

Carnine, D. (1991). Curricular interventions for teaching higher order thinking to all students: Introduction to the special series. *Journal of Learning Disabilities, 24,* 261–269.

Carnine, D. (1997). Instructional design in mathematics for students with learning disabilities. *Journal of Learning Disabilities, 30*(2), 130–141.

Carnine, D., Silbert, J., and Kame'enui, E. J. (1997). *Direct instruction reading* (3rd ed.). Columbus, OH: Merrill.

Carpenter, D., and Miller, L. J. (1982). Spelling ability of reading disabled LD students and able readers. *Learning Disability Quarterly, 5*(1), 65–70.

Carr, E. G., Dunlap, G., Horner, R. H., Koegel, R. L., Turnbull, A. P., Sailor, W., Anderson, J., Albin, R. W., Koegel, L. K., and Fox, L. (2002). Positive behavior support: Evolution of an applied science. *Journal of Positive Behavior Interventions, 4,* 4–16.

Carr, E., and Ogle, D. (1987). K-W-L plus: A strategy for comprehension and summarization. *Journal of Reading, 30,* 626–631.

Carr, S. C., and Thompson, B. (1996). The effects of prior knowledge and schema activation strategies on the inferential reading comprehension of children with and without learning disabilities. *Learning Disability Quarterly, 19,* 48–61.

Carrekar, S. (1999). Teaching spelling. In J. R. Birsh (Ed.), *Multisensory teaching of basic language skills* (pp. 217–256). Baltimore: Brookes.

Carroll, J. (1964). *Language and thought.* Englewood Cliffs, NJ: Prentice Hall.

Carrow, E. (1973). *Test of auditory comprehension of language.* Austin, TX: Urban Research Group.

Carrow-Woolfolk, E. (1999). *Test for auditory comprehension of language* (3rd ed.). Austin, TX: PRO-ED.

Carter, E. W., and Kennedy, C. H. (2006). Promoting access to the general curriculum using peer support strategies. *Research and Practice for Persons with Severe Disabilities, 31,* 284–292.

Casby, M. (1992). An intervention approach for naming problems in children. *American Journal of Speech-Language Pathology, 1*(3), 35–42.

Case, L. P., Speece, D. L., and Molloy, D. E. (2003). The validity of a response-to-instruction paradigm to identify reading disabilities: A longitudinal analysis of individual differences and contextual factors. *School Psychology Review, 32,* 557–582.

Cassady, J. K. (1998). Wordless books: No-risk tools for inclusive middle-grade classrooms. *Journal of Adolescent and Adult Literacy, 41,* 428–433.

Catts, H. W., Fey, M. E., Tomblin, J. B., and Zhang, X. (2002). A longitudinal investigation of reading outcomes in children with language impairments. *Journal of Speech, Language, and Hearing Research, 45*(6), 1142–1157.

Catts, H. W., and Kamhi, A. G. (Eds.). (1999). *Language and reading disabilities.* Boston: Allyn & Bacon.

Cavanaugh, C. L., Kim, A., Wanzek, J., and Vaughn, S. (2004). Kindergarten reading interventions for at-risk students: Twenty years of research. *Learning Disabilities: A Contemporary Journal, 2*(1), 9–21.

Cawley, J. (2002). *My Math* (computer software). Unpublished computer software. Storrs, CT.

Cawley, J. F. (1984). An integrative approach to needs of learning disabled children: Expanded use of mathematics. In J. F. Cawley (Ed.), *Developmental teaching of mathematics for the learning disabled.* Rockville, MD: Aspen.

Cawley, J. F., and Miller, J. H. (1986). Selected views on metacognition, arithmetic problem solving, and learning disabilities. *Learning Disabilities Focus, 2*(1), 36–48.

Cawley, J. F., and Miller, J. H. (1989). Cross-sectional comparisons of the mathematical performance of children with learning disabilities: Are we on the right track toward comprehensive programming? *Journal of Learning Disabilities, 22,* 250–254, 259.

Cawley, J. F., Foley, T. F., and Doan, T. (2003). Giving students a voice in selecting arithmetical context. *Teaching Exceptional Children, 36,* 8–17.

Cawley, J. F., Parmar, R. S., Yan, W., and Miller, J. H. (1998). Arithmetic computation performance of students with learning disabilities: Implications for curriculum. *Learning Disabilities Research and Practice, 13*(2), 68–74.

Cawley, J., Fitzmaurice, A. M., Goodstein, H., Lepore, A., Sedlak, R., and Althaus, V. (1976). *Project Math.* Tulsa, OK: Educational Progress Corporation.

Ceci, S. (1985). A developmental study of learning disabilities and memory. *Journal of Experimental Child Psychology, 39,* 202–221.

Chalfant, J. C. (1987). Providing services to all students with learning problems: Implications for policy and programs. In S. Vaughn and C. Bos (Eds.), *Research in learning disabilities: Issues and future trends* (pp. 239–251). Boston: College-Hill, Little Brown.

Chalfant, J. C. (1989). Learning disabilities: Policy issues and promising approaches. *American Psychologist, 44,* 392–398.

Chalfant, J. C., and Pysh, M. V. (1981). Teacher assistance teams—A model for within-building problem solving. *Counterpoint, 16*–21.

Chalfant, J. C., and Pysh, M. V. (1989). Teacher assistance teams: Five descriptive studies on 96 teams. *Remedial and Special Education, 10*(6), 49–58.

Chalfant, J. C., and Pysh, M. V. (1993). Teacher assistance teams: Implications for the gifted. In C. J. Maker (Ed.), *Critical issues in gifted education: Vol. 3. Gifted students in the regular classroom* (pp. 32–48). Austin, TX: PRO-ED.

Chalfant, J. C., Pysh, M. V., and Moultrie, R. (1979). Teacher assistance teams: A model for within-building problem-solving. *Learning Disability Quarterly, 2,* 85–96.

Chamberlain, S. P. (2005). Recognizing and responding to cultural differences in the education of culturally and linguistically diverse learners. *Intervention in School and Clinic, 40,* 195–211.

Chamot, A. (1998). Effective instruction for high school English language learners. In R. M. Gersten and R. T. Jimenez (Eds.), *Promoting learning for culturally and linguistically diverse students* (pp. 187–209). Belmont, CA: Wadsworth.

Chamot, A., and O'Malley, J. M. (1994a). The CALLA Handbook: How to implement the cognitive academic language learning approach. In K. Spangenberg-Urbschat and R. Pritchard (Eds.), *Kids come in all languages: Reading instruction for ESL students* (pp. 82–103). Newark, DE: International Reading Association.

Chamot, A., and O'Malley, J. M. (1994b). *The CALLA handbook: Implementing the cognitive academic language learning approach.* Reading, MA: Addison-Wesley.

Chan, L. K. S. (1991). Promoting strategy generalization through self-instructional training in students with reading disabilities. *Journal of Learning Disabilities, 24,* 427–433.

Chapman, J. W., and Boersman, F. J. (1980). *Affective correlates of learning disabilities.* Lisse, Netherlands: Swets & Zeitlinger.

Chard, D. J., and Dickson, S. V. (1999). Phonological awareness: Instructional and assessment guidelines. *Intervention in Clinic and School, 34*(5), 261–270.

Chard, D. J., Vaughn, S., and Tyler, B. (2002). A synthesis of research on effective intervention for building reading fluency with elementary students with learning disabilities. *Journal of Learning Disabilities, 35*(5), 386–406.

Cheek, E. H., Jr., and Lindsey, J. D. (1986). Principal's roles and teacher conflict: A recapitulation. *Journal of Learning Disabilities, 19*(5), 280–284.

Chen, H. C., and Graves, M. F. (1996). Effects of previewing and providing background knowledge on Taiwanese college students' comprehension of American short stories. *TESOL Quarterly, 29,* 663–686.

Cherkes-Julkowski, M. (1985). Metacognitive considerations in mathematics for the learning disabled. In J. Cawley (Ed.), *Cognitive strategies and mathematics for the learning disabled* (pp. 22–67). Rockville, MD: Aspen.

Children's Educational Services, Inc. (1987). *Test of oral reading fluency.* Minneapolis, MN: Author.

Chomsky, C. (1969). *The acquisition of syntax in children from 5 to 10.* Cambridge, MA: MIT Press.

Chomsky, C. (1976). After decoding: What? *Language Arts, 53,* 288–296.

Christ, T. J., Burns, M. K., and Ysseldyke, J. E. (2005). Conceptual confusion within response-to-intervention vernacular: Clarifying meaningful differences. *NASP Communiqué, 34*(3). Retrieved December 14, 2007, from www.nasponline.org/publications/cq/cq343rti.aspx.

Christian, B. T. (1983). A practical reinforcement hierarchy for classroom behavior modification. *Psychology in the Schools, 20,* 83–84.

Ciborowski, J. (1992). *Textbooks and the students who can't read them: A guide to teaching content.* Boston: Brookline.

Cimbolic, P. and Jobes, D. A. (1990). Youth suicide: The scope of the problem. In P. Cimbolic and D. A. Jobes (Eds.), *Youth suicide: Issues, assessment, and intervention* (pp. 3–32). Springfield, IL: Charles C. Thomas.

Clark, D. B., and Uhry, J. K. (1995). *Dyslexia: Theory and practice of remedial instruction.* Baltimore: York.

Clark, F. L., Deshler, D. D., Schumaker, J. B., Alley, G. R., and Warner, M. M. (1984). Visual imagery and self-questioning: Strategies to improve comprehension of written materials. *Journal of Learning Disabilities, 17*(3), 145–149.

Clark, G. M. (1998). *Assessment for transitions planning.* Austin, TX: PRO-ED.

Clark, G. M. (2007). *Assessment for transitions planning* (2nd ed.). Austin: PRO-ED.

Clark, G. M., and Patton, J. R. (1997). *Transition planning inventory.* Austin, TX: PRO-ED.

Clark, G. M., Patton, J. R., and Moulton, R. (2001). *Informal assessments in transition planning.* Austin, TX: PRO-ED.

Clark, J. O. (1990). *Harrup's dictionary of English idioms.* London: Harrup.

Clark, J., and Klecan-Aker, J. S. (1992). Therapeutic strategies for language disordered children: The impact of visual imagery on verbal encoding in vocabulary instruction. *Journal of Childhood Communication Disorders, 14*(2), 129–145.

Clarke, B., and Shinn, M. R. (in press). A preliminary investigation into the identification and development of early mathematics curriculum-based measurement. *School Psychology Review.*

Coffland, J. A., and Baldwin, R. S. (1985). *Wordmath.* St. Louis: Milliken.

Cohen, J. (1986). Learning disabilities and psychological development in childhood and adolescence. *Annals of Dyslexia, 36,* 287–300.

Coie, J. D., Dodge, K. A., and Coppotelli, H. (1982). Dimensions and types of social status: A cross-age perspective. *Developmental Psychology, 18,* 557–570.

Coldwell, J., (1997). *Introducing word families through literature.* Greensboro, NC: Carson-Dellosa.

Cole, J. (1989). *Anna Banana: 101 jump rope rhymes.* New York: Morrow Junior Books.

Cole, J. (1999). *Patty's cake: A describing game.* East Moline, IL: LinguiSystems.

Cole, J. (2000). *Gram's cracker: A grammar game.* East Moline, IL: LinguiSystems.

Cole, J., and Calmenson, S. (1990). *Miss Mary Mack and other children's street rhymes.* New York: Morrow Junior Books.

Compton, D. L., Fuchs, D., Fuchs, L. S., and Bryant, J. D. (2006). Selecting at-risk readers in first grade for early intervention: A two-year longitudinal study of decision rules and procedures. *Journal of Educational Psychology, 98,* 394–409.

Connolly, A. J. (1998). *Key math-revised: A diagnostic inventory of essential mathematics.* Circle Pines, MN: American Guidance Service.

Conte, K. L., and Hintze, J. M. (2000). The effects of performance feedback and goal setting on oral reading fluency within curriculum-based measurement. *Diagnostique, 25,* 85–98.

Conte, R., and Humphreys, R. (1989). Repeated readings using audiotaped material enhances oral reading in children with reading difficulties. *Journal of Communication Disorders, 22,* 65–79.

Cook, B. G. (2002). Inclusive attitudes, strengths, and weaknesses of pre-service general educators enrolled in a curriculum infusion teacher preparation program. *Teacher Education and Special Education, 25,* 262–277.

Cooper, D. H., Roth, F. P., Schatschneider, C., and Speece, D. L. (2002). The contribution of oral language skills to the development of phonological awareness. *Applied Psycholinguistics, 23,* 399–416.

Cooper, H., and Nye, B. (1994). Homework for students with learning disabilities: The implications of research for policy and practice. *Journal of Learning Disabilities, 27,* 470–479.

Cooper, P., and Bilton, K. M. (2002). *Attention Deficit/Hyperactivity Disorder: A Practical Guide for Teachers* (2nd ed.). Great Britain: David Fulton Publishers Ltd.

Corkill, A. J. (1992). Advance organizers: Facilitators of recall. *Educational Psychology Review, 4,* 33–67.

Cornwall, A. (1992). The relationship of phonological awareness, rapid naming, and verbal memory to severe reading and spelling disability. *Journal of Learning Disabilities, 25,* 532–538.

Cortiella, C. (2006). *A parent's guide to response to intervention.* National Center for Learning Disabilities. Retrieved December 14, 2007, from www.ncld.org/images/stories/downloads/parent_center/rti_final.pdf.

Coterell, G. (1972). A case of severe learning disability. *Remedial Education, 7,* 5–9.

Council for Exceptional Children. (1993). *CEC Statement on Inclusion.* Reston, VA: Author.

Council for Exceptional Children. (2006–2007). *Response-to-intervention: The promise and the peril.* Retrieved December 14, 2007, from www.cec.sped.org/AM/Template.cfm?Section=Home&CONTENTID=8427&TEMPLATE=/CM/ContentDisplay.cfm.

Cox, A. R. (1992). *Foundations for literacy: Structures and techniques for multisensory teaching of basic written English language skills (Alphabetic Phonics).* Cambridge, MA: Educators Publishing Service.

Cox, C., and Many, J. E. (1992). Towards an understanding of the aesthetic stance towards literature. *Language Arts, 66,* 287–294.

Coyne, M. D., Kame'enui, E. J., Simmons, D. C. (2001). Prevention and intervention in beginning reading: Two complex systems. *Learning Disabilities: Research and Practice, 16,* 62–73.

Cronin, M. E., and Patton, J. R. (1993). *Life skills instruction for all students with special needs: A practical guide for integrating real-life content into the curriculum.* Austin, TX: PRO-ED.

Cronin, M. E., Patton, J. R., and Wood, S. (2007). *Life skills instruction: A practical guide for integrating real-life content into the curriculum at the elementary and secondary levels for students with special needs or who are placed at risk.* Austin: PRO-ED.

Cullinan, B. E. (Ed.). (1992). *Invitation to read: More children's literature in the reading program.* Newark, DE: International Reading Association.

Culp, A. M., Clyman, M. M., and Culp, R. E. (1995). Adolescent depressed mood, reports of suicide attempts, and asking for help. *Adolescence, 30,* 827–837.

Cummings, R. W., and Maddux, C. D. (1985). *Parenting the learning disabled: A realistic approach.* Springfield, IL: Charles C. Thomas.

Cummins, J. (1981). *Bilingualism and minority language children.* Ontario: Ontario Institute for Students in Education.

Cummins, J. (1984). *Bilingualism and special education: Issues in assessment and pedagogy.* San Diego, CA: College Hill.

Cummins, J. (1989). A theoretical framework for bilingual special education. *Exceptional Children, 56,* 111–119.

Cummins, J. (1991a). Empowering minority students: A framework for intervention. In M. Minami and B. Kennedy (Eds.), *Language issues in literacy and bilingual/multicultural education,* Series 22. Boston: Harvard Education Review.

Cummins, J. (1991b). Interdependence of first- and second-language proficiency in bilingual children. In E. Bialystok (Ed.), *Language processing in bilingual children.* Cambridge, England: Cambridge University Press.

Cunningham, P. M. (1991). *Phonics they use: Words for reading and writing.* New York: HarperCollins.

Cunningham, P. M. (2000). *Phonics they use: Words for reading and writing* (3rd ed.). New York: Longman.

Cunningham, P. M., and Hall, D. P. (1994a). *Making words.* Parsippany, NJ: Good Apple.

Cunningham, P. M., and Hall, D. P. (1994b). *Making big words.* Parsippany, NJ: Good Apple.

Dahl, K., Scharer, P., Lawson, L., and Grogan, P. (1999). Phonics teaching and student achievement in whole language first grades. *Reading Research Quarterly, 34*(3), 312–341.

Dahl, K. L., and Scharer, P. L. (2000). Phonics teaching and learning in whole language classrooms: New evidence from research. *The Reading Teacher, 53,* 584–594.

Dale, E., and Chall, J. S. (1948). A formula for predicting readability. *Educational Research Bulletin, 27,* 37–54.

Dale, P. S. (1996). Parent–child book reading as an intervention technique for young children with language delays. *Topics in Early Childhood Special Education, 16,* 213–235.

Daniel, S. S., Walsh, A. K., Goldston, D. B., Arnold, E. M., Reboussin, B. A., and Wood, F. B. (2007). Suicidality, school dropout, and reading problems among adolescents. *Journal of Learning Disabilities, 39*(6), 507–514.

Darch, C., and Carnine, D. (1986). Approaches to teaching learning-disabled students literal comprehension during content area instruction. *Exceptional Children, 53*(3), 240–246.

Darling-Hammond, L. (1995). Inequality and access to knowledge. In J. A. Banks and C. A. Banks (Eds.), *The handbook of multicultural education* (pp. 465–483). New York: MacMillan.

Davison, A. (1984). Syntactic markedness and the definition of sentence topic. *Language, 60,* 797–846.

deFur, S., and Williams, B. T. (2002). Cultural considerations in the transition process and standards-based education. In C. A. Kochhar-Bryant and D. S. Bassett (Eds.), *Aligning transition and standards-based education: Issues and strategies* (pp. 105–123). Arlington, VA: Council for Exceptional Children.

De La Paz, S. (1999). Teaching writing strategies and self-regulation procedures to middle school students with learning disabilities. *Focus on Exceptional Children, 31*(5), 1–16.

De La Paz, S., Swanson, P., and Graham, S. (1998). Contribution of executive control to the revising problems of students with writing and learning difficulties. *Journal of Educational Psychology, 90,* 448–460.

de Villiers, J., and de Villiers, P. (1978). *Language acquisition.* Cambridge, MA: Harvard University Press.

Delquadri, J., Greenwood, C. R., Whorton, D., Carta, J. J., and Hall, R. V. (1986). Classwide peer tutoring. *Exceptional Children, 52,* 532–542.

DeMaster, V. K., Crossland, C. L., and Hasselbring, T. S. (1986). Consistency of learning disabled students' spelling performance. *Learning Disability Quarterly, 9*(1), 89–96.

Dembinski, R. J., and Mauser, A. J. (1977). What parents of the learning disabled really want from professionals. *Journal of Learning Disabilities, 10,* 578–584.

Deno, S. L. (1998). Academic progress as incompatible behavior: Curriculum-based measurement (CBM) as intervention. *Beyond Behavior, 9*(3), 12–17.

Deno, S. L., Fuchs, L. S., Marston, D., and Shin, J. (2001). Using curriculum-based measurement to establish growth standards for students with learning disabilities. *School Psychology Review, 30,* 507–524.

Deno, S., Lembke, E., and Reschly Anderson, A. (no date). *Progress monitoring: Study group content module.* Retrieved December 14, 2007, from http://cehd.umn.edu/EdPsych/Projects/cbmMOD1.pdf.

Denton, C. A., Anthony, J. L., Parker, R., and Hasbrouck, J. (2004). The effects of two tutoring programs on the English reading development of Spanish-English bilingual students. *The Elementary School Journal, 104,* 289–305.

Deschenes, C., Ebeling, D. G., and Sprague, J. (1994). *Adapting curriculum and instruction in inclusive classrooms: A teacher's desk reference.* Bloomington, IN: ISDD-CSCI.

Deshler, D. D., and Schumaker, J. B. (1986). Learning strategies: An instructional alternative for low-achieving adolescents. *Exceptional Children, 52*(6), 583–590.

Deshler, D. D., Ellis, E. S., and Lenz, B. K. (1996). *Teaching adolescents with learning disabilities: Strategies and methods* (2nd ed.). Denver: Love.

Deshler, D. D., Schumaker, J. B., and McKnight, P. C. (1997). *The survey routine.* Lawrence: University of Kansas Press.

Dettmer, P., Dyck, N., and Thurston, L. P. (1999). *Consultation, collaboration, and teamwork for students with special needs.* Boston: Allyn & Bacon.

Dettmer, P., Thurston, L. P., and Dyck, N. (1993). *Consultation, collaboration, and teamwork: For students with special needs.* Boston: Allyn & Bacon.

Dettmer, P., Thurston, L. P., and Selberg, N. J. (2004). *Consultation, collaboration, and teamwork for students with special needs* (5th ed.). Boston: Allyn and Bacon.

Devine, T. G. (1987). *Teaching study skills: A guide for teachers* (2nd ed.). Boston: Allyn & Bacon.

Di Vesta, F. J., and Smith, D. A. (1979). The pausing principle: Increasing the efficiency of memory for ongoing events. *Contemporary Educational Psychology, 4*(3), 288–296.

Diamond, S. (1993). *Language lessons in the classroom.* Phoenix, AZ: ECL Publications.

Diaz, S., Moll., L. C., and Mehan, H. (1986). Sociocultural resources in instruction: A context-specific approach. In *Beyond language: Social and cultural factors in schooling language minority students* (pp. 187–229). Sacramento, CA: Bilingual Education Office, California State Department of Education.

Diaz-Rico, L., and Weed, K. (1995). *The crosscultural language and academic development handbook.* Boston: Allyn & Bacon.

Dieker, L. A. (2001). What are the characteristics of "effective" middle and high school co-taught teams for students with disabilities? *Preventing School Failure, 48*(1), 14–23.

Dixon, C., and Nessel, D. (1992). *Meaning making: Directed reading and thinking activities for second language students.* Englewood Cliffs, NJ: Prentice Hall Regents.

Dixon, R. (1976, 1991). *Morphographic spelling.* Toronto: SRA.

Dixon, R. C., Carnine, D. W., Lee, D. S., Wallin, J., and Chard, D. (1998). Report to the California State Board of Education and addendum to principal report: Review of high-quality experimental mathematics research. Retrieved from http://idea.uoregon.edu/~ncite/documents/math/math.html.

Dixon, R. C., Isaacson, S., and Stein, M. (2002). Effective strategies for teaching writing. In E. J. Kame'enui, D. W. Carnine, R. C. Dixon, D. C. Simmons, and M. D. Coyne (Eds.), *Effective teaching strategies that accommodate diverse learners.* Upper Saddle River, NJ: Merrill Prentice Hall.

Dole, J. A., Brown, K. J., and Trathen, W. (1996). The effects of strategy instruction on the comprehension performance of at-risk students. *Reading Research Quarterly, 31,* 62–88.

Dole, J. A., Valencia, S. W., Greer, E. A., and Wardrop, J. L. (1991). Effects of two types of reading instruction on the comprehension of narrative and expository text. *Reading Research Quarterly, 26,* 142–159.

Donahue, M., Pearl, R., and Bryan, T. (1980). Learning disabled children's conversational competence: Responses in inadequate messages. *Applied Psycholinguistics, 1,* 387–403.

Donovan, M. S., and Cross, C. T. (2002). *Minority students in special and gifted education.* Washington, DC: National Academy Press.

Dorval, B., McKinney, J. D., and Feagans, L. (1982). Teacher interaction with learning disabled children and average achievers. *Journal of Pediatric Psychology, 7*(3), 317–330.

Dowhower, S. L. (1987). Effects of repeated reading on second-grade transitional readers' fluency and comprehension. *Reading Research Quarterly, 22,* 389–406.

Dowhower, S. L. (1994). Repeated reading revisited: Research into practice. *Reading and Writing Quarterly, 10,* 343–358.

Doyle, W. (1979). Making managerial decisions in classrooms. In D. L. Duke (Ed.), *Classroom management.* Seventy-eighth yearbook of the National Society for the Study of Education, Part 2. Chicago: University of Chicago Press.

Doyle, W. (1986). Classroom organization and management. In M. C. Wittrock (Ed.), *Handbook of research on teaching* (3rd ed., pp. 392–431). New York: Macmillan.

Duffy, G., Lanier, J. E., and Roehler, L. R. (1980). *On the need to consider instructional practice when looking for instruction implications.* Paper presented at the Reading Expository Materials. University of Wisconsin–Madison.

Duling, W. P. (1999). Literacy development of second language learners with technology and LEA. In O. G. Nelson and W. M. Linek (Eds.), *Practical classroom applications of language experience: Looking back, looking forward* (pp. 248–256). Boston: Allyn & Bacon.

Dunn, L. M., Smith, J. O., Horton, K. B., and Smith, D. D. (Rev. Ed. 1981). *Peabody language development kits.* Circle Pines, MN: American Guidance Service.

Dunst, C. J. (2002). Family-centered practices: Birth through high school. *Journal of Special Education, 36,* 139–147.

Duran, R. P. (1989). Assessment and instruction of at-risk Hispanic students. *Exceptional Children, 56,* 154–159.

Durkin, D. D. (1978–79). What classroom observations reveal about reading comprehension instruction. *Reading Research Quarterly, 14*(4), 481–533.

Dweck, C. S., and Kamins, M. L. (1999). Person versus process praise and criticism: Implications for contingent self-worth and coping. *Developmental Psychology, 35*(3), 835–847.

Echevarria, J., and Graves, A. (1998). *Sheltered content instruction: Teaching English-language learners with diverse abilities.* Boston: Allyn & Bacon.

Echevarria, J., and McDonough, R. (1996). An alternative reading approach: Instructional conversations in a bilingual special education setting. *Learning Disabilities Research and Practice, 10,* 108–119.

Edmonds, M. S., Vaughn, S., Wexler, J., Reutebuch, C. K., Cable, A., Tackett, K., et. al. (in press). A synthesis of reading interventions and effects on reading outcomes for older struggling readers. *Review of Educational Research.*

Eggen, P. D., and Kauchak, D. (1992). *Educational psychology: Classroom connections.* New York: Macmillan.

Ehren, B. J., Montgomery, J., Rudebusch, J., and Whitmire, K. (2006). *Responsiveness to intervention: New roles for speech-language pathologists.* Retrieved from www.asha.org/members/slp/schools/prof-consult/NewRolesSLP.htm

Ehri, L. C. (1989). The development of spelling knowledge and its role in reading acquisition and reading disability. *Journal of Learning Disabilities, 22*(6), 356–365.

Ehri, L. C. (1998). Grapheme-phoneme knowledge is essential for learning to read words in English. In J. Methsala and L. Ehri (Eds.), *Word recognition in beginning literacy* (pp. 3–40). Mahwah, NJ: Erlbaum.

Ehri, L. C. (2004). *Teaching phonemic awareness and phonics: An explanation of the National Reading Panel meta-analyses.* Baltimore: Brookes.

Ehri, L. C., and Wilce, L. S. (1983). Development of word identification speed in skilled and less skilled beginning readers. *Journal of Education Psychology, 75,* 3–18.

Ehri, L. C., Nunes, S. R., Schuster, B. V., Shanahan, T., Willows, D. M., and Yaghoub-Zadeh, Z. (2001). Phonemic awareness instruction helps children learn to read: Evidence from the National Reading Panel's meta-analysis. *Reading Research Quarterly, 36,* 250–287.

Elam, S. M., and Gallup, A. M. (1989). The 21st annual Gallup poll of the public's attitudes toward the public schools. *Phi Delta Kappan, 71,* 41–54.

Elbaum, B. (2007). Effects of an oral testing accommodation on the mathematics performance of secondary students with and without learning disabilities. *Journal of Special Education, 40*(4), 218–229.

Elbaum, B. E., Schumm, J. S., and Vaughn, S. (1997). Urban middle-elementary students' perceptions of grouping formats for reading instruction. *Elementary School Journal, 97*(5), 475–500.

Elbaum, B., and Vaughn, S. (2001). School-based interventions to enhance the self-concept of students with learning disabilities: A meta-analysis. *The Elementary School Journal, 101,* 303–329.

Elbaum, B., and Vaughn, S. (2003). For which students with learning disabilities are self-concept interventions effective? *Journal of Learning Disabilities, 36,* 101–108.

Elbaum, B., Vaughn, S., Hughes, M., and Moody, S. W. (1999). Grouping practices and reading outcomes for students with disabilities. *Exceptional Children, 65*(3), 399–415.

Eldredge, J. L., and Quinn, D. W. (1988). Increasing reading performance of low-achieving second graders with dyad reading groups. *Journal of Educational Research, 82*(1), 40–46.

Elias, M. J., and Clabby, J. F. (1989). *Social decision-making skills: A curriculum guide for the elementary grades.* Rockville, MD: Aspen.

Elkonin, D. B. (1973). U.S.S.R. In J. Downing (Ed.), *Comparative reading* (pp. 551–579). New York: Macmillan.

Ellis, E. (1991). *SLANT: A starter strategy for participation.* Lawrence, KS: Edge Enterprises.

Ellis, E. S. (1996). Reading strategy instruction. In D. D. Deshler, E. S. Ellis, and B. K. Lenz, *Teaching adolescents with learning disabilities: Strategies and methods* (2nd ed., pp. 61–126). Denver: Love.

Emery, D. W. (1996). Helping readers comprehend stories from the characters' perspectives. *The Reading Teacher, 49,* 534–541.

Emmer, E. T., Evertson, C. M., Sanford, J. P., Clements, B. S., and Worsham, M. E. (1989). *Classroom management for secondary teachers* (2nd ed.). Englewood Cliffs, NJ: Prentice Hall.

Engelhardt, J. M., Ashlock, R. B., and Wiebe, J. H. (1984). *Helping children understand and use numerals* (pp. 89–149). Boston: Allyn & Bacon.

Engelmann, S., Bruner, E. C., Hanner, S., Osborn, J., Osborn, S., and Zoref, L. (1995). *Reading mastery: Rainbow edition.* Columbus, OH: SRA/McGraw-Hill.

Engelmann, S., Carnine, D., and Steely, D. G. (1991). Making connections in mathematics. *Journal of Learning Disabilities, 24*(5), 292–303.

Engelmann, S., Carnine, D., and Steely, D. (2005). *Corrective mathematics.* Columbus, OH: McGraw Hill.

Engelmann, S., Meyer, L., Carnine, L., Becker, W., Eisele, J., and Johnson, G. (1999). *Corrective reading program.* Columbus, OH: SRA/-McGraw-Hill.

Engelmann, S., and Osborn, J. (1987). *DISTAR Language I.* Chicago: SRA/McGraw-Hill.

Engelmann, S., and Osborn, J. (1999). *Language for Learning.* DeSoto, TX: SRA/McGraw-Hill.

Englert, C. S. (1992). Writing instruction from a sociocultural perspective: The holistic, dialogic, and social enterprise of writing. *Journal of Learning Disabilities, 25,* 153–172.

Englert, C. S., and Mariage, T. (1990). Send for the POSSE: Structuring the comprehension dialogue. *Academic Therapy, 25,* 473–487.

Englert, C. S., and Mariage, T. V. (1991). Making students partners in the comprehension process: Organizing the reading "POSSE." *Learning Disability Quarterly, 14,* 123–138.

Englert, C. S., and Raphael, T. E. (1988). Constructive well-formed prose: Process, structure, and metacognitive knowledge. *Exceptional Children, 54,* 513–520.

Englert, C. S., and Thomas, C. C. (1987). Sensitivity to text structure in reading and writing: A comparison between learning disabled and non-learning disabled students. *Learning Disability Quarterly, 10*(2), 93–105.

Englert, C. S., Garmon, A., Mariage, T., Rozendal, M., Tarrant, K., and Urba, J. (1995). The early literacy project: Connecting across the literacy curriculum. *Learning Disability Quarterly, 18,* 253–277.

Englert, C. S., Raphael, T. E., and Anderson, L. M. (1992). Socially-mediated instruction: Improving students' knowledge and talk about writing. *Elementary School Journal, 92*(4), 411–449.

Englert, C. S., Raphael, T. E., Anderson, L. M., Anthony, H. M., and Stevens, D. D. (1991). Making strategies and self-talk visible: Writing instruction in regular and special education classrooms. *American Educational Research Journal, 23,* 337–372.

Englert, C. S., Raphael, T. E., Fear, K. L., and Anderson, L. M. (1988). Students' metacognitive knowledge about how to write informational texts. *Learning Disability Quarterly, 11,* 18–46.

Englert, C. S., Rozendal, M. S., and Mariage, M. (1994). Fostering the search for understanding: A teacher's strategies for leading cognitive development in "zones of proximal development." *Learning Disability Quarterly, 17,* 187–204.

Ericcson, K. A., and Kintsch, W. (1995). Long-term working memory. *Psychological Review, 102,* 211–245.

Erickson, R., and Schultz, J. (1981). When is a context? Some issues and methods in the analysis of social competence. In J. L. Green and C. Wallat (Eds.), *Ethnography and language in educational settings.* Norwood, NJ: Ablex.

Esterreicher, C. A. (1995). *SCAMPER strategies: FUNdamental activities for narrative development.* Eau Claire, WI: Thinking Publications.

Exceptional Parent. (1984, March). Parent advocacy. *Exceptional Parent, 14*(2), 41–45.

Fairbanks, S., Sugai, G., Guardino, D., and Lathrop, M. (2007). Response to intervention: Examining classroom behavior support in second grade. *Exceptional Children, 73*(3), 288–310.

Farmer, T. W., Pearl, R., and Van Acker, R. M. (1996). Expanding the social skills deficit framework: A developmental synthesis perspective, classroom social networks, and implications for the social growth of students with disabilities. *Journal of Special Education, 30*(3), 232–256.

Fauke, J., Burnett, J., Powers, M., and Sulzer-Azaroff, B. (1973). Improvement of handwriting and letter recognition skills: A behavior modification procedure. *Journal of Learning Disabilities, 6,* 25–29.

Fearn, L., and Farnan, N. (1998). *Writing effectively: Helping children master the conventions of writing.* Boston: Allyn and Bacon.

Ferguson, P. M. (2002). A place in the family: An historical interpretation of research on parental reactions to having a child with a disability. *The Journal of Special Education, 36,* 124–130.

Fernald, G. M. (1943). *Remedial techniques in basic school subjects.* New York: McGraw-Hill.

Fernald, G. M. (1988). *Remedial techniques in basic school subjects.* (L. Idol, Ed.). Austin, TX: PRO-ED (original edition 1943).

Fielding, L., and Roller, C. (1992). Making difficult books accessible and easy books acceptable. *The Reading Teacher, 45,* 678–682.

Figula, D. (1992). *Friendzee: A social skills game.* East Moline, IL: LinguiSystems.

Finn, J. D. (1989). Withdrawing from school. *Review of Educational Research, 59,* 117–142.

Fitzsimmons, R. J., and Loomer, B. M. (1978). *Spelling: Learning and instruction.* (Report No. CS 205 117). Des Moines: Iowa State Department of Public Instruction. (ERIC Document Reproduction Service No. ED 176 285).

Flavell, J. H. (1976). Metacognitive aspects of problem solving. In L. B. Resnick (Ed.), *The nature of intelligence.* Hillsdale, NJ: Erlbaum.

Fleischner, J. E., Nuzum, M. G., and Marzola, E. S. (1987). Devising an instructional program to teach arithmetic problem-solving skills to students with learning disabilities. *Journal of Learning Disabilities, 20*(4), 214–217.

Fletcher, J. M. (1989). Nonverbal learning disabilities and suicide: Classification leads to prevention. *Journal of Learning Disabilities, 22,* 176–179.

Flexar, R. W., Baer, R. M., Luft, P., and Simmons, T. J. (2008). *Transition planning for secondary students with disabilities* (3rd ed.). Upper Saddle River, NJ: Pearson.

Foorman, B. R., and Ciancio, D. J. (2005). Screening for secondary intervention: Concept and context. *Journal of Learning Disabilities, 38*(6), 494–499.

Foorman, B. R., Fletcher, J. M., Francis, D. J., and Schatschneider, C. (1998). The role of instruction in learning to read: Preventing reading failure in at-risk children. *Journal of Education Psychology, 90,* 37–55.

Forness, S. R. (1973). The reinforcement hierarchy. *Psychology in the Schools, 19,* 168–177.

Foster, S. L., and Ritchey, W. C. (1979). Issues in the assessment of social competence in children. *Journal of Applied Behavior Analysis, 12,* 625–631.

Fountas, I. C., and Pinnell, G. S. (1999). *Matching books to readers: Using leveled books in guided reading, K–3.* Portsmouth, NH: Heinemann.

Fowler, G. L., and Davis, M. (1985). The story frame approach: A tool for improving reading comprehension of EMR children. *Teaching Exceptional Children, 17*(4), 296–298.

Fox, C. (1989). Peer acceptance of learning disabled children in the regular classroom. *Exceptional Children, 56*(1), 50–57.

Fox, L., Vaughn, B. J., Wyatte, M. L., and Dunlap, G. (2002). "We can't expect other people to understand": Family perspectives on problem behavior. *Exceptional Children, 68,* 437–450.

Francis, D. J., Rivera, M., Rivera, H., Lesaux, N., and Kieffer, M. (2006). Research-based recommendations for instruction and academic interventions. Retrieved from Center on Instruction Website: www.centeroninstruction.org.

Frayer, D. A., Frederick, W. C., and Klausmeier, H. J. (1969). *A schema for testing the level of concept mastery* (Working Paper No. 16). Madison: University of Wisconsin, Wisconsin Research and Development Center for Cognitive Learning.

Frederickson, N., and Turner, J. (2003). Utilizing the classroom peer group to address children's social needs: An evaluation of the Circle of Friends intervention approach. *Journal of Special Education, 36,* 234–246.

Freppon, P. A., and Dahl, K. L. (1998). Theory and research into practice: Balanced instruction: Insights and considerations. *Reading Research Quarterly, 33,* 240–251.

Friend, M. (2000). Perspectives: Collaboration in the twenty-first century. *Remedial and Special Education, 20,* 130–132, 160.

Fries, C. C. (1963). *Linguistics and reading.* New York: Holt, Rinehart and Winston.

Frith, G. H., and Armstong, W. W. (1986). Self-monitoring for behavior disordered students. *Teaching Exceptional Children, 18*(2), 144–148.

Frith, U. (1980). *Cognitive processes in spelling.* London: Academic Press.

Fromkin, V., and Rodman, R. (1998). *An instruction to language* (6th ed.). Orlando, FL: Harcourt Brace.

Fry, E. B. (1977). Fry's readability graph: Clarifications, validity, and extension to level 17. *Journal of Reading, 21,* 242–252.

Fry, E. B., Fountoukidis, D. L., and Polk, J. K. (1985). *The new reading teacher's book of lists.* Englewood Cliffs, NJ: Prentice Hall.

Fuchs, D., and Fuchs, L. S. (1994). Inclusive school movement and radicalization of special education reform. *Exceptional Children, 60,* 294–309.

Fuchs, D., and Fuchs, L. S. (1995). What's "special" about special education? *Phi Delta Kappan, 76,* 522–530.

Fuchs, D., and Fuchs, L. S. (2006). Introduction to response to intervention: What, why, and how valid is it? *Reading Research Quarterly, 41,* 92–99.

Fuchs, D., Fuchs, L. S., and Bahr, M. W. (1990). Mainstream assistance teams: A scientific basis for the art of consultation. *Exceptional Children, 57,* 128–139.

Fuchs, D., Fuchs, L. S., and Burish, P. (2000). Peer-assisted learning strategies: An evidence-based practice to promote reading achievement. *Learning Disabilities Research and Practice, 25,* 85–91.

Fuchs, D., Fuchs, L. S., Harris, A., and Roberts, P. H. (1996). Bridging the research-to-practice gap with Mainstream Assistance Teams: A cautionary tale. *School Psychology Quarterly, 11,* 244–266.

Fuchs, D., Fuchs, L. S., and Mathes, P. G. (1994). Importance of instructional complexity and role reciprocity to classwide peer tutoring. *Learning Disabilities Research and Practice, 9,* 203–212.

Fuchs, D., Fuchs, L. S., Mathes, P. G., and Simmons, D. C. (1997). Peer-assisted learning strategies: Making classrooms more responsive to diversity. *American Educational Research Journal, 34,* 174–206.

Fuchs, D., Fuchs, L. S., Thompson, A., Al Otaiba, S., Yen, L., Yang, N. J., Braun, M., and O'Connor, R. E. (2003). Exploring the importance of reading programs for kindergartners with disabilities in mainstream classrooms. *Exceptional Children, 68,* 295–311.

Fuchs, D., Mock, D., Morgan, P. L., and Young, C. L. (2003). Responsiveness to intervention: Definitions, evidence, and implications for the learning disabilities construct. *Learning Disabilities Research and Practice, 18,* 172–186.

Fuchs, L. S., Bahr, C. M., and Rieth, H. J. (1989). Effects of goal structures and performance contingencies on the math performance of adolescents with learning disabilities. *Journal of Learning Disabilities, 22,* 554–560.

Fuchs, L. S., and Deno, S. L. (1991). Paradigmatic distinctions between instructionally relevant measurement models. *Exceptional Children, 57,* 488–500.

Fuchs, L. S., and Fuchs, D. (1996). Combining performance assessment and curriculum-based measurement to strengthen instructional planning. *Learning Disabilities Research and Practice, 11,* 183–192.

Fuchs, L. S., Fuchs, D., Compton, D. L., Bryant, J. D., Hamlett, C. L., and Seethaler, P. M. (2007). Mathematics screening and progress monitoring at first grade: Implications for responsiveness to intervention. *Exceptional Children, 73*(3), 311–330.

Fuchs, L. S., Fuchs, D., and Hamlett, C. L. (1989). Effects of instructional use of curriculum-based measurement to enhance instruction programs. *Remedial and Special Education 10*(2), 43–52.

Fuchs, L. S., Fuchs, D., Hamlett, C. L., and Allinder, R. M. (1991). The contribution of skills analysis to curriculum-based measurement in spelling. *Exceptional Children, 57,* 443–452.

Fuchs, L. S., Fuchs, D., Hamlett, C. L., Phillips, N. B., and Karns, K. (1995). General educators' specialized adaptation for students with learning disabilities. *Exceptional Children, 61*(5), 440–459.

Fuchs, L. S., Fuchs, D., Hamlett, C. L., Phillips, N. B., Karns, K., and Dutka, S. (1997). Enhancing students' helping behavior during peer-mediated instruction with conceptual mathematical explanations. *The Elementary School Journal, 97,* 223–249.

Fuchs, L. S., Fuchs, D., Hamlett, C. L., Walz, L., and Germann, G. (1993). Formative evaluation of academic progress: How much growth can we expect? *School Psychology Review, 22*(1), 27–48.

Fuchs, L. S., Fuchs, D., and Speece, D. L. (2002). Treatment validity as a unifying construct for identifying learning disabilities. *Learning Disability Quarterly, 25,* 33–45.

Fuchs, L. S., Hamlett, C., and Fuchs, D. (1990). *Monitoring basic skills progress: Basic math.* Austin, TX: PRO-ED.

Fujiki, M., Brinton, B., and Todd, C. M. (1996). Social skills of children with specific language impairment. *Language, Speech, and Hearing Services in Schools, 27,* 195–202.

Fulk, B. J. M., Mastropieri, M. A., and Scruggs, T. E. (1992). Mnemonic generalization training with learning disabled adolescents. *Learning Disabilities Research and Practice, 7,* 2–10.

Fulk, B. M., and Stormont-Spurgin, M. (1995). Spelling interventions for students with disabilities: A review. *Journal of Special Education, 28,* 488–513.

Furner, B. (1969a). The perceptual-motor nature of learning in handwriting. *Elementary English, 46,* 886–894.

Furner, B. (1969b). Recommended instructional procedures in a method emphasizing the perceptual-motor nature of learning in handwriting. *Elementary English, 46,* 1021–1030.

Furner, B. (1970). An analysis of the effectiveness of a program of instruction emphasizing the perceptual-motor nature of learning in handwriting. *Elementary English, 47,* 61–69.

Gajria, M., and Salend, S. J. (1995). Homework practices of students with and without learning disabilities: A comparison. *Journal of Learning Disabilities, 28,* 291–296.

Gajria, M., and Salvia, J. (1992). The effects of summarization instruction on text comprehension of students with learning disabilities. *Exceptional Children, 58,* 508–516.

Galambos, S., and Goldin-Meadow, S. (1990). The effects of learning two languages on metalinguistic development. *Cognition, 34,* 1–56.

Ganske, K. (2000). *Word journeys: Assessment-guided phonics, spelling, and vocabulary instruction.* New York: Guilford Press.

Garcia, E. E. (1991). Effective instruction for language minority students: The teacher. *Journal of Education, 173,* 130–141.

Gaskins, I. W. with Cress, C., O'Hara, C., and Donnelly, K. (1998). *Word detectives: Benchmark extended word identification program for beginning readers.* Media, PA: Benchmark Press.

Gaskins, I. W., Anderson, R. C., Pressley, M., Cunicelli, E. A., and Satlow, E. (1993). Six teachers' dialogue during cognitive process instruction. *Elementary School Journal, 93,* 277–304.

Gast, D., Ault, M., Wolery, M., Doyle, P., and Belanger, S. (1988). Comparison of constant time delay and the system of least prompts in teaching sight word reading to students with moderate retardation. *Education and Training in Mental Retardation, 23,* 117–128.

Gerber, A. (1993). *Language related learning disabilities: Their nature and treatment.* Baltimore: Brookes.

Gerber, M. M., and Hall, R. J. (1989). Cognitive-behavioral training in spelling for learning handicapped students. *Learning Disabilities Quarterly, 12,* 159–171.

Gerber, M., and Kauffman, J. (1981). Peer tutoring in academic settings. In P. Strain (Ed.), *Utilization of classroom peers as behavior change agents* (pp. 155–187). New York: Plenum.

German, D. J. (1987). Spontaneous language profiles of children with word-finding problems. *Language, Speech, and Hearing Services in Schools, 18,* 217–230.

German, D. J. (1992). Word-finding intervention for children and adolescents. *Topics in Language Disorders, 13*(1), 33–50.

German, D. J. (1994). *The word finding intervention program.* Tucson, AZ: Communication Skill Builders.

German, D. J. (2001). *It's on the tip of my tongue.* Chicago: Word Finding Materials.

Gersten, R., and Baker, S. (2001). Teaching expressive writing to students with learning disabilities: A meta-analysis. *Elementary School Journal, 101*(3), 251–272.

Gersten, R., and Chard, D. (1999). Number sense: Rethinking arithmetic instruction for students with mathematical disabilities. *Journal of Special Education, 33*(1), 18–28.

Gersten, R., and Geva, E. (2003). Teaching reading to early language learners. *Educational Leadership, 60*(7), 44–49.

Gersten, R., Carnine, D., and Woodward, J. (1987). Direct Instruction research: The third decade. *Remedial and Special Education, 8*(6), 48–56.

Gersten, R., Schiller, E. P., and Vaughn, S. (2000). *Contemporary special education research: Syntheses of knowledge bases in critical instructional issues.* Mahwah, NJ: Erlbaum.

Gersten, R., Williams, J. P., Fuchs, L. S., and Baker, S. (in press). Teaching reading comprehension strategies to students with learning disabilities: A review of research. *Review of Educational Research.*

Gersten, R., Williams, J., Fuchs, L., and Baker, S. (1998). *Improving reading comprehension for children with learning disabilities.* (Final Report: Section 1, U.S. Department of Education Contract HS 921700.) Washington, DC: U.S. Department of Education.

Gertsen, B., and Baker, S. (2000). What we know about effective instructional practices for English-language learners. *Exceptional Children, 66,* 454–470.

Gettinger, M. (1984). Applying learning principles to remedial spelling instruction. *Academic Therapy, 20*(1), 41–48.

Gettinger, M., Bryant, M. D., and Fayne, H. R. (1982). Designing spelling instruction for learning disabled children: An emphasis on unit size, distributed practice, and training for transfer. *Journal of Special Education, 16*(4), 439–448.

Gibb, G. S., and Dyches, T. T. (2000). *Guide to writing quality individualized educational programs: What's best for students with disabilities?* Boston: Allyn & Bacon.

Gibbs, R. W. (1987). Linguistic factors in children's understanding of idioms. *Journal of Speech and Hearing Research, 54,* 613–620.

Giddan, J. J., Bade, K. M., Rickenberg, C., and Ryley, A. T. (1995). Teaching the language of feelings to students with severe emotional and behavioral handicaps. *Language, Speech, and Hearing Services in Schools, 26,* 3–10.

Gillam, R. B., and Pearson, N. (2004). *Test of Narrative Language.* Austin, TX: PRO-ED.

Gillingham, A., and Stillman, B. W. (1973). *Remedial training for children with specific disability in reading, spelling, and penmanship.* Cambridge, MA: Educators Publishing Service.

Ginsburg, H. P. (1997). Mathematics learning disabilities: A view from developmental psychology. *Journal of Learning Disabilities, 30*(1), 20–33.

Ginsburg-Block, M. D., Rohrbeck, C. A., and Fantuzzo, J. W. (2006). A meta-analytic review of social, self-concept, and behavioral outcomes of peer-assisted learning. *Journal of Educational Psychology, 98*(4), 732–749.

Glatthorn, A. A. (1990). Cooperative professional development: Facilitating the growth of the special education teacher and the classroom teacher. *Remedial and Special Education, 11*(3), 29–35.

Glick, B., and Goldstein, A. P. (1987). Aggression replacement training. *Journal of Counseling and Development, 65*(7), 356–362.

Gold, V. (1976). *The effect of an experimental program involving acquisition of phoneme-grapheme relationships incorporating criterion referenced tests with evaluative feedback upon spelling performance of third grade pupils.* Unpublished doctoral dissertation, University of Southern California, Los Angeles.

Goldman, S. R., Hasselbring, T. S., and the Cognition and Technology Group at Vanderbilt (1997). Achieving meaningful mathematics literacy for students with learning disabilities. *Journal of Learning Disabilities, 30*(2), 198–208.

Goldstein, A. P., Sprafkin, R. P., Gershaw, N. J., and Klein, P. (1980). *Skillstreaming the adolescent.* Champaign, IL: Research Press.

Goldstein, S. (1995). *Understanding and managing children's classroom behavior.* New York: Wiley.

Good, R. H., and Kaminski, R. (2003). *DIBELS 6th edition: Dynamic Indicators of Basic Early Literacy Skills.* Longmont, CO: Sopris West.

Good, R. H., and Kaminski, R. A. (Eds.). (2002). *Dynamic indicators of basic early literacy skills* (6th ed.). Eugene, OR: Institute for the Development of Educational Achievement. Retrieved from http://dibels.uoregon.edu.

Good, R. H., Bank, J., and Watson, J. (2004). *IDEL: Indicadores dinámicos del éxito en la lectura.* Longmont, CO: Sopris West.

Good, T. L., and Brophy, J. E. (1997). *Looking in classrooms* (7th ed.). New York: Addison-Wesley, Longman.

Goodman, K. (1986). *What's whole in whole language?* Portsmouth, NH: Heinemann.

Goodman, K. S. (1984). Unity in reading. In A. C. Purves and O. Niles (Eds.), *Becoming readers in a complex society* (pp. 79–114). Eighty-third yearbook of the National Society for the Study of Education. Chicago: University of Chicago Press.

Goodman, K. S. (1996). *On reading.* Portsmouth, NH: Heinemann.

Goodman, K. S., and Goodman, Y. M. (1980). Linguistics, psycholinguistics, and the teaching of reading: An annotated bibliography. Newark, DE: International Reading Association.

Goodman, Y. M., Watson, D. J., and Burke, C. L. (1996). *Reading strategies: Focus on comprehension* (2nd ed.). Katonah, NY: Richard C. Owens.

Goodstein, H. A. (1981). Are the errors we see the true errors? Error analysis in verbal problem solving. *Topics in Learning and Learning Disabilities, 1*(3), 31–45.

Gordon, J., Vaughn, S., and Schumm, J. S. (1993). Spelling intervention: A review of literature and implications for instruction for students with learning disabilities. *Learning Disabilities Research and Practice, 8,* 175–181.

Gorman-Gard, K. A. (1992). *Figurative language: A comprehensive program.* Eau Claire, WI: Thinking Publications.

Goswami, U. (1998). Rime-based coding in early reading development in English: Orthographic analogies and rime neighborhoods. In D. Hulme and R. M. Joshi, (Eds.), *Reading and spelling: Development and disorders* (pp. 69–86). Mahwah, NJ: Erlbaum.

Goswami, U., and Bryant, P. E. (1990). *Phonological skills and learning to read.* Mahwah, NJ: Erlbaum.

Gough, P. B. (1996). How children learn to read and why they fail. *Annals of Dyslexia, 46,* 3–19.

Graham, S. (1983). The effect of self-instructional procedures on LD students' handwriting performance. *Learning Disability Quarterly, 6*(2), 231–244.

Graham, S. (1990). The role of production factors in learning disabled students' compositions. *Journal of Educational Psychology, 82,* 781–791.

Graham, S. (1999). Handwriting and spelling instruction for students with learning disabilities: A review. *Learning Disability Quarterly, 22*(2), 78–98.

Graham, S., and Freeman, S. (1986). Strategy training and teacher- vs. student-controlled study conditions: Effects on LD students' spelling performance. *Learning Disability Quarterly, 9,* 15–22.

Graham, S., and Harris, K. R. (1989). Components analysis of cognitive strategy instruction: Effects on learning disabled students' compositions and self-efficacy. *Journal of Educational Psychology, 81,* 353–361.

Graham, S., and Harris, K. R. (1993). Teaching writing strategies to students with learning disabilities: Issues and recommendations. In L. Meltzer (Ed.), *Strategy assessment and instruction for students with learning disabilities: From theory to practice* (pp. 271–292). Austin, TX: PRO-ED.

Graham, S., and Harris, K. R. (1994). Implications of constructivism for teaching writing to students with special needs. *Journal of Special Education, 28,* 275–289.

Graham, S., and Harris, K. (2005). *Writing better: Effective strategies for teaching students with learning difficulties.* Baltimore: Brookes.

Graham, S., and Miller, L. (1979). Spelling research and practice: A unified approach. *Focus on Exceptional Children, 12*(2), 1–16.

Graham, S., and Miller, L. (1980). Handwriting research and practice: A unified approach. *Focus on Exceptional Children, 13*(2), 1–16.

Graham, S., and Perin, D. (2007). *Writing next: Effective strategies to improve writing of adolescents in middle and high schools: A report to Carnegie Corporation of New York.* Washington, DC: Alliance for Excellent Education.

Graham, S., and Voth, V. (1990). Spelling instruction: Making modifications for students with learning disabilities. *Academic Therapy, 25,* 447–457.

Graham, S., Berninger, V., and Weintraub, N. (1998). The relationship between handwriting style and speed and legibility. *Journal of Educational Research, 91,* 290–297.

Graham, S., Harris, K. R., and Loynachan, C. (1996). The directed spelling thinking activity: Application with high-frequency words. *Learning Disabilities Research and Practice, 1,* 34–40.

Graham, S., Harris, K. R., and MacArthur, C. A. (1995). Introduction to special issue: Research on writing and literacy. *Learning Disability Quarterly, 18,* 250–252.

Graham, S., Harris, K., and Troia, G. (1998). Writing and self-regulation: Cases from the self-regulated strategy development model. In D. Schunk and B. Zimmerman (Eds.), *Self-regulated learning: From teaching to self-reflective practice* (pp. 20–41). New York: Guilford.

Graham, S., MacArthur, C. A., Schwartz, S., and Page-Voth, V. (1992). Improving the comprehension of students with learning disabilities using a strategy involving process and product goal setting. *Exceptional Children, 58,* 322–334.

Graham, S., MacArthur, C., and Schwartz, S. (1995). Effects of goal setting and procedural facilitation on the revising behavior and writing performance of students with writing and learning problems. *Journal of Educational Psychology, 87,* 230–240.

Graves, A. W. (1986). Effects of direct instruction and metacomprehension training on finding main ideas. *Learning Disabilities Research, 1*(2), 90–100.

Graves, A. W. (1995). Teaching students who are culturally and linguistically diverse. *Teacher Educator's Journal, 15*(3), 32–40.

Graves, A. W., Valles, E. C., and Rueda, R. (2000). Variations in interactive writing instruction: A study in four bilingual special education settings. *Learning Disabilities Research and Practice, 15*(3), 1–9.

Graves, D. H. (1983). *Writing: Teachers and children at work.* Portsmouth, NH: Heinemann.

Graves, D. H. (1985). All children can write. *Learning Disability Focus, 1*(1), 36–43.

Graves, D. H., and Hansen, J. (1983). The author's chair. *Language Arts, 60,* 176–183.

Graves, M. F., Juel, C., and Graves, B. B. (2001). *Teaching reading in the 21st century* (2nd ed.). Boston: Allyn & Bacon.

Greaney, U. K. T., Tunmer, W. E., and Chapman, J. W. (1997). Effects of rime-based orthographic analogy training on the word recognition skills of children with reading disability. *Journal of Education Psychology, 89,* 645–651.

Green, S. K. (2001). Use of CBM oral reading in the general education classroom. *Assessment for Effective Intervention, 26,* 1–13.

Greene, J. R. (1996). Language: The effects of an individualized structured language curriculum for middle and high school students. *Annals of Dyslexia, 38,* 258–275.

Greenham, S. (1999). Learning disabilities and psychosocial adjustment: A critical review. *Child Neuropsychology, 5,* 171–196.

Greenwood, C. R., Delquadri, J. C., and Hall, R. V. (1989). Longitudinal effects of classwide peer tutoring. *Journal of Educational Psychology, 81,* 371–383.

Gregory, R. P., Hackney, C., and Gregory, N. M. (1982). Corrective reading programme: An evaluation. *British Journal of Educational Psychology, 52,* 33–50.

Gresham, F. M. (1982). Misguided mainstreaming: The case for social skills training with handicapped children. *Exceptional Children, 48,* 422–433.

Griffiths, D. (1991). *An analysis of social competence training with persons with developmental handicaps.* Unpublished doctoral dissertation, University of Toronto.

Grimm, J. A., Bijou, S. W., and Parsons, J. A. (1973). A problem solving model for teaching remedial arithmetic to handicapped children. *Journal of Abnormal Child Psychology, 1,* 26–39.

Grossen, B. (1999). *The research base for corrective reading.* Columbus, OH: SRA/McGraw-Hill.

Grossman, H. (1995). *Special education in a diverse society.* Boston: Allyn & Bacon.

Grottenthaler, J. A. (1970). *A comparison of the effectiveness of three programs of elementary school spelling.* Unpublished doctoral dissertation, University of Pittsburgh.

Guetzloe, E. C. (1989). *Youth suicide: What the educator should know.* Reston, VA: The Council for Exceptional Children.

Gunn, B., Biglan, A., Smolkowski, K., and Ary, D. (2000). The efficacy of supplemental instruction in decoding skills for Hispanic and non-Hispanic students in early elementary school. *The Journal of Special Education, 34*(2), 90–103.

Gunning, T. G. (1998). *Assessing and correcting reading and writing difficulties.* Boston: Allyn & Bacon.

Gunning, T. G. (2000). *Creating literacy instruction for all children* (3rd ed.). Boston: Allyn & Bacon.

Gunning, T. G. (2001). *Building words: A resource manual for teaching word analysis and spelling patterns.* Boston: Allyn & Bacon.

Gunning, T. G. (2006). *Closing the literacy gap.* Boston: Pearson/Allyn & Bacon.

Gurney, D., Gersten, R., Dimino, J., and Carnine, D. (1990). Story grammar: Effective literature instruction for high school students with learning disabilities. *Journal of Learning Disabilities, 23,* 335–342.

Guszak, F. J. (1972). *Diagnostic reading instruction in the elementary school.* New York: Harper & Row.

Hacker, D. J., Dunlosky, J., and Graesser, A. C. (1998). *Metacognition in educational theory and practice.* Mahwah, NJ: Erlbaum.

Hadaway, N. L., and Mundy, J. (1999). Children's informational picture books visit a secondary ESL classroom. *Journal of Adolescent and Adult Literacy, 42,* 464–475.

Hagin, R. A. (1983). Write right or left: A practical approach to handwriting. *Journal of Learning Disabilities, 16*(5), 266–271.

Hake, S., and Saxon, J. (2004a). *Saxon math 5/4* (3rd ed.). Norman, OK: Saxon.

Hake, S., and Saxon, J. (2004b). *Saxon math 6/5* (3rd ed.). Norman, OK: Saxon.

Hake, S., and Saxon, J. (2004c). *Saxon math 7/6* (3rd ed.). Norman, OK: Saxon.

Hake, S., and Saxon, J. (2004d). *Saxon math 8/7* (3rd ed.). Norman, OK: Saxon.

Haley, M. H., and Austin, T. Y. (2004). *Content-based second language teaching and learning: An interactive approach.* Boston: Allyn & Bacon.

Hall, R. V., and Hall, M. L. (1998). *How to use planned ignoring (Extinction)* (2nd ed.). Austin, TX: PRO-ED.

Hallahan, D. P., Keller, C. E., McKinney, J. D., Lloyd, J. W., and Bryan, T. (1988). Examining the research base of the regular education initiative: Efficacy studies and the adaptive learning environments model. *Journal of Learning Disabilities, 21,* 29–35, 55.

Hallahan, D. P., Lloyd, J., Kosiewicz, M. M., Kauffman, J. M., and Graves, A. W. (1979). Self-monitoring of attention as a treatment for learning disabled boy's off-task behavior. *Learning Disability Quarterly, 2,* 24–32.

Hallowell, E. M., and Ratey, J. J. (1995). *Driven to distraction: Recognizing and coping with attention deficit disorder from childhood through adulthood.* New York: Touchstone.

Halperin, M. S. (1974). Developmental changes in the recall and recognition of categorized word lists. *Child Development, 45,* 144–151.

Halpern, A. S. (1994). The transition of youth with disabilities to adult life: A position statement of the Division on Career Development and Transition, The Council for Exceptional Children. *Career Development for Exceptional Individuals, 17,* 115–124.

Halpern, A. S., Herr, C. M., Doren, B., and Wolf, N. K. (2000). *Next S.T.E.P.: Student transition and evaluation planning* (2nd ed.). Austin, TX: PRO-ED.

Halpern, N. (1981). Mathematics for the learning disabled. *Journal of Learning Disabilities, 14*(9), 505–506.

Hamayan, E. V., and Damico, J. S. (Eds.). (1991). *Limiting bias in the assessment of bilingual students.* Austin, TX: PRO-ED.

Hamstra-Bletz, L., and Blote, A. W. (1993). A longitudinal study on dysgraphic handwriting in primary school. *Journal of Learning Disabilities, 26,* 689–699.

Hanover, S. (1983). Handwriting comes naturally? *Academic Therapy, 18,* 407–412.

Hansen, J., and Pearson, P. D. (1983). An instructional study: Improving the inferential comprehension of good and poor fourth grade readers. *Journal of Educational Psychology, 75*(6), 821–829.

Harniss, M. K., Epstein, M. H., Bursuck, W. D., Nelson, J., and Jayanthi, M. (2001). Resolving homework-related communication problems: Recommendations of parents of children with and without disabilities. *Reading & Writing Quarterly, 17,* 205–225.

Harper, G. F., Mallete, B., and Moore, J. (1991). Peer-mediated instruction: Teaching spelling to primary school children with mild disabilities. *Reading, Writing, and Learning Disabilities, 7,* 137–151.

Harris, K. R. (1985). Conceptual, methodological, and clinical issues in cognitive behavior assessment. *Journal of Abnormal Child Psychology, 13,* 373–390.

Harris, K. R., and Graham, S. (1992). *Helping young writers master the craft.* Cambridge, MA: Brookline.

Harris, K. R., and Pressley, M. E. (1991). The nature of cognitive strategy instruction: Interactive strategy construction. *Exceptional Children, 57,* 392–404.

Harry, B. (1992). *Cultural diversity, families, and the special education system.* New York: Teachers College Press.

Harry, B. (2002). Trends and issues in serving culturally diverse families of children with disabilities. *The Journal of Special Education, 36,* 131–138, 147.

Harry, B., Allen, N., and McLaughlin, M. (1995). Communication versus compliance: African-American parents' involvement in special education. *Exceptional Children, 6*(4), 364–377.

Harry, B., and Klingner, J. K. (2006). *Why are so many minority students in special education? Understanding race and disability in schools.* New York: Teachers College Press.

Harste, J. C., Short, K. G., with Burke, C. (1988). *Creating classrooms for authors: The reading-writing connection.* Portsmouth, NH: Heinemann.

Hartas, D., and Donahue, L. M. (1997). Conversational and social problem-solving skills in adolescents with learning disabilities. *Learning Disabilities Research and Practice, 12*(4), 213–220.

Hasbrouck, J. E., and Tindal, G. (1992). Curriculum-based oral reading fluency norms for students in Grades 2 through 5. *Teaching Exceptional Children, 24*(3), 41–44.

Hasbrouck, J. E., Ihnot, C., and Rogers, G. H. (1999). "Read naturally": A strategy to increase oral reading fluency. *Reading Research and Instruction, 39*(1), 27–38.

Hasselbring, T., Goin, L., and Bransford, J. (1987). Developing automaticity. *Teaching Exceptional Children, 19,* 30–33.

Hawaii Transition Project. (1987). Honolulu: Department of Special Education, University of Hawaii.

Hazel, J. S., Schumaker, J. B., Sherman, J. A., and Sheldon, J. (1982). Application of a group training program in social skills and problem solving to learning disabled and non-learning disabled youth. *Learning Disability Quarterly, 5,* 398–409.

Hazel, J. S., Schumaker, J. B., Sherman, J. A., and Sheldon-Wildgen, J. (1981). *ASSET: A social skills program for adolescents.* Champaign, IL: Research Press.

Heath, N. L., and Wiener, J. (1996). Depression and nonacademic self-perceptions in children with and without learning disabilities. *Learning Disability Quarterly, 19,* 34–44.

Helmke, L. M., Havekost, D. M., Patton, J. R., and Polloway, E. A. (1994). Life skills programming: Development of a high school science course. *Teaching Exceptional Children, 26*(2), 49–53.

Hembree, R. (1986). Research gives calculators a green light. *Arithmetic Teacher, 34*(1), 18–21.

Hennessey, B. A. (2007). Promoting social competence in school-aged children: The effects of the open circle program. *Journal of School Psychology, 45,* 349–360.

Henry, C. S., Stephenson, A. L., Hanson, M. F., and Hargett, W. (1993). Adolescent suicide and families: An ecological approach. *Adolescence, 28,* 291–308.

Henry, M. (1996). *Patterns for success in reading and spelling: A multisensory approach to teaching phonics and word analysis.* Austin, TX: PRO-ED.

Henry, M. (1997). The decoding/spelling curriculum: Integrated decoding and spelling instruction from pre-school to early secondary school. *Dyslexia, 3,* 178–189.

Herman, P. A., Anderson, R. C., Pearson, P. D., and Nagy, W. E. (1987). Incidental acquisition of word meaning from expositions with varied text features. *Reading Research Quarterly, 22,* 263–284.

Heron, T. E., Welsch, R. G., and Goddard, Y. L. (2003). Applications of tutoring systems in specialized subject areas. *Remedial and Special Education, 24*(5), 288–300.

Herzog, P. R. (1998). *PhonicsQ: The complete cueing system.* Available from www.phonicsq.com

Heward, W. L. (2003). Ten faulty notions about teaching and learning that hinder the effectiveness of special education. *Journal of Special Education, 36,* 186–205.

Hickman, P., Pollard-Durodola, S., and Vaughn, S. (2004). Storybook reading: Improving vocabulary and comprehension for English language learners. *The Reading Teacher, 57*(8), 720.

Hicks, B. B. (1990). *Youth suicide: A comprehensive manual for prevention and intervention.* Bloomington, IN: National Education Service.

Hiebert, E. H. (2002). *Quickreads: A research-based fluency program.* Parsippany, NJ: Modern Curriculum Press.

Higgins, E. L., and Raskind, M. H. (1995). An investigation of the compensatory effectiveness of speech recognition on the written composition performance of postsecondary students with learning disabilities. *Learning Disability Quarterly, 18,* 159–174.

Hirsch, E., and Niedermeyer, F. C. (1973). The effects of tracing prompts and discrimination training on kindergarten handwriting performance. *Journal of Educational Research, 67*(2), 81–86.

Holdaway, D. (1979). *The foundations of literacy.* Portsmouth, NH: Heinemann.

Hoover, J., and Stenhjem, P. (2003). Bullying and teasing of youth with disabilities: Creating positive school environments for effective inclusion. *Issue Brief: Examining current challenges in secondary education and transition, 2*(3), 1–6.

Hoover, J. J., and Patton, J. R. (2007). *Teaching study skills to students with learning problems: A teacher's guide for meeting diverse needs.* Austin: PRO-ED.

Hoover, J. H., and Salk, J. (2003). *Bullying: Bigger concerns.* St. Cloud State University, Department of Special Education.

Horowitz, E. C. (1981). Popularity, decentering ability, and role-taking skills in learning disabled and normal children. *Learning Disability Quarterly, 4,* 23–30.

Horton, S. V., Lovitt, T. C., and Bergerud, D. (1990). The effectiveness of graphic organizers for three classifications of secondary students in content area classes. *Journal of Learning Disabilities, 23,* 12–22, 29.

Hoskins, B. (1987). *Conversations: Language intervention for adolescents.* Allen, TX: Developmental Learning Materials.

Hoskins, B. (1990). Language and literacy: Participating in the conversation. *Topics in Language and Language Disorders, 10*(2), 46–62.

Hoskisson, K., and Krohm, B. (1974). Reading by immersion: Assisted reading. *Elementary English, 5,* 831–836.

Howard, K. A., and Tryon, G. S. (2002). Depressive symptoms in and type of classroom placement for adolescents with LD. *Journal of Learning Disabilities, 35*(2), 185–190.

Howe, M. L., Brainerd, C. J., and Kingma, J. (1985). Storage-retrieval process of normal and learning disabled children: A stages-of-learning analysis of picture-word effects. *Child Development, 56,* 1120–1133.

Howe, M. L., O'Sullivan, J. T., Brainerd, C. J., and Kingma, J. (1989). Localizing the development of ability differences in organized memory.

Contemporary Education Psychology, 14, 336–356.

Hudson, F., Ormsbee, C. K., and Myles, B. S. (1994). Study guides: An instructional tool for equalizing student achievement. *Intervention in School and Clinic, 30*(20), 99–102.

Hudson, P., Lignugaris-Kraft, B., and Miller, T. (1993). Using content enhancements to improve the performance of adolescents with learning disabilities in content classes. *Learning Disabilities Research and Practice, 8,* 106–126.

Hudson, R. (1996). *Gramopoly.* East Moline, IL: LinguiSystems.

Huefner, D. S. (1988). The consulting teacher model: Risks and opportunities. *Exceptional Children, 54,* 403–414.

Hughes, C. A. (1996). Memory and test-taking strategies. In D. D. Deshler, E. S. Ellis, and B. K. Lenz (Eds.), *Teaching adolescents with learning disabilities: Strategies and methods* (2nd ed., pp. 209–266). Denver: Love.

Hughes, C. A., and Schumaker, J. B. (1991). Test-taking strategy instruction for adolescents with learning disabilities. *Exceptionality, 2,* 205–221.

Hughes, C. A., Ruhl, K. L., Deshler, D. D., and Schumaker, J. B. (1995). *The assignment completion strategy.* Lawrence, KS: Edge Enterprises.

Hughes, C. A., Schumaker, J. B., and Deshler, D. D. (2001). *The essay test-taking strategy.* Lawrence, KS: Edge Enterprises.

Hughes, C. A., Schumaker, J. B., Deshler, D. D., and Mercer, C. D. (1993). *The test-taking strategy* (rev. ed.). Lawrence, KS: Edge Enterprises.

Hughes, M. T., Schumm, J. S., and Vaughn, S. (1999). Home literacy activities: Perceptions and practices of Hispanic parents of children with learning disabilities. *Learning Disabilities Quarterly, 22,* 224–235.

Hutchinson, N. L. (1993a). Effects of cognitive strategy instruction on algebra problem solving of adolescents with learning disabilities. *Learning Disability Quarterly, 16*(1), 34–63.

Hutchinson, N. L. (1993b). Integrative strategy instruction: An elusive ideal for teaching adolescents with learning disabilities. *Journal of Learning Disabilities, 26*(7), 428–432.

Hutchinson, N. L. (1993c). Second invited response: Students with disabilities and mathematics education reform—Let the dialogue begin. *Remedial and Special Education (RASE), 14*(6), 20–23.

Hynd, G. W., Obrzut, J. E., and Bowen, S. M. (1987). Neuropsychological basis of attention and memory in learning disabilities. In H. L. Swanson (Ed.), *Advances in learning and behavior disabilities: Memory and learning disabilities* (pp. 175–201). Greenwich, CT: JAI Press.

Idol, L. (1987a). A critical thinking map to improve content area comprehension of poor readers. *Remedial and Special Education, 8*(4), 28–40.

Idol, L. (1987b). Group story mapping: A comprehension strategy for both skilled and unskilled readers. *Journal of Learning Disabilities, 20*(4), 196–205.

Idol, L. (1997). Key questions related to building collaborative and inclusive schools. *Journal of Learning Disabilities, 30*(4), 384–394.

Idol, L., Nevin, A., and Paolucci-Whitcomb, P. (2000). *Collaborative consultation* (3rd ed.). Austin, TX: PRO-ED.

Idol, L., Paolucci-Whitcomb, P., and Nevin, A. (1986). *Collaborative consultation.* Austin, TX: PRO-ED.

Ikeda, M. J., Rahn-Blakeslee, A., Niebling, B. C., Allison, R., and Stumme, A. (2006). *Evaluating evidence-based practice in response-to-intervention systems.* NASP *Communiqué, 34*(8). Retrieved December 14, 2007, from www.nasponline.org/publications/cq/index .aspx?Vol=34&Issue=8.

Imber, S. C., Imber, S. C., and Rothstein, C. (1979). Modifying independent work habits: An effective teacher-parent communication program. *Exceptional Children, 46,* 218–221.

Irvine, J. J. (1991). *Black students and school failure: Policies, practice, and prescriptions.* New York: Praeger.

Isaacson, S. (1988). Assessing the writing product: Qualitative and quantitative measures. *Exceptional Children, 54,* 528–534.

Isaacson, S., and Gleason, M. M. (1997). Mechanical obstacles to writing: What can teachers do to help students with learning problems? *Learning Disabilities Research and Practice, 12*(3), 188–194.

Jackson, H. J., and Boag, P. G. (1981). The efficacy of self-control procedures as motivational strategies with mentally retarded persons: A review of the literature and guidelines for future research. *Australian Journal of Developmental Disabilities, 7,* 65–79.

Janney, R., and Snell, M. E. (2000). *Behavioral support.* Baltimore: Brookes.

Jarvis, P. A., and Justin, E. M. (1992). Social sensitivity in adolescents and adults with learning disabilities. *Adolescence, 27*(108), 977–988.

Jenkins, J. R., Antil, L. R., Wayne, S. K., and Vadasy, P. F. (2003). How cooperative learning works for special education and remedial students. *Exceptional Children, 69,* 279–292.

Jewell, T. A., and Pratt, D. (1999). Literature discussions in the primary grades: Children's thoughtful discourse about books and what teachers can do to make it happen. *The Reading Teacher, 52,* 842–850.

Jiménez, R. T., and Gersten, R. (1999). Lessons and dilemmas derived from the literacy instruction of two Latina/o teachers. *American Educational Research Journal, 36,* 265–301.

Jitendra, A. K., Hoff, K., and Beck, M. M. (1999). Teaching middle school students with learning disabilities to solve word problems using a schema-based approach. *Remedial and Special Education, 20*(1), 50–64.

Johns, B. H., Crowley, E. P., and Guetzloe, E. (2002). Planning the IEP for students with emotional and behavioral disorders. *Focus on Exceptional Children, 32*(9), 1–12.

Johnson, C. J., Beitchman, J. H., Young, A., Escobar, M., Atkinson, L., Wilson, B. Brownlie, E. B., Douglas, L., Taback, N., Lam, I., and Wang, M. (1999). Fourteen-year follow-up of children with and without speech/language impairments: Speech/language stability and outcomes. *Journal of Speech, Language, and Hearing Research, 42,* 744–760.

Johnson, D. D., and Pearson, P. D. (1984). *Teaching reading vocabulary* (2nd ed.). New York: Holt, Rinehart and Winston.

Johnson, D. D., Pittelman, S. D., and Heimlich, J. E. (1986). Semantic mapping. *The Reading Teacher, 39*(8), 778–783.

Johnson, D. J., and Myklebust, H. R. (1967). *Learning disabilities: Educational principles and practices.* New York: Grune & Stratton.

Johnson, D. W., and Johnson, R. T. (1975). *Learning together and alone*. Englewood Cliffs, NJ: Prentice Hall.

Johnson, D. W., and Johnson, R. T. (1984a). Classroom learning structure and attitudes toward handicapped students in mainstream settings: A theoretical model and research evidence. In R. Jones (Ed.), *Special education in transition: Attitudes toward the handicapped*. Reston, VA.: ERIC Clearinghouse on Handicapped and Gifted Children, Council for Exceptional Children.

Johnson, D. W., and Johnson, R. T. (1984b). Building acceptance of differences between handicapped and nonhandicapped students: The effects of cooperative and individualistic problems. *Journal of Social Psychology, 122,* 257–267.

Johnson, D., Johnson, R., and Holubec, E. (1993). *Cooperation in the classroom*. Edina, MN: Interaction.

Johnson, R. T., and Johnson, D. W. (1986). Action research: Cooperative learning in the science classroom. *Science and Children, 24,* 31–32.

Johnson Santamaria, L., Fletcher, T. V., and Bos, C. S. (2002). Scaffolded instruction: Promoting biliteracy for second language learners with language/learning disabilities. In A. Artiles and A. Ortiz (Eds.), *English language learners with special education needs: Identification, assessment, and instruction*. Washington, DC: Center for Applied Linguistics.

Johnston, L. D., O'Malley, P. M., and Bachman, J. G. (2003). *Monitoring the future national results on adolescent drug use: Overview of key findings, 2002* (NIH Publication No. 03–5374). Bethesda, MD: National Institute on Drug Abuse.

Jones, D. J., Fox, M. M., Haroutun-Babigian, H. M., and Hutton, H. E. (1980). Epidemiology of anorexia nervosa in Monroe County, New York: 1960–1976. *Psychosomatic Medicine, 42*(6), 551–558.

Jordan, N. C., and Hanich, L. B. (2003). Characteristics of children with moderate mathematics deficiencies: A longitudinal perspective. *Learning Disabilities Research and Practice, 18*(4), 213–221.

Juel, C. (1983). The development and use of mediated word identification. *Reading Research Quarterly, 18,* 306–327.

Juel, C. (1994). *Learning to read and write in one elementary school*. New York: Springer-Verlag.

Juvonen, J., and Bear, G. (1992). Social adjustment of children with and without learning disabilities in integrated classrooms. *Journal of Educational Psychology, 84*(3), 322–330.

Kail, R., and Leonard, L. B. (1986). Word-finding abilities in language-impaired children. *ASHA Monograph Number 25*. Rockville, MD: American Speech-Language-Hearing Association.

Kalafat, J. (1990). Adolescent suicide and the implications for school response programs. *The School Counselor, 37,* 359–369.

Kame'enui, E. J., and Carnine, D. W. (1998). *Effective teaching strategies that accommodate diverse learners*. Upper Saddle River, NJ: Prentice Hall.

Kame'enui, E. J., Simmons, D. C., Baker, S., Chard, D., Dickson, S., Gunn, B., Smith, S., Sprick, M., and Lin, S. (1998). Effective strategies for teaching beginning reading. In E. J. Kame'enui and D. W. Carnine (Eds.), *Effective teaching strategies that accommodate diverse learners* (pp. 45–70). Columbus, OH: Merrill.

Kamhi, A. G. (1999). To use or not to use: Factors that influence the selection of new treatment approaches. *Language, Speech, and Hearing Services in Schools, 30,* 92–98.

Kaminski, R. A., and Good, R. H. (1996). Toward a technology for assessing basic early literacy skills. *School Psychology Review, 25*(2), 215–227.

Kandel, D. B. (2002). *Stages and pathways of drug involvement: Examining the gateway hypothesis*. New York: Cambridge University Press.

Karp, N. (1996). Individualized wrap-around services for children with emotional, behavior, and mental disorders. In G. H. S. Singer, L. E. Powers, and A. L. Olson (Eds.), *Redefining Family Support* (pp. 291–312). Baltimore: Brookes.

Katz-Leavy, J. W., Lourie, I. S., Stroul, B. A., and Ziegler-Dendy, C. (1992, July). *Individualized services in a system of care*. Washington, DC: CASSP Technical Assistance Center, Center for Child Health and Mental Health Policy, Georgetown University Child Development Center.

Kauffman, J. M. (1995). Why we must celebrate diversity of restrictive environments. *Learning Disabilities Research and Practice, 10,* 225–232.

Kauffman, J. M. (2001). *Characteristics of children's behavior disorders* (7th ed.). Columbus, OH: Merrill.

Kauffman, J., Hallahan, D., Haas, K., Brame, T., and Boren, R. (1978). Imitating children's errors to improve spelling performance. *Journal of Learning Disabilities, 11,* 33–38.

Kaufmann, L., Handl, P., and Thony, B. (2003). Evaluation of a numeracy intervention program focusing on basic numerical knowledge and conceptual knowledge: A pilot study. *Journal of Learning Disabilities, 36,* 564–573.

Kavale, K., and Forness, S. R. (1996). Social skill deficits and learning disabilities: A meta-analysis. *Journal of Learning Disabilities, 29*(3), 226–237.

Kazdin, A. E. (1989). *Behavior modification in applied settings* (4th ed.). Pacific Grove, CA: Brooks/Cole.

Kelly, B., Gersten, R., and Carnine, D. (1990). Student error patterns as a function of curriculum design: Teaching fractions to remedial high school students and high school students with learning disabilities. *Journal of Learning Disabilities, 23,* 23–29.

Kiewra, K. A. (1985). Providing the instructor's notes: An effective addition to student notetaking. *Educational Psychologist, 20,* 33–39.

Kim, A. (2002). *Effects of Computer-Assisted Collaborative Strategic Reading (CACSR) on reading comprehension for students with learning disabilities*. Unpublished doctoral dissertation, University of Texas, Austin.

Kim, A., Vaughn, S., Klingner, J. K., Woodruff, A. L., Klein, C., and Kouzekanani, K. (2003). *Improving the reading comprehension of middle school students with reading disabilities through Computer-Assisted-Collaborative Strategic Reading*. Manuscript submitted for publication.

Kim, A., Vaughn, S., Wanzek, J., and Wei, S. (2004). Graphic organizers and their effects on the reading comprehension of students with LD: A synthesis of research. *Journal of Learning Disabilities, 37*(2), 105–118.

King, C. M., and Parent Johnson, L. M. (1999). Constructing meaning via reciprocal teaching. *Reading Research and Instruction, 38*(3), 169–186.

King-Sears, M. E., Mercer, C. D., and Sindelar, P. T. (1992). Toward independence with key word mnemonics: A strategy for science vocabulary instruction. *Remedial and Special Education, 13*(5), 22–33.

Kirk, S. A., and Chalfant, J. (1984). *Academic and developmental learning disabilities*. Denver: Love.

Kirk, S. A., Kirk, W. D., and Minskoff, E. H. (1985). *Phonic remedial reading lessons*. Novato, CA: Academic Therapy Publications.

Kirk, S. A. (1962). *Educating exceptional children*. Boston: Houghton Mifflin.

Kirkpatrick, E. M., and Schwarz, C. M. (Eds.). (1982). *Chambers idioms*. Edinburgh, Scotland: Chambers.

Kistner, J., and Osborne, M. (1987). A longitudinal study of LD children's self-evaluations. *Learning Disability Quarterly, 10,* 258–266.

Klausmeier, H. J., and Sipple, T. S. (1980). *Learning and teaching concepts: A strategy for testing applications theory*. New York: Academic Press.

Klingner, J. K., and Edwards, P. (2006). Cultural considerations with response-to-intervention models. *Reading Research Quarterly, 41,* 108–117.

Klingner, J. K., Méndez Barletta, L., and Hoover, J. (in press). Response to intervention models and English language learners. In J. K. Klingner, J. Hoover, and L. Baca (Eds.), *English Language Learners who struggle with reading: Language acquisition or learning disabilities?* Thousand Oaks, CA: Corwin Press.

Klingner, J. K., and Solano-Flores, G. (2007). Cultural responsiveness in response-to-intervention models. In *Accommodating students with disabilities: What works?* Educational Testing Service.

Klingner, J. K., and Vaughn, S. (1996). Reciprocal teaching of reading comprehension strategies for students with learning disabilities who use English as a second language. *Elementary School Journal, 96,* 275–293.

Klingner, J. K., and Vaughn, S. (1998). Using collaborative strategic reading. *Teaching Exceptional Children, 30*(6), 32–37.

Klingner, J. K., and Vaughn, S. (1999a). Promoting reading comprehension, content learning, and English acquisition through collaborative strategic reading (CSR). *The Reading Teacher, 52*(7), 738–747.

Klingner, J. K., and Vaughn, S. (1999b). Students' perceptions of instructional practice. *Exceptional Children, 66,* 23–37.

Klingner, J. K., and Vaughn, S. (2000). The helping behaviors of fifth graders while using collaborative strategic reading during ESL content classes. *TESOL Quarterly, 34*(1), 69–98.

Klingner, J. K., and Vaughn, S. (2002). Joyce: The changing roles and responsibilities of an LD specialist. *Learning Disability Quarterly, 25,* 19–32.

Klingner, J. K., Vaughn, S., Argüelles, M. E., Hughes, M. T., and Ahwee, S. (in press). Collaborative strategic reading: "Real world" lessons from classroom teachers. *Remedial and Special Education.*

Klingner, J. K., Vaughn, S., and Boardman, A. (2007). *Teaching reading comprehension to students with learning disabilities*. New York: Guilford.

Klingner, J. K., Vaughn, S., Dimino, J., Schumm, J. S., and Bryant, D. P. (2001). *From clunk to click: Collaborative Strategic Reading*. Longmont, CO: Sopris West.

Klingner, J. K., Vaughn, S., and Schumm, J. S. (1998). Collaborative strategic reading during social studies in heterogeneous fourth-grade classrooms. *Elementary School Journal, 99,* 3–22.

Klingner, J. K., Vaughn, S., Schumm, J. S., Cohen, P., and Forgan, J. W. (1998). Inclusion or pull-out: Which do students prefer? *Journal of Learning Disabilities, 32*(2), 148–158.

Kloomok, S., and Cosden, M. (1994). Self-concept in children with learning disabilities: The relationship between global self-concept, academic discounting, nonacademic self-concept, and perceived social support. *Learning Disability Quarterly, 17*(2), 140–153.

Knoff, H. M. (2003). *The stop & think social skills program.* Longmont, CO: Sopris West.

Konopka, G. (1973). Requirements for the healthy development of adolescent youth. *Adolescence, 8*(31), 2–25.

Kosc, L. (1981). Neuropsychological implications of diagnosis and treatment of mathematical learning disabilities. *Topics in Learning and Learning Disabilities, 1*(3), 19–30.

Kosiewicz, M. M., Hallahan, D. P., Lloyd, J. W., and Graves, A. W. (1982). Effects of self-instruction and self-correction procedures on handwriting performance. *Learning Disability Quarterly, 5*(1), 71–78.

Koskinen, P. A., and Blum, I. H. (1984). Paired repeated reading: A classroom strategy for developing fluent reading. *The Reading Teacher, 40,* 70–75.

Koskinen, P. S., Blum, I. H., Bisson, S. A., Phillips, S. M., Creamer, T. S., and Baker, T. K. (1999). Shared reading, books, and audiotapes: Supporting diverse students in school and at home. *The Reading Teacher, 52,* 430–444.

Kozulin, A., and Presseisen, B. Z. (1995). Mediated learning experience and psychological tools: Vygotsky's and Feuerstein's perspectives in a study of student learning. *Educational Psychologists, 30,* 67–75.

Krashen, S. (1985). *The input hypothesis: Issues and implications.* London: Longman.

Kress, R. A., and Johnson, M. S. (1970). Martin. In A. J. Harris (Ed.), *Casebook on reading disability* (pp. 1–24). New York: David McKay.

Kronik, D. (1977). A parent's thought for parents and teachers. In N. Haring and B. Bateman (Eds.), *Teaching the learning disabled child.* Englewood Cliffs, NJ: Prentice Hall.

Krug, R. S. (1983). Substance abuse. In C. E. Walker and M. C. Roberts (Eds.), *Handbook of clinical child psychology* (pp. 853–879). New York: Wiley.

Kucer, S. B. (1986). Helping writers get the "big picture." *Journal of Reading, 30*(1), 18–25.

Kuder, S. J. (1997). *Teaching students with language and communication disabilities.* Boston: Allyn & Bacon.

Kuhn, M. R., and Stahl, S. (2003). Fluency: A review of developmental and remedial practices. *Journal of Educational Psychology, 95,* 3–21.

Kuhne, M., and Wiener, J. (2000). Stability of social status of children with and without learning disabilities. *Learning Disability Quarterly, 23*(1), 64–75.

LaBerge, D., and Samuels, S. J. (1974). Toward a theory of automatic information processing in reading. *Cognitive Psychology, 6,* 293–323.

Ladson-Billings, G. (1995). Toward a theory of culturally relevant pedagogy. *American Educational Research Journal, 32,* 465–491.

LaGreca, A. M. (November 1982). Issues in the assessment of social skills with learning disabled children. In *Children's social skills: Future directions,* S. Beck (Chair). Paper presented at the annual meeting of the Association for the Advancement of Behavior Therapy, Los Angeles, CA.

Lahey, M., and Edwards, J. (1999). Naming errors of children with specific language impairment. *Journal of Speech, Language, and Hearing Research, 42,* 196–202.

Lancelotta, G. X., and Vaughn, S. R. (1989). Relation between types of aggression and sociometric status: Peer and teacher perceptions. *Journal of Educational Psychology, 81*(1), 86–90. In W. R. Borg, *Applying educational research,* (1993), New York: Longman.

Landrum, T. J., Tankersley, M., and Kauffman, J. M. (2003). What is special about special education for students with emotional or behavioral disorders? *Journal of Special Education, 37,* 148–156.

Langan, J. (1982). *Reading and study skills* (2nd ed.). New York: McGraw-Hill.

Langdon, H. W. (1992). Speech and language assessment of LEP/bilingual Hispanic students. In H. W. Langdon and L. L. Cheng (Eds.), *Hispanic children and adults with communication disorders* (pp. 201–271). Gaithersburg, MD: Aspen.

Langer, J. A. (1981). From theory to practice: A prereading plan. *Journal of Reading, 25*(2), 152–156.

Langer, J. A., and Nicolich, M. (1981). Prior knowledge and its effects on comprehension. *Journal of Reading Behavior, 13,* 375–378.

Lankford, F. G. (1974). *Some computational strategies in seventh grade pupils.* Unpublished manuscript, University of Virginia.

Lardieri, L. A., Blacher, J., and Swanson, H. L. (2000). Sibling relationships and parent stress in families of children with and without learning disabilities. *Learning Disability Quarterly, 23*(2), 105–116.

Larkin, M. J., and Ellis, E. S. (1998). Adolescents with learning disabilities. In B. Y. L. Wong (Ed.), *Learning about learning disabilities* (2nd ed., pp. 557–584). San Diego, CA: Academic Press.

Larsen, S. C., Parker, R., and Trenholme, B. (1978). The effects of syntactic complexity upon arithmetic performance. *Learning Disability Quarterly, 1*(4), 80–85.

Larsen-Freeman, D. (2001). Teaching grammar. In M. Celce-Murcia (Ed.), *Teaching English as a second or foreign language* (pp. 251–266). Boston: Heinle & Heinle.

Larson, N. (2004a). *Saxon math 2* (2nd ed.). Norman, OK: Saxon.

Larson, N. (2004b). *Saxon math 3* (2nd ed.). Norman, OK: Saxon.

Larson, N. (2004c). *Saxon math 4.* Norman, OK: Saxon.

Larson, N. (2004d). *Saxon math K* (2nd ed.). Norman, OK: Saxon.

Lazar, R. T., Warr-Leeper, G. A., Nicholson, C. B., and Johnson, S. (1989). Use of figurative language in classrooms. *ELT Journal, 50,* 43–51.

Lazzari, A. M. (1995). *HELP for grammar.* East Moline, IL: LinguiSystems.

Lazzari, A. M. (1999). *HELP for vocabulary.* East Moline, IL: LinguiSystems.

Lazzari, A. M., and Peters, P. M. (1988). *Help 3.* East Moline, IL: LinguiSystems.

Lazzari, A. M., and Peters, P. M. (1989). *Help 4.* East Moline, IL: LinguiSystems.

Lazzari, A. M., and Peters, P. M. (1991). *Help 5.* East Moline, IL: LinguiSystems.

Lazzari, A. M., and Peters, P. M. (1994a). *HELP for auditory processing.* East Moline, IL: LinguiSystems.

Lazzari, A. M., and Peters, P. M. (1994b). *HELP for word finding.* East Moline, IL: LinguiSystems.

Leadholm, B., and Miller, J. (1992). *Language sample analysis: The Wisconsin guide.* Madison, WI: Bureau for Exceptional Children, Wisconsin Department of Public Education.

Lederer, J. M. (2000). Reciprocal teaching of social studies in inclusive elementary classrooms. *Journal of Learning Disabilities, 33,* 51–106.

Legenza, A. (1974). *Questioning behavior of kindergarten children.* Paper presented at the 19th Annual Convention, International Reading Association.

Leinwand, S., and Burrill, G. (2001). *Improving mathematics education: Resources for decision-making.* Washington, DC: National Academy Press.

LeMare, L., and de la Ronde, M. (2000). Links among social status, service delivery mode, and service delivery preference in LD, low-achieving, and normally achieving elementary-aged children. *Learning Disability Quarterly, 23*(1), 52–62.

Lennox, C., and Siegel, L. S. (1996). The development of phonological rules and visual strategies in average and poor spellers. *Journal of Experimental Child Psychology, 62,* 60–83.

Lennox, C., and Siegel, L. S. (1998). Phonological and orthographic processes in good and poor spellers. In C. Hulme and R. M. Joshi (Eds.), *Reading and spelling development and disorders* (pp. 395–404). Mahwah, NJ: Erlbaum.

Lenz, B. K. (1983). Promoting active learning through effective instruction: Using advance organizers. *Pointer, 27*(2), 11–13.

Lenz, B. K., Alley, G. R., and Schumaker, J. B. (1987). Activating the inactive learner: Advance organizers in the secondary content classroom. *Learning Disability Quarterly, 10*(10), 53–67.

Lenz, B. K., and Bulgren, J. A. (1995). Promoting learning in content classes. In P. A. Cegleka and W. H. Berdine (Eds.), *Effective instruction for students with learning problems* (pp. 385–417). Boston: Allyn & Bacon.

Lenz, B. K., and Hughes, C. A. (1990). A word identification strategy for adolescents with learning disabilities. *Journal of Learning Disabilities, 23*(3), 149–158, 163.

Lenz, B. K., Bulgren, J. A., and Hudson, P. (1990). Content enhancement: A model for promoting the acquisition of content by individuals with learning disabilities. In T. E. Scruggs and B. L. Y. Wong (Eds.), *Intervention research in learning disabilities* (pp. 122–165). New York: Springer-Verlag.

Lenz, B. K., Ellis, E. S., and Scanlon, D. (1996). *Teaching learning strategies to adolescents and adults with learning disabilities.* Austin, TX: PRO-ED.

Lenz, B. K., Schumaker, J., Deshler, D., and Beals, V. (1993). *The word identification strategy.* Lawrence: University of Kansas.

Leon, J. A., and Pepe, H. J. (1983). Self-instructional training: Cognitive behavior modification for remediating arithmetic deficits. *Exceptional Children, 50*(1), 54–60.

Lerner, J. W. (2000). *Learning disabilities: Theories, diagnosis, and teaching strategies* (8th ed.). Boston: Houghton Mifflin.

Levine, M. P. (1987). *Student eating disorders: Anorexia nervosa and bulimia.* Washington, DC: National Education Association.

Levy, B. A., and Lysynchuk, L. (1997). Beginning word recognition: Benefits of training by segmentation and whole word methods. *Scientific Studies of Reading, 1,* 359–387.

Lewis, S. K., and Lawrence-Patterson, E. (1989). Locus of control of children with learning disabilities and perceived locus of control by significant others. *Journal of Learning Disabilities, 22,* 255–257.

Lian M. J., and Aloia, G. F. (1994). Parental responses, roles, and responsibilities. In S. K. Alper, P. J. Schloss, and C. N. Schloss, *Families of students with disabilities* (pp. 51–94). Boston: Allyn & Bacon.

Licht, B. G. (1983). Cognitive-motivational factors that contribute to the achievement of learning disabled children. *Journal of Learning Disabilities, 16,* 483–489.

Linan-Thompson, S., and Vaughn, S. (2007). *Research-based methods of reading instruction for English language learners.* Alexandria, VA: ASCD.

Linan-Thompson, S., Cirino, P. T., and Vaughn, S. (2007). Determining English language learners' response to intervention: Questions and some answers. *Learning Disabilities Quarterly, 30*(3), 185–196.

Linan-Thompson, S., Vaughn, S., Hickman-Davis, P., and Kouzekanani, K. (2003). Effectiveness of supplemental reading instruction for second-grade English language learners with reading difficulties. *Elementary School Journal, 103*(3), 221–238.

Linan-Thompson, S., Vaughn, S., Prater, K., and Cirino, P. T. (2006). Response to intervention for English language learners. *Journal of Learning Disabilities, 39,* 390–398.

Lindamood, P. A., and Lindamood, P. (1998). *The Lindamood phoneme sequencing program for reading, spelling, and speech: The LiPS program.* Austin, TX: PRO-ED.

LinguiSystems Staff. (1997). *WORDopoly: A play with words game.* East Moline, IL: LinguiSystems.

Link, D. (1980). *Essential learning skills and the low achieving student at the secondary level: A rating of the importance of 24 academic abilities.* Unpublished master's thesis, University of Kansas, Lawrence.

Lipson, M. Y., Mosenthal, J. H., and Mekkelsen, J. (1999). The nature of comprehension among grade 2 children: Variability in retellings as a function of development, test, and task. In T. Shanahan and F. Rodgrigues-Brown (Eds.), *National reading conference yearbook 48.* Chicago: National Reading Conference.

Loftus, G., and Loftus, E. R. (1976). *Human memory.* Hillsdale, NJ: Erlbaum.

LoGiudice, M., and LoGiudice, C. (1997). *100% grammar.* East Moline, IL: LinguiSystems.

Lovett, M. W., Borden, S. L., Warren-Chaplin, P. M., Lacerenza, L., DeLuca, T., and Giovinazzo, R. (1996). Text comprehension training for disabled readers: An evaluation of reciprocal teaching and text analysis training programs. *Brain and Language, 54,* 477–480.

Lovitt, T. C., and Horton, S. V. (1994). Strategies for adapting science textbooks for youth with learning disabilities. *Remedial and Special Education, 15,* 105–116.

Lovitt, T., Rudsit, J., Jenkins, J., Pious, C., and Benedetti, D. (1985). Two methods of adaptive science materials for learning disabled and regular seventh graders. *Learning Disability Quarterly, 8,* 275–285.

Lovitt, T., Rudsit, J., Jenkins, J., Pious, C., and Benedetti, D. (1986). Adapting science materials for regular and learning disabled seventh graders. *Journal of Remedial and Special Education, 7,* 31–39.

Lucangeli, D., Galderisi, D., and Cornoldi, C. (1995). Specific and general transfer effects following metamemory training. *Learning Disabilities Research and Practice, 10,* 11–21.

Lucyshyn, J. M., Dunlap, G., and Albin, R. W. (Eds.) (2002). *Families and positive behavior support.* Baltimore: Brookes.

Lucyshyn, J. M., Horner, R. H., Dunlap, G., Albin, R. W., and Ben, K. R. (2002). Positive behavior support with families. In J. M. Lucyshyn, G. Dunlap, and R. W. Albin (Eds.), *Families and positive behavior support* (pp. 3–43). Baltimore: Brookes.

Lundberg, I. (1995). The computer as a tool of remediation in the education of students with reading disabilities: A theory-based approach. *Learning Disabilities Quarterly, 18*(2), 89–99.

Lyerla, K. D., Schumaker, J. B., and Deshler, D. D. (1994). *The paragraph writing strategy* (rev. ed.). Lawrence, KS: Edge Enterprises.

Lynch, E. W., and Stein, R. (1982). Perspectives on parent participation in special education. *Exceptional Education Quarterly, 3*(2), 56–63.

Lyon, G. R. (1998). *Congressional testimony: Reading Research.* Washington, DC: Committee on Labor and Human Resources.

Lyon, G. R., Fletcher, J. M., Shaywitz, S. E., Shaywitz, B. A., Torgesen, J. K., Wood, F. B., Schulte, A., and Olson, R. (2001). Rethinking learning disabilities. In C. E. Finn, Jr., A. J. Rotherham, and C. R. Kokanson, Jr. (Eds.), *Rethinking special education for a new century* (pp. 259–288). Washington, DC: Thomas B. Fordham Foundation.

Lysynchuk, L., Pressley, M., and Vye, N. (1990). Reciprocal teaching improves standardized reading-comprehension performance in poor comprehenders. *The Elementary School Journal, 90*(5), 469–484.

MacArthur, C. A. (Winter 1988). Computers and writing instruction. *Teaching Exceptional Children,* 37–39.

MacArthur, C. A., Schwartz, S. S., Graham, S., Molloy, D., and Harris, K. (1996). Integration of strategy instruction into a whole-language classroom: A case study. *Learning Disabilities Research and Practice, 11,* 168–176.

MacArthur, C., Graham, S., and Schwartz, S. (1991). Knowledge of revision and revising behavior among learning disabled students. *Learning Disability Quarterly, 14,* 61–73.

MacArthur, C., Graham, S., Schwartz, S., and Schafer, W. D. (1995). Evaluation of a writing instruction model that integrated a process approach, strategy instruction, and word processing. *Learning Disability Quarterly, 18,* 278–291.

Maccini, P., and Gagnon, J. C. (2002). Perceptions and application of NCTM standards by special and general education teachers. *Exceptional Children, 68,* 325–344.

Macrorie, K. (1980). *The I search paper.* Portsmouth, NH: Heinemann.

MacWilliams, L. J. (1978). Mobility board games: Not only for rainy days. *Teaching Exceptional Children, 11*(1), 22–25.

Madelaine, A., and Wheldall, K. (1999). Curriculum-based measurement of reading: A critical review. *International Journal of Disability, Development and Education, 46,* 71–85.

Maheady, L., Harper, G. F., and Mallette, B. (2001). Peer-mediated instruction and interventions and students with mild disabilities. *Remedial and Special Education, 22,* 4–14.

Maheady, L., Harper, G. F., and Sacca, M. K. (1988). Peer mediated instruction: A promising approach to meeting the needs of learning disabled adolescents. *Learning Disability Quarterly, 11,* 108–113.

Malone, L. D., and Mastropieri, M. A. (1992). Reading comprehension instruction: Summarization and self-monitoring training for students with learning disabilities. *Exceptional Children, 58,* 270–279.

Mandler, J. M., and Johnson, N. S. (1977). Remembrance of things passed: Story structure and recall. *Cognitive Psychology, 9,* 111–151.

Mandoli, M., Mandoli, P., and McLaughlin, T. F. (1982). Effects of same-age peer tutoring on the spelling performance of a mainstreamed elementary learning disabled student. *Learning Disability Quarterly, 5*(2), 185–189.

Mann, V. (1991). Language problems: A key to early reading problems. In B. Y. L. Wong (Ed.), *Learning about learning disabilities* (pp. 129–162). San Diego, CA: Academic Press.

Manzo, A. V. (1969). The request procedure. *Journal of Reading, 13,* 123–126.

Manzo, A. V., and Manzo, U. C. (1990). *Content area reading: A heuristic approach.* Columbus, OH: Merrill.

Manzo, A. V., and Manzo, U. C. (1993). *Literacy disorders: Holistic diagnosis and remediation.* Fort Worth, TX: Harcourt Brace Jovanovich.

Margalit, M., Raviv, A., and Ankonina, D. B. (1992). Coping and coherence among parents with disabled children. *Journal of Clinical Child Psychology, 21*(3), 202–209.

Mariage, T. V. (2000). Constructing educational possibilities: A sociolinguistic examination of meaning-making in "sharing chair." *Learning Disability Quarterly, 23,* 79–103.

Markham, L. (1976). Influence of handwriting quality on teacher evaluation of written work. *American Educational Research Journal, 13,* 277–283.

Marsh, L. G., and Cooke, N. L. (1996). The effects of using manipulatives in teaching math problem solving to students with learning disabilities. *Learning Disabilities Research and Practice, 11,* 58–65.

Marston, D., Muyskens, P., Lau, M., & Canter, H. (2003). Problem solving model for decision-making with high-incidence disabilities: The Minneapolis experience. *Learning Disabilities Research and Practice, 18*(3), 187–200.

Martin, J. E., and Marshall, L. H. (1995). Choicemaker: A comprehensive self-determination transition program. *Intervention in School and Clinic, 30,* 147–156.

Martin, J. H., and Friedberg, A. (1986). *Writing to read. A parent's guide to the new, early learning program for young children.* New York: Warner.

Martinez, M., and Teale, W. H. (February 1988). Reading in a kindergarten classroom library. *The Reading Teacher,* 568–572.

Martinez-Roldan, C. M., and López-Robertson, J. M. (2000). Initiating literature circles in a first-grade bilingual classroom. *The Reading Teacher, 53,* 270–281.

Mason, D. J., Humphreys, G. W., and Kent, L. S. (2003). Exploring selective attention in ADHD: Visual search through space and time. *Journal of Child Psychology and Psychiatry, 44*(8), 1158–1176.

Massaro, D. W., and Cowan, N. (1993). Information processing models: Microscopes of the mind. *Annual Review of Psychology, 44,* 383–425.

Mastropieri, M. A., and Scruggs, T. E. (1989). Reconstructive elaborations: Strategies that facilitate content learning. *Learning Disabilities Focus, 4,* 73–77.

Mastropieri, M. A., and Scruggs, T. E. (1997). Best practices in promoting reading comprehension in students with learning disabilities: 1976–1996. *Remedial and Special Education, 18,* 197–213.

Mastropieri, M. A., and Scruggs, T. E. (1998). Constructing more meaningful relationships in the classroom: Mnemonic research into practice. *Learning Disabilities Research and Practice, 13*(3), 138–145.

Mastropieri, M. A., Leinart, A., and Scruggs, T. E. (1999). Strategies to increase reading fluency. *Intervention in School and Clinic, 34*(5), 278–283.

Mastropieri, M. A., Scruggs, T. E., and Shiah, S. (1991). Mathematics instruction for learning disabled students: A review of research. *Learning Disabilities Research and Practice, 6,* 89–98.

Mastropieri, M. A., Scruggs, T. E., Bakken, J. P., and Whedon, C. (1996). Reading comprehension: A synthesis of research in learning disabilities. *Advances in Learning and Behavioral Disabilities, 10B,* 201–227.

Mastropieri, M. A., Scruggs, T. E., Hamilton, S. L., Wolfe, S., Whedon, C., and Canevaro, A. (1996). Promoting thinking skills of students with learning disabilities: Effects on recall and comprehension of expository prose. *Exceptionality, 6,* 1–11.

Mastropieri, M. A., Scruggs, T. E., Spencer, V., and Fontana, J. (2003). Promoting success in high school world history: Peer tutoring versus guided notes. *Learning Disabilities Research and Practice, 19*(1), 52–65.

Mastropieri, M. A., Sweda, J., and Scruggs, T. E. (2000). Putting mnemonic strategies to work in an inclusive classroom. *Learning Disabilities Research and Practice, 15*(2), 69–74.

Mathes, P. A., and Fuchs, L. S. (1994). The efficacy of peer tutoring in reading for students with mild disabilities: A best-evidence synthesis. *School Psychology Review, 23,* 59–80.

Mathes, P. G., Grek, M. L., Howard, J. K., Babyak, A. E., and Allen, S. H. (1999). Peer-assisted learning strategies for first-grade readers: A tool for preventing early reading failure. *Learning Disabilities Research and Practice, 14,* 50–60.

Mathes, P. G., Torgesen, J. K., and Howard, A. J. (2001). The effects of peer-assisted literacy strategies for first-grade readers with and without additional computer-assisted instruction in phonological awareness. *American Educational Research Journal, 38*(2), 371–410.

Mathinos, D. A. (1987). *Communicative abilities of disabled and nondisabled children.* Paper presented at the biennial meeting of the Society for Research in Child Development, Baltimore, MD.

Matthews, D. D. (Ed.). (2003). *Learning disabilities sourcebook.* Detroit, MI: Omnigraphics.

Matuszny, R. M., Banda, D. R., and Coleman, T. J. (2007, Mar./Apr.). A progressive plan for building collaborative relationships with parents from diverse backgrounds. *Teaching Exceptional Children,* 24–31.

Maxwell, J. C., and Liu, L. Y. (1998). *Texas school survey of substance use among students: Grades 7–12.* (ERIC Document Reproduction No. 429256). Austin: Texas Commission on Alcohol and Drug Abuse.

Mayer, R. E. (1979). Twenty years of research on advance organizers: Assimilation theory is still the best predictor of results. *Instructional Science, 8,* 133–167.

Mayes, S. D., Calhoun, S. L., and Crowell, E. W. (2000). Learning disabilities and ADHD: Overlapping spectrum disorders. *Journal of Learning Disabilities, 33,* 417–424.

McCardle, P., and Chhabra, V. (2004). *The voice of evidence in reading research.* Baltimore: Brookes.

McCauley, J. K., and McCauley, D. S. (1992). Using choral reading to promote language learning for ESL students. *The Reading Teacher, 45,* 526–533.

McCormick, S., and Cooper, J. O. (1991). Can SQ3R facilitate secondary learning disabled students' literal comprehension of expository text? Three experiments. *Reading Psychology, 12,* 239–271.

McDonald, M., and Shaw-King, A. (1994). *Listening in room 14.* East Moline, IL: LinguiSystems.

McDonough, K. M. (1989). Analysis of the expressive language characteristics of emotionally handicapped students in social interactions. *Behavior Disorders, 14,* 127–139.

McGregor, K. K., and Leonard, L. B. (1989). Facilitating word-finding skills of language-impaired children. *Journal of Speech and Hearing Disorders, 54,* 141–147.

McIntosh, R., Vaughn, S., and Bennerson, D. (1995). FAST social skills training for students with learning disabilities. *Teaching Exceptional Children, 28,* 37–41.

McIntosh, R., Vaughn, S., and Zaragoza, N. (1991). A review of social interventions for students with learning disabilities. *Journal of Learning Disabilities, 24*(8), 451–458.

McIntosh, R., Vaughn, S., Schumm, J., Haager, D., and Lee, O. (1993). Observations of students with learning disabilities in general education classrooms: You don't bother me and I won't bother you. *Exceptional Children, 60,* 249–261.

McIntyre, C. W., and Pickering, J. S. (1995). *Clinical studies of multisensory structured language education for students with dyslexia and related disorders.* Poughkeepsie, NY: Hamco.

McKeown, M. G., and Beck, I. L. (2004). Transforming knowledge into professional development resources: Six teachers implement a model of teaching for understanding text. *The Elementary School Journal, 104,* 391–408.

McKeown, M. G., Beck, I. S., Sinatra, G. M., and Loxterman, J. A. (1992). The contribution of prior knowledge and coherent text to comprehension. *Reading Research Quarterly, 27,* 78–93.

McKinley, N., and Larson, V. L. (1991, November). *Seven, eighth, and ninth graders' conversations in two experimental conditions.* Paper presented at the annual convention of the American Speech-Language-Hearing Association, Atlanta, GA.

McKinney, J. D., and Hocutt, A. M. (1982). Public school involvement of parents of learning disabled and average achievers. *Exceptional Education Quarterly, 3*(2), 64–73.

McKinney, J. D., and Hocutt, A. M. (1988). Policy issues in the evaluation of the regular education initiative. *Learning Disabilities Focus, 4,* 15–23.

McKinney, J. D., McClure, S., and Feagans, L. (1982). Classroom behavior of learning disabled children. *Learning Disabilities Quarterly, 5,* 45–52.

McLoughlin, J. A., and Senn, C. (1994). Siblings of children with disabilities. In S. K. Alper, P. J. Schloss, and C. N. Schloss (Eds.), *Families of students with disabilities* (pp. 95–122). Boston: Allyn & Bacon.

McNaughton, D., Hughes, C., and Ofiesh, N. (1997). Proofreading for students with learning disabilities: Integrating computer and strategy use. *Learning Disabilities Research and Practice, 12*(1), 16–28.

Meichenbaum, D. (1977). *Cognitive-behavior modification: An integrative approach.* New York: Plenum.

Meichenbaum, D. (1985). *Stress inoculation training: A clinical guidebook.* Elmsford, NY: Pergamon.

Meichenbaum, D., and Biemiller, A. (1998). *Nurturing independent learners: Helping students take change of their learning.* Cambridge, MA: Brookline.

Meltzer, L., Ranjini, R., Sales Pollica, L., Roditi, B., Sayer, J., and Theokas, C. (2004). Positive and negative self-perceptions: Is there a cyclical relationship between teachers' and students' perceptions of effort, strategy use, and academic performance? *Learning Disabilities Research and Practice, 19*(1), 33–44.

Menke, P. J., and Pressley, M. (1994). Elaborative interrogation: Using "why" questions to enhance the learning from text. *Journal of Reading, 37,* 642–645.

Menyuk, P. (1971). *The acquisition and development of language.* Englewood Cliffs, NJ: Prentice Hall.

Mercer, C. D., and Mercer, A. R. (1989). *Teaching students with learning problems* (3rd ed.). Columbus, OH: Merrill.

Mercer, C. D., and Mercer, A. R. (1993). *Teaching students with learning problems* (4th ed.). New York: Merrill/Macmillan.

Mercer, C. D., and Mercer, A. R. (2005). *Teaching students with learning problems.* Upper Saddle River, NJ: Merrill/Prentice-Hall.

Mercer, C. D., Mercer, A. R., and Bott, D. A. (1984). *Self-correcting learning materials for the classroom.* Columbus, OH: Merrill.

Merrell, K. W., and Stein, S. (1992). Behavior problems of learning-disabled, low-achieving, and average boys: A comparative study with the Conners Teacher Ratings Scales-28. *Journal of Psychoeducational Assessment, 10,* 76–82.

Merritt, D. D., and Culatta, B. (1998). *Language intervention in the classroom.* San Diego, CA: Singular.

Mesmer, H. A. E. (1999). Scaffolding a crucial transition using text with some decodability. *The Reading Teacher, 53*(2), 130–142.

Meyer, M. S., and Felton, R. H. (1999). Repeated reading to enhance fluency: Old approaches and new directions. *Annals of Dyslexia, 49,* 283–306.

Miller, R. J., Lombard, R. C., & Corbey, S. A. (2007). *Transition assessment: Planning transi-*

tion and IEP development for youth with mild to moderate disabilities. Boston: Pearson.

Mills, H., O'Keefe, T., and Stephens, D. (1992). *Looking closely: Exploring the role of phonics in one whole language classroom.* Urbana, IL: National Council of Teachers of English.

Miranda, A., Presentacion, M. J., and Soriano, M. (2002). Effectiveness of a school-based multicomponent program for the treatment of children with ADHD. *Journal of Learning Disabilities, 35*(6), 546–562.

Moats, L. C. (1995). *Spelling: Development, disability, and instruction.* Baltimore: York.

Moats, L. C. (1999). *Teaching reading is rocket science: What expert teachers of reading should know and be able to do.* Washington, DC: American Federation of Teachers. (ERIC Document Reproduction Service No. ED445323).

Moats, L. C. (2000). *Speech to print: Language essentials for teachers.* Baltimore: Paul H. Brookes.

Moll, L. C. (1990). Introduction. In L. C. Moll (Ed.), *Vygotsky and education: Instructional implications and applications of sociohistorical psychology* (pp. 1–27). Cambridge: Cambridge University Press.

Moll, L. C. (1994). Literacy research in community and classrooms: A sociocultural approach. In R. B. Ruddell, M. R. Ruddell, and H. Singer (Eds.), *Theoretical models and processes of reading* (pp. 179–207). Newark, DE: International Reading Association.

Moll, L. C., and Greenberg, J. (1990). Creating zones of possibilities: Combining social contexts for instruction. In L. C. Moll (Ed.), *Vygotsky and education* (pp. 319–348). Cambridge: Cambridge University Press.

Montague, M., and Bos, C. S. (1986a). The effect of cognitive strategy training on verbal math problem-solving performance of learning-disabled adolescents. *Journal of Learning Disabilities, 19,* 26–33.

Montague, M., and Bos, C. S. (1986b). Verbal math problem solving and learning disabilities: A review. *Focus on Learning Problems in Math, 8*(2), 7–21.

Montague, M., and Bos, C. S. (1990). Cognitive and metacognitive characteristics of eighth grade students' mathematical problem solving. *Learning and Individual Differences, 2,* 371–388.

Montague, M., and Leavell, A. G. (1994). Improving the narrative writing of students with learning disabilities. *Remedial and Special Education, 15,* 21–33.

Montague, M., and Rinaldi, C. (2001). Classroom dynamics and children at risk: A follow-up. *Learning Disability Quarterly, 24*(2), 75–83.

Montague, M., and van Garderen, D. (2003). A cross-sectional study of mathematics achievement, estimation skills, and academic self-perception in students of varying ability. *Journal of Learning Disabilities, 36,* 437–447.

Moody, S. W., Vaughn, S., and Schumm, J. S. (1997). Instructional grouping for reading: Teachers' views. *Remedial and Special Education 18*(6), 347–356.

Moore, J., and Fine, M. J. (1978). Regular and special class teachers' perceptions of normal and exceptional children and their attitudes toward mainstreaming. *Psychology in the Schools, 15*(2), 253–259.

Morgan, D., and Guilford, A. (1984). *Adolescent Language Screening Test (ALST).* Austin, TX: PRO-ED.

Morgan, H. (1980). How schools fail black children. *Social Policy, 10*(4), 49–54.

Morgan, S. R. (1986). Locus of control in children labeled learning disabled, behaviorally disordered, and learning disabled/behaviorally disordered. *Learning Disabilities Research, 2,* 10–13.

Morgan, S. R., and Reinhart, J. A. (1991). *Interventions for students with emotional disorders.* Austin, TX: PRO-ED.

Morocco, C. C., Dalton, B., and Tivnan, T. (1992). The impact of computer-supported writing instruction on 4th grade students with and without learning disabilities. *Reading and Writing Quarterly: Overcoming Learning Disabilities, 8,* 87–113.

Morrison, G. M. (1985). Differences in teacher perceptions and student self-perceptions for learning disabled and nonhandicapped learners in regular and special education settings. *Learning Disabilities Research, 1,* 32–41.

Morrison, G. M., Walker, D., Wakefield, P., and Solberg, S. (1994). Teacher preferences for collaborative relationships: Relationship to efficacy for teaching in prevention-related domains. *Psychology in the Schools, 31,* 221–231.

Morrow, L. M. (1992). The impact of a literature-based program on literacy achievement, use of literature, and attitudes of children from minority backgrounds. *Reading Research Quarterly, 25,* 251–275.

Mosberg, L., and Johns, D. (1994). Reading and listening comprehension in college students with developmental dyslexia. *Learning Disabilities Research and Practice, 9,* 130–135.

Most, T., and Greenback, A. (2000). Auditory, visual, and auditory-visual perception of emotions by adolescents with and without learning disabilities, and their relationship to social skills. *Learning Disabilities Research and Practice, 15*(4), 71–78.

Muma, J. (1986). *Language acquisition: A functional perspective.* Austin, TX: PRO-ED.

Muniz-Swicegood, M. (1994). The effects of metacognitive reading strategy training on the reading performance and student reading analysis strategies of third grade bilingual students. *Bilingual Research Journal, 18*(1–2), 83–97.

Murawski, W. A., and Swanson, L. (2001). A meta-analysis of co-teaching research: Where are the data? *Remedial and Special Education, 22*(5), 258–267.

Murphy, J., Hern, C., Williams, R., and McLaughlin, T. (1990). The effects of the copy, cover, compare approach in increasing spelling accuracy with learning disabled students. *Contemporary Educational Psychology, 15,* 378–386.

Murray, D. (1984). *Write to learn.* New York: Holt, Rinehart and Winston.

Murray, D. (1985). *A writer teaches writing.* Boston: Houghton Mifflin.

Muter, V., and Snowling, M. (1998). Concurrent and longitudinal predictors of reading: The role of metalinguistic and short-term memory skills. *Reading Research Quarterly, 33,* 320–337.

Muth, K. D. (1987). Teachers' connection questions: Prompting student to organize text idea. *Journal of Reading, 31,* 254–259.

Nagel, B. R., Schumaker, J. B., and Deshler, D. D. (1994). *The FIRST-letter mnemonic strategy* (rev. ed.). Lawrence, KS: Edge Enterprises.

Nagy, W., Berninger, V., Abbott, R., Vaughan, K., and Bermeulen, K. (2003). Relationship of morphology and other language skills to literacy skills in at-risk second-grade readers and at-risk fourth-grade writers. *Journal of Educational Psychology, 95,* 730–742.

Nancy, A., and Dill, M. (1997). *Let's write.* NY: Scholastic.

National Association of School Psychologists (2006). New roles in response to intervention: Creating success for schools and children. Retrieved December 14, 2007, from www.nasponline.org/advocacy/New%20Roles%20in%20RTI.pdf.

National Association of State Directors of Special Education. (2006). *Response to intervention: Policy considerations and implementation.* Retrieved from www.nasdse.org.

National Center for Learning Disabilities (2006). *A parent's guide to response to intervention.* Retrieved from www.ncld.org.

National Council on Disability. (2000). *Back to school on civil rights: Advancing the federal commitment to leave no child behind.* Washington, DC: Author.

National Institute for Literacy. (2001). *Put reading first: The research building blocks for teaching children to read.* Washington, DC: U.S. Government Printing Office.

National Institute of Mental Health. (1999). *Questions and answers.* NIMH Multimodal Treatment Study of Children with ADHD. Bethesda, MD: Author.

National Mental Health Association. (2003). *Adolescent depression: Helping depressed teens.* Washington, DC: Author.

National Reading Panel. (2000). *Teaching children to read: An evidence-based assessment of the scientific research literature on reading and its implications for reading instruction.* Bethesda, MD: National Institute of Child Health and Human Development, National Institutes of Health.

National Research Council. (1989). *Everybody counts: A report to the nation on the future of mathematics education.* Washington, DC: National Academy Press.

National Research Council. (2001). *Adding it up: Helping children learn mathematics.* Division of Behavioral and Social Sciences and Education. Washington, DC: National Academy Press.

Neisser, U. (1967). *Cognitive psychology.* New York: Appleton.

Nelson, A. (1998). *A long hard day on the ranch.* Buffalo, NY: Firefly Books Limited.

Nelson, J. R., Babyak, A., Gonzalez, J., and Benner. G. J. (2003). An investigation of the types of behavior problems exhibited by K–12 students with emotional or behavioral disorders in public school settings. *Behavioral Disorders, 28*(4), 348–359.

Nelson, J. R., Smith, D. J., Young, R. K., and Dodd, J. M. (1991). A review of self-management outcome research conducted with students who exhibit behavioral disorders. *Behavioral Disorders, 16,* 169–179.

Nelson, J. S., Jayanthi, M., Epstein, M. H., and Bursuck, W. D. (2000). Student preferences for adaptations in classroom testing. *Remedial and Special Education, 21*(1), 41–52.

Nelson, N. W. (1998). *Childhood language disorders in context: Infancy through adolescence* (2nd ed.). Boston: Allyn & Bacon.

Nelson, O. G., and Linek, W. M. (Eds.). (1999). *Practical classroom applications of language experience: Looking back, looking forward.* Boston: Allyn and Bacon.

Nevin, A. (1998). Curricular and instructional adaptations for including students with disabilities in cooperative groups. In J. W. Putnam (Ed.), *Cooperative Learning and strategies for inclusion* (pp. 49–66). Baltimore: Brookes.

Newcomer, P. (2001). *Diagnostic Achievement Battery–Third Edition.* Austin, TX: PRO-ED.

Newcomer, P. L., and Hammill, D. D. (1997). *Test of language development: Primary* (3rd ed.). Austin, TX: PRO-ED.

Newland, E. (1932). An analytic study of the development of illegibilities in handwriting from the lower grades to adulthood. *Journal of Educational Research, 26,* 249–258.

Nippold, M. A. (1992). The nature of normal and disordered word finding in children and adolescents. *Topics in Language Disorders, 13*(1), 1–14.

Nippold, M. A. (1993). Adolescents language developmental markers in adolescent language: Syntax, semantics, and pragmatics. *Language, Speech, and Hearing Services in Schools, 24,* 21–28.

Nippold, M. A. (1998). *Later language development: The school-age and adolescent years.* Austin, TX: PRO-ED.

Nowicki, E. A. (2003). A meta-analysis of the social competence of children with learning disabilities compared to classmates of low and average to high achievement. *Learning Disability Quarterly, 26,* 171–188.

Nulman, J. H., and Gerber, M. M. (1984). Improving spelling performance by imitating a child's errors. *Journal of Learning Disabilities, 17,* 328–333.

Oakes, J., Franke, M. L., Quartz, K. H., and Rogers, J. (2002). Research for high-quality urban teaching: Defining it, developing it, assessing it. *Journal of Teacher Education, 53,* 228–234.

Obiakor, F. E. (2007). Multicultural special education: Effective intervention for today's schools. *Intervention in School and Clinic, 42*(3), 148–155.

O'Brien, D. G., Stewart, R. A., and Moje, E. B. (1995). Why content literacy is difficult to infuse into the secondary school: Complexities of curriculum, pedagogy, and school culture. *Reading Research Quarterly, 30,* 442–465.

O'Connor, R. E., and Jenkins, J. R. (1995). Improving the generalization of sound/symbol knowledge: Teaching spelling to kindergarten children with disabilities. *Journal of Special Education, 29,* 255–275.

O'Connor, S. C., and Spreen, O. (1988). The relationship between parents' socioeconomic status and education level, and adult occupational and educational achievement of children with learning disabilities. *Journal of Learning Disabilities 21*(3), 148–153.

Ogle, D. M. (1986). K-W-L: A teaching model that develops active reading of expository text. *The Reading Teacher, 39,* 564–570.

Ogle, D. M. (1989). The know, want to know, learn strategy. In K. D. Muth (Ed.), *Children's comprehension of text: Research into practice* (pp. 205–233). Newark, DE: International Reading Association.

Okolo, C. M. (1992). The effects of computer-based attribution retraining on the attributions, persistence, and mathematics computation of students with learning disabilities. *Journal of Learning Disabilities, 25,* 327–334.

Okrainec, J. A., and Hughes, M. J. (July, 1996). *Conversational interactions between intellectually disabled and normal progress adolescents during a*

problem-solving task. Paper presented at the meeting of the World Congress of IASSD, Helsinki, Finland.

Olweus, D. (1993). *Bullying at school: What we know and what we can do.* Cambridge, MA: Blackwell.

O'Malley, J. M., and Chamot, A. U. (1990). *Learning strategies in second language acquisition.* New York: Cambridge University Press.

Opitz, M. F. (1998). Children's books to develop phonemic awareness—For you and parents, too! *Reading Teacher, 51*(6), 526–528.

Orosco, M. J. (2007). *Response to intervention with Latino English language learners: A school-based case study.* Doctoral dissertation, University of Colorado at Boulder.

Orton, S. T. (1937). *Reading, writing, and speech problems in children.* New York: W. W. Norton.

O'Shaughnessy, T. E., and Swanson, H. E. (2000). A comparison of two reading interventions for children with reading disabilities. *Journal of Learning Disabilities, 33*(3), 257–277.

O'Shea, D. J., Williams, A., and Sattler, R. O. (1999). Collaboration across special education and general education: Pre-service teacher's views. *Journal of Teacher Education, 50*(2), 147–158.

Ovander, C. J., and Collier, V. P. (1998). *Bilingual and ESL classrooms: Teaching in multicultural contexts.* Boston: McGraw-Hill.

Owens, R. E., Jr. (1999). *Language disorders: A functional approach to assessment and intervention* (3rd ed.). New York: Merrill/Macmillan.

Owens, R. E., Jr. (2001). *Language development: An introduction* (5th ed.). Boston: Allyn and Bacon.

Owens, R. E., Jr. (2005). *Language development: An introduction* (6th ed.). Boston: Allyn & Bacon.

Palincsar, A. S. (1982). *Improving the reading comprehension of junior high students through the reciprocal teaching of comprehension-monitoring.* Unpublished doctoral dissertation, University of Illinois, Urbana.

Palincsar, A. S. (1986). The role of dialogue in providing scaffolded instruction. *Educational Psychologist, 21*(1–2), 73–98.

Palincsar, A. S. (1988). *Reciprocal teaching instructional materials packet.* East Lansing: Michigan State University.

Palincsar, A. S., and Brown, A. L. (1984). Reciprocal teaching of comprehension fostering and comprehension monitoring activities. *Cognition and Instruction, 1*(2), 117–175.

Palincsar, A. S., and Brown, A. L. (1986). Interactive teaching to promote independent learning from text. *The Reading Teacher, 39*(8), 771–777.

Palincsar, A. S., and Brown, D. A. (1987). Enhancing instructional time through attention to metacognition. *Journal of Learning Disabilities, 20*(2), 66–75.

Palmatier, R. A., and Ray, H. L. (1989). *Sports talk: A dictionary of sports metaphors.* New York: Greenwood.

Parker, R., Hasbrouck, J. E., and Denton, C. (2002). How to tutor students with reading problems. *Preventing School Failure, 47,* 42–44.

Parmar, R. S., and Cawley, J. F. (1997). Preparing teachers to teach mathematics to students with learning disabilities. *Journal of Learning Disabilities, 30*(2), 188–197.

Parmar, R. S., Cawley, J. F., and Miller, J. H. (1994). Differences in mathematics performance between students with learning disabili-

ties and students with mild retardation. *Exceptional Children, 60,* 549–563.

Parsons, J. A. (1972). The reciprocal modification of arithmetic behavior and program development. In G. Semb (Ed.), *Behavior analysis and education.* Lawrence: University of Kansas, Department of Human Development.

Partington, G. (1998, April). *Power, discipline and minority students in high school.* Paper presented at the 1998 annual meeting of the American Educational Research Association, San Diego, CA.

Pastor, P. N., and Reuben, C. A. (2002). Attention deficit disorder and learning disabilities: United States, 1997–1998. National Center for Health Statistics. *Vital Health Statistics, 10*(206).

Paterson, K. (1978). *The great Gilly Hopkins.* New York: Crowell.

Patton, J. R., and Dunn, C. (1998). *Transition from school to young adulthood: Basic concepts and recommended practices.* Austin, TX: PRO-ED.

Patton, J. R., Cronin, M. E., and Jairrels, V. (1997). Curricular implications of transition: Life skills instruction as an integral part of transition education. *Remedial and Special Education, 18,* 294–306.

Patton, J. R., Cronin, M. E., and Wood, S. (1999). *Infusing real-life topics into existing curricula at the elementary, middle, and high school levels: Recommended procedures and instructional examples.* Austin, TX: PRO-ED.

Patton, J. R., Cronin, M. E., Bassett, D. S., and Koppel, A. E. (1997). A life skills approach to mathematics instruction: Preparing students with learning disabilities for the real-life math demands of adulthood. *Journal of Learning Disabilities, 30*(2), 178–187.

Patton, J. R., and Trainor, A. (2002). Using applied academics to enhance curricular reform in secondary education. In C. A. Kochhar-Bryant and D. S. Bassett (Eds.), *Aligning transition and standards-based education: Issues and strategies* (pp. 55–75). Arlington, VA: Council for Exceptional Children.

Pauk, W. (2001). *Essential study strategies.* Columbus, OH: Prentice Hall.

Paulson, F. L., Paulson, P. R., and Meyer, C. A. (1991). What makes a portfolio a portfolio? *Educational Leadership, 48*(5), 60–63.

Pavri, S., and Monda-Amaya, L. (2000). Loneliness and students with learning disabilities in inclusive classrooms: Self-perceptions, coping strategies, and preferred interventions. *Learning Disabilities Research and Practice, 15*(1), 22–33.

Pearl, R., Bryan, T., Fallon, P., and Herzog, A. (1991). Learning disabled students' detection of deception. *Learning Disabilities Research and Practice, 6,* 12–16.

Pearson, P. D., and Camperell, K. (1994). Comprehension of text structures. In R. B. Ruddell, M. R. Ruddell, and H. Singer (Eds.), *Theoretical models and process of reading* (4th ed., pp. 448–568). Newark, DE: International Reading Association.

Pearson, P. D., and Fielding, L. (1991). Comprehension instruction. In R. Barr, M. L. Kamil, P. Mosenthal, and P. D. Pearson (Eds.), *Handbook of reading research* (Vol. 2, pp. 815–860). White Plains, NY: Longman.

Pearson, P. D., and Johnson, D. D. (1978). *Teaching reading comprehension.* New York: Holt, Rinehart and Winston.

Pecyna-Rhyner, P., Lehr, D., and Pudlas, K. (1990). An analysis of teacher responsiveness to communicative initiations of children with handicaps. *Language, Speech, and Hearing Services in Schools, 21,* 91–97.

Pehrsson, R. S., and Robinson, H. A. (1985). *The semantic organizer approach to writing and reading instruction.* Rockville, MD: Aspen.

Perez, B., and Torres-Guzman, M. E. (1992). *Learning in two worlds.* New York: Longman.

Perfect, K. A. (2000). Rhyme and reason: Poetry for the heart and head. *The Reading Teacher, 52,* 728–737.

Perry, R. P. (1999). Teaching for success: Assisting helpless students in their academic development. *Education Canada, 39*(1), 16–19.

Personkee, C., and Yee, A. (1971). *Comprehensive spelling instruction: Theory, research, and application.* Scranton, PA: Intext Educational.

Peters, T., and Austin, N. (1985). *A passion for excellence.* New York: Random House.

Pfeffer, C. R. (1986). *The suicidal child.* New York: Guilford Press.

Pinel, J. P. J. (1993). *Biopsychology* (2nd ed.). Boston: Allyn & Bacon.

Pittman, K. (1991). *Promoting youth development: Strengthening the role of youth serving and community organizations.* Washington, DC: Academy for Educational Development, Center for Youth Development and Policy Research.

Platt, J. J., and Spivack, G. (1972). Social competence and effective problem solving thinking in psychiatric patients. *Journal of Clinical Psychiatry, 28,* 3–5.

Podhajski, B. (1999). *Time for teachers: What teachers need to know about what children need to know to learn to read.* Williston, VT: Stern Center for Language and Learning.

Polloway, E., Epstein, M., Polloway, C., Patton, J., and Ball, D. (1986). Corrective reading program: An analysis of effectiveness with learning disabled and mentally retarded students. *Remedial and Special Education, 7,* 41–47.

Pompa, D. (1998, March). *Testimony for the House Appropriations Subcommittee on Labor, Health & Human Services and Education on the fiscal year 1999 budget request.* Washington, DC: Office of Bilingual Education and Minority Languages Affairs.

Popenhagen, M. P., and Qualley, R. M. (1998). Adolescent suicide: Detection, intervention, and prevention. *Professional School Counseling, 1*(4), 30–35.

Powell, T. H., and Ogle, P. A. (1985). *Brothers and sisters: A special part of exceptional families.* Baltimore: Brookes.

Powers, L. E. (1996). *TAKE CHARGE transition planning project.* (Grant No. HH158U50001 from the U.S. Department of Education and Oregon Health Sciences). Portland: Oregon Health Sciences University.

Premack, D. (1959). Toward empirical behavior laws. *Psychological Review, 66*(4), 219–233.

President's Commission on Excellence in Special Education. (2002). *A new era: Revitalizing special education.* Washington DC: U.S. Department of Education.

Pressley, M. (1998). *Reading instruction that works: The case for balanced teaching.* New York: Guilford.

Pressley, M. (2000). What should comprehension instruction be the instruction of? In M. L. Kamil, P. B. Mosenthal, P. D. Pearson, and R. Barr (Eds.), *Handbook of reading research,* (vol. III, pp. 545–561). Mahwah, NJ: Erlbaum.

Pressley, M., and Rankin, J. (1994). More about whole language methods of reading instruc-

tion for students at risk for early reading failure. *Learning Disabilities Research and Practice, 9,* 156–167.

Pressley, M., Brown, R., El-Dinary, P. B., and Afflerbach, P. (1995). The comprehension instruction that students need: Instruction fostering constructively responsive reading. *Learning Disabilities Research and Practice, 10,* 215–224.

Pressley, M., El-Dinary, P. B., Gaskins, I., Schuder, T., Bergman, J., Almasi, L., and Brown, R. (1992). Beyond direct explanation: Transactional instruction of reading comprehension strategies. *Elementary School Journal, 92,* 511–554.

Prillaman, D. (1981). Acceptance of learning disabled students in the mainstream environment: A failure to replicate. *Journal of Learning Disabilities, 14,* 344–346.

Progress in math. (2000). New York: Sadlier.

Prutting, C. (1982). Pragmatics as social competence. *Journal of Speech and Hearing Disorders, 47,* 123–124.

Pugach, M. C., and Johnson, L. J. (1995). *Collaborative practitioners, collaborative schools.* Denver: Love.

Purkey, S. C., and Smith, M. S. (1985). School reform: The district policy implications of the effective schools literature. *Elementary School Journal, 85,* 353–389.

Putnam, M. L. (1992a). The testing practices of mainstream secondary classroom teachers. *Remedial and Special Education, 13*(5), 11–21.

Putnam, M. L. (1992b). Characteristics of questions on tests administered by mainstream secondary classrooms teachers. *Learning Disabilities Research and Practice, 7,* 129–136.

Putnam, M. L., Deshler, D. D., and Schumaker, J. S. (1993). The investigation of setting demands: A missing link in learning strategy instruction. In L. S. Meltzer (Ed.), *Strategy assessment and instruction for students with learning disabilities* (pp. 325–354). Austin, TX: PRO-ED.

Radencich, M. C., Beers, P. C., and Schumm, J. S. (1993). *A handbook for the K–12 reading resource specialist.* Boston: Allyn & Bacon.

RAND Reading Study Group (2002). *Reading for Understanding: Toward an R&D Program in Reading Comprehension.* Washington, DC: RAND.

Raphael, T. E. (1982). Question-answering strategies for children. *The Reading Teacher, 36,* 188.

Raphael, T. E. (1984). Teaching learners about sources of information for answering comprehension questions. *Journal of Reading, 27,* 303–311.

Raphael, T. E. (1986). Teaching question-answer relationships revisited. *The Reading Teacher, 39*(6), 516–523.

Raphael, T. E. (2000). Balancing literature and instruction: Lessons from the book club project. In B. M. Taylor, M. F. Graves, and P. Van den Broek (Eds.), *Reading for meaning: Fostering comprehension in the middle grades* (pp. 70–94). Newark, DE: International Reading Association.

Raphael, T. E., and Pearson, P. D. (1982). *The effect of metacognitive awareness training on children's question-answering behavior.* (Tech. Rep. No. 238). Urbana: University of Illinois, Center for Study of Reading.

Rashotte, C. A., and Torgesen, J. K. (1985). Repeated reading and reading fluency in learning disabled children. *Reading Research Quarterly, 20*(2), 180–188.

Rasinski, T. V. (1990a). Effects of repeated reading and listening-while-reading on reading fluency. *Journal of Education Research, 83,* 147–150.

Rasinski, T. V. (1990b). Investigating measures of reading fluency. *Educational Research Quarterly, 14*(3), 37–44.

Rathvon, N. (2004). *Early reading assessment: A practitioner's handbook.* New York: Guilford.

Rea, P. J., McLaughlin, V. L., and Walther-Thomas, C. (2002). Outcomes for students with learning disabilities in inclusive and pull-out programs. *Exceptional Children, 68*(2), 203–222.

Read, C. (1975). *Children's categorization of speech sounds in English.* Research Report No. 17. Urbana, IL: National Council of Teacher of English.

Readence, J. E., Bean, T. W., and Baldwin, R. S. (1995). *Content area reading: An integrated approach* (5th ed.). Dubuque, IA: Kendall/Hunt.

Readence, J. E., Bean, T. W., and Baldwin, R. S. (1998). *Content and literacy.* Dubuque, IA: Kendall/Hunt Publishing Company.

Reed, A. J. S. (1994). *Comics to classics: A parent's guide to books for teens and preteens.* Newark, DE: International Reading Association.

Reed, V. A. (1994). *An introduction to children with language disorders* (2nd ed.). New York: Macmillan.

Reichardt, P. (1992). *Concept building: Developing meaning through narratives and discussion.* Eau, Claire, WI: Thinking Publications.

Renik, M. J. (April 1987). *Measuring the relationship between academic self-perceptions and global self-worth: The self-perception profile for learning disabled students.* Presented at the Society for Research in Child Development, Baltimore, MD.

Reutzel, D. R., and Hollingsworth, P. M. (1993). Effects of fluency training on second graders' reading comprehension. *Journal of Educational Research, 86,* 325–331.

Reyes, E. I., and Bos, C. S. (1998). Interactive semantic mapping and charting: Enhancing content area learning for language minority students. In R. Gersten and R. Jimenez (Eds.), *Innovative practices for language minority students* (pp. 133–150). Pacific Grove, CA: Brooks/Cole.

Reyes, E. I., Duran, G. Z., and Bos, C. S. (1989). Language as a resource for mediating comprehension. In S. McCormick and J. Zutell (Eds.), *Cognitive and social perspectives for literacy research and instruction* (Thirty-eighth yearbook of the National Reading Conference, pp. 253–260). Chicago: National Reading Conference.

Richards, G. P., Samuels, S. J., Turnure, J., and Ysseldyke, J. (1990). Sustained and selective attention in children with learning disabilities. *Journal of Learning Disabilities, 23,* 129–136.

Richards, M. (2000). Be a good detective: Solve the case of oral reading fluency. *The Reading Teacher, 53,* 534–539.

Ridley, C. A., and Vaughn, S. R. (1982). Interpersonal problem solving: An intervention program for preschool children. *Journal of Applied Developmental Psychology, 3,* 177–190.

Ritchey, K. D., and Goeke, J. L. (2006). Orton-Gillingham and Orton-Gillinham-based reading instruction: A review of the literature. *The Journal of Special Education, 40*(3), 171–183.

Rivera, D. P., and Smith, D. D. (1997). *Teaching students with learning and behavior problems* (3rd ed.). Boston: Allyn & Bacon.

Rivera, D. P., Smith, R. G., Goodwin, M. W., and Bryant, D. P. (1998). Mathematical word problem solving: A synthesis of intervention research for students with learning disabilities. In T. E. Scruggs and M. A. Mastropieri (Eds.), *Advances in learning and behavioral disabilities* (vol. 12, pp. 245–285). Greenwich, CT: JAI Press.

RMC Research Corp. (1995). *Communicating with parents. Training guides for the Head Start Learning Community.* (ERIC Document Reproduction Service No. ED 407 138).

Roberts, G. H. (1968). The failure strategies of third grade arithmetic pupils. *The Arithmetic Teacher, 15,* 442–446.

Roberts, J. M. (1999). *Effective study skills: Maximizing your academic potential.* Columbus, OH: Prentice Hall.

Roberts, J., and Crais, E. (1989). Assessing communication skills. In D. Bailey and M. Wolery (Eds.), *Assessing infants and preschoolers with handicaps* (pp. 337–389). New York: Macmillan.

Roberts, R., and Mather, N. (1995). The return of students with learning disabilities to regular classrooms: A sellout. *Learning Disabilities Research and Practice, 10,* 46–58.

Robertson, H. M. (1999). LEA and students with special needs. In O. G. Nelson and W. M. Linek (Eds.), *Practical classroom applications of language experience: Looking back, looking forward* (pp. 221–223). Boston: Allyn and Bacon.

Robinson, F. P. (1946). *Effective study.* New York: Harper and Brothers.

Rogers, B. (2002). *Classroom Behaviour: A practical guide to effective teaching, behaviour management, and colleague support.* Thousand Oaks, CA: Sage.

Rogoff, B. (1990). *Apprenticeship in thinking.* New York: Oxford University Press.

Roller, C. M. (2002). Accommodating variability in reading instruction. *Reading and Writing Quarterly, 18,* 17–38.

Rooney, K. J., and Hallahan, D. P. (1985). Future directions for cognitive behavior modification research: The quest for cognitive change. *Remedial and Special Education, 6*(2), 46–51.

Roos, P. (1985). Parents of mentally retarded children: Misunderstood and mistreated. In H. R. Turnbull and A. P. Turnbull (Eds.), *Parents speak out: Then and now* (pp. 245–257). Columbus, OH: Merrill.

Rose Simms, S., Barrett, M., Huisingh, R., Zachman, L., Blagdon, C., and Orman, J. (1992). *The listening kit.* East Moline, IL: Lingui-Systems.

Rose, T. L. (1984). The effect of two prepractice procedures on oral reading. *Journal of Learning Disabilities, 17,* 544–548.

Rose, T. L., and Beattie, J. R. (1986). Relative effects of teacher-directed and taped previewing on oral reading. *Learning Disability Quarterly, 9,* 193–199.

Rosenblatt, L. (1978). *The reader, the text, the poem: The transactional theory of the literary work.* Carbondale: Southern Illinois University Press.

Rosenshine, B. (1997). Advances in research in instruction. In J. W. Lloyd, E. J. Kame'enui, and D. Chard (Eds.), *Issues in educating students with disabilities.* Mahwah, NJ: Erlbaum.

Rosenshine, B., and Meister, C. (1994). Reciprocal teaching: A review of the research. *Review of Education Research, 64,* 479–530.

Rossman, M. (1983). The cheese: An essay on method in science teaching. *Phi Delta Kappan, 64,* 632–634.

Rothman, H. R., and Cosden, M. (1995). The relationship between self-perception of a learning disability and achievement, self-concept and social support. *Learning Disability Quarterly, 18,* 203–212.

Rourke, B. (1993). Arithmetic disabilities, specific and otherwise: A neuropsychological perspective. *Journal of Learning Disabilities, 26*(4), 214–226.

Rourke, B. P., and Fuerst, D. R. (1992). Psychological dimensions of learning disability subtypes: Neuropsychological studies in the Windsor Laboratory. *School Psychology Review, 21*(3), 361–374.

Rourke, B. P., Young, G. C., and Leenaars, A. A. (1989). A childhood learning disability that predisposes those afflicted to adolescent and adult depression and suicide risk. *Journal of Learning Disabilities, 22*(3), 169–175.

Routh, D. K. (1979). Activity, attention, and aggression in learning disabled children. *Journal of Clinical Child Psychology, 8,* 183–187.

Rubin, H. (1988). Morphological knowledge and early writing ability. *Language and Speech, 31,* 337–355.

Rubin, H., Patterson, P. A., and Kantor, M. (1991). Morphological development and writing ability in children and adults. *Language, Speech, and Hearing Services in School, 22,* 228–235.

Ruddell, M. R. (1994). Vocabulary knowledge and comprehension: A comprehension process view of complex literacy relationship. In R. B. Ruddell, M. R. Ruddell, and H. Singer (Eds.), *Theoretical models and processes of reading* (4th ed., pp. 414–447). Newark, DE: International Reading Association.

Rudolph, S., and Luckner, J. L. (1991). Social skills training for students with learning disabilities. *Journal of Humanistic Education and Development, 29*(4), 163–171.

Ruedy, L. R. (1983). Handwriting instruction: It can be part of the high school curriculum. *Academic Therapy, 18*(4), 421–429.

Ruhl, K. L. (1996). Does nature of student activity during lecture pauses affect notes and immediate recall of college students with learning disabilities? *Journal of Postsecondary Education and Disability, 12*(2), 16–27.

Ruhl, K. L., Hughes, C. A., and Gajar, A. H. (1990). Efficacy of the pause procedure for enhancing learning disabled and nondisabled college students' long- and short-term recall of facts presented through lecture. *Learning Disability Quarterly, 13,* 55–64.

Ruhl, K. L., Hughes, C. A., and Schlos, P. J. (1987). Using the pause procedure to enhance lecture recall. *Teacher Education and Special Education, 10,* 14–18.

Ruiz, N. T., and Figueroa, R. A. (1995). Learning-handicapped classrooms with Latino students: The optimal learning environment (OLE) project. *Education and Urban Society, 27,* 463–483.

Ruiz, N. T., Figueroa, R. A., and Boothroyd, M. (1995). Bilingual special education teacher's shifting paradigms: Complex responses to educational reform. *Journal of Learning Disabilities, 28,* 622–635.

Ruiz, N. T., Garcia, E., and Figueroa, R. A. (1996). *The OLE curriculum guide: Creating optimal learning environments for students from diverse backgrounds in special and general education.* Sacramento, CA: Specialized Program Branch, California Department of Education.

Rumelhart, D. E. (1977). *Introduction to human information processing.* New York: Wiley.

Rumelhart, D. E. (1980). Schemata: The building blocks of cognition. In R. J. Spiro, B. C. Bruce, and W. F. Brewer (Eds.), *Theoretical issues in reading comprehension* (pp. 33–58). Hillsdale, NJ: Erlbaum.

Rumelhart, D. E. (1985). Toward an interactive model of reading. In H. Singer and R. B. Ruddell (Eds.), *Theoretical models and processes of reading* (3rd ed.). Newark, DE: International Reading Association.

Rupley, W. H., Logan, J. W., and Nichols, W. D. (1998). Vocabulary instruction in a balanced reading program. *The Reading Teacher, 52,* 338–346.

Ryan, J. B., Sanders, S., Katsiyannis, A., and Yell, M. L. (2007). Using time-out effectively in the classroom. *Teaching Exceptional Children, 39*(4), 60–67.

Saenz, L. M., Fuchs, L. S., and Fuchs, D. (2005). Peer-assisted learning strategies for English language learners with learning disabilities. *Exceptional Children, 71,* 231–247.

Salend, S. J. (1995). Modifying tests for diverse learners. *Intervention in School and Clinic, 31*(2), 84–90.

Salend, S. J. (2000). *Effective mainstreaming: Creating inclusive classrooms* (3rd ed.). New York: Macmillan.

Salend, S. J., and Lutz, J. G. (1984). Mainstreaming or mainlining: A competency based approach to mainstreaming. *Journal of Learning Disabilities, 17*(1), 27–29.

Salend, S. J., and Nowak, M. R. (1988). Effects of peer-previewing on LD students' oral reading skills. *Learning Disability Quarterly, 11,* 47–53.

Salend, S. J., Duhaney, D., Anderson, D. J., and Gottschalk, C. (2004). Using the internet to improve homework communication and completion. *Teaching Exceptional Children, 36,* 64–73.

Salend, S. J., Gordon, J., and Lopez-Vona, K. (2002). Evaluating cooperative teaching teams. *Intervention in School and Clinic, 37,* 195–200.

Salend, S. J., Jantzen, N. R., and Giek, K. (1992). Using a peer confrontation system in a group setting. *Behavioral Disorders, 17,* 211–218.

Samuels, S. J. (1979). The method of repeated readings. *The Reading Teacher, 32,* 403–408.

Samuels, S. J. (1987). Information processing abilities and reading. *Journal of Learning Disabilities, 20*(1), 18–22.

Samuels, S. J. (1997). The method of repeated reading. *The Reading Teacher, 50,* 376–381. Originally published in *The Reading Teacher* in January 1979 (vol. 32).

Sanger, D., Maag, J. W., and Shapera, N. R. (1994). Language problems among students with emotional and behavioral disorders. *Intervention in School and Clinic, 30,* 103–108.

Sawyer, V., Nelson, J. S., Jayanthi, M., Bursuck, W., and Epstein, M. H. (1996). Views of students with learning disabilities of their homework in general education classes: Student interviews. *Learning Disability Quarterly, 19,* 70–85.

Sax, C. L., and Thoma, C. A. (2002). *Transition assessment: Wise practices for quality lives.* Baltimore: Paul Brookes.

Saxon, J. (2001a). *Advanced mathematics* (2nd ed.). Norman, OK: Saxon.

Saxon, J. (2001b). *Algebra ½* (3rd ed.). Norman, OK: Saxon.

Saxon, J. (2003a). *Algebra 1* (3rd ed.). Norman, OK: Saxon.

Saxon, J. (2003b). *Algebra 2* (3rd ed.). Norman, OK: Saxon.

Scanlon, D. J., and Anders, P. L. (1988 December). *Conceptual complexity and considerateness of vocation textbooks.* Paper presented at the annual meeting of the National Reading Conference, Tucson, AZ.

Scanlon, D. J., Duran, G. Z., Reyes, E. I., and Gallego, M. A. (1992). Interactive semantic mapping: An interactive approach to enhancing LD students' content area comprehension. *Learning Disabilities Research and Practice, 7,* 142–146.

Scanlon, D., Deshler, D. D., and Schumaker, J. B. (1996). Can a strategy be taught and learned in secondary inclusive classrooms? *Learning Disabilities Research and Practice, 11,* 41–57.

Scarborough, H. S. (2001). Connecting early language and literacy to later reading (dis)abilities: Evidence, theory, and practice. In S. Neuman and D. Dickinson (Eds.), *Handbook for research in early literacy* (pp. 97–110). New York: Guilford Press.

Schank, R. C., and Abelson, R. (1977). *Scripts, plans, goals, and understanding.* Hillsdale, NJ: Erlbaum.

Scheuermann, B., Jacobs, W. R., McCall, C., and Knies, W. C. (1994). The personal spelling dictionary: An adaptive approach to reducing the spelling hurdle in written language. *Intervention in School and Clinic, 29,* 292–299.

Schifini, A. (1994). Language, literacy, and content instruction: Strategies for teachers. In K. Spangenberg-Urbschat and R. Pritchard (Eds.), *Kids come in all languages: Reading instruction of ESL students* (pp. 158–179). Newark, DE: International Reading Association.

Schloss, P. J., Smith, M. A., and Schloss, C. N. (2001). *Instructional methods for adolescents with learning and behavior problems* (3rd ed.). Boston: Allyn & Bacon.

Schmidt, P. R. (1999). KWLQ: Inquiry and literacy learning in science. *The Reading Teacher, 52,* 789–792.

Schrag, J. A., and Henderson, K. (1996). *School-based intervention assistance teams and their impact on special education.* Alexandria, VA: National Association of State Directors of Special Education.

Schultz, J. B., and Turnbull, A. P. (1984). *Mainstreaming handicapped students: A guide for classroom teachers* (2nd ed.). Boston: Allyn & Bacon.

Schultz, T. (1974). Development of the appreciation of riddles. *Child Development, 45,* 100–105.

Schumaker, J. B., and Deshler, D. D. (1988). Implementing the regular education initiative in secondary schools: A different ball game. *Journal of Learning Disabilities, 21,* 36–42.

Schumaker, J. B., Denton, P. H., and Deshler, D. D. (1993). *The paraphrasing strategy* (rev. ed.) (Learning Strategies Curriculum). Lawrence: University of Kansas.

Schumaker, J. B., Deshler, D. D., Alley, G. R., Warner, M. M., and Denton, P. H. (1982). Multipass: A learning strategy for improving reading comprehension. *Learning Disability Quarterly, 5*(3), 295–304.

Schumaker, J. B., Nolan, S. M., and Deshler, D. D. (1994). *The error monitoring strategy* (rev. ed.). Lawrence: Center for Research on Learning Disabilities, University of Kansas.

Schumaker, J. D., Wildgen, J. S., and Sherman, J. A. (1982). Social interaction of learning disabled junior high school students in their regular classrooms: An observational analysis. *Journal of Learning Disabilities, 11,* 98–102.

Schumm, J. S. (2001). *School power: Study skill strategies for succeeding in school.* Minneapolis, MN: Free Spirit.

Schumm, J. S., and Mangrum, C. T. (1991). FLIP: A framework for textbook thinking. *Journal of Reading, 35,* 120–124.

Schumm, J. S., Moody, S. W., and Vaughn, S. (2000). Grouping for reading instruction: Does one size fit all? *Journal of Learning Disabilities, 33*(5), 477–488.

Schumm, J. S., and Post, S. A. (1997). *Executive learning: Successful strategies for college reading and studying.* Columbus, OH: Prentice Hall.

Schumm, J. S., and Strickler, K. (1991). Guidelines for adapting content area textbooks: Keeping teachers and students content. *Intervention in School and Clinic, 27,* 79–84.

Schumm, J. S., and Vaughn, S. (1991). Making adaptations for mainstreamed students: General classroom teachers' perspectives. *Remedial and Special Education, 12*(4), 18–27.

Schumm, J. S., and Vaughn, S. (1992a). Planning for mainstreamed special education students: Perceptions of general classroom teachers. *Exceptionality, 3,* 81–98.

Schumm, J. S., and Vaughn, S. (1992b). Reflections on planning for mainstreamed special education students. *Exceptionality, 3,* 121–126.

Schumm, J. S., and Vaughn, S. (1995). *Using Making Words in heterogeneous classrooms.* Miami, FL: School Based Research, University of Miami: unpublished manuscript.

Schumm, J. S., Vaughn, S., Haager, D., McDowell, J., Rothlein, L., and Saumell, L. (1995a). General education teacher planning: What can students with learning disabilities expect? *Exceptional Children, 61*(4), 335–352.

Schumm, J. S., Vaughn, S., Haager, D., McDowell, J., Rothlein, L., and Saumell, L. (1995b). Teacher planning for individual student needs: What can mainstreamed special education students expect? *Exceptional Children, 61,* 335–352.

Schumm, J. S., Vaughn, S., and Harris, J. (1997). Pyramid power for collaborative planning. *Teaching Exceptional Children, 29*(6), 62–66.

Schumm, J. S., Vaughn, S., and Leavell, A. G. (1994). Planning pyramid: A framework for planning for diverse student needs during content area instruction. *The Reading Teacher, 47,* 608–615.

Schumm, J. S., Vaughn, S., and Saumell, L. (1992). What teachers do when the textbook is tough: Students speak out. *Journal of Reading Behavior, 24,* 481–503.

Schunk, D. H. (1996). Goal and self-evaluative influences during children's cognitive skill learning. *American Education Research Journal, 33,* 359–382.

Schuster, J. W., Stevens, K. B., and Doak, P. K. (1990). Using constant time delay to teach word definitions. *Journal of Special Education, 24,* 306–318.

Schwartz, N. H., Ellsworth, L. S., Graham, L., and Knight, B. (1998). Assessing prior knowledge to remember text: A comparison of advance organizers and maps. *Contemporary Educational Psychology, 23*(1), 65–89.

Schwartz, S. E., and Budd, D. (1981). Mathematics for handicapped learners: A functional approach for adolescents. *Focus on Exceptional Children, 13*(7), 1–12.

Schwartz, S., and Doehring, D. (1977). A developmental study of children's ability to acquire knowledge of spelling patterns. *Developmental Psychology, 13,* 419–420.

Scott, C. M., and Stokes, S. L. (1995). Measures of syntax in school-age children and adolescents. *Language, Speech, and Hearing Services in Schools, 26,* 309–319.

Scruggs, T. E., and Mastropieri, M. A. (1988). Are learning disabled students "test-wise"? A review of recent research. *Learning Disabilities Focus, 3,* 87–97.

Scruggs, T. E., and Mastropieri, M. A. (1989a). Mnemonic instruction of LD students: A field-based evaluation. *Learning Disability Quarterly, 12,* 119–125.

Scruggs, T. E., and Mastropieri, M. A. (1989b). Reconstructive elaborations: A model for content area learning. *American Educational Research Journal, 26,* 311–327.

Scruggs, T. E., and Richter, L. (1985). Tutoring learning disabled students: A critical review. *Learning Disability Quarterly, 8*(4), 286–298.

Seidel, J. F., and Vaughn, S. (1991). Social alienation and the LD school dropout. *Learning Disabilities Research and Practice, 6*(3), 152–157.

Seigle, P., Lange, L., and Macklem, G. (1997). *Open Circle Curriculum.* Wellesley, MA: Reach Out to Schools Social Competency Program, The Stone Center, Wellesley College.

Seligman, M. E. P. (1975). *Helplessness: On depression, development, and death.* San Francisco: Freeman.

Seuss, Dr. (1974). *There's a wocket in my pocket.* New York: Random House.

Sexton, M., Harris, K. R., and Graham, S. (1998). Self-regulated strategy development and the writing process: Effects on essay writing and attributions. *Exceptional Children, 64*(3), 290–291.

Seymour, P. H. K., Aro, M., and Erskine, J. (2003). Foundation literacy acquisition in European orthographies. *British Journal of Psychology, 94,* 143–174.

Shand, M. (1993). *The role of vocabulary in developmental reading disabilities* (Technical Report No. 576). Urbana, IL: Center for the Study of Reading. (ERIC Document Reproduction Service No. 356 458).

Shannon, P., Kame'enui, E., and Baumann, J. (1988). An investigation of children's ability to comprehend character motives. *American Educational Research Journal, 25,* 441–462.

Shany, M. T., and Biemiller, A. (1995). Assisted reading practice: Effects on performance for poor readers in grades 3 and 4. *Reading Research Quarterly, 30,* 382–395.

Shapero, S., and Forbes, C. R. (1981). A review of involvement programs for parents of learning disabled children. *Journal of Learning Disabilities, 14*(9), 499–504.

Shapiro, E. G., Lipton, M. E., and Krivit, W. (1992). White matter dysfunction and its neuropsychological correlates: A longitudinal study of a case of metachromatic leukodystrophy. *Journal of Clinical and Experimental Neuropsychology, 14*(4), 610–624.

Share, D. L., and Stanovich, K. E. (1995). Cognitive processes in early reading development: A model of acquisition and individual differences. *Issues in Education: Contributions from Education Psychology, 1*, 1–57.

Shaywitz, S. (2003). *Overcoming dyslexia: A new and complete science-based program for reading problems at any level.* New York: Knopf.

Shaywitz, S., and Shaywitz, B. (November, 1996). *State of the art: Functional MRI of the brain during reading.* Paper presented at the annual meeting of the Orton Dyslexia Society, Boston, MA.

Shea, T. M., and Bauer, A. M. (1991). *Parents and teachers of children with exceptionalities: A handbook for collaboration.* Boston: Allyn and Bacon.

Sheras, P. L. (1983). Suicide in adolescence. In E. Walker and M. Roberts (Eds.), *Handbook of clinical child psychology.* New York: Wiley.

Shinn, M. R. (Ed.). (1989). *Curriculum-based measurement: Assessing special children.* New York: Guilford.

Shipley, K. G., and Banis, C. J. (1989). *Teaching morphology developmentally.* Tucson, AZ: Communication Skill Builders.

Shippen, M. E., Simpson, R. G., and Crites, S. A. (2003). A practical guide to functional behavioral assessment. *Teaching Exceptional Children, 35*, 36–44.

Shondrick, D. D., Serafica, F. C., Clark, P., and Miller, K. G. (1992). Interpersonal problem solving and creativity in boys with and boys without learning disabilities. *Learning Disability Quarterly, 15*(2), 95–102.

Shore, K. (2003). *Elementary teacher's discipline problem solver: A practical A–Z Guide for managing classroom behavior problems.* San Francisco: Jossey-Bass.

Short, K. (1997). *Literature as a way of knowing.* York, ME: Stenhouse.

Short, K. G., Harste, J. C., with Burke, C. (1995). *Creating classrooms for authors and inquirers.* Portsmouth, NH: Heinemann.

Shure, M. B., and Spivack, G. (1978). *Problem solving techniques in child-rearing.* San Francisco: Jossey-Bass.

Shure, M. B., and Spivack, G. (1979). Interpersonal cognitive problem solving and primary prevention: Programming for preschool and kindergarten children. *Journal of Clinical Child Psychology, 8*, 89–94.

Shure, M. B., and Spivack, G. (1980). Interpersonal problem solving as a mediator of behavioral adjustment in preschool and kindergarten children. *Journal of Applied Developmental Psychology, 1*, 29–44.

Silver, A. A., and Hagin, R. A. (2002). *Disorders of learning in childhood* (2nd ed.). New York: Wiley.

Simeonsson, R. J., and Simeonsson, N. E. (1993). Children, families and disability: Psychological dimensions. In J. L. Paul and R. J. Simeonsson (Eds.), *Children with special needs* (pp. 25–50). Orlando, FL: Harcourt, Brace, Jovanovich.

Simmons, D. C., and Kame'enui, E. J. (1998). *What reading research tells us about children with diverse learning needs.* Mahwah, NJ: Erlbaum.

Simmons, D. C., Kame'enui, E. J., Stoolmiller, M., Coyne, M. D., and Harn, B. (2003). Accelerating growth and maintaining proficiency: A two-year intervention study of kindergarten and first-grade children at risk for reading difficulties. In B. F. Foorman (Ed.), *Preventing and remediating reading difficulties: Bringing science to scale* (pp. 199–228). Baltimore: York.

Simmons, D., Fuchs, D., Fuchs, L. S., Hodge, J. P., and Mathes, P. G. (1994). Importance of instructional complexity and role reciprocity to classwide peer tutoring. *Learning Disabilities Research and Practice, 9*, 203–212.

Simon, C. S. (Ed.). (1985). *Communication skills and classroom success: Assessment of language-learning disabled students.* San Diego, CA: College-Hill.

Simpson, R. (1990). *Conferencing parents of exceptional children* (2nd ed.). Austin, TX: PRO-ED.

Simpson, R. L. (1982). *Conferencing parents of exceptional children.* Rockville, MD: Aspen.

Simpson, R. L. (1988). Needs of parents and families whose children have learning and behavior problems. *Behavioral Disorders, 14*(1), 40–47.

Singer, H., and Donlan, D. (1989). *Reading and learning from text* (2nd ed.). Hillsdale, NJ: Erlbaum.

Siperstein, G. N., and Goding, M. J. (1985). Teachers' behavior toward learning disabled and non-learning disabled children: A strategy for change. *Journal of Learning Disabilities, 18*, 139–144.

Siperstein, G. N., Bopp, M. J., and Bak, J. J. (1978). Social status of learning disabled children. *Journal of Learning Disabilities, 11*, 217–228.

Sitlington, P. L. (2007). Transition to living: The neglected components of transition programming for individuals with learning disabilities. *Journal of Learning Disabilities, 29*, 31–39, 52.

Sitlington, P. L., Frank, A., and Carson, R. (1993). Adult adjustment among graduates with mild disabilities. *Exceptional Children, 59*, 221–233.

Sitlington, P. L., Neubert, D. A., Begun, W., Lombard, R. C., and Leconte, P. J. (1996). *Assess for success: Handbook on transition assessment.* Reston, VA: Division on Career Development and Transition, Council for Exceptional Children.

Skinner, M. E. (1991). Facilitating parental participation during individualized education program conferences. *Journal of Educational and Psychological Consultation, 2*, 285–289.

Skutnabb-Kangas, T. (February, 1981). *Linguistic genocide and bilingual education.* Paper presented at the California Association for Bilingual Education, Anaheim, CA.

Slavin, R. E. (1984). Team assisted individualization: Cooperative learning and individualized instruction in the mainstreamed classroom. *Remedial and Special Education, 5*(6), 33–42.

Slavin, R. E. (1987). Cooperative learning: Where behavioral and humanistic approaches to classroom motivation meet. *Elementary School Journal, 88*, 29–37.

Slavin, R. E. (1991). Synthesis of research on cooperative learning. *Educational Leadership, 48*(5), 71–82.

Slavin, R. E. (2000). *Educational psychology: Theory and practice.* Boston: Allyn & Bacon.

Slavin, R. E., Madden, N. A., Karweit, N. L., Dolan, L., and Wasik, B. A. (1992). *Success for all: A relentless approach to prevention and early intervention in elementary schools.* Arlington, VA: Educational Research Service.

Slavin, R. E., Stevens, R. J., and Madden, N. A. (1988). Accommodating student diversity in reading and writing instruction: A cooperative learning approach. *Remedial and Special Education, 9*(1), 60–66.

Smith, E. M., and Alley, G. R. (1981). *The effect of teaching sixth graders with learning difficulties a strategy for solving verbal math problems* (Research Report No. 39). Institute for Research in Learning Disabilities.

Smith, F., and Goodman, K. S. (1971). On the psycholinguistic method of teaching reading. *Elementary School Journal, 71*, 177–181.

Smith, M. K. (1941). Measurement of the size of general English vocabulary through the elementary grades and high school. *Genetic Psychological Monographs, 24*, 311–345.

Smith, T. J., and Adams, G. (2006). The effect of comorbid AD/HD and learning disabilities on parent-reported behavioral and academic outcomes of children. *Learning Disability Quarterly, 29*, 101–112.

Snell, M. E., and Janney, R. J. (2000). *Collaborative teaming.* Baltimore: Brookes.

Snow, C. E., Burns, M. S., and Griffin, P. (Eds.). (1998). *Preventing reading difficulties in young children.* Washington, DC: National Academy Press.

Sobol, M. P., Earn, B. M., Bennett, D., and Humphries, T. (1983). A categorical analysis of the social attributions of learning disabled children. *Journal of Abnormal Child Psychology, 11*(2), 217–228.

Soenksen, P. A., Flagg, C. L., and Schmits, D. W. (1981). Social communication in learning disabled students: A pragmatic analysis. *Journal of Learning Disabilities, 14*, 283–286.

Solomon, R. N., and Rhodes, A. (2001). *Strong images and practical ideas: A guide to parent engagement in school reform.* Baltimore, MD: Annie E. Casey Foundation.

Spargo, E., Williston, G. R., and Browning, L. (1980). *Time readings: Book one.* Providence, RI: Jamestown Publishers.

Spear-Swerling, L. (2006). *The importance of teaching handwriting.* Retrieved August 10, 2006, from www.ldonline.org/spearswerling/10521.

Spear-Swerling, L., and Sternberg, R. J. (1996). *Off track: When poor readers become "learning disabled."* Boulder, CO: Westview Press.

Special Education Report. (1997). *More IDEA students receiving mainstream instruction.* Alexandria, VA: Capitol Publications.

Spector, J. E. (1995). Phonemic awareness training: Applications of principles of direct instruction. *Reading and Writing Quarterly: Overcoming Learning Difficulties, 11*, 37–51.

Speece, D. L., MacDonald, V., Kilsheimer, L., and Krist, J. (1997). Research to practice: Preservice teachers reflect on reciprocal teaching. *Learning Disabilities Research and Practice, 12*, 177–187.

Spencer, S. (1998). *Definition play by play.* East Moline, IL: LinguiSystems.

Spivack, G., Platt, J. J., and Shure, M. B. (1976). *The problem solving approach to adjustment: A guide to research and intervention.* San Francisco: Jossey-Bass.

Sridhar, D., and Vaughn, S. (2000). Bibliotherapy for all. *Teaching Exceptional Children, 33*(2), 74–82.

Stahl, S. A. (1999). *Vocabulary development.* Cambridge, MA: Brookline.

Stahl, S. A. (2004). What do we know about fluency? In P. McCardle and V. Chhabra, *The voice of evidence in reading research* (pp. 187–211). Baltimore: Brookes.

Stahl, S. A., and Kuhn, M. R. (2002). Making it sound like language: Developing fluency. *Reading Teacher, 55*(6), 582–584.

Stahl, S. A., and Miller, P. D. (1989). Whole language and language experience approaches for beginning reading: A quantitative research synthesis. *Review of Educational Research, 59,* 87–116.

Stahl, S. A., and Shiel, T. G. (1992). Teaching meaning vocabulary: Productive approaches for poor readers. *Reading and Writing Quarterly: Overcoming Learning Difficulties, 8*(2), 223–241.

Stahl, S. A., Pagnucco, J. R., and Suttles, C. W. (1996). First graders' reading and writing instruction in traditional and process-oriented classes. *The Journal of Educational Research, 89,* 131–144.

Stainback, S., and Stainback, W. (1992). *Curriculum consideration in inclusive classrooms: Facilitating learning for all students.* Baltimore: Brookes.

Stallings, J. (1975). *Relationships between classroom instructional practices and child development* (Rep. No. PLEDE-C-75). Menlo Park, CA: Stanford Research Institute. (ERIC Document Reproduction Service No. ED 110 200).

Stanovich, K. (1986). Cognitive processes and the reading problems of learning-disabled children: Evaluating the assumption of specificity. In J. K. Torgesen and B. Y. L. Wong (Eds.), *Psychological and educational perspectives on learning disabilities* (pp. 85–131). Orlando, FL: Academic Press.

Stanovich, K. I. (1992). Speculations on the causes and consequences of individual differences in early reading acquisition. In P. B. Gough, L. D. Ehri, and R. Treiman (Eds.), *Reading acquisition* (pp. 307–342). Mahwah, NJ: Erlbaum.

Stauffer, R. G. (1969). *Directing reading maturity as a cognitive process.* New York: Harper & Row.

Stauffer, R. G. (1970). *The language-experience approach to the teaching of reading.* New York: Harper & Row.

Stauffer, R. G. (1976). *Teaching reading as a thinking process.* New York: Harper & Row.

Stein, N. L., and Glenn, C. G. (1979). An analysis of story comprehension in elementary school children. In R. O. Freedle (Ed.), *New directions in discourse processing* (vol. 2, pp. 53–120). Norwood, NJ: Ablex.

Stephens, T. (1977). *Teaching skills to children with learning and behavior problems.* Columbus, OH: Merrill.

Stern, C., Stern, M. B., and Gould, T. S. (1998). *Structural arithmetic.* Cambridge, MA: Educators Publishing Service.

Stevens, K. B., and Schuster, J. W. (1987). Effects of a constant time delay procedure on the written spelling performance of a learning disabled student. *Learning Disability Quarterly, 10,* 9–16.

Stevens, K. B., and Schuster, J. W. (1988). Time delay: Systematic instruction for academic tasks. *Remedial and Special Education, 9*(5), 16–21.

Stevens, R. J., and Slavin, R. E. (1995). Effects of cooperative learning approach in reading and writing on academically handicapped and nonhandicapped students. *Elementary School Journal, 95*(3), 1–25.

Stewart, J. C. (1986). *Counseling parents of exceptional children* (2nd ed.). Columbus, OH: Merrill.

Stires, S. (1983). Real audiences and contexts for LD writers. *Academic Therapy, 18*(5), 561–568.

Stires, S. (Ed.). (1991). *With promise: Redefining reading and writing for "special students."* Portsmouth, NH: Heinemann.

Stokes, S. M. (1989). LD students and language experience. *Journal of Language Experience, 10*(2), 19–23.

Stokes, T. F., and Baer, D. M. (1977). An implicit technology of generalization. *Journal of Applied Behavior Analysis, 10,* 349–367.

Stone, W. C., and LaGreca, A. M. (1984). Comprehension of nonverbal communication: A reexamination of the social competencies of learning disabled children. *Journal of Abnormal Child Psychology, 12*(4), 505–518.

Stone, W. L., and LaGreca, A. M. (1990). The social status of children with learning disabilities: A reexamination. *Journal of Learning Disabilities, 23*(1), 32–37.

Stratton, B. D., Grindler, M. C., and Postell, C. M. (1992). Discovering oneself. *Middle School Journal, 24,* 42–43.

Strecker, S., Roser, N., and Martinez, N. (1998). Toward understanding oral reading fluency. In T. Shanahan and F. Rodriquez-Brown (Eds.), *Forty-seventh yearbook of the National Reading Conference* (pp. 295–310). Chicago: National Reading Conference.

Strickland, D. S., Ganske, K., and Monroe, J. (2002). *Supporting struggling readers and writers: Strategies for classroom intervention, 3–6.* Portland, ME: Stenhouse.

Stuart, M. (1999). Getting ready for reading: Early phoneme awareness and phonics training improves reading and spelling in inner-city second language learners. *British Journal of Educational Psychology, 69*(4), 587–605.

Stuebing, K. K., Fletcher, J. M., LeDoux, J. M., Lyon, G. R., Shaywitz, S. E., and Shaywitz, B. A. (2002). Validity of IQ-discrepancy classifications of reading difficulties: A meta-analysis. *American Educational Research Journal, 39,* 469–518.

Sugai, G., and Horner, R. (2001, June). *School climate and discipline: Going to scale.* Paper presented at National Summit on the Shared Implementation of IDEA, Washington, DC.

Sugai, G., Horner, R. H., Dunlap, G., Hieneman, M., Lewis, T. J., Nelson, C. M., et al. (2000). Applying positive behavior support and functional assessment in schools. *Journal of Positive Behavior Interventions, 2,* 131–143.

Sugai, G., Horner, R., and Gresham, F. M. (2002). Behaviorally effective school environments. In M. Shinn, H. Walker, and G. Stoner (Eds.), *Interventions for achievement and behavior problems II: Preventive and remedial approaches* (pp. 315–350). Bethesda, MD: National Association of School Psychologists. (ERIC Document Reproduction Service No. ED 462 655).

Sullivan, P. (1992). *ESL in context.* New York: Corwin Press.

Sulzby, E., and Teale, W. H. (1991). Emergent literacy. In R. Barr, M. L. Kamil, P. B. Mosenthal, and P. D. Pearson (Eds.), *Handbook of reading research* (2nd ed., pp. 727–757). New York: Longman.

Sulzer-Azaroff, B., and Mayer, G. R. (1991). *Behavior analysis for lasting change.* Fort Worth, TX: Holt, Rinehart and Winston.

Sundbye, N. (1987). Text explicitness and inferential questioning: Effects on story understanding and recall. *Reading Research Quarterly, 22,* 82–98.

Suritsky, S. K., and Hughes, C. A. (1996). Notetaking strategy instruction. In D. D. Deshler, E. S. Ellis, and B. K. Lenz (Eds.), *Teaching adolescents with learning disabilities* (2nd ed., pp. 267–312). Denver: Love.

Sussman, S., and Ames, S. L. (2001). *The social psychology of drug abuse.* Buckingham, UK: Open University Press.

Suydam, M. N. (1982). *The use of calculators in precollege education: Fifth annual state-of-the-art review.* Columbus, OH: Calculator Information Center. (ERIC Document Reproduction Service No. ED206454).

Swafford, K. M., and Reed, V. A. (1986). Language and learning-disabled children. In V. A. Reed (Ed.), *An introduction to children with language disorders* (pp. 105–128). New York: Macmillan.

Swanson, H. L. (1985). Verbal coding deficits in learning disabled readers. In S. J. Ceci (Ed.), *Handbook of cognitive, social and neuropsychological aspects of learning disabilities* (vol. 1, pp. 203–228). Hillsdale, NJ: Erlbaum.

Swanson, H. L. (1991). Learning disabilities, distinctive encoding, and hemispheric resources: An information-processing perspective. In J. E. Obrzut and G. W. Hynd (Eds.), *Neuropsychological foundations of learning disabilities* (pp. 241–280). San Diego, CA: Academic Press.

Swanson, H. L. (1996). Information processing: An introduction. In D. K. Reid, W. P. Hresko, and H. L. Swanson (Eds.), *Cognitive approaches to learning disabilities* (3rd ed., pp. 251–286). Austin, TX: PRO-ED.

Swanson, H. L. (1999a). Reading research for students with LD: A meta-analysis of intervention outcomes. *Journal of Learning Disabilities, 32,* 504–532.

Swanson, H. L. (1999b). Instructional components that predict treatment outcomes for students with learning disabilities: Support for a combined strategy and direct instruction model. *Learning Disabilities Research and Practice, 14*(3), 129–140.

Swanson, H. L., and Cooney, J. B. (1991). Learning disabilities and memory. In B. Y. L. Wong (Ed.), *Learning about learning disabilities* (pp. 104–127). New York: Academic Press.

Swanson, H. L., and Cooney, J. B. (1996). Learning disabilities and memory. In D. K. Reid, W. P. Hresko, and H. L. Swanson (Eds.), *Cognitive approaches to learning disabilities* (3rd ed., pp. 287–315). Austin, TX: PRO-ED.

Swanson, H. L., and Trahan, M. F. (1992). Learning disabled readers' comprehension of computer-mediated text: The influence of working memory, metacognition, and attribution. *Learning Disabilities Research and Practice, 7,* 75–86.

Swanson, H. L., with Hoskyn, M., and Lee, C. (1999). *Intervention for students with learning disabilities: A meta-analysis of treatment outcomes.* New York: Guilford.

Swanson, M., McBurnett, K., Wigal, T., Pfiffner, L., Lerner, M., Williams, L., Christian, D., Tamm, L., Willcutt, E., Crowley, K., Clevenger, W., Khouzam, N., Woo, C., Crinella, F., and Fisher, T. (1993). Effect of stimulant medication on children with attention deficit disorder: A "review of reviews." *Exceptional Children, 60,* 154–162.

Talbott, E., and Fleming, J. (2003). The role of social contexts and special education mental health problems of urban adolescents. *The Journal of Special Education, 37*(2), 111–123.

Tarver, S. G., Hallahan, D. P., Kauffman, J. M., and Ball, D. W. (1976). Verbal rehearsal and selective attention in children with learning disabilities: A development lag. *Journal of Experimental Child Psychology, 22*, 375–385.

Teicher, J. D. (1973). A solution to the chronic problem of living: Adolescent attempted suicide. In J. C. Schoolar (Ed.), *Current issues in adolescent psychiatry* (pp. 129–147). New York: Brunner/Mazel.

Tharp, R. G., and Gallimore, R. (1988). *Rousing minds to life: Teaching, learning, and schooling in social context.* New York: Cambridge University Press.

Tharp, R., Estrada, P., Dalton, S. S., and Yamauchi, L. (1999). *Teaching transformed: Achieving Excellence, Fairness, Inclusion, and Harmony.* Boulder, CO: Westview Press.

Thibadeau, S. (1998). *How to use response cost.* Austin, TX: PRO-ED.

Thomas, A. (1979). Learned helplessness and expectancy factors: Implications for research in learning disabilities. *Review of Education Research, 49*(2), 208–221.

Thomas, C. C., Englert, C. S., and Gregg, S. (1987). An analysis of errors and strategies in the expository writing of learning disabled students. *Remedial and Special Education, 8*(1), 21–30.

Thomkins, G. E., and Friend, M. (1986). On your mark, get set, write! *Teaching Exceptional Children, 18*(2), 82–89.

Thompson, M. (1977). *The effects of spelling pattern training on the spelling behavior of primary elementary students.* Unpublished doctoral dissertation, University of Pittsburgh.

Thorne, M. T. (1978). "Payment for reading": The use of the *Corrective Reading* scheme with junior high maladjusted boys. *Remedial Education, 13*(2), 87–90.

Thornton, C. A. (1978). Emphasizing thinking strategies in basic fact instruction. *Journal for Research in Mathematics Education,* 215–227.

Thornton, C. A., and Toohey, M. A. (1985). Basic math facts: Guidelines for teaching and learning. *Learning Disabilities Focus, 1*(1), 44–57.

Thornton, C. A., Tucker, B. F., Dossey, J. A., and Bazik, E. F. (1983). *Teaching mathematics to children with special needs.* Menlo Park, CA: Addison-Wesley.

Thorpe, H. W., and Borden, K. F. (1985). The effect of multisensory instruction upon the on-task behavior and word reading accuracy of learning disabled students. *Journal of Learning Disabilities, 18*, 279–286.

Tierney, R. J., and Readence, J. E. (2000). *Reading strategies and practices: A compendium* (5th ed.). Boston: Allyn & Bacon.

Tierney, R. J., Carter, M. A., and Desai, L. E. (1991). *Portfolio assessment in the reading-writing classroom.* Norwood, MA: Christopher-Gordon.

Tikunoff, W. J. (1983). *Compatibility of the SBIF features with other research instruction of LEP students.* San Francisco: Far West Laboratory.

Tilly, W. D. III, Reschly, D. J., and Grimes, J. (1999). Disability determination in problem solving systems: Conceptual foundations and critical components. In D. J. Reschly, W. D. Tilly, and J. P. Grimes (Eds.), *Special education in transition: Functional assessment and noncategorical programming* (pp. 221–251). Longmont, CO: Sopris West.

Tindal, G. A., and Marston, D. B. (1990). *Classroom-based assessment: Evaluating instructional outcomes.* New York: Merrill/Macmillan.

Tindal, G., and Nolet, V. (1996). Serving students in middle school content classes: A heuristic study of critical variables linking instruction and assessment. *Journal of Special Education, 29*, 414–432.

Toolan, J. M. (1981). Depression and suicide in children: An overview. *American Journal of Psychotherapy, 35*(3), 311–323.

Topping, K., and Eli, S. (1998). *Peer-assisted learning.* Mahwah, NJ: Erlbaum.

Torgesen, J. K. (1982). The learning disabled child as an inactive learner: Educational implications. *Topics in Learning and Learning Disabilities, 2*(1), 45–52.

Torgesen, J. K. (1985). Memory processes in reading disabled children. *Journal of Learning Disabilities, 18*(6), 350–357.

Torgesen, J. K. (1999). Assessment and instruction for phonemic awareness and word recognition skills. In H. W. Catts and A. G. Kamhi (Eds.), *Language and reading disabilities* (pp. 128–153). Boston: Allyn & Bacon.

Torgesen, J. K. (2000). Individual differences in response to early interventions in reading: The lingering problem of treatment resisters. *Learning Disabilities Research and Practice, 15*, 55–64.

Torgesen, J. K. (2002). The prevention of reading difficulties. *Journal of School Psychology, 40*, 7–26.

Torgesen, J. K., and Barker, T. A. (1995). Computers as aids in the prevention and remediation of reading disabilities. *Learning Disability Quarterly, 18*, 76–88.

Torgesen, J. K., and Burgess, S. R. (1998). Consistency of reading-related phonological processes throughout early childhood: Evidence from longitudinal, correlational and instructional studies. In J. Metsala and L. Ehri (Eds.), *Word recognition in beginning literacy* (pp. 161–188). Mahwah, NJ: Erlbaum.

Torgesen, J. K., and Licht, B. G. (1983). The learning disabled child as an inactive learner: Retrospect and prospects. In J. D. McKinney and L. Feagans (Eds.), *Current topics in learning disabilities.* Norwood, NJ: Ablex.

Torgesen, J. K., Rashotte, C. A., Greenstein, J., Houck, G., and Portes, P. (1987). Academic difficulties of learning disabled children who perform poorly on memory span tasks. In H. L. Swanson (Ed.), *Advances in learning and behavioral disabilities* (Supplement 2, pp. 305–333). Greenwich, CT: JAI Press.

Torgesen, J. K., Wagner, R. K., and Rashotte, C. A. (1994). Longitudinal studies of phonological processing and reading. *Journal of Learning Disabilities 19*, 623–630.

Torgesen, J. K., Wagner, R. K., and Rashotte, C. A. (1997). Approaches to the prevention and remediation of phonologically based reading disabilities. In B. Blachman (Ed.), *Foundations of reading acquisition and dyslexia: Implications for early intervention.* Mahwah, NJ: Erlbaum.

Torgesen, J. K., Wagner, R. K., Rashotte, C. A., Alexander, A. W., and Conway, T. (1997). Preventive and remedial interventions for children with severe reading disabilities. *Learning Disabilities: A Multidisciplinary Journal, 8*(1), 51–61.

Tournaki, N. (2003). The differential effects of teaching addition through strategy instruction versus drill and practice to students with

and without learning disabilities. *Journal of Learning Disabilities, 36*, 449–458.

Towell, J., and Wink, J. (1993). *Strategies for monolingual teachers in multilingual classrooms.* Turlock: California State University, Stanislaus (ERIC Document Reproduction Service No. ED 359 797).

Townsend, M. A. R., and Clarihew, A. (1989). Facilitating children's comprehension through the use of advance organizers. *Journal of Reading Behavior, 21*, 15–36.

Trainor, A. A., and Patton, J. R. (2008). Culturally responsive transition planning and instruction from early childhood to postsecondary life. In J. J. Hoover, J. K. Klingner, L. M. Baca, and J. M. Patton (Eds.), *Methods for teaching culturally and linguistically diverse exceptional learners* (pp. 342–367). Upper Saddle River, NJ: Pearson.

Tralli, R., Colombo, B., Deshler, D., and Schumaker, J. B. (1996). The strategies intervention model: A model for supported inclusion at the secondary level. *Remedial and Special Education, 17*, 204–216.

Treder, D., Morse, W., and Ferron, J. (2000). The relationship between teacher effectiveness and teacher attitudes toward issues related to inclusion. *Teacher Education and Special Education, 53*, 202–210.

Trelease, J. (1995). *The new read-aloud handbook* (3rd ed.). New York: Penguin.

Trelease, J. (2001). *The read-aloud handbook* (5th ed.). New York: Penguin.

Trent, S., Artilles, A. J., and Englert, C. S. (1998). From deficit thinking to social constructivism: A review of theory, research, and practice in special education. In P. D. Pearson and A. Iran-Nejad (Eds.), *Review of research in education* (pp. 277–307). Washington, DC: American Educational Research Association.

Troia, G. A., and Graham, S. (2002). The effectiveness of a highly explicit, teacher-directed strategy instruction routine: Changing the writing performance of students with learning disabilities. *Journal of Learning Disabilities, 35*, 290–305.

Troia, G. A., Graham, S., and Harris, K. R. (1999). Teaching students with learning disabilities to mindfully plan when writing. *Exceptional Children, 65*(2), 235–252.

Tulving, E. (1993). What is episodic memory? *Current Directions in Psychological Science, 2*, 67–70.

Tur-Kaspa, H. (2004). Social-information-processing skills of kindergarten children with developmental learning disabilities. *Learning Disabilities Research and Practice, 19*(1), 3–11.

Tur-Kaspa, H., and Bryan, T. (1994). Social information-processing skills of students with learning disabilities. *Learning Disabilities Research and Practice, 9*(1), 12–23.

Turnbull, A. P., and Turnbull, H. R. (1990). *Families, professionals, and exceptionality: A special partnership* (2nd ed.). Columbus, OH: Merrill.

Turnbull, H. R., Turnbull, A. P., and Wheat, M. J. (1982). Assumptions about parental participation: A legislative history. *Exceptional Education Quarterly, 3*(2), 1–8.

Tylka, T. L., and Subich, L. M. (1999). Exploring the construct validity of the eating disorder continuum. *Journal of Counseling Psychology, 46*, 268–276.

U.S. Congress. (1975). *Education for all Handicapped Children Act of 1975.* Washington, DC: U.S. Government Printing Office.

U.S. Congress. (1990). *Individuals with Disabilities Education Act.* Washington, DC: U.S. Government Printing Office.

U.S. Congress. (1997). *Individuals with Disabilities Education Act Amendments of 1997.* Washington, DC: U.S. Government Printing Office.

U.S. Department of Education. (2006a). "Assistance to states for the education of children with disabilities and preschool grants for children with disabilities: Final rule," 34 CRF Parts 300 and 301, *Federal Register* 71: 156 (Aug. 14, 2006): 46540–46845. Retrieved February 14, 2007, from www.idea.ed.gov/download/final-regulations.pdr.

U.S. Department of Education. (2006b, April). *Twenty-sixth annual report to congress on the implementation of the Individuals with Disabilities Education Act.* Washington, DC: U.S. Department of Education.

U.S. Department of Education, Office of Special Education and Rehabilitative Services, Office of Special Education Programs. (2003). *Identifying and Treating Attention Deficit Hyperactivity Disorder: A Resource for School and Home.* Washington, DC: U.S. Department of Education.

Ulanoff, S. H., and Pucci, S. L. (1999). Learning words from books: The effects of read aloud on second language vocabulary acquisition. *Bilingual Research Journal, 23,* 319–332.

Ulman, J. G. (2005). *Making technology work for learners with special needs: Practical skills for teachers.* Boston: Allyn & Bacon.

University of Texas Center for Reading and Language Arts. (1999). *Enhancing vocabulary instruction for secondary students.* Austin, TX: UT System/Texas Education Agency.

University of Texas Center for Reading and Language Arts. (2000a). *Establishing an intensive reading and writing program for secondary students.* Austin, TX: UT System/Texas Education Agency.

University of Texas Center for Reading and Language Arts. (2000b). *First grade teacher reading academy.* Austin, TX: UT System/Texas Education Agency.

University of Texas Center for Reading and Language Arts. (2001a). *Effective instruction for elementary struggling readers: Research-based practices.* Austin, TX: UT System/Texas Education Agency.

University of Texas Center for Reading and Language Arts. (2001b). *Second grade teacher reading academy.* Austin, TX: UT System/Texas Education Agency.

University of Texas Center for Reading and Language Arts. (2002). *Effective instruction for secondary struggling readers: Research-based practices.* Austin, TX: UT System/Texas Education Agency.

University of Texas Center for Reading and Language Arts. (2003a). *Fourth grade teacher reading academy.* Austin, TX: UT System/Texas Education Agency.

University of Texas Center for Reading and Language Arts. (2003b). *Third Grade Teacher Reading Academy.* Austin, TX: UT System; Texas Education Agency; Education Service Center Region XIII; Education Service Center Region IV.

Vacca, R. T., and Vacca, J. A. (1999). *Content area reading: Literacy and learning across the curriculum.* New York: Longman.

Van Luit, J. E. H., and Naglieri, J. A. (1999). Effectiveness of the MASTER program for teaching children multiplication and division. *Journal of Learning Disabilities, 32,* 98–107.

Van Reusen, A. K., and Bos, C. S. (1990). I PLAN: Helping students communicate in planning conferences. *Teaching Exceptional Children, 22,* 30–32.

Van Reusen, A. K., Bos, C. S., Schumaker, J. B., and Deshler, D. D. (1994). *The self-advocacy strategy for education and transition planning.* Lawrence, KS: Edge Enterprises.

Van Wagenen, M. A., Williams, R. L., and McLaughlin, T. F. (1994). Use of assisted reading to improve reading rate, word accuracy, and comprehension with ESL Spanish-speaking students. *Perceptual and Motor Skills, 79,* 227–230.

Vaughn, S. R. (1987). TLC—Teaching, learning, and caring: Teaching interpersonal problem solving skills to emotionally disturbed adolescents. *Pointer, 31,* 25–30.

Vaughn, S. R., and Bos, C. S. (1987). Knowledge and perception of the resource room: The students' perspective. *Journal of Learning Disabilities, 20,* 218–223.

Vaughn, S. R., Bos, C. S., Harrell, J., and Lasky, B. (1988). Parent participation in the initial placement/IEP conference ten years after mandated involvement. *Journal of Learning Disabilities, 21,* 82–89.

Vaughn, S., Bos, C. S., and Schumm, J. S. (1997). *Teaching mainstreamed, diverse, and at-risk students in the general education classroom.* Boston: Allyn & Bacon.

Vaughn, S., Bos, C. S., and Schumm, J. S. (2007). *Teaching students who are exceptional, diverse, and at risk in the general education classroom* (4th ed.). Boston: Allyn & Bacon.

Vaughn, S., Cirino, P. T., Linan-Thompson, S., Mathes, P. G., Carlson, C. D., Cardenas-Hagan, E., et al. (2006). Effectiveness of a Spanish intervention and an English intervention for English language learners at risk for reading problems. *American Educational Research Journal, 43*(3), 449–487.

Vaughn, S., Cohen, J., Fournier, L., Gervasi, J., Levasseur, T., and Newton, S. (1984). *Teaching interpersonal problem solving to behavior disordered adolescents.* Paper presented at Council for Exceptional Children, Washington, DC.

Vaughn, S., Elbaum, B. E., and Schumm, J. S. (1996). The effects of inclusion on the social functioning of students with learning disabilities. *Journal of Learning Disabilities, 29,* 598–608.

Vaughn, S., Elbaum, B. E., Schumm, J. S., and Hughes, M. T. (1998). Social outcomes for students with and without learning disabilities in inclusive classrooms. *Journal of Learning Disabilities, 31*(5), 428–436.

Vaughn, S., and Fuchs, L. S. (2003). Redefining learning disabilities as inadequate response to treatment: The promise and potential problems. *Learning Disabilities Research and Practice, 18*(3), 137–146.

Vaughn, S., and Fuchs, L. S. (2006). A response to "Competing views: A dialogue on response to intervention": Why response to intervention is necessary but not sufficient for identifying students with learning disabilities. *Assessment for Effective Intervention, 32*(1), 58–61.

Vaughn, S., Gersten, R., and Chard, D. J. (2000). The underlying message in LD intervention research: Findings from research syntheses. *Exceptional Children, 67*(1), 99–114.

Vaughn, S., Haager, D., Hogan, A., and Kouzekanani, K. (1992). Self-concept and peer acceptance in students with learning disabilities: A four to five year prospective study. *Journal of Educational Psychology, 84,* 43–50.

Vaughn, S., and Hogan, A. (1990). Social competence and learning disabilities: A prospective study. In H. L. Swanson and B. K. Keogh (Eds.), *Learning Disabilities: Theoretical and research issues* (pp. 175–191). Hillsdale, NJ: Erlbaum.

Vaughn, S., Hogan, A., Kouzekanani, K., and Shapiro, S. (1990). Peer acceptance, self-perceptions, and social skills of LD students prior to identification. *Journal of Educational Psychology, 82*(1), 1–6.

Vaughn, S., and Klingner, J. (1999). Teaching reading comprehension through collaborative strategic reading. *Intervention in School and Clinic, 34*(5), 284–292.

Vaughn, S., and Klingner, J. K. (2004). Teaching reading comprehension to students with learning disabilities. In K. Apel, B. J. Ehren, E. R. Silliman, and C. A. Stone (Series Eds.) & C. A. Stone, E. R. Silliman, B. J. Ehren, and K. Apel (Vol. Eds.), *Challenges in language and literacy; Handbook of language and literacy: Development and disorders* (pp. 541–555). New York: Guilford Press.

Vaughn, S., and Klingner, J. K. (2007). Response to Intervention (RtI): A new era in identifying students with learning disabilities. In D. Haager, J. Klingner, and S. Vaughn (Eds.), *Validated reading practices for three tiers of intervention* (pp. 3–9). Baltimore: Brookes.

Vaughn, S., Klingner, J. K., and Schumm, J. S. (1996). *Collaborative strategic reading.* Miami, FL: School-Based Research, University of Miami.

Vaughn, S., and LaGreca, A. M. (1992). Beyond greetings and making friends: Social skills from a broader perspective. In B. Y. L. Wong (Ed.), *Contemporary intervention research in learning disabilities: An international perspective* (pp. 96–114). New York: Springer-Verlag.

Vaughn, S., and Lancelotta, G. X. (1990). Teaching interpersonal skills to poorly accepted students: Peer-pairing versus non-peer-pairing. *Journal of School Psychology, 28,* 181–188.

Vaughn, S., Lancelotta, G. X., and Minnis, S. (1988). Social strategy training and peer involvement: Increasing peer acceptance of a female LD student. *Learning Disabilities Focus, 4*(1), 32–37.

Vaughn, S. R., Levine, L., and Ridley, C. A. (1986). *PALS: Problem solving and affective learning strategies.* Chicago: Science Research Associates.

Vaughn, S., and Linan-Thompson, S. (2003). What is special about special education for students with learning disabilities? *Journal of Special Education, 37,* 140–147.

Vaughn, S., and Linan-Thompson, S. (2004). *Research-based methods of reading instruction.* Alexandria, VA: ASCD.

Vaughn, S., Linan-Thompson, S., and Hickman, P. (2003). Response to instruction as a means of identifying students with reading/learning disabilities. *Exceptional Children, 69*(4), 391–409.

Vaughn, S., Linan-Thompson, S., Kouzekanani, K., Bryant, D. P., Dickson, S., and Blozis, S. A. (2003). Reading instruction grouping for students with reading difficulties. *Remedial and Special Education, 24*(5), 301–318.

Vaughn, S., Linan-Thompson, S., Mathes, P. G., Cirino, P. T., Carlson, C. D., Pollard-Durodola,

S. D., et al. (2006). Effectiveness of Spanish intervention for first-grade English language learners at risk for reading difficulties. *Journal of Learning Disabilities, 39*(1), 56–73.

Vaughn, S., Mathes, P. G., Linan-Thompson, S., Cirino, P. T., Carlson, C. D., Pollard-Durodola, S. D., et al. (2006). First-grade English language learners at-risk for reading problems: Effectiveness of an English intervention. *Elementary School Journal, 107*(2), 153–180.

Vaughn, S., McIntosh, R., Schumm, J. S., Haager, D., and Callwood, D. (1993). Social status and peer acceptance revisited. *Learning Disabilities Research and Practice, 8*, 82–88.

Vaughn, S., McIntosh, R., and Spencer-Rowe, J. (1991). Peer rejection is a stubborn thing: Increasing peer acceptance of rejected students with learning disabilities. *Learning Disabilities Research and Practice, 6*(2), 83–88, 152–157.

Vaughn, S. R., Ridley, C. A., and Bullock, D. D. (1984). Interpersonal problem solving skills training with aggressive young children. *Journal of Applied Developmental Psychology, 5*, 213–223.

Vaughn, S. R., Ridley, C. A., and Cox, J. (1983). Evaluating the efficacy of an interpersonal skills training program with children who are mentally retarded. *Education and Training of the Mentally Retarded, 18*(3), 191–196.

Vaughn, S., and Schumm, J. S. (1994). Middle school teachers' planning for students with learning disabilities. *Remedial and Special Education, 15*, 152–161.

Vaughn, S., and Schumm, J. S. (1995). Responsible inclusion for students with learning disabilities. *Journal of Learning Disabilities 28*(5), 264–270.

Vaughn, S., and Schumm, J. S. (1996). Classroom ecologies: Classroom interactions and implications for inclusion of students with learning disabilities. In D. L. Speece and B. Keogh (Eds.), *Research on classroom ecologies: Implications for inclusion of children with learning disabilities* (pp. 107–124). Mahwah, NJ: Erlbaum.

Vaughn, S., Schumm, J. S., and Arguelles, M. E. (1997). The ABCDE's of co-teaching. *Teaching Exceptional Children, 30*(2), 4–10.

Vaughn, S., Schumm, J. S., Jallad, B., Slusher, J., and Saumell, L. (1996). Teachers' views of inclusion. *Learning Disabilities Research and Practice, 11*(2), 96–106.

Vaughn, S., Schumm, J. S., Klingner, J., and Saumell, L. (1995). Students' views of instructional practices: Implications for inclusion. *Learning Disability Quarterly, 18*, 236–248.

Vaughn, S., Schumm, J. S., and Kouzekanani, K. (1993). What do students with learning disabilities think when their general education teachers make adaptations? *Journal of Learning Disabilities, 26*, 545–555.

Vaughn, S., Schumm, J. S., Niarhos, F., and Daugherty, T. (1993). What do students think when teachers make adaptations? *Teaching and Teacher Education, 9*, 107–118.

Vaughn, S., Schumm, J. S., Niarhos, F. J., and Gordon, J. (1993). Students' perceptions of two hypothetical teachers' instructional adaptations for low achievers. *Elementary School Journal, 94*, 87–102.

Vaughn, S., Zaragoza, N., Hogan, A., and Walker, J. (1993). A four year longitudinal investigation of the social skills and behavior problems of students with learning disabilities. *Journal of Learning Disabilities, 26*, 353–424.

Veatch, J. (1991). *Whole language and its predecessors: Commentary.* Paper presented at the annual meeting of the College Reading Association (ERIC Document No. 341–035).

Vellutino, F., Scanlon, D. M., Sipay, E. R., Small, S. G., Pratt, A., Chen, R., et al. (1996). Cognitive profiles of difficult-to-remediate and readily remediated poor readers: Early intervention as a vehicle for distinguishing between cognitive and experiential deficits as basic causes of specific reading disability. *Journal of Educational Psychology, 88*, 601–638.

Vellutino, F. R., and Scanlon, D. M. (1987). Phonological coding, phonological awareness, and reading ability: Evidence from a longitudinal and experimental study. *Merrill-Palmer Quarterly, 33*, 321–363.

Vellutino, F. R., Scanlon, D. M., Small, S. G., Fanuele, D. P., and Sweeney, J. (2007). Preventing early reading difficulties through kindergarten and first grade intervention: A variant of the three-tier model. In D. Haager, J. Klingner, and S. Vaughn (Eds.), *Validated reading practices for three tiers of intervention.* Baltimore: Brookes.

Vitale, M., Medland, M., Romance, N., and Weaver, H. P. (1993). Accelerating reading and thinking skills of low-achieving elementary students: Implications for curricular change. *Effective School Practices, 12*(1), 26–31.

Voltz, D. L., Elliott, R. N., and Cobb, H. B. (1994). Collaborative teacher roles: Special and general educators. *Journal of Learning Disabilities, 27*, 527–535.

Vygotsky, L. S. (1978). *Mind in society: The development of higher psychological processes.* Cambridge, MA: Harvard University Press.

Waggoner, K., and Wilgosh, L. (1990). Concerns of families of children with learning disabilities. *Journal of Learning Disabilities, 23*, 97–98, 113.

Wagner, M., Blackorby, J., Cameto, R., Habbleler, K., and Newman, L. (1993). *The transition experiences of young people with disabilities: A summary of findings from the National Longitudinal Transition Study of Special Education Students.* Menlo Park, CA: SRI International.

Wagner, R. K., Torgesen, J. K., and Rashotte, C. A. (1994). The development of reading-related phonological processing abilities: New evidence of bi-directional causality from a latent variable longitudinal study. *Developmental Psychology, 30*, 73–87.

Walker, H. M., Golly, A., Kavanagh, K., Stiller, B., Severson, H. H., and Feil, E. G. (2003). *First Step to Success.* Longmont, CO: Sopris West.

Wallace, G., and Kauffman, J. M. (1986). *Teaching students with learning and behavior problems* (3rd ed.). Columbus, OH: Merrill.

Wallace, T., Shin, J., Bartholomay, T., and Stahl, B. J. (2001). Knowledge and skills for teachers supervising the work of paraprofessionals. *Exceptional Children, 67*, 520–534.

Wallach, G. P., and Miller, L. (1988). *Language intervention and academic success.* Boston: Little, Brown–College-Hill.

Walther-Thomas, C., and Brownell, M. (2000). An interview with Dr. Janice Bulgren. *Intervention in School and Clinic, 35*, 232–236.

Wannan, G., and Fombonne, E. (1998). Gender differences in rates and correlates of suicidal behavior amongst child psychiatric outpatients. *Journal of Adolescence, 21*(4), 371–381.

Wanzek, J., Vaughn, S., Wexler, J., Swanson, E. A., and Edmonds, M. (2006). A synthesis of spelling and reading outcomes for students with learning disabilities. *Journal of Learning Disabilities, 39*(6), 528–543.

Warger, C. L., and Pugach, M. C. (1996). Forming partnerships around curriculum. *Educational Leadership, 53*(5), 62–65.

Warren, J. (1970). *Phonetic generalizations to aid spelling instruction at the fifth-grade level.* Unpublished doctoral dissertation, Boston University.

Watkins, T. J. (1997). Teacher communications, child achievement, and parent traits in parent involvement models. *Journal of Educational Research, 91*(1), 3–14.

Watson, D. (1997). Beyond decodable texts: Supportable and workable literature. *Language Arts, 74*, 635–643.

Weaver, C. (1990). *Understanding whole language: Principles and practices.* Portsmouth, NH: Heinemann.

Weaver, C. (Ed.). (1998). *Reconsidering a balanced approach to reading.* Urbana, IL: National Council of Teachers of English.

Wehmeyer, M. L., and Kelchner, K. (1995). *Whose future is it anyway? A student-directed transition planning program.* Arlington, TX: Arc National Headquarters.

Weintraub, N., and Graham, S. (1998). Writing legibly and quickly: A study of children's ability to adjust their handwriting to meet common classroom demands. *Learning Disability Research and Practice, 13*(3), 146–152.

Weiss, M. P., and Lloyd, J. (2003). Conditions for co-teaching: Lessons from a case study. *Teacher Education and Special Education, 26*(1), 27–41.

Weiss, M. P., and Lloyd, J. W. (2002). Congruence between roles and actions of secondary special educators in co-taught and special education settings. *The Journal of Special Education, 36*, 58–68.

Welch, M. (1992). The PLEASE strategy: A metacognitive learning strategy for improving the paragraph writing of students with mild learning disabilities. *Learning Disability Quarterly, 15*, 119–128.

Wells, G. (1973). *Coding manual of the description of child speech.* Bristol, England: University of Bristol School of Education.

Weltmann Begun, R. (Ed.). (1995). *Ready-to-use social skills lessons and activities for grades 1–3.* West Nyack, NY: Center for Applied Research.

West, G. F. (1978). *Teaching reading skills in content areas: A practical guide to the construction of student exercises.* Oviedo, FL: Sandpiper.

West, J. F., and Cannon, G. S. (1988). Essential collaborative consultation competencies for regular and special educators. *Journal of Learning Disabilities, 21*, 56–63.

West, J. F., and Idol, L. (1990). Collaborative consultation in the education of mildly handicapped and at-risk students. *Remedial and Special Education, 11*(1), 22–31.

West, J. F., Idol, L., and Cannon, G. (1989). *Collaboration in the schools: An inservice and preservice curriculum for teachers, support staff, and administrators.* Austin, TX: PRO-ED.

Westwood, P. (2003). *Commonsense methods for children with special educational needs* (4th ed.). New York: Routledge Falmer.

Wexler, J., Vaughn, S., Edmonds, M., and Klein-Reutebuch, C. (in press). A synthesis of fluency interventions for secondary struggling readers. *Reading and Writing: An Interdisciplinary Journal*.

Whinnery, K. W. (1995). Perceptions of students with learning disabilities: Inclusion versus pull-out services. *Preventing School Failure, 40*(1), 5–9.

White, B. (1975). Critical influences in the origins of competence. *Merrill-Palmer Quarterly, 2,* 243–266.

White, T. G., Power, M. A., and White, S. (1989). Morphological analysis: Implications for teaching and understanding vocabulary growth. *Reading Research Quarterly, 24,* 283–304.

White, T. G., Sowell, J., and Yanagihara A. (1989). Teaching elementary students to use word-part clues. *The Reading Teacher, 42*(4), 302–308.

Whitehurst, G. J., and Lonigan, C. J. (2001). Emergent literacy: Development from pre-readers. In S. B. Neuman and D. K. Dickinson (Eds.), *Handbook of early literacy research* (pp. 11–29). New York: Guilford Press.

Wicks-Nelson, R., and Israel, A. L. (1984). *Behavior disorders of childhood.* Englewood Cliffs, NJ: Prentice Hall.

Wiener, J. (2002). Friendship and social adjustment of children with learning disabilities. In B. Y. L. Wong and M. L. Donahue (Eds.), *The social dimensions of learning disabilities: Essays in honor of Janis Bryan* (pp. 93–114). Mahwah, NJ: Erlbaum.

Wiener, J., and Harris, P. J. (1997). Evaluation of an individualized, context-based social skills training program for children with learning disabilities. *Learning Disabilities Research and Practice, 12*(1), 40–53.

Wiener, J., and Tardif, C. Y. (2004). Social and emotional functioning of children with learning disabilities: Does special education placement make a difference? *Learning Disabilities Research and Practice, 19*(1), 20–32.

Wiig, E. H. (1982). *Let's talk: Developing prosocial communication skills.* Columbus, OH: Merrill.

Wiig, E. H. (1992). Strategy training for people with language-learning disabilities. In L. Meltzer (Ed.), *Strategy assessment and training for students with learning disabilities: From theory to practice* (pp. 167–194). Austin, TX: PRO-ED.

Wiig, E. H., and Bray, C. M. (1983). *Let's talk for children.* Columbus, OH: Merrill.

Wiig, E. H., and Secord, W. A. (1998). Language disabilities in school-age children and youth. In G. H. Shames, E. H. Wiig, and W. A. Secord (Eds.), *Human communication disorders* (5th ed., pp. 212–247). New York: Merrill.

Wiig, E. H., and Semel, E. M. (1984). *Language assessment and intervention for the learning disabled* (2nd ed.). Columbus, OH: Merrill.

Wiig, E. H., and Wilson, C. C. (1994). Is a question a question? Passage understanding by preadolescents with learning disabilities. *Language, Speech, and Hearing Services in Schools, 25,* 241–249.

Wilkinson, I. A. G., and Anderson, R. C. (1995). Sociocognitive processes in guided silent reading: A microanalysis of small-group lessons. *Reading Research Quarterly, 30*(4), 710–740.

Will, M. (1984). *OSERS programming for the transition of youth with disabilities: Bridges from school to working life.* Washington, DC: Office of Special Education and Rehabilitative Services.

Williams, J. P. (1998). Improving the comprehension of disabled readers. *Annals of Dyslexia, 48,* 213–238.

Williams, J. P., Brown, L. G., Silverstein, A. K., and deCani, J. S. (1994). An instructional program in comprehension of narrative themes for adolescents with learning disabilities. *Learning Disability Quarterly, 17,* 205–221.

Williamson, G. V., and Shields, S. S. (1997). *WordBURST.* East Moline, IL: LinguiSystems.

Williamson, G. V., and Shields, S. S. (1999). *Rocky's mountain: A word-finding game.* East Moline, IL: LinguiSystems.

Willig, A. C., and Ortiz, A. A. (1991). The nonbiased individualized educational program: Linking assessment to instruction. In E. V. Hamayan and J. S. Damico (Eds.), *Limiting bias in the assessment of bilingual students* (pp. 281–302). Austin, TX: PRO-ED.

Willman, A. T. (1999). "Hello, Mrs. Willman, it's me!" Keep kids reading over the summer by using voice mail. *The Reading Teacher, 52,* 788–789.

Wilson, C. C. (1993). *Room 14.* East Moline, IL: LinguiSystems.

Wilson, C. L., and Sindelar, P. T. (1991). Direct instruction in math word problems: Students with learning disabilities. *Journal of Learning Disabilities, 23*(1), 23–29.

Wilson, D. R., and David, W. J. (1994). Academic intrinsic motivation and attitudes toward school and learning of learning disabled students. *Learning Disabilities Research and Practice, 9,* 148–156.

Winton, P. J., and Turnbull, A. P. (1981). Parent involvement as viewed by parents of preschool handicapped children. *Topics in Early Childhood Special Education, 1,* 11–19.

Wolery, M., Cybriwsky, C. A., Gast, D. L., and Boyle-Gast, K. (1991). Use of constant time delay and attentional responses with adolescents. *Exceptional Children, 57,* 462–474.

Wolford, P. L., Heward, W. L., and Alber, S. H. (2001). Teaching middle school students with learning disabilities to recruit peer assistance during cooperative learning group activities. *Learning Disabilities Research and Practice, 16*(3), 161–173.

Wong, B. Y. L. (1979). Increasing retention of main ideas through questioning strategies. *Learning Disability Quarterly, 2*(2), 42–47.

Wong, B. Y. L. (1986). A cognitive approach to teaching spelling. *Exceptional Children, 53,* 169–173.

Wong, B. Y. L. (1987). Directions in future research on metacognition in learning disabilities. In H. L. Swanson (Ed.), *Memory and learning disabilities: Advances in learning and behavioral disabilities* (Supplement 2, pp. 335–356). Greenwich, CT: JAI Press.

Wong, B. Y. L. (1996). *The ABCs of learning disabilities.* San Diego, CA: Academic Press.

Wong, B. Y. L., and Jones, W. (1982). Increasing metacomprehension in learning disabled and normally achieving students through self-questioning training. *Learning Disability Quarterly, 5,* 228–240.

Wong, B. Y. L., and Wong, R. (1980). Role taking skills in normal achieving and learning disabled children. *Learning Disability Quarterly, 3,* 11–18.

Wong, B. Y. L., Butler, D. L., Ficzere, S. A., and Kuperis, S. (1997). Teaching adolescents with learning disabilities and low achievers to plan, write, and revise compare-and-contrast essays. *Learning Disabilities Research and Practice, 12*(1), 2–15.

Wong, B. Y. L., Wong, R., Perry, N., and Sawatsky, D. (1986). The efficacy of a self-questioning summarization strategy for use by underachievers and learning disabled adolescents in social studies. *Learning Disabilities Focus, 2*(1), 20–35.

Wood, K. D., Lapp, D., and Flood, J. (1992). *Guiding readers through the text: A review of study guides.* Newark, DE: International Reading Association.

Woodcock, R. W., Clark, C. R., and Davies, C. O. (1969). *The Peabody rebus reading program.* Circle Pines, MN: American Guidance Service.

Woodward, A., and Elliott, D. L. (1990). Textbook use and teacher professionalism. In D. L. Elliott and A. Woodward (Eds.), *Textbooks and schooling in the United States* (Eighty-ninth yearbook of the National Society for the Study of Education, Part I, pp. 178–193). Chicago: University of Chicago Press.

Woodward, J. (1995). Technology-based research in mathematics for special education. *Focus on Learning Problems in Mathematics, 17*(2), 3–23.

Worthy, J. (1996). A matter of interest: Literature that hooks reluctant readers and keeps them reading. *The Reading Teacher, 50,* 204–212.

Worthy, J., and Broaddus, K. (2002). Fluency beyond the primary grades: From group performance to silent, independent reading. *Reading Teacher, 55*(4), 334–343.

Wylie, R. E., and Durrell, D. D. (1970). Teaching vowels through phonograms. *Elementary English, 47,* 787–791.

Wysocki, K., and Jenkins, J. R. (1987). Deriving word meanings through morphological generalization. *Reading Research Quarterly, 22,* 66–81.

Xin, Y. P., and Jitendra, A. K. (1999). The effects of instruction in solving mathematical word problems for students with learning problems: A meta-analysis. *The Journal of Special Education, 32*(4), 207–225.

Yauman, B. E. (1980). Special education placement and the self-concepts of elementary school age children. *Learning Disability Quarterly, 3,* 30–35.

Yee, A. (1969). Is the phonetic generalization hypothesis in spelling valid? *Journal of Experimental Education, 37,* 82–91.

Yell, M. L. (2006). *The law and special education* (2nd ed.) Upper Saddle River, NJ: Merrill/Prentice Hall.

Yopp, H. K. (1992). Developing phonemic awareness in young children. *The Reading Teacher, 45,* 696–703.

Yopp, H. K. (1995). A test for assessing phonemic awareness in young children. *The Reading Teacher, 49*(1), 20–29.

Zaragoza, N., and Vaughn, S. (1992). The effects of process instruction on three second-grade students with different achievement profiles.

Learning Disabilities Research and Practice, 7(4), 184–193.

Zeno, S. M., Ivens, S. H., Millard, R. T., and Duvvuri, R. (1995). *The educator's word frequency guide.* Brewster, NY: Touchstone Applied Science Associates.

Zigmond, N. (2001). Special education at a crossroads. *Preventing School Failure, 45*(2), 70–74.

Zigmond, N. (2003). Where should students with disabilities receive special education services? Is one place better than another? *The Journal of Special Education, 37,* 193–199.

Zigmond, N., and Baker, J. M. (1994). Is the mainstream a more appropriate educational setting for Randy? A case study of one student with learning disabilities. *Learning Disabilities Research and Practice, 9,* 108–117.

Zigmond, N., and Magiera, K. (2002). Coteaching. *Current Practice Alerts, 6,* 1–4.

Zinberg, N. E. (1984). *Drug, set, and setting.* New Haven, CT: Yale University Press.

Zirkel, P. A. (2007). What does the law say? *Teaching Exceptional Children, May/June,* 65–67.

Zorfass, J., Corley, P., and Remz, A. (1994). Helping students with disabilities become writers. *Educational Leadership, 51*(5), 62–66.

Zutell, J. (1993). *Directed spelling thinking activity: A developmental, conceptual approach to advance spelling word knowledge.* Paper presented at the First International and 19th National Conference of the Australian Reading Association, Melbourne, Australia.

Zutell, J., and Rasinski, T. V. (1991). Training teachers to attend to their students' oral reading fluency. *Theory into Practice, 30,* 211–217.

Koskinen, P. A., 304
Koskinen, P. S., 301
Kottman, T., 126
Kouzekanani, K., 113, 115, 153, 272, 430
Kozulin, A., 51
Krashen, S., 54
Kress, R. A., 282
Krist, J., 337
Krohm, B., 303
Kronik, D., 177
Krug, R. S., 127
Kucan, L., 410
Kucer, S. B., 372
Kuhn, M. R., 294, 298, 303
Kuhne, M., 113
Kuperis, S., 375

LaBerge, D., 57, 298
LaGreca, A. M., 113, 117, 139
Lancelotta, G., 118, 119, 129, 130
Landrum, T. J., 3
Langan, J., 441
Lange, L., 135
Langer, J. A., 319, 320, 321
Lanier, J. E., 316
Lankford, F. G., 482
Lapp, D., 431
Lardieri, L. A., 174
Larkin, M. J., 437, 439, 440
Larsen, S. C., 487
Larsen-Freeman, D., 309
Laskey, B., 179
Lathrop, M., 111
Lathuliere, E., 463
Lau, M., 71
Lawrence-Patterson, E., 122
Lawson, L., 346
Leavell, A. G., 162, 372
Leconte, P. J., 521
Lederer, J. M., 337
LeDoux, J. M., 6
Lee, D., 493
Lee, D. S., 466
Lee, O., 153
Leenaars, A. A., 125
Legenza, A., 325
Lehman, J., 526
Leinart, A., 300
LeMare, L., 113, 115
Lembke, E., 76
Lennox, C., 382
Lenz, B. K., 46, 49, 50, 414, 415, 416, 421, 422, 423, 424, 429
Leon, J. A., 492
Lerner, J. W., 46, 57
Lesaux, N., 300
Levine, L., 128
Levine, M. P., 126
Levy, B. A., 268
Lewis, S. K., 122
Lian, M. J., 174
Licht, B. G., 446
Lignugaris-Kraft, B., 429
Linan-Thompson, S., 3, 8, 71, 77, 277, 341
Lindamood, P., 247, 255
Lindamood, P. A., 247, 255
Lindsey, J. D., 188
Linek, W. M., 277
Lipson, M. Y., 310
Lipton, M. E., 115
Liu, L. Y., 127
Lloyd, J., 17, 160

Lloyd, J. W., 153, 157, 395
Loftus, E. R., 57
Loftus, G., 57
Logan, J. W., 408
Lonigan, C. J., 298
Loomer, B. M., 387
López-Robetson, J. M., 346
Lopez-Vona, K., 152
Lourie, I. S., 176
Lovett, M. V., 337
Lovitt, T., 430
Lovitt, T. C., 428, 487
Loxterman, G. A., 312
Loynachan, C., 386
Lucangeli, D., 61
Luckner, J. L., 118
Lucyshyn, J. M., 108
Luft, P., 526
Lutz, J. G., 187
Lyerla, K. D., 49
Lynch, E. W., 181
Lyon, G. R., 6, 241, 272
Lysynchuk, L., 268, 337

MacArthur, C., 45, 47, 362, 374
MacArthur, C. A., 44, 380, 381
McCall, C., 387
McCardle, P., 245
McCauley, D. S., 303
McCauley, J. K., 303
Maccini, P., 463
McClure, S., 116
McCormick, S., 443
MacDonald, V., 337
McDonough, R., 54
McDowell, J., 151, 153, 156
McGuire, M., 437
McIntosh, R., 102, 113, 114, 116, 130, 137, 139, 152, 153
McIntyre, C. W., 273, 275
McKeown, M. G., 312, 328, 329, 410, 416
McKinney, J. D., 116, 153, 181
Macklem, G., 135
McKnight, P. C., 444
McLaughlin, M., 12
McLaughlin, T. F., 303, 387
McLoughlin, J. A., 174
McNaughton, D., 380
Macrorie, K., 398
MacWilliams, L. J., 96
Madden, N. A., 89, 251
Maddux, C. D., 174, 177
Madelaine, A., 17
Magiera, K., 151
Maheady, L., 89, 90, 480
Mallette, B., 89, 90, 391
Malone, L. D., 334
Mandler, J. M., 329
Mandoli, M., 387
Mandoli, P., 387
Mangrum, C. T., 418
Mann, V., 244
Mann-Rinehart, P., 128
Many, J. E., 315
Manzo, A. V., 324, 336
Manzo, U. C., 324, 336
Margalit, M., 174
Mariage, M., 47
Mariage, T., 48
Mariage, T. V., 50, 51, 335, 341
Markham, L., 391
Marsh, L. G., 491
Marston, D., 17, 71
Marston, D. B., 190

Martin, J. H., 279
Martinez, M., 299
Martinez, N., 300
Martinez-Roldan, C. M., 346
Marzola, E. S., 489
Mason, D. J., 120
Massaro, D. W., 53
Mastropieri, M. A., 47, 58, 300, 313, 316, 328, 329, 334, 348, 415, 447, 448, 491, 492
Mather, N., 159
Mathes, P. A., 304
Mathes, P. G., 45, 89, 247, 255, 303, 305, 370
Mathinos, D. A., 117
Matuszny, R. M., 166
Mauser, A. J., 179
Maxwell, J. C., 127
Mayer, G. R., 38
Mayer, R. E., 421
Medland, M., 269
Mehan, H., 48
Meichenbaum, D., 41, 44, 45, 46, 47, 492
Meister, C., 335, 337
Mekkelson, J., 310
Meltzer, L., 113
Méndez Barletta, L., 79
Menke, P. J., 323
Mercer, A. R., 86, 94, 102, 468
Mercer, C. D., 86, 94, 102, 131, 468
Merrell, K. W., 120
Mesmer, H. A. E., 265
Meyer, C. A., 20
Meyer, L., 255
Meyer, M. S., 300
Michalove, B., 347
Mikulincer, M., 113
Milich, R., 119
Millard, R. T., 262
Miller, D. E., 502
Miller, H., 490
Miller, J. H., 463, 465
Miller, K. G., 118
Miller, L., 385, 387, 393
Miller, L. J., 384
Miller, P. D., 279
Miller, R. J., 521
Miller, T., 429
Mills, H., 347
Minnis, S., 119
Minskoff, E. H., 247, 255
Moats, L. C., 252, 275
Mock, D., 72
Molina, B., 131
Moll, L. C., 47, 48, 50
Molloy, D., 45
Molloy, D. E., 71
Monda-Amaya, L., 123
Monroe, J., 375
Montague, M., 46, 60, 113, 461, 486, 489
Montague, M. A. G., 372
Montgomery, J., 226
Moody, S. W., 89, 429, 430
Moore, J., 113, 391
Morgan, D., 227
Morgan, P. L., 72
Morocco, C. C., 380
Morrison, G. M., 121
Morrow, L. M., 347
Mosberg, L., 293
Mosenthal, J. H., 310
Most, T., 117

Moulton, R., 522
Murawski, W. A., 159
Muter, V., 246
Muth, K. D., 330
Muyskens, P., 71
Myklebust, H. R., 384, 388, 389, 392, 463
Myles, B. S., 432

Nagel, B. R., 49, 447
Nagy, W. E., 418
Nancy, A., 399
National Association of School Psychologists, 76
National Association of State Directors of Special Education (NASDSE), 26, 69
National Center for Health Statistics, 126
National Institute for Literacy, 413
National Mental Health Association, 125
National Reading Panel, 241, 245, 256, 257, 264, 298, 300, 313, 314, 316, 318, 335, 347, 408, 409, 411, 412
National Research Council (NRC), 466
Neisser, U., 57
Nelson, D. R., 46
Nelson, J., 434
Nelson, J. R., 111
Nelson, J. S., 435
Nelson, L. L., 171
Nelson, O. G., 277
Nessel, D., 345
Neubert, D. A., 521
Nevin, A., 89, 153, 155
Newcomer, P. L., 227
Newman, L., 511
Niarhos, F., 153, 430, 435
Nicholich, M., 321
Nichols, W. D., 408
Niebling, B. C., 74
Niedermeyer, F. C., 393
Nolan, S. M., 49
Nolen, S. B., 364
Nolet, V., 408
Nowak, M. R., 299
Nowicki, E. A., 115
Nuzum, M. G., 489
Nye, B., 434

Oakes, J., 73
Obrzut, J. E., 57
O'Connor, R., 159
O'Connor, R. E., 385
O'Connor, S. C., 184
Ofiesh, N., 380
Ogle, D., 323, 354, 411
Ogle, D. M., 319, 322, 323, 398
Ogle, P. A. 175
O'Hara, C., 255
O'Keefe, T., 347
Okolo, C. M., 477
Okrainec, J. A., 117
Olweus, D., 119
O'Malley, J. M., 429
O'Malley, P. M., 126, 127
Opitz, M. F., 248
Ormsbee, C. K., 432
Orosco, M. J., 79
Orton, S. T., 273
Osborn, J., 268

Subject Index